International Marketing

SECOND EDITION

RAKESH MOHAN JOSHI

Professor (International Business and International Marketing)
Indian Institute of Foreign Trade
New Delhi

OXFORD

UNIVERSITY PRESS

OXFORD
UNIVERSITY PRESS

Oxford University Press is a department of the University of Oxford.
It furthers the University's objective of excellence in research, scholarship,
and education by publishing worldwide. Oxford is a registered trade mark of
Oxford University Press in the UK and in certain other countries.

Published in India by
Oxford University Press
YMCA Library Building, 1 Jai Singh Road, New Delhi 110001, India

ISBN-13: 978-0-19-807702-2
ISBN-10: 0-19-807702-5

Typeset in Times New Roman
by Ideal Publishing Solutions, Delhi
Printed in India by Tara Art Printers (P) Ltd, Noida

Third-party website addresses mentioned in this book are provided
by Oxford University Press in good faith and for information only.
Oxford University Press disclaims any responsibility for the material contained therein.

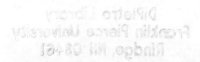

To my
parents, Smt. Subhadra Sharma and Late Dr Chandra Mohan Sharma
wife, Dr Indu Joshi
and children, Vidhu and Chandrika
for
their deep emotional support and sacrifices for my academic achievements

Acknowledgements

The quest to achieve excellence in writing this book entailed enormous fortitude, diligence, perseverance, and forgoing numerous social and other opportunities not only for me but for my entire family. I owe a deep sense of gratitude to my family, especially my wife Dr Indu Joshi and children Vidhu and Chandrika, for their sustained forbearance, support, and unflinching faith in me to write a world-class text.

I am deeply indebted to numerous authors, researchers, intellectuals, and my teachers and colleagues whose research and writings have greatly influenced my thought process and contributed towards developing and reinforcing my concepts on the subject. I owe all the participants of my management development programmes with whom I interacted and taught in various parts of the world for their constructive criticism, suggestions, and inputs for improvements.

I am highly grateful to all the professors, professionals, and students from all parts of the world for adopting the book for their teaching, learning, and reference and sending me their valuable ideas and comments.

I am grateful to Dr Surajit Mitra, Director, Indian Institute of Foreign Trade, for providing generous support for my research and writings.

Special thanks are due to my research associates, Akanksha Dua, Renu Sharma, and Surbhi Malhotra, personal assistants—Monica Saini and Lalita Gupta—and other supporting staff for their unrelenting support in preparing an excellent manuscript.

Last but not least, I highly appreciate the unstinting support of the OUP editorial team in bringing out an outstanding text.

Rakesh Mohan Joshi

Preface to the First Edition

Marketing activity carried out by a firm for profit in more than one country is referred to as international marketing. Since the firm has to carry out its marketing operations in more than one nation, the task of marketing becomes much more complex compared to domestic marketing. As in the case of domestic marketing, international marketing involves identifying the needs and wants of customers, conceptualizing and developing products, pricing, promotion and distribution of goods and services, and coordinating marketing activities in international markets.

Though the fundamentals of marketing are the same as those in domestic markets, in international markets, a variety of environmental factors combine to make the marketing decisions of a business organization more challenging. Also known as 'uncontrollable elements', these are social, economic, political, legal, and technological factors over which a marketer can exercise little influence. The challenge in international marketing thus lies in managing the controllable elements of the marketing mix—product, price, distribution, and promotion—and adapting to environmental uncontrollables to ensure marketing success.

During the last few decades, the marketing environment across the world has witnessed unprecedented changes, which have metamorphosed the entire approach to marketing. Increase in income levels in nearly all parts of the world, except in Sub-Saharan Africa, has accelerated the growth of global markets. Reduction in tariffs and prohibition of explicit non-tariff marketing barriers under the WTO framework has contributed to the opening up of international markets. Economic integration of the entire world through the removal of trade barriers, increase in capital mobility, and diffusion of knowledge and information have significantly contributed to the process of globalization. Even countries with state-driven marketing systems, such as CIS and China, are fast moving towards free markets.

Thus, in the emerging marketing scenario, developing a thorough understanding of international marketing has become not only necessary for the firms operating in international markets but also a precondition of success even for operating domestically. Recent developments in the world economy have led to the emergence of international marketing as one of the key areas of marketing. The subject adopts a multi-disciplinary approach, borrowing from diverse disciplines such as marketing, international trade, international economics, international business environment, international supply chain and logistics management, and international finance. All this has contributed to making it a strategically important field of study.

About the Book

The book has been designed to serve as a comprehensive text on international marketing that especially meets the requirements of MBA students specializing in marketing. The book is written with a specific focus on international marketing as compared to a generalized trade focus. It provides a detailed coverage and in-depth analysis of international markets specifically based on Indian and developing countries' perspectives with regard to their economic, political, and legal environments. The book responds to a long-standing need for a textbook whose approach to international marketing is significantly different from that of developed countries in terms of their financial resources, infrastructure, logistics, etc. It also serves as a handy reference book for international marketing practitioners and entrepreneurs looking at vast opportunities in the emerging global market.

Pedagogical Features

The book discusses recent developments and best practices in international marketing, using examples and case studies of world-class business organizations, such as Indian Oil Corporation, Cipla, Essel Propack,

Gillette, and the Export-Import Bank of India. Also discussed are cases on international marketing opportunities for medical services, automobiles, tea, rice, mangoes, diamond jewellery, and floriculture products. Each topic is approached step by step to enable students to relate conceptual understanding to real-life situations.

Other features of the book include review questions at the end of each chapter that help students to revisit the main concepts discussed in that particular chapter. Interesting practicals—classroom and fieldwork-based projects—provide an opportunity for students to internalize learning by critically examining concepts in the classroom and then applying them to real-life situations.

The book is accompanied by a CD-ROM containing select forms of international trade transactions. Annexures include key data on India's foreign trade, text of the Agreement on South Asian Free Trade Area (SAFTA), ranking of the top 100 global brands, and highlights of India's foreign trade policy 2004–2009, which are discussed in Chapters 2, 4, 9, and 13.

The Instructors' Manual, which is available to instructors on demand, provides notes on teaching international marketing and solutions to review questions, project assignments, and case study questions.

Acknowledgements

I thankfully acknowledge the inputs received from my students and numerous participants of various management development programmes conducted by me.

I am grateful to Mr Prabir Sengupta, Director, Indian Institute of Foreign Trade, for his generous support and cooperation in writing the book. My gratitude is due to Prof. B. Bhattacharyya, whose insightful suggestions have greatly contributed to my conception of the book. I also thank my colleague Dr Vijaya Katti and the library personnel of the Indian Institute of Foreign Trade, especially Ms B. Pankti and Mr R.S. Meena, for making the latest publications readily available to me. My secretary Lalita deserves special thanks for her secretarial assistance, especially in typing the manuscript.

My sincere thanks are due to the editorial team of Oxford University Press for their consistent follow-up, patience, and creative suggestions during the course of writing.

I am highly indebted to Mrs Nirmla, Mr Rajesh Dixit, and Mr Mayank Mohan Joshi for the support provided by them to my family during the making of the book.

I will be grateful to the readers if they could send their suggestions to improve the book at the following email ID: rmjoshi2000@yahoo.com

Rakesh Mohan Joshi

Brief Contents

Detailed Contents

PART I DECISION TO INTERNATIONALIZE 1

PART II SCANNING INTERNATIONAL MARKETING ENVIRONMENT 49

PART IV   ENTRY MODE DECISIONS   283

PART V   MARKETING MIX DECISIONS   323

PART VI EXPORT–IMPORT MANAGEMENT   501

PART VII   CONTEMPORARY ISSUES   687

List of Exhibits and Case Studies

PART I
Decision to Internationalize

1. The Concept of International Marketing

The Concept of International Marketing

INTRODUCTION

Selling goods to international markets is not new to India and other Asian countries. The existence of international trade is traceable to 3000 BC in India (Exhibit 1.1) when the Indian goods reached the markets of Persia, Mesopotamia, Egypt, and other parts of South East Asia. The Silk Road from Xian to Rome connected the Eastern and the Western markets for regular trade and commerce.

During the last century, marketing activities around the world witnessed an unprecedented change. It was only during the latter half of the 20th century when large US, European, and Japanese companies expanded their markets as well as production facilities beyond national borders. The breakthroughs in information and communication technology and means of transport have contributed to the convergence in tastes and preferences of the consumers around the world. Besides consumers, competitors too have become global in their outlook and approach to business and are ready to experiment and adopt different competitive marketing strategies in various markets. All these developments have led to interdependency in international trade between nations.

Income growth has triggered the consumers' desire for more and newer varieties of goods, thereby creating markets for foreign products. All these factors have reinforced one another in the international market. Lower trade barriers have triggered a new global organization of production to take advantage of diversity in comparative advantage across the world. Desire for new products and search for new markets have provided strong incentives for lower trade barriers. Besides, technological progress and income growth have been spurred by increased global competition and efficiency gains through global networks.

International trade has over-performed world output in recent years. World output during 1994–2003 grew at an average rate of 3.4 per cent, whereas the world trade grew at 6.9 per cent during

Learning Objectives

- To highlight the significance of international marketing
- To understand globalization and its marketing implications
- To explain the concept of international marketing
- To delineate the evolutionary process of global marketing
- To develop a theoretical background of international trade
- To identify the reasons for entering international markets
- To expound the international marketing framework

Exhibit 1.1   India's march towards international markets through the ages

The tradition of international trade can be traced back to the days of Indus valley civilization in 3000 BC when trade between India, Mesopotamia, and Egypt was a regular phenomenon. The merchant class was wealthy and evidently played an important role. There was a colony of Indian merchants living at Memphis in Egypt around 5th century BC as the discovery of modelled heads of Indians there has shown. Probably, India traded with the island countries of South East Asia also.

Gordon Childe writes, 'Manufactures from the Indus cities reached even the markets on the Tigris and Euphrates. Conversely, a few Sumerian devices in art, Mesopotamia toilet sets, and a cylinder seal were copied on the Indus. Trade was not confined to raw materials and luxury articles; fish, regularly imported from the Arabian Sea coasts augmented the food supplies of Mohenjodaro.'[1]

Moreover, Childe's observation, 'It would seem to follow that the craftsmen of the Indus cities were, to a large extent, producing "for the market"' reveals their market-oriented approach, which was little known to the rest of the world at that time.

Throughout the first millennium of the Christian era, India's trade activities became widespread and Indian merchants controlled many foreign markets. It was a dominant force in the Eastern markets and it also reached out to the Mediterranean markets. Pepper and other spices were exported from India or via India to the West, often on Indian and Chinese boats, and it is said that Alaric the Goth took away 3,000 pounds of pepper from Rome. Roman writers bemoaned the fact that gold flowed from Rome to India and other Eastern countries in exchange for various luxury articles.

Source: Adapted from Nehru, Jawahar Lal, *The Discovery of India*, The Signet Press, Calcutta, 1946.

this period. In the following decade, during 2004–2013, world trade output increased at the rate of 3.9 per cent, whereas world trade grew at 5.4 per cent (Fig. 1.1). Growing importance of trade in world economy is indicative of increasing global integration. As a result, exports have gained increasing significance for national economies and companies alike, making international marketing crucial not only for growth but also for their survival.

The process of liberalization and the integration of national economic policies with the World Trade Organization (WTO) framework have accelerated the process of internationalization for home-based companies and have created marketing opportunities for overseas firms in the home market. Innovative marketing tactics such as cross-subsidization of production, neo-marketing

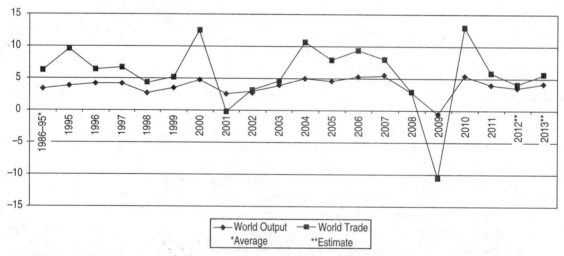

Fig. 1.1   Faster growth of world trade vis-à-vis world output implies growing significance of international marketing

Source: 'Overview of the World Economic Outlook Projections', *World Economic Outlook*, International Monetary Fund, January 2011.

---

[1] Childe, Gordon, *What Happened in History*, Pelican Books, 1943, p. 112.

barriers, marketing strategies to circumvent the same, and global market segments have become the order of the day. Under the emerging marketing scenario, the significance of developing a thorough understanding of international marketing has become crucial for not only those who operate in international markets but also for those operating domestically.

In the last decade, the number of Indian firms venturing into international markets rose consistently. With the liberal foreign exchange policies, Indian firms are moving towards establishing foreign operations and international acquisitions. The global recognition of Indian products and brands not only facilitate India's positive image worldwide, but also in turn gives recognition to them back home in India.

The present chapter delineates the concept of globalization and its marketing implications. Unprecedented integration in telecommunication, travel, transport, technology, and a move towards reduction of international marketing barriers have resulted in the opening up of marketing opportunities across the borders. Consequently, an increasing number of firms have established their manufacturing and marketing operations at the most competitive locations. In the recent years, the focus of international marketing has shifted from selling to marketing with greater emphasis on identifying and satisfying customers' needs and wants across the national borders. The chapter also clarifies the distinction between various terms such as foreign marketing, comparative marketing, international trade, international business, international marketing, and global or world marketing. The basic distinction in making decisions for international markets vis-à-vis domestic market lies in the environmental challenges a firm comes across, which vary to a much greater extent in cross-border markets compared to domestic markets. The process of internationalization has also been explained with the help of ethnocentric, polycentric, regiocentric, and geocentric (EPRG) model to show how a purely domestic firm enters international markets and subsequently becomes global in operation. The significance of adaptation, which is a critical success factor for international markets, has also been emphasized.

Theories of international trade such as theory of mercantilism, absolute advantage, factor endowment theory, product life cycle, and theory of competitive advantage have also been explained. The reasons for entering international markets such as growth, profitability, economies of scale, risks spread, spreading R&D cost, and access to imported inputs have also been discussed.

The chapter also brings out a conceptual framework of international marketing, which provides a blueprint for a firm's march towards the global markets. At the end of the chapter, a brief account of growing significance of emerging economies has also been given.

GLOBALIZATION AND ITS MARKETING IMPLICATIONS

In today's world, it is hard to imagine one's daily routine without the involvement of an 'international' component. Customers worldwide use a computer, tab, or laptop with a US, Japanese, or Korean brand, made in China, using software patented in the US, developed by an Indian engineer based at Hong Kong or Singapore. The entire value chain of the products has become so global that it becomes often too difficult to identify the real 'country of origin' of the product. Irrespective of the country one is located in, people begin a typical day by using a 'Colgate', 'Crest', or 'Pepsodent' toothpaste locally manufactured by transnational corporations, Colgate-Palmolive, Proctor & Gamble, or Unilever, respectively. Personal care brands of everyday use such as 'Lux', 'Lifebuoy', 'Dettol', 'Ariel', 'Gillette', 'Pantene', 'Olay', 'Whisper', 'Oral-B' 'L'Oreal', and 'Revlon' have gained popularity and are being used worldwide (Fig. 1.2). Frequent calls are made by customers across the world using mobile phones made by 'Nokia', 'samsung', 'Apple', 'Blackberry', 'Motorola', or 'Ericsson'. We often use consumer electronics including

Fig. 1.2 Marketing across borders made several products household names worldwide

Sources: http://all-free-download.com/free-photos/aluminum_can_coca_236719_download.html; http://all-free-download.com/free-photos/old_mobile_phone_201593_download.html; http://www.flickr.com/photos/justusbluemer/6045397356/in/photostream/; http://all-free-download.com/free-photos/digital_slr_185877.html; and http://commons.wikimedia.org/wiki/File:Cadbury_Dairy_Milk_2006.jpg, all accessed on 2 April 2014.

an air-conditioner, refrigerator, microwave, washing machine, TV, camera, etc. made by multi-national firms such as Sony, Philips, Panasonic, Toshiba, LG, Samsung, and Haier with global operations and supply chains networks. Readers would find it difficult even to imagine their daily lives without 'foreign' component making our lives de facto 'global'.

Understanding Globalization

In management circles, globalization is widely understood to imply 'economic globalization' by way of free movement of factor inputs (both labour and capital) as well as output between countries. In real sense, globalization is much more than merely economic integration of countries, as it also comprises various other aspects, such as financial, cultural, and political integration across the world, as depicted in Fig. 1.3. Thus, taking a holistic view, Joshi defines globalization[2] as 'the process of integration and convergence of economic, financial, cultural, and political systems across the world brought about by breakthroughs in information and communication technology (ICT) and means of transport and the breaking down of artificial barriers to the flow of goods and services, capital, knowledge, and (to a lesser extent) people across the borders'. It is a historical process of moving at different speeds in different countries and in different sectors.

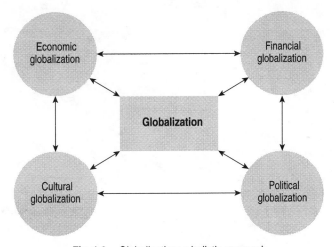

Fig. 1.3 Globalization: a holistic approach

Source: Joshi, Rakesh Mohan, *International Business*, Oxford University Press, New Delhi, 2009, p. 9.

From the perspective of a marketer, globalization refers to 'the increasing economic integration and interdependence of national economies across the world through a rapid increase in cross-border movement of goods, service, technology, and capital'.[3] It is indeed a process of economic integration of the entire world through the removal of barriers to free trade and capital mobility as well as through the diffusion of knowledge and information. Globalization is characterized by growing interdependence of various facets. For instance, foreign direct investment (FDI) is accompanied by transfer of technology and know-how, along with the movement of capital (equity, international loans, repatriation of profits, interest, royalties, etc.) generating exports of goods and services from the investor countries. Global firms rely on technological innovation to enhance their capabilities. In this sense, technology is both driven by and is a driver of globalization.

---

[2] Joshi, Rakesh Mohan, *International Business*, Oxford University Press, New Delhi, 2009, p. 9.

[3] Joshi, Rakesh Mohan, *International Business*, Oxford University Press, New Delhi, 2009, p. 9.

The process of globalization for a firm mainly consists of globalization of production and globalization of markets.

Globalization of production

Globalization of production has led to multinational origin of product components, services, and capital as a result of transnational collaborations among business enterprises. The firms evaluate various locations worldwide for manufacturing activities so as to take advantage of local resources and optimize their manufacturing competitiveness. The firms from the USA, the EU, and Japan manufacture at overseas locations more than three times of their exports output produced in their home country. The intra-firm export–import transactions constitute about one-third of their international trade. Toyota, one of the world's leading automakers, has its operations worldwide and manages its supply-chain on global basis. It has a total of 51 overseas manufacturing companies in 26 countries and markets (Fig. 1.4) and markets cars worldwide through its overseas network consisting of more than 170 importers/distributors[4] and numerous dealers.

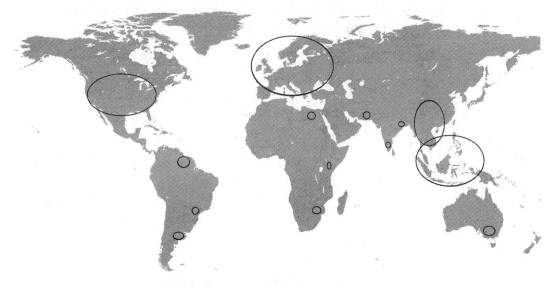

Number of distributors (as of May 2013)

Region	Manufacturing companies	Distributors
North America	11	5
Latin America	4	41
Europe	8	30
Africa	3	44
Asia (excluding Japan)	24	16
Oceania	1	15
Middle East	1	16
Overseas total	**52**	**167**

Fig. 1.4   Toyota's worldwide marketing and manufacturing operations

[4] As per company sources, March 2012.

Globalization of markets

Marketing gurus in the last two decades have extensively argued over the benefits of globalization of markets over customized marketing strategies. Prof. Theodore Levitt in his path-breaking paper[5] 'Globalization of Markets' strongly argued in favour of the emergence of global markets at a previously unimagined magnitude. Technology as the most powerful force has driven the world towards converging commonality. Technological strides in telecommunication, transport, and travel have created a new consumer segment in the isolated places of the world. Prof. Kenichi Ohmae also advocates the concept of a borderless world and need for universal products for global markets.[6] Standardized products are increasingly finding markets across the globe. The products from global brands such as Nokia, Coke, Kodak, Colgate, Sony, General Electric, and Benetton are few of the several brands preferred and bought by the consumers around the world. Such globalization of the world market has increased the scope for marketing activities internationally and has also increased the competitive intensity of the global brands in the market.

Measuring Globalization

Although quantifying globalization is difficult, a number of approaches have been used to measure it. As marketing managers are especially concerned about economic globalization that affects businesses the most, it can be measured based on the trade openness of a country, FDI inflows and outflows, capital account restriction, trade barriers, etc.

Trade openness

The trade openness of a country can be measured as the percentage share of total trade (imports plus exports) in the total GDP. Smaller countries with limited resources and relatively higher level of economic liberalization such as Luxemburg, Singapore, and Hong Kong tend to rank higher in terms of their trade openness, whereas countries with large domestic economies such as the USA, China, Brazil, Japan, and India rank lower. Countries with higher degree of trade openness generally grew relatively faster compared to those with low trade openness. Switzerland is home to the largest number of the world's top global companies in relation to its population followed by the USA, Scandinavia, Britain, Belgium, Netherlands, and France.[7] Developing economies have become more open,[8] as their ratio of total trade to total GDP rose considerably from 34 per cent in 1990 to 62 per cent in 2008.

Globalization index

A holistic approach to assess globalization is adopted under the KOF overall index of globalization based on three sub-indices, which are as follows.

Economic globalization This refers to the long-distance flows of goods, capital, and services as well as information and perceptions that accompany market exchanges.

Social globalization This is characterized by the spread of ideas, information, images, and people.

Political globalization This is expressed as a diffusion of government policies.

Each of the above indices is allocated different weights: economic globalization (36%), social globalization (38%), and political globalization (26%). In constructing the indices of globalization, each of the aforementioned variables is transformed to an index on a scale of one to hundred,

---

[5] Levitt, Theodore, 'Globalization of Markets', *Harvard Business Review*, May/June 1983.

[6] Ohmae, Kenichi, *Harvard Business Review*, May/June 1989.

[7] 'Tomorrow the World', *The Economist*, 10 February 2007, pp. 5–6.

[8] *World Development Indicators*, World Bank, 2011.

where hundred is the maximum value for a specific variable over the period 1970 to 2008, and one is the minimum value. Higher values denote higher degree of globalization. The indices enable empirical comparison of globalization trends during the period.[9]

Belgium tops in overall globalization with a score of 92.76 under the KOF index of globalization, as shown in Table 1.1, followed by Ireland (91.95), Netherland (90.94), Austria (90.55), and Singapore (89.18), whereas the UK ranks at 14th place with a score of 85.54, the USA at 35th (74.88), China at 73rd (59.37), India at 110th (51.88), and Virgin Islands (USA) ranks at the last.

Table 1.1   KOF index of globalization, 2012

Rank	Country	Overall globalization index	Economic globalization	Social globalization	Political globalization
1	Belgium	92.76	92.15	89.75	97.91
2	Ireland	91.95	93.27	91.43	90.86
3	Netherlands	90.94	91.91	87.87	93.99
4	Austria	90.55	85.98	90.28	97.31
5	Singapore	89.18	97.39	91.04	75.10
6	Sweden	88.23	88.98	82.13	95.86
14	UK	85.54	77.73	85.50	96.43
15	Canada	85.53	76.05	88.72	94.16
18	France	84.12	72.41	85.65	98.21
21	Australia	81.60	76.26	79.65	91.77
22	Germany	81.53	72.52	82.16	93.15
29	Malaysia	77.43	76.38	73.11	85.05
33	United Arab Emirates	75.69	88.74	77.91	54.40
35	USA	74.88	60.83	76.24	92.47
47	Russian Federation	67.35	54.56	66.96	85.69
53	South Africa	64.42	65.81	46.83	87.52
55	Japan	64.13	45.84	64.57	88.91
61	Saudi Arabia	62.34	NA	69.37	52.33
73	China	59.37	51.25	48.09	86.70
74	Brazil	59.36	53.54	40.69	94.02
75	Egypt	59.35	48.80	45.31	94.02
110	India	51.88	43.73	31.67	91.98
162	Tanzania	39.42	43.46	21.78	58.90
176	Myanmar	33.57	50.96	15.42	35.23
208	Virgin Islands (USA)	NA	NA	NA	2.66

Source: KOF Swiss Economic Institute, Zurich, 2012.

---

[9] Axel, Dreher, Noel Gaston, and Pim Martens, *Measuring Globalization—Gauging Its Consequence*, Springer, New York, 2008.

Impact of Globalization on Present-day Marketing

In the earlier era of restrictive trade and investment regimes with much lower degree of interconnectedness among countries, companies solely operating in their home markets were generally protected and isolated from the vagaries of upheavals in the international marketing environment. Globalization tends to erode national boundaries and integrates national economies, cultures, technologies, and governance leading to complex relations of mutual interdependence.

In fact, globalization is a matter of necessity when a country is a flyweight. Reaching out beyond national borders is the only way to find new opportunities for tiny countries. Countries such as Singapore and the Netherlands lack natural resources. Small countries, such as Ireland and Denmark, can hardly rely upon their domestic markets to sustain large scale production the way the USA, India, and China can. Thus, these countries hardly have an option other than to open up their economies and attract trade and investment to be globally competitive. Globalization not only opens up new opportunities, but also offers numerous challenges with worldwide implications to business enterprises as follows.

Breaking down of marketing boundaries

Breakthroughs in the means of transport and communication technology in the last few decades have made international communication, transport, and travel much cheaper, faster, and more frequent. The changes induced by the dynamics of trade, capital flows, and transfer of technology have made markets and production of different countries increasingly interdependent.

The establishment of World Trade Organization in 1995 resulted into significant increase in market-access for cross-border trade, reduction of tariffs, and a rule-based multilateral trading system. Companies, whose output had long been limited by the size of their domestic market, now have the chance to reap greater advantages from economies of scale by 'being global'. Economic liberalization especially in trade and invest regulations has greatly facilitated marketing of goods at global scale.

Intensifying competition

The opening up of national economies after 1990s, especially in the emerging markets by way of considerable reduction in tariffs and rationalization restrictions, has led to influx of foreign products in hitherto protected markets. Moreover, domestic firms are increasingly challenged from multinationals. This has greatly intensified the market competitions.

Simultaneous competition in markets between numerous new competitors across the world is intensifying. Such globalization of competition has resulted in the emergence of new strategic transnational alliances among companies across the world. Increasingly, more firms need to compete with new international players in their own markets as well as foreign ones. To cope with global competition, firms need to simultaneously harness the skills and generate synergy by a broad range of specialized skills, such as technological, financial, industrial, commercial, cultural, and administrative skills, located in different countries or even different continents. This offers tremendous challenge to existing business competitiveness of firms compelling them to globalize and make rapid structural changes.

The growing intensity of international competition has increased the need for cross-border strategic interactions, necessitating companies to organize themselves into transnational networks.

Rising economic instability and market volatility

Increased integration between various economies has made countries more prone to economic upheavals elsewhere in the world leading to increased instability in the markets. As the forces of integration between various countries continue to grow, national economies are likely to become more instable in future and volatility of markets is likely to be ever increasing. If marketers expect anything to be certain in future, it is the ever-rising level of uncertainty in the markets across the world. Therefore, the secret of survival in the present-day marketing is the ability of businesses to anticipate the forthcoming challenges as precisely as possible and reorient their marketing strategies.

Ever-increasing customer sophistication

The increase in the disposable income of the consuming class the world over has made the customers identify with their distinctive needs and wants. Customers are becoming more and more demanding in terms of product features and quality. This has exerted tremendous pressure on marketers to bring out quality products with additional features so as to meet the growing customer aspirations.

Growing fragmentation of markets

Contrary to the fact that customer preferences are conversing at global scale, customers are getting increasingly demanding and want products and services to be tailored and delivered to their specific requirements. This would require a fundamental shift in firms' strategies from mass marketing to mass customization.

Increased product diversification

In quest to compete in the market, companies are compelled to bring out a large range of products to cater to all segments of the customers. Intensifying competition has forced marketers to conceptualize positioning a product against those of their competitors. This has led to proliferation of products in the markets to the extent that even the marketers hardly hesitate to confuse the customers in case they fail to convince them.

Shortening of product life cycles

In quest to compete in the marketplace as a strategic response to growing insatiable customer aspirations, companies are developing and launching new products much more frequently than ever before. Product obsolescence is often built-in or induced by the companies as a part of their strategic intent. Bringing out newer and newer products that too at amazingly higher frequency vis-à-vis competitors has led to shortening of product life cycles. To illustrate, computers, mobiles, IT applications, and luxury items are increasingly having shorter life cycles.

Proliferation of global brands

Global reach of marketing, significant rise in spending power, and sophistication of customers worldwide has led to increase in demand for global brands than ever before. Branding has become a strategic edge to the marketers. Since commodities as common as drinking water, salt, milk, editable oils, sugar, tea, spices, etc. are increasingly getting branded, to compete with the rivals, companies are launching new brands too frequently to the extent that there has been virtual 'commoditization' of brands in the market. Successful companies are those that could build brands with worldwide reach.

Growing pervasiveness of e-marketing

The widespread use of Internet, computers, and mobile devices with numerous applications is not only 'user friendly', but has also become too 'customer fascinating' to abstain. The revolution in ICT in the last two decades has also made communication much cheaper and faster. The transaction costs of transferring ideas and information have decreased enormously and the arrival of the Internet has accelerated this trend. Innovations in on-line banking systems and payment gateways have contributed to rapid penetration of e-marketing globally.

CONCEPT OF INTERNATIONAL MARKETING

International marketing is a sub-system of marketing. With changes in the discipline of marketing, it has evolved both as a concept and as a branch of study, and has become more complex and interesting.

Marketing Fundamentals

In the mid 1950s, the orientation of markets shifted from selling to marketing. Earlier, under the selling concept, the focus was on selling products through aggressive selling and sales promotion programmes leading to sales maximization, which in turn was expected to maximize a firm's profit earnings. On the other hand, under the marketing concept, the target market is the starting point and the focus is on customers' needs. The profit maximization under the marketing concept is achieved through customer satisfaction by way of integrated marketing efforts. Prof. Theodore Levitt explains this distinction by stating that selling focuses on the needs of the sellers, whereas marketing focuses on the needs of the buyers. Selling is preoccupied with the seller's need to convert his product into cash; marketing involves the idea of satisfying the needs of the customers by means of the product and the whole cluster of things associated with creating, delivering, and finally consuming it.[10] However, Prof. Peter Drucker opines that there would always be need for some selling. But the aim of marketing is to make selling superfluous. The aim of marketing is to know and understand a customer so well that the product or service satisfies him and sells itself. Ideally, marketing should result in a customer who is ready to buy. All that is needed then is to make the product or service available.[11]

The marketing guru Philip Kotler defines marketing as 'the human activity directed at satisfying needs and wants through exchange processes'. Achieving customer satisfaction is given the utmost importance in the marketing concept as getting a new customer costs much more (estimated to be five times) than retaining an existing one.[12] It is likely to cost 16 times as much to bring the new customer to the same level of profitability as the lost customer.[13] Emphasizing exchange processes, the *American Marketing Association* defines marketing as the process of planning and executing the conception, pricing, promotion, and distribution of ideas, goods, and services to create exchanges that satisfy individual and organizational goals. With manifold increase in competitive intensity in the present marketing era, the focus is shifting fast to market orientation. Under the traditional concept, a responsive marketer finds a stated need and fulfils it. A step further is the anticipative marketer who looks ahead at the customer's needs in the near future. However, a creative marketer discovers and produces solutions that a customer did not ask for but would enthusiastically respond to. Products such as Walkman, VCRs, CDs, ATMs, and mobile phones are illustrations of creative marketing.

International Marketing: The Concept

The fundamental principles of marketing, especially related to its technical aspects in domestic and international markets, remain more or less the same. However, the differences in marketing environment make international marketing a distinct discipline. In simple terms, international marketing is defined as the marketing activities carried out across national boundaries. Every firm has to operate in a given set of environmental factors on which it has little control. Although the fundamentals of marketing remain the same and have universal applicability, the flexibility of

[10] Levitt, Theodore, 'Marketing Myopia', *Harvard Business Review*, September–October 1975, pp. 26–48.
[11] Drucker, Peter, *Management: Tasks, Responsibilities, Practices*, Harper and Row, New York, 1973, pp. 64–65.
[12] Sellers, Patricia, 'Getting Customers to Love You', *Fortune*, 13 March 1989, pp. 38–49.
[13] Kotler, Philip, *Marketing Management*, 11th Edition, Prentice Hall of India Pvt. Ltd, New Delhi.

marketing decisions is limited by a variety of uncontrollable factors, such as social, economic, political, legal, and technological environment. These environmental factors are known as uncontrollable elements on which a marketer hardly has any influence, but the marketing challenge is to adapt the controllable elements of marketing mix, that is, product, price, distribution, and promotion, so as to ensure marketing success.

Cateora and Graham (2002) defines international marketing as the performance of business activities designed to plan, price, promote, and direct the flow of company's goods and services to consumers or users in more than one nation for a profit.[14] International marketing takes place when marketing/trade is carried out 'across the border' or between 'more than one nation'. Global marketing is the process of focusing the resources and objectives of an organization on global marketing opportunities and needs.[15] International marketing is all about identifying and satisfying global customers' needs better than the competitors, both domestic and international, and coordinating marketing activities within the constraints of the global environment.[16]

Consequent to economic liberalization, a firm operating in domestic market can no longer rely upon its home market because the firm's home market is now an export market for everybody else. It was believed earlier that in order to compete in the international markets, a firm needs to be competitive in the domestic market. But in view of the liberal economic policies, the Indian firms are now required to compete with international firms in the domestic market also. Therefore, in order to remain domestically competitive, a firm needs to be internationally competitive. As a strategic response to globalization of markets, Indian firms need to follow a proactive approach and learn to transform the emerging marketing threats and challenges to their benefit. It makes international market relevant even for firms operating solely in domestic markets.

Thus, international marketing would involve

- identifying needs and wants of customers in international markets;
- taking marketing mix decisions related to product, pricing, distribution, and communication keeping in view the diverse consumer and market behaviour across different countries on one hand and firms' goals towards globalization on the other hand;
- penetrating into international markets using various modes of entry; and
- taking decisions in view of dynamic international marketing environment.

The distinction between international and domestic marketing mainly arises due to the differences in the challenges a firm has to face in the marketing environments, which are invariably much more grave than what a firm faces while operating exclusively in domestic markets. Since the environmental challenges are beyond the control of a marketer, the key to success in international markets lies in responding competitively by adopting an effective marketing strategy.

Terms in International Marketing

The readers should develop a thorough understanding of the nuances of commonly used terms[17] in international marketing, which are sometimes used interchangeably. Some of these terms are as follows.

Domestic marketing   These are the marketing practices within the domestic markets.

---

[14] Cateora, Philip R. and John L. Graham, *International Marketing*, 11th Edition, Tata McGraw-Hill, New Delhi, 2002.

[15] Keegan, Warren J., *Global Marketing Management*, Pearson Education (Singapore) Pvt. Ltd, New Delhi, 2002.

[16] Terpstra, Vern and Ravi Sarathy, *International Marketing*, Harcourt Asia Pte Ltd, New Delhi, 2000.

[17] Adapted from Onkvisit, Sak and J. John Shaw, *International Marketing—Analysis and Strategy*, Prentice Hall of India Private Limited, New Delhi, 1997.

to a varying degree by the Uppsala model. The evolution of marketing across national boundaries has five identifiable stages,[22] which are as follows.

Domestic Marketing

In the initial stages, most companies focus solely on their domestic markets (Fig. 1.6). The marketing mix decisions are invariably based on the needs and wants of the domestic customers. These decisions are taken so as to respond competitively and effectively to the domestic environmental factors. With the implementation of liberal trade policies, the Indian market also has domestic as well as foreign competitors. The marketing of most companies in the initial stages tend to be ethnocentric, paying little attention to changes taking place in the international marketing environment as a result of the arrival of new products and brands in the market, the effect of tastes and preferences of international customers on the domestic market, and the emergence of new market segments. Ethnocentrism is defined as the predisposition of a firm to be predominantly concerned with its viability and legitimacy only in its home country. The strategic actions of such companies are similar to domestic responses in such situations. This ethnocentric approach makes domestic companies vulnerable to changes forced upon them by foreign competition. Neglect of competition from low-cost Japanese manufacturers of consumer electronics by the US manufacturers in the 1960s and 1970s as a result of their ethnocentric approach was the major reason behind their inability to cope with forced competition in the US market.

Domestic marketing	
Market focus	Domestic
Orientation	Ethnocentric
Marketing mix decisions	Focused on domestic customers

Fig. 1.6 Evolution of global marketing (Stage I)

Export Marketing

The stage models suggest that generally a firm focused on domestic markets begins to export (Fig. 1.7) unintentionally by receiving unsolicited orders from overseas markets. The firm tries to fulfil such orders reluctantly with little strategic orientation. Thus, the initial entry of a firm

Export marketing	
Marketing focus	Overseas (Targeting and entering foreign markets)
Orientation	Ethnocentric
Marketing mix decisions	• Focused mainly on domestic customers • Overseas marketing—generally an extension of domestic marketing • Decisions made at headquarters

Fig. 1.7 Evolution of global marketing (Stage II)

---

[22] Adapted from Chakravarthy, Bajaj S. and Howard V. Perlmutter, 'Strategic Planning for a Global Business', *Columbia Journal of World Business*, Summer 1985; Douglas, S.P. and C. Samuel Craig, 'Evolution of Global Marketing Strategy: Scale, Scope and Synergy', *Columbia Journal of World Business*, Fall 1989; and Kotabe, Masaaki and Kristiaan Helsen, *Global Marketing Management*, Second Edition, John Wiley & Sons Inc., Singapore, 2001.

in international markets may be characterized as a consequence of responding to unsolicited export enquiries. However, the positive experience in fulfilling such overseas market requirements serves as a stimulus to look for repeat orders.

The motivating factors that lead to increased interest in the overseas markets include additional marketing outlets for the firm, less dependence on the domestic markets, risk spread, and increased profitability. The impact of these motivators may differ depending upon the characteristics of domestic markets such as size, maturity, and competitive intensity.

Initially, a firm solely focused on the domestic market has little exposure and experience to operate in international markets. Therefore, assistance from an export market intermediary, such as trading houses, is generally sought, which is popularly known as indirect exporting. As a result of operating in overseas markets indirectly, in due course, the firm develops backward linkages and product customization to suit the foreign market need. It also gains the know-how and experience of operating in international markets, and eventually it exports directly without the help of any market intermediary. However, the approach of the firm still remains ethnocentric as it uses the marketing mix strategies similar to the domestic markets. Foreign markets are considered just an extension of the domestic market. The major marketing decision areas at this stage include market identification and selection, timing, and sequencing of entry and selection of an appropriate entry mode. The marketing mix decisions are primarily made at the headquarters.

International Marketing

Over a period of time, the exporting company starts catering to the specific needs of a few overseas markets (Fig. 1.8) and establishes noticeable share in the market. The growing prominence of the company triggers the existing market players to devise and implement fiercely competitive marketing strategies so as to maintain their presence and supremacy in the market. Besides, the physical distance of an exporting firm also increases the psychic distance and the local companies are in a better position to respond to the market forces vis-à-vis foreign competitors due to their proximity to the market. This necessitates the adaptation of different marketing strategies for different markets to face the marketing challenges of the specific markets. It is known as polycentric orientation, in which product and promotional adaptations are often made.

International marketing	
Marketing focus	Differentiation in country markets by way of developing or acquiring new brands
Orientation	Polycentric
Marketing mix decisions	• Developing local products depending upon country needs • Decisions by individual subsidiaries

Fig. 1.8 Evolution of global marketing (Stage III)

Thus, polycentric orientation refers to the predisposition of a firm to the existence of significant cultural variations across the markets. It recognizes the differences among markets and the need to respond to the market forces with market-specific strategies. The polycentric strategy has a strong orientation towards the target markets. The products are manufactured in the home country with separate product adaptation for different markets. However, the marketing decisions, such as decisions about product development, branding, distribution, pricing, and promotion, are taken independently by the marketing department in each country.

The extreme form of international marketing is multi-domestic marketing, in which a company establishes an independent foreign subsidiary in each and every foreign market. The foreign subsidiaries operate independently without any measurable control from the headquarters.[23] Each subsidiary is free to take decisions about product development, manufacturing, pricing, distribution, product positioning, and market promotion. Since there is little synergy in a company's international operations, economies of scale is hardly achieved. Therefore, multi-domestic marketing is viable and effective only when differences among the markets justify individual market strategies for each market in terms of increased market share, sales volume, or profit.

Multinational Marketing

Once a company establishes its manufacturing and marketing operations in multiple markets (Fig. 1.9), it begins to consolidate its operations on regional basis so as to take advantage of economies of scale in manufacturing and marketing mix decisions. Various markets are divided into regional sub-segments on the basis of their similarity to respond to marketing mix decisions. It is known as multinational marketing, in which marketing mix decisions are standardized within the region but not across the region. Marketing mix decisions are based on regional basis, which brings economies of scale.

Multinational marketing	
Marketing focus	• Consolidation of operations on regional basis • Gains from economies of scale
Orientation	Regiocentric
Marketing mix decisions	• Product standardization within regions but not across them • On regional basis

Fig. 1.9   Evolution of global marketing (Stage IV)

Global Marketing

The extreme view of global marketing (Fig. 1.10) refers to the use of a single marketing method across the international markets with little adaptation. As promulgated by Levitt,[24] the globalization of markets leads to

- reduction of cost inefficiencies and duplication of efforts among national and regional subsidiaries;
- opportunities for the transfer of products; brands, and other ideas across subsidiaries
- emergence of global customers; and
- improved linkages among national marketing infrastructures leading to the development of a global marketing infrastructure.

In practice, global marketing hardly means complete standardization of the marketing mix decisions, but it increasingly means a strategic approach to have a global perspective to have economies of scale. Higher volumes of production and sales result into reduction in cost per unit due to 'experience curve' effects and increased efficiency in activities mainly related to

---

[23] Kotabe, Masaaki and Kristiaan Helsen, *Global Marketing Management*, Second Edition, John Wiley & Sons Inc., Singapore, 2001.
[24] Levitt, Teodore, 'The Globalization of Markets', *Harvard Business Review*, 61, May–July 1983, pp. 92–102.

	Global marketing
Marketing focus	Consolidating firm's operations on global basis
Orientation	Geocentric
Marketing mix decisions	• Globalization of marketing mix decisions with local variations • Joint decision-making across firm's global operations

Fig. 1.10   Evolution of global marketing (Stage V)

production, resource management, and marketing. Economies of scope refer to the synergy effect as a result of the firms catering to global markets as far as feasible to meet the challenges of the global markets. The objective is to find out some commonality in the customers' needs and strive for a uniform marketing strategy as far as feasible in various country markets.

Towards GLOCAL Marketing

The process of internationalization, summarized in Fig. 1.11, follows an evolutionary process. The internationalization process appears to be evolutionary in nature emanating from domestic marketing. As a firm gets motivated to enter international markets as a result of several factors described in Fig. 1.5, it enters international markets initially by way of exporting. Generally, indirect exports precede the direct exports till the time the firm builds up its own capability to handle export marketing. The complexity in handling overseas markets increases as compared to domestic markets. The gains in terms of increased profitability, market share, or strategic advantage in the overseas markets act as a positive stimulus. This draws the competitors' attention, who initiate a fiercely competitive marketing strategy in the country markets. It necessitates the firm to adopt individual marketing approaches in different markets. Such polycentric approach increases the marketing complexity for the firm and the company adopts international marketing. However, over a period, the firm consolidates its gains in the international markets and adopts a regiocentric approach, wherein the marketing

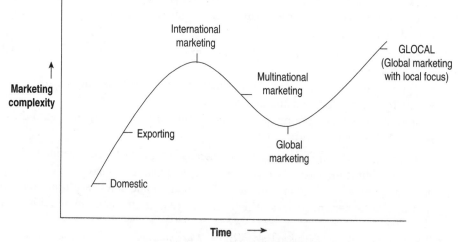

Fig. 1.11   Process of internationalization

strategies are standardized within the regions but not across the regions, and this is known as multinational marketing. It reduces the marketing complexity and adds some synergy to the marketing mix decisions.

The gains in multinational marketing are further consolidated when the firm tries to identify the similarities in various markets across the globe and standardize the marketing mix as far as feasible. Under this geocentric orientation, the firm follows global marketing with standardization of marketing mix to the extent possible with a few local variations. It may be observed that the complexity of marketing tasks varies with the type of marketing practised and the economies of scale achieved. As achieving greater market share and improved profitability is more critical to a firm rather than achieving economies of scale, the global marketing firm finds it difficult to overlook the local expectations and finer marketing nuances. Besides, the growing level of expectations of the target market necessitates the global firms to give more attention to the customers in view of their local requirements. Thus, the term GLOCAL refers to global marketing with a local focus. One needs to stop thinking of home-country market mindset and start playing by the rules of the target market. This in turn increases the marketing complexity for a firm, but helps it to fulfil the customer expectations more competitively and secure greater market share.

ADAPTATION: THE CRITICAL SUCCESS FACTOR IN INTERNATIONAL MARKETS

A firm operating in international markets is subjected to environmental factors that are substantially different from the domestic market and also among overseas markets. Therefore, the key to success in international markets lies in a marketer's ability to adapt the company's strategies to the requirements of the overseas markets. An international marketing manager has to make a conscious effort to anticipate the effect of both domestic and foreign uncontrollable environmental factors on a marketing mix and then adjust the marketing mix accordingly to enable the firm to compete in the overseas market successfully, as explained in Exhibit 1.2.

However, the ability of an international marketer to have an objective evaluation of environmental factors on the marketing mix is severely affected by his cultural conditioning and understanding of the nuances of another culture. The self-reference criterion (SRC) is an unconscious reference to one's own cultural values, experiences, and knowledge as a basis for decision-making. A person from one culture is often not aware that reaction to any situation is influenced by one's own cultural background and is interpreted in different cultural situations in different perspectives. Market relativism is in fact a subtle and unintended result of cultural conditioning.

When one is faced with a specific set of marketing situations overseas, one is prone to misjudge and erroneously react to the marketing situation. For instance, an Indian firm planning to operate in the Chinese market may apparently find the Chinese market quite huge.

In order to arrive at an objective marketing decision, one has to isolate the influences of SRC while carrying out a cross-cultural analysis as discussed in Chapter 5.

The largest global fast food marketer McDonald's faced quite a few challenges while entering the Indian market. Besides statutory provisions to prohibit cow slaughter in most Indian states, consumption of beef is unacceptable and is an extremely sensitive social issue in India. India is also home to the second largest Muslim population, which considers pork impious and its consumption is not permitted by religion. As a result, McDonald's does not serve either beef or pork in the Indian market. Moreover, the concept of vegetarianism in India is the most complex in the world wherein the slightest interchange even of the cooking and serving utensils is shunned. Therefore, India is the only country where McDonald's has got separate kitchen area as well as

Exhibit 1.2   Domestic marketing experience hardly works in international markets

Domestic marketing experiences often interfere in international markets. The past marketing experiences and strategies may actually act as a deterrent in international marketing efforts. The sheer gravity of one's memory of the domestic market keeps one pulling down towards set thinking and set procedures. Therefore, an international marketer needs to train himself to operate from a clear mind. One should venture into a new market without any preconceived notions and fill the mind with first-hand experiences and feelings, as every overseas market is unique, the people are different, and cultural responses are diverse too. However, the fundamentals remain the same—consumers 'behave'—but the way they behave varies from country to country. To illustrate this point, let us take the case of the Chinese market. The favourable growth factors in the Chinese market captivate the Indian companies to follow a low-price mass marketing strategy. For example, in the detergent powder product segment, Indian companies believe that as both are oriental countries, have similar markets, and similar backgrounds, they would also have similar needs for washing clothes, similar drives for wanting whiteness, and similar economic aspirations.

However, past experiences in mass marketing reveal that marketing strategies adopted in India can hardly be replicated without any adaptation in an apparently similar overseas market. For instance, the popular Indian detergent Nirma created marketing history in India by shifting the product category of detergents to the low-price segment from the high-price market segment, which is difficult to work in the Chinese market. The unique selling proposition (USP) of Nirma in the Indian market was its bottom down prices. Any reduction in product pricing so as to replicate Nirma's mass marketing experiment in the Chinese market would necessitate some compromise in the quality of the product. Moreover, in the Chinese market, a good-quality detergent is available to its customers through government-controlled marketing channels at a low price. Therefore, the marketing situation provides little flexibility for any compromise in the quality of the product as the customers are habituated to get the product virtually at no price. Such a situation poses a real challenge before an international marketer, which is not easy to overcome.

In India, shampoos and detergents are available in sachet packs mainly to induce trial among the non-existing customers and also to offer the convenience of a smaller pack. However, in the Chinese market, the market penetration for the product is already between 85 and 95 per cent and, therefore, such a strategy aimed at bringing new consumers into the ambit of the product users' category hardly serves any purpose. It may be interesting to note that the price of a sachet pack for detergent or shampoo in the Indian market is surprisingly cheaper than bigger packs, which are contrary to the basic marketing logic of quantity discounts. Under the Indian economic policy framework, the excise duty on packaging material for small-scale industries (SSI) sector is lower, which contributes to reduced cost of package.

The Indian experience also reveals that a consumer often attempts to emulate the behaviour of its peer group. The emotive side of the Indian consumer induces them to aspire to do better than their peers. But in China, the only recognized superiority is age. Moreover, there appears to be an extremely high level of contentment among the Chinese people. So the competitive side of life is missing there. It is quite confounding. The people hardly attempt to create or recognize some sort of difference between themselves. Culturally and socially, they have grown up in an environment where it is deeply ingrained that it is only time that will bring one prosperity or betterment vis-à-vis another, that one cannot be prosperous before one becomes old, and that one can be superior to one's neighbour only if one is elder. In such a scenario, there are no takers for the *Rin* kind of rhetoric, *Bhala uski sari meri sari se safed kaise?* (How can her cloth be whiter than mine?). Moreover, it does not appeal to the sensibilities of the Chinese people.

In this kind of an environment, advertisements such as *Safedi aisi ki nazar lag jaaye (Whiteness that creates envy)* and *Neighbour's envy, owner's pride* would lead to cognitive dissonance. Privately, one may feel good that her clothes look better, but socially such superiority is not acceptable in China. In a socially responsible environment, no marketer would want to exploit this overtly as it would be seen by the establishment, which still controls the business activities, as a defiance of the ethos that they have protected for decades. Therefore, comparative advertising is difficult to pursue in China.

Two markets that appear to be similar may actually be very different in terms of their behaviour and marketing dynamics. The marketing strategies that work in the domestic market are hardly going to work in the overseas markets. Marketing strategies should be implemented in the international markets after careful study.

utensils for cooking vegetarian and non-vegetarian preparations. Even among the non-vegetarian Indian consumers, red meat is not preferred which has compelled McDonald's to serve chicken burger. In response to the liking of Indian consumers for spicy food, McDonald's not only serves more spices in its preparations but it also serves sauces such as McMasala and McImli customized for the Indian palate. Moreover, in order to compete with popular Indian preparations, McDonald's also introduced McMaharaja and Chicken Tikka Burger in the Indian market.

EPRG Concept

The orientation of a company's personnel affects the ability of a company to adapt to any foreign marketing environment. The behavioural attributes of a firm's management in casual exports to global markets can be described under the ethnocentric, polycentric, regiocentric, and geocentric (EPRG) approach.[25] A key assumption underlying the EPRG framework is that the degree of internationalization to which the management is committed or willing to move affects the specific international strategies and decision rules of the firm.

Ethnocentric orientation

The belief that considers one's own culture as superior to others is termed as ethnocentric orientation. It means that a firm or its managers are so obsessed with the belief that the marketing strategy that has worked in the domestic market would also work in the international markets. Thus, ethnocentric companies ignore the environmental differences between markets. These companies generally indulge in domestic marketing. A few companies that do carry out export marketing consider it as an extension of domestic marketing. These companies believe that just like domestic marketing, export marketing too requires the minimum level of efforts to adapt the marketing mix to the needs of the overseas market. Generally, an exporting firm in the initial phases of internationalization relies too heavily on product expansion in international markets. For instance, most Indian handicraft exporters who are primarily from the small and medium-sized enterprises (SME) sector hardly appreciate the cultural differences and realize the need to adapt a marketing strategy in different countries.

Ethnocentric orientation may be of the following types:

* The firm becomes so accustomed to certain cause and effect relationships in import activities that certain cultural factors in overseas markets are overlooked. Managers need to analyse the cultural variables so as to consider all the major factors before taking a decision. For instance, most Indian handicraft exporters, which are primarily from the SME sector, hardly appreciate the market differences and need for adaptation of marketing strategy.
* The environmental differences are recognized by the management, but marketing strategy focuses on achieving home-country objectives rather than international or worldwide objectives. It leads to a decline in the long-term competitiveness of the firm as the firm fails to compete effectively against its competitors and show any resistance to their overseas marketing practices. The large size of the Indian market provides little motivation to firms to venture into the overseas market, or, even if overseas marketing is undertaken by them, the company tries to find the market for similar products and consumers with similar tastes and preferences.

Ethnocentrism considers overseas operations as a means of disposing the surplus production, thereby giving a secondary or subordinate treatment. Usually, in ethnocentric approach, goods are manufactured at the home base and decisions are taken at the headquarters. Generally, in the initial stages of internationalization, most companies adopt ethnocentric orientation, but this approach becomes difficult to sustain once a sizeable market share is achieved.

Multinationals' all-know attitude often hampers them to bring out a timely strategy to the changing needs of a foreign market, whereas the local companies often have an edge in understanding domestic customers and responds to their needs much quickly. For instance, the Finnish multinational Nokia grossly underestimated the growing popularity of dual SIM and low-cost QWERTY key phones in India and lost its market share from 65 per cent in 2001 to 36 per cent in 2010.

---

[25] Adapted from Perlmutter, Howard, 'The Torturous Evolution of Multinational Corporation', *Columbia Journal of World Business*, January–February 1969; and Wind, Yoram, Susan P. Douglas, and Howard V. Perlmutter, 'Guidelines for Developing International Marketing Strategy', *Journal of Marketing*, April 1973, pp. 14–23.

Polycentric orientation

It is based on the belief that substantial differences exist among various markets. Each market is considered unique in terms of its market environment, such a political, cultural, legal, economic, consumer behaviour, and market structure. The marketing mix decisions as well as product development strategies, pricing strategies, etc. involve local experts and are different for different countries. The key to success in international markets is to participate in the formats relevant to that market as opposed to transpose the home country portfolio on an 'as is' basis. The decentralization of marketing activities is highest in polycentric orientation.

The HSBC Bank, with its network in six continents, total assets worth US$1,000 million, and serving over 100 million customers worldwide, advertises with the punchline 'The World's Local Bank'. The bank focuses on the cultural differences between countries. HSBC's classic advertisement campaign reveals that body tattoos are considered to be trendy in the East, whereas colourful, glittery *mehendi* is a popular tradition in India. On the other hand, Indian mehendi seems trendy to the Western world, whereas body tattoos are considered traditional. Similarly, contrary perceptions do prevail among cultures about the medicinal effects of traditional herbs and modern allopathic drugs. Thus, HSBC emphasizes upon its adaptation of products offered and marketing strategies used across the countries.

Although polycentric approach is highly market oriented, it generally needs more corporate resources, little coordination among various affiliates, and duplication of certain activities. Besides, economies of scale are hardly achieved in any corporate house.

Regiocentric orientation

A firm treats a region as a uniform market segment and adapts a similar marketing strategy within the region but not across the region. Depending upon the convergence of market behaviour on the basis of geographical regions, a similar marketing strategy is used.

Geocentric orientation

The geocentric approach considers the whole world as a single market and attempts to formulate integrated marketing strategies. A geocentric orientation identifies similarities between various markets and formulates a uniform marketing strategy. The companies that follow the geocentric approach strive to analyse and manage the marketing strategy with integrated global marketing programmes.

THEORETICAL BACKGROUND OF INTERNATIONAL TRADE

The theories of international trade provide an insight into the fundamental principles as to why international trade and investment take place. They also help in understanding the basic reasons behind the evolution of a country as a supply base or a market for specific products. The principles of regulatory framework of national governments and international organizations are also influenced to a varying extent by these basic economic theories. Therefore, an international marketing manager should have a conceptual understanding of these theories.

Theory of Mercantilism

The theory of mercantilism attributes and measures the wealth of a nation by the size of its accumulated treasures. The accumulated wealth is usually measured in terms of gold, as in the earlier days gold and silver were considered to be the currency of international trade. Nations should accumulate financial wealth in the form of gold by encouraging exports and discouraging imports. The theory of mercantilism[26] aims at creating trade surplus which in turn contributes to accumulation of a nation's wealth. During 1500–1800 AD, the European colonial powers actively pursued international trade so as to increase their treasury of goods, which were in turn invested to build a powerful army and infrastructure.

The international trade pursued by colonial powers was primarily for the benefit of their respective mother countries, which treated their colonial nations as exploitable resources. The first ship of the East India Company arrived at the port of Surat, India, in 1608, primarily to carry out trade with India and take advantage of its rich resources of spices, cotton, finest muslin cloth, etc. Other European nations such as Germany, France, Portugal, Spain, Italy, and the East Asian country Japan actively set up colonies to exploit their natural and human resources.

Mercantilism was implemented by active government interventions, which focused on maintaining trade surplus and expansion of colonization. The national governments imposed restrictions on imports through tariffs and quotas, whereas the exports were promoted by subsidizing production. These colonies served as a cheap source for primary commodities such as raw cotton, grains, spices, herbs and medicinal plants, tea, coffee, and fruits, for consumption and also as raw material for industries. Thus, the policy of mercantilism greatly assisted and benefited the colonial powers in accumulating wealth.

The limitations of the theory of mercantilism are as follows:

- Under this theory, accumulation of wealth takes place at the cost of another trading partner. Therefore, it treats international trade as a win–lose game resulting virtually in no contribution to the global wealth. Thus, international trade becomes a zero-sum game.
- In case all countries follow restrictive trade policies, which promote exports and restrict imports and create several trade barriers in the process, it would ultimately result in a highly restrictive environment for international trade.
- Mercantilist policies were used by colonial powers as a mean of exploitation, whereby they charged higher prices from their colonial markets for their finished industrial goods and bought raw materials at a much lower cost from their colonies. Developmental activities in their colonies were restricted to create minimum infrastructure to support international trade for their own interest and the colonies remained poor.

Presently, the terminology used is new mercantilism, which aims at creating favourable trade balance and has been employed by a number of countries to create trade surplus. Japan is a fine example of a country that tried to equate political power with economic power and economic power with trade surplus.

Theory of Absolute Advantage

An Inquiry into the Nature and Causes of the Wealth of Nations by Adam Smith, published in 1776, critically evaluated the mercantilist trade policies and found that wealth of a nation does not lie in building huge stockpiles of gold and silver in its treasury, but the real wealth of a nation is measured by the level of improvement in the quality of living of its citizens reflected by the per capita income.

Smith emphasized on productivity and advocated free trade as a means of increasing global efficiency. The country's standards of living can be enhanced by international trade with other countries by buying goods not produced by them or by producing large quantities of goods through specialization.

---

[26] Vaggi, Gianni, *A Concise History of Economic Thought: From Mercantilism to Monetarism*, Palgrave Macmillan, New York, 2002.

Absolute advantage is the ability of a nation to produce a product more efficiently and cost-effectively than any other country. Thus, instead of producing all the products, each country would like to specialize in manufacturing products that can be produced with competitive advantage. Such efficiency is gained through the following ways:

- Repetitive production of a product increases the skills of the labour force.
- Labour time is saved in switching production from one produce to another.
- Long product runs provide incentives to develop more effective work methods over a period of time.

Therefore, a country should use the increased production to export and acquire more goods by way of imports, which would in turn improve the living standards of its people. A country's advantage may be either natural or acquired.

Natural

Natural factors such as a country's geographical and agro-climatic conditions, mineral, or other natural resources, or specialized manpower, contribute to a country's natural advantage in certain products. For instance, the agro-climatic condition in India is an important factor for sizeable export of agro-produce such as spices, cotton, tea, and mangoes. The availability of relatively cheap labour contributes to India's edge in export of labour-intensive products. Till recent years, Bangladesh was heavily dependent on its export of jute and jute products, which was primarily attributed to natural advantage.

Acquired advantage

Today, international trade is moving from the traditional agro-products to industrial products and services, especially in developing countries like India. It is the acquired advantage in either a product or its processed technology that plays an important role in creating such advantage. The ability to differentiate or produce a different product is termed as an advantage in product technology, whereas the ability to produce a homogeneous product more efficiently is termed as an advantage in process and technology. Some of the export centres in India for precious and semi-precious stone in Jaipur, Surat, Navasari, and Mumbai have come up not because of their raw material resources but because of the skills they have developed in processing imported raw stones.

Theory of Comparative Advantage

In *Principles of Political Economy and Taxation*, Ricardo (1817) promulgated the theory of comparative advantage, wherein a country benefits from international trade even if it is less efficient than other nations in production of both commodities. Comparative advantage may be defined as the inability of a nation to produce a product more efficiently than other nations, but its ability to produce it more efficiently than it does in any other goods. Thus, even if a country is at absolute disadvantage with respect to production of both the commodities, the absolute disadvantage is lower in one commodity than another. Therefore, the country should specialize in the production and export the commodity in which absolute disadvantage is less than another or, in other words, the country has got a comparative advantage in terms of more production efficiency.

Limitations of theories of specialization

The limitations of the theories of specialization are as follows:

- The theories of comparative and absolute advantage lay emphasis on specialization with an assumption that countries are driven only by maximization of production and consumption.

However, attainment of economic efficiency in a specialized field may not be the only goal of countries. For instance, Middle East countries have spent enormous resources and pursued a sustained strategy in developing their agriculture and horticulture sector in which these countries have very high absolute and comparative disadvantage so as to become self-reliant.

- Specialization in one commodity or product may not necessarily result in efficiency gains. Production and export of more than one product often have synergistic effect on developing the overall efficiency levels.
- These theories assume that production takes place under full employment conditions and labour is the only resource used in the production process, which is not a valid assumption.
- The division of gains is often unequal among the trading partners, which may alienate the partner perceiving or getting lower gains, who may forgo absolute gains to prevent relative losses.
- The original theories have been proposed on the basis of two countries–two commodities situation. However, even when experimented with multiple-commodities and multiple-countries situations, the same logic applies.
- Logistics cost is overlooked in these theories, which may defy the proposed advantage of international trading.
- The size of economy and production runs is not taken into consideration.

Factor Endowment Theory

Earlier theories of absolute and comparative advantages provided little insight into the type of products in which a country can have an advantage. Heckscher (1919) and Ohlin (1933) developed a theory to explain the reasons for differences in relative commodity prices and competitive advantage between two nations. According to this theory, a nation will export the commodity whose production requires intensive use of the nation's relatively abundant and cheap factors and import the commodity whose production requires intensive use of the nation's scarce and expensive factors. Thus, a country with abundance of cheap labour would export labour-intensive products and import capital-intensive goods and vice versa. It suggests that the patterns of trade are determined by factor endowment rather than productivity. The theory suggests three types of relationships.

Land–Labour relationship

A country would specialize in production of labour-intensive goods if the labour is in abundance (i.e., relatively cheaper) as compared to the cost of land (i.e., relatively costly). This is mainly due to the ability of a labour-abundant country to produce something more cost-efficiently compared to a country where labour is scarcely available and therefore expensive.

Labour–Capital relationship

In countries where the capital is abundantly available and labour is relatively scarce (therefore, more costly), they would tend to achieve competitiveness in the production of goods requiring large capital investments.

Technological complexities

As the same product can be produced by adopting various methods or technologies of production, its cost competitiveness would have great variations. In order to minimize the cost of production and achieve cost competitiveness, one has to examine the optimum way of production in view of technological capabilities and constraints of a country.

To sum up, a country with relatively cheaper cost of labour would export labour-intensive products, whereas a country where the labour is scarce and capital is relatively abundant would export capital-intensive goods.

Empirical evidence on factor proportion theory

Wassily Leontief carried out an empirical test of the Heckscher–Ohlin model in 1951 to find out whether the USA, which has abundant capital resources, exports capital-intensive goods and imports labour-intensive goods. He found that the USA exported more labour-intensive commodities and imported more capital-intensive products, which was contrary to the results of the Heckscher–Ohlin model of factor endowment.

Country Similarity Theory

The relative costs of production and factor endowments determined trade especially in natural resource-based industries. However, in case of manufactured goods, costs are generally determined by similarity in product demands across countries rather than by relative production costs or factor endowments.[27]

It has been observed that a majority of trade occurs between nations that have similar characteristics. The major trading partners of most developed countries are other developed industrialized countries. The country similarity theory is based on the following principles:

- If two countries have similar demand patterns, then their consumers would demand the same goods with similar degrees of quality and sophistication. This phenomenon is also known as *preference similarity*. Such similarity leads to enhanced trade between two developed countries.
- The demand patterns in countries with higher level of per capita income are similar to those in other countries with similar income levels, as their residents would demand more sophisticated, high-quality, 'luxury' consumer goods, whereas countries with lower per capita income would demand low-quality, cheaper consumer goods as a part of their 'necessity'. Since developed countries would have a comparative advantage in manufacture of complex, technology-intensive luxury goods, they would find export markets in other high-income countries.
- Since most products are developed on the demand patterns in the home market, other countries with similar demand patterns due to cultural or economic similarity would be their natural trade partners.
- Countries with proximity of geographical locations would also have greater trade compared to the distant ones. This can also be explained by various types of similarities, such as cultural and economic, besides cost of transportation.

The country similarity theory goes beyond cost comparisons; therefore, it is also used in international marketing.

New Trade Theory

Countries do not necessarily trade only to benefit from their differences, but they also trade so as to increase their returns, which in turn enable them to benefit from specialization. International trade enables a firm to increase its output due to its specialization by providing a much larger market that results in enhancing its efficiency. The theory helps explain the trade patterns when markets are not perfectly competitive or when economies of scale are achieved by production of specific products. A decrease in the unit cost of a product resulting from large-scale production is termed as economies of scale. Since fixed costs are shared over an increased output, the economies of scale enable a firm to reduce its per-unit average cost of production and enhance its price competitiveness.

---

[27] Linder, S.B., *An Essay on Trade and Transformation*, Wiley, New York, 1961.

Higher economies of scale lead to increase in returns, enabling countries to specialize in production of such goods and trade with countries with similar consumption patterns. Besides intra-industry trade, the theory also explains intra-firm trade between the multinational enterprises (MNEs) and their subsidiaries with a motive to take advantage of scale economies and increase their returns.

Theory of International Product Life Cycle

International markets follow a cyclical pattern[28] over a time due to a variety of factors, which explains the shifting of markets as well as location of production. The pattern of international product life cycle depends upon the market size of the innovating country. In case the innovating country has a large market size, as in case of the USA, India, China, etc., it can support mass production for domestic sales. This mass market also facilitates the producers based in these countries to achieve cost-efficiency, which enables them to become internationally competitive. However, in case the market size of a country is too small to achieve economies of scale from the domestic market, the companies from these countries can also achieve economies of scale by setting up their marketing and production facilities in other cost-effective countries. Thus, it is the economies of scope that assists in achieving the economies of scale by expanding into international markets.

The product life cycle explains the emerging pattern of international markets, but it has got its own limitations in the present marketing era with fast proliferation of market information, wherein products are launched more or less simultaneously in various markets.

Theory of Competitive Advantage

As propounded by Michael Porter in his book *The Competitive Advantage of Nations*, the theory of competitive advantage[29] emphasizes on a firm's home country environment as the main source of competencies and innovations. The model is often referred to as the diamond model, wherein four determinants interact with each other. Porter's diamond consists of the following attributes.

Factor (input) conditions

It refers to how well-endowed a nation is as far as resources are concerned. These resources may be created or inherited, which include human resources, capital resources, physical infrastructure, administrative infrastructure, information infrastructure, scientific and technological infrastructure, and natural resources. The efficiency, quality, and specialization of underlying inputs that firms draw while competing in international markets are influenced by a country's factor conditions. The inherited factors in case of India, such as abundance of arable land, water resources, large work force, round-the-year sunlight, bio-diversity, and variety of agro-climatic conditions do not necessarily guarantee a firm's international competitiveness. Rather the factors created by meticulous planning and implementation, such as physical administrative information and scientific and technological infrastructure, play a greater role in determining a firm's competitiveness.

Demand conditions

The sophistication of demand conditions in the domestic market and the pressure from domestic buyers are the critical determinants for a firm to upgrade its product and services. The major

---

[28] Vernon, Raymond, 'International Investment and International Trade in Product Life Cycle', *Quarterly Journal of Economics*, May 1996.

[29] Porter, M.E., *The Competitive Advantage of Nations*, The Free Press, New York, 1990.

characteristics of the domestic demand include the nature of demand, the size and growth patterns of domestic demand, and the way a nation's values are spreading across foreign markets. As the Indian market had long been a sellers' market, it exerted little pressure on Indian firms to strive for quality upgradation in the home market.

Related and supporting industries

The availability and quality of local suppliers and related industries and the state of development of clusters play an important role in determining the competitiveness of a firm. These determine the cost-efficiency, quality, and speedy delivery of inputs, which in turn influence a firm's competitiveness. This explains the development of industrial clusters such as IT industries around Bengaluru, textile industries around Tirupur, and metal handicrafts around Moradabad.

Firm strategy, structure, and rivalry

It refers to the extent of corporate investment, type of strategy, and the intensity of local rivalry. Differences in management styles, organizational skills, and strategic perspectives create advantages and disadvantages for firms competing in different types of industries. Besides, the intensity of domestic rivalry also affects a firm's competitiveness. In India, the management system is paternalistic and hierarchical in nature. In a system of mixed economy with protectionist and monopolistic regulations, the intensity of competition was almost missing in major industrial sectors. It was only after economic liberalization that Indian industries were exposed to market competition. The quality of goods and services has remarkably improved as a result of increased intensity of market competition.

Two additional external variables of Porter's model for evaluating national competitive advantage include chance and government.

Chance

Occurrences that are beyond the control of firms, industries, and usually governments have been termed as chance, which plays a critical role in determining competitiveness. It includes wars and their aftermath, major technological breakthroughs, innovations, exchange rates, shifts in factor or input costs (e.g., rise in petroleum prices), etc. Some of the major chance factors in the context of India include disintegration of the erstwhile USSR and the collapse of the communist system in Eastern Europe, opening up of the Chinese market, the Gulf War, etc.

Government

The government has an important role to play in influencing the determinants of a nation's competitiveness. The government's role in formulating policies related to trade, foreign exchange, infrastructure, labour, product standards, etc. influences the determinants in the Porter's diamond.

REASONS FOR ENTERING INTERNATIONAL MARKETS

The reasons for entering international markets (Fig. 1.12) vary from firm to firm and country to country depending upon the market characteristics. However, firms often decide to enter into international markets due to the following reasons.

Growth

Firms enter international markets when the domestic market potential saturates and they are forced to explore alternative marketing opportunities overseas. However, given the size of the Indian market, enormous opportunities for most of the practices exist in the domestic market

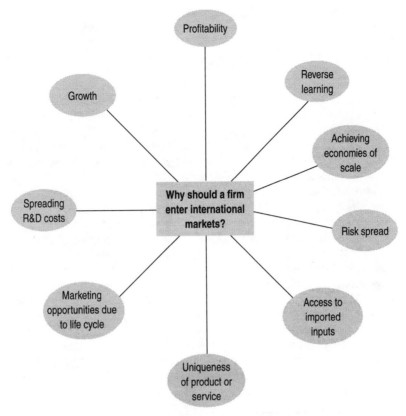

Fig. 1.12 Reasons for entering international markets

itself. Therefore, growth is the motive of only a few select companies to internationalize. This is also true for large market economies such as the USA and China. It may also be observed that countries with smaller market size, such as Singapore, Hong Kong, and Scandinavian countries, had no other option but to internationalize. Markets in the developed countries especially the USA and the Europe were hit the hardest during the economic slowdown; emerging markets such as India, China, and Brazil have shown considerable growth. The US president has asked American business leaders at several forums to aggressively pursue the huge middle class in India and China to increase their export (Exhibit 1.3), thus creating hundreds and thousands of jobs in the country[30].

Profitability

The price differential among markets also serves as an important incentive to internationalize. Exporters benefit from the higher profit margins in the foreign markets. Sometimes, strong competition in domestic market limits a firm's profitability in that market. Price differentials and enhanced profits in the international markets are some of the fundamental motives for exporting. Some of the policy incentives such as exemption from indirect taxes and duties, several incentives by the governments for export-oriented production, and marketing support schemes contribute to enhance the profitability of firms in international marketing.

---

[30] 'Target India & China: Obama Tells Corporate America', *The Economic Times*, New Delhi, 9 February 2011, p. 14.

Exhibit 1.3 US President asks corporate America to market internationally

Consequent to the global economic slowdown, developed countries have realized the need to emphasize on an economic framework that is based not on what they consume and borrow from other nations but what make and sell around the world. As most developed economies growing at a rate of about 2 per cent or even less by 2010, growth in export markets has become imperative for most developed countries even to sustain their domestic economies and to create new jobs in the future. Since 95 per cent of the world's customer and fastest growing markets are beyond the US borders, it needs to compete aggressively for those customers in order to find new growth streams for the US economy. The US President, Barrack Obama, consistently emphasizes on competing in emerging markets aggressively and fight for every job, every industry, and every market everywhere.

No company can afford to be truly global unless it has some sort of operations in countries such as India and China. As a strategic intent virtually all Fortune 500 companies have set up their shops in India. The employee strength of many global technology companies in India is the largest outside their home country. However, a number of companies especially in the IT sector have reversed the equation by hiring more employees in India

than its home country. IBM and Accenture have more employees in India than in the USA. Capgemini, the French IT consulting major, employed about 30,000 people in India by December 2010, which constituted approximately 30 per cent of its global workforce, whereas it employed nearly 20,000 employees in France[31]. Indian subsidiary of L'Oreal, the world's largest cosmetics and beauty firm with brands such as Maybelline, Matrix, Garnier, L'Oreal, Kiehl's, and Lancome has become the fastest-growing subsidiaries in the world, growing at over 30 per cent annually.

Obama's India visit in 2010 highlighted the role American business played in India and took the opportunity to export American goods to one of the fastest growing markets in the world. The US President visited India with a fleet of CEOs of corporate America and made several deals worth nearly US$10 billion in exports ranging from Boeing jets and GE engine to medical and mining equipment, which was projected to support more than 50 thousand jobs in the USA. President Obama's effort to strike deals for tariff reduction for American companies in South Korea was projected to boost export of American goods up to US$11 billion, which is projected to support over 70 thousand American jobs including opening up of the large Korean services markets.

Source: 'Deals with India will Support More than 50,000 American Jobs', *Swadeshi Patrika*, 2011, p. 34; 'Target India and China: Obama Tells Corporate America, *The Economic Times*, 8 February 2011.

Reverse Learning

Expanding into international market is not only critical to growth and expansion of a firm but it also provides opportunity to firms for reverse learning. For instance, the Indian firm Marico launched Parachute hair cream in the international market first, as it had significant presence in the Middle East and Bangladesh, and brought this to India later.

In China, everyone drinks soup but not packaged soup. The Chinese love the taste of long-boiled soup. So, Unilever innovated the Knorr jelly cube for China and created a product format that was disruptive. It gained huge success in China and the same format was rolled across the world and the entire knowledge of savoury category of Unilever[32] was made use of.

Achieving Economies of Scale

Large-scale production capacities necessitate domestic firms to dispose of their goods in international markets once the domestic markets become saturated. One of the basic reasons behind the internationalization of Great Britain during the Industrial Revolution was domestic market saturation.

Risk Spread

A company operating in domestic markets is highly vulnerable to economic upheavals in the home market. Overseas markets provide an opportunity to reduce their dependence on one market and spread the market risks.

[31] 'Capegemini has More Staff in India than at HQ', *The Times of India*, 3 December 2010.

[32] 'We Want to Think Local and Act Global', *The Economic Times*, 27 May 2010.

Access to Imported Inputs

The national trade policies provide for import of inputs used for export production, which are otherwise restricted. Besides, there are a number of incentive schemes that provide duty exemption or remission on import of inputs for export production, such as advance licensing, duty drawback, duty exemption, export promotion, and capital goods scheme. It helps the companies in accessing imported inputs and technical know-how to upgrade their operations and increase their competitiveness.

Uniqueness of Product or Service

The products with unique attributes are unlikely to meet any competition in the overseas markets and enjoy enormous opportunities in international markets. For instance, herbal and medicinal plants, handicrafts, value-added business process outsourcing (BPO) services, and software development at competitive prices provide Indian firms an edge over other countries and smoothen their entry into international markets.

Marketing Opportunities due to Life Cycles

Each market shows a different stage of life cycle for different products, which varies widely across country markets. When a product or service gets saturated in the domestic or an international market, a firm may make use of such challenges and convert them into marketing opportunities by operating into international markets. Strategies to launch new products in the existing markets or identify new markets for existing products may be adopted.

Spreading R&D Costs

By way of spreading the potential market size, a firm recovers quickly the costs incurred on research and development (R&D). It is especially true for products involving higher costs of R&D, where use of price-skimming strategies necessitates faster recovery of costs incurred, such as software, microprocessors, and pharmaceutical products. International markets facilitate speedy recovery of such costs because of the large market size and also due to larger coverage of the right market segments in international markets.

INTERNATIONAL MARKETING FRAMEWORK

The process of internationalization calls for a variety of interrelated set of international marketing decisions which have long-term repercussions. In order to facilitate readers' understanding of the concepts and processes involved in international marketing, the schematic framework is presented in Fig. 1.13, which is self-explanatory and provides a synoptic view of decisions required to be made while approaching international markets.

Once a firm decides to enter international markets, it needs to set objectives as to what it intends to achieve out of its international marketing operations. The next important challenge is to identify marketing opportunities, evaluate them, and select the most appropriate one so as to meet its objectives. The firm has to scan the international marketing environment, which includes economic, political, legal, and socio-cultural aspects. 'How to enter international markets?' is the next big challenge considering the relevant resource constraints, risks, and marketing opportunities.

In view of the external environmental factors, the key decisions related to the marketing mix, that is, product, pricing, distribution, and marketing communications, have to be made. Taking such decisions is much more complex in the international context. Managing export–import operations,

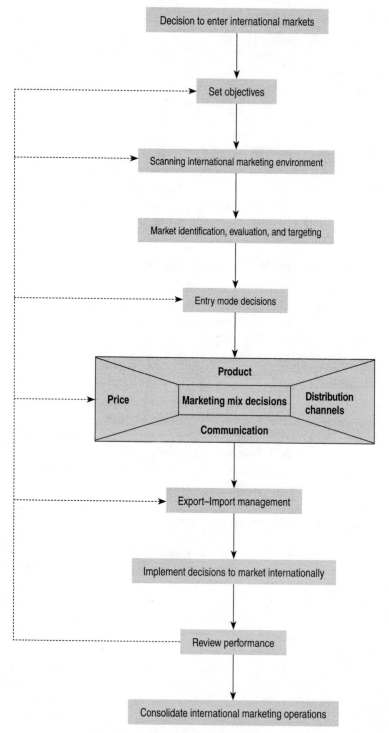

Fig. 1.13   International marketing framework

Source: Based on Joshi, Rakesh Mohan, *International Business*, Oxford University Press, New Delhi, 2009, p. 584.

which include institutional framework, trade policy issues, export procedures and documentation, international shipping and trade logistics, modes of payment, and international trade finance and risk management are the key to achieve efficiency in trade operations across borders. Once these decisions are implemented and the firm begins international marketing operations, the performance, primarily in terms of sales, profits, or market share, needs to be reviewed and remedial measures taken, if required. Ending strategies to integrate ICT with marketing significantly facilitates in achieving competitive edge in international marketing. The firm further consolidates its international marketing operations from a long-term perspective and becomes an established player in global markets. Marketers also need to keep them abreast of contemporary issues in international marketing so as to anticipate and respond effectively to emerging challenges.

Decision to Internationalize

The initial stimuli for entering international markets include any one or several motivational factors, such as growth, profitability, reverse learning, achieving economies of scale, risk spread, access to imported inputs, uniqueness of product or service, marketing opportunities due to life cycles, and spreading R&D costs.

The significance of these stimuli varies among the firms, which may assign them respective weights to carry out a cost–benefit analysis, as shown in Fig. 1.14. Subsequently, a firm is required to carry out a strengths weaknesses opportunities threats (SWOT) analysis to assess its capability to internationalize and identify the issues and factors need special attention while taking international marketing decisions. The analysis may vary from company to company; however, a typical SWOT analysis made for a small- or medium-sized company in a developing country like India may appear similar to what is shown in Fig. 1.14.

Strengths	Opportunities
• Specialize technical skills, namely, IT or any other skills • Competent human resources • Adequate production facilities	• High growth in overseas markets • Emerging new market segments • Substantial difference in price realization
Weaknesses	**Threats**
• Little expertise in international marketing • No prior experience in overseas markets • Financial constraints	• High competitive intensity • Increasing non-tariff barriers • Increased market risk

Fig. 1.14　SWOT analysis for a medium-sized company for internationalization

Once a firm's strengths and weaknesses are carefully examined, decisions to enter into international markets are taken. The marketing decision is made by adopting appropriate strategies to take benefit of emerging marketing opportunities and suitable measures to respond to the threats of international markets.

Setting Marketing Objectives

Once a firm decides to enter international markets, it needs to set its short- as well as long-term objectives. The objectives vary widely from one business enterprise to another and even for a company from one market to another. The objectives to be achieved from international marketing operations may include

- increase in total sales turnover;
- percentage of revenue earned from international markets to the company's domestic sales, market share;
- market share in the target markets;
- increased profitability;
- optimal utilization of production capacity;
- increased geographical spread of the company's marketing operations;
- brand promotion in target markets; or
- any other strategic objectives.

An empirical evaluation of this is to be carried out so as to decide upon one or a combination of objectives to be achieved from international marketing operations.

Based on various components of the international marketing framework, the book has been broadly divided into seven parts covering each one in different chapters. The present chapter examines the concept of international marketing in view of various changes that have taken place as a result of globalization. All the other constituents of the framework have been covered in the subsequent chapters in a comprehensive and an analytical manner.

Summary

Although existence of international trade is traceable to 3000 BC in India, it is only during the last century that marketing activities around the world underwent an unprecedented change. It was during the latter half of the 20th century when large US, European, and Japanese companies expanded their markets and production facilities across national borders. The globalization of markets accelerated by liberalization in economic policies around the world and their integration with WTO has remarkably increased the significance of international marketing. The revolutionary breakthroughs in the modes of communication and transport have assisted men to conquer time and distance to a great extent. This has also contributed to convergence in the consumer tastes and preferences across national borders and has significantly affected the tools and techniques used in reaching international markets.

In simple terms, 'international marketing' means marketing activities across the national borders. Various definitions of international marketing have been examined in the chapter. In order to facilitate readers' understanding of terminological jargons such as foreign marketing, comparative marketing, international trade, international business, international marketing, and global/world marketing have also been explained. International marketing is much more complex than domestic marketing because a marketer has to operate in a foreign business environment wherein the uncontrollable factors such as economic, political, socio-cultural, legal, and geographical factors, competition, and logistics vary substantially in the international markets vis-à-vis the domestic market. Besides, these environmental differences get more complex when a firm is operating in a number of foreign markets. The marketing practices that have been effective in the domestic market may not succeed in foreign markets and the domestic marketing experiences and strategies serve as a deterrent in international marketing efforts.

The ability of an international marketer to have an objective evaluation of the influence of the environmental factors on the marketing mix is severely affected by one's own cultural conditioning in understanding the nuances of another culture. Such unconscious reference to one's own cultural values, experiences, and knowledge as a basis for decision-making is termed as self-reference criterion. Adaptation of the marketing mix to the overseas marketing environment is the secret of success in international markets.

The identifiable stages of such evolutionary process include domestic marketing, export marketing, international marketing, multinational marketing, and global marketing. The marketing orientation of a company may have several forms, such as ethnocentric, polycentric, regiocentric, and geocentric. The ethnocentric approach is highly oriented towards the domestic market, wherein the domestic marketing strategy is extended to foreign markets with little adaptation. The polycentric approach is highly market-oriented, which recognizes significant differences among various markets and develops individually customized strategies for different markets. In the regiocentric approach, a similar market strategy is followed within the region but not across the region, whereas the geocentric approach views the whole world as a single market and attempts to formulate integrated marketing strategies.

Various theories have evolved to explain the raison d'etre for international trade. The earliest theory of mercantilism emphasized on accumulated treasures of wealth and the creation of trade surpluses by encouraging exports and discouraging imports. The subsequent theory of absolute advantage advocates that a country should export goods in which it has got absolute advantage and use export proceeds to acquire more goods by way of imports. However, the theory of comparative advantage suggests that in case a country does not have absolute advantage for production of any of the goods, it can benefit by exporting the goods, wherein it does have comparative advantage, that is, production of a product more efficiently than it does any other product. Heckscher and Ohlin recommended in their factor endowment theory that a nation will export the commodity whose production requires intensive use of the nation's relatively abundant and cheap factors and import the commodity whose production requires the intensive use of the nation's scarce and expensive factors. Raymond Vernon found that international markets follow a cyclical pattern over a time period due to a variety of factors, which explains the shifting of markets as well as location for their production.

The reasons for entering international marketing include growth, profitability, reverse learning, achieving economies of scale, risk spread, access to imported inputs, and uniqueness of product or service, marketing opportunities due to stages in the life cycle, and spreading R&D costs. The evolution of marketing across national boundaries has generally followed a gradual process that takes place in stages.

The suggested framework of international marketing includes decisions to enter international markets, setting objectives, scanning international marketing environment, market identification, evaluation and targeting, entry mode decisions, marketing mix decisions, export–import management and implementing, and reviewing and consolidating international marketing operations. The chapterization plan of the book is based on various components of international marketing framework.

Key Terms

Comparative marketing Comparative study of two or more marketing systems to find out the differences and similarities.

Ethnocentric orientation The belief that considers one's own culture as superior to others and views overseas marketing as an extension of domestic marketing.

Export marketing Manufacturing in home country and selling in foreign markets.

Factor endowment theory A nation should export the commodity whose production requires the intensive use of its relatively abundant and cheap factors and import the commodity whose production requires the intensive use of its scarce and expensive factors.

Foreign marketing Methods and practices used in the home market and applied in the overseas markets with little adaptation

Geocentric orientation The approach that treats the whole world as a single market and attempts to formulate integrated marketing strategies

International marketing Firm-level marketing practices used across the border, including market identification and targeting, entry mode selection, marketing mix, and strategic decisions to compete in the international markets.

International trade A macroeconomic term used at the national level with a focus on flow of goods, services, and capital across national borders.

Polycentric orientation A strongly market-oriented approach recognizing substantial market differences among various markets and providing for decentralized decision-making in each of the markets.

Regiocentric orientation The approach that considers a region as a uniform market segment, and a firm following this approach adapts a similar marketing strategy within the region but not across the region.

Self-reference criterion An unconscious reference to one's own cultural values, experiences, and knowledge as a basis for decision-making.

Theory of absolute advantage A nation should export the goods that it produces more efficiently than elsewhere, which would enable the nation to acquire more goods by way of imports.

Theory of international product life cycle The cyclical pattern followed by the international markets over a time due to a variety of factors that explain the shift in the markets as well as manufacturing bases of the firms.

Theory of mercantilism Attributes wealth of a nation by the size of its accumulated treasures, usually measured in terms of gold. This theory holds that nations should accumulate financial wealth in the form of gold by encouraging exports and discouraging imports.

Concept Review Questions

1. 'Globalization has been a powerful driving force that has brought convergence in the tastes and preferences of the consumers around the world. Despite this fact, transposing techniques from domestic market may not necessarily yield results even if the new market seems very similar.' Critically evaluate the statement. Identify the major hindrances in formulating global marketing strategies and means to overcome them.
2. Critically evaluate the impact of globalization on present-day marketing.
3. 'Operating in international markets is much more complex than marketing domestically.' Critically evaluate the statement with suitable examples.

4. Describe various reasons for a firm to enter international markets.
5. Explain the concept of EPRG model in the evolution of global marketing with the help of suitable examples.
6. How do self-reference criteria (SRC) interfere in making international marketing decisions? What steps would you take to minimize the impact of SRC?
7. Differentiate between the following:
   (a) Absolute advantage and comparative advantage
   (b) International trade and international business
   (c) Export marketing and foreign marketing
   (d) International marketing and global marketing

Project Assignments

1. Visit a firm near your place and find out the factors that have motivated it to enter international markets. Compare these motives with what you have already been taught and present them before the class. You may also compare your findings with your other colleagues who have visited other exporting companies.
2. Visit a multinational fast food chain operating in your city and meet some senior marketing officer. Try to explore the mistakes

the company has made in designing its marketing mix in the Indian market and the steps taken to compete vis-à-vis Indian food retailers. How do these mistakes relate to self-reference criteria?
3. Browse the Internet and identify two companies that have different orientations towards international marketing as explained in the EPRG schema. Do you find some overlaps in their differences or find them mutually exclusive?

CASE STUDY: ESSEL PROPACK—WORLD'S LARGEST MANUFACTURER OF LAMINATED TUBES

Often billion dollar companies dominate the leadership position in global markets due to their enormous clout, financial as well as worldwide reach. To name a few are Walmart, Coca-Cola, Pepsi, Procter & Gamble (P&G), McDonald's, Sony, Toshiba, Apple, Nestlé, Ford, etc. Moreover, such multinational corporations (MNCs) also dominate the illustrations and cases in management textbooks. The present case demonstrates very effectively how a little known firm from India became a global market leader.

Interestingly, a low-key Indian company, Essel Propack Limited, established in 1982, became the world's largest manufacturer of laminated tubes. If one looks at the laminated tube used in the packaging of toothpaste, medicines, or cosmetics, the chance is that one in three of such packaging worldwide is manufactured by Essel.

With a global market share of over 33 per cent, Essel Propack is the world's largest manufacturer of laminated tubes with operations in India, USA, UK, China, Russia, Indonesia, Egypt, Germany, Poland, Mexico, Columbia, and Philippines (Fig. C1.1).

Presently, Essel Propack is a US$342 million enterprise, making over 5.5 billion tubes a year. Essel has 24 state-of-the-art manufacturing facilities in 12 countries across five continents employing 2,600 people representing 25 different nationalities serving over 3,000 customers in more than 68 countries.

Tubes in Packaging

Tubes are specialized form in nature, used in packaging a variety of semi-liquid products and gels. These serve the packaging needs of oral care, health care, cosmetics, toiletries, hair care, pharmaceutical, food products, and industrial products. Tubes used in packaging can broadly be classified into three categories: aluminium, plastic, and laminated.

Use of tubes as a form of packaging began with use of aluminium tubes, which had long been in use worldwide. Traditionally, toothpaste tubes were made of aluminium, but those tubes were not the best solution for packaging toothpastes and many cosmetic creams. However, the advent of laminated and extruded tubes about two decades ago gave rise to systematic replacement of

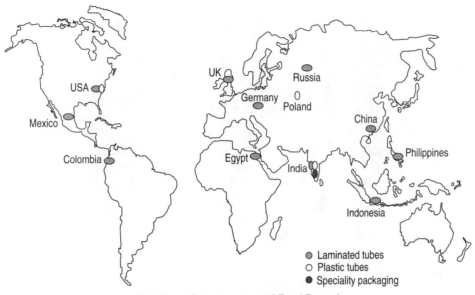

Fig. C1.1 Global presence of Essel Propack

Source: Essel Propack, 2013.

aluminium tubes. These laminated plastic tubes had plastic layers at the top and bottom, adhesive layers in between, and a thin aluminium layer in the middle to preserve fragrance and taste. The laminated plastic tubes offer the following advantages over aluminium tubes:

- Excellent barrier properties
- High standard of manufacturing hygiene, in a firmly controlled environment
- Highly flexible and squeezable
- Remain soft and smooth at any stage of use
- Value addition to products through enhanced shelf appeal and superior aesthetics

Cosmetics and toiletries was the first industry to switch over from aluminium to extruded plastic tubes. Subsequently, oral care products (i.e., toothpaste) began conversion to laminated tubes. Presently, oral care products in most of the world markets are packed in laminated tubes. More and more toiletries, hair care, pharmaceuticals, food, and industrial products have switched to laminated tubes with technological advancement, whereas extruded plastic tubes remain preferred for premium cosmetic products.

Among the end-use segments, toothpaste leads to metal replacement by laminated tubes (Fig. C1.2). Geographically, laminated tube penetration is concentrated in the USA and Western Europe. Emerging economies are increasingly following the trend.

Essel Propack's Pioneered Manufacturing Laminated Tubes in India

Essel Propack was started by Subhash Chandra, who is more known as a promoter of media and entertainment firms, that is, Zee TV and Essel World, became the first company to introduce laminated tubes in India. Though account for 75 per cent share of Essel Propack's revenue, it is now also present in the business of co-extruded plastic tubes (12.5%), speciality packaging, and plastic films (12.5%), as shown in Fig. C1.3.

EPL's first plant was established at Vasind in 1984 with a capacity of 57 million tubes per annum with technical collaboration with American National Can Company of USA, Karl Magerle Kunscht (KMK) of Switzerland, and Kaito Chem of Japan. These collaborations were one-time transfer of technology and after absorption of technology, EPL has not renewed it. In 1991, Essel introduced a polyester-based product called EP9190, which is still very popular among brands like Pond's. EPL's second plant came up at Murbad in 1992, third plant in Wada in April 1994, fourth plant at Goa, and fifth plant at Silvassa in 1998. Essel set up another plant at Nalagarh in Himachal Pradesh in 2005 for manufacturing laminated tubes.

In 2006, Essel acquired Packaging India Pvt. Ltd, one of the largest manufacturers of speciality packaging materials. The second plant of Packaging India based in Uttarakhand started its commercial production in 2007, whereas the third plant is located at Cuddalore. In 2012, two Indian companies, Ras Propack Lamipack Limited and Ras Extrusions Limited, in

Fig. C1.2   EPL's laminated tubes are widely used by global oral care firms

Source: Essel Propack.

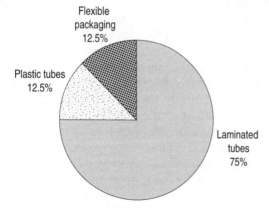

Fig. C1.3   Essel Propack's product profile, 2013

Source: *Annual Report*, Essel Propack, 2013.

India, merged with Essel Propack, which gave Essel access to their manufacturing facility in Chakan, Maharashtra.

EPL's pioneering efforts to introduce and popularize the laminated tubes in the domestic markets were full of hurdles. In the initial years, the demand for laminated tubes in the domestic market was low and the adverse foreign exchange fluctuations increased the project cost by almost 50 per cent. Till 1988, the company was being run in loss. The company started earning profits only from 1988 with a meagre profit after tax as US$0.4 million to US$9.75 million in 2012 (Table C1.1).

Essel's Global Footprints

Essel went on a worldwide expansion spree by way of international alliances, acquisitions, and greenfield operations as well. The firm entered into international markets with its first overseas

Table C1.1   Essel Propack's financial performance (in US$ million)

Year	Total assets	Sales	Profit after tax	Total income	Total foreign exchange earnings	Foreign exchange earnings as % of total income
1988	13.25	10.61	0.4	10.74	0.04	0.37
1989	13.82	19.83	1.04	20.11	0.01	0.05
1990	13.31	13.42	0.9	13.67	1.82	13.31
1991	9.46	10.92	1.07	11.21	0.4	3.57
1992	8.96	8.34	0.94	8.52	0.07	0.82
1993	22.61	16.38	2.79	16.77	0.93	5.55
1994	51.03	25.32	4.93	26.67	0.86	3.22
1995	77.58	33.23	5.99	36.66	1.19	3.25
1996	75.41	42.59	5.51	45.46	1.25	2.75
1997	84.19	45.56	6.35	48.33	2.1	4.35
1998	73.88	43.8	5.8	46.0	1.8	3.91
1999	65.09	57.38	8.4	59.66	4.55	7.63
2000	91.76	56.38	9.17	59.88	7.13	11.91
2001	155.62	40.81	6.18	44.46	3.59	8.07
2002	157.16	53.41	9.99	60.9	9.21	15.12
2003	166.83	56.89	8.74	61.76	4.29	6.95
2004	175.6	58.42	9.3	62.82	6.71	10.68
2005	179.87	62.31	10.07	67.51	6.43	9.52
2006	201.06	69.95	9.2	76.61	10.41	13.59
2007	264.84	85.94	9.45	96.41	15.99	16.59
2008	252.63	73.19	5.59	84.56	18.32	21.67
2009	258.69	98.75	7.59	117.32	21.59	18.40
2010	259.11	97.76	9.8	110.7	17.7	15.99
2011	263.85	105.28	9.75	114.58	13.81	12.05
2012	263.85	105.28	9.75	114.58	13.81	12.05

Source: *Annual Report*, Essel Propack, 2013.

joint venture in Egypt in 1993, which became first in the world to introduce tubes using barrier liver technology. In April 1994, Essel Overseas Ltd was incorporated, a 100 per cent subsidiary of the company, to mainly deal in its export business. The company's globalization spree began with induction of a group of professions led by its erstwhile CEO Cyrus Bagwadia in 1995 who was a seasoned manager with stints at DuPont and Voltas. In 1997, the company entered China with a greenfield facility at Guangzhou. In 1999, Essel set up a joint venture in Dresden, Germany. EPL set up a wholly owned subsidiary in Nepal in the year 2000.

A major breakthrough came in 2000 with acquisition of Switzerland's Propack AG, which was then the world's fourth largest company. Propack lacked in captive web making; it had tubes-making mastery with recent development of very sophisticated PP/340 technology and geographic presence including single largest contract for supplying 0.50 billion tubes per annum to Unilever in China. EPL's business model primarily involved centralized production of web in India and then transferring the same to subsidiaries/JVs for conversion. In return for US$11 million in cash and 6.87 million equity shares, Essel gained access to the Latin American, Indonesian, and Chinese markets and an annual capacity of 600 million units. Besides, it got proprietary technology in the form of PP340, a high speed machine that slashed costs by 30 per cent.

Another major thrust in its effort in international markets came in 2001–2002 as the company received a five-year contract with Cincinnati-based fast-moving consumer goods (FMCG) giant P&G to supply its tube requirements for the entire North American market. In 2003, Essel set up a 1,00,000 square feet plant in the town of Danville, North Carolina, USA, at the cost of US$20 million to service P&G, North America.

In a strategic move, to cater to European market, EPL acquired a UK-based company Arista Tubes through its Mauritius-based wholly owned subsidiary Lamitube Technologies Ltd, Mauritius, in 2004. Artista Tubes UK was founded in 1998, which manufactured plastic seamless tubes for cosmetics, personal care, toiletries, and pharmaceutical segments. The company had a turnover of US$20 million and a 30 per cent market share in UK and Ireland with an integrated facility at Stevenage near London. With acquisition of Arista Tubes, EPL consolidated its marketing efforts in Europe.

In 2004, Essel also built up its own greenfield facility in Russia. In 2005, the company commissioned a state-of-the-art Caps and Closures manufacturing facility in Danville, USA, for supplying laminated tubes for P&G's North American operations. In the same year, it also acquired Telcon Packaging, a UK-based manufacturer of laminated tubes in 2005.

In 2006, the company forayed into the medical devices business by acquiring Tacpro Inc. in USA and Avalon Medical Services in Singapore. These two companies were the manufacturers of medical devices such as catheters and balloons.

In December 2006, the company started commercial production of co-extruded plastic tubes in Danville, Virginia, USA. In 2007, the company commissioned a state-of-the-art plant in Poland to cater to the requirement of their customers in Europe for plastic tubes under the brand name Arista Tubes, UK.

Essel commenced a state-of-the-art facility to handle high-volume manufacturing in Singapore in the business of medical devices. In March 2008, the company expanded their footprint in the USA with the acquisition of Catheter and Disposables Technology, Inc. in Minneapolis, USA. In September 2008, the company, through its step-down subsidiary, Tacpro Inc., USA, acquired 74 per cent equity holding of Medical Engineering and Design Inc, a company based in Minneapolis, USA, and a supplier of specialized disposable medical devices.

Essel Packaging (Guangzhou) Limited Tianjin Branch (EPKB) was established in 2009. It is located at the Jin Nan Development Zone in the city of Tianjin. EPTB is a footprint of EP in north of China. In 2010, Essel Propack China (EP China) started production in its new plant in Tianjin, North East China, which is the metropolis in North China and one of the five national central cities. The plant is geographically close to South Korea and Japan and it will be used to spearhead the exports to these countries. With a view to improve cost structure, Essel Propack Limited, UK, closed its manufacturing operations in the end of 2011 and will source its sales requirements from other Essel Propack's group companies in Europe. In 2012, Essel Propack merged with Ras Propack Lamipack Limited and Ras Extrusions Limited.

International Marketing Challenges

Essel's global market share witnessed a considerable decline from 38 per cent in 2005 to 33 per cent in 2012 in view of stiff market competition. Moreover, Essel's total foreign exchange earnings also grew significantly from US$0.4 million to US$21.59 million in 2009, but fell subsequently to US$13.81 million in 2012.

The laminated tubes had been a niche segment of the tube market characterized by high growth and high margins. Conversion from aluminium tubes to laminated tubes has contributed to significant growth globally.

The tube packaging industry operates in a highly competitive marketing environment and during the recent years has undergone the following changes:

- Capacity consolidation by customers as a result of their global sourcing strategies so as to take advantage of manufacturing cost arbitrage. Due to the emerging international market scenario, the regional players are being marginalized. They would either have to merge with large players or emerge as niche players in certain market segments. In international market, the rule of three—only three large global players—is fast emerging.
- This has resulted into intense competition and rise in cost cutting by customers leading to pressure on pricing.
- The global laminated tube market is facing a glut due to oversupply, whereas prices have witnessed continued decline over the years.
- Constant technology upgradation and innovation are required to maintain growth.

In international market, Essel Propack faces competition from other major manufacturers such as Adams Packaging Ltd, Kranson Industries, Excelisor Technologies Ltd, Advanced Packaging Solutions, RPC Group Plc, and Alexir Packaging Ltd.

Innovation and Diversification of Products and Markets: The Secret of Success

Overdependence on a few products and markets is the key challenge the company is facing. To cope with this challenge, Essel is increasingly focusing on diversification strategy, both for products as well as markets what it terms as 'multiply' not only to meet the ever-growing competition but for its future growth.

Innovation

'Innovation' is the strategic tool to sustain and improve Essel's competitive edge in a fiercely competitive market. Essel's strategy to innovate is not limited to its products, but it transcends to its processes as well as sustainability. The company makes concerted efforts to leverage upon its capability to bring out newer designs and decorations so as to make its product offerings appear fresh and contemporary. To improve market competitiveness, some of the recent innovations by Essel include the following:

Etain A fully recyclable plastic packaging tube made from a combination of virgin and recycled plastic material with an objective to reduce virgin plastic in tube packaging. Etain is fully recyclable and contains up to 40 per cent polymerase chain reaction high density polyethylene (PCR HDPE) plastic material.

Egnite It is a high-lustre, metallic-finish plastic barrier laminated tube, available in a variety of colour shades that facilitate complex printing and noble colour effects. The metallic finish makes the foil-blocking process easier and also offers advantages of striking product differentiation.

Inviseam It is also called non-visible seam, which caters to a large volume of personal care product and is therefore opening up new segments in cosmetics and hair colourant segments. The overlapping of the two ends of the laminate is kept as little as possible so that the seam is virtually 'invisible' after the manufacture.

Application aid/chemical clock It offers customer-specific AppAid buttons on specific locations on tube. When pressed by consumers while dispensing, it will start the time clock. It also offers decoration of a cartoon character on kids oral care tubes, which can be used to motivate kids for brushing teeth for recommended durations.

High-definition printing This is a new innovative offering of high-definition printing on laminated tubes from Danville, North America, that offers customers high-definition reproduction of images/artwork on laminated tubes. Brands are taking advantage of this technology, as this provides them with unprecedented shelf appeal.

The company is innovating into manufacture of 'closures' (caps for tubes as well as other packaging media), which is estimated at US$32 billion global market. It is setting up a state-of-the-art closure manufacturing units in USA and one in Murbad, India. The vertical integration into caps has enabled the company to provide one-stop shop convenience to customers besides greatly adding to value proposition through innovative designs and other functionalities. Essel has also developed anti-counterfeiting foiling, that is, tamper evident foiling. The company is focusing on R&D as a means to create a leading edge for itself and has been filing several patents in the recent years developing a range of caps, closures, dispensing systems, and sealing (Fig. C1.4). Essel leverages on its relationship with large global MNCs to provide closures along with tubes that would enable foolproof packaging solutions.

Product diversification

Essel needs to understand its limitation of over-reliance on the laminated tube category and a few buyers of oral-care sector (Fig. C1.5). Essel attempted to explore opportunities to find growth potential by way of increasing FMCG penetration, developments in modern retail formats, and proliferation of products and their new forms especially in personal care, such as fairness creams, skin care and other cosmetics, and pharmaceuticals.

Essel partners with a large number of FMCG players. It got its first major order from Hindustan Unilever Limited (HUL, which was earlier Hindustan Lever), which was a turning point for the company. Over the years, EPL has become a trusted supplier to major customers worldwide such as Colgate, Palmolive, Unilever, P&G, GlaxoSmithKline, Revlon, and Oriflame.

As oral care segment accounts for about 70 per cent of the total worldwide output, the market for lamitubes is characterized by oligopsony, wherein the buyer has considerable bargaining power. Therefore, size of operation and establishing strong relationship with the clients become critical to the success even in the home market. As toothpaste manufacturers were consolidating their operations worldwide, it became pertinent for the tube manufacturers to competitively cater to their clients in those markets.

The global oral care market is growing worldwide at an estimated 4 per cent per annum in volume terms. Though the developed markets have attained the maturity stage, the developing and emerging economies are on a growth stage primarily due to new customers using the toothpaste as well as increased frequency of use. While the per capita consumption of toothpaste in India at 138 grams is only half the Asian average, growth in the domestic oral care market has slowed down to 3–4 per cent per annum. So, from the oral care segment, which made up the lion's share (over 75%) of EPL's sales in 2002, the company was forced to diversify its client base as well as explore opportunities in non-oral care segment. As indicated in Fig. C1.6, Essel is making inroads into non-oral care market segment, wherein its share has significantly increased from 24 per cent in 2002 to 49 per cent in 2012.

A key emerging growth area for tube manufactures besides targeting non-oral care applications could be the small tubes/toothpaste sachet, which is an effective solution for low-cost

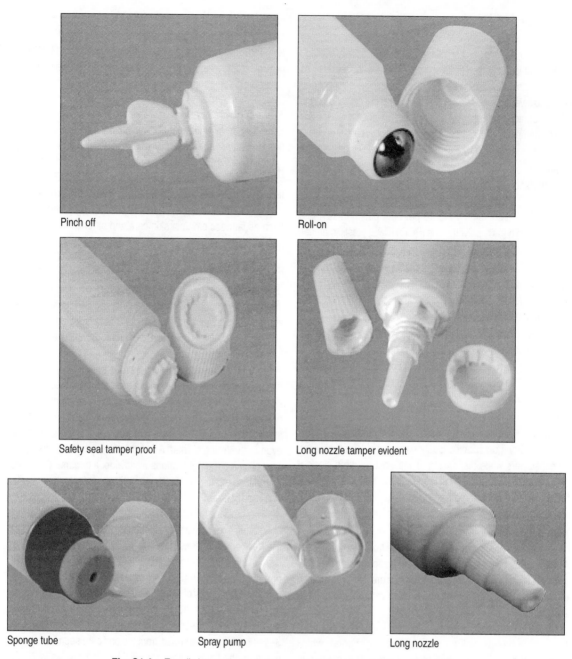

Fig. C1.4   Essel's innovative caps, closures, dispensing systems, and sealing

Source: Essel Propack, 2013.

manufacture of small tubes, which are emerging as a key growth opportunity.

Market diversification

The markets served by Essel have witnessed considerable changes over the years. AMESA (Africa, Middle East, and South Asia) that include India and Egypt became more prominent accounting for 47 per cent of Essel's total revenues in 2013 compared to 35 per cent in 2005. The share of America remained 22 per cent, whereas that of East Asia Pacific fell from 24 per cent in 2005 to 18 per cent in 2013 and that of Europe fell from 18 per cent to 13 per cent during the same period, as shown in Fig. C1.7.

The Concept of International Marketing

Fig. C1.5 Essel's product diversification in non-oral care segment

Source: Essel Propack, 2013.

Presently, Essel's key business in plastic packaging material is managed by four geographical segments:

1. America (with operations in USA, Mexico, and Colombia)
2. Europe (with operations in UK, Germany, and Poland))
3. AMESA (with operation in Egypt and India)
4. East Asia Pacific (EAP) (with operations in China, Philippines, and Indonesia)

Essel Propack gained market leadership in the laminated tube segment in a large number of markets such as China, India, Egypt, Philippines, Indonesia, and Singapore and became a dominant player in several other markets across the world, as shown in Table C1.2.

The high growth of Chinese economy leading to rise in consumerism makes it a promising market especially in pharmaceuticals

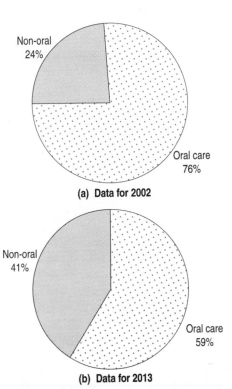

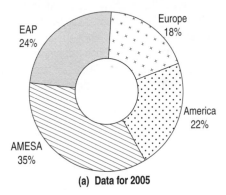

(a) Data for 2005

(a) Data for 2002

(b) Data for 2013

(b) Data for 2013

Fig. C1.6 Changes in Essel's revenue share

Source: *Annual Report*, Essel Propack, 2013.

Fig. C1.7 Geographic share of Essel's revenue

Source: *Annual Report*, Essel Propack, 2012–2013.

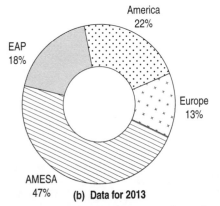

Table C1.2 Essel dominates a large number of laminated tube markets

Geographies	Countries	Market share (%) (2013)	Leadership status	CAGR (%) (2005–2013)
AMESA	Egypt and India	58	Market leader	16
EAP	China, Philippines, Singapore, and Indonesia	33	Market leader	8
America	USA, Mexico, and Columbia	28	Market leader	12
Europe	UK, Germany, Russia, Poland	16	Fourth largest player	7

Source: *Annual Report*, Essel Propack, 2013.

and high-value cosmetic packaging. Though Essel has a relatively small base in Europe, it focuses on leveraging its capabilities both in oral and non-oral care sectors. The USA being a mature market offers much lower opportunities for organic growth in volume terms. Therefore, Essel emphasizes on improving profitability by bringing in more efficiency to its operations, introducing high-value decoration tubes targeting the cosmetics and beauty care category.

EPL's secret of success lies in being very efficient and competitive producers of customized printed co-extruded web (the main input for making lamitubes) that is capital intensive and its efficient conversion into tubes. In the global markets, integrated lamitube manufacturers are less than half a dozen, whereas the rest are pure converters. Besides, Essel has to focus on diversification of its product segments and markets as well.

Questions

1. What were the reasons that led Essel Propack Limited to enter into international markets?
2. Find out the key reasons for success of EPL in international markets.
3. Identify the benefits and risks for EPL in operating into a niche market segment of laminated tubes. Suggest measures to leverage its strengths and manage the risks identified by you.
4. In view of the intensifying competition among laminated tube manufacturers on one hand and rise in customers negotiating power on the other, how should EPL tackle with these marketing challenges so as to retain its market leadership in lamitubes in the next few years?

PART II
Scanning International Marketing Environment

Scanning the International Economic Environment

INTRODUCTION

The international marketing decisions are influenced, to a large extent, by international economic environment. To operate in international markets, one needs to develop a broad understanding of various factors affecting economic environment both at the international level and in the target markets.

This chapter provides a broad framework of international economic institutions and trade groups. Major international and multilateral organizations that have come up under the aegis of the UN system include the World Trade Organization (WTO), World Bank Group, International Monetary Fund (IMF), World Intellectual Property Organization (WIPO), United Nations Conference on Trade and Development (UNCTAD), and International Trade Centre (ITC). These institutions influence the international business scenario in a variety of ways. Among the various economic institutions, the WTO has been the most significant one, as it deals with a large number of issues such as gradual reduction and binding of import tariffs, elimination of non-tariff barriers such as quantitative restrictions, most-favoured-nation (MFN) treatment to all member countries, anti-dumping, etc., which have been dealt separately in Chapter 3.

The systems of trade preferences such as the Generalized System of Preferences (GSP)—tariff concessions extended by developed countries to developing countries on unilateral and non-reciprocal basis—and the Global System of Trade Preferences (GSTP) among developing countries influence the international market selection process and price competition.

Almost all the countries in the world have entered into some form of trade agreements, either bilaterally or multilaterally, consisting of a select group of countries. Such trade agreements have proliferated speedily during the last few decades. RTAs include European Union (EU), North American Free Trade Area (NAFTA), MERCOSUR, Gulf Cooperation Council (GCC), Asia-Pacific Economic Cooperation

Learning Objectives

- To explain the significance of economic organizations and trade groups in international marketing
- To describe the international economic institutions under the UN system
- To understand the conceptual framework of international economic integration
- To explain the major regional trading agreements (RTAs)
- To examine India's participation in RTAs

(APEC), Association of Southeast Asian Nations (ASEAN), etc. India has also entered into various economic cooperation agreements with Thailand, Sri Lanka, ASEAN, Afghanistan, Bay of Bengal Initiative for Multi-sectoral Technical and Economic Cooperation (BIMSTEC), South Asian Preferential Trade Agreement (SAPTA), and South Asian Free Trade Area (SAFTA). Since these trade agreements affect a firm's international marketing efforts in a number of areas, such as market access, modes of entry, competitiveness, and other marketing-mix decisions, the marketers should develop a thorough understanding of these agreements.

WORLD ECONOMIC OUTLOOK

The world output, which increased to 5.3 per cent in 2010, decreased to 3.9 per cent in 2011, which was again expected to decrease to 3.5 per cent in 2012 and rise to 4.1% in 2013, as shown in Table 2.1. The growth of world output is likely to decrease to 6 per cent in emerging markets and developing economies as compared to 2 per cent in advanced economies by 2013. The growth in world-trade volume of goods and services decreased[1] from 12.9 per cent in 2010 to 5.8 per cent in 2011, which is further likely to decrease to 5.6 per cent in 2013.

Strongly supported by growing exports and domestic investment, China continues to remain the main driver of economic momentum in developing Asia. India has contributed with 7.2 per cent growth in its output in 2011, which is projected at 6.9 per cent in 2012 and 7.3 per cent in 2013.

Table 2.1 World economic outlook: an overview (annual % change)

	Projections			
	2010	**2011**	**2012**	**2013**
World output[1]	5.3	3.9	3.5	4.1
Advanced economies	**3.2**	**1.6**	**1.4**	**2.0**
USA	3.0	1.7	2.1	2.4
Germany	1.9	1.4	−0.3	0.9
France	3.6	3.1	0.6	1.5
Itlay	1.4	1.7	0.5	1.0
Spain	1.8	0.4	−1.9	−0.3
Japan	−0.1	0.7	−1.8	0.1
UK	4.4	−0.7	2.0	1.7
Canada	2.1	0.7	0.8	2.0
Other advanced economies[2]	3.2	2.5	2.1	2.2
Newly industrialized Asian economies	5.8	3.2	2.6	3.5
Emerging and developing economies[3]	**8.5**	**4.0**	**3.4**	**4.2**
Central and Eastern Europe	7.5	6.2	5.7	6.0
Commonwealth of Independent States	4.5	5.3	1.9	2.9
Russia	4.8	4.9	4.2	4.1
Excluding Russia	4.3	4.3	4.0	3.9
Developing Asia	6.0	6.2	4.6	4.6
China	9.7	7.8	7.3	7.9

[1] *World Economic Outlook*, International Monetary Fund, April 2012.

	Projections			
	2010	**2011**	**2012**	**2013**
India	10.4	9.2	8.2	8.8
ASEAN-5[4]	10.6	7.2	6.9	7.3
Latin America and the Caribbean	7.0	4.5	5.4	6.2
Brazil	6.2	4.5	3.7	4.1
Mexico	7.5	2.7	3.0	4.1
Middle East and North Africa (MENA)	5.5	4.0	3.6	3.7
Sub-Saharan Africa	4.9	3.5	4.2	3.7
South Africa	5.3	5.1	5.4	5.3
Memorandum	2.9	3.1	2.7	3.4
European Union	2.0	1.6	0	1.3
World growth based on market exchange rates	4.2	2.8	2.7	3.3
World trade volume (goods and services)	**12.9**	**5.8**	**4.0**	**5.6**
Imports				
Advanced economies	11.5	4.3	1.8	4.1
Emerging and developing economies	15.3	8.8	8.4	8.1
Exports				
Advanced economies	12.2	5.3	2.3	4.7
Emerging and developing economies	14.7	6.7	6.6	7.2

Note: Real effective exchange rates were assumed to remain constant at the levels prevailing from 13 February to 12 March 2012.
[1]The quarterly estimates and projections account for 90% of the world purchasing-power-parity weights.
[2]Excludes the G7 (Canada, France, Germany, Italy, Japan, UK, USA) and Euro Area countries.
[3]The quarterly estimates and projections account for approximately 80% of the emerging and developing economies.
[4]Indonesia, Malaysia, Philippines, Thailand, and Vietnam.
Source: *World Economic Outlook*, International Monetary Fund, April 2012.

INTERNATIONAL ECONOMIC INSTITUTIONS

Under the UN system, a number of international economic organizations (Fig. 2.1) have been set up to facilitate and promote trade by way of multilateral framework. These institutions play a vital role in significantly influencing the international marketing environment.

The major international economic institutions include the World Bank Group, that is, International Bank for Reconstruction and Development (IBRD), International Development Association (IDA), International Finance Corporation (IFC), Multinational Investment Guarantee Corporation (MIGA), and International Centre for Settlement of Trade Disputes (ICSTD), and some other prominent economic institutions of the UN system, such as IMF, WIPO, UNCTAD, and ITC.

World Bank Group

The World Bank Group consists of five closely associated institutions (Fig. 2.2), all owned by member countries that carry the ultimate decision-making power. Each institution plays a distinct role in their broad mission to fight poverty and improve living standards for people in the developing world. The term 'World Bank Group' encompasses all five institutions whereas the term 'World Bank' refers specifically to IBRD and IDA.

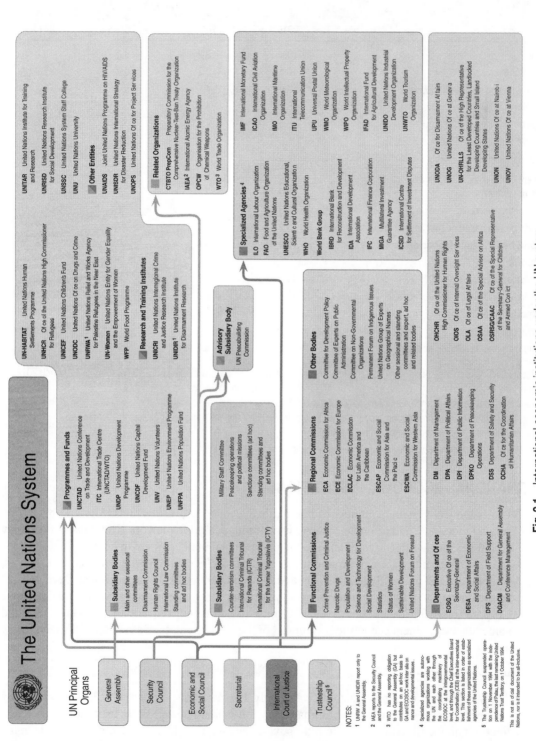

Fig. 2.1 International economic institutions under the UN system

Source: United Nations, http://www.un.org/en/aboutun/structure/org_chart.shtml, accessed on 18 October 2013.

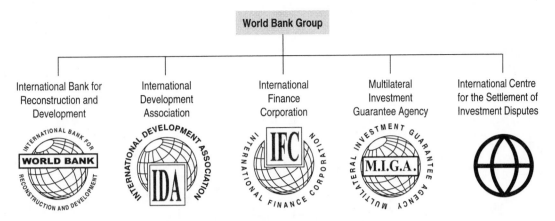

Fig. 2.2   The World Bank Group

Source: World Bank, http://go.worldbank.org/D2ALRSK6O0, accessed on 18 October 2013.

World Bank

The World Bank is a vital source of financial and technical assistance to developing countries around the world. It is made up of two unique development institutions owned by its member countries— IBRD and IDA. Each institution plays a different but supportive role in its mission to reduce global poverty and improve living standards. The IBRD aims to reduce poverty in middle income and creditworthy poor countries, whereas the IDA focuses on the poorest countries in the world. Together, these institutions provide low-interest loans, interest-free credit, and grants to developing countries for education, health, infrastructure, communication, and many other purposes.

The World Bank is run like a cooperative with 188 member countries as its shareholders. The number of shares a country has is based roughly on the size of its economy. The USA is its single largest shareholder with 16.41 per cent of votes, followed by Japan (7.87%), Germany (4.49%), the UK (4.31%), and France (4.31%). The rest of the share is divided among its other member countries.

The IBRD and IDA are run on similar lines. They share the same staff and headquarters, report to the same president, and evaluate projects with the same rigorous standards. But they draw on different resources for their lending. A country must be a member of the IBRD before it can join the IDA.

International Bank for Reconstruction and Development   Established in 1944, initially to help Europe recover from the devastation of World War II, the IBRD is the oldest of the World Bank Group institutions. Subsequently, it shifted its attention to developing countries. It aims to reduce poverty in middle-income and creditworthy poorer countries by promoting sustainable development through loans, guarantees, risk-management products, and (non-lending) analytic and advisory services. The income that IBRD has generated over the years has allowed it to fund developmental activities and ensure its financial strength, enabling it to borrow in capital markets at low cost and offer good borrowing terms to clients. The 24-member board of IBRD is made up of five appointed and 35 elected executive directors who represent the institution's member countries.

The IBRD helps clients gain access to capital and financial risk management tools in larger volumes, on better terms, at longer maturities, and in a more sustainable manner than they could receive from other sources. Unlike commercial banks, the IBRD is driven by development impact rather than profit maximization.

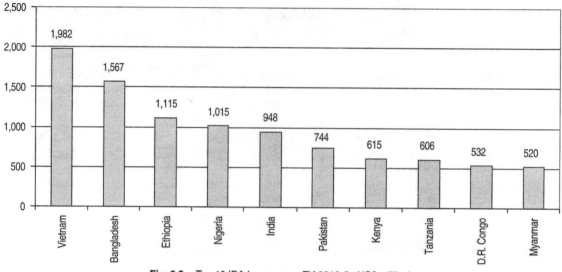

Fig. 2.3 Top 10 IDA borrowers—FY 2013 (in US$ million)

Source: World Bank

International Development Association   Established in 1960, the IDA helps support country-led poverty reduction strategies in key policy areas, including raising productivity, providing good governance, improving the private investment climate, and improving access to education and health care to poor people (Fig. 2.3). It provides interest-free credits and grants to the poorest developing countries in order to boost their economic growth and improve people's living conditions. The IDA funds help these countries deal with complex challenges they face in striving to meet the Millennium Development Goals (MDGs). It helps reduce inequalities both across and within countries by allowing more people to participate in the mainstream economy, reducing poverty, and promoting more equal access to the opportunities created by economic growth. The IDA complements the World Bank's other lending arm, IBRD. Presently, it has 172 members.

The IDA depends on the contributions from its wealthier member countries for most of its financial resources. The other important source is from repayment of outstanding credits, by countries that received IDA assistance in the past but have since 'graduated' from the IDA. Since its inception, IDA credits and grants have directed the largest share, about 50 per cent to Africa.

International Finance Corporation

The IFC promotes economic development through the private sector. It was established in 1956 as the private sector arm of the World Bank Group. It provides finance to markets deemed too risky by commercial investors in the absence of IFC participation and adds value to the projects it finances through its corporate governance, environmental, and social expertise. Working with business partners, it invests in sustainable private enterprises in developing countries without accepting government guarantees.

The IFC coordinates its activities with other institutions of the World Bank Group but is legally and financially independent. Its share capital is provided by its member countries, which vote in proportion to the number of shares held. The IFC is owned by its 179 member countries with an authorized capital of US$2.45 billion.

The IFC promotes private businesses in developing countries by providing loans and making equity investments, helping companies mobilize financing in the international financial markets, and providing advice and technical assistance to businesses and governments. It charges market rates for its products and does not accept government guarantees. Financial products and services to client companies include

- long-term loans in major currencies at fixed or variable rates;
- equity investments;
- quasi-equity instruments (subordinated loans, preferred stock, and income notes);
- guarantees and standby financing;
- risk management tools; and
- structured finance products.

The IFC's investments are funded out of its net worth, the total of paid-in capital and retained earnings. To ensure the participation of investors and lenders from the private sector, IFC limits the finance provided of a project to 25 per cent of total estimated costs; it does not normally hold more than a 35 per cent stake or be the largest shareholder. For all new investments, the IFC articulates the expected impact on sustainable development, and, as the projects mature, it assesses the quality of the development benefits realized.

Multilateral Investment Guarantee Agency

Established in 1988, the MIGA was aimed at promoting foreign direct investment in developing countries by providing guarantees to investors against noncommercial risks, such as expropriation, currency inconvertibility and transfer restrictions, war and civil disturbance, and breach of contract. Its capacity to serve as an objective intermediary and its ability to influence the resolution of potential disputes enhances investors' confidence that they will be protected against these risks. Presently, it has 172 members.

The MIGA provides noncommercial guarantees (insurance) for foreign direct investment in developing countries. It addresses concerns about investment environments and perceptions of risk, which often inhibit investment, by providing political risk insurance. It also provides advisory services to help countries attract and retain foreign investment, mediates investment disputes to keep current investments intact and to remove possible obstacles to future investment, and disseminates information on investment opportunities to the international business community. Since its inception, the MIGA has issued more than US$24 billion in political risk insurance for project in wide variety of sectors, covering all regions of the world.

Cross-border investments and new investment contributions associated with the expansion, modernization, or financial restructuring of existing projects are also eligible for guarantee, as are acquisitions that involve the privatization of state-owned enterprises. Types of foreign investments that can be covered include equity, shareholder loans, and shareholder loan guarantees, provided the loans have a minimum maturity period of three years. Loans to unrelated borrowers can be insured, provided shareholders' investment in the project is insured concurrently or has already been insured. Other forms of investment, such as technical assistance and management contracts, and franchising and licensing agreements, may also be eligible for coverage.

The MIGA provides private investors the confidence and comfort they need to make sustainable investments in developing countries. As part of the World Bank Group, and having shareholders of both host countries and investor countries, the MIGA brings security and credibility to an investment that is unmatched. Its presence in a potential investment can literally transform a 'no-go' into a 'go'. The MIGA acts as a potent deterrent against government actions that may adversely affect investments. Even if disputes arise, leverage with host governments frequently enables resolving differences to the mutual satisfaction of all parties.

Investors may choose a combination of any of the four types of coverages. Equity investments can be covered up to 90 per cent and debt up to 95 per cent, with coverage typically available for up to 15 years, and in some cases, for up to 20 years. The MIGA may insure up to US$220 million and, if necessary, more can be arranged through syndication of insurance. Pricing is determined on the basis of both country and project risk, with the effective price varying depending on the type of investment and industry sector. An investor has the option to cancel a policy after three years.

The MIGA offers comparative advantages in areas ranging from unique packaging of products and ability to restore the business community's confidence to ongoing collaboration with the public and private insurance market to increase the amount of insurance available to investors. The guarantee programme of MIGA complements national and private investment insurance schemes through co-insurance and re-insurance arrangements. It provides investors a more comprehensive investment insurance coverage worldwide.

International Centre for Settlement of Investment Disputes

The International Centre for Settlement of Investment Disputes (ICSID) was established in 1966 with the basic objective to establish an institutional mechanism specially designed to facilitate the settlement of investment disputes between governments and foreign investors to help promote increased flow of international investment. The ICSID provides facilities for the conciliation and arbitration of disputes between member countries and investors who qualify as nationals of other member countries. Recourse to ICSID conciliation and arbitration is entirely voluntary. However, once the two parties have consented to arbitration under the ICSID convention, neither can unilaterally withdraw its consent. Moreover, all ICSID contracting states, whether or not parties to the dispute, are required by the convention to recognize and enforce ICSID arbitral awards. Many international agreements concerning investment refer to the arbitration facilities of ICSID.

The ICSID is headquartered at Washington, DC and has an administrative council and a secretariat. The administrative council is chaired by the World Bank's president and consists of one representative from each state ratified by the convention.

Since 1978, for providing conciliation and arbitration, the centre has a set of additional facility rules authorizing the ICSID secretariat to administer certain types of proceedings between states and foreign nationals, which fall outside the scope of convention. These include conciliation and arbitration proceedings where either the state party or the home state of the foreign national is not a member of the ICSID.

Arbitration under the auspices of the ICSID is one of the main mechanisms for the settlement of investment disputes under four recent multilateral trade and investment treaties, such as the North American Free Trade Agreement, the Energy Charter Treaty, the Cartagena Free Trade Agreement, and the Colonia Investment Protocol of MERCOSUR. During recent years, the caseload of the ICSID has increased considerably, mainly due to the proliferation of international investment treaties. The ICSID also conducts research and carries on publishing activities in the areas of arbitration law and foreign investment law.

International Monetary Fund

The International Monetary fund, also known as the IMF or simply the 'Fund', was conceived at a UN conference convened in Bretton Woods, New Hampshire, USA in July 1944 with an objective to build a framework for economic cooperation that would avoid a repetition of the disastrous economic policies that had contributed to the Great Depression of the 1930s. Broadly, the IMF is responsible for ensuring the stability of the international monetary and financial system—the system of international payments and exchange rates among national currencies that enable trade to take place between countries.

The main responsibilities of the IMF include

- promoting international monetary cooperation;
- facilitating the expansion and balanced growth of the international trade;
- promoting exchange stability;
- assisting in the establishment of a multilateral system of payments; and
- making its resources available, under adequate safeguards to members experiencing balance of payments difficulties.

The Fund seeks to promote economic stability and prevent crises, to help resolve crises when they do occur, and to promote growth and alleviate poverty. To meet these objectives, it employs three main functions, as follows.

Surveillance   It is the main policy dialogue and policy advice that the IMF offers to each of its members. Generally once a year, the IMF conducts in-depth appraisals of each member country's economic situation. It discusses with the country's authorities the policies that are most conducive to stable exchange rates and a growing and prosperous economy. In its oversight of member countries' economic policies, the IMF looks mainly at the performance of an economy as a whole—often referred to as its macroeconomic performance. This comprises total spending (its major components like consumer spending and business investment), output, employment, and inflation, as well as the country's balance of payments, that is, the balance of a country's transactions with the rest of the world.

Technical assistance   The objective of IMF technical assistance is to contribute to the development of the productive resources of member countries by enhancing the effectiveness of economic policy and financial management. Technical assistance and training are offered mostly free of charge within its IMF resource constraints to help member countries strengthen their capacity to design and implement effective policies. The IMF offers technical assistance in several areas, including fiscal policy, monetary and exchange rate policies, banking and financial system supervision and regulation, and statistics.

In case member countries experience difficulties in financing their balance of payments, the IMF also helps in recovery. About three-quarters of the Fund's technical assistance go to low- and lower-middle income countries, particularly in sub-Saharan Africa and Asia, and post-conflict countries.

The IMF is accountable to the governments of its member countries. At the apex of its organizational structure is its Board of Governors, which consists of one governor from each of its member countries. All governors meet once each year at the IMF–World Bank Annual Meetings.

Lending   Even the best economic policies cannot eradicate instability or avert crises. In the event that a member country does experience financing difficulties, the IMF can provide financial assistance to support policy programmes that will correct underlying macroeconomic problems, limit disruptions to the domestic and global economies, and help restore confidence, stability, and growth. IMF financing instruments can also support crisis prevention.

The IMF's resources are provided by its member countries, primarily through payment of quotas, which broadly reflect the economic size of each country. The annual expenses of running the Fund are met mainly by the difference between interest receipts on outstanding loans and interest payments on quota 'deposits'.

Special Drawing Right   The Special Drawing Right (SDR) is an international reserve asset introduced by the IMF in 1969 due to concern among IMF members that the current stock and prospective growth of international reserves might not be sufficient to support the expansion of world trade. The main reserve assets were gold and US dollars, and members did not want global reserves to depend on gold production, with its inherent uncertainties and the continuing US balance of payments deficits, which would be needed to provide continuing growth in US dollar reserves. The SDR was introduced as a supplementary reserve asset, which the IMF could 'allocate' periodically to its members when the need arose, and cancel, as necessary.

SDRs, sometimes known as 'paper gold' although they have no physical form, have been allocated to member countries (as bookkeeping entries) as a percentage of their quotas. Readers should note that the SDR is neither a currency, nor a claim on the IMF. However, the IMF member countries may use SDRs in transactions among themselves, with 'institutional' holders of SDRs, and with the IMF. The SDR is also the unit of account of IMF. A number of other international and regional organizations and international conventions use it as a unit of account or as a basis for a unit of account.

The value of the SDR was initially defined as equivalent to 0.888671 g of fine gold, which at the time was also equivalent to one US dollar. After the collapse of the Bretton Woods System in 1973, the SDR was redefined as a basket of currencies. The value of the SDR is set daily using a basket of four major currencies: the euro, Japanese yen, pound sterling, and US dollar. The composition of the basket is reviewed every five years to ensure that it is representative of the currencies used in international transactions, and that the weights assigned to the currencies reflect their relative importance in the world's trading and financial systems.

The distinguishing features of IMF and World Bank are shown in Exhibit 2.1.

Exhibit 2.1   IMF vs World Bank

IMF	World Bank
• Oversees the international monetary system	• Seeks to promote the economic development of the world's poorer countries
• Promotes exchange stability and orderly exchange relations among its member countries	• Assists developing countries through long-term financing of development projects and programmes
• Assists all members—both industrial and developing countries that find themselves in temporary difficulties of balance of payments—by providing short- to medium-term credits	• Provides to the poorest developing countries whose per capita GNP is less than US$865 a year special financial assistance through the IDA
• Supplements the currency reserves of its members through the allocation of SDRs in proportion to their quotas	• Encourages private enterprises in developing countries through its affiliate IFC
• Draws its financial resources principally from the quota subscriptions of its member countries	• Acquires most of its financial resources by borrowing on the international bond market
• Has at its disposal fully paid-in quotas now totalling SDR 145 billion (about US$215 billion)	• Has an authorized capital of US$184 billion, of which members pay in about 10%
• Has a staff of over 2,600, drawn from 146 member countries	• Has a staff of over 10,000, drawn from all its 185 member countries

Source: IMF and World Bank publications.

United Nations Conference on Trade and Development

In the early 1960s, growing concerns about the place of developing countries in international trade led many of these countries to call for the convening of a full-fledged conference specifically devoted to tackling these problems and identifying appropriate international actions. The UNCTAD was established in 1964, aimed at creating development-friendly integration of developing countries into the world economy. The basic functions of UNCTAD are as follows:

- Serve as the focal point within the UN for the integrated treatment of trade and development and the interrelated issues in the areas of finance, technology, investment, and sustainable development.
- Serve as a forum for intergovernmental discussions and deliberations, supported by discussions with experts and exchanges of experience, aimed at consensus-building.
- Undertake research, policy analysis, and data collection in order to provide substantive inputs for the discussions of experts and government representatives.
- Facilitate cooperation with other organizations and donor countries and to provide technical assistance tailored to the needs of the developing countries, with special attention to the needs of the least developed countries and countries with a transitional economy.

The UNCTAD is the most visible symbol of the UN's assurance to promote the economic and social advancement of all people of the world and this remains equally relevant in the changing world economic order. It continues to be an important resource base for the South and it provides a forum for various nations to network and form issue-based coalitions with like-minded countries, especially the developing countries. UNCTAD has played a valuable role in educative, early warning, and watchdog functions vis-à-vis interests of the developing countries in the working of the WTO.

The technical cooperation programmes of the UNCTAD in trade efficiency, trade points, harmonization of customs procedure, database on trade information (TRAINS), debt management programmes, etc. have been found extremely useful by the developing countries.

The UNCTAD secretariat works together with member governments and interacts with organizations of the UN system and regional commissions, as well as with governmental institutions, nongovernmental organizations, and the private sector, including trade and industry associations, research institutes, and universities worldwide. The Ministerial Conference which meets every four years is the highest decision-making body of the UNCTAD, which sets priorities and guidelines for the organization and provides an opportunity to debate and evolve policy consensus on key economic and development issues.

Over the years, the UNCTAD has focused its analytical research on the linkages between trade, investment, technology, and enterprise development. It has put forward a positive agenda for developing countries in international trade negotiations, designed to assist developing counties in better understanding the complexity of the multilateral trade negotiations and in formulating their positions. Moreover, it has expanded and diversified its technical assistance, which today covers a wide range of areas, including training trade negotiators, and addressing trade-related issues, debt management, investment policy reviews and the promotion of entrepreneurship, commodities, competition law, policy, trade, and environment.

The UNCTAD has continued to play a critical role in emphasizing the development dimension of issues in the fields of international trade and investment and related areas. In particular, it has been addressing the imbalances of globalization and the need to overcome the supply constraints of developing countries, so as to ensure development gains and poverty reduction.

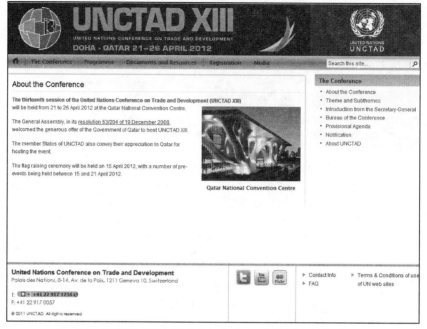

Qatar National Convention Centre

Fig. 2.4 UNCTAD XIII held at Doha in Qatar during 21–26 April 2012

Source: United Nations Conference on Trade and Development (UNCTAD), http://unctadxiii.org, accessed on 18 October 2013.

UNCTAD XIII   In view of the significance of rapid globalization, the theme of UNCTAD XIII held during 21–26 April 2012 at Doha, Qatar[2] (Fig. 2.4) was 'Development-centred globalization: towards inclusive and sustainable growth and development'.

The sub themes of UNCTAD XIII were as follows:

• Enhancing the enabling economic environment at all levels in support of inclusive and sustainable development
• Strengthening all forms of cooperation and partnerships for trade and development, including North–South, South–South, and triangular cooperation
• Addressing persistent and emerging development challenges as related to their implications for trade and development and interrelated issues in the areas of finance, technology, investment, and sustainable development
• Promoting investment, trade, entrepreneurship and related development policies to foster sustained economic growth for sustainable and inclusive development

India wants UNCTAD to focus on certain aspects, such as enhanced and predictable market access for agriculture and better terms of trade, removal of market entry barriers to trade, financial support, volatility in the capital market, trade diversification and moving up the value chain into technology intensive manufactured exports, greater policy space to develop local industries, strengthening of technological capacity, and the need for a more benign and development sensitive international technology and Intellectual Property Rights (IPR) regime.

The Generalized System of Preferences (GSP), International Commodities Agreements, Code of Conduct for Liner Conferences, Control of Restrictive Business Practices, and Global System of Trade Preferences (GSTP) among developing countries are some of the major agreements launched under the UNCTAD.

---

[2] *Civil Society Declaration to UNCTAD XIII*, 13th Session, Doha, Qatar, 21–26 April 2012.

Generalized System of Preferences

The GSP is a noncontractual instrument by which preferential tariff treatment is granted on a nonreciprocal and nondiscriminatory basis by most developed countries unilaterally to exports from developing countries, with MFN treatment duties reduced or eliminated. The GSP was formally accepted in 1968 by UN members at the second UNCTAD conference in New Delhi. The general underlying principles of the scheme are nondiscrimination and nonreciprocity. The GSP offers developing countries tariff reductions, and in some cases, duty-free concessions for their manufactured exports and certain agricultural exports as well. The GSP is a tariff instrument, which is autonomous and complementary to the General Agreement on Tariffs and Trade (GATT). Its aim is to grant developing countries tariff preferences over developed countries, thus allowing their exports easier access to the market.

Common Fund for Commodities

A Common Fund for Commodities (CFC) was established in 1989 with the following objectives:

- Serve as a key instrument in attaining the agreed objectives for the integrated programme for commodities adopted by the UNCTAD.
- Facilitate the conclusion and functioning of International Commodity Agreements (ICAs), particularly concerning commodities of special interest to developing countries.

In order to fulfil these objectives, the fund has been authorized to exercise the following functions:

- Contribute, through its First Account to the financing of international buffer stocks and internationally coordinated national stocks, all within the framework of ICAs.
- Finance, through its Second Account, measures in the field of commodities other than stocking.
- Promote coordination and consultation through its Second Account with regard to measures in the field of commodities other than stocking, and their financing, with a view to provide commodity focus.

The resources of the common fund are derived from subscription of shares of directly contributed capital paid in by the member countries. The interest earned by the capital of the First Account is used to finance projects under the First Account Net Earning initiative and to cover the administrative expenses of the Fund. Therefore, member countries do not need to pay annual membership fees. Commodity development measures of the common fund are financed by either loans or grants or a combination of both. The capital resources of the Second Account can only be used for loans, whereas the voluntary contributions are available for grants and/or loans.

Since the conception of the Fund in 1970s, certain elements of commodity trade have changed dramatically, in particular the shift away from market regulating instruments to a liberalized system of market forces. Due to this, the Common Fund has not been able to put into operation the First Account capital, which was primarily meant for the financing of international buffer stocks and internationally coordinated national stocks within the framework of the ICAs.

Global System of Trade Preference among developing countries

The agreement on the GSTP among developing countries was established in 1988 as a framework for the exchange of trade preferences among developing countries in order to promote intra-developing-country trade. The idea received its first political expression at the 1976 ministerial meeting of the Group of 77 (G77) in Mexico City and was further promoted at the G77 ministerial meeting in Arusha (1979) and Caracas (1981).

The GSTP establishes a framework for the exchange of trade concessions among the members of G77. It lays down rules, principles, and procedures for conduct of negotiations and for implementation of results of the negotiations. The coverage of the GSTP extends to arrangements in the area of tariffs, nontariff measures, and direct trade measures including medium and long-term contracts and sectoral agreements. One of the basic principles of the agreement is that it is to be negotiated step by step, improved upon, and extended in successive stages.

The agreement in its present form is too modest; the concessions in scope and quality are few, limited, and insufficiently attractive to motivate greater trade among countries of the South. Additional efforts, additional instruments, additional participating countries, additional stimulus, and concessions are therefore, required for the system to fully gain ground. Presently, 44 countries have acceded to the agreement including India, Pakistan, Bangladesh, Brazil, Indonesia, Malaysia, Philippines, Singapore, Sri Lanka, Thailand, and Tanzania.

Participants may convene rounds of negotiations in order to broaden and deepen the scope of trade preferences. Three rounds of negotiations have so far been launched: the first in Brasilia (1986), the second in Tehran (1992), and the third in Sao Paulo (2004). On 2 December 2009, modalities were adopted at the end of the negotiations in Geneva agreeing to apply an across the board, line-by-line, linear cut of at least 20 per cent on minimum 70 per cent of their all dutiable tariff lines.[3] During UNCTAD XIII held on 23 April 2012 at Doha, Qatar, the negotiating parties reaffirmed their commitment to boost South–South cooperation.[4]

World Intellectual Property Organization

The WIPO was established in 1970 as a specialized agency of the UN headquartered at Geneva, dedicated to ensure that the rights of the creators and owners of intellectual property (IP) are protected worldwide and that inventors and authors are recognized and rewarded for their ingenuity. The WIPO facilitates a balanced and accessible international IP system, which rewards creativity, stimulates innovation, and contributes to economic development while safeguarding public interest. It also facilitates providing a stable environment to market IP products internationally.

The WIPO treats IP as an important tool for the economic, social, and cultural development of all countries. This shapes its mission to promote the effective use and protection of IP worldwide. Strategic goals are set out in a four yearly medium-term plan and refined in the biennial programme and budget document. The five strategic goals defined by WIPO are as follows:

- Promote an IP culture
- Integrate IP into national development policies and programmes
- Develop international IP laws and standards
- Delivery quality services in global IP protection systems
- Increase the efficiency of the management and support processes of WIPO

    The major functions of WIPO include providing

- advice and expertise in the drafting and revision of national legislation, which is particularly important for the WIPO member states with obligations under the agreement on Trade-Related Aspects of Intellectual Property (TRIPS);

---

[3] *Sao Paulo Round of the Global System of Trade Preferences among Developing Countries*, Special Session at Ministerial Level, Geneva, 2 December 2009.
[4] *Global System of Trade Preferences among Developing Countries*, GSTP High Level meeting, Doha, Qatar, 23 April 2012.

- comprehensive education and training programmes at national and regional levels for
  - officials dealing with IP, including those concerned with management of rights and enforcement; and
  - traditional and new groups of users, on the value of IP and how to create their own economic assets through better use of the IP system;
- extensive computerization assistance to help developing countries acquire the information technology resources (both in human and material terms) to streamline administrative procedures for managing and administering their own IP resources, and to participate in the global information network of the WIPO; and
- financial assistance to facilitate participation in WIPO activities and meetings, especially those concerned with the progressive development of new international norms and practices.

The WIPO derives its fundamentals of protecting IP from Paris (1896) and Berne (1886) conventions, but the subsequent treaties have widened and deepened the system of protection. In 2002, the WIPO Copyright Treaty (WCT) and the WIPO Performances and Phonograms (WPPT) came into force, which entail basic rules updating the international protection of copyright and related rights in the Internet age. The WIPO is carrying out a major project to develop and establish a global IP network called WIPOnet, which is likely to facilitate economic integration of developing countries in the international digital environment, narrowing down the information gap that exists between developing and developed countries.

United Nations Industrial Development Organization

The United Nations Industrial Development Organization (UNIDO), set up in 1966, is headquartered in Geneva and became a specialized agency of the UN in 1985. It aims to promote industrialization in developing countries and in countries with economies in transition. The UNIDO helps these countries in their fight against marginalization in today's globalized world. It mobilizes knowledge, skills, information, and technology to promote productive employment, a competitive economy, and a sound environment.

The assistance of UNIDO is delivered through two core functions, as follows.

As a global forum　The UNIDO generates and disseminates knowledge related to industrial matters and provides a platform to various stakeholders to enhance cooperation, establish dialogue, and develop partnership.

As a technical cooperation agency　It designs and implements programmes to support the industrial development efforts of its clients. It also offers tailor-made specialized support for programme development.

These two core functions of the UNIDO are complementary and mutually supportive. On one hand, experience gained in the technical cooperation work of UNIDO can be shared with policy makers; on the other hand, the organization's analytical work shows where technical cooperation will have the greatest impact by helping define priorities.

Asian Development Bank

The Asian Development Bank (ADB) is a multilateral financial institution that aims to improve the welfare of the people in Asia and the Pacific, particularly the 1.8 billion who live on less than US$2 per day. It is owned by 67 member countries, 48 from the region, and 19 from other parts of the world. Japan and the US are coequally the largest shareholders, each with 12.8 per cent of total subscribed capital. The ADB has an important role to play in making the region free of poverty, as Asia and the Pacific region are home to two-thirds of the world's poor. The main instruments for providing help to its developing member countries (DMCs) include policy dialogue, loans, technical assistance, grants, guarantees, and equity investments.

The major functions of the bank are as follows:

- Extend loans and equity investments to its DMCs for their economic and social development
- Provide technical assistance for planning and execution of development projects and programmes and for advisory services
- Promote and facilitate investment of public and private capital and development
- Respond to requests for assistance in coordinating development policies and plans of its DMCs

The priorities of the ADB's projects and programmes include economic growth, human development, gender and development, good governance, environmental protection, private sector development, and regional cooperation. Pro-poor sustainable economic growth, inclusive social development, and good governance are the three pillars of the poverty reduction strategy of ADB.

The ADB lends to governments and to public and private enterprises in its DMCs. Loans and technical assistance are its principal tools which are provided to governments for specific, high-priority development projects and programmes. Its lending both supports and promotes investment for development, based on a country's priorities.

United Nations Economic and Social Commission for Asia and the Pacific

The Economic and Social Commission for Asia and the Pacific (ESCAP) is the most comprehensive of the five regional commissions of the UN, which are aimed at developing the Asia-Pacific region. It was established in 1947 with headquarters in Bangkok, Thailand. India is one of the founding members of the ESCAP. The main mandate of the ESCAP is to foster cooperation between its 62 member countries. It provides the strategic link between global- and country-level programmes and issues. It supports governments of the regions in consolidating regional positions and advocates regional approaches to meet the region's unique socioeconomic challenges in a globalizing world.

Trade and investment is one of the eight sub-programmes of ESCAP that aims to benefit the region through the globalization process with the help of increased global and regional trade and investment flows. The trade and investment division assists countries to

- understand trade and investment agreements, their implications, and economics;
- facilitate trade and investment flows, including trade finance and e-commerce;
- promote regional trade agreements (RTAs) in conformity with the multilateral trading system;
- understand the economics of trade policy;
- negotiate accession to the WTO, especially for least developed countries and economies in transition;
- formulate more effective policies and strategies for foreign direct investment promotion and facilitation;
- develop small- and medium-sized enterprises and promote entrepreneurship; and
- access trade and investment-related information.

Trade facilitation, trade and investment information, RTAs, Doha development agenda, investment promotion and facilitation, and enterprise development are its areas of focus.

INTERNATIONAL ECONOMIC INTEGRATIONS

Economic integrations among countries significantly influence a firm's strategic decisions in international markets. The preferential treatment granted to member countries affects the competitiveness of goods in different country markets. The elimination of import tariffs by the member countries of a trade group encourages sourcing of goods from cost-efficient production locations. However, discriminatory tariff against nonmembers results in trade diversion to member countries, even at the cost of production efficiency. International marketing managers should develop a thorough insight into the concept and impact of international economic integrations, various forms of trade groups, major trade groups and their legitimacy under the multilateral trade regime of WTO.

Subsequent to World War II, economic integration has become a widespread phenomenon that has greatly affected the operations of international markets. In the post-WTO era, the sluggish movement of trade negotiations at the WTO has led to frustration among its member countries to a varying extent and has contributed to the rapid proliferation of preferential trade agreements (PTAs). Despite the fundamental conflict of PTAs with multilateralism, these are legally permitted as a perception under Article XXIV of WTO. It is estimated that about 60 per cent of world trade is conducted on preferential basis rather than on MFN basis.

Such economic integrations have widely been referred to as RTAs. However, in the present scenario, since a considerable number of these agreements for preferential trade are not necessarily on a contiguous-region basis, the term 'regional' in the 'RTAs' has lost its connotation and the term 'preferential' is preferred over 'regional'. However, in the WTO terminology, the term RTA is used interchangeably for all types of economic groupings, such as PTA, free trade area (FTA), and RTA.

Conceptual Framework of International Economic Integration

The basic theories explaining the concept of trade agreements suggest that economic cooperation among member countries not only increases their trade, but also improves the quality of their citizens' lives. The formation of an FTA is believed to bring in the following impacts of trade:

Trade creation effect Increase in consumption opportunities by making low-cost goods available due to reduced tariffs

Trade diversion effect Shift of trade to the member partner countries from more efficient nonmember countries even at the cost of efficiency

The coverage and depth of preferential treatment varies from one PTA to another. Present-day PTAs are not exclusively those linking the most developed economies, rather they tend to go far beyond tariff-cutting exercises. They provide for increasingly complex regulations governing intra-trade (e.g., with respect to standards, safeguard provisions, and customs administration) and they often also provide for a preferential regulatory framework for mutual services trade. The most sophisticated PTAs go beyond traditional trade policy mechanisms, to include regional rules on investment, competition, environment, and labour.

As shown in Fig. 2.5, the level of integration among the countries increases as it moves from PTA to a political union, which needs much greater commitment on the part of member countries. Generally, the form of economic groupings as shown inside the smaller boxes precedes those shown in outer boxes. The basic attributes of such economic groupings are as follows.

Preferential trading agreement (PTA) Member countries in a PTA lower tariff barriers to imports of identified products from one another. Examples of such associations include the

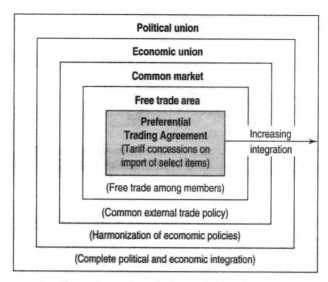

Fig. 2.5 Conceptual framework of international economic integration

Economic Community of West African States (ECOWAS), the Bangkok Agreement, the Global System of Trade Preferences (GSTP) among developing countries, and the Common Market for Eastern and Southern Africa (COMESA).

Free trade area (FTA)　This is the basic form of economic integration in which member countries seek to remove all tariffs and nontariff barriers among themselves. However, the members are free to maintain their own tariffs and nontariff barriers with nonmember countries. Member countries strive to remove all tariffs and nontariff barriers for cross-border trade of goods and services. Since, in case of free trade area, marketing firms from nonmember countries may evolve ways to take benefit of tariff differentials among members, it may result in parallel trade unless checked by effective legislation and implementation.

Customs union (CU)　In a customs union, countries not only eliminate tariff barriers among themselves but also apply common external import tariffs for nonmembers. CUs include the Caribbean Community and Common Market (CARICOM) and the Central American Common Market (CACM)

Common market (CM)　In addition to free trade among members and uniform tariff policy for nonmembers in a common market, such an arrangement ensures all restrictions on cross-border investment, movement of labour, technology transfer, management, and sharing of capital resources are eliminated. Common markets include the Common Market for Eastern and Southern Africa (COMESA) and the Southern Cone Common Market (MERCOSUR), among others.

Economic union (EU)　An economic union, such as the EU enjoys much greater level of economic integration where free exchange of goods and services takes place. The member countries in an economic union maintain a fiscal discipline, stability in exchange, and interest rates by way of unified monetary and fiscal policies.

Political union (PU)　As a culmination of economic integration, the member countries strive to harmonize their security and foreign policies. A common parliament is created with representatives of member countries who work in synchronization with an individual country's legislature.

At this stage, the member countries are willing to dilute their national identities to a considerable extent and become a part of the union.

While the most common category is the FTA, which accounts for 70 per cent of all RTAs, the configuration of RTAs is diverse and is becoming more complex with overlapping RTAs and networks of RTAs spanning across continents.

MAJOR TRADE GROUPS

There has been a sharp proliferation in RTAs in the last 50 years. WTO members, similar to earlier contracting parties of GATT, are bound to notify the RTAs in which they participate. During 1948–1994, the GATT received 124 notifications of RTAs relating to trade in goods, whereas since the creation of WTO in 1995, over 240 additional agreements covering trade in goods and services have been notified. A total of 511 RTAs had been notified by the WTO by January 2012. Of these, 319 were in force.

The major trade groups are shown in Exhibit 2.2.

The European Union

After World War II, the idea of European integration was conceived to prevent such killing and destruction from ever happening again. In 1948, the Organization for European Economic Cooperation (OEEC) was established, mainly to administer Marshall Plan aid from the USA that paved the way for deeper economic integrations in the future. Six European nations, that is, West Germany, France, Italy, Belgium, the Netherlands, and Luxembourg, joined hands to establish the European Coal and Steel Community (ECSC) to establish a common market in coal, steel, and iron ore.

The idea of the European Union (EU) was first proposed by the French foreign minister Robert Schumann, in a speech on 9 May 1950, which is still celebrated as Europe Day, the birthday of the present EU. The European Community (EC) was formed in 1967, as a result of a merger of ECSC, EEC, and the European Atomic Energy Community (EURATOM). Denmark, Ireland, and the UK joined the EU on 1 January 1973 raising the number of member states to nine. Subsequently, Greece joined the EU in 1981, Spain and Portugal in 1986, and Austria, Finland, and Sweden in 1995.

The Single European Act, signed in 1987, paved the way to create the 'single Market'. European countries came closer following the collapse of communism across Central and Eastern Europe. The Single Market was accomplished through a 'four freedom', that is, freedom, of movement of goods, services, people, and money. The 'Maastricht treaty', signed in 1992 by all (then) 12 member countries of the EC resulted in the creation of the EU, which became operational on 1 January 1994. Ten new countries, that is, the Czech Republic, Cyprus, Estonia, Hungary, Poland, Slovenia, Slovakia, Latvia, Lithuania, and Malta joined the EU in 1994. Consequent to 11 September 2001, political dealings between East and West Europe diminished considerably. Two more countries from Eastern Europe, Bulgaria and Romania, joined the EU on 1 January 2007, bringing its membership to 27 states. Additionally, Croatia, the former Yugoslav Republic of Macedonia, and Turkey are also candidates for future membership.

In the early years, much of the cooperation between EU countries was about trade and the economy, but now the EU also deals with many other subjects, such as citizens' rights; ensuring freedom, security, and justice; job creation; regional development; environmental protection; and promoting globalization.

Exhibit 2.2 Summary of major trade groups

Trade groups	Member countries
High-, low-, and middle-income economies	
European Union	Austria, Belgium, Denmark, Finland, France, Germany, Greece, Ireland, Italy, Luxembourg, the Netherlands, Portugal, Spain, Sweden and the UK, Czech Republic, Cyprus, Estonia, Hungary, Poland, Slovenia, Slovakia, Latvia, Lithuania, Malta, Bulgaria, and Romania
North American Free Trade Area (NAFTA)	Canada, Mexico, and the USA
Asia Pacific Economic Cooperation (APEC)	Australia, Brunei Darussalam, Canada, Chile, People's Republic of China, Hong Kong, China, Indonesia, Japan, Republic of Korea, Malaysia, Mexico, New Zealand, Papua New Guinea, Peru, the Philippines, The Russian Federation, Singapore, Chinese Taipei, Thailand, USA, and Vietnam
Latin America and the Caribbean	
Association of Caribbean States (ACS)	Antigua and Barbuda, the Bahamas, Barbados, Belize, Colombia, Costa Rica, Cuba, Dominica, the Dominican Republic, El Salvador, Grenada, Guatemala, Guyana, Haiti, Honduras, Jamaica, Mexico, Nicaragua, Panama, St Kitts and Nevis, St Lucia, St Vincent and the Grenadines, Suriname, Trinidad and Tobago, and Venezuela
Andean community	Bolivia, Colombia, Ecuador, Peru, and Venezuela
Group of three	Colombia, Mexico, and Venezuela
Latin American Integration Association (LAIA) (formerly Latin American Free Trade Area)	Argentina, Bolivia, Brazil, Chile, Colombia, Ecuador, Mexico, Paraguay, Peru, Uruguay, and Venezuela
Southern Cone Common Market (MERCOSUR)	Argentina, Brazil, Paraguay, Uruguay, and Venezuela
Africa	
Common Market for Eastern and Southern Africa (COMESA)	Angola, Burundi, Comoros, the Democratic Republic of Congo, Djibouti, the Arab Republic of Egypt, Eritrea, Ethiopia, Kenya, Libya, Madagascar, Malawi, Mauritius, Namibia, Rwanda, Seychelles, Sudan, Swaziland, Uganda, Tanzania, Zambia, and Zimbabwe
Economic Community of West African States (ECOWAS)	Benin, Burkina, Faso, Cape Verde, Cote d'Ivoire, the Gambia, Ghana, Guinea, Guinea-Bissau, Liberia, Mali, Mauritania, Niger, Nigeria, Senegal, Sierra Leone, and Togolese
Southern African Development Community (SADC), formerly Southern African Development Coordination Conference	Angola, Botswana, the Democratic Republic of the Congo, Lesotho, Malawi, Mauritius, Mozambique, Namibia, Seychelles, South Africa, Swaziland, Tanzania, Zambia, and Zimbabwe
Middle East and Asia	
Association of Southeast Asian Nations (ASEAN)	Brunei, Cambodia, Indonesia, the Lao People's Democratic Republic, Malaysia, Myanmar, the Philippines, Singapore, Thailand, and Vietnam
Asia Pacific Trade Agreement (APTA) (Bangkok Agreement)	Bangladesh, India, the Republic of Korea, the Lao People's Democratic Republic, the Philippines, Sri Lanka, Thailand, and China
Bay of Bengal Initiative for Multi-sectoral Technical and Economic Cooperation (BIMSTEC)	Bangladesh, India, Sri Lanka, Thailand, Myanmar, Nepal, and Bhutan
East Asian Economic Caucus (EAEC)	Brunei, China, Hong Kong (China), Indonesia, Japan, the Republic of Korea, Malaysia, the Philippines, Singapore, Taiwan (China), and Thailand
Gulf Cooperation Council (GCC)	Bahrain, Kuwait, Oman, Qatar, Saudi Arabia, and the United Arab Emirates (UAE)
South Asian Free Trade Agreement (SAFTA)	Bangladesh, Bhutan, India, Maldives, Nepal, Pakistan, and Sri Lanka

Presently, the EU includes 502.4 million people and has 23 official languages. Each member country, when it joins the EU, has to stipulate which language or languages it wants to be declared as the official language or languages of the EU. There are five EU institutions, each playing a specific role:

- European parliament (elected by the people of the member sates)
- Council of the European Union (representing the governments of the member states)
- Presidency (rotates every six months among member countries)
- European commission (driving force and executive body)
- Court of justice (ensuring compliance with the law)
- Court of auditors (controlling and managing the EU budget)

The first direct elections of the European parliament were held in June 1979, 34 years after the World War II. The 1992 Maastricht Treaty and the 1997 Amsterdam Treaty have transformed the European parliament from a purely consultative assembly into a legislative parliament exercising powers similar to the national parliaments. The 785 members of the European parliament represent the citizens of the member countries. The members are elected to the parliament once every five years by voter-right across the 27 member states.

All EU decisions and procedures are based on the treaties, which are agreed upon by all the EU countries. The treaties are flanked by five other important bodies:

- The European Economic and Social Committee (expresses the opinions of organized civil society on economic and social issues)
- Committee of the Regions (expresses the opinions of regional and local authorities)
- European Central Bank (responsible for monetary policy and managing the euro)
- European Ombudsman (deals with citizens' complaints about maladministration by any EU institution or body)
- European Investment Bank (helps achieve EU objectives by financing investment projects)

North American Free Trade Area

The first ever reciprocal economic integration between two developed countries, that is, the US and Canada and a developing country, Mexico, took effect on 1 January 1994. It created a market for 360 million people having a combined purchasing power of US$6.5 trillion. The agreement has facilitated elimination of trade barriers related to industrial goods and services, besides separate agreement on agriculture, IP rights, labour adjustment, and environmental protection. Under the NAFTA agreement, all three countries were required to remove all tariffs and barriers to trade over 15 years but each country will have its own tariff arrangements with non-member countries. Under the NAFTA country of origin rules, most products should have 50 per cent of North American content, whereas for most automobiles, the stipulated local content requirement is 62.5 per cent. This has resulted in the shift of US investment from Asian countries to Mexico. The benefits accrued to various member countries in the NAFTA have always been debated but this has significantly transformed the trade patterns in the region.

MERCOSUR

The Southern Common Market, MERCOSUR, was created in March 1991 by Brazil, Argentina, Paraguay, and Uruguay with the signing of the Treaty of Asuncion. Common external tariffs were implemented by the MERCOSUR in 1995 and the tariffs on intra-group trade were abolished in 1996. Consequent to Chile and Bolivia joining in MERCOSUR in 1996, Latin America became the third largest business area of the world with 220 million people and a combined GDP of US$1 trillion. This common market is expected to allow free movement of goods, capital labour, and services with a common uniform external tariff among member countries.

Gulf Cooperation Council

Officially known as the Cooperation Council for the Arab States of the Gulf, the Gulf Cooperation Council (GCC) was established on 25 May 1981 with an aim to promote stability and economic cooperation among Persian Gulf nations. Its members are Bahrain, Kuwait, Oman, Qatar, Saudi Arabia, and the UAE. The principle objectives of GCC include

- formulating similar regulations in various fields, such as economy, finance, trade, customs, tourism, legislation, and administration;
- fostering scientific and technical progress in industry, mining, agriculture, water, and animal resources;
- establishing scientific research centres;
- setting up joint ventures;
- encouraging cooperation of the private sector; and
- strengthening ties between their people.

An aid fund was also established to promote development in Arab states.

Asia-Pacific Economic Cooperation

The APEC was established in 1989 to enhance economic growth and prosperity for the region and to strengthen the Asia-Pacific community. It is the only inter-governmental grouping in the world operating on the basis of non-binding commitments, open dialogue, and mutual respect. Unlike the WTO or other multilateral trade bodies, APEC has no treaty obligations required of its participants. Decisions made within APEC are reached by consensus and commitments and undertaken on a voluntary basis.

It works in three broad areas to meet the broader goals of free and open trade and investment in the Asia-Pacific region for both developed and developing economies. Known as the 'three pillars' of APEC, the key areas of focus are as follows:

- Trade and investment liberalization
- Business facilitation
- Economic and technical cooperation

APEC has 21 members referred to as 'member economies', which account for about 40 per cent of the world's population, approximately 56 per cent of world GDP, and about 48 per cent of world trade. Its member economies include Australia, Brunei Darussalam, Canada, Chile, People's Republic of China, Hong Kong (China), Indonesia, Japan, the Republic of Korea, Malaysia, Mexico, New Zealand, Papua New Guinea, Peru, the Republic of the Philippines, the Russian Federation, Singapore, Chinese Taipei, Thailand, the USA, and Vietnam. It represents the most economically dynamic region in the world, having generated nearly 70 per cent of global economic growth in its first 10 years.

Association of Southeast Asian Nations

The ASEAN was established on 8 August 1967 in Bangkok by five original member countries, namely Indonesia, Malaysia, Philippines, Singapore, and Thailand. Subsequently, Brunei Darussalam joined on 8 January 1984, Vietnam on 28 July 1995, Laos and Myanmar on 23 July 1997, and Cambodia on 30 April 1999. The ASEAN region has a population of about 500 million, a total area of 4.5 million square km, a combined GDP of about US$700 billion, and a total trade of US$850 billion. The major objectives of ASEAN include the following:

- Accelerate economic growth, social progress, and cultural development in the region through joint endeavours.
- Promote regional peace and stability through abiding respect for justice and the rule of law in the relationship among countries in the region and adherence to the principles of the UN charter.

Institutional mechanism

The highest decision-making organ of the ASEAN is the meeting of the ASEAN Heads of State and Government. The ASEAN summit is convened every year. The ASEAN Ministerial Meeting is also held on an annual basis. Also held are Ministerial Meetings on several other sectors, such as agriculture and forestry, economics, energy, environment, finance, information, investment, labour, law, regional haze, rural development and poverty alleviation, science and technology, social welfare, transnational crime, transportation, tourism, youth, and the AFTA Council. Supporting these ministerial bodies are 29 committees of senior officials and 122 technical working groups.

In January 2004, the Southeast Asian economic ministers agreed to 11 industry sectors, that is, air travel, tourism, automotive, textile, electronics, agriculture, infotech, fisheries, health care, wood, and rubber. This is considered as an important catalyst in creating a single market covering 530 million people by 2020.

Economic and functional cooperation

When ASEAN was established, trade among member countries was insignificant. Estimates between 1967 and the early 1970s showed that the share of intra-ASEAN trade from the total trade of the member countries was between 12 and 15 per cent. In order to promote inter-group trade, the Preferential Trading Arrangement, 1977, accorded tariff preferences for trade among ASEAN economies. The Framework Agreement on Enhancing Economic Cooperation was adopted at the fourth ASEAN summit in Singapore in 1992, which included the launching of a scheme toward an ASEAN free trade area or AFTA. The strategic objective of AFTA is to increase the ASEAN region's competitive advantage as a single production unit. The fifth ASEAN summit held in Bangkok in 1995 adopted the Agenda for Greater Economic Integration, which included the acceleration of the timetable for the realization of AFTA from the original 15-year timeframe to 10 years.

In addition to trade and investment liberalization, regional economic integration is being pursued through the development of the trans-ASEAN transportation network consisting of major inter-state highway and railway networks, principal ports and sea lanes for maritime traffic, inland waterway transport, and major civil aviation links. Building of Trans-ASEAN energy networks, which consist of the ASEAN power grid and the trans-ASEAN gas pipeline projects, are also being developed. ASEAN cooperation has resulted in greater regional integration.

INDIA'S PARTICIPATION IN PREFERENTIAL TRADE AGREEMENTS

While these PTAs could serve to open up markets for India's exports, there could be scope for cost reduction through economies of scale, and sourcing materials and components from partner countries as well. Indian companies could also find it easier to set up projects in partner countries to cater to local and regional customers. Investments becoming more industry- or product-specific than country-specific in today's world, a lot of transnational FDI takes place across countries. It may promote FDI in India along with other member countries.

South Asian Association for Regional Cooperation (SAARC) was established in 1985 comprising India, Bangladesh, Bhutan, Maldives, Nepal, Pakistan, and Sri Lanka. Afghanistan became its eighth member in 2007. India, Pakistan, and Sri Lanka are categorized as non-least developed contracting states (NLDCSs) and Afghanistan, Bangladesh, Bhutan, Maldives, and Nepal are categorized as least developed contracting states (LDCs). In April 1993, these countries signed a PTA named SAPTA, effective from 7 December 1995 that graduated into the SAFTA which became operational from 1 January 2006. India has also been instrumental in forming BIMSTEC, the 'Bay of Bengal' initiative PTA. Besides, India's other PTAs include comprehensive economic partnership with ASEAN, a Comprehensive Economic Cooperation Agreement (CECA) with Singapore, and separate PTAs with Afghanistan and Thailand.

SAARC Preferential Trading Agreement

SAPTA has been notified under the enabling clause of the WTO, the participating countries being the developing countries of South Asia. The agreement establishing the SAARC Preferential Trading Arrangement (SAPTA) was signed on 11 April 1993 at the Seventh SAARC Summit held in Dhaka. The agreement was signed by all seven SAARC countries, namely India, Pakistan, Nepal, Bhutan, Bangladesh, Sri Lanka, and the Maldives. It initially focused on soft issues, such as social issues, culture, youth, and sports, and trade cooperation did not figure in its agenda. Creating a regional trading arrangement came up only in 1997, almost after 12 years of its formation. It was only during the fourth special session of the SAARC Standing Committee held in Kathmandu during 9–10 July 2003 that bilateral negotiations between India and Pakistan were revived.

SAPTA provides a framework for the exchange of tariff concessions with a view to promoting trade and economic cooperation among the SAARC member countries. SAPTA extends to arrangements in the area of tariffs, nontariff measures, and direct trade measures.

SAPTA's constraints in promoting regional trade   Trade within the South Asian region has been limited by a host of economic and political factors. Although there is substantial informal trading, official trade among SAARC countries today accounts for only about 5.5 per cent of total trade in 2011. The pace of regional cooperation among the SAARC countries has been slow owing to the poor state of physical and human infrastructure, the relatively underdeveloped states of economy of some member countries, and several policy-induced impediments. The existence of trade barriers and inadequate trade facilitation mechanism has further impeded the cooperation efforts. Besides, the region as a whole has a competitive, rather than complementary nature of product mix.

SAARC member countries have not been a major player in world trade because of their long-standing policies of inward orientation. The inability of the region to diversify its export structure in favour of more modern products has resulted in slower export growth and lower value realization. There is an urgent need to diversify and sharpen the global competitiveness of exports of the region by value addition in traditional exports. As all member countries are import-dependent and exports from the region suffer low value addition, SAARC countries should collectively try to tap the global market than out-compete each other.

India's comparative advantage in a range of products has resulted in asymmetric trade relations with her neighbours, hindering regional integration. Regional trade has also perhaps not taken off because all the countries in the region had been pursuing, until the late 1980s, import substitution policies aimed at promoting domestic industries. Lastly, low growth and demand within the region itself, and historical trade links with developed countries, have resulted in extra-regional patterns of trade.

South Asian Free Trade Agreement

During the twelfth SAARC summit on 4 January 2004 at Islamabad, the historic agreement on SAFTA was signed by all the SAARC members. SAFTA has come into force from 1 January 2006 and supersedes SAPTA. Under the agreement, India, Pakistan, and Sri Lanka are categorized as NLDCS and Bangladesh, Bhutan, and Nepal as LDCS. SAFTA anticipates completion of the whole process of instituting free trade in 10 years. Measures for economic cooperation and integration of economies include removal of barriers to intra-SAARC investment, harmonization of customs classifications, transit facilities for efficient intra SAARC trade, and simplification of procedures for business visas, customs procedures, import licensing, insurance, and competition rules.

The highlights of the agreement are as follows:

Trade liberalization programme (TLP)   The agreement provides for trade liberalization as per this schedule.

Non-least developed country (Non-LDC) members of SAARC (India, Pakistan, and Sri Lanka) Non-LDC countries would reduce their existing tariffs to 20 per cent within a time frame of two years from the date of coming into force of the agreement. If the actual tariff rates are below 20 per cent then there shall be an annual reduction of 10 per cent on margin-of-preference basis for each of the two years. The subsequent tariff reductions from 20 per cent or below to 0–5 per cent shall be enacted within a period of five (for Sri Lanka, six) years, beginning from the third year from the date of coming into force of the agreement.

Least developed country (LDC) members of SAARC (Bangladesh, Bhutan, Maldives, and Nepal) The LDC member countries would reduce their existing tariff to 30 per cent within a time frame of two years from the date of coming into force of the agreement. If actual tariff rates are below 30 per cent, there will be an annual reduction of 5 per cent on margin-of-preference basis for each of the two years. The subsequent tariff reductions from 30 per cent or below to 0–5 per cent shall be achieved within a period of eight years beginning from the third year from the date of coming into force of the agreement.

> Besides, the Non-LDC member states have agreed to reduce their tariffs to 0–5 per cent for the products of the LDC member states within a period of three years beginning from the date of coming into force of the agreement.

Sensitive list   Tariff reduction shall be carried out on the basis of the negative list approach. Keeping in mind the interests of the domestic stakeholders, the agreement provides for a sensitive list to be maintained by each country (subject to a maximum ceiling) which will be finalized after negotiations among the contracting countries with provision that the LDC contracting states may seek derogation in respect of products of their export interest. The sensitive lists are subject to review after every four years or earlier with a view to reducing the number of items which are to be traded freely among the SAARC countries.

Non-tariff barriers   The agreement also provides for elimination of non-tariff and para-tariff barriers with a view to facilitate trade among members.

Trade facilitation   Keeping in view the increasing importance of trade facilitation measures, the agreement provides for harmonization of standards, reciprocal recognition of tests and accreditation of testing laboratories, simplification and harmonization of customs procedures, customs classification of harmonized system (HS) coding system, import-licensing and registration procedures, simplification of banking procedures for import financing, transit facilities for efficient intra-SAARC trade, microeconomic consultations, development of communication systems and transport, infrastructure, and simplification of business visas.

Institutional mechanism   The agreement also provides for an institutional mechanism to facilitate the implementation of its provisions, which includes safeguard measures in case of surge in imports of products covered under SAFTA concessions that threaten or cause a serious injury to the domestic industry. It also provides a dispute settlement mechanism for the interpretation and application of the provisions of this agreement or any instrument adopted within its framework concerning the rights and obligations of the contracting states.

The SAFTA ministerial council consists of commerce or trade ministers of all the member countries. It has a committee of experts for the administration and implementation of the agreement. The dispute settlement mechanism is also modelled along the lines of the WTO dispute settlement mechanism. The SAFTA agreement envisages amicable settlement of all disputes pertaining to interpretation and application of SAFTA provisions regarding rights and obligations of its member states through bilateral consultations under the auspices of the SAFTA forum.

Special provisions   The agreement provides for special provisions for LDCs, such as longer phase-out schedule, longer sensitive lists and revenue compensation mechanism while considering the application of anti-dumping and/or countervailing measures. Maldives has been given special dispensation to retain the special provisions accorded to LDCs even after its graduation, and Sri Lanka has been given one year more for its trade TLP.

Implementation   The agreement on SAFTA came into force on 1 January 2006. The applied MFN rate existing since 1 January 2006 has been considered as the base rate for the purpose of tariff reduction.

Since SAFTA was signed post-WTO, it is designed to be compatible with WTO provisions in all its forms and contents. It leans heavily on WTO institutions and practices which get reflected in dispute settlement, safeguard measures, BOP exceptions, and special and differential treatment to least developed countries. Any member country will have the right to pull out of the treaty at any time by giving a six-month notice in writing to the Secretary General of the SAARC.

In view of the different budget periods of the member states, the members decided to carry out phased liberalization from 1 July 2006 instead of 1 January 2006 (Nepal from 1 August 2006) with the condition that trade liberalization process for the first two years was to be completed by December 2007. The SAARC Agreement on Trade in Services (SATIS) was signed in April 2010 in the 16th SAARC meeting held at Thimpu in Bhutan expanding the scope of SAFTA agreement. The sixth meeting of the SAFTA Ministerial Council held at Islamabad in February 2012 agreed on further relaxation of visa regimes for SAARC countries as free movement of people was considered crucial to promote intra-region trade[5]. Various measures to reduce para-tariff and non-tariff measures were considered and the member countries agreed to issue their respective customs notifications[6] at least for the years 2012.

Comprehensive Economic Cooperation Agreement between India and Singapore

The India–Singapore CECA was signed on 29 June 2005 and came into force on 1 August 2005. The India–Singapore CECA has been notified at the WTO on 3 May 2007 under GATT article XXIV and GATS article V. Besides trade in goods, the CECA also covers investment, services, mutual recognition agreements, and customs cooperations. Under the agreement, Singapore has eliminated duties on all products originating from India from 1 August 2005 and the tariff concessions offered by India have been completed by 1 April 2009. India has

---

[5] 'Pak to Keep SAFTA Sensitive List to Protect Local Industry', *Business Line*, 6 May 2012.

[6] *The Express Tribune*, 17 February 2012.

approved tariff reduction/elimination on 539 products which was included in the amendment to India–Singapore CECA on 20 December 2007. These concessions are likely to be completed by December 2014.

Framework Agreement on Comprehensive Economic Cooperation between ASEAN and India

India has had close cultural and economic ties with Southeast Asian countries throughout history. The political and strategic importance of ASEAN in the larger Asia-Pacific region and its potential to become a major partner of India in the area of trade and investment has encouraged India to seek closer linkages with these countries. India's engagement with ASEAN started with its 'look east policy' in 1991. India became a sectoral dialogue partner of ASEAN in 1992 and full dialogue partner in 1996. The ASEAN–India relationship was upgraded to summit level in November 2001. The first ASEAN economic ministers (AEM)–India consultations were held in Brunei on 15 September 2002. An ASEAN–India economic linkages task force was set up to study and prepare a draft agreement for the next AEM–India consultations in 2003 through senior economic officials for further consideration and follow-up action.

The framework agreement on comprehensive economic cooperation between ASEAN and India was signed on 8 October 2003 during the second ASEAN India summit in Bali, Indonesia. It covers gradual tariff reductions leading to formation of FTA in goods, liberalization in services and investment, other areas of economic cooperation, such as trade facilitation measures, sectors of cooperations and trade, investment promotion measures and early harvest programmes covering areas of economic cooperation, and a common list of items for exchange of tariff concessions as a confidence building measure. The ASEAN–India trade negotiating committee has also been set up to carry out the programme of negotiations of necessary agreements and other instruments thereof to establish the ASEAN–India Regional Trade and Investment Area (RTIA) in accordance with the provisions set out in the framework agreement.

The Trade and Goods Agreement was signed between India and ASEAN on 13 August 2009 under the broader framework of CECA. The agreement has been fully implemented between the ASEAN member states and India. The Agreement on Trade in Services and Investments is currently being negotiated.

Bay of Bengal Initiative for Multi-sectoral Technical and Economic Cooperation

The initiative to explore economic cooperation on a sub-regional basis involving contiguous countries of Southeast and South Asia grouped around the Bay of Bengal was taken by Thailand in 1994. On 6 June 1997, the subgroup was renamed Bangladesh–India–Sri Lanka–Thailand Economic Cooperation (BISTEC). Myanmar was admitted in December 1997 as a full member and the name of the group was changed to BIMSTEC. Subsequently, Nepal and Bhutan received full membership in 2003. During the summit in Bangkok on 31 July 2004, the name was again changed to Bay of Bengal Initiative for Multi-sectoral Technical and Economic Cooperation (BIMSTEC).

BIMSTEC provides a unique link between South Asia and Southeast Asia, bringing together about 21 per cent of the world population having considerable amount of complementarities. During the first meeting of economic/trade ministers of BIMSTEC which was held in Bangkok in August 1998, it was agreed that BIMSTEC should aim and strive to develop into an FTA and should focus on activities that facilitate trade, increase investment, and promote technical cooperation among member countries. It was further reiterated that BIMSTEC activities should be designed to form a bridge linking ASEAN and SAARC. Six areas were identified for cooperation, namely trade and investment, technology, transportation and communication, energy, tourism, and fisheries.

The framework agreement on the BIMSTEC FTA was signed on 8 February 2004 in Phuket, Thailand by Bangladesh, India, Myanmar, Nepal, Sri Lanka, and Thailand, which includes provisions for negotiations on FTA in goods, and services and investment. The major highlights of the framework agreement are as given here.

FTA in goods   The negotiations for tariff reduction/elimination for FTA in goods commenced in July 2004 and concluded by December 2005.

Fast track   Products listed in the fast track by the party on its own accord shall have their respective applied MFN tariff rates gradually reduced/eliminated in accordance with specified rates to be mutually agreed by the parties, within the following time frame:

Countries	For developing country parties	For LDC parties
India, Sri Lanka, and Thailand	1 July 2006 to 30 June 2009	1 July 2006 to 30 June 2007
Bangladesh and Myanmar	1 July 2006 to 30 June 2011	1 July 2006 to 30 June 2009

Normal track   Products listed in the normal track by a party on its own accord shall have their respective applied MFN tariff rates gradually reduced/eliminated in accordance with specified rates to be mutually agreed by the parties, within the following time frame:

Countries	For developing country parties	For LDC parties
India, Sri Lanka, and Thailand	1 July 2007 to 30 June 2012	1 July 2007 to 30 June 2010
Bangladesh and Myanmar	1 July 2007 to 30 June 2017	1 July 2007 to 30 June 2015

FTA in services and investments   For trade in services and trade in investments, the negotiations on the respective agreements commenced in 2005 and was planned to be concluded by 2007.

Identification, liberalization, among others of the sectors of services/investments shall be finalized for implementation subsequently, in accordance with the time frames to be mutually agreed, (a) taking into account the sensitive sectors of the parties; and (b) with special and differential treatment and flexibility for the LDC parties.

The second BIMSTEC summit held in November 2008 at New Delhi found the process made in the negotiations for FTA in goods satisfactory. In the 19th session of BIMSTEC Trade Negotiating Committee (TNC), the areas covered included tariff concessions on trade in goods, customs cooperation, services and investments. Negotiations on Agreement on Trade in Goods were agreed to conclude by 2011 and implement the tariff concessions by July 2012. However, negotiations on Agreement on Services and Investment were to continue.

Indo-Sri Lanka Free Trade Agreement

An FTA between India and Sri Lanka was signed on 28 December 1998 in New Delhi. The agreement envisages phasing out of tariffs on all products except for a limited number of items in the negative list and tariff rate quota (TRQ) items over a period of time. The implementation of the agreement started on 1 March 2000. As prescribed in the agreement, India has eliminated tariffs on all items other than those in the negative list or under TRQ with effect from 18 March 2003 and Sri Lanka was scheduled to phase out the tariffs by the year 2008 except for items in the negative list.

The rules of origin specify that domestic value addition requirement should be 35 per cent for products to qualify for preferential treatment under the agreement. If the raw material/inputs are sourced from each other's country, the value addition requirement is reduced to 25 per cent within the overall limit of 35 per cent. The criterion of 'substantial transformation' has been provided in the rules. The goods must undergo transformation at four-digit level of harmonized system.

The agreement provides for establishment of a joint committee at the ministerial level which shall meet at least once a year to review the progress made in the implementation of this agreement and to ensure that the benefits of trade expansion emanating from this agreement accrue to both countries equitably. India and Sri Lanka have initiated negotiations to enter into a Comprehensive Economic Partnership Agreement (ECPA) and to deepen and widen the coverage by including trade in services, investment cooperation, etc.

Negotiations are under way for a Comprehensive Economic Partnership Agreement (CEPA). Consequent to the ISLFTA coming into force, the bilateral trade between India and Sri Lanka has grown from US$2.7 billion in 2006–2007 to US$4.54 billion in 2010–2011.

Asia-Pacific Trade Agreement (Bangkok Agreement)

Under the auspices of ESCAP, the first agreement on trade negotiations was signed in 1975 among the DMCs of ESCAP. India is a founder signatory to this preferential trading arrangement along with Bangladesh, Laos, Philippines, South Korea, Sri Lanka, and Thailand. It is essentially a PTA designed to liberalize and expand trade progressively in the ESCAP region through mutually agreed concessions by member countries. ESCAP functions as a secretariat for the agreement. The Bangkok agreement was approved by the GATT council in March 1978. China acceded to this agreement in 2001. On 2 November 2005, this agreement was renamed as the Asia Pacific Trade Agreement (APTA). This agreement is operational among five countries, namely Bangladesh, China, India, Republic of Korea, and Sri Lanka.

Three rounds of negotiations have been concluded under this agreement and the third round has been implemented from 1 September 2006. The 35th session of the Standing Committee and the third session of Ministerial Council were held in Seoul, Republic of Korea in December, 2009 to move forward the fourth round of negotiations. Mongolia was also invited to participate as an observer to the session. Framework agreements were finalized in the areas of trade facilitation, trade and services, promotion and liberalization of investments. Besides, a framework agreement on non-tariff measures was also being considered.

Framework Agreement for Establishing Free Trade between India and Thailand

The framework agreement for establishing an FTA between India and Thailand was signed on 9 October 2003 in Bangkok. The key elements of the framework agreement cover FTA in goods, services and investment, and areas of economic cooperation. The framework agreement also provides for an early harvest scheme (EHS) under which common items have been agreed for elimination of tariffs on a fast-track basis. The highlights of the various components of the framework agreement are as follows:

FTA in goods
- Negotiations to commence in January 2004 and conclude by March 2005
- Establishment of FTA (zero-duty imports) by 2010

FTA in services
- Negotiations to commence in January 2004 and concluded by January 2006

FTA in investments
- Negotiations to commence in January 2004 and conclude by January 2006

Areas of economic cooperation
- Areas of economic cooperation to include trade facilitation measures; sectors identified for cooperation; and trade and investment promotion measures

Early Harvest Scheme
- Both sides to agree to have a common list of 84 items (6-digit HS level) for exchange of tariff concessions
- Tariffs on these items to be phased out in two years' time frame starting from 1 March 2004

The early harvest items covering 82 items for exchange of concessions between India and Thailand has been implemented with effect from 1 September 2004 and became zero from 1 September 2006. Negotiations on a comprehensive FTA are underway by the TNC, which include trade in goods, trade in services, investment, rules of origin, dispute settlement mechanism, etc. A second protocol was signed on 25 January 2012 to amend the framework agreement.

Bilateral Preferential Trading Agreement with Afghanistan

The Preferential Trade Agreement between India and Afghanistan, which was signed on 6 March 2003, provide for establishing a PTA between the two countries to promote harmonious development of the economic relations and free movement of goods through reduction of tariffs. The objective is to provide for grant or concessions on a range of products of export interest to Afghanistan, as a part of India's endeavour to strengthen trade and economic relations between the two countries. The Agreement is WTO-compatible.

Products covered under the agreement shall be eligible for preferential treatment,[7] provided they satisfy the rules of origin laid down under the agreement. India is granting Afghanistan 50–100 per cent tariff concession on 38 items of dry fruits, fresh fruits, seeds, medicinal herbs, and precious stones and in turn India is receiving duty-free access on eight tariff lines of our export interest, which include black tea, pharmaceutical products, Ayurvedic and Homeopathic medicines, refined sugar, cement, etc. The agreement would remain in force till either party gives notice to the other for termination of the agreement.

India–MERCOSUR PTA

A PTA was signed between India and MERCOSUR on 19 March 2005 aimed to expand and strengthen existing trade relations by granting reciprocal fixed trade preferences with the ultimate objective of creating an FTA. The PTA consists of five annexure including lists of products on which the two sides have agreed to extend tariff preferences to each other, rules of origin, safeguard measures, and dispute settlement procedure. The PTA became operational on 1 June 2009. Under this PTA, India and MERCOSUR have agreed to extend tariff concessions ranging from 10–100 per cent on 450–452 tariff lines, respectively.

India-Chile Framework Agreement on Economic Cooperation

A framework agreement on economic cooperation was signed between India and Chile on 20 January 2005 that envisages a PTA between the two countries. The negotiations on PTA have been concluded and the agreement was signed on March 2006, which became operational in September 2007. Both the sides agreed for further expansion of trade relations in the third meeting held in July 2011.

Indo-Gulf Cooperation Council FTA

This agreement is of special significance to India as GCC is the largest trading partner of India in the world with a bilateral trade estimated at US$ 113 billion during 2010–2011. Moreover, it is crucial to India's energy security as it imports 40 per cent of its crude oil requirements from GCC countries.

A framework agreement between India and Gulf Cooperation Council was signed on 25 August 2004. The GCC side agreed to include services as well as investment and general economic

---

[7] *Annual Report*, 2011–2012, Ministry of Commerce and Industry, Government of India, New Delhi.

cooperation along with goods in the proposed agreement during the first round of negotiations held in Riyadh in March 2006. Proposed tariff liberalization schedules were further discussed during the second round of negotiations in September 2008 at Riyadh.

India-Malaysia Comprehensive Economic Cooperation Agreement

A CECA was signed between India and Malaysia on 18 February 2011, which came into effect from 1 July 2011. Key items on which Malaysia has offered market access to India include basmati rice, mango, egg, trucks, motorcycles, and cotton garments whereas India has offered market access to Malaysia on fruits, cocoa, palm oil product, and synthetic textiles. For refined palm oil (RPO) exports by Malaysia into India, as compared to the concessions under the India-ASEAN Trade in Goods (TiG) Agreement, only advancement of timeline from 2019 to 2018–19 is offered by India, retaining the end-tariff rate of 45 per cent.

India-Korea Comprehensive Economic Partnership Agreement

A CEPA between India and the Republic of Korea was signed on 7 August 2009 which came into force from 1 January 2011.

India-Japan CEPA

A CEPA between India and Japan was signed on 16 February 2011, which came into force from 1 August 2011.

India's Other Economic Cooperation Agreements under Negotiation

India is also in the process of negotiating with several trade groups and countries, which include the following:

- India is in the process of negotiating a PTA with South African Customs Union (SACU), the oldest custom union of the world, comprising South Africa, Lesotho, Swaziland, Botswana, and Namibia.
- India–New Zealand FTA/CEPA have taken place, for which six round of negotiations have been held so far. The sixth round of negotiation was held in August 2011.
- A CECA between India and Indonesia is being negotiated covering substantially all trade in goods and services, investment, trade facilitation, and other areas of economic cooperation, as a 'single undertaking'.
- A Comprehensive Economic Cooperation and Partnership Agreement (CECPA) between India and Mauritius is under negotiation.

RTAS UNDER THE WTO: THE MULTILATERAL TRADING SYSTEM

The multilateral initiative culminating in the signing of the general agreement on tariffs and trade and ultimately leading to the formation of the WTO rests on the principle of non-discrimination, the two main pillars being the MFN treatment and the national treatment. RTAs are an exceptional situation under the multilateral trading system enunciated within the WTO. Any regional trading arrangement is bound to have certain trade distortion effects. This trade distortion arises because of the discriminatory treatment advanced to the non-members of the regional trading arrangement vis-à-vis is the members. This discriminatory treatment arises because of the increased market access granted to the members of the same regional block. Certain conditions are imposed to ensure minimization of such distortion effects. However, even the most stringent of the conditions cannot absolutely erase out the distortion effect, as that itself is the driving force behind the benefits available to the members of an RTA.

The MFN treatment calls for non-discrimination among the members, whereas national treatment ensures non-discrimination between domestically produced items and imported ones. An RTA implies a higher degree of liberalization within the region as compared to the rest of the world. This in turn implies increased market access for the member countries of that particular RTA, vis-à-vis is the nonmembers, that is, the other WTO members. Thus, a case of violation of the MFN treatment can be found inbuilt in the regional trading arrangements. The basic reason for granting such exception amounts to the belief that the RTAs would act as the building blocks for forming a liberalized and fair global trading system.

RTAs are thus allowed under the multilateral trading system as an exception to the MFN principle of the WTO on the belief that they would facilitate the trade liberalization at the multilateral level. The idea is that regionalism would gradually expand, leading to multilateral trade liberalization. As such, it would facilitate the formation of a liberalized and fair global trading regime. However, because of the discriminatory environment created by its formation, any regional trading arrangement is bound to result in some amount of trade diversion.

This chapter provides an overview of international economic environment and elucidates various international economic institutions and trade groups so as to provide a broad understanding of economic environment. Major international economic institutions are also discussed. Besides, conceptual framework of economic integration and their various forms are elucidated. This chapter also discusses major trade groups and also those with India's involvement.

Summary

The chapter provides a basic understanding of international economic environment including economic institutions and regional trading blocks in international marketing as it influences decisions related to selection of international markets, mode of entry, determining market competitiveness, and pricing strategies.

The major international economic institutions of the World Bank Group include the International Bank for Reconstruction and Development (IBRD), the International Development Association (IDA), the International Finance Corporation (IFC), the Multilateral Investment Guarantee Agency (MIGA), and the International Centre for Settlement of Investment Disputes (ICSID). The International Monetary Fund (IMF) plays an important role in achieving the UN's vision to fight poverty and improve standard of living of the people in the developing world by way of economic growth. The International Monetary Fund offers regular dialogue and policy advice to each of its members and promotes exchange stability. The Special Drawing Rights (SDRs) created by IMF as an international reserve asset supplement the existing official reserves of the member countries.

The United Nations Conference on Trade and Development (UNCTAD) provides an institutional framework for creating development friendly integration of developing countries into the world economy. The tariff concessions extended by developed countries on the basis of non-reciprocity and unilaterally under the Global Scheme of Preference (GSP) and among developing countries under the Generalized Scheme of Trade Preferences (GSTP) affect the market competitiveness of exports. The World Intellectual Property Organization (WIPO) is a specialized agency of the UN aimed at developing the balanced and accessible international IP system.

United Nations Industrial Development Organization (UNIDO) promotes industrialization in developing countries and in countries with economies in transition. The Asian Development Bank (ADB) aims to improve the welfare of the people in Asia and the Pacific. The Economic and Social Commission for Asia and the Pacific (ESCAP) of the UN aims at developing the Asia-Pacific region.

The forms of economic integration, also known as RTAs, vary from merely extending tariff concessions in import of select items under preferential trading arrangement (PTA) to complete political and economic integration under a political union. The major RTAs include the European Union (EU), North American Free Trade Area (NAFTA) MERCOSUR, Gulf Cooperation Council (GCC), Asia-Pacific Economic Cooperation (APEC), and Association of Southeast Asian Nations (ASEAN). India is involved in economic integration with RTAs such as ASEAN, besides Bangkok Agreement, GCC, and South Asian Association for Regional Cooperation (SAARC). The South Asian Free Trade Area (SAFTA) is significant for economic integration of South Asian countries and offer new marketing opportunities.

Although PTAs do have a fundamental conflict with multilateralism being built on discrimination with non-members while liberalizing trade, they are legally permitted under Article XXIV of GATT 1994 of the WTO agreement.

Key Terms

Common market All restrictions on cross-border investment, movement of labour, technology transfer, management, and sharing of capital resources are eliminated to form a common market.

Customs union In addition to eliminating trade barriers among member countries, a common external trade policy is adopted for non-members.

Economic union Involves much greater level of economic integration with harmonization of monetary and fiscal policies.

Free trade area (FTA) Member countries remove all tariffs and non-tariff barriers among themselves but are free to maintain their own tariffs and non-tariff barriers with non-member countries.

Fund A name used for International Monetary Fund (IMF)

Generalized System of Preferences (GSP) A non-contractual instrument by which developed countries unilaterally and on the basis of non-reciprocity extend tariff concessions to developing countries.

Global System of Trade Preference (GSTP) A framework for the exchange of trade preferences among developing countries in order to promote intra-developing-country trade.

Political union The highest level of integration with political and economic harmonization wherein the member countries are willing to dilute their national identities to a considerable extent.

Preferential trading agreement (PTA) Member countries reduce import tariffs on identified products from one another.

Regional trading agreement (RTA) Some form of economic cooperation among two or more countries.

SAFTA The agreed free trade area in South Asia consisting of India, Bangladesh, Sri Lanka, Pakistan, Nepal, Bhutan, and Maldives.

Special Drawing Right An international reserve asset created by the IMF to supplement the existing official reserves of member countries, also known as 'paper gold'.

The Millennium Development Goals Goals to reduce world poverty by half by 2015 as signed under the Millennium Declaration at a meeting at the UN in 2000 by most of the countries of the world.

Trade creation impact Expansion of consumption opportunity by making low cost goods available.

Trade diversion impact Shift of trade from non-member countries to member countries as a result of tariff elimination or preferential treatment.

World Bank Group A group of five institutions, that is, the International Bank for Reconstruction and Development (IBRD), International Development Association (IDA), International Finance Corporation (IFC), the Multilateral Investment Guarantee Agency (MIGA), and the International Centre for Settlement on Investment Disputes (ICSID).

Concept Review Questions

1. Differentiate between International Monetary Fund and World Bank.
2. Describing the role of the International Centre for Settlement on Investment Disputes (ICSID), critically evaluate its effectiveness under the present context.
3. Differentiate between GSTP and GSP.
4. Evaluate the effectiveness of World Intellectual Property Organization (WIPO) in view of the TRIPs agreement.
5. Explain the conceptual framework of various types of regional trade agreements (RTAs).
6. Evaluate EU as the most powerful economic integration. Evaluate its impact on the marketing of Indian products in European countries.
7. Briefly evaluate India's participation in PTAs.
8. Write short notes on the following:
   (a) Special Drawing Rights (SDRs)
   (b) NAFTA
   (c) BIMSTEC
   (d) ASEAN
   (e) MERCOSUR

Critical Thinking Questions

1. Explore the UNCTAD website (www.unctad.org) and list out the trade information provided by it. Find out its uses and limitations.
2. Carry out a comparative analysis of intra-group trade among member countries of major economic groups.

Project Assignments

1. Carry out the trade analysis of your country and identify major trading partners. Find out the impact of economic integration on trade patterns and relate it with the concepts learnt in this chapter.
2. In view of India's trade patterns with SAFTA countries, critically evaluate the concerns of the member countries in trade liberalization under SAFTA. Prepare your arguments in the assigned group and discuss in the class as role-play.
   Make your recommendations to address the concerns of various stakeholders for effective implementation of SAFTA.
3. Due to India's comparative advantage in the region, formation of such Asia Free Trade Area opens up enormous marketing opportunities for Indian products. Identify the products and services with high marketing potential under the FTA.
4. As RTAs discriminate among members and non-members, it makes sense to treat them in contrary to WTO's basic principle of MFN. Write down your arguments and conduct a debate in the class.

CASE STUDY: EMERGING MARKETING OPPORTUNITIES AND BRICS

Introduction

BRICS stand for the acronym of the group of five nations, that is, Brazil, Russia, India, China, and South Africa, fast emerging as multilateral grouping that has considerable potential to influence the political and economic scenario of the world. The acronym BRIC, coined by Jim O'Neil, Goldman Sachs, identified Brazil, Russia, India, and China (BRIC) as rapidly emerging economic powers. Subsequently, the foreign ministers of the BRIC nations met in New York in September 2006 and formed a political organization to seek out opportunities in trade, investment, infrastructure development, and other areas. This led to the beginning of high level summits among BRIC nations. The first formal BRIC summit was held at Yekaterinburg, Russia in

June 2009 when the world was going through global economic downturn. The focus of the summit was to increase the role of emerging economies and developing nations in global financial institutions and to improve international trade and investment environment. South Africa became the fifth member nation to join the grouping in 2010 and the acronym became BRICS representing extended membership of the group. The subsequent summits were held in Brazil, China, India, and South Africa.

The five BRICS nations represent 40 per cent of the land area and as a result own vast natural resources. 45 per cent of the world's population accounting for 25 per cent of the global GDP in 2012 (Table C2.1) and is expected to perform even better in the near future.[8] As an economic bloc, BRICS has contributed

Table C2.1 BRICS: A comparative overview

	Brazil	Russia	India	China	South Africa	Total
Area (in km^2)	8.5	17	3.2	9.6	1.2	39.5
Population (in millions)	195	141.9	1,241	1,347	50.5	2,941.9
GDP at current prices (US$ trillions)	2.5	1.85	1.84	7.31	0.4	13.73
GDP at PPP (US$ trillions)	2.29	2.38	4.4	11.3	0.5	20.87
GDP per capita, current prices (US$)	12,788	12,993	1,513	5,416	8,078	–
GDP growth (%)	2.7	4.3	6.9	9.3	3.1	–
Exports (value in US$ billions)	256	478	301	1,898	92	3,025
Imports (value in US$ billions)	226	284	462	1,743	100	2,815
Trade balance (value in US$ billions)	30	194	–161	155	–7	–
Annual growth in Exports (%) 2007–2011	10	5	18	10	7	–
Annual growth in imports (%) 2007–2011	14	7	17	15	4	–
Share in world exports (%)	1.4	2.7	1.7	10.6	0.5	17
Share in world imports (%)	1.2	1.6	2.5	9.6	0.5	15.5

Source: World Economic Outlook database, 2013; Trade Map.

---

[8] 'Power of 5', *The Times of India*, 1 April 2012.

almost 50 per cent to the global economic growth, which makes it the principal driver of global economic development. The five BRICS nations are still amongst the fastest growing nations in the world and their economic influence is consistently on the rise. By 2050, the BRICS combined economies could eclipse the combined economies of the current richest countries of the world.

Exploring Marketing Opportunities with BRICS

With an aggregate population of 2.9 billion, the BRICS nations represent a huge market size that is still untapped besides its vast geographical area. As an economic bloc, it also exerts considerable economic influence on world trade. The BRICS nations accounted for 17 per cent and 15.5 per cent of the world exports and imports, respectively, in 2011. While exports from BRICS to the rest of the world has increased from US$494 billion in 2001 to US$3 trillion in 2011, its imports have increased from US$417.2 billion in 2001 to 2.8 trillion in 2011. Moreover, Intra-BRICS trade was recorded at US$230 billion in 2011 and is projected to increase[9] to US$500 billion by 2015.

Country-wise trade-analysis reveals that Brazil, India, and China have shown better performance in annual growth between 2007 and 2011 in exports as well as imports (Fig. C2.1). Brazil's exports have increased from US$58 billion in 2001 to US$256 billion in 2011, whereas its imports have increased from US$56 billion to US$226 billion during the same period. Russia's exports have increased from US$100 billion in 2001 to US$478 billion in 2011, whereas its imports have increased from US$42 billion to US$285 billion during the same period. India's exports have increased from US$44 billion in 2001 to US$301 billion in 2011, whereas its imports have increased from US$51 billion to US$462 billion during the same period. China's exports have increased from US$266 billion in 2001 to US$1898 billion in 2011, whereas its imports have increased from US$244 billion to US$1743 billion during the same period. South Africa's exports have increased from US$26 billion in 2001 to US$93 billion in 2011, whereas its imports have increased from US$26 billion to US$100 billion during the same period (Fig. C2.1).

The strength of the BRICS nations arises from strong domestic demand-driven economies of India and Brazil and

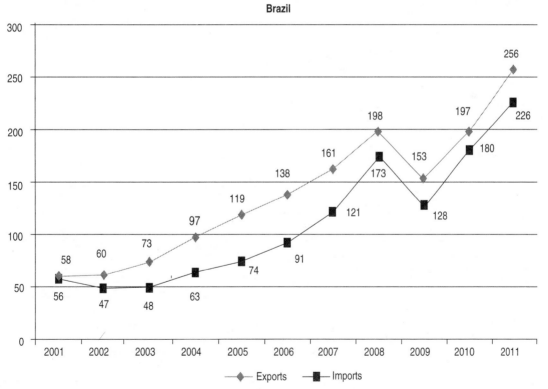

Brazil

Fig. C2.1   BRICS: Country-wise international trade patterns (*Contd*)

Source: Trade Map, 2012.

---

[9] 'BRICS Targets $500 Billion Intra-group Trade by 2015', *India Today*, 28 March 2012.

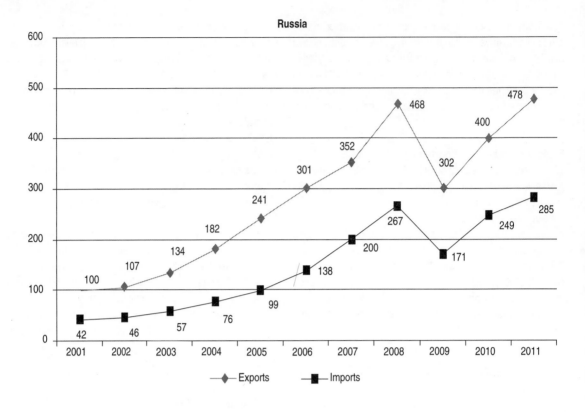

Russia

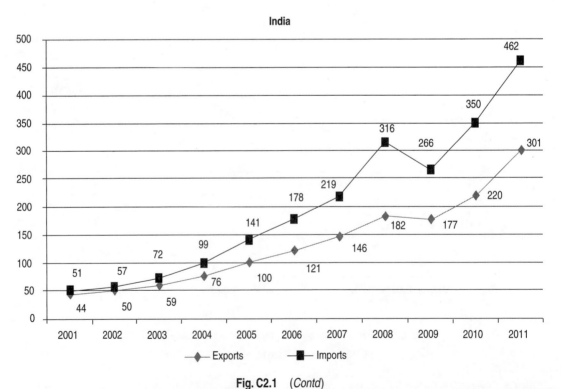

India

Fig. C2.1 *(Contd)*

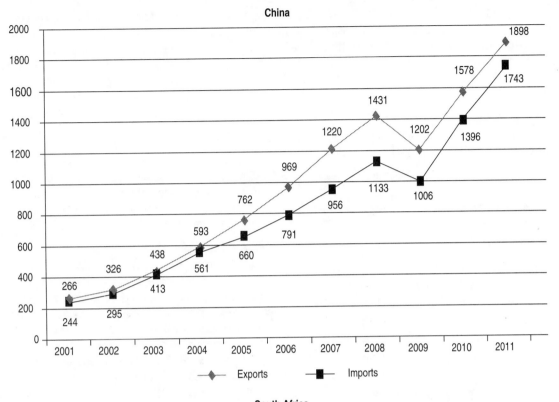

China

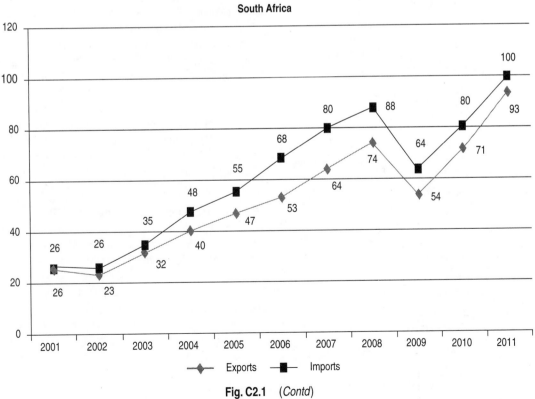

South Africa

Fig. C2.1 (*Contd*)

significant outward linkages of China and Russia. The strength of South Africa lies in its large resource base and proximity to untapped growth potential of the African continent. The sustained economic reforms and improved macroeconomic environment contributed to the improved growth performance of the BRICS in the current decade.

BRICS' Major Trading Partners

Trade analysis of BRICS reveals that China is a major trading partner of all the BRICS nations (Table C2.2). It has grown

Table C2.2 Major trade partners of BRICS countries

Country	Major markets	Major importers
Brazil	China (17.3%)	USA (15.1%)
	USA (10.1%)	China (14.4%)
	Argentina (8.8%)	Argentina (7.4%)
	Netherlands (6.7%)	Germany (6.7%)
	Japan (3.6%)	Republic of Korea (4.5%)
Russia	Netherlands (12.8%)	China (16.9%)
	China (7.2%)	Germany (13.2%)
	Italy (5.8%)	Ukraine (7%)
	Germany (4.8%)	Japan (5.3%)
	Poland (4.4%)	Italy (4.7%)
India	China (11.9%)	UAE (12.3%)
	UAE (7.6%)	USA (10.9%)
	Switzerland (6.7%)	China (5.5%)
	Saudi Arabia (6.1%)	Singapore (5.1%)
	USA (4.8%)	Hong Kong, China (4.1%)
China	USA (17.1%)	Japan (11.1%)
	Hong Kong, China (14.1%)	Republic of Korea (9.3%)
	Japan (7.8%)	Chinese Taipei (7.1%)
	Republic of Korea (4.3%)	USA (7%)
	Germany (4%)	Germany (5.3%)
South Africa	China (13.3%)	China (14.2%)
	USA (8.9%)	Germany (10.6%)
	Japan (8.2%)	USA (7.9%)
	Germany (5.9%)	Japan (4.7%)
	UK (4.2%)	Saudi Arabia (4.4%)

from having a negligible role in world trade to being one of the world's largest exporters. Its exports represent 10.63 per cent of world exports[10] making its ranking number one in world exports, whereas its imports represent 9.61 per cent of world imports making its ranking number three during 2011. China has become the second largest economy and the biggest exporter in the world.

The major trading partners of Brazil include China, USA, Argentina, Germany, Netherlands, Korea, and Japan. The major trading partners of Russia are China, Netherlands, Germany, Italy, Ukraine, Germany, Japan, and Poland, whereas those of India are China, UAE, USA, Switzerland, Saudi Arabia, and Singapore. The major trading partners of China are USA, Japan, Hong Kong, Korea, and Germany, whereas those of South Africa are China, USA, Germany, Japan, UK, Germany, and Saudi Arabia.

BRICS' Major Products Traded

Country-wise trade analysis of BRICS indicates that mineral fuels and machinery are major products traded by most BRICS nations. Each of the BRICS countries has its specific strengths and, therefore, enjoys tremendous potential for trade expansion. Brazil with an agricultural area of 31.2 per cent of the total land area has abundance of coffee, sugar cane, soya bean, etc. Russia has massive deposits of oil, natural gas, and minerals. India is the most sought-after service provider in the world, with a rising manufacturing base and capability to process mineral fuels and precious stones. China has a competitive edge in its highly skilled workforce and relatively low-wage costs with major exports of electronic items and machinery. South Africa holds the world's largest known reserves of chromium, platinum group metals, manganese, vanadium, and alumina-silicates. Interestingly, South Africa generates 45 per cent of Africa's electricity and the South African power supplier provides the fourth cheapest electricity in the world. Its major exports include precious stones, ores, and mineral fuels.

Intra-BRICS trade is dominated by China's demand for raw materials and this has led to trade imbalances. This has raised doubts about the economic sustainability of the bloc. The major products traded by BRICS countries is given in Table C2.3.

Exploring Marketing Opportunities with BRICS

Given its population, size, and rapid pace of growth of its domestic market, global dominance in the field of information technology and democratic form of government makes India one of the economies with highest potential in the world. Coming together of countries with multiple similarities under the BRICS boosts their collective bargaining power and political-economic clout. The South–South cooperation in BRICS also aids to strengthen economic and political ties among the member countries. This also facilitates a closer cooperation in the fields of energy and food security,

---

[10] Trade Map, http://www.trademap.org/, accessed on 18 October 2013.

Table C2.3 Major products traded by BRICS countries

Country	Major products exported	Major products imported
Brazil	Ores (17.2%)	Mineral fuels (18.6%)
	Mineral fuels (12.3%)	Machinery (14.9%)
	Oil seeds and fruits (6.4%)	Electronic equipment (11.7%)
	Sugars and sugar confectionery (5.9%)	Vehicles other than railways (10%)
	Machinery (5.5%)	Organic chemicals (4.2%)
Russia	Mineral fuels (59%)	Machinery (18.1%)
	Iron and steel (4.5%)	Vehicles other than railway (13.2%)
	Fertilizers (2.1%)	Electrical, electronic equipment (10.8%)
	Pearls and precious stones (2%)	Pharmaceutical products (4.6%)
	Inorganic chemicals	Plastics and articles thereof (3.5%)
India	Mineral fuels (18.7%)	Mineral fuels (34%)
	Pearls and precious stones (16.5%)	Pearls and precious stones (20.2%)
	Electronic equipment (3.8%)	Machinery (7.6%)
	Organic chemicals (3.6%)	Electronic equipment (6.9%)
	Machinery (3.5%)	Organic chemicals (3%)
China	Electronic equipment (23.4%)	Electronic equipment (20.1%)
	Machinery (18.6%)	Mineral fuels (15.8%)
	Articles of apparel knit or crochet (4.2%)	Machinery (11.4%)
	Articles of apparel, not knit or crochet (3.3%)	Ores, slag, and ash (8.6%)
	Optical and technical apparatus (3.1%)	Optical and other technical apparatus (5.6%)
South Africa	Pearls and precious stones (22.3%)	Mineral fuels (21.2%)
	Ores, slag, and ash (15.3%)	Machinery (15.1%)
	Mineral fuels (10.4%)	Electronic equipment (9.3%)
	Iron and steel (8.5%)	Vehicles other than railway (9%)
	Vehicles other than railway (7.7%)	Optical and other technical apparatus (2.4%)

Source: Trade Map, http://www.trademap.org/, accessed on 18 October 2013.

as well as tapping into the potential of other sectors, such as trade and investment, science and technology, and infrastructure. The economic cooperation among the BRICS countries helps to increase their mutual trade. India's export to BRICS nations is US$28.3 billion while its imports are US$72.5 billion[11] in 2011.

The recent global economic crisis that engulfed the US and the European economies also adversely affected the BRICS nations, mainly due to increasing economic interdependence especially on trade and investment. Despite the adverse global economic conditions, BRICS economies, especially India and China, not only withstood the economic slump, but have also shown impressive growth in the real GDP. The other BRICS economies have also come out of the crisis swiftly.

Inadequacies and deficiencies of the present day international monetary order got exposed after the recent financial crisis. An overdependence on the world's most used currency 'US dollar' in international transactions caused serious concern worldwide, especially in view of increasing trade and budget deficits of the USA. Several countries including China diversified into euros so as to reduce their dollar dependency. The BRICS nations also called for stronger regulation of commodity derivatives to dampen excessive volatility in food and energy prices which they said pose new risks for the recovery of the world economy. The development banks of the five nations agreed in principle to establish mutual credit lines denominated in their local currencies in a move designed

---

[11] Trade Map, http://www.trademap.org/, accessed on 18 October 2013.

to reduce dollar-dependency. The BRICS nations are also exploring possibility of a broad-based international reserve currency system that provides stability and certainty against dollar volatility. Notwithstanding euphoria and optimism, the BRICS economies should learn lessons from the economic glitches faced by the USA and Europe, particularly on issues of structural reform.

Trade promotion, both within BRICS countries as well as with the rest of the world, remains the key agenda of BRICS cooperation. During the BRICS summit 2012 held in India, the member countries signed the Master Agreement on Extending Credit Facility in Local Currency and the Multilateral Letter of Credit Confirmation Facility Agreement to replace the US dollar as the main unit of trade between them. The proposal to extend credit facility in local currency would help reduce the demand for fully convertible currencies for transactions among BRICS nations. The BRICS countries also aspire to have their own development bank aimed at mobilizing domestic savings so as to co-fund the infrastructure projects in developing regions. This will directly help in reducing transaction costs and facilitate credit. The BRICS Summit 2013 held in South Africa emphasized on increasing partnership of BRICS with Africa.

Questions

1. Evaluate the significance of BRICS as a country grouping. In your opinion, to what extent, BRICS can exert its economic influence on world trade.
2. A glance over the major trade partners of BRICS reveals that China is the common country as the major trade partner of all other BRICS countries. Critically examine the dominant status of China and its gains from BRICS vis- is other member countries.
3. Critically study the major products traded by BRICS countries. To what extent, you find these products competing or complementary to each other? Assess its influence on trade among the member countries.
4. Assess the impact of BRICS on India, especially on its international trade.

World Trade Organization: International Marketing Implications

INTRODUCTION

The World Trade Organization (WTO) is the only international organization dealing with global rules of trade between nations. It came into existence on 1 January 1995 as a successor of General Agreements on Tariffs and Trade (GATT). Whereas GATT had mainly dealt with trade in goods, the WTO and its agreements now cover trade in services, and in traded inventions, creations, and designs (intellectual property). Its major function is to ensure smooth flow of international trade as predictably and freely as possible. It is a multilateral trade organization aimed at evolving a liberalized trade regime under a rule-based system. Essentially, WTO is

- an organization for opening up trade;
- a forum for governments to negotiate trade agreements;
- a place for countries to settle trade disputes; and
- a place where member governments try to sort out the trade problems they face with each other.

The national governments of all member countries have negotiated under the Uruguay Round to improve access to international markets so as to enable business enterprises to convert trade concessions into new marketing opportunities. The basic objective behind strengthening the rule-based system of international trade under the WTO is to ensure that the international markets remain open and their access is not disrupted by sudden and arbitrary imposition of import restrictions. Moreover, the emerging legal systems not only confer benefits on manufacturing industries and business enterprises but also create rights in their favour. An international marketer needs to develop a thorough understanding of the new opportunities opened up by multilateral trading system[1] under the WTO regime. The major implications of the WTO's multilateral trade regime are as follows.

---

[1] *Understanding WTO*, Fifth Edition, WTO, 2011.

Learning Objectives

- To explain the significance of studying WTO in international marketing
- To briefly explain the functions and structure of WTO
- To describe the principles of multilateral trading system under WTO
- To give an overview of WTO agreements
- To explain the dispute settlement system under WTO
- To explore the WTO implications for international marketing

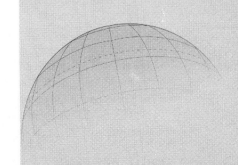

Security of Access to International Markets

In addition to tariff reductions agreed under the Uruguay Round, a large number of tariff lines in trade in goods among the member countries have been bound against further increases. Such bindings ensure that improved access to international markets resulting from tariff reductions is not disrupted by sudden increases in the rates of import duties or imposition of other restrictions by importing countries. In trade in services, the member countries have made binding commitments not to restrict access to service products and foreign-service suppliers beyond the conditions and limitations specified in their national schedules. Thus, the bindings enable international marketing firms to prepare investment and production plans under conditions of certainty resulting from secured access to international markets.

Stability of Access to International Markets

The WTO system also provides stability of access to international markets by instructing all member countries to apply at their respective borders the uniform set of rules proposed in various agreements. Thus, countries are under obligation to ensure that their rules for determining dutiable value for customs purposes, for inspecting products to ascertain conformity to mandatory standards, or for the issue of import licences conform to the provisions of the relevant agreements. The adoption of such uniform rules helps international marketing firms by eliminating dissimilarities in the requirements of different markets.

Implications for Importers of Raw Materials and Other Inputs

A firm operating in international markets often has to import raw materials and intermediate products and services for export production purposes. The WTO agreements require that imports are allowed upon payment of duties and obligation, if any, without any further restrictions. This ensures that the other national regulations applied at the border conform to the uniform rules laid down under the agreements so as to facilitate imports. These rules give exporting firms some assurance that the importing firm will obtain these requirements without delay and at competitive costs. Besides, the general increase in tariff bindings under the agreements indicates to importers that their importing costs will not be inflated by the imposition of higher customs duties.

FROM GATT TO WTO

After World War II, over 50 countries came together to create the International Trade Organization (ITO) as a specialized agency of the United Nations (UN) to manage the business aspect of international economic cooperation. The draft ITO charter was ambitious and extended beyond world trade discipline to rules on employment, commodity agreements, restrictive business practices, international investment, and services. However, the attempts to create the ITO were aborted, as the USA did not ratify it and other countries found it difficult to make it operational without US support.

The combined package of trade rules and tariff concessions negotiated and agreed by 23 countries out of 50 participating countries came to be known as the GATT—an effort to salvage from the aborted attempt to create the ITO. India was also a founder member of GATT, a multilateral treaty aimed at trade liberalization. The GATT provided a multilateral forum during 1947–1994 to discuss the trade problems and reduction of trade barriers.

The GATT was provisional for almost half a century, but it succeeded in promoting and securing liberalization of world trade. As shown in Exhibit 3.1, its membership increased from

Exhibit 3.1 Multilateral trade rounds under GATT

Year	Round/Name	Subjects covered	Countries	Average tariff cut (%)
1947	Geneva	Tariffs	23	35
1949	Annecy	Tariffs	13	NA
1951	Torquay	Tariffs	38	25
1956	Geneva	Tariffs	26	NA
1960–61	Dillon	Tariffs	26	NA
1964–67	Kennedy	Tariffs and anti-dumping measures	62	35
1973–79	Tokyo	Tariffs, non-tariff measures, framework agreements	102	33
1986–94	Uruguay	Tariffs, non-tariff measures, rules, services, intellectual property, dispute settlement, textiles, agriculture, creation of WTO, etc.	123	36
2001–present	Doha	Tariffs on goods, non-agricultural market access (NAMA), special and differential treatment, trade facilitation, etc.	159*	

*As on 1 March 2013.
Source: WTO, as on 14 October 2013.

23 countries in 1947 to 123 countries in 1994. During its existence from 1947 to 1994, the average tariffs on manufactured goods in developed countries declined from about 40 per cent to a mere 4 per cent. It focused on tariff reduction till 1973. It was only during Tokyo and Uruguay Rounds that non-tariff barriers were discussed under GATT. With the increasing use of non-tariff barriers and the increasing significance of service sector in the economies, the need was felt to bring non-tariff barriers and intellectual property (IP) under the purview of multilateral trade.

The WTO was born out of negotiations, and everything the WTO does is the result of negotiations. The bulk of the current work of the WTO comes from the 1986–1994 negotiations called Uruguay Round and earlier negotiations under the GATT. The WTO is currently host to new negotiations, under the 'Doha Development Agenda' launched in 2001.

FUNCTIONS OF WTO

The WTO has nearly 153 members accounting for over 90 per cent of world trade. About two-third of the membership of WTO are developing countries. Around 30 others are negotiating membership. Decisions are made by the member countries through the consensus approach. A majority vote is also possible, but it has never been used in the WTO, and was extremely rare even during the GATT era. The WTO agreements have been ratified in the parliaments of all member countries. The basic functions of WTO are as follows:

- It facilitates the implementation, administration, and operation of the trade agreements.
- It provides a forum for further negotiations among member countries on matters covered by the agreements as well as on new issues falling within its mandate.
- It is responsible for the settlement of differences and disputes among its member countries.
- It is responsible for carrying out periodic reviews of the trade policies of its member countries.

- It assists developing countries in trade policy issues through technical assistance and training programmes.
- It encourages cooperation within international organizations.

Where countries have faced trade barriers and wanted them lowered, the negotiations have helped to open markets for trade. But the WTO is not just about opening markets, and in some circumstances, its rules support maintaining trade barriers, for example, to protect the consumers or prevent spread of disease.

The system's overriding purpose is to help trade flow as freely as possible, as long as there are no undesirable side effects, because this is important for economic development and well-being, which partly means removing obstacles. It also means ensuring that individuals, companies, and governments know what the trade rules are around the world, and giving them the confidence that there will be no sudden changes of policy. In other words, the rules have to be 'transparent' and predictable.

STRUCTURE OF WTO

The structure of the WTO is summarized[2] in Fig. 3.1. The top-level decision-making body of the WTO is the Ministerial Conference, which meets at least once every two years. At the next level is the General Council (normally consists of ambassadors and heads of delegation in Geneva, but sometimes officials sent from members' capitals), which meets several times a year at the Geneva headquarters. At the next level are the Goods Council, the Services Council, and the Intellectual Property (TRIPS) Council, which report to the General Council. The General Council also meets as the Trade Policy Review Body and the Dispute Settlement Body.

Numerous specialized committees, working groups, and parties deal with individual agreements and other areas such as the environment development, membership applications, and regional trade agreements. All WTO members may participate in all councils except Appellate Body, Dispute Settlement panels, Textiles Monitoring Body, and plurilateral committees.

The WTO has a permanent Secretariat based in Geneva and is headed by a Director General. It does not have branch offices outside Geneva. Since decisions are taken by the members themselves, the Secretariat does not have the decision-making power as opposed to other international bureaucracies. The Secretariat's main duties are to supply technical support to the various councils and committees and the ministerial conference, to provide technical assistance to developing countries, to analyse world trade, and to explain WTO concerns to the public and media. The Secretariat also provides legal assistance in the dispute settlement process and advises non-member governments wishing to become members of the WTO.

PRINCIPLES OF MULTILATERAL TRADING SYSTEM UNDER THE WTO

It is difficult for an international marketer to go through all the WTO agreements, which are lengthy and complex, because these are legal texts covering a wide range of issues and activities. The agreements deal with a wide range of subjects related to international trade such as agriculture, textiles and clothing, banking, telecommunications, government purchases, industrial standards and product safety, food sanitation regulations, and IP. However, a manager dealing with international markets needs to have an understanding of the basic principles of the WTO, which form the foundations of multilateral trading system. These principles are as follows.

---

[2] *Annual Report*, 2012, WTO, Geneva.

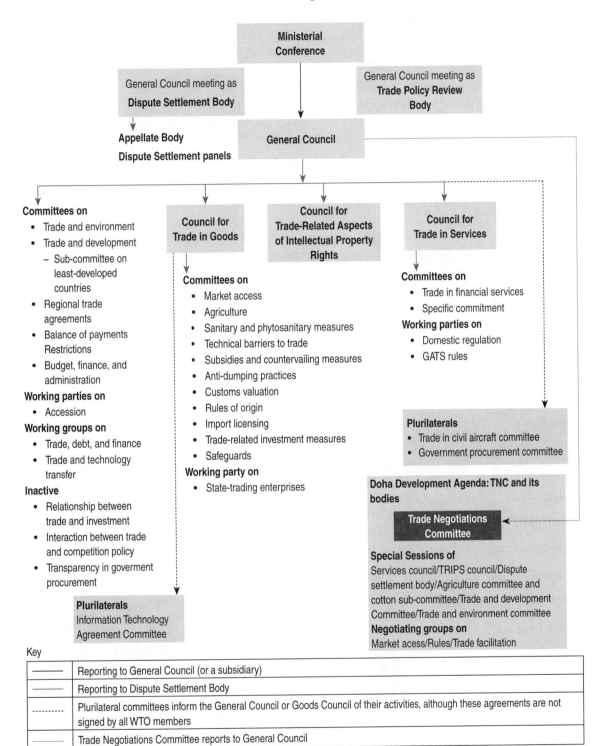

Ministerial Conference

General Council meeting as **Dispute Settlement Body**

General Council meeting as **Trade Policy Review Body**

Appellate Body
Dispute Settlement panels

General Council

Committees on
- Trade and environment
- Trade and development
  - Sub-committee on least-developed countries
- Regional trade agreements
- Balance of payments Restrictions
- Budget, finance, and administration

Working parties on
- Accession

Working groups on
- Trade, debt, and finance
- Trade and technology transfer

Inactive
- Relationship between trade and investment
- Interaction between trade and competition policy
- Transparency in goverment procurement

Plurilaterals
Information Technology Agreement Committee

Council for Trade in Goods

Committees on
- Market access
- Agriculture
- Sanitary and phytosanitary measures
- Technical barriers to trade
- Subsidies and countervailing measures
- Anti-dumping practices
- Customs valuation
- Rules of origin
- Import licensing
- Trade-related investment measures
- Safeguards

Working party on
- State-trading enterprises

Council for Trade-Related Aspects of Intellectual Property Rights

Council for Trade in Services

Committees on
- Trade in financial services
- Specific commitment

Working parties on
- Domestic regulation
- GATS rules

Plurilaterals
- Trade in civil aircraft committee
- Government procurement committee

Doha Development Agenda: TNC and its bodies

Trade Negotiations Committee

Special Sessions of
Services council/TRIPS council/Dispute settlement body/Agriculture committee and cotton sub-committee/Trade and development Committee/Trade and environment committee

Negotiating groups on
Market acess/Rules/Trade facilitation

Key

———	Reporting to General Council (or a subsidiary)
———	Reporting to Dispute Settlement Body
- - - - - -	Plurilateral committees inform the General Council or Goods Council of their activities, although these agreements are not signed by all WTO members
··············	Trade Negotiations Committee reports to General Council

The General Council also meets as the Trade Policy Review Body and Dispute Settlement Body.

Fig. 3.1 The WTO structure

Source: WTO.

Trade without Discrimination

Under the WTO principles, a country cannot discriminate between its trading partners and its own and foreign products and services.

Most-favoured-nation treatment   Under the WTO agreements, countries cannot normally discriminate between their trading partners. In case a country grants someone a special favour (such as a lower rate of customs for one of its products), then it has to do the same for all other WTO members. The principle is known as most-favoured-nation (MFN) treatment. Its importance can be gauged from the fact that it is the first article of the GATT, which governs trade in goods. The MFN is also a priority in the General Agreement on Trade in Services (GATS, Article 2) and the Agreement on Trade Related Aspects of Intellectual Property Rights (TRIPS, Article 4), although in each of the agreements the principle is handled slightly differently. Together these three agreements cover the three main areas of trade handled by the WTO.

Some exceptions to the MFN principle are allowed, which are as follows:

- Countries can set up a free trade agreement that applies only to goods traded within the group—discriminating against goods from outside.
- Countries can give developing countries special access to their markets.
- A country can raise barriers against products that are considered to be traded unfairly from specific countries.
- In case of services, countries are allowed, in limited circumstances, to discriminate.

But the agreements permit these exceptions only under strict conditions. In general, MFN means that every time a country lowers a trade barrier or opens up a market, it has to do so for the same goods or services for all its trading partners—whether rich or poor, weak or strong.

National treatment   The WTO agreements stipulate that imported and locally produced goods should be treated equally—at least after the foreign goods have entered the market. The same should apply to foreign and domestic services, and to foreign and local trademarks, copyrights, and patents. This principle of 'national treatment' (giving others the same treatment as one's own nationals) is also found in all the three main WTO agreements, that is, Article 3 of GATT, Article 17 of GATS, and Article 3 of TRIPS. The principle, however, is handled slightly differently in each of these agreements. National treatment only applies once a product, service, or item of IP has entered the market. Therefore, charging customs duty on an import is not a violation of national treatment even if locally produced products are not charged an equivalent tax.

Gradual Move towards Freer Markets through Negotiations

Lowering trade barriers is one of the most obvious means of encouraging international trade. Such barriers include customs duties (or tariffs) and measures, such as import bans or quotas, that restrict quantities selectively. Since the creation of the GATT in 1947–48, there have been eight rounds of trade negotiations. Initially, these negotiations focused on lowering tariffs (customs duties) on imported goods. As a result of the negotiations, by the mid-1990s, the industrial countries' tariff rates on industrial goods had fallen steadily to less than 4 per cent. But by the 1980s, the negotiations had expanded to cover non-tariff barriers on goods and to new areas such as services and IP. The WTO agreements allow countries to introduce changes gradually, through 'progressive liberalization'. Developing countries are usually given a longer period to fulfil their obligations.

Increased Predictability of International Marketing Environment

Sometimes, promising not to raise a trade barrier can be as important as lowering one because the promise gives businesses a clearer view of their future market opportunities. With stability and predictability, investment is encouraged, jobs are created, and consumers can fully enjoy the benefits of competition—more choice and lower prices. The multilateral trading system is an attempt by the governments to make the business environment stable and predictable.

One of the achievements of the Uruguay Round of multilateral trade talks was to increase the amount of trade under binding commitments. In the WTO, when countries agree to open their markets for goods or services, they 'bind' their commitments. For goods, these bindings amount to ceilings on customs tariff rates. A country can change its bindings, but only after negotiating with its trading partners, which could mean compensating them for loss of trade. All agricultural products, for example, now have bound tariffs. This has resulted in a substantially higher degree of market security for traders and investors.

The trading system under WTO attempts to improve predictability and stability in other ways as well. One way is to discourage the use of quotas and other measures used to set limits on quantities of imports, as administering quotas can lead to more red-tape and accusations of unfair play. Another way is to make countries' trade rules as clear and public ('transparent') as possible. Many WTO agreements require governments to disclose their policies and practices publicly within the country or by notifying the WTO. The regular surveillance of national trade policies through the trade policy review mechanism provides a further means of encouraging transparency both domestically and at the multilateral level.

Promoting Fair Competition in International Markets

The WTO is sometimes described as a 'free trade' institution, but that is not entirely correct. The system does allow tariffs and, in limited circumstances, other forms of protection. More accurately, it is a system of rules dedicated to open, fair, and undistorted competition.

The rules on non-discrimination—MFN and national treatment—are designed to secure fair conditions of trade. It also sets rules on dumping and subsidies, which adversely affect fair trade. The issues are complex and the rules try to establish what is fair or unfair, and how governments can respond, in particular, by charging additional import duties calculated to compensate for damage caused by unfair trade. Many of the other WTO agreements aim to support fair competition such as in agriculture, intellectual property, services, and other areas. The Agreement on Government Procurement (a 'plurilateral' agreement because it is signed by only a few WTO members) extends the competition rules to purchases made by thousands of government entities in many countries.

WTO AGREEMENTS: AN OVERVIEW

The WTO agreements are often referred to as trade rules and WTO is often described as a 'rule-based' system. These rules are essentially agreements negotiated and signed by the bulk of the world's trading nations; these documents provide the legal ground rules for international commerce. They are essentially contracts, binding governments to keep their trade policies within agreed limits. Although negotiated and signed by governments, the goal is to help producers of goods and services, exporters, and importers conduct their business, while allowing governments to meet social and environmental objectives.

The WTO agreements fall in a broad structure of six main parts (Exhibit 3.2) as follows:

- An umbrella agreement (the agreement establishing WTO)
- Agreements for each of the broad areas of trade covered by WTO
  - Goods
  - Services
  - Intellectual property (IP)

- Dispute settlement
- Review of governments' trade policies

Exhibit 3.2   Structure of WTO agreements

Umbrella	Agreement establishing WTO		
	Goods	**Services**	**Intellectual property**
Basic principles	GATT	GATS	TRIPS
Additional details	Other goods agreements and annexes	Services annexes	
Market access commitments	Countries' schedules of commitments (and MFN exemptions)	Countries' schedules of commitment	
	Dispute settlement		
Transparency		Trade policy reviews	
Source: WTO.			

The WTO agreements cover two basic areas—goods and services, and IP. The agreements for goods under GATT deal with the sector-specific issues such as agriculture, health regulations for farm products (sanitary and phytosanitary, SPS), textiles and clothing, product standards, investment measures, anti-dumping measures, customs valuation methods, pre-shipment inspection, rules of origin, import licensing, subsidies and counter-measures, and safeguards. The specific issues covered by GATS include movement of natural persons, air transport, financial services, shipping, and telecommunications. The major WTO agreements are summarized in this chapter.

Increasing Opportunities for Goods in International Markets

The GATT has significantly widened the access to international markets, besides providing a legal and institutional framework. Under the WTO regime, countries can break the commitment (i.e., raise the tariff above the bound rate), but only with difficulty. To do so, a member country is required to negotiate with the countries most concerned, and that could result in compensation for trading partners' loss of trade.

Creating marketing opportunities in the industrial sector

The market access schedules under GATT include commitments of member countries to reduce the tariffs and not to increase the tariffs above the listed rates—the rates are bound. For developed countries, bound rates are the rates generally charged. Most developing countries have bound the rates somewhat higher than the actual rates charged so that the bound rates can serve as a ceiling.

Reduction in tariffs   The individual member countries have listed their commitments to reduce the tariff rates in schedules annexed to Marrakesh Protocol in the General Agreement on Tariffs and Trade, 1994, which is a legally binding agreement. As per these commitments, the developed countries were required to cut the average tariff levels on industrial products by 40 per cent in five equal instalments from 1 January 1995. However, the percentage of tariff reduction on some products of export interest to developing countries, such as textiles and clothing and leather and leather products, was much lower than the average, as they were considered sensitive. A number of developing countries and economies in transition agreed to reduce their tariffs by nearly two-thirds of the percentage achieved by the developed countries. As a result, the weighted average level of tariffs applicable to industrial products is now expected to fall from the present level of

- 6.3–3.8 per cent in developed countries;
- 15.3–12.3 per cent in developing countries; and
- 8.6–6 per cent in the transition economies.

Additional commitments were made under the Information Technology Agreement in 1997, wherein 40 countries, accounting for more than 92 per cent of trade in information technology products, agreed to eliminate import duties and other charges on most of these products by 2000 and on a handful of the products by 2005. As with the other tariff commitments, each participating country is applying its commitments equally to exports from all WTO members, that is, on an MFN basis, even from the members that did not make the commitments.

Tariffs bindings   Binding of tariff lines has substantially increased the degree of market security for traders and investors. Developed countries increased the number of imports whose tariff rates were 'bound' (committed and difficult to increase) from 78 per cent of the product lines to 99 per cent. For developing countries, the increase was considerable, from 21 to 73 per cent. Economies in transition (centrally planned economies) increased their bindings from 73 to 98 per cent.

Creating Fairer Markets in Agriculture Sector

Although the earlier rules of GATT did apply to agriculture-related trade, it contained certain loopholes. Some developed countries protected their costly and inefficient production of temperate zone agricultural products (e.g., wheat and other grains, meat, and dairy products) by imposing quantitative restrictions and variable levies on imports in addition to the high import tariffs. This level of protection often resulted in increased domestic production which, because of high prices, could be disposed of in the international markets only under subsidy. Such subsidized sales depressed international market prices of these agro-products. It also resulted in the reduction of legitimate market share of competitive producers in the same sector.

As a result, the international trade in agriculture became highly 'distorted', especially with the use of export subsidies, which would not normally have been allowed for industrial products. Trade is termed as 'distorted' if prices are higher or lower than normal and if quantities produced, bought, or sold are also higher or lower than the normal levels that usually exist in a competitive market.

The Uruguay Round produced the first multilateral agreement dedicated to the agriculture sector. The objective of the Agreement on Agriculture (AoA) is to reform trade in agriculture and to make policies more market-oriented. This is likely to improve predictability and security for both importing and exporting countries. The salient features of the AoA (Exhibit 3.3) are as follows.

Elimination of non-tariff measures through the tariffication process

Subsequent to the Uruguay Round, quotas and other types of trade-restrictive measures were replaced by tariffs that provide, more or less, equivalent level of protection. This process of converting quotas and other types of non-tariff measures (NTMs) to tariffs is termed as *tariffication*. The member countries agreed under the Uruguay Round that developed countries would

Exhibit 3.3 Reduction of subsidies and protection under AoA

	Developed countries 6 years: 1995–2010	Developing countries Years: 1995–2004
Tariffs		
Average cut for all agricultural products	36%	24%
Minimum cut per product	15%	10%
Domestic support		
Total AMS cuts for sector (Base period: 1986–88)	20%	13%
Exports		
Value of subsidies	36%	24%
Subsidized quantities (Base period: 1986–90)	21%	14%
Least-developed countries do not have to make commitments to reduce tariffs or subsidies.		
Source: WTO.		

cut the tariffs by an average of 36 per cent in equal steps over six years, whereas the developing countries would make 24 per cent cuts over 10 years. Several developing countries also used the option of offering ceiling tariff rates in cases where duties were not 'bound' before the Uruguay Round. Least developed countries did not have to cut their tariffs.

For products whose non-tariff restrictions have been converted to tariffs, the governments are allowed to take special emergency actions called 'special safeguards' in order to prevent swiftly falling prices or surges in imports from hurting their farmers.

Binding against further increase of tariffs

In addition to the elimination of all NTMs by tariffication, all countries have also bound all the tariffs applicable to agricultural products. In most cases, developing countries have given bindings at rates that are higher than their current applied or reduced rates.

Domestic support National policies that support domestic prices or subsidized production often encourage over-production. This squeezes out imports or leads to export subsidies and low-price dumping in international markets. Under the AoA, domestic policies that have a direct effect on production and trade have to be cut back. The domestic support in the agriculture sector is categorized by green, amber, and blue boxes, as shown in Exhibit 3.4.

The member countries quantified the support provided per year for the agriculture sector, termed as 'total aggregate measurement of support' (total AMS) in the base years of 1986–88. Developed countries agreed to reduce the total AMS by 20 per cent over six years starting from 1995, while the developing countries agreed to make 30 per cent cut over 10 years. Least developed countries were not required to make any cuts in AMS. The AMS is calculated on a product-by-product basis by using the difference between the average external reference price for a product and its applied administered price multiplied by the quantity of production. To arrive at AMS, non-product-specific domestic subsidies are added to the total subsidies calculated on a product-by-product basis.

Exhibit 3.4   Categories of domestic support in agriculture sector

Green Box   All subsidies that have little or, at most, minimal trade distorting effects and do not have the 'effect of providing price support to producers', are exempt from reduction commitments. The subsidies under the green box include

- government expenditure on agricultural research, pest control, inspection, and grading of particular products, marketing, and promotion services;
- financial participation by government in income insurance and income safety net programmes;
- payments for natural disaster;
- structural adjustment assistance provided through
  - producer retirement programmes designed to facilitate the retirement of persons engaged in marketable agricultural production,
  - resource retirement programmes designed to remove land and other resources, including livestock, from agricultural production,

  - investment aids designed to assist the financial or physical restructuring of a producer's operations;
- payments under environmental programmes; and
- payments under regional assistance programmes.

Amber Box   This category of domestic support refers to the amber colour of traffic lights, which means 'slow down'. The agreement establishes a ceiling on the total domestic support that a government may provide to its domestic producers.

Blue Box   Certain categories of direct payment to farmers are also permitted in cases where farmers are required to limit production. This also includes government assistance programmes to encourage agricultural and rural development in developing countries, and other support on a small scale when compared with the total value of the product or products supported (5% or less in the case of developed countries and 10% or less for developing countries).

Source: WTO.

Export subsidies   The AoA prohibits export subsidies on agricultural products unless the subsidies are specified in a member's list of commitments. Where they are listed, the agreement requires WTO members to cut both the amount of money they spend on export subsidies and the quantities of exports that receive subsidies. Taking averages for 1986–90 as the base level, developed countries agreed to cut the value of export subsidies by 36 per cent over a period of six years starting from 1995 (24% over 10 years for developing countries). Developed countries also agreed to reduce the quantities of subsidized exports by 21 per cent over six years (14% over 10 years for developing countries). Least developed countries were not required to make any cuts. During the six-year implementation period, developing countries were allowed under certain conditions to use subsidies to reduce the costs of marketing and transporting.

Opening up Marketing Opportunities in Textiles

World trade in textiles and clothing has been subject to a large number of bilateral quota arrangements over the past five decades. The range of products covered by quotas extended from cotton textiles under the short-term and long-term arrangements of the 1960s and the early 1970s to an ever-increasing list of textile products made from natural and man-made fibres under the five expansions of the Multi-fibre Agreement. From 1974, until the end of the Uruguay Round, international trade in textiles was governed by the Multi-fibre Arrangement (MFA). This was a framework for bilateral agreements or unilateral actions that established quotas limiting imports into countries whose domestic industries were facing serious damages from rapidly increasing imports.

The quota system under MFA conflicted with GATT's general preference for customs tariffs instead of measures that restricted quantities. The quotas were also exceptions to the GATT principle of treating all trading partners equally because they specified how much the importing country was going to accept from individual exporting countries.

Since 1995, the ATC of the WTO has taken over from the MFA. The schedule of integration into GATT is shown in Exhibit 3.5.

Exhibit 3.5 Integration schedule under Agreement of Textile and Clothing (ATC)

Step	Percentage of products to be brought under GATT (including removal of any quota)	How fast remaining quotas should open up, if 1994 rate was 6%
Step 1: 1 January 1995 (to 31 December 1997)	16% (minimum, taking 1990 imports as base)	6.96% per year
Step 2: 1 January 1998 (to 31 December 2001)	17%	8.7% per year
Step 3: 1 January 2002 (to 31 December 2004)	18%	11.05% per year
Step 4: 1 January 2005	49% (maximum)	No quotas left

Source: WTO.

STANDARDS AND SAFETY MEASURES FOR INTERNATIONAL MARKETS

Article 20 of the GATT allows governments to act against a particular trading activity in order to protect human, animal, or plant life or health, provided no discrimination is made and it is not used as disguised protectionism. In addition, there are two specific agreements, which lay down product standards to ensure food safety and animal and plant health and safety.

The Agreement on Sanitary and Phytosanitary (SPS) Measures sets out the basic rules on food safety and plant health standards. This allows the countries to set their own standards, which should have a scientific basis and should be applied only to the extent necessary to protect human, animal, or plant life or health. These regulations should not arbitrarily or unjustifiably discriminate between countries where identical or similar conditions prevail. Member countries are encouraged to use international standards such as FAO/WHO Codex Alimentarius Commission for food, International Animal Health Organization for animal health, etc. However, the agreement allows countries to set higher standards with consistency. The agreement includes provisions for control, inspection, and approval procedures. The member governments must provide advance notice of new or changed SPS regulations and establish a national enquiry point to provide information. As indicated in Exhibit 3.6, an international marketer needs to know about health and sanitary regulations so as to prepare his marketing plan and product adaptation framework as per the requirements of the target market.

Exhibit 3.6 Planning for international markets requires knowledge of health and sanitary regulations

A firm planning to enter international markets needs to know the health and sanitary regulations in international markets so as to make product adaptation strategy and design international marketing strategy. A number of major importers of fresh fruits and vegetables have strict regulations on plant protection. These countries require fresh commodities from countries with specific pests, especially the fruit fly of the Tephridiate family, to be treated to prevent the pests from entering their territories. In the past, ethylene dibromide (EDB) was widely used for the fumigation of such produce prior to importation. The prohibition of EDB by the USA, Japan, and other countries jeopardized trade in fresh fruits and vegetables originating from tropical and semi-tropical countries. Alternative treatments to EDB fumigation such as vapour and dry heat treatment, hot water dips, refrigeration at near 0°C for a specific duration, and treatment with other chemicals such as methyl bromide, phosphine, and cyanide, are now used with varying degrees of success.

Source: Business Guide to Uruguay Round, International Trade Centre, *UNCTAD/WTO.*

The Agreement on Technical Barriers to Trade (TBT) tries to ensure that regulations, standards, testing, and certification procedures do not create unnecessary obstacles to trade. This agreement complements the Agreement on Sanitary and Phytosanitary (SPS) measures. Firms engaged in international marketing and manufacturing products for international markets need to know about the latest standards in their prospective markets. All WTO member countries are required to set up national enquiry points to make this information available.

Bringing International Trade in Services under Multilateral Framework

The GATS is the first and only set of multilateral rules governing international trade in services. Negotiated in the Uruguay Round, it was developed in response to the strong growth of the services economy over the past three decades and the greater potential for marketing services internationally brought about by the communications revolution. The GATS has three elements:

- The main text containing general obligations and disciplines
- Annexes dealing with rules for specific sectors
- Individual countries' specific commitments to provide access to their markets and also indicating sectors where countries are temporarily not applying the MFN principle of non-discrimination

General obligations and disciplines

The agreement covers all internationally traded services, for example, banking, telecommunications, tourism, professional services, etc. It also defines four ways or modes of trading services internationally.

Mode 1: Services supplied from one country to another (e.g., international telephone calls), officially known as 'cross-border supply'

Mode 2: Consumers or firms making use of a service in another country (e.g., tourism), officially known as 'consumption abroad'

Mode 3: A foreign company setting up subsidiaries or branches to provide services in another country (e.g., foreign banks setting up operations in a country), officially known as 'commercial presence'

Mode 4: Individuals travelling from their own country to supply services in another (e.g., fashion models or consultants), officially known as 'presence of natural persons'

There is a lot of debate over full implementation of GATS wherein all modes of trading services internationally become available. In view of highly competent, high-proficiency medical and other technical skills (Exhibit 3.7), the agreement is likely to open up tremendous opportunities in international market for medical trade.

Most-favoured-nation treatment

MFN also applies to the services sector wherein a member country's trading partners are treated equally as per the principle of non-discrimination. Under GATS, if a country allows foreign competition in a sector, equal opportunities in that sector should be given to the service providers from all other WTO members. This applies even if the country has made no specific commitment to provide foreign companies access to its markets under the WTO. MFN applies to all services, but some special temporary exemptions have been allowed to countries that already have preferential agreements in services with their trading partners. Such exemptions are expected to last not more than 10 years.

Commitments on market access and national treatment

Individual countries' commitments to open markets in specific sectors and the extent of their openness has been the outcome of the Uruguay Round of negotiations. The commitments appear

Exhibit 3.7 GATS: Emerging opportunities in medical trade

Medical travel is the most visible face of India's increasing global trade in health-care services, but the WTO expects three other modes to become equally significant over a period of time.

The first one is dubbed as the 'cross-border delivery of trade.' It covers everything from shipment of laboratory samples, diagnosis, and clinical consultation via traditional mail channels to the electronic delivery of health services. The latter, especially, is expected to become a significant movement because of the advances in telecommunications.

Telemedicine holds out big potential simply because it allows one to offer medical services without investing heavily in infrastructure. Some hospitals in the USA have started offering tele-consultation services to hospitals in Central America and the eastern Mediterranean region. Some Indian hospitals are offering similar services to their counterparts in Nepal and Bangladesh.

The third mode (medical travel is considered Mode 2 by the WTO) covers the setting up of hospitals, clinics, and diagnostic centres in a country by a medical group that has its base in another country. It could also involve the taking over of a hospital chain by a foreign group.

The final mode of trade involves the movement of health personnel—physicians, specialists, nurses, paramedics, and other health professionals—from one country to another. For instance, many Indian doctors and nurses move to the UK, and countries such as Cuba and China often send their health-care personnel to other countries, especially to Africa, on short-term contracts. The most prominent source countries for health personnel are India, the Philippines, and South Africa, while Australia, the UK, the USA, and the Eastern Mediterranean countries provide the biggest outlet for such staff.

Source: 'How the Medical Trade will Grow', *Business World*, 22 December 2003.

in 'schedules' that list the sectors being opened, the extent of market access being given in those sectors (e.g., whether there are any restrictions on foreign ownership), and any limitations on national treatment (whether some rights granted to local companies will not be granted to foreign companies). For instance, if a government commits itself to allow foreign banks to operate in its domestic market, it is a market-access commitment. And if the government limits the number of licences it will issue, it is a market-access limitation. If it also says foreign banks are only allowed to open one branch while domestic banks are allowed to open numerous branches, it is an exception to the national treatment principle.

These clearly defined commitments are 'bound'. Like bound tariffs for trade in goods, they can only be modified after negotiations with affected countries. As 'unbinding' is difficult, the commitments are virtually guaranteed conditions for foreign exporters and importers of services and investors in the services sector.

Government services are explicitly placed in the agreement and there is nothing in GATS that forces a government to privatize service industries. The carve-out is an explicit commitment by WTO member governments to allow publicly funded services in core areas of their responsibility. Government services are defined in the agreements as those that are not supplied commercially and do not compete with other suppliers. These services are not subject to any GATS disciplines nor are they covered by negotiations and commitments on market access, and the principle of national treatment does not apply to them.

Transparency

GATS stipulates that governments must publish all relevant laws and regulations and set up enquiry points within their bureaucracies. Foreign companies and governments can then use these inquiry points to obtain information about regulations in any service sector. Also, they have to notify the WTO of any changes in regulations that apply to the services that come under specific commitments.

Objectivity and reasonability of regulations

Since domestic regulations are the most significant means of exercising influence or control over the services trade, the agreement says that governments should regulate services reasonably, objectively, and impartially. When a government makes an administrative decision that affects a service, it should also provide an impartial means for reviewing the decision (e.g., tribunal). GATS does not require any service to be deregulated. Commitments to liberalize do not affect governments' right to set levels of quality, safety, or price, or to introduce regulations to pursue any other policy objective they deem fit. A commitment to national treatment, for example, would only mean that the same regulations would apply to foreign suppliers as to nationals. Governments naturally retain their right to set qualification requirements for doctors or lawyers, and to set standards to ensure consumer health and safety.

Recognition

When two or more governments enter into agreements recognizing each other's qualifications (e.g., the licensing or certification of service suppliers), GATS states that other members must also be given a chance to negotiate comparable pacts. The recognition of other countries' qualifications must not be discriminatory and it must not amount to protectionism in disguise. These recognition agreements must be notified to the WTO.

International payments and transfers

Once a government has made a commitment to open a service sector to foreign competition, it must not normally restrict money being transferred out of the country as payment for services rendered (current transactions) in that sector. The only exception is when there are difficulties in balance of payments, but even then the restrictions must be temporary and subject to other limits and conditions.

Progressive liberalization

As the Uruguay Round was only the beginning, GATS required more negotiations, which began in early 2000 and formed part of the Doha Development Agenda. The goal was to take the liberalization process further by increasing the level of commitments in schedules.

Complexity of international trade in services

International trade in goods is a relatively simple idea to grasp—a product is transported from one country to another. Trade in services is much more diverse. Telephone companies, banks, airlines, and accountancy firms provide their services in quite different ways. The GATS annexes cover some of the diversity as follows.

Movement of natural persons   This annex deals with negotiations on individuals' rights to stay temporarily in a country for the purpose of providing a service. It specifies that the agreement does not apply to people seeking permanent employment or to conditions for obtaining citizenship, permanent residence, or permanent employment.

Financial services   Instability in the banking system affects the whole economy. The financial services annex gives governments wide latitude to take prudential measures, such as those for the protection of investors, depositors, and insurance policy holders, and to ensure the integrity and stability of the financial system. The annex also excludes from the agreement services provided when a government exercises its authority over the financial system, for example, central banks' services.

Telecommunications   The telecommunications sector has a dual role. It is a distinct sector of economic activity and is an underlying means of supplying other economic activities (e.g., electronic money transfers). The annex says governments must ensure that foreign-service suppliers are given access to the public telecommunications networks without discrimination.

Air transport services   Under this annex, traffic rights and directly related activities are excluded from GATS's coverage. These are handled by other bilateral agreements. However, the annex establishes that GATS will apply to aircraft repair and maintenance services, marketing of air transport services, and computer reservation services.

Protection and Enforcement of Intellectual Property Rights

Knowledge and ideas are rapidly gaining increased significance in market offerings. Most of the value of technology-intensive products and medicines lies in the amount of invention, innovation, research, design, and testing involved. Films, music recordings, books, computer software, and online services are bought and sold because of the information and creativity they contain, not usually because of the plastic, metal, or paper used to make them. The objects of IP are creation of the human mind—the human intellect. Creators can be given the right to prevent others from using their inventions, designs, or other creations—and to use that right to negotiate payment in return for those using them. These are intellectual property rights (IPRs). They take a number of forms. For example, books, paintings, and films come under copyright regulations; inventions can be patented; brand names and product logos can be registered as trademarks; and so on.

The extent of protection and enforcement of these rights varies widely around the world. Besides, tax or ineffective enforcement of such rights in a number of world markets may encourage trade in counterfeit and pirated goods, thereby damaging the legitimate commercial interests of manufacturers who hold or have acquired those rights. Conflicting views on IP protections[3] are depicted in Fig. 3.2, wherein developed countries are interested in raising the levels of IP

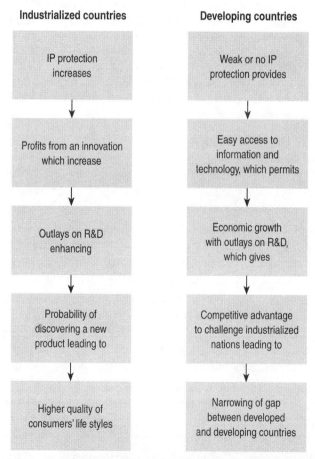

Fig. 3.2 Conflicting views on IP protection

[3] Jain, Subhash C., Problems in International Protection of Intellectual Property Rights, *Journal of International Marketing*, 4(1), 1996, pp. 9–32.

Exhibit 3.8   Turmeric patents in the US

Turmeric (*Curcuma longa*) is a plant of the ginger family yielding saffron-coloured rhizomes used traditionally as a spice for flavouring Indian cooking. Its unique properties also make it an effective ingredient in medicines, cosmetics, and as a colour dye. As a medicine, it is traditionally used in India to heal wounds and rashes.

In March 1995, two expatriate Indians at the University of Mississippi Medical Centre, Jackson (Suman K. Das and Hari Har P. Cohly), were granted a US patent (patent number 5,401,504) for turmeric to be used to heal wounds. The Indian Council for Scientific and Industrial Research (CSIR) filed a case with the US Patent Office challenging the patent on the grounds of 'prior art,' that is, existing public knowledge. CSIR said turmeric has been used for thousands of years for healing wounds and rashes, and therefore its use as a medicine was not a new invention.

- Inventions can only be patented if they satisfy the following three criteria:
  - Novelty—only inventions that are genuinely new, and not part of existing knowledge, can be patented.
  - Nonobviousness—if the new invention is obvious, that is, anyone familiar with the subject could easily anticipate the invention, then it cannot be patented.
  - Utility—the invention has to work in practice.
- The claim had to be backed by written documentation claiming traditional wisdom. CSIR went so far as to present an ancient Sanskrit text and a paper published in 1953 in the Journal of the Indian Medical Association. The US Patent Office upheld the objection on the grounds of novelty and cancelled the patent.

Source: India Case Study—Local Species and Intellectual Property, Trade and Development Centre.

protection so as to keep higher profits leading to higher outlays for research and development. On the other hand, laxity in legislative framework and enforcement of IPRs provides developing countries an easy access to information and technology, which in turn contributes to economic growth with little investment on research and development (R&D). It provides competitive advantage to developing countries to challenge industrialized nations resulting in narrowing of the gap between developed and developing countries. The new rules related to product patent are likely to affect the pharmaceutical industry in developing countries, which had so far been able to produce and supply drugs at very competitive prices.

Farmers and consumers in developing countries are highly apprehensive of misuse of patent laws by the developed countries. Patents in developed countries related to turmeric (Exhibit 3.8), *neem*, Darjeeling tea, and basmati rice (Fig. 3.3) have generated a lot of controversy in India and other South Asian countries.

Fig. 3.3   Texmati Rice given patent by US Patent and Trademark Office
Source: www.riceselect.com/contact.aspx, accessed on 15 October 2013.

Such ineffective enforcement of protection to the intellectual property leading to high incidence of piracy has been the key reason for knowledge-based firms like Blockbuster Video, the world market leader in rented video market, to refrain from large potential markets in developing countries. The WTO's agreement on Trade-Related Aspects of Intellectual Property Rights (TRIPS), negotiated in the 1986–94 Uruguay Round, introduced IP rules in the multilateral trading system for the first time. The TRIPS agreement lays down minimum standards for the protection of IPRs as well as the procedures and remedies for their enforcement. It establishes a mechanism for consultations and surveillance at the international level to ensure compliance with these standards by member countries at the national level.

The TRIPS agreement of the WTO attempts to narrow the gaps in the way these rights are protected around the world and to bring them under common international rules. It establishes minimum levels of protection that each government has to give to the IP of fellow WTO members. The trade disputes over IPRs may also be dealt with the dispute settlement system of the WTO.

As in the other two agreements of GATT and GATS, the principles of non-discrimination, that is, national treatment and MFN, feature prominently in the TRIPS agreement. Besides, IP protection is expected to contribute to technical innovation and transfer of technology. This is especially significant while marketing technology-intensive and knowledge-based products. The structure of the agreement is built on the existing international conventions dealing with IPRs such as

- the Paris Convention for the Protection of Industrial Property (patents, industrial designs; etc.) and
- the Berne Convention for the Protection of Literary and Artistic Works (copyright).

Its provisions apply to the following IPRs related to patents, copyright and related rights, trademarks, industrial designs, layout designs of integrated circuits, undisclosed information and trade secrets, and geographical indications. The minimum periods of protection for IPRs are given in Table 3.1.

Table 3.1 Minimum period for IPR protection

Types	Minimum period
Patents	20 years from the date of filing of the application for a patent (TRIPS, Article 33)
Copyright	Work other than cinematographic or photographic: 50 years from the date of authorized publication or life of the author plus 50 years
	Cinematographic work: 50 years after the work has been made available to the public or, if not made available, after the making of such work
	Photographic work: 25 years after the making of the work.
Trademarks	Seven years from initial registration and each renewal of registration; registration is renewable indefinitely (TRIPS, Article 18)
Performers and producers of phonograms	Fifty years from the end of the calendar year in which the fixation (phonogram) was made or the performance took place (TRIPS, Article 14:5)
Broadcasting	Twenty years from the end of the calendar year in which the broadcast took place (TRIPS, Article 14:5)
Industrial designs	At least 10 years (TRIPS, Article 26:3)
Layout designs of integrated circuits	10 years from the date of registration or, where registration is not required, 10 years from the date of first exploitation (TRIPS, Article 38:2 and 3)

In order to ensure that the rights available to patent holders are not abused, it provides for compulsory licensing. The agreement also lays down procedures for consultations between governments when one party has reasons to believe that the licensing practices or conditions of an enterprise from another member country constitute an abuse of the agreement or have adverse effects on competition.

The countries were given one year to ensure that their laws and practices conform to the TRIPS agreement. Developing countries and (under certain conditions) transition economies were given five years until 2000. Least developed countries have 11 years until 2006—now extended to 2016—for pharmaceutical patents.

Curbing Unfair Marketing Practices

While making pricing decisions for international markets, a thorough understanding of 'unfair trade practices' under WTO agreements is required so as to assess their implications in the target markets. Subsidies may play an important role in developing countries and in the transformation of centrally planned economies to market economies. The pricing strategy should be designed to deal with threats of anti-dumping and countervailing duties while using differential pricing strategies.

International market competitions get distorted mainly by unfair trade practices as follows:

- If the exported goods benefit from the subsidies
- If exported goods are dumped in overseas markets

The agreements on Anti-Dumping Practices (ADP) and on Subsidies and Countervailing Measures (SCM) authorize importing countries to levy compensatory duties on import of products.

Agreements on Anti-dumping Practices

The WTO agreement on anti-dumping allows governments to act against dumping where there is genuine (material) injury to the competing domestic industry. A product is considered to be dumped if

- the export price is less than the price charged for the like product in the exporting country; or
- it is sold for less than its cost of production.

In order to initiate anti-dumping action, the government should be able to show that dumping has taken place, calculate the extent of dumping (how much lower the export price is compared to the exporter's home market price), and show that dumping is causing injury or threatening the local industry. Typically, anti-dumping action means charging extra import duty on a particular product from the particular exporting country in order to bring its price closer to the 'normal value' or to remove the injury to domestic industry in the importing country.

There are many ways of calculating whether a particular product is being dumped heavily or only lightly. The agreement narrows down the range of possible options. It provides three methods to calculate a product's 'normal value'. The main one is based on the price in the exporter's domestic market. When this cannot be used, two alternatives are available—the price charged by the exporter in another country or a calculation based on the combination of the exporter's production costs, other expenses, and normal profit margins. The agreement also specifies how a fair comparison can be made between the export price and the normal domestic price.

Anti-dumping measures can only be applied if the dumping is hurting the industry in the importing country. Therefore, first a detailed investigation has to be conducted according to specified rules. The investigation must evaluate all relevant economic factors that have a bearing on the state of the industry in question. If the investigation shows that dumping has indeed taken place and domestic industry has been hurt, the exporting company can undertake to raise its price to an agreed level in order to avoid anti-dumping import duty.

Detailed procedures are set out on how anti-dumping cases are to be initiated, how the investigations are to be conducted, and the conditions for ensuring that all interested parties are given an opportunity to present evidence. Anti-dumping measures must expire five years after the date of imposition, unless an investigation shows that ending the measure would lead to injury.

Anti-dumping investigations are to end immediately in cases where the authorities determine that the margin of dumping is insignificantly small (defined as less than 2% of the export price of the product.) Besides, the investigations also have to end if the volume of dumped imports is negligible, that is, if the volume from one country is less than 3 per cent of the total imports of that product—although investigations can proceed if several countries, each supplying less than 3 per cent of the imports, together account for 7 per cent or more of total imports.

The member countries are required to inform the committee on ADP about all preliminary and final anti-dumping actions, promptly and in detail. When differences arise, members may consult each other and use the dispute settlement procedure of the WTO.

The use of contingent protection measures like anti-dumping duties increased to its peak by 2000 but declined subsequently. India has been a leading user[4] of anti-dumping instrument (Table 3.2) followed by the USA, European Union (EU), Argentina, Brazil, Australia, South Africa, China, Canada, and Turkey.

Table 3.2   Top 10 users of anti-dumping measures, 1995–2012

Country	1995	2001	2005	2010	2012*	1995–2012*
India	6	79	28	41	7	663
USA	14	77	12	3	7	465
EU	33	28	24	15	7	444
Argentine	27	28	12	14	10	301
Brazil	5	17	6	37	26	258
Australia	5	24	7	7	6	241
South Africa	16	6	23	0	0	216
China	0	14	24	8	4	195
Canada	11	25	1	2	10	165
Turkey	0	15	12	2	6	154
All countries	157	372	201	172	114	4,125

*Up to June 2012.
Source: WTO, *Economic Survey*, 2012–13.

Agreement on Subsidies and Countervailing Measures

This agreement administers the use of subsidies and regulates the actions that countries can take to counter the effects of subsidies. The importing country can use the dispute settlement procedure of the WTO to seek the withdrawal of the subsidy or the removal of its adverse effects. It can launch its own investigation and ultimately charge extra duty (known as 'countervailing duty') on subsidized imports that are found to be hurting domestic producers.

The agreement contains two categories of subsidies as follows.

Prohibited subsidies   These are the subsidies that require recipients to meet certain export targets, or to use domestic goods instead of imported goods. They are prohibited because they are

---

[4] *Economic Survey*, 2011–12, Ministry of Finance, Government of India, New Delhi.

specifically designed to distort international trade, and are therefore likely to hurt other countries' trade. They can be challenged in the WTO dispute settlement procedure where they are handled under an accelerated timetable. If the dispute settlement procedure confirms that the subsidy is prohibited, it must be withdrawn immediately. Otherwise, the complaining country can take counter measures. If domestic producers are hurt by imports of subsidized products, countervailing duty can be imposed. The agreement's illustrative list of prohibited export subsidies includes the following:

- Direct subsidies based on export performance
- Currency-retention schemes involving a bonus on exports
- Provision of subsidized inputs for use in the production of exported goods
- Exemption from direct taxes (e.g., tax on profits related to exports)
- Exemption from, or remission of, indirect taxes (e.g., value-added tax, VAT) on exported products in excess of those borne by these products when sold for domestic consumption
- Remission of drawback of import charges (e.g., tariffs and other duties) in excess of those levied on inputs consumed in the production of exported goods
- Export-guarantee programmes at premium rates inadequate to cover the long-term costs of the programme
- Export credits at rates below the government's cost of borrowing, where they are sued to secure a material advantage in export credit items

Actionable subsidies   In this category, the complaining country has to show that the subsidy has an adverse effect on its interest. Otherwise the subsidy is permitted. The agreement defines the following three types of damages by such subsidies:

- One country's subsidies can hurt a domestic industry in an importing country.
- It can hurt rival exporters from another country when the two compete in a third market.
- The domestic subsidies in one country can hurt exporters trying to compete in the subsidizing country's domestic market.

If the Dispute Settlement Body rules that the subsidy does have an adverse effect, the subsidy must be withdrawn or its adverse effects must be removed. Again, if domestic producers are hurt by imports of subsidized products, countervailing duty can be imposed.

The agreement originally contained a third category, that is, non-actionable subsidies. This category existed for five years, ending in December 1999, and was not extended. Some of the disciplines are similar to those of the anti-dumping agreement. Countervailing duty (the parallel of anti-dumping duty) can only be charged after the importing country has conducted a detailed investigation similar to that required for anti-dumping action. The subsidized exporter can also agree to raise its export prices as an alternative to its exports being charged countervailing duty.

Emergency Protection from Imports

A WTO member may restrict imports of a product temporarily (take 'safeguard' actions) if its domestic industry is seriously injured or threatened with injury caused by a surge in imports. Safeguard measures were always available under GATT (Article 19); however, they were infrequently used. A number of countries preferred to protect their domestic industries through 'grey area' measures—using bilateral negotiations outside GATT's auspices. They also persuaded exporting countries to restrain exports 'voluntarily' or to agree to other means of sharing markets. Agreements of this kind were reached for a wide range of products among countries, for example, automobiles, steel, and semi-conductors.

The WTO agreement on safeguards prohibits 'grey-area' measures and sets time limits (a sunset clause) on all safeguard actions. According to the agreement, members must not seek, take, or maintain any voluntary export restraints, orderly marketing arrangements, or any other similar measures on the export or the import side. The bilateral measures that were not modified to conform to the agreement were phased out at the end of 1998. Countries were allowed to keep one of these measures an extra year (until the end of 1999), but only the EU——for restrictions on imports of cars from Japan—made use of this provision.

Industries or companies may request safeguard actions by their respective governments. The WTO agreement sets out requirements for safeguard investigations by national authorities. The emphasis is on transparency and on following established rules and practices avoiding arbitrary methods. A safeguard measure should be applied only to the extent necessary to prevent or remedy serious injury and to help the industry concerned to adjust. Where quantitative restrictions (quotas) are imposed, they normally should not reduce the quantities of imports below the annual average for the last three representative years for which statistics are available, unless clear justification is given that a different level is necessary to prevent or remedy serious injury.

In principle, safeguard measures cannot be targeted at imports from a particular country. A safeguard measure should not last for more than four years, although it can be extended up to eight years under special circumstances. When a country restricts imports in order to safeguard its domestic producers, in principle it must give something in return. To some extent, developing countries' exports are shielded from safeguard actions. An importing country can apply a safeguard measure to a product from a developing country only if the developing country is supplying more than 3 per cent of the imports of that product, or if the developing member countries with less than 3 per cent import share collectively account for more than 9 per cent of total imports of the product concerned.

The WTO's Safeguards Committee oversees the operations of the agreement and is responsible for the surveillance of members' commitment. Member governments have to report each phase of a safeguard investigation and related decision-making, and then the committee reviews these reports.

Attempts to Reduce Non-tariff Marketing Barriers

In addition to import tariffs, an international marketing firm faces a number of bureaucratic and legal issues in the target markets, which hinders smooth flow of trade. Such barriers often lack transparency and are often criticised as arbitrary to block market entry. Growing use of unconventional NTMs such as health and safety measures, technical regulations, environmental controls, customs valuation procedures, and labour laws by developed countries has become a major barrier to market access to exports from developing countries. Such market barriers are considerably stiffer for products with lower value addition and technological content (agricultural products, textiles, leather products, etc.), which are of major interest to countries like India.

Non-tariff marketing barriers on imports imposed by various countries are summarized here.

USA Advance manifest rules imposed by US customs, American provisions to promote US-made iron foundry products, refusal of import consignments by the United States Food and Drugs Administration (USFDA) for simple reasons, registration documentation and customs procedures, levies and charges, standards and other technical requirements.

EU Lack of harmonization and common standards, labelling rules and regulations, NTMs related to SPS conditions, pesticides residues, subsidies, health and hygiene conditions, and testing and certification requirements for electric vehicles.

Japan Authorization requirement in the import of goods, large-scale retail store law, import quotas in respect of squid, seaweed, mackerel, sardine, herring and scallop, impractical and strict quarantine procedure, Japanese standards affecting food additives, etc.

Australia   Holding up of samples for phyto-sanitary clearance, quarantine and inspection process, pesticide residues, prohibition of imports of milk-based items, SPS standards, import restrictions, health inspection in the case of items shipped.

West Asia and North Africa (WANA)   Legalization of documents, health-related non-tariff barriers (NTBs), government monopoly, strict packaging and labelling requirements, and regional trading arrangements (RTAs).

Brazil   Fixation of minimum price to prevent under-invoicing, marking of 'EN-METRO' on tyres, requirement for bio-availability and bio-equivalence studies, extensive labelling and marketing requirements, and charges for clearance at port and the merchant marine renewal tax, etc.

Argentina   Cumbersome certificate of origin requirements, burdensome labelling requirement standard, listing, etc., and cumbersome regulations for product re-testing.

Mexico   'NORM-MEXICO' certificate for each and every tyre, strict general customs law, imposition of a special certificate of origin and levy of custom user fee, stringent and cumbersome rules on standards and technical requirements relating to wooden packing, and complicated testing procedure for electrical equipment.

Colombia   Improper tariff schedule classification, issue of improper address or typing mistake, registration of imports with MINCOMEX in a specific application, sanitary registration and discriminatory certification requirements.

Venezuela   Heavy fines imposed on importer and the forfeiture of goods in case of under-invoicing of goods.

Sri Lanka   Import restriction on essential/sensitive items.

Turkey   Quantitative restrictions and import licenses, imposition of anti-dumping duty on polyester-texturized yarn.

Chile   Salmonella inspection requirement on exports of fresh and frozen uncooked poultry.

China   Restrictions on imports, standardization regulations, registration requirements, commodity inspection, quarantine rules, and tax-related barriers like VAT.

Central Europe and Baltic countries   Stringent health rules for spices and microbiological count, mold count to be free from salmonella and e-coil bacteria.

The various non-tariff marketing barriers dealt under WTO framework include the following.

Import licensing procedures

Import licensing procedures are generally considered as complex and non-transparent with little predictability, and have often been used to block market entry of foreign products. The Agreement on Import Licensing Procedures attempts to simplify and bring transparency to the import procedures. The agreement requires governments to publish sufficient information for international traders to know how and why the licences are granted. It also describes how countries should notify the WTO when they introduce new import licensing procedures or change existing procedures. The agreement offers guidance on how governments should assess applications for licences. The agreement sets criteria for automatic issuance of some licenses so that the procedures used do not restrict trade. Here, the agreement tries to minimize the importers' burden in applying for licences so that the administrative work does not in itself restrict or distort imports. The agreement says that the agencies handling licensing should not normally take more than 30 days to deal with an application. However, 60 days are permitted when all applications are considered at the same time.

Customs valuation

For importers, the process of estimating the value of a product at customs presents problems that can be as high as the actual duty rate charged. The WTO agreement on customs valuation aims for a fair, uniform, and neutral system for the valuation of goods for customs purposes—a system that conforms to commercial realities, and which outlaws the use of arbitrary or fictitious customs values. The agreement provides a set of valuation rules, expanding and giving greater precision to the provisions on customs valuation in the original GATT.

The basic aim of the agreement is to protect the interests of the firms engaged in international marketing by requiring that customs should accept for determining dutiable value the price actually paid by the importer in a particular transaction. This applies to both arms-length and related-party transactions. The agreement recognizes that the prices obtained by different importers for the same range of products may vary. The mere fact that the price obtained by a particular importer is lower than that at which other importers have imported the product cannot be used as a ground for rejecting the transaction value. Customs can reject the transaction value in such situations only if it has reasons to doubt the truth or accuracy of the declared price of the imported goods. Even in such cases, it has to give importers an opportunity to justify their price and if this justification is not accepted, to give them in writing the reasons for rejecting the transaction value and for determining the dutiable value by using other methods. Furthermore, by providing importers the right to be consulted throughout all stages of the determination of value, the agreement ensures that the discretionary power available to customs for scrutinizing declared value is used objectively.

The agreement also requires national legislation on the valuation of goods to prove the following rights to importers:

- Right to withdraw imported goods from customs, when there is likely to be a delay in the determination of customs value, by providing sufficient quantities, in the form of surety or a deposit, covering the payment of customs duties for which the goods may be liable
- Right to expect that any information of a confidential nature that is made available to customs shall be treated as confidential
- Right to appeal, without fear of penalty, to an independent body within the customs administration and to judicial authority against decisions taken by customs

Pre-shipment inspection

Pre-shipment inspection is the practice of employing specialized private companies (or independent entities) to check shipment details—essentially price, quantity, and quality—of goods ordered overseas. The basic purpose of pre-shipment inspection is to safeguard national financial interests (for instance, preventing capital flight, commercial fraud, and customs duty evasion) and to compensate for inadequacies in administrative infrastructures.

The Pre-shipment Inspection Agreement places obligations on governments, which use pre-shipment inspection such as non-discrimination, transparency, protection of confidential business information, avoiding unreasonable delay, the use of specific guidelines for conducting price verification, and avoiding conflicts of interest by the inspection agencies. The obligations of exporting members towards countries using pre-shipment inspection include non-discrimination in the application of domestic laws and regulations, prompt publication of those laws and regulations, and, wherever requested, the provision of technical assistance.

The agreement establishes an independent review procedure administered jointly by the International Federation of Inspection Agencies (IFIA), representing inspection agencies, and the International Chamber of Commerce (ICC), representing exporters. Its purpose is to resolve disputes between an exporter and an inspection agency.

Rules of origin

Rules of origin are used as the criteria to define where a product was made. They are an essential part of trade rules because a number of policies discriminate between exporting countries such as quotas, preferential tariffs, anti-dumping actions, countervailing duty (charged to counter export subsidies), etc. Rules of origin are also used to compile trade statistics, and for 'made in … ' labels that are attached to products. This is complicated by globalization and the way a product can be processed in several countries before it is ready for the market.

The Agreement on Rules of Origin requires WTO members to ensure that their rules of origin are transparent and that they do not have restricting, distorting, or disruptive effects on international trade. They are administered in a consistent, uniform, impartial, and reasonable manner. For the longer term, the agreement aims for common (harmonized) rules of origin among all WTO members, except in some kinds of preferential trade—for example, countries setting up a free trade area are allowed to use different rules of origin for products traded under their free-trade agreement.

Promoting Cross-border Investments

When investment is the mode of entry in international markets, the host governments often impose conditions on foreign investors to encourage investments in accordance with their certain national priorities. The Agreement on Trade-Related Investment Measures (TRIMs) recognizes that certain measures can restrict and distort trade. It stipulates that no member shall apply any measure that discriminates against foreigners or foreign products (i.e., violates 'national treatment' principles of GATT). It also outlaws investment measures that lead to restrictions in quantities (violating another principle of GATT) and measures requiring particular levels of local procurement by an enterprise (local content requirements). It also discourages measures that limit a company's imports or set targets for the company to export (trade balancing requirements).

Under the agreement, countries must inform fellow members through the WTO of all investment measures that do not conform to the agreement. Developed countries had to eliminate these in two years (by the end of 1996); developing countries had five years (by the end of 1999); and the least developed countries had seven. In July 2001, the Goods Council agreed to extend this transition period on the request of developing countries.

However, countries are not prevented from imposing export performance requirements as a condition for investment. They are also not prohibited from insisting that a certain percentage of equity should be held by local investors or that a foreign investor must bring in the most up-to-date technology or must conduct a specific level or type of R&D locally.

Plurilateral Agreements

All the WTO agreements except four originally negotiated under the Tokyo Round became multilateral agreements. These four agreements are known as plurilateral agreements, as they had a limited number of signatories.

Fair trade in civil aircraft

The Agreement on Trade in Civil Aircraft came into force on 1 January 1980, which presently has 30 signatories. The agreement eliminates import duties on all aircraft and its parts and components other than military aircraft. It also contains disciplines on government-directed procurement of civil aircraft and inducements to purchase with government financial support for the civil aircraft sector.

Opening up of competition in government procurement

In most countries, the government and its agencies are together the biggest purchasers of goods of all kinds, ranging from basic commodities to high-technology equipment. At the same time, the political pressure to favour domestic suppliers over their foreign competitors can be very strong. It poses considerable barrier to international marketing firms in these countries.

An Agreement on Government Procurement (GPA) was first negotiated during the Tokyo Round and came into force on 1 January 1981 with a view to open up as much of this business as possible to international competition. It was designed to make laws, regulations, procedures, and practices regarding government procurement more transparent, and to ensure they do not protect domestic products or suppliers, or discriminate against foreign products or suppliers. A large part of the general rules and obligations is about tendering procedures.

The GPA under the WTO became effective on 1 January 1996. It extends coverage to services (including construction services), procurement at the sub-central level (e.g., states, provinces, departments, and prefectures), and procurement by public utilities. It also reinforces rules guaranteeing fair and non-discriminatory conditions of international competition. For instance, governments are required to put in place domestic procedures by which aggrieved private bidders can challenge procurement decisions and obtain redress in the event such decisions were made inconsistently with the rules of the agreement. The agreement applies to contracts worth more than specified threshold values.

The International Dairy Agreement and the International Bovine Meat Agreement, other two plurialteral agreements, were scrapped at the end of 1997. Countries that had signed the agreements decided that the sectors were better handled under the agriculture and SPS agreements.

Ensuring Transparency in Trade Policy

An international marketing firm needs to know, as much as possible, the conditions of trade in the target market. The Trade Policy Review Mechanism (TPRM) aims to achieve transparency in regulations[5] in the following ways:

- Governments have to inform the WTO and its fellow members about specific measures, policies, or laws through regular 'notifications'.
- The WTO conducts regular reviews of individual countries' trade policies—the trade policy reviews.
- The objectives of trade policy review include the following:
  - Increase the transparency and understanding of countries' trade policies and practices through regular monitoring
  - Improve the quality of public and inter-governmental debate on the issues
  - Enable a multilateral assessment of the effects of policies on the world trading system

The reviews focus on members' own trade policies and practices. But they also take into account the countries' wider economic and developmental needs, their policies and objectives, and the external economic environment that they face. These 'peer reviews' by other WTO members encourage governments to follow more closely the WTO rules and disciplines and to fulfil their commitments. These reviews enable outsiders to understand a country's policies and circumstances, and they provide feedback to the reviewed country on its performance in the system.

Over a period of time, all WTO members are to come under scrutiny. The frequency of the reviews depends on the country's size:

- The four biggest traders—the EU, the USA, Japan, and Canada (the Quad)—are examined approximately once every two years.
- The next 16 countries (in terms of their share of world trade) are reviewed every four years.
- The remaining countries are reviewed every six years with the possibility of a longer interim period for the least developed countries.

---

[5] *Trade Policy Review, India*, WTO, Geneva, 2002, 2007, 2011, pp. iii and vii–ix.

For each review, two documents are prepared: a policy statement by the government under review and a detailed report written independently by the WTO Secretariat. These two reports, together with the proceedings of the Trade Policy Review Body's meetings, are published, which may be consulted while making strategic decisions about the markets.

SETTLEMENT OF INTERNATIONAL TRADE DISPUTES

Trade relations often involve conflicting interests. Agreements, including those painstakingly negotiated in the WTO system, often need interpreting. The most harmonious way to settle these differences is through some neutral procedure based on an agreed legal foundation. That is the basic purpose behind the dispute settlement process under the WTO agreements.

Although trade disputes were handled by GATT, it had no power to enforce its decisions. The process of dispute settlement often stretched on for years and the losing party was entitled to ignore its rulings. Due to its ineffectiveness in resolving trade disputes, GATT was often criticized as 'General Agreement to Talk and Talk.'

Dispute settlement is a unique contribution of the WTO, which provides effectiveness to the rule-based multilateral trading system. Its procedure to settle dispute makes the trading system more secure and predictable. A classic case on dispute settlement under the WTO is given in Exhibit 3.9 regarding a dispute related to discrimination in the enforcement of environmental legislation between member countries, wherein the USA had to lose the case. The system is based on clearly defined rules, with timetables for completing a case. First rulings are made by a panel and endorsed (or rejected) by full membership of the WTO.

Exhibit 3.9 Dispute settlement under WTO

Seven species of sea turtles have been identified as those that are distributed around the world in subtropical and tropical areas. They spend their lives in sea, and they migrate between their foraging and nesting grounds. Sea turtles have been adversely affected by human activity, either directly (their meat, shells, and eggs have been exploited) or indirectly (incidental capture in fisheries, destroyed habitats, polluted oceans).

The US Endangered Species Act of 1973 listed as endangered or threatened the five species of sea turtles that are found in the US waters, and prohibited their 'take' within the USA, in its territorial sea, and the high seas. ('Take' means harassment, hunting, capture, killing, or attempting to do any of these.) Under the Act, the USA required US shrimp trawlers to use 'turtle excluder devices' (TEDs) in their nets when fishing in areas where there is a significant likelihood of encountering sea turtles.

Section 609 of US Public Law 101–102, enacted in 1989, dealt with imports. It said, among other things, that shrimp harvested with technology that may adversely affect certain sea turtles may not be imported into the US—unless the harvesting nation was certified to have a regulatory programme and an incidental take-rate comparable to that of the USA, or that the particular fishing environment of the harvesting nation did not pose a threat to sea turtles.

In practice, countries that had any of the five species of sea turtles within their jurisdiction, and harvested shrimp with mechanical means, had to impose on their fishermen requirements comparable to those borne by US shrimpers if they wanted to be certified to export shrimp products to the USA. Essentially this meant the use of TEDs at all times.

In early 1997, India, Malaysia, Pakistan, and Thailand brought a joint complaint against a ban imposed by the USA on the imports of certain shrimp and shrimp products.

In this report, the Appellate Body made clear that under WTO rules, countries have the right to take trade action to protect the environment (in particular, human, animal or plant life and health, and endangered species and exhaustible resources). The WTO does not have to 'allow' them this right.

It also said measures to protect sea turtles would be legitimate under GATT Article 20, which deals with various exceptions to the WTO's trade rules, provided certain criteria such as non-discrimination were met.

The USA lost the case not because it sought to protect the environment but because it discriminated between WTO members. It provided countries in the western hemisphere—mainly in the Caribbean—technical and financial assistance and longer transition periods for their fishermen to start using TEDs. It did not give the same advantages, however, to the four Asian countries (India, Malaysia, Pakistan, and Thailand) that filed a complaint with the WTO.

Source: WTO.

The priority is to settle disputes through consultations, if possible. If two members believe that the fellow members are violating trade rules, they can use the multilateral system of settling disputes instead of taking actions unilaterally. This means abiding by the agreed procedures and respecting judgements. A dispute arises when one country adopts a trade policy measure or takes some action that one or more fellow WTO members consider to be breaking the WTO agreements, or to be a failure to live up to the obligations. A third group of countries can declare that they have an interest in the case and enjoy some rights.

The Uruguay Round agreement introduced a more structured process with more clearly defined stages in the procedure. It introduced greater discipline regarding the length of time a case should take to be settled, with flexible deadlines set in various stages of the procedure. The agreement emphasizes that prompt settlement is essential if the WTO is to function effectively. It sets out in considerable detail the procedures and the timetable to be followed in resolving disputes. The indicated time taken at each stage of dispute settlement is given in Table 3.3.

The target time schedules are flexible under the agreement. However, if a case runs its full course to a first ruling, it should not normally take more than about one year—15 months if the case is appealed.

Table 3.3   Time taken at different stages of dispute settlement

Time taken	Stages
60 days	Consultations, mediation, etc.
45 days	Panel set up and panellists appointed
6 months	Final panel report to parties
3 weeks	Final panel report to WTO members
60 days	Dispute Settlement Body adopts report (if no appeal)
Total	**One year (without appeal)**
60–90 days	Appeal resort
30 days	Dispute Settlement Body adopts appeals report
Total	**15 months (with appeal)**

The Uruguay Round agreement also made it impossible for the country losing a case to block the adoption of the ruling. Under the previous GATT procedure, rulings could only be adopted by consensus, meaning that a single objection could block the ruling. Now, rulings are automatically adopted unless there is a consensus to reject a ruling—any country wanting to block a ruling has to persuade all other WTO members (including its adversary in the case) to share its view.

Procedure of Dispute Settlement

Settling disputes is the responsibility of the Dispute Settlement Body (The General Council in another guise), which consists of all WTO members. The Dispute Settlement Body has the sole authority to establish 'panels' of experts to consider the case, and to accept or reject the panels' findings or the results of an appeal. It monitors the implementation of the rulings and recommendations, and has the power to authorize retaliation when a country does not comply with a ruling. The dispute settlement mechanism is summarized in Fig. 3.4.

- First stage, consultation (up to 60 days): Before taking any other actions, the countries involved in the dispute have to talk to each other to see if they can settle their differences by themselves. If that fails, they can also ask the WTO Director General to mediate or try to help in any other way.

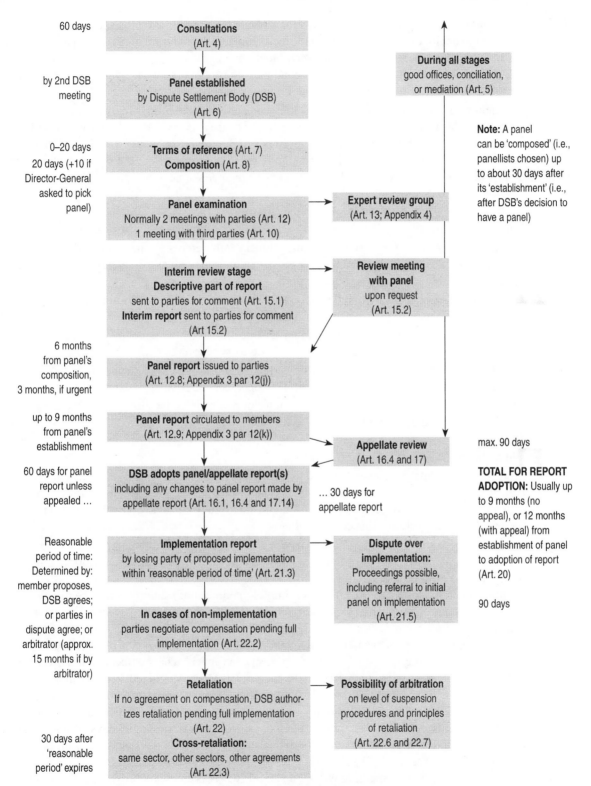

Fig. 3.4   WTO's dispute settlement process

Source: WTO, 2013.

- Second stage, the panel (up to 45 days for a panel to be appointed, plus six months for the panel to conclude): If consultations fail, the complaining country can ask for a panel to be appointed. The country 'in the dock' can block the creation of a panel once, but when the Dispute Settlement Body meets for a second time, the appointment can no longer be blocked (unless there is a consensus against appointing the panel).

Officially, the panel helps the Dispute Settlement Body to make rulings for recommendations. But because the panel's report can only be rejected by consensus in the Dispute Settlement Body, its conclusions are difficult to overturn. The panel's findings have to be based on the agreements cited. The pane's final report should normally be given to the parties to the dispute within six months. In cases of urgency, including those concerning perishable goods, the deadline is shortened to three months.

The main stages of the panel process are as follows:

Before the first hearing   Each side in the dispute presents its case in writing to the panel.

First hearing: the case for the complaining country and defence   The complaining country (or countries), the responding country, and those that have announced an interest in the dispute make their case at the panel's first hearing.

Rebuttals   The countries involved submit written rebuttals and present oral arguments at the panel's second meeting.

Expert   If one side raises scientific or other technical matters, the panel may consult experts or appoint an expert review group to prepare an advisory report.

First draft   The panel submits the descriptive (factual and argument) sections of its report to the two sides, giving them two weeks to comment. This report does not include findings and conclusions.

Interim report   The panel then submits an interim report, including its findings and conclusions, to the two sides, giving them one week to ask for a review.

Review   The period of review must not exceed two weeks. During that time, the panel may hold additional meetings with the two sides.

Final report   A final report is submitted to the two sides, and three weeks later, it is circulated to all WTO members. If the panel decides that the disputed trade measure does break a WTO agreement or an obligation, it recommends that the measure be made to conform to WTO rules. The panel may suggest how this could be done.

The report becomes a ruling   The report becomes the Dispute Settlement Body's ruling or recommendations within 60 days unless a consensus rejects it. Both sides can appeal against the report (and in some cases both sides do).

Either side can appeal against a panel's ruling. Sometimes both sides do so. Appeals have to be based on points of law such as legal interpretation. However, they cannot re-examine existing evidence or examine new issues.

Three members of a permanent seven-member Appellate Body, set up by the Dispute Settlement Body and broadly representing WTO members, hear each appeal. The members of the Appellate Body have a four-year term. They have to be individuals with recognized standing in the field of law and international trade, and should not be affiliated with any government.

The appellate body can uphold, modify, or reverse the panel's legal findings and conclusions. Normally, appeals should not last more than 60 days, with a maximum of 90 days. The Dispute Settlement Body has to accept or reject the appeals report within 30 days, and rejection is only possible by consensus.

If a country has done something wrong, it should swiftly correct its fault, and if it continues to break an agreement, it should offer compensation or suffer a suitable penalty that has some bite. Even once the case has been decided, there is more to be done before trade sanctions (the conventional form of penalty) are imposed. The priority at this stage is for the losing 'defendant' to bring its policy into line with the rulings or the recommendations.

WTO: OVER THE YEARS

The WTO began its life on 1 January 1995 as a result of the Marrakesh Agreement signed on 15 April 1994 at Marrakesh in Morocco. The timeline of various milestones achieved by the WTO is given in Exhibit 3.10. The WTO has significantly contributed in promoting trade by lowering tariff barriers like customs duties and measures like import bans or quotas that restrict quantities selectively. Besides, it attempted to evolve a multilateral trade regime of non-discrimination between its trading partners and also between the products, services, and nationals of a member country and that of foreign origin.

Ministerial Conferences, the highest decision-making body under the WTO, have contributed considerably in phased opening up of trade and removing obstacles, and also generated considerable debate and controversies across the world. Developed countries often take advantage of escape routes and loopholes in the agreements. For instance, the Agreement

Exhibit 3.10   WTO: over the years

1994	**April**	2004	**July**
	The Marrakesh Agreement establishing the WTO is signed.		Ministerial discussions on the Doha Round take place in Geneva.
	GATT 1994 is incorporated in the WTO's umbrella treaty for trade in goods.	2005	**December** Sixth Ministerial Conference takes place in Hong Kong, China. Aid for Trade initiative is launched.
1995	**January** The WTO is born on 1 January.		Hong Kong Declaration is approved.
1996	**February**	2006	**June**
	The WTO General Council creates the Regional Trade Agreements Committee.		Ministerial discussions on the Doha Round take place in Geneva.
	December		**September**
	First Ministerial Conference takes place.		First WTO public forum takes place in Geneva.
1997	**December**	2007	**November**
	70 WTO members reach a multilateral agreement to open their financial services sector.		First global review of Aid for Trade takes place in Geneva
1998	**May**	2008	**July**
	Second Ministerial Conference held in Geneva.		Ministerial discussions on the Doha Round take place in Geneva.
1999	**November**	2009	**September**
	Third Ministerial Conference takes place in Seattle, USA.		First WTO open day held in Geneva.
2000	**January**		**November**
	Negotiations on services begin.		Seventh Ministerial Conference takes place in Geneva.
	March	2010	**June**
	Negotiations on agriculture begin.		Thinking Ahead on International Trade (TAIT),
2001	**November**		second conference on 'Climate Change, Trade and
	Fourth Ministerial Conference in Doha, Qatar, Doha Development Agenda is launched.		Competitiveness: Issues for the WTO' held in Geneva.
2003	**September**	2011	**December** Eighth Ministerial Conference scheduled in Geneva.
	Fifth Ministerial Conference held in Cancun, Mexico.		

Source: WTO.

on Textiles was back-loaded and left the choice of products to the importing countries. As developed countries were importers and had been imposing restraints, they chose only such products for liberalization that were not under import restraints without significantly liberalizing their textile imports until the end of 2004 when the agreement was automatically abolished. Similarly, developed countries could fulfil their obligation of reduction of subsidiary in agriculture despite actually increasing considerably the absolute quantum of subsidiary.

Developed countries significantly influence the decision-making process as they possess enormous resources to make elaborate preparations for the negotiating process. Substantial negotiations are carried out in small groups where developing countries are not present. Countries who have not participated are expected to agree when the results are brought forth in larger groups. It is difficult to stop decision-making at this stage as any such move by developing countries would mark them as obstructionists and have political repercussions. As views of developed countries are put forth effectively and strongly, the issues of their interest take centre stage leading to frustration among developing countries.

Major developed countries continue to give high amount of subsidies to their farmers. Interestingly, developed countries have fulfilled their obligation of reduction in reducible subsidy in technical terms despite increasing the absolute amount of subsidy. Besides, the EU and the USA continue to give export subsidies. Ironically, developed countries are pressurizing developing countries to reduce their tariffs substantially. This poses a threat to the domestic farming sector of developing countries, which has got serious socio-economic and political implications. This makes negotiations in agriculture extremely complex. On the other hand, developed countries are keen on market access for their industrial products.

The Doha Round of negotiations, which began in November 2001 during the Fourth Ministerial Conference in Doha, Qatar, missed the original deadline of 1 January 2005 despite intensive negotiations. The deadlock between the members especially on the most contentious issues such as agriculture and non-agriculture (industrial) market access (NAMA) continues to hamper the consensus among the members and thus widen the divide between the rich and the poor countries. In April 2011, the WTO Director General, Pascal Lamy, termed NAMA gaps as 'non-bridgeable'.

However, despite vast differences among the interests of member countries, the WTO remains the only international organization that provides a multilateral framework for international trade. Besides trade in goods, it covers a number of issues related to international trade, such as services, intellectual property rights, anti-dumping, safeguards, non-tariff barriers, dispute settlement, etc., making its approach highly comprehensive.

IMPLICATIONS OF WTO ON INTERNATIONAL MARKETING

An international marketer needs to understand the marketing implications of WTO agreements. The major areas of interest to international marketers include binding of concessions and commitments leading to secure access in international markets.

The other areas of interest to international marketers include customs valuation, pre-shipment inspection services, and import licensing procedures wherein the emphasis is laid on transparency of the procedures so as to restrain their use as non-tariff marketing barriers. Besides, the agreements also stipulate the rights of exporters and domestic producers to initiate actions against dumping of foreign goods. Therefore, a thorough understanding of these agreements is critical to firms operating in international markets.

The implications of the WTO on various strategic decisions of the international marketing framework, discussed in Chapter 1, are shown in Fig. 3.5. The broad agreements under the GATT and GATS affect in general the entire marketing process.

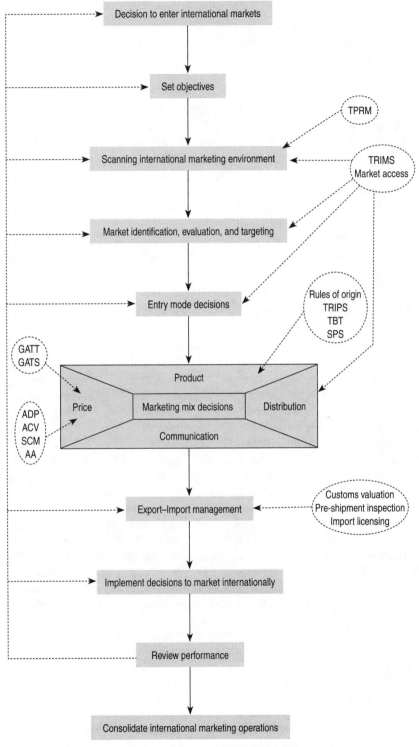

Fig. 3.5 WTO implications on international marketing

The TPRM, which provides for periodic review of economic policies of member countries, needs to be taken into account while scanning the international marketing environment. Market selection, entry mode, and distribution decisions are often influenced by the TRIMS and the market-access agreements.

Product decisions in international markets are affected by the Agreement on Rules of Origin, TRIPS, TBT, and SPS measures. The WTO agreements on customs valuations and pre-shipment inspection on import licensing play a significant role in managing export–import operations.

This chapter explains the multilateral trade regime under the WTO framework. Besides liberalizing trade and providing level playing field for all the member countries, the WTO also provides an in-built mechanism for implementation and monitoring of the WTO agreements and facilitates multilateral trade negotiations. It provides a platform for settlement of disputes among the member countries.

The functions and structure of WTO and the principles of the multilateral trading system are dealt at length. This chapter explains the major WTO agreements including GATT, AoA, ATC, GATS, TRIPS, ADP, SCMs, TRIMs, and TPRM; agreements on standard and safety measures, emergency protection from imports, import licensing procedures, customs valuation, pre-shipment inspection, and rules of origin; and the plurilateral agreements. Moreover, the dispute settlement mechanism is also explained in detail. This chapter also makes a critical evaluation of WTO over the years and its implications on international marketing.

Summary

The WTO is the only international organization dealing with global rules of trade between the nations. It came into existence on 1 January 1995 as a successor of the GATT. Its major function is to ensure flows of international trade as smoothly, predictably, and freely as possible. This is a multilateral trade organization aimed at evolving a liberalized trade regime under a rule-based system. The multilateral system under WTO affects security and stability of market access. Besides dealing with various tariff and non-tariff marketing barriers, an international marketing manager needs to develop a thorough understanding of WTO legislations.

Presently, nearly 153 WTO members account for over 90 per cent of the world trade and about 30 others are negotiating its membership. Ministerial Conference is the top-level decision-making body of the WTO, which meets once in every two years. The General Council headquartered in Geneva is below the Ministerial Conference, which meets several times a year and is represented by ambassadors and heads of delegations in Geneva. The General Council also meets as the Trading Policy Review Body and Dispute Settlement Body. The WTO has a permanent Secretariat based in Geneva, which is headed by a director general.

The principles of multilateral trading system under WTO include trade without discrimination wherein a member country cannot discriminate between its trading partners and its own and foreign products and services. Besides, the WTO attempts to reduce tariff and non-tariff marketing barriers so as to facilitate freer trade among its members. Binding of commitments and transparency in trade rules under the WTO contribute to increase in the predictability of the international marketing environment. It also helps to promote fair competition in international markets. The WTO agreements are often referred to as trade rules, as it is described as a rule-based system. The main agreement under the WTO includes an umbrella agreement for establishing the WTO, and agreements on goods, services, intellectual property, dispute settlement, and review of government's trade policy. The agreement for goods under GATT deals with sector-specific issues such as agriculture, health regulations for farm products (SPS), textiles and clothing, product standards, investment measures, anti-dumping measures, customs valuation methods, pre-shipment inspection, rules of origin, import licensing, subsidies, and counter-measures and safeguards. The WTO also attempts to create fairer markets in the agriculture sector by way of addressing issues related to trade distortions with extensive use of export and production subsidies, especially by developing countries. The international trade in textile, which had been governed from 1974 to 1995 by the Multi-fibre Agreement (MFA), has been brought under GATT.

The agreement on services under GATS deals with specific issues. It includes movement of natural persons, air transport, financial services, shipping, and telecommunications. The trade in services has been brought under the multilateral framework of GATS, which is likely to provide greater market access in the services sector such as telecommunication, air transport, financial services, and movement of natural persons. The agreement on

TRIPS deals with protecting creators' rights for patents, copyright and related rights, trademarks, industrial designs, layout designs of integrated circuits, undisclosed information and trade secrets, and geographical indicators.

The WTO attempts to curb unfair marketing practices by way of agreements on ADP, subsidies, and countervailing measures, which authorize importing countries to levy compensatory duties on import of goods. In recent years, India has emerged as the world's top user of anti-dumping measures. Besides, attempts to reduce non-tariff marketing barriers such as import-licensing procedures, customs valuation, pre-shipment inspection, and rules of origin have also been dealt with. Various non-tariff marketing barriers for India's exports in major markets have also been discussed in the chapter. At the end of the chapter, the WTO's implications on international marketing have also been summarized so as to enable readers to take care while developing an international marketing plan.

Key Terms

Appellate body An independent seven-person body that, upon request by one or more parties to the dispute, reviews findings in panel reports.

Counterfeit Unauthorized representation of a registered trademark carried on goods identical or similar to goods for which the trademark is registered with a view to deceive a purchaser into believing that he is buying the original goods.

Countervailing measures Action taken by an importing country, usually in the form of increased duties, to offset subsidies given to producers or exporters in the exporting country.

Distortion It arises when prices and production are higher or lower than the levels that would usually exist in a competitive market.

Dumping It occurs when goods are exported at a price less than their normal value, generally meaning they are exported for less than the price that they are sold in the domestic market or third country markets, or at less than the production cost.

GATT The General Agreement on Tariffs and Trade, which has been superseded as an international organization by the WTO. An updated general agreement is now one of the agreements of the WTO.

Geographical indicators Place name (or words associated with a place) used to identify products (e.g., 'Champagne', 'Tequila', or 'Roquefort'), which have a particular quality, reputation, or other characteristic because they come from that place.

Integration programme The phasing out of MFA restrictions in four stages, which started on 1 January 1995 and ended on 1 January 2005.

Intellectual property rights Ownership of ideas, including literary and artistic works (protected by copyright), inventions (protected by patents), signs for distinguishing goods of an enterprise (protected by trademarks), and other elements of industrial property.

MFA Multi-fibre Arrangement (1974–94) under which countries whose markets are disrupted by increased imports of textiles and clothing from another country were able to negotiate quota restrictions.

MFN The principle of most-favoured-nation treatment, meaning not discriminating between one's trading partners.

National treatment The principle of giving others the same treatment as one's own nationals. Article 3 of GATT requires that imports be treated no less favourably than the same or similar domestically produced goods once they have passed customs. GATS Article 17 and TRIPS Article 3 also deal with national treatment for services and intellectual property (IP).

NTMs Non-tariff measures such as quotas, import licensing systems, sanitary regulations, and prohibitions.

Piracy Unauthorized copying of materials protected by IP rights (such as copyright, trademarks, patents, geographical indications, etc.) for commercial purposes and unauthorized commercial dealings in copied materials.

Quantitative restriction Specific limits on the quantity or value of goods that can be imported (or exported) during a specific time period.

SPS regulations Sanitary and phyto-sanitary regulations— the standards set by a government to protect human, animal, and plant life and health to help ensure that food is safe for consumption.

Tariff binding Commitment not to increase a rate of duty beyond an agreed level. Once a rate of duty is bound, it may not be raised without compensating the affected parties.

Tariffication Procedures relating to the agricultural market access provision in which all non-tariff measures are converted into tariffs.

Tariffs Customs duties on merchandise imports levied either on an ad valorem basis (percentage of value) or on a specific basis (e.g., $5 per 100 kg). Tariffs give price advantage to similar locally produced goods and raise revenues for the government.

Uruguay Round Multilateral trade negotiations launched at Punta del Este, Uruguay, in September 1986, concluded in Geneva in December 1993, and signed by ministers in Marrakesh, Morocco, in April 1994.

Concept Review Questions

1. Why is it necessary for an international marketing manager to understand various legislations under WTO?
2. Explain in brief the functions of the WTO. What are the major principles of multilateral trading system?
3. Explain the major provisions of the Agreement on Agriculture (AoA). Critically analyse its implications on export of agro-products from India.
4. Describe the dispute settlement process under WTO. Justify its effectiveness with examples.
5. 'Reduction in import tariffs has resulted in bringing up new non-tariff marketing barriers by developed countries.' Critically examine the statement with the help of illustrations from trade.

Critical Thinking Questions

1. Canada and Norway have granted duty-free access to Bangladeshi garments w.e.f. 1 January 2003. The Canadian buyers are looking for Bangladeshi garments of Indian fabrics. It would result in export of fabrics from India to Bangladesh rather than export of garments from India to Canada and reduction of export of value-added products from India. Under the WTO framework of MFN treatment, are such concessions to a particular country justified? Suggest remedial measures and discuss in the class.
2. The concept of product patents for pharmaceutical products is likely to make the life-saving medicines beyond the reach of the poor and deprived section of the society around the world. A number of African countries have been the worst hit by the spectre of AIDS. Cipla, an Indian pharmaceutical company, has offered to market anti-AIDS medicine at one-tenth the costs at which it is sold by global pharmaceutical firms. However, due to the product patent laws, substantial controversy has been generated around the globe on ethical grounds. In your opinion, is it correct to deprive the needy population of the latest scientific inventions crucial for saving human life? Prepare and discuss a strategic plan to deal with the issue.

CASE STUDY: DARJEELING TEA—GLOBAL INFRINGEMENT AND WTO

India is one of the largest producers and exporters of tea with an estimated annual production of about 100 million kg of tea. The district of Darjeeling is situated in the state of West Bengal in India, which is known for growing exclusive 'Darjeeling tea' at altitudes ranging from 600 to 2,000 metres (Fig. C3.1). Since about 1935, tea has been cultivated, grown, and produced in tea gardens of Darjeeling and geographically nearby areas in India. The cool and moist climate, the soil, the rainfall, and the sloping terrain, all combine to give Darjeeling its unique muscatel flavour (a desirable character in Darjeeling tea denoting a grapey taste) and exquisite bouquet. The combination of natural factors that has given Darjeeling tea its unique distinction is not found anywhere else in the world. Hence, this finest and most delicately flavoured of all types of tea has over the years acquired the reputation of being the 'champagne of teas'.

Since less than 1 per cent of all the tea harvested in the world is Darjeeling tea, it always commands a higher price in international markets. Darjeeling's exclusive taste and quality, as well as the fact that it cannot be replicated anywhere else in the world, make it one of the most sought after tea in the world. Besides, Darjeeling tea is acknowledged as the superlative standard for flavour, unmatched by tea grown anywhere else in the world. Jacksonville Tea Company based in Florida communicates in its promotional literature, 'Darjeeling is to tea, what champagne is to wine.'

There is a vast difference in auction price and retail price of Darjeeling tea. For instance, the auction price of organic Darjeeling tea is only around US\$3–5 per kg, while it is sold in retail at US\$350 per kg in Japan, at US\$100 per kg in the USA, US\$40 kg in Germany, US\$200 per kg in the UK, and US\$150 per kg in France.

It is not uncommon that other varieties of tea, usually inferior, are also branded as Darjeeling tea—either by blending with Darjeeling tea or by itself. It is noteworthy that although just 10 million kg of Darjeeling tea is produced every year, 40 million

Fig. C3.1 Tea bushes carpeting Darjeeling hillside in India

Source: Tea Board.

Fig. C3.2　Darjeeling Lingerie at Rue du Faubourg in Paris

Source: www.darjeeling.fr, accessed on 15 October 2013.

kg of tea is sold as Darjeeling tea worldwide. Tea produced in countries such as Kenya, Sri Lanka, and Nepal have often been passed of as Darjeeling tea around the world. Besides, misleading the international consumer whether she is buying 100 per cent Darjeeling tea or a blend of some other inferior tea in the name of Darjeeling tea, it also results into serious economic loss to marketers and planters from India.

In view of the strong brand equity 'Darjeeling,' it is not uncommon to find non-tea products using the name. In France, the fashionable *Rue du Faubourg*, St Antoine, in Paris, one may find Darjeeling greeting at *Megasin 74*. One should not be surprised that instead of the exquisite variety of India's Darjeeling tea, one finds piles of lingerie[6] labelled 'Darjeeling' (Fig. C3.2). In Norway, telecom products under the brand name Darjeeling may be obtained. A whole host of services and products such as perfumes, coffee, and soft

drinks sell under the Darjeeling brand name around the world (Exhibit C3.1). Such misuse and infringement of 'Darjeeling' around the world have severe implications in international marketing from Darjeeling industry.

Under the TRIPS agreement, issues related to international protection of geographical indicators were included and the member countries of the WTO were bound to comply within their national legislations. Besides, it was supported by a strong dispute settlement mechanism under the WTO system, which could ensure the enforcement of such legal provisions.

Given such a legally binding status, the TRIPS agreement did have the potential to ensure effective protection for geographical indicators. However, even with the TRIPS agreement in place, the current status of international protection for all geographical indications is far from adequate. Though the TRIPS agreement contains a single, identical definition for all geographical

Exhibit C3.1　Instances of infringement of 'Darjeeling'

Country	Forms of use	Product and services
France	Darjeeling	Perfumes, lingerie, telecommunication
Germany	Darjeeling logo	Device applications
Japan	Divine Darjeeling/Darjeeling with India map/Darjeeling	Coffee, cocoa, tea, soft drinks
Norway	Darjeeling	Telecommunication
Russia	Darjeeling/Darjeeling logo	Tea
Sri Lanka	Sakir Darjeeling	Tea
USA	Darjeeling Noveau	Tea

---

[6] *Le Groupe Chantelle*, Publication literature.

Fig. C3.3   India's tea board's logo for Darjeeling tea
Source: Used with the kind permission of Tea Board.

indicators irrespective of product categories, it mandates a two-level system of protection for geographical indicators:

(i) The general or basic protection applicable to geographical indicators associated with all products in general (under Article 22)

(ii) The additional (absolute) protection applicable only for the geographical indicators denominating wines and spirits (under Article 23)

European wines and spirits such as Champagne, Cognac, and Sherry are effectively the only geographical indicators under TRIPS. Article 22 merely stipulates the general standards of protection that must be available for all geographical indications against deceptive or misleading business practices and other acts of unfair competition. The second clause of this article provides that in respect of geographical indications, members shall provide the legal means for interested parties to prevent the use of any means in the designation or presentation of a good that indicates or suggests that the good in question originates in a geographical area other than the true place of origin in a manner that misleads the public as to the geographical origin of the good. It further prohibits any use, which constitutes an act of unfair competition within the meaning of Article 10 b of the Paris Convention (1967).

Under the TRIPS agreement, there is no obligation on the part of member countries to protect any geographical indication which has fallen into disuse or cease to be protected in its country of origin. In recognition of mandatory statutory regime, the Indian Parliament has passed the necessary law [i.e., General Indications of Goods (Registration and Protection) Act, 1999] for registration and protection of geographical indications.

In stark contrast with Article 22, Article 23 of TRIPS stipulates an additional protection only for the geographical indicators designating wines and spirits, which requires member countries to prevent any abusive application of such geographical indicators irrespective of whether the consumers are misled or whether it constitutes an act of unfair competition. Under Article 23.1, using a geographical indicator identifying wines/

spirits for wines/spirits not originating in the place indicated by the geographical indicators concerned is prohibited, even where the true origin of the wine/spirit concerned is indicated and/or a translation is used and/or the indication is accompanied by expressions such as 'kind', 'type', 'style', 'imitation', or the like. Competitors, not producing in the geographical region purported in geographical indications associated with wines or spirits are also not allowed to use such an indication in their trademarks (Article 23.2). In contrast, the refusal or invalidation of registration of a trademark for any other goods (than wines and spirits), on similar ground, is conditional on the 'misleading test' (Article 22.3). To facilitate the protection of geographical indicators for wines and spirits, Article 23.4 further provides for negotiations for the establishment of a multilateral system of notification and registration for such geographical indicators.

The additional level of protection under Article 23, however, is subject to certain exceptions and concessions (contained in Article 24), which recognize the so-called 'acquired rights' prior to TRIPS, such as

- use in good faith or use of more than 10 years standing (Article 24.4);
- rights acquired through trademarks (Articles 24.5 and 24.7);
- existence of generic name or the use of the names of grape variety with a geographical significance (Article 24.6); and
- patronymic geographical names (Article 24.8).

Russia is a non-WTO country with civil law jurisprudence. The tea board's application for registration of Darjeeling in Russia was objected due to a prior registration of an identical word in the name of a company called Akorus. Cancellation proceedings were filed against Akorus, but it filed an assignment deed, assigning the registration to a company in Siliguri called Kamasutra Tea Ltd (KTL). The cancellation action was disallowed, as registration in the name of KTL as a Darjeeling-based company would not confuse or deceive a proposed customer. However, KTL turned out to be a fictitious company and the Russian Patent Office had to cancel the trademark. France put its might behind protecting the word 'Champagne' and Scotland had been fiercely protective about the 'Scotch' Whisky brand. It is noteworthy that 'Scotch' constitutes UK's most significant component of liquors' exports that dominate in a large number of foreign markets.

Thus, under the present framework of TRIPS, it is difficult to protect 'Darjeeling' as a geographical indicator for tea, which has got severe marketing implications. This hinders marketers and plantation growers from Darjeeling making use of its brand equity in product positioning and price realization in international markets.

Questions

1. Divide the class in the following three groups.
   (a) International marketing managers from leading Darjeeling tea firms
   (b) International marketing managers from overseas firms exporting non-Indian tea under the 'Darjeeling' brand name
   (c) Representatives of various interest groups in WTO (these groups may be decided in the class by mutual consent)
2. Discuss the following issues in the class and try to evolve a consensus on the issue of registering 'Darjeeling' tea as a geographical indicator.

   (a) Should 'Darjeeling' be used exclusively to Darjeeling grown tea in India? Give reasons for your answer.
   (b) Should the brand name 'Darjeeling' be extended to other product categories such as garments including lingerie and soft drinks? Justify.
   (c) Chalk out a detailed plan with suitable arguments to register 'Darjeeling' tea as a geographical indicator.

Prepare a comprehensive report on your suggestions and forward your proposals to the stakeholders in the industry and government for further consideration.

International Political and Legal Environment

4

Learning Objectives

- To explain the significance of the political and legal environment in international marketing
- To discuss various forms of political systems
- To explicate different types of legal systems
- To elucidate the principles of international law

INTRODUCTION

Markets in different countries necessitate a firm to deal with diverse political and legal frameworks that, at times, conflict with its home country. International managers often make value judgement from the home country's perspective and tend to have an ethnocentric approach to political and legal environments prevailing in other countries. Such value judgements made from the perspective of the home country considerably hinder objective decision-making in the diverse international scenario. Therefore, managers marketing internationally should develop a thorough conceptual understanding of political and legal environments so as to assess their implications on marketing.

The various players in international markets have diverse and sometimes conflicting business interests that considerably influence their political agendas and constraints. For instance, foreign multinationals often use diplomatic channels to get a favourable climate for foreign investment, whereas domestic firms often build up political pressure to oppose foreign investment to put off competition from foreign firms. Importers use political pressure to increase market access with little tariffs, whereas the domestic manufacturers lobby to obstruct imports so that they continue to operate in a protected domestic environment. Exporters are concerned about the removal of all restrictions on exports and demand higher level of export incentives so that exports remain attractive.

Political cataclysm and upheavals such as those in Libya, Egypt, Syria, Russia, and Myanmar in 2012, bifurcation of Sudan in 2011, attack by the USA on Iraq in 2003, the Kosovo crisis in Yugoslavia in 1999, the Gulf War in the 1990s, the break-up of the USSR, the Iranian Revolution in the 1980s, and the Cuban crisis in the 1960s have severely affected business operations of foreign multinationals in these countries. Political considerations in the 1970s significantly influenced international fruit trade in bananas that

Exhibit 4.1   The end of the Banana Wars

Bananas are the fourth most important crop in terms of gross value production after rice, wheat, and maize. The EU is the world's largest banana market and more than 70 per cent of the yellow fruit sold in the EU comes from Latin America. The importance of banana trade in Latin America can be understood from the case of Guatemala. A 1954 coup d'etat in the country, broadly supported by the United Fruit Company, nowadays known as Chiquita, plunged it into a 40-year period of dictatorship and civil war, costing the lives of over 2,00,000 citizens.

In the Africa, Caribbean, and Pacific (ACP) countries, bananas are produced mainly on family owned farms in contrast to its production by multinationals in Latin American countries. Interestingly, two-third of world trade in bananas is controlled by three US companies, namely Chiquita, Dole, and Del Monte. Due to over-riding problems of size, climate, and terrain, Caribbean banana producers cannot compete on price with the vast, flat plantations and more fertile soil of Latin America, where production and marketing are highly integrated.

But Caribbean banana production was able to flourish under the protective regime historically operated by the UK for their benefit. These arrangements continued following the UK accession to the European Community, alongside similar arrangements operated by France. These traditional benefits were guaranteed under successive Lome Conventions, running from 1975 to 2000, between the EU and ACP countries. These countries were allocated an exclusive quota and provided with duty free access to the rest of import quota.

The 'Banana Trade War' began in 1993 when the EU established a preferential policy for imports from former British and French colonies, but earlier tensions date back as far as the 1970s. The system has enabled the ACP producers to compete with the US multinationals and trade in a commodity that would otherwise have been impossible. Nevertheless, the WTO repeatedly found the preferences in breach of international trade rules, even authorizing the USA to retaliate and slap tariffs on some EU products from Scottish cashmere to French cheese.

On 15 December 2009, a deal on trade in bananas, sponsored by the WTO, was made between the USA, the EU, and the Latin American banana producing states. Under the new accord, the EU was set to gradually end its preferential treatment of banana exporters in the ACP countries. In exchange, Latin American countries agreed to drop their complaints against the EU at the WTO and not to see further tariff card in the Doha Round.

The deal would see the EU gradually cut its import tariff on bananas from Latin America in eight stages, from €176 a tonne at the outset to €114 in 2017. On the other hand, bananas from ACP countries would continue to enter the EU market duty free. Furthermore, the main ACP banana-producing countries were to receive help from the EU budget, up to €200 million, to help them adjust to stiffer competition from Latin America. The deal would probably mean lower prices for European consumers as competition would intensify between ACP and Latin American producers. On the other hand, the deal has been slammed by the farmers' organizations of ACP countries. On 17 January 2011, the European Parliament's International Trade Committee also supported the deal putting an end to the world's longest running 16-year-old trade dispute.

Source: 'Decades-long "Banana War" Ends', *EU Business,* 3 February 2011; 'Banana War at an End...Hopefully', *Jamaica Observer*, 7 February 2011.

led to the famous 'Banana Wars' (Exhibit 4.1). The major cause behind this crisis was that most EU countries have been importing bananas with concessional market access to their former colonies in the Caribbean, Africa, and Asia, whereas bananas imported by the world's largest banana firm based in the USA, Chiquita Brands International, were subjected to quotas and tariffs. In 2011, the Members of the European Parliament supported the deal to trade in bananas reached in 2009 between the European Union (EU), the USA, and the Latin American banana producing countries to end its preferential treatment to Africa, Caribbean, and Pacific (ACP) countries that would make it easier for big multinationals to sell the Latin American bananas to the EU ending a 16-year-old international trade war.

This chapter discusses the significance of political environment in international marketing. Political ideologies based on economic and political systems and governmental structures have been elaborated. Trade embargoes and sanctions are often used as instruments of foreign policy to achieve political rather than economic objectives. In the era of globalization, the impact of sectarian violence, terrorism, or erratic political decisions taken by any country is felt beyond national boundaries, affecting business operations.

Judicial independence and efficiency, which vary widely across countries, are crucial to fair treatment in foreign locations of business operations. Managers operating in international markets need to develop conceptual understanding of the major types of the prevailing legal systems, such as common law, civil law, and theocratic law, and adapt their business strategies accordingly.

INTERNATIONAL POLITICAL ENVIRONMENT

The political environment of the country of operation becomes increasingly important for an internationalizing firm as it moves from exports to foreign direct investment (FDI) as the mode of international market entry. Exporting firms use political pressure tactics to have free export-ability of the products in their domestic regulations, hassle free procedures, and legislative requirements and export incentives. Besides, diplomatic channels are utilized to get improved market access for imported goods in the target foreign country markets, reduced import tariffs, compatible quality regulations, etc. The dispute settlement mechanism, legal framework, and judicial independence are also critical to fair treatment expected in international markets. Cordial political relations between the firm's home country and the host countries have a direct favourable impact on FDIs. As a firm expands internationally and begins to operate in multiple countries, the political and legal issues become increasingly complex.

Consequent to economic liberalization in the People's Republic of China, multi-level marketing firms, such as Amway, Avon, Tupperware, and Mary Kay Cosmetics grew rapidly. By 1997, Amway had approximately 80,000 sales representatives who generated $178 million in sales, and Avon had nearly 50,000 representatives who produced $75 million. It was reported that some other companies using the so-called 'pyramid schemes' were cheating consumers. Consequently, the Chinese government banned direct selling in April 1998. As a result, the direct marketing companies were prohibited to operate their business model in China.[1] Avon was compelled to open its own stores called Beauty Boutiques. It was only after diplomatic pressures and negotiations between the US and the Chinese governments that the policy was reversed.

Firm-level economic and political interests of the home and the host countries may differ widely. International managers need to understand the significance of political decision-making in the host country that may severely influence its overseas operations. International business relations between the firms are greatly affected by 'affinity' or 'animosity' among the countries based on historical or political reality. For instance, India's political affinity with Sri Lanka and Mauritius has led to high level of trade and investment, whereas the reverse situation exists in case of Indo-Pak trade. A large number of Islamic countries have restricted trade relations with Israel, which provides ample scope for third country trade and innovative marketing strategies.

International Political Systems and Ideologies

International political and economic systems hardly function independently. The two are mutually interdependent. Political and diplomatic relations between two countries greatly influence their economic relations. The *political system* of a country comprise various stakeholders, such as the government, political parties with different ideologies, labour unions, religious organizations, environmental activists, and various non-governmental organizations (NGOs). Each of these players in a political system has its own unique sets of beliefs and aspirations and exerts its influence upon political decisions. The acquisition, development, securing, and

---

[1] Normandy, Madden, 'China's Direct Sales Ban Stymies Marketers', *Advertising Age*, 18 May 1998, p. 56.

use of power in relation to other entities, where power is viewed as the capacity of the social actors to overcome the resistance of the other actors, is termed as *political behaviour*.[2]

Ideology is a set of beliefs or ideas as to how the society or group should be organized, politically, economically, or morally. *Political ideology* is a set of ideas or beliefs that people hold about their political regime and its institutions about their position and role in it.[3] The ideologies of different groups or political parties are often conflicting and they keep on challenging each other. In democratic countries, such as India, the USA, and the UK, the shift in the political parties and their ideologies puts pressure on business operations of foreign firms.

The power exerted by different pressure groups also varies from country to country. For instance, communist or socialist parties in countries such as Russia and China hardly face any challenge, whereas such parties exert sizeable political pressure in countries such as India, Sweden, Italy, and Greece. On the other hand, these parties hardly have any political viability in the USA. Most religious organizations are apparently politically neutral in India, whereas the Catholic church played a crucial role in overthrowing Ferdinand Marcos in Philippines and in the liberation of Poland from Soviet domination. Islamic religious leaders in Iran greatly influence political decision-making.

Principal political ideologies may be categorized by way of economic systems, political systems, and governance structure, as follows.

Types of government: economic systems

Based on economic systems being followed, governments may be categorized as communist, socialist, and capitalist.

Communism   Based on Karl Marx's Theory of Social Change directed at the idea of a classless society, all the major factors of production in a country under communism are owned by the government and shared by all the people rather than profit-seeking enterprises, for the benefit of the society. Since the government controls all the productive resources and industrial enterprises, it exerts significant control on determining production quantity, price, employment, and practically everything else. The focus of communism is on human welfare rather than profit-making.

Typically communism involves seizure of power by a political party, maintaining the power by a suppression of any opposition and commitment to achieve the ultimate goal of a worldwide communist state. After the Bolshevik Revolution in 1917 in Russia, the government overtook all the private businesses and this was repeated after each communist takeover of a country.

Countries following the communist philosophy had non-market and weak economies and the governments had an active role in economic planning. These countries had rigid and bureaucratic political and economic systems and indulged in huge foreign debts. Countries, such as China, the former Soviet Union, Eastern European countries, North Korea, and Vietnam, are also referred to as 'centrally planned economies'. However, there exists marked difference between the communist countries too. Since there had been lack of incentive and motivation to workers and managers under communism to improve productivity, the system suffered from gross inefficiencies. For instance, the former Soviet Union and China follow the same basic communism ideology, but under the new type of communism, Chinese citizens are allowed to work for themselves and keep the profit. Despite economic liberalization in China, the state's permission is needed for operation of 'free markets'.

---

[2] Astley, W.G. and P.S. Sachdeva, *Structural Sources of International Organisational Power: A Theoretical Synthesis*, Academy of Management Review 9, 1984, pp. 104–113.

[3] Macridis, Roy C., *Contemporary Political Ideologies*, Fifth Edition, Harper Collins, New York, 1992. p. 2.

Socialism   In a socialist form of government, basic and heavy industries are operated by the government, whereas small businesses may be privately owned. Basic industries, such as mining, oil exploration, steel, ship building, railways, roads, and airlines, are kept under government control. The extent of government control under socialism is lower than that under communism. Countries following the socialist system include Sweden, France, India, Poland, etc. However, the socialist countries too differ from each other in terms of the degree of public and private ownership.

Capitalism   In stark contrast to communism, capitalism is the economic system in which there is a complete freedom of private ownership of productive resources and industries. Thus, there is full freedom to both the business enterprises and the consumer that provides for a 'free market economy'. Under capitalism, individuals are allowed to produce goods and services under competitive conditions giving rise to a 'market-oriented system'. Market prices are determined by the forces of demand and supply. As individuals are motivated by private gains, it leads to product innovation, quality upgradation, increase in efficiency, and lower market prices. Capitalism too differs among countries. For instance, the USA is highly capitalistic compared to Japan. Although business enterprises in Japan are privately owned, the Japanese Government meticulously supervises their activities and, therefore, exerts indirect control.

The prevalence of the purest form of capitalism, laissez-faire, wherein the economic activity is left to the private sector with no government interference, is rare. Governments significantly influence a country's economic system. There is hardly any country that allows complete ownership either by the private sector or by the government. Thus, the pure form of capitalism or communism hardly exists.

Types of government: political systems

On the basis of political systems being followed, governments may be categorized as democratic and totalitarian.

Democracy   The word 'democracy' is derived from the Greek term *demokratia*, which means rule of the people or government by the people where citizens are directly involved in decision-making. Over a period of time, there has been proliferation of population across the world and societies have become more complex. This has led to decision-making by people's elected representatives in democratic countries. The most comprehensive definition[4] of democracy is the government 'of the people, for the people, and by the people'. India is the largest democracy in the world.

Totalitarianism   It is a dictatorial form of centralized government that regulates every aspect of the state and exhibits centralized behaviour. Power is centralized in the hands of a dictator who operates through a mixture of cultivating a devoted following and terrorizing those who do not agree with its policies. Citizens in a totalitarian state are generally deprived of their basic rights of freedom of expression, organizing meetings, free media, tolerance, and elections, which are available under democracy. The major forms of totalitarianism include the following.

Secular totalitarianism   In secular totalitarianism, the government uses military power to rule.

Fascist totalitarianism   Fascism is a right-wing nationalistic political ideology fundamentally opposed to democracy with a totalitarian and hierarchical structure. The term 'fascism' is derived from the Latin world *fasces*, which refers to the bundle of rods bound around a

---

[4] Basler, Roy P., (ed.), *The Collected Works of Abraham Lincoln*, vol. 7, 1953–1955, p. 22.

projecting axe-head as a symbol of power and authority. In Italian, the word fascism refers to radical political groups of many different and sometimes opposing orientations. Fascist totalitarianism prevailed in Italy under Mussolini, Germany under Hitler, Spain under Franco, and Portugal under Salazar.

Authoritarian totalitarianism　Authoritarianism aims to control both the minds and souls of people and to convert them to its own faith, whereas totalitarianism aspires to just rule people. Chile under Pinochet and South Africa prior to apartheid are examples of such authoritarian totalitarianism.

Communist totalitarianism　This is the most widespread form of secular totalitarianism, which advocates that socialism can be achieved only through totalitarian dictatorship. It is the left-wing totalitarianism that believes in equal distribution of wealth and complete government ownership and control on national resources. Since 1989, communist dictatorships in the former USSR and East European countries have collapsed and the former communist countries are moving gradually towards democracy. Moreover, countries, such as China, North Korea, Cuba, Vietnam, and Laos that follow communism also exhibit the signs of decline in the political monopoly enjoyed by communist power.

Theocratic totalitarianism　Religious leaders also assume political leadership in theocratic totalitarianism, for instance, in the Islamic Republic of Iran.

Types of government: structure

Based on the governance structure, governments may be classified as parliamentary, monarchy, and theocracy.

Parliamentary　The government consults its citizens from time to time and the parliament has power to formulate and execute laws. The British parliamentary system is one of the oldest in the world, whereas in the USA, the Congress passes the law and the executive branch of the government is independent. India follows a Westminster form of parliamentary democracy. The major forms of government are as follows.

Parliamentary republics　In parliamentary republics, the prime minister is the executive head of the government and also the leader of the legislature. The president is more of a titular head of the state with little executive power. India, Singapore, Finland, Italy, Germany, Austria, Greece, etc. represent parliamentary republics.

Semi-presidential system　Under such systems, a president and a prime minister coexist. The president has genuine executive authority, unlike in a parliamentary republic. But the prime minister is the head of the legislature and also heads the government. Systems followed in France, Russia, Pakistan, and the Republic of Korea fall under this category.

Fully presidential system　The president is both head of the state and head of the government in fully presidential systems and there is no prime minister. This type of system is followed in the USA, Philippines, Mexico, Indonesia, Brazil, Tanzania, etc.

Commonwealth countries　These countries represent constitutional monarchies that recognize the British monarch as head of the state over an independent government. A governor-general to each country other than the UK is appointed by the Queen as a representative. However, the active head of the executive branch of the government and also the leader of the legislature is the prime minister, such as in the UK, Australia, New Zealand, Canada, and Jamaica.

Monarchies

There could be either constitutional or absolute monarchies.

Constitutional monarchies   A constitutional monarch is the active head of the executive branch of the government and also the leader of the legislature who exercises power with the consent of the government and its representatives, as in Japan, Thailand, Spain, the Netherlands, Denmark, Sweden, Belgium, etc.

Absolute monarchies   It includes countries that have monarchs as the executive heads of government, exercising all powers, such as in the UAE, Saudi Arabia, Oman, Qatar, Bhutan, and Swaziland.

Theocracy   It is derived from the Greek word *theokratia*, which means the rule of God. The civil leader is believed to have a direct personal connection with God in a pure theocracy. For instance, the religious leadership in Iran exerts considerable political influence.

Trade Embargoes and Sanctions

Trade embargoes and sanctions are often used as hostile political measures rather than being based on economic considerations. Trade embargoes prohibit trade completely with a country so as to economically isolate it and exert political pressure on its government. For instance, the UN imposed a trade embargo on Iraq, following its invasion on Kuwait in the 1990s. During the discriminatory apartheid regime, the UN also had an embargo on trade with South Africa. Following the fall of Muammar Gaddafi, the UN dropped sanctions in September 2011 on two Libyan oil companies and eased restrictions on four banks.[5] Consequent to North Korea's conducting its first nuclear weapon test in 2006, the UN Security Council imposed a ban on trade with North Korea in 'luxury' goods, some conventional armaments, and materials 'related' to nuclear weapons and ballistic missile programmes.[6] In June 2009, additional economic sanctions and trade and arms embargo on North Korea was imposed.[7]

Trade sanctions are used to impose selective coercive measures to restrict trade with a country. Under Section 301 of the Trade Act of 1974, the US government exercises its authority to impose trade sanctions on foreign countries on the grounds of violation of trade or maintaining laws and practices that are either considered unjustifiable or restrict US trade. The use of trade sanctions as an instrument of foreign policy has always been debated in terms of achieving economic or political objectives. The imposition of trade sanctions has proliferated during recent years but their effectiveness has considerably declined. Since 1993, the USA has imposed more than 40 trade sanctions against about three dozen foreign countries. The US president's Export Council estimated that these sanctions did cost American exporters US$15 billion to US$19 billion in lost overseas sales. For instance, the sanctions under the Nuclear Proliferation Act failed to deter India and Pakistan from testing nuclear weapons in May 1994. Moreover, US sanctions have utterly failed to change the basic behaviour of governments in Cuba, Myanmar, Iran, Nigeria, Yugoslavia, and a number of other target countries.[8]

Bureaucracy

The term 'bureaucracy' refers to the form of administration based on hierarchical structure, governed by a set of written rules and established procedures. Since the officials in a bureaucratic

---

[5] Varner, Bill, 'UN Drops Sanctions on Libyan Oil Companies, Eases Restrictions on Banks', *Bloomberg*, 17 September 2011.

[6] 'UN Slaps Trade, Travel Sanctions on North Korea', *CNN World*, 14 October 2006.

[7] 'UN Approves "Unprecedented" Sanctions against North Korea over Nuclear Test', *The Guardian*, 12 June 2009.

[8] 'Unilateral Sanctions', Centre for Trade Policy and Research, Washington DC, 2007.

system derive authority by virtue of their official position rather than their own personal traits or competence, it leads to an impersonal approach to administration and too much reliance on rules and routine regulations. In the present context, the term bureaucracy is often used to describe inefficient and obstructive administrative process and red-tapism. The Indian bureaucracy has become apt at the art of shunning any direct responsibility in decision-making leading to avoidable delays. An international firm often finds it difficult to deal with a foreign bureaucratic system.

For instance, local political interests in Japan overweigh those in the rest of the country. Therefore, Japanese bureaucracy is difficult to streamline as politicians are interested in the affairs of their own districts rather than the country as a whole.

Terrorism, Crime, and Violence

The term 'terrorism' refers to systematic use of violence to create fear among the general public with an objective to achieve a political goal or convey a political message. Thus, terrorism is a political tactic that uses threat or violence, usually against civilians, so as to frighten them and build political pressure on the government. International terrorist activities may range from mere threat or physical assault to vandalism, mass killing, kidnapping, hijacking, and bombing.

Although isolated acts of terror have been witnessed in the past too, these were generally confined to a country and region. Technological breakthroughs and emerging globalization have led to globalization of terrorism as well. Organized terrorist groups now conceptualize and accomplish worldwide acts of terror. Terrorism has become endemic and has gained increased global attention consequent to 11 September 2001 widely referred to as 9/11.

The global reach of mass media, transport, and telecommunication has made even the considerably immune Western countries vulnerable to terrorist attacks. This has considerably influenced US business interests in a large number of countries where such terror groups are active. Following the US 'war on terror' and the attack on Afghanistan in October 2001, the perception of American companies operating in Islamic countries has suffered drastically; often franchises have come under assault with reported incidence of violence. In order to mitigate the negative perception, US companies have had to proactively adapt to local sensitivities.

Politically motivated use of computers and the Internet has led to the emergence of 'cyber-terrorism' that uses computers as weapons or as targets so as to create destructive or disruptive effects comparable to the physical form of terrorism. Since international business firms are highly integrated with the computer networks, they become increasingly susceptible to 'cyber-terrorism' that impinges across national boundaries.

Incidence of crime and violence, such as street mugging and looting, imposes considerable costs on the international operations of a firm as well. The business cost of crime and violence (Fig. 4.1) is the lowest in Qatar at 6.6 on a seven-point scale compared to UAE (6.5), Finland (6.4), Singapore (6.1), Germany (5.8), Japan (5.4), France (5.3), the UK (5.3), India (5), China (4.8), against the global average of 4.7, whereas it is below global average in the USA (4.5), Russian Federation (4.5), Burundi (3.6), Kenya (3.5), Brazil (3.5), Egypt (3.0), South Africa (2.9), El Salvador (1.9), and Guatemala (1.9).

There appears a negative correlation between economic freedom and terrorism: the higher the level of economic freedom, the lesser is the possibility of terrorism in a country. Besides, countries with greater degree of economic freedom are also economically more developed with higher per capita income.

The Index of Economic Freedom measures and ranks 177 countries across 10 specific freedoms, namely business, trade, fiscal, government size, monetary, investment, financial, property

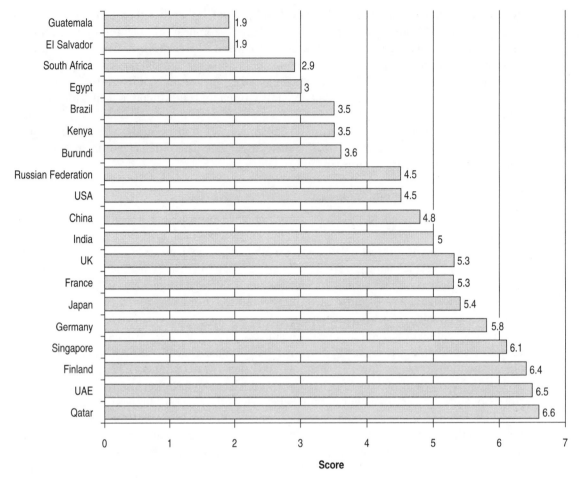

Fig. 4.1 Business costs of crime and violence

1 = to a great extent; 7 = not at all

Source: The Global Competitiveness Report, 2012–13, World Economic Forum, Geneva, p. 402.

rights, corruption, and labour freedoms. The overall scores given in Fig. 4.2 reveal that Hong Kong, Singapore, Australia, New Zealand, Switzerland, and Canada are the countries with highest levels of economic freedom, whereas North Korea, Cuba, Zimbabwe, Venezuela, Eritrea, Libya, and Burma are the most economically repressed. The Indian economy is assessed to possess 55.2 per cent of economic freedom, whereas China has 51.9 per cent freedom. Thus, India is the world's 119th freest economy, whereas China at 136th has been classified under the 'mostly unfree' category. India enjoys strong fiscal freedom (78.3%), freedom from government spending (77.9%), and monetary freedom[9] (65.3%).

The top individual and corporate tax rates are moderate, and overall tax revenue is not excessive as a percentage of gross domestic product (GDP) but government price controls hinder market forces. The highest rate of income tax rate in India is 30.9 per cent, whereas the top corporate tax rate is 33.99 per cent in 2013. The overall tax burden equals 7.4 per cent of total domestic income, whereas the government spending is equivalent to 27.1 per cent of GDP. The

---

[9] *2013 Index of Economic Freedom*, The Heritage Foundation.

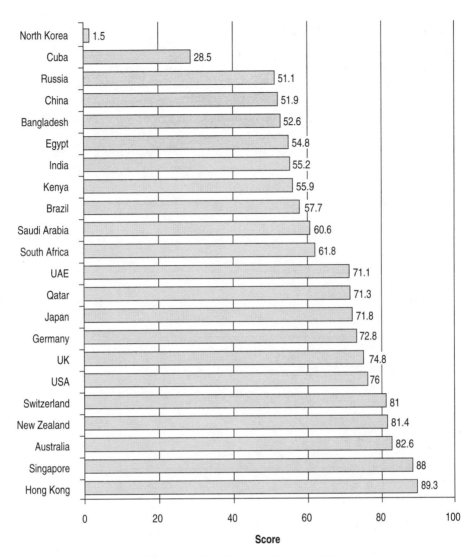

Fig. 4.2 Index of Economic Freedom, 2012

Source: 2013 Index of Economic Freedom, The Heritage Foundation Washington; and *Wall Street Journal,* New York, 2013.

Indian economy also enjoys considerable labour freedom (73.6%), trade freedom (63.6%), and freedom of property rights (50%), whereas financial freedom (40%), business freedom (37.3%), investment freedom (35%), and freedom from corruption (31%) are relatively low.

INTERNATIONAL LEGAL ENVIRONMENT

Firms operating internationally face major challenges in conforming to different laws, regulations, and legal systems in different countries. The legal framework to protect small and medium enterprises (SMEs) mainly to achieve social objectives adversely influences the expansion of manufacturing capacities and achieving economies of scale in certain countries. International managers need to develop basic understanding of the types of legal systems followed in the countries of their operations before entering into legal contracts.

Judicial Independence and Efficiency

The independence of a country's judicial system from political influences of the members of governments, citizens, or firms is crucial for the fair treatment a firm receives in its overseas operations. A fair judicial system also reduces political risks in overseas markets. The level of judicial independence and efficiency differs widely among countries. New Zealand had the highest level of judicial independence (Fig. 4.3) with a score of 6.7 on a seven-point scale compared to Finland (6.5), Germany (6.2), the UK (6.2), Japan (5.8), UAE (5.4), South Africa (5.3), France (4.9), the USA (4.9), India (4.5), Egypt (4.1), China (3.9), Brazil (3.8), Uganda (3.5), Kenya (3.4), Russian Federation (2.6), Burundi (1.7), and the lowest in Venezuela (1.3).

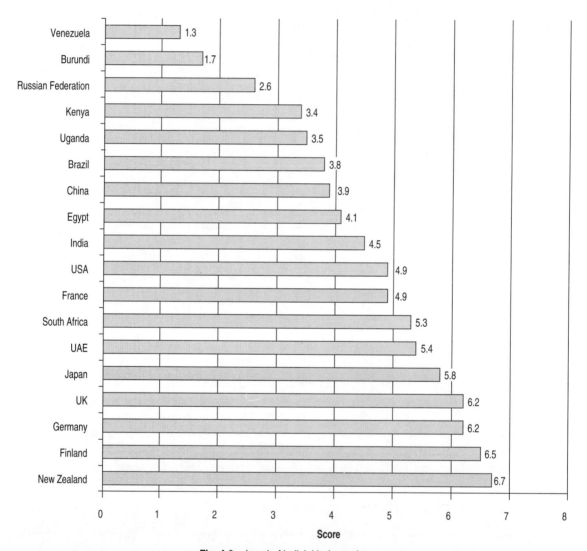

Fig. 4.3 Level of judicial independence

1 = heavily influenced; 7 = entirely independent

Source: The Global Competitiveness Report, 2012–13, World Economic Forum, Geneva, p. 393.

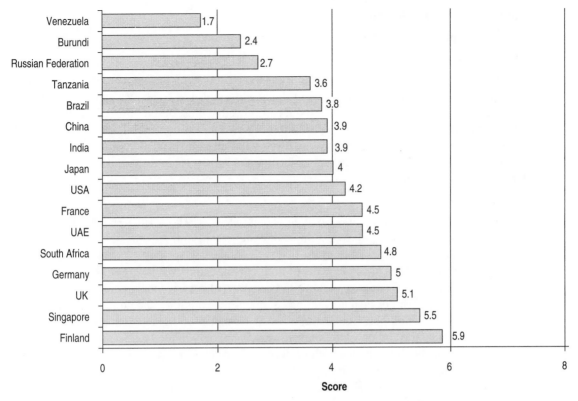

Fig. 4.4   Efficiency of legal framework in challenging regulations

1 = extremely inefficient; 7 = highly efficient

Source: *The Global Competitiveness Report*, 2012–13, World Economic Forum, Geneva, p. 398.

The efficiency of legal framework for private businesses to settle dispute and challenge the legality of government actions or regulations also varies widely. A cross-country comparison as shown in Fig. 4.4 on a seven-point scale indicates that Finland (5.9) had the highest level of efficiency of legal framework, followed by Singapore (5.5), the UK (5.1), Germany (5.0), South Africa (4.8), the UAE (4.5), France (4.5), the USA (4.2), Japan (4), India (3.9), China (3.9), Brazil (3.7), Russian Federation (2.7), and Burundi (2.4). The legal framework was the least efficient in Venezuela (1.7).

The extent of separation of judicial powers between the judiciary and the public authorities varies considerably across nations. China, for instance, has generally followed 'rule by man and not by law', the tradition of which still remains despite the country developing a model legal system. The efficiency of enforcement of legal system is also lax in many low-income countries.

In countries like Japan, reliance on courts for conflict resolution is much lower compared to USA, which is considered to be one of the most litigious societies in the world. On the other hand, Japan is considered to be a 'non-contractual' society where contracts signed represent general understanding and are subject to change depending upon the circumstance. There is heavy reliance on settling disputes through third-party negotiations rather than courts.

International Legal Systems

The major types of legal systems are briefly mentioned here.

Common law

It is based on traditions, past practices, and legal precedents set by the courts through interpretation of statutes, legal legislations, and past rulings. It depends less on written statutes and codes. Common law originated from England and it is followed in most of the former British colonies, such as India, the UK, USA, Canada, Australia, and New Zealand. In general, the greater the level of economic development of a country, the more elaborate is its legislative framework. India is an exception as it has the most voluminous income-tax legislation in the world, whereas it ranks ninth[10] in terms of GDP.

Civil law

Also known as code or civil law, it is based on a comprehensive set of written statutes. It is derived from the Roman law and is followed in most of continental Europe, Japan, and Latin America. The elaborate legislative codes embody the main rules of the law, spelling out every circumstance.

Laws of most countries have elements of both common and civil law. The complications in a meeting out of non-performance of a business contract also vary widely among the common- and civil-law countries. For instance, in the common-law countries, the non-performance of a contract due to an 'act of God' may include floods, earthquakes, lightening, or similar happenings, whereas under the civil law, non-performance is not only limited to 'acts of God', but also includes 'unavoidable interference with performance, whether resulting from forces of nature or unforeseeable human acts', including such factors as labour strikes and riots.

The distinction between the common law and civil law is more in theory rather than in practice. Many common law countries, including the USA and India have adapted commercial codes to govern business.

The most significant difference in the common law and the civil law countries is in the protection of intellectual property. Ownership is established by use in common law countries, whereas it requires registration in the civil law countries. It is extremely important for certain agreements in civil law countries to get registered, in order to be enforceable, whereas in common law countries, as long as the proof of the agreement can be established, an agreement is binding.

Although there is significant overlapping in practice under the two systems, laws are much more rigid in the countries with civil-law system compared to common-law systems. In civil law countries, judges have to strictly follow the 'letter of the law', giving them low flexibility in judicial decisions, whereas in common-law countries, greater reliance is placed on the previous rulings and interpretations by other judges in similar cases. Business contracts tend to be detailed and specific with all contingencies elaborated in civil-law countries, whereas contracts tend to be shorter and less specific in common-law countries. The judiciary tend to be less adversarial in civil-law countries, whereas little significance is accorded to legal precedence and traditions compared to common-law countries.

Socialistic law

This law is derived from the Marxist socialist system and continues to influence legal framework in former communist countries, such as the Commonwealth of Indian States (CIS), China, North Korea, Vietnam, and Cuba. Socialist law traditionally advocates ownership of most property by the state or state-owned public enterprises, prohibiting free entry to foreign firms.

---

[10] World Development Indicators Database, World Bank, 2011.

Theocratic law

Theocratic law is the legal system based on religious doctrine, precepts, and beliefs. For instance, the Hebrew law and the Islamic law are derived from religious doctrines and their scholarly interpretations. Unlike the countries dominated by Christianity, Hinduism, and Buddhism where either common or civil law is followed, a large number of Islamic countries integrate their legal system based on the Sharia. The legal system in a number of Islamic countries, including Saudi Arabia and Iran, is integrated with Sharia.

In Arabic, 'Sharia' means the clear, well-trodden path to water. In Islam, Sharia is used to refer to the matters of religion that God has legislated for His Servants. Sharia is the canonical law derived from a combination of sources, such as the Koran, the holy book of Islam, the Sunna, teachings and practices of the prophet Mohammed, and the fatwas, the rulings of the Islamic scholars. The Sharia regulates all human actions and places them in five categories, that is, obligatory, recommended, permitted, disliked, or forbidden. Classic Sharia manuals are divided in four parts: laws related to personal acts of worship, laws related to commercial dealings, laws related to marriage and divorce, and penal laws.

The major similarities between the Sharia and secular laws are that in both

- all people are equal before the law;
- a person is innocent unless proved guilty;
- the burden of proof is on the plaintiff; and
- written contracts have a sanctity and legitimacy of their own.

The salient features of Islamic law concerned to business are that

- contracts should be fair to all parties. Partnership is preferred over hierarchical claims;
- *gharar*, the transaction involving fundamental uncertainty or speculation is prohibited. Gambling is not liked in Islamic countries, but futures and currency hedging also involves speculation. International managers need to be aware of such situations;
- interest on money is prohibited but allows management fees and services. All business transactions must avoid *riba*, that is, excessive profit, loosely defined as interest;
- business involving forbidden products or activity such as alcohol, pork, or gambling is prohibited;
- normally award of damages is in line with practicality but not as inflated as is often the case in the West. In other words, the damages to property will be actual sums relating to repair and replacement of the property. The loss of opportunity cost of money is not compensated under the Sharia; and
- compassion is required when a business is in trouble. In a country with Islamic legal structure, it is not considered appropriate to put pressure in the event of bankruptcy of one's business partner.

The major difference between Sharia law and the Western law is the idea of reference to a precedent. A ruling issued by a judge is not binding on other judges or on him in later cases. While doing business in Islamic countries, international managers need to appreciate the intertwining of religion and Islamic law and take care never to mention the Palestine-Israeli situation.

After independence from erstwhile colonial rulers, most Islamic countries have grappled with the problem of replacing colonial legal systems with the Sharia. The implications of Islamic law vary in terms of degree among the Islamic countries. In most countries it is applied in conjunction with the common and the civil law.

Islamic finance

Under the Islamic law, Western style finance is *haram*, or forbidden, to devout Muslims. The interest-bearing accounts and loans, which fall under the strict *riba* rules, most futures and options, which are considered speculative and *gharar*, and insurance, because the outcome of the contract can no way be determined beforehand[11] are all *haram*. In order to enable Islamic investors to benchmark their investment on a regional basis and give product providers the opportunity to develop structured products tailored to the Islamic market, Standard & Poor's (S&P) brings out Sharia indices that include only those stocks that comply with Sharia law. This provides investors with a comparable investable portfolio while adopting explicit investment criteria defined by the Sharia. All S&P indices constituents are monitored on a daily basis to ensure that the indices maintain strict Sharia compliance. A substantial amount of oil-money is invested in Sharia-compliant funds. As the index provides for benchmarking with Sharia, some of these funds may be invested as per the Sharia indices.

Principles of International Law

International law is less coherent compared to domestic law since it embodies a multiplicity of treaties (bilateral, multilateral, or universal) and conventions (such as the Vienna Convention of Diplomatic Security, Geneva Convention on Human Rights, etc.) besides the laws of individual countries. International managers need to understand the basic principles that govern the conduct of international law. These are as follows.

Principle of sovereignty

A 'sovereign' state is independent and free from all external control or enjoys complete legal equality with other states. It governs its own territory, has the right to select and implement its own political, economic, and social systems, and has the power to enter into bilateral or multilateral agreements with other nations. Thus, a sovereign state exercises powers over its own members and in relation to other countries. This also implies that courts of a sovereign country cannot be used to rectify its injustices on other countries.

International jurisdiction

Under international law, there are three basic types of jurisdictional principles, as follows.

Nationality principle   Every country has jurisdiction over its citizens, irrespective of their locations. For instance, an Indian citizen travelling abroad may be given a penalty by a court in India.

Territoriality principle   Every country has the right of jurisdiction within its own legal territory. Therefore, a foreign firm involved in illegal business practices in India can be sued under Indian law.

Protective principle   Every nation has jurisdiction over conduct that adversely affects its national security even if such behaviour occurs outside the country. For instance, an Italian firm that sells India's defence secrets can be booked under the Indian law.

Doctrine of comity

As a part of international customs and traditions, there must be mutual respect for the laws, institutions, and the government system of other countries in the matter of jurisdiction over their own citizens.

---

[11] 'Finance and Economics: West Meets East: Islamic Finance', *The Economist,* London, 25 October 2003.

Act of state doctrine

Under this jurisdiction principle of international law, all acts of other governments are considered to be valid by a country's court, even if such acts are not appropriate in the country. For instance, foreign governments have the right to impose restrictions related to financial repatriation to other countries.

Treatment and rights of aliens

Nations have the right to impose restriction upon foreign citizens on their rights to travel and stay, their conduct, or area of business operations. A country may also refuse entry to foreign citizens or restrict their travel. As a result of rise in terrorism during the last decade, the USA and many European countries have imposed restrictions on foreigners.

Forum for hearing and settling disputes

Courts can dismiss cases at their discretion, brought before them by foreigners. However, courts are bound to examine issues, such as the place from where evidence must be collected, location of the property under restitution, and the plaintiff. For instance, after the disaster of Union Carbide's pesticide plant located at Bhopal in India, the New York Court of Appeals sent back the case to India for resolution.

United Nations Commission on International Trade Law

The United Nations Commission on International Trade Law (UNCITRAL) was established in 1966 by the UN General Assembly with the aim to reduce obstacles in international trade. Its general mandate is to harmonize and unify the laws of international trade. 'Harmonization' and 'unification' of the law of international trade refer to the process through which the law facilitating international trade is created and adopted.

The commission is composed of 60 member states elected by the General Assembly. Membership is structured so as to be representative of the world's various geographic regions and its principal economic and legal systems. Members of the commission are elected for terms of six years, the term of half-members expiring every three years. Presently, UNCITRAL has six working groups for areas, such as procurement, international arbitration and conciliation, transport law, electronic commerce, insolvency law, and security interests. It has prepared a wide range of conventions, model laws, and other instruments dealing with the substantive law that governs trade transactions or other aspects of business law influencing international trade.

It is pertinent for managers operating internationally to develop a thorough understanding of political and legal environments in the target countries as it significantly influences the marketing decisions. This chapter elaborates different forms of international political systems that need to be understood while formulating marketing strategies across markets. Besides, various types of legal systems and prevailing international law are also discussed that need to be followed for international operations.

Summary

International political and economic systems are mutually interdependent. As a firm expands internationally, it needs to operate in multiple countries with diverse politico-economic environments. Understanding the basic dynamics of international, political, and legal environments is crucial for effective decision-making in international markets. The set of ideas or beliefs people hold about political regime and its institutions, known as political ideology, influences marketing environment considerably. The types of political ideologies may be categorized by way of economic systems (communism, socialism, and capitalism), political systems (democracy and totalitarianism), and structure (parliamentary, commonwealth, monarchies, and theocracy).

Trade embargoes and sanctions are often used as hostile political measures rather than being based on economic considerations. The extent of bureaucracy, the inefficient and obstructive administrative process, and red-tapism adversely affect the smooth conduct of business operations. Technological breakthroughs in means of transport and communications have led to globalization of terrorism, crime, and violence. The correlation between terrorism and degree of economic freedom between nations appears to be negative. Commercial, economic, and political risks adversely affect international marketing operations.

The extent of judicial independence and efficiency considerably mitigates political risks in international markets, which varies significantly across the countries. The principal legal systems followed include common law, civil law, socialist law, and theocratic law. Unlike the countries dominated by Christianity, Hinduism, and Buddhism where either common or civil law is followed, a large number of Islamic countries integrate their legal systems based on the Sharia, the Islamic law. The basic principles of international law include the principle of sovereignty, international jurisdiction, doctrine of comity, act of state doctrine, treatment and rights of aliens, forum for hearing and settling disputes. The UNCITRAL aims to harmonize and unify the laws of international trade.

Key Terms

Act of state doctrine   All acts of other governments are considered to be valid by a country's court, even if such acts are not appropriate in the country.

Bureaucracy   Form of administration based on hierarchical structure governed by a set of written rules and established procedures. The term is often used to describe inefficient and obstructive administrative process and red-tapism.

Capitalism   An economic system that provides complete freedom of private ownership of productive resources and industries.

Civil law   Law based on a comprehensive set of written statutes, also known as code or civil law.

Common law   Law based on tradition, past practices, and legal precedents set by the courts through interpretation of statutes, legal legislations, and past rulings that depends less on written statutes and codes.

Commonwealth countries   Countries representing constitutional monarchies, which recognize Queen Elizabeth II as head of the state over an independent government.

Communism   Theory based on the concept of a classless society, all the major factors of production being owned by the government and shared by all the people rather than profit-seeking enterprises, for the benefit of the society.

Democracy   Government by the people where citizens are directly involved in decision-making.

Doctrine of comity   There must be mutual respect for the laws, institutions, and the government systems of other countries in the matter of jurisdiction over their own citizens.

Nationality principle   Every country has jurisdiction over its citizens irrespective of their locations.

Parliamentary   The government consults its citizens from time to time and the parliament has power to formulate and execute laws.

Political ideology   A set of ideas or beliefs that people hold about their political regime and its institutions.

Political system   A system that comprises various stakeholders, such as the government, political parties with different ideologies, labour unions, religious organizations, environmental activists, and various NGOs.

Principle of sovereignty   A 'sovereign' state is independent and free from all external controls and enjoys complete legal equality with other states.

Protective principle   Every nation has jurisdiction over conduct that adversely affects its national security even if such behaviour occurred outside the country.

Sharia law   Canonical law based on combination of teachings, mainly from Islamic religious books such as the Koran and the Sunna.

Socialism   A form of government where basic and heavy industries are operated by the government so as to ensure social welfare objectives, whereas small business may be privately owned.

Territoriality principle   Every country has the right of jurisdiction within its own legal territory.

Terrorism   Systematic use of violence to create fear in general public with an objective to achieve a political goal or convey a political message.

Theocracy   The rule of God where the civil leader is believed to have a direct personal connection with God.

Theocratic law   Legal system based on religious doctrine, precepts, and beliefs.

Totalitarianism   Dictatorial form of centralized government, usually in the hands of a dictator who regulates every aspect of state.

Trade embargoes   Prohibiting trade completely with a country so as to economically isolate it and apply political pressure on its government.

Trade sanctions   Imposing selective coercive measures to restrict trade from a country.

Concept Review Questions

1. Explain the significance of political environment in international marketing with suitable examples.
2. Describe various forms of government systems on the basis of economic systems and its impact on international marketing decisions with suitable illustrations.
3. Distinguish between common law and civil law and overlaps in the two legal systems. What are the major implications of these legal systems on international marketing decisions?

4. Critically examine the basic principles of international law.
5. Write short notes on the following:
   (a) UNCITRAL
   (b) BERI Index
   (c) MIGA

Critical Thinking Questions

1. Carry out an analysis of trade of your country with Iraq for the last 20 years and assess the impact of UN embargo imposed on Iraq in 1991 and of the US attack on Iraq in 2003 on the international marketing activities.

2. Visit the website of a Western bank operating in Saudi Arabia and identify the adaptations made to operate under the Sharia law.

Project Assignment

Visit a firm operating in a country with considerable influence of Islamic law. Discuss with its international managers and find out the key difference in the legal framework that necessitated adaptation of marketing strategy in Islamic law countries vis-à-vis countries following common or civil law.

CASE STUDY: HOMOLOGATION OF 'MOTOR VEHICLES' IN INTERNATIONAL MARKETS

India: Emerging Global Hub for Small Cars

India is the world's second fastest growing passenger car manufacturing hub with a CAGR of 16.6 per cent in the world after China (31.1%) during 2000–12, whereas there has been a decline in some of the world's major car manufacturing countries such as France (–4.4%), Spain (–3.5%), the USA (–2.5%), and the UK (–0.9%). In terms of total passenger cars manufactured in 2012, India ranked sixth with 3.29 million passenger cars compared to 15.52 million in China, 8.55 million in Japan, 5.39 million in Germany, 4.17 million in South Korea, and 4.11 million[12] in the USA (Fig. C4.1). India is estimated to manufacture 9 million passenger cars[13] by 2020.

In terms of passenger car sales, India is also the second fastest growing market in the world with a CAGR of 14 per cent during 2005–12 after China (21.5%) ahead of Brazil (11%), Russia (8.9%), whereas the sales have declined in other major markets such as the UK (–2.5%), France (–1.5%), Germany (–1.1%) the USA (–0.8%), and Japan (–0.5%), though India remains the sixth largest passenger car market in 2012 with 2.8 million

cars sold compared to 15.5 million in China, 7.2 million in the USA, 4.6 million in Japan, 3.1 million in Germany, 2.9 million in Brazil, 2.8 million in Russia, 2 million in the UK, and 1.9 million in France (Fig. C4.2).

India is not just a low cost production destination for passenger cars, but also a leader in engineering services. It ranks fourth after China, Germany, and the USA and is likely to be the second most competitive country in the world in the next five years in terms of its manufacturing competitiveness.[14] India has also got competitive advantage in research and development, low cost production, availability of both skilled and unskilled labour, a strong and well-developed auto-component industry and well-established local OEM suppliers. Besides, India's strategic edge in its competence and experience of indigenous car development, excellence in the manufacturing sector, and strong auto component industry makes it a rapidly emerging prominent manufacturing and export hub of small cars.

Presently, India is estimated to manufacture over 30 per cent (Fig. C4.3) of world's small cars and it is set to topple Japan

---

[12] *India: Mecca of Small Car*, India Brand Equity Foundation, 2013.

[13] Society of Indian Automobile Manufacturers (SIAM) as updated up to 2013.

[14] *Global Manufacturing Competitiveness Index*, Deloitte, 2013.

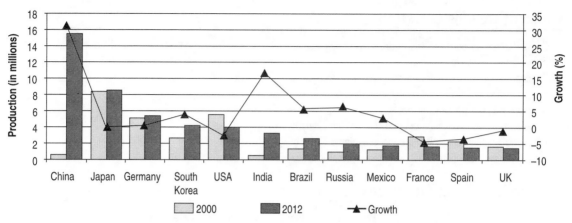

Fig. C4.1   World's top car manufacturing countries

Source: International Organization of Motor Vehicle Manufacturers (OICA), 2013.

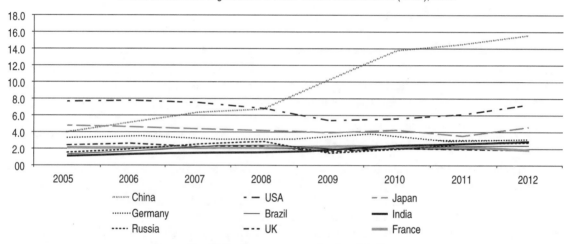

Fig. C4.2   Passenger car sales (in million)

Source: International Organization of Motor Vehicle Manufacturers (OICA), 2013.

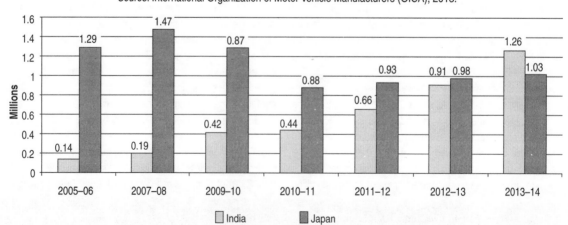

Fig. C4.3   India rapidly emerging as the world's largest small car exporter

Source: *India: Mecca of Small Car*, India Brand Equity Foundation, 2013.

by 2016 as the world's largest small car producer.[15] Small cars manufactured in India are exported worldwide including to the UK, Italy, Germany, Netherlands, South Africa, Singapore, Latin America, and several other East Asian countries. Singapore has been a fast growing market where the demand of Indian cars has grown seven times over the last four years. Considering an average growth of 40–50 per cent in small car exports, India is likely to overtake Japan by 2014 as the largest exporter of small cars.

India's first small car Maruti 800 launched by Maruti Suzuki in 1983 was indigenized over 70 per cent in less than five years of its launch to reduce production costs. The company followed much greater level of indigenization of 80–90 per cent in its future models of Zen and WagonR. Hyundai, the second largest automotive manufacturer in India, exports 50 per cent of its India production. A number of small cars developed, manufactured, and launched in India by various manufacturers such as Tata Motors, Maruti Suzuki, Hyundai, Ford, Renault Nissan, Chevrolet, and Fiat are exported internationally (Table C4.1).

Table C4.1 World-class small cars developed and manufactured in India

Car manufacturers	Cars
Tata Motors	Indica, Nano
Maruti Suzuki	Maruti 800, Alto, Zen
Hyundai	Santro, i10, i20
Ford	Figo
Renault-Nissan	Micra
Chevrolet	Beat, Spark, Aveo U-VA
Fiat	Palino, Punto
Toyota	Etios

Source: India: Mecca of Small Car, India Brand Equity Foundation, 2013.

In 1999, India's first indigenously designed and manufactured car Tata Indica was launched by Tata Motors. The launch of Tata Nano completely developed and manufactured in India by Tata Motors in 2009 surprised the automobile pundits across the world and demonstrated India's extraordinary capability in small car design and development.

Growing barriers to international markets
Apparently, high import tariffs make imported cars more expensive compared to domestically manufactured cars, whereas non-tariff barriers pose even more formidable obstacles to market entry. Though import tariffs are low in most developed countries on passenger cars, ranging from 0 per cent in Japan to 5.6 per cent in South Korea, 6.5 per cent to 10 per cent in the EU, and 10 per cent in the USA but remains considerably high in developing country markets varying from 25 per cent in Russia and China, 30 per cent in Malaysia, 35 per cent in Brazil and Argentina, 50 per cent in Indonesia, 75 per cent in India, and 83 per cent in Vietnam.[16]

Non-tariff barriers take different forms that are difficult to fully eliminate. A variety of product requirements continues to affect price competitiveness of automobiles significantly in foreign markets. The growing gap between auto regulations in exporting countries and their target market regulations often results in significant costs for car exporters especially from developing countries to developed country markets. A number of countries are introducing their own national standards. For instance, exports to Indonesia require certification by Indonesian National Standards (SNI) for car components (such as braking systems) and for completely built cars (such as tyre and windscreen certifications).

Homologation of motor vehicles
'Homologation', derived from the Greek word *homologeo* meaning 'to agree', is a technical term to signify granting of approval by a public authority. In the automobile industry, the term 'automotive homologation' refers to the process of certifying vehicles or a particular component of a vehicle that it has satisfied the requirements set by various statutory regulatory bodies. Thus, homologation is the process certifying that a particular car is roadworthy and matches certain specified criteria laid out by the government of a country for all vehicles made or imported into that country. Such processes and certifications are also known as 'type approvals'. It is an acceptable practice worldwide and is mandatory worldwide to export automobile products and components.

Exporters of automobiles and spare parts including their manufacturers and suppliers have to comply with homologation regulations of the country of destination or use. With the growing emphasis on passenger safety and environment, the number of rules and norms applying to automobiles has considerably increased across the world.

All original models running in any country including India have to be homologated. It includes either cars of Tata developed in India, such as the Tata Indica and Nano, or cars imported as a completely built unit and sold in India like the Tata Etios. It also includes any variants that the company may later introduce which would affect emission or safety parameters. For

---

[15] *India: Mecca of Small Car*, India Brand Equity Foundation, 2013.

[16] *The EU Automotive Sector in a Globalised Market*, European Union, 2012.

instance, if the company introduces a new engine in an existing model, the engine would need to be homologated. However, the ancillary manufacturers also validate their products, so if the variant only uses a validated ancillary there is no need for fresh homologation of the entire vehicle.

Homologation normally costs around ₹1 to ₹1.5 million, depending on the number of tests necessary to ensure road-worthiness. Normally, the process takes around three months, which is also the international average. In India, this clearance is given by the Pune-based Automotive Research Association of India (ARAI) or the Vehicle Research and Development Establishment (VRDE), Ahmednagar (Maharashtra), and by the Central Farm Machinery Training and Testing Institute, Budni (Madhya Pradesh), for tractors. Essentially, the homologation tests ensure that the vehicle matches the requirements of the Indian market in terms of emission and safety standards and roadworthiness as per the Central Motor Vehicle Rules.

A car that is tuned to the fuel condition and road conditions of a more developed market need not necessarily work in developing countries including India. For instance, the fuel quality in devel-oping countries may be so poor that manufacturers often need to tweak their engines to make them country worthy including checking its worthiness to Indian conditions. Also, each country has separate homologation laws and not all of them are relevant to India. According to the government notification after the 2001 Exim Policy phased out quantitative restriction on new and used car imports, every original car model brought into the country by an individual or a manufacturer has to have local homologation clearance. Once a model or prototype is homologated, other similar cars do not need to be separately certified.

There had been consistent pressure for a long time on the government to relax the norms by influential groups and persons including Sachin Tendulkar, Amitabh Bachchan, Shah Rukh Khan, Lalit Suri, and Mukesh Ambani using high market segment cars.[17] Consequently, the government has exempted homologation (test for roadworthiness) to imported new cars that have an FOB value of US$40,000 (which translates to ₹3.60 million after 102 per cent peak imported duty) or more, imported either by 'an individual or company or firm under EPCG scheme' subject to approval certificate from an interna-tionally accredited agency that deals with ECE regulations.[18] The Automotive Research Association of India (ARAI) and the Society of Indian Automobile Manufactures (SIAM) are critical of the government's decisions to relax the homologa-tion norms on high-end imported cars, which fear mushroom growth of imported cars.

There has been a worldwide move towards greater reciprocity in recognizing each other's standards. Till recently, there had not been any reciprocal arrangement between ARAI and its European or American counterparts. Since they did not recognize ARAI certification, ARAI did not recognize their certification either. Now, ARAI has joined hands with TUV Rhineland, the German multinational, for testing and homologation.

Though homologation aims at improving active and passive car safety, environment protection as well as quality of products, and production processes, it is not uncommon to use technical regulations under homologation as market entry barriers. For instance, motor vehicles imported in China are subjected to more than one type approval or homologation requirements by different regulatory agencies with little coordination. Moreover, the 2002 China Compulsory Certification System imposes additional burden on importers as it requires each automotive product and component to be re-tested in Chinese laboratories even if is tested earlier in the exporting country. India's largest car exporting company Hyundai that exports to over 100 countries had to shelve its plan to export i10 passenger car to the USA due to homologation requirements.[19]

As evident from the case, the homologation norms for automobiles are significant barriers to international markets for manufactures from developing countries as the developed countries do not recognize the quality standards and testing norms of ARAI. Despite India's superiority in developing technol-ogy intensive products, such regulations and testing methods related to product quality and specification are going to be a major barrier for Indian firms in marketing their products in international markets.

Questions

1. Critically evaluate India's growing competence in export of small passenger cars and identify the reasons for the same.

2. Explore reasons as to why the legal regulations are increas-ingly being used as formidable barriers for exports especially for small cars. Carry out a cross-country comparison of such barriers.

3. 'A large number of countries especially developed ones employ "homologation" as a market entry barrier by most countries rather than ensuring passenger safety.' Do you agree with the statement? Express your opinion in a debate in front of your class.

4. India is the emerging hub for manufacture and export of small cars. Find out the impact of homologation requirements on export of small cars from India.

---

[17] 'Big B, SRK in Sachin's Company', *The Times of India*, 30 November 2003.

[18] 'Cars above $40,000 can Forget Homologation', *The Economic Times*, 29 January 2004.

[19] 'Hyundai i10 Faces US Homologation Hurdle', *The Economic Times*, 3 November 2008.

International Cultural Environment

INTRODUCTION

A firm operating internationally comes across a wide range of diverse cultural environments, which significantly influence international marketing decisions. Managers operating in international markets need to appreciate the differences among cultural behaviours of their business partners and consumers across various countries. As a matter of basic principle, an international manager visiting overseas is expected to follow local customs and a seller needs to adapt to the buyer's requirements.

This chapter brings out the significance of understanding culture in international markets. When international managers are faced with a set of marketing situations overseas, they are prone to misjudge or erroneously react due to perceptual differences of cross-cultural nuances. In order to effectively manage cross-cultural differences in international markets, one has to

- develop a conceptual understanding of one's own cultural biases and assumptions;
- explore the reasons as to why the way of doing things in different cultures makes sense in view of their cultural assumptions; and
- treat ways of doing things and cultural assumptions as starting points that need to be integrated in developing culture-specific competitive solutions.

International managers need to develop cultural sensitivities in the countries of their operations and adapt their marketing strategies accordingly. The failure of Euro Disneyland is a classic example of the failure to understand a foreign culture and is often described as a 'Cultural Chernobyl'. Disney's insensitivity to French culture in terms of product designs, consumer habits, and local norms made the company enter into troubled waters in its French venture. For instance, alcoholic beverages are out of place in Disney's US 'family restaurants', whereas in most parts of Europe alcoholic drinks form an integral part of their meals.

Learning Objectives

- To understand the significance of culture in international marketing decisions
- To elucidate the concept of culture and its constituents
- To explain comparisons of cross-cultural behaviour
- To discuss cultural orientation in international marketing
- To explicate self reference criteria and ethnocentrism

Another example of cultural insensitivity was witnessed in May 2001 when a wave of anger erupted among vegetarian and Hindu consumers across the world, especially in India, within hours of receiving the news of McDonald's using beef extract for cooking its fries.[1] Over 80 per cent of India's one billion population is Hindu, for whom the cow is highly sacred and worshipped. Angry mobs in Mumbai vandalized McDonald's outlets. To combat public ire, McDonald's adopted a comprehensive approach integrating use of public relations, media publicity, and employing police security. It sent samples of the fries to leading Indian laboratories for testing on the same day the news broke in India, the results of which were published in leading dailies. Besides, McDonald's displayed prominent posters in its outlets stating '100 per cent Vegetarian French Fries in McDonald's India' and 'No flavours with animal products/extracts are used for preparing any vegetarian products in India'. Consequently, It emphasized on adapting a more vegetarian-friendly menu and became more sensitive to Indian culture.

The perception and behaviour of people varies widely across cultures. Summarily, culture represents the collective or group behaviour of people that makes them different from others. Various constituents of culture, such as value system, norms, aesthetics, customs and traditions, language and religion have also been elaborated along with their implications in international marketing.

This chapter also elucidates the major types of cultural classifications so as to facilitate a comparison of cross-cultural behaviour. Major cultural orientations such as parochialism and simplification are also explained.

THE CONCEPT OF CULTURE

The word 'culture' is derived from the Latin word *cultura*, which is related to cult or worship. Culture is the way of life of people, including their attitudes, values, beliefs, arts, sciences, modes of perception, and habits of thought and activity. The Oxford Encyclopaedic English Dictionary defines culture as 'the art and other manifestations of human intellectual achievement regarded collectively; the customs, civilization, and achievement of a particular time or people; the way of life of a particular society or group'.

Culture is the collective programming of the mind, which distinguishes the members of one group or category from those of another.[2] Hofstede's model indicates three levels of uniqueness in human mental programming.[3] Culture lies between human nature on one side and individual personality on the other, as shown in Fig. 5.1. Each person has several layers of cultural 'programming', from basic values to practices at corporate level.

The Encyclopaedia Britannica defines culture as an integrated pattern of human knowledge, belief, and behaviour that is both a result of and integral to the human capacity for learning and transmitting knowledge to succeeding generations. Culture thus consists of language, ideas, beliefs, customs, taboos, codes, institutions, tools, techniques, works of art, rituals, ceremonies, and symbols.

The characteristics of culture[4] may be summarized as follows.

Learned   Culture is not inherited or biologically based; it is acquired by learning and experience.

Shared   People as members of a group, organization, or society share culture; it is not specific to a single individual.

---

[1] Gupte, Sarika, 'McDonald's Avert a Crisis: Crisis Management Teams Reverse Damages to the Fast Food Giants in India', *Advertising Age Global*, 1 July 2000.

[2] Hofstede, Geert, 'National Cultures Revisited', *Asia Pacific Journal of Management*, September 1984, pp. 22–24.

[3] Hofstede, G., *Cultures and Organisations: Software of the Mind*, McGraw-Hill, London, 1991.

[4] Luthans, Fred, *Organization Behaviour*, Seventh edition, McGraw-Hill, New York, 1995, pp. 33–55

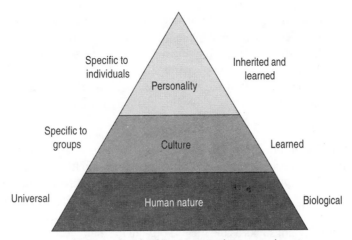

Fig. 5.1　Levels of human mental programming

Trans-generational　Culture is cumulative, passed down from one generation to the next.

Symbolic　Culture is based on the human capacity to symbolize or use one thing to represent another.

Patterned　Culture has structure and is integrated; a change in one part will bring changes in another.

Adaptive　Culture is based on the human capacity to change or adapt, as opposed to the more genetically driven adaptive process of animals.

The process of adjusting and adapting to a new culture is known as *acculturation*, which is crucial to one's success in international markets.

Constituents of Culture

As culture is an integrated sum of learned behaviour shared by a group of people that differentiates them from others, it becomes imperative to understand various constituents that contribute to the sum total of learned behaviour. Although a variety of learned traits that influence human behaviour can contribute to the culture of a social group, only the major constituents such as value system, norms, aesthetics, customs and traditions, language, and religion are discussed here.

Value system

Values are shared assumptions of a group about how things ought to be or abstract ideas about what a group believes to be good, desirable, or right. Market behaviour is considerably affected by a country's value systems. Values are basic convictions of a group regarding what is good or bad, right or wrong, and important or unimportant. Values are learnt by a person while being reared in a culture that significantly influences one's behaviour. Value patterns vary among managers across countries, for instance, US managers are high-achievement- and competition-oriented and emphasize on profit maximization, organizational efficiency, and high productivity, whereas Japanese managers have strong emphasis on size and growth and high-value for competence and achievement. Indian managers have moral orientation and strong focus on organizational compliance and competence.

In an advertisement used by Proctor & Gamble (P&G) for Camay soap, a man meeting a woman for the first time compares her skin to that of a fine porcelain doll; this worked well in Europe and South America, but failed miserably in Japan, where it was considered to be unsophisticated or rude to a Japanese woman. Another Camay ad that showed a man walking onto his bathing wife who begins to tell him about her new beauty soap, worked well in Europe but not in Japan as it is considered bad manners for a husband to intrude upon his wife there. Thus, one needs to be culturally sensitive while marketing in foreign countries.

Cultural values tend to change over time. For instance, the Japanese business value system that lays high emphasis on life-time employment, group-orientation, formal authority, seniority, and paternalism has witnessed considerable change over the years.

Norms

Norms are guidelines or social rules that prescribe appropriate behaviour in a given situation. For instance, in Japan aggressive selling is not perceived in the positive spirit. Many companies, including Dell computers emphasize on the benefits in terms of lower price by direct selling instead of using aggressive selling tactics. Cultural norms affect consumption patterns and habits too. Indian and other South Asians generally use spoons of different sizes while eating. Chinese and Japanese use Chopsticks as the meat is pre-cut to small pieces but Europeans and Americans use knives and forks to cut the meat on the dining table.

International managers should be able to differentiate between what is acceptable or unacceptable in a foreign culture and familiarize themselves with cultural tolerance to business customs that may be grouped as follows.

Cultural imperatives   It refers to the norms that must be followed or must be avoided in a foreign country. Adherence to such business customs and expectations is crucial to one's success in foreign cultures. In relationship-focused oriental cultures, one is expected to develop mutual trust and rapport as a precondition to success in international markets.

To market effectively in cross-country business situations, international managers need to develop a broad understanding of cultural imperatives that need to be followed in one culture and avoided in another. For instance, a prolonged eye contact is considered to be offensive in Japan and, therefore, needs to be avoided. On the other hand, unless you establish strong eye contact in Latin America and Gulf countries, you are likely to be perceived as untrustworthy and evasive. Therefore, one needs to establish a strong eye contact while negotiating with an Arab. It should be remembered at the same time that establishing eye contact with a woman in Islamic Middle East is frowned upon.

Cultural exclusives   It refers to behaviour patterns or social customs which are appropriate for locals and foreigners are expected not to participate. For instance, foreign visitors should stay away from entering into any controversial discussions on the host country's internal politics, social customs, and practices.

Cultural adiaphora   It refers to social customs or behaviour in which a foreigner may conform to or participate but it is not imperative to do so. Thus, it is the discretion of the international manager either to participate or avoid such social customs. For instance, the ritual of bowing among Japanese is a complex protocol and foreigners are not expected to follow the same. However, an attempt to follow a symbolic bowing by foreigners is taken positively and reflects sensitivity to Japanese culture. A foreigner has an option to refuse an offer to eat or drink on personal, health-related, or religious grounds.

Therefore, international managers need to appreciate the social norms either to be followed or excluded in foreign cultures so as to avert occasional cultural mistakes in marketing overseas.

Aesthetics

Ideas and perceptions that a cultural group upholds in terms of beauty and good taste is referred to as aesthetics. It includes areas related to music, dance, painting, drama, architecture, etc.

Colours have different manifestation across cultures. For African consumers, bright colours are favourites, while in Japan pastels are considered to express softness and harmony and are preferred over bright colours. America's corporate colour blue is associated with evil in many African countries. In China, red is a lucky colour, whereas it is associated with death and witch-craft in a number of African countries. Green is often associated with disease in countries that have dense, green jungles, but is associated with cosmetics by the French, Dutch, and Swedes. Various colours represent death. Black signifies death to Americans and many Europeans, while in Japan and many other Asian countries white represents death. Latin Americans generally associate purple with death, but dark red is the appropriate mourning colour among the Ivory Coast. And even though white is the colour representing death in some countries; it expresses joy to those living in Ghana.

Traditions and customs

The word 'tradition' is derived from the Latin world *traditio* which means 'to hand down' or 'to hand over'. Traditions are the elements of culture passed down from generation to generation. An established pattern of behaviour within a society is known as a custom. It is an accepted rule of behaviour that is regulated informally by the social group. Since customs and traditions in a social group are passed on from one generation to another over thousands of years, they become ingrained into the social system.

Social environment also affects the motives behind a buying decision and communication strategies needs to be customized as per the varied social traits for different markets. Social beliefs and aspirations also vary significantly among countries and the marketing mix has to be tailor-made to suit the social norms of the target market.

The concept of Indian vegetarianism is too complex for outsiders to comprehend, where even the interchange between utensils in which vegetarian and non-vegetarian food, respectively, is cooked and served is frowned upon. Therefore, exclusive vegetarian food outlets, such as Haldiram and MTR thrive on a huge market segment. Kentucky Fried Chicken (KFC), synonymous with crispy chicken across the world, offers an exclusive vegetarian menu in India. Even McDonald's has adapted separate cooking facilities for vegetarian and non-vegetarian food and Pizza Hut has experimented with opening some exclusive vegetarian outlets in India.

In India and other South Asian countries, ghee (milk fat) is the most important constituent of milk and sells at premium price. Besides, it is used in preparation of a variety of Indian sweets and other cooking. On the other hand, in the majority of developed countries, defatted milk is preferred and costs higher than milk with fat. International mangers need to learn customs and traditions of the cultures being dealt with, appreciate them, and integrate the strategic response in the marketing strategy.

Language

Language can be described as a 'systematic means of communicating ideas or feelings by the use of conventionalized signs, gestures, marks, or especially articulate vocal sounds'.[5] Language is the most important element that sets human beings apart from the animals. Moreover, it is the most obvious difference among cultures. As languages evolve over considerable time, it also reveals several aspects about the nature and value of a culture. Sanskrit and Latin are the two major literary languages of the world from which a large number of languages have emanated over time. Besides, a number of modern languages are descendents of classical Chinese, ancient Greek, Persian, and Biblical Hebrew. Richness of vocabulary and grammar of a language reveals

---

[5] Webster's Dictionary.

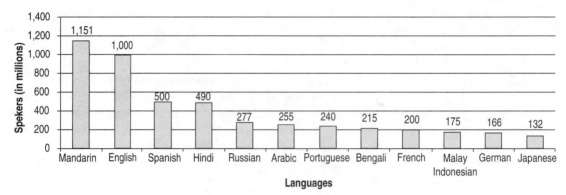

Fig. 5.2 World's most widely spoken languages

Source: KryssTal, 2010, www.krysstal.com/spoken.html, accessed on 18 October 2013.

significant attributes of a culture. As depicted in Fig. 5.2, Mandarin is the most widely used language in the world, followed by English, Spanish, and Hindi.

Languages differ very widely among nations and even regions. Language reflects the nature and value system of a culture. There have been several incidences worldwide of resistance towards communicating in foreign languages, which is often viewed as cultural imperialism. It was the difference in languages and love of the natives' for their mother tongue—Bangla—that gave rise to a conflict leading to the separation of Bangladesh from Pakistan. The French majority in the Québec Province of Canada forced upon a constitution amendment in 1992 to declare French as the official language, banning the use of foreign words in 1994. There is considerable resistance among Germans to learn French, which is perceived as cultural imperialism.

Ethnologue lists 6,909 living languages[6] in the world. 90 per cent of the world's languages are spoken by less than 1,00,000 speakers. Asia, with 61 per cent of total speakers in the world, account for 33.6 per cent of the total languages, whereas Europe, with 26.1 per cent of speakers, has merely 3.4 per cent of the world's total languages. Africa, with 12.2 per cent of speakers, has 30.5 per cent of the languages; America, with 0.8 per cent of speakers, has 14.1 per cent of languages; and the Pacific, with 0.1 per cent speakers, has 18 per cent of the languages.

Despite linguistic differences, English has become a lingua franca to communicate among non-English speaking people around the world. Conducting cross-country market research in English often fails to provide non-verbal cues to the respondents. Besides, issues related to translation of questionnaires or the uses of interpreters need to be addressed so as to ensure data compatibility. Therefore, use of natives and communicating in local languages are of extreme importance in international market research across regions with linguistic diversity.

Religion

Religion is a vital constituent of culture that significantly influences people's behaviour. It is imperative to understand the 'meaning' and 'significance' of religion across cultures. Religion encompasses three distinct elements,[7] which are as follows.

Explanation God seen as a 'first cause' behind the creation of the universe

---

[6] *Ethnologue: Languages of the World*, 16th Edition, SIL International, USA, 2009.

[7] Diamond, Jared, 'The Religious Success Story', *New York Review of Books*, 7 November 2002, pp. 30–31.

A standard organization   Consisting of places of worships and rituals

Moral rules of good behaviour   Concerning principles of right and wrong in human behaviour

Religious beliefs considerably influence international marketing decisions. In Southeast Asia, *feng shui*, which means wind-water, an ancient Chinese philosophy, plays an important role in designing and placement of retail space and construction of corporate buildings. Designs conforming to *feng shui* are considered to allow free flow of cosmic energy and keep away evil spirits. Major religious festivals, such as Christmas in Europe and the US, Ramadan in Islamic countries, Chinese New Year in East Asia, and Diwali in India and Nepal provide good marketing opportunities. Besides, the religious holidays also need to be considered while scheduling international business trips.

Generally, the consumption patterns are influenced considerably by religious beliefs. As most Indians do not eat beef and India has the second largest Muslim (who do not consume pork) population in the world, McDonald's serves neither beef nor pork in India. Besides, Indian vegetarianism is too difficult for foreigners to understand, where even an exchange of cooking utensils between the two groups is frowned upon. As a result and in an effort to respect the sensibilities of the two large consumer groups, India is perhaps the only country where McDonald's has separate kitchens for vegetarian and non-vegetarian food.

All advertisements need to be cleared by Islamic censoring authorities in Iran. Since Islam prohibits its followers from shaving, Gillette found it difficult to place an advertisement for its Gillette Blue II razor in Iran. After much effort, Gillette could convince the advertising manager of a local newspaper to this end by arguing that sometimes shaving becomes essential, for instance, in case of head injuries resulting from an accident.[8]

Christianity is the largest religion in the world with 2.1 billion adherents accounting for 33 per cent of the total population (Table 5.1), whereas Islam with 1.3 billion (21%) ranks second and Hinduism with 900 million (14%) ranks third.[9] About 1.1 billion people (16%) hardly follow any religion. Chinese traditional religion is followed by 394 million (6%), Buddhism by 376 million (6%), and Sikhism by 23 million (0.6%). Other religions followed include Judaism (14 million), Bahai (7 million), Jainism (4.2 million), and Shinto (4 million).

Islam is the fastest growing religion in the world with 1.84 per cent growth rate, followed by Bahai (1.70%), Sikhism (1.62%), Jainism (1.57%), Hinduism (1.52%), and Christianity (1.38%). Hinduism, followed by over 80 per cent of India's population, is the only surviving major ancient religion that has no founder. Hinduism had strong cultural influence on several other countries (Exhibit 5.1) too.

Marketing in Islamic countries   Religions, such as Christianity, Buddhism, and Hinduism largely remain in the private domain. On the other hand, in Islamic countries, business is considerably influenced by the religion.

Islamic cultures greatly affect the behaviour of women consumers and emphasize upon separation of males and females in public places. Consequently, it is difficult to conduct field surveys or personal selling to women consumers by male researchers. Therefore, it is better to engage women in business activities when interaction with women is needed in Islamic countries. In Arabian countries, the dolls Sara and Leila that compete with Barbie have 'brother dolls' and not 'boyfriend dolls' as the concept of having a boyfriend may not be acceptable to

---

[8] 'Smooth Talk Wins Gillette Ad Space in Iran', *Advertising Age International*, 8 November 1993, pp. 1–21.
[9] www.adherants.com, assessed on 1 June 2012.

Table 5.1   Major religions of the world

	Christianity	Islam	Hinduism	Buddhism
Number of followers (%)	2.1 billion	1.3 billion	900 million	376 million
Founder	Jesus Christ	Muhammad	No founder	Gautam Buddha
Year and place of foundation	AD 30, Jerusalem	AD 570, Mecca (Saudi Arabia)	Dates to pre-historic times, oldest religion in the world	4th or 5th century BC, India
Number of gods	One	One	Numerous	None, but there are enlightened beings (Buddhas)
Holy book	Bible	Koran	No single holy book, the four Vedas are most ancient	Many including the Tripitaka, the Mahayana Sutras, Tantra and Zen texts
Types	Christians separated in 1054 into the Eastern Orthodox Church and the Roman Catholic Church. Major Protestant groups separated in 1500s. Subsequently, a variety of other groups also developed.	Sunnis (90%) and Shiites (10%). In 632, when Muhammad died, Shiites split from the Sunnis.	No single belief system unites Hindus. A Hindu can believe in only one god, in many, or in none.	Theravada (Way of the Elders) and Mahayana (Greater Vehicle).
Region	Christianity has spread to most parts of the world through its missionary activity.	Middle East, Asia and the North of Africa	India (81%), Nepal (81%), Maurititius (48%), Fiji (38%), Guyana (35%), Suriname (27%), Bhutan (25%)	East Asia

Exhibit 5.1   Global reach of Indian deities

Many Hindu and Buddhist deities worshipped in India are also revered in other countries. Ganesha, the destructor of all obstacles, is a true global Indian deity known as Sho-ten in Japan, Ho Tei in China, and Virakosha in Mexico. Ganesha (Sho-ten) in Japan symbolizes the joy of life that rises from the power rooted in the virtues of wisdom and compassion. Elderly people worship the deity to get prosperity and money (Fig. 5.3), whereas the young Japanese boys and girls worship Him to achieve success in love. In Indonesia, the country with the world's largest Muslim population, Ganesha has been depicted even on currency notes and shares space along with the Indonesian President Ki Hadjar Dewantara, as shown in Fig. 5.4.

Three of the seven lucky gods worshipped in Japan, that is, Daikoku-ten (Mahakala/Maheshvara), Benten/Benzai-ten (Saraswati), and Bishamon-ten (Kuber/Kuvera), have an Indian origin from Hinduism. Besides, the 'seed mantra' used in many worships in Japan still continues to be from their original Sanskrit name. Some other Hindu gods and goddesses worshipped in Japan include the sea-god Varuna (Suiten), the king of gods Indra (Taishakuten),

the goddess of fortune Lakshmi (Kichijoten), and the divine architect Vishvakarma (Bishukatsuma). The four lokpalas (Shitenno) of Hindu mythology, that is, Kuber (Bishamon), Yama (Zouchoten), Indra (Jikokuten), and Varuna (Koumokuten) also find place among Japanese deities. Some of the Hindu deities with multiple roles are split into multiple Japanese deities, each having a specific role. The Siddham script used by Shingon Buddhists in Japan for Sanskrit mantras/sutras has its lineage from the Sanskrit script.

Saraswati is believed to be the goddess for learning and is also the name of a river in India. Saraswati is referred to as Benzaiten or Benten in Japan and is almost always associated with water. She is considered to be a beautiful goddess of fortune and is depicted holding a traditional Japanese musical instrument biwa (a Japanese counterpart of Indian veena). Her shrines are built either on beautiful lakesides or seasides. Interestingly, the vahana (vehicle) of Indra, the elephant Airavata, has been reduced in size to a horse in Japanese mythology, perhaps due to the fact that the ancient Japanese never had an opportunity to see a real living elephant.

(Contd)

Exhibit 5.1 (*Contd*)

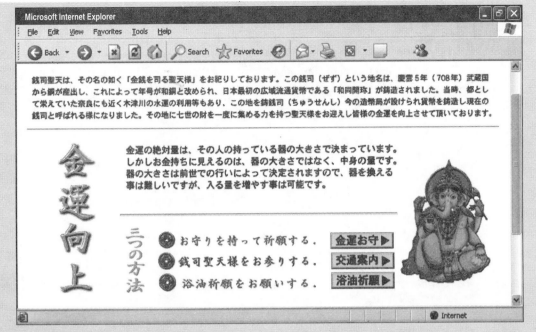

Fig. 5.3 The global Ganesha (Sho-ten) as a revered deity in Japan

Source: www.z-shoten.or.jp, accessed on 18 October 2013.

Fig. 5.4 Islamic Indonesia's currency with Hindu deity Ganesha

Source: Wikimedia Commons, http://commons.wikimedia.org/wiki/File:Indonesia_1998_20000r_o.jpg, accessed on 18 October 2013.

Indra, Ganesha, Saraswati, Mahakala, Bodhisattva Manjusri, Bodhisattva Avalokitesvara or Lokesvara, Sakyamuni Buddha, and Amitabha Buddha are some of the examples which have widely attracted the worship of the Japanese people. The Hindu gods and goddesses worshipped in Japan today were originally introduced to Japan from China as an integral part of the Buddhist pantheon. These Vedic and Hindu deities had undergone certain transformations in terms of their appellations, characteristics, and even appearances in China in the course of acceptance, especially through the process of translating sutras and transliterating Buddhist terminology from Sanskrit to classical Chinese.

Sources: 'Ganesha: A Global Indian', *The Times of India*, 9 September 2006; Okabe, Takamichi, 'Nepalese Deities in Japan', Embassy of Japan, Nepal; Atjeh, Hidayat, 'Ancient Ganesha in Indonesia', Socio-Culture and Information Indonesian Consulate General in Mumbai.

Islamic families. Implications of Islam on international marketing decisions are summarized in Exhibit 5.2.

All Muslims are expected to consume meat obtained through the 'halal' method of slaughter. Therefore, restaurants in Islamic countries highlight in their marketing communication that only halal meat is used for cooking food. Islamic countries also require a certificate from exporting countries along with the meat consignments certifying that genuine halal process has been used in slaughtering the animals.

Exhibit 5.2   Implications of Islam in international marketing decisions

Elements	Implications for marketing
I. Fundamental Islamic concepts	
A. Unity (concept of centrality, oneness of God, harmony in life)	Product standardization, mass media techniques, central balance, unity in advertising copy and layout, strong brand loyalties, a smaller evoked size set, loyalty to company, opportunities for brand-extension strategies.
B. Legitimacy (fair dealings, reasonable level of profits)	Less formal product warranties, need for institutional advertising and/or advocacy advertising, especially by foreign firms, and a switch from profit maximizing to a profit satisfying strategy.
C. *Zakaat* (2.5% per annum) compulsory tax binding on all classified as 'not poor'	Use of 'excessive' profits, if any, for charitable acts: corporate donations for charity, institutional advertising.
D. Usury (cannot charge interest on loans. A general interpretation of this law defines 'excessive interest' charged on loans as not permissible.)	Avoid direct use of credit as a marketing tool. Establish a consumer policy of paying cash for low-value products; for high-value products, offer discounts for cash payments and raise prices of products on an installment basis. Sometimes it is possible to conduct interest transactions between local/foreign firms in other non-Islamic countries; banks in some Islamic countries take equity in financing ventures, sharing resultant profits (and losses).
E. Supremacy of human life (compared to other forms of life, objects, human life of supreme importance)	Pet food and/or products are less important. Avoid use of statues and busts interpreted as forms of idolatry. Symbols in advertising and/or promotion should reflect high human values. Use floral designs and artwork in advertising as representation of aesthetic values.
F. Community (all Muslim should strive to achieve universal brotherhood, with allegiance to the 'one God'. One way of expressing community is the required pilgrimage to Mecca for all Muslims at least once in their lifetime, if able to do so.)	Formation of an Islamic economic community; development of an 'Islamic consumer' served with Islamic-oriented products and services, for example, 'kosher' meat packages, gifts exchanged at Muslim festivals, and so forth; development of community services; need for marketing of non-profit organizations and skills.
G. Equality of people	Participative communication systems; roles and authority structures maybe rigidly defined but accessibility at any level to be relatively easy.
H. Abstinence (During the month of Ramadan, Muslims are required to fast without food or drink from the first streak of dawn to sunset—a reminder to those who are more fortunate to be kind to the less fortunate and as an exercise in self-control. Consumption of alcohol and pork is forbidden; so is gambling.)	Products that are nutritious, cool, and digested easily to be formulated for *Sehr* and *Iftar* (beginning and end of the fast). Opportunities for developing non-alcoholic items and beverages (for example, soft drinks, ice cream, milk shakes, fruit juices) and non-chance social games, such as Scrabble; food products to use vegetable or beef shortening.

(Contd)

Exhibit 5.2 (*Contd*)

I. Environmentalism (The universe created by God was pure. Consequently, land, air, and water should be held as sacred elements.)	Anticipate environmental, anti-pollution acts; opportunities for companies involved in maintaining a clean environment; easier acceptance of pollution-control devices in the community.
J. Worship (five times a day; timing of prayers varied)	Need to take into account the variability and shift in prayer timings in planning sales calls, work schedules, business hours, customer traffic, and so forth.
II. Islamic culture	
A. Obligations to family and tribal traditions	Importance of respected members in the family or tribe as opinion leaders; word-of-mouth communication, customer referrals may be critical; social or clan allegiances, affiliations, and associations may be possible surrogates for reference groups; advertising home-oriented products stressing family roles may be highly effective, for example, that of electronic games.
B. Obligations towards parents are sacred	Image of functional products to be enhanced with advertisements that stress parental advice or approval; even with children's products, less emphasis on children as decision-makers.
	Product designs that are symbols of hospitality outwardly open in expression; rate of new product acceptance may be accelerated and erased by appeals based on community.
C. Obligation to extend hospitality to both insiders and outsiders	More colourful clothing and accessories are worn by women at home, so promotion of products for use in private homes to be more intimate—such audiences to be reached effectively through women's magazines; avoid use of immodest exposure and sexual implications in public settings.
D. Obligation to conform to codes of sexual conduct and social interaction. These may include	Access to female consumers often gained only through women as selling agents, salespeople, catalogues, home demonstrations, and women's speciality shops.
1. modest dress for women in public	
2. separation of male and female audiences in some cases	
E. Obligations to religious occasions (Two major religious observances, celebrated as Eid-ud-Fitr and Eid-ul-Adha)	Purchase of new shoes, clothing, and sweets and preparation of food items for family reunions and Muslim gatherings; practice of giving money in place of gifts increasingly changing to more gift-giving; due to lunar calendar, festival dates not fixed.

Source: Mushtaq, Luqumain, Zahir A. Quraeshi, and Linda Delene, 'Marketing in Islamic Countries: A Viewpoint', *MSU Business Topics*, Summer 1980, pp. 20–21.

CULTURAL GLOBALIZATION

Convergence of cultures across the world is often termed as cultural globalization. India's rich cultural heritage has a glorious history of globalization (Exhibit 5.3) which is evident even today by its profound impact on people and their lives. Globalization has led to the development of global pop culture. Coca Cola is sold in more countries than the United Nations has members. 'Coke' is claimed to be the second-most universally understood word after 'OK'. McDonald's has more than 30,000 local restaurants serving 52 million people everyday in more than 100 countries. Levi's jeans are sold in more than 110 countries. Ronald McDonald is second only to Santa Claus in name recognition for most school children.

Exhibit 5.3 India's cultural globalization

In the 16th century, at a time when North India was reeling under waves of conquests and cultural stagnation, people from South India were exporting Indianness to Southeast Asia. It was an anonymous task carried out not by warrier heroes blazing across land bearing swords of conquest, but by individuals who had come in peace, to trade, to teach, and to persuade. Their impact was profound. Even to this day, the kings of Thailand are only crowned in the presence of Brahmin priests; Muslims in Java still sport Sanskrit names, despite their conversion to Islam, a faith whose adherents normally bear names originating in Arabia; Garuda is Indonesia's best selling airline, and Ramayana its best selling brand of clove cigars; even the Philippines has produced a pop-dance ballet about Rama's quest for his kidnapped queen Sita.

Angkor Wat, perhaps the greatest Hindu temple ever built in the world, is in Cambodia, not in India. The exquisite sculptures in the temple recount tales from the great Indian epics, the Ramayana and the Mahabharata. At the site, Cambodian guides earnestly explain the significance of the symbols protecting the shrine—the *naga*, the *shimha*, and the *garuda*, corresponding to present-day navy, army, and air force. The marvel at the epic scale of the Hindu temple as impressive as the finest cathedral or mosque anywhere in the world is also a marvel at the extraordinary reach of the Indian culture beyond its own shores.

Hinduism was brought to Cambodia by merchants and travellers more than a millennium ago, and has long since disappeared, supplanted by Buddhism that was also an Indian export. But, at its peak, Hinduism influenced the culture, music, dance, and mythology of the Cambodian people.

Right at the entrance of Thailand's Suvarnabhoomi International Airport in Bangkok is a fascinating sculpture depicting the Hindu mythological story of the 'Churning of the Oceans' between the demons and the gods on the other evidences India's deep-rooted cultural globalization. 'Yoga', essentially an Indian culture export, is widely practised across the globe, with over 16 million persons practising Yoga in the US alone (Fig. 5.5) that nearly tripled from

Fig. 5.5 Yoga in Times Square

Source: http://www.flickr.com/photos/familyclan/8409525969/ sizes/c/in/photostream/, accessed on 2 April 2014.

6 million in 1994. The Yoga market in the US alone is estimated at US$6 billion.

Indian culture can be characterized by its exceptional capability to imbibe align cultures, and this feature distinguishes it from the rest of the world. India's present day civilization draws heavily from Islam and Christianity consequent to Muslim invasions and British colonial rules. A Hindu bridegroom invariably puts on a Sherwani during the wedding ceremony, a practice which did not exist before the Muslim invasion of India. The alien cricket is India's virtual national sport. In selecting the 'seven new wonders of the world', Indians voted cynically for the Taj Mahal, constructed by Mughal king Shah Jahan and not for the Angkor Wat, the most magnificent architect of the Hindu religion, a fact which testifies to the uniqueness of Indian culture.

Diversity of Indian culture and its extraordinary capability not only to imbibe but also adapt to foreign cultures adds to its worldwide acceptability and makes it more relevant than ever before in the era of political, social, and economic turmoil across countries.

Source: Based on Tharoor, Shashi, 'Let's Promote the Great Indic Civilisation', *The Times of India*, New Delhi, 21 October 2007; 'Yoga as an Olympic Sport?', CNN, 27 May 2012; 'Yoga: American Style', *New York Times*, 1 March 2012.

COMPARISON OF CROSS-CULTURAL BEHAVIOUR

Attempts have been made to carry out cross-country comparisons of cultural behaviour so as to develop better understanding among cultures. An appreciation of cultural differences facilitates international managers to conceptualize and implement marketing strategies in view of culture sensitivities in various countries. Major types of cross-cultural classifications are discussed here.

Hofstede's Cultural Classification

The most widely used tool to study cross cultural behaviour is the Hofstede's classification, which identified cross-cultural differences based on a massive survey of 1,16,000 respondents from 70 countries working in IBM subsidiaries. Hofstede's classification involves the following.

Power distance

The degree of inequality among people that is viewed equitable is known as 'power distance'. It is the extent to which less powerful members of an institution accept that power is distributed unequally. As indicated in Fig. 5.6, power distance in Malaysia is the highest while it is the lowest in case of Austria. Power distance in India is on a higher side. In the UK and Scandinavian and Dutch countries, managers expect their decision-making to be challenged, while the French consider the authority to take decisions as their right. Germans feel more comfortable in formal hierarchies, while the Dutch have a relaxed approach to their authorities.

In countries with large power distance, hierarchical organizational structures are based on inequality among superiors and subordinates and juniors blindly follow the orders of their superiors. Generally, high social inequalities are tolerated in cultures with wide differences in power and income distribution. Small power distance is characterized by egalitarian societies, in which superiors and subordinates consider each others more equal. Organizations are relatively flatter and decision-making is decentralized.

Power distance greatly affects the international marketing decision-making process. In view of the power distance, an international manager has to assess the organizational dynamics, identify the key decision-makers, and accordingly formulate their marketing strategy for different countries.

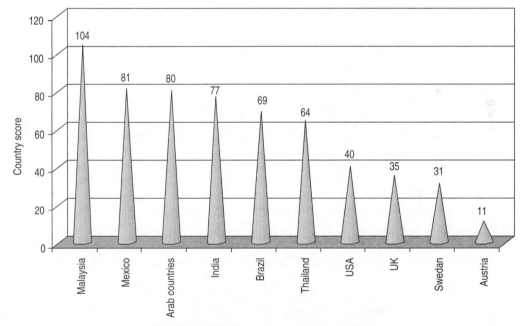

Fig. 5.6   Hofstede's value survey: power distance

Source: Hofstede, Geert, *Culture's Consequences: International Differences in Work-related Values*, Sage Publications, Beverly Hills, CA, 1980.

Individualism vs collectivism

The tendency of people to look after themselves and only their immediate family is termed as individualism. Societies with high level of individualism tend to have strong work ethics, promotions are based on merit, and involvement of employees in the organizations is primarily calculative. The ability to be independent of others is considered to be the key criterion for success in individualistic

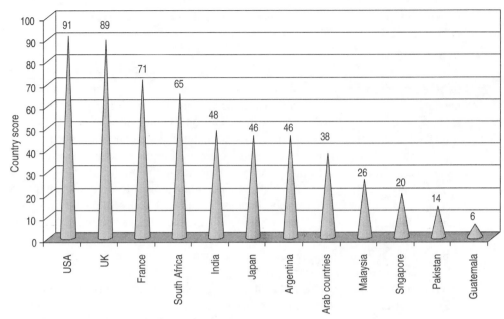

Fig. 5.7 Hofstede's value survey: individualism

Source: Hofstede, Geert, *Culture's Consequences: International Differences in Work-related Values*, Sage Publications, Beverly Hills, CA, 1980.

societies. Collectivism is referred to the tendency of people to belong to groups and to look after each other in exchange for loyalty. The interests of groups have precedence over individual interests.

As indicated in Fig. 5.7, the USA, the UK, and France have highly individualistic societies, while Guatemala, Pakistan, Singapore, and Malaysia show high level of collectivism. International marketing strategy is greatly influenced by individualism versus collectivism in terms of decision-making and market communication. For a product to be successful in collective societies, such as Guatemala, Ecuador, Panama, Venezuela, Malaysia, and Japan, it should have group acceptability unlike in individualistic societies of the USA, Australia, UK, and Canada.

Masculinity vs femininity

In masculine societies, the dominant values emphasize on work goals, such as earnings, advancement, success, and material belongings. On the other hand, the dominant values in a feminine society are achievement of personal goals, such as quality of life, caring for others, friendly atmosphere, getting along with boss and others. Summarily, in masculine societies, people 'live to work', while in feminine societies, people 'work to live'.

As indicated in Fig. 5.8, Scandinavian countries such as Sweden, Norway, and Denmark are highly feminine, while Japan is highly masculine. India falls in between, indicating a balanced emphasis on personal and work goals. In feminine societies, such as Sweden, Norway, Netherlands, and Denmark, the gender equality is much greater compared to that in masculine societies such as Japan, Austria, Venezuela, Italy, and the USA.

Uncertainty avoidance

Uncertainty avoidance refers to lack of tolerance for ambiguity and need for formal rules. It measures the extent to which people feel threatened by ambiguous situations. As indicated in Fig. 5.9, Greece, Poland, and Japan are the most uncertainty avoidance societies, while Singapore, Denmark, and India are the least uncertainty avoidance societies.

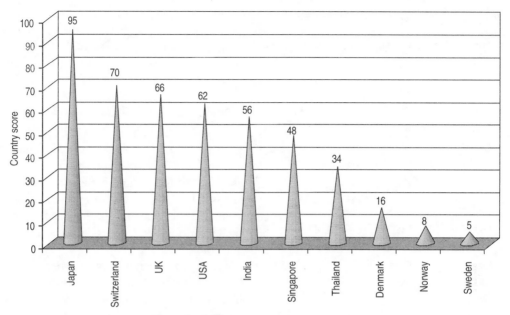

Fig. 5.8   Hofstede's value survey: masculinity

Source: Hofstede, Geert, *Culture's Consequences: International Differences in Work-related Values*, Sage Publications, Beverly Hills, CA, 1980.

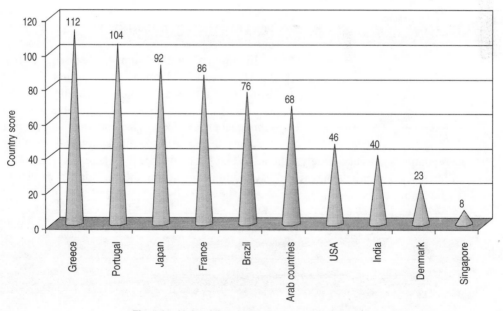

Fig. 5.9   Hofstede's value survey: uncertainty avoidance

Source: Hofstede, Geert, *Culture's Consequences: International Differences in Work-related Values*, Sage Publications, Beverly Hills, CA, 1980.

Table 5.2 Trompenaars' voluntary abbreviations

Abbreviation	Country
ARG	Argentina
AUS	Austria
BEL	Belgium
BRZ	Brazil
CHI	China
CIS	Former Soviet Union
CZH	Former Czechoslovakia
FRA	France
GER	Germany (excluding former East Germany)
HK	Hong Kong
IDO	Indonesia
ITA	Italy
JPN	Japan
MEX	Mexico
NL	Netherlands
SIN	Singapore
SPA	Spain
SWE	Sweden
SWI	Switzerland
THA	Thailand
UK	United Kingdom
USA	United States
VEN	Venezuela

In high uncertainty avoidance societies, such as Japan, Portugal, and Greece, lifetime employment is more common, whereas in low uncertainty avoidance societies, such as Singapore, Denmark, India, and the USA, job mobility is more common.[10]

Trompenaars' Cultural Classification

The Dutch researcher, Fons Trompenaars, conducted research over a ten-year period administering questionnaires to over 15,000 managers from 28 countries and published the findings in 1994. Each of the cultural dimensions of Trompenaars' research is defined on the basis of the usable responses received from at least 500 managers in each country. The abbreviated terms for 23 countries, included in his report, are shown in Table 5.2.

Trompenaars' five cultural dimensions address the way in which people deal with each other. This helps in explaining the cultural differences and offers practical ways in which MNCs can market in various countries.

Universalism vs particularism

Universalism is the belief that ideas and practices can be defined and applied everywhere without modification. On the contrary, particularism is the belief that unique circumstances and relationships, rather than abstract rules, are more important considerations that determine how ideas and practices should be applied.

In cultures with high universalism (Fig. 5.10), such as the USA, Austria, Germany, Sweden, and the UK, the focus is more on formal rules than on relationships. Whereas in particularist cultures, such as Venezuela, CIS, Indonesia, China, Hong Kong, and Thailand, the focus is more on relationships than on rules. In high universalism cultures, business contracts are very closely adhered to and 'a deal is a deal', whereas in high particularism cultures, legal contracts may readily be modified honouring the changing circumstances based on the reality of the situation.

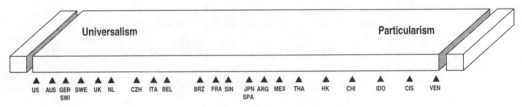

Fig. 5.10 Universalism vs particularism

---

[10] Adler, N.J. and S. Bartholomeu, 'Managing Globally Competent People', *Academy of Management Executive*, 1992, vol. 6, pp. 52–65.

Individualism vs communitarianism

Trompenaars' communitarianism seems to be an analogue of Hofstede's collectivism. Individualism refers to people regarding themselves as individuals, whereas communitarianism refers to people regarding themselves as part of a group. Societies with high individualism make more frequent use of 'I' and 'me'; decisions are typically made on the spot by a representative during business negotiations; and achievement and responsibility are also personal. On the contrary, in collectivist societies, 'we' is used more frequently than 'I'; business decisions are typically referred back to the organization; achievement is considered to be a group achievement; and managers believe in joint responsibility. The USA, Czechoslovakia, Argentina, the CIS, Mexico, and the UK rank high on individualism (Fig. 5.11), whereas Singapore, Thailand, Japan, and Indonesia rank high on communitarianism.

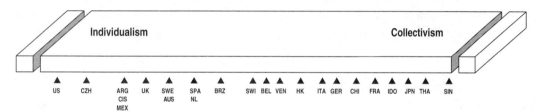

Fig. 5.11   Individualism vs collectivism

Neutral vs affective

All human beings have emotions but this dimension deals with the different contexts and ways in which emotions are expressed by various cultures. In affective cultures, emotions are expressed openly and are more 'natural', whereas in neutral cultures, people tend to hold in check their emotions and try not to explicitly exhibit their feelings. Neutral cultures often consider anger, delight, or intensity in the workplace as 'unprofessional', whereas affective cultures regard holding back of emotions by colleagues to signify 'emotionally dead' or a 'mask of deceit'. In affective cultures, people often smile, laugh, talk loudly, and exhibit a great deal of enthusiasm in greeting each other. Managers from neutral cultures such as the UK, Japan, Singapore, and Australia (Fig. 5.12) need to be open to the emotional behaviour displayed in affective cultures, such as Mexico, Netherlands, Switzerland, China, and Brazil.

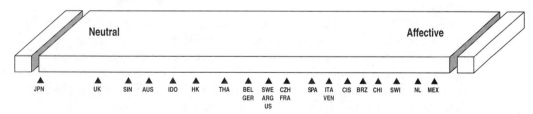

Fig. 5.12   Neutral vs affective

Specific vs diffuse

The degree of involvement, that is, how comfortable individuals are in dealing with other people varies across cultures. Individuals have various levels to their personality—from a more public or outer layer to a more private or inner level. The relative size of people's public and private 'spaces' and the degree to which individuals feel comfortable sharing them with others differs considerably among cultures. In specific cultures, individuals tend to have a large public space and a smaller private space. They readily share public space, whereas the personal life is kept separate, closely guarded, and shared only with close friends and associates. On the contrary, in diffuse cultures, public and private space is more or less similar and public space is guarded more carefully because entry into public space gives more accessibility to individuals' private space.

Work and private lives are separate in specific cultures, whereas these are closely linked in diffuse cultures. Countries such as Australia, the UK, the USA, and Switzerland (Fig. 5.13) are characterized by a small, intimate private layer that is well separated from more public outer layers. On the other hand, in Venezuela, China, and Spain, personality structures have large private areas separated from a relatively small public layer. Doing business in cultures more diffused compared to one's own is considered highly time consuming. 'Work' is set apart from the rest of life in specific cultures, whereas everything is connected to everything else in diffused cultures. Therefore, it is important to invest time and resources and build relationships for operating in countries with diffused cultures.

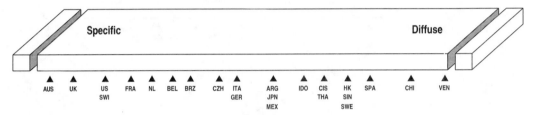

Fig. 5.13   Specific vs diffuse

Achievement vs ascription

Cultures differ in the way how status and power in a society are determined. Such social status and power may be attributed either to a person's own efforts and achievements or as a birthright. In achievement cultures, people are evaluated and accorded social status based on how well they perform their allocated functions. In ascription cultures, status is accorded to individuals who 'naturally' evoke admiration from others, such as the elderly, seniors in the organization, and highly qualified and skilled people. Status in ascription cultures is generally independent of a task or specific functions and society tends to show respect to such distinguished people who are not easily compared with others.

Austria, the USA, Switzerland, the UK, Sweden, and Mexico (Fig. 5.14) possess high achievement cultures, whereas Venezuela, Indonesia, China, the CIS, and Singapore have ascription cultures. Managers from ascription cultures doing business with achievement cultures need to emphasize upon facts and figures, data analysis, and sound technical strength. On the other hand, managers from achievement cultures doing business with ascription cultures need to be careful to show due respect to the elderly, seniors, and formal position holders.

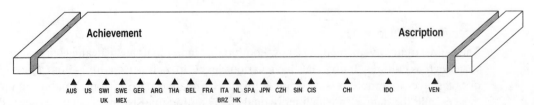

Fig. 5.14   Achievement vs ascription

Other Cross-cultural Classifications

Other forms of cross-cultural classifications, such as those based on cultural context, homogeneity, focus on relationship versus focus on business deal, formality, time, and communications also provide a useful insight into international marketing decisions.

High context vs low context

The context of a culture has crucial implications[11] in communicating and interpreting verbal and non-verbal messages. Different cultures interpret verbal and non-verbal cues differently. The cultural context influences marketing decisions in several ways, especially in different marketing communication situations.

In high context cultures, implicit communications such as non-verbal and subtle situational cues are extremely important. On the other hand, in low context cultures, communication is more explicit and relies heavily on words to convey the meaning. In high context cultures, the relationship is long lasting, while in low context cultures the relationship is shorter in duration. Verbal commitments are given high sanctity in high context cultures, while commitments in low context cultures are written. Figure 5.15 indicates cultural context[12] for select cultures.

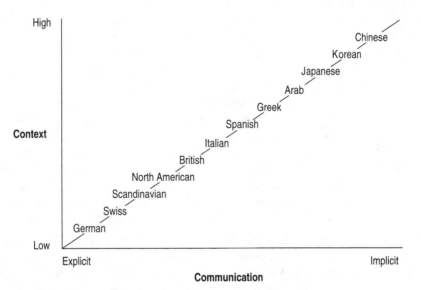

Fig. 5.15 Cultural context of various countries

Source: Duleck, R.E., J.S. Fielden, and J.S. Hall, 'International Communication: An Exclusive Premier', *Business Horizons*, January–February 1991.

The market promotion and advertising has to be subtle in high-context cultures, while it should focus on explicit display of information and facts in low-context cultures. The marketing firms rotate sales teams more frequently in low-context cultures. However, in high context cultures where building relationships with the clients is extremely important, the sales force tend to have longer duration of operation in assigned territories.

---

[11] Hall, E.T., *Beyond Cultures*, Anchor Press/Doubleday, New York, 1976, pp. 1–16.

[12] Duleck, R.E., J.S. Fielden, and J.S. Hall, 'International Communication: An Exclusive Premier', *Business Horizons*, January–February 1991.

Homophilous vs heterophilous

On the basis of homogeneity, culture may be divided into the following subsets.

Homophilous   Cultures where people share the same beliefs, speak the same language, and practise the same religion are referred to as homophilous. Japan, Korea, and Scandinavian countries generally have homophilous cultures. Diffusion of new products takes much less time in homophilous cultures, in which relatively uniform marketing mix decisions can be adopted.

Heterophilous cultures   In countries with heterophilous cultures, there is a fair amount of differentiation in language, beliefs, and religions followed. India and China are countries with heterophilous cultures, wherein the variations in culture within provinces are significant. The marketing communication strategies, in such cases, will have to incorporate new changes and adapt to given sets of cultural norms from region to region.

Relationship-focused vs deal-focused

Relationship-focused cultures lay heavy emphasis on human relationship, whereas deal-focused cultures are task-oriented. When managers from deal-focused cultures do business with relationship-focused cultures, conflicts often arise. This is beacuse relationship-focused people find deal-focused people aggressive, offensive, and even blunt, whereas deal-focused managers find relationship-focused people vague, slack, and enigmatic. The fundamental differences between the two kinds of cultures determine one's success in international markets.

In China, *guanxi*, which means 'relationships', 'connections', or 'networks', is crucial to success. Establishing a *guanxi* relationship makes a person feel obligated to help the other. Essence of *guanxi* lies in a strong emotional relationship that is often overlooked by outsiders. Building trust, understanding, and personal relationship is vital to developing economic relationship, not only in China but also in other Asian countries. *Guanxi* can be established by having some commonalities, called *tong,* like being in the same industry, company, school or university, or coming from the same region. Sometimes, *guanxi* is also established through exchanging gifts or personal favours. In Egypt, *wastah*, an intermediary or personal contact, in Russia, *blat* and in many Latin American countries, *palanca* are used to express similar connotations. Although it takes considerable time, patience, and commitment to establish personal relationships, such social contacts often help one in the time of need in relationship-focused cultures.

Relationship-focused   In relationship-focused cultures, people have strong orientation towards building relationships and developing mutual trust. Relationship-focused cultures include India, Bangladesh, Indonesia, Malaysia, Japan, China, Vietnam, Thailand, Philippines, South Korea, Singapore, Saudi Arabia, UAE, Egypt, Brazil, Mexico, and Russia. The key features of relationship-focused cultures include

- reluctance to approach strangers for marketing, use of intermediaries, use of trade shows and exhibitions to meet prospects;
- high emphasis on building relationship and establishing rapport;
- indirect, polite, and high-context communication;
- face-to-face negotiations and meetings;
- importance given to 'saving face', dignity, and respect;
- lawyers kept in the background during negotiations; and
- verbal deals emphasized over written contracts.

Therefore, it is important to establish personal rapport in relationship-focused cultures, which are hesitant to conduct business with strangers. Marketing managers get things done in relationship-focused cultures through intricate networks of personal contacts. Managers from relationship-focused cultures prefer to deal with acquaintances, friends, and family members with greater trust. Thus, it is important to have a thorough understanding of prospective business partners in relationship-focused cultures before entering into business deals with strangers, especially foreigners.

Deal-focused　Managers from deal-focused cultures, such as the USA and the Nordic countries are open to discuss business prospects with strangers. Making appointments is easy and quick in deal-focused cultures, whereas in relationship-focused cultures one has to establish indirect contacts through acquaintances or a third party introduction. Trade missions and embassies are often considered in high esteem and are effective for getting initial contacts. Countries, such as France, Belgium, Italy, Spain, and Hungary form part of moderately deal-focused cultures whereas Britain, the USA, Germany, Denmark, Australia, Canada, Finland, the Netherlands, and the Czech Republic have deal-focused cultures. Key features of deal-focused cultures include

- openness to talking business with strangers;
- directly approaching prospective clients;
- clarity of understanding, given more importance than harmony;
- direct, frank, low-context communication;
- communication via telephone, email, and faxes;
- little or no concept of 'saving face';
- lawyers forming part of negotiation; and
- reliance on written agreements and contracts.

Formal vs informal

When informal business managers from relatively egalitarian cultures interact with their formal counterparts from hierarchical cultures, there is a fear that their informality may offend status-conscious people from formal societies.

Formal　Countries such as India, Bangladesh, Indonesia, Malaysia, Vietnam, Thailand, Philippines, Saudi Arabia, UAE, Egypt, Greece, Brazil, Russia, Poland, Romania, Japan, China, South Korea, Singapore, France, Belgium, Italy, Spain, Hungary, Britain, Germany, Denmark, Finland, the Netherlands, and Czech Republic are classified as possessing formal cultures. In formal cultures,

- formality is used to show respect;
- status differences are large and valued;
- counterparts are addressed by title or family name; and
- protocol rituals are numerous and elaborate.

Informal　The USA, Canada, and Australia are among countries with an informal culture. In informal cultures,

- informal behaviour is not considered disrespectful;
- status differences are not valued;
- counterparts are addressed by first name; and
- protocol rituals are few and simple.

Polychronic (fluid time) vs monochronic (rigid time)

Based on adherence of time schedules, cultures may be classified as polychronic or monochronic.

Polychronic (fluid time)　In polychronic cultures, people have a relaxed approach to time schedules, punctuality, and meeting deadlines, which makes managers from rigid time cultures often frustrated. The word 'tip' is derived from the phrase 'to insure promptness' in such cultures.

India, Bangladesh, Indonesia, Malaysia, Vietnam, Thailand, Philippines, Saudi Arabia, UAE, Egypt, Greece, Brazil, Russia, Poland, and Romania may be classified under fluid time (polychronic) cultures. Key attributes of polychronic culture are that

- people and relationships are more important than punctuality and precise scheduling;
- schedules and deadlines are flexible; and
- meetings are frequently interrupted.

In polychronic cultures, people often avert rigid deadlines. For instance, the Arabian term *Insha'Allah* frequently used in the Middle East means 'god willing', that is, things will happen if the Almighty wishes so. Thus, it is God and not man who is in-charge of what is going to happen. In oriental countries, such as India and Singapore, business meetings usually start within five to ten minutes of the scheduled time, whereas social functions, such as a dinner, a birthday, or a wedding party may begin even one to two hours late.

Monochronic (rigid time)   France, Belgium, Italy, Spain, and Hungary form part of moderately monochronic cultures, whereas the USA, Japan, China, South Korea, Singapore, Britain, Canada, Australia, Germany, Denmark, Finland, and the Netherlands have rigid time (monochronic) cultures. The salient features of monochronic culture include

- primacy of punctuality and schedules;
- rigid schedules and deadlines; and
- seldom interrupted meetings.

Therefore, international managers from polychronic cultures scheduling business meetings in monochronic cultures need to be extra punctual about time since any delay is considered to be rude. On the other hand, international managers from monochronic cultures when interacting with their counterparts from polychronic cultures need to have patience.

Expressive vs reserved cultures

Communication patterns in expressive cultures are radically different from their reserved counterparts. This is true for all types of communications, such as non-verbal, para-verbal, and verbal. This can lead to major confusions and problems in international marketing activities.

Expressive   Saudi Arabia, UAE, Egypt, Greece, Brazil, Mexico, France, Belgium, Italy, Spain, and Hungary possess expressive cultures, whereas the USA, Russia, Poland, Romania, Australia, and Canada may be said to have variably expressive cultures. The key characteristics of expressive cultures are that

- people speak louder, interrupt frequently, and are uncomfortable with silence;
- interpersonal space is half an arm's length;
- there is considerable physical contact;
- there is direct eye contact; and
- there are lively facial expressions and gesturing.

Reserved   The cultures of India, Bangladesh, Indonesia, Malaysia, Vietnam, Thailand, Philippines, Japan, China, South Korea, Singapore, Britain, Germany, Denmark, Finland, the Netherlands, and the Czech Republic may be said to be reserved. In reserved cultures,

- people speak softly, interrupt less, and are comfortable with silence;
- interpersonal space is arm's length;
- there is little physical contact;
- eye contact is indirect; and
- facial expressions and gesturing are restrained.

CULTURAL ORIENTATION IN INTERNATIONAL MARKETING

The orientation of its international managers, such as parochialism versus simplification, affects the ability of a company to adapt to any foreign business environment.

Parochialism vs Simplification

International managers need to understand contrasting cultural orientations while operating in international markets.

Parochialism

Parochialism is the belief that views the rest of the world with one's own cultural perspectives. This notion is found in all cultures of the world. The tendency to view the rest of the world with one's own perspective creates problems in international marketing situations. The domestic marketing experiences of international managers often interfere in alien cultures. The tendency of one's culture to persuade thinking and behaviour without one being aware of is generally known as 'cultural baggage'. Cultural baggage often becomes a liability when international managers encounter new cultures. The sheer gravity of one's memory of the domestic marketing experience pulls one down towards set thinking and set procedures. Therefore, an international manager needs to train her mind to operate from a zero base for which she virtually needs an eraser. One should go to overseas markets with a clear mind and fill it with first-hand experience and feelings.

Simplification

Simplification is the process of exhibiting the same cultural orientation towards different cultural groups, for instance, a manager's behaviour while doing business with Swedish, Middle East, and Japanese managers, overlooking cultural differences.

As overseas markets are unique, people are different and so are their cultural responses. Although the fundamental remain the same—people 'behave'—the way they behave varies from country to country. Therefore, it is extremely important for international marketing managers to understand the cultural differences between countries and prepare themselves to meet marketing challenges.

SELF-REFERENCE CRITERION AND ETHNOCENTRISM: MAJOR OBSTACLES IN INTERNATIONAL MARKETING DECISIONS

The ability of an international manager to objectively evaluate environmental factors is severely affected by his own cultural conditioning in understanding the nuances of another culture. A self-reference criterion is an unconscious reference to one's own cultural values, experiences, and knowledge as a basis for decision-making. A person from one culture is often not aware that reaction to any situation is influenced by one's own cultural background and is interpreted in different cultural situations in different perspectives. Market relativism is in fact a subtle and unintended result of cultural conditioning.

Ethnocentrism is a belief that considers one's culture as superior to others and contemplates that the marketing strategies that work in one's home country will work as well in foreign countries too. Most Indians find it difficult to understand how westerners eat the meat of the cow, which gives milk and is revered as the mother of mankind. Korea and other East Asian countries' love for food such as bloodworm soup, snake, and dog meat is not easy for outsiders to rationalize. Sometimes, even consumers believe that buying foreign-made goods is wrong because it hurts domestic economy, causes loss of jobs and, is therefore, unpatriotic. This phenomenon is known as *consumer ethnocentrism*.[13]

In order to arrive at an objective marketing decision, one has to isolate the influences of self-reference criteria (SRC) while carrying out a cross-cultural analysis. James Lee (1966) has suggested a four-step approach to eliminate SRC:

Step 1: Define the marketing problem or goal in home-country traits, habits, or norms.

Step 2: Define the marketing problem or goal in foreign country cultural traits, habits, or norms. Make no value judgements.

Step 3: Isolate the SRC influence in the problem and examine it carefully to see how it complicates the problem.

Step 4: Redefine the problem without the SRC influence and solve for the optimum marketing goal situation.[14]

This chapter brings out the significance of the cultural environment in international marketing decisions. The conceptual understanding of various constituents of culture, such as value systems, norms, aesthetics, customs and traditions, language and religion, and their implications help in increasing appreciation to culture and in formulating effective marketing strategy. Cross-cultural classifications, as discussed in this chapter, facilitate international marketing managers to prepare challenges encountered in cross-cultural marketing situations.

Summary

International marketing decisions are considerably influenced by the socio-culture environment of the country of its operation. Therefore, international managers need to develop a thorough conceptual understanding of cross-cultural differences and sensitivities. Even the largest of international firms have committed blunders due to lack of understanding and appreciation of foreign cultures.

Culture is the way of life of people, including their attitudes, values, beliefs, arts, sciences, modes of perception, and habits of thought and activity. It is the collective programming of the mind, which distinguishes the members of one group or category from those of another. Culture is learned, shared, trans-generational, symbolic, and patterned; human beings have tremendous capacity for cultural adaptations. Various constituents of culture, such as value system, norms, aesthetics, customs and traditions, language, and religion considerably influence international marketing decisions.

Hofstede's and Trompenaars's cultural classifications are useful tools for carrying out comparison of cross-cultural behaviour. Besides, other cross-cultural classifications such as high versus low context, homophilous versus heterophilous, relationship versus deal focused, formal versus informal, polychronic versus monochromic, and expressive versus reserved cultures provide useful insight into cross-cultural behaviours. Cultural orientations such as parochialism versus simplification do affect one's ability to adapt to a foreign environment. The ability of an international manager to objectively evaluate environmental factors is severely affected by his/her own cultural conditioning and limitations in understanding the nuances of another culture. In order to arrive at objective marketing decisions, international managers need to isolate the influences of their own cultural conditioning.

Key Terms

Achievement culture   Culture in which status is accorded to high achievers and high performers.

Aesthetics   Ideas and perceptions that a cultural group upholds in terms of duty and good taste.

Affective culture   Culture where emotions are expressed openly.

Ascription culture   Culture in which status is accorded to those who 'naturally' evoke admiration from others such as elderly, seniors, highly qualified, and skilled people.

Cultural adiaphora   Social customs or behaviour in which a foreigner may participate but the participation is not imperative.

---

[13] Shimp, Terence A. and Subhash Sharma, 'Consumer Ethnocentrism: Construction and Validation of the CETSCALE', *Journal of Marketing Research*, August 1987, vol. 24, no. 3, pp. 280–289.

[14] Lee, James A., 'Cultural Analysis in Overseas Operations', *Harvard Business Reviews*, March–April 1966, pp. 106–111.

Cultural exclusives Behaviour patterns or social customs that are appropriate for locals, and foreigners are not expected to participate.

Cultural imperatives Norms that must be followed or must be avoided in a foreign country.

Culture Derived from the Latin word *cultura*, collective programming of mind that distinguishes members of one group or category from those of another.

Deal-focused culture Task-oriented culture with openness to hold direct business talks with strangers.

Diffused culture Culture in which public and private space is more or less similar and public space is guarded more carefully.

Ethnocentrism A belief that considers one's own culture superior to others and expects marketing strategies used in the home country to work overseas.

Feminine culture Culture in which the dominant social values are achievement of personal goals such as quality of life, caring for others, and friendly atmosphere.

Heterophilous culture Culture in countries that have a fair amount of differentiation in languages, beliefs, and religions followed.

High context culture Culture in which high significance is given to implicit communications, such as non-verbal and subtle situational cues.

Homophilous culture Culture where people share beliefs, speak the same language, and practise the same religion.

Individualism The tendency of people to look after themselves and only their immediate family.

Language Systematic means of communicating ideas or feelings by the use of conventionalized signs, gestures, marks, or especially articulate vocal sounds.

Low context culture Culture in which communication is more explicit with heavy reliance on words to convey the meanings.

Masculine culture Culture in which the dominant values emphasize work goals such as earnings, advancement, and success and material belongings.

Monochronic culture Culture with rigid time schedules and deadlines with high emphasis on punctuality.

Neutral culture Culture in which people tend to hold back their emotions and try not to exhibit their feelings.

Norms Guidelines for social rules that prescribe appropriate behaviour in a given situation.

Parochialism Belief that views the rest of the world from one's own cultural perspective.

Particularism Belief that unique circumstances and relationships, rather than abstract rules, are more important considerations that determine how ideas and practices should be applied.

Polychronic culture Culture in which time schedules and deadlines are flexible and relationships take precedence.

Power distance The degree of inequality among people that is viewed as equitable.

Regiocentric orientation An approach that considers the region as a uniform cultural segment and adapts a similar marketing strategy within but not across the region.

Relatioship-focused culture Culture with strong orientation towards building relationships and developing mutual trust.

Self-reference criterion An unconscious reference to one's own cultural values, experiences, and knowledge as a basis for decision–making.

Simplification Exhibiting same cultural orientation towards different cultural groups.

Specific culture Culture in which individuals tend to have a large public space and a smaller private space and public space is readily shared.

Uncertainty avoidance The extent to which people feel threatened by ambiguous situations.

Universalism Belief that same ideas and practices can be defined and applied everywhere without modification.

Values Shared assumptions of a group on how things ought to be or abstract ideas that a group believes to be good, desirable, or right.

Concept Review Questions

1. Explain the significance of culture in international marketing decisions.
2. Critically evaluate the concept of culture.
3. Marketing firms across the world have committed blunders in translating from one language to another. As an international marketing manager, how would you cope with such mistakes?
4. Critically evaluate Hofstede's cross-cultural classification and its implications on international marketing decisions.
5. How do self-reference criteria (SRC) become an obstacle in international marketing decisions? How would you minimize

the influence of SRC? Substantiate your answer with suitable examples.
6. Differentiate between the following:
   (a) Homophilous vs heterophilous cultures
   (b) Universalism vs particularism
   (c) Individualism vs collectivism
   (d) Relationship-focused vs deal-focused cultures
   (e) Polychronic (fluid time) vs monochronic (right time) cultures

Critical Thinking Questions

1. Explore the website of McDonald's and identify the cultural adaptations it has to make in different countries.
2. You are scheduled to visit Japan, Saudi Arabia, Sweden, and the USA on a business trip. Based on the cross-cultural classification

learnt in this chapter, prepare a checklist of cultural challenges you are going to face. Discuss your observations in class.

Project Assignments

1. Based on your foreign visits or interactions with foreigners in your own country, identify the differences in major cultural practices. Categorize such cultural norms under categories of cultural imperatives, exclusives, and adiaphora. Share your observations in class.
2. Identify a few mistakes made by foreign firms in India and Indian firms abroad due to lack of cultural understanding and appreciation. Discuss your findings in class.

3. Visit an internationally operating company based in your city/ country and interact with its managers. Explore the cultural differences the company is facing in its international operations and identify the strategy to cope with these cultural issues.

CASE STUDY: CROSS-CULTURAL MISAPPREHENSIONS OVER THE SWASTIKA IN THE WEST

Confusions leading to severe problems in international business often arise due to lack of understanding of cross-cultural issues. The swastika (Fig. C5.1) is the most ancient surviving symbol, which dates to prehistoric times. The word 'swastika' is derived from the Sanskrit word *svastika*: from the roots, *su* or good, *asti*, meaning 'to be', and *ka* as a suffix. *Svasti* connotes well-being and is a widely used religious symbol in Hinduism, Buddhism, and Jainism. The Thai greeting *sawasdee* is also derived from the same root and carries the same implication. Over the years, the swastika symbol became common in various cultures around the world, with some modifications. It is known as *swastika* and *hakenkreuz* in Germany, *svastika* in Denmark

Fig. C5.1   Swastika: An ancient symbol of well-being, love, and luck in Hinduism and other oriental cultures

and Sweden, *svastica* in Italy, *wan* in China, *manji* in Japan, *fylfot* in England, *tetraskelion* and *gammadion* in Greece, and *swastika* in India.

The British author Rudyard Kipling was so strongly influenced by Indian culture that he had a swastika inscribed on all his books until the rise of Nazism made this inappropriate. The swastika was also a symbol used by Scouts in Britain, although it was taken off Robert-Baden Powell's 1922 Medal of Merit after complaints in the 1930s.

In the 1800s, countries around Germany were growing larger and forming empires; yet Germany was not a unified country until 1871. To counter the feeling of vulnerability and the angst of the youth, German nationalists in the mid-19th century adopted the swastika for its ancient Aryan origins, to represent a long Germanic/Aryan history. By the end of the 19th century, the swastika could be found on nationalist German volkisch periodicals and was the official emblem of the German Gymnasts' League.

In the beginning of the 20th century, the swastika was a common symbol of German nationalism and was placed in a multitude of places such as the emblem for the *Wandervogel*, a German youth movement, on Joerg Lanz von Liebenfels' antisemitic periodical *Ostara*; on various *Freikorps* units; and as an emblem of the Thule Society.

On 7 August 1920, the swastika (*Hakenkreuz*)[15] was formally adapted by the Nazi Party at the Salzburg Congress. This

---

[15] 'Origins of the Swastika', *BBC News*, 18 January 2005.

symbol became the official emblem of the Nazi Party and was used on the party's flag, badge, and armband. In *Mein Kempf*, Adolf Hitler described the Nazi's new flag as 'in red we see the social idea of the movement, in white the nationalistic idea, in the swastika, the mission of the struggle for the victory of the Aryan man, and, by the same token, the victory of the idea of creative work, which as such always has been and always will be anti-Semitic'.

Thus, from a symbol of well-being, love, and luck, the swastika was transformed by the Nazis into a symbol of hate, anti-Semitism, and death. The British documentary *Swastika*, directed by Philippe Mora and released in 1973, focused on German history during the Nazi era. The post-world war criminal codes in Germany and Austria made the public showing of the swastika (*hakenkreuz*), except for scholarly purpose, illegal and punishable. However, the swastika on Hindu, Buddhist, and Jain temples are exempt as no religious symbol can be banned in Germany.

Due to cross-cultural confusion over the swastika, Nintendo confessed that what is appropriate in one culture may not be for another. It had to withdraw a Pokemon Trading Card featuring *manji* (swastika) in 1999 from Western markets following a complaint by the Anti-Defamation League.

In December, 2002, Christmas crackers imported from China by Walpert Industries in Canada were found to display the swastika on miniature panda bears.[16] The swastika mark was placed on the toy pandas due to lack of cross-cultural understanding by the Chinese manufacturer. Walpert personally called some of the people who received the bears with the swastika symbol and apologized. It also assured more stringent quality measures in the future.

In December 2003, Microsoft faced a problem with its Bookshelf Symbol 7 as the font's array of graphic symbols resembled the swastika. Microsoft offered an apology for its 'unintentional oversight' that caused two swastikas to be included in a font in its new Office suite. Microsoft also released a utility that allowed its users to remove the offending fonts.

In January 2005, the photographs of British prince Harry in a costume with a swastika armband taken at a birthday party in Wiltshire created a furore and the prince had to issue a statement apologizing for the offence caused.[17] In 2006, a court in Stuttgart fined a 32-year-old man more than 7,000 euros (8,700 dollars) for selling anti-Nazi badges that showed a swastika with a line through it.[18] The fashion firm Esprit was forced to recall 2,00,000 catalogues and came under investigation in Germany in October 2006 after accusations that British-made-buttons appearing in their new collection had swastika designs.

Handbags made by an Indian supplier, which had swastika symbol on it, had to be withdrawn from its stores[19] in 2007 by the Spanish fashion chain Zara after a customer in Britain complained and asked for a refund when she spotted swastikas on her bag. Zara, owned by the world's second largest fashion retailer Inditex, which has more than 3,330 stores across 66 countries, had to apologize to everyone whom it offended.

In 2012, the singer Madonna sparked a controversy during a concert in Paris with swastika superimposed on her forehead.[20] The video with swastika had already appeared in her 30-nation MDNA tour. A major French political party threatened to sue Madonna who had to later drop the swastika from video footage and replaced it with a question mark.[21]

Recent attempts to ban the swastika in the European Union have witnessed severe opposition from various socio-cultural groups, especially the Hindus, the Buddhists, the Jains, and other oriental religious groups.[22]

Questions

1. Carry out a cross-country comparison of the differences in perceptions and cultural implications of the swastika.
2. Critically evaluate how the use of swastika by the Nazis transformed its common perception to a symbol of hate rather than a symbol of well-being, love, and luck.
3. In your opinion, is the proposed ban on swastika on commercial products in the European Union justified? Discuss your views with your classmates.

---

[16] 'Toy Pandas Bearing Swastikas, a Cultural Mix-up', *CBC News*, 30 December 2002.

[17] 'Call for Europe-wide Swastika Ban', *BBC New*, 17 January 2005.

[18] 'Prosecutors Drop Probe into Swastika Buttons', *Expatica*, 19 October 2006.

[19] 'Fashion Chain Zara Withdraws Swastika Handbag', *Reuters*, 21 September 2007.

[20] 'Madonna Explains Use of Swastika during MDNA Tour', *BBC News*, 25 July 2012.

[21] 'Madonna's Swastika Controversy Calmed', *The Riviera Times*, 22 August 2012.

[22] 'Swastika Ban Left Out of EU's Racism Law', *Scotsman*, 30 January 2007.

PART III
Market Identification, Evaluation, and Selection

International Marketing Research

INTRODUCTION

Market research plays a critical role in determining the success or failure of international marketing decisions. Consequent to reduction in marketing barriers and an increasing level of integration in international markets, firms from developing countries, too, are rapidly expanding into international markets. A firm desirous of expanding internationally needs to carry out research so as to spot marketing opportunities, evaluate various countries, and select the most attractive target markets. As the commitment of resources for international expansion is much larger than that for operating in domestic markets, the role of international marketing research is fast gaining significance. This chapter elucidates the significance of conducting research in international markets.

Unilever introduced iced tea in India after seeing the success of this brand in various other countries like the USA. Although this concept was successful in other countries, it failed in India primarily due to poor market research. Besides, the introduction of the product was based on the fact that 60 per cent of the people in other countries liked iced tea. It was envisaged that India being a typical country with a much longer summer season, people would prefer iced tea. However, Unilever faltered in the fact that in India, most of the people are fond of hot tea. Even in peak summers, Indians prefer to take hot tea instead of iced tea, and hence the concept failed in India.

Kraft introduced an orange energy drink concentrate Tang in India a few years ago on the basis of the findings of an extensive market research, which indicated there was an identified need for an energy drink like the Tang. Kraft India, a 100 per cent subsidiary of Phillip Morris, USA, accordingly went ahead and launched Tang in India. It tied up with Dabur for its distribution. The product, however, failed miserably in the local markets. The chief reason for the failure of Tang was its comparatively higher prices in relation to other energy drink substitutes like Glucon-D.

Learning Objectives

- To appreciate the significance of research in international marketing
- To understand the concept of international marketing research
- To explain the process of international marketing research
- To analyse the problems of equivalence in international marketing research
- To evaluate emic versus etic dilemma in international marketing research

Exhibit 6.1 Introduction of new Coke: the classic marketing blunder

One has to carefully monitor the international marketing research, as even the best-known companies of the world can make classic marketing blunders. Coca Cola, which had long been a market leader, witnessed decline in its market share in the late 1970s despite its superior distribution channels across the international markets. As Pepsi's advertisement campaign 'Pepsi Generation' in the mid-1960s rejuvenated the brand through projecting youth vitality and idealism. As a result, Pepsi was making inroads and taking away Coke share. The company management decided to carry out research to evaluate the product itself. Blind test conducted indicated that consumers generally preferred Pepsi to Coke, which gave strong evidence that the taste of the Coke was responsible for its decline. Subsequently, the project 'Kansas' was launched with an objective of scrapping the original Coke formula. In 10 major markets, approximately 2,000 people were interviewed to explore the willingness of the consumer to accept the different coke. Research indicated that the respondents favoured a sweeter less-fizzy cola that had a sticky taste due to high sugar content. Once again a blind test was conducted and there was an overwhelming reaction to the entry of the new coke.

A majority of the respondents subjected to the test preferred the new coke to Pepsi.

On 23 April 1985, the new Coke was launched. Millions of people across the world became aware within 24 hours that the Coke had changed its classic formula. The sales of Coke jumped as an initial market response.

On the contrary, the success of the new Coke was short-lived. Complaints poured from around the world. The media reports added fervour to the problem and the consumers began talking of an old friend who had suddenly betrayed them. The sales of the new Coke started dropping.

Within four months of introducing the new flavour, finally on 11 July 1985, the company management apologized to the public for withdrawing the Coke. The company's message stated that those who wanted the old Coke would get it back, and at the same time those who enjoyed the taste of new Coke could continue to do so. The market reacted very favourably to the return of classic Coke. Thus, Coke ended up with a classic marketing blunder in view of the above problems related to market research.

Source: Hartley, Robert, 'Coca Cola's Classic Blunder', *Marketing Mistakes*, John Wiley & Sons, Inc., New York, 1998, pp. 160–176.

Even companies enjoying one of the highest brand equities in the world like Coca Cola made classic marketing blunders due to shortcomings in conducting marketing research. As illustrated in Exhibit 6.1, based on the research findings, the company withdrew its age-old Coke from the market and introduced a new Coke formula on 23 April 1985. The company had to withdraw its decisions within four months and had to re-introduce the classic Coke.

The basic reasons for market failure of the new Coke were primarily due to shortcomings in conducting market research, as follows:

• The results of the research were solely based on blind tests, but the participants were not aware that they are choosing a new flavour, which would mean that they would lose the other.

• The research overlooked the emotional attachment of the consumers with Coke's 100-year formula.

• The group of respondents for the blind test was young who generally prefer sweet taste. However, the taste for sweet things diminishes with age.

This chapter elucidates the process of conducting international marketing research in a step-by-step manner including problem identification, deciding research methodology, working out information requirements and information sources, preparing research design, primary data collection, analysing information, and evaluation and interpretation of research.

The concept of international marketing research that involves carrying out research across the borders to gain an insight into various cultures is explained. In cross-country research studies, various types of equivalences, such as construct measurement and data collection and analysis, have significant influences on the international marketing research process; hence, these are being dealt with in detail.

INTERNATIONAL MARKETING RESEARCH

In simple terms, international marketing research is a study conducted to assist making marketing decisions in more than one country. Market research is the function that links an organization to its markets through information collection and analysis. It involves the systematic gathering, recording, and analysing of data about problems related to marketing of goods and services.[1] This information is used to identify and define marketing opportunities and problems; generate, refine, and evaluate marketing actions; monitor marketing performance; and improve the understanding of marketing as a process.

International marketing research can be defined as research that crosses national borders and involves respondents and researchers from different countries and cultures.[2] It may be conducted simultaneously in multiple countries or sequentially over a period of time. The major objectives of international marketing research are as follows:

- Carry out country screening and selection.
- Evaluate a country's market potential.
- Identify problems that would not require a country's listing for further consideration.
- Identify aspects of the country's environment that needs further study.
- Evaluate the components of marketing mix for possible adoption.
- Facilitate in developing a strategic marketing plan.

Process of Marketing Research

The process of international marketing research involves problem identification, deciding research methodology, working out information requirements, identifying sources of information, preparing research designs, and collecting primary information and its analysis, evaluation, and interpretation, as shown in Fig. 6.1. However, the process of marketing research should be developed taking into consideration the nature of the problem to be addressed.

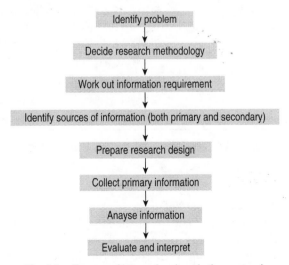

Fig. 6.1   Process of international marketing research

---

[1] American Marketing Association, http://www.marketingpower.com/AboutAMA/pages/DefinitionofMarketing.aspx, accessed on 18 October 2013.

[2] Craig, Samuel and Susan P. Douglas, *International Marketing Research*, John Wiley & Sons Ltd, Singapore, 2003, pp. 1–8.

Since research is conducted across national borders, it involves respondents and researchers from different countries and cultures. It may be conducted simultaneously in multiple countries or sequentially over a period of time.

Problem identification

It is the first step of the international marketing research process and is very crucial. It has to be as precise as possible. It may include one or many of the following:

- Deciding whether to remain in domestic market or enter into international markets
- Product identification for international markets
- Deciding international markets for entry
- Deciding upon mode of entry into international markets
- Decisions related to international marketing mix
- Decisions for implementing and controlling the strategic international marketing plans

Deciding research methodology

As indicated in Table 6.1, different marketing decisions require different kinds of marketing research.

Table 6.1   International marketing research and marketing decisions

Marketing mix decision	Type of research
Product policy	Focus groups and qualitative research to generate ideas for new products
	Survey research to evaluate new product ideas
	Concept testing, test marketing
	Product benefit and attitude research
	Product formulation and feature testing
Pricing distribution	Pricing sensitivity studies
Distribution	Survey of shopping patterns and behaviour
	Consumer attitudes toward different store types
	Survey of distributor attitudes and policies
Advertising	Advertising pre-testing
Advertising post-testing, recall scores	Surveys of media habits
Sales promotion	Surveys of response to alternative types of promotion
Sales force	Tests of alternative sales presentations

Source: Douglas, Susan P. and C. Samuel Craig, *International Marketing Research*, Prentice Hall Inc., New Jersey, 1983, p. 32.

Working out information requirement

Once the problem is identified and the methodology is decided for the market research, detailed information requirement needs to be worked out. It helps in identifying information sources and compilation of information. The basic information requirements for international marketing research are as follows:

- *Decision regarding whether to operate in domestic market or enter international markets*
  - Analysing basic trade statistics related to the firm's products
  - Assessment of international market demand
  - Competitiveness of the firm's products in domestic and international market

- *Estimating market size*
  - Total sales in the market: last three years' growth rate as well as the projected sales growth
  - Total imports of the product into the country: last three years' growth rate as well as the projected rate of growth (both in value and volume terms)
  - Sources of imports by country, shares of each country, change in shares in the last three years (special focus on whether and how much imports are from India)
  - Domestic production: last three years' growth rate as well as the projected production growth
  - Balance of payments: last three years
  - Foreign exchange reserves: trend and present amount
- *Assessing market access*
  - Import policy: control mechanisms
  - Import licensing: banned, restricted, open
  - Tariff regime: *ad valorem*, specific, mixed—MFN, preferential, tariff quota
  - Basis for duty valuation
  - Exchange rate: convertible, non-convertible
  - Foreign exchange controls, foreign exchange authorizations
- *Market selection*
  - Prioritizing international markets on the basis of market size
  - Tariff barriers
  - Non-tariff barriers
  - Political risks and relationship with India (or home country)
  - Cultural affinity
  - Communication facilities
  - Logistics
- *International marketing mix decisions*
  - Competition analysis
  - Consumer behaviour
  - Pricing strategy and exchange rate
  - Marketing channels
  - Promotional and advertising decisions
- *Decisions for implementing and controlling the strategic international marketing plans*
  - Turnover and profit analysis
  - Market share and profit growth analysis
  - Analysis of marketing expenses

Identifying sources of information

Secondary information plays an important role in international marketing research. Since carrying out overseas field surveys involves considerable cost and time, the secondary information results into a considerable saving in cost and time. Besides, there may be situations when conducting field survey is either difficult or not feasible due to the resource constraints of a firm. A researcher, in such a case, has to heavily rely upon secondary data. At times, the secondary data related to market estimation, competitors' turnover, and profit, etc. may be more reliable than the data collected through independent market research. Often the secondary data related to a country's business environment, market estimation, regulatory framework, tariffs and taxation, etc. may be more reliable than what a firm can obtain through independent research. Specific data from secondary sources may also be obtained from outside agencies in lieu of payment.

Major desk research sources of international marketing information are depicted in Exhibit 6.2.

Exhibit 6.2 Desk research sources of international marketing information

Information	Examples of sources
Import statistics	UN, Organization for Economic Cooperation and Development (OECD) trade statistics, national trade statistics (from embassies)
Production statistics	Official statistical sources (from embassies), trade associations, UN Statistical Yearbook and Monthly Bulletin of Statistics
Tariff and quotas	Embassies, chambers of commerce
Currency restrictions	Banks, embassies
Sanitary restrictions	Embassies
Political situation	Banks, press reports
Economic situation	Banks, economic and financial journals and newspapers, IMF and OECD reports
Consumption (of a product)	Official statistics, trade journals and commodity reviews, trade associations
Identification of agents, importers, producers	Trade directories, trade associations, articles, and advertisements in trade journals
Information about specific companies	Banks, trade directories, press articles and advertising, company literature
Credit terms	Banks
Transport costs	Freight forwarders
Packing requirements	Letters to purchasing offices of industrial users, to department store/supermarket buyers, importers, etc.
Prices	Catalogues and price lists, advertising trade press reports
Features of competing	Press advertising, catalogues and product literature, trade journal products reports
Leading trade journals	Press and media directories
Population	Almanacs, statistical yearbooks
Geographic features	Atlases, encyclopedias

Source: International Trade Centre, Export Market Research, http://www.intracen.org, accessed on 18 October 2013.

Limitations of secondary data

The major limitations of secondary data such as its availability, reliability, comparability, and validity are discussed here.

Availability The kind of secondary data needed for marketing decisions at times may not be available for all countries. Generally, availability of detailed secondary data is directly proportional to the state of economic development in a particular country (Fig. 6.2). For instance, in countries such as Japan, the USA, Singapore, and in some European countries, comprehensive market data are available on wholesalers, retailer, manufacturers, and traders, which is hardly available in many developing and least-developed countries. However, the general data on demographic profile compiled by national governments and UN organizations are readily available.

Reliability In order to take marketing decisions confidently, the information needs to be accurate and reliable. However, it is observed that the secondary data available from various agencies is influenced by various environmental and cultural factors in the country. For instance, the data collected by revenue and taxation authorities understate the sales and profitability figures due to fear of increased incidence of taxation. However, the data furnished by consumers in individual surveys by nongovernmental agencies and even the data collected by government agencies are sometimes inflated as a manifestation of individual or national pride. It is reflected in the enormous size of parallel economies operating in several countries, especially in developing and least-developed

Fig. 6.2   Japan External Trade Organization provides exhaustive market information on Japanese markets

Source: http://www.jetro.go.jp/en/reports/market/, accessed on 19 October 2013.

countries. It adversely affects the accuracy and reliability of data. Further, the secondary data available, at times, may not be updated, which requires additional collection of primary data.

Comparability   The data collected from secondary sources by various agencies across nations may not be comparable, depending upon the methodology used in data collection. For instance, there is a wide variation in trade statistics collected by various agencies within a city, such as by the Directorate General of Commercial Intelligence and Statistics (DGCIS) and the Reserve Bank of India (RBI), mainly due to the different methods used in data collection. Besides, differences in classification of various terminologies, like consumer classifications, also contribute to difficulties in comparison of cross-country research data.

Validity   The secondary data collected from two sources should be consistent for assessing validity of the data. The validity of data depends on a number of factors[3] including the following:

- Who collected the data? Would there be any reason for purposely misrepresenting the facts?
- For what purposes were the data collected?
- How were the data collected? (methodology)
- Are the data internally consistent and logical in light of known data sources or market factors?

Generally, the availability and accuracy of secondary data increases with increase in level of the country's economic development. However, India is an exception, which has accurate and

---

[3] Cateora, Philip R. and John L. Graham, *International Marketing*, 11th edition, Tata McGraw Hill, New Delhi, 2002.

relatively complete government collected data, despite its lower level of economic development than many other countries.

Preparing research design

Research design is the specification of methods and procedures for acquiring the information needed to structure or solve problems. It is the arrangement of conditions for collection and analysis of data in a manner that aims to combine relevance of research purpose with economy in procedures. Thus, research design is the conceptual structure within which research is conducted; it constitutes the blueprint for the collection, measurement, and analysis of data. It includes an outline of what the researcher will do: from writing the hypothesis and its operational implications to the final analysis of data.

Types of research designs

The major types of research designs, such as exploratory, descriptive, and causative, are discussed here.

Exploratory research   This type of marketing research is conducted to gather preliminary information to help define problems and suggest hypothesis in a better way. It is used when one is seeking insight into the general nature of a problem, the possible research alternatives, and relevant variables that need to be considered.

Descriptive research   This kind of marketing research is carried out to better describe marketing problems, situations, or markets such as the market potential for a product or the demographics and attitudes of consumers. It is used to provide accurate snapshots of some aspects of the market environment.

Causative research   This type of marketing research is conducted to test the hypothesis and to establish a cause and effect relationship between the variables. It is widely used to identify interrelationship among various constituents of marketing strategy. Therefore, the results under the causative research are unambiguous and often sought for in research.

Collecting primary information

The information collected by the researcher for the first time is termed as primary information. Although it is comparatively costlier to collect primary data in comparison to secondary research, it is important to get information specific to the research project. However, in view of the much higher costs and complexity involved in collecting primary data, the researcher should first collect as much secondary information as feasible and identify the information gaps. Such information gaps may be filled up by collecting primary information. Further, the cost-benefit analysis of collecting primary information should also be carried out. Firms operating internationally also collect primary information on a regular basis for monitoring their marketing strategy. Primary information may be collected by conducting field surveys, observation, or conducting experiments. Various tools used to conduct field surveys include telephone interviews, mail surveys, electronic surveys, and personal surveys.

Types of field surveys   Field survey is a commonly used method of conducting primary research in international markets. Field surveys may be classified into the following major categories.

Telephone interviews   With the advent of telecommunication, conducting interviews telephonically is a cost-effective alternative to personal field survey in international markets. However, the level of penetration of telephones varies widely across countries.

A cross-country comparison reveals that China with 294.4 million has the highest number of fixed telephone subscriptions followed by USA (151.17), Germany (45.7), Russia (44),

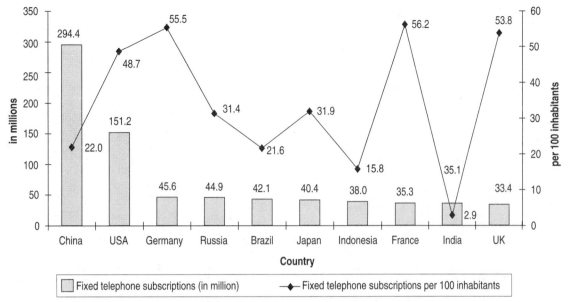

Fig. 6.3 Countries with highest fixed telephone subscriptions vis-à-vis penetration (2010)

Source: International Telecommunication Union, December 2011.

Brazil (42.1), Japan (40.42), Indonesia (38), France (35.3), India (35.09), and the UK (33.3), as shown in Fig. 6.3.

Although India has 35.1 million fixed telephone subscriptions, the per capita penetration is miserably low at 2.9 fixed telephones per 100 inhabitants compared to 56.2 in France, 53.8 in the UK, 55.4 in Germany, 48.7 in the USA, 31.94 in Japan, 31.42 in Russia, 21.95 in China, 21.62 in Brazil, and 15.83 in Indonesia. This presents wide variations in use of fixed telephone for conducting market surveys.

The number of mobile subscribers has also increased rapidly in recent years. As shown in Fig. 6.4, significant differences exist among various countries. Interestingly, India, with 752 million mobile subscribers, ranks only second after China (859 millions) in terms of numbers and an impressive penetration of 61.4 mobiles per 100 inhabitants, whereas it presents a contrast with fixed telephone penetration at merely 2.9 fixed telephones per 100 inhabitants (Fig. 6.3). Besides, there is a wide variation in mobile penetration within India among urban and rural inhabitants and income groups. Therefore, surveys on mobile become effective in India especially for most products marketed. Moreover, the target market segments in most countries for a large number of products marketed internationally is in the form of market clusters where telephonic and mobile interviews can be conducted.

However, cultural factors also influence the willingness of the respondents to participate in telephonic interviews. For instance, telephonic interviews are very popular in the Netherlands, which tops the list of countries with the highest number of personal interviews, while Germans have a lot of issues against telephonic interviews. In a number of countries, the number of unlisted telephones is high, making it difficult for an international marketer to approach the target population. In case of cellular mobiles, published directories are generally not available and the issue of breach of privacy is also involved. Sampling techniques used in telephonic interviews include random digit-dialling and systematic random digit-dialling with pre-defined criteria.

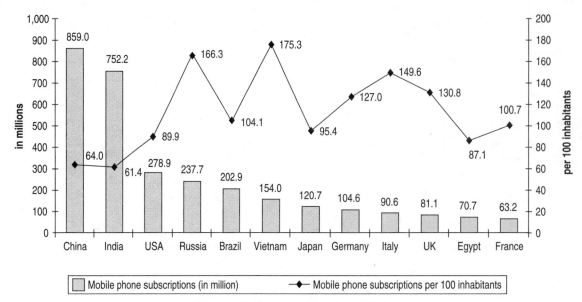

Fig. 6.4 Mobile phone subscribers (2010)

Source: International Telecommunication Union, December 2011.

Mail surveys Under this method, a questionnaire is mailed to the respondents, who fill in the questionnaire and mail it back. A researcher has to obtain a mailing list and use a sampling technique for selecting the mailing addresses. The interviews are commonly used in countries where the literacy rate is high and the postal system is well developed. Mail interviews are very common in countries such as Finland, Japan, Switzerland, and Singapore, where postal system is highly efficient. The postal system is hardly reliable in countries such as Venezuela, Nigeria, and Philippines, where mail surveys are difficult to use.

Electronic surveys With the development of information and computer technology, the use of electronic surveys has increased by leaps and bounds in the last decade.

Though China has the highest number of Internet users at 513.1 million, which is far ahead the USA (245.2 million), India (121 million), Japan (101.2 million), Brazil (81.7), Germany (67.3), Russia (61.4), Indonesia (55), UK (52), and France (50.2), Internet penetration of China and India remains comparatively lower at 38.4 and 10.2 per cent of population respectively compared to the UK (84.1%), Germany (82.7 %), Japan (80%) and the USA (78.3%). Though Internet penetration is rising rapidly, its use for mass market research is presently limited to a select number of countries. However, it may be employed with stratified sampling for select market segments even in low-income countries.

With the large-scale mobile penetration and cyber cafe revolution in India, the Internet has touched the lives of a greater number of people than that depicted in Fig. 6.5. Business and institutional surveys are gaining popularity even in the developing countries. The sample surveyed may not be representative of the population and may lead to faulty inferences. Therefore, due care should be taken while selecting a sample for an electronic survey. Electronic surveys are cost-effective and quick.

Personal surveys Interviewing the respondents personally is not only the costliest but also the most flexible method of obtaining information. Besides, the incidence of non-response is negligible as is in the case of other mailing methods. An interviewer also has an opportunity to clarify any doubts with the respondents.

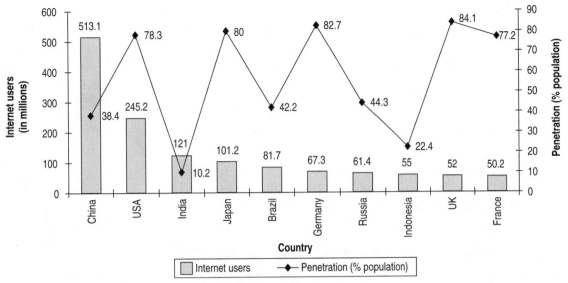

Fig. 6.5   Top 10 countries with highest number of Internet users

Source: Internet World Statistics, 31 March 2012.

A researcher has to make thorough preparations, well in advance, for field visits and get himself sensitized to the sociocultural behaviour of the respondents, which has already been discussed in detail in this chapter.

The benefits and limitations of survey methods[4] have been summarized in Table 6.2, which is self-explanatory.

Table 6.2   Evaluation of survey methods used in international marketing research

Criteria	Telephone	Personal	Mail
High sample control	+	+	−
Difficulty in locating respondents at home	+	−	+
Inaccessibility of homes	+	−	+
Unavailability of large pool of trained interviewers	+	−	+
Large population in rural areas	−	+	−
Unavailability of current telephone directory	−	+	−
Unavailability of mailing lists	+	+	−
Low penetration of telephones	−	+	+
Lack of an efficient postal system	+	+	−
Low level of literacy	−	+	−
Face-to-face communication culture	−	+	−

Note: + denotes an advantage; − denotes a disadvantage

Source: Malhotra, N.K., J. Agrawal, and M. Peterson, 'Methodological Issues in Cross Cultural Marketing Research', *International Marketing Review*, 13(6), 1997, pp. 7–43.

---

[4] Malhotra, N.K., J. Agrawal, and M. Peterson, 'Methodological Issues in Cross Cultural Marketing Research', *International Marketing Review*, 13(6), 1997, pp. 7–43.

Analysis of information

Although the data analysis techniques in international marketing research remain similar to that used in domestic marketing research, they depend upon the nature of the problem and the type of data. Univariate techniques, such as cross-tabulation and *t* test, and multivariate techniques, such as analysis of variance, discriminant analysis, conjoint analysis, factor analysis, cluster analysis, and multidimensional scaling, can be used. However, a researcher should check the multicountry data for various equivalences, as explained in detail later in the chapter, and prepare the data for analysis.

Evaluation and interpretation

Based on data analysis, the research results should be evaluated in view of the equivalences and constraints in obtaining cross-country information. One should also take care to eliminate the influence of self-reference criteria (SRC) while interpreting and presenting the research findings.

Major Challenges to Successful International Marketing Research

A researcher should be aware of the challenges for carrying out international marketing research with meaningful outcomes. Some of these are as follows:

- Overlooking cross-cultural market behaviour
- Employing standardized research methodologies across the international markets
- Using English as a standard language for market communication
- Inappropriate sample selection
- Misinterpretation of cross-country data
- Failure to use locals to conduct field surveys

Adequate measures should be taken to address these issues while conducting international marketing research. As cross-cultural profile of consumers in international markets plays a significant role in marketing behaviour, it has been separately discussed in Chapter 5.

Cross-cultural Marketing Behaviour and Research

A researcher conducting cross-country research needs to appreciate the variations in cultural behaviour of respondents and consumers in overseas market. These cultural aspects need to be examined while preparing the international marketing research plan. A firm operating in international markets comes across different types of socio-cultural variations that influence its marketing-mix decisions.

However, the problem identification in international markets is influenced by the marketer's SRC,[5] which is an unconscious reference to one's own cultural values, experiences, and knowledge as a basis for decision-making. Thus, one's own cultural background often influences the decision-making and interpretation of market research problem while conducting cross-country research. For instance, it is difficult for a Japanese consumer to say no; rather Japanese consumers use more subtle expressions for indicating their disagreement. Therefore, research conducted in Japanese market can be misleading at times. A four-step approach may be used to eliminate SRC, which consists of the following:

- Defining the market research problem in the home country's trade, habits, or norms
- Defining the problem in the target markets, cultural values, habits, or norms without any value judgement

---

[5] Lee, J.A., 'Cultural Analysis in Overseas Operations', *Harvard Business Review*, 1966, 44 (March–April), pp. 106–114.

- Isolating the influence of SRC in the research problem and carefully examining its impact in complicating the problem
- Re-defining the research problem without the SRC influence

Equivalences in cross-country research

Equivalences in cross-country research (Fig. 6.6) refer to whether the particular concept being studied is understood and interpreted in the same manner by people in different cultures. As discussed earlier, it is the cultural background that determines the acceptability or unacceptability of family values. An advertisement copy that is considered sensual in the Middle East may fail to convey a similar message in Europe, as discussed in Chapter 14. Even the demographics, which appear to have universal appeal, may be very different. Thus, these concepts specific to a culture have varied implications in international marketing.

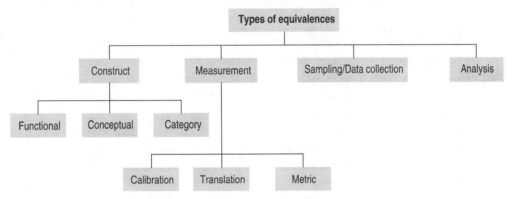

Fig. 6.6   Equivalences in cross-country research

Source: Joshi, Rakesh Mohan, *International Business*, Oxford University Press, 2009, p. 392.

Construct equivalence

Construct equivalence refers to whether the marketing constructs (that is, product functionality, interpretation of marketing stimuli, and classification schemes) under the study have same meaning across countries. The forms of construct equivalence are explained here.

Functional equivalence   It refers to whether the function or purpose served or performed by a given concept or behaviour is the same across the national markets. For instance, sewing machine in developing countries with low per capita income is primarily a means of saving or adding to household incomes, while in high-income countries, it is a means of recreation or hobby. Similarly, a bicycle is a means of transport in low-income countries, while it is used as a means of recreation in high-income countries. Possessing a car or air-conditioner is a necessity and no longer a status symbol in high-income countries, while it is considered to be a symbol of prestige or status in low-income countries. Thus, the role or functions served by a bicycle or a sewing machine are different in different country markets. Therefore, for valid and meaningful comparison of the research data across nations, the functional differences in the use of a product or service need to be taken into consideration in the measuring instrument.

Conceptual equivalence   The extent of variation in individual interpretation of objects, stimuli, or behaviour across cultures is termed as conceptual equivalence. This significantly affects interpretation of the marketing stimuli. The contextual background of cultures plays an important role in understanding such behaviour. In eastern societies, acceptance by group, unwillingness to express explicit disagreements, and giving each other the chance to save face are important cultural traits, which is hardly the case with Western cultures. Thus, the conceptual equivalence is important in interpretation of cross-country market behaviour of products, brands, consumer behaviour, and promotional campaigns.

Classification or category equivalence   It refers to the category in which the relevant objects or other stimuli are placed. The definition of product class may vary from country to country. The demographic classifications also vary among nations. Such category variation may be due to consumer perception or by official law-enforcing authorities. In a number of Mediterranean countries, beer is considered a soft drink, while it is an alcoholic beverage in most of the countries. Definition of 'urban' varies widely among nations. In Iceland, localities with more than 200 inhabitants are classified as urban, while in Canada, places with more than 1,000 inhabitants and in Japan, places with more than 50,000 inhabitants are categorized as urban. Therefore, while conducting cross-country marketing research, the researcher has to take into account such differences in demographic classifications.

Measurement equivalences

Measurement equivalences refer to establishing equivalence in terms of procedures used to measure concepts or attitudes.[6] There are significant differences in measuring methods or instruments as far as their applicability and effectiveness from one culture to another are concerned.

Calibration equivalence   The system of calibration includes monitory units, measure of weight, distances, volume, and perceptual cues, such as colour, shape, and forms, used to interpret visual stimuli. It requires establishing equivalence of scale or scoring procedure and equivalence of response to a given measure in different countries. For instance, in India and the USA, a five- or seven-point scale is normally used, while there are countries where the scale has 15–20 categories. The Japanese generally avoid giving opinions; therefore, a scale used in Japan does not have a neutral point.

Translation equivalence   The translation of the instrument used should be such that it can be understood by respondents in different countries and has equivalent meaning in each research context. An exact translation of the instrument is often difficult, as it may have different connotations in different country markets. In India, a unit can refer to parents, spouses, and children, whereas in the USA, a family refers to only a couple and their children. In India, Italy, and Pakistan, separate words are used for paternal and maternal uncles and aunts. Considerable differences exist even in the English used in various countries.

As indicated in Exhibit 6.3, significant differences can be seen even in the English used in the USA and the UK.

The following incidence at the UN World Conference on population development held in Cairo illustrates how translation can create equivalence problems:

> *At this conference, the Americans raised the concept of 'reproductive health'. This was translated into German, as the equivalent of 'health of propagation', into Arabic as 'spouses take a break from each other after childbirth'. The equivalent in Russian became 'the whole family goes on holiday' and in Mandarin as 'a holiday at the farm'.*

Even in an English-speaking country, like the USA, nearly 200 languages are spoken. Papua New Guinea, a small country, has the highest number of 830 languages, followed by Indonesia

---

[6] Crimp, Margaret, and Len Tiu Wright, *The Marketing Research Process*, Fourth edition, Prentice Hall, Herefordshire, 1995, p. 63.

Exhibit 6.3   American English vs British English

American English	British English
Diaper	Nappy
Dessert	Sweet
Elevator	Lift
Long-distance call	Trunk call
Lawyer	Solicitor
Truck	Lorry
Balcony	Gallery
Band-aid	Elastoplasts
Coffee with or without cream	Black or white coffee
Druggist	Chemist
Flashlight	Torch
French-fried potatoes	Chips
Instalment buying	Hire purchase
Kerosene	Paraffin
Line	Queue
Mail box	Pillar box
Mezzanine	Dress circle
Monkey wrench	Spanner
Mutual fund	Unit trust
Radio	Wireless
Raincoat	Mackintosh
Round-trip ticket	Return ticket
Scotch tape	Cello tape
Second floor	First floor
Sidewalk	Pavement
Subway	Underground
Superhighway	Motorway
Underwear	Smalls
Vacation	Holiday
Sales	Turnover
Inventory	Stock
Stock	Shares
President	Managing director

(719 languages), Nigeria (514 languages), India (438 languages), and China (292 languages), as shown in Fig. 6.7. The ratio between the number of languages and the population of a country, known as the Languages Diversity Index, is also the highest in Papua New Guinea with 0.99, followed by Congo (0.95), India (0.94), Nigeria (0.87), and Philippines (0.86). The score may be employed to infer the probability that two citizens from the country will share the same mother tongue. Operating in linguistically diverse countries, like India, makes marketing communications and conducing market research much more complex compared to those with low linguistic diversity such as the USA.

Unlike in China, where a majority of the population communicates in Mandarin, the exceedingly large number of languages used in India poses a challenge to the marketers. Even the Reserve Bank of India (RBI), India's central bank, uses 15 other languages in addition to English and Hindi on its currency notes (Fig. 6.8) to communicate with the people of the country. Therefore, while conducting field surveys, especially in rural areas, local languages have to be used in questionnaires and local field surveyors have to be used for effective communication. For instance, Arunachal Pradesh, an Indian state in the North East with a population of about 1.1 million, has 26 major tribes and a number of sub-tribes with their own dialects, ethos, and cultural identities. The number of dialects and their distinction from each other in the state are so varied that the people adopted Hindi as the common language of the state to communicate with each other.

A questionnaire used for international market research needs to be written perfectly and reviewed by a native of that particular country. In order to minimize translation errors in the research instrument used for international markets, techniques such as back translation, parallel translation, and decentring, as discussed in Chapter 14, may be employed.

Metric equivalence   Equivalence of scale or procedure to establish as measure and equivalences of responses of given measure in different countries are termed as metric equivalence. In different countries and cultures, the effectiveness of scales and scoring procedures varies widely. In English-speaking countries, a five- or seven-point scale is common, whereas 10- or 20-point scale is very common in many other countries.[7] Further, the non-verbal response from across countries and cultures needs to be considered for comparability.

[7] Douglas, S.P. and P. Le Maire, 'Improving Quality and Efficiency of Life-Style in Research, *The Challenges Facing Market Research: How Do We Meet Them?* XXV ESOMAR Congress, Hamburg, 1974.

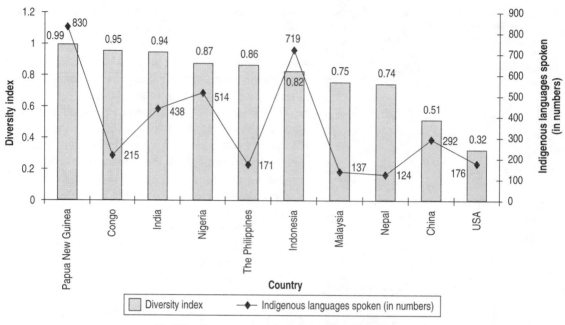

Fig. 6.7 Cross-country comparison of linguistic diversity

Note: 1 = Total diversity (where no two people meeting at random would have the same mother tongue)
Source: *The Economic Times*, 21 February 2012; Ethnologue.com.

Fig. 6.8 Use of 15 regional languages in the currency notes of India

Sampling equivalence

The major forms of sampling equivalence include comparability and its representativeness to the population, as follows.

Comparability of samples The sampling methods among various countries need to be comparable for cross-country market research. For instance, the process of the decision to purchase varies due to role variation among family members. In China and India, children have relatively much higher pester power to influence the buying decision as compared to their Western counterparts. In the USA, the decision-making for buying durables and major investments is collaborative, whereas in the Middle East, womenfolk have little say in such decision-making. It influences the sample selection for carrying out cross-country market surveys.

Sample's representativeness to the population   A sample should be representative of the population surveyed. Generally, availability and accuracy of customer database are proportional to the level of the country's development. For instance, the database in Japan, Singapore, and the USA is far more detailed and precise compared to those available in developing and least-developed countries. In a country, like India, there are wide variations among the regional and urban countries; therefore, uniform sampling techniques within the country are hardly representative of the population surveyed.

Equivalence of data analysis

The country–culture biases need to be taken into account while carrying out data analysis. The emphasis and expression of disagreement vary widely among cultures. As the Japanese find it very difficult to say 'No' and face-saving is an important cultural trait in Eastern cultures unlike the West, these factors need to be considered while applying uniform analytical techniques.

EMIC VS ETIC DILEMMA: CULTURAL UNIQUENESS VS PAN-CULTURALISM

Emic and *etic* are the approaches that represent two different streams of thought at polar extremes of cross-country marketing decision-making and research methodology. Emic emphasizes cultural uniqueness while etic emphasizes pan-culturalism in the behavioural patterns and the research process.

The Emic Approach

The emic school holds that attitudes, interests, and behaviour are unique to a culture and best understood in their own terms. It emphasizes studying the marketing research problem in each country's specific context and identifying and understanding its unique facets. Subsequently, cross-cultural differences and similarities are made in qualitative terms. As the motive to buy differs substantially across cultures, the multi-country research may call for an emic approach.

The Etic Approach

The etic school emphasizes identifying and assessing universal attitudinal and behavioural concepts and developing 'pan-cultural' measures. Thus, etic is basically concerned with measuring universal behavioural and attitudinal traits. The assessment of such phenomenon needs unbiased measures. For instance, there appears to be convergence in preferences across cultures.

Operationalization of Emic and Etic

An international firm focuses on identifying similarities across national markets, as it offers opportunities to transfer the products and services and integration of marketing strategies across the borders. Therefore, an international firm generally prefers etic strategy. While conducting cross-country research, emphasis is placed on identifying and developing constructs that are feasible across countries and cultures.

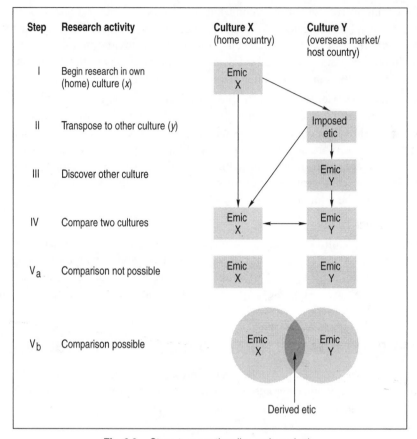

Fig. 6.9 Steps to operationalize emic and etic

Source: Adapted from Berry, J.W., 'Imposed Etics—Emics-derived Etics: The Operationalisation of a Compelling Idea', *International Journal of Psychology*, vol. 24, 1989, pp. 721–735.

An approach to resolve the emic versus– etic dilemma was proposed by Berry[8] as shown in Fig. 6.9. Under this approach, research is first conducted in one's own cultural context X and then the construct or instrument developed for cultural context is applied to another culture, that is, of the host country, which is known as 'imposed etic.' Using an emic approach, the market behaviour is studied in the second culture from within. Then, the results of the emic and the 'imposed etic' approach are examined and compared. No comparison is possible if no commonality is identified between the two and the cultures are to be studied under the emic elements. In case some commonality is identified based on common aspects/features, a 'derived etic' comparison between the cultures is possible.

INTERNATIONAL MARKETING RESEARCH AND HUMAN JUDGEMENT

Despite the advances in research techniques across the globe, one should always keep in mind that international marketing research is not a substitute for human intellect. Exhibit 6.4 illustrates

---

[8] Adapted from Berry, J.W., 'Imposed Etics–Emics-Derived Etics: The Operationalisation of a Compelling Idea', *International Journal of Psychology*, 1989, vol. 24, pp. 721–735.

Exhibit 6.4 Market research is not a substitute to human intellect and judgement in decision-making

Market research is hardly a substitute for human intellect in decision-making. As cited by Akio Morita,18 the idea of developing the 'walkman' took shape when one of his colleagues Ibuka came to his office with one portable stereo tape recorder and a pair of standard-size head phones. He complained of the weight of the system and was unhappy with it. Besides, Ibuka expressed his desire to listen to music without disturbing others and not sitting at the same place for the whole day. Ibuka wanted to take the whole system with him wherever he went, but it was too heavy. Akio Morita after listening to Ibuka's problems ordered his engineers to take one of Sony's reliable small cassette tape recorders, strip out the recording circuit and the speaker, and replace them with a stereo amplifier and improved a very light headphone. In a short time, the first experimental unit with new miniature headphones was delivered. In Akio Morita's words, 'Instead of doing a lot of market research, we refine our thinking on a product and its use, and try to create a market for it by educating and communicating with the public. I do not believe that any amount of market research could have told us that the Sony Walkman would be successful, not to say a sensational hit that would spawn many imitators.'

Source: Morita, Akio, *Made in Japan*, Dutton, 1986, pp. 87–91.

the classic case of Sony's 'Walkman', which was conceived by intuition and judgment of Akio Morita and created history in the global markets.

As discussed in the chapter, marketing research plays a crucial role in international marketing decisions such as country screening and market selection, entry decisions, decisions regarding marketing mix, competitive analysis, and designing and monitoring marketing strategy. As international marketing decisions require much higher level of commitment of a firm's resources, any marketing failure has serious repercussions. There is no dearth of illustrations in the marketing history about marketing failures due to ineffective market research. Even the global companies with mighty resources and battalions of top-notch marketing professionals could not escape from mistakes in marketing strategy.

Although the technical aspects of international marketing research are more or less similar to the marketing research carried out in the home market, a variety of factors including inappropriate sample selection, linguistic barriers, and cross-cultural behaviour of the respondents and the consumers have been key differentiators. Culture plays an important role in determining the consumers' behaviour, perception, and reaction to marketing stimuli. On the other hand, inability of a researcher in making unbiased judgement in different cultural contexts is often hindered by one's own cultural experiences termed as SRC. It constitutes a major barrier in the researcher's evaluation and response to international marketing situation.

The researcher should develop the process of marketing research taking into consideration the nature of problem to be addressed. Secondary data are extremely important in conducting international marketing research due to cost and speed of collecting market information. It is advisable to source the specific data from outside agencies in lieu of payment. Therefore, the researcher should also acquaint himself with various sources of desk research for compiling secondary information. The major limitations of secondary data relate to its availability, reliability, comparability, and validity. Telephone interviews, mail surveys, and electronic surveys are important tools to collect primary information from international markets in terms of both speed and cost. However, while collecting, compiling, and interpreting the information thus collected, various types of equivalences such as construct, measurement, data collection, and analysis need to be taken care of. The researcher needs to design appropriate operational strategies to resolve the emic versus etic dilemma, whether to emphasize developing different constructs for different markets or identifying and developing uniform tools that can be used across the countries.

Summary

A firm desirous of entering international markets needs to carry out market research to assess the feasibility of its products in the overseas markets and to map and analyse the market dynamics in target markets. This chapter provides various instances of market failures due to bottlenecks associated with conducting market research, resulting in loss of financial and other resources of the international firm. Research carried out across the national borders involving different cultures and countries has been referred to as international market research. Major challenges while conducting international market research include overlooking the cross-cultural market behaviour, inappropriate sample selection, and misinterpretation of cross-country data. The cultural traits influence the marketing research process at all the stages and influence significantly the cross-country market behaviour, which needs to be understood. The process of international marketing research involves problem identification, deciding research methodology, working out information requirements, identifying sources of information, preparing research designs, collecting primary information, its analysis, evaluation, and interpretation.

Whether a particular study is understood and interpreted in the same manner in various countries refers to equivalences in international marketing. The major types of equivalences in international marketing research include construct, measurement, data collection, and analysis. Construct equivalence refers to whether the marketing constructs (i.e., product functionality, interpretation of marketing stimuli, and classification schemes) under the study have the same meaning across the countries. Measurement equivalence refers to establishing equivalences in measuring methods and instruments such as measurement equivalence, translation equivalence, and metric equivalence. Sampling equivalence refers to comparability and representativeness of the samples drawn. Equivalence of data analysis involves taking into account various cultural biases while applying uniform analytical techniques to cross-country information.

Etic and emic refer to two polar schools of thoughts of cross-country research methodology. The etic emphasizes cultural uniqueness, while the emic emphasizes pan-culturalism in behavioural patterns and research process. While conducting cross-country market research, emphasis is placed on identifying similarities across the national markets and developing constructs that have wide feasibility and applicability.

Key Terms

Back translation Questionnaire is translated from one language to another and then a second party translates it back into the original.

Calibration equivalence Equivalence in the system of calibration such as monetary units, measure of weight, distances, and volume.

Causative research Marketing research to test hypothesis to establish cause and effect relationship.

Classification or category equivalence Variation in the category or product class from country to country.

Conceptual equivalence The extent of variation in individual interpretation of objects, stimuli, or behaviour across the cultures.

Construct equivalence Whether the marketing constructs (i.e., product functionality, interpretation of marketing stimuli, and classification schemes) under the study have the same meaning across the countries.

Decentring A hybrid of back translation, wherein a successive process of translation and retranslation of a questionnaire is used each time, by a different translator, till there is no perceptible difference in the two versions.

Descriptive research Marketing research to better describe marketing problems, situations, or markets.

Emic Holds that attitudes, interests, and behaviour are unique to a culture and best understood in their own terms, and emphasizes studying the research problem in each country's specific context.

Equivalence of data analysis Equivalence of the country–culture biases while carrying out data analysis.

Equivalences Whether the particular concept being studied is understood and interpreted in the same manner by people of various cultures.

Etic Emphasizes identifying and assessing universal attitudinal and behavioural concepts and developing 'pan-cultural' measures.

Exploratory research Marketing research to gather preliminary information that will help to better define problems and suggest hypothesis.

Functional equivalence Whether the function or purpose served or performed by a given concept or behaviour is the same across the national markets.

International marketing research Market research that crosses national borders and involves respondents and researchers from different countries and cultures.

Measurement equivalence Equivalence in terms of procedures used to measure concepts or attitudes.

Metric equivalence Equivalence of scale or procedure to establish as measure and equivalences of responses of the given measure in different countries.

Parallel translation   Using more than two translators for the back translation and subsequently the results are compared, differences discussed, and the most appropriate translation is selected.

Process of international marketing research   The planned, systematic, and comprehensive approach to carry out international marketing research.

Research design   The specification of methods and procedures for acquiring the information needed to structure or to solve problems.

Translation equivalence   Equivalence in meaning while translation of the instrument across different languages.

Concept Review Questions

1. 'Effective international marketing research is crucial to prevent marketing failures.' Justify the statement with suitable examples.
2. Briefly describe the process of international marketing research.
3. Briefly examine the distinction between construct and measurement equivalence.

4. Critically evaluate the emic versus etic dilemma in international marketing research. Suggest techniques for its operationalization.

Critical Thinking Questions

1. A Jaipur-based firm is engaged in importing rough stones from Africa and polishing and selling precious stones in the international market. The firm has recently started polishing Tanzanite—stones imported from Tanzania. As recently appointed head of the firm's International Market Development Division, prepare a research plan detailing out the requirement for secondary information and possible sources of collecting information.

2. Compile an exhaustive list of sources providing commercial intelligence in your country.
3. Work out a research plan to explore market potential and consumer behaviour for an Indian herbal fairness cream for the Middle East. How does primary data collection in the Middle East differ from that in India?

Project Assignments

1. Visit the nearby library having information on international markets and compile a detailed list of various sources of information that can be used for conducting international marketing research.
2. Surf the Internet and list various resources from where you could get information that can be used for conducting international marketing research. Critically comment on the limitations of each of the information source from the Internet. Discuss your findings in groups in class.

3. Contact an office of a multinational firm in your town and discuss with the company's marketing manager about the different research techniques adopted by them in different countries. Identify the differences in research techniques adopted in India vis-à-vis other countries.

Exploring International Trade Opportunities

Learning Objectives

- To explain the significance of international trade patterns in marketing decisions
- To provide an overview of world trade
- To critically evaluate India's foreign trade
- To identify key issues in India's exports growth
- To explain the concepts of balance of payment (BoP) and balance of trade (BoT)
- To explain the concept of terms of trade
- To discuss strategic measures to promote India's exports

INTRODUCTION

A marketing manager needs to keep a constant watch on the dynamics of international markets and work out suitable strategies to identify and penetrate into countries with high market potential. The past patterns of international trade not only help in analysing various factors related to international marketing environment, which cause changes in the flow of goods and services, but also facilitate in developing an insight into various types of products marketed across the countries.

World trade has undergone considerable changes, from unrestricted trade prior to World War I, followed by several barriers to trade imposed by various nations, to the subsequent era of globalization with an emphasis on systematic removal of trade barriers under the multilateral trade regime of the WTO. Today, a large volume of goods and services are traded across national borders, as a result of which international marketing has emerged as a crucial management discipline.

The growth of world trade has generally been faster than the growth of world output over the years. It is evident from the fact that during 1986–95 the world output grew at an average rate of 3.3 per cent, while the world trade grew at 6.2 per cent. In the following decade, during 1995–2004, world output increased at the rate of 3.6 per cent, whereas the trade grew at 7 per cent. During 2005–2014, world trade is likely to grow at 4.7 per cent compared to world output growth at 3.7 per cent. It means that more goods and services have been traded across borders than their worldwide output and will continue to do so. Therefore, international marketing has a significant role to play in such a scenario.

A marketing manager needs to develop a thorough understanding of the patterns of international trade so as to carry out a macro-analysis for identifying marketing opportunities overseas. This chapter aims at providing an overview of the past and present trends in world trade including the composition and the direction of international trade. It also provides an insight into various issues related to world trade and particularly India's foreign trade sector. The upheavals in international trade have also been critically examined to identify the reasons for changing trade patterns. Future patterns of world output and trade have also been projected.

The outflow and inflow of funds through trade and investment in a country are often reflected in its BoP accounts, whereas the BoT reveals differences between a country's net foreign exchange flow and its exports and imports. Though India's exports have grown considerably over the last decades in absolute terms, its export performance has been much lower compared to a number of Southeast Asian countries. This chapter brings out the strategic measures to promote exports in India.

BACKGROUND OF INTERNATIONAL TRADE PATTERNS

The integration of a country's economy with the rest of the world is associated with faster growth. It is observed that the countries that trade more grow faster.[1] Rapid integration of economies in terms of trade flows, movement of capital, and migration of people took place during the pre-World War I period of 1870 to 1914 and witnessed the growth of globalization mainly led by technological forces in the field of transport and communication. There were fewer barriers to flow of trade and people across geographical boundaries. In fact, there were no passports and visa requirements and very few non-tariff barriers and restrictions on fund flows.[2]

However, between World Wars I and II, the pace of globalization decelerated. Various rules to restrict free movement of goods and services were introduced during the inter-war period. Under high protective walls, most economies recorded higher growth. After World War II, it was resolved by all leading countries that earlier mistakes committed by them to isolate themselves should not be repeated. Moreover, after 1945, there was a drive to increase integration and cooperation among countries in the area of trade and commerce, which took a long time to reach the pre-World War I level. In terms of the percentage of imports and exports to total output, the USA could reach the pre-World War I level of 11 per cent only around 1970. Most of the developing countries that gained independence from colonial rule in the immediate post-World War II period followed an import substitution strategy to promote local industries. The countries from Soviet Bloc shielded themselves from the process of global economic integration.

An overview of India's foreign trade reveals that in value terms India's exports have grown from US$1.01 billion in 1949–50 to US$304.6 billion in 2011–12 before declining to US$300 billion in 2012–13, but India's share in world exports declined considerably from 2.53 per cent in 1947 to 0.43 per cent in 1980. But, thereafter its share has increased to 1.6 per cent in 2012.

WORLD TRADE: AN OVERVIEW

World trade has grown significantly over the years. The world merchandise exports grew from US$59 billion in 1948 to US$18.32 trillion in 2012, whereas the imports grew from US$62 billion to US$18.56 trillion during the same period. The export of services grew more rapidly compared to merchandise exports from US$390.8 billion in 1980 to US$4.34 trillion in 2012, whereas the imports of services grew from US$431.8 billion to US$4.10 trillion during the same period. Commercial services accounted for 19.2 per cent, whereas the merchandise exports

---

[1] The World Bank, *Global Economic Prospects*, Washington D.C., 2004, pp. 38–42.
[2] Streeten, Paul, 'Globalization: Threat or Salvation?', *Globalization, Growth and Marginalization*, (ed.) A.S. Bhalla, International Development Research Centre, Ottawa, 1998.

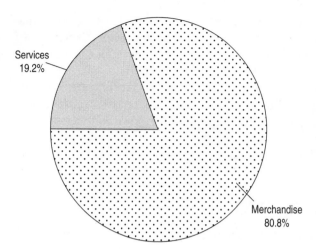

Fig. 7.1 Composition of world trade, 2012

Source: International Trade Statistics, 2013, WTO.

accounted for 80.8 per cent of world trade in 2012, as indicated in Fig. 7.1.

World Merchandise Trade

A cross-country comparison of share of world merchandise exports (Table 7.1) reveals that the share of the USA in the world merchandise exports significantly decreased from 21.7 per cent in 1948 to 8.4 per cent in 2012, whereas the share of the UK declined from 11.4 per cent in 1948 to 2.6 per cent in 2012. The share of Japan and China increased significantly from 0.4 per cent and 0.9 per cent in 1948 to 4.6 per cent and 11.2 per cent, respectively in 2012. While the share of Asian countries, such as China and Japan, grew remarkably in the world merchandise exports, India's share in world trade declined from 2.2 per cent in 1948 to 1.1 per cent by 1963 and further to 0.5 per cent in 1973. The erosion was lowest at 0.42 per cent in 1980. However, it subsequently increased sluggishly to a 1.6 per cent share of world trade in 2012 (Fig. 7.2).

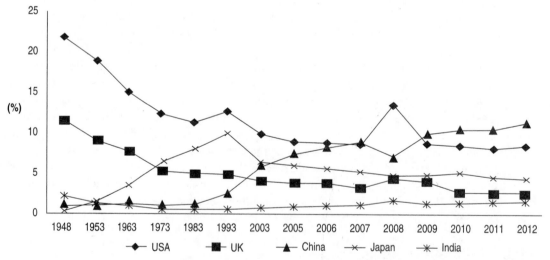

Fig. 7.2 Cross-country comparison of share in world merchandise exports

Source: International Trade Statistics, 2013, WTO.

High-income countries account for more than three-quarters of the world's gross domestic product (GDP) and for three-quarters of the world trade. Besides, these high-income countries also remain the major markets for low- and middle-income countries. With the re-strengthening of the US economy and the growth prospects for emerging markets, especially developing Asia, it is expected that the growth of world output as well as trade volumes would be higher in emerging markets and developing countries as compared to advanced economies. China became the largest exporter, whereas the USA was the largest importer of world merchandise trade in 2012.

Table 7.1 Cross-country comparison of share in world merchandise exports (in %)

	1948	1953	1963	1973	1983	1993	2003	2006	2008	2009	2011
World	100.0	100.0	100.0	100.0	100.0	100.0	100.0	100.0	100.0	100.0	100.0
North America	28.3	24.9	19.9	17.3	16.8	18.0	15.8	14.2	18.1	13.2	12.8
USA	21.7	18.8	14.9	12.3	11.2	12.6	9.8	8.8	13.5	8.7	8.3
Canada	5.5	5.2	4.1	4.3	4.2	4.0	3.7	3.3	2.6	2.6	2.5
Mexico	1.0	0.7	0.6	0.4	1.4	1.4	2.2	2.1	2.0	1.9	2.0
South and Central America	12.3	10.5	7.0	4.7	4.4	3.0	3.0	3.6	3.7	3.8	4.2
Brazil	2.0	1.8	0.9	1.1	1.2	1.0	1.0	1.2	1.1	1.3	1.4
Argentina	2.8	1.3	0.9	0.6	0.4	0.4	0.4	0.4	0.4	0.5	0.5
Europe	31.5	34.9	41.4	45.4	43.5	45.4	45.9	42.1	42.3	41.2	37.1
Germany[a]	1.4	5.3	9.8	12.5	9.2	10.3	10.2	9.4	7.5	9.2	8.3
France	3.5	4.8	5.1	6.1	5.2	6.0	5.3	4.2	4.4	4.0	3.3
UK	11.4	9.0	7.6	5.2	5.0	4.9	4.1	3.8	3.9	3.3	2.9
Italy	1.9	1.8	3.2	3.8	4.0	4.6	4.1	3.5	3.4	2.9	2.7
Commonwealth of Independent States (CIS)[b]	–	–	–	–	–	1.5	2.6	3.6	3.1	3.7	4.4
Africa	7.3	6.5	5.7	4.8	4.5	2.5	2.4	3.1	2.9	3.2	3.3
South Africa[c]	2.0	1.7	1.5	1.0	1.0	0.7	0.5	0.5	0.6	0.5	0.5
Middle East	2.0	2.7	3.2	4.1	6.8	3.5	4.1	5.5	3.6	5.7	7.0
Asia	13.6	13.1	12.4	14.9	19.1	26.1	26.2	27.8	26.4	29.4	31.1
China	0.9	1.2	1.3	1.0	1.2	2.5	5.9	8.2	7.0	9.9	10.7
Japan	0.4	1.5	3.5	6.4	8.0	9.9	6.4	5.5	4.7	4.8	4.6
India	2.2	1.3	1.0	0.5	0.5	0.6	0.8	1.0	1.8	1.3	1.7
Australia and New Zealand	3.7	3.2	2.4	2.1	1.4	1.5	1.2	1.2	1.5	1.5	1.7
Six East Asian traders	3.0	2.7	2.4	3.4	5.8	9.7	9.6	9.6	8.9	9.6	9.8

[a] Figures refer to the Fed. Rep. of Germany from 1948 through 1983.
[b] Figures are significantly affected by changes in the country composition of the region and major adjustment in trade conversion factors between 1983 and 1993.
[c] Beginning with 1998, figures refer only to South Africa and no longer to the Southern Africa Customs Union.
Source: International Trade Statistics, 2012, WTO.

The USA has also been the highest exporter as well as importer in commercial services trade in 2012. India was the 19th largest exporter and the 10th largest importer of world merchandise trade in 2012, whereas it was the sixth largest exporter and seventh largest importer of commercial services in 2012.

The growth of world merchandise trade in 2012 was much lower than one would have expected given the rate of world GDP growth for the year. Under normal conditions, the growth rate for trade is usually around twice that of GDP, but in 2012 the ratio of trade growth to GDP growth fell to 1:1.

Direction of world merchandise trade

'Direction of trade' is often referred to describe the statistical analysis of the set of a country's trading partners and their significance in trade. The set of countries where the goods are exported and their significance on a country's exports is known as 'direction of exports'. On the other hand, the set of countries from where the goods are imported and their significance on a country's imports is known as 'direction of imports'.

The world exports have primarily been dominated by the developed market economies having 66.8 per cent share in 1980, which increased to 72.5 per cent in 1990, while their share declined to 52.7 per cent in 2011 (Fig. 7.3). The share of developing countries decreased from 29.2 per cent in 1980 to 24.3 per cent in 1990. However, its share increased to 42.7 per cent in 2011, while the share of economies in transition declined from 4 per cent in 1980 to 3.2 per cent in 1990, which further increased to 4.5 per cent in 2011 (Table 7.2). This change has been mainly because of economic and political upheavals in economies in transition. It is noteworthy that the annual average growth rate of exports of 6.35 per cent in developed countries in 1980–90 declined to 5.80 per cent in 2000–09.

A regionwise comparison indicates that the share of North America in world merchandise export declined significantly from 28.3 per cent in 1948 to 12.8 per cent in 2011, whereas the share of South America and Central America fell from 12.3 per cent in 1948 to 4.2 per cent in 2011 and the share of Africa dropped from 7.3 per cent in 1948 to 3.3 per cent in 2011. The share of Europe in world merchandise exports increased from 31.1 per cent in 1948 to 37.1 per cent in

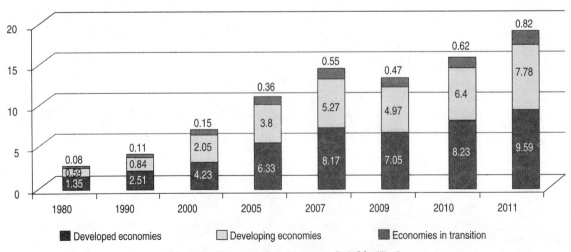

Fig. 7.3   Direction of world exports (in US$ trillion)

Source: UNCTAD Handbook of Statistics, United Nations, Geneva, New York, 2012.

Table 7.2 Direction of world exports (FOB US$ trillion)

Year	Developed economies	Developing economies	Economies in transition
1980	1.35	0.59	0.08
1990	2.51	0.84	0.11
2000	4.23	2.05	0.15
2005	6.33	3.8	0.36
2007	8.17	5.27	0.55
2009	7.05	4.97	0.47
2010	8.23	6.4	0.62
2011	9.59	7.78	0.82

Source: *UNCTAD Handbook of Statistics*, United Nations, Geneva, New York, 2012.

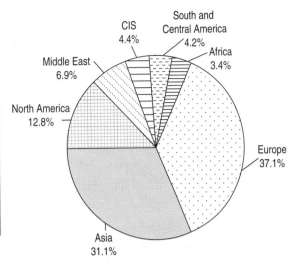

Fig. 7.4 Direction of world merchandise exports, 2011

Source: *International Trade Statistics*, 2012, WTO.

2011, the share of Middle East rose from 2.2 per cent to 7 per cent, whereas that of Asia grew considerably from 14 per cent to 31.1 per cent during the same period (Fig. 7.4).

Europe with US$6.85 trillion (Fig. 7.5) accounted for 38.1 per cent of world merchandise imports in 2011, followed by Asia with US$5.56 trillion (30.9%), North America with US$3.09 trillion (17.2%), South and Central America with US$727 billion (4%), Middle East with US$665 billion (3.7%),) CIS with US$540 billion (3%), and Africa with US$555 billion (3.1%).

China was the leading exporter in 2012 with US$2.04 trillion (Table 7.3) accounting for 11.2 per cent share of world exports, followed by the USA (8.4%), Germany (7.7%), Japan (4.4%), and the

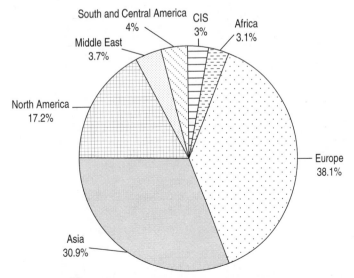

Fig. 7.5 Direction of world merchandise imports, 2011

Source: *International Trade Statistics*, 2012, WTO.

Table 7.3   Leading exporters and importers in world merchandise trade, 2012

Rank	Exporters	Value (US$ billion)	Share (%)	Rank	Importers	Value (US$ billion)	Share (%)
1	China	2,049	11.2	1	USA	2,335	12.6
2	USA	1,547	8.4	2	China	1,818	9.8
3	Germany	1,407	7.7	3	Germany	1,167	6.3
4	Japan	799	4.4	4	Japan	886	4.8
5	Netherlands	656	3.6	5	UK	680	3.7
6	France	569	3.1	6	France	674	3.6
7	Korea, Republic	548	3.0	7	Netherlands	591	3.2
8	Russian Federation	529	2.9	8	Hong Kong China	554	3.0
9	Italy	500	2.7		retained imports	140	0.8
10	Hong Kong, China	493	2.7	9	Korea, Repulic of	520	2.8
	Domestic exports	22	0.1	10	India	489	2.6
	Re-exports	471	2.6	11	Italy	486	2.6
11	UK	468	2.6	12	Canada	475	2.6
12	Canada	455	2.5	13	Belgium	435	2.3
13	Belgium	446	2.4	14	Mexico	380	2.0
14	Singapore	408	2.2	15	Singapore	380	2.0
	Domestic exports	228	1.2		Retained imports	199	1.0
	Re-exports	180	1.0	16	Russian Federation	335	1.8
15	Saudi Arabia, Kingdom of	386	2.1	17	Spain	332	1.8
16	Mexico	371	2.0	18	Taipei, Chinese	270	1.5
17	Taipei, Chinese	301	1.6	19	Australia	261	1.4
18	UAE	300	1.6	20	Thailand	248	1.3
19	**India**	**293**	**1.6**	21	Turkey	237	1.3
20	Spain	292	1.6	22	Brazil	233	1.3
21	Australia	257	1.4	23	UAE	220	1.2
22	Brazil	243	1.3	24	Switzerland	198	1.1
23	Thailand	230	1.3	25	Malaysia	197	1.1
24	Malaysia	227	1.2	26	Poland	196	1.1
25	Switzerland	226	1.2	27	Indonesia	190	1.0
26	Indonesia	188	1.0	28	Austria	178	1.0
27	Poland	183	1.0	29	Sweden	162	0.9
28	Sweden	172	0.9	30	Saudi Arabia, Kingdom of	144	0.8
29	Austria	166	0.9		**Total of above**	**15,270**	**82.3**
30	Norway	160	0.9		**World**	**18,565**	**100.0**
	Total of above	**14,870**	**81.2**				
	World	**18,325**	**100.0**				

Source: International Trade Statistics, 2013, WTO.

Netherlands (3.6%). The USA remained the single largest importer with US$2.33 trillion accounting for 12.6 per cent share of world imports, followed by China (9.8%), Germany (6.3%), Japan (4.8%), the UK (3.7%), and France (3.9%). India ranked at the 19th position with US$293 billion accounting for 1.6 per cent share in world mercandise exports, whereas it ranked at the 10th position with US$489 billion with 2.6 per cent share in world merchandise imports in 2012.

Composition of world merchandise trade

The statistical analysis of a country's product groups in its international trade is often referred to as 'composition of trade'. This can be carried out for the trade with all the countries in the world collectively or individually, with a group of countries, or a particular country. Such an analysis carried out for product groups exported is known as 'composition of exports', whereas the analysis carried out for product groups imported is known as 'composition of imports'.

Transformation in the composition of product mix of exports, as shown in Fig. 7.6, has been remarkable. The manufactured goods which accounted for 49.8 per cent in 1965 increased to 73.9 per cent in 2000, but later declined to 63.5 per cent in 2011. The share of agricultural raw materials came down significantly from 7.8 per cent in 1965 to 1.7 per cent in 2011. Food items that constituted 18.2 per cent of world merchandise exports in 1965 declined to 6.2 per cent in 2008 with a marginal increase of 7.7 per cent in 2011. The exports of ores and metals decreased substantially from 12 per cent in 1965 to 3 per cent in 2001 but thereafter it increased to 11 per cent in 2009 but later declined to 6.7 per cent in 2011. The world exports of fuel increased sharply from 9.3 per cent in 1970 to 24 per cent in 1980, which later declined to 9.4 per cent in 2002. However, it increased to 17.4 per cent in 2011. Figure 7.7 gives the changing patterns of composition of world merchandise exports for the years 1965–2011. Developing countries derived 70 per cent of merchandise export revenue from sales of primary commodities—agriculture and energy—two decades ago, whereas presently 80 per cent of their revenue comes from export of manufactured goods. Developing countries now rely less on the shipments of primary commodities than on manufactured goods.

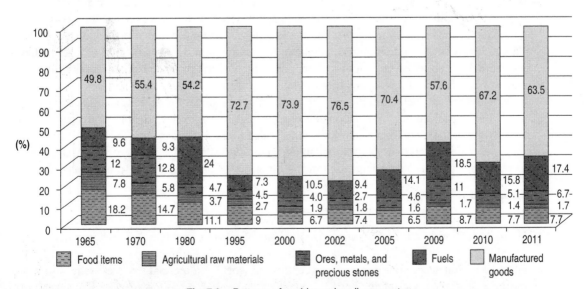

Fig. 7.6 Patterns of world merchandise exports

Source: UNCTAD Handbook of Statistics, United Nations, Geneva, New York, 2012.

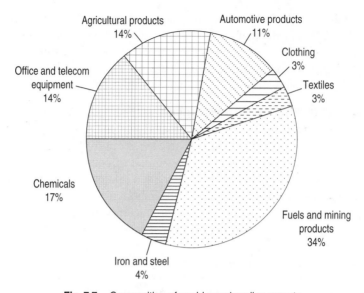

Fig. 7.7 Composition of world merchandise exports

Source: UNCTAD Handbook of Statistics, United Nations, Geneva, New York, 2012.

The effect of export composition will continue to influence the overall growth during the coming decade as the share of manufactured products continues to rise further. The factors responsible for the change in the composition of exports include policy reforms, structural changes in global production process, and global economic trends.

The policy reforms that started in East Asia in the 1970s were later initiated in other regions culminating in a rapid acceleration of reforms during the 1990s. Reduction of trade barriers in manufacturing had been the key element of policy reforms—unilaterally, regionally, or multilaterally. But in all successful cases, broader institutional reforms played a crucial role.

The developments in the field of technology lowered transportation costs, improved communications and business practices, and made it possible to build global production networks. This radically altered geographic specialization patterns and intensified trade in intermediate products. The continued growth of real per capita income triggered consumers' desire for more and newer varieties of goods, creating markets for foreign goods.

Moreover, these factors reinforced one another; for example, lower trade barriers triggered a new global organization of production to take advantage of the diversity in comparative advantage across the world. Desire for new products and a search for new markets provided a strong incentive for lower trade barriers. Besides, the technological development and income growth got spurred by increased intensity of global competition and the efficiency gains through global production networks.

World Services Trade

The world commercial services exports increased rapidly from US$390.8 billion in 1980 to US$4.34 trillion in 2012. A countrywise analysis of world commercial services as delineated in Table 7.4 reveals that the USA was the largest exporter of commercial services in 2012 with US$614 billion accounting for 14.1 per cent of the world commercial services trade, followed by the UK (6.4%), Germany (5.9%), France (4.8%), and China (4.4%). The USA was also the largest importer of services with US$406 billion accounting for 9.9 per cent, followed by Germany (6.9%), China (6.8%), UK (4.3%), and Japan (4.2%). India ranked at the sixth position

Table 7.4   Leading exporters and importers in world commercial services trade, 2012

Rank	Exporters	Value (US$ billion)	Share (%)	Rank	Importers	Value (US$ billion)	Share (%)
1	USA	614	14.1	1	USA	406	9.9
2	UK	278	6.4	2	Germany	285	6.9
3	Germany	255	5.9	3	China	281	6.8
4	France	208	4.8	4	UK	176	4.3
5	China	190	4.4	5	Japan	174	4.2
6	**India**	**148**	**3.4**	6	France	171	4.2
7	Japan	140	3.2	7	**India**	**125**	**3.0**
8	Spain	140	3.2	8	Singapore	117	2.8
9	Singapore	133	3.1	9	Netherlands	115	2.8
10	Netherlands	126	2.9	10	Ireland	110	2.7
11	Hong Kong, China	126	2.9	11	Canada	105	2.6
12	Ireland	115	2.6	12	Korea, Republic of	105	2.6
13	Korea, Republic of	109	2.5	13	Italy	105	2.6
14	Italy	104	2.4	14	Russian Federation	102	2.5
15	Belgium	94	2.2	15	Belgium	90	2.2
16	Switzerland	88	2.0	16	Spain	90	2.2
17	Canada	78	1.8	17	Brazil	78	1.9
18	Sweden	76	1.7	18	Australia	65	1.6
19	Luxembourg	70	1.6	19	Denmark	57	1.4
20	Denmark	65	1.5	20	Hong Kong China	57	1.4
21	Austria	61	1.4	21	Sweden	55	1.3
22	Russian Federation	58	1.3	22	Thailand	53	1.3
23	Australia	53	1.2	23	UAE	50	1.2
24	Norway	50	1.2	24	Saudi Arabia, Kingdom of	49	1.2
25	Thailand	49	1.1	25	Norway	49	1.2
26	Taipei, Chinese	49	1.1	26	Switzerland	44	1.1
27	Macao, China	45	1.0	27	Austria	43	1.1
28	Turkey	42	1.0	28	Taipei, Chinese	42	1.0
29	Brazil	38	0.9	29	Malaysia	42	1.0
30	Poland	38	0.9	30	Luxumbourg	41	1.0
	Total of above	**3,640**	**83.7**		**Total of above**	**3,285**	**80.0**
	World	**4,345**	**100.0**		**World**	**4,105**	**100.0**

Source: *International Trade Statistics*, 2013, WTO.

with US$148 billion accounting for 3.4 per cent share in export of world commercial services, whereas it ranked seventh with US$125 billion with 3 per cent share in services imports in 2012.

Since the commercial services data are derived from BoP statistics, it does not include the sales of majority-owned foreign affiliates abroad. 'Other commercial services' that include software, education, health, financial services, etc. has been the fastest growing category. India has a strategic edge in services trade and continues to excel in its expansion.

Direction of world commercial services trade

Europe with US$1.9 trillion accounted for 47.3 per cent of total world commercial services exports (Fig. 7.8) worth US$4.15 trillion, in 2011. It was followed by Asia with US$1.09 trillion

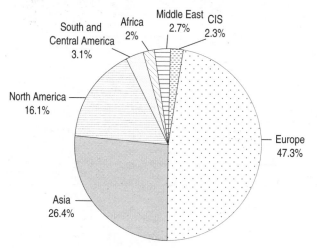

Fig. 7.8 Direction of world commercial services: exports, 2011

Source: World Trade Report, 2012.

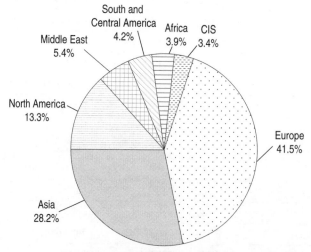

Fig. 7.9 Direction of world commercial services: imports, 2011

Source: World Trade Report, 2012.

(26.4%), North America with US$668 billion (16.1%), South and Central America with US$130 billion (3.1%), Africa with US$85 billion (2%), Middle East with US$111 billion (2.7%), and CIS with US$96 billion (2.3%).

Europe was also the highest importer of world commercial services (Fig. 7.9) with US$1.60 trillion (41.5%) in 2011, followed by Asia with US$1.09 trillion (28.2%), North America with US$516 billion (13.3%), Middle East with US$210 billion (5.4%), Africa with US$149 billion (3.9%), South and Central America with US$163 billion (4.2%), and CIS with US$133 billion (2.4%) of the total imports of world commercial services worth US$3.86 trillion.

Composition of world commercial services trade

The categorywise break-up of commercial services of exports in Fig. 7.10 indicates that travel accounted for US$1.06 trillion (25.5%), transport for US$885 billion (20.4%), and other commercial services for US$2350 billion (54.1%) in 2012. It is interesting to note that other commercial services are not only the largest category, but also the fastest growing category.

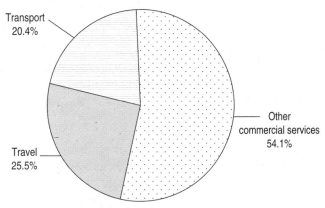

Fig. 7.10   Composition of world commercial services trade

Source: International Trade Statistics, 2013, WTO.

INDIA'S FOREIGN TRADE: AN OVERVIEW

India's foreign trade has grown significantly as shown in Fig. 7.11. India's exports increased from US$1.26 billion in 1950–51 to US$304.6 billion in 2011–12 but declined to US$300 billion in 2012–13, while the imports increased much rapidly from US$1.27 billion in 1950–51 to US$491.4 billion in 2012–13. The exports witnessed a negative growth during a number of years as it declined sharply by 18.6 per cent during 1952–53. Moreover, there had been a significant fall in India's exports by 8.1 per cent in 1953–54, 7 per cent in 1957–58, 9.9 per cent in 1985–86, 5.1 per cent in 1998–99, 1.6 per cent in 2001–02, 3.5 per cent in 2009–10, and 1.3 per cent in 2012–13. India's exports grew at about 20 per cent in phases: during 1950–52, 1972–77, 1987–90, 1993–96, and 2000–08 and increased at its record growth of 40.5 per cent in 2010–11 but exhibited a negative growth during 2012–13.

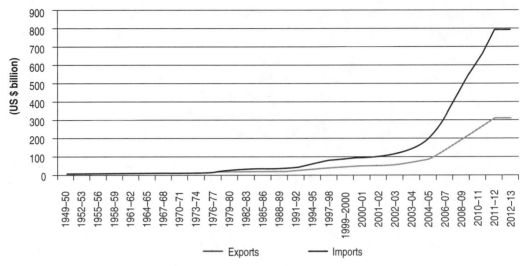

Fig. 7.11 India's foreign trade

Source: Based on DGCI&S data, 2013.

Most developing countries, including India, are relatively smaller players and have little ability to influence the demand and pricing patterns in the international markets. Unless a country commands a significant share in international markets, it has to heavily depend upon the prevailing market prices and get affected by strategic moves of major players in the international markets.

Direction of India's Merchandise Trade

While identifying international markets, the direction of trade patterns facilitates in carrying out macro-analysis of flow of goods and services across borders. Such direction of international trade is also highly dynamic in nature. The share of the top 15 trading partners increased by 5.5 per cent points to 60.3 per cent in 2007–08 compared to 2000–01. However, it did not change much as the top 15 countries continue to hold a share of around 60 per cent even in 2012–13 (April–November). But, the top 15 countries have themselves changed over the years. The major changes are the entry of developing countries such as Indonesia, Korea, Iraq, Kuwait, and Nigeria in the new list in place of Italy, Malaysia, the UK, France, and Australia.

Interestingly, the USA that had long been India's largest trading partner till 2007–08 was relegated to the third position in 2008–09 with the UAE becoming India's largest trading partner, followed by China. Till 2010–11, the UAE remained India's largest trading partner primarily due to India's significant trade of gems and jewellery items followed by petroleum, oil, and lubricants (POL) with UAE. The rising trade with the UAE may also be, to some extent, due to circular trading. However in 2011–12, UAE was relegated to the second position first by China and China in turn was relegated to the second position by the UAE in 2012–13 (April–November).

Exports

A destination-wise analysis reveals that India's exports have undergone a significant change over the years. The share of the Organization for Economic Cooperation and Development (OECD) countries in value terms declined from 59 per cent in 1987–88 to 32.84 per cent in 2011–12, as indicated in Fig. 7.12. Exports to the European Union (EU) have gone down considerably

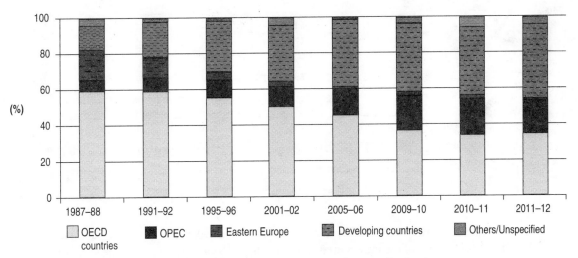

Fig. 7.12 Direction of India's foreign trade: exports (% share)

Source: Based on DGCI&S data, 2013.

from 36.2 per cent in 1960–61 to 17.3 per cent in 2011–12. The UK that accounted for 26.9 per cent of India's exports in 1960–61 decreased to 2.8 per cent in 2011–12. USA's share in India's exports declined from 16 per cent in 1960–61 to 11.1 per cent in 1980–81 and later increased substantially to 20.7 per cent in 2002–03 but thereafter declined to 11.3 per cent in 2011–12. India's exports to Japan have exhibited a fluctuating trend as it increased from 5.5 per cent in 1960–61 to 13.3 per cent in 1970–71, but thereafter declined to 2.1 per cent by 2011–12.

India's export share to the Organization of the Petroleum Exporting Countries (OPEC) has grown from 4.1 per cent in 1960–61 to 19.04 per cent in 2011–12. Its exports to Saudi Arabia increased from 0.5 per cent in 1960–61 to 1.8 per cent in 2011–12. India's exports to Eastern Europe increased rapidly from 7 per cent in 1960–61 to 21 per cent in 1970–71 but later declined substantially to 1.06 per cent in 2011–12. India's exports to Russia increased substantially from 4.5 per cent in 1960–61 to 18.3 per cent in 1980–81, which declined sharply after the break-up of the former USSR from 16.1 per cent in 1990–91 to 3.3 per cent in 1995–96, which further decreased to 0.6 per cent in 2011–12. India's share of exports to other less developed countries increased from 14.8 per cent in 1960–61 to 40.7 per cent in 2011–12, which reveals considerable diversification in its export markets.

Imports

India's dependence on imports from OECD has substantially decreased from 60 per cent in 1987–88 to 29.6 per cent in 2011–12, as shown in Fig. 7.13. There has been a significant reduction in its imports from EU from 37.1 per cent in 1960–61 to 11.7 per cent in 2011–12. This had largely been due to a significant decline in India's imports from the UK from 19.4 per cent in 1960–61 to 7.8 per cent in 1970–71, which had further gone down to 1.6 per cent in 2011–12.

The share of India's imports from North America decreased significantly from 31 per cent in 1960–61 to 10.7 per cent in 2010–11, which was mainly due to a decline in share of imports from the USA. Although the share of the USA has declined substantially from 29.2 per cent in 1960–61 to 4.8 per cent in 2011–12, it remained the largest exporter to India till 2003; thereafter China became the largest exporter to India. India's imports from Canada that increased initially

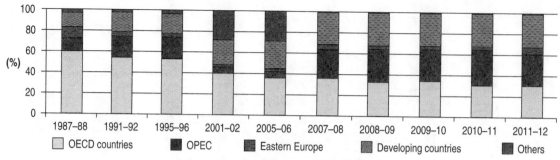

Fig. 7.13 Direction of India's trade: imports (% share)

Source: Based on DGCI&S data, 2013.

from 1.8 per cent in 1960–61 to 7.2 per cent in 1970–71 have subsequently gone down to 0.5 per cent in 2011–12. One of the important developments had been the increase in the share of India's imports from OPEC from 4.6 per cent in 1960–61 to its peak 35.4 per cent in 2011–12, as a result of a steep hike in India's oil bill.

Composition of India's Merchandise Trade

The product mix of exports and imports, widely known as 'composition of trade' has undergone a significant change over the last decades due to change in demand and competitiveness in international markets. It is remarkable to note that the agricultural and allied products that constituted 44.2 per cent of India's exports in 1960–61 only contributed about 14 per cent to India's exports during 2012–13 (April–November). However, export share of manufactured goods increased from 45.3 per cent in 1960–61 to 80.7 per cent during 1999–2000, but its share declined in the following years to 64.5 per cent in 2012–13 (April–November). It indicates a shift in India's market competitiveness from agro-based products to manufactured goods and value added products. Even among manufactured products, the share of gems and jewellery increased from 0.1 per cent in 1960–61 to 20.4 per cent in 1999–2000, which is indicative of India's capacity development, especially related to processing skills of raw stones and manufacturing of jewellery. However, its share declined in the following years to 12.6 per cent in 2008–09 but increased later to 23.9 per cent in 2012–13 (April–November). The ready-made garments segment has emerged as another star performer, whose share increased from 0.1 per cents in 1960–61 to 12.5 per cent in 2000–01. But, thereafter its share declined to 6.7 per cent in 2012–13 (April–November). These trends indicate the dynamic nature of international markets. Therefore, it is necessary for a manager to analyse international trade patterns while assessing international markets.

Exports

A positive development on the export front has been the steady rise in the share of manufactured goods in India's total exports, as shown in Fig. 7.14. The share of manufactured goods rose from 45.3 per cent in 1960–61 to 78 per cent in 2000–01. The 1980s was particularly remarkable in raising this share from 55.8 per cent in 1980–81 to 74.6 per cent in 1989–90 and further to 80.7 per cent in 1999–2000. However, this share has declined to 64.5 per cent in 2012–13 (April–November). Another remarkable development has been the decline in the share of exports of agricultural and allied products from 44.2 per cent in 1960–61 to 31.7 per cent in 1970–71 and further to 13.5 per cent in 2001–02. This share decreased to 9.7 per cent

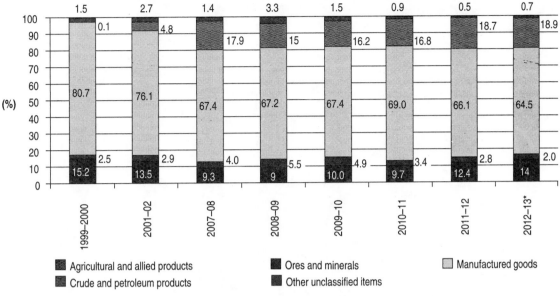

Fig. 7.14   Composition of India's trade: exports (% share)

*Refers to April–November
Source: Based on DGCI&S data, 2013.

in 2010–11 before increasing to 14 per cent in 2012–13 (April–November). The share of crude and petroleum products in India's exports increased from 0.1 per cent in 1999–2000 to 18.9 per cent in 2012–13 (April–November). The rising domestic refining capacity enabled continued robust growth in exports of petroleum products. The share of ores and minerals increased from 2.5 per cent in 1999–2000 to 4.9 per cent in 2009–10 but declined to 2 per cent in 2012–13 (April–November).

In 2012–13, export growth became broad based both in commodity groups and manufacturing goods. The manufacturing sector was the major contributor to this rise. Major traditional exports such as textiles (including garments), gems and jewellery, engineering goods (especially iron and steel, non-ferrous metals, transport equipment, and projects goods), chemicals and related products, and electronic goods contributed to the bulk of such increase in manufactured goods exports. The manufactured goods category (Fig. 7.15) consisted of gems and jewellery (22.9%), ready-made garments (6.7%), cotton yarn fabrics (3.9%), pharmaceuticals and fine chemicals (7.8%), machinery and instruments (8.1%), manufacture of metals (5.6%), primary and semi-finished iron and steel (2.5%), handicrafts (0.2%), leather and manufactures (1.7%), electronic goods (4.7%), transport equipment (9.8%), dyes, intermediates, coal tar (2.3%), and leather footwear (0.9%). The share of gems and jewellery exports increased from 0.1 per cent in 1960–61 to 20.4 per cent in 1999–2000, however, its share declined to 16.6 per cent during 2003–04 (April–January) and further to 12.6 per cent in 2008–09 before increasing to 23.9 per cent in 2012–13 (April–November). The ready-made garments segment has been another star performer, whose share increased from 0.1 per cent in 1960–61 to 12.5 per cent in 2000–01, which subsequently declined to 7 per cent in 2008–09 and further to 6.7 per cent in 2012–13 (April–November).

In spite of a drought, exports of agricultural and allied commodities recorded a sharp turnaround, contributed mainly by enhanced exports of cereals (mainly non-basmati rice), marine products,

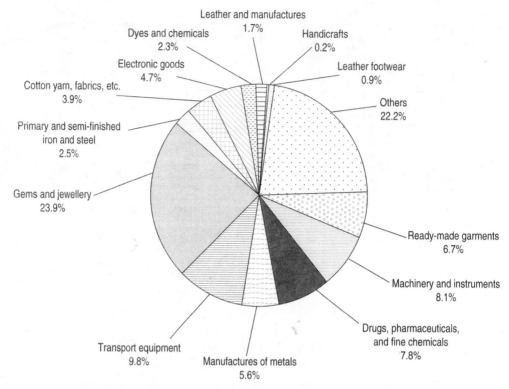

Fig. 7.15 Composition of India's exports of manufactured goods (2012–13*)

*Refers to April–November.
Source: Based on DGCI&S data, 2013.

spices, tobacco, cashew nuts, processed foods, meat and meat preparations, and floriculture products. India's exports of agricultural and allied products (Fig. 7.16) in 2012–13 (April–November) comprise of cereals (23.6%), marine products (10.2%), cashew nuts (2.4%), tea (2.4%), coffee (2.4%), spices (8.7%), fruits and vegetables (3.9%), and oil meals (4.7%).

Imports

A significant shift has taken place in India's imports since independence. Petroleum, oil, and lubricants that accounted for only 27.4 per cent in 1999–2000 rose to 38 per cent (Fig. 7.17) in 2012–13 (April–November). The import of fertilizers also grew from 1.1 per cent in 1960–61 to 5.2 per cent in 1970–71, and remained around 5 per cent in 1989–90. It decreased to 2.8% in 1999–2000. However, as a result of India's marked increase in fertilizer production, its imports came down to 1% during 2002–03. But thereafter, it increased to 1.9% in 2007–08 and further to 2.2 % during 2012–13 (April–November).

The share of cereal imports had gone down from 16.1 per cent in 1960–61 to 0.8 per cent in 1980–81 due to remarkable achievements domestically in increasing its agricultural production as a result of green revolution in India. Presently, India has become a net exporter of food grains. However, India's imports of edible oil rose significantly from 0.3 per cent in 1960–61 to 5.4 per cent in 1980–81 due to higher increase in demand as compared to its production. This declined to 0.6 per cent in 1989–90 as a result of a strategic measure taken to increase oil seed production, but it is again showing a rising trend. It increased to 3 per cent during 2002–03 but after that fell

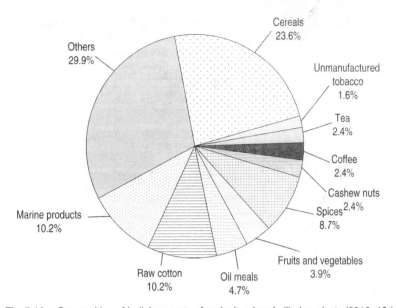

Fig. 7.16   Composition of India's exports of agricultural and allied products (2012–13*)

*Refers to April–November.
Source: Based on DGCI&S data, 2013.

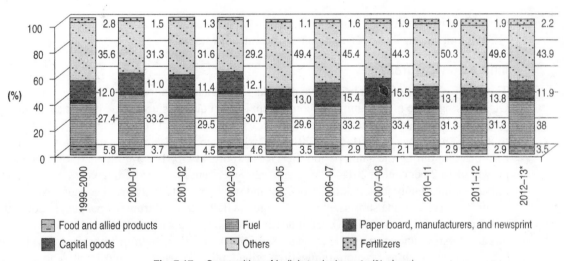

Fig. 7.17   Composition of India's trade: imports (% share)

*Refers to April–November.
Source: Based on DGCI&S data, 2013.

to 1.9 per cent during 2008–09 before increasing to 2 per cent in 2012–13 in (April–November). The import of capital goods has also declined substantially from 31.7 per cent in 1960–61 to 11 per cent in 2000–01 mainly because of India's own capacity building in production of capital goods and equipment but increased in the following years to 15.8 per cent in 2005–06, but thereafter declined to 11.9 per cent in 2012–13 (April–November). Other product categories in India's imports in 2012–13 comprised (Fig. 7.18) pearls, precious and semi-precious stones

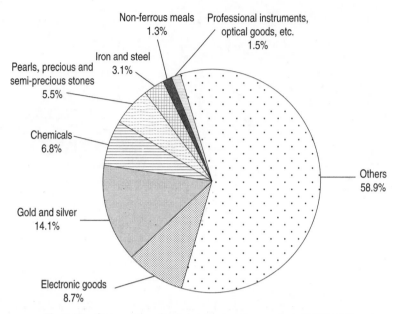

Fig. 7.18   Composition of India's imports: other products (2012–13*)

*Refers to April–November.
Source: Based on DGCI&S data, 2013.

(5.5%), gold and silver (14.1%), chemicals (6.8%), professional instruments, optical goods, etc. (1.5%), iron and steel (3.1%), and non-ferrous metals (1.3%).

India's Services Trade

The services sector in India has grown remarkably and accounts for over 55 per cent of India's GDP making it the most significant component of the country's economy. India's services export grew faster than the merchandise exports with the export of services growing at a CAGR of 23.6 per cent during 2001–02 to 2011–12, while merchandise exports grew at a CAGR of 21.4 per cent during the same period. Services exports at US$142.3 billion exhibited a lower growth of 14.2 per cent in 2011–12 as against 29.8 per cent in the preceding year, reflecting the impact of uncertainty in the global economy and weak growth in advanced economies.

India's services trade surplus as a percentage of GDP increased from 0.7 per cent in 2001–02 to 4.7 per cent in 2008–09. However, it declined to 2.8 per cent of the GDP in 2009–10 mainly due to global financial crisis. There had been considerable growth in transport, travel, and other services such as telecommunications, financial, construction, and legal. The exports of these services were matched by corresponding imports. Therefore, the software services were mainly responsible for surplus in services trade. Surplus on account of India's services exports has been a cushioning factor for financing a large part of the merchandise trade deficit in recent years. From 2006–07 to 2011–12, surplus in services exports, on an average, financed around 38 per cent of merchandise trade deficit. During 2011–12, net surplus on account of services exports at US$64.1 billion stood significantly higher than that in 2010–11 and financed 33.8 per cent[3] of trade deficit. During 2012–13, with slower growth in services exports and rise in services imports, the surplus was relatively lower compared to the previous year. In

---

[3] *Economic Survey*, 2012–13, Government of India.

the near future, downward risks to export of services persist as global economic conditions remain less conducive.

Over the years, the composition of services exports from India has undergone considerable change. Transportation accounted for 49.7 per cent of India's total services exports in 1970–71 and declined to 11.7 per cent in 2009–10 before increasing to 12.1 per cent in 2012–13 (April–September). Besides, the share of travel increased from 16.8 per cent in 1970–71 to 43.5 per cent in 1980–81, (Fig. 7.19 and Table 7.5) but declined later to 10.7 per cent in 2012–13 (April–September). There were hardly any software exports from India till 1990–91, which rapidly became the largest

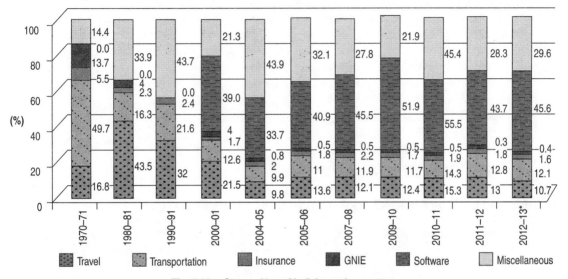

Fig. 7.19 Composition of India's services exports

*Refers to April–November.

Source: *Economic Survey*, 2012–13, Government of India.

Table 7.5 Composition of India's services exports

Year	Amount (US$ billion)	% share in total services exports					
		Travel	Transportation	Insurance	GNIE	Software	Miscellaneous**
1970–71	0.29	16.8	49.7	5.5	13.7	0	14.4
1980–81	2.8	43.5	16.3	2.3	4	0	33.9
1990–91	4.55	32	21.6	2.4	0.3	0	43.7
2000–01	16.26	21.5	12.6	1.7	4	39	21.3
2004–05	51.32	9.8	9.9	2	0.8	33.7	43.9
2005–06	57.65	13.6	11	1.8	0.5	40.9	32.1
2007–08	90.1	12.1	11.9	2.2	0.5	45.5	27.8
2009–10	95.8	12.4	11.7	1.7	0.5	51.9	21.9
2010–11	132.9	15.3	14.3	1.9	0.5	55.5	45.4
2011–12	142.3	13	12.8	1.8	0.3	43.7	28.3
2012–13*	n.a.	10.7	12.1	1.6	0.4	45.6	29.6

*Refers to April–September.

**Refers to 'excluding non-software service'.

Source: *Economic Survey*, 2012–13, Government of India.

constituent of India's services exports with 48.9 per cent share in 2003–04 and further increased to 55.5 per cent in 2010–11 but decreased to 45.6 per cent in 2012–13 (April–September). The exports of the miscellaneous services category, which comprises business services, financial services, and commercial services, grew remarkably from 14.4 per cent in 1970–71 to 45.4 per cent in 2010–11 but declined to 29.6 per cent in 2012–13 (April–September).

An in-depth analysis of services exports from India reveals that the largest services segment, software and IT-enabled services, has graduated to newer services such as packaged software implementation, systems integration, network infrastructure management, and IT consulting. There remains a huge untapped potential for IT-enabled services.

Under the miscellaneous services segment, India's entertainment industry, with export earnings of about US$230 million annually, is likely to grow by 70–80 per cent over the next five to ten years. It covers films, music, broadcast, television, and live entertainment and is basically an intellectual property-driven sector with small to large players spread across India. Education process outsourcing (EPO) includes imparting online education, training, coaching, and other related services through the Internet and has emerged as a significant segment for services exports. India's cost competitiveness as an education service provider (ESP) is reflected by an average billing rate in India of about US$12 per hour in India compared to US$25 per hour in the USA, which is expected to be the largest consumer of EPO. The travel and tourism sector has also shown significant growth in recent years.

INDIA'S SLUGGISH EXPORT PERFORMANCE: AN EVALUATION

When India gained independence in 1947, it accounted for 2.53 per cent of the world exports and 2.33 per cent of the world imports. Despite significant growth in India's exports in value terms, India's share in world exports declined to 1.03 per cent in the 1960s and further to 0.60 per cent in 1970. The decline was the lowest in 1980 at 0.42 per cent. Although India's share in world exports exhibited growth in the later years and its share gradually increased to 1.6 per cent in 2012, the growth achieved by other Asian countries, such as China and Japan,which was an increase from 0.9 per cent and 0.4 per cent respectively in 1948 to 11.2 per cent and 4.4 per cent in 2012, is highly impressive. It reveals that although India's export growth during this period had been comparable to the growth of world trade, some of the Southeast Asian countries' share in world trade had increased dramatically. It is obvious from this that India's exports have been much lower compared to other Southeast Asian countries and its export potential could hardly be harnessed optimally.

India's foreign trade was largely determined by the strategic needs of the British colonial powers prior to its independence in 1947. Like other colonies, India too was a supplier of raw materials and agricultural commodities to Britain and other industrial countries and it used to import the manufactured goods from Britain. The dependence of colonial India on Britain for manufactured goods hindered the process of industrialization and obliterated the indigenous handicraft and cottage industries.

As a part of British strategy, India had to export more than its imports prior to World War II so as to meet the unilateral transfer of payments to Britain by way of the salaries and pensions of the British officers, both military and civil, dividends on British capital invested in India, and interest on sterling loans. This helped India achieve a favourable trade balance. In April 1946, India was able to build a huge sterling balance of ₹17.33 billion. Even after paying the sterling debt, the anxiety of the then Government of India was to utilize these balances as early as possible.

As a result, after independence, the imports grew much rapidly compared to exports primarily due to the following reasons:

- Scarcity of food grains and basic raw materials such as cotton and jute consequent to partition
- Rapid increase in import of capital goods for India's developmental activities
- Rise in post-war demands

The share of raw materials in India's exports declined from 45 per cent in 1938–39 to 31 per cent in 1947–48, whereas the share of manufactured goods increased from 30 per cent in 1938–39 to 49 per cent in 1947–48.

It was only after independence that India's trade patterns began to change in view of its developmental needs. India, as a newly independent country, had to import equipment and machinery that could not be manufactured domestically, in order to create new production capacity and build infrastructure, known as developmental imports. It also had to import intermediate goods and raw materials so as to make full use of its production capacity, known as maintenance imports. Moreover, as a newly developing country, it had to import consumer goods such as food grains that were in short supply domestically, in order to curb inflationary pressures. Such heavy dependence on imports adversely influenced the country's balance of trade. It also necessitated the need to expand exports so as to finance its imports.

The basic reasons for such a sluggish export performance may be summarized as follows:

- India was such a small player at the beginning of this period that its slide over the next three decades essentially reflected further slip in the competitiveness on cost and quality grounds.
- As the dependence on imports only intensified over time, the sluggish export performance adversely affected India's ability to achieve a positive trade balance.

In the face of what was seen in the mid-1960s as an unprecedented deterioration in the current account, the government resorted to rupee devaluation in a bid to improve the country's export competitiveness. The 1966 devaluation, while not resulting in the expected improvement in trade deficit due to a combination of circumstances, brought to the fore problems stemming from an overvalued exchange rate. The export growth through the 1960s averaged just 4 per cent in value and volume.

Also, the two wars with Pakistan and the oil shocks of 1973 and 1979 were the exogenous factors that resulted in the overall slowdown of the economy. The 1970s was also the period when the emphasis was mainly on the import substitution rather than export promotion. The foundation of a systematic and scientific foreign trade policy was actually laid down in the third five-year plan when some changes in the attitude towards exports became perceptible.

The fourth five-year plan period stressed on the 'import more and export more' philosophy. The national commitment to exports manifested itself for the first time in the 1970 Export Policy Resolution. The resolution aimed at expanding and reorienting export production. The export house scheme was also introduced in the fourth five-year plan period. The international market also experienced a boom and the Indian export sector was able to take advantage by realizing higher unit values for a wide variety of export items. The emergence of Bangladesh and west Asian markets provided opportunities for trade diversification.

In 1980–81, recognizing the severe strains on the BoP front and the urgent need to expand exports, the government introduced a number of measures aimed at promoting exports. These included enabling the setting up of 100 per cent export oriented units (EOUs) anywhere in India with facilities similar to those available in the free trade zones, the setting up of an Exim Bank to handle foreign trade finance, linking supplies of raw materials with export production to ensure timely deliveries, paying attention on a priority basis to transport problems, and bottlenecks inhibiting exports, etc. These measures helped raise India's share in world exports to 0.45 per cent in 1985 and further to 0.53 per cent in 1989. Since 1985, the policy framework has been systematically structured to improve the competitiveness of India's exports.

India was a closed economy till the 1990s. There were stringent restrictions on imports and foreign investment. However, a major programme of economic reform and liberalization was introduced in 1991 with emphasis on external sector. The Indian government emphasized on opening up the trade and foreign investments with a view to reaping the potential benefits from external liberalization and greater integration with the world economy which marked a significant departure from the earlier policy of import substitution. The measures of external liberalization, combined with robust growth of world trade, improved the export performance during the reform period. As a result, India's share in world exports improved from 0.52 per cent in 1990 to 1.6 per cent in 2011.

BALANCE OF PAYMENTS

A country's BoP is defined as the summary of all its economic transactions that have taken place between the country's residents and the residents of other countries during a specified time period. It is used as an indicator of a country's political and economic stability. A consistently positive BoP reflects more foreign investment and money coming into the country and not much of its currency being exported. On the other hand, adverse or negative BoP indicates more outflows of money compared to inflows. Thus, a surplus or positive BoP implies that a country has more funds from trade and investment coming in compared to what it pays out to other countries. It has a positive impact on the country's currency appreciation. Conversely, deficit BoP implies an excess of imports over exports, dependence on foreign investors, and an overvalued currency. A country needs to make deficit BoP by exporting its hard currency foreign exchange reserves or gold.

The BoP is generally computed on monthly, quarterly, or yearly basis. The BoP includes both visible and invisible transactions. The BoP reports the country's international performance in trading with other nations and the volume of capital flowing in and out of the country. The BoP accounting uses the system of double-entry bookkeeping, which means that every debit or credit in the account is also represented as a credit or debit somewhere else. In a BoP sheet, currency inflows are recorded as credits (plus signs), whereas outflows are recorded as debits (minus signs). The accounts used for computing BoPs include the following.

Current account   It includes import and export of goods and services and unilateral transfer of goods and services.

Capital account   It includes transactions leading to changes in financial assets and liabilities of the country.

Reserve account   It includes only 'reserve assets' of the country. These are the assets which the monetary authority of the country uses to settle the deficits and surpluses that arise on the other two categories taken together.

The BoP profile reveals some interesting trends at a micro level. In recent years, the deficits in the trade account have been more than made up by large invisibles surpluses sustained by large inflows of private transfers and non-factor services resulting in positive current account balances. On the other hand, the growing strength of the capital account has risen largely from

Table 7.6 Summary of India's BoP (in US$ million)

	1990-91	2000-01	2001-02	2002-03	2003-04	2004-05	2005-06	2006-07	2007-08	2008-09	2009-10	2010-11	2011-12	2012-13*
1. Exports	18,477	45,452	44,703	53,774	66,285	85,206	1,05,152	1,28,888	1,66,162	1,89,001	1,82,442	2,56,159	3,09,774	1,46,549
2. Imports	27,915	57,912	56,277	64,464	80,003	1,18,908	1,57,056	1,90,670	2,57,629	3,08,521	3,00,644	3,83,481	4,99,533	2,37,221
3. Trade balance	-9,438	-12,460	-11,574	-10,690	-13,718	-33,702	-51,904	-61,782	-91,467	-1,19,520	-1,18,203	-1,27,322	-1,89,759	-90,672
4. Invisibles (net)	-242	9,794	14,974	17,035	27,801	31,232	42,002	52,217	75,731	91,605	80,022	79,269	1,11,604	51,699
5. Non-factor service	980	1,692	3,324	3,643	10,144	15,426	23,170	29,469	38,853	53,916	36,016	44,081	64,098	29,572
6. Income	-3,752	-5,004	-4,206	-3,446	-4,505	-4,979	-5,855	-7,331	-5,068	-7,110	-8,038	-17,952	-15,988	-10,510
7. Pvt. transfers	2,069	12,854	15,398	16,387	21,608	20,525	24,493	30,079	41,945	44,798	52,045	53,140	63,494	32,637
8. Goods and services balance	-8,458	-10,768	-8,250	-7,047	-3,574	-18,276	-28,734	-32,313	-52,614	-65,604	-82,187	-83,241	-12,5661	-61,100
9. Current account balance	-9,680	-2,666	3,400	6,345	14,083	-2,470	-9,902	-9,565	-15,737	-27,915	-38,181	-48,053	-78,155	-38,973
10. External assistance (net)	2,204	410	1,117	-3,128	-2,858	1,923	1,702	1,775	2,114	2,441	2,890	4,941	2,296	15
11. Commercial borrowing (net)	2,254	4,303	-1,585	-1,692	-2,925	5,194	2,508	16,103	22,609	7,862	2,000	12,160	10,344	1,726
12. Non-resident deposits (net)	1,534	2,316	2,754	2,978	3,642	-964	2,789	4,321	179	4,290	2,922	3,238	11,918	9,397
13. Foreign investment (net) of which	103	5,862	6,686	4,161	13,744	13,000	15,528	14,753	43,326	5,785	50,362	42,127	39,231	18,608
(i) foreign direct invest (net)	97	3,272	4,734	3,217	2,388	3,713	3,034	7,693	15,893	19,816	17,966	11,834	22,061	12,812
(ii) Portfolio	6	2,590	1,952	944	11,356	9,287	12,494	7,060	27,433	-14,031	32,396	30,293	17,170	5,796
14. Other flows (net)	1,090	-4,356	-615	8,321	5,735	9,476	-180	4,047	10,847	-4,090	-13,259	-12,484	-7,008	-4,769
15. Capital account total (net)	7,188	8,535	8,357	10,640	17,338	28,629	24,629				51,634	63,740	67,755	39,989
16. Reserve use (-increase)	1,278	-5,842	-11,757	-16,985	-31,421	-26,159	-26,159	-36,606	-92,164	20,080	-13,441	-13,050	12,831	-363

*Refers to April–September.

Source: Economic Survey, 2012–13.

steady growth in non-debt creating foreign investment inflows. External commercial borrowings and external assistance have been showing net outflows in recent years. The trends indicate the fast-growing invisibles and non-debt creating foreign investment inflows are the main factors behind accumulation of foreign exchange reserves.

When India launched its economic planning in the early 1950s, the BoP position was more or less comfortable. But in 1951–52, there was a huge trade deficit and as a result, there was over-all deficit on the current and capital accounts, despite net surplus invisible transfers and capital account surplus mainly due to long-term loans, which was met by the official reserves account. The situation did not improve in the 1960s and the 1970s. The trade and current account deficits continued to increase sharply due to large scale imports of food grains, machinery, and equipment. During the 1980s, issues relating to BoP became crucial in terms of India's macroeconomic management. The second oil price hike shock in 1979 had a far more severe impact on the country's BoP than that of the first shock in 1973–74. In 1990, the Gulf crisis led to a sharp increase in oil prices, which led to an increase in the import bill of POL. It was at this juncture that the Government of India introduced a number of measures for fiscal correction and structural reforms through radical changes in trade and industrial policies and overall economic liberalization. To finance the BoP requirements, the government resorted to borrowings from the International Monetary Fund (IMF), the World Bank, and the Asian Development Bank as well as from bilateral donors. After 1993, there was a distinct improvement in the BoP position. A significant growth in exports, the fall in international prices of crude oil, and the slack in the growth of non-POL imports in the following years resulted in a sharp contraction in trade deficit.

India's current account balance witnessed surpluses from 2001–02 to 2003–04 but exhibited a reverse trend (Table 7.6) since 2004–05 of current account deficit along with a burgeoning trade deficit primarily due to steep rise in prices of petroleum products. In spite of large re-payments of India Millennium Deposits (IMD) under external commercial borrowings, India was able to maintain a strong balance in the capital account even after financing the current account deficit. Foreign investments, both direct and portfolio and inflow of non-resident deposits, were on the rise. The invisibles (net), comprising of non-factor services (such as travel, transportation, software, and business services), investment income, and transfers traditionally compensated, to a large extent, the trade deficit. As a per cent of GDP, India's current account balance improved from a deficit of 3.1 per cent in 1990–91 to a surplus of 2.3 per cent in 2003–04 but declined subsequently to a deficit of 10.2 per cent in 2011–12. India's invisibles balance grew remarkably from a deficit of 0.1 per cent of GDP in 1990–91 to a surplus of 6 per cent of GDP in 2011–12.

BALANCE OF TRADE

The difference between the value of exports and that of imports is termed as the BoT. After independence, India had a positive trade balance only during two financial years, that is, a balance of US$134 million in 1972–73 and US$77 million in 1976–77. India's trade deficit increased from US$4 million in 1950–51 to US$12.8 billion in 1999–2000, as shown in Fig. 7.20. However, it declined to US$5.9 billion in 2000–01 but increased considerably in the following years. There has been a considerable rise from US$8.69 billion in 2002–03 to US$ 118.40 billion in 2008–09 and it increased steeply further to burgeoning US$191 billion in 2012–13. India recorded sustained trade deficits due to low exports base and inflexibility in its imports of coal, petroleum, fertilizers, and edible oils.

India had trade surplus with four countries namely the UAE, USA, Singapore, and Hong Kong in 2008–09 to 2011–12. However, in 2012–13 (April–November) India's trade surplus with

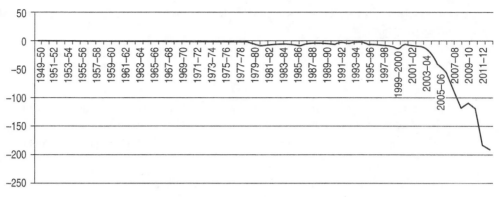

Fig. 7.20　India's trade balance (in US$ billion)
Source: Based on DGCI&S data, 2013.

the UAE has turned into deficit mainly due to rising oil prices. India's trade balance improved further with the USA and Hong Kong. There is also high trade deficit of India with China and Switzerland, which increased from US$28 billion and US$24.1 billion in 2010–11 respectively, to US$39.4 billion and US$31.3 billion respectively in 2011–12 (April–November) mainly due to rising imports of machinery from China and gold from Switzerland.

GAINS FROM INTERNATIONAL TRADE

To measure the benefits derived by a nation from international trade, trade indices are widely used instruments. Trade indices facilitate in assessing the impact of trade volume and/or unit value realization of a country's gains from trade. For instance, without any increase in the quantity of goods imported, the rise in the total value of imports implies only a financial burden for a country. In order to measure gains from international trade, net, gross, and income, terms of trade are often used. The 'terms of trade' is a measure of relative changes in export and import prices of a nation. It reflects the quantity of imports that a given quantity of exports can buy.

Concept of Terms of Trade

The 'terms of trade' of a country are defined as the ratio of the price of its export commodity to the price of its import commodity. In case of a hypothetical assumption of a two-nation world, the export of a country equals its trade partner's imports wherein the terms of trade of a country are equal to the inverse of the terms of trade of its trade partner. Since, in the real world, numerous commodities are traded, the terms of trade of a nation are expressed by the ratio of price index of a country's exports to the price index of its imports. This ratio is usually multiplied by 100 in order to express the terms of trade in percentage. These terms of trade are often referred to as 'commodity' or 'net barter' terms of trade.

The terms of trade are mainly of the following three types:

1. Net terms of trade: It implies unit value index of exports expressed as a percentage of unit value index of imports.

$$\text{Net value terms of trade } (N) = \frac{\text{Unit value index of exports}}{\text{Unit value index of imports}} \times 100$$

$$N = (Px/Pm) \times 100$$

2. Gross terms of trade: It implies volume index of imports expressed as a percentage of volume index of exports.

$$\text{Gross terms of trade } (G) = \frac{\text{Volume index of imports}}{\text{Volume index of exports}} \times 100$$

$$G = (Qm/Qx) \times 100$$

3. Income terms of trade: It implies the product of net terms of trade and volume index of exports expressed as a percentage. It reflects a nation's capacity to import.

$$\text{Income terms of trade } (I) = \text{Net terms of trade} \times \text{Volume index of exports} \times 100$$

$$I = Px/Pm \times Qx \times 100$$

In addition, single and double factorial terms of trade are also used to make adjustments for productivity changes, as follows.

Single factorial terms of trade   Net barter terms of trade adjusted for changes in productivity of exports

Double factorial terms of trade   Net barter terms of trade adjusted for changes both in productivity of exports and imports

Since developing countries considerably rely upon imported capital goods for their industrialization and development activities, the income terms of trade assume high significance.

Terms of Trade: Developed, Developing, and Transition Economies

The measures of trade volume are expressed by the volume indices of exports and imports. The volume indices of exports for developed economies increased from 34 in 1980 to 139 in 2008, thereafter it declined to 118 in 2009 but increased to 140 in 2011, whereas it increased for developing economies very significantly from 24 in 1980 to 194 in 2008, declined to 107 in 2009, but grew rapidly to 216 in 2011 (Table 7.7). Besides, the volume indices of imports also grew from 34 in 1980 to 138 in 2008 but declined to 118 in 2009 before increasing to 136 in 2011 for developed economies and from 25 to 201 for developing economies during 2008 but thereafter it fell to 182 in 2009 before increasing to 231 in 2011.

The unit value indices, which measure the average price realization, indicate a significant improvement in unit value indices of exports for developed economies, rising from 88 in 1980 to 155 in 2008 but significantly declining thereafter to 146 in 2010 before increasing to 161 in 2011, whereas they have shown considerable deterioration for developing economies from 120 in 1980 to 92 in 2002. However, by 2008, it improved to 158 in 2008 but it declined to 138 in 2009 before increasing to 176 in 2011. The unit value indices of imports grew considerably from 91 in 1980 to 158 in 2008 but thereafter it declined to 139 in 2009 before increasing to 165 in 2011 for developed economies, whereas it increased from 103 in 1980 to 149 in 2008 for developing economies. However, it declined to 134 in 2009 before increasing to 164 in 2011.

Table 7.7   Trade indices: developed, developing, and transition economies (Base year 2000 = 100)

Year	Developed economies	Developing economies	Transition economies
2002	102	97	97
2003	103	98	104
2004	103	98	117
2005	101	103	138
2006	100	105	153
2007	101	159	159
2008	98	106	190
2009	102	104	154
2010	100	107	169
2011	98	107	192

Source: UNCTAD Handbook of Statistics, United Nations, Geneva, New York, 2012.

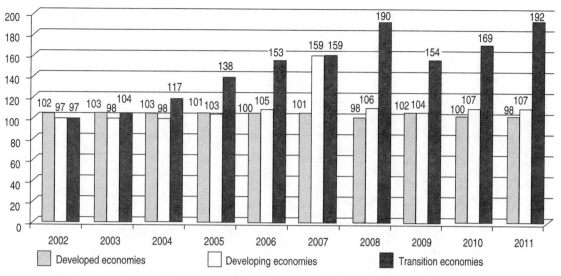

Fig. 7.21 Terms of trade (Base year 2000 = 100)

Source: Based on data from *UNCTAD Handbook of Statistics*, United Nations, New York, Geneva, 2012.

The terms of trade for developed economies improved from 97 in 1980 to 102 in 2009 but deteriorated to 98 in 2011, whereas it deteriorated for developing economies from 117 in 1980 to 107 in 2011, as shown in Fig. 7.21. This is because the exports basket of most developing countries comprises agricultural products or raw materials wherein the price rise is much slower compared to manufactured goods. Besides, the growth in demand is also much slower compared to industrial growth. Moreover, developing countries generally market primary products as commodities, whereas manufactured goods are marketed as branded products. The price realized from commodities in international markets is prone to heavy price fluctuations. In case of such products, any cost cutting measure used by the producers is passed on to importers. Therefore, a country whose exports are mainly dependent on agricultural commodities and primary goods tends to require more volumes of exports to buy the same amount of finished goods. This explains the inherent problem in lower gains by developing countries compared to developed countries.

The reasons for deterioration in terms of trade for developing countries may be summarized as follows:

- International demand for export of manufactured goods by developed countries tends to increase at a much faster rate compared to demand for agricultural commodities and primary goods as the income elasticity of manufactured goods is much higher than agricultural commodities and primary goods.
- Any productivity gain in manufactured goods by developed countries is generally passed on to its workers in the form of higher wages and income, whereas such gains in productivity of agricultural commodities and primary products by developing countries are reflected in price decline. This leads to a consistent deterioration in the collective terms of trade of developing countries.

Most economic models suggest that a large increase in exports would be followed by a substantial decline in export prices, as countries export more and more of the same products. Past experiences suggest that successful exporters of manufactured products can avoid the problems of declining terms of trade. The terms of trade of the developing countries whose exports have grown rapidly have deteriorated only moderately and not to the extent predicted by most economic models. Since the 1980s, China and India have made efforts to integrate with the global economy. The decline in their terms of trade has been much more modest than what would be.

The terms of trade of mineral and oil exporting economies continued their rebound from the export price collapse in 2009. In contrast, the terms of trade for economies relying on manufactured exports have deteriorated on average. In 2011, mineral exporting countries experienced strongly improved terms of trade, in part since prices of some precious metals increased sharply due to heightened global economic uncertainty that raised their importance as a store of value.

India's Terms of Trade

India's terms of trade deteriorated, as shown in Fig. 7.22, from 94 in 2000–01 to 77 in 2006–07, considering 1999–2000 as the base year, but improved to 92 in 2010–11 before deteriorating steeply to 67 in 2011–12. The resurgence of international crude oil prices has been the major reason for deterioration in the net terms of trade.

However, the income terms of trade that measures the import purchasing power of exports improved continuously during the last decade from 118 in 2000–01 to 280 in 2010–11, except 2001–02, on account of the strong growth of exports in volume terms. The capacity to import based on exports improved due to several factors including recovery in international commodity prices, movements in cross-currency exchange rates, a faster repatriation of export proceeds, and various policy initiatives for export promotion and market diversification. However, it declined by 20.7 per cent to 222 in 2011–12 reflecting an unfavourable situation for the country.

The unit value index for imports, as shown in Table 7.8, rose from 109 in 2000–01 to 425 in 2011–12 compared to the corresponding rise in unit value index of exports from 102 to 268 during the same period. It implies that the rise in the value of imports was much more than the quantity of goods imported, which added to India's financial burden. A detailed analysis of unit value and volume indices reveals that relative inelasticity of India's import demands for petroleum

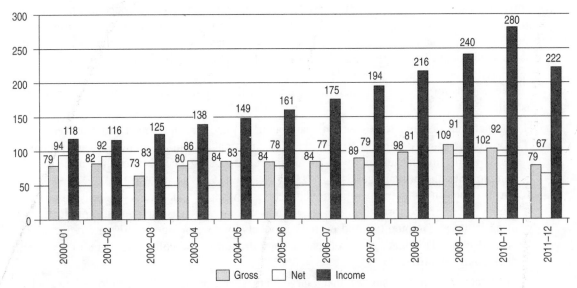

Fig. 7.22   India's terms of trade (Base year 1999–2000 = 100)

Source: DGCI&S Kolkata, 2013.

Table 7.8 India's terms of trade (Base year 1999–2000 = 100)

	Unit value index		Volume index		Terms of trade		
	Exports	Imports	Exports	Imports	Gross	Net	Income
2000–01	102.0	109.0	125.0	99.0	79	94	118
2001–02	103.0	112.0	126.0	103.0	82	92	116
2002–03	106.0	128.0	150.0	109.0	73	83	125
2003–04	114.0	132.0	161.0	128.0	80	86	138
2004–05	131.0	157.0	179.0	150.0	84	83	149
2005–06	139.0	179.0	206.0	174.0	84	78	161
2006–07	158.0	206.0	227.0	191.0	84	77	175
2007–08	166.0	210.0	245.0	218.0	89	79	194
2008–09	194.0	239.0	267.0	262.0	98	81	216
2009–10	196.0	215.0	264.0	288.0	109	91	240
2010–11	223.0	243.0	304.0	311.0	102	92	280
2011–12	268.0	425.0	331.0	246.0	79	67	222

Source: DGCI&S, Kolkata, 2013.

products, food grains, fertilizers, oilseeds, and capital goods constrained India in making any substantial cuts on imports.

The volume index of India's exports grew from 125 in 2000–01 to 331 in 2011–12 considering 1999–2000 as the base year, whereas the volume index of imports increased from 99 in 2000–01 to 246 in 2011–12. The gross term of trade improved significantly from 79 in 2000–01 to 109 in 2009–10 but declined to 79 in 2011–12.

STRATEGIC MEASURES TO PROMOTE INDIA'S EXPORTS

After independence, the focus of India's economic planning was on import substitution and achieving self-sufficiency. Till that time the basic philosophy of the government was to achieve self-reliance rather than promoting international trade. However, in the later years, India's imports of industrial goods including plant and machinery and components thereof, petroleum products, fertilizers, edible oil, etc. grew significantly, which necessitated the country to earn foreign exchange for financing its burgeoning imports.

This compelled the Indian government to promote exports that became overriding priority for the country. The government initiated a number of steps to facilitate exports, such as a variety of schemes for duty exemption or remission for import of goods, for export production, and some sector-specific schemes for gems and jewellery so as to make available the raw materials and capital goods to the exporting units at international prices. Schemes to set up free trade zones or special economic zones (SEZs) and export oriented units (EOUs) were conceived so as to facilitate export production. Other measures such as exemption of export profits from taxes and provision of bank finance at lower rates of interest also contributed to enhance the profitability of export operations.

With the liberalization of various world economies, the exports function acquired a prime place in the country's economy and was considered as the engine of growth. Therefore, a number of proactive measures were taken to boost exports including gradual removal of quantitative restrictions and an export promotion approach focused on identified international markets.

These measures had only a limited impact on India's exports and growth rate of India's exports remained far below the other Southeast Asian economies. The key issues that have restrained India's growth in international trade[4] and the measures to overcome these barriers are as follows.

Developing a Proactive Approach to International Trade

India's approach to international trade had generally been to look at the negative side and miss out on the opportunities to benefit from globalization. Evidence suggests that countries that opened up early, such as Hong Kong and Singapore (Exhibit 7.1), achieved much higher economic growth compared to countries that followed protectionist economic policies. In contrast, China had an unequivocal acceptance that growth of exports is beneficial for the economy and

Exhibit 7.1   Lessons from free trade in Hong Kong and Singapore

Singapore and Hong Kong have been the most open economies in the world during the last 50 years. While the former went through a brief import substitution period during the 1960s, the latter has been entirely free of trade barriers throughout this period.

The domestic markets in Singapore and Hong Kong were too small. Reliance on exports was a natural response to this small size of the internal market. With a population of 2 million in 1950 and relatively high per capita income derived from trading activities, Hong Kong had a larger domestic market for manufactured goods than the majority of the developing countries. Yet, many of these developing countries embarked on industrialization behind high protective barriers. For example, Tunisia had a home market smaller than that of Hong Kong but it went on to establish small local plants to serve the domestic market behind a protective wall that remained in existence for decades.

An alternative explanation for the victory of free-trade policies in Hong Kong and Singapore is offered in their geography. They are both island economies that stood to benefit from large volumes of trade that free-trade policies may generate. For example, Singapore was a natural port to serve as a way station for storage and final processing of goods destined to and originating from the neighbouring countries in Southeast Asia. While this feature of geography may have played some role, by itself it is insufficient to explain why pro-export interests won over import-competing interests in these economies but not elsewhere. Sri Lanka, Mauritius, and Madagascar were all island economies but fell prey to protectionist policies for achieving industrialization.

The failure of protectionist interests to assert themselves in Hong Kong and Singapore during the latter part of the last century can be explained in terms of two other mutually reinforcing factors.

Historical reasons

By 1950, both Singapore and Hong Kong had accumulated a long history of free trade. Singapore had become a British colony under the Straits Settlement in 1867. The British gave it free-trade status. Likewise, after colonizing it, the British adopted free trade policies in Hong Kong, as early as 1840s. Free-trade status of these economies resulted in a large expansion of re-export trade. In 1960–67, the share of re-exports in total exports in Singapore had reached 85.6 per cent. This large share of re-exports made trade barriers costly and thus strengthened the hands of pro-export interests.

Absence of significant agricultural activity

In 1970, only 3.78 per cent of Singapore's labour force was engaged in agriculture, fishing, and quarrying. As much as 23.44 per cent of the labour force was engaged in trade and 21.98 per cent in manufacturing. The remaining 50.8 per cent of population was engaged in construction, utilities, transport, communications, financial, business, and other services. Thus, the pressure for transformation from a principally rural, agrarian economy to an industrial or service economy that other developing countries faced during the early part of the last half century was essentially absent in Singapore and Hong Kong. With industry and exports already having a significant presence, the pressure for achieving industrialization behind a high protective wall was contained.

In 2012, re-exports from Hong Kong and Singapore accounted for 2.6 per cent and 1 per cent of world trade respectively, despite much smaller sizes of the countries with limited resource. In view of the free trade experiences of Singapore and Hong Kong reflected by their economic growth, countries with high barriers to trade may overcome their fear of free trade and learn lessons.

Source: Panagariya, Arvind, 'India Needs Free Trade', *The Economic Times*, 20 June 2002; *International Trade Statistics*, 2013, WTO.

---

[4] Prabhu, P.P., 'Planning for a Revolutionary Growth of India's Foreign Trade', *RITES Journal*, March 2004, pp. 22.1–12.

needs to be pursued relentlessly at all costs. Knowing well that joining the WTO would open up its domestic markets and such liberalizations would cost domestic products, enterprises, and industries to face more intense competition, China consistently pursued its case to join the WTO. The membership of WTO provides both a challenge and an opportunity. China's approach was to accept the challenge and grasp the opportunity and take benefits of globalization. There had always been a fear in India that some parts of the domestic economy will be controlled by external factors. In India, it is very often referred to as the 'East India Company syndrome'. However, the transnational companies have increasingly realized not to act in a manner that is inconsistent with the policies of a country in which the investment is made.

Therefore, it became pertinent for India to be proactive rather than defensive in its approach to economic liberalization and multilateral trade negotiations. Its interest lies in the promotion of multilateralism in international trade and in securing better market access during multilateral negotiations for items of export interest to India.

Promoting Foreign Direct Investments

Investment and technology are crucial to economic growth and competitiveness in international trade. One of the reasons for the phenomenal success of China in manufacturing is the huge foreign direct investment that it has been attracting, especially in export-oriented production. Nearly 50 per cent of exports of China emanate from foreign enterprises. The importance of foreign investment can be appreciated from the fact that nearly a third of world trade today is between transnationals and their affiliates.

Access to technology is also an important condition for higher growth of exports. Though there are no restrictions on import of technology now, there have been, among foreign companies, some reservations regarding free flow of technology to India on account of the nature and extent of protection provided to intellectual property. With the enactment of the new Patent Act, such suspicion has declined considerably.

Of late, India's approach to foreign investment has become positive, but a lot is still required to be done. Enunciation of clear and transparent policies and norms for foreign direct investment and not linking it to specific approvals would be necessary to attract investment in manufacturing and infrastructure. Also, there is a need to evolve and implement a composite approval system that would accord all approvals simultaneously, including the approvals required from different state-level agencies.

Foreign investments for export production will come in only if exports become profitable, the climate for foreign investment becomes positive and favourable, and the country's legal system is able to settle commercial disputes speedily. India has a bad reputation for corruption and that is a handicap. Transparency in policies and even greater and progressive liberalization is a fitting reply to all these ills.

Abolition of Indirect Taxes in Certain Sectors for Export Production

Abolition of all indirect taxes on inputs relevant to the selected industries to give total freedom to import any inputs required at most competitive prices and in the quickest of time and export any type of product demanded by the market would be an essential initiative that would pay rich dividends in terms of attracting investment for export production. It would not be possible to provide within the existing schemes of duty exemption or remission the required freedom to the exporters to import any inputs and export the resultant products without the intervention of government machinery, by way of inspection, etc. Such interventions often act as a disincentive to exporters. Hence, one way to go about achieving the objective of eliminating the government controls would be to remove all indirect taxes on specific inputs pertaining to such industries so that both imports and exports can be free from inspections and verification by central excise and custom authorities, which is the normal cause for delays in clearance of imported inputs and hold up of export consignments. It may appear that such a move may cause loss of revenue, but as the government is already committed to substantial reduction in the level of indirect taxes to the ASEAN level, the abolition of duties in selected sectors, such as electronics and textiles, etc., should not result in any appreciable loss of revenue. The actual incidence of loss will, in fact, be much lower as the present outgo on account of payment of drawback to exporters will then cease. Also, the scope for frauds that exists in the present dispensation in these areas will vanish and only genuine enterprises will flourish. It would also result in considerable lowering of transaction costs and thereby contribute to competitiveness.

Entrepreneurship Facilitation

India's major asset is the entrepreneurship of the Indian people. Economic history tells us about the extensive and successful trading relationships built by India. It is worth noting that even at the time of independence, India was a major trading nation. It is the anti-international trade bias in India's policy and the emasculation of entrepreneurship after independence that have been responsible for its dismal performance in international trade since then. The biggest constraint to India's economic progress in the decades before reforms was the thwarting of entrepreneurship. The success of the gems and jewellery sector in recent years is an example of the vast strides that India could have made had the entrepreneurship of our people not been shackled. This industry has to import all the inputs—diamonds, gold, etc.—and the entire market is in the rich countries. However, the industry has been able to capture most of the world market for diamond jewellery, with only limited support from the government, mainly due to the entrepreneurship of the industry and business. Similar success stories abound in sectors such as handicrafts, garments, software, and business process outsourcing (BPO).

Competition encourages and fosters efficiency, and entrepreneurship is the key to success in business. During the licence-permit regime, there was little incentive for efficiency as there was no competition; only a favoured coterie of businessmen enjoyed all the benefits at the cost of the Indian consumers. The knowledge industry like software and the space or atomic energy programmes could succeed only because they were left alone by the government. On the contrary, the growth of electronic hardware industry was stunted because of too much of bureaucratic controls and operational constraints.

Infrastructure Development

Of the various handicaps, the state of infrastructure in India is the biggest problem for exporters and it has significant impact on costs. An important reason for the success of China in manufacture exports is the great strides it has been making in its infrastructure, well ahead of demand. China's present standard of infrastructure is superior to India, whether in railway freight carrying capacity or road infrastructure, availability and quality of power, or communication facilities. In India, inland movement of goods to ports take enormous time, the port infrastructure is weak, and delays due to port congestion and demurrage charges are a common occurrence.

Privatization and modernization of berths, total freedom to build additional berths, facilitating competition in other infrastructure sectors also to spur efficiency are some of the essential and urgent policy measures needed to bring about the much desired improvement in the availability, adequacy, efficiency, and quality of infrastructure that is the basic condition for growth of exports as well as the economy.

Promoting Services' Exports

Apart from merchandise exports, export of commercial services offers enormous opportunities. The world trade in commercial services has been steadily growing and reached US$4.34 trillion in 2012. Tourism and transport services are well known as important commercial services. Many small, less-endowed countries receive millions of tourists, while India seems to be satisfied with the increase in tourist arrivals by just two million. Apart from modernizing the airports, increasing the number of flights, developing specific tourist destinations as per the international standards of cleanliness and hygiene, facilitating a sharp increase in the number of hotel rooms, and enabling them to charge affordable tariffs, as in Malaysia, Thailand, etc., are some of the measures urgently needed to be taken. Achievement of rapid growth in this vital sector is extremely important.

The exports of software and, of late, BPO have been doing well and the prospects are also promising due to India's competitive advantage. Fortunately, the improvement in communication technologies has been a boon. The regulatory measure in no case should be allowed to undermine our competitive advantage in this sector. Construction is another major area in which Indian firms can become an important player in the world with some support from the government. There are other commercial services, such as financial services, accountancy, and health care, which have great export potential. Most commercial services are knowledge intensive and particularly suit India's capabilities.

This chapter elucidates the significance of understanding international trade patterns so as to facilitate exploring opportunities in international markets. The trade patterns of the world and India as well have undergone significant change over the years both in terms of its direction and composition that helps exploring new opportunities in international markets. Interestingly, both trade and output in developing countries grew much faster than in the developed ones. Inflexibility of India's import requirements especially for petroleum products, fertilizers, and edible oil on one hand and several limiting factors to enhance its exports on the other have been the key reasons for the country's growing trade deficit in recent years.

A country's international performance in trading with other nations and the volume of capital flowing in and out of the country is often reported through BoP, as elaborated in the chapter. The BoP reports the country's international performance in trading with other nations and the volume of capital flows in and out of the country. At the end, the chapter suggests some strategic measures to promote exports from India.

Summary

To explore, evaluate, and identify emerging opportunities in international markets, a manager has to develop a thorough understanding of existing patterns of international trade. The chapter provided an insight into various issues related to world trade and India's foreign trade so as to facilitate the readers to analyse and take decisions on country identification and developing appropriate strategies for international markets.

World trade has undergone various upheavals from unrestricted trade prior to World War I, followed by several barriers to trade imposed by various nations and a subsequent era of globalization with an emphasis on systematic removal of trade barriers under the multilateral trade regime under the WTO. International marketing has gained increased significance during the last decades as the growth of world trade has been substantially higher than the overall growth in world output.

The world merchandise exports grew from US$59 billion in 1948 to US$18.32 trillion in 2012, whereas the imports grew from US$62 billion to US$18.56 trillion during the same period. The export of services grew more rapidly compared to merchandise exports from US$ 390.8 billion in 1980 to US$4.34 trillion in 2012, whereas the imports of services grew from US$431.8 billion to US$4.10 trillion during the same period.

The 'direction of trade' is often referred to describe the statistical analysis of the set of a country's trading partners and their significance in trade. The set of countries where the goods are exported and their significance on a country's exports is known as 'direction of exports'. On the other hand, the set of countries from where the goods are imported and their significance on a country's imports is known as 'direction of imports'. China ranked as the leading exporter in 2012 with US$2.04 trillion accounting for 11.2 per cent share of world exports, followed by the USA (8.4%), Germany (7.7%), Japan (4.4%), and the Netherlands (3.6%). India ranked at the 19th position with US$293 billion accounting for 1.6 per cent share in world mercandise exports, whereas it ranked at the 10th position with US$489 billion with 2.6 per cent share in world merchandise imports in 2012.

The statistical analysis of a country's product groups in its international trade is often referred to as 'composition of trade'. This can be carried out for the trade with all the countries in the world collectively or individually, with a group of countries, or a particular country. Such an analysis carried out for product groups exported is known as 'composition of exports', whereas the analysis carried out for product groups imported is known as 'composition of imports'. The composition of product mix of world exports, known as composition of trade, has undergone a significant change. The manufacturing goods which accounted for 49.8 per cent in 1965 increased to 76.5 per cent in 2002 but declined subsequently to 63.5 per cent in 2011, while the share of agricultural raw materials, food items, and ores and metals significantly came down.

India's foreign trade increased in value terms from US$1.02 billion in 1949–50 to US$304.6 billion in 2011–12, while the imports increased at a much higher pace from US$1.29 billion in 1949–50 to US$489.1 billion 2011–12. As a result, India's trade deficit increased significantly from US$4 million in 1950–51 to US$184.5 billion in 2011–12. India's share in world exports declined considerably from 2.53 per cent in 1947 to 0.43 per cent in 1980 but thereafter its share increased to 1.6 per cent in 2012.

The share of OECD countries in India's exports declined from 66.1 per cent in 1960–61 to 33.8 per cent in 2011–12, whereas there had been a significant rise in the share of India's imports from OPEC from 4.6 per cent in 1960–61 to its peak 35.4 per cent in 2011–12.

Over the years, the composition of India's exports has undergone a significant transformation as the share of manufactured goods exports grew from 45.3 per cent in 1960–61 to 64.5 per cent in 2012–13 (April–November), whereas exports of agricultural and allied products declined from 44.2 per cent in 1960–61 to 14 per cent in 2012–13 (April–November).

The outflow and inflow of funds through trade and investment in a country are often reflected in its BoP accounts, whereas the BoT reveals differences between a country's net foreign exchange flow from exports and imports.

To measure the benefits derived by a nation from international trade, trade indices are widely used instruments. India's terms of trade deteriorated from 94 in 2000–01 to 67 in 2011–12, mainly due to a quantum steep rise in import of petroleum, edible oils, and fertilizers. Although the net terms of trade deteriorated, the income terms of trade that measure import purchasing power of exports improved from 118 in 2000–01 to 222 in 2011–12.

Though India's exports have grown considerably over the last decades in absolute terms, but its export performance had been much lower compared to a number of Southeast Asian countries. Strategic measures used to promote India's exports include developing a proactive approach to international trade, promoting foreign direct investments, promoting competitiveness, facilitating entrepreneurship, developing infrastructure, and promoting exports of services.

Key Terms

Balance of payment　All economic transactions between the country's residents and residents of other countries during a specified time period.

Balance of trade　Difference between the value of exports and imports of a country.

Capital account　Transactions leading to changes in financial assets and liabilities of a country.

Commercial service exports　Total service exports minus exports of government services not included elsewhere.

Composition of exports　Product mix of exports.

Composition of imports　Product mix of imports.

Current account　Includes import and export of goods and services and unilateral transfer of goods and services.

Direction of exports　Composition of destinations for exports.

Direction of imports　Composition of exporting countries for imports.

Gross domestic product (GDP)　Sum of value added by all resident producers plus any product taxes (less subsidies) not included in the valuation of output.

Gross terms of trade　Volume index of imports expressed as a percentage of volume index of exports.

Income terms of trade　Product of net terms of trade and volume index of exports expressed as a percentage.

Merchandise exports　Freight on board (FOB) value of goods provided to the rest of the world.

Merchandise imports　Cost, insurance and freight (CIF) value of goods purchased from the rest of the world.

Net terms of trade　Unit value index of exports expressed as a percentage of unit value index of imports.

Reserve account　Includes only 'reserve assets' of the country.

Trade in goods as a share of GDP　Sum of merchandise exports and imports divided by the value of GDP.

Concept Review Questions

1. Briefly describe the trends in world trade. Explain the reasons for such changes.
2. What do you understand by 'composition of trade'? Critically analyse the changes in the composition of India's exports over the last decade.
3. Explain the term 'direction of trade'. Critically analyse the changes that have taken place in the direction of India's exports and imports over the last three decades.
4. Carry out a critical analysis of India's growth of exports in international markets vis-à-vis select Asian countries. Identify the reasons for variations among them.
5. Identify the major constraints in India's exports growth. Suggest suitable measures that can be integrated in the strategy to promote exports.

Project Assignments

1. Identify the organizations involved in collection of international trade statistics located near your place. Visit their offices and discuss about the mechanism of data compilation and limitations thereof, if any. Share your observations and discuss your findings in the class.
2. On the basis of export–import data from secondary sources, identify 10 major products and major markets for India's exports in the last decade and the current financial year separately. Compare the two and comments on the findings.
3. Collect data on terms of trade of other emerging Asian markets and carry out a comparative analysis vis-à-vis India's terms of trade. Identify the reasons for such differences and discuss in the class.

CASE STUDY: EMERGING OPPORTUNITIES IN INTERNATIONAL DAIRY TRADE AND INDIA

Introduction

The vast majority of world's milk never crosses the border as evident by the fact that the share of world dairy trade in the global milk pool was just over 7 per cent in 2009. Thus, the focus of dairy industry remains local rather than global or at the most regional. The expected growth in production and consumption of dairy products in developing countries would further reduce the ratio of international dairy trade to global milk production[5] to 6 per cent in the next decade. However, during the last decade, the international trade volumes grew at an average of 3 per cent per annum and overtook dairy production that increased at about 2.4 per cent per year during the period. This reveals the growing significance of international trade and its rapidly rising integration of global production patterns and markets.

The globalization of the dairy industry has led to a paradigm shift in international dairy markets from being supply driven to demand driven. Thus, the international dairy market is getting increasingly responsive to market signals and changing consumer preferences, rather than merely by excess production and depressed world prices. The dairy sector has become among the highest gross value sectors in agriculture with higher prices and correspondingly higher value of milk production. The prospects of sustained high prices for dairy products is creating incentives for investment expansion and restructuring of local dairy industries. Milk production, international demand patterns, and economic development in various parts of the world impact the world dairy trade.[6]

The establishment of the multilateral trading system under the WTO that came into existence on 1 January 1995 led to a new trade order in the world. The WTO opened up opportunities in international trade by increased market access and worldwide reduction in import tariffs. Though WTO aims at eliminating non-tariff barriers which include quota restriction, direct subsidies both for production and exports, quality issues etc. but in practice, these are being used as potent tools especially by developed countries such as the USA and the EU not only to obstruct entry of goods from developing countries but also distort the free and fair operation in the international markets.

Global Milk Production and India

World milk production[7] is projected to increase at an average of 1.9 per cent during the next 10 years compared to 2.1 per cent average annual growth experienced in the past decade. It

---

[5] *OECD–FAO Agricultural Outlook 2012–21*, p.161.
[6] Joshi, Rakesh Mohan, 'Emerging Challenges under WTO to International Dairy Trade with Special Reference to India', *Transnational Corporations Review, Canada*, 4 (3), 2012, pp. 59–76.
[7] *OECD–FAO Agricultural Outlook 2012–21*.

increased at an average of 2.4 per cent in 2011 as a result of good returns and excellent fodder and pasture conditions. The world milk production is projected to increase by 154 million ton, out of which 70 per cent of additional milk production is expected to come from developing countries especially, India and China, which alone account for 40 per cent of global gains. The share of developed countries in the global milk production is expected to fall below 50 per cent by 2021. After years of double digit growth in milk production in China, the melamine crisis shattered the consumer confidence in domestically produced dairy products. The Chinese focus has shifted from increasing milk quantity to improving milk quality and the milk production is expected to grow at an average of 3.3 per cent per annum.

The milk production predominantly based on low cost pasture systems in Oceania has become less prone to feed price fluctuations but has become more dependent on weather conditions. Thus, the international prices of dairy products are likely to be affected considerably by the weather conditions in the Oceania. The Indian subcontinent is among the few regions in the world where consumption of milk and milk products is historically imbibed in its culture unlike China and several other countries in Asia and Africa where consumption of milk products is a recent phenomenon.

The livestock sector in India has been regarded as one of the most pro-poor sectors with considerable positive development translating into increased income and employment to millions of people across the country. Milk production and selling is crucial to livelihood of over 600 million people in rural India with a herd size of 1–3 milch animals unlike large scale dairy farms in Europe. Over the last four decades, while India has made considerable progress in industrial sector, the growth in the agriculture sector has hovered around 3 per cent. The contribution of agriculture to the country's GDP[8] has also declined steadily from 50 per cent in 1947, the year of India's independence, to 13.9 per cent in 2011–12. On the other hand, the contribution of the livestock sector to the overall GDP remained at about 5 per cent during the last three decades. The dairy and livestock sector contribute over 25 per cent to the GDP of agriculture.[9] Within the livestock sector, dairy farming has emerged as an important source of income and employment. The sector has excellent forward and backward linkages, which promotes many industries and increases income of vulnerable groups in rural areas, especially for marginal and small farmers, and contributes to a third of the gross income of rural households and nearly half for the landless.

The milk revolution in India reveals an exceptional success story as the milk production increased remarkably from 17 million tonnes in 1950–51 to 121.8 million tonnes in 2010–11 and emerged as the largest milk producer in the world, much ahead of the second largest producer—the USA. Moreover, India's milk production[10] is expected to grow to 166 million tonnes by 2021 and become very close to the total milk production of the entire EU. This has been achieved through ingenious organizations of a large number of small milk producers spread across the rural areas of the country. Operation Flood, one of the world's largest dairy development programmes, played a crucial role in achieving transformation of the dairy industry in India. In addition to being the largest milk producer, India also has the distinction to be the lowest cost milk producer. More interestingly, there is a wide gap in the next highest producers: the USA (87 million tonnes), China (43 million tonnes), and Russia (32 million tonnes) (Fig. C7.1).

This phenomenal growth in milk production has been due to demand side development on one hand and supply side promotions on the other. The per capita availability has also increased from 130 gm/day in 1950–51 to 281 gm/day in 2010–11 (Fig. C7.2).

Despite India being the largest milk producer in the world, its yield continues to remain miserably low (Fig. C7.3) at one per tonne per head during 2009–11. The USA has the world's highest milk yield with 9.6 tonnes per head, followed by EU (6.4 tonnes per head) during the same period. The enormous gap in milk yields and reliance on other animals for milk purpose, such as sheep, goats, and camels, which inherently have lower milk yields compared to milch cows is responsible, to a large extent, for huge disparity between the share of milk production and inventories between developed and developing countries, especially India.

Emerging International Dairy Trade Scenario

International trade is often used to bridge the gap between demand and supply. Figure C7.4 reveals that world dairy exports have increased from US$28 billion in 2001 to US$66 billion in 2008 before falling to US$51.92 billion in 2009. The global economic crisis during the recent years led to sluggishness of trade volumes in the beginning of 2009. However, dairy exports increased to US$75 billion in 2011 (Fig. C7.4). Consequent to the melamine crisis in 2008 in China, the demand for imported dairy products in China soared as domestically produced milk products were perceived as health hazards. The Chinese demand has considerably boosted the international dairy trade especially for the whole milk powder.

---

[8] *Economic Survey*, 2012–13

[9] Bhasin, N.R., *Indian Dairyman*, November, 2011, pp. 14–15.

[10] *OECD–FAO Agricultural Outlook 2012–21.*

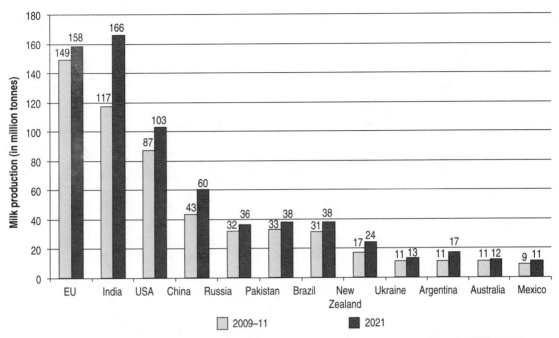

Fig. C7.1   India: The largest milk producing country in the world would even take over the entire EU by 2021

Source: OECD–FAO Agricultural Outlook 2012–21.

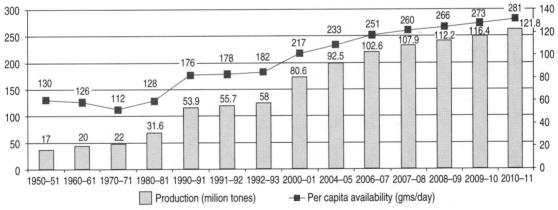

Fig. C7.2   Production and per capita availability of milk in India

Source: Department of Animal Husbandry, Dairying and Fisheries, Ministry of Agriculture, Government of India.

Germany remains the largest exporter of dairy products;[11] however, its share decreased from 16 per cent in 2011 to 14 per cent in 2011. The share of France and Netherlands also decreased from 13 per cent in 2001 to 11 per cent in 2011 and 12 per cent to 11 per cent during the same period respectively, though the trade volumes increased in absolute terms.

Interestingly, the share of New Zealand increased from 10 per cent in 2001 to 13 per cent in 2011. On the other hand, there has been a remarkable growth in the share of other countries from 17 per cent in 2001 to 21 per cent in 2011(Figs C7.5 and C7.6).

Cheese was the highest traded product globally in 2011 (Figs C7.7 and C7.8) with 39 per cent share of world exports,

[11] Trade Map, 2012.

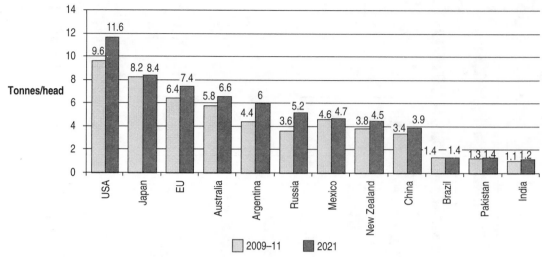

Fig. C7.3 Milk yield in India continues to remain miserably low

Source: OECD–FAO Agricultural Outlook 2012–21.

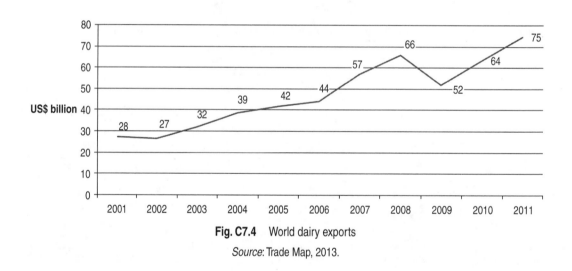

Fig. C7.4 World dairy exports

Source: Trade Map, 2013.

followed by whole milk powder(13.4 %), skimmed milk powder (10.1%), milk not concentrated (7.8%), butter (7.6%), fermented milk products (5.6%), whey and whey products (4.8%), and milk fat and oil (2.9%).

Price Trends in Dairy Industry

The prices of global dairy products increased to its peak in 2011 and are expected to rise in nominal terms while they are likely to remain flat in real terms, as indicated in Figs C7.9–C7.12. High production costs are expected to moderate the price fall despite the fact that food prices are likely to decrease over the short run. World market prices are expected to be 10 per cent

higher for SMP and 30 per cent higher for butter during the present decade ending 2021.

Emerging Trends in India's International Dairy Trade

India remains the largest milk producing country in the world contributing about 15 per cent of the total world milk production. But, due to its large and rapidly growing domestic demand especially in view of increase in population and rising income levels, it has become the net dairy importer in the recent years. India's share in global milk exports is merely 1.7 per cent in 2011, whereas its share in milk imports is 2.5 per cent. This trade pattern is attributed to consumption

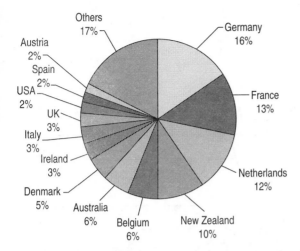

Fig. C7.5 World's major dairy exporting countries (2001)

Source: Trade Map, 2013.

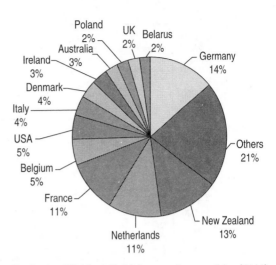

Fig. C7.6 World's major dairy exporting countries (2011)

Source: Trade Map, 2013.

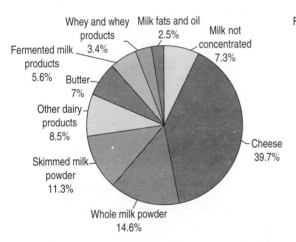

Fig. C7.7 Composition of world dairy exports (2001)

Source: Trade Map, 2013.

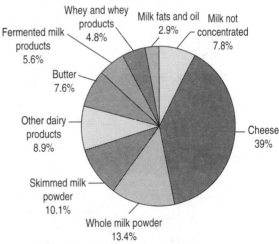

Fig. C7.8 Composition of world dairy exports (2011)

Source: Trade Map, 2013.

of milk in bulk and produced in liquid form by the producer households.

India's dairy exports have exhibited highly fluctuating trend mainly due to fluctuations in dairy production, domestic demand, and prices in international markets. Traditionally, India has been a net importer of dairy products till Operation Flood began showing results. The trend for imports continued till 1993, when for the first time, India's dairy exports exceeded imports. However, between 1993 and 1999, imports and exports kept edging each other out, and by 2000–2001, India became a net exporter of dairy products. Its exports continued to increase almost consistently from a meagre

US$3.45 million in 1996 to US$270 in 2008 but declined subsequently to US$88.95 million in 2009 before increasing to US$115 million in 2010. However, it declined subsequently to US$75 million. Also, with increasing income levels in urban centres, the demand for processed dairy products has gone up leaving little surpluses for exports. On the other hand, the rapidly growing domestic demand led to increase in India's dairy imports from a meagre US$1.48 in 1996 to US$177 million in 2010. As a result, India became a net importer of milk products (Fig. C7.13) by 2011.

The composition of India's dairy trade has undergone drastic change over the last decade. The share of skimmed

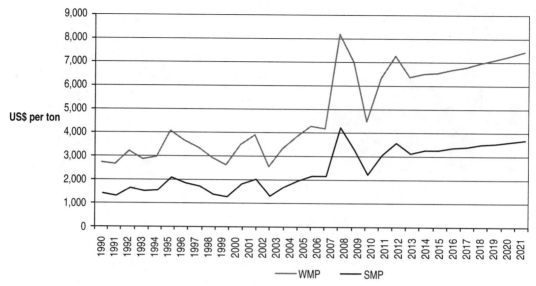

Fig. C7.9   Trends in international WMP and SMP prices (in nominal terms)

Source: OECD–FAO Agricultural Outlook 2012–21.

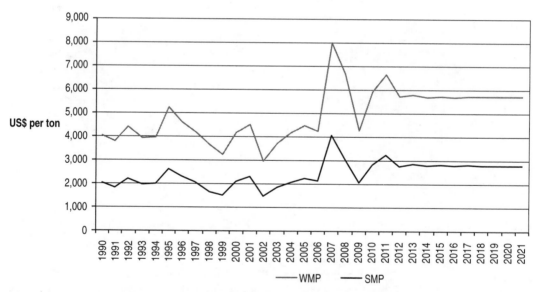

Fig. C7.10   Trends in international WMP and SMP prices (in real terms)

Source: OECD–FAO Agricultural Outlook 2012–21.

milk powder and whole milk powder in India's dairy exports has decreased from 65.6 per cent and 15.1 per cent in 2001 to 44.1 per cent and 8.2 per cent in 2010 and further declined to 12.1 per cent and 2.6 per cent respectively in 2011(Figs C7.14, C7.16, and C7.18). On the other hand, milk fats and butter increased from 10.9 per cent and 1.8 per cent in 2001 to 22.6 per cent and 12.4 per cent in 2010 and further rose

to 45.8 per cent and 18.8 per cent, respectively in 2011. Interestingly, there has been a remarkable increase in the share of India's cheese exports from a meagre 0.8 per cent in 2001 to 11.1 per cent in 2011.

The share of skimmed milk powder in India's dairy imports has increased from 1 per cent in 2001 to 30.7 per cent in 2010 and further increased to 69.5 per cent in 2011. On the other hand,

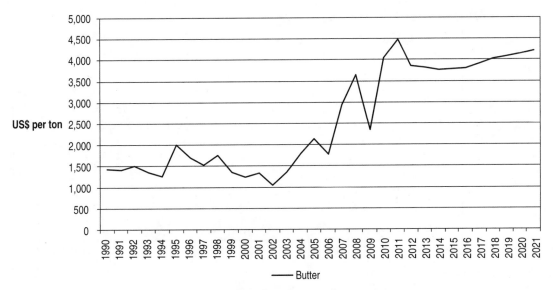

Fig. C7.11   Trends in international butter prices (in nominal terms)

Source: *OECD–FAO Agricultural Outlook 2012–21*.

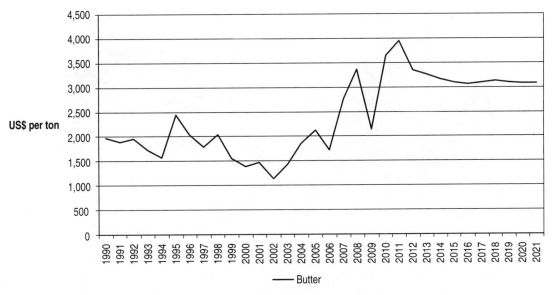

Fig. C7.12   Trends in international butter prices (in real terms)

Source: *OECD–FAO Agricultural Outlook 2012–21*.

milk fats increased from 41.5 per cent in 2001 to 39.9 per cent in 2010 and further rose to 1.2 per cent in 2011. The import share of whole milk powder increased from 11.7 per cent in 2001 to 18 per cent in 2010 but subsequently declined to 11.5 per cent in 2011. Despite increase in absolute value of cheese imports from US$968,000 in 2001 to US$7.4 million in 2011, its share in India's dairy imports declined from 19.9 per cent to 4.2 per cent during the same period (Figs C7.15, C7.17, and C7.19).

Asian and African countries remain the major destinations for India's dairy exports. In the Asian region, neighbouring countries

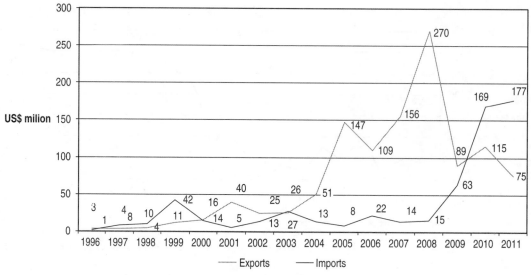

Fig. C7.13   India's dairy trade

Source: Trade Map, 2013.

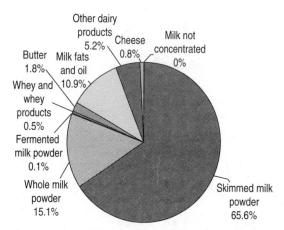

Fig. C7.14   Composition of India's dairy exports (2001)

Source: Trade Map, 2013.

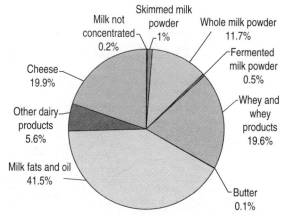

Fig. C7.15   Composition of India's dairy imports (2001)

Source: Trade Map, 2013.

in South Asia and the Middle East are the main buyers. UAE and Egypt are the largest markets of Indian dairy products accounting for 23 per cent and 15 per cent share (Figs C7.20 and C7.21) respectively in 2011. Despite several efforts, India has not been able to penetrate into the markets of Europe and North America, while the markets in South America also remain untapped. Unless India enhances exports of its value added products with higher shelflife, it would be difficult to have any significant increase in its dairy exports.[12]

The sourcing of dairy imports by India has witnessed a significant shift from France (33.6%) and Australia (21.3%) in 2001 to New Zealand (30%) and Australia (20.1%) in 2011 (Figs C7.22 and C7.23). Interestingly, the share of New Zealand has increased from 14.8 per cent in 2001 to 30 per cent in 2011.

Distortions in international dairy trade

International diary trade is often distorted by employing a number of non-tariff marketing barriers such as obstructions

---

[12] Joshi, Rakesh Mohan, 'India in Relation to Emerging International Dairy Trade', *Indian Dairying: Perspective 2020*, February 2012.

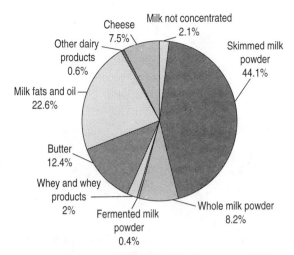

Fig. C7.16 Composition of India's dairy exports (2010)

Source: Trade Map, 2013.

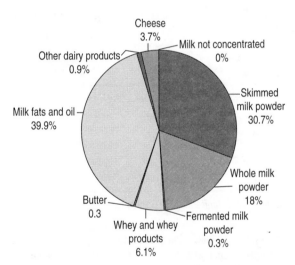

Fig. C7.17 Composition of India's dairy imports (2010)

Source: Trade Map, 2013.

in market access, several types of subsidies on production as well as exports, and legal obstructions related to health and hygiene.

Market access

Market access in developed countries is hampered by their maintaining high tariffs on products of interest to developing countries. In addition to elimination of all non-tariff measures by *tariffication*, all countries have bound all the tariffs applicable to agricultural products. In most cases, developing countries have given binding at rates that are higher than their current applied or reduced rates. There

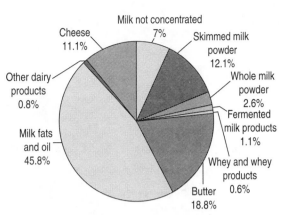

Fig. C7.18 Composition of India's dairy exports (2011)

Source: Trade Map, 2013.

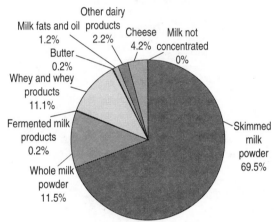

Fig. C7.19 Composition of India's dairy imports (2011)

Source: Trade Map, 2013.

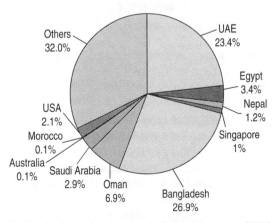

Fig. C7.20 International markets for India's dairy exports (2001)

Source: Trade Map, 2013.

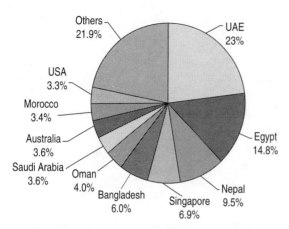

Fig. C7.21   International markets for India's dairy exports (2011)

Source: Trade Map, 2013.

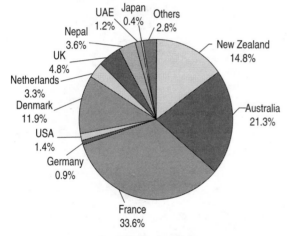

Fig. C7.22   Countries for sourcing India's dairy imports (2001)

Source: Trade Map, 2013.

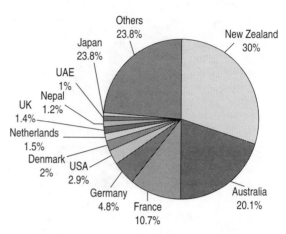

Fig. C7.23   Countries for sourcing India's dairy imports (2011)

Source: Trade Map, 2013.

Table C7.1   Cross-country comparison of tariff structure for dairy product (2011)

Country	Average bound (%)	Average applied (%)
Canada	218.5	126.6
Japan	118.1	93.3
EU	50.5	48.3
India	65.0	33.7
US	19.8	20.3

Source: *WTO Tariff Profile*, WTO, 2011.

is a huge disparity in tariffs on dairy products in India and other developed countries. The tariffs on dairy products are almost three times higher in most developed countries than in India (Table C7.1).

Canada and Japan apply very high rate of tariffs at an average of 126.6 per cent and 93.3 per cent respectively. The average applied tariff in the EU and USA is 48.3 per cent and 20.3 per cent respectively. India's applied tariff rate of 33.7 per cent is much lower than its average bound tariff of 65 per cent unlike most other developed countries.

On one hand, this tariff peaks continue to block developing countries' exports to developed world, whereas on the other, due to reduction in tariffs by developing countries, the domestic

markets would have been flooded with cheap and highly sub-sidized products, which would only lead to large-scale resent-ment. SPS also continues to be a major barrier for developing countries in diversifying their exports in horticulture, meat, and dairy products.

Subsidies by developed countries

The agreement on agriculture prohibits export subsidies on agricultural products unless the subsidies are specified in a member's lists of commitments. The level of domestic support continues to be very high in form of input subsidies such as foodgrains, irrigation, interest on loan, and insurance. Where they are listed, the agreement requires the WTO members to cut both the amount of money they spend on export subsidies and the quantities of exports that receive subsidies. Taking averages for 1986–90 as the base level, developed countries agreed to cut the value of export subsidies by 36 per cent over the six years starting 1995 (24% over 10 years for developing countries). Developed countries also agreed to reduce the quantities of subsidized exports by 21 per cent over the six years (14% over 10 years for developing countries). Least developed countries were not required to make any cuts. During the six-year implementation period, developing countries were allowed under certain conditions to use subsidies to reduce the costs of exports marketing and transporting.

The developed countries continue to provide high export subsidy to dispose of their large agricultural surplus in other countries of the world. The EU gives subsidy of more than US$550 per tonne on skimmed milk powder (SMP), US$850 per tonne on full cream milk powder and US$12 per tonne on butter and butter oil. Export subsidies on dairy products have been eliminated by the EU except small subsidies for storing butter under the Private Storage Aid (PSA) scheme, but that too is high.

International food laws and growing health concerns

The trend of tightening food law legislations and the debate over the issue is also a matter of concern. For instance, an EU proposal asked for an indication on a package as to whether a product has ever been frozen, in order to improve transparency, which also includes dairy products such as butter and cheese. Denmark implemented a tax on saturated fat in October 2011, which also concerns certain dairy products, as a measure to reduce the incidence of cardiovascular diseases and obesity. To develop effective strategic responses to newly evolving regulations would remain the key challenge in international marketing of dairy products.

The growing concern about health and nutrition is likely to bring opportunities as well as challenges to the dairy industry. The perceived benefits among the consumers of various bacteria strains have made probiotic sector among the fastest growing dairy business. Though the health claims of functional dairy products are being revisited in several countries, it provides tremendous marketing opportunities for high value added dairy products.[13]

Questions

1. Critically evaluate the impact of globalization on world dairy trade.
2. Explore the reasons for paradigm shift in world's major dairy exporters.
3. Critically examine product composition of India's dairy exports in view of the product composition of world dairy exports. Identify the reasons for the same.
4. 'A number of trade distorting practices adopted by developed countries is adversely affecting competitiveness of developing countries in international dairy trade.' Do you agree with this statement? Put forth your arguments to support your opinion.
5. Despite being the largest milk producer in the world, India has been only a marginal player in international dairy markets. Identify the reasons and work out a strategy to promote dairy exports from India.

---

[13] Joshi, Rakesh Mohan, *Promoting Dairy Exports from India: Emerging Challenges*, Publication on National Seminar on an Integrated Approach for Enhancing the Productivity Quality and Safety of Indian Food Products, National Productivity Council, 2013, pp. 25–38.

Identification, Segmentation, and Targeting of International Markets

Learning Objectives

- To explain the significance of segmentation and targeting of international markets
- To discuss identification of international markets
- To elucidate various methods of segmenting international markets
- To delineate selection of international markets
- To explicate tools and techniques for evaluation and selection of international markets

INTRODUCTION

International expansion of a firm's activities requires identification of marketing opportunities across the borders, evaluating, and selecting one or a few countries for its operations. A business enterprise needs to employ its finite resources most gainfully in countries where it gets optimum returns to fulfil its goals and objectives. However large a business enterprise, it is always faced by the limitation of resources for expansion into new activities and geographical areas. Therefore, an internationalizing company should carefully evaluate the marketing environment and select the most appropriate location for its expansion where it can operate and compete most effectively.

This chapter examines various issues related to market identification, segmentation, and selection. Generally, the process of internationalization gets initiated in a firm by a reactive approach to unsolicited enquiries from overseas markets. However, a systematic proactive approach often helps a firm in its efforts to reach foreign markets. The chapter explains various forms of market segmentation, such as geographic, demographic, and psychographic, based on the stages of development and international marketing opportunities and market attractiveness.

The managers operating in international markets need to develop a conceptual understanding of various tools and techniques employed for market evaluation and selection. For identifying marketing opportunities, scanning the global economic environment provides useful insight. Preliminary screening of international markets may be carried out so as to access the market size, its accessibility, and overall market potential. Countries may further be evaluated and selected using various tools such as trade analysis and analogy methods, opportunity-risk analysis, products-country matrix strategy, growth-share matrix, and market attractiveness-company strength matrix. A separate set of criteria is often used for locating services, as discussed later in the chapter.

IDENTIFICATON OF INTERNATIONAL MARKETS

To expand internationally, a firm may adopt either a reactive or a proactive approach and identify and evaluate marketing opportunities, as follows.

Reactive approach

Most firms, particularly small and medium enterprises (SMEs), internationalize as an unintended response to an international marketing opportunity in the form of unsolicited export orders. In doing so, the positive stimulus in terms of increased profitability, turnover, market share, or image leads to catering to overseas markets as a repeat activity. Over a period, the firm takes up overseas marketing on a regular basis. Consequently, carrying out marketing across the borders becomes an integral part of the firm's marketing strategy.

Systematic approach

A systematic proactive approach is generally adopted by larger companies with relatively higher level of resources in country identification, evaluation, and selection. A firm has to carry out the preliminary screening of various countries before a refined analysis is carried out for country selection.

Institutes Facilitating Identification of International Markets

Trade statistics available from secondary sources may be used for preliminary market scanning. One can use published data from multilateral organizations, such as United Nations Conference on Trade and Development (UNCTAD), World Bank, International Monitory Fund (IMF), World Trade Organization (WTO) and national organizations like India's Directorate General of Commercial Intelligence and Statistics (DGCI&S). Import promotion organizations like Centre for Promotion of Import from Developing Countries (CBI) and import promotion offices from a number of high-income countries, such as the UK, Finland, Norway, and Japan also provide enormous information and services for investors.

Besides, information provided by commercial banks, countries' missions overseas and foreign missions in the home country, newspapers, magazines, and periodicals, and research reports are also helpful for identifying and evaluating international marketing opportunities.

Import promotion organizations

Many countries are substantially dependent on imports due to limited availability of their resources. Besides, companies in Japan import heavily due to heavy trade surpluses. These countries have set up institutional frameworks to promote imports so as to develop competitive supplier base for its importing firms. Such import promotion organizations also facilitate the foreign exporting firms to explore marketing opportunities and identify importers. Exhibit 8.1 indicates some major import promotion organizations.

Established in 1971, the Centre for Promotion of Imports from Developing Countries (CBI) (Fig. 8.1) facilitates imports into European countries. The major services offered by the CBI include

- market information and matchmaking;
- export development of business;
- training; and
- institutional development of business support opportunities.

Its clients include companies willing to export to Europe, business support organizations in developing countries, and companies from Europe who wish to buy from developing countries.

Exhibit 8.1 Import promotion organizations

Australia
Pacific Islands Trade and Investment Commission (PITIC)
Website: http://www.pitic.org.au

Canada
Trade Facilitation Office Canada (TFOC)
Website: http://www.tfoc.ca

Denmark
Danish Import Promotion Office for Products from
Developing Countries (DIPO)
Website: http://www.dipo.dk

Germany
*Deutsche Gesellschaft für Technische
Zusammenarbeit (GTZ) GmbH*
Website: http://www.gtz.de/english

Italy
*Département de la coopération, des
investissements et des relations UE & OMC
Istituto Nazionale per il Commercio Estero (ICE)*
Website: http://www.italtrade.com

Japan
Japan External Trade Organization (JETRO)
Website: http://www.jetro.go.jp

Netherlands/EU
Centre for the Promotion of Imports from Developing
Countries (CBI)
Website: http://www.cbi.nl

Sweden
Association of Swedish Chambers of Commerce
Website: http://www.cci.se

Switzerland
Swiss Import Promotion Programme (SIPPO)
Website: http://www.sippo.ch

Norway
Norwegian Agency for Development Cooperation (NORAD)
Website: http://www.norad.no

Fig. 8.1 Centre for Promotion of Imports from Developing Countries facilitates imports to EU

Source: Centre for Promotion of Imports from Developing Countries, www.cbi.eu.

SEGMENTATION OF INTERNATIONAL MARKETS

Market segmentation refers to dividing the market of potential customers into homogeneous sub-groups. Segmentation is needed because substantial differences exist in response of market to a particular marketing strategy. A small firm can compete more effectively in specific market segments as it concentrates its resources on the target segment. For a market segment to be effective,[1] it must be

- *measurable*; the size, purchasing power, and characteristics of the segments can be measured.
- *substantial*; the segments are large and profitable enough to serve. A segment should be the largest possible homogeneous group worth going after with a tailored marketing programme.
- *accessible*; the segments can be effectively reached and served.
- *differentiable*; the segments are conceptually distinguishable and respond differently to different marketing-mix elements and programmes.
- *actionable*; effective programmes can be formulated for attracting and serving the segments.

International market segmentation is defined as the process of identifying and dividing the customers around the world into distinct subsets that respond to a particular marketing strategy. As the customers of a particular segment have similar needs that can be addressed through a uniform marketing strategy, it is advisable to adopt differentiated marketing strategies for different market segments. While making decisions for international markets, major types of segmentation are used, which are as follows.

Geographic Segmentation

Under geographic segmentation, the markets are divided into geographical subsets. Although geographical segmentation is easier to monitor and measure, it does not always ensure uniformity in customer habits among the consumers due to geographical proximity. For instance, Myanmar is the next-door neighbour of India but the market structure and consumption patterns are entirely different. Table 8.1 depicts classification of markets on the basis of their geographical location, besides income. However, for segmenting international markets, geography has been ranked as the lowest criteria.[2]

Demographic Segmentation

Segmentation of international markets on the basis of demographic characteristics such as age, gender, family size, and education is known as demographic segmentation. This type of market segmentation has reasonable accuracy in measurement and is easy to access. Besides, demographic information is readily available, updated, and relatively accurate in most countries.

Country segmentation on the basis of income

The World Bank segments countries on the basis of income for operational and analytical purposes. Each economy is divided on the basis of income. The criteria used as in July 2011, for classifying countries by the World Bank on the basis of per capita gross national income (GNI) are as follows (see also Table 8.1):

- Low-income countries: US$1,005 or less
- Lower middle-income countries: US$1,006–3,975

---

[1] Kotler, Phillip, *Marketing Management*, 11th Edition, Prentice Hall of India, New Delhi, 2002, p. 286.
[2] Hermann, Simon, *Hidden Champions: Lessons from 500 of the World's Best Unknown Companies*, Harvard Business Press, Boston, 1996, pp. 9–48.

Table 8.1 Classification of economies by income and region (April 2012)

Income group	Sub-group	Sub-Saharan Africa		Asia		Europe & Central Asia		Middle East & North Africa		America
		East & Southern Africa	West Africa	East Asia & Pacific	South Asia	Eastern Europe & Central Asia	Rest of Europe	Middle East	North Africa	
Low income		Burundi	Benin	Korea, Dem. Rep.	Afghanistan	Kyrgyz Rep.				Haiti
		Comoros	Burkina Faso	Myanmar	Bangladesh	Tajikistan				
		Congo, Dem. Rep.	Central African Rep.	Combodia	Nepal					
		Eritrea	Chad							
		Ethiopia	Gambia, The							
		Kenya	Guinea							
		Madagascar	Guinea-Bissau							
		Malawi	Liberia							
		Mozambique	Mali							
		Rwanda	Niger							
		Somalia	Sierra Leone							
		Tanzania	Togo							
		Uganda								
		Zimbabwe								
Lower middle income		Angola	Cameroon	Indonesia	Bhutan	Armenia		Iraq	Djibouti	Belize
		South Sudan	Cape Verde	Kiribati	India	Kosovo		Syrian Arab Rep.	Egypt, Arab Rep.	Bolivia
		Sudan	Lesotho	Lao PDR	Pakistan	Georgia		West Bank and Gaza	Morocco	Guyana
		Swaziland	Congo, Rep.	Fiji	Sri Lanka	Moldova		Yemen, Rep.		Honduras
		Zambia	Cote d'Ivoire	Marshall Islands		Turkmenistan				El Salvador
			Ghana	Micronesia, Fed. Sts.		Ukraine				Guatemala
			Mauritania	Mongolia		Uzbekistan				Nicaragua
			Nigeria	Papua New Guinea						Paraguay
			Sao Tome and Principe	Philippines						
			Senegal	Samoa						
				Solomon Islands						
				Timor-Leste						
				Tonga						
				Tuvalu						
				Vanuatu						
				Vietnam						

(Contd)

Table 8.1 *(Contd)*

Income group	Sub-group	Sub-Saharan Africa		Asia		Europe & Central Asia		Middle East & North Africa		America
		East & Southern Africa	West Africa	East Asia & Pacific	South Asia	Eastern Europe & Central Asia	Rest of Europe	Middle East	North Africa	
Upper middle income		Mauritius Mayotte Namibia Seychelles South Africa	Botswana Gabon	American Samoa China Malaysia Palau Thailand	Maldives	Albania Belarus Bosnia and Herzegovina Bulgaria Kazakhstan Latvia Lithuania Macedonia, FYR Azerbaijan Montenegro Romania Russian Federation Serbia Turkey		Jordan Lebanon Iran, Islamic Rep.	Algeria Libya Tunisia	Antigua and Barbuda Argentina Brazil Jamaica Chile Colombia Costa Rica Cuba Dominica Dominician Republic Ecuador Grenada Mexico Panama Peru St. Kitts and Nevis St. Lucia St. Vincent and the Grenadines Suriname Uruguay Venezuela, RB
High income	OECD			Korea, Rep. Australia Japan New Zealand		Poland Hungary Czech Republic Estonia	Denmark Austria Belgium Luxembourg Germany Netherlands Slovak Rep. Slovenia Finland France Iceland Ireland Greece Norway Portugal Sweden Spain			Canada USA

(Contd)

Table 8.1 *(Contd)*

Income group	Sub-group	Sub-Saharan Africa		Asia		Europe & Central Asia		Middle East & North Africa		America
		East & Southern Africa	West Africa	East Asia & Pacific	South Asia	Eastern Europe & Central Asia	Rest of Europe	Middle East	North Africa	
							UK Switzerland Italy			
High income	Non-OECD			Brunei Darussalam Oman		Croatia	Andorra		Malta	Virgin Islands
							Channel Islands	Bahrain		Northern Mariana Islands
				French Polynesia Guam			Cyprus	Kuwait		Puerto Rico
							Faeroe Islands	Qatar		Aruba
				Hong Kong SAR, China Macao SAR, China New Caledonia Singapore			Greenland	UAE		Bahamas, The
							Isle of Man	Israel		Barbados
							Liechtenstein	Equatorial Guinea		Bermuda
							Monaco			Cayman Islands
				Taiwan, China			San Marino			
							Curacao Gibraltar			

Source: *The Global Competiveness Report*, 2011–12.

- Upper middle-income countries: US$3,976–12,275
- High-income countries: US$12,276 or more
  Source: World Bank, 2011.

Lower income and middle-income countries are sometimes referred to as developing economies. The country classification on the basis of per capita income facilitates preliminary screening of international markets and provides broad inferences on the consumption patterns.

Segmentation of Indian market on the basis of household income

On the basis of household income, the Indian market may be segmented as upper middle class having a household income of over ₹8.5 lakh (1 lakh = 100,000) per year that comprise 14 per cent of the total population, middle class with a income range of ₹3 to ₹8.5 lakhs (23% of the population), emerging middle class with income range of ₹1.5 to ₹3 lakhs (42% of the population) and poor with income below ₹1.5 lakhs comprising 21 per cent of the population. As indicated in Fig. 8.2, the number of poor is likely to decline from 460 million in 2010 to 290 million in 2021, whereas the number of people in all other categories is likely to increase offering tremendous opportunities to market to these segments.

Interestingly, business fortunes for mass marketing lie in the category above the bottom of the pyramid, that is, emerging middle, which is still the largest category with 470 million

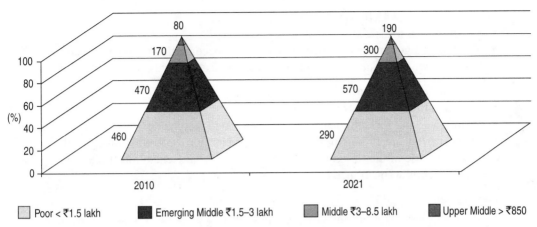

Fig. 8.2 Segmentation of Indian market on the basis of household income (no. of people in million)

Note: 1 lakh = 100,000

Source: 'The Fortune Just above the Bottom', *The Economic Times*, 6 March 2012.

Table 8.2 Projected market size of different sectors by 2021

Sector	Market size by 2021 ($ billion)
Misc. goods and services	200–250
Food and beverages	180–230
Housing and utilities	135–185
Transport and communication	170–220
Medicare and health-care services	60–80
Apparel	55–75
Education and recreation	40–50

Source: 'The Fortune Just above the Bottom', *The Economic Times*, 6 March 2012.

people comprising 42% of Indian population and is expected to further grow to 570 billion by 2021. After adjusting to purchasing power parity, by 2021, the market size is estimated to be as shown in Table 8.2.

As this class becomes a conspicuous consumer, the emerging middle class market is likely to grow from US$450 billion in 2011 to US$1 trillion by 2021 their representation in GDP to grow form US$1,843 billion to US$3,625 billion during the corresponding period. International companies do formulate their marketing strategies keeping in view the needs of various customer segments in India and developed innovative products and marketing strategy as well to harness its market potential.

Segmentation of markets on the basis of age

The consumption patterns within a country are significantly influenced by age. The demographic classification of Chinese market[3] on the basis of age indicates the following three distinct segments.

---

[3] Masaru, Ariga, Yasue Mariko, and Wen Gu Xiang, 'China's Generation III', *Marketing and Research Today*, February 1997, pp. 17–24.

Generation I (Age 45 to 59)
- Generation of the socialistic society
- The talented got university education and have become high-ranking government officials, but many work for state-owned enterprises. Some are already retired.

Generation II (Age 30 to 44)
- Lost opportunity to get proper education
- Mainly working for state-owned enterprises where income does not reflect job performance
- Those married are willing to spend as much as possible for 'Little Emperor', their only child, at the expense of their pleasures. In many cases, what Generation II purchases is based on what the child wants or needs.

Generation III (Age 18 to 29)
- Good educational background, with opportunity to work for foreign-affiliated firms.
- They are blessed with a good aspect of the market economy system that promises a brighter future for people who earn enough money.

For international marketers, Generation III is the most attractive market segment, also known as *s*-generation (single child generation), which has the following common characteristics.[4]

Luxury principle   They spend a disproportionate amount of money on one thing at the expense of others. They have a strong drive towards a high personal consumption level.

Consumption of Western feeling   Material goods are a medium for them to experience Western culture.

Aspiration of big names   They tend to be very fond of famous brand name products.

Newer-the-better syndrome   They like to go after the newest products.

One-cut-above-the-rest mentality   They like to impress others.

Once segmentation is complete, the priority is to focus on those target markets that generate the greatest revenue at the least investment.

Psychographic Segmentation

Dividing the consumers into different groups on the basis of lifestyle, personality, or values is termed as psychographic segmentation. Consumers within the same demographic clusters may have different psychographic profiles. As psychographic market segments go beyond national boundaries, it facilitates in developing an international marketing strategy.

Segmentation of international markets on the basis of core values

As core values are associated much deeper than behaviour and attitudes, they affect the consumer desires and choices over the long term. Consumer attitude and behaviour is greatly influenced by belief systems, known as core values. International markets can be segmented on the basis of core values[5] as follows.

Strivers (12%)   Place higher emphasis on material and professional goals and slightly more likely to include men than women. One third of Asians are strivers.

---

[4] Masaru, Ariga, Yasue Mariko, and Wen Gu Xiang, 'China's Generation III', *Marketing and Research Today*, February 1997, pp. 17–24.

[5] Miller, Tom, 'Global Segments from "Strivers" to "Creatives"', *Marketing News*, 20 July 1998, p. 11.

Devouts (22%) Place more value on traditions and duty and include more women than men. In developing Asia, Middle East, and Africa, devouts are more common, but rarely found in Western Europe and developed Asia.

Altruists (18%) They are more interested in social issues and social welfare and consist of slightly more women than men of older age with a median age of 44. Latin America and Russia have more altruists than any other country.

Intimates (15%) Place more value on close personal relationships and family above all, and include men and women almost equally. One fourth of American and Europeans are intimates compared to only 7 per cent in developing Asia.

Fun seekers (12%) The youngest group with a male–female ratio of 54:56, found in disproportionate numbers in developing Asia.

Creatives (10%) This market segment has strong interest in education, knowledge, and technology. Creatives are more common in Latin America and Western Europe.

The core-value-based segmentation of international markets is based on interviews conducted by Roper Reports of 1,000 people in 35 countries. As the people in each segment differ in terms of their activities, product, preference and use, and media use, understanding the dominance of these segments in various countries facilitates decision-making in international markets.

Psychographic segmentation of Indian youth

Indian youth in the age group of 15 to 24 constitutes 60 per cent of India's population. It is the generation that matured in the aftermath of liberalization and had exposure to the West through the media. A survey to study the psychographic profile of Indian youth on the basis of their values, icons, rituals, and symbols was carried out by MTV and presents the following distinct segments.[6]

Homebodies
- Form 16 per cent of the total audience, but their overall share has fallen.
- Largely traditional, have low individuality.
- Duty and morality at the core of their values.
- Not into brands, last to pick up on trends and fashion.
- Very few aspirations for self.
- Uneasy with the opposite sex.
- Focused on education/job but not career; what others would call 'bookworm'.

Two-faced
- 16 per cent of the target segment.
- Inwardly traditional, outwardly modern.
- Body tattoos co-exist with *Kyunki Saas Bhi Kabhi Bahu Thi* (Because the mother-in-law was also a daughter-in-law, once).
- Once married, they know they will have to abide by prescribed norms. Hence, the need to 'enjoy life' to the fullest.
- Openness with the opposite sex.
- Need to be aggressive to get ahead in life.

Wannabes
- The largest cluster, the massive mainstream.
- Materialistic, show-offs.

---

[6] 'India Youth', *The Marketing White Book, Business World (2003–04)*, Kolkata, p. 108.

- Desperate to be part of a crowd, trend followers who aggressively seek out lifestyle cues and adapt them to feel more confident and be perceived as 'cool' by others.
- High desire to attract opposite sex, while chances of comfort with the opposite sex are low.
- Extremely competitive.

Rebels
- With 23 per cent of the target segment, this is the second largest cluster.
- Their parents are very traditional.
- Their rebellion need not be overt.
- Perhaps first generation educated professionals, experiencing winds of change—education as the means of a career, wealth, change in lifestyle, independence.
- Responses guarded—unsure/do not wish to express/commit.
- Heavy reliance on friends—not understood by parents.

Cool guys
- Influencers, who all others want to be.
- Work hard–play hard types.
- Confident, strong individuality.
- Friends are very important.
- West is a dream for studies.
- Lots of aspirations.
- Experimentative.
- Liberal/Westernized.
- Enjoy life in the fast lane.
- Brand and label conscious.

Such psychographic segmentation is extremely useful for transnational corporations looking at marketing of trendy, luxury, and branded products in India.

Segmentation on the Basis of Stages of Development

Countries are classified under various stages of development[7] based on the level of GDP per capita at market exchange rates, which is a widely available measure used as proxy for wages and the extent to which countries are factor-driven. Share of exports of primary goods in total exports is used as a proxy and countries that export more than 70 per cent of primary products are, to a large extent, assumed to be factor-driven. Countries falling between the two stages are considered to be in transition, as indicated in Table 8.3. The stages of development are generally employed as a constituent to assess a country's competitiveness.

Moreover, this segmentation based on the stages of development may be used to develop entry strategy in various country markets.

Segmentation on the Basis of International Marketing Opportunity

The stage of demand for products and services varies significantly in countries. On the basis of opportunity, international markets can be classified[8] as follows.

Existing markets

These are the markets that are already serviced by existing suppliers and where customer needs are known. Marketing opportunities can be assessed by estimating the consumption rates and

---

[7] *The Global Competitiveness Report*, 2011–12, World Economic Forum, Geneva, p. 11.
[8] Gilligan, C. and M. Hird, *International Marketing*, Routledge, 1985.

Table 8.3 Country classification based on stages of development

Stage 1: Factor-driven (37 economies)	Transition from stage 1 to stage 2 (24 economies)	Stage 2: Efficiency-driven (28 economies)	Transition from stage 2 to stage 3 (18 economies)	Stage 3: Innovation-driven (35 economies)
Bangladesh	Algeria	Albania	Argentina	Australia
Benin	Angola	Belize	Barbados	Austria
Bolivia	Armenia	Bosnia and Herzegovina	Brazil	Bahrain
Burkina Faso	Azerbaijan	Bulgaria	Chile	Belgium
Burundi	Botswana	Cape Verde	Croatia	Canada
Cambodia	Brunei Darussalam	China	Estonia	Cyprus
Cameroon	Egypt	Colombia	Hungary	Czech Republic
Chad	Georgia	Costa Rica	Latvia	Denmark
Cote d'Ivoire	Guatemala	Dominican Republic	Lebanon	Finland
Ethiopia	Guyana	Ecuador	Lithuania	France
Gambia, The	Honduras	El Salvador	Mexico	Germany
Ghana	Iran, Islamic Rep.	Indonesia	Oman	Greece
Haiti	Jamaica	Jordan	Poland	Hong Kong SAR
India	Kazakhstan	Macedonia, FYR	Russian Federation	Iceland
Kenya	Kuwait	Malaysia	Slovak Republic	Ireland
Kyrgyz Republic	Mongolia	Mauritius	Trinidad and Tobago	Israel
Lesotho	Paraguay	Montenegro	Turkey	Italy
Madagascar	Philippines	Morocco	Uruguay	Japan
Malawi	Qatar	Namibia		Korea, Rep.
Mali	Saudi Arabia	Panama		Luxemburg
Mauritania	Sri Lanka	Peru		Malta
Moldova	Syria	Romania		Netherlands
Mozambique	Ukraine	Serbia		New Zealand
Nepal	Venezuela	South Africa		Norway
Nicaragua		Suriname		Portugal
Nigeria		Swaziland		Puerto Rico
Pakistan		Thailand		Singapore
Rwanda		Tunisia		Slovenia
Senegal				Spain
Tajikistan				Sweden
Tanzania				Switzerland
Timor-Leste				Taiwan, China
Uganda				UAE
Vietnam				UK
Yemen				USA

Source: *The Global Competitiveness Report*, 2011–12, World Economic Forum, Geneva, p. 11.

import patterns in these countries. Since competing suppliers are already in the market, the market entry is difficult unless a superior product is offered.

Latent markets

These markets have recognized potential customers but no company has so far offered a product to fulfil the latent needs; therefore, there is no existing market. As the market demand potential is known and there is no direct competition in the market, market entry is relatively easier once a firm is able to convince the customers about the benefits of its market offerings.

Incipient markets

There is no demand at present in the market, but the conditions and trends that indicate future emergence of needs can be identified. The incipient markets have the potential to become existing markets once the need is identified, created, and customers are persuaded to use the product resulting in market creation.

As indicated in Fig. 8.3, the marketing opportunities may be classified in three distinct product types as follows.

Competitive product   Competitive product is one that has no significant advantage over those already on offer. It is a 'me too' market offering.

Improved product   Although an improved product is not unique, it provides some improvement over the presently available market offering.

Breakthrough product   It represents significant differentiation with innovation and therefore has considerable competitive advantage.

The demand patterns are different for these three types of products. In existing markets, a product needs to be breakthrough or superior so as to offer a high competitive strength. Since there is no direct competition in latent markets, an improved product may also succeed. In incipient markets, as demand for the product is yet to be generated, competitive products in other markets may also be launched. However, breakthrough products offer considerable competitive advantage if market need is identified or created.

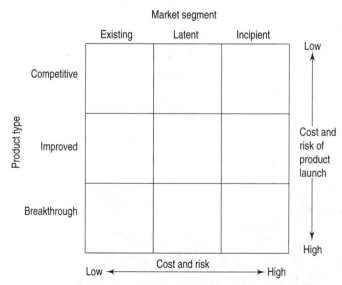

Fig. 8.3   Opportunities-based segmentation of international markets

Segmentation on the Basis of Market Attractiveness

The overall attractiveness of the market depends on market size and growth, risk, government regulations, competitive intensity, and physical and institutional infrastructure. Markets can be classified on the basis of overall market attractiveness[9] under the following five categories:

- *Platform countries* can be used to gather intelligence and establish a marketing network. Examples include Singapore and Hong Kong.
- *Emerging markets* include Vietnam and the Philippines. Here, the major goal is to build up an initial presence, for instance, via a liaison office.
- *Growth markets* such as China, India, Thailand, Indonesia, Malaysia, and the Philippines can offer early mover advantages. These often encourage companies to build up a significant presence in order to capitalize on future market opportunities.
- *Maturing markets* such as Taiwan and Korea offer far fewer growth prospects than the other types of markets. Many a time, the local competitors are well entrenched. On the other hand, these markets have a sizeable middle-class and solid infrastructure. The prime task here is to look for ways to further develop the market via strategic alliances, major investments, or acquisitions of local or smaller foreign players.
- *Established markets* such as Japan. Similar to maturing markets, the growth prospects are much lower than the other types of markets. An international firm often enters into these markets by way of joint ventures or acquisitions and integrates into regional or global operations as a part of its consolidation strategy.

PRELIMINARY SCREENING FOR SELECTION OF INTERNATIONAL MARKETS

Since a firm has limited resources, it has to focus on a few foreign markets. Besides, proper selection of markets avoids wastage of the firm's time and resources so that it can concentrate on a few fruitful markets. Market selection is a process of evaluating various market segments and focusing marketing efforts on a country, region, or a group of people that has significant potential to respond. A firm should identify those consumers that can be reached most effectively and efficiently.

Before arriving at a country or group of countries as the target market/s, a preliminary screening of countries may be carried out employing various criteria as follows.

Market Size

A firm looking forward to entering the international market needs to assess the present market size and future potential. It should be borne in mind that developed countries are not always the largest markets. Market size depends on a number of factors, which will be discussed here.

Population

The population of the market broadly gives a rough estimate of market size, though it has to be used with some other indicators as discussed later in the chapter. China with a population of about 1.3 billion is the most populous country in the world, followed by India with a population of over 1.2 billion (Fig. 8.4). The other most populous countries include the USA, Indonesia, Brazil, Pakistan, Nigeria, Bangladesh, the Russian Federation, and Japan. It does not always mean that the most populous countries are the largest markets in the world. However, for 'necessary goods' with low unit value such as food products, health-care items, educational products, bicycles, etc., population provides a gross indicator of market size.

---

[9] Lasserre, Philippe, 'Corporate Strategies for the Asia Pacific Region', *Long Range Planning*, vol. 28, no. 1, 1995, pp. 13–30.

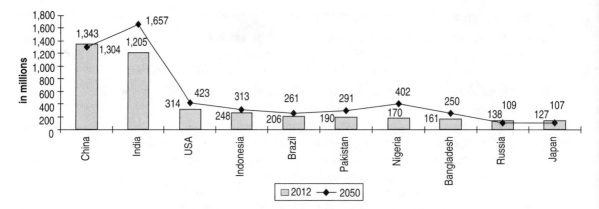

Fig. 8.4 World's most populated countries

Source: US Census Bureau, 2013.

The growth rate in population is an indicator of the future market potential. The World Bank estimates that between 2001 and 2015, approximately one billion people will be added to the world. Ninety-seven per cent will be born in low and middle-income countries and concentrated mainly in urban areas. The fastest growing region will be Sub-Saharan Africa, but the largest number of people will be added in Asia. The population of some high-income and Eastern European countries is likely to decline. However, for high-value products and luxuries the population figure is often misleading.

The ease of reach to a market is often determined by the density of population. The higher the population density, the easier it is to reach the market. It becomes difficult to maintain marketing channels in sparsely populated countries.

Income

Consumers need money to buy the products in a market. The GDP of a country provides a better estimate of the market size as compared to population. The USA has the highest GDP (purchasing power parity, PPP) of US$15,094 billion followed by China with US$11,300 billion. India ranks third with US$4,458 billion in terms of total GDP (PPP) (Fig. 8.5), ahead of Japan, Germany, Russia, Brazil, UK, and France.

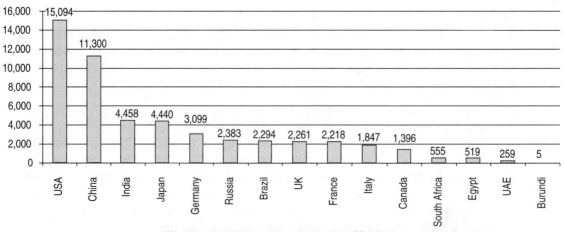

Fig. 8.5 World's largest economies (in US$ billion)

[Gross domestic product based on purchasing-power-parity (PPP) valuation of country GDP (in US$ billions)]

Source: World Economic Outlook Database, April 2012.

The growth rate per capita GDP facilitates in the estimation of future market potential. Per capita income is a better indicator of purchasing power of the residents of a country. The per capita income calculation assumes that the country's income is evenly distributed. India has a sizeable middle class but there are a number of countries that have a bimodal income distribution with no middle class. This indicates the existence of different market segments within a country. The purchasing power of money varies very significantly across countries, which significantly influences the cost of living.

Therefore, purchasing power needs to be taken into consideration. The GDP per capita in India works out to US$3,694 in terms of purchasing power parity (Fig. 8.6).

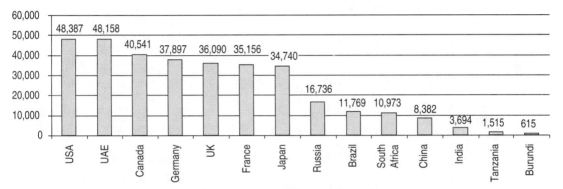

Fig. 8.6   GDP per capita purchasing power parity (PPP), 2011 (in US$ billion)

Source: World Economic Outlook Database, April 2012.

In terms of overall size, the USA is the largest market with a score of 6.92 on a seven-point scale followed by China (6.77), India (6.16), Japan (6.12), Germany (6.0), UK (5.77), France (5.74), and Russia (5.73), as shown in Fig. 8.7.

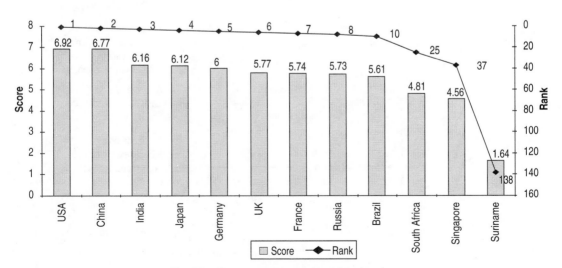

Fig. 8.7   Crosscountry comparison of market size

Note: 1 = least, 7 = highest (size of market)

Source: *The Global Competitiveness Report*, 2011–12, World Economic Forum, pp. 20–21.

Accessibility to International Markets

The market needs to be accessed in terms of various marketing barriers which include tariffs, non-tariff measures, and financial controls. A high-potential profitable market may not be attractive due to a variety of marketing barriers. A summarized diagrammatic depiction of marketing barriers[10] is given in Fig. 8.8.

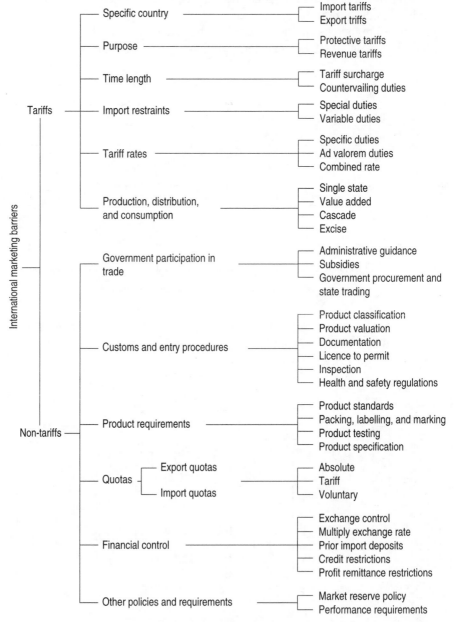

Fig. 8.8   International marketing barriers

---

[10] Onkvisit, Sak and J. John Shaw, 'Marketing Barriers in International Trade', *Business Horizons*, vol. 31, May–June 1988, pp. 64–72; *International Marketing: Analysis and Strategy*, Third Edition, Prentice Hall, 1997, New Delhi, pp. 84–110.

Tariff barriers

These are official constraints on import of certain goods and services and are levied in the form of customs duties or tax on products moving across borders. The tariff instruments may be classified as follows.

On the basis of direction of trade—import vs exports tariffs Tariffs may be imposed on the basis of direction of product movement, that is, either on exports or imports. Generally, import tariffs or customs duties are more common than tariffs on exports. However, countries sometimes resort to impose export tariffs to conserve their scarce resources. Such tariffs are generally imposed on raw materials or primary products rather than on manufactured or value-added goods.

On the basis of purpose—protective vs revenue tariffs The tariff imposed to protect the home industry, agriculture, and labour against foreign competitors is termed as protective tariff which discourages foreign goods. Historically, India had very high tariffs so as to protect domestic industry against foreign competition. A tariff rate of 200 to 300 per cent, especially on electronic and other consumer goods, created formidable barriers for foreign products to enter the Indian market.

The government may impose tariffs to generate tax revenues from imports that are generally nominal. For instance, the UAE imposes 3–4 per cent tariffs on its imports, which may not be termed as protective tariffs.

On the basis of time length—tariff surcharge vs countervailing duty On the basis of duration of imposition, tariffs may be classified either as surcharge or countervailing duty. Any surcharge on tariffs represents a short-term action by the importing country, while countervailing duties are more or less permanent in nature. The raison d'etre for imposition of countervailing duties is to offset the subsidies provided by the exporting countries governments. Countervailing duties have already been discussed in detail in Chapter 3.

On the basis of tariff rates—specific, ad-valorem, and combined Duties fixed as a specific amount per unit of weight or any other measure are known as specific duties. For instance, these duties are in terms of rupees or dollars per kg weight or per metre or per litre of the product. The c.i.f. value, product cost, or prices are not taken into consideration while deciding specific duties. Specific duties are considered to be discriminatory but effective in protection of cheap-value products because of their lower unit value.

Duties levied 'on the basis of value' are termed *ad-valorem* duties. Such duties are levied as a fixed percentage of the dutiable value of imported products. In contrast to specific duties, it is the percentage of duty that is fixed. Duty collection increases or decreases on the basis of value of the product. Ad-valorem duties help protect against any price increase or decrease for an import product.

A combination of specific and ad-valorem duties on a single product is known as combined or compound duty. Under this method, both specific and ad-valorem rates are applied to an import product.

On the basis of production and distribution points
Single stage sales tax Tax collected only at one point in the manufacturing and distribution chain is known as single stage sales tax. Single stage sales tax is generally not collected unless products are purchased by the final consumer.

Valued added tax (VAT) It is a multi-stage non-cumulative tax on consumption levied at each stage of production, distribution system, and value addition. A tax has to be paid at each time the product passes from one hand to the other in the marketing channel. However, the tax collected at each stage is based on the value addition made during the stage and not on the total value of the product till that point. VAT is collected by the seller in the marketing channel from a buyer, deducted from the VAT amount already paid by the seller on purchase of the product and remitting the balance to the government. Since VAT applies to the products sold in domestic markets and imported goods, it is considered to be non-discriminatory. Besides, VAT also conforms to the WTO norms.

Cascade tax   Taxes levied on the total value of the product at each point in manufacturing and distribution channel, including taxes borne by the product at earlier stages, are known as cascade taxes. India had a long regime of cascade taxes wherein the taxes were levied at a later stage of marketing channel over the taxes already borne by the product. Such a taxation system adds to the cost of the product making goods non-competitive in the market.

Excise tax   Excise tax is a one-time tax levied on the sale of a specific product. Alcoholic beverages and cigarettes in most countries tend to attract more excise duty.

Turnover tax   In order to compensate for similar taxes levied on domestic products, a turnover or equalization tax is imposed. Although the equalization or turnover tax hardly equalizes prices, its impact is uneven on domestic and imported products.

Non-tariff marketing barriers

Contrary to tariffs, which are straightforward, non-tariff barriers are non-transparent and obstruct trade on discriminatory basis. As the WTO regime calls for binding of tariffs wherein the member countries are not free to increase the tariffs at their will, non-tariff barriers in innovative forms are emerging as powerful tools to restrict imports on discriminatory basis. The major non-tariff policy instruments include the following.

Government participation in trade   State trading, governments' procurement policies, and providing consultations to foreign companies on a regular basis are often used as disguised protection of national interests and barrier to foreign firms. A subsidy is a financial contribution provided directly or indirectly by a government that confers a benefit. Various forms of subsidies include cash payment, rebate in interest rates, value added tax, corporate income tax, sales tax, insurance, freight and infrastructure, etc. As subsidies are discriminatory in nature, direct subsidies are not permitted under the WTO trade regime.

Customs and entry procedure   Custom classification, valuation, documentation, various types of permits, inspection requirements, and health and safety regulations are often used to hinder free flow of trade and discriminate among the exporting countries. These constitute an important non-tariff barrier. However, WTO legislation attempts to rationalize these barriers as discussed in Chapter 3.

Product requirements   Product standards and specifications, regulations related to packaging, labelling and marking, and product testing are frequently used as innovative barriers to trade mainly by high income countries. The insistence of the EU countries on banning the azo dyes had severely hampered India's exports of cotton textiles and ready-made garments to Europe and the firms had to resort to the use of vegetable dyes. The US Consumer Product Safety Commission in August 1994 imposed a ban on the import of Indian-made rayon and cotton-blended skirts on the grounds of fire hazard as they were considered to be highly inflammable. The Commission banned Indian skirts without any reported incidence of fire on preventive grounds. It may be noted that sales of synthetic skirts, called *ghagras,* increased enormously from 63,000 dozen in 1992 to 1.2 lakh dozen in the first six months of 1994. This makes it obvious that the objective behind the ban on Indian skirts was to protect their domestic industry by hampering the growing popularity of Indian products in the US market.

Quotas   Quotas are the quantitative restrictions on exports/imports intended at protecting local industries and conserving foreign exchange. The various types of quotas are as follows.

Absolute quotas   These quotas are the most restrictive, limiting in absolute terms, the quantity imported during the quota period. Once the quantity of the import quota is fulfilled, no further imports are allowed.

Tariff quotas   They allow import of specified quantity of quota products at reduced rate of duty. However, excess quantities over the quota can be imported subject to a higher rate of import duty. Using such a combination of quotas and tariffs facilitates some import, but at the same time discourages, through higher tariffs, excessive quantities of imports.

Voluntary quotas   Voluntary quotas are unilaterally imposed in form of a formal arrangement between countries or between a country and an industry. Such agreements generally specify the import limit in terms of product, country, and volume.

The Multi-Fibre Agreement (MFA) had been the largest voluntary quota arrangement wherein developed countries forced an agreement on economically weaker countries so as to provide artificial protection to their domestic industry. However, with the integration of the MFA with the WTO, the quota regime got scrapped by 1 January 2005. Summarily, all sorts of quotas have a restrictive effect on free flow of goods across countries.

Other trade restrictions   Other trade restrictions include minimum export price, wherein the government may fix a minimum price for exports so as to safeguard the interests of domestic consumers. Presently, India's trade policy does not impose any restrictions of minimum export price (MEP).

Financial controls

Governments often impose a variety of financial restrictions to conserve the foreign currencies restricting their markets. Such restrictions include exchange control, multiple exchange rates, prior import deposit, credit restrictions, and restriction on repatriation of profits. India had long followed a stringent exchange control regime to conserve foreign currencies.

Profitability

A market needs to be evaluated in terms of profitability in addition to market potential and growth. Profitability of a market can be significantly affected by the cost of logistics, government subsidies to local firms, price controls, import tariffs, and other statutory provisions of the target market. Besides, various types of risks associated with stability in the target markets, exchange rate, and payment ability of the importing firm. Despite being a high-potential and accessible market, Latin America is not always profitable due to higher logistic costs.

However, the selection criteria for a firm may also be product/market specific. A handicraft exporter from a low-income country needs to target a market with higher levels of disposable income (profitability), large size of population with aesthetic inclination and leisure time (market size), and few trade barriers (accessibility).

Assessing Market Potential

Firms tend to invest more resources in countries with high market potential. Although market size and its estimated growth rates provide useful insight, the determination of overall market potential of a country is arrived at by eight dimensions and each of these dimensions is allocated weights to contribute to the overall market potential index as given in Exhibit 8.2.

Exhibit 8.2 Computation of market potential indicators

Dimension	Weight	Measures used
Market size	10/50	Urban population (million), 2010[1]
		Electricity consumption (billion kwh), 2007[2]
Market growth rate	6/50	Average annual growth rate of primary energy use (%), between years 2004 and 2008[2]
		Real GDP growth rate (%), 2010[1]
Market intensity	7/50	GNI per capita estimates using PPP (US$), 2010[1]
		Private consumption as a percentage of GDP (%), 2010[1]
Market consumption capacity	5/50	Percentage share of middle-class in consumption/income, (2009)3[1]
Commercial infrastructure	7/50	Main telephone lines (per 100 habitants), 2010[3]
		Cellular mobile subscribers (per 100 habitants), 2010[3]
		Number of PCs (per 1000 habitants), 2010[4]
		Paved road density (km per million people), 2010[4]
		Internet users (per 100 habitants), 2010[3]
		Population per retail outlet, 2010[4]
		Percentage of households with TV, 2010[4]
Economic freedom	5/50	Economic Freedom Index, 2011[5]
		Political Freedom Index, 2011[6]
Market receptivity	6/50	Per capita imports from US (US$), 2010[7]
		Trade as a percentage of GDP (%), 2010[1]
Country risk	4/50	Country risk rating, March 2011[8]

Sources: [1] World Bank, *World Development Indicators*, 2009.
[2] US Energy Information Administration, *International Energy Annual*, 2008, published in December 2008.
[3] International Telecommunication Union, *ICT Indicators*, 2009.
[4] Euromonitor International, *Global Market Information Database*, accessed in August 2009.
[5] Heritage Foundation, *The Index of Economic Freedom*, 2010.
[6] Freedom House, *Survey of Freedom in the World*, 2010.
[7] US Census Bureau Foreign Trade Division, *Country Trade Data*, 2009.
[8] Euromoney, *Country Risk Survey*, March 2010.

Emerging markets comprise more than half of the world's population, account for a large share of world output and have very high growth rates, which means enormous market potential. India is the second largest market in terms of size after China among the emerging markets.[11] However, due to relatively lower ranking on other parameters that measure market potential, such as market growth rate, market intensity, market consumption capacity, commercial infrastructure, economic freedom, market receptivity, country risk, India has been ranked as the world's sixth most attractive market, while China is ranked as the third most attractive market, as shown in Exhibit 8.3.

---

[11] *Market Potential Indicators for Emerging Markets*, globalEDGE, 2011.

Exhibit 8.3   Cross-country comparison of market potential indicators

Overall rank	Country	Market size	Market growth rate	Market intensity	Market consumption capacity	Commercial infrastructure	Economic freedom	Market receptivity	Country risk	Overall score
1	Singapore	1	100	72	65	83	80	100	100	63
2	Hong Kong	1	29	100	59	100	93	86	95	58
3	China	100	93	1	67	36	7	4	55	55
4	South Korea	10	41	59	92	88	83	16	71	49
5	Czech Republic	1	18	45	100	92	89	14	76	45
6	India	38	83	35	67	17	50	2	42	41
7	Israel	1	17	63	76	73	81	20	61	40
8	Poland	4	21	60	79	73	80	5	69	40
9	Hungary	1	4	65	83	81	83	17	47	40
10	Turkey	6	70	66	65	49	60	4	43	38
11	Brazil	20	57	47	42	51	58	1	54	36
12	Mexico	10	40	59	47	46	65	18	45	35
13	Argentina	4	65	62	64	59	51	3	18	35
14	Malaysia	3	41	29	59	61	53	22	57	34
15	Chile	2	21	44	43	53	100	11	74	34
16	Peru	2	67	49	58	36	72	4	42	34
17	Indonesia	12	69	25	70	28	53	3	45	34
18	Thailand	4	53	26	61	45	46	14	54	32
19	Russia	23	20	39	62	64	15	3	42	32
20	Egypt	4	53	67	77	41	28	3	18	32
21	Saudi Arabia	4	26	19		55	29	12	58	28
22	Philippines	5	28	49	59	28	48	6	38	28
23	Colombia	3	35	53	32	42	61	3	46	28
24	Pakistan	6	52	62	74	1	32	1	1	26
25	Venezuela	3	1	48	66	41	1	4	15	20
26	South Africa	6	23	35	1	17	68	4	47	19

Source: GlobalEDGE, 2013.

TOOLS FOR INTERNATIONAL MARKET EVALUATION AND SELECTION

Analytical tools for market evaluation and selection also facilitate firms to develop and adopt differentiated marketing strategies for different country segments. Widely used techniques such as trade analysis and analogy methods, opportunity-risk analysis, products-country matrix strategy, growth-share matrix, and market attractiveness-company strength matrix are as follows.

Trade Analysis Method

One of the easiest and relatively quick methods of estimating market size for a country is by way of analysis of its trade data. In simple terms, the market size of a country may be determined by subtracting the exports of a product from the sum total of its production and imports.

$$\text{Market size} = \text{Production} + \text{Imports} - \text{Exports}$$

Changes in stocks need to be taken into consideration while arriving at an effective market size. One can arrive at market size by using data based on HS (ITC) code classifications up to eight digits for specific product categories. Published data on exports and imports can be obtained through international sources, such as the WTO, International Trade Centre, and the UNCTAD. National governments comply trade statistics through customs and central banks, for instance, in India, through the Directorate General of Commercial Intelligence and Trade Statistics (DGCI&S) and the Reserve Bank of India. Production statistics are generally available through government organizations for broad product categories, such as agricultural commodities, textiles, steel, cement, and minerals. More product-specific statistics are compiled by commodity organizations and trade associations.

Analogy Methods

For new product categories, with little consumption and production in the past, various types of analogy methods are employed. In the analogy method, a country at similar stage of economic development and comparable consumer behaviour is selected whose market size is known. Besides, a surrogate measure is also identified, which has similar demand to the product for the international market. Alternatively, the analogy method for different time periods, which may be compared with similar demand patterns in two different countries, may also be used.

Opportunity-risk Analysis

Carrying out a cross-country analysis of opportunities and risks provides a useful tool to compare and evaluate various investment locations based on a company's objectives and marketing environment. The internationalizing firm may choose variables both for opportunities (market size, growth, future potential, tax regime, costs, etc.) and risks (political, economic, legal, operational, etc.). Moreover, values and weights may be assigned to each of these variables depending upon their perceived significance by the firm. Thus, it provides an opportunity to a company to evaluate each country on the weighted indicators.

On the basis of marketing opportunities and risks, ranking of various countries may be made for investment. Countries with low-risks and high-returns are often preferred investment destinations. In addition, such grids may also be used for future projections. Although, such grids (Exhibit 8.4 and Fig. 8.9) serve as useful tools for cross-country comparison of opportunity and risk, it hardly provides any insight into relationships among the investment destinations.

Exhibit 8.4   Opportunity-risk grid for cross-country evaluation

Variable	Weight	Country			
		A	B	C	D
Opportunities • Market size • Growth • Competitive intensity • Operations costs • Marketing efficiency • Tax rates **Risks** • Political • Commercial • Economic • Operational					

Source: Joshi, Rakesh Mohan, *International Business*, Oxford University Press, New Delhi, 2009, p. 432.

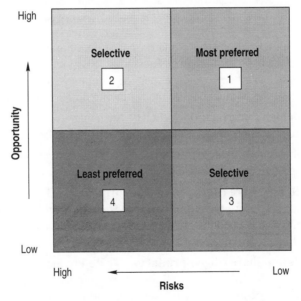

Fig. 8.9   Opportunity-risk matrix for country evaluation

Countries for investment can also be plotted in form of a matrix, as shown in Fig. 8.9, to indicate opportunities and risks. Besides, the countries can be placed for a pre-defined future time, both for opportunities and risks. In addition to inter-country evaluation, the country placements and its benchmarking with the global average opportunities and risks may also be carried out.

Growth-share (Boston Consulting Group) Matrix

The technique offers a useful tool to evaluate countries for different product categories based on their market share and growth rate. Products are classified under four categories on the lines of

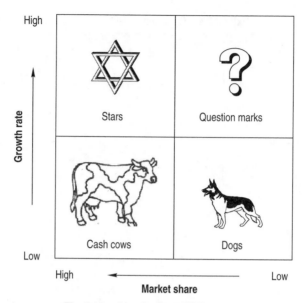

Fig. 8.10 Growth-share (BCG) matrix

Source: Adapted from the BCG Portfolio Matrix from the 'Product Portfolio Matrix'.

Copyright: Boston Consulting Group, 1970.

Boston Consulting Group (BCG) matrix based on a model[12] developed by Boston Consulting Group for classification of strategy business units (SBUs) of an organization, as shown in Fig. 8.10.

Such a matrix can be prepared either for a country's or a firm's exports so as to facilitate segmentation of the products under the following broad categories:

High growth high share (stars) products   Such markets offer high growth potential but require lot of resources to maintain the share in high growth markets.

Low growth high share (cash cows) products   Products under this category bring higher profits, though they have a slow market growth rate.

High growth low share (question marks) products   These are the products under high risk category with an uncertain future, sometimes called *problem children*. A highly competitive strategic marketing decision is required to invest resources to bring it to the category of stars by achieving a higher market share.

Low growth low share (dogs) products   These products have low growth and low market share, therefore generally do not call for investing much resources.

The growth-share matrix may be used for working out differentiated strategies for international marketing of each product category. Similar matrix can also be prepared country-wise for formulating country specific marketing strategies.

Country Attractiveness–Company Strength Matrix

An analysis may be carried out for country evaluation and strategy development based on market attractiveness of countries and the competitive strength of the company. Various factors, such as market size, market growth, customers' buying power, average trade margins, seasonality and

---

[12] *The Experience Curve Reviewed: IV. The Growth Share Matrix of the Product Portfolio*, Boston Consulting Group, Boston, 1973.

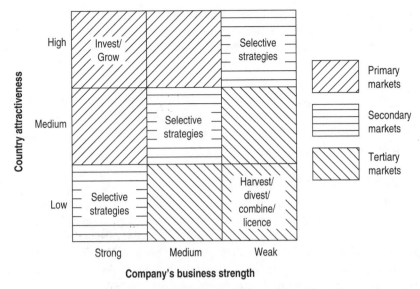

Fig. 8.11   Country attractiveness–company strength matrix

fluctuations in the market, marketing barriers, competitive structures, government regulations, economic and political stability, infrastructure, and psychic distance may be taken into account to assess country attractiveness. The competitive strength of a firm is often determined by its market share, familiarity and knowledge about the country, price, product-fit to the market, demands, image, contribution margin, technology position, product quality, financial resources, access to distribution channels, and their quality. An analysis can be carried out in the form a matrix, assigning weight to each of these factors. Based on this analysis, a matrix may be drawn as in Fig. 8.11.

The countries depicted in the matrix may be segmented as follows.

Primary markets

These countries offer the highest marketing opportunities and call for a high level of marketing commitments. The firms often strive to establish permanent presence in these markets.

Secondary markets

In these countries, the perceived political economic risks are too high to make long-term irrevocable business commitments. A firm has to explore and identify the perceived risk factors or the firm limitations in these markets and adopt individualized marketing strategies like joint ventures so as to take care of the marketing limitations.

Tertiary markets

In these markets the perceived political-economic risks are too high to make long-term irrevocable commitments. Generally, a firm does not have any long-term commitment in such countries and opportunistic marketing strategies like licensing are often followed.

Based on the above analysis, a firm should focus its market targeting and expansion strategies in countries at the top left of the matrix where the country attractiveness and the competitive strengths of the company are very high. On the other hand, the firm should focus on harvesting/divesting its resources from countries where the country attractiveness and company strength both are very low. However, a firm may use licensing as a mode of business operation with little resource commitment but continue to receive royalties. Countries at the extreme right top of the matrix signify higher country attractiveness but lower company strength. A firm should identify its competitive weaknesses in these countries and strive to gain the competitive strength. It may also enter into joint venture with other firms, which most of the time are local and have complementarities to gain competitive strength. In countries where a firm has medium competitive strength and country attractiveness needs to carefully study the market condition and adopt appropriate strategy. Ford tractors used the country attractiveness company strength matrix and placed India under the extreme right top of the matrix wherein the country attractiveness was very high but the competitive strength of the company was low.

Country Evaluation for Locating Services

Advents of telecommunication and transports technology have paved way for global expansion of services. Moving operations to low-cost countries offers a variety of advantages from reduced wages for qualified workers to historically lower costs of businesses. In order to strategically choose global locations, the decisions should be based on maximizing the long-term benefits of offshoring while offsetting rising wages and other developments. Rather than offshoring *per se*, companies often succeed in their offshore strategies by use of a holistic approach and focusing on global delivery models.

Key emerging markets in Southeast Asia, Latin America, and Eastern Europe are becoming more attractive in terms of talent, industry experience, quality certifications, and regulatory environment. As the relative cost advantage of leading offshore destinations has continually declined over the recent years, the key to maintain and enhance long-term competitiveness, for both developed and developing countries lies in skills development, infrastructure, and investment and regulatory environment rather than in attempts to control wages. In the fast-moving remote services businesses, the failure to improve the skills of the workforce would lead to loss of competitiveness.

The top 50 locations worldwide that provide the most common remote functions, including IT services and support, contact centres and back-office support have been analysed and ranked by A.T. Kearney's Global Services Location Index (GSLI). Each country's score is composed of a weighted combination of relative scores on 43 measurements, which are grouped into three categories: financial attractiveness, people and skills availability, and business environment. The weight distribution for the three categories is 40:30:30. Financial attractiveness is rated on a scale of 0–4 and the categories for people and skill availability and business environment are on a scale of 0–3.

India is the most preferred country to locate services in the world as it offers an unbeatable mix of low costs, deep technical and language skills, mature vendors, and supportive government policies. After India, the other most preferred services locations include China, Malaysia, Thailand, Brazil, and Indonesia (Fig. 8.12). Although the double digit growth rate has fuelled wage inflation by around 30 per cent in China and 20 per cent in India, the cost escalation have been matched by corresponding increases in skills apply and quality. In terms of language skills and vendor maturity, India maintains a strong lead, which makes a large number of Western companies increasingly outsource services. For instance, in 2007, Citigroup Inc. announced to move as many as 8,000 positions to India, particularly in equity research, investment banking, and back-office transaction related activities, in addition to its 12,000 strong workforce in the BPO division. India's continued competitiveness can also be credited to in-country shifts of resources from expensive tier-one cities to tier-two and tier-three cities, with higher quality of life and lower costs. Developed nations rank poorly on the financial attractiveness of services; therefore, they need to focus on moving up the value chain.

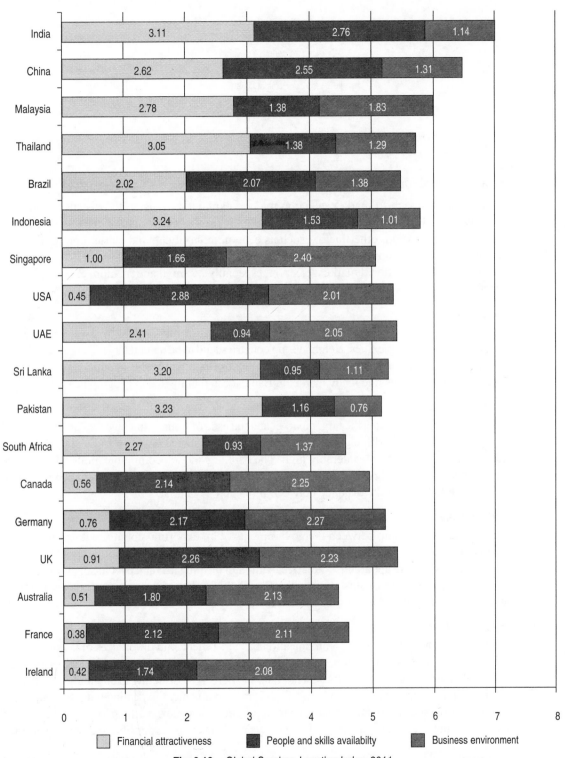

Fig. 8.12 Global Services Location Index, 2011

Source: 'Off-shoring for Long-term Advantage', *A.T. Kearney's Global Services Location Index*, Chicago, 2011.

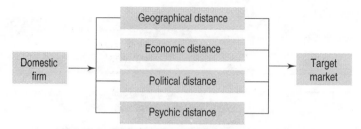

Fig. 8.13 Various hurdles in reaching a target market

Distance Model for Selection of International Markets

A pragmatic approach to market selection may be explained by using the distance model, as shown in Fig. 8.13. Though countries with geographic proximity are natural markets for a firm's international expansion, other factors such as economic, political, and cultural proximity also assume considerable significance.

This kind of international market selection, especially by small and medium exporting firms, comes from countries with relatively less distances[13] to cover, as follows.

Geographical distance

Countries with geographical proximity tend to be natural target markets due to lower physical distances and logistic complexities. Neighbouring countries tend to be natural target markets especially for products with lower unit value. Despite a number of political and economic barriers, a wide range of Indian products find ready market in Bangladesh mainly due to geographical proximity.

Economic distance

The final cost of a product in the target market and the ease of transacting business are determined by economic distance. Although there is little physical distance between India and Myanmar, the economic distance is considerably high. The banking and telecommunication infrastructure in Myanmar is far from adequate. On the other hand, the economic distance between India and UK is much lower than the distance between India and Myanmar.

Political distance

The political relationship between the governments of an exporting country with an importing country considerably influences the selection of target markets. Adverse political relations may hinder markets that are apparently attractive. Although the physical and psychic distance is much lower between India and Pakistan, it is the formidable political distance that makes Pakistan hardly the preferred market for most Indian firms.

Psychic distance

Psychological gaps often create communication barriers reflected in differences of languages, life styles, cultural orientation, awareness levels, political ideologies, or the level of technical skills. As a result, the uncertainty about foreign markets and perceived difficulty in obtaining information about foreign markets is lower and a firm finds it more convenient in dealing with firms in countries with fewer such barriers. The narrowing of psychological gaps has helped China increase its trade with Southeast Asian countries. Lower psychic distance is responsible for significant trade

---

[13] Johanson, J. and E. Vahlne, 'The Internationalization Process of the Firm: A Model of Knowledge Development and Increasing Foreign Market Commitment', *Journal of International Business Studies*, vol. 8, no. 1, 1977, pp. 23–32.

between China and other East Asian countries. The large Indian ethnic population in Middle East, Singapore, the UK, the USA, and Canada constitutes sizeable markets for Indian products.

As depicted in Fig. 8.13, the international market selection is determined by a combination of these distances such as geographical, psychic, economic, and political. It is also obvious from the above that though geographical proximity influences market selection considerably, but it does not always ensure the most preferred market.

Decisions to expand business across national boundaries require much higher level of commitment of company's resources as any business failure may have serious repercussions. By way of effective evaluation and selection of countries, the internationalizing firm avoids wastage of time and resources and it can focus its efforts on a few fruitful locations. This chapter highlights approaches to identification and evaluation of marketing opportunities and provides insight into the international market research. Various options available with the firm for country evaluation are also discussed. This chapter also examines various tools for country evaluation and selection.

Summary

Identification of international marketing opportunities, evaluating various countries, and targeting right markets is crucial to the success of a firm in its internationalization efforts. This chapter describes identification, segmentation, selection, and targeting of international markets. Small and medium firms with limited resources often use a reactive approach for identifying opportunities, whereas a systematic proactive approach is adapted by larger companies. Cross-country research is employed for objective evaluation of marketing opportunities and country selection.

A firm can make use of information and services from various export promotion agencies, DGCI&S, the World Bank, and the WTO in identifying markets. The methods of segmenting international markets include geographic, demographic, and psychographic segmentation. International markets can also be segmented on the basis of marketing opportunities under categories of existing, latent, and incipient markets, which represent marketing opportunities for three distinct product types, such as competitive products, improved products, and breakthrough products. Platform countries, emerging markets, growth markets, maturing markets, and established markets represent various segments of international markets on the basis of market attractiveness.

The selection of international markets is divided into two phases: preliminary screening and final analysis for selecting and targeting. The methods used for estimating market size for preliminary screening include estimation of market size, accessibility, and profitability. For final selection of the target market, micro analysis is required for estimating product specific market size. Trade analysis and market analogy are the widely used techniques for estimating market size. Final selection and strategy development for international markets, growth-share, and market portfolio matrices serve as useful analytical tools.

Trade analysis and analogy methods, opportunity-risk analysis, products–country matrix strategy, growth-share matrix, and market attractiveness–company strength matrix serve as useful analytical tools for country evaluation and market selection. Besides, the distance model requires a firm to overcome various distances, namely geographical, psychic, economic, and political, to reach the target markets, which serves as a handy tool in market selection.

Key Terms

Absolute quota   Restricts the quantity imported during the quota period beyond which no further imports are allowed.

Ad-valorem duties   Duties levied 'on the basis of value'.

Breakthrough product   Represents products with significant differentiation and innovation, and, therefore has considerable competitive advantage.

Cascade tax   Taxes levied on the total value of the product at each point in a manufacturing and distribution channel including taxes borne by the product at earlier stages.

Competitive product   A competitive product is one that has no significant advantage over those already on offer.

Countervailing duty   Duty imposed to offset the subsidies provided by the exporting countries' governments. Countervailing duties are more or less permanent in nature.

Demographic segmentation   Market segmentation on the basis of demographic characteristics such as age, gender, family size, and education.

Existing markets   The markets that are already serviced by existing suppliers and where customer needs are known.

Geographic segmentation   Division of markets into geographical subsets.

Improved product   Not a unique product, but provides some improvement over the presently available market offering.

Incipient markets   There is no existing demand in the market but the conditions and trend can be identified to indicate future emergence of needs.

International market selection   The process of evaluating various market segments and focusing marketing efforts on a country, region, or a group of people that has significant potential to respond.

Latent markets   The markets that have recognized potential customers but where no company has so far offered a product to fulfil the latent need; therefore, there is no existing market.

Market segmentation   Dividing the market of potential customers into homogeneous sub-groups.

Non-tariff barriers   Contrary to tariff barriers, which are straightforward, non-tariff barriers are non-transparent and inhibit trade on a discriminatory basis.

Psychic distance   The differences in language, culture, political system, and level of education among the countries.

Psychographic segmentation   Dividing consumers into different groups on the basis of lifestyle, personality, or values.

Quotas   Quantitative restrictions on exports intended to protect local industries and to conserve foreign currencies.

Single stage sales tax   Tax collected only at one point in the manufacturing and distribution chain.

Specific duty   Duties fixed as a specific amount per unit of weight or any other measure.

Tariff barriers   The official constraints on import of certain goods and services in the form of customs duties on products moving across the borders.

Tariff quotas   Allows import of specified quantity of quota products at reduced rate of duty permitting excess quantities over the quota to be imported subject to a higher rate of import duty.

Tariff surcharge   A short-term duty by the importing country.

Valued added tax (VAT)   A multi-stage non-cumulative tax on consumption levied at each stage of the production and distribution system and each stage of value addition.

Voluntary quotas   Unilaterally imposed quantitative restrictions in the form of a formal arrangement between countries or between a country and an industry.

Concept Review Questions

1. 'Markets with geographic proximity are not always the most preferred markets.' Examine the statement critically and give suitable examples.
2. Explaining the significance of market selection in international marketing, discuss the major approaches used to identify and select foreign markets.
3. Explain various types of marketing barriers.
4. Write short notes on the following:
   (a) Assessing market potential
   (b) Country classification based on stages of developments
   (c) Country attractiveness–company strength matrix

Critical Thinking Questions

1. A US firm identified India as a high opportunity market but the company has little competitive strength in the market. Explain, with the help of a portfolio matrix, the types of marketing strategies the firm should adopt in India.
2. Work out a market segmentation plan for exports of fresh fruits from India or your country.
3. How would you proceed to explore market potential for the export of ladies' causal wear from your country?

Project Assignments

1. Visit the website of the International Trade Centre (ITC), Geneva (www.intracen.com). List out the services provided by ITC. Identify its limitations and discuss in class.
2. Contact a local firm and find out how it first identified an overseas market. Explore the types of segmentation used by the firm, if any.
3. A US-based IT firm is looking at options to off-shore some of its services. Prepare a list of parameters you would use to evaluate various countries and suggest the most suitable location.
4. An Indian pharmaceutical company primarily engaged in manufacturing and marketing bulk drugs domestically is looking at setting up manufacturing operations overseas. Select a few countries for its business expansion based on your evaluation, using risk-opportunity analysis. Discuss your findings in class.

CASE STUDY: IDENTIFYING INTERNATIONAL MARKETING OPPORTUNITIES IN MEDICAL SERVICES

Emergence of International Market for Medical Tourism

Historically, wealthy people from developing countries used to travel to developed countries for medical treatments primarily due to superiority of the skills of their medical professionals and the state-of-the-art technology. The UK, the USA, Germany, Japan, and France fascinated riches from across the world for medical treatment. With the advent of widespread adaptation of modern technology, education and training in modern medical sciences, developing countries including India increasingly achieved the competence to offer medical services at a fraction of the cost of similar services in developed countries. Patients especially the old, sick, poor, or those not covered under health insurance schemes or public healthcare systems in the wealthy countries desperately explore options for affordable medical care. As a result, the trend of patients travelling from developing to developed countries witnessed a reversal in the 21st century with increasing number of visitors from developed countries travelling to low-cost medical destinations.

The advent of Internet facilitated increased and speedy flow of information about diseases and their remedies across borders among patients, doctors, and other stakeholders. Rising frequency of international travel with decreasing fares and liberal visa regimes especially aimed at travel for medical purposes has given rise to new patterns of production and consumption of healthcare services. This has led to emergence of an 'international market' for patients who are viewed as 'customers' rather than 'citizens'.

The WTO has significantly contributed to liberalization of trade in healthcare services. Under the aegis of WTO, the General Agreement on Trade in Services (GATS) aims at liberalizing trade in medical services under the following four delivery modes.

Medical travel   Wherein people travel across borders with an intent to get healthcare, also known as 'medical tourism', it is the most visible face of the increasing global trade in healthcare services.

Cross-border delivery of trade   It covers everything from shipment of laboratory samples, diagnosis and clinical consultation via traditional mail channels, to the electronic delivery of health services. This mode of medical trade is expected to become a significant movement because of the advances in telecommunications. Tele-medicine holds out big potential simply because it allows offering the services without investing very heavily in infrastructure. Some hospitals in the USA have started offering tele-consultation services to hospitals in Central America and the eastern Mediterranean region. Some Indian hospitals are offering similar services to their counterparts in Nepal and Bangladesh.

Setting up of health-care services overseas   It covers setting up of hospitals, clinics, and diagnostic centres in a country by a medical group that has its base in another country. It could also involve the taking over of a hospital chain by a foreign group.

Movement of health-care personnel from one country to other   It includes the movement of physicians, specialists, nurses overseas, for instance Indian doctors, nurses, physiotherapists, etc. to the UK and other countries for offering medical services.

The international market demand for medical services is likely to witness a progressive increase as the proportion of elderly (60 years and above) population vis-à-vis total population is rapidly increasing in the USA, UK, Japan, and many other European countries. The number of people aged 65 years and above is expected to double in the USA in the next 15 years. In the UK, the people aged 60 years and above will form 25 per cent of the population in the next 30 years—up from the current 16 per cent. Similar trends are likely to be expected in all west European countries. Besides, the average life expectancy is steadily growing across countries over the years. On the other hand, the healthcare systems in the USA, Japan, and UK are under tremendous pressure to take care of the increasing demand. The number of doctors and nurses joining the medical workforce in both the USA and the UK is not keeping pace with growing demand of the ageing population.

The financial crisis in the Europe and the USA has led to reduced public healthcare provisions and has necessitated search for alternate places for low cost treatment. As the treatment costs are increasingly becoming prohibitive in developed countries such as Japan, the USA, and the UK, more and more patients are looking for destinations with cost effective treatments. As a result of all these factors, there is likely to be a big surge in demand for international healthcare.

International medical tourism market: a brief overview

The global medical travel market is estimated at US$30–40 billion with approximate 750 million patients travelling worldwide and is likely to grow annually at 20 per cent. India, Thailand, Jordan, Malaysia, South Africa, and Cuba have emerged as preferred destinations for international medical tourism. Depending upon the country competence, the range of healthcare services offered in the international medical tourism market includes the following:

- Cardiac surgery: Coronary Artery Bypass Graft (CABG), valve replacement
- Orthopaedic surgery: hip replacement, knee-replacement, joint surgery, restructuring
- Bariatric surgery: gastric by-pass, gastric banding
- Transplantation surgery: organ transplantation, stem cell
- Fertility/Reproductive system: Gender reassignment, IVF
- Eye surgery
- Cosmetic surgery: face, breast, liposuction
- Dentistry: reconstruction and cosmetic
- Diagnostics and check-ups

International destinations for medical tourism include India, Malaysia, Singapore, and Thailand in Asia; South Africa and Dubai in Middle East; Brazil, Costa Rica, Cuba, and Mexico in South and Central America; and a range of European countries. A summary of international markets of medical tourism is given in Table C8.1. Thailand has emerged as the largest destination for medical tourism, which receives patients mainly from the USA and the UK for cosmetic surgery, organ transplant,

dental treatment, and joint replacements. Jordan mainly attracts patients from Middle East primarily for organ transplant, fertility treatment, and cardiac care. Malaysia has primarily specialized in cosmetic surgery attracting travellers from the USA, Japan, and developing countries. Travellers from the USA and the UK visit South Africa mainly for cosmetic surgery, and eye (Lasik) and dental treatment. India offers a range of medical treatment services from cardiac surgery to joint replacement and cosmetic surgery.

With a large fleet of highly proficient and skilled doctors, such world class surgery is available in India at a fraction of cost as compared to high-income countries as shown in Table C8.2. The cost for heart bypass surgery in India is available at US$10,000 compared to its cost of US$1,13,000 in the USA, US$13,921 in the UK. The hip replacement costs merely US$9,000 in India vis-à-vis US$47,000 in the USA. Breast implants in India costs US$2,200 compared to US$6,000 in the USA and US$4,350 in the UK.

In view of high treatment costs in most high-income countries, the source country is bound to benefit from outflow of patients in terms of their employers' and employees' contribution to health plans and public health insurance systems. The potential savings range from 75 per cent to 90 per cent reduction in prices compared with the US in-patient prices depending upon the type of procedures and the location. It is estimated that if one in ten patients in the USA choose to travel abroad for treatment, it could lead to a saving of US$1.4 billion annually.[14] By way of sending patients to India, substantial savings could accrue to the UK in alleviating its waiting lists and saving financial costs estimated to about £200 million annually.[15] Moreover, long waiting time in a large number of developed countries is likely to further boost international medical tourism as patients search for alternative medical treatment destinations with little waiting time that too at much lower costs, especially for emergency healthcare requirements.

Table C8.1 International travellers' flow for medical treatment

Destination country	Country of origin	Healthcare strengths
Thailand	USA, UK	Cosmetic surgery, organ transplants, dental treatment, joint replacements
Jordan	Middle East	Organ transplants, fertility treatment, cardiac care
India	Middle East, UK, Bangladesh, developing countries	Cardiac care, joint replacements, Lasik, cosmetic surgery
Malaysia	USA, Japan, developing countries	Cosmetic surgery
South Africa	USA, UK	Cosmetic surgery, Lasik, dental treatment
Cuba	Latin America, USA	Vitiligo, night blindness, cosmetic surgery

International medial tourism: customers' behaviour

Medical service providers across the world directly target patients or 'customers' through the Internet, who pay out of their own pockets. Unlike most public health schemes, the patients or the customers become the key decision-makers as to what treatment they wish to undergo, at what place and when, and evaluates options available across the globe initially through the Internet. Stakeholders with commercial interests in medical tourism include providers of healthcare services, insurance companies, brokers, travel agencies, financing institutions, and websites.

---

[14] Mattoo, A. and R. Rathindran, 'How Health Insurance Inhibits Trade in Health Care', *Health Affairs*, 25, 2006, pp. 358–368.
[15] *Medical Tourism: Treatments, Markets and Health System Implications: A Scoping Review*, OECD, 2011, pp. 31–32.

Table C8.2 Surgery prices* in select countries (in US$)

Procedure	USA	Thailand	Singapore	Malaysia	Mexico	Poland	UK	India
Hear bypass (CABG**)	1,13,000	13,000	20,000	9,000	3,250	7,140	13,921	10,000
Compared to India (in times)	(11.3)	(1.3)	(2.0)	(0.9)	(0.3)	(0.7)	(1.4)	
Angioplasty	47,000	10,000	13,000	11,000	15,000	7,300	8,000	11,000
Compared to India (in times)	(4.3)	(0.9)	(1.2)	(1.0)	(1.4)	(0.7)	(0.7)	
Hip replacement	47,000	12,000	11,000	10,000	17,300	6,120	12,000	9,000
Compared to India (in times)	(5.2)	(1.3)	(1.2)	(1.1)	(1.9)	(0.7)	(1.3)	
Knee replacement	48,000	10,000	13,000	8,000	14,650	6,375	10,162	8,500
Compared to India (in times)	(5.6)	(1.2)	(1.5)	(0.9)	(1.7)	(0.8)	(1.2)	
Rhinoplasty	4,500	2,500	4,375	2,083	3,200	1,700	3,500	2,000
Compared to India (in times)	(2.3)	(1.3)	(2.2)	(1.0)	(1.6)	(0.9)	(1.8)	
Tummy tuck	6,400	3,500	6,250	3,903	3,000	3,500	4,810	2,900
Compared to India (in times)	(2.2)	(1.2)	(2.2)	(1.3)	(1.03)	(1.2)	(1.7)	
Breast reduction	5,200	3,750	8,000	3,343	3,000	3,146	5,075	2,500
Compared to India (in times)	(2.1)	(1.5)	(3.2)	(1.3)	(1.2)	(1.3)	(2.0)	
Breast implants	6,000	2,600	8,000	3,308	2,500	5,243	4,350	2,200
Compared to India (in times)	(2.7)	(1.2)	(3.6)	(1.5)	(1.1)	(2.4)	(2.0)	
Crown	385	243	400	250	300	246	330	180
Compared to India (in times)	(2.1)	(1.4)	(2.2)	(1.4)	(1.7)	(1.4)	(1.8)	
Dental implants	1,188	1,429	1,500	2,636	950	953	1,600	1,100
Compared to India (in times)	(1.1)	(1.3)	(1.4)	(2.4)	(0.9)	(0.9)	(1.5)	

*Includes hospital and doctor charges

**Coronary Artery Bypass Graft

Source: 'Medical Tourism: Treatments, Markets and Health System Implications: A Scoping Review', OECD, 2011.

Internet is the single-most important technological break-through that has provided a platform to patients who are considered 'customers' of medical services to assess healthcare information from anywhere in the world and interact with various stakeholders to explore a solution to their medical problem anywhere on the earth. Such websites may be portals of healthcare providers that are focused on providing treatment information, media sites, consumer driven sites, consumer related sites of various stakeholders providing ancillary services, government sites or websites of healthcare professionals. The formats and functionalities of such sites vary considerably, which include advertisements, discussion forums, posting information and sharing experience, online virtual tours, and facilitating purchase decisions and making online bookings.

Factors affecting choice of a country for medical treatment include price advantage, quality of medical facilities, country familiarity, geographical proximity, cost of travel, etc. For instance, a large number of Indian diaspora overseas travelling back to India to get treatment, where they also have family support, also shows under international medical tourism. Patients undertake international travel to cope up with bio-ethical regulations such as abortion, gender selection, and issues related to fertility and euthanasia services.

Promoting international medical tourism

Governments across the countries, both developing and developed, as also private business sectors have engaged themselves in promoting 'medical tourism' and even forging international linkages. A number of emerging medical tourism destinations are actively promoting medical tourism. For instance, Dubai markets its Dubai Health Care City, whereas Singapore promotes its Biomedical City especially aimed at international medical tourists. In India, medical tourism is considered as 'deemed exports', therefore, extended certain fiscal incentives, including concessional import duties, allotment of prime land at subsidized rates and tax rebates.

India has emerged as a major destination for cost-effective medical services. During the late 1980s and early 1990s, most medical travellers coming to India were from Arab countries, Africa, and Southeast Asia, but today a significant number of travellers are coming from the UK, the USA, CIS countries, and Afghanistan for treatment. So far, little organized efforts have been made to market India as a healthcare destination.

India has got an edge over his competitors as it provides holistic treatment for a variety of chronic problems. About 20,000 doctors pass out every year in India and some of India's healthcare facilities are comparable to the best of the world. India provides medical treatment facilities comparable to the best in the world in cardiac surgery, orthopaedic, neurosurgery, and Lasik (eye) surgeries. The competency of Indian doctors is acknowledged worldwide. Besides, the Indian system of medicines (*Ayurveda*) is also viewed with high esteem around the world and medical travellers from around the world are keen to visit India for a holistic treatment.

Countries promoting medical tourism need to focus on upgrading skills and regular training programmes of their doctors and other paramedical staff to develop and retain their core-competence in providing world-class treatment. Besides, use of cutting-edge technology in the surgical procedures and hospitals is crucial to attract international patients especially from high income countries. Accreditations from international agencies such as the US-based Joint Commission International (JCI), Australian Council for Healthcare Standards, the Canadian Council on Health Services, and Society for International Healthcare Accreditation help in boosting patients' confidence in the selection of a hospital. Improving infrastructure, not only of the hospitals but also roads, transport, and telecommunications significantly influence international patients' decision-making in choice of a country for their medical treatment.

Questions

1. Identify the factors contributing to the emergence of international markets for medical services.

2. Identify the areas wherein India or your home country has got strategic edge in healthcare services vis-à-vis other competing destinations for medical tourism.

3. Explore the Web and carry out a cross-country analysis of the major destinations of medical tourism and identify the range of specialized services offered along with their strengths and weaknesses.

4. Prepare a step-by-step flow diagram of the selection process of medical tourism destination for overseas patients.

5. Identify various factors that influence a patient's decision for choice of a country and the hospital for medical treatment. Prioritize various factors and assign weights so as to arrive at a decision.

Entering International Markets

INTRODUCTION

Once a firm decides to expand overseas, it becomes necessary to explore and evaluate various options available to enter international markets. Entry modes are specific forms of entering a foreign country so as to have international presence and achieve the firm's strategic goals. In order to succeed in international markets, the decision to select an appropriate entry mode is a crucial and integral part of the firm's international marketing strategy.

This chapter explains the concept of entry modes for international markets. Entry modes are broadly divided under two heads: production in home country and production in foreign countries. In the initial phases of internationalization, when a firm's ability and willingness to commit resources and take risks is limited, it generally expands only in international markets having production facilities in the home country, by way of exports or providing offshore services.

Though expanding in international markets with home-based production requires low commitment to resources, involves minimal risks, and provides greater flexibility to exit from the country or switching over to another entry mode, this keeps a firm at considerable distance, both operational and marketing, and provides only a limited insight into the markets served.

To effectively respond to emerging competition in foreign markets and increase its control, the firm begins production at overseas locations. Such entry modes are broadly divided into contractual and investment modes. This chapter discusses at length various contractual entry modes such as international licensing, international franchising, overseas turnkey projects, international leasing, international management contracts, international strategic alliance, and international contract manufacturing. To gain increased control, in overseas operations, the firm invests in a foreign country, which may range from mere assembly operations or overseas joint ventures to wholly owned foreign subsidiaries.

Learning Objectives

- To explain the concept of international market entry modes
- To discuss modes of entry involving production in the home country
- To elucidate modes of entry involving production in foreign countries
- To understand various tools affecting the selection of entry mode
- To arrive at the right entry mode mix for international markets

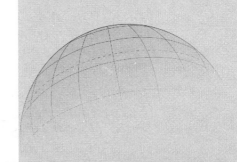

The selection of the entry mode is one of the most crucial decisions a firm takes in the process of internationalization, as it involves commitment of resources with long-term financial and structural implications. A firm needs to evaluate trade-offs in selecting entry modes based on several parameters explained in the chapter such as its ability and willingness to commit resources and take risks, expected returns, extent of control needed, and the desired flexibility. Various factors affecting selection of entry modes, both external and internal, also need to be evaluated. The firm may also make use of the model for decision-making as discussed later in the chapter for selecting international market entry modes. Finally, the firm needs to choose the right entry mode mix for international markets.

CONCEPT OF INTERNATIONAL MARKET ENTRY MODES

Mode of entry may be defined as an institutional mechanism by which a firm makes its products or services available to consumers in international markets. To successfully compete in the international market, it is extremely important for a firm to make its products and services available in an effective and competitive manner keeping in view the firm's own resources and capabilities as elaborated later in the chapter.

Stage models of internationalization like the Uppsala model[1] (1975) and subsequent research identify five stages of internationalization as follows:

- Domestic operation and marketing activities
- Infrequent exports
- Exports through independent representatives or agents
- Establishment of sales subsidiaries
- Foreign production and manufacturing

As already explained, a firm's internationalization process follows a gradual pattern. A purely domestic firm, especially a small and medium enterprise (SME), expands its operations overseas by reluctantly fulfilling unsolicited export orders it gets through friends, acquaintances, or other business firms. Consequent to successfully fulfilling such unsolicited export orders, positive stimuli, such as higher profitability, incremental revenue, or achievement of strategic goals makes the firm to further pursue its export plans. This transforms a purely domestic firm into a regular exporter. In order to consolidate its gains in the market, it further shifts its production facilities overseas employing various types of contractual entry modes and strategic alliances. Once the market potential and viability is assured, the firms invest overseas to gain complete ownership and control.

Thus, by way of operating in a country over a period, a firm's uncertainty is gradually abridged and it becomes willing to commit more resources for extension of existing activities. For example, as a part of international market entry strategy, Heineken initially accesses a foreign market by way of exports. If Heineken finds a considerable market potential, it uses the contractual entry mode by way of licensing to some local brewery in the identified target country. This provides flexibility to Heineken to exit the country if it is not found lucrative enough to operate. Operating into a foreign country through exports and later by licensing provides the firm enough insights into the country's marketing opportunities and its operational environment. Heineken eventually acquires its own licensee or some other brewer using investment entry mode to have a long-term strategic market commitment.

---

[1] Johanson, J. and P. Wiedersheim-Paul, 'The Internationalisation of the Firm: Four Swedish Cases', *Journal of Management Studies*, 12(3), 1975, pp. 305–322.

A market entry strategy for international markets may be defined as a comprehensive plan that sets forth the objectives, goals, resources, and policies that guide a company's international business operations over a future period long enough to achieve sustainable growth in world markets.[2]

MODES OF ENTRY IN INTERNATIONAL MARKETS

Various modes of international market entry, summarized in Fig. 9.1, may be broadly classified as production facility in its home country or locating it in a foreign country.

In order to facilitate international managers to develop a thorough understanding of the concept, each of the entry modes is elaborated in detail with suitable illustrations in the following sections of the chapter.

Production in Home Country

Selling goods and services produced in the home country to overseas customers is the most common form of entering international markets in the initial phases of a firm's internationalization. Production in the home country requires relatively lower risk and offers flexibility to

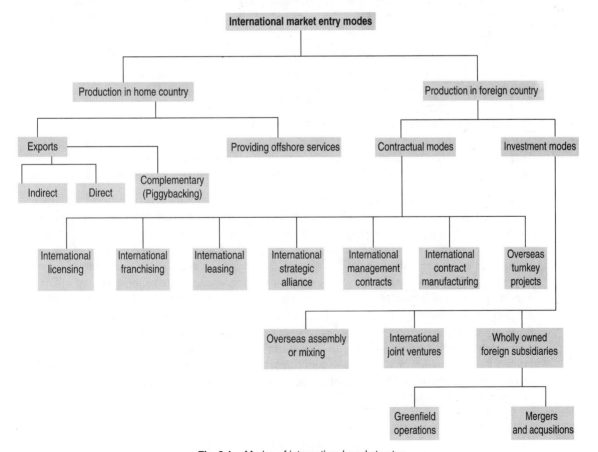

Fig. 9.1   Modes of international market entry

---

[2] Root, Franklin R., *Entry Strategies for International Markets*, Lexington, New York, 1994, p. 4–16.

exit the country or switching over to another entry mode. Moreover, it offers opportunity only to domestic firms to enter international markets with low resource commitment. Such entry modes are highly suitable for simultaneous expansion in geographically diverse countries. As entry modes involving production in home country do employ some form of trade with foreign countries, these are also termed as 'trade-related' modes.

A firm has to substantially rely upon external agencies for its international expansion under such entry modes. Moreover, when production is based in home countries, considerable distance, both operational and marketing, is maintained between the internationalizing firm and the target country market. Major forms of such entry modes, namely exports, piggybacking or complementary exports, and providing off-shore services, are discussed next.

Exports

The term 'export' is derived from the conceptual meaning of shipping goods and services out of the port of a country. The seller of such goods and services is referred to as an 'exporter' who is based in the country of export, whereas the overseas based buyer is referred to as an 'importer'. 'Exports' may be defined as manufacturing the goods in the home country or a third country and shipping them for sales to a country other than the country of production.[3] Export is the most common initial mode of entry into foreign markets as it involves much lower risks and is a low cost and simple mode of entry. Besides, exports are also used as strategic options to dispose of surplus production in overseas markets.

In the export development process, the following distinct stages[4] may be identified:

Stage I: Firm is not interested in exporting; ignores unsolicited business.
Stage II: Firm supplies unsolicited business; does not examine the feasibility of active exporting.
Stage III: Firm actively examines the feasibility of exporting.
Stage IV: Firm exports on experimental basis to a country of close business distance.
Stage V: Firm becomes an experienced exporter to that country.
Stage VI: Firm explores feasibility of exporting to countries with greater business distance.

Research indicates that a firm's progress from one stage to another depends on its international orientation, its perception of attractiveness of exports, and the management's confidence in its ability to successfully compete overseas. This framework indicates that unsolicited export orders are critical to a firm to become an experimental exporter. The quality and dynamics of the management also influence the movement between the stages. At Stage V, the proportion of output to be sold in the overseas markets will depend on the firm's perception of the expected effect the export operation will have on profit and growth. However, such models of export development are criticized on the grounds that they lack explanatory power and movement from one stage to the next cannot be clearly predicted.[5] But such models provide an intuitive appreciation of the decision mechanism in the process of internationalization. Many a time, internal behavioural influences within a firm may be more significant than direct stimuli such as unsolicited orders and economic incentives. Management's predisposition to export is also an important determinant of a firm's response to export stimuli.

---

[3] Joshi, Rakesh Mohan, *International Business*, Oxford University Press, New Delhi, 2009, p. 444.

[4] Bilkey, W.J. and G. Tesar, 'The Export Behaviour of Small Wisconsin Manufacturing Firms', *Journal of International Business Studies*, vol. 8, no. 2, 1977, pp. 93–98.

[5] Andersen, O., 'On the Internationalization Process of Firms: A Critical Analysis', *Journal of International Business Studies*, vol. 24, no. 2, 1993, pp. 209–231.

Exhibit 9.1 Japanese trading houses

In Japan, the top *Soga Shoshas* control about 60 per cent of the country's exports. *Soga Shosha* in Japanese means a general or an integrated company. A *Soga Shosha* handles an exceptionally wide range of products and services, which virtually encompasses all sectors of business and can assume a variety of functions. Therefore, it is defined as a general or an integrated company.

In the 1850s, Westerners handled about 95 per cent of Japan's international trade. In an attempt to control their own economic future, the Japanese created national companies to ensure that industry obtained the raw materials and equipment it needed from overseas markets as well as the distribution network for its finished products in national and international markets. The major trading houses,

which are still active, such as Mitsui (1876), Mitsubishi (1889), and Nichimen (1892), came up subsequently. These companies soon became successful. By 1920, they controlled 70 per cent of Japanese exports and 90 per cent of imports. The major Japanese *Soga Shoshas* include Mitsui, Mitsubishi, Itoh, Marubeni, Sumitomo, Nissho Iwai, Toyo Menka, Kanematsu, and Nichimen.

Besides, there are approximately 8,000 *Semen Shoshas* in Japan, which are smaller than general trading houses and deal in highly specialized products such as textiles and raw materials. The *Semen Shoshas* are also involved in export and domestic distribution and their strategic strength lies in their ability to trade standardized products such as commodities and raw materials.

Source: *Trading Houses, What are They?* Ontario Association of Trading Houses (OATH), http://www.oath.on.ca/publications/PDF_En/EN_TradingHousesWhat.pdf, accessed on 24 October 2013.

Small firms with limited financial and other resources find exports the most suitable international market entry mode. Even the larger firms use exports as an entry mode suitable under the following situations:

- Primarily assessing potential for new markets
- Countries with relatively smaller market potential or infrequent demand patterns

Though exports require minimum foreign market operational experience, it generates the lowest levels of profit. In countries with high market complexities of operating business, such as political, economic, or other uncertainties, it is not advisable to commit substantial resources. Thereby, exports become strategically the most suitable option for expanding business in such countries.

Indirect export   Indirect export can be defined as the process of selling products to an export intermediary in the company's home country, who would in turn sell the products in overseas markets. When a firm does not have much exposure to foreign markets, and has limited resources to invest in export development, indirect exporting is the recommended strategy for entering international markets. Indirect exports may occur using either of the following ways:

- Selling to a foreign firm or a buying agent in the home country
- Exports through a market intermediary such as exports house or trading house

International market intermediaries involved in trading operations are known by different names in different countries such as *Soga Shosha* and *Semen Shosha* in Japan (Exhibit 9.1), *Comercializadoras* in Latin America, *Operateur Specialise en Commerce Exterieur* in France, export management company and export trading company in the USA, export houses in India, and trading houses in Canada, Hong Kong, and India.

As indirect exports offer a simple and low-cost entry mode to foreign countries, they enable companies to test international markets before plunging into a more proactive market entry mode. As the firm is not required to deal directly in the overseas markets, indirect exports offer the following advantages over other entry modes:

- Since the firm has to deal with a market intermediary in the domestic market, it needs little investment and marketing experience.
- Indirect exports provide low-cost opportunity to test products in the international markets.

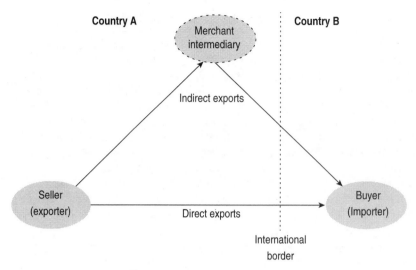

Fig. 9.2   Indirect vs direct exports

However, indirect exports have certain limitations as well, as follows:

- As the firm has to heavily depend upon domestic market intermediary, its feedback from the ultimate customers is limited.
- The firm has to part with relatively higher share of its profit margins by way of commissions and other payments.
- The firm gets little insight into the markets served even after operating for several years.
- The firm does not develop its own contacts with the buyers in the overseas market.

Direct exports   In direct exports, a firm's products are sold directly in foreign markets to importers without employing any market intermediary in the home country (Fig. 9.2). Direct export does not mean selling products directly to the end-users. Direct exports are accomplished through foreign-based independent market intermediaries such as agents or distributors. Direct exporting is far more complex than indirect exporting as a firm has to carry out its own market research, select markets, identify buyers, establish contacts, handle documentation and transportation, and decide on the marketing mix for different overseas markets.

Agents generally work on a commission basis, do not take title to the goods, and assume no risks or responsibilities. An agent represents the exporting company in the given market and finds wholesalers and retailers for its products. Agents may be exclusive, semi-exclusive, or non-exclusive. An exclusive agent has exclusive rights to sell the company's products in the specified sales territories; a semi-exclusive agent handles exporters' goods along with other companies' non-competing goods; and a non-exclusive agent handles a wide variety of goods including competing products. In case of an overseas agent, cargo is directly shipped to the importer and terms of credit, shipment, finance, and promotion are decided between the exporter and the importer. However, overseas agents do provide market intelligence and information on the financial position of importers. The range of commission paid to overseas agents varies widely depending upon market characteristics and services provided.

An overseas distributor is a foreign-based merchant who buys the products on his own account and resells them to wholesalers and retailers to make profit. Distributors are generally the sole importers of the firm's product in the market. Thus, the exporting firm has to deal with one distributor in a country market.

Unlike indirect exports, direct exports need more experience and resources on the part of the internationalizing company, but they offer the following benefits over indirect exports:

- As no intermediary is involved, the exporter gets more profit.
- The firm operating directly collects marketing intelligence about the pricing of competing or substitute products in the markets and therefore eliminates the possibility of receiving lower prices from the merchant exporter.
- Over a period of time, the firm involved directly in exports develops in-house skills for export operations.
- As the company directly comes in contact with the overseas importers, it establishes its own rapport/brand image in the foreign market.
- The exporting firm gains knowledge about markets, competitors, and competing products.

The disadvantages of direct exporting include higher commitment of resources as considerable investment is needed for marketing, logistics, and administrative costs, and higher risk exposure. Therefore, transition from indirect to direct exporting has to be well-planned and gradual depending upon the availability of resources of internationalizing firm.

Complementary exporting (piggybacking)

In case of complementary or piggybacking exports, overseas distribution channels of another firm are used by the internationalizing firm to make its product available in the overseas market. Thus, piggyback exporting provides immediate access to the well-developed distribution channels of another company. In piggybacking arrangements, the exporting company, known as 'rider', with inadequate experience of operating marketing channels overseas, makes use of a foreign company, which has well-established distribution network in the foreign market, known as 'carrier'. The 'carrier' either acts as an agent for a commission or as an independent distributor by buying the products on outright basis. Normally, the piggybacking arrangement is made for products from unrelated companies that are complementary (allied) but non-competitive.

In piggybacking exports, the branding and market promotion arrangements may differ. The 'carrier' may buy the products outright and sell them under its own brand name. However, as a matter of common practice, the 'rider' retains its brand name and the market promotion activity is carried out with mutual consent. There is an increasing trend in international markets of piggybacking taking various forms of strategic alliance.

Piggybacking arrangements allow a 'rider' to access overseas markets without establishing its own distribution channels. Besides, it also gives the 'rider' a chance to learn and understand the entire process, which later on assist it in setting up its own distribution channels. On the other hand, piggybacking facilitates to fill up gaps in the product line of the 'carrier' by way of offering a wider product range. It also benefits the 'carrier' by way of designing more attractive sales packages and increasing economies of scale by getting more revenue without any additional investment in its distribution channel.

Foreign companies accustomed to operating through large supermarkets/department stores in developed countries find it operationally unfamiliar and difficult to develop distribution channels in developing countries. For instance, an Indian confectionery firm Parry's distribution network was used in a piggybacking arrangement by Wrigley's—a US-based chewing gum company—to enter the Indian market. It provided immediate access to over 2,50,000 retail outlets. It is to be observed that Parry's has a complementary product mix of hard-boiled sugar confectionery. Therefore, the marketing of chewing gum had a complementary effect on its marketing channels. Tanishq sells its jewellery in India exclusively through company-controlled retail outlets, whereas it has tied up with High glow, a jewellery retail chain in the USA, to utilize the latter's distribution channels. In spite of considerable efforts to make a dent in the Indian market even after investing ₹20 million in Indian operations, Fiat decided to use the extensive nationwide network of Tata Motors to market and service its passenger cars.

The limitations of a piggybacking arrangement for the 'carrier' include its concern about the quality and warranty of the product and continuity of supply from the 'rider'. For the 'rider', piggybacking arrangements in overseas market means handing over control of its sales and distribution activities to the 'carrier', which may not be compatible with the firm's long-term marketing goals. Besides, the carrier's commitment to selling the rider's goods is also a matter of concern to the 'rider'.

Providing offshore services

A company being based in its home country can provide offshore services to overseas clients with the help of information and telecommunication technology. The business process out-sourcing (BPO) includes such activities as maintenance of accounts, audit sales, telemarketing, managing human resource databases, logistics, and handling customer complaints. Developing countries including India enjoy a distinct cost advantage in providing offshore services. Besides, the slowdown of the global economy has forced transnational corporations to seek innovative ways to slash costs. The cost benefits of shifting a routine work from USA to India may result in savings of up to 30–40 per cent, as a skilled worker in India earns around US$6–8 a day as opposed to US$12 in the USA.

The basic reasons for the growing interest in global outsourcing[6] are as follows:

- *Industry drivers*
  - New forms of emerging global competition
  - Obsolete contracting approaches
  - Changing success criteria
  - Innovation becoming a differentiator
- *IT drivers*
  - Competitive pressure to improve service levels
  - Enhanced IT effectiveness
  - Supplementary IT resources
  - Shortened implementation time
- *Business drivers*
  - Focus on core competencies
  - Alignment of IT strategy with business goals
  - Improvement in overall competitiveness
  - Cost savings

The business sectors that provide opportunities for offshore services include the following:

- *Insurance*: Claim processing, call centres
- *Banking and finance*: Loan processing, call centres
- *Airlines*: Revenue accounting, call centres
- *Telecom*: Billing, customer relations, call centres
- *Automotive*: Engineering and design, accounts
- *Other sectors*: Transportation, direct manufacturing, manufacturing, utilities, etc.

It opens tremendous opportunities for developing countries and great potential for India to become the back office of the world.

---

[6] Marriott, Ian, 'The Changing Shape of Outsourcing', *Gartner Research*, June 2003, p. 13.

Production in a Foreign Country

Despite ease of market entry, low level of commitment, and need for little international experience, exporting continues to keep a firm distanced from overseas consumers. Besides, the exporting firms often receive below average profits. As a market entry strategy, exporting is highly production-oriented rather than market-oriented with little adaptation of marketing strategy as per the diverse needs of the markets served. A firm shifts its manufacturing operations in foreign countries to

- effectively respond to market competition;
- take advantage of host country incentives;
- gain access to host country resources to be used as inputs;
- shift manufacturing operations overseas to a relatively cost effective location;
- have manufacturing base in market proximity;
- circumvent host country regulations such as trade restrictions and prohibitive import duties; and/or
- minimize logistics cost, which offers considerable cost disadvantage especially for geographically distant countries or low unit value products.

For instance, import duty on cigarettes in China is exorbitantly high. Besides, local governments also favour licensing as compared to other market entry modes. Therefore, a number of international tobacco companies have entered the Chinese market using international licensing.

Exporting is generally more suitable when the home currency is weak. As the currency of the home country strengthens, it makes sense to relocate production facilities in more cost-effective locations with weak currencies besides production efficiency. It also explains why Japanese companies have shifted their manufacturing facilities to other countries with weaker currencies rather than manufacturing and exporting from their Japanese home base. As the home currency strengthens, it makes sense for a number of home-based companies to enter into international joint ventures and offshore acquisitions.

Production facilities are generally shifted to foreign markets through contractual alliances or foreign direct investment (FDI) as discussed next.

Contractual entry modes

Firms having high-tech manufacturing facilities but no access to foreign markets may use a foreign partner that is well established and has got a strong distribution and marketing network in the foreign market. They may enter international markets using the synergistic effect of the partner firm and make use of its resources. Such contractual arrangements are often complementary in nature and have mutually beneficial effect on a firm's overseas operations as it provides access to new technology and markets.

In case of contractual modes of entry and strategic alliances such as licensing, franchising, contract manufacturing, management contract, and joint venture, a firm is required to select an overseas partner for cooperation. The following factors should be kept in mind while selecting an alliance partner:

- The alliance partner should have some strength that can be translated into business values for the alliance.
- The alliance partners should be committed to cooperative goals.
- The alliance between the two firms should be based on mutual trust.
- It is preferable that the alliance partner should have multi-cultural working environment.

Contractual modes are often preferred over other modes of international market entry under the following circumstances:

- Reluctance to invest considerable resources in a target country
- High level of perceived or actual risks due to unstable political and economic environment
- Differences in marketing environment where a local partner adds considerable value to a firm's operations
- High tariff on imported goods
- Sociocultural differences
- Policy restrictions that prohibits use of other market entry modes such as investment

Major forms of contractual entry modes such as international licensing international franchising, international leasing, international strategic alliances, international management contracts, international contract manufacturing, and turnkey projects are discussed next.

International licensing   A company that possesses technical know-how, design, a competitive manufacturing process, and marketing expertise may enter into international markets by way of international licensing with minimum involvement of financial resources. In this mode of entry, the domestic company allows the foreign company to use its intellectual property, such as patents, trademarks, copyright, process technology, design, or specific business skills. The overseas recipient firm pays compensation to the domestic firm in lieu of use of the latter's intellectual property which is termed as royalty. The royalty in international licensing agreements may vary between one-eighth of 1 per cent and 15 per cent. The firm transferring the intellectual property is termed as the 'licenser', while the recipient firm is known as the 'licensee'.

As a part of international licensing agreements, a licensee usually performs the following functions:

- Production of the licenser's products covered by rights
- Marketing these products in the assigned territory
- Paying royalty to the licenser for using the intellectual property

However, Lowe and Crawford (Fig. 9.3) indicate that licensing in technology improves the net cash flow position of the licensee but lowers profits in the long term. The immediate benefits of licensing include quick access to new technology, lower developmental costs, and relatively early positive cash flows.

The major benefits of using international licensing for market entry are as follows:

- It facilitates rapid penetration in international markets for technology intensive products and processes.
- It provides access to markets with high levels of tariff and non-tariff barriers.
- It reduces political and economic risk associated with international markets and therefore provides opportunities to venture into more sensitive markets.
- It helps the international licenser to rapidly expand into international markets and amortize the expenditure incurred on research and development.
- In the case of developing and least developed countries wherein forged products are in high circulation in the market, licensing helps in curtailing the duplicate products' market.
- Since only intangibles are exported in case of international licensing, the exit cost from the market is very low.

Firms with superior technological competence but limited financial resources can rapidly enter into international markets through international licensing and in the process earn extra profits with little additional investment. Since developed countries enjoy a competitive advantage in proprietary technology and own a majority of the most powerful global brands, they are the

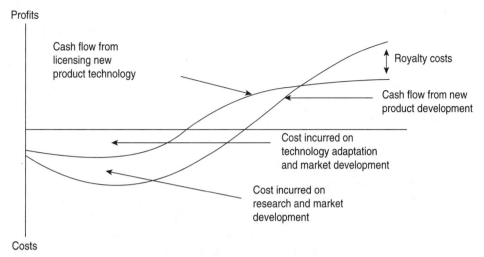

Fig. 9.3 Life cycle of benefits of licensing

Source: Lowe, J. and N. Crawford, 'Technology Licensing and the Small Firm', in Frank Bradley, *International Marketing Strategy*, Fourth Edition, Pearson Education Limited, 2002. First Published by Harlow and Prentice Hall.

major beneficiaries of international licensing arrangements. However, as a result of highly skilled and talented manpower, international licensing offers opportunities for firms from developing countries including India.

However, like all other contractual modes of entry, the international licenser also has to part with his profit. Besides, the following limitations are also associated with international licensing:

- The product quality and its consistency are mainly left to the overseas licensee. Lack of commitment on the part of the licensee may adversely affect the brand image of the international licenser.
- Since the licensee is given exclusive rights to manufacture and market the products in the assigned territory, it may restrict the licenser's own marketing activities in those countries.
- By way of making process technology and other skills available to the overseas licensee, the firm may unknowingly create a potential competitor in the market.

Types of licensing arrangements Licensing may involve either process or trademark licensing agreement, as discussed here.

Process licensing The licensee gets the right to manufacture, produce, and market the product in the defined market area.

Trademark licensing The licensee also gets the rights to use trademarks/tradenames, besides using the process know-how. Trademark licensing is used as an effective strategy to control counterfeit products in the market. However, over-licensing may damage the firm's interest in the long run. For instance, the brand equity of Pierre Cardin was affected adversely consequent to its licensing about 800 brands.

The licensee makes a payment of royalties to the licensor in exchange for intellectual property by any one or a combination of following methods:

- A lump-sum payment made in the beginning after initial transfer of intangible assets, such as know-how, drawings and designs, blueprint, spare parts, and machinery, not related to the output of production processes

- A minimum annual royalty guaranteed to the licensor
- Continued royalty computed as a percentage of sales revenue or amount per unit of output

While expanding to countries with unstable marketing environment by way of high political and economic risks, higher initial payment and shorter duration of agreement is preferred. International licensors need to adopt a competitive strategy to gain market share in relatively low-risk countries with sizeable markets. Licensing arrangements from CIS countries do involve other forms of payments, such as technical and management fee and conversion of royalties into equity.

International licensing facilitates foreign-based firms to access established products, processes, and brand names with little investment in in-house R&D. It also enables them to access the know-how and technology that is otherwise not available due to government restrictions on inward foreign investment. The US firm Qualcomm owns the bulk of the intellectual property behind the code division multiple access (CDMA) standards and thus earns substantial profits from royalty when companies like Nokia make CDMA products.

The Indian pharmaceutical company Dr Reddy's licenses its anti-diabetic molecules DRF 2593 (Balaglitazone) and DRF 2725 (Ragaglitazar) to Novo Nordisk, a Danish firm that is the world leader in diabetes care. Asian Paints adopted technology and brand licensing for its international expansion.

The limitations of international licensing include problems related to maintaining product quality by the licensee, leading to sullying the brand image of the licensor. Licensing may also restrict the licensor's future activities in the country. Besides transferring know-how and technology outside the firm may nurture a future competitor, thus having an adverse impact on the firm's long-term interests.

Cross-licensing It is a form of licensing involving mutual exchange of intangible assets that may not involve a cash payment. In cross-licensing, companies swap their intellectual property for mutual benefit. Thus, cross-licensing is the mutual sharing of patents between two companies without exchange of licensing fee. It is used extensively by software companies to pile up more licenses.

International franchising The term 'franchising' is derived from the French word *francorum rex*, which means 'freedom from servitude'. In the service sector, where the transfer of intellectual property and other assistance is required for an extended period, international franchising is used as a preferred mode of entry. In international franchising, the home company, known as the franchiser, provides an overseas company (the franchisee) intellectual property and other assistance over an extended period of time. Under the franchising agreement, the franchisee acquires the right to market the producer's products and services in a prescribed fashion using the franchiser's brand name, processing and production methods, and marketing guidelines.

Franchising is also a form of licensing wherein transfer of intellectual property rights takes place. But the two processes are different from each other in a number of ways, which have been summarized in Exhibit 9.2.

International franchising is also a low-cost, low-risk mode of entry, which provides a firm the opportunity to rapidly penetrate overseas where it has little market knowledge and strength. Besides, transfer of business know-how is an ongoing process. A company exerts higher control on the franchisee operations, which ensure uniform quality and service standards across markets. The internationalizing firm exerts much higher control over its franchisee so as to ensure quality standards across countries. Besides, transfer of business know-how is also an ongoing

Exhibit 9.2   Licensing vs franchising

Licensing	Franchising
The term 'royalty' is normally used.	'Management fees' is regarded as the appropriate term.
Products are the major source of concern.	Covers all the aspects of business including know-how, intellectual property rights, goodwill, trademarks, and business contacts. (Franchising is all-encompassing whereas licensing concerns just one part of the business.)
Licenses are usually taken by well-established businesses.	Tends to be a start-up situation, certainly as regards the franchisee.
Terms of 16–20 years are common, particularly when they are related to technical know-how, copyright, and trademarks. The terms are similar for patents.	The franchise agreement is normally for 5 years, sometimes extending to 10 years. Franchises are frequently renewable.
Licensees tend to be self-selecting. They are often established businesses and can demonstrate that they are in a strong position to operate the license in question. A licensee can often pass its license to an associate or sometimes unconnected company with little or no reference back to the original licenser.	The franchisee selected by the franchiser, and its eventual replacement is controlled by the franchiser.
Usually concerns specific existing products with very little benefit from ongoing research being passed on by the licenser to its licensee.	The franchiser is expected to pass on to its franchisees the benefits of its ongoing research programme as part of the agreement.
There is no goodwill attached to the license as it is totally retained by the licenser.	Although the franchiser does retain the main goodwill, the franchisee picks up an element of localized goodwill.
The licensee enjoys a substantial measure of free negotiation. As bargaining tools, they can use their trade muscle and their established position in the marketplace.	There is a standard fee structure and any variation within an individual franchise system would cause confusion and mayhem.

Source: Perkins, J.S., 'How Licensing and Franchising Differ', *Les Nouvelles*, vol. 22, no. 4, 1987, pp. 155–158.

process. Franchising is widely used in international business expansion of fast food chains and the hotel industry.

Some of the major franchisers include McDonald's, Carrefour (hypermarket), Pizza Hut (burgers, pizzas), KFC (chicken), Benetton, etc. International franchising is the preferred mode of entry of Benetton, one of the leading marketers of garments in the world. Under international franchising guidelines, the franchisers need to achieve the minimum sales target, follow the marketing guidelines, and must adhere to a standard shop layout. However, the franchisers are not required to pay any franchising fees. Coca-Cola controls its trademark, recipe, and advertising single-handedly, while its independent bottlers around the world prepare the soft drink from the concentrate supplied to them under strict specifications. Coca-Cola has franchised about 400 million vending machines in India for marketing its hot beverage brand, Georgia.

OSIM International Limited, the Singapore-based manufacturer of lifestyle products primarily expands internationally through franchising. OSIM has entered into a master franchisee agreement (MFA) with an Indian manufacturer of surgical products, Paramount Surgimed Limited, to import and trade OSIM products in India and Nepal.

However, franchising also has its own limitations for the internationalizing firm:

- Restrictive host country regulations
- Problems in identifying and selecting right franchisees

- Franchisor gets 'franchising fee' rather than sharing the profits
- Lack of direct control over franchisee operations
- Adverse effect on the brand equity if quality is lowered by the franchisee
- Uncertainties and conflicts in receiving franchising fee
- Franchisor not gaining market knowledge even after firm's overseas presence for a considerable time

Sometimes, due to limitations in controlling the performance of the franchisee's operations in terms of consistency in maintaining desired product and service quality, international franchisers take more control of the franchising operations and enter into equity participation. Due to cultural differences, marketing distance, and higher political and economic risk, Blockbuster Video entered into the Latin American market through an international franchising arrangement. However, dissatisfaction over the performance of its franchisees in 1995, led Blockbuster Video to set up joint ventures in Mexico and Brazil.

In many developing and least developed countries, the concept of franchising hardly exists and the international marketers find it difficult to identify and select franchising partners. However, the international franchisers sometimes find it difficult to coordinate and control a large number of franchises.

International leasing   In low-income countries, manufacturers often do not possess enough financial resources or necessary foreign currency to pay for equipment and machinery. A firm can expand its business by leasing out new and used equipment to a manufacturing firm in such countries. The ownership of the property retains with the leasing firm (i.e., lessor) throughout the lease period during which the foreign-based user (i.e., lessee) pays leasing fee. Leasing provides international marketing opportunities by rapid market access using idle and obsolete equipment in an efficient manner. It also benefits low-income country-based manufacturers to reduce cost of getting machinery and equipment from overseas and reduces investment and operational risks.

International Lease Finance Corporation (ILFC), headquartered in Los Angles, is the largest aircraft lessor by value that had an inventory of about 1,000 aircraft by 2012. It leases Airbus and Boeing aircraft to airlines worldwide, such as Emirates, Lufthansa, Air France, KLM, American Airlines, Continental, Vietnam Airlines, etc.

International strategic alliances   A firm has to be globally cooperative, to be globally competitive. International strategic alliances refer to the relationship between two or more firms that cooperate with each other to achieve common strategic goals but do not form a separate company (Fig. 9.4). Such strategic alliances are long-term formal relationships for mutual benefit. Rapid growth in global strategic alliance among large and small firms around the world highlights its growing significance. Due to increased competitive pressures, most firms prefer to focus on their core competencies rather than spreading themselves too thin. Therefore, the scope for international strategic alliances is on the rise.

The benefits of international strategic alliances are as follows:

- They encourage cooperation with competitors to make use of their specific strengths.
- The cost of investment for international market entry is shared.
- They give access to the distribution channels of the partner firm.
- Since a strategic alliance is a shared venture, it reduces the individual risk of the firm while operating in international markets.

The Star Alliance launched on 14 May 1997, a strategic alliance in the airlines industry, is the largest in the world that runs about 18,100 daily flights to 975 airports in 162 countries, having

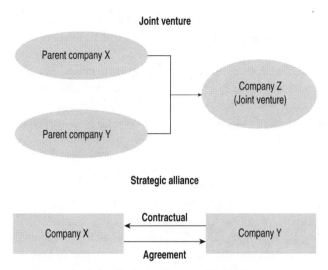

Fig. 9.4 Strategic alliance vs joint venture

a total fleet of 3,360 aircraft carrying about 510 million passengers annually. It includes major airlines, such as Air Canada, USA Airways, United Airlines, All Nippon Airways, Lufthansa, Air New Zealand, Asiana Airline, Austrian, BMI, South African Airways, Swiss International, Thai Airways, Singapore Airline, and Scandinavian Airlines.

Shilla Hotels and Resorts of Korea forged a marketing alliance with India's Taj hotels to develop cross-promotional opportunities for both companies to harness each other's strengths in their respective markets of dominance. Tata Motors has launched its range of Indica cars in the UK under the brand name City Rover using the marketing channels of the MG Rover Group. The company has also forged a strategic alliance with Honda Motor Co. Ltd, Japan, to manufacture its 'Accord' model of car in India. Similarly, in order to develop the medicine market in Poland, Ranbaxy has forged a strategic alliance for marketing its products with Glaxo Smithkline and Schnarz Pharma. Nestlé has also entered into a strategic alliance with Coca-Cola to market its ready-to-drink coffee and tea under the brand names Nescafé and Nestea.

However, the major limitations of international strategic alliances include difference of opinion and conflicts with an alliance partner and giving access to the company's resources and information to alliance partners, which are capable of becoming future competitors.

International management contracts In international management contracts, a company provides its technical and managerial expertise for a specific duration to an overseas firm. Management contracts are used in a variety of business activities, such as managing hotels, catering services, and operation of power plants. A management contract is a feasible option when a company provides superior technical and managerial skills to an overseas company that needs such assistance to remain competitive in the market or to improve its productivity or performance.

Entering into international markets by way of management contracts is a low-risk low-cost mode of entry. Besides earning foreign exchange and optimally utilizing its skilled manpower, the professional manpower of the company also gets international exposure. International management contracts also give overseas companies a chance to upgrade the professional skill levels of their manpower. There is little transfer of physical assets to the overseas country but since skilled manpower is deputed overseas, there is a certain degree of risk.

There is a good market for management contracts in African and Latin American countries, which are at a lower stage of development as compared to India. For instance, Indian companies have a large reservoir of skilled manpower and a great potential to undertake international management contracts by way of transferring the technical expertise of its professional manpower to other countries.

The Indian Oil Corporation received a contract to manage aviation stations in Bhutan and the Maldives. Engineers India Ltd (EIL) got a project management contract for providing project consultancy[7] for the revamp and upgradation of the Skikda Refinery in Algeria in February 2005 and for upgradation of tank farm area in Abu Dhabi in August 2005.

Management contracts are common in the hotel industry, especially in Asia so as to take advantage of economies of scale, brand equity, and global reservation system. International expansion strategy of Global Hyatt Corporation is primarily based on managing over 216 hotels across 44 countries through management contracts. In order to prevent dilution of quality and hence brand erosion, it ensures that all the properties under its management contract follow and maintain rules, regulations, benchmark practices, and standards as per its corporate policy. Similarly, India's Taj hotels have also employed management contracts for international entry securing management contracts at Palm Island, Jumeirah in Dubai, Langkawi in Malaysia, and Thimpu in Bhutan.

International contract manufacturing Under contract manufacturing the manufacturing operations of an international firm are carried out at offshore locations on a contractual basis. A number of global companies outsource their manufacturing activities to low-cost locations. International sub-contracting arrangements may involve supply of inputs, such as raw materials, semi-finished goods, components and technical know-how to a local manufacturer in a foreign country. A processing fee is paid to a foreign-based manufacturer who is primarily responsible for processing or assembly. Overseas-based contract manufacturers are often expected to supply the goods directly to the firm's clients and invoice for processing fee to the internationalizing firm, as elucidated in Fig. 9.5. The firm in turn directly raises invoice for finished goods to its customer. The international firm takes care of marketing in international markets, whereas the contracted manufacturer limits itself to production activities.

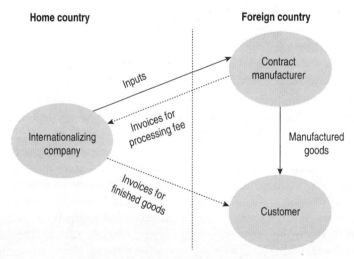

Fig. 9.5 International contract manufacturing

Source: Joshi, Rakesh Mohan, *International Business*, Oxford University Press, New Delhi, 2009, p. 459.

---

[7] 'EIL Secures PMC Contract from Algeria', *The Hindu Business*, 25 February 2005.

The major advantages of contract manufacturing are as follows:

- A firm with a competitive edge in international marketing may concentrate its resources on marketing including quality assurance, managing channels of distribution, and market promotion and communication.
- The international marketer need not invest its resources in manufacturing.
- The manufacturing operations can be done at competitive cost-effective locations.
- Since the exit cost of contract manufacturing is very low, it provides the international firm with an opportunity to change contracted manufacturers to improve quality and cost competitiveness.

Contract manufacturing has also been used as a strategic tool for economic development in a number of countries, such as Korea, Mexico, Thailand, and China. For instance, Taiwan is a world leader in semi-conductor manufacturing. China produces 30 per cent of air conditioners, 24 per cent of washing machines, and 16 per cent of refrigerators sold in the USA.

Nike, the leading international shoe brand, does not own a single production facility and gets its manufacturing done through contract manufacturing throughout the world. It provides raw materials and manufacturing know-how to contract manufacturers for manufacturing shoes in Asian countries, such as China, Vietnam, Indonesia, Thailand, and Bangladesh for payment of processing fees. However, Nike maintains its proprietary rights over materials and products, and exerts stringent control over production processes and product quality.

Indian pharmaceutical companies find contract manufacturing an effective tool for maintaining a high growth rate in view of limited resources for research and development. Ranbaxy and Lupin Laboratories were among the first Indian companies to get manufacturing contracts from multinational companies, Eli Lilly and Cynamid. When Ranbaxy developed an alternative process for manufacturing Eli Lilly's patented drug Cefaclor, the American company became concerned that the low-cost drug manufactured by the Indian company would take away its market share in countries which do not recognize product patents. Subsequently, Wockhardt India, Cadila Health Care, Sun Pharma, and Dr Reddy's Laboratories Ltd have also entered into contract manufacturing with several overseas firms.

Globalization of technology and increasing pressure on international firms to be globally competitive in their costs, product offerings, speed in bringing new products into the market, quality, and customer service have been the primary driving forces of international contract manufacturing. A number of global companies outsource their manufacturing activities to low-cost locations. A substantial part of manufactured exports comes from such activities.

Contract manufacturing provides an excellent opportunity to firms located in developing countries, including India, to take advantage of their strategic strength of low labour cost and ample availability of skilled and semi-skilled human resources to make their product available in international markets. This opens up new avenues, especially for firms with strong production bases but limited resources and skills to market the products internationally.

Overseas turnkey projects Conceptually 'turnkey' means handing over a project to the client, when it is complete in all respect and is 'ready to use' on 'turning the key'. In case of international turnkey projects, a firm conceptualizes, designs, installs, constructs, and carries out preliminary testing of a production facility or engineering structure for the overseas client organization. It often includes providing training to the client's personnel to operate the plant. Companies with core competencies in setting up engineering infrastructure, plants or manufacturing facilities such as dams and bridges can utilize their technical expertise to enter international markets.

Contracts for large-scale turnkey projects are generally awarded on the basis of competitive international bidding. A firm has to take great care while preparing the bid and follow various guidelines while formulating the price quotation. Generally, pre-screening is done by the importer to shortlist the number of bidding companies on the basis of their resources, market image, and relevant experience in executing similar projects. In developing countries, large projects are often funded by international financial institutions such as Asian Development Bank and World Bank. Therefore, firms need to keep track of various funding options available for the project. The contract for turnkey projects is a complex legal document and unique for every case.

The major variants of turnkey projects include the following:

Build and transfer (BT) The firm conceptualizes, designs, builds, carries out primary testing, and transfers the project to the owner. Important issues negotiated with the overseas firm include design specifications, price, make and source of equipment, man specifications, performance schedules, payment terms, and buyer's support system.

Build, operate, and transfer (BOT) The exporting firm not only builds the project but also manages it for a contracted period before transferring it to the foreign owner. During the operational period, the functional viability of the project is established and the technical and managerial staff of the buyer may be trained during this period. However, the exporting company needs additional resources and competence to run this type of a project.

Build, operate, and own (BOO) The exporting firm is expected to buy the project once it has been built, which results in FDI after a certain time period. For executing projects on a BOO basis, the exporting company has to be highly integrated, providing exports and management services besides having experience in owning and controlling infrastructure projects.

Entering into international markets by way of turnkey projects allows firms to take advantage of their core competencies and exploit export opportunities. One of the world's premier engineering, construction, and project management companies, Bechtel, with a fleet of 40,000 employees and 40 offices around the world has completed more than 22,000 projects on turnkey and contractual basis in more than 140 countries. Overseas Construction Council of India is the nodal Indian export promotion agency for project exports.

India has an edge over other countries when it comes to the efficient handling of turnkey projects in other developed and developing countries. The air conditioning of the Hong Kong airport as well as the Etisalat building in Sharjah was done by Voltas. Engineers India Ltd (EIL), Metallurgical and Engineering Consultants (India) Ltd (MECON), and Larsen and Toubro (L&T) have also handled a number of offshore projects. However, political relations between countries play a major role in getting turnkey projects in international markets.

INVESTMENT ENTRY MODES

If a country is found to be attractive enough to justify a firm's long-term commitment, investment modes of entry are often employed. Major forms of investment modes, such as overseas assembly or mixing, joint ventures, and wholly owned subsidary are discussed next.

Assembly or Mixing in Overseas Markets

In order to avoid the high cost of shipping and high import tariffs, counter non-tariff barriers for import, or to take advantage of cheap labour in overseas markets, a company exports various components of the product in completely knocked down (CKD) condition and assembles them overseas. In the case of medicines and food products, the equivalence of assembling is mixing the ingredients while importing from the home country.

Most of the Japanese automobile companies entered the European market by establishing their assembling operations in Europe to overcome import barriers. These operations were also described as screwdriver operations. However, due to insistence on value addition norms, the Japanese automobile companies had to increase the use of local resources for production in Europe. Tata Motors forged a strategic alliance with Nita Company Ltd, Bangladesh, for assembly and sale of its commercial vehicles in Bangladesh.

International Joint Ventures

When a firm is willing to take complete control of its overseas operations in the international markets, it opts for equity participation with an overseas firm. A joint venture involves more than two firms in equity participation. In joint ventures, the two or more companies involved provide a complementary competitive advantage for the formation of a new company (Fig. 9.4). Thus, in joint ventures, the participating firms contribute their complementary expertise and resources. The basic difference between a joint venture and a strategic alliance is that unlike a joint venture, a strategic alliance has no equity participation from the two firms.

The basic reasons for formation of international joint ventures are as follows:

- To overcome foreign investment barriers especially in developing and least developed countries (LDCs)
- To manage emerging new opportunities with complementary technology or management skills provided by joint venture partners
- To overcome operational barriers—for example, by establishing contacts with government and local officials—and thereby enter international markets quite easily and in a speedy way
- To achieve competitive advantage in global operations with low investment

International joint ventures offer the following benefits:

- Provide access to international markets with high tariff and other import barriers.
- Provide access to the strengths of local firms including their supply chain and distribution channels in foreign markets.
- Provide instant access to operational knowledge so that the company has a perception of being local in foreign markets.
- Reduce political and economic risk
- Provide opportunities to Indian firms with strength in technical and process know-how to enter international markets
- Provide access to foreign capital markets
- Facilitate shifting of manufacturing operations to low production countries
- Provide greater control over production and marketing functions
- Facilitate firms to strengthen their competitive position in international markets

The Japanese consumer electronics company Sony Corporation and Swedish telecommunication firm Ericsson merged to establish a 50:50 joint venture headquartered in London in 2001 to combine Ericsson's technological leadership in telecommunication and Sony's global marketing strengths to make mobile phones. Both companies have stopped making their own mobile phones in 1995.Sony Ericsson also introduced Walkman branded w-services music phones. In the first quarter of 2006, Sony Ericsson was the fourth largest manufacturer of mobile phones in the world with 7 per cent global market share after Samsung, Motorola, and Nokia. Similarly, in June 2006, Nokia's Network Business Group and Siemens AG's communication division also announced its merger by way of a 50:50 joint venture to form a new company, Nokia Siemens Networks. The new JV entity would have a synergistic effect to make it the largest telecommunication company of the world. Also in the oil and gas industry, international joint venture is a common phenomenon where one or more international firms often cooperate with a local firm.

However, the limitations associated with joint ventures are as follows:

- Involve greater risk as compared to modes of entry without equity participation.
- Opportunistic behaviour of partner firms adds to high rate of dissolution of international joint ventures.
- Conflict between partners may adversely affect a joint venture's performance.

Despite the above limitations, joint ventures provide an effective way of entering international markets by assisting in overcoming trade, investment, and operational barriers.

Wholly Owned Foreign Subsidiaries

A firm expands internationally to have complete control over its overseas operations by way of 100 per cent ownership in the new entity, known as wholly owned subsidiary. Besides ownership and control, wholly owned subsidiaries help the internationalizing firm protect its technology and skills from external sharing.

Therefore, for successful operation of a wholly owned subsidiary, one has to take care to

- actively involve indigenous people at all levels of managerial and operational decision-making and
- ensure extensive use of local marketing and supply channels, to the extent possible.

The major benefits of wholly owned subsidiaries are as follows:

- The firm exerts complete control over its foreign operations.
- The trade secrets, proprietary technology, and other firm specific advantages (FSAs) retain within the company.

Tata Tea, which entered into a joint venture with Tetley Group, UK, in 1994, acquired Tetley in 2000 to become one of the largest integrated branded tea companies in the world (Exhibit 9.3). Asian Paints Group has a presence in 24 countries located in the Indian subcontinent, south-east Asia, the Far East, the Middle East, the South Pacific, the Caribbean, Africa, and Europe, and 27 manufacturing plants across these countries. The Aditya Birla Group pioneered the establishment of wholly owned subsidiaries in Southeast Asia so as to expand its manufacturing base and take advantage of better opportunities in view of prevailing restrictive policies of the Indian government. It has wholly owned manufacturing operations of rayon, acrylic fibre, textiles, rubber, edible oil, etc. in Thailand, the Philippines, Indonesia, Malaysia, and Egypt besides a number of

Exhibit 9.3   Tilda Rice: success story of market-oriented processing facilities

Tilda Rice, owned by a Gujarati family from East Africa, which was thrown out of Uganda during civil war, is one of the world's largest brands in basmati rice. The India-based company United Riceland Ltd sells 85 per cent of its produce to the parent company Tilda Rice under the mechanism of transfer pricing. Tilda Rice established a world-class milling facility at the banks of the river Thames in London, whereas the competitors from Indian basmati industry did not have any milling facility in the European Union (EU). The preferential import duty structure in the EU basically aimed at protecting the local milling industry in EU of which Tilda was also a part has given the company a competitive edge vis-à-vis its competitors. Thus, the company could import brown rice, process it at its milling facility at London and then cater to the EU and the US market. The subsequent integration policies of the EU have given a competitive edge to Tilda Rice vis-à-vis its competitors due to its own milling facility in the EU. In addition to the EU, the company also exports to the USA, Saudi Arabia, UAE, Kuwait, Europe, etc. and has established itself among the world's largest brands in basmati rice.

Source: www.tilda.com, accessed on 20 March 2013.

joint ventures. Tilda Rice could establish itself as one of the leading brands of basmati rice only because it had market-oriented production facilities in the UK (Exhibit 9.3).

However, the limitations of wholly owned foreign subsidiaries are as follows:

- They need substantial financial and other operational resources which are beyond the capability of smaller companies.
- In order to cope with operational difficulties, companies need substantial international exposure before having a wholly owned subsidiary.
- Complete control over the operations is associated with exposure to high risk.

However, lessons should be learnt from Enron, which had to wind up its operations in India after building a power plant in Maharashtra due to differences between the company and the Indian government over the power purchase agreement.

Wholly owned subsidiaries often face numerous prejudices in host countries, which may be summarized here:

- Completely owned operations are generally not allowed in vital and sensitive industrial sectors such as defence, nuclear energy, media, and select infrastructure.
- Since virtually there is little control over wholly owned foreign subsidiaries, the host country's governments generally set stricter scrutiny and operational norms, such as pollution control, foreign exchange administration, and technology level.
- There exists high vulnerability to criticism by various social activists, NGOs, political parties, and other interest groups in the host country.

As discussed earlier, firms may invest overseas either by way of greenfield operations or mergers and acquisitions (M&As). The choice of FDI mode is largely influenced by industry-specific factors, as greenfield investment is the preferred mode of entry in technology-intensive industries. The choice may also be influenced by institutional, cultural, and transaction cost factors, in particular the attitude towards takeovers, conditions in capital markets, liberalization policies, privatization, regional integration, currency risks, and the role played by intermediaries (e.g., investment bankers) actively seeking acquisition opportunities and taking initiatives in making deals.

Since the global economic crisis in 2008, the total project value of greenfield investments has been much higher than that of cross-border M&As (Fig. 9.6). Investors from developing economies are becoming increasingly important players in cross-border M&A markets, which were previously dominated by developed country players. Cash rich multinationals especially from emerging markets have also created new acquisition opportunities for cross-border M&As.

Developing and transition economies tend to prefer greenfield investments rather than cross-border M&A. More than two-third of the total value of greenfield investments is directed to these economies, while only 25 per cent of cross-border M&As are undertaken there.

Greenfield operations

Creating production and marketing facilities on a firm's own from scratch is termed as greenfield operations. Greenfield operations are preferred over M&As under the following situations:

- In all least developing and some developing countries where right targets for acquisition are barely available
- When smaller firms do not possess required finances for acquisition
- When attractive incentives are offered by the host country to encourage foreign investment leading to increased financial viability.
- When expanding in countries with regulatory barriers to international acquisition

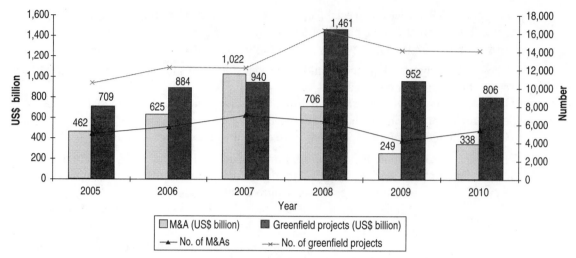

Fig. 9.6 Cross-border M&As and greenfield projects

Source: World Investment Report, 2011.

Table 9.1 World's top 10 greenfield investments (2006–2010)

Year	Value (US$ million)	Host economy	Investing company	Industry	Home economy
2006	18,725	Pakistan	Emaar Properties PJSC	Real estate	UAE
2010	16,000	Australia	Petroliam National Berhad	Oil and natural gas	Malaysia
2007	14,000	Tunisia	Dubai Hoding LLC	Real estate	UAE
2006	9,000	China	Kuwait Petroleum Corporation	Oil and natural gas	Kuwait
2006	6,000	Turkey	Indian Oil Corporation Ltd	Oil and natural gas	India
2010	5,800	Cuba	China National Petroleum Corporation	Oil and natural gas	China
2010	5,740	Nigeria	China State Construction Engineering Corporation	Oil and natural gas	China
2008	5,000	Morocco	International Petroleum Investment Company PJSC	Coal, oil, and natural gas	UAE
2010	5,000	Cameroon	GDF Suez SA	Oil and natural gas	France
2008	4,700	USA	AREVA Group	Renewable energy	France

Source: World Investment Report, 2011.

Top 10 greenfield investments during 2006–2009 were dominated in energy and real estate sectors by companies from the UAE, China, France, India, and Kuwait, as shown in Table 9.1.

Mergers and acquisitions

Transfer of existing assets of a domestic firm to a foreign firm lead to mergers and acquisitions (M&As). In cross-border mergers, a new legal entity emerges by way of merging assets and operations of firms from more than one country. Cross-border acquisition involves transferring management control of assets and operations of a domestic company to a foreign firm. As a result, the local firm becomes an affiliate of the foreign company. Generally, mergers occur in friendly settings wherein two firms come together to build a synergy. On the other hand, acquisitions can be hostile takeovers by purchasing the majority of shares of a firm from the open market.

Mergers and acquisitions (M&As) are preferred over greenfield investments due to the following reasons:

- They provide a rapid entry of the firm's business in foreign countries. Therefore, M&As become crucial when speed of market entry is important.
- The acquiring firm gets ready access to tangible and intangible assets of the target firm overseas. In addition to acquisition of manufacturing and other physical facilities, the target firm's brand equity, marketing channels skilled manpower, and patents and trademarks do have strategic significance for market entry.
- The investing firm also acquires technical know-how, process, and management skills that add to its operational efficiency overseas.

Acquisitions can be of the following three types:

Minority   When a foreign firm acquires 10 per cent to 49 per cent interest in a firm's voting stock

Majority   When a foreign firm acquires 50 per cent to 99 per cent voting interest

Full outright stake   When a foreign firm acquires 100 per cent of voting stock

The top 10 cross-border acquisitions during 2006–10, as shown in Table 9.2, have been dominated by energy and electric services, logistics, and information technology by companies from France, China, Japan, Saudi Arabia, UAE, Switzerland, and Singapore. Certain industries, such as energy, telecommunications, pharmaceuticals, and financial services have exhibited a high level of cross-border M&A activity. In contrast to the M&A boom of the late 1990s and early 2000s, which was largely driven by takeovers in the information and communication technology (ICT) industries, the current M&As were in the consumer goods and service industries (including financial services) and in energy supply and basic materials. Besides, in the previous M&A boom, transactions were to a large extent financed by the exchange of shares. Recent cross-border M&A transactions have been carried out primarily through cash and debt financing.[8] For instance, in large deals, including many in mining and oil industries, cash is now the standard payment method. Emerging economies awash with petrodollars (West Asia) and foreign exchange (China) have become very active in cash-based cross-border acquisitions. The increasing role of debt financing in cross-border acquisitions may be explained by the fact that the cost of equity capital remains significantly higher than the cost of debt financing. This reflects a corporate strategy of not holding excessive equity capital and instead using borrowings and internal funds in investment to attain high managerial efficiency.

M&As by Indian firms   Setting up a subsidiary and attempting to grow organically could take years. Moreover, major costs are to be incurred in building up marketing channels and brands. In high-cost economies, such as Europe with stringent labour and environment regulations, the synergy of a local distribution network and low-cost manufacturing in India makes strategic sense. As companies grow, have surplus funds, and want to expand their markets, they find the virtues of foreign acquisition.

India's deepening integration into the global economy led to corporate restructuring and significant growth in M&As, especially in high-tech, energy, and core industries. India's net purchase through cross-border M&As increased impressively from US$1.9 billion in 2005 to

---

[8] *World Investment Report*, 'Transnational Corporations, Extractive Industries and Development', United Nations, New York and Geneva, 2007, pp. 3–16.

Table 9.2 World's top 10 cross-border mergers and acquisitions (2006–2010)

Year	Value (US$ million)	Host economy	Acquired company	Industry	Acquiring company	Home economy	Shares acquired (%)
2009	16,938	UK	British Energy Group PLC	Electric services	EDF	France	73
2007	14,684	UK	Gallaher Group PLC	Cigarettes	Japan Tobacco Inc	Japan	100
2007	11,600	USA	GE Plastics	Plastics and synthetic resins	SABIC	Saudi Arabia	100
2009	7,157	Switzerland	Addax Petroleum Corp	Petroleum and natural gas	Sinopec Group	China	100
2010	7,111	Brazil	Repsol YPF Brasil SA	Petroleum and natural gas	Sinopec Group	China	40
2006	6,899	UK	Peninsular & Oriental Steam Navigation Co	Shipping	Dubai World	UAE	100
2008	6,086	UK	British Energy Group PLC	Electric services	EDF	France	26
2007	5,483	Italy	FASTWEB SpA	Information services	Swisscom AG	Switzerland	82
2009	4,500	USA	Constellation Energy Nuclear Group LLC	Electric services	EDF	France	50
2006	4,388	Hong Kong, China	Hutchison Port Holdings Ltd	Marine cargo handling	PSA Corp Ltd	Singapore	20

Source: World Investment Report, 2011.

US$29 billion in 2007 but declined subsequently to US$26.4 billion[9] in 2010. During the recent years, there had been significant M&As in commodities, such as steel, aluminum, metals and ores, telecom, and power and energy. The ability of many Indian companies to raise money cheaply due to prevailing market conditions in India seems to be an enabling factor driving overseas acquisitions. The factors that enabled Indian companies to go on an acquisition spree include the following:

- Major Indian companies had surplus cash reserves that were to be better invested in the production facilities.
- The financial reform process has simplified the process of overseas acquisitions by removing the cap of US$100 million on foreign investment in 2001.
- The rupee is strong in international markets and it makes better sense to invest outside.
- Balance of payments surplus ensured that the dollar is available easily.
- Exposure to the international competitive environment underlined the need to incorporate professional work environment available in the developed countries.

---

[9] *World Investment Report,* 'Non-equity Modes of International Production and Development', United Nations, New York and Geneva, 2011, p. 197.

Reasons for international acquisitions by Indian firms   Opening up of the domestic market to foreign companies has the potential to obliterate the difference between the domestic market and the international market. Domestic players with substantial market share have been forced to increase their standards to international levels to survive even in the domestic market in the long-run. Such internationalization can best be brought about by taking the M&A route to rope in foreign firms. The major objectives of the acquisitions abroad are as follows:

- Increase productivity levels to internationally accepted standards.
- Raise the profitability by achieving economies in logistics, transportation, etc.
- Improve their competitiveness in the global market by strategic location of the manufacturing facilities closer to the user markets.
- Get better access to foreign markets especially when there are strong entry barriers in the shape of sanitary and phytosanitary (SPS) restrictions and environmental constraints.

The main motives for Indian companies to undertake cross-border M&As were to gain access to new technologies and competencies, and to build stronger positions in global markets. The acquisition of the European Steel company Arcelor by the Mittal Steel Company, a company of Indian origin headquartered in the Netherlands, for $32 billion, was the world's largest cross-border M&A transaction in 2006, and the largest deal ever made by a company with origins in a developing country. In the same year, Tata Group in India acquired the Corus Group (UK/Netherlands), also in the steel industry, for $9.5 billion. Broadly, the acquisition strategy followed by Indian firms was to

- acquire companies in the developed countries which are facing mounting costs and falling profit levels;
- turn them around through a synergy of a local distribution network and low-cost manufacturing based in India, which makes the companies financially viable and competitive;
- develop the developed country markets through a barrier-free entry riding on the brands of the foreign 'acquired' firms; and
- protect the developing country markets by sustaining the existing distribution network and by introducing premier products of the 'acquired' firm.

SELECTION OF INTERNATIONAL MARKET ENTRY MODES

A firm has to choose from various alternative entry modes as discussed in the previous section to expand in foreign markets. Selecting an appropriate mode of market entry is an important decision, having both short- and long-term operational and strategic ramifications on a firm's success in its internationalization process. Although it is difficult to make a ready-made prescription about the most appropriate entry mode, a firm has to critically evaluate strategic trade-offs and various internal and external factors and may use the decision model, as follows, before deciding upon the entry mode mix.

In order to minimize international market entry risk, Walt Disney entered into a contractual agreement in 1979 with a Japanese land reclamation company—Oriental Land Company—in partnership with Mitsui Real Estate and Keisei Railway Company. Under the contract, Oriental Land was the owner and licensee, while Walt Disney was the designer and licenser. In Tokyo Disneyland, Walt Disney received as a management fee 10 per cent on admissions and corporate sponsorship agreements besides 5 per cent royalties from gross revenues on food and merchandise from Oriental Land Company. The investment of Walt Disney in Tokyo Disneyland was only US$2.5 million in a total estimated project of US$250 million. Although Walt Disney had complete control on design and significant control over its operations through a series of well-documented operating manuals, it did not have any ownership. Subsequently, Tokyo Disneyland became a highly successful theme park attracting more visitors than the US parks.

Encouraged by its success in its Japanese venture 'Tokyo Disneyland', the US company Walt Disney decided to enter into the European market through owned subsidiaries, investing 49 per cent equity in the operating company Euro Disney SEA and the balance being raised through a public issue and through loans. However, due to a variety of factors such as sociocultural differences, local labour laws, and unrealistic project estimates, Euro Disney had financial problems between 1992 and 1994 and incurred huge losses. However, major financial and operational restructuring was undertaken, which included a change of name from Euro Disney to Disneyland Paris, so as to make the park profitable.

This example illustrates the significance of the decision of international market entry. A flawed or incorrect decision may cause much trouble; a case in point being that of Michael Eisner, the legendary CEO of Walt Disney, who had to go through such difficult times. Therefore, a company should decide on its market entry mix only after a thorough evaluation of entry mode alternatives, as follows, to effectively and strategically serve its international markets.

Strategic Trade-offs in Selecting Entry Modes

Given an ideal situation, hardly any firm would like to share the control and returns of its international operations and would like to internalize entire operating processes within the company. However, such an entry mode would require high commitment of resources for foreign entry associated with considerably high risk as depicted in Fig. 9.7. Moreover, high resource commitment in a country by way of investment increases a firm's exit cost and provides much lower flexibility.

Selecting an entry mode is an important decision for a firm since it involves long-term strategic implications and considerable commitment of resources. Besides, it involves considerable operational complexities and resources to switch over to another entry mode from the existing one. A firm has to choose from a variety of entry modes depending upon the following:

- Ability and willingness to commit resources in the target country
- Magnitude of risk the firm is willing to take in its international expansion
- Types of return anticipated from overseas operations
- Extent of control to be exerted in the firm's foreign operations
- Level of externalization of the firm's resources including its intellectual property
- Desired flexibility of entry modes

However large a firm may be, its resources are limited and need to be optimally employed so as to derive maximum returns. Therefore, when the market potential is not proven or the market size is not large enough to invest considerable resources, the firm has to make a trade-off between various benefits and costs as indicated in Fig. 9.7 and reconcile with entry modes that share control and returns. Small and medium enterprises (SMEs) generally adopt trade-related modes to enter international markets. Large companies do adopt trade-related modes for expanding their markets internationally to unfamiliar countries to get first-hand experience.

Factors Affecting Selection of Entry Modes

The internationalizing firm may evaluate both external factors, such as market growth, government regulations, competition, physical infrastructure, risks associated, and production and shipping costs, and internal factors, which may include the firm's objectives, resource availability, level

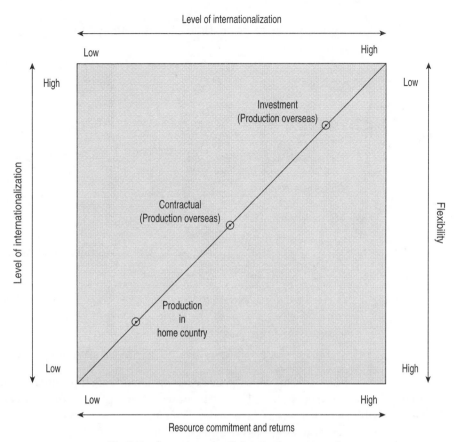

Fig. 9.7   Strategic trade-offs in selecting entry modes

Source: Based on Joshi, Rakesh Mohan, *International Business*, Oxford University Press,
New Delhi, 2009, p. 442.

of commitment, international experience, and flexibility. Figure 9.8 shows the factors that affect selection of international market entry mode.

External factors

Market size   Market size is one of the key factors an international marketer has to keep in mind when selecting an entry mode. Countries with a large market size justify the modes of entry with long-term commitment requiring higher level of investment, such as wholly owned subsidiaries or equity participation.

To take advantage of market size and growth potential, a number of Indian companies are in the process of committing more resources to the Chinese market. Ranbaxy, as a pioneering Indian company to enter the Chinese market in 1990, entered into a joint venture in 1994 and emerged as a market leader with brand Cifran.

Market growth   Most of the large, established markets, such as the US, Europe, and Japan, have more or less reached a point of saturation for consumer goods such as automobiles and consumer electronics (TVs, refrigerators, washing machines, etc.). Therefore, the growth of markets in these countries is showing a declining trend. For instance, the overall growth in most of the US and European markets is about 7 per cent, while in emerging markets like India and

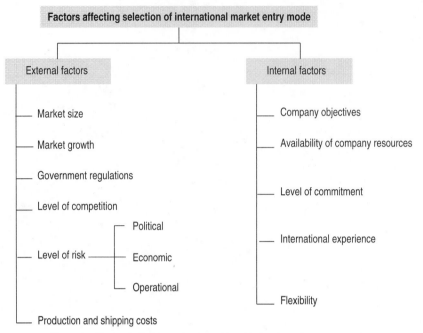

Fig. 9.8 Factors affecting selection of international market entry mode

China it is over 30 per cent, which indicates tremendous market potential in the time to come. Therefore, from the perspective of long-term growth, firms invest more resources in markets with high growth potential such as China, India, Thailand, Indonesia, Malaysia, and the Philippines. These markets are also termed as emerging markets.

Government regulations   The selection of a market entry mode is to a great extent affected by the legislative framework of the overseas market. The governments of most of the Gulf countries have made it mandatory for foreign firms to have a local partner. For instance, the UAE is a lucrative market for Indian firms but most firms operate there with a local partner.

   Trade barriers such as ecological regulations and local content requirements also affect the mode of entry. It has been a major reason for increased foreign investment in Mexico, which is a part of the North American Free Trade Agreement (NAFTA), in order to cater to the US market. Japanese automobile firms set up their units in the EU mainly due to local content requirements. It was primarily due to a high import tariff on automobiles that foreign firms were forced to set up manufacturing units, especially in the automobile sector, in China.

Level of competition   Presence of competitors and their level of involvement in an overseas market is another crucial factor in deciding on an entry mode so as to effectively respond to competitive market forces. This is one of the major reasons behind automobile companies setting up their operations in India and other emerging markets so as to effectively respond to global competition.

Physical infrastructure   The level of development of physical infrastructure such as roads, railways, telecommunications, financial institutions, and marketing channels is a pre-condition for a company to commit more resources to an overseas market. The level of infrastructure development (both physical and institutional) has been responsible for major investments in Singapore, Dubai, and Hong Kong. As a result, these places have developed as international marketing hubs in the Asian region.

Level of risk   From the point of view of entry mode selection, a firm should evaluate the following risks.

Political risk   Political instability and turmoil dissuades firms from committing more resources to a market. Companies have greater inclination to invest resources in countries with stable governments and transparent legal systems. Broadly, the political system in developed countries, such as the USA, the UK, Japan, and Australia, is more or less stable. Besides, the judiciary is largely independent of political interference in developed countries.

On the other hand, the political system is unstable and turbulent in many developing countries such as Brazil, Pakistan, Argentina, and Fiji. The legal system is highly influenced by those in power especially in autocratic forms of government.

Economic risk   Economic risk may arise due to volatility of exchange rates of the target market's currency, upheavals in balance of payments situations that may affect the cost of other inputs for production, and marketing activities in foreign markets. International companies find it difficult to manage their operations in markets wherein the inflation rate is extremely high (i.e., in a state of hyper-inflation). For instance, companies have experienced such a situation in the Commonwealth of Independent States (CIS), Argentina, and Brazil. This explains why most companies prefer to enter these markets by way of licensing and franchising rather than equity participation. Thus, a firm would be willing to invest more resources in countries with higher levels of economic stability.

Operational risk   In case the marketing system in an overseas country is similar to that of the firm's home country, the firm has a better understanding of operational problems in the foreign market in question. For instance, the absence of an organized retailing system in India provides Indian exporters a strategic edge when operating in other developing countries, which do not have organized retailing systems. This is also true for marketing promotion and communication strategies in countries with less developed marketing systems.

Production and shipping costs   Markets with substantial cost of shipping as in the case of low-value high-volume goods may increase the logistics cost. The increased shipping cost may not only be due to the longer distance but also because of the lack of availability of competitive shipping lines as in case of shipping goods from India to most African and Latin American countries.

Lower cost of production may also be one of the key factors in firms deciding to establish manufacturing operations in foreign countries. Many transnational companies establish their manufacturing bases in developing countries, such as India, China, and Brazil, in order to take advantage of lower production costs. Such a strategy to manufacture locally or in countries with low production cost gives multinational companies a competitive edge in terms of cost competitiveness in international markets.

Internal factors

Company objectives   Companies operating in domestic markets with limited aspirations generally enter foreign markets as a result of a reactive approach to international marketing opportunities. In such cases, companies receive unsolicited orders from acquaintances, firms, and relatives based abroad, and they attempt to fulfil these export orders. This casual approach to entering international markets by way of producing in the home market and exporting overseas translates into regular exporting if the firm has positive experience in its exports operations.

However, the strategic objectives of proactive companies make them enter into international markets through investment modes of entry.

Availability of company resources   Venturing into international markets needs substantial commitment of financial and human resources and therefore choice of an entry mode depends upon the financial strength of a firm. It may be observed that Indian firms with good financial strength have entered international markets by way of wholly owned subsidiaries or equity participation.

Level of commitment   In view of the market potential, the willingness of the company to commit resources in a particular market also determines the entry mode choice. Companies need to evaluate various investment alternatives for allocating scarce resources. However, the commitment of resources in a particular market also depends upon the way the company is willing to perceive and respond to competitive forces.

International experience   A company well exposed to the dynamics of the international marketing environment would be at ease when making a decision regarding entering into international markets with a highly intensive mode of entry such as joint ventures and wholly owned subsidiaries. It may be observed that only those Indian companies such as Ranbaxy, Tata Tea, and Asian Paints that have substantial experience in foreign markets have opted for equity participation or wholly owned subsidiaries in international markets.

Flexibility   Companies should also keep in mind exit barriers when entering international markets. A market which presently appears attractive may not necessarily continue to be so, say over the next 10 years. It could be due to changes in the political and legal structure, changes in the customer preferences, emergence of new market segments, or changes in the competitive intensity of the market. Therefore, the markets that are difficult to forecast may necessitate an exit strategy over a period of time and therefore may need to be approached by way of strategic alliances, such as licensing and franchising, where the companies' stakes are low and the exit is easy.

Decision-making Model for Selecting International Market Entry Modes

The entry mode strategy should aim at achieving a firm's strategic goals. It should take into consideration the firm's long-term goals so as to establish its international presence. A company is believed to possess some core competencies or advantages that are specific to the firm and hardly available to its competitors. As depicted in Fig. 9.9, the firm may exploit its existing core competencies in the domestic market or focus its resources to develop new competitive advantages for the home country. In case the opportunities to exploit such competencies in the home country are limited, the firm decides to expand overseas. Firms often decide to pursue international market expansion as a strategic goal in addition to exploiting home country market.

Cost of logistics, depending upon geographical distances and unit value realization of goods, forms a significant constituent of price competitiveness in the target country. Besides, various trade restrictions and import tariffs of host country governments considerably affect a firm's competitiveness. Expanding through exports is suitable for countries having low transportation cost and lower import tariffs and other import restrictions.

The firm needs to begin overseas production, if expanding through exports adversely affects its competitiveness either due to prohibitive costs of logistics or imports restrictions, including tariff and non-tariff barriers. The choice of entry mode may be made, depending upon the availability and willingness to commit financial and other resources. For rapid expansion into multiple markets with little financial commitments, licensing or franchising serve as effective expansion tools so as to exploit a firm's core competence internationally. Although licensing

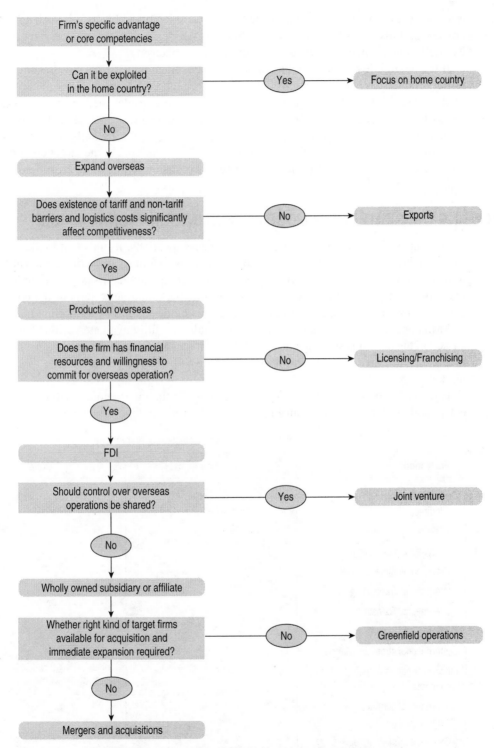

Fig. 9.9 Decision tree for selection of international market entry modes

Source: Joshi, Rakesh Mohan, *International Business*, Oxford University Press, New Delhi, 2009, p. 478.

is a low-cost entry mode, it requires the firm to share its intangible assets, such as technology, processes, skills, and know-how, with its business partner. A firm's strategy to have control over its intellectual property serves as key determinant in licensing.

If the intangible assets are not amenable to licensing and the firm wants to commit sizeable resources overseas and exert control, it expands through FDI. It is the extent of control desired, likely risks, ability and willingness to commit resources, besides the long-term business prospects of the host country that determine the extent of investment. In case the firm is not willing to share control and ready to assume complete risk, it opts for a wholly owned subsidiary. If the right kind of target firm with goal compatibility is available in the target country, M&A is a preferred strategy that also facilitates speedy expansion. Otherwise, greenfield investment is adopted.

CHOOSING THE RIGHT ENTRY MODE MIX FOR INTERNATIONAL MARKETS

As a company expands its operations into overseas locations, it finds that market conditions, such as market size, growth potential, government regulations, competitive intensity, physical infrastructure, uncertainties—political, economic, and operational risks—vary among different markets. A sum of all these factors determines the market attractiveness of the country under consideration. Therefore, companies adopt various modes of entry for different markets.

Firms operating in international markets should carefully evaluate various factors, as discussed in the previous section, and select the right entry strategy for a market. An international marketing manager may use the framework in Exhibit 9.4 to select a mode of international market entry.

However, companies with a significant presence in the international market may opt for an entry mode in a particular country market based on its strategic decisions to serve the global

Exhibit 9.4 Framework for selection of entry mode

Entry mode	Pros	Cons
Export		
– Indirect		
– Direct		
Piggybacking exporting		
Providing offshore services		
International franchising		
International licensing		
International leasing		
International strategic alliance		
International management contracts		
International contract manufacturing		
Overseas turnkey projects		
International joint ventures		
Wholly owned subsidiaries		

Exhibit 9.5   International market entry mode mix

Entry market / Country mode	Exports	International licensing	International franchising	Overseas contract manufacturing	Overseas assembly or mixing	Joint ventures	Wholly owned subsidiary
Country I							
Country II							
Country III							
Country IV							
Country V							
Country VI							

market. The international marketing manager may use Exhibit 9.5 for analysing the international market entry mix.

In an attempt to reach out to Indians living abroad, ICICI Bank entered the international market in 2003 using a mix of entry modes. It has established subsidiaries in London and Toronto with an investment of US$50 million and US$20 million, respectively, offshore branches in Singapore and Bahrain, representative offices in Dubai, Shanghai, and Hong Kong. These different modes of entry have been adopted by ICICI Bank because of differing governmental regulations, as a number of countries require banks to first run either representative offices or offshore branches for a few years before a subsidiary is allowed.[10]

Dr Reddy's Laboratory has gone in for wholly owned subsidiaries in the USA, France, Singapore, the Netherlands, and Hong Kong because of large market size, potential for growth, and lower risk factors. Russia and China offer huge market potential, but because of the level of difficulty involved in responding to local environment conditions and risks, the company has entered into joint ventures with local partners. Markets with relatively lower potential, such as Ukraine, Romania, Kazakhstan, Vietnam, and Sri Lanka are being served by resident offices.

This chapter brings out the concept of entry modes in international market and elaborates various types of entry modes under two heads: production in the home country and production in foreign countries. Entry modes based on production in home country, such as exports, piggybacking, and providing offshore services, generally need much lower level of resource commitment and provide greater flexibility to switch over to other entry modes. Therefore, these are highly suitable for smaller firms with limited resources and even for larger firms for preliminary market assessment. However, such modes generally offer much lower profit and control.

A firm may locate its production facilities overseas and enter into a contractual agreement with another firm in the target country. Depending upon a firm's business goals and strategy, it may choose from one or more contractual entry modes, such as international strategic alliances, contract manufacturing, management contracts, turnkey projects, international leasing, international licensing, and international franchising. Markets with considerable size and growth potential require long-term commitment and firms strategically cater to such markets by way of FDI. Selection of entry modes is a crucial decision. Various tools employed for selection of modes of international market entry are discussed in the chapter.

---

[10] Rajadhyaksha, Niranjan, 'The Global Gambit', *Business World*, 13 October 2003, pp. 36–38.

Summary

The institutional mechanism by which a firm expands its markets overseas is termed as entry mode. International market entry modes vary from low-risk low-control modes with minimum resource commitment, such as indirect exports to high-risk high-control modes with a much higher level of commitment by establishing its own manufacturing facilities in the overseas market.

Indirect exporting is the easiest way to make the products available in the international market with the help of international marketing intermediaries who perform several export-related functions. Once a company acquires adequate information on export-related activities, it begins to export on its own to gain market knowledge and generate more profits. A firm may also piggyback on the distribution channels of an overseas firm with a strong marketing network to penetrate into overseas markets. Outsourcing offshore services is rapidly growing in developed countries due to significant differences in wage patterns. It opens up tremendous scope for developing countries especially for Indian companies, due to their large reservoir of skilled and qualified manpower at competitive prices.

A company with a strong production base, technical know-how, design, and marketing expertise may enter into international markets by way of licensing, while services firms find it more appropriate to have international franchising as an international market entry mode. Turnkey projects, management contracts, international strategic alliances, and contract manufacturing are other contractual modes of entry. In order to have greater control over its overseas operations, a company may have equity participation in joint ventures or have a wholly owned subsidiary.

Selection of entry mode is an important decision as it involves both short- and long-term ramifications in the internationalization process of a firm. The strategic trade-offs in selecting various entry modes provide an insight for evaluation and selection of entry modes. The factors affecting the choice of an entry mode include external factors, such as market size, market growth, government regulations, level of competition, physical infrastructure, level of political, economic, and operational risks, production and shipping costs, and internal factors, such as company objectives, availability of company resources, level of commitment, international experience, and flexibility.

A self-explanatory decision tree given at the end of the chapter serves as a useful tool for selecting an appropriate international market entry mode. A firm has to evaluate various alternatives and choose a mix of international market entry modes as a part of its strategic decisions in order to serve diverse international markets.

Key Terms

Brownfield investment Expansion or re-investment in existing foreign affiliates or sites.

Buyback Often used as a marketing tool to sell plant and equipment wherein the payment is recovered by way of output from plant and equipment sold.

Clearing arrangement Transaction of goods and services extends over an agreed period of time.

Contract manufacturing A contractual arrangement under which a firm's manufacturing operations are carried out in foreign countries.

Counter purchase A deal involving two separate transactions payable in hard currency, each with its own cash value.

Counter-trade Various forms of trade arrangements wherein the payment is in form of reciprocal commitments for other goods and services rather than an exclusive cash transaction.

Direct exports The process of selling the firm's products directly to an importer in the overseas market.

Export intermediary One who buys the products from a firm in the domestic market and in turn sells to an overseas importer. Also known as a merchant exporter.

Exports Manufacturing the goods in the home market or a third country and shipping them to a country other than the country of production. It is also a mode of international market entry wherein production is carried out in the home country and subsequently the goods are shipped to overseas markets for sale.

Greenfield operations The establishment of production and marketing facilities by a firm on its own from scratch.

Indirect exports The process of selling products to an export intermediary in the company's home country who in turn sells the products in the overseas markets.

International assembly Exports of components, parts or machinery in completely knocked down (CKD) condition and assembling these parts at a site in a foreign country.

International franchising A special form of licensing in which intangible assets are transferred to a foreign firm along with methods of doing business in a prescribed manner and other assistance over an extended period of time in return for a franchising fee. It involves the transfer of intellectual property and other assistance over an extended period of time with greater control compared to licensing.

International licensing The process by which a domestic company allows a foreign company to use its intellectual property, such as patents, trademarks, copyright, process technology, design, and specific business skills for a compensation called royalty.

Joint venture   Equity participation of two or more firms resulting in formation of a new entity.

Management contract   Providing managerial and technical expertise to an overseas firm on contractual basis.

Mode of entry   Institutional mechanism by which a company makes its products or services available in overseas markets.

Naïve rule   Using same entry mode for all foreign markets ignoring the heterogeneity of different foreign markets and entry conditions.

Offset   Partial payment is made by the importer in hard currency, besides promising to source inputs from the importing country and also make investment to facilitate production of such goods.

Piggybacking (complementary exporting)   Business expansion in a foreign country using the distribution network of another company. It involves the use of established distribution channels of a firm in the target market.

Pragmatic rules   Using a low-risk entry mode for initial market entry followed by a workable entry mode if the initial entry mode is not feasible or profitable.

Simple barter   Direct and simultaneous exchange of goods without use of money.

Strategic alliance   The cooperation between two or more international firms to achieve strategic goals without the formation of a separate company.

Strategy rule   Systematically comparing and evaluating all alternative entry modes before a decision is made.

Switch trading   Trading involving a third party, known as switch trader in the transaction to facilitate buying of unwanted goods from the importer and make payment by cash or barter to the exporter.

Turnkey projects   To conceptualize, design, install, construct, and carry out primary testing of manufacturing facilities or engineering structures for an overseas client organization.

Concept Review Questions

1. Selection of a market entry mode is the key decision companies have to take while expanding into overseas markets because it involves risk and a certain level of control. Explain how risk and control are affected by different entry methods.
2. In view of the disadvantages associated with indirect exports, critically examine the reasons for firms opting for indirect exports as a mode of entry over direct exports.
3. Explain the concept of contract manufacturing. Illustrate with the help of suitable examples how companies in developing countries can gain access to international markets by way of contract manufacturing.
4. Critically evaluate various strategic trade-offs a firm is required to make in selecting modes of international market entry.

5. A family run handmade manufacturing unit located in Sanganer near Jaipur is desirous of international expansion. The entrepreneur has little knowledge about international markets and ways to enter. In your opinion, which mode of entry should be adopted? Give reasons to justify your answer.
6. Differentiate between management contracts and contract manufacturing for international market expansion.
7. Why should a firm make direct investments abroad when low investment modes of entry like licensing are available?
8. Write short notes on the following:
   (a) International franchising
   (b) International licensing
   (c) Piggybacking
   (d) Greenfield operations

Critical Thinking Questions

1. Select an Indian company that has made international acquisitions. Critically evaluate the reasons for such acquisitions and their marketing implications.

2. Critically evaluate entry mode strategy of an identified company using the decision tree approach.

Project Assignments

1. Visit a company in your city, which has been engaged in international marketing activities. Discuss the company's performance and growth in the field with a responsible officer engaged in its international marketing operations. Record your observations and carry out the following:
   (a) List out the country markets the company has entered into.
   (b) What are the modes of entry used in different markets?
   (c) Give reasons for using various modes of entry in these markets.
2. Identify an international trading company located near your place and contact it. Make a list of its activities and countries of operations. Critically evaluate the pros and cons of indirect exports through a trading company vis-à-vis direct exports.

3. Collect information from secondary sources about a foreign company engaged in franchising operations in India. Meet one of the local franchisees and list its activities. Find out the problems faced by the franchisee and the remedial actions taken to meet international quality and service requirements.

4. Form groups in class where each group should identify one firm from your country operating overseas and one foreign firm operating in your country adopting one of the following entry modes:
   (a) Overseas turnkey projects
   (b) International management contracts
   (c) International strategic alliance
   (d) International contract manufacturing

5. Critically examine the market entry strategy used by a firm, including the following parameters:
   (a) Brief about the firm
   (b) Reasons for using the entry strategy
   (c) Effectiveness of market entry strategy
   Make a group presentation of your findings and discuss in class.

CASE STUDY:　INDIAN OIL CORPORATION'S INTERNATIONALIZATION STRATEGY

Background

India is the fourth largest oil consumer in the world after USA, China, and Japan, whereas it has limited resources to meet its rapidly rising petroleum demand. India imports most of its crude oil requirements, which makes it the world's fourth largest oil importer. Petroleum products take special significance in the Indian economy due to limited domestic resources and exploration fields and over-dependence on imports. This has significant impact on India's import bill and the country's trade deficit. Moreover, availability of petroleum products is crucial to India's oil security and therefore takes extreme strategic significance in the country's political and economic diplomacy.

Soon after India's independence in 1947, the country focused on regaining control over its oil and gas sector that was hitherto dominated by Western companies, primarily the British. Aimed at achieving oil security, Indian Oil Corporation (IOC) and Oil and Natural Gas Commission (ONGC) were created for downstream and upstream oil sectors respectively under India's Industrial Policy Resolution in 1956. The hydrocarbon sector in India witnessed nationalization in the 1970s and the process was completed by 1981 wherein upstream blocks for exploration were allocated to state owned oil companies on a nomination basis limiting participation of private players only through joint ventures. In 1999, the New Exploration and Licensing Policy (NELP) paved way for 100 per cent foreign and private participation for award of oil exploration blocks through competitive bidding. As a result, state-owned oil companies both in upstream and downstream sectors that operated under a protected business environment by the government were gradually exposed to market forces and were compelled to come up with new strategies to remain competitive.

Indian Oil Corporation (IOC) has the distinction of being India's largest company with an annual sales turnover of US$85 billion and profits of US$825 million in 2012 and a strong workforce of over 34,000. It is the 18th largest petroleum company in the world and ranked in various international listings including at 83rd place in the *Fortune* 'Global 500' in 2012.

India's downstream petroleum sector is dominated by publicly owned three oil marketing companies (OMCs): Indian Oil Corporation Ltd (IOCL), Bharat Petroleum Corporation Ltd (BPCL), and Hindustan Petroleum Corporation Ltd (HPCL) that together account for over 98 per cent of operational retail outlet in the country and over 50 per cent of domestic refining.[11] Unable to compete with state-owned oil marketing companies that are the only authorized entities to sell subsidized fuel, Essar Oil had to close its 1,250 filling stations in 2005 and even India's largest private oil company, Reliance petroleum had to shut down all of its 1,432 filling stations in 2008.

IOCL has the largest share of 31 per cent in the country's refining capacity owning 10 of the 22 refineries in India with a combined capacity of 1.2 million barrels per day (bpd) against the country's total refining capacity of 4.3 million bpd. In the downstream sector, IOCL is the single largest player with a market share of over 50 per cent in domestic marketing and retail of oil and petroleum products.

International Market Entry of Indian Oil

Expansion in international markets was a strategic decision for Indian Oil primarily to sustain and grow as domestic markets were constrained owing to a number of factors. Phased de-regulation of the Indian market exposed IOC to free market competition; therefore, expanding in international markets facilitated the company to maintain reasonable returns on its operations while fulfilling social responsibility at home. Due to entry of private sector and MNCs in oil business, prospects for growth in refining capacity and sales volume for Indian oil were under threat. Besides, excess refining capacity in India vis-à-vis petroleum consumption was leading to a reduction in refining capacity

[11] Clarke, Kiran, *India's Downstream Petroleum Sector*, OECD/International Energy Agency, 2010, p. 28.

utilization. In order to maintain economies of scale of operations, exports to neighbouring countries was a strategic option. Internationalization was also a strategic response to mitigate business risks domestically and increase its competitiveness so as to enable IOC to effectively face the challenges of private sector and transnational oil firms in India. Indian Oil could also leverage its professional expertise and core competences developed at home in international markets. Moreover, being a state owned enterprise of the Indian government, Indian Oil has a broad objective to help India in its energy security efforts. Thus, IOC's decision to enter international markets was a strategic move.

International market entry modes

IOC used a mix of entry modes for expanding into international markets as follows.

Exporting Indian Oil's expansion in international markets began with exporting of its petroleum products and Servo lubricants to a number of overseas markets including Bangladesh and Sri Lanka.

Strategic alliance For providing aviation fuel and refueling facility at SSR International Airport in Mauritius, IndianOil Mauritius Ltd (IOML) formed a strategic alliance with existing players such as Shell, Caltex, and ESSO.

Turnkey projects IOC constructed a port oil terminal on turnkey basis at Mer Rouge in Mauritius and formed a wholly owned subsidiary, M/s Indian Oil Tanking Ltd, Mauritius, in October 2002.

International joint ventures IOCL collaborated with a number of foreign companies to form joint ventures as summarized next:

- Avi-Oil India Pvt. Ltd (NYCO SA, France and Balmer Lawrie & Co. Ltd): Blending, manufacturing, and selling synthetic, semi-synthetic and mineral-based lubricating oils, greases and hydraulic fluids, related products and specialities for defence and civil aviation uses.
- Indo Cat Pvt. Limited (Intercat, USA): Manufacturing and marketing of FCC catalysts and additives.
- IOT Infrastructure and Energy Services Ltd (Oiltanking GmbH, Germany.): Building and operating terminalling services for petroleum products.
- Indian Oil Petronas Private Ltd (Petronas, Malaysia): Constructing and importing facilities for LPG import at Haldia and engaging in parallel marketing of LPG.
- Indian Oil Skytanking Limited (IOT Infrastructure and Energy Services Ltd, Skytanking GmbH, Germany): Designing, financing, constructing, operating, and maintaining aviation fuel facility projects.

- Indian Synthetic Rubber Limited (TSRC Taiwan and Marubeni Japan): Implementing Styrene Butadiene Rubber Project at Panipat
- Lubrizol India Private Limited (Lubrizol Inc., USA): Manufacturing and marketing of chemicals for use as additives in fuels, lubricants, and greases.
- Suntera Nigeria 205 Limited: Investments in oil and gas industry, especially in the upstream sector.

Wholly owned subsidiaries IOC expanded in certain international markets with long-term perspective with wholly owned subsidiaries as briefly outlined next.

IndianOil Mauritius Ltd Mauritius is a small island in the Afrcian sub-continent where people of Indian origin account for about 70 per cent of its total population. This has made significant impact on every walk of life in the island nation's culture, education, and businesses. Hindi and Bhojpuri are widely spoken languages and about 50 per cent of its population follows Hinduism.[12] India is the single largest exporter accounting for 22.5 per cent of total imports to Mauritius.[13] All these factors contribute to highly conducive environment for trade and business between the two countries.

Initially to provide aviation fuel and refueling facility at SSR International Airport in Mauritius, Indian Oil Mauritius Ltd (IOML) was registered as a wholly owned subsidiary in October 2001 commencing its marketing operations in January 2004. IOML had 25 per cent equity in the new petroleum terminal at Sir Seewoosagar Ramgoolam International Airport, created by a consortium at an investment of US$16 million. It has set up a modern state of art 24,000 metric tons storage facility with eight tanks at Mer Rouge in Port Louis.

Presently, IOML competes with other multinationals operating in Mauritius for the last five decades and markets automotive, aviation, and marine fuels besides SERVO lubricants. IOML has established its own retail network with over 18 filling stations in Mauritius, whereas distributors to unorganized sectors, that is, workshops, garages, and service stations. As Mauritius has only about 170 filling stations, there is enormous scope for expansion of IOML. The company has become the major supplier of aviation fuel with 49 per cent market share and holds 24 per cent overall market share in across all petroleum products in Mauritius.[14]

Market entry to Mauritius is of strategic significance for the company as it provides marketing opportunities to enter the African market and other island countries in the region. Being a free port entity in Mauritius, IOML gets various tax breaks for operating from Mauritian ports for exports to Africa.

---

[12] Joshi, Rakesh Mohan, 'Without Connectivity an Airline Cannot Prosper', *Weekly L'Express*, Mauritius, 2 March 2012.

[13] Based on Trade Map, 2013.

[14] 'Indian Oil Plans Fresh Investment in Mauritius: Eyes Africa', *Deccan Herald*, 26 May 26 2013.

Lanka IOC Pvt. Ltd (LIOC) India is the largest source of imports to Sri Lanka accounting for 19.7 per cent of its total imports,[15] whereas India had been the country's third largest export market with a share of 6.4 per cent. Moreover, geographical, cultural, and political proximity made Sri Lanka a natural choice for IOCL's international expansion.

IOC formed a wholly owned subsidiary in Sri Lanka, known as Lanka IOC Pvt. Ltd (LIOC) in 2002. In order to facilitate operations of LIOC, the government of Sri Lanka has extended the following concessions:

- A tripartite agreement signed between the Sri Lankan government, CPC, and LIOC guarantees that only three retail players (including CPC and LIOC) will operate in the Sri Lankan market for the next five years.
- LIOC has also been allowed income tax exemption for 10 years from the date of commencement of operations and a concessional tax of 15 per cent thereafter against the prevailing rate of 35 per cent.
- The Indian Oil subsidiary has also been granted customs duty exemption for import of project-related plant, machinery, and equipment during the project implementation period of five years, besides free transfer of dividend/income to India.

Lanka IOC is involved in importing, blending, distribution, and selling of petroleum products and bunkering in Sri Lanka. It holds one third share in Ceylon Petroleum Storage Terminals Ltd, the common user facility in Sri Lanka for storage and distribution of petroleum products. It acquired China Bay tank-farm, which is the largest tank-farm located between the Middle East and Singapore, and is of high historic and strategic significance since it connects to Trincomalee harbour.

LIOC is the only privately owned company besides the state-owned Ceylon Petroleum Corporation (CPC) that operates retail petrol stations in Sri Lanka. Over the years, the company has developed a very efficient marketing distribution network, owning over 150 petrol and diesel stations in the island country. LIOC took over 100 retail outlets owned by Ceylon Petroleum Corporation in February 2003. Subsequently, it also took over 59 dealer owned franchise retail outlets. Lanka IOC is ranked number one among the island nation's leading listed companies.

IOC Middle East FZE India is the largest source of imports to UAE accounting for 17.8 per cent of its total imports[16] whereas India has been the country's second largest export market with a share of 19 per cent. As UAE is among the largest markets for most Indian products, IOC entered this market by forming a wholly owned subsidiary, IOC Middle East FZE in 2006 with an objective to market SERVO lubricants and other petroleum products in the Middle East, Africa, and CIS region. Besides UAE, lubricants are being marketed in Oman, Bahrain, Qatar, Yemen, Nepal, etc. through IOC Middle East FZE.

IOC Sweden AB With a strategic intent to promote and facilitate overseas exploration and production investments, IOC incorporated a wholly owned subsidiary, IOC Sweden AB in 2010. The Swedish subsidiary acquired 3.5 per cent stake in the heavy oil project, Carabobo, in Venezuela along with five other international oil companies. Production of oil from the Carabobo project commenced in December 2012 and it is expected be about 2–3 million barrels during 2013 wherein IOC is likely to have about 95,000 barrels.

IOCL (USA) Inc. To invest in shale gas projects in the USA, a wholly owned subsidiary IOCL (USA) Inc. was formed in the USA in 2012. The subsidiary acquired 10 per cent stake in a Texas-based company, Carrizo Oil and Gas Inc, in its liquid-rich shale assets in Denever-Julesburg basin in Colorado along with Oil India Ltd that also acquired 20 per cent assets. With the US acquisition, the company has a strategic intent to enter the American region especially in upstream exploration.

The world's major oil producing countries witnessed considerable geopolitical and economic upheavals that have led to increased uncertainty and risks especially for countries having high level of import dependence that too with little flexibility owing to rising demand on one hand and limited capability to enhance their indigenous production on the other. In view of the emerging global scenario, IOC's expansion in international markets is not only of strategic significance but is likely to have long-term implications both for the company and energy security needs of India as a country.

Questions

1. Identify the main reasons behind Indian Oil Corporation's (IOC) entry into international markets.
2. IOC has adopted a mix of entry modes for approaching international markets. Critically evaluate the factors affecting IOC's selection of these entry modes.
3. Find out the reasons for IOC's entry into Mauritius and UAE by forming wholly owned subsidiaries. Identify similarities and differences in the marketing objectives and strategies of the company in the two countries.
4. In view of the emerging economic-political scenario, evaluate IOC's entry into Sri Lanka as a wholly owned subsidiary.
5. Critically evaluate IOC's entry strategy in Sweden and the USA as wholly owned subsidiaries.

---

[15] Based on Trade Map, 2013.
[16] Based on Trade Map, 2013.

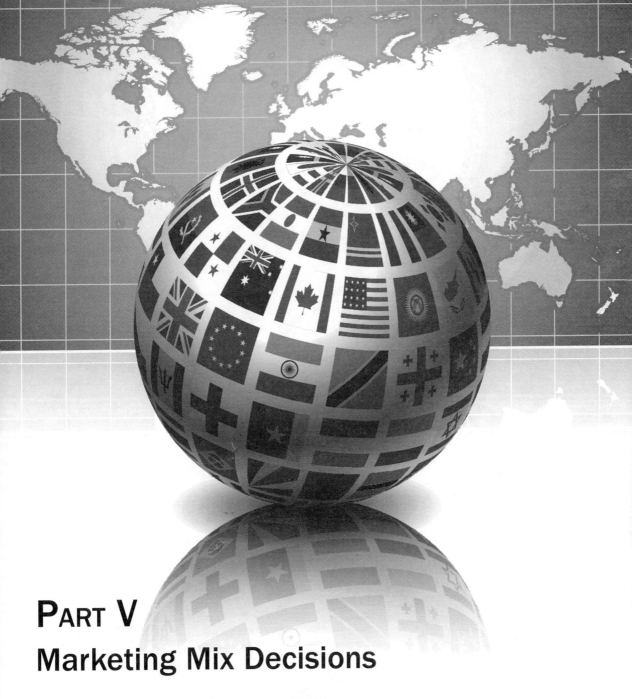

PART V
Marketing Mix Decisions

Product Strategy for International Markets

INTRODUCTION

Product decisions are crucial to a firm's success in international markets as the basic purpose of any marketing activity revolves around satisfying the customers' needs in a superior manner vis-à-vis competitors. Perceptions and expectations about products differ to a varied extent across countries, as already discussed in Chapter 5, which makes decision-making about products much more complex in international markets. This chapter brings out the concept of a product and the implications of product decisions in international markets.

A product is anything that can be offered to a market[1] to satisfy a want or need. Products that are marketed include physical goods, services, experiences, events, persons, places, properties, organizations, information, and ideas. The following components form an integral part of a product.

Core component   The core benefit or the problem-solving services offered by the product

Packaging component   The features, quality, design, packaging, branding, and other attributes integral to a product's core benefit

Augmented component   Support services and other augmented components, such as warrantees, guarantees, and after-sales service

A firm operating in international markets should not only identify the products for various markets but should also evolve suitable strategies for developing such products. Whether a single standardized product can be offered worldwide or a customized product needs to be developed for each market is the most significant product decision that a firm has to make while operating in international markets. This chapter examines the factors

Learning Objectives

- To elucidate the concept of product decisions for international markets
- To discuss product standardization versus adaptation in international markets
- To describe the quality, packaging, and labelling decisions in international markets
- To explicate the process of new product launch and diffusion in international markets
- To examine international product-promotion strategies
- To examine the concept of international product life cycle (IPLC)

---

[1] Philip, Kotler, *Marketing Management*, 11th Edition, 2002, Prentice Hall, New Delhi, p. 407.

that influence the product decision to market standardized versus customized products. In international markets, decisions related to quality, packaging, and labelling of products require special attention and consideration. Product diffusion in international markets is often influenced by cultural context, as is discussed in this chapter. A new product may be launched in international markets either sequentially or simultaneously, which is also discussed at length in this chapter. The patterns of demand in international markets exhibit cyclical variations, which are explained in the section on the concept of international product life cycle. The international competitive posture matrix in terms of product strength and geographical expansion can be used as a tool for determining international product strategies. Various alternatives related to product promotion strategies in international markets are also dealt with in this chapter.

IDENTIFICATION OF PRODUCTS FOR INTERNATIONAL MARKETS

The firm has to carry out preliminary screening, that is, identification of markets and products by conducting market research. The consumption patterns of a country often provide an idea of its product requirements. One can also use a preliminary trade analysis on six digit HS (ITC) code to find out the products exported and imported and trade balance can be used to assess a country's product demand. Besides, the supplying countries, their export volumes, unit value realization for the products supplied provide useful insight into competitors. Once the target country and the products to be marketed is identified, as explained in Chapters 6, 7, and 8, a detailed evaluation of consumption pattern in the targeted market needs to be made.

A poorly conceived product often leads to marketing failures. It was not a smooth sailing in the Indian market for a number of transnational food companies after the initial short-lived euphoria among Indian consumers. Kellogg's, Pizza Hut, McDonald's, and Domino's Pizza have all run into trouble in the Indian market at one point of time or the other. The basic mistakes that these firms made were as follows:

Gross overestimation of spending patterns of Indian consumers Despite the ability to buy products, while spending, the customers in South Asia are very cautious and selective. They look for value for money in their purchase decisions far more than their Western counterparts do.

Gross overestimation of the strength of their transnational brands These MNCs estimated their brand image very high in the international markets and the globalization of markets was considered to be a very potent factor for getting a large number of customers for their products, as happened in African and other East Asian countries.

Gross underestimation of the strength of ethnic Indian products As Indian food is traditionally prepared on a small scale, and mass manufacturing and organized mass marketing of Indian products was missing, it was wrongly believed that the food products manufactured by the multinationals would change the traditional eating habits of the Indian consumers. They failed to recognize the variety and strength of ethnic Indian food. India is not only the largest producer of milk in the world[2] with an 11 million metric ton output, that is, about 22 million tons ahead of the USA, but also home to hundreds of varieties of sweets.

---

[2] Joshi, Rakesh Mohan, 'India in Relation to Emerging International Dairy Trade, Souvenir', *Indian Dairying: Prospects 2020*, New Delhi, February 2012, pp. 3–17.

DEVELOPING PRODUCTS FOR INTERNATIONAL MARKETS

Various approaches followed for developing products for international markets are as follows.

Ethnocentric Approach

This approach is based on the assumption that consumer needs and market conditions in foreign markets are more or less similar to domestic markets. Such firms market their products that are primarily developed for the home market with little adaptation to international markets.

Generally, companies with ethnocentric orientation attempt to market their products in countries where the demand is similar to the domestic market or the indigenous products are acceptable to the consumers in those markets. For instance, a number of Indian products sold abroad, such as garments like salwar kurtas and *sarees*, food items, such as dosa mix, idli mix, *vada* mix, *sambhar* mix, *gulab jamun* mix, *papad*, and Indian sweets, primarily target the ethnic Indian population. Trade statistics also reveal that these products find major markets, such as Dubai, Singapore, London, and Canada, which have a sizeable ethnic Indian or South Asian population. This marketing strategy can be used in South Asian markets as well, where consumer tastes and preferences resemble to a large extent.

Such market extension approach of product development facilitates cost minimization in various functional areas facilitating a firm to gain rapid entry into international markets. However, the ethnocentric approach does not always lead to maximization of market share and profits in international markets since the local competitors are in a relatively better position to satisfy consumers' needs.

Polycentric Approach

Contrary to ethnocentric, the polycentric approach recognizes cross-cultural differences in the target countries and therefore, is strongly market-oriented. An international firm is aware of the fact that each country market is significantly different from the other. It, therefore, adopts separate approaches for different markets. In a polycentric approach, products are developed separately for different markets to suit local marketing conditions.

The HSBC Bank, with its network in six continents, advertises worldwide with the punchline 'the world's local bank'. The bank focuses on the cultural differences between countries. HSBC's classic advertisement campaign reveals that body tattoos are considered to be trendy in the East, whereas colourful, glittery *mehendi* is a popular tradition in India. On the other hand, Indian *mehendi* seems trendy to the Western world, whereas body tattoos are considered traditional. Similarly, contrary perceptions do prevail among cultures in different parts of the world about the medicinal effects of traditional herbs and modern allopathic drugs. Thus, HSBC lays emphasis on the importance of local knowledge and market differences. It makes adaptation of products offered and marketing strategies used across the countries employing polycentric approach.

Regiocentric Approach

Once an international firm establishes itself in various markets the world over, it attempts to consolidate its gains and tries to ascertain product similarity within market clusters. Generally, such market clusters are based on geographical and psychic proximity.

All Muslims are expected to consume only halal meat and abstain from pork. Therefore, restaurants and hotels in the Islamic countries prominently highlight in their marketing communication the fact that they serve only halal meat. Islamic countries also require a certificate from exporting countries along with meat consignments certifying that the meat is halal. India's second largest manufacturer of hard gelatine capsules, Medi-Caps Limited (MCL), an ISO 9002 certified

Fig. 10.1   McDonald's serves only halal menu in Islamic countries

Source: McDonald's.

company with an annual capacity of 3,500 million capsules, has a turnover of over ₹200 million. For Muslim consumers, availability of genuine halal products is a very sensitive issue in food and pharmaceutical products. Suppliers of genuine halal products are limited. In order to cater to Islamic markets, Medi-Caps manufactures Hala-Caps especially for Muslims[3] across the world. The Muslim community traditionally consumes only animals of bovine sources, slaughtered according to Islamic procedure (Shariah). Since gelatine is derived from animals, Muslims have to ensure that these are not just halal, but also slaughtered accordingly. Medi-Caps manufactures Hala-Caps only from halal gelatine procured from Halagel, Malaysia. Moreover, Medi-Caps also gets certifications of genuine halal process from the Islamic Development Department of Malaysia, and halal certificates from Majelis Ulama Indonesia (MUI), the Islamic Central Committee of Thailand (ICCT). Besides, the process of manufacturing the halal gelatine capsules has also been certified by the Jamiat Ulama-e-Maharashtra. The company has witnessed considerable success in marketing its halal products in Islamic countries, especially in the Middle East.

McDonald's strategy (Fig. 10.1) to not serve pork and to slaughter animals through the halal process is followed only in the Middle East or Muslim-dominated countries and can be termed as regiocentric.

Geocentric Approach

Instead of extending the domestic products into international markets, a firm tries to identify similarities in consumption patterns that can be targeted with a standard product around the world.

---

[3] Basu, Sirshendu, 'Halal Gelatin Capsules' in *Product Brochure*, Medi-Caps Limited, 2012.

Psychographic segmentation is often helpful in identifying consumer profiles beyond national borders. In a geocentric approach to product development, there is a high degree of centralization and coordination of marketing and production activities, resulting in higher economies of scale in the various constituents of the marketing mix. However, it needs meticulous and consistent researching of international markets.

The *Harry Potter* series of books is a classic example of geocentric orientation, wherein the author J.K. Rowling has brought out a series of fictions appealing to global readers, and marketed it globally using a highly integrated marketing strategy.

PRODUCT STANDARDIZATION VS ADAPTATION IN INTERNATIONAL MARKETS

A firm operating in international markets has to make a crucial decision about whether it sells a uniform product across countries, or customizes products in view of individual market requirements. Although no readymade solution can be prescribed for the decision to standardize or adapt a product in international markets, firms are required to carry out a careful cost-benefit analysis before arriving at a decision. The cost incurred in product adaptation should justify the benefits achieved, such as increase in total sales, market share, and higher price realization. It has been observed that most firms attempt to project a uniform product image across global markets but often customize the perceived value of the product to suit the target market customers. While retaining its brand name as common, firms attempt to customize the augmented product components, such as features, packaging, and labelling. Support service components, including warrantees, guarantees, delivery schedule, installation, and payment terms are most often adapted to suit the needs of the target market.

Generally, industrial products and services are insensitive to cross-country preferences and may be marketed as standardized products, whereas foods, trends, fashions, and styles are highly sensitive, and customer preferences for these items vary widely among markets. Such products often require a much higher level of customization.

Product Standardization

Product standardization refers to marketing a product in the overseas markets with little change except for some cosmetic changes such as modifying packaging and labelling. Generally, products with high technological intensity such as heavy equipment, plants and machinery, microprocessors, hard disks, and projectors are marketed as standardized products across the world. Some of the consumer products with global appeal, namely Big Mac, Coke, Budweiser, Heineken, etc., are also marketed as globally standardized products. The benefits associated with using standardized products in international markets include the following:

- Projecting a global product image
- Catering to the global customers moving across countries
- Cost savings in terms of economies of scale in production
- Economy in designing and monitoring various components of the marketing mix
- Facilitates in developing the product as a global brand

Major factors favouring product standardization

High level of technology-intensity   Products with high-technology content are marketed as standardized products to maintain uniform international standards and reduce confusion across international markets. Besides, using standard specifications facilitates product compatibility internationally. For instance, computer servers, micro- and macro-processors, value added networks (VAN), etc. are marketed worldwide as standard products.

Fig. 10.2   Perfume marketers often emphasize on its 'Paris' origin so as to create a high-end user imagery

Source: www.ysl.com; www.bourjois.fr; www.yvesdorgeval.com, all accessed on 21 October 2010.

Formidable adaptation costs   The nature of product and market size determines the cost of adaptation that may be too high to recover. A number of foreign books and motion pictures are primarily sold as standardized products worldwide. Only a few books written in the foreign context are adapted or even translated due to prohibitive adoption costs that are difficult to recover.

Convergence of customer needs worldwide   Customers in diverse country markets increasingly exhibit convergence of their needs and preferences, resulting into growing psychographic market segments across the borders. It has resulted in an increase in demand for similar goods across the world. Products such as Levi's jeans, MTV, and McDonald's have become increasingly popular among international consumers as a result of growing convergence worldwide. Besides, the rapid growth of transport and telecommunication has resulted in increase in transnational travel among people who exhibit similar tastes and preferences across the markets.

Country-of-origin (CoO) impact   Customers' perception of products differs on the basis of the country of their origin. For instance, consumer electronic durables from Japan, fashion designs from Italy, fragrances from France (Fig. 10.2), instruments from Germany, computer software from India, and herbal products from China and India are perceived to be superior in quality and fetch a premium price in international markets. The international firms attempt to retain their CoO image and market, at least the augmented product, with little customization.

Product Adaptation

Making changes in the product in response to the needs of the target market is termed as product adaptation or customization. In view of local consumption requirements, the product for international market is often customized. The adaptation of a product may vary from major modifications in the product itself to minor alterations in its packaging, logo, or brand name. A thorough market research needs to be conducted so as to identify the customers' requirements in the target market. Customizing products for international markets offers a number of benefits, as follows:

- It enables a firm to tap markets that are not accessible due to mandatory requirements.
- It competitively fulfils the needs and expectations of customers in varied cultures and environments.
- It helps in gaining market share.
- It increases sales leading to economies of scale.

The secret of the success of Japanese goods in international markets lies in the capacity of Japanese manufacturers to develop a thorough understanding of customer demand in its target market and customizing products accordingly. In recent years, China emerged as the global hub to manufacture goods to suit diverse needs and preferences of the customers in different countries (Exhibit 10.1).

Mandatory Factors Influencing Product Adaptation

Product adaptation includes mandatory product modifications that a firm has to carry out in international markets, not as a matter of choice but compulsion. The major factors influencing product modification are as follows.

Government regulations   A firm needs to adapt its products in various markets in order to comply with government regulations. The differing quality specifications in different markets also require marketers to follow up the quality norms, such as approval by the Food and Drug Administration (FDA) for marketing a product in the USA, or following codex standards for European Union. The ban on the use of azo-dyes in Europe requires use of natural dyes in all products. Maps are a sensitive issue all over the world and the exporting company needs to follow the regulations of the importing country. Toy-globes made in China that depicted the northern territory of Kashmir in a different colour than the rest of India were found offensive by an Indian court, and their imports were banned.[4]

The product standards in target markets have caused Indian exporters to modify their production process to meet regulatory requirements. For instance, in the early 1980s, Indian shipments of marine products were detained on account of salmonella contamination. Production methods had to be changed quickly to meet importers' standards. A ban on pentachlorophenol (PCP), a fungicide used by the leather industry that was initiated by Germany, resulted in a short-term setback for Indian leather exports.[5] The Indian leather industry had to go through dramatic alternations in its changeover to substitute chemicals, and these PCP substitutes were roughly 10 times costlier.[6]

Standards for electric current   The electric current standards also vary from country to country. In India, the standard electric current supply is 220 volts with a frequency of 50 Hz, while the values in the USA are 110–120 volts with 60 Hz. Electrical equipment need to be modified for use in the target countries, depending upon the prevailing electrical standards.

Operating systems   Differences in operating systems influence the product designs that need to be adapted to suit the target market. In India, China, UK, Singapore, Pakistan, UAE, and Tanzania, televisions operate on Phase Alternating Lines (PAL) while in the USA, Japan, Philippines, and South Korea they work on National Television Systems Committee (NTSC) standards. Televisions operate on System Electrique Pour Couleur Avec Mémoire (SECAM) in France, Vietnam, Russia, and Mauritius. Therefore, a television operating on PAL System in India is unsuitable in countries that have different operating systems, such as the USA, Japan, and France. Thus, in order to market televisions in countries with incompatible operating systems, suitable adaptations are mandatory.

---

[4] 'India Court Bans Kashmir Globes', *BBC News*, 11 November 2004.

[5] Vasantha, Bharucha, 'The Impact of Environmental Standards and Regulations Set in Foreign Markets on India's Exports', *Trade Environment and Sustainable Development: A South Asian Perspective*, Macmillan, London, 1999.

[6] Mattoo, Aditya and Robert M. Stern (eds), *India and the WTO*, World Bank and Oxford University Press, New York, 2003, p. 313.

Exhibit 10.1   Chinese firms: the masters in product adaptation

Chinese firms have become masters in product adaptation that cater to the varied needs of customers' tastes and preferences in various parts of the world. Gifts and souvenirs 'made in China' accounted for a lion's share of 627 items out of nearly 900 items sold on the London Olympics 2012 website. This included Olympic mascots Wenlock, Mandeville, and Pride the Lion, besides models of London buses and taxies, emblazoned with the Union Jack. The host country for Olympics 2012 accounted only for 16 per cent of the gifts sold. One can easy find 'made in China' key-chains, purses, T-shirts, other apparels, toys, and even replicas of local monuments across the world (Fig. 10.3). International travellers often come across Chinese souvenirs and gifts at airports, historical monuments and tourist places, irrespective of which part of the world they are.

The product adaptation by Chinese manufacturers and marketers is exemplary. 'Made in China' idols of Hindu gods and goddesses in all shapes, colours, and sizes, even with fitted electronic gadgets and pre-recorded devotional music in most Indian languages apart from Hindi and Sanskrit, swamp the Indian markets during festive seasons. Idols of god Ganesha made in China during the Ganpati festival in Maharashtra, goddess Durga during the Puja festival in West Bengal, and goddess Lakshmi and a host of other Indian deities during Diwali are a common sight. Moreover, these are far more attractive and cost-effective than their traditional counterparts.

The modus-operandi of Chinese manufactures is to send a team of experts to the target market who pick up the locally-made items which are in high demand, either during festival season or otherwise. The Chinese visiting team takes back a variety of samples of locally manufactured popular products. Extensive innovations are made by the Chinese manufacturers and similar products are manufactured in bulk and sold in foreign markets at much lower rates than the domestically manufactured products. To illustrate, a few years back, a team of Chinese experts visited Mumbai to pick up specimens of clay Ganesha idols. Back in China, the team manufactured idols in different materials, such as papier-mache, plastic, fibre, and glass, and innovated them with the latest electronic technology. The Chinese idols looked far more attractive and life-like, and at the same time were cheaper too.

Consumer durables made in China of the value of over ₹1 million are sold every day in India. Goods made in China have established a vast retail network all over India down to the remotest villages without the help of media hype or publicity campaigns. Concerns about quality and adverse impact on indigenous manufacturing industries hardly deter Indian consumers and the market intermediaries from falling in love with Chinese goods. The customer is delighted to get Western-styled goods at much lower costs. Besides, such goods are available in wide ranges and the compromise in quality hardly impacts the customer. On the other hand, the rapid influx of low-cost Chinese goods has created considerable concern among manufacturers across the world.

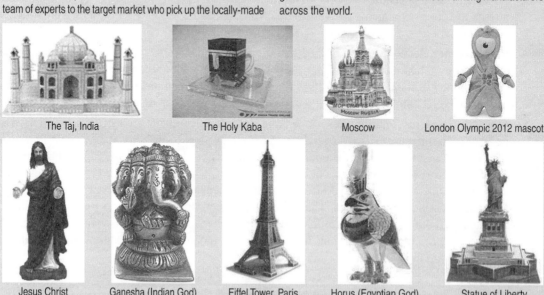

| The Taj, India | The Holy Kaba | Moscow | London Olympic 2012 mascot |

| Jesus Christ | Ganesha (Indian God) | Eiffel Tower, Paris | Horus (Egyptian God) | Statue of Liberty |

Fig. 10.3   Exceptional agility in product adaptation facilitated 'Made in China' products to flood the gifts and souvenir markets worldwide

Source: 'Olympic Fury as 84% Gifts Made Abroad', *The Sun*, London, 9 April 2012; 'Made in China, Sold in India', *Business Economics*, 1–15 October, 2006, pp. 27–31; 'Guru Nanak Looks Chinese in China-made Idols, *The Times of India*, 13 August 2007.

Measurement systems   Product design is influenced by the measurement systems followed in a country. India follows the metric system with kilograms, metre, or litre as measurement units, whereas the USA follows the imperial system of measurement using pound, feet, and gallons. Therefore, the packaging size, weights, and measures of the product need to be modified, depending upon the measurement system followed in the target market.

Packaging and labelling regulations   Each country prescribes separate regulations for packaging and labelling, which have to be adhered to by an international marketing firm. Due to the sensitive vegetarianism issue, regulations in India require food packages to exhibit a mark, that is, vegetarian or non-vegetarian, so as to explicitly inform the consumers about their contents. Most countries in the Middle East emphasize the use of Arabic. Similar linguistic regulations are also required in a number of European countries. In India, food products generally bear the duration for use of a product. In most developed countries, the date of expiry is also mentioned explicitly. Even regulations requiring magazines to display the date after which they should not remain on bookstands are not uncommon in a number of high-income countries.

Voluntary factors influencing product adaptation

Product modifications that are not compulsory but based on the international marketer's own decision to meet the marketing challenges competitively are known as voluntary factors. The major factors influencing product adaptation by exporters' own choices in the international market are as follows.

Culture   Cultural factors such as local tastes, traditions, and religious beliefs considerably affect the product decisions for international markets, as discussed in detail in Chapter 5. However, the sensitivity to culture varies with product categories. Food items and clothing are generally more sensitive to culture, whereas products with high technical intensity such as software, electronic goods, plant, and machinery are hardly sensitive.

Women's apparel designed for customers in the Middle East are likely to get little attention in European markets. In another instance, camera sales in Saudi Arabia were historically low. Sales boomed with the advent of Polaroid instant photography as this allowed Arab men to photograph their wives and daughters in the privacy of their homes without the need of strangers handling the film in a processing lab. In Arabian countries, the dolls Sara and Leila that compete with Barbie have brother dolls and not boyfriend dolls as counterparts, as the concept of having a boyfriend is not acceptable to Islamic families.

Traditional Indian products, such as the *saree,* the salwar kurta, and Indian ethnic foodstuff are exported to the international markets that have sizeable Indian ethnic populations. Similarly, Chinese foodstuff, goods of worship, and Chinese traditional medicinal and herbal products find easy market in countries with sizeable population of ethnic Chinese, especially in East Asian countries.

The leading fast food giant McDonald's serves a variety of customized products in different markets to satisfy customers' needs and expectations (Fig. 10.4). It serves *hamburgers* in the USA, *chicken tatsuta, teriyaki chicken,* and *teriyaki McBurger* in Japan, and has replaced its traditional *Big Mac* with the *Maharaja Mac* in India. Despite its image of a family restaurant, McDonald's serves beer as well as *McCroissants* in Germany. In New Zealand, McDonald's serves its *Kiwiburger* with beetroot sauce and an optional apricot pie. In Singapore, it serves fries with chilli sauce besides chicken rice. It also uses vegetable oil in food preparation in the Singapore market. The Dutch veggie burger, made of spiced potatoes, peas, carrots, and onions is served in the Dutch market. *McPalta*, made from avocados in Chile, curry potato pie, shake fries, red bean sundae in Hong Kong, and a variety of salads featuring Mediterranean flavours in Italy, reflect careful product adaptation by McDonald's to address the varied needs of international customers.

Vegetarian burger (India)

Maharaja Mac (India)

Aloo Tikki burger (India)

McArabia (Middle East)

The Big Mac (Global)

Mega Teriyaki (Japan)

Farm fresh chicken burger (China)

Beef burger (Spain)

Rice burger (Philippines)

Fig. 10.4   Product adaptation by McDonald's in international markets

Source: McDonald's.

As Jewish law forbids cooking, serving, or eating meat and milk products together, in Jerusalem, McDonald's has both kosher and non-kosher restaurants. The kosher restaurants of McDonald's do not have milkshakes, ice creams, and cheeseburgers. McDonald's serves beer and wine in some countries, such as France, UK, Germany, and Brazil. The McDonald's in Brazil has a 'happy hours' with a salsa band playing. It offers soup and fried rice to cater to Japanese eating habits as well.

Table 10.1   The evolution of Gillette blades

Product	Year introduced
• Gillette manufactures first safety razor with disposable blades	1903
• Blue blade	1932
• Thin blade	1938
• Super blue blade	1960
• Coated super stainless steel blade	1963
• Platinum-plus blade with platinum chromium coating	1969
• Trac II, world's first twin blade shaving system	1971
• Good News, first twin blade disposable razor	1976
• ATRA, first razor with a pivotal head	1977
• ATRA Plus, first razor with a lubricating strip	1985
• Good News Plus, first disposable razor with a lubricating strip	1985
• Sensor, first razor with spring mounted twin blades	1989
• Sensor Excel, with five flexible microfins	1994
• MACH3, first triple-blade shaving system	1998
• MACH3 Turbo, with 10 micro-fins and a lubrication strip	2001
• Sensor, triple-bladed disposable razor	2003
• Sensor 3, refillable triple-bladed razor	2004
• Gillette Fusion, a Five blade razor	2005
• Gillette Fusion ProGlide razor and power shaving systems	2010

10 micro-fins and a lubrication strip in 2001. Triple-bladed disposable razor was introduced in 2003 in Sensor and made refillable in 2004. Gillette introduced a five-blade razor, Fusion in 2005 which was upgraded to Gillette Fusion ProGlide razor and power shaving systems in 2010, each of the subsequent products claiming to offer a better shaving experience than earlier. Similar strategies of replacing one's own products with a superior product have also been followed by manufacturers of computer hardware, such as micro-processors, macro-processors, hard disks, and computer memory.

Depending upon the market and product attributes, a firm may adapt one of the following strategies for launching its products in international markets.

Waterfall Approach

Under this approach, the products trickle down in the international markets in a cascading manner, as depicted in Fig. 10.7, and are launched in a sequential manner. In the waterfall approach, generally a longer duration is available for a product to customize in a foreign market before it is launched in another market. This strategy had long been followed in international marketing. It took a long time for a number of firms, which are now global, to launch their products in international markets. For instance, it took almost 22 years for McDonald's to market outside the USA, whereas Coca-Cola took about 20 years and Marlboro about 35 years to market overseas.

The waterfall approach is generally more suitable for firms that have limited resources and find it difficult to manage multiple markets simultaneously. In case the size of the target market and its growth potential are not sufficient to commit its resources, product launch may be carried out in a phased manner.

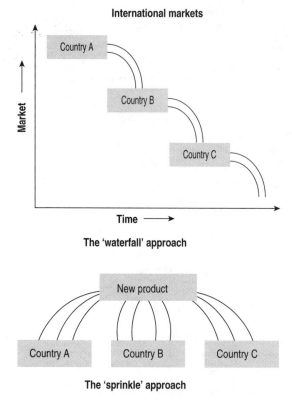

Fig. 10.7 Product launch approaches for international markets

Sprinkler Approach

Under this approach, the product is simultaneously launched in various countries. The sprinkler approach of simultaneous market entry is preferred under the following circumstances:

- The competitive intensity of the market is very high with strong and fierce competitors.
- The life cycle of the product is relatively short.
- The markets have high potential such as
  - large market size;
  - rapid growth; and
  - relatively less cost of entry.
- The firm has large resources to manage simultaneous product launch in multiple markets.

Firms catering to international markets are increasingly segmenting markets on the basis of the psychographic profiles of their customers. Such market segments extend beyond national borders and need to be approached at the same time. In case of luxury consumer goods wherein the fashion trends rapidly change across international markets, simultaneous product launch is preferred. IT software like Microsoft products are launched across the world simultaneously as there is no time lag between markets. Growing competitive pressure in international markets and the decreasing market gap has encouraged simultaneous product launch.

---

[8] Wills, J.I., A.C. Samli, and L. Jacobs, 'Developing Global Products and Marketing Strategies: A Construct and a Reach Agenda', *Journal of the Academy of Marketing Science*, vol. 19, Winter 1991, pp. 1–10.

NEW PRODUCT DIFFUSION IN INTERNATIONAL MARKETS

New product diffusion is the process by which innovations spread throughout a social system over time. The rate of product diffusion is influenced significantly by the cultural contexts,[8] as depicted in Fig. 10.8. Among the countries with high context culture, the new product diffusion is faster in Japan and Southeast Asian countries compared to India and the rest of Asia. The USA, Canada, and the Scandinavian countries have a faster rate of new product diffusion among the low context countries as compared to the UK and Eastern Europe. While designing new product launch strategies, a firm should take care of the cross-cultural differences (Fig. 10.8).

Diffusion rate	
High context/Fast diffusion South-east Asia Japan	**High context/Slow diffusion** India Asia
Low context/Fast diffusion Scandinavia USA Canada	**Low context/Slow diffusion** UK Eastern Europe

Fig. 10.8   Interrelationship between cultural context and diffusion

Source: Wills, J.I., A.C. Samli, and L. Jacobs, 'Developing Global Products and Marketing Strategies; A Construct and a Reach Agenda', *Journal of the Academy of Marketing Science*, vol. 19, Winter 1991, pp. 1–10.

It has been observed that in the Oriental countries, the response patterns of the consumers differ widely as compared to their counterparts in the West. Under the influence of the peer group, the customers are cautious while buying new products, which leads to a slight delay in new product diffusion as compared to Western markets. Similarly, at the maturity stage of the product in Oriental countries, consumers discontinue the product use at a relatively rapid pace. It calls for significant adjustments in product launch strategies in international markets.

CONCEPT OF INTERNATIONAL PRODUCT LIFE CYCLE THEORY

International markets tend to follow a cyclical pattern[9] due to a variety of factors over a period of time, which explains the shifting of markets as well as location of production. The level of innovation and technology, resources, size of market, and competitive structure influence the trade patterns. In addition, the gap in technology, preference, and ability of the customers in international markets also determine the stage of international product life cycle (IPLC) (Exhibit 10.4).

In case the innovating country has a large market size, as in case of the USA, India, China, etc., it can support mass production or domestic sales. This mass market also facilitates the producers based in these countries to achieve cost efficiency, which enables them to become internationally competitive. However, in case the market size of a country is too small to achieve economies of

---

[9] Vernon, Raymond, 'International Investment and International Trade in Product Life Cycle', *Quarterly Journal of Economics*, May 1996, p. 199.

Exhibit 10.4 Stages of IPLC

	IPLC stages			
	Introduction	**Growth**	**Maturity**	**Decline**
Production	In country of innovation due to • availability of technical know-how • manpower • frequent product modifications	In innovating and other developed countries	Multiple locations	Mainly in developing countries
Pricing strategy	Products marketed at premium prices in other countries	Beginning of price competition and competition determines prices	Product differentiation pricing	Intense competition base
Product attributes	Emphasis on customer feedback and frequent modification of product	Standardization of product attributes	Emphasis on creating product differentiation. Innovating company Establishes production in other developed countries to face local competition	Product attributes get well established and offered by several competitors
Marketing strategy	Marketed primarily in home country; beginning of exports to other developed countries	Export grows to other developed countries and some developing countries	The innovating company begins marketing from its production in other bases developed countries	Market develops in other developing and least developed countries besides, other firms marketing from developed countries

scale from the domestic market, the companies from these countries can alternatively achieve economies of scale by setting up their marketing and production facilities in other cost-effective locations. Thus, it is the economies of scope that assists in achieving the economies of scale by expanding into international markets.

The theory explains the variations and reasons for change in production and consumption pattern among various markets over a time period as depicted in Fig. 10.9. The IPLC has the following four distinct (Exhibit 10.4) identifiable stages that influence demand structure, production, marketing strategy, and international competition as follows.

Stage 1: Introduction   Generally, it is high-income or developed countries wherein majority of new product inventions take place. Since product invention requires substantial resources on R&D activities, which needs speedy recovery of initial cost incurred by way of market skimming pricing strategies. Since, in the initial stages, the price of a new product is relatively higher, it is only within the means and capabilities of the customers in high-income countries to buy the product. Therefore, a firm finds markets for new products in other developed countries in the initial stages.

Stage 2: Growth   The demand in the international markets exhibits an increasing trend and the innovating firm gets better opportunities for exports. Moreover, as the markets begin to develop in other developed countries, the innovating firm faces increased international competition in the target market. In order to defend its position in international markets, the firm establishes its production locations in other developed countries.

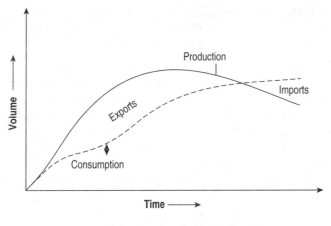

(a) Country of product innovation

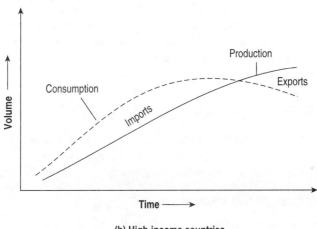

(b) High-income countries

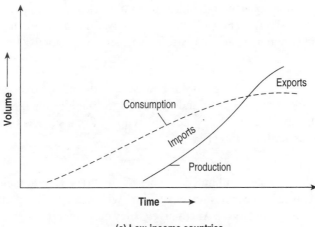

(c) Low-income countries

Fig. 10.9   The IPLC

Stage 3: Maturity As the technical know-how of innovative process becomes widely known, the firm begins to establish its operations in middle- and low-income countries in order to take advantage of resources available at competitive prices.

Stage 4: Decline The major thrust of marketing strategy at this stage shifts on price and cost competitiveness, as the technical know-how and skills become widely available. Therefore, the emphasis of the firm is on most cost-effective locations rather than producing themselves. Besides other developing countries, the production also intensifies in least developed countries. As a result, it has been observed that the innovating country begins to import such goods from other developing countries rather than manufacturing itself.

The UK, which was once the largest manufacturer and exporter of bicycles, now imports it in large volumes. Bicycles are at the declining stage of its life cycle in industrialized countries, whereas it was still at a growth or maturity stage in a number of developing countries. Besides, the chemical and hazardous industries are shifting from high-income countries to low-income countries as a part of their increasing concern on environmental issues exhibiting a cyclical pattern in international markets.

The firm may adopt the strategy of positioning its products at different stages of the life cycle in different countries. Although the product life cycle explains the emerging pattern of international markets, it has got its own limitations in the present marketing era with fast proliferation of market information, wherein products are launched more or less simultaneously in various markets to meet ever-growing market competition.

INTERNATIONAL PRODUCT STRATEGY

Competitive product strategy for operating in international markets may be explained making use of international competitive posture matrix. This matrix classifies firms under four categories depending upon their product strength and geographical coverage, as follows.

International Competitive Posture Matrix

The resources available with a firm for expansion of international markets and strengthening the product features are limited. Product strengthening is necessary to create and maintain a product's competitive position in the markets. At the same time, a firm has to peruse its geographical expansion so as to grab global opportunities and respond to competitors in international markets, as shown in Fig. 10.10. Accordingly, firms may be categorized as kings, barons, crusaders, and commoners and may use various strategic options.[10]

Kings

Firms with a strong product portfolio and wide geographic coverage are termed as kings. These firms have strong products and expanded geographic coverage. For an effective global strategy, such firms are in the best position. Global firms such as Coke, Pepsi, McDonald's, and Sony fall under this category.

Barons

Such companies operate in a limited number of countries. Due to their high product strength, geographical expansion becomes attractive. Firms with weak product portfolios in foreign markets tend to be their takeover targets. Alternatively, they may enter into some sort of strategic alliance

---

[10] Gogel, R. and J.C. Larreche, 'The Battlefield for 1992: Product Strength and Geographical Coverage', *European Journal of Management*, vol. 17, 1989, p. 289.

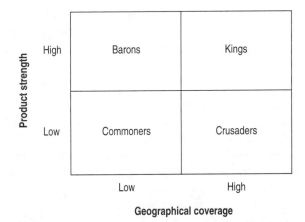

Fig. 10.10 The international competitive posture matrix

with such firms in foreign markets. Ispat International, founded in 1976 by Lakshmi Narayan Mittal of Indian origin focused on steel business, and set up a greenfield plant PT Ispat Indo at Indonesia. In 1989, the company became international by setting up its operations in Trinidad and Tobago. Thereafter, the company went into a buying spree and acquired a number of companies in America, Europe, Africa, and Asia. In 2004, it merged with LNM Group (also owned by Lakshmi Mittal) and International Steel Group to form Mittal Steel Company that became the largest steel company in the world. Mittal's quest for transnational acquisition did not stop here. In 2006, Mittal Steel went for the world's largest cross-border mergers and acquisitions (M&A) deal for US$32 billion by acquiring the world's second largest steel producer, Arcelor and became ArcelorMittal. Presently, the steel baron operates in 60 countries and employs about 2,60,000 people worldwide.

Crusaders

Despite a weak product base, these are the firms that expand globally. Such firms are highly prone to global competitors. Outsourcing, acquisition, or international product development is required by firms to consolidate their product portfolio in international markets.

Commoners

Firms with low product strength and limited geographical coverage are termed as commoners. Such firms sustain themselves in the domestic market or to a limited extent in the overseas markets due to protectionist regulations that act as barriers to free market competition. Generally, their expansion in overseas markets is opportunistic in nature. These firms need to strengthen their portfolios before expanding into international markets.

FRAMEWORK FOR PRODUCT-PROMOTION STRATEGIES FOR INTERNATIONAL MARKETS

The widely used method for international product strategies has primarily five alternatives.[11] It includes expansion into international markets without any change in the product, customizing the product or developing new products depending upon product function or need satisfied, and conditions of product used and buying ability of target customers.

---

[11] Keegan, Warren J., 'Multinational Product Planning: Strategic Alternatives', *Journal of Marketing*, January 1969, pp. 58–62.

Under the first four marketing situations, potential customers have the ability to purchase the product, while in the fifth option, the customers do not have the ability to buy. Based on this matrix, a firm has to select from the five strategic alternatives, which are as follows.

Straight Extension

In countries where the product function or needs satisfied and the condition of product use is the same, the straight or dual extension strategy is used. The soft drink firm Coca-Cola and Unilever for its Lux brand of soaps use the straight extension strategy in international markets. The same product is used with minor customization in marketing communication. The leading beer firm Heineken uses a standardized product and promotional approach (Fig. 10.11) the world over to maintain and communicate the uniform product quality of premium beer.

The straight adaptation of product and promotion strategies for global markets resulted in enormous cost savings for the firms on R&D for product development, market research, and

Fig. 10.11   Global standardized product and promotion by Heineken

Source: www.heineken.com

marketing communication. Besides, a continued approach also helped to create global awareness of the brands and customer base.

Product Extension–Promotion Adaptation

In markets where the product function and the needs satisfied are different but the conditions of product use are same, the product extension–promotion adaptation strategy is used. For instance, bicycles are cost-effective and affordable means of transport for the rural population in low-income countries, whereas it is the means for recreation and healthcare in high-income countries. Similarly, in low-income countries sewing machines are generally perceived as a means to economize the household expenditure on stitching, and are widely gifted in rural areas as a utility item, whereas in high-income countries, sewing machines are considered to be a recreational item. To tap the Indian customers' need for traditional styles and imagery, Reid & Taylor features the Bollywood icon Amitabh Bachhan in its promotional campaign in a typical Jodhpuri ethnic costume.

In India, chewing gum is viewed primarily as a children's product, whereas it is considered to be a substitute for smoking in the USA. It is supposed to provide dental benefits in Europe, while considered beneficial for facial fitness in Far Eastern countries. Under such situations, no changes are made in the product, whereas the promotional strategy is customized so as to address customers' needs.

Product Adaptation–Promotion Extension

In markets where the conditions of product use are different but the product performs the same function or satisfies the same needs, the strategy of product adaptation–promotion extension is employed. Around the world, detergent is primarily used for washing and cleaning clothes. Nevertheless, the washing habits of the people vary widely in various markets. Indian housewives use lukewarm water, whereas the French wash their cloths in scalding hot water and the Australians use cold water. Indians and the French generally use top-loading washing machines, while most Europeans use front-loading washing machines. The differences in electrical voltage require product modifications in electrical appliances marketed in countries such as India and the USA. Due to differences in TV operating systems, Japanese consumer electronics firms customize their products to market them in countries that do not use NTSC systems, namely India, Pakistan, the UK, the UAE, and Russia. Under such situations, the promotional strategy remains the same but the product modification is made depending upon the customers' need in different markets.

Dual Adaptation

In countries where the functions of the product and the needs satisfied are different and the conditions of the product use are also different, a firm has to customize both the product and the promotional strategies. Clothing in low-income countries serves the basic purpose of physical protection, whereas in high-income countries or even in urban centres of medium- and low-income countries, it symbolizes the personality and status of the user. Therefore, a firm has to customize both the product and its promotion.

Developing New Product

In markets where the product function and the need satisfied remain the same but the conditions of product use differ and the consumers do not possess the necessary ability to pay for the product, new product invention and development of new marketing communication are required. For instance, in countries with very low income, specifically in rural areas in Africa, Asia, and Latin America, the buying power of the people is limited. Therefore, firms have to develop technologies suitable to the target markets. The conditions in Africa necessitated the firms developing hand-powered washing machines for African markets. Philips India introduced a hand-wound radio in 2003, primarily to address the needs of rural India where the electricity supply is erratic and constant use of batteries makes the radio expensive. The product has done exceedingly well in the rural markets.[12]

In the aftermath of economic recession in the developed world, both MNCs and consumers across the world are hunting for value. Consumers even in developed markets are exhibiting a shift in their behaviour; there is a lifestyle change not to over-spend and to seek the same value at lower prices. So far, customers in developed countries were hardly given an option of low-cost products. The entire cost structure in developed markets prevented the customers from having access to product's price economically. Products designed and developed in emerging markets like India are finding their way to the rest of the world (Exhibit 10.5).

Exhibit 10.5   Products made in India for the world

Toyota Etios   The Japanese car-maker Toyota did not have small cars in its portfolio and was keen to have a product in the volume segment. Since major markets in Europe, the USA, and Japan were not growing much, the company kept a close watch on its Indian subsidiary Toyota Kirloskar. After examining several options from the company's current global portfolio, Toyota decided to build a car in India and take it to the rest of the world. And that is how Etios was born. Nearly 2,000 engineers from India and Japan were given a clear brief to make a good quality, low-cost car. They worked for over four years on developing the car. Most of the components were sourced from India. Etios was launched in the domestic market in early 2011, followed by Brazil in 2012, and thereafter, in South Africa and China.

Ford Figo   A thousand Ford engineers worked to build the Figo. It will be sold in 50 countries including Mexico, North Africa, and the Middle East. Ford follows a geocentric marketing strategy: One Ford, sell the same model, built the same way, in all the same markets. While this strategy helps reduce errors, it is a viable one as consumers the world over are coming closer, demanding the same standards of value, safety fuel efficiency and service. The strategy has helped keep costs 20–30 per cent low and improve quality. Since 2012, the auto major has started taking the India-made subcompact car to 50 new markets, including Mexico, North Africa, and West Asia.

Nokia's learn english application   The service, developed for the Indian market, has 6 million users worldwide. The application relates to the consumer in an intimate way—it teaches her conversational English in her mother tongue. When a consumer subscribes to the tools, she gets a word each day phonetically in her phone. This means, she is taught the structure of the word and how to pronounce it. The consumer

is also tested at the end of the course. The company is looking to take it to new consumers, such as the Hispanic population in the USA. It also plans to replicate its tie-up with IGNOU, the Indian universities primarily aimed at distance learning, globally. The next set of application may be in any language in any country.

HP's SiteOnMobile   The company's Indian research arm introduced a service that enables web access from low-end phones. It also worked on hand gestures for computer interfaces. HP plans to make this technology global.

Nestlé Maggi Masala-ae-Magic   The high-nutrient and low-cost variant of Maggi noodles, developed for the rural poor at ₹2 per pack in India and Pakistan, is on its way to Australia and New Zealand.

Pepsi Kurkure and Nimbooz   After tasting success in India, PepsiCo plans to launch these products globally. With these, it will reverse its process of innovating in emerging markets and distributing products in developed markets.

McDonald's Aloo Tikki Burger   With vegetarianism catching on globally, the market is ripe for Big Mac's very 'Indian' burger. There are plans to introduce the product across Europe and the Middle East.

KFC Krushers   The range of chilled drinks was developed in India with a unique combination of chocolate, cookie bits, coffee, dairy, and ice. KFC now plans to take it to other markets.

Tata Swach   The mass-market water purifier was initially meant for the Indian market, but will soon be exported to African countries with similar climatic conditions, and even the USA and UK.

---

[12] Sadagopan, S., 'Enter, Made for India Product', *The Economic Times*, 1 April 2004.

This framework of product-promotion strategies serves as a useful tool in developing broad understanding about the adaptation-standardization decisions related to product and promotion in international markets. However, firms need to make further evaluation of market situations before formulating their specific strategies.

As the basic purpose of any marketing activity is to satisfy the customers' needs in a superior manner vis-à-vis competitors, product decisions become vital for success in international markets. A firm has to carry out preliminary screening of the markets, and in-depth market research so as to find out the customers' expectations and needs before identifying products for international markets. The approach to product development for international markets may vary from ethnocentric, wherein the domestic product is extended to international markets, to polycentric, wherein products are customized individually for each market. Based on the cost-benefit analysis, a firm has to decide upon the extent of product customization needed for international markets. The support service and augmented component of the product are often more adapted as compared to the core component of a product. Product standardization facilitates higher economies of scale in production and various components of marketing mix, besides projecting a global product image and facilitating development of a global brand, whereas an adaptation positions a product at an advantageous position vis-à-vis competitors. The factors influencing product adaptation are both mandatory and voluntary, as discussed at length in this chapter.

The chapter also discusses various approaches to new product launch in international markets. The interrelationship of cultural context and product diffusion in the international markets reveals that new product diffusion takes slightly longer in Eastern countries than it does in Western countries. This is primarily due to a much stronger peer group influence. Even among the high context countries new product diffusion is relatively faster in Japan and Southeast Asia as compared to India and the rest of Asia. Among the low context countries, product diffusion is relatively slower in the UK and Eastern Europe as compared to the USA, Canada, and Scandinavian countries.

The concept of product life cycle that reveals the changes in patterns in international markets is discussed in this chapter. Various options for international product strategy based on the product strength and geographic coverage and product-promotion strategies for international markets are critically examined, which may be used by the readers in working out product strategies for international markets.

Summary

In international markets, customers' perceptions and needs differ to a varied extent from one country to other. Therefore, product decisions become a crucial component of any international marketing strategy. Identification and development of products for international markets are the two most critical decisions that a firm has to take. Various approaches adopted for product development for international market include ethnocentric, polycentric, regiocentric, and geocentric approaches. A firm has to make a decision whether to offer a standardized product across markets or customize the products separately for different markets based upon a cost-benefit analysis. The major factors favouring product standardization include technology intensity, cost of adaptation, customer convergence, and country of origin. Product adaptation is influenced by mandatory factors such as government regulations, electric current standards, operating systems, measurement systems, and packaging and labelling requirements. The voluntary factors for product adaptation include consumer demographics, culture, local customs and traditions, conditions of use, and price. Firms have to pay special attention to product quality, packaging, and labelling issues for international markets.

A firm has an option to select either waterfall or sprinkler approach for product launch in the international markets depending upon its assessment of international markets. The cyclical patterns followed by the international markets have been explained with the help of IPLC. The technology gap and willingness and ability to pay for new products influence the demand patterns in international markets. A firm may position its products at different stages of the product life cycle in different markets. Besides, it may cause its own products to move to another stage of the life cycle by introducing innovative products—as is being done by firms such as Gillette, whose products are positioned on the basis of functional superiority.

The international product strategy may be based on product strength and geographical coverage of the international markets. The product-promotion matrix for standardization versus adaptation decisions for products and promotion serves as a useful tool for evolving international product and promotional strategies.

Key Terms

Augmented components   These include the support services and other augmented components such as warranties, guarantees, and after-sales services.

Core components   These refer to the core benefits or the problem-solving services offered by the products.

Country-of-origin (CoO) impact   Customers' perception of the product on the basis of the country of its origin.

International product life cycle (IPLC)   The patterns followed by a product in international markets in terms of its production and market demand.

Kings   Theses are firms with a strong product portfolio and wide geographic coverage.

Packaging components   These include the features, quality, design, packaging, branding, and other attributes of the product, which are integral to offering a product's core benefit.

Product adaptation   Modification of products for international markets.

Product quality   Set of features and characteristics of a good or service that determines its ability to satisfy needs.

Product standardization   Marketing a product in the overseas markets with little change except for some cosmetic changes such as modifying packaging and labelling

Product   A product is anything that can be offered to a market to satisfy a want or need. It may include physical goods, services, experiences, events, persons, places, properties, organizations, information, and ideas.

Sprinkler approach   Simultaneous product launch in various international markets.

Waterfall approach   The launch of a new product in international markets in a phased manner.

Concept Review Questions

1. Explain the significance of product decisions in international markets.
2. 'An international marketer has to find out a trade-off between standardized and customized product as it is difficult to evolve a global product.' Do you agree with the statement? Justify your answer with suitable examples.
3. Distinguish between 'waterfall' and 'sprinkler' strategies for launching new products in international markets. Identify the strengths and weaknesses of these approaches.
4. Explain the concept of IPLC. Does it apply at industry or product level? Evaluate the relevance of the concept for the following:
   (a) Bicycles
   (b) Generic pharmaceutical products
5. Critically evaluate various product promotion strategies in international markets with suitable examples.

Practice Exercise

Go through Exhibit 10.5 and identify a few products that were developed for emerging markets and subsequently marketed internationally.

Project Assignments

1. Visit the website of a transnational firm and find out the product adaptations in different markets.
2. Find out the quality, packaging, and labelling requirements for marketing fresh mangoes in Japan.
3. Contact a local firm operating in international markets. Explore whether the firm is marketing standardized or customized products in different markets. Find out the implications of the firm's product decision.
4. Visit an organization engaged in quality assurance and certification for international market. Select a product and identify its major quality-related issues for international markets.

CASE STUDY: BARBIE FACES ISLAMIC DOLLS

Barbie, so named by businesswoman-inventor Ruth Handler after daughter Barbara's nickname, became the world's most popular fashion doll. Handler found that young girls enjoyed playing out their dreams in adult roles when she saw her daughter Barbara playing with a paper doll and imagining it as a grown up. Most children's dolls available at that time represented infants. This gave rise to an idea of a teenage doll, Barbie. Handler co-founded Mattel, a Southern California toy company with her husband Elliot Handler, and spearheaded the introduction of the doll. Barbie's physical appearance was modelled on the German *Bild Lilli* doll, a risqué gag gift for a man, based upon the cartoon character featured in the West German newspaper *Bild Zeitung*. Barbie made its debut in the American International Toy Fair in New York on 9 March 1959. This date is also considered to be Barbie's official birthday.

Barbie sells over £1 billion annually across 150 countries. It is estimated that three Barbie dolls are sold every second.[13] Although Barbie was positioned as the ultimate American girl, it was never manufactured in the US, primarily to avoid higher production costs. The first Barbie dolls were manufactured in Japan with their clothes hand-stitched by Japanese home-workers. In the first year of production, around 350,000 Barbie dolls were sold. The Mattel-owned four factories, two in China and one each in Malaysia and Indonesia,[14] produce over 100 million Barbie dolls a year. However, a number of other companies produced Barbie-licensed products.

The process of Barbie production is very complex, which includes shipping the dolls from one country to another for different processes. To illustrate, the US ships the cardboard packaging, paint pigments, and moulds to manufacturing facilities in China that provides the factory space, labour, electricity, and cotton cloth for Barbie dresses. Taiwan refines the oil into ethylene for plastic pellets for Barbie's body whereas Japan attaches the nylon hair. International shipping operations are carried out by Hong Kong-based managers.

Barbie is a plastic vinyl doll with the figure of an adult woman whose full name is Barbie Millicent Robert. Initially, Barbie was marketed as a glamorous, physically developed teenage fashion model with a range of fashion accessories. With her hair in a ponytail, and dressed in a black and white stripped bathing suit and sunglasses, Barbie proved an instant and phenomenal marketing success among young girls. Barbie has had over 40 pets, including 21 dogs, 14 horses, 6 cats, parrot, chimpanzee, panda, lion cub, giraffe, and a zebra. In response to consumer demand, in 1961, Mattel brought out Barbie's ultimate 'accessory'—her boyfriend, the fashion conscious Ken. Unlike other baby-like dolls, Barbie did not teach nurturing. Barbie has no parents or offspring.

Over the years Barbie has become very popular among young girls. She has been the subject of numerous books and controversies, besides, being the star in her own movies. Young girls love Barbie because she continually evolves as girls change. Barbie remains paramount in the hearts and minds of girls and moms alike because she reflects the interests, activities, and aspirations of present-day girls. Barbie offers a way for girls to play out their dreams and fantasies in a way that is relevant to today's girls. She is also credited to have provided many young girls an alternative to restrictive fifties' gender roles. She demonstrates girls that they can be anything they want to be—a princess, a teacher, an Olympic athlete, a doctor, a pilot, or even an astronaut. The doll became a role model for financial self-sufficiency, outfitted with career paraphernalia.

Barbie's marketing strategy involved meticulous product customization to suit diverse cultures across the world. The dolls are customized to represent varied cultures, regions, and occasions. It is estimated that since 1959, over a billion Barbie dolls representing over 45 nationalities and 80 occupations have been sold worldwide.

The Chinese Barbie evokes the exotic Far East with a costume inspired by those of the Qing Dynasty. The Egyptian Barbie wears a serpent ornament with a stunning golden crown inspired by the royalty of ancient Egypt. The Moja Barbie perfectly reflects the grandeur of the African continent. Mattel has customized the Barbie doll for India as well by cladding her in the conventional sari and traditional jewellery especially designed to appeal to Indian masses.

Barbie dolls have also been designed to symbolize various festivals across the world. Indian Barbie symbolizes Diwali; Kwanzaa Barbie, the African-American celebrations kwanza, meaning the first fruit of the harvest; Carnival Barbie, the week-long joyous Brazilian celebrations of music, dance, sequins, and feathers at Rio de Janeiro; Chinese new-year Barbie, the ancient festival of Chinese new year beginning with the new moon on the first day of the year that ends the evening of the full moon on the 15th day, called the Lantern festival, etc.

---

[13] 'Vintage Barbie Struts Her Stuff', *BBC News*, 22 September 2006.

[14] Ritz, Ashish, 'Introducing: Slave Barbie', available at http://ihscslnews.org/view_article.php?id=187, December, 2006; 'The Creation of a Barbie', available at http://www.lclark.edu/~soan221/97/Barbie5.html, accessed on 21 April 2010.

Barbie is also known as the 'most collectible doll in the world'. Through the years, she has developed from a teenage fashion model to a trendsetter and fashion adventurer. The four major types of Barbie collectors include pink, silver, gold, and platinum label Barbies. Packaged in pink-trimmed boxes, Pink Label Barbies are widely available and not limited to production numbers. Silver Label Barbies, packaged in silver-trimmed boxes are only available at select retailers and can be produced at only 50,000 per edition. Gold Label barbies are even more difficult to find as only 25,000 of each edition can be produced worldwide.

Despite Barbie's diverse product portfolio, considerable competition has evolved from new dolls like the funky Bratz, the long-term UK rival Sindy, and the Islamic dolls.

Barbie's Criticism and the Islamic Markets

In many countries, Barbie's curvaceous body and revealing garments are perceived to promote sexuality and promiscuity. The standard size of the Barbie doll, 11.5 inches, corresponds to a real height of 5 feet 9 inches at 1/6 scale. Barbie's vital statistics have been estimated at 36 inches (chest), 18 inches (waist), and 33 inches (hips). Barbie has been criticized for unrealistic body proportions and for promoting materialism associated with amassing cars, houses, and clothes. Girls tend to develop an inferiority complex, as they grow up, if they can't look exactly like Barbie. The desire to attain the physical appearance and lifestyle similar to Barbie has been termed as 'Barbie syndrome'. Although pre-teen and adolescent females are more prone to the Barbie syndrome, it is applicable to any age group.

Barbie came under fire in Russia and was banned in 2002 because the doll was thought to awaken sexual impulses in the very young, and encourage consumerism among Russian children.[15] The Commission for the Propagation of Virtue and Prevention of Vice, known as moral police or *mutaween* in Saudi Arabia, declared Barbie dolls a threat to morality and offensive to Islam.[16] Barbie was banned in Saudi Arabia[17] in 2003 as Saudi Arabia's religious police found the Jewish Barbie dolls with their revealing clothes and shameful postures, accessories, and tools, as a symbol of the decadence of the West.

Dolls for the Islamic World

Product adaptation to cultural sensitivities is crucial to success in international markets. Mattel markets a Moroccan Barbie and collectors' doll Leyla that represent Muslim women. Leyla's elaborate costume and the backstory of being enslaved in the court of a Turkish sultan were intended to convey the tribulations

of a popular Muslim character from the 1720s. However, Mattel's portrayal of the Middle Eastern Barbie as the stereotype of a belly dancer or a concubine hardly appealed to present-day Muslim customers.

A number of dolls have been launched for Islamic markets (Fig. C10.1) not only to fill the marketing void but also to offer Muslim girls someone they can relate to. Therefore, most Muslim buyers identify more closely with Islamic dolls as one of them rather than with the stranger Barbie. Islamic dolls generally show young girls that the *hijab* (veil) is a normal part of a woman's life. If the girls put scarves on their dolls when they are young, the parents believe it might be easier to do so for themselves in real life, when their time comes. Sometimes, it is difficult for girls to put on the hijab. They feel it is the end of their childhood. Muslim parents often prefer to buy Islamic dolls over Barbie as it expresses their way of life. Islamic dolls are conceptualized to be the role model for children in Islamic cultures, representing how most Muslim buyer like their daughters to dress and behave.

Islamic dolls launched in the market, include Sara from Iran, Fulla form Syria, Razanne by a Michigan-based US Company, Saghira from Morocco, and Salma from Indonesia.

Fulla

Conceptualized by a Damascus-based Syrian toy manufacturer, New Boy Toys, Fulla was aimed at children in Islamic markets across the world. The concept to bring out an Islamic doll evolved around 1999 and was carefully honed. Fulla's creators have gone to great length to make her modest and conservative. It took 50 animators, artists, and psychologists 18 months to design her face. Like any Western ad agency with a product or politician to sell, Fulla's creators turned to focus groups to test their progress. The product development team considered 10 different faces before settling on the Fulla look: large brown eyes and long, coal-black hair streaked with auburn.

Fulla, an alternative to Barbie for children in the Islamic countries, hit stores in late 2003. Within a couple of years of its launch, Fulla became the dream of every Arab girl and the hottest-selling doll in the Middle East. Over the years, the product profile of Fulla and her accessories have grown manifold. Now there is a 'singing Fulla' and a 'Talking Fulla' pushing a luggage cart with suitcases to hold the dozens of seasonal outfits that crowd their closets. The product catalogue runs to almost 80 pages and includes 150 Fulla-licensed items, ranging from cameras to CD players to inflatable chairs and swimming

---

[15] 'Barbie Is Banned from Russia, Without Love', *The Observer*, 24 November 2002.

[16] 'Barbie Deemed Threat to Saudi Morality', *US Today*, 10 September 2003.

[17] 'Saudi Bans Female Doll Imports', *Guardian*, 18 December 2003.

| Little Farah | Razanne (In–Out) | Fulla |

Fig. C10.1 Dolls for the Islamic markets

Source: www.noorart.com; www.simplyislam.com; www.desidollcompany.com, all accessed on 31 May 2013.

pools. Girls from Beirut to Bahrain carry Fulla umbrellas, wear Fulla watches, ride Fulla bicycles, and eat Fulla corn-flakes.

The name Fulla is derived from a fragrant jasmine flower found only in the Middle East. Like Barbie, she is 11½ inch tall, but unlike Mattel's products, she is visibly less bosomy. There is no such thing as a single Arab look, but broader features and heavier figures are more the norm among Arab women. However, Fulla's button nose, bow mouth, and svelte figure testify to the internationalization of Western standards of beauty, superceding indigenous ideas of beauty. Fulla's complexion is olive compared to Barbie's peaches-and-cream skin-tone, her hair is much thicker than Barbie's blonde mane and her face is fuller than[18] that of the typical American, but otherwise she is much the same.

To make her more acceptable in Saudi Arabia, one of the richest and most conservative Islamic countries, she was initially dressed in a black abaya and headscarf, but without the veil most Saudi women wear. The manufacturer did not go to the extremes of covering the face of the little girl. Although, Fulla was dressed in a black abaya and headscarf for the Saudi market, it had no veil in other markets. For relatively liberal Islamic countries, such as Syria and Lebanon, Fulla has a white scarf and pastel coat making her outdoor clothes more colourful. Since Muslim women do not show much skin unlike their Western counterparts, Fulla's shoulders are always covered and the skirt always falls below her knees. The carefully drawn marketing strategy could

maintain the brand identity of a conservative girl rather than being just another doll trying to reflect Barbie.

The toy capitalizes on the Islamization of cultural life in the Arab world as evidenced in a heightened focus on dress and rituals. Like most Muslims in the Arab world, Fulla has two sets of clothes. Form-fitting, revealing outfits are sported at home, while items that cover the arms, legs, neck, and often the hair are donned in public (Fig. C10.1). This concept of two wardrobes and especially that of the conservative 'outdoor' outfits is what mainly distinguishes the Arab dolls from their Western counterparts. Fulla's clothes include cloaks and prayer outfits that conceal her long dark-brown hair. She also has her own prayer mat,[19] in pink felt.

With her two wardrobes, Fulla taps into the Arab Muslim market by combining religious identity with femininity. The skirts in Fulla's 'home' wardrobe may not rise north of the knee, but many of her tops are close fitting and brightly coloured. Nowadays, many Arab women sport these 'home' outfits outdoors, topped with a scarf.

The brand personality of Fulla is designed to be 'loving, caring, honest, and respectful to her parents. She is honest and does not lie. Fulla has two friends, Yasmeen and Nada, as well a little brother and sister. Fulla has an older protective brother too. Fulla would never have a boyfriend unlike her Western counterpart, Barbie, as this is frowned upon in Islam.

Even the commercials for dolls in the Middle East are designed to represent Islamic values. For instance, in Saudi Arabia,

---

[18] 'Fulla—The Arab World's Barbie', *Khaleej Times*, 25 November 2006.
[19] 'Barbie hasn't a Prayer against Devout Islamic Doll,' *The Sunday Times*, 22 January 2006.

Barbie is shown to offer her prayers as the sun rises, bake a cake to surprise her friend, or read a book at bedtime. Fulla is also depicted to be family-oriented promoting modest outfits. Commercials even promote, 'when you take your Fulla out of the house, don't forget her new spring abaya'.

Barbie vs Fulla

Barbie and Fulla offer contrasting role models to customers. Although both Barbie and Fulla have a wide range of costumes, jewellery, furniture, and other accessories, the outdoor clothes of Fulla do not include swimwear or anything revealing. Besides, Fulla has a smaller chest, is skinnier compared to Barbie's curves, large breasts and shapely legs. An average Barbie is designed to have blond hair, blue eyes, and fair skin whereas Fulla has dark hair, brown eyes, and olive skin. New Boy also introduced dolls with lighter hair and eyes, assuming they would be popular in Mediterranean regions where blue-eyed blonds are not unknown. However, both the dolls have been criticized for presenting the same unrealistic idea of beauty, a certain image for women to conform to.

Fulla is differentiated from Barbie in terms of her lifestyle and appearance. Shopping, spending time with her friends, cooking, reading, and praying are Fulla's favourite activities whereas Barbie has a wide range of hobbies and careers. Unlike Barbie, a perennial job-hopper for about last half a century, who has been everything from an astronaut to the US president, Fulla remains a traditional Arab woman, whose life revolves around the family, serving as a role model for Muslim girls. Fulla has also been designed to be a doctor and a teacher, the two most respected careers in the Islamic world.

A large number of Fulla items are manufactured in the same Chinese factories that turn out Barbie and her related products. That's partly because the items are identical and partly because these factories meet the safety standards set by the United Arab Emirates, through which the Fulla line is distributed.

Other dolls for the Islamic markets

Dolls aimed at the Islamic markets also include Sara, Razanne, Saghira, and Salma. The Iranian doll Sara was introduced as an alternative to Barbie in 2002 by the Institute for the Intellectual Development of Children and Young Adults, a government agency affiliated with the Ministry of Education. She has a brother doll Dara unlike Barbie's boyfriend, Ken (Fig. C10.2). The dolls have a distinct 'eastern look' complete with Iranian clothes. The siblings help each other to solve problems and turn to their loving parents for guidance. The children are supposed

Fig. C10.2   Instead of a beau, Iranian doll Sara has a brother doll Dara

Source: www.dara-sara.com, accessed on 4 June 2013.

to be eight years old, young enough under the Islamic law for Sara to appear in public without a headscarf. But each model of Sara comes with a white scarf to cover her brown or black hair. In the first round of production, 1,00,000 dolls were made by a manufacturer in China.

Razanne was created as an alternative to Barbie for American Muslim girls by Ammar and Sherrie Saadeh at their toy company NoorArt based in Livonia, Michigan, outside of Detroit. Razanne has long-sleeved dresses, a head scarf, and a not-so-buxom bustline. Unlike Barbie, Razanne, with her modest dress and a removable hijab, exemplifies the virtues of a proper, young Muslim woman, such as modesty, piety, and humility. Moreover, the doll is more than a toy. It is a tool for young Muslim girls to learn the value of things like education and religious piety instead of focusing on their bodies as the most significant aspect of their lives. Razanne has the body of a pre-teen. The doll comes in various types: fair-skinned blonde, olive-skinned with black hair, or black skin and black hair. Her aspirations represent a modern Muslim woman. Praying Razanne, who comes complete with a long *hijab* and a modest prayer gown, is aimed to attract Saudi Arabia and other Islamic markets. There's In–Out Razanne (Fig. C10.1), whose wardrobe also includes a short, flowery dress she can wear at home, in view of the men in her family only.[20]

Saghira was created by a Moroccan manufacturer in 2005–06 and launched in January 2007 in the Morocco market. She has a mix of both authentic traditional and Western attire, but her accessories, even if Western versions, are based on the articles usually found in Arabic and Muslim households. The dolls come both in veiled and unveiled models, the later representing Saghira within her home or in a family environment. Each model has a

---

[20] 'Muslim Doll Offers Modest Alternative to Barbie', *CNN*, 8 October 2003.

different Arabic girl's name: Amira (princess), Doaa (Prayer), Aya, Abir, Ahd, Shada, Nada, Dahab, Najma, Nour, Lina, etc.

Little Farah is designed to recite some most commonly used Islamic phrases (Fig. C10.1) in Arabic and English. For instance: 'Welcome, *Assalamu*'; '*Alaikum* peace be upon you'; 'Lets begin, *Bismillah* in the name of Allah'; 'I promise, *Inshallah* if Allah wills'. An Indonesian businesswoman, Sukmawati Suryaman, created Salma,[21] which means 'peace' in Arabic, targeted at young Muslim girls. The toy is marketed as the 'Muslim Barbie Doll' on the net.

The world's bestselling doll, Barbie, which enchanted little girls across the globe, is being elbowed off the toy shelves in the Middle East markets by Islamic playmates. The new dolls aimed at Islamic markets strive to create a character that parents and teachers want children to relate to. These represent that Muslim girls too have options, goals, and dreams and also the ability to realize them unlike the stereotype Barbie aimed at Muslim consumers. Moreover, the surge in sales of Muslim girls' toys, including the veiled dolls, comes amid new enthusiasm among Muslim women for wearing the veil.[22]

Questions

1. Explore the secret of Barbie's success that made it the dream-toy for girls across the world.

2. Sensitivity to culture is crucial to success in international markets. Evaluate Barbie's product adaptation for different markets.

3. Barbie has been criticized for its curvaceous, unrealistic body and materialism, leading to controversies and its ban in some countries, such as Saudi Arabia and Russia. On the other hand, Islamic dolls are criticized for promoting gender stereotypes and restrictive roles. In your opinion, to what extent are such criticism and bans justified?

4. Despite adaptation to represent vast ethnic groups, nationalities, and occasions, Barbie dolls have been jostled out from the Islamic markets. Identify the key reasons.

5. In view of the fast-growing popularity of Islamic dolls among Muslim customers across the world, suggest a marketing plan for Barbie to address the specific needs of the Islamic markets. Also evaluate the impact of suggested plan on the brand image of Barbie in other markets.

---

[21] 'Barbie Inspires Modest, Muslim Alternative', *Reuters*, UK, 10 October 2007.

[22] 'Barbie Looses Out to Veiled Rival', *BBC News*, 12 January 2006.

Building Brands in International Markets

Learning Objectives

- To explain the concept of branding
- To describe various types of branding
- To discuss the concepts of brand equity and brand identity
- To examine brand-building strategies
- To evaluate branding strategies for global markets

INTRODUCTION

The owners of products/animals in ancient times used some sort of identifying marks to distinguish their property from that of others. The word 'brand' is derived from the Norse word *brandr* meaning 'to burn', traditionally used in branding livestock to declare ownership. Even today the basic purpose of branding is to differentiate one's products in the market. However, the ways and means of branding at present have much higher levels of sophistication and include intangibles associated with the brand.

Branding undifferentiated generic products provides marketers an opportunity to differentiate their offerings from their competitors' by way of value addition that may be rational or emotional. Human beings are hardly rational in their decision-making. The concept of brand building centres around the fact that both rational and emotional factors affect a customer's decision-making. It is important to understand that so long as the customers perceive the firm's intended value projections as a benefit, it hardly matters whether such a benefit is objectively relevant or not. For instance, a shampoo brand claims that the use of silk as an ingredient makes consumers' hair silky. However, the two are completely irrelevant and unrelated aspects of the claim, and it is difficult to support the claims empirically. So long as the customer feels that she can have silky hair by using the brand due to the silk content in the product, such a perception can contribute to an increase in sales and profit margins. The marketer may use and build brands around such benefits.

Developing countries market most products as undifferentiated commodities. The only competitive advantage these products have in the market is their price competitiveness, which is difficult to sustain in the long run; whereas, products from developed countries compete on the basis of brand image built over the years as a distinct identity for the product in terms of quality and credibility.

Therefore, it is pertinent for marketing managers operating in developing countries to learn the concept and tactics of branding to leverage themselves in their international marketing efforts. Since the penetration of Indian and other brands from developing countries is limited, this chapter discusses and examines the international branding strategies of firms from high-income countries so that lessons can be learnt from their experience in international markets.

This chapter explains the concept of branding and demonstrates how it can be effectively used as a marketing tool to exploit a firm's competitive strength. Various types of brands such as private brands, manufacturers' brands, local brands, and global brands are also described. The key concepts related to strategic brand management such as brand equity, brand identity, brand positioning, and strategies for building brands are also dealt with. Various strategies for managing brands in the international markets in the various phases of their life cycles are critically examined.

CONCEPT OF BRANDING

Branding creates differentiation between the firm's and competitors' products, and provides marketing edge to the brands to price them relatively higher than competitors' and get better margins. Besides, brands also facilitate coping with market competition and increasing the life of the product. In present times when the mobility of the consumers, including transnational travel, is rapidly growing, branding serves as an important tool in international marketing as the image of the brand crosses national boundaries. Brands also facilitate consumers by forging an emotional relationship with them and help in their buying decisions by enhancing their confidence while purchasing their favourite brand. With the increased competitive intensity in the market, even basic commodities such as rice, tea, edible oils, salt, and petroleum are branded widely.

Jeans, as a product, were historically used by mining labourers because of their inherent product qualities such as ruggedness, durability, and low cost of maintenance (Fig. 11.1). Branding jeans as Levi's added intangible benefits to the product and caused it to metamorphose into a product of high aspiration among the youth (Fig. 11.2). Moreover, the brand Levi's signifies personality traits such as youthful, rebellious, individualistic, free, strong, sexy, and different.

A brand may be defined as a name, term, sign, symbol, or design, or a combination of these, intended to identify the goods or services of one seller or a group of sellers and to differentiate them from those of competitors.[1] Thus, a brand identifies and differentiates a seller's or a maker's goods and services from the goods and services of the other sellers. Under the Trademark Law, a seller is granted exclusive rights to use the brand name forever. Brand name differs from other assets, such as patents and copyrights, which exist for specific periods and have expiration dates.

Michael Eisner, the legendary CEO of Walt Disney, views brand as a living entity, enriched or undermined cumulatively over time, a product of a thousand small gestures. A brand is nothing but a way of creating an identity; almost like identifying a specific person within a large crowd.[2] A brand is the name of a marketable unit to which a unique, relevant, and motivating set of associations and benefits, both functional and emotional, have been attached.[3]

It is the intangible aspect of brand that wraps around a product and makes the brand special or unique. When consumers think of a product or a service, they only compare the basic attributes

---

[1] American Marketing Association, www.marketingpower.com, accessed on 24 April 2012.

[2] K. Choudhury, Pran, *Successful Branding*, Universities Press (India) Ltd, Hyderabad, 2003, pp. 2–3.

[3] Sen, Shunu, 'Foreword' in Pran K. Choudhury, *Successful Branding*, Universities Press (India) Ltd, Hyderabad, 2001, pp. ix–x.

Fig. 11.1 Jeans were initially
meant for mining labourers

Fig. 11.2 Branding jeans as Levi's makes the product highly
desirable among youth the world over

Source: www.levi.com, accessed on 18 October 2013.

and features with those of their competitors, whereas branding a product adds an emotional dimension to the product–consumer relationship and creates a bond between the two.

Thus, brands also facilitate the forging of an emotional relationship between consumers and products, helping a buyer to arrive at a decision supported by the credibility of a particular brand. Today, when the mobility of consumers, both within a country and overseas, is rapidly growing, brands serve as an important tool in international marketing as the image of the brand crosses national boundaries.

BRANDING ALTERNATIVES FOR INTERNATIONAL MARKETS

The product decision varies from selling products as undifferentiated commodities without any brand name to multiple worldwide brands. Based on the branding strategy used by a firm, the major types of brands are elucidated here.

No Brand or Branding the Product

A firm has to make an initial decision whether it should sell the product as an undifferentiated, generic commodity, or sell it in a branded form. Selling an unbranded product reduces the cost of production, packaging, selling, and legal costs, besides providing the firm flexibility in production. Nevertheless, marketing of an unbranded generic product fails to establish its identity in the market even after a long period of supply and it primarily competes on price parameters. Besides, generic products are highly prone to international competitive pressures and find it difficult to sustain their competitiveness in the long term (Exhibit 11.1).

A firm has to first identify those features and attributes of the product that can be differentiated while building the brand image. In case a company fails to identify differentiable attributes

Exhibit 11.1 Benefits of branding

Marketing parameter	Unbranded commodity	Brand
Firm's perception of customer's need	Generic	Differentiated
Target customers	All	Segmented
Market offerings	Similar	Customized
Competitive leverage	Lower prices	Value creation by adding benefits
Competitive intensity	Head-to-head	Emphasis on differentiation
Customer loyalty	Low, decreasing	Increasing, long-term
Investment	Generic	Targeted
Scope	Cost	Service
Marketing focus	Quality	Quality
Margins	Low	High
Future outlook on market share & profitability	Difficult to sustain, decreasing	Sustainable, growing

in its products, branding becomes difficult. However, the present-day marketing protagonists have successfully branded basic commodities such as water, milk, edible oils, sugar, salt, tea, rice, pulses, flour (*atta*), and petroleum products. Since it is difficult to differentiate in terms of functionality in basic products, such as water, soft drinks, and beverages, brand building based on intangible components is widely used.

Firms from developing countries often find it difficult to build brands, especially with international reach. Their products compete on the basis of price in international markets. For instance, India is among the largest suppliers of generic medicines in the world market, but Indian firms have little presence in branded market.

Manufacturer's Own Brand or a Private Brand

Generally, large companies have substantial goodwill in the market and have built their own brand image over the years. It facilitates realizing higher prices, increases the brand loyalty of their products, and provides better control over distribution channels. It is difficult for a consumer goods retail outlet to operate without well-known brands from Unilever, Procter and Gamble, and Nestlé, because these brands have a strong pull factor in the market. Manufacturers' own brands increase the effectiveness of marketing communication and lead to economies of scale.

With smaller firms that do not have a desired level of brand recognition, the retailers do enjoy enormous negotiating power, and generally use their own private label. Supermarkets such as Walmart, Carrefour, Marks and Spencer, and Sainsbury's use their own private labels on a majority of the products sold by them. A large number of suppliers from developing countries including India and China often sell generic products to large retailers.

Local, National, or Global Brand

A firm operating in international markets has to examine the size of potential markets and identify differences in its various markets of operation. In case the size of a market operation is large enough to justify, the brand may be expanded to have national or worldwide coverage.

The magnitude of differences in the target market in terms of its segments (psychographic or demographic) determines the decision to have single, global, or local brands for different markets.

Single or Multiple Brands

The inter-country differences in terms of customer segments, whether demographic or geographic, determine a firm's decision to have a single brand for its markets or numerous brands for multiple market segments. As multiple brands for international markets respond competitively in a superior way to a uniform branding strategy, this facilitates fighting competition with local brands. However, it needs much greater commitment of resources to manage such a large portfolio of brands in international markets.

Branding alternatives for international markets that include no brand, branding, private brands, manufacturer's brand, multiple brands, single brand, local brands, and worldwide brands are summarized in Exhibit 11.2.

Exhibit 11.2 Branding alternatives for international markets

Advantages	Disadvantages
No Brand	
Lower production cost	Severe price competition
Lower marketing cost	Lack of market identity
Lower legal cost	
Flexible quality and quantity control	
Branding	
Better identification and awareness	Higher production cost
Better chance for product differentiation	Higher marketing cost
Possible brand loyalty	Higher legal cost
Possible premium pricing	
Private brands	
Better margins for dealers	Severe price competition
Possibility of larger market share	Lack of market identity
No promotional problems	
Manufacturer's brands	
Better price due to more price inelasticity	Difficulty for small manufacturers with unknown
Retention of brand loyalty	brand offering
Better bargaining power	Brand promotion required
Better control of distribution	
Multiple brands (in one market)	
Market segmented for varying needs	Higher marketing cost
Competitive spirit created	Higher inventory cost
Negative connotation of existing brand avoided	Loss of economies of scale
More retail shelf space gained	
Existing brand's image not damaged	
Single brand (in one market)	
Marketing efficiency	Market homogeneity assumed
More focused marketing permitted	Existing brand's image when trading up/down
Brand confusion eliminated	Limited shelf space
Advantage for product with good reputation (halo effect)	

(Contd)

Exhibit 11.2 *(Contd)*

Advantages	Disadvantages
Local brands	
Meaningful names	Higher marketing cost
Local identification	Higher inventory cost
Avoidance of taxation on international brand	Loss of economies of scale
Quick market penetration by acquiring local brand	Diffused image
Variations of quantity and quality across markets allowed	
Worldwide brands	
Maximum marketing efficiency	Market homogeneity assumed
Reduction of advertising costs	Problems with black and grey markets
Elimination of brand confusion	Possibility of negative connotation
Advantage for culture-free product	Quality and quantity consistency required
Advantage for prestigious product	Opposition and resentment in less developed countries
Easy identification/recognition for international travellers	Legal complications
Uniform worldwide image	

STRATEGIES FOR BUILDING BRANDS

Branding decisions are generally based on the basic marketing principle of identifying and satisfying the needs and wants of consumers that differ widely. As discussed in Chapter 10, under the strategic framework for international product promotion, the product function or needs have to be satisfied, and conditions of product use differ among various market segments; therefore the need to be responded to by different marketing strategies. Product extension-communication adaptation strategy is used in situations where the conditions of product use remain the same but the need satisfied differs. Since consumers do not behave in a rational manner for their purchase decisions, marketers have to identify the emotional aspects of their decision-making process and develop a framework for brand building. The basic concept of brand building is based on the rational and emotional aspects of the product.

Brand Based on Tangible Product Component

Under this approach, the brand is built around the core benefits of a product that emphasize its functional characteristics (Fig. 11.3). The differentiation in building the brand is created on the basis of functional superiority of the product or service.

As discussed in Chapter 10, Gillette has adapted a strategy to introduce a new brand on the basis of its functional superiority over the previous brands. The new brands introduced by Gillette on the basis of superior performance by adding more blades to its razor, compete with its own previous brands, making them obsolete over a period of time. Intel has also adopted a strategy of introducing a new version of microprocessor that is superior in performance to the earlier versions. Such a strategy is adopted to compete in the market where it is feasible to achieve an edge in product function to gain a competitive advantage in the market.

Japanese consumer electronics firms such as Sony, Panasonic, and Casio emphasize core product benefits, and their brands are generally built around these benefits, such as quality, reliability, service, and reputation relevant to the core product.

Generally, the marketing mix decisions under brands based on tangible aspects are emphasized on product, price, and/or place. However, sustaining functional superiority in the market vis-à-vis competitors is a key challenge in marketing such brands. In the beginning of this century, the price competitiveness per unit of talk time was the key differentiator in the Indian mobile

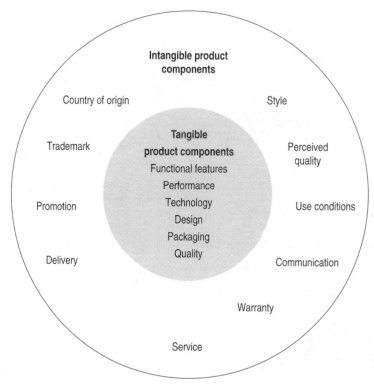

Fig. 11.3   Brand based on tangible product component

market. Since mobile operators found it difficult to create and sustain further price competitiveness, their brands were repositioned to intangible superiority.

Brand Based on Intangible Product Component

Most customers hardly understand all functional benefits and attributes of a product available in the market. Despite this, they have a preference for one brand over the other. It is the emotional need of the consumers that determines their preference for the brand. Thus, the secret of branding is in adding value, especially psychological value, to products, services, and companies in the form of intangible benefits—the emotional associations, beliefs, values, and feelings that people relate to the brand. It is this aspect of the product/service, and not the features and attributes, that can strongly distinguish one brand from another in consumers' minds. This can be achieved by building a strong identity or personality for the brand and strategically positioning it in the minds of the target audience. This is not an easy or quick process, but it is absolutely vital to brand success.

In situations where core product benefits are difficult to differentiate and consumers find it difficult to evaluate quality, brands are built around intangible benefits rather than the core benefits of the product (Fig. 11.4). Soft drinks, mineral water, alcoholic beverages, etc. use this approach to brand building. Besides, for products having higher levels of visibility than others, such as readymade garments, cars, and shoes, brands are generally centred on intangible product benefits.

The key criterion of differentiation in such brands is their image, which is perceived by the buyers as offering a unit set of associations. The marketing strategy emphasizes communication to create the desired image for such brands. Brands centred around intangible benefits fulfil the social and esteem needs of the buyers, generally, in moderate to high involvement products. The basic types of brand images are created in the following manner.

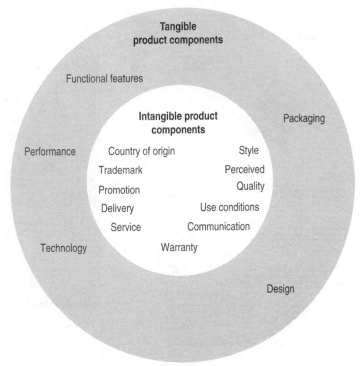

Fig. 11.4 Brand based on intangible product component

Feature based Such brands are based on the distinctive product features to create user imagery. 'Waterman' pens are depicted as heirlooms by emphasizing that the product may be handed down from one generation to another. Similarly, diamonds have been positioned in India by De Beers as being transferred from one generation to another generation, similar to gold jewellery. This approach is also being used in its marketing communications, for example, 'A Diamond is Forever'. Therefore, diamonds have been positioned in the Indian market as being as good as gold jewellery, which is primarily used as a gift from parents to their daughters. Sustaining and balancing the brand image in a competitive environment and within a cultural context is the key marketing challenge for such brands.

User imagery based Images of the user of a brand represent the brand characteristics in the minds of the user. Celebrities are generally used in brand building, based on the concept of user imagery as they instantly pass their qualities to the brand. In India, use of celebrities has special significance, where stars are viewed as superhuman beings. Soft drink companies use a number of celebrities such as Kareena Kapoor, Shah Rukh Khan, Aishwarya Rai, and Sachin Tendulkar. The legendary film star Amitabh Bachchan is a celebrity who endorses Parker pens (Fig. 11.5) unlike in Western markets.

Advertising campaigns are also used to create vivid associations for the brand. Cigarettes and automobiles are advertised creating fantasy associations around the brand.

Balance Brand Based on Tangible–Intangible Product Component

Indian and other Asian consumers emphasize both tangible and intangible aspects of the brand. It is also known as the Yin-Yang model in East Asia, wherein maintaining harmony between the two is of utmost significance. Therefore, the brands need to emphasize both the tangible and intangible product components, as indicated in Fig. 11.6.

Fig. 11.5 Contrasting branding strategies in Western and Indian markets

Source: www.parkerpen.com, accessed on 27 December 2010.

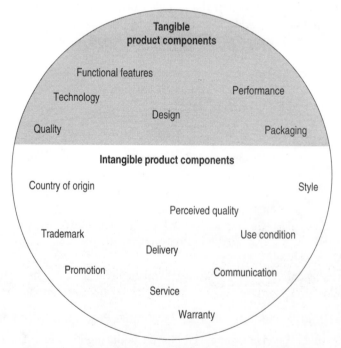

Fig. 11.6 Brand based on tangible–intangible product component

However, the composition of the two components may be altered depending upon the market situation. Both the tangible and intangible components should work together in harmony.

BRANDING OF SERVICES

Services are characterized by their perishable nature, which is created at the time of consumption with the active participation of those who consume them. Such brands are also termed as 'experiential brands'. Since the brand experience is co-created by the brand and the consumer at the time of consumption, it becomes unique and highly personal. If a product is a part of an experiential brand, its ownership can never be transferred to the consumer. In an experiential brand, the products, environment, and services are combined to create temporary, multi-sensory encounters with a brand. As a result, the 'place and people' become key components of service delivery that is used for building a strong experiential brand. Amusement parks and airlines use the strategy of experiential branding.

The basis of creating differentiation among experiential brands centres around the uniquely engaging experience at the time of brand consumption. Therefore, the marketer has to pay special attention to maintaining consistency of delivery and consistent innovation so as to overcome the risk of consumer satiation. Amusement parks and restaurants strive to add innovative offerings to their existing product line so as to deal with the problem of 'boredom' among loyal customers.

STRATEGY FOR BUILDING GLOBAL BRANDS

Developing a global brand requires enormous resources and enduring commitment. Therefore, most global brands come from developed or high-income countries, whereas developing or low-income countries often sell unbranded generic products that fetch relatively much lower prices. Price competitiveness is the major competitive advantage for generic products and commodities, making such products highly prone to market competition. Such a lack of differentiation in market offerings by developing countries consistently keeps them at the lower end of the market.

Exhibit 11.3 presents a classic case of transforming a traditional herbal remedy used for generations in Oriental countries into a global brand.

A global brand should have a minimum level of geographical spread and turnover in various global markets. However, in the fields of information and communication technology, a lot of leapfrogging has taken place and a number of IT companies in India have targeted global markets and are building global brands with little presence domestically. Quelch identifies the following six traits[4] for a brand to be global:

- Dominates the domestic market, which generates cash flow to enter new markets.
- Meets a universal consumer need.
- Demonstrates balanced country-market coverage.
- Reflects a consistent positioning worldwide.
- Benefits from positive country of origin effect.
- Focus is on the product category.

For global firms such as Nike, Apple, Ikea, and BMW, brand value exceeds 75 per cent of their market capitalization. The longevity of branded goods is much higher than that of unbranded generics. A number of brands such as Kellogg's in breakfast cereals, Kodak in cameras, Eveready in batteries, Wrigley in chewing gums, Gillette in razors, Singer in sewing machines, Ivory in

---

[4] Quelch, J., 'Global Brands: Taking Stock', *Business Strategy Review*, vol. 10, no.1, 1999, pp. 1–14.

Exhibit 11.3   Tiger Balm: from a herbal remedy to a global brand

Herbal remedies are not only popular, but also believed to be quite effective in most of East Asia. Clove oil, camphor, and menthol are widely used ingredients in Asia's traditional medicinal systems including Ayurveda (the science of life in India) and the Chinese system. Tiger Balm owes its origins to a soothing herbal balm prepared for Chinese emperors who suffered from aches and pains. Chinese herbalists and healers used it for their patients as an analgesic rub blended with natural ingredients. However, it was only Tiger Balm that packaged these ingredients to make it popular in more than a 100 countries as an effective pain reliever for body aches and pains such as headaches, rheumatism, arthritic pains, muscle strains, and sprains. A Hakka herbalist from China named Aw Chu Kin left China and established a medicine shop in Rangoon in Burma in the late 1870s where he developed and sold the balm. He had two sons, Aw Boon Haw (meaning gentle tiger) and Aw Boon Par (meaning gentle leopard). The brand name 'Tiger' is derived from Boon Haw's name. The present name of the company Haw Par Corporation Limited is derived from the names of both the brothers. After the death of his father, Aw Boon Haw marketed the balm under the brand name Tiger Balm and moved its production to Singapore in the 1920s along with his brother Aw Boon Par.

Aw Boon Haw, a marketing genius, made a success of selling Tiger Balm in Singapore, Malaysia, Hong Kong, Thailand, and China. In order to cater to the large and growing international demand, Tiger Balm is manufactured in various factories licensed by Haw Par Healthcare Limited. It has manufacturing facilities in Singapore, Malaysia, and China and contract manufacturers in Indonesia, Thailand, Taiwan, India, and the USA.

Tiger Balm is actively marketed in more than a 100 countries across five continents from Hammerfest, Norway (about three degrees from the Arctic Circle), the northern-most point, to Bluff, South Island of New Zealand, the southern-most point. In most countries, Tiger Balm is sold as an over-the-counter (OTC) drug.

Fig. 11.7   A traditional herbal remedy bottled as Tiger Balm that became a global brand

Source: www.tigerbalm.com, accessed on 6 April 2013.

This means that it can be purchased without prescription from drug stores, pharmacies, medical halls, and even department stores. Presently, Tiger Balm comes in two versions, the mint oil-scented Tiger Balm white, and Tiger Balm red with its comforting aroma of cinnamon oil. The brand Tiger Balm has now been extended (Fig. 11.7) to Tiger Balm Medicated Plaster and Tiger Balm Muscle Rub, Kwan Loong oil, ethical pharmaceuticals, and dietary supplements.

Tiger Balm has exhibited exemplary consistency in its brand building approach since the beginning. Clove oil, camphor, menthol, and cajuput oil continue to constitute the active ingredients of Tiger Balm. The old photographs of the two brothers with their names in Chinese and English are still retained. The brand has used the springing tiger as its logo from the very beginning. This consistency of brand identity has evoked a very high level of brand awareness in the international market. Small hexagonal jars and round-shaped cans make the product look distinctive, and remind the customers of the product's heritage.

Source: Based on information released by Haw Par Corporation Limited.

soaps, Coca-Cola in soft drinks, Lipton in tea, and Goodyear in tyres category were the leading brands in 1925. They have continued to maintain their brand leadership even 60 years later.[5]

Selecting Brand Names for International Markets

It is important to understand the cultural traits of the target markets while selecting brand names. Mistakes have been made by some of the most valuable brands in the world in deciding brand names in target markets. In 1920, the Coca-Cola entered the Chinese market as Coca-Cola, which is pronounced in Chinese as 'Kou-Ke-Kou-La'. In Chinese, this translates as 'a thirsty mouth and full of candle wax' or 'bite the wax tadpole', which was not accepted by the Chinese consumers

---

[5] Wurster, Thomas S., *The Leading Brands: 1925–1985 Perspectives*, The Boston Consulting Group, 1987.

Fig. 11.10 McDonald's mascot Ronald McDonald in Macy's Thanksgiving Day Parade, New York City

Source: McDonald's.

Brand packaging

It includes the brand name, symbol, or product package, which play a significant role in enhancing and maintaining brand equity and serve as a barrier to competitors. The distinctive Coca-Cola bottle has become such an integral part of the brand that the firm could not part with its associations on the label of its brand of bottled drinking water, Kinley or on the Coke can. Even distribution channels get associated to a brand, such as the retail outlets created by Titan watches around the world.

Brand Identity

It refers to the unique set of brand associations that a firm aspires to create or maintain. Brand associations should represent what the brand stands for and imply its promise to the customers. Aaker defines brand identity as the sum of the brand expressed as a product, organization, person, and symbol. Brand identity may be represented through six interrelated components of brand identity as a hexagonal prism—physique, personality, culture, self-image, reflection, and relationship[9] (Fig. 11.11).

Brand physique

It refers to the physical qualities of the brand. These are the tangible aspects of the brand and include its core features and attributes. A brand's physique is its backbone, around which the intangible components are created. As without a strong foundation, the building collapses no matter how impressive it appears. Therefore, a firm has to carefully and meticulously conceptualize and

---

[9] Kapferer, Jean-Noël, *Strategic Brand Management: Creating and Sustaining Brand Equity Long Term*, Second Edition, Kogan Page India P. Ltd, New Delhi, 2000.

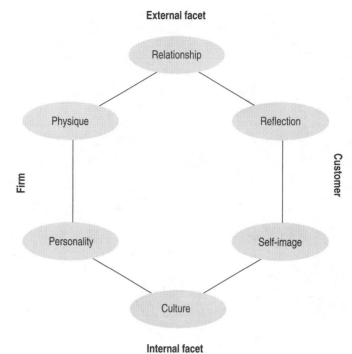

Fig. 11.11 Concept of brand identity

Source: Adapted from Kapferer, Jean-Noël *Strategic Brand Management: Creating and Sustaining Brand Equity Long Term*, Second Edition, Kogan Page India P. Ltd, New Delhi, 2000.

develop the tangible part of the brand in terms of superior quality, performance, and durability. Any brand coming out of Tata's stable provides a promise of trust to its consumers that needs concrete and long-lasting efforts in providing and maintaining the core component of the brand. Even after shifting from traditional glass bottles to family size PET bottles and cans, Coca-Cola still uses the picture of its traditional glass bottles of bright red Coca-Cola that reminds customers of the root of the product and reconfirms the original 'Real Thing'.

Brand personality

Like living creatures, brands also have a personality that distinguishes them from competing brands. Similar to human personality, brand personality is a summation of all the tangible and intangible aspects of a brand. The basic difference between the human and brand personality is that human beings develop their own personality by way of their deeds and behaviour, while the personalities of brands are built by marketing protagonists. Marketing communication and promotion are the major tools used for building brand personality.

Personality traits in human beings such as demographic personality traits, such as gender, age, socio-economic status; subtle traits such as youthfulness, happiness, seriousness, social concern, emotionality, warmth, and anger also form important components of brand personality. A brand may be young, spirited, and exciting like Pepsi and can also be old, but the original 'Real Thing' like Coke. It may be feminine like Pantene or Sunsilk or masculine like Denim and Musk. Mysore Sandal, Hamam, and Sunlight are perceived to be old, while Fair Glow is new. Brands are also differentiated on the basis of psychographics such as Van Heusen for the upper class, whereas Nirma for the lower market segment. Cars such as Indigo and Esteem are sophisticated, Scorpio and Land Cruiser are rugged, while Maruti 800, Alto, and Nano are economic and affordable. Cartier watches are upscale, while Sonata from Titan is downscale.

Like human beings, brands also have strong capability to develop over a period of time. Soft drinks such as Pepsi reflect fun, energy, youth, and a rebellious attitude to the consumer. One of the easiest ways of rapidly creating brand personality is to give the brand a spokesperson or a figure-head; real or symbolic. Shah Rukh Khan's personal traits, such as his being a popular actor, smart, fast, innovative, energetic, and youthful, transmits to the endorsed brand. Similarly, Lalitaji who is perceived as a symbol of wit and experience, passed on her personality traits to the brand Surf. Indian customers tend to believe Lalitaji's endorsement *Surf ki kharidari mein hi samjahdari hai* (It makes sense to buy Surf). With the growing competitive intensity in the market, firms have to evolve a distinct brand personality and forge a bond of relationship with the customers to last longer.

Culture

It symbolizes the country of origin, the organization, and the values for which the brand stands. The cultural aspects of a brand refer to the basic principles governing the brand and its outward aspects, including marketing communications. The culture of the organization is passed on to the brand, especially when the brand bears the same name. For instance, footwear is so closely associated with the brand Bata that it is difficult for the company to disassociate itself from footwear and hard for customers to imagine that it may sell Bata butter to the market. Similarly, milk and milk products have become so integral a part of the brand Amul that it is difficult for Amul to even dream of selling Amul shoes. The degree of freedom of a brand is often reduced by its corporate culture, which is its most visible outward sign. It was because of the corporate culture of trust, quality, reliability, and seriousness that Nestlé could not communicate to its customers the image of a food brand with fun and frolic, unlike the US brands, such as Coke, Pepsi, and McDonald's.

The country of origin forms an integral part of the brand culture. The country of manufacture, assembly, or design influences the consumer's positive or negative perception of a product. Buyers often associate the image of a country, type of product, and the firm's image with the brands in the market. French wines and perfumes, Swiss chocolates and watches, New Zealand dairy products (Fig. 11.12), Italian fashions, Japanese consumer electronics, Indian spices, Chinese herbs, etc. evoke an outstanding perception of product quality. Similarly, engineering goods from Germany have a positive consumer perception of precision and accuracy. The German Mercedes is considered to be stable and rugged even on uneven roads. Heritage-based and ethnic market offerings from India evoke a good response in international markets. Indian firms, such as Himalaya, Dabur, Balsara, and Zhandu, reflect this traditional strength in their international market strategy.

Self-image

The inward reflection of a brand to the consumer is known as its self-image. A customer develops an inner relationship with a brand by perception of self-image in it. Using a Parker pen may give inner satisfaction and confidence to the customer. A customer rationalizes while using Surf that she is not only using the cheapest product available in the market but it is also value for money. This influences her purchase decision as she includes herself among the class of witty women who supposedly purchase the product.

Reflection

Reflection is the target customers' perception of their external image. A brand facilitates the communication of the users' image to the outside world. The brand may reflect the user as young, mature, a show-off, beautiful, or handsome. Brand protagonists should keep in mind that the customer is not the target while reflecting the brand image, rather the brand should reflect the image of the

French wine   **New Zealand milk**

Fig. 11.12 Country of origin influences the brand image significantly

Source: www.domainebellevue.fr; www.meadowfresh.co.nz, both accessed on 19 October 2010.

person she wishes to be as a result of using the brand. A customer does not like to be portrayed as she actually is, but would like to be seen as how she would become after using the brand. Although a lady may not be beautiful, she would always like to see the most beautiful models endorsing the brand, anticipating that she would become similar to the model soon after using the brand.

Lux has been consistent in its market communication in using film stars around the world. Allen Solly positions itself to reflect the typical young executive although the brand may not be exclusively targeted to this customer group, which is very wide. MTV targets youth between the age of five and 24 years, and its music attempts to identify with their value system and reflect their personality.

Relationship

Over a period, a brand forges relationships with its customers on the basis of tangible or intangible attributes. Thus, the brand becomes a friend that the customer does not want to lose. 'Just do it' is the slogan used by Nike to encourage its customers not to lose the brand and develop an enduring relationship based on its strong values and cultural traits related to sports.

Brand Essence

The basic idea behind the brand when it is conceptualized is termed as brand essence. A brand should first decide upon its brand essence, which translates into the anticipated benefits that are later converted into specific product attributes. The brand essence of Elanza luggage from VIP is 'top of the line', which translate into a sophisticated product. The material used for manufacturing Elanza luggage is of premium quality, which is its specific brand attribute. Raaga watches have been conceptualized with a 'lady like' brand essence transforming into the product 'elegance'. Therefore, the watches are designed to match the colour and design of the consumers' *sarees* and other garments. 'Macho' is the essence of Marlboro cigarettes translating it into a socially admired brand by the customers using strong tobacco as its ingredient.

while selecting a brand name for international markets and due attention has to paid to cultural and linguistic issues.

Impressions created by a brand on the consumers' psyche, termed as brand image, are extremely important for brand building. The set of brand assets and liabilities linked to the brand—including its name and symbol—that add to or subtract from the value provided by a product or service to a firm and/or to the firm's customers are referred to as its brand equity. These brand assets include brand awareness, perceived quality, brand association, brand loyalty, and brand packaging. The attachment of a customer to a brand is termed as brand loyalty. The way a firm wants the brand to be perceived by the customer is known as brand identity, while how the customers perceived it is termed as brand image. The brand's identity and value proposition in relation to its competitors is known as brand positioning.

This chapter discusses three alternative methods to build brands. In products where the firms can create functional differentiation, the brands may be built around the core product components known as tangible product component based brand. In case of products such as soft drinks, alcoholic beverages, and mineral water where firms find it difficult to differentiate on the basis of functional aspects, brands are built around intangible components termed as intangible product component based brand. However, Indian and other Asian consumers give emphasis to both emotional and rational aspects of the products that need to be carefully imbibed while building brands for these markets. Such brands are termed as tangible–intangible product component balanced brands.

For a brand to be global it should have a minimum level of market penetration in diverse markets, dominate the domestic market so as to generate cash flows to enter new markets, meet a universal consumer need, reflect a consistent market positioning worldwide, and focus on the product category. However, in categories such as information and communication technology, the leapfrogging effect plays an important role in brands going global. This is highly significant in the Indian context where brands have attained leadership in global markets in a number of information technology related off-shore services.

The life cycle concept for product categories and individual brands exhibits different stages of market development in different markets that require separate branding strategies. This analysis of different stages of market development has further been transformed in the form of a matrix, and various branding strategies are discussed.

Summary

Developing countries including India sell most of their products in international markets as undifferentiated commodities. In the case of unbranded products, the key marketing leverage is price competitiveness, which is difficult to sustain in the long run. Brands refer to name, term, sign, symbol, or design, or a combination of these, intended to identify the goods or services of one seller or a group of sellers and to differentiate them from those of their competitors.

This chapter provides an in-depth discussion of the conceptual framework of brands and brand building. Various concepts of branding discussed in the chapter include brand image, brand equity, brand loyalty, brand awareness, brand association, brand identity, brand personality, and brand essence. How a firm wants the brand to be perceived by the customers is known as brand identity, whereas how the brand is perceived by the customers is the brand image. Competitive pressures, communication noise, bias, and market distortions play a key role in determining the perceptual filter between the firm and the customers. Brand positioning is that part of brand identity and value proposition that is actively communicated to target customers in relation to the competitors.

Strategies for building brand include tangible product component based approach, intangible product component based approach, and tangible–intangible product component based approach. Brands follow different life cycle patterns in different markets that need differentiated strategies. Developments of the product category and brand penetration are two major parameters for determining branding strategies for international markets.

Key Terms

Brand   A name, term, sign, symbol, or design, or a combination of these, intended to identify the goods or services of one seller or a group of sellers and to differentiate them from those of competitors.

Brand association   Anything that is a link in the memory of a customer to the brand.

Brand awareness   Ability of potential buyers to recognize or recall a brand as a member of a certain product category.

Brand development index (BDI)   Per capita sales of the brand category in a particular country to its per capita sales in the world.

Brand equity   Brand assets and liabilities linked to a brand, its name, and symbol that add to or subtract from the value provided by a product or service to a firm and/or to that firm's customers.

Brand essence   Basic idea behind the brand for its conceptualization.

Brand extension   Extending the brand into other categories either related or unrelated.

Brand identity   A unique set of brand associations that a firm aspires to create or maintain.

Brand image   The way a brand is perceived by the customers.

Brand loyalty   Attachment of the customer to the brand.

Brand personality   Submission of all tangible and intangible aspects of a brand.

Brand positioning   Creation of a distinct image for the brand in the minds of the customers.

Brand repositioning   Changing the existing position of a brand and modifying marketing communication accordingly.

Brand revitalization   Reviving a brand in order to revitalize sales revenue and maintain its market share.

Category development index (CDI)   Per capita sales of the product category in a particular country to its per capita sales in the world.

Global brand   A brand that reflects a consistent positioning worldwide and has balanced global market coverage.

Perceived quality   Customers' perception of the overall quality or superiority of a product or service with respect to its intended purpose.

Concept Review Questions

1. In view of the fact that most of the products marketed by developing countries are unbranded, give reasons why a marketer from India or other developing countries should learn about building brands.
2. Discuss various types of branding decisions for domestic and international markets.

3. Explain the concept of brand equity with suitable examples.
4. Distinguish between brand identity, brand image, and brand positioning.
5. Describe various brand-building alternatives. Identify the situations that influence selection of these brand-building alternatives.
6. Differentiate between BDI and CDI.

Project Assignments

1. Visit the nearest Titan showroom and list the brands available. Find out the positioning of Titan brands vis-à-vis imported watches.
2. Study the branded Indian golden jewellery available in the market and work out a strategy for launching these brands in international markets.

3. Compare the milk product brands Nestlé and Amul, and critically evaluate their brand positioning strategy for international markets.
4. Select an Indian brand and analyse its branding strategies in international markets.

CASE STUDY: BUILDING FORMIDABLE INDIAN BRANDS IN DIAMOND JEWELLERY

Ingression of Diamond Jewellery in the World's Largest Gold Jewellery Market

India has the distinction of being the largest gold jewellery market in the world. The privately held gold in India, largely in form of jewellery, is estimated over US$200 million, that is,

about one-fifth of all the gold ever mined in the world. In India, jewellery account for about 75 per cent of the total gold demand compared to world average demand for jewellery[10] of 49 per cent.

Though India had been the world's leading centre for diamond processing accounting for polishing approximately 90 per

---
[10] Average of 2008–2012; World Gold Council, 2013.

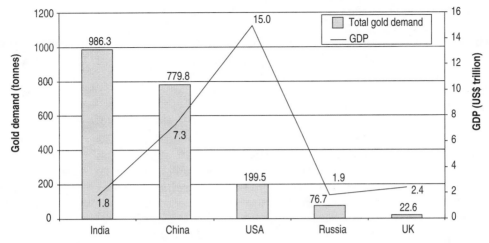

Fig. C11.1   India's obsession for gold is revealed by its consumer demand for gold vis-à-vis GDP (2011)

Source: World Gold Council and UNCTAD, 2013.

cent of world's rough diamonds representing more than 50 per cent of their total value, its market for diamond jewellery was almost insignificant about two decades ago. Branded jewellery segment was dominated by global players such as De Beers, Tiffany, and Cartier around the world with hardly any Indian brand present in the market. Rising income, especially in urban India and increasing Western influence on consumer lifestyles was paving the way for new designs and trendy jewellery in Indian markets. Owing to the large size of Indian market and its potential for growth, global luxury players were eyeing the Indian market as a goldmine for global brands in the diamond jewellery segment.

Margins in the retail segment of diamond jewellery are much higher compared to polishing rough diamonds, and Indian players too spotted the opportunity to build indigenous brands and compete with global players. In a market obsessed with gold, it was not easy to compete with gold jewellery. Interestingly, Indian diamond jewellery brands not only succeeded in building formidable Indian brands, but very impressively, India became the only market today among the world's major diamond jewellery markets where the branded segment is not dominated by any of the global brands (Fig. C11.8), rather Indian brands such as Tanishq and Nakshatra have become synonymous with diamond jewellery.

Gold: India's national obsession

Gold is a national obsession in India accounting for nearly one-third of total world demand for gold. Consumer demand for gold in India is 26.5 per cent more than that of China, whereas India's GDP is just 24.6 per cent of China and 12 per cent of the USA (Fig. C11.1). India has one of the highest saving rates in the world, estimated at 30 per cent of total income of which 10 per cent is invested in gold. Merely 21 per cent rural India has access to formal finances that leads to heavy gold purchases.

Interestingly, despite being the largest importer of gold in the world, its share in the total forex reserves is 10 per cent, much lower than that of the USA (76%) and the UK (16%), though higher than Japan (3%) and China[11] (2%). India with 557.7 million tonne of official gold reserves that account for 10 per cent of official reserves ranks 10th in the world.

In the Indian sub-continent, gold is considered to be the best possible protection, both economic and political, not only for government treasuries and businesses but households as well, unlike the West. Certain attributes of gold that make it a desirable investment option include

- liquidity;
- universal acceptance;
- insurance against instability and risks; and
- deep cultural affinity towards gold purchase.

India imports most of its gold requirements as domestic production of gold is very limited. In terms of percentage, gold and silver combined are the second most imported commodity only behind petroleum products,[12] much higher than the industrial raw materials such as coal, iron, and steel. The passion of Indians for buying gold has made even the Indian government worry about its impact on country's foreign exchange reserves, compelling it to explore policy measures to restrict gold imports. However, the obsession of the Indians for gold seems too difficult to contain.

[11] Data for 2011, World Gold Council.

[12] In 2010–2011, based on DGCI&S data.

India: the undisputed home to world's first diamonds

India has been the undisputed home to the world's first diamond mines. No place on earth has as long or close an association with diamonds as India. As far back as 3,000 years, some of the Indian Sanskrit texts made the world's first written reference to the diamonds and its commerce. A number of legendary diamonds including the *Koh-i-Noor* and the Hope excavated from India, were fascinating for their size and brilliance. They not only became world famous, but even made a mark for their colourful and notorious history. Even today, the controversies of ownership of some of these diamonds refuse to die down. In 2013, the British Prime Minister declined to hand over the *Koh-i-Noor* to India,[13] which passed on from Hindu Rajputs to Mughals, then to Iranians and Sikhs, before becoming the pride of the British Crown jewels in 1850.

Till the 19th century, India has been the undisputed principal source of diamonds in the world before discovery of diamonds in Brazil and South Africa. Presently, all mines of diamond in India are depleted except one, but the knowledge and skill of cutting and polishing that evolved over centuries makes India the global hub of diamond processing. Indian merchants, especially in places such as Surat, Navsari, Jaipur, and Mumbai, specialize in processing of rough stones. They procure these stones from around the world including Africa, and carry out cutting and polishing and re-export it as unbranded generic products. Diamond business in India is characterized by typical family-run enterprisers. However, the Indian diamond industry had limited itself till the late 1990s to trading diamonds in international markets as a commodity rather than diamond jewellery brands.

Diamond jewellery market in India

India has emerged as the world's third largest market for diamond jewellery with total annual sales[14] of US$8.5 billion in 2011 that surpass Japan, the EU, and the Gulf region. The world's three largest diamond markets, namely the USA, China, and India, account for about 60 per cent of global demand. India's share in global diamond jewellery market increased from merely 3 per cent in 2000 to 4 per cent in 2005 and reached 12 per cent in 2011 (Fig. C11.2). Diamonds are India's second fastest growing discretionary purchase only after mobile phones, but ahead of clothing, motor vehicles, and packaged holidays.

India's growth of 22 per cent in diamond jewellery market during 2005–11 is quite impressive only behind China's growth of 32 per cent but much ahead of Russia (18%) and the Gulf (16%), whereas the markets in the EU (–2%), the USA (–3%), and Japan (–9%) have experienced negative growth rates during

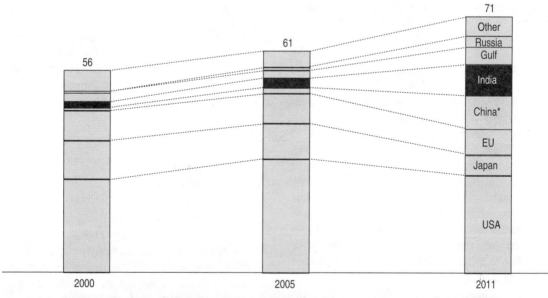

Fig. C11.2   India: emerging as the world's fastest growing diamond jewellery market after China (Global Gold Jewellery Market, US$ billion)

Source: Jewellery Retail Chains 2012, RBC Research; *The Global Diamond Industry: 2012*, Bain & Company and Antwerp World Diamond Centre (AWDC).

[13] 'Britain to India: Diamond in Royal Crown is Ours', *Reuters*, 20 February 2013.
[14] International Diamond and Jewellery Exchange, 2012.

this period. Though the diamond jewellery market in India initially declined from US$3 billion in 2005 to US$2 billion in 2006, but grew subsequently to US$9 billion in 2011 compared to total growth of global diamond jewellery market for US$11 billion to US$31 billion during the same period.

Rise in personal income, rapid urbanization, and growing influence of Western customs and traditions have contributed to increase market demand for diamond jewellery both in India and China and these markets are likely to grow much rapidly compared to other developed markets. Though total disposable income in value terms of the USA, Europe and Japan are much higher presently compared to China and India (Fig. C11.3), but over the next decade China and India are projected to grow (CAGR) at a much higher rate of 6.5 per cent and 4.8 per cent respectively compared to the USA (2.1%), Europe (1.8%), and Japan (1.8%).

Diamond share in the Indian jewellery market grew significantly from 24 per cent in 2005 to 27 per cent in 2011, compared to overall growth of 19 per cent in the jewellery market. Though the share of diamond jewellery in India at 27 per cent (Fig. C11.4) is lower than Japan (51%), the USA (49%), and Russia (36%), it is higher than the EU (18%) and China (14 %).

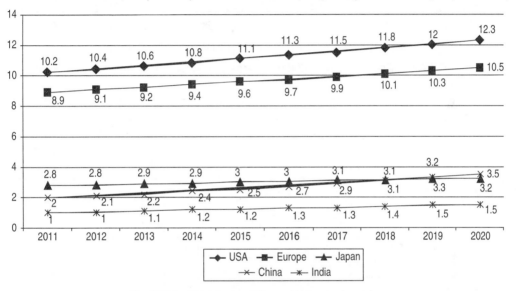

Fig. C11.3   Total personal disposable income by region

Source: *The Global Diamond Industry: 2012*, Bain & Company and Antwerp World Diamond Centre (AWDC).

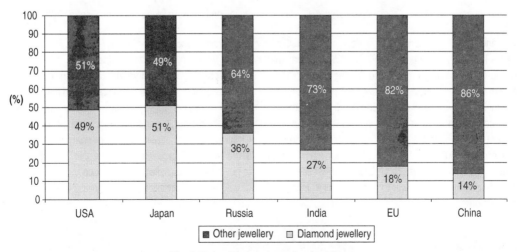

Fig. C11.4   Diamond vs other jewellery

Source: *The Global Diamond Industry: 2012*, Bain & Company and Antwerp World Diamond Centre (AWDC).

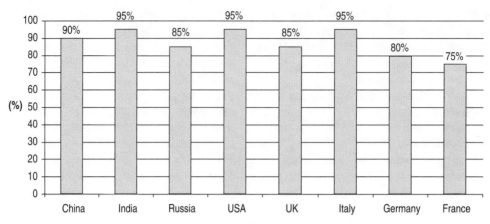

Fig. C11.5 Penetration rate of diamonds for highest income group

Source: *The Global Diamond Industry: 2012*, Bain & Company and Antwerp World Diamond Centre (AWDC).

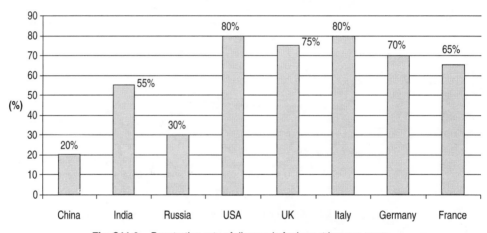

Fig. C11.6 Penetration rate of diamonds for lowest income group

Source: *The Global Diamond Industry: 2012*, Bain & Company and Antwerp World Diamond Centre (AWDC).

The penetration rate of diamond jewellery in India at 95 per cent in the highest income group[15] (Fig. C11.5) is at par with that of the USA and Italy compare to 90 per cent in China, 85 per cent in Russia and the UK, 80 per cent in Germany, and 75 per cent in France. However, diamond jewellery penetration in lowest income group[16] (Fig. C11.6) in India is much lower at 55 per cent compared to the USA (80%), Italy (80%), the UK (75%), Germany (70%), and France (65%) but much higher than Russia (30%) and China (20%). Diamond jewellery is yet to penetrate deeply among lower income groups in India and China which outnumber the rich by a large margin.

Long-term secure investment: key to jewellery purchase by Indians

To the psyche of most Indians, the use of gold in jewellery provides additional incentive of a secure and reliable investment. Diamonds are bought especially for investment motive in India by 50 per cent of the customers, compared to 45 per cent in China, 25 per cent in Russia, 20 per cent in Italy, 15 per cent in the UK and France, and 10 per cent in Germany. Compared to gold, the value of diamonds is much more complex in terms of valuation, financial, and other characteristics as shown in Table C11.1, which offers a formidable challenge to promote

---

[15] Households with annual disposable income of over US$1,00,000 in developed countries, whereas of over US$60,000 in developed countries.

[16] Households with annual disposable income of below US$50,000 in developed countries, whereas of over US$5,000 in developed countries.

Table C11.1 Diamonds are more complex to value than gold

	Specific features	Gold	Diamonds
Valuation	Homogeneous quality	Yes	No
	Value is preserved during division or reshaping	Yes	No
	Objective and direct valuation	Yes	No
Financial characteristics	Easy transportation and convenient storage	Yes	Yes
	Volume sufficient for use as currency	Yes	No
	Relatively high liquidity	Yes	No
	Limited reserves	Yes	Yes
	Sport price	Yes	In process
Others	Infeasible to economically mass produce	Yes	No
	Aesthetic value	Yes	Yes

Source: *The Global Diamond Industry: 2012*, Bain & Company and Antwerp World Diamond Centre (AWDC).

diamond as a category vis-à-vis gold jewellery. To penetrate and develop these markets especially in India and China, it becomes imperative to develop a market for investment in diamond jewellery.

Besides, pricing of gold jewellery is highly transparent as this takes into account the gold cost based on spot market prices and making or crafting charges plus a gross margin of about 5 to 20 per cent. On the other hand, margins are much higher across the diamond value chain. For instance, rough diamonds produced worldwide in 2011 worth US$15 billion become US$ 24 billion in polish diamonds, which in turn go into diamond jewellery with a retail market value of US$71 billion. In addition, lack of transparency in diamond jewellery allows for higher margins where gross profit margins are even higher at 50 to 65 per cent in mass products, compared to 30 to 40 per cent on high-end gem jewellery. As a result, diamonds and other gem jewellery are usually sold at a fixed price per piece, especially by branded players.

As Indian customers are highly obsessed with gold jewellery, major elements of marketing strategy for promoting diamond jewellery in India may be

- to persuade the trader to increase the stocking and display of diamond jewellery, in addition to the gold jewellery they were already showing; and
- to persuade consumers to include diamonds in their gold jewellery purchases as an add-on, rather than as a direct substitution.

Peeping into Indian consumer's psyche

The gift of gold in one's daughter's marriage is a matter of social status so much so that sometimes it becomes an inevitable necessity. As a result, the purchase of gold in most families starts with the birth of a daughter, which is a symbol of 'parental love' unlike most jewellery gift in the West as a symbol of 'romantic love'. Even if a gold jewellery is bought and gifted by a husband to the wife, it is under this tacit understanding, that when need arises this gold would serve as a security or pass on as a gift to the daughter or daughter-in-law. Unlike most Western countries, gift of gold jewellery to a girlfriend in India makes an insignificant part of the entire jewellery market.

To evolve a marketing strategy, the total jewellery market in India may be segmented in three distinct segments as follows:

- The wedding segment: targeting the newly-wed and marriage-related purchases
- The non-bridal segment: Singles and post-marital acquisition
- The elite segment: The few super-rich who acquire high value pieces on a regular basis

There may be a few key opportunities for promoting diamonds:

- The single largest opportunity for acquisition in Indian market was wedding opportunity extending to occasional acquisitions that started from the moment a daughter is born. This acquisition was clearly in the form of a gift from the parents to their daughter.
- Post-marital opportunity generally as a romantic surprise from the husband to the wife although constituted much lower share of total acquisition.

Among the aforementioned three, the wedding segment constitutes the largest market segment. In 81 per cent of the cases, parents and relatives of the bride and groom arrange their marriage; therefore the purchase decision for jewellery is made by them. Decision on purchase of jewellery by the groom or bride is rare in India. Even in the post-marital segment, the largest purchase without any special occasion takes place eventually for a daughter's wedding, as and when the cash happens to be available.

Customers in India exhibit distinct motives for buying gold and diamond jewellery. The competitive positioning of gold

Exhibit C11.1 Market positioning of gold vs diamond jewellery in India

Gold	Diamonds
Traditional	Modern
Common	Special
Old-fashioned	Young
Investment	Eternal
	Ultimate gift of love

and diamond jewellery in Indian market may be depicted in Exhibit C11.1.

Wedding being the largest marketing opportunity, diamond jewellery is targeted as a special gift to symbolize a young, modern, and confident Indian woman as widely depicted in advertisements (Fig. C11.7). Diamonds are also gaining popularity as gifts even on religious festivals, birth of a child, or Valentine's Day, one of the many Western cultural imports that have caught up very quickly in India.

Buying behaviour of Indian customers

Indian women have well-developed tastes in diamonds, and are very particular while shopping. Different designs are favoured depending upon the occasion of purchase: trendy designs for light hearted occasions such as birthdays and Valentine's Day, evergreen designs with classy looks that are neither too trendy nor too traditional for everyday wear, whereas traditional designs for their wedding jewellery.

The design of the jewellery is what matters most to a woman in most part of the world. Clarity is the next most important considerations ahead of the size and colour of the stones. The price and the brand of the diamond or jewellery and the stones' country of origin are often secondary consideration in purchase decision.

The first piece of diamond jewellery to an Indian woman is a ring or a pair of earrings. Her repertoire is further enhanced over a period with pendants, necklace, and bracelets usually by way of purchase or a gift received for her engagement, wedding, marriage anniversary, or birth of a child. Over the last 10–20 years, diamond engagement ring on the left hand is increasingly and proudly being used to showcase a girl's to-be-bride status.

Indian women are far more directly involved in selection of the stones, their settings, and jewellery designs, though the payments are often made by their parents or groom's families and sometimes by their fiancées or husbands. By way of Indian tradition, jewellery is gifted to the newly-weds, both the bride's and the groom's families

Fig. C11.7 Diamond jewellery positioned as a special wedding gift for a young, modern, and confident Indian woman

Source: nakshatradiamonds.in, accessed on 17 January 2012.

signifying each family's affluence. Similarly, Chinese women also take charge of the selection process, unlike American and Russian women who like to be surprised by their husbands or boyfriends who perform the actual purchase of the jewellery.

In India, China, and Russia, the top determinant of shoppers' store choice is the availability of quality certificates, whereas in developed markets such as the USA and the UK where trust in retailers and consumer protection are relatively stronger, service quality is the main criteria for choice of a diamond jewellery store.

To astonish any global marketer, India is home to over 3,00,000 jewellery stores, seven times more than in the USA and six times more than in China. Local jewellers account for over 95 per cent of jewellery sales in the highly fragmented Indian retail market. A typical Indian customer is highly loyal to their local jewellers who have been patronized by their families for generations. Large Indian organized retail chains that account only 1 per cent of diamond sales by number of outlets and 5 per cent sales by value are slowly but steadily making inroads. Geetanjali, Cygnus, and Diti are large retail chain stores.

Young working women especially from the emergent middle class are aggressively targeted with new product categories such as 'everyday diamonds' even by neighbourhood jewellery retailers offering financing schemes with instalment payment plans so as to facilitate purchase.

Brand positioning of diamond jewellery in India

Since the jewellery market in India has so far largely been for non-branded generic jewellery, the concept of branded jewellery had been not very popular among the jewellers. Besides, even diamond as a category is moving from a nascent to a growing stage in the Indian market.

Building brands of diamond jewellery is based on one common psychological association of the women around the world: expression of a way to say 'love'. Diamond is the most preferred gift a woman will like to receive in most countries across the world including India, China, the UK, Russia, Germany, and France. Interestingly, in the USA, diamond as a preferred gift for women ranks third behind cash and vacation trips.

Though diamonds carry a strong positive emotional association for women across the world, but the emotions vary across cultures. For Indian women, diamond means 'expensive', that is, its monetary value, and is also closely associated with conspicuous wealth similar to their American counterparts, unlike the Chinese women who associate diamonds with the feeling of 'eternity'. Tanishq, India's most prestigious diamond brand, frequently emphasizes on 'expensive and beautiful' in their advertisements.

Across the globe, diamond is associated with a powerful symbol of love, engagement, and wedding. In the USA and the UK, the idea of proposing marriage without offering a diamond ring is difficult to imagine for most couples. The Western practice of use of diamond rings in formalizing an engagement is rapidly gaining popularity in emerging markets such as India, China, and Russia with rise in their economic status.

The international positioning of diamond as 'a symbol of love' has also been found appropriate and motivating in positioning diamond jewellery. However, in India, the two different target segments require different marketing communication for the international positioning, 'symbol of love'. As the major marketing opportunity existed in the wedding segment wherein the jewellery was gifted from the parents to the daughter, the marketing communication had to convey the symbol of 'parental love' to their daughter who is perceived to be a working, confident, and capable women. The other marketing opportunity in post-marital segment had to be addressed by way communicating 'symbol of romantic love' wherein the relationship of the couple and the specialty of the occasion was to be conveyed. These two communication strategies for positioning diamond as a category were used.[17]

Branding Indian diamond jewellery

India had primarily been a market obsessed with gold jewellery that too mostly unbranded. On the other hand, international luxury brands do have global exposure and experience and are market leaders in the major diamond jewellery markets across the world. Global leaders of the luxury category such as Tiffany and Cartier dominate most markets in the world. Tiffany has the largest share of the women's preference in the USA, the UK, and Russia, whereas the Cartier has the edge in France, Italy, and China (Fig. C11.8).

International players target India for diamond and other designer jewellery and are usually not focused on gold, but to their utter despair, they found it extremely difficult to assess the strengths of local brands and displace them. Indian players in the branded diamond jewellery segment spotted the opportunity not only to promote diamond jewellery as a category, but also to build strong Indian brands by developing a deep understanding into customers' psyche and their buying behaviour.

To evoke public fascination towards diamond jewellery in India, leading producers, retailers, and industry associations have sponsored lavish advertising campaigns featuring top film stars and beauty queens of India. There has been a remarkable rise in ad spending of top retailers as the industry

---

[17] Choudhury, Pran K., *Successful Branding*, Universities Press, Hyderabad, 2001, pp. 69–79.

China

1. Chow Tai Fook
2. Cartier
3. Tiffany
4. Chow Sang Sang
5. Kimberlite

India

1. Tanishq
2. Nakshatra
3. Ddamas
4. Asmi
5. De Beers

Russia

1. Tiffany
2. Cartier
3. Bulgari
4. Sunlight
5. Chopard

France

1. Cartier
2. Maty
3. Boucheron
4. Mauboussin

US

1. Tiffany
2. Kay Jewelers
3. Zales
4. De Beers

UK

1. Tiffany
2. De Beers
3. H. Samuel

Italy

1. Damiani
2. Cartier
3. Bulgari
4. Tiffany

Germany

1. Christ
2. Tiffany
3. Cartier
4. Bulgari

Fig. C11.8   India is the world's only major market where indigenous diamond jewellery brands dominate and are at the customers' 'top of the mind' (Order of names shows frequency of mentioning)

Source: Based on online consumer survey.

has witnessed an increase in demand and revenue. The collective annual expenditure on advertising and promotion by four largest retailers in India—Tanishq, Tribhovandas Bhimji Zaveri (TBZ), Geetanjali, and P C Jewellers (PCJ)—is about US$100 million.

As a result, India became an illustrious exception to the dominance of global brand where the international names are surprisingly absent from the market. Local brands such as Tanishq and Nakshatra are not only at the top of the mind of Indian customers, but entrenched so deeply in public consciousness that they are not so easy to be dislodged by international players.

Questions

1. Identify the challenges in marketing diamond jewellery in India where gold is a national obsession.

2. Critically examine India's potential for marketing diamond jewellery vis-à-vis other parts of the world.

3. Assess opportunities and challenges in promoting diamond jewellery as a product category in Indian market.

4. Prepare a market segmentation plan to target branded jewellery in India.

5. Critically evaluate customer behaviour for purchase of diamond jewellery in India compared to other markets and prepare a strategy for building Indian brands for international markets.

6. How would you position branded Indian diamond jewellery in international markets? Analyse the brand positioning strategy for a few selected markets using the life cycle approach.

Pricing Decisions for International Markets

INTRODUCTION

Pricing is the only component of marketing-mix decisions, which is often adapted in international markets with least commitment of the firm's resources. In view of intense market competition from suppliers worldwide, pricing decisions become crucial to a firm's success in international markets. Moreover, pricing for international markets is extremely significant especially for small and medium enterprises (SMEs) and also for most firms from low-income countries primarily because of their inability to influence prices in international markets.

Developing countries and companies are often at disadvantageous positions in terms of their pricing options in international markets mainly due to the following reasons:

- The lower production and technology base often results in higher cost of production.
- As the market share of developing countries is relatively much lower and these countries are marginal suppliers in most product categories, they have little bargaining power to negotiate. This compels them to often sell their products in international markets at prices below the total cost of production.
- Since the majority of products from developing and least developed countries are sold in international markets as commodities with marginal value addition, there is limited scope for realizing optimal prices.

This chapter brings out the concept of pricing decisions with special reference to international markets. The major pricing approaches for international markets such as cost-based pricing and market-based pricing have been examined. The concepts of marginal cost pricing vis-à-vis full cost pricing have also been dealt with so as to provide a sound understanding of international pricing concepts. Various factors influencing pricing decisions in international markets such as cost, competition, buyer's purchasing power, and foreign exchange fluctuations have also been explained.

Learning Objectives

- To discuss the significance of pricing in international markets
- To elucidate the concept of pricing in international markets
- To examine various pricing approaches in international markets
- To delineate various terms of delivery
- To discuss various terms of payment
- To explicate counter trade and its various forms
- To understand the concept of dumping in international markets
- To describe transfer pricing in international markets
- To explain the concept of grey marketing

The terms of delivery widely known as International Commercial Terms (INCOTERMS), which forms an integral part of an international price quotation, have been dealt with in detail in the chapter. Alternative payment options in international trade transactions, popularly known as 'terms of payment' have also been elucidated. This chapter discusses various forms of countertrade, such as barter, counter purchase, buy-back, and offset.

Dumping is a widely used marketing tool in international business as it makes strong economic sense to sell goods at lower prices in international markets than in the domestic market. The concept of dumping has been explained, besides major variants of dumping. Non-cash commitments are also prevalent as a part of pricing decisions under the practice of countertrade. The price of an international transaction between related parties, often referred to as transfer price, has also been dealt with in detail. The firm has to take care of grey marketing channels while fixing prices as they can otherwise defeat the firms' strategic intent of international pricing. This chapter also examines various issues related to grey marketing and its types.

CONCEPT OF PRICING IN INTERNATIONAL MARKETS

The price of a product or a service is the sum of values received from the customer. We generally refer to price in terms of amount of money, but it may also include other tangible and intangible items of utility. In view of the fiercely competitive markets and complex pricing strategies adopted by multinational marketers, formulation of appropriate pricing strategies with innovation becomes a pre-condition for success in international markets. Moreover, it needs little resources to adapt pricing for different markets unlike other components of international marketing mix.

It should thus be made clear that determination of price is seldom a function of cost. The cost of suppliers in the international markets varies widely, whereas the price has to be set in view of the prevailing market prices of competing products or close substitutes. The price in international markets is often influenced by a number of factors such as competition, market demand, costs, buyers' purchasing power, and foreign exchange fluctuation. However, costs serve as an important parameter for determining the firms' profit margins.

As the intensity of competition is much higher in international markets, firms often use the marginal cost pricing approach. As explained later in this chapter, it makes sound economic sense to adopt the marginal costing approach; nevertheless, it carries the risk of anti-dumping action in the importing country. Hence, it needs to be used carefully as a strategic tool to penetrate international markets.

The market-based pricing approach often pays as it takes into account the prevailing prices in the market. A top-down calculation approach is suggested to estimate the cost of production, which may be subsequently followed by bottom-up calculations. Such an approach often suggests that rather than cost deciding the price, it is the other way round, wherein the cost of production is often decided by the price. The terms of delivery (INCOTERMS) define the costs, risks, and obligations of buyers and sellers in an international transaction. This forms an integral part of a price quotation and facilitates the formulation of pricing decisions for international markets.

For tapping markets with hard currency shortage and balance of payment (BOP) problems, countertrade is a highly effective tool. One has to be careful in making pricing decisions so that the products meant for a given market do not pass through unauthorized channels, giving rise to grey marketing. Proactive and reactive approaches to combat grey marketing may also be employed.

PRICING APPROACHES FOR INTERNATIONAL MARKETS

Pricing decisions for international markets are often made based either on costs—full or marginal—or prevailing market prices as delineated next.

Cost-based Pricing

Costs are widely used by firms to determine prices in international markets, especially in the initial stages. New exporters often determine export prices on 'ex-works' price level, and add a certain percentage of profit and other expenses, depending upon the term of delivery used. However, such cost-based pricing methods are not optimal and the reasons are as follows:

- The price quoted by the exporter on the basis of cost calculations may be too low vis-à-vis competitors that allow importers to earn huge margins.
- The price quoted by the exporters may be too high to make their goods uncompetitive resulting in the outright rejection of the offer.

Cost-based pricing approaches may either be based on full or marginal costs as discussed next.

Full cost pricing

Pricing based on full cost is the most common pricing approach used by exporters in the initial stages of their internationalization. It includes adding a mark-up on the total cost to determine price. The major benefits of the full cost pricing approach are as follows:

- Widely used by exporters in the initial phases of their internationalization
- Useful for firms that are mainly dependent upon international markets and have very low or negligible sales in domestic markets
- Speedy recovery of investments
- Ease of operations and implementation

Nevertheless, certain bottlenecks are also associated with full cost pricing approach. They are as follows:

- It often overlooks the prevailing price structure in international markets that may either make the product uncompetitive or deprive the firm from charging higher prices.
- As competitors often use price-cutting strategies to penetrate or gain share in international markets, the full cost pricing approach fails to withstand the price competition.

Marginal cost pricing

In view of the huge size of international markets compared to the domestic market, exports are considered to be outlets to dispose of surplus production that a firm finds difficult to sell in the domestic market. As the intensity of competition in international markets is much higher than that in the domestic market, competitive pricing becomes a pre-condition for success. Therefore, a large number of firms adopt the marginal costing approach for pricing decisions in international markets.

Marginal cost is the cost of producing and selling one more unit. It sets the lower limit to which a firm can reduce its price without affecting its overall profitability. Under the marginal cost approach, the firm realizes its fixed cost from domestic markets and uses variable costing approach for international markets (Fig. 12.1). The major reasons for adopting pricing based on marginal cost are as follows:

- In cases where foreign markets are used to dispose of the surplus production, marginal cost-based pricing provides an alternative marketing outlet.

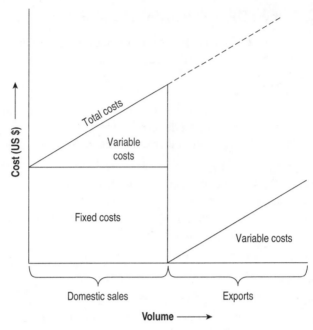

Fig. 12.1 Marginal vs full cost pricing

- As products from developing countries seldom compete on brand image or unique value, marginal costing is used as a tool to penetrate and compete in international markets.
- Selling on marginal cost-based pricing provides some contribution, which the firm would forego in case it decides not to export at marginal cost-based price.

Thus, using marginal costs for international pricing makes sound commercial sense as elucidated in Exhibit 12.1.

Exhibit 12.1 Why does it make sense to use marginal costing in export pricing?

Twinkle Illuminations is a Kolkata-based firm with an installed capacity of producing 10,000 units of designer lamps per annum with a fixed cost of US$5,00,000. The variable cost is US$100 per unit. It sells 5,000 units in the domestic market at ₹230 per unit. Using the total cost approach, per unit cost can be worked out as follows:

Total cost = Fixed cost + Variable cost
= US$5,00,000 + US$5,000 × 100
= US$5,00,000 + US$5,00,000
= US$10,00,000
Therefore, Total cost per unit = US $10,00,000/5,000
= US$200

The firm receives an export order for 40,000 units @ US$130 per unit. Apparently, it does not cover the total cost of US$200 per unit as depicted above. Now, the firm has to decide whether it would be able to export 40,000 units at US$130 per unit. The implications of accepting this order are as follows:

- The firm would receive a contribution of US$30 per unit for export

Contribution = Selling price − Variable cost
= US$130 − US$100
= US$30

It works out to a total contribution on 40,000 units as US$12,00,000. It would lose this contribution in case the firm does not accept the export order.

- The firm finds it difficult to sell beyond 5,000 units in the domestic market; so it has to look for alternate marketing opportunities overseas.
- There is idle installed capacity of 5,000 units after meeting the domestic demand of 5,000 units.

Therefore, it makes sound commercial sense to export using the marginal cost pricing approach till full capacity utilization is achieved.

However, the major limitations associated with marginal cost-based pricing approach are as follows:

- In case the firm is selling most of its output in international markets, it cannot use marginal cost-based pricing as the fixed cost is also to be recovered.
- Pricing based on marginal cost may be treated as dumping in overseas markets and is liable to anti-dumping action subject to investigations.
- Such pricing tends to trigger price wars in overseas markets and lead to price undercutting among the suppliers.
- Use of marginal cost-based price with little information on prevailing market prices leads to unrealistic low-price quotations.

Market-based Pricing

It is a popular myth that costs alone determine the price. In fact, it is the interaction of a variety of factors such as costs, competitive intensity, demand structure, and consumer behaviour that contribute to price determination in international markets. However, costs serve as useful indicators of the profitability of a firm. Therefore, a market-based pricing approach is generally preferred to a cost-based pricing approach.

As developing countries are marginal suppliers of goods in most markets, they hardly have market shares large enough to influence prices in international markets. Hence, the exporters in developing countries are generally price followers rather than price setters. Besides, the products offered by them are seldom so unique to enable them to dictate prices. Under such market situations, the pricing decisions by price followers from developing countries involve assessment of prevailing prices in international markets and working out prices based on top-down calculations[1] as follows:

- Establish the current market price for comparative and/or substitute products in the target market.
- Establish all the elements of the market price, such as VAT, margins for the trade and the importer, import duties, and freight and insurance costs.
- Make a top-down calculation, deducting all the elements of the expected market price of the product(s) in order to arrive at the 'ex-works', 'ex-factory', or 'ex-warehouse' price.
- Assess if this can be met.
- If not, re-calculate the cost price by finding ways to decrease costs in the factory or organization or to decrease the marketing budget, which also burdens export-market price.
- Estimate total sales over a three-year period, add total planned expenses, including those of the export department and the travelling, and canvassing efforts.
- Make a bottom-up calculation per product item, dividing the supporting budgets over the total number of items to be sold.
- Set the final market price.
- Test the price through market research.

Such top-down calculations enable a firm to determine if it can meet competitors' market prices at the cost price level. In this calculation, the 'ex-works' price, that is, US$330 is 28.4 per cent of the price paid by the consumer, which is US$1160. It works out to a 'multiplier' of 3.5. This 'multiplier' is used as a calculating aid while offering price quotations in international

---

[1] Laman, Johan F., M.A. Trip, *CBI Export Planner—A Comprehensive Guide for Prospective Exporters in Developing Countries*, Third Edition, CBI Rotterdam, The Netherlands, 1997.

Exhibit 12.2 Top-down calculations for international pricing

Consumer price:	1,160		
VAT*	160	+	16%**
Market price minus VAT:	1,000		
Margin retailer:	250	=	25%**
Price to retailer:	750		
Margin wholesaler:	90	+	12%**
Price to wholesaler:	660		
Margin to importer	33	+	5%**
Landed-cost price:	627		
Import duties:	110	+	20%**
Other costs (storage, banking):	17**		
CIF (port of destination):	500		
Transportation costs:	130**		
Insurance costs:	6**		
FOB (port of shipment):	364		
Transportation costs factory to port:	34**		
Export price ex-works (EXW):	330		
Factory cost price:	300**		
Export profit (per unit):	30		

*Note that VAT is calculated as a percentage of the price without VAT. Trade margins are usually calculated as a percentage of the trade selling price. The trade margins for some sectors are calculated as a percentage of trade buying prices.
**Figures based on assumptions.

markets. However, the firms should estimate their total sales in the planned year and also carry out bottom-up calculations for preparing a price quotation based on an estimated 'ex-works' price. This may be followed up by carrying out a 'feasibility calculation' so as to assess the export feasibility on the basis of the price estimates as given in Exhibits 12.2 and 12.3.

Thus, the firm may estimate the gross profits from exports based on the market size, share, growth, and various expenses. Based on this, suitable modifications may be done in the product design, costs, and price before deciding upon entering overseas markets.

FACTORS INFLUENCING PRICING DECISIONS

Various factors influencing pricing decisions in international markets include cost, competition, buyer's purchasing power, and foreign exchange fluctuations.

Cost

A large number of exporters in their initial stages of their business use cost-based pricing, which is hardly the best way to determine price in international markets. However, the cost is often the key determinant of the profitability of a firm in selling the product. Firms located in different countries do have significant variations in their costs of production and marketing but the price in international markets is determined by market forces. Therefore, the profitability among international firms varies widely, depending upon their costing. In general, the 'ex works' cost is only about 20 per cent to 30 per cent of the price the consumer pays for the product; any savings in cost of production is likely to have a multiplier effect on the final price paid by the consumer.

Exhibit 12.3 Assessing export feasibility

Country/Market

(In units/$1,000)

Plan year	0	1	2	3
Market size	100	102	104.0	107.2
Change/annum (%)	+2	+2	+3	
Market share (%)	0	1.5	4	5
Gross turnover				
1. At market prices				
2. At EXW prices				
–/– Commissions				
–/– Bonuses				
–/– Claims, returns				
Net sales	0			
–/– Export marketing costs	0			
Contribution to export department				
–/– Indirect costs				
Export dept. (Travelling, etc.)				
Contribution to export overheads				
–/– Overheads export				
department (Salaries, rent, etc.)				
Contribution to corporate overheads				
(Actual export profit)				
Same, cumulative	0			
–/– Corporate overheads				
(Corporate salaries, R&D, warehousing,				
administration, etc.)				
Gross profit				
(Before taxes)				

Source: Johan F. Laman Trip M.A., *CBI Export Planner—A comprehensive Guide for Prospective Exporters in Developing Countries*, Third Edition, CBI Rotterdam, The Netherlands, 1997.

Since the cost incurred on logistics forms a substantial part of the final consumer price, the efficiency and cost-cutting on logistics considerably influence a firm's price competitiveness in international markets.

Competition

The level of competition is much higher in international markets compared to the domestic markets. The nature of competition and its intensity vary widely in international markets. On a seven-point scale, wherein the highest point of the scale '7' indicates that the competition in the local markets is intense in most industries and the lowest point '1' indicates that the market competition is limited in most industries, intensity of local competition is highest in Netherlands (6.1), compared to Japan (6.0), Taiwan (6.0), Belgium (6.0), UK (6.0), Germany (5.8), UAE (5.7), France (5.5), India (5.4), China (5.3), Brazil (5.1), South Africa (5.1), Egypt (4.0), Venezuela (3.3), and Algeria (3.1) as shown in Fig. 12.2. A firm should carefully assess the market competition while making pricing decisions in international markets.

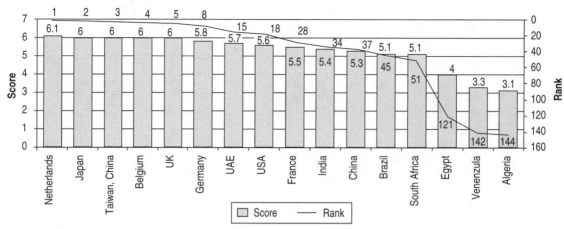

Fig. 12.2 Intensity of local competition

7 = Intense in most industries   1 = Limited in most industries
Source: Based on data from *The Global Competitiveness Report*, 2012–13, World Economic Forum, Geneva, 2012, p. 450.

Purchasing Power

The purchasing power of customers varies widely among countries. A firm operating in international markets should take into consideration the ability of buyers to pay while making pricing decisions. A company has leverage to provide additional product features and charge relatively higher prices in countries with high purchasing power.

Gross domestic product (GDP) per capita, as discussed in Chapter 8, serves as a broad indicator for purchasing power. The Big Mac Index and the CommSec iPad Index also serve as useful tools to carry out a cross-country comparison and assess purchasing power.

Big Mac Index

Big Mac is considered a global product, which involves similar inputs and processes in its preparation across the world. McDonald's prices its products in international markets depending upon the country's purchasing power, as indicated in Exhibit 12.4. The theory of purchasing power parity

Exhibit 12.4 The Big Mac Index

Country	Big Mac prices in local currency	Big Mac prices in $*	Implied PPP of the dollar	Actual dollar exchange rate, 11 January 2012	Under (–)/Over (+) valuation against the dollar (%)
USA‡	$4.20	4.20	–	–	–
Argentina	Peso 20.0	4.64	4.77	4.31	10
Australia	A$4.80	4.94	1.14	0.97	18
Brazil	Real 10.25	5.68	2.44	1.81	35
Britain	£2.49	3.82	1.69¶	1.54	–9
Canada	C$4.73	4.63	1.13	1.02	10
Chile	Peso 2,050	4.05	488	506	–3

(Contd)

TERMS OF DELIVERY (INCOTERMS) IN INTERNATIONAL TRANSACTIONS

In export–import transactions, prices are generally quoted using internationally accepted terms of delivery, known as INCOTERMS, used to describe the rights and responsibilities of the buyers and the sellers with regard to sale and transport of goods. Uniform rules interpreting INCOTERMS have been developed by the International Chamber of Commerce (ICC) in Paris so as to define the costs, risks, and obligations of the buyers and the sellers in international transactions. These INCOTERMS were first published in 1936 and had subsequently been revised to account for changing modes of transport and document delivery. INCOTERMS 2010 are the current version in force from 1 January 2011. Although it is difficult to cover all possible legal and transportation issues in an international transaction, INCOTERMS provide a sort of contractual shorthand among various parties.

INCOTERMS 2010 facilitate the contracting parties:

- To complete sale of goods
- To indicate each contracting party's costs, risks, and obligations with regard to the delivery of goods as follows:
  - When is the delivery completed?
  - How does a party ensure that the other party has met that standard of conduct?
  - Which party must comply with requisite licences and government-imposed formalities?
  - What are the modes and terms of carriage?
  - What are the delivery terms and what is required as proof of delivery?
  - When is the risk of loss transferred from the seller to the buyer?
  - How will transport costs be divided between the parties?
  - Who is responsible for taking insurance cover?
  - What notices are the parties required to give to each other regarding the transport and transfer of the goods?
- To establish the basic terms of transport and delivery in a short format

INCOTERMS 2010 comprise a set of eleven delivery terms as shown in Exhibit 12.5, categorized based on their applicability to the mode of transport vis-à-vis main carriage unpaid and paid used for departure and shipment.

Exhibit 12.5   INCOTERMS 2010 and their applicability

Category	Applicable for sea and inland waterways transport only	Applicable for all modes of transport (including water)
Departure terms		EXW (ex works)
Shipment terms, main carriage unpaid	FAS (free alongside ship) FOB (free on board)	FCA (free carrier)
Shipment terms, main carriage paid	CFR (cost and freight) CIF (cost, insurance, and freight)	CPT (carriage paid to) CIP (carriage and insurance paid to)
Delivery terms		DAT (delivered at terminal)
		DAP (delivered at place)
		DDP (delivered duty paid)

A self-explanatory depiction of transfer of costs and risks from sellers to buyers based on INCOTERMS 2010 is shown in Fig. 12.5.

Charges/Fees	Any transport mode		Sea/Inland waterway transport				Any transport mode				
	EXW	FCA	FAS	FOB	CFR	CIF	CPT	CIP	DAT	DAP	DDP
	Ex works	Free carrier	Free alongside ship	Free on board	Cost & freight	Cost insurance & freight	Carriage paid to	Carriage insurance paid to	Delivered at terminal	Delivered at place	Delivered duty paid
Packaging	Buyer or Seller	Seller	Seller	Seller	Seller	Seller	Seller	Seller	Seller	Seller	Seller
Loading charges	Buyer	Seller*	Seller	Seller	Seller	Seller	Seller	Seller	Seller	Seller	Seller
Delivery to port/place	Buyer	Seller	Seller	Seller	Seller	Seller	Seller	Seller	Seller	Seller	Seller
Export duty & taxes	Buyer	Seller	Seller	Seller	Seller	Seller	Seller	Seller	Seller	Seller	Seller
Origin terminal charges	Buyer	Buyer	Seller	Seller	Seller	Seller	Seller	Seller	Seller	Seller	Seller
Loading on carriage	Buyer	Buyer	Buyer	Seller	Seller	Seller	Seller	Seller	Seller	Seller	Seller
Carriage charges	Buyer	Buyer	Buyer	Buyer	Seller	Seller	Seller	Seller	Seller	Seller	Seller
Insurance						Seller		Seller			
Destination terminal charges	Buyer	Buyer	Buyer	Buyer	Buyer	Buyer	Seller	Seller	Seller	Seller	Seller
Delivery to destination	Buyer	Buyer	Buyer	Buyer	Buyer	Buyer	Buyer	Buyer	Buyer	Seller	Seller
Import duty & taxes	Buyer	Buyer	Buyer	Buyer	Buyer	Buyer	Buyer	Buyer	Buyer	Buyer	Seller

* Seller is responsible for loading charges, if the term states FCA at seller's facility

Fig. 12.5 INCOTERMS 2010: transfer of costs and risks from sellers to buyers

INCOTERMS for Sea and Inland Waterways

FAS (Free alongside Ship) at named port of shipment The seller passes the risk to the buyer, including payment of all transportation and insurance costs, when the goods are delivered alongside the vessel at the named port of shipment by the seller. The seller also gets the goods clear for exports.

FOB (Free on Board) at named port of shipment The seller passes the risk to the buyer, including payment of all transportation and insurance costs, when the goods are placed on board the ship at the named port. It is a step further from FAS.

CFR (Cost and Freight) to named port of shipment The seller delivers goods and passes the risk to buyers when the goods are placed on board the vessel at the port of export. It is a step further from FOB. The seller must pay the costs and freight necessary to bring the goods to the named port of destination.

CIF (Cost, Insurance, and Freight) to named port of shipment   the seller passes the risk to the buyer when goods are placed on board the ship at the port of export. The seller arranges and pays cost and freight for bringing the goods to the named port of destination. The seller also has to procure marine insurance against the buyer's risk of loss of or damage to the goods during the carriage.

INCOTERMS for Any Mode or Modes of Transportation

EXW (Ex Works) at named place   The seller makes goods available to the buyer at the seller's premises or another named place (i.e., works, factory, warehouse, etc.) not cleared for export and not loaded on any collecting vehicle. Long held as the most preferable term for new-to-export because it presents minimum liability to the seller.

FCA (Free Carrier) at named place of departure   The seller delivers the goods to the carrier named by the buyer at the specified place and may be responsible for clearing the goods for export.

CPT (Carriage Paid to) to named place of destination   The seller shifts the risk to the buyer by delivering goods to the carrier at an agreed place and also pays cost of bringing good to the named place of destination. The seller also clears the goods for export.

CIP (Carriage and Insurance Paid to) to named place of destination   The seller shifts the risk to the buyer by delivering goods to the carrier at an agreed place and pays cost of bringing good to the named place of destination. The seller also obtains insurance against the buyer's risk of loss or damage during carriage and clears the goods for exports.

DAT (Delivered at Terminal) at named terminal or port or place of destination   The seller bears cost, risk, and responsibility until goods are unloaded at named quay, warehouse, yard, or terminal at destination. Demurrage or detention charges may apply to the seller. The seller clears goods for export, not import. DAT replaces DEQ and DES.

DAP (Delivered at Place) at named place of destination   The seller bears cost, risk, and responsibility for goods until they are made available to the buyer at the named place of destination. The seller clears goods for export, not import. DAP replaces DAF and DDU.

DDP (Delivered Duty Paid) at named place of destination   The seller bears cost, risk, and responsibility for delivering cleared goods at the named place of destination at the buyer's disposal. The buyer is responsible for unloading. The seller is responsible for import clearance, duties, and taxes; so the buyer is not 'importer of record'.

The rights and obligations of buyers and sellers indicating their responsibility in an international sales transaction have been indicated in Exhibit 12.6. Ex-work (EXW) involves lowest obligation while the delivered duty paid (DDP) involves highest obligation for a seller. However, one has to decide upon the delivery term in view of the prevailing trade practices and competitive structure of the market.

As major limitations, INCOTERMS do not
- apply to contracts for services;
- define contractual rights and obligations other than for delivery;
- specify details of the transfer, transport, and delivery of the goods;
- determine how title to the goods will be transferred;
- protect a party from his/her own risk of loss;
- cover the goods before or after delivery; and
- define the remedies for breach of contract.

Exhibit 12.6 Division of responsibilities under INCOTERMS 2010

INCOTERMS used in price quotation	Expenses to be included	Additional cost (in ₹)	Total price to be quoted (in ₹)
EXW	Ex-works Jaipur: Export packing, marking crates with shipping marks	200	5,000
FCA	Free on carrier at Jaipur station: Carriage and insurance for delivery to railway station by road transport including insurance	150	5,350
FAS	Free alongside ship at Kandla: Rail transport to port (including insurance) and getting goods on the quay alongside ship	400	5,750
FOB	Free on board Kandla: Dock dues, loading goods on board ship, preparing shipping documents	120	5,870
CFR	Cost and freight: Sea freight to Singapore (nearest port to Singapore)	230	6,100
CIF	Cost, insurance, and freight: Sea freight plus marine insurance (port to port)	100	6,200
DAP	Delivered at place in Singapore: Inland transport charges at Singapore	80	6,280
DDP	Delivered duty paid at the buyer's place in Singapore • Import duties for 1000 pieces of greeting cards	720	7,000

TERMS OF PAYMENT IN INTERNATIONAL TRANSACTIONS

While making a price quotation to an overseas importer, an exporting firm has to decide the payment terms mutually agreeable both to the importer as well as the exporter. The terms of payment also known as modes of payment indicate as to how and when the money is transferred from the importer to the exporter. Managers involved in international markets need to develop a thorough understanding of various payment terms used in export–import transactions and apply them aptly so as to suit their requirements.

Though, various modes of payments are discussed in detail in Chapter 15, a brief description is given here from the perspective of international pricing. As the problem faced in realizing the payment varies from case to case, terms of payment differ widely, depending upon the nature of market competition, type of products dealt in, credit worthiness of buyers, and exporters' relationship and experience with the importer. Various factors affecting the terms of payment include the risk associated, speed, security, cost, and the market competition. The major terms of payment used in international markets are as follows.

Advance Payment

Exporters would always like to receive the payment in advance as this involves little risk for them and is devoid of any complexities. The payment under the advance payment term is remitted by the buyer in advance either by a draft, email, or telegraphic transfer (TT). It involves the highest level of risk for the buyer. Therefore, advance payment is used only in cases where the exporter is in a position to dictate terms. For example, if the product supplied is unique or has some sort of monopolistic power, such mode of payment can be used. However, such a form of payment is common usually in case of overseas affiliates of the exporting firm.

Open Account

Foreign affiliates or subsidiary companies of multinationals or overseas importers, which have longstanding relations with the exporting firms, often agree to make payments without documents.

Payments under open accounts are generally settled after the exports are made and even the importer takes delivery of the goods. Though there is enormous ease operation settling the accounts, there are tremendous risks to the exporter. Therefore, such accounts are permitted by most countries' regulatory authorities between the related firms or their offshoots.

Consignment Sales

In cases of consignment sales, even price is often quoted only once the buyer physically examines the product. For high value products such as diamonds, tanzanite, sapphire, ruby and most other gems pricing is made only after the overseas buyer examines the product and is satisfied. Flowers being highly perishable are also sold on consignment sales in international flower auctions. It involves certain additional costs such as warehousing charges, insurance, interest, and commission of the agents. The exporter has to bear the liability and risks of the consignment unless it is sold. As the period to receive the payment is uncertain till the products are finally sold, the exporter's funds are blocked. Depending upon the product attributes and the buyer's satisfaction, there is also a possibility of realizing higher prices.

Documentary Credit

In a typical international transaction, an exporter deals with an overseas buyer who is situated in a significantly different regulatory and business environment. The exporter is unwilling to part with his goods unless s/he is assured of receipt of the payment from the importer. The importer is unwilling to part with the money unless he is assured of receiving the payment. In such situations, the bank plays a crucial role of an intermediary providing assurance to both the importer and the exporter in an international transaction. A documentary credit may be with or without letter of credit (L/C) which is governed by the Uniform Customs and Practices for Documentary Credits (UCPDC) of the ICC as elaborated in Chapter 15.

COUNTER TRADE

Counter trade is a practice where price setting and trade financing are tied together in one transaction. It is a generic term that refers to various forms of trade arrangements wherein the payment is in the form of reciprocal commitments for other goods or services rather than an exclusive cash transaction. Modern forms of counter trade are sophisticated forms of the ancient practice of simple barter of goods and services to accommodate present-day business needs.

Contrary to general belief, counter trade has grown over the recent years. About 15 countries were believed to be involved in counter trade in 1972, which increased to 27 countries in 1979, and by the beginning of 1990s around 100 countries used counter trade.[3] It is estimated that about 20 to 30 per cent of the world trade takes place in the form of counter trade and is likely to increase in the future.

In situations where the importer is not able to make payment in hard currencies, some other forms of counter trade take place. Various factors contributing to counter trade include the following:

- Importing country's inability to pay in hard currency
- Importing country's regulations to conserve hard currency
- Importing country's concern about balance of trade
- Exploring opportunities in new markets
- Gaining access to capital goods markets in countries with shortage of hard currency

---

[3] Vertariu, P., 'Trends and Development in International Counter Trade', *Business America*, 2 November 1992, pp. 2–6.

Counter trade is classified on the basis of reciprocal commitments mode.[4] The major types of counter trade are discussed here.

Simple Barter

Barter is the simplest and the most ancient form of counter trade in which direct and simultaneous exchange of products of equal value takes place. Since one product is exchanged for another in barter trade, the role of money as a medium of exchange is eliminated. Barter makes international trade transactions possible between cash-constrained countries.

In simple barter, there is no involvement of money, and goods are exchanged for other goods (Fig. 12.6). This type of barter has been in practice for centuries right from the ancient civilizations of Indus Valley, Mesopotamia, Greek, and Rome, wherein spices, grains, metals, olive oil, wine, and cosmetics were exchanged.

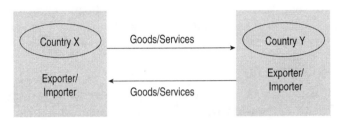

Fig. 12.6   Simple barter

Source: Hennart, Jean-Francois, 'Some Empirical Dimensions of Counter Trade', *Journal of International Business Studies*, Second Quarter, 1990, p. 245.

PepsiCo entered one of the largest barters with Russia valued at US$3 billion. PepsiCo had been engaged in business with Russia since 1974, shipping soft drinks syrup, bottling it as Pepsi Cola, and marketing it within Russia. In 1999, PepsiCo's sales volume amounted to US$300 million comprising about 40 million cases from about 26 bottling plants in Russia. PepsiCo found it difficult to take out the profits from Russia, as the hard currency was just not available. Therefore, PepsiCo entered into an agreement to export Stolichnaya vodka to the USA, where it was sold through an independent liquor company. In 1990, a new deal was also signed, which included the sale or the lease of at least 10 Russian tanker ships ranging from 28,000 to 65,000 tonnes. The proceeds of these transactions were to be used to expand the ongoing PepsiCo business in Russia by expanding Pepsi Cola through national distribution channels and to fund the expansion of the Pizza Hut restaurant chain.[5]

In 2000, India and Iraq agreed on an 'oil for wheat and rice' barter deal, subject to UN approval under Article 50 of the UN Gulf War sanctions to facilitate 3,00,000 barrels of oil delivered daily to India at a price of US$6.85 a barrel, while Iraq oil sales into Asia were valued at about US$22 a barrel. In 2001, India agreed to swap 1.5 million tonnes of Iraqi crude oil under the oil for food programme.[6]

Air India signed a counter-trade agreement[7] with the European aircraft manufacturer Boeing in January 2006 for purchase of 68 aircraft at an estimated cost of ₹350 billion. As a part of

[4] Hennart, Jean-Francois, 'Some Empirical Dimensions of Countertrade', *Journal of International Business Studies*, Second Quarter 1990, p. 245.

[5] 'Pepsi will be Bartered for Ships and Vodka in Deal with Soviets', *New York Times*, 9 April 1990, p. 1.

[6] 'India to Barter Wheat for Iraq's Crude Oil', *Indian Express*, Mumbai, 11 November 2000.

[7] 'AI Sings Deal for 68 Boeing Aircraft-Boeing to Invest US$185 million for Various Facilities', *Business Line*, 12 January 2006.

the deal, Boeing is committed to invest US$100 million in setting up an MRO (maintenance, repair, and overhauling) facility, US$75 million in a pilot training institute, and US$10 million in other facilities. Besides, Boeing would also buy goods and services worth ₹85 billion from Indian companies.

Since it is not always possible to find a perfect match of mutual needs of the buyer and the seller, other forms of counter trade are also involved.

Clearing Arrangement

Under the clearing arrangements, the transaction of goods and services extends over a long time. Generally, under such agreements, the governments of exporting and importing countries enter into an agreement to purchase the goods and services over an agreed period of time, as indicated in Fig. 12.7. Besides, the currency of transaction, such as Rupee or Rouble, is also agreed upon. Such a form of counter trade existed between India and the erstwhile USSR under the Rupee Payment Agreement with an objective to preserve hard currency and facilitate bilateral trade. The Soviet Union also had such clearing arrangements with Morocco.

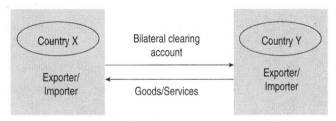

Fig. 12.7 Clearing arrangement

Switch Trading

Switch trading involves third parties in the transactions, as depicted in Fig. 12.8. In case an importer in country Y has neither the goods that can be used for barter nor the capability to make payment in hard currency, a switch trader is involved in the third country. The switch trader in country Z imports the goods or services from the importer in country Y and makes payment either in cash or by way of barter in terms of goods and services to the exporter in country X.

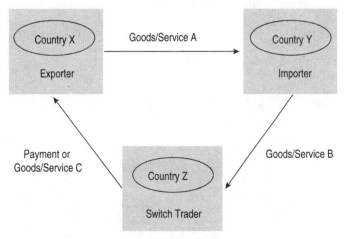

Fig. 12.8 Switch trading

Counter Purchase

It is also known as parallel barter wherein two contracts or a set of parallel cash sales agreements take place, each payable in cash. Counter purchase, unlike barter, involves two separate transactions (Fig. 12.9), each with its own cash value. Brazil has long been exporting vehicles, steel, and farm products to oil producing countries, from which it buys oil in return.

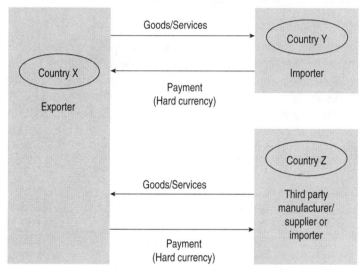

Fig. 12.9   Counter purchase

Buy-back (Compensation)

While supplying capital goods or technology in international markets, firms often enter some sort of buy-back arrangements (Fig. 12.10) wherein the output of the equipment and plants is taken back. A large number of industrial units that buy such capital goods and machinery especially in low-income countries often find it difficult to arrange finances for such large investments. Therefore, the buy-back arrangements not only serve as an important tool for financing their capital goods investment but also assure them of a market outlet for their resultant output. Hence, buy-back arrangements are very common in international marketing of capital goods and technology. Such buy-back arrangements may involve full

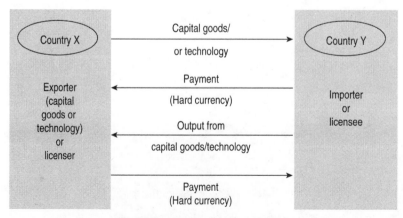

Fig. 12.10   Buy-back (compensation)

compensation by way of purchasing the output from the capital goods supplied or it may be partial wherein a part payment is received in hard currency, whereas the balance is compensated by way of purchasing the output.

Offset

Generally, in large government purchases such as public utilities or defence equipment purchases, offset is particularly common due to the difficulties faced by the importer or the importer's government to make payment in hard currency and issues related to balance of payment. Under the offset arrangements (Fig. 12.11), the importer makes partial payment in hard currency besides promising to source inputs from the importing country and also makes investment to facilitate production of such goods.

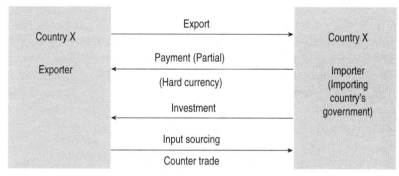

Fig. 12.11 Offset

Both exporters and importers find counter trade a useful tool in international transactions. Exporters favour it because counter trade

- provides an opportunity to access the markets that do not have capability to pay in hard currency;
- facilitates higher capacity utilization;
- helps in finding alternate markets for their goods;
- establishes long-term relationship with international buyers; and
- increases profits and market share.

Since importers in low-income countries often face paucity of foreign exchange to finance their imports, counter trade is frequently used. Importers favour counter trade because of the following reasons:

- It is an effective source of finance for their purchase.
- It facilitates conservation of foreign exchange.
- It is used to cope with statutory requirements related to foreign currency.
- It helps them to reduce their debt liability.
- It serves as an effective instrument for industrial growth in countries with constraint foreign exchange.
- It helps them to establish a long-term relationship with the suppliers.

Despite several benefits, just discussed, counter trade is not free of criticisms:

- It has a distorting effect on the free market competition as considerations other than currency payments are involved.
- As only a limited number of exporting firms are willing to enter counter trade, importers often have restricted choice and generally tend to pay higher than the free market price.

- Counter trade seldom improves the foreign exchange of importing countries that are generally low or medium-income countries.
- Large international firms often engage in dumping the obsolete technology and plant and machinery in low- and medium-income countries by way of counter trade.

DUMPING

Dumping is a widely used competitive strategy in international markets. Dumping means selling of a product or commodity below the cost of production or at a lower price in overseas markets compared to domestic markets. Dumping is considered as an 'unfair' trade practice by the World Trade Organization (WTO). Anti-dumping duties can be levied on imports of such products under the Agreement on Anti-dumping Practices. A product is considered to be dumped if its export price is less than either its cost of production or the selling price in the exporting country. Besides, for taking anti-dumping action, there should be genuine 'material' injury to the competing domestic industry. The government in the importing country should assess the extent of dumping and estimate the injury cost to prove dumping.

Though dumping is considered to be 'unfair' in international markets, it makes sound economic sense as a profit maximization strategy. For dumping to occur, the following conditions need to be satisfied.

- The industry must be imperfectly competitive so that the firm acts as a price setter rather than a price taker.
- Markets must be so segmented as to make it difficult for the domestic buyers to purchase goods intended for overseas markets.

Figure 12.12 indicates that a monopolistic firm has a demand curve D_d in the domestic market. It is assumed that foreign markets are highly responsive to price. D_f is the demand curve in the

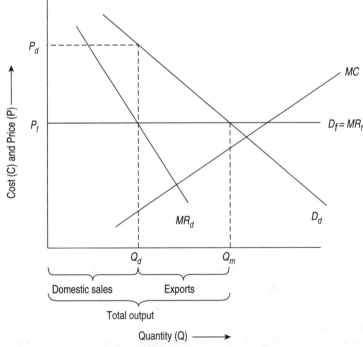

Fig. 12.12 Concept of dumping

foreign market indicating that the firm can sell as much as it wants at price P_f. It is also assumed that the markets are segmented; so, the firm can charge a higher price in domestic market and a lower price in the foreign markets. MC indicates the marginal cost curve for total output that can be sold in either of the markets. In order to maximize profit, the firm should set marginal revenue equal to marginal cost in each market. For domestic sales, marginal revenue is defined by the curve MR_d, which lies below the domestic demand curve D_d. Since export sales take place at a constant price P_f, the marginal revenue for an additional unit exported equals P_f.

The firm has to produce the quantity Q_m so as to set the marginal cost equal to the marginal revenue, to sell Q_d in domestic market, and to export the remaining quantity $Q_m - Q_d$. The cost of producing an additional unit equals price P_f in the foreign market, the marginal revenue from exports, which in turn is equal to the marginal revenue for domestic sales. The firm sells quantity Q_d in domestic market at price P_d while the remaining output $Q_m - Q_d$ is exported at price P_f. The price P_d in domestic market is higher than the price P_f in foreign markets for producing and selling total output Q_m for maximizing profits.[8] Hence, it makes strong economic sense to sell goods at lower prices in foreign markets than in the domestic market. Therefore, firms often engage in dumping.

Forms of Dumping

Dumping may be of various forms, as follows.

Sporadic dumping

The practice of occasionally selling excess goods or surplus stock in overseas markets at lower prices than the domestic price or below the cost is termed as sporadic dumping. In sporadic dumping, the basic objective of a firm is to liquidate the excessive inventories without initiating a price war by reducing the price in the home market. This form of dumping is least detrimental.

Predatory dumping

The basic objective of such intermittent dumping by way of predatory pricing is used to force the competitors to leave the market, thus enabling the predator to raise the price in the long run.[9] The practice of predation is more common where the predator firm operates in numerous markets or where the potential competitors, who are the ultimate victims of predatory prices, and their national governments do not have sufficient information to prove occurrence of predation. The regulatory framework regarding predatory pricing varies widely among the countries. Anti-dumping actions against such dumping practices are often justified. The European countries have long been accused of dumping agricultural products with huge farm subsidies, and Japan is often accused for dumping consumer electronics. As the strategic objective of predatory dumping is to force competitors to leave the market, this form of dumping is highly detrimental. Moreover, once the competitors become redundant, the predator increases the price.

Persistent dumping

It refers to the consistent tendency of a firm to sell goods at lower prices in international markets. Since such form of dumping is most common, it is highly detrimental to the competing firms. However, as depicted in Fig. 12.12, firms generally sell the product using the marginal cost pricing approach at lower prices in foreign markets. The Chinese consumer goods firms

---

[8] Krugman, Paul R. and Obstfeld Maurice, *International Economics—Theory and Policy*, Sixth Edition, Pearson Education (Singapore), New Delhi, 2003, pp. 142–144.

[9] OECD, *Predatory Pricing*, Organization for Economic Cooperation and Development, Paris, 1989.

are accused of persistent dumping internationally primarily with an objective to utilize their large-scale production capacities.

TRANSFER PRICING

Transfer pricing refers to the price between related parties in an international transaction (Fig. 12.13). With globalization, corporates are making use of differential rates of transfer pricing to optimize their profitability in low-tax regimes at the expense of high-tax regimes. The concept of transfer pricing, which was earlier limited to foreign multinational companies, is becoming increasingly significant for companies from emerging economies such as India, China, Brazil, and Russia as a result of their increasing internationalization. Firms from emerging economies often enter international markets by way of joint ventures, wholly owned subsidiaries, etc. Companies own distribution systems in international markets, which make transfer pricing crucial for formulating an international pricing strategy. The objectives of transfer pricing[10] are as follows:

- Maximizing overall after-tax profits
- Reducing incidence of customs duty payments
- Circumventing the quota restrictions (in value terms) on imports
- Reducing exchange exposure, circumventing exchange controls, and restricting profit repatriation so that transfer firms' affiliates to the parent can be maximized
- Transferring of funds in locations so as to suit corporate working capital policies
- 'Window dressing' operations to improve the apparent (i.e., reported) financial position of an affiliate so as to enhance its credit ratings

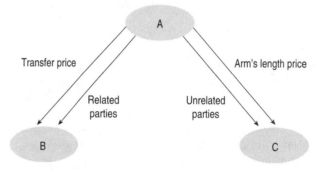

Fig. 12.13   Concept of transfer pricing

International transactions based on intra-company transfer pricing involves conflicting interests of various stakeholders. Therefore, in view of the diverse interests of stakeholders, transfer-pricing decisions become a formidable task. The factors influencing transfer pricing[11] include the following:

- Market conditions in the foreign country
- Competition in the foreign country
- Reasonable profit for the foreign affiliate
- Home country income taxes

---

[10] Apt, P.G., *International Financial Management*, Tata McGraw Hill, New Delhi, 2000, p. 547.
[11] Burns, Jane, 'Transfer Pricing Decisions in U.S. Multinational Corporations', *Journal of International Business Studies*, 11(2), Fall 1980, pp. 23–39.

- Economic conditions in the foreign country
- Import restrictions
- Customs duties
- Price controls
- Taxation in the host country, for example, withholding taxes
- Exchange controls, for example, repatriation of profits

A number of transnational corporations have re-invoicing centres at low tax countries (popularly known as tax heavens) such as Jamaica, Cayman Islands, and Bahamas to coordinate transfer pricing around the world. These re-invoicing centres are used to carry out intra-corporate transactions between two affiliates of the same parent company or between the parent and the affiliate companies. These re-invoicing centres take title of the goods sold by the selling unit and resell it to the receiving units. The prices charged to the buyer and the prices received by the seller are determined so as to achieve the transfer pricing objectives. In such cases, the actual shipments of goods take place from the seller to the buyer while the two-stage transfer is shown only in documentation. The basic objective of such transfer pricing is to siphon profits away from a high-tax parent company or its affiliate to low-tax affiliates and allocate funds to locations with strong currencies and virtually no exchange controls.

Types of Transfer Pricing

Market-based transfer pricing It is also referred to as arm's length pricing, wherein the sales transactions occur between two unrelated (arm's length) parties. Arm's length pricing is preferred by taxation authorities. Transfer pricing comes under the scrutiny of tax authorities when it is different from the arm's length price to unrelated firms.

Non-market pricing Pricing policies that deviate from market-based arm's length pricing are known as non-marketing based pricing.

Pricing at direct manufacturing costs It refers to the intra-firm transactions that take place at the marketing cost.

The purpose of transfer price apparently seems simple allocation of profits among the subsidiaries and the parent company, but the differences in the taxation patterns in various markets make it a complex phenomenon. Transfer prices come under scrutiny of taxation authorities when it is different from the arm's length price to unrelated parties. Transfer pricing involves several stakeholders, such as parent company, foreign subsidiary or joint venture or any other strategic alliance, strategic alliance partners, home country and overseas mangers, home country governments, and host country government. International transactions based on intra-company transfer pricing involve conflicting interests of various stakeholders.

Legal Framework of Transfer Pricing

With globalization, companies are making use of differential rates of transfer pricing to optimize their profitability in low-tax regimes at the expense of high-tax regimes. Globally about 60 per cent transactions are carried out at the firm level. Countries use transfer-pricing laws to stop the outflow of income from their jurisdiction by ensuring that the price at which related parties transact is at fair market value or arm's length price.

In India the detailed law on transfer pricing was introduced through the Finance Act, 2001. The transfer pricing law encompasses all multinational companies (MNCs) that transfer goods and services across borders. For instance, an MNC A's Indian arm B undervalues its export of goods or services to A. This would fall under the ambit of transfer pricing law as the firm books more profits in the books of A (headquartered abroad) than in that of B (situated in India). This transfer pricing phenomenon deprives India of its share of taxes on that income.

The law requires companies to submit details of their own transactions with related parties along with comparable data of similar transactions by others to justify their transfer pricing to tax authorities. The institutional set-up for transfer pricing taxation is headed by a director general of income tax, who is assisted by a number of directors in Delhi, Mumbai, Kolkata, Bengaluru, and Chennai.

GREY MARKETING

Grey marketing refers to import or export of goods and their distribution through unauthorized channels. International brands with high price differentials and low cost of arbitrage constitute typical grey market goods. The arbitrage costs of grey market goods include transportation, customs tariffs, taxes, and in a few cases, cost towards product modification, generally changing the language of instructions. If the transportation costs are relatively lower than price differences between two markets, grey marketing channels often become attractive. Therefore, companies marketing in multiple countries need to carefully control the prices of similar products sold in multiple markets.

Types of Grey Marketing Channels

Alternate channels of grey marketing include parallel importing, re-importing, and lateral re-importing.

Parallel importing   This type of grey marketing takes place when a product is sold at a higher price to the authorized importer in the overseas market than the price at which the product is available in the home market. This makes parallel importing directly through unauthorized marketing channels attractive as compared to buying from authorized importers or market intermediaries.

Re-importing   Re-importing becomes an attractive means of grey marketing when a product is priced lower in overseas market as compared to home market.

Lateral re-importing   Products are sold from one export market to another through parallel importing when the price differences exist in different markets that make such grey marketing channels attractive.

The difference between prices of automobiles in the USA and Canada is substantial. As Canadian prices are relatively cheaper and there is hardly any customs tariff between the two countries, the Canadian distributors often engage in selling to the US market, for which they are not authorized by the company.

Grey marketing channels adversely affect the established distribution channels of the firm. Products are sold through grey marketing channels at prices lower than that of legitimate importers and distributors. Therefore, firms need to carefully control the prices of similar products sold in multiple markets. A firm has to adapt reactive and proactive strategies (Exhibit 12.7) to combat grey marketing activities. Reactive strategies include strategic confrontation, participation, price-cutting, supply interference, promotion of grey market product limitations, and collaboration and acquisition, whereas proactive strategies include product or service differentiation and availability, strategic pricing, dealer development, marketing information systems, long-term image reinforcement, establishing legal precedence, and lobbying.[12]

---

[12] Causgil, S. Tamer and Ed Sikora, 'How Multinationals can Counter Grey Market Imports', *Columbia Journal of World Business*, vol. 23, Winter 1988, pp. 75–85.

Exhibit 12.7 How to combat grey market activities

A. Reactive strategies to combat grey market activities

Type of strategy	Implemented by	Cost of implementation	Difficulty of implementation	Does it curtail grey market activity at source?	Does it provide immediate relief to authorized dealers?	Long-term effectiveness	Legal risks to manufacturers or dealers	Company examples
Strategic confrontation	Dealer with manufacturer support	Moderate	Requires planning	No	Relief in the medium term	Effective	Low risk	Creative merchandising by Caterpillar and auto dealers
Participation	Dealer	Low	No difficulty	No	Immediate relief	Potentially damaging reputation of manufacturer	Low risk	Dealers wishing to remain anonymous
Price cutting	Jointly by manufacturer and dealer	Costly	No difficulty	No, if price cutting is temporary	Immediate relief	Effective	Moderate to high risk	Dealers and manufacturers remain anonymous
Supply interference	Either party can engage	Moderate at the wholesale level; high at the retail level	Moderately difficult	No	Immediate relief or slightly delayed	Somewhat effective if at wholesale level; not effective at retail level	Moderate risk at wholesale level; low risk at retail	IBM, Hewlett-Packard, Lotus Corp., Swatch Watch USA, Charles of the Ritz Group, Ltd., Leitz, Inc., NEC Electronic
Promotion of grey market product limitations	Jointly, with manufacturer leadership	Moderate	No difficult	No	Slightly delayed	Somewhat effective	Low risk	Komatsu, Seiko, Rolex, Mercedes-Benz, IBM
Collaboration	Dealer	Low	Requires careful negotiations	No	Immediate relief	Somewhat effective	Very high risk	Dealers whish to be anonymous
Acquisition	Dealer	Very costly	Difficult	No	Immediate relief	Effective if other gray market brokers don't creep in	Moderate to high risk	No publicized cases

(Contd)

Exhibit 12.7 *(Contd)*

B. Proactive strategies to combat grey market activity

Product/service differentiation and availability	Jointly, with manufacturer leadership	Moderate to high	Not difficult	Yes	No; impact felt in medium to long term	Very effective	Very low risk	General Motors, Ford, Porsche, Kodak
Strategic pricing	Manufacturer	Moderate to High	Complex; impacts overall profitability, needs monitoring	Yes	Slightly delayed	Very effective	Low risk	Prosche
Dealer development	Jointly, with manufacturer leadership	Moderate to high	Not difficult; requires close dealer participation	No	No; impact felt in the long term	Very effective	No risk	Caterpillar, Canon
Marketing information systems	Jointly, with manufacturer leadership	Moderate go high	Not difficult; requires dealer participation	No	No; impact felt after implementation	Effective	No risk	IBM, Caterpillar, Yamaha, Hitachi, Komatsu, Lotus, Development, insurance companies
Long-term image reinforcement	Jointly	Moderate	Not difficult	No	No; impact felt in the long term	Effective	No risk	Most manufacturers with strong dealer networks
Establishing legal precedence	Manufacturer	High	Difficult	Yes, if fruitful	No	Uncertain	Low risk	COPIAT, Coleco, Charles of the Ritz Group Ltd
Lobbying	Jointly	Moderate	Difficult	Yes, if fruitful	No	Uncertain	Low risk	COPIAT, Duracell, Porsche

Source: Cavusgil, S. Tamer, and Ed Sikora, 'How Multinationals can Counter Market Imports', *Columbia Journal of World Business*, 23, Winter 1988, pp. 75–85.

Moreover, legitimate products are also distributed through unauthorized channels in grey markets. These grey marketing channels can also facilitate distribution of counterfeit products, both knowingly and unknowingly. Since grey market distributors have no way to distinguish between the genuine and fake products, sudden influxes of counterfeit products also take place through unauthorized distributors.

The chapter brings out the significance of pricing decisions in international markets. Pricing decisions in international markets are extremely significant for SMEs and companies from low-income countries due to their limited pricing options. Price determination becomes much more complex compared to domestic market due to numerous environmental factors influencing international pricing decisions.

This chapter explicates the concept of price in international markets and its main approaches. Major factors are also discussed. INCOTERMS, often used to describe transfer of responsibilities and risks from the seller to the buyer while making price quotation in international trade, are dealt with. Terms of payments used in export–import transactions also form an integral part of export price quotation. This chapter also provides an overview of key concepts such as counter trade, dumping, transfer pricing, and grey marketing, related with international pricing.

Summary

Price is the sum of value received from the customer for the product or service. It is often adapted in international markets. Besides, price adaptation involves least commitment on the part of the firm's resources. Pricing approaches for international markets such as cost-based pricing (full cost and marginal cost pricing) and market-based pricing have been discussed with illustrations. As export sales are often considered as alternate marketing outlets to dispose of surplus production and utilize the installed capacities, marginal cost pricing is often adopted. Costs, competition, buyer's purchasing power, and foreign exchange fluctuations often influence international pricing decisions.

Exporters find advance payment as the simplest and the least risky method of receiving payment, but one which involves a high level of risk on the part of the importer. Therefore, importers are unwilling to remit advance payment unless the exporter enjoys monopolistic power in the market. Other modes of payment involve open account, consignment, and documentary credits. From exporters' point of view, a confirmed, irrevocable, and payable at sight letter of credit is considered highly secure. The costs, risks, and obligations of buyers and sellers in international transactions are defined by uniform rules set under the International Commercial Terms of the ICC. INCOTERMS 2010 are categorized on the basis of mode of transport and departure, shipment, and delivery. Selling a product in the overseas market below the cost of production or at a lower price than in the domestic price is termed as dumping. Such price discrimination is often used as an international marketing tool. Sporadic, predatory, and persistent dumping are major types of dumping, which have been discussed in this chapter. Counter trade is an international marketing practice where price setting and trade financing are tied together in one transaction. It is an important instrument to enter international markets and helps in overcoming problems related to hard currency and balance of payment. The major forms of counter trade include barter, counter purchase, buy-back, and offset.

The price of an international transaction termed as transfer price is used as a powerful pricing tool to maximize a firm's after-tax profits and circumvent the regulatory framework in different countries of operation. Market-based (arm's length) transfer pricing, non-market pricing, and pricing at direct manufacturing cost are major variants of transfer pricing. A firm has to carefully develop markets so as to ensure that goods do not flow through unauthorized marketing channels. Parallel importing, re-importing, and lateral re-importing are widely used forms of grey marketing channels.

Key Terms

Arm's length pricing Pricing wherein the sales transaction occurs between two unrelated (arm's length) parties.

Consignment Shipment of goods to an overseas consignee retaining the title and risk of goods with the exporter until it is finally sold.

Counter trade A practice where price setting and trade financing are tied together in one transaction, often involving reciprocal commitments other than cash payments.

Dumping   Selling a product or commodity below the cost of production or at a lower price in overseas markets as compared to its price in domestic markets.

Grey marketing   Import and export of goods and their marketing through unauthorized channels.

INCOTERMS   International Commercial Terms that set uniform rules defining costs, risks, and obligations of sellers and buyers in international transactions.

Marginal cost   Cost of producing and selling one more unit.

Non-market pricing   Pricing policies that deviate from market-based arm's length pricing.

Persistent dumping   Consistent tendency of a firm to sell goods at lower price in international markets than in domestic markets.

Predatory dumping   Intermittent dumping using predatory pricing practices so as to force the competitors to leave the market, thus enabling the predator to raise the price in the long run.

Price   Sum of values takenfrom the customer for the product or service.

Simple barter   Exchange of goods and services without any involvement of money.

Sporadic dumping   The practice of occasionally selling goods or surplus stock in overseas markets at a lower price than its price in the domestic markets or its cost of production.

Transfer pricing   Price of an international transaction between related parties.

Concept Review Questions

1. Discuss the significance of pricing decisions in international markets with specific reference to SMEs and companies from emerging economies.
2. Explain the concept of marginal cost pricing. Give reasons for its implications in international marketing vis-à-vis domestic marketing.
3. Critically evaluate the factors influencing international pricing decisions.
4. Explain the concept of transfer pricing. How do firms use it as a tool to circumvent statutory provisions of the countries where they operate?

Practice Exercises

1. Contact a local exporting firm and find out its pricing strategy for international markets.
2. Visit a local market and identify a few imported products in the local market, which are sold through unauthorized marketing channels. Carry out a detailed investigation of the pricing implications that led to grey marketing.

Project Assignments

1. Prepare a price quotation for export of a product of your choice. Make suitable assumptions.
2. Find out illustrations for each type of counter trade discussed in this chapter in which a firm from India or your country is involved.

CASE STUDY: PRICING MEDICINES: PROFITS, PATENTS, AND POOR CUSTOMERS

It is a myth[13] that costs determine price. In practice, 'charge what customer can pay' seems to be an unwritten code for strategic pricing in international markets rather than an exception, especially for those who enjoy one or the other form of monopolistic competition. To garner hefty profits by pricing medicines at exorbitantly high rates, multinational pharmaceutical companies reiterate such pricing practices. Multinationals often argue that prices for new drugs are generally determined by the value they offer to the patients mostly in comparison to the other competing medicines available in the market. Higher prices are often justified on the grounds that they need the revenue to pay for further innovations. However, companies invariably refuse to provide details on how much they have invested in research and development of new drugs on the pretext of trade secrets. In the absence of free-market competition, consumers hardly have any option but are compelled to pay higher prices. Enormity of profit margins of transnational firms and the oligopolistic price structure make the consumer the ultimate loser.

Access to basic healthcare and medicines is the fundamental right of every human being. Countries with low income are

---

[13] Joshi, Rakesh Mohan, 'Cost Determines Price: Just a Myth', *Gulf Log*, October–December 2007, Dubai, pp. 16–17.

home to most diseases and people lack both awareness and affordability of the required medicines. About 1.2 billion people live in extreme poverty on less than US$1.25 a day, mainly concentrated in sub-Saharan Africa (33%), India (33%), and China[14] (13%) for whom bearing the cost of medical treatment is a dream. The prohibitively high costs of treatment worsen the condition as it is hardly affordable by the majority of poor patients worldwide who are the ultimate target consumers.

Moreover, multinational corporations adopt differential pricing policy for medicines with vast price variations across the countries. A comparative analysis reveals that the price of Diclofenac Sodium, a commonly used non-steroidal anti-inflammatory painkiller, which costs merely ₹4 in India for a strip of 10 tablets costs ₹5 in Pakistan and ₹675 in the USA, which makes its price 193 times in the USA compared to India. A strip of 10 tablets of 500 mg each of Ciprofloxacin HCL, a widely used antibiotic, costs about ₹29 in India, whereas it costs the US consumer about ₹2,353. The difference in price between the two countries is about 81 times (Table C12.1).

Cost of ingredients is hardly responsible for such price differences. Rather, such wide price variations are often attributed to regulatory practices like the patent regime where an inventor is awarded the monopoly of the said product for a given period. This prevents new market entrants, and in near monopolistic market conditions, consumers are forced to pay sky-high prices.

The Indian Patent Act, 1970 did not provide product patent protection for medicines and food. It only provided 'process patent', which does not prevent manufactures from making products by using alternate processes. Indian firms mastered the art and science of 'reverse engineering' to manufacture 'generic drugs' by using their own processes and developed an outstanding capability to produce even the most complex drugs of high quality at a fraction of costs compared to their Western counterpart. A generic drug is identical (bio equivalent) to a branded drug in dosage form, safety, strength, route of administration, quality, performance, characteristics, and intended use. As a result, India became the largest supplier of generic drugs in the world and exports about US$10 billion of generic medicines every year. India, widely known as 'the pharmacy of the world', continues to provide quality generic medicines at affordable prices to millions of people around the world.

HIV remains the most dreaded epidemic of the present times, which has infected over 70 million people across the world, and about 35 million people have died of AIDS. Worldwide, about 34 million people were living with HIV at the end of 2011. An estimated 0.8 per cent of adults aged 15–49 years worldwide are living with HIV. Every hour, 300 people globally are contracted with the disease. Sub-Saharan Africa is the worst-hit with nearly one in every 20 adults (4.9%) living with HIV and accounting for 59 per cent of the people living with HIV worldwide.[16]

The issue of supplying HIV/AIDS medicines at affordable costs to developing countries, which has extremely limited paying capacity, has been a matter of serious concern for development agencies, various social groups, and patients across the globe. Pricing medicines at astronomically high rates makes the situation extremely grave, especially for the needy patients. A large majority of them hardly have any means to afford the treatment. For example, till 2000, antiretroviral (ARV) drugs used to treat AIDS were priced between US$12,000–13,000 annually per person by the USA multinationals, around the world.

Table C12.1 Cross-country comparison of drug prices[15] (in ₹)

Drugs	India	Pakistan	Indonesia	UK	USA
Ciprofloxacin HCL 500 mg × 10 tabs	29	424	393	1186	2353
Costlier to India by... times		15	14	41	81
Diclofence sodium 50 mg × 10 tabs	4	85	60	61	675
Costlier to India by... times		24	17	18	193
Ranitidine 150 mg × 10 tabs	6	74	178	247	864
Costlier to India by ... times		23	13	39	91

---

[14] 'The State of the Poor: Where are the Poor and Where are They Poorest?', The World Bank, 17 April 2013.

[15] Sharma, Sanchita, 'Tripping Over Drug Prices', *Hindustan Times*, 28 November 2004, p. 16.

[16] World Health Organization, as on 4 July 2013.

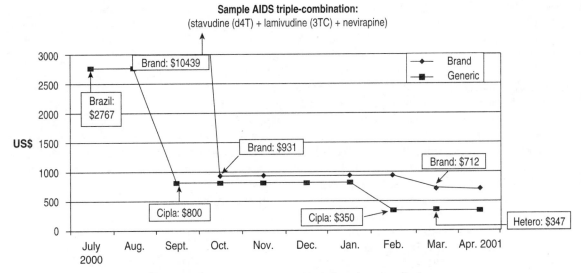

Fig. C12.1 Generic versions introduced by Indian pharmaceutical company
Cipla drastically slashed international prices of ARV drugs

Source: Hoen, Ellen B., 'Affordable Medicines for Developing Countries', WHO-WTO Workshop on
Differential Pricing and Financing of Essential Drugs, Hosbjor, Norway, 8–11 April 2001, p. 15.

Conceptually unilateral price reduction by a single player may trigger a price war in the markets. When Cipla, an Indian company introduced generic versions of ARV drugs, the international prices of drugs used for HIV treatment fell drastically to US$800 in September 2000 (Fig. C12.1). Besides, three more Indian pharmaceutical companies—Delhi-based Ranbaxy Laboratories, Hyderabad-based Matrix Laboratories, and Bengaluru-based Hetero—further pushed down the prices. The sharp price cut from about US$12,000 to US$800 per person's annual dose (i.e., 93% reduction) for ARV drugs in less than four months revealed the exorbitant margins earned by multinational enterprises (MNEs).

The fall in drug prices promoted governments of Brazil, South Africa, China, and India to announce free HIV/AIDS treatment to anyone who needed it. Clinton Foundation played a vital role in controlling HIV and bought the ARV drugs in bulk quantities from Indian manufacturers to treat over one million poor worldwide. By 2013, such ARV drugs are sold by a few Indian companies to some NGOs for as little as US$100–120 annually per person to treat millions of poor patients around the world. Low-cost generics from India contributed to dramatically lessen the medical costs worldwide and provided critical support to global AIDS relief programmes. At present, India supplies 80 per cent of the world's anti-retroviral drugs. As a result, the prices of ARV

dropped more than 99 per cent over the last decade primarily due to generic competition.

In 2013, there are more than nine million people in developing countries survive by receiving antiretroviral therapy (ART), including more than seven million in Africa,[17] primarily due to availability of generic medicines at affordable prices from India, which enabled treatment scale-up on a large scale. But, many more are still waiting to be treated as WHO estimates that around 25 million people could be in need of the treatment[18] in 2012. It is anticipated that by 2030 about 55 million people would need ARV therapy.

However, the progress achieved in controlling diseases including HIV is now again under threat as the key generic manufacturing countries especially India need to comply with their international obligations like the WTO for new patents granted on medicines. As the current medicines lose their effectiveness and newer patented replacements are required for treatment, which is priced at astronomically higher rates and is out of bounds of patients across the world except a wealthy few.

The newer ARVs are already patented by a few multinationals in developed countries, which restrict production of generics, keeping monopoly prices high. The prices of third line ART is about 14.5 times higher than the first line and 6.6 times the second generation ART regime representing prohibitive treatment

---

[17] Press Release, UNAIDS, 21 May 2013.

[18] *The Strategic Use of Antiretrovirals to Help end the HIV Epidemic*, World Health Organization, July 2012.

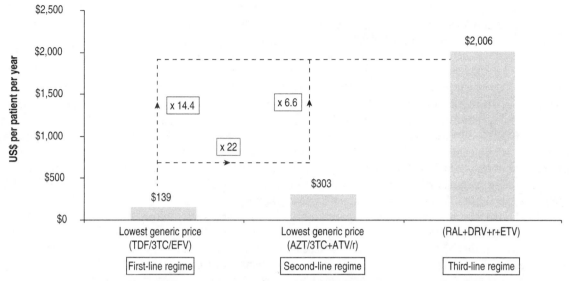

Fig. C12.2   Price comparison of first-, second-, and possible third-line ARV treatment regimes (2012)

Source: Untangling the Web of Antiretroviral Price Reductions, Medicines Sans Frontiers, July 2013.

costs (Fig. C12.2). It is critical to ensure availability of ARVs to millions of patients who need treatment regimes for life.

Under the WTO's TRIPS agreement, member countries are required to give exclusive rights of manufacturing to the patent owner for 20 years. TRIPS prescribes universal minimum protection to intellectual property, such as trademarks, copyrights, geographical indications, patents, industrial designs, plant varieties, topography of integrated circuits, and trade secrets. It is often argued that such product patents are necessary for recovery of investments made on research and development (R&D) and to motivate firms to invest on innovation.

However, as a part of the TRIPS agreement, India had to introduce product patent protection in January 2005. Consequently, new drugs discovered after 1995 are to be sold by Indian manufacturers at international prices, which are exorbitantly high and a large segment of population, not only in India but also in other markets including sub-Saharan Africa, is feared to be deprived of low-cost medicines.

To balance enforcement of IP policy with public health needs, the TRIPS agreement under the WTO offers all member countries important policy and legal choices, known as TRIPS flexibilities. The Doha Declaration, signed in 2001, both by the Indian government and the US, reiterate the right to use legal tools—TRIPS flexibilities, to promote generic competition to save lives. Compulsory licences (CLs) like legal tools wherein a government allows someone else to produce the patented

product or process without consent of the patent owner as legally recognized means under international trade rules it is to overcome barriers in accessing affordable medicines.

Rising longevity and changing lifestyle has led to rapid increase of cancer in high- and low-income countries as well. Access to effective cancer medicines is limited in low-income countries and medicines are out of reach as most patients pay out-of-pocket for most of their medicines. Cancers that are preventable in wealthy nations are death sentences in low-income countries. For instance, 90 per cent of children with leukaemia in high-income countries get cured, whereas 90 per cent of those with the disease in low-income countries die of it.

To illustrate, 'sorafenib tosylate', a drug patented by the German pharmaceutical company Bayer, used to treat last-stage kidney and liver cancers, is marketed as Nexavar at an astronomically high price of US-$5,500 (₹2,80,000). Bayer too justified its high prices putting an R&D price tag of US$1 billion on the drug, however, which was called 'one of the great myths of the industry' by GSK Chief Andrew Witty. In May 2010, the National Institute for Health and Clinical Excellence, UK's watchdog, rejected use of Nexavar by National Health Service (NHS) on the grounds of its too high price to justify its use as the drug was reported to extend the lives of liver cancer patients by an average of 2.8 months.[19] The decision was widely slammed publicly by the families of cancer patients in the UK.

---

[19] *Liver Cancer Drug Not Recommended for the NHS*, Press Release, National Institute for Health and Clinical Excellence, 26 May 2010.

In India where over half of its 1.23 billion population lives on less than US$1 per day, poor patients had no choice but to pay for this exorbitant sum of US$5,500 (₹2,80,000) for patented Nexvar. In order to secure an affordable alternative in the interest of public health, in March 2012, the Indian government issued its first-ever compulsory licence (CL) under section 92 of the Indian Patent Act allowing Natco to legally make and sell a low-cost version of Nexavar. The Indian Controller of Patents said that Bayer did not make Nexavar publicly available at a reasonably affordable price or manufactured the drug sufficiently in India and granted Natco a non-exclusive licence to legally make and sell generic version of Nexavar, until 2020, when Nexavar's patent expires. Natco was ordered to charge not more than US$175 (₹8,800) per patient per month[20] against Bayer's US$5,500 (₹2,80,000) and pay Bayer a royalty of 6 per cent. Bayer appealed against the licence, but the Intellectual Property Appellate Board (IPAB) dismissed Bayer's appeal against the compulsory licence in March 2013 but increased the 6 per cent royalty by 1 per cent. The landmark decision has not only brought down the price of the medicine by 97 per cent but also paved way for making available affordable medicines in future too. In addition to India, Indonesia, Philippines, and China also amended their pharmaceutical patent laws making it easier to take measures similar to India.

Moreover, there are serious concerns about 'evergreening' of patents over the same drug, the abusive practices, often used to extend monopolies, keeping prices high for as long as possible. It is common that multinational firms get several patents on a single medicine because a patent protects the invention and not the medicine. Apart from the new molecule (active medical ingredient), they get patents for formulations, isomers, polymorphs, combinations, new delivery devices, new use, manufacturing process, etc. By patenting these features at different points of time, MNEs effectively tend to extend the monopoly beyond the 20 years of the first patent.

'Imatib', a drug which is very effective against the form of cancer known as chronic myeloid leukaemia (CML), made by a Swiss pharmaceutical company Novartis, marketed under the brand name Gleevec (or Glivec), which costs US$70,000 in the USA, costs just US$ 2,500 in India.[21] Having denied a patent on the application in 2006 covering a beta crystalline form of 'imatib', Novartis took the Indian government to court over Section 3 (d), because it wanted granting a more extensive protection for its products than offered by the Indian law. It also claimed that the Act did not meet rules set down by the WTO and was in violation of the Indian constitution. Novartis lost the case in 2007, but launched a subsequent appeal before the Supreme Court of India in a bid to weaken the interpretation of the law. In a landmark judgement on 1 April 2013, the Supreme Court upheld IPAB's decision to deny patent protection to Novaratis on the grounds that this modification did not satisfy the standard of inventiveness required under Indian Patent Law. The Supreme Court also affirmed that India adopted a standard of pharmaceutical patenting that is stricter than that followed by the USA and the EU. Having a stricter inventive law is also allowed by international law and the TRIPS agreement under the WTO.

Thus, India's action to make available affordable medicines to the masses by way of compulsory licensing and adopting stricter standards for patentability has put pressure on global pharmaceutical companies to reduce their prices drastically not only in low-income countries but also wealthy countries so as to make medicines available to the poor patients in world's wealthiest nations. A number of social activist groups across the world have been vociferous in their concern about continued supply of life-saving drugs from India (Fig. C12.3) at affordable prices.

The generic drug industry of India has compelled several US and European pharmaceutical companies to make a significant cut on their profit margins. Even in the USA, there has been a considerable decline in market share of branded drugs from about 50 per cent in 2000 to 16.3 per cent in 2012 in favour of generic drugs, which led to an estimated saving for consumers of more than US$1 trillion over a decade.[22] Interestingly, India and China account for producing more than 80 per cent of the active ingredients of all drugs used in the USA.[23] Multinational pharmaceutical companies, especially in the developed world, lobby with their full might against such generic drugs on the ground of investments made in R&D. Poor countries maintain they have a moral obligation to make cheaper generic drugs available to their population by limiting patents in some cases.

To cope up with the growing resistance with the existing medicines and emerging new diseases, innovation is critical for their treatment, control, and management. But innovation is of little use if patients who need the medicines cannot afford exorbitantly high priced medicines. In developing countries, the affordability of medicines had long been a crucial issue but now

[20] 'Patients Lose out to Patients and Profits', *The Hindu*, 2 September 2012.
[21] 'Why Chemotherapy that Costs US$70,000 in the US Costs US$2,500 in India', *The Atlantic*, 10 April 2013.
[22] 'Drugstores Press for Pricing Data', *The Wall Street Journal*, 27 March 2013.
[23] 'Low Cost Drugs in Poor Nations Get a Lift in Indian Court', *New York Times*, 1 April 2013.

Fig. C12.3 Worldwide protests in support of affordable medicines from India: the pharmacy of the world
Copyright: Stop AIDS Campaign, 2011.

even in developed countries with aging population, dwindling economies, and falling healthcare budgets, the issue of affordable medicines has become increasingly important. We need to find out a system where prices of medicines are kept close to the cost of production to the extent possible, whereas a mechanism is evolved to reward innovation separately.

Questions

1. 'Costs determine the price is a myth.' Do you agree with this statement? Critically evaluate.
2. Identify the factors contributing to wide price variations of pharmaceutical products in international markets.
3. 'The consumer is the ultimate looser especially in the developed countries as she hardly has access to the products at internationally competitive prices.' Give reasons to substantiate your answer.
4. The population living in extreme poverty on an earning less than US$1.25 per day is the worst-hit by AIDS and other infectious diseases. Moreover, resistance to the existing drugs is rising fast. Buying high cost drugs is beyond the purchasing power of this segment. In view of the new patent regime, should the needy population be deprived of life-saving medicines? Justify your answer and discuss in the class in form of a debate.
5. The wide price difference of drugs in international markets conceptually gives rise to proliferation of counterfeit products and grey marketing. Assess the size of grey markets and counterfeit products in your region or country and its impact on the healthcare scenario. Discuss your findings in the class.
6. Supply of affordable drugs from India is also under renewed threat because of strong lobbing from multinational companies and their governments as well. Do you agree with India's approach of using compulsory licensing and its stand on 'evergreening' of patents under the TRIPS flexibility provided under the WTO agreement? Present your point of view with suitable arguments.

International Distribution

Learning Objectives

- To explain the concept of distribution channels in international markets
- To discuss various types of international distribution channels
- To delineate various channel intermediaries
- To elucidate the structure of distribution channels in international markets
- To explicate international retailing and related issues
- To discuss private labels and their growing significance

INTRODUCTION

Making products and services available to the ultimate customers in international markets in an effective and competitive manner is crucial to the success of a firm in its internationalization process. A firm expanding in international markets is required to employ a number of market intermediaries so as to ensure smooth flow of its products to the target customers overseas. The chapter elucidates the concept of distribution channels in international markets. International managers need to develop a thorough understanding of the differences in distribution channels across countries. Moreover, it is much more complex to conceptualize and manage distribution channels in international markets compared to domestic market as the marketing system varies considerably from country to country and an exporting firm has little insight into overseas marketing systems.

An international marketing firm has an option to choose either an indirect or a direct marketing channel. In case of an indirect marketing channel, a firm does not come in direct contact with an overseas marketing intermediary, whereas it deals directly with an overseas market intermediary while using a direct marketing channel. One also needs to evaluate alternative channel intermediaries available such as agents and the merchants and decide upon the most suitable ones for its operations. The breakthroughs in information and communication technology have revolutionized the international marketing channels and facilitated direct marketing through e-channels.

A firm may select a marketing channel depending upon its objectives in international markets, financial resources, organizational structure, resources, experience in international markets, existing distribution system, channel availability in target market, required speed of market entry, legal implications, and specific product need, if any.

This chapter carries out a cross-country evaluation of the structure of distribution channels in international markets. The European and American channels are relatively shorter, whereas the Japanese marketing channels are characterized by multi-level market intermediaries at horizontal level. Thus, the distribution system in Japan is viewed as a considerable marketing barrier.

This chapter also elucidates the concept of international retailing, various types of retail outlets, and the growing significance of organized retailing across the world. The global trend indicates a decline in the number of retail outlets but an increase in their average size. India has a low penetration of organized retail at 5–6 per cent, making it one of the most promising markets for strategic investments by international retail players. Various tools such as global retail development index and retail talent index have also been explained to carry out a cross-country evaluation for investment in the retail sector. An international marketer has to develop a thorough understanding of the retail structures in the target market and the strength of the private labels, which has also been dealt with at the end of the chapter.

CONCEPT OF INTERNATIONAL DISTRIBUTION CHANNELS

Once a firm has decided to expand overseas and identifies the markets and the products, it has to ensure smooth flow of goods from the place of manufacture to the ultimate customers. For making the goods available from the producer or manufacturer in one country to an overseas customer, a number of market intermediaries are involved for physical transfer of goods. Besides, the firm receives the payments through a channel of such intermediaries. Channels of distribution play a crucial role in making the products or services reach the end consumer.

Channels of international distribution may be defined as a 'set of interdependent organizations networked together to make the product or services available to the end consumer in international markets'.[1] The major functions performed by distribution channels include

- physical flow of goods from the producer or manufacturer to the ultimate customer;
- transfer of ownership to the ultimate customer;
- realizing payment that flows from ultimate customer through market intermediaries to the producer or manufacturer;
- regular flow of information from the ultimate customer and within the channel intermediaries; and
- promotion flow from the manufacturer to the end customer and receiving feedback.

The control of local companies over international distribution and marketing varies considerably across countries. It is the highest in Japan with a score of 5.7 on a seven-point scale where 7 indicates complete ownership and control by local companies, whereas 1 implies complete control by foreign companies, followed by Germany (5.3), Switzerland (5.3), the USA (5.1), UAE (4.9), France (4.8), the UK (4.8), South Africa (4.6), China (4.4), India (4.2), Egypt (3.8), Uganda (3.6), Russian Federation (3.6), and Burkina Faso (2.7), as shown in Fig. 13.1.

Managing distribution channels in international markets is much more complex than domestic market due to a number of factors:

- The distribution system in international markets varies significantly from one country to another. Therefore, the firm has to develop a thorough understanding of the distribution channels in target markets. For instance, prior to Perestroika, the marketing channels in the erstwhile USSR were controlled by the government. The Foreign Trade Organization

---

[1] Joshi, Rakesh Mohan, *International Business*, Oxford University Press, New Delhi, 2009, p. 607.

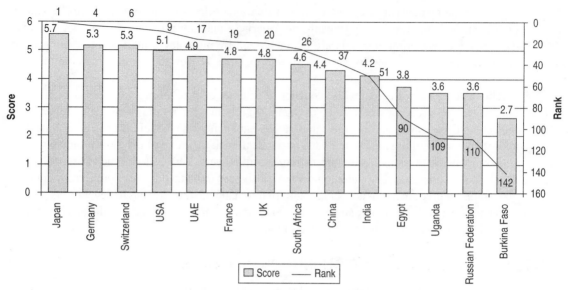

Fig. 13.1 Control of international distribution

1 = not at all controlled by domestic companies, controlled by foreign companies

7 = Extensively owned and controlled by domestic companies

Source: Based on data from *The Global Competitiveness Report*, 2011–12, World Economic Forum, Geneva, p. 509.

(FTO), the enormous government body, was involved in bulk import and distribution through a government-controlled distribution network. However, after the disintegration of USSR, it was found that the private distribution channels were largely non-existent in the Commonwealth of Independent States (CIS) markets and the international firms were required to create their own distribution networks.

- Firms are more familiar with the system of marketing channels in their home market; therefore, selection of distribution channels in overseas market is often a complex decision.
- Collecting information about distribution channels in overseas markets requires greater resources, both managerial and financial.
- In addition to the considerable physical distance in managing the overseas distribution channels, the marketing systems' distance is also much higher.
- Since a firm commits substantial resources for its overseas marketing operations, the long-term commitment of channel members is an important but difficult to assess aspect in channel design.

TYPES OF INTERNATIONAL DISTRIBUTION CHANNELS

International distribution channels may broadly be divided into two categories—direct and indirect channels. In indirect channels, a firm deals with only a home-based intermediary and does not come in direct contact with the overseas-based market intermediary as shown in Fig. 13.2.

Indirect Channels

In indirect channels, an international marketing firm has to deal with domestic agents or market intermediaries without any direct dealing with a foreign-based firm. The home-based market intermediary may include agents, such as broker/commission agent, importer's buying agents,

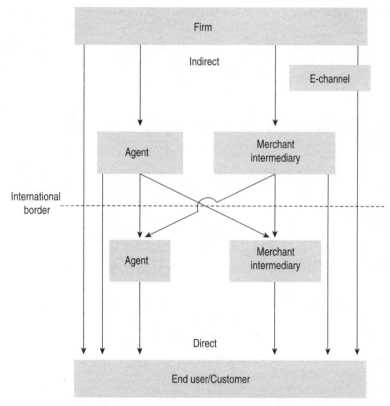

Fig. 13.2 International distribution channels

country-controlled buying agents, and buying offices of overseas firms or merchant intermediaries, such as merchant exporters, international trading companies, and export/trading houses. As the firm is not required to deal directly in overseas markets, indirect marketing channels offer the following benefits:

- Since the firm has to deal with the market intermediary in the domestic market, it needs relatively lower investment and marketing experience.
- Indirect distribution channels provide low-cost opportunity to test products in the international market.

However, indirect channels have certain limitations, which are as follows:

- As the firm has to heavily depend upon domestic market intermediary, its feedback from the ultimate customers is limited.
- The firm has to part with relatively higher share of its profit margins by way of commissions and other payments.
- The firm gets little insight into the market even after operating for several years.
- The firm does not develop its own contacts with the buyers in the overseas market.

Direct Channels

As depicted in Fig. 13.2, direct marketing channels involve selling of goods directly to a market intermediary based overseas. The major benefits of using direct channels are as follows:

- The firm develops a closer relationship with overseas buyers as it comes in direct contact with them.
- The firm develops an insight into the markets of operations, which helps in restructuring its marketing strategies as per the market requirements.
- The firm's control over the export process is greater in direct marketing channels compared to indirect marketing channels.

CHANNEL INTERMEDIARIES IN INTERNATIONAL MARKETS

Channel intermediaries in international markets, as indicated in Fig. 13.3, can be divided into two categories—agents and merchant intermediaries. The agents do not take title of the goods and represent the principal firms rather than themselves, whereas the merchant intermediaries take title of the goods and buy and sell it on their own account. Agents work for a commission, whereas merchant intermediaries work on margins.

A brief description of various channel members in the international market is given next.

Indirect Channels

Agents

Merchant intermediaries do not take the title of the goods and operate on behalf of principal firms, rather they themselves work on commission basis. In indirect marketing channels, the various agents in the home market are as follows.

Brokers/commission agents   The basic function of a broker is to bring the buyer and the seller together. Generally, brokers specialize in one or a few commodities and keep themselves in constant touch with major exporters and importers throughout the world. Brokers serve on commission basis known as brokerage. Home-country brokers generally deal in commodities such as soybean, oilseed, and spices.

Importer's buying agents   A large number of international firms send their agents in overseas market to procure supplies. These agents work on commission basis for the overseas firms and procure samples and subsequent supplies from competing producers. The buying agents are highly useful, especially for small exporters as they come to their doorsteps and assess the suitability of their products for exports to their principals. Such importers' buying agents are common in handicraft, handloom, and garment sectors.

Country-controlled buying agents   The country-controlled buying agents are appointed by an overseas government or a government organization. They identify countries and importers for supply of their requirements. Such agents make frequent visits to the suppliers' countries or establish their base there.

Buying offices   Overseas firms make their permanent presence in the suppliers' countries by way of establishing a permanent buying office. This indicates a long-term commitment on the part of the international firm to source supplies from such markets. For instance, a number of garment firms have established their buying offices in India.

Additionally, in view of India's strength as a low-cost manufacturing hub, global retail chains are sourcing a wide variety of products from India. These global retail chains not only provide a marketing outlet for Indian firms but also facilitate manufacturers of Indian goods to become globally competitive. Due to the renewed interest in sourcing from India, vendors are becoming more confident about investing in new product lines for Western consumers. Liberty Shoes, an Indian company, is in the process of developing a range of non-leather beachwear and sports footwear for American retail giant Walmart.

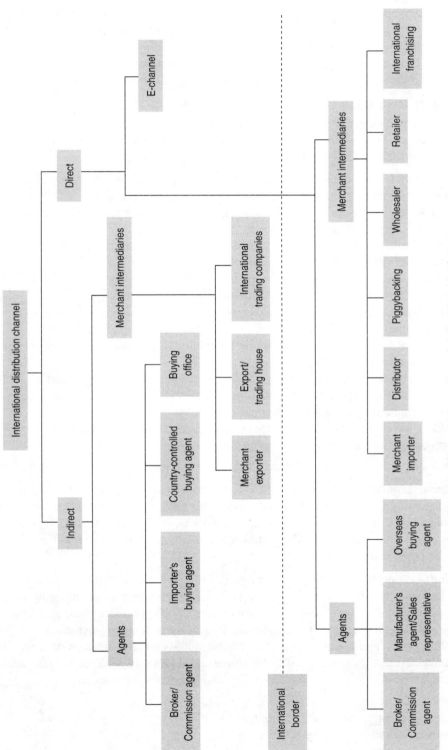

Fig. 13.3 Channel intermediaries in international markets

Global retail chains such as J.C. Penny and Target have set up their sourcing offices in India. Marks and Spencer, the UK based retailer with over 700 stores in the UK and over 300 stores across Europe, Middle East, and Asia also has sourcing centre in Bengaluru. A few years ago, Bentonville-based Walmart used to source its merchandise through the Hong Kong-based Pacific Resource Export. Now, it directly sources a variety of products such as diamond, pens, shrimps, towels, and shoes from India through its procurement offices in Bengaluru.

Merchant intermediaries

Market intermediaries that buy and sell goods for a profit and take title of the goods and assume risks thereof are known as merchant intermediaries. The advantages of using a merchant exporter to enter international markets are as follows:

- Firms mainly operating in domestic markets with limited volumes for export can enter international markets through a merchant exporter or trading house.
- Since a merchant exporter consolidates shipment from a number of manufacturers, he may get more competitive price for exports.
- A merchant exporter often takes care of various risks associated with exports, such as commercial risk, transit risk, and credit risk.
- As operational cost of cargo shipment is spread over a number of clients served by the merchant exporter, it results in saving operational cost per unit.
- Generally, a merchant exporter makes payment against purchase of goods. Hence, the manufacturer's capital is not blocked.
- A merchant exporter has better negotiating capability to get lower shipping rates as he carries out consolidated shipments.
- As a merchant exporter substantially invests his resources in gathering marketing intelligence and in setting up export departments/foreign branches, it results in considerable savings in financial and other operational resources of the manufacturer.
- Since a merchant exporter has a significant presence in foreign markets, it may have a synergistic effect on exporting complimentary products to overseas markets.

The major types of merchant intermediaries are discussed here.

Merchant exporters   The merchant exporters collect produces from several producers or manufacturers and export directly in their own name. Generally, merchant exporters have long-standing relationships with their suppliers and work on profit margins. Home-based merchant exporters are easy to access and help in avoiding the hassles related to direct dealing with an overseas-based market intermediary.

Trading or export houses   Home country-based firms involved in international trading activities, often known as trading/exports houses, serve as important merchant intermediary for exports. Conceptually, trading houses are service companies, which provide an exporting firm with the agility and flexibility needed to operate simultaneously in multiple markets and in handling more than one line of merchandise. Since trading houses serve as intermediaries to a number of manufacturers, they need to justify their intervention by way of value addition through the services. Some of the functions carried out by trading houses are as follows:

- Market selection and market research
- Customer identification and evaluation
- Commercial and technical negotiations
- Vendor development
- Product/Packaging adaptation and technology upgradation

- Imports, particularly, of items required for export production
- Financial arrangements including securing credit
- Counter trading
- Provide protection against export risks, including insurance
- Ensuring timely payments
- Export documentation and shipping
- Managing crises and disasters
- Dealing with claims
- After-sales service and spare parts availability
- Project exports, consortia, and tender business
- Creating distribution networks abroad
- Fostering special relations with the government

Since the export/trading houses are of the home country (i.e., Indian) origin, firms are familiar with the system and have a sense of security in transacting with them. Besides, the relations with export/trading houses are relatively on a long-term basis. The major bottleneck in exporting through export/trading houses is price realization and lack of knowledge about international markets.

As a part of export development strategies, most countries facilitate such trading/exports houses. Certain incentives are available to these trading companies under India's foreign trade policy to assist them in their international marketing efforts. Merchants as well as manufacturer exporters, service providers, export oriented-units (EOUs) and units located in special economic zones (SEZs), agri-export zones (AEZs), electronic hardware technology parks (EHTPs), software technology parks (STPs), and bio-technology parks (BTPs) are also eligible to obtain the status as star export houses. Based on their exports performance, the Government of India recognizes theses firms as export houses and allocates them various types of star status.

The State Trading Corporation (STC) and Metals and Minerals Trading Corporation (MMTC) are among India's largest export/trading houses. India's largest international business company Tata International offers value-added services and international trading expertise and has stakes in a variety of businesses. Its trading operations are organized into five global business units (GBU), such as leather, steel, engineering, minerals, bulk commodities, and chemicals, each of which leverages the Tata Group's wide range of products and services and also sources from other non-Tata companies worldwide.

In India, the concept of export houses gained ground as a result of government policy to encourage trading companies, which were expected to acquire a strategic marketing edge vis-à-vis international trading companies. However, the experience of many trading houses in India has not been very encouraging. For instance, Ganpati Exports, which ranked among the top three export houses in India in 1995–96, ended up in turmoil. A life cycle pattern may be observed in the majority of trading houses in India, the span of which varies widely between various trading houses.

The major factors responsible for stagnation or decline of Indian trading/export houses are as follows:

- Small scale of operations and hence lack of operating leverage
- Lack of professional management
- Focus on exports ignoring imports
- Restrictive government policies such as quantitative restrictions
- Lack of spread of international markets
- Absence or low level of trade in the domestic market

International trading companies International trading companies are generally large companies that accumulate, transport, and distribute goods in various country markets. Traditionally, trading companies have been in operation for centuries as pioneers of international trade. The British East India Company (1600), the Dutch East India Company (1602), and the French *Compagnie des Indes Orientales* (1664) were supported by their governments and enjoyed not only trading rights but also military protection in exchange for tax and payments. The basic objective of these trading companies was to find markets for their industrial production and sell them at higher prices while sourcing raw materials and inputs for their manufacturing units.

Earlier, large family-based businesses comprising financial and manufacturing capabilities in Japan were called *Zaibatsu*, which were engaged in trading since 1700. After World War II, the large Japanese trading companies, *sogo shoshas*, came into existence as trading arms of large manufacturing firms, called *keiretsus*. As the Japanese trading companies are very large, their presence is omnipresent within Japan. Therefore, for entering into Japanese distribution channels, these firms provide an easy and effective route. The world's top trading companies include Mitsubishi, Mitsui, Marubeni, Sumitomo, Sinochem, Itochu, SHV Holdings, Samsung, COFCO, and S.K. Networks. As the international trading companies operate globally, they often have presence in the exporting firm's home country and provide an easy access to international markets.

Direct Channels

In direct marketing channels, the market intermediaries are located in overseas markets. Direct marketing channels provide better understanding of the target market and bring the firm closer to the customer overseas. The exporting firm also gains knowledge about the ultimate buyers and the prices at which goods are sold. In case of direct channels, the firm comes in direct contact with foreign market intermediaries, which include agents, such as overseas-based commission agents or brokers, manufacturers' export agents or sales representatives, overseas-based buying agents, or merchant intermediaries, such as merchant importers, distributors, wholesalers, and retailers.

Agents

Located in overseas markets, agents do not take title of the goods and operate on behalf of the principal.

Overseas-based commission agents/brokers Generally, in commodities and food products, overseas-based brokers provide matchmaking services to the importers and the exporters. Since these brokers are based in overseas markets and are in constant touch with both the buyers and the sellers, they facilitate international transactions. These brokers generally specialize in a few commodity or markets. They work on the basis of one-time brokerage on a deal-to-deal basis.

Manufacturers' export agents or sales representatives The individual intermediaries who operate on a commission basis and travel frequently in overseas markets are known as export agents. These agents specialize in one or a few markets and offer their services to a number of manufacturers for non-competing products. These agents carry out the business in the name of the firm rather than their own name. In the recent years, professionals with wide exposure and market specialization are increasingly working as export agents. Such export agents are generally employed by small manufacturers, who do not have their own distribution networks in overseas markets primarily due to

- small size of operations;
- lack of experience in overseas markets;
- resource constraints; and
- too small a presence in target market to justify the presence of a large sales force.

As an export agent does not take ownership of goods and operates on behalf of the principals, the producing firm bears the risk of any loss. Besides, they do not provide after-sales services such as installations, complaint handling, and repairs as these are passed on to the principal firm.

Overseas-based buying agents   Some foreign companies have exclusive contract arrangements with agents to perform their business. Generally, these agents are paid on the basis of a specific percentage of profit and the costs incurred. Such agents in some countries are also termed as compradors. These agents have an ongoing relationship with buyers but not sellers. As these agents represent the buyers, they deal in all types of goods for their principals.

A firm may get information for identification of overseas-based agents through

- foreign embassies located in India;
- Indian embassies located abroad;
- commercial agents associations like International Union of Commercial Agent;
- import promotion organizations such as Centre for Promotion of Import from Developing countries (CBI) and Japanese External Trade Organisation (JETRO);
- specialized magazines and journals; and
- bank directories.

Merchant Intermediaries

Merchant intermediaries are located in a foreign country, which makes onward sales for a profit margin. Merchants take title of the goods from the sellers, bear handling costs, and also assume associated risks.

Merchant importers   Merchant importer is an overseas-based trader who imports products and further sells them to a wholesaler or a retailer for profit. Generally, merchant importers are overseas-based trading firms that take possession and title of the goods, and, therefore, assume risks and responsibilities. For bulk commodities, especially agricultural goods and some industrial goods, these merchant exporters serve as an effective marketing channel to reach international markets.

Distributors   The distributors in the target markets buy goods and subsequently sell them to either a market intermediary or the ultimate customers. Thus, the distributors take title of the goods and assume full risk and responsibility for the goods. The distributors have contractual agreements with the exporting manufacturers and deal with them on a long-term basis. Under the contract, distributors are authorized to represent the manufacturers and sell their goods in the assigned foreign territory. A firm has the following alternative distribution strategies in terms of market coverage.

Exclusive distribution   The firm opts for a single or a few distributors.

Selective distribution   The firm has limited coverage of the market in terms of area and has a select number of distributors.

Intensive distribution   The firm deals with as many distributors and outlets in the market as possible.

A distributor is generally appointed for exclusively marketing the firm's products in the contracted overseas market territory. The distributor operates on margins. As the distributor has long-standing relationship with the exporter, the level of control by the principal is relatively higher. The basic functions of distributors in international markets are as follows:

- Estimating market demand
- Conducting customers' need analysis and providing consistent market feedback

- Breaking bulk, meaning to buy goods in large quantities from the parent firm and breaking them up for market intermediaries
- Processing orders, and proper documentation and billing
- Storing goods and maintaining inventories
- Providing low-cost storage and delivery
- Transporting goods
- Undertaking sales promotion and advertising
- Offering market credit and capital for financing inventory
- Handling complaints, guarantees, maintenance, after-sales service, repairs, and instructions for use on behalf of the supplier

Contract for distributorship in international markets Once a distributor is selected in a target market, the firms enter into a formal contract. The following points are to be covered while making an agreement for agency or distributorship:

- Details of contracting parties
- Products contracted
- Territories to be covered
- Whether the contract is exclusive or not
- Target customers to be handled
- Duration of contract
- Whether agencies are authorized to accept or reject the order
- Responsibility for local promotion and advertising
- Sales targets
- After-sales services to be offered, if any
- Performance parameters
- Provision for renewal or termination of contract

Selection of an overseas distributor A firm may select an overseas distributor based on several factors such as the firm's size, its financial strength, type of products offered in markets covered, synergy with the firm's products, experience in dealing with similar products, physical infrastructure such as transport, warehousing, market goodwill, ability and willingness to carry the inventory, and public relations. However, an overall rating may be made depending upon the weights assigned, as given in Exhibit 13.1, as per the firm's objectives in the market.

Piggybacking A firm may expand in a foreign country by using the distribution network of another company, which is termed as piggybacking. SMEs that have limited resources may get access to a well-established distribution channel of a larger company in a foreign country. A company that is not willing to commit its own resources for creating its own distribution channel often prefers piggyback.

Thus, the exporting firm 'rides' at the back of the 'carrier' through the latter's well-established distribution channel and gets immediate access to the market with little investment. Piggybacking is generally used for related but non-competitive products of unrelated companies, which are complementary to the distributors' existing product lines.

To the carrier, piggybacking offers quick access to an outsider's product, which fills gaps in its product line. This helps the carrier in widening its product range without investing in new product development and manufacturing. However, as the carrier has little control over continuity of supply and the quality and warranty of the products, it may adversely affect its brand name.

Exhibit 13.1 Criteria for selecting a distributor in international markets

Firm characteristics	1 Very poor	2 Poor	3 Medium	4 Good	5 Very good	% Weight factor	Result (Grading x weight)
Firm size							
Financial strength							
Products dealt							
Area coverage							
Compatibility							
Experience							
Physical infrastructure							
Performance record with other clients							
Strength of sales organization							
Willingness and ability to carry inventory							
Market reputation							
Relations with local authorities							
Overall rating						100	

The exporting firm makes use of the experience of carrier's marketing channels with little investment. If the country market is attractive enough to pump more resources, the exporting firm may develop its own distribution channel. Since under the piggybacking arrangement, marketing of product is controlled by an outside agency, the exporting firm has little control over carrier's marketing commitment and distribution efficiency.

In piggybacking exports, the branding and market promotion arrangements may differ. The carrier may buy the product outright and sell it under its own brand name. However, as a matter of common practice, the rider retains its brand name and the market promotion activity is carried out with mutual consent. There is an increasing trend in international markets of piggybacking taking various forms of strategic alliance.

Wholesaler Overseas-based wholesalers purchase goods from merchant exporters or distributors and generally sell them to retailers. Wholesalers in international markets play an important role as they buy the goods in bulk and break them in small parts for subsequent sales to retailers. In high-income countries, a limited number of large wholesalers serve a larger number of retailers. Unlike India where thousands of wholesalers serve numerous small retailers, in Finland, the largest wholesaler, Kesko, serves more than 11,500 retailers across the country. In Japan, vertical marketing channels are also common wherein a large wholesaler sells goods to a smaller one and makes profit out of that, as explained later in this chapter.

Retailers Retailers buy goods from wholesalers or distributors and sell them to the ultimate customers in the international market. Retailers perform the crucial function of carrying inventories, displaying products at the sales outlets, point-of-purchase promotion, and extending credit. Retailers do provide market feedback to the firms, which are keen on reviewing their marketing decisions. The retailing system and the legal framework also vary significantly among countries. In Japan, France, Italy, and Belgium, the legal framework serves as a deterrent in market entry of new large-scale retailers. International retailing is discussed in detail later in this chapter.

International Franchising

International franchising is gaining popularity for market expansion and projecting uniform retailing image of the firms in the international markets. A firm's retailing practices are transferred to the franchisees, which are expected to put them in practice and the process is monitored by the parent firm. McDonald's, Pizza Hut, Benetton, and Kentucky Fried Chicken (KFC) have extensively used franchising to reach international markets.

E-channels

The breakthrough in information technology has revolutionized the international marketing channels. It has facilitated in overcoming logistics barriers such as distance, speed, and cost of transport to international markets, especially in sectors related to services.

Amazon.com grew its sales at a very faster rate than other retailers, with 93 per cent annual growth rate. Its virtual marketing channel (Fig. 13.4) made it 'the earth's biggest book store' in July 1995; since then it has expanded into a wide range of product lines.

Dell sells personal computers (PCs) directly through the Internet to its global customers on 'build to order' basis rather than 'build to forecast' basis. However, the firm has a very efficient supply chain management system so as to ship PCs on a local or regional basis.

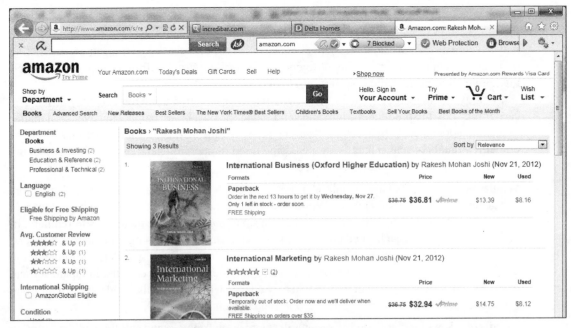

Fig. 13.4 Amazon.com—'the earth's biggest book store'

Source: www.amazon.com, accessed on 12 August 2012.

Over recent years, e-channels have revolutionized international marketing channels, overcoming the barriers of distance, speed, and transportation cost, thereby opening enormous marketing opportunities, especially in the service sectors, for countries like India. A firm now has the option to make its products available in the international market through either the channels or a combination thereof.

SELECTING CHANNELS OF INTERNATIONAL DISTRIBUTION

The selection of a distribution channel is one of the most crucial decisions a firm has to make while entering international markets. A firm may use the following criteria for the selection of channels of international distribution:

- International marketing objectives of the firm
- Financial resources
- Organizational structure
- Experience in international markets
- The firm's marketing image
- Existing marketing channels of the firm
- Channel availability in the target market
- Speed of market entry required
- Legal implications
- Specific product need, if any
- Synergy with other elements of marketing mix

Depending upon the firm's objectives and need, appropriate weights may be assigned to each of the criteria listed and final ratings based on weightage may be arrived at for final selection of an appropriate international distribution channel.   .

STRUCTURE OF DISTRIBUTION CHANNELS IN INTERNATIONAL MARKETS

Distribution channels vary considerably from country to country. For instance, distribution channels in Japan are considered to be the most effective non-tariff marketing barriers. The distinguishing features of Japanese distribution system[2] are as follows.

High Density of Middlemen

The Japanese distribution system is characterized by high density of middlemen wherein a lot of horizontal transactions take place. Japanese consumers often make small frequent purchases at small and conveniently located stores. There is a chain of primary, secondary, regional, and local wholesalers before the goods pass on to the retailers and subsequently to the consumers. In Japan, small stores (95.1% of all retail food stores) account for 57.7 per cent of retail foods sales, whereas small stores (69.8% of all retail food stores) generate 19.2 per cent of food sales in the USA. A disproportionate percentage of non-food sales are generated in small stores in Japan. In the USA, small stores (81.6% of all stores) sell 32.9 per cent of non-food items; in Japan, small stores (94% of all stores) sell 50.4 per cent.[3] The small Japanese stores serve the

---

[2] Cateora, Philip R. and John L. Graham, 'International Marketing Channels', *International Marketing*, 11th Edition, Tata McGraw-Hill, New Delhi, 2002, p. 404.

[3] Japan Research Institute Limited, 'Food Trends in 2000', JETRO Japanese Market Report—Regulations and Practices—Spices, *The Japan Food Journal*, No. 56 (AG-81), March 2001, pp. 17–18.

specific needs of Japanese consumers and function in accordance with the characteristics of the consumer segment such as its high population density, the tradition of frequent trips to the stores, and an emphasis on services, freshness, and quality.

Channel Control

Wholesalers perform a variety of functions such as financing, physical distribution, warehousing, inventory, promotion, and payment collection for which large manufacturers generally depend upon wholesalers. All the market intermediaries including the wholesalers are tied to manufacturers by a set of practices and incentives to get their marketing support. Wholesalers are expected not to keep the competitors' products, and getting away from the channel is not viewed favourably.

Business Culture

The unique business culture of Japan emphasizes loyalty, harmony, and friendship, which strengthens the business relationships and dependency among the channel members. The suppliers' relationship with the dealers is long-term and supported by Japan's value system. However, the channel structure in Japan is largely responsible for the increase in consumer prices of goods and services. It is reported that the consumer goods in Japan are the highest priced in the world.

Legal System

The large-scale retail store law *Daitenho* governs and controls the competition posed by large retail stores in Japan and is designed to protect small retailers from large retailers. The law requires that any store larger than 5,382 sq ft (500 sq m) must have approval from the prefecture government to be 'built, expanded, stay open later in the evening, or change the days of the month they must remain closed'. All proposals for new 'large' stores are first judged by the Ministry of International Trade and Industry (MITI). The plan has to be unanimously agreed by all the local retailers failing which it is returned for further clarification and modification. The process takes several years for approval.

India is a major producer and exporter of spices. The marketing channels for spices differ significantly among the countries. For instance, the distribution channels of spices from crude spice procurement to final product sales in Japan are complicated,[4] as indicated in Fig. 13.5. Though crude spices are imported mainly by specialized importers and partly by general trading companies, spice makers and processed food makers also import directly from overseas sources. Final products ready for retail sales account for a very small portion of all the spices imported. The majority of imported spices go to spice makers and processed food makers for blending, packaging, and seasoning. Roughly, 50 per cent of crude spices procured by major spice manufacturers are directly imported by the spice manufacturers themselves and the remainder are domestically procured through importers, from fellow spice makers, and as domestically produced products.

One reason for spice distribution routes being complicated is that spice manufacturers buy unprocessed and processed spices from fellow spice companies. The sales ratio (in volume) by type of business (consumers) in Japan has been reported to be 6.3 per cent of processed spices and 16.6 per cent of unprocessed spices, which are traded between fellow spice companies.

---

[4] *Spices and Herbs—A Survey of the Netherlands and Other Major Markets in the European Union*, Centre for the Promotion of Imports from Developing Countries, Rotterdam, July 1996, pp. 44–46.

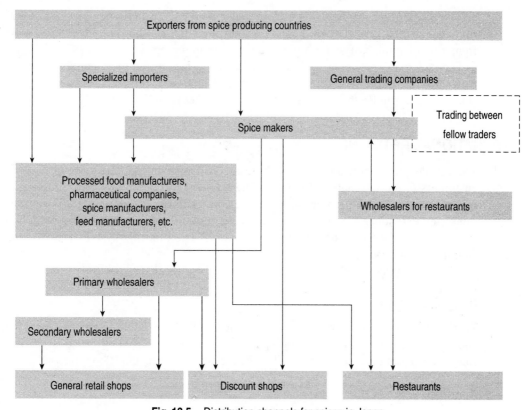

Fig. 13.5 Distribution channels for spices in Japan

Source: Centre for Promotion of Imports from Developing Countries, accessed on 19 November 2012.

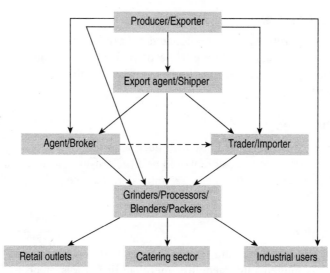

Fig. 13.6 Distribution channel for spices in the Netherlands

Source: Centre for Promotion of Imports from Developing Countries,
accessed on 9 January 2013.

The distribution channels of spices in the Netherlands, which often serves as a gateway to European market, are relatively shorter, as indicated in Fig. 13.6. The spices are traded in bulk from a small number of major brokers and traders/importers.

For new exporters, bulk trade of non-ground spices is the most common trade channel. Nowadays, the direct trade between medium- and large-sized producers/exporters in developing countries and grinders/processors in consumer market is on the rise.

INTERNATIONAL RETAILING

The retailer buys the goods from wholesalers or distributors and sells it to the ultimate customers in the international market. The retailers serve the important function of carrying inventories, displaying products at sales outlets, providing points for purchase promotions, and extending credit. Retailers provide market feedback to the firm, which is highly significant in reviewing its marketing decisions. The retailing system varies widely from country to country.

The retail outlets in international markets may be classified as follows.

Department Stores

These stores have several product lines—typically clothing, home furnishings, and household goods—with each line operated as a separate department managed by specialist buyers or merchandisers. Examples include Sears, J.C. Penney, Nordstrom, and Bloomingdale's.

Supermarkets

These are relatively large, low-cost, low-margin, high-volume, and self-service operations designed to serve all needs related to food, laundry, and household products. Examples are Kroger, Food Emporium, and Jewel.

Convenience stores

These are relatively small stores located near residential areas, open for long hours, seven days a week, and carry a limited line of high-turnover convenience products at slightly higher prices plus takeaway sandwiches, coffee, soft drinks, etc. Examples include 7-Eleven and Circle K.

Speciality Stores

These have narrow product lines with deep assortment. A clothing store would be a single-line store; a men's clothing store would be a limited-line store; and a men's custom-shirt store would be a super speciality store. Examples are Athlete's Foot, Tall Men, The Limited, and The Body Shop.

Discount Stores

These sell standard merchandise at low prices with low margins and high volumes. Discount retailing has moved into speciality merchandise stores, such as discount sporting-goods stores, electronics stores, and bookstores. Examples include Walmart, Kmart, and Crown Bookstores.

Superstores

These are about 35,000 sq ft of selling space traditionally aimed at meeting consumers' needs for routinely purchased food and non-food items plus services such as laundry, dry cleaning, shoe repair, check cashing, and bill paying. Examples are IKEA, Home Depot, PETsMART, and Staples.

Hypermarkets

They range between 80,000 and 2,20,000 sq ft and combine supermarket, discount, and warehouse retailing. Product assortment includes furniture, large and small appliances, clothing, and many other items. They feature bulk display and minimum handling by store personnel, with discounts for customers who are willing to carry heavy appliances and furniture out of the store. Hypermarkets originated in France. Examples include Carrefour and Casino (France); Pyrca, Continente, and Alcampo (Spain); and Meijer's (Netherlands).

A firm may develop its own retail outlets that have synergy with the company's strategy, as indicated in Exhibit 13.2. Bata, one of the world's leading footwear retailers and manufacturers,

Exhibit 13.2 Bata's international retail stores

Bata operates over 5,000 retail stores with a presence in over 70 countries to serve over one million customers per day employing more than 50,000 people. It aims at consistently being the most satisfying store to shop for well-priced and fashionable footwear. Bata operates four core formats of stores as follows.

Bata city stores Bata operates stores in many of the world's fashion capitals. Bata city stores (Fig. 13.7) offer urban customers the best in today's fashion footwear and accessories. These stores are in prime locations and provide a high level of customer service and exclusive fashion shoe lines with good shopping environments to discerning shoppers.

Bata superstores Bata superstores (Fig. 13.8) offer a wide assortment of fashion, casual, and athletic footwear for the entire family. Located primarily in urban and suburban shopping malls,

Fig. 13.7 Bata city store

(Contd)

Exhibit 13.2 (*Contd*)

these stores offer high value by providing good-quality shoes at great prices in a service-assisted shopping environment.

Bata family stores Bata is the world's leading family footwear chain. The Bata family stores (Fig. 13.9) offer a wide assortment of comfortable, durable, and fashionable footwear for the entire family at reasonable prices. The products are primarily of the Bata brand, but the stores do have a carefully selected assortment of articles from both local and international brands including footwear, handbags, hosiery, and shoe care products.

Bata value stores Bata has built its reputation by providing high value to the consumers in the region where it operates. Bata value stores (Fig. 13.10)—outlet centres, Bata Bazaar stores, and depots—offer a wide assortment of affordable footwear for the entire family. The shopping environment is of a self-service format to ease the shopping process. Attractive, durable, and specifically selected and sourced footwear are displayed to meet the needs of the value-conscious consumers.

Fig. 13.8 Bata superstore

Fig. 13.9 Bata family store

(*Contd*)

Exhibit 13.2 *(Contd)*

Fig. 13.10 Bata value store

has operations across five continents. It operates four core formats of retail stores: city stores, superstores, family stores, and value stores around the world, which facilitate in projecting a uniform worldwide image.

Thus, a firm operating in international markets may evolve its own system of retail stores so as to project a uniform market image globally. The growing strength of retailers empowers them for tough negotiations with the manufacturers as they buy in bulk.

Organized retailing is gaining significance across the world and has, therefore, emerged as a powerful marketing channel. The global trend indicates a decline in the number of retail outlets but an increase in their average size. As the size of retail outlets increases, the emphasis shifts to market expansion and efficient management of international logistics. The large retailers start their operations in international markets and evolve supply chain systems in an internationally integrated manner so as to achieve efficiency.

In the USA, 85 per cent of retail activities are performed by organized modern channels compared to 81 per cent in Taiwan, 55 per cent in Malaysia, 40 per cent in Thailand, 36 per cent in Brazil, 30 per cent in Indonesia, 20 per cent in Poland, 20 per cent in China, and 5–6 per cent in India.

Walmart is the world's largest retailer with retail sales of US$4,18,952 million in 2010 followed by Carrefour SA (France), Tesco (UK), Metro (Germany), Kroger (USA), Schwarz (Germany), Costco (USA), the Home Depot (USA), Walgreen Co. and Aldi Einkauf, as shown in Exhibit 13.3.

Exhibit 13.3 Top 10 global retailers

Rank	Name	Country of origin	Retail sales (US $ million)	Group revenue* (US $ million)	Retail sales growth (%)	Net profit margin (%)	Return on assets (%)	Dominant operational format	Countries of operation	Retail sales CAGR** (2005–10) (%)
1	Walmart	USA	4,18,952	4,21,849	3.4	4.0	9.4	Hypermarket, supercentre, superstore	16	6.0
2	Carrefour	France	1,19,642	1,21,519	4.8	0.6	1.1	Hypermarket, supercentre, superstore	33	3.9
3	Tesco	UK	92,171e	94,244	6.7	4.4	5.7	Hypermarket, supercentre, superstore	13	9.3
4	Metro	Germany	88,931	89,311	2.8	1.4	2.7	Cash and carry/warehouse club	33	3.8
5	Kroger	USA	82,189	82,189	7.1	1.4	4.8	Supermarket	1	6.3
6	Schwarz	Germany	79,119e	79,119e	9.4	n/a	n/a	Discount store	26	9.8
7	Costco	USA	76,255	77,946	9.1	1.7	5.6	Cash and carry/warehouse club	9	8.0
8	The Home Depot	USA	67,997	67,997	2.8	4.9	8.3	Home improvement	5	–2.5
9	Walgreen Co.	USA	67,420	67,420	6.4	3.1	8.0	Drug store/pharmacy	2	9.8
10	Aldi Einkauf	Germany	67,112e	67,112e	5.2	n/a	n/a	Discount store	18	6.0

*Group revenue and net income may include results from non-retail operations
**CAGR = Compound annual growth rate
n/a = not available
e = estimate
Source: Global Powers of Retailing 2012, Deloitte, London, 2012.

It may be observed that of the top 10 retailers, five are from the USA and five from Europe. Kroger, which ranks as the fifth largest retailers globally, do not have any operations outside the USA.

The top 250 retailers accounted for aggregate sales of US$3.94 trillion in 2010, whereas their composite net profit margin was 3.8 per cent and only 23.4 per cent sales was from their foreign operations.[5] Figure 13.11 indicates that 32 per cent of the top 250 retailers are from the USA, 15 per cent from Japan, 6 per cent from the UK, 8 per cent from Germany, 5 per cent from France, 4 per cent from Canada, 17 per cent from other European countries, 4 per cent from Latin America, 3 per cent from Africa/Middle East, and 6 per cent from other Asian/Pacific countries in 2010. However, retailers from the USA accounted for 41.7 per cent of the retail sales, Germany for 11.1 per cent, France for 9.5 per cent, the UK for 6.4 per cent, Japan for 8.8 per cent, Canada for 2.6 per cent, other European countries for 11.6 per cent, Africa/Middle East for 1.2 per cent, Latin America for 1.8 per cent, while the retailers from other Asian/Pacific countries accounted a meagre 5.4 per cent sales, as indicated in Fig. 13.12.

Among the top 250 retailers, as indicated in Fig. 13.13, FMCG comprise 66.6 per cent, hardlines and leisure products 15.6 per cent, diversified products 9.8 per cent, and fashion products 8 per cent.

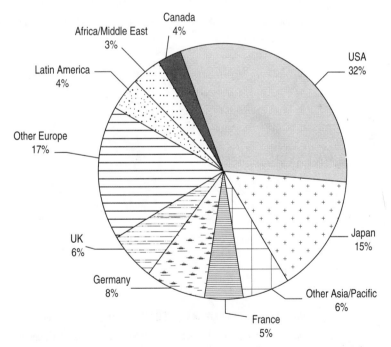

Fig. 13.11   Share of top 250 retailers by region/country of origin, 2010

Source: Switching Channels: Global Powers of Retailing 2012, Deloitte, London, 2012, p. G11.

---

[5] *Global Powers of Retailing 2012*, Deloitte, London, 2012.

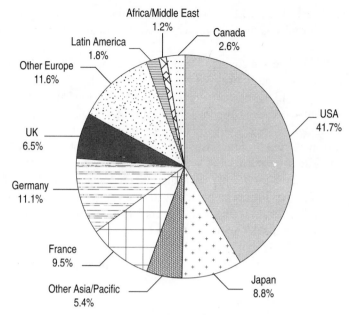

Fig. 13.12   Sales share of top 250 retailers by region/country, 2010

Source: *Switching Channels: Global Powers of Retailing 2012*, Deloitte, London, 2012, p. G11.

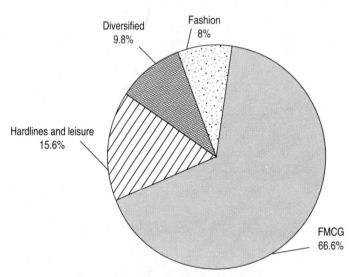

Fig. 13.13   Sales share of top 250 retailers by product categories, 2010

Source: *Switching Channels: Global Powers of Retailing 2012*, Deloitte, London, 2012, p. G11.

RETAILING IN INDIA

India's retail sector is estimated at US$350 billion and expected to grow by 15 per cent to 20 per cent on an annual basis. The retail sector in India contributes to 14 per cent of India's national GDP and employs 7 per cent of India's total workforce. India has a low organized retail penetration (ORP) of 5–6 per cent, which makes it one of the last unconsolidated retail sectors of a significant size left in the world. India has the highest shopping density in the world with

11 shops per 1,000 people. It has 12 million shops employing over 40 million people. Of these, 95 per cent of small shops are run by self-employed people.[6]

Popular formats of organized retail in India include the following:

Malls Malls in suburbs are increasing in number. Developers are even beginning to launch mall chains, trying to build brands.

Discount malls These sometimes offer both premium and mass fashion brands. Promotional activities are common in order to increase traffic. Value malls that offer large food courts, cinemas, or other family entertainment are doubling traffic and driving sales.

Hypermarkets Increasing in popularity with cash-and-carry operators, as well as food and grocery. Non-food sales help improve margins, and most of these have a 60 per cent non-food/ 40 per cent food product mix. One large food and grocery operator plans to open more than 20 hypermarkets in the next two to three years.

Luxury malls India's luxury malls include DLF Emporio (Delhi), UB City (Bengaluru), and the Palladium (Mumbai). These malls offer luxury shopping environments; however, in some luxury malls premium brands exist side by side with true luxury brands.

High streets Always a part of the traditional Indian shopping experience, these are now also offering a range of premium Indian and global brands.

Five-star hotels These are a favourite for luxury brands. India's affluent customers gather at hotels for meals, celebrations, festivals, etc.

Key organized retailers in India in major product categories, as shown in Exhibit 13.4, reveal growing interest of both global and local players in the Indian market. Thus, India's retail sector is an evolving market, which is expected to grow and develop over the next four to six decades as the consuming class in India is growing, more foreign retailers are entering the market, and operations are expanding in India. Consumers' buying patterns and shopping habits would also eventually evolve.

Opening up of Indian Retail Sector for Foreign Players

The penetration of organized retail in India remains low at 5–6 per cent indicating ample scope of future growth. India remains a high potential market with accelerated retail growth of 15–20 per cent expected over the next five years. The Global Retail Development Index (GRDI) developed by A.T. Kearney facilitates international retailers to identify the most promising markets for strategic investments. The GRDI is computed based on the weighted average of market attractiveness, country risk, market saturation, and time pressure. Brazil becomes the hottest investment destination for global retailers as it ranks at the top of the index followed by Chile, China, Uruguay, India, and Georgia as indicated in Table 13.1.

The long-term success of retailers in their international expansion especially in developing countries hinges on availability of a skilled, reliable, and affordable local workforce. To assess talent for retail internationalization, the Retail Talent Index based on talent availability, labour regulations, and labour costs for in-store employees may be used as an empirical tool. Malaysia ranks at the top in the index with a score of 75 followed by China (68.5), Chile (65.4), Indonesia (65.4), Azerbaijan (65), India (62.5), Lebanon (62), Saudi Arabia (61.9), UAE (61.8), and Sri Lanka (61.5), as shown in Table 13.2.

Opening up of retail trade to foreign players witnessed significant resistance from various interest groups in India and there has been considerable debate over the impact of FDI in retail

---

[6] Who is Afraid of FDI in Retail?, *The Times of India*, 29 November 2011.

Exhibit 13.4 Organized retailers in India: global vs domestic players

Food and grocery		Luxury products	
Global	**Indian**	**Global**	**Indian**
Carrefour	Bharti-Walmart	Chanel	Amrapali
Max Hypermarket-SPAR	Food Bazaar	Christian Dior	Manish Arora
Metro	More	L'ladro	Rohit Bal
Tata Tesco	Nature's Basket	LVMH	Ritu Kumar
	Reliance Fresh	Mont Blanc	Tarun Tahiliani
	Spencer's		Titan Nebula
Consumer electronics/durables		**Footwear**	
Global	**Indian**	**Global**	**Indian**
Bang and Olufsen	Croma	Aldo	Catwalk
Bose	eZone	Bata	Inc. 5
LG	Pal Electronics	Charles & Keith	Reliance Footprint
Samsung	Reliance Digital	Hush Puppies	Woodland
Sony	The Electronics Store	Nike	
Whirlpool	Vivek's	Nine West	
Apparel		**Watches**	
Global	**Indian**	**Global**	**Indian**
Diesel	Chemistry	Baume & Mercier	Ethos
Esprit	Dolphin	Cartier	Fastrack
Levi's	Lilliput	Chopard	Helios
Mango	Mustard Seed	Citizen	Titan
Marks & Spencer	Provogue	Longines	Watches and More
	Wills Lifestyle	Omega	

Source: Winning in India's Retail Sector: Factors for Success, PricewaterhouseCoopers India, 2012, p. 12.

sector. This has witnessed a stiff opposition from small shop owners, *kirana* (mom and pop) stores, and political parties. Major pros and cons often debated for opening up FDI in the retail trade in India are discussed here.

Pros

- FDI in retail would benefit the consumer by offering her more choice, better services, wider access, easier credit, and a better shopping experience.
- Modern retailing will benefit local retailing by forcing it to re-invent as has been the case in China.
- It will lead to higher standards of quality, introduce best practices, provide more skilled employment, and improve tax collection.
- FDI in retail would lead to less wastage of agri-produce due to improved food processing techniques and cold storage facilities.
- Agricultural activities in India are typically carried out by small farmers with little resources and capability to sell their produce and are often exploited by middlemen who expect better prices.
- FDI would involve upgradation of infrastructure, logistics, and support services and make supply chains more efficient.

Table 13.1   Global retail development

Rank (2012)	Country	Market attractiveness	Country risk	Market saturation	Time pressure	GRDI score
1	Brazil	100.0	85.4	48.2	61.6	73.8
2	Chile	86.6	100.0	17.4	57.1	65.3
3	China	53.4	72.6	29.3	100.0	63.8
4	Uruguay	84.1	56.1	60.0	52.3	63.1
5	India	31.0	66.7	57.6	87.9	60.8
6	Georgia	27.0	68.7	92.6	54.0	60.6
7	UAE	86.1	93.9	9.4	52.9	60.6
8	Oman	69.3	98.3	17.4	50.4	58.9
9	Mongolia	6.4	54.4	98.2	75.1	58.5
10	Peru	43.8	55.5	62.9	67.2	57.4

	0 = Low attractiveness	0 = High risk	0 = Saturated	0 = No time
	100 = High attractiveness	100 = Low risk	100 = Not saturated	pressure
				100 = urgency to enter

Source: 'Global Retail Expansion: Keeps on Moving', *The A.T. Kearney Global Retail Development Index*, Chicago, 2012, p. 3.

Table 13.2   Retail talent index

Country	Talent availabiity (40%)	Labour regulation (20%)	Labour costs (40%)	Score
Malaysia	62.8	77.9	85.7	75.0
China	56.5	71.3	79.0	68.5
Chile	66.7	56.7	68.5	65.4
Indonesia	51.0	55.9	84.5	65.4
Azerbaijan	42.1	95.9	72.5	65.0
India	48.5	64.2	75.6	62.5
Lebanon	56.1	74.8	61.4	62.0
Saudi Arabia	57.4	93.5	50.8	61.9
UAE	67.7	94.2	39.6	61.8
Sri Lanka	48.7	49.4	80.5	61.5

Source: A.T. Kearney analysis, 2012.

- It would help Indian products get global recognition.
- It will help increase the supply of processed food, apparel, and handicrafts.
- Elimination of multiple middlemen would reduce transaction costs related to inventory, delivery, and handling, which would be beneficial for producers and consumers.

Cons

- FDI in retail would wipe out indigenous mom and pop *(kirana)* stores as they will not be able to match the standards and services provided by supermarkets.

- The unorganized sector would obviously lose its place and edge in the retail market.
- Global retail giants often resort to predatory pricing to create monopoly/oligopoly, which may result in control of essentials including food supply by foreign organizations.
- Consumers have larger options while markets are fragmented, whereas consolidated markets make consumers captive. Allowing foreign players with deep pockets lead to market consolidation. Consequently, international retailers displace existing markets rather than creating additional markets.
- Retail FDI would also introduce competitive pricing, forcing a lot of domestic players out of the game.
- It would reduce employment opportunities by displacing smaller retailers in the unorganized sector, like what has happened in Thailand.
- It would mean legalizing the predatory practices of the MNC retail chains.
- FDI in retail will promote a 'standardized' form of global foreign culture.
- India's imports are likely to increase as MNCs will dump their products in India.
- Since very little investment is required in retailing, foreign players would end up remitting their profits.

In view of its impact on structure and the consumers, the Indian government has been cautious in opening up retail trade for foreign investors. The process of liberalization to retail trade in India began in 1997 when the Indian government allowed 100 per cent FDI in cash-and-carry wholesale trading with case by case clearance, as given in Exhibit 13.5.

Despite FDI restrictions, a large number of international players, such as Walmart, Gap, IKEA, and Tesco made their initial entry by way of sourcing from India and opened up buying offices. India has emerged as an important supplier of textiles, apparels, home products, and jewellery to Walmart, the world's largest retailer, which has developed a network of suppliers across the country.

Exhibit 13.5   Liberalization of retail trade in India

January 1997
100 per cent FDI allowed in cash-and-carry wholesale trading, with case-by-case clearance.

August 2001
N.K. Singh Committee on FDI set up ahead of preparation of the 10th Five Year Plan.

August, 2002
N.K. Singh Committee favours ban on FDI in retail.

December 2002
10th Plan document drops proposal to recommend FDI in retail after initially including it in the draft.

October 2003
Germany's Metro becomes the first foreign company to set up cash-and-carry wholesale store in Bengaluru (then Bangalore).

January 2006
FDI allowed in single brand retail with 51 per cent foreign ownership cap; cash-and-carry wholesale trading approvals eased.

August 2007
Walmart announces agreement with Bharti Enterprises to set up wholesale joint venture.

August 2008
Tesco enters into an exclusive franchise agreement with Trent, retail arm of the Tata Group.

May 2009
Bharti Walmart opens its first cash-and-carry wholesale store in Amritsar.

July 2010
Discussion paper on FDI in multi-brand retail trading published, evokes mixed response.

December 2010
Carrefour opens its cash-and-carry wholesale store in Delhi.

March 2011
Inter-ministerial group recommends allowing FDI in multi-brand retail.

January 2012
Government permits 100 per cent FDI in single brand retail trade.

Consequent to FDI liberalization in cash-and-carry wholesale retail trading, global retail giants such as Walmart, Carrefour, and Metro have set up wholesale outlets in India in their efforts to capture a slice of the growing retail market. Walmart announced an agreement with Bharti Enterprises in August 2007 to establish a joint venture, Bharti Walmart Private Limited, for wholesale cash-and-carry and back-end supply chain management operations in India. A typical wholesale cash-and-carry facility stands between 50,000 and 1,00,000 sq ft and sells a wide range of fruits and vegetables, groceries and staples, stationery, footwear, clothing, consumer durables, and other general merchandise items. Walmart's first best price Modern Wholesale opened in May 2009. The store offers an assortment of approximately 6,000 items, including food and non-food items, which are available at competitive wholesale prices to retailers and institutional buyers.

In January 2012, the Indian government permitted 100 per cent FDI in single brand-retail trade with government approval subject to the following conditions:

- For proposals of more than 51 per cent FDI at least 30 per cent of the value of products sold must come from Indian small industries. A small industry is defined as one that has a total investment in plant and machinery of not more than US$1 million.
- Products to be sold should be only of a single brand.
- Products should be sold under the same brand internationally (i.e., under the same brand in one or more countries other than India).
- Covers only products that are branded during manufacturing.
- The foreign investor must be the owner of the brand.

A number of retail chains that offer their products under single brand (Table 13.3) are ready to enter the Indian market with the opening up of FDI in single brand retail trade.

Table 13.3 Global single brand retail chains keen to enter India

Name of company	Product category	Country of origin
Apple Stores	Electronics	USA
IKEA	Furniture and furnishing	Sweden
Gap	Apparel/Footwear	USA
Polo Ralph Lauren	Apparel/Footwear	USA
Banana Republic	Apparel/Footwear/Jewellery/Accessories	USA
Best Buy	Electronics	USA
H&M (Hennes & Mauritz)	Apparel/Footwear	Sweden
RadioShack	Electronics	USA
Abercrombie & Fitch	Apparel/Footwear	USA
Uniqlo	Apparel speciality	Japan
Topshop	Apparel/Footwear/Cosmetics/Accessories	UK

Single brand retailers waiting to set up shops in India include American fine jewellery brand Tiffany & Co., French label Emanuel Ungaro, American clothing chain Gap, Italian knitwear brand Missoni, American women's wear, lingerie, and beauty product brand Victoria's Secret, and Italian luxury brand Blumarine. FDI in multi-brand retail has so far been not permitted in India.

INTERNATIONAL RETAILING AND PRIVATE LABELS

As large retail stores account for a considerable share of overall sales, they create their own set of loyal customers by displaying private labels. As private labels generate much higher gross margins at 60–70 per cent against 30 per cent earned from international and national brands, retailers actively push their private brands. The development of private labels is not based on the successful targeting of cost-conscious customers alone. Private labels grow fastest in the following socio-economic conditions:

- High concentration of organized retail
- High penetration of international players
- High penetration of discounters
- Strong centralized distribution network

- Overcapacity in manufacturing facilities
- Fragmented retail brands
- Low brand loyalty
- Commodity markets

Private labels often offer tough competition to the manufacturers of branded products. Manufacturers, who do not hold the number one or two national brand positions, are being knocked off the shelves by private labels. For example, in Germany while private labels grew by 50 per cent between 1995 and 2005, brand share declined by 8–30 per cent.[7]

The penetration of private labels varies across countries depending upon the country's buying habits and structure of its retail trade besides, pricing and brand recognition. Switzerland has the highest private label penetration at 46 per cent compared to 41 per cent in the UK, 33 per cent in Germany, 30 per cent in France, 21 per cent in the USA, 11 per cent in India, 9 per cent in Japan, 4 per cent in China, and 3 per cent in Russia (Fig. 13.14).

Private labels' contribution to modern trade in urban India is estimated[8] at 5.7 per cent and its year-on-year growth is 42 per cent compared to 38 per cent growth in modern trade. Top level label categories in India include packaged rice with a share of 38 per cent in modern trade, followed by floor cleaners (32%), glass cleaners (29%), phenyls (23%) and jams-jelly-marmalade (21%).

Retailers often use private labels to increase profits and gain customer loyalty. The strategy in introducing a private brand is not to be number one in the product category but it is to be on the retail shelves along with national and international brands so as to attract new customers towards it by sheer pricing and quality consistency. Retailers are often keen to introduce more private brands to offer new product categories at new price points, which are increasing their gross margins. Recent slowdown in the global market has made shoppers hunt for lower-cost options generating increased interest in private labels. Interestingly, a majority of customers often continue to buy retailers' brands even after the economy recovers.

This chapter brings out the concept of distribution channels in international markets. Various types of international distribution channels and intermediaries are discussed at length. Firms operating in international markets may evaluate various channel alternatives and select the most appropriate ones to suit their resources and meet their objectives. Managers operating in international markets also need to understand the differences in marketing channels across countries.

As the share and role of global retailers is also on the rise, it strengthens their capability to negotiate with the suppliers and build their own brands. Countries with higher level of organized

---

[7] *The Private Labels Revolution*, PricewaterhouseCoopers, Russia, 2011, p. 4.

[8] 'Private Unlimited Labels', *The Economic Times*, 21 January 2011.

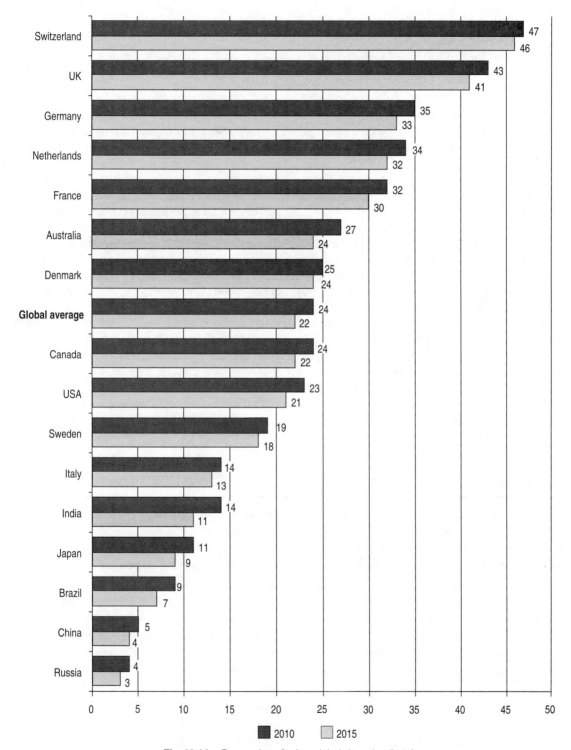

Fig. 13.14 Penetration of private labels by value (in %)

Source: The Private LabelsRevolution, PriceWaterhouseCoopers, 2010.

retailing may be explored for direct supply to the retailers. Besides, the large retailers are also on a constant lookout for reliable quality suppliers for contract manufacturing for the products marketed by them under their private labels.

Summary

To ensure smooth flow of goods and services to the ultimate customers in the target markets, a firm needs to employ a number of market intermediaries. A set of interdependent organizations, involved in the process of making a product or service available to the ultimate customers across national boundaries, is termed as channels of international distribution.

Broadly, distribution channels may either be indirect or direct. In indirect channels, a firm does not come in direct contact with the overseas market. The home-based intermediaries include agents such as broker/commission agent, importers' buying agents, country-controlled buying agents, and buying offices of overseas firms, or the merchant intermediary such as merchant exporters, export/trading houses and international trading companies. In direct channels, a firm deals with an overseas-based market intermediary. The foreign market intermediaries include agents such as overseas-based commission agent or broker, manufacturers' export agents or sales representatives, overseas-based buying agents, or merchant intermediaries such as merchant importer, distributor, piggybacking, wholesaler, retailer, and international franchising.

Over the recent years, e-channels have revolutionized the international marketing channels overcoming the barriers of distance, speed, and transportation cost, thereby offering good marketing opportunities especially in service sectors for countries like India.

A cross-country comparison of distribution channels reveals significant differences. The Japanese distribution system is characterized by the presence of a large number of middlemen, channel control by large manufacturers, business culture based on loyalty, harmony, and relationship, and the legal system favouring small retail outlets. Thus, the distribution channels in Japan are characterized by multi-layer of market intermediaries vis-à-vis relatively shorter marketing channels in the USA and the Europe.

Organized retailing, though varies considerably among countries, is considerably growing across the world. Various types of retail outlets in international markets include department store, supermarket, convenience store, speciality store, discount store, superstore, and hypermarket. Despite being one of the largest markets in the world, India had been reluctant to open up its retail sector for foreign players.

The rising strength of international retailers has given rise to growth of private labels.

Key Terms

Agent A market intermediary that does not take title of the goods and represents the principal firm and works on commission basis.

Direct channels Distribution channels wherein a firm has to deal with overseas-based market intermediaries.

Distributor Generally appointed on long-term basis in the target market who takes titles of the goods, assume full risk and responsibility and sell it either to a market intermediary or the ultimate customer.

Exclusive distribution The firm opts for a single or a few distributors.

Indirect channels Distribution channels wherein market intermediaries are based in the home country.

Intensive distribution The firm deals with as many distributors and outlets in the target market as possible.

International distribution channels A set of interdependent organizations networked together to make the products or services available to the end consumers in international markets.

International trading company A large company that accumulates transports and distributes goods in various countries.

Merchant exporter An exporter who collects produce from several manufacturers and exporters and exports directly in its own name.

Merchant intermediary A channel member that buys the goods and takes its title and sells it to his own account working on margins.

Private label Own brands created by a large retail store, which gives them much higher margins compared to national or international brands.

Retailer One who buys goods from wholesalers or distributors and sells them to the ultimate customers.

Selective distribution The firm has limited coverage of the market in terms of area and has a select number of distributors.

Wholesaler One who purchases goods from merchant exporters or distributors and generally sells them to retailers.

Concept Review Questions

1. Explain the concept of distribution channels in international markets. Why is it more complex to manage distribution channels in international markets compared to domestic ones?
2. Distinguish between indirect and direct distribution channels in international markets.
3. Identify the key differences in distribution channels in Japan vis-à-vis the Western markets.

4. Write short notes on the following:
   (a) Agents
   (b) Merchant intermediary
   (c) Export house
   (d) International trading company
   (e) Wholesaler
   (f) Retailer

Critical Thinking Questions

1. As the international marketing manager of a bicycle exporting firm to Tanzania, identify alternative channels of distribution for bicycles in Tanzania. Develop criteria for selecting the most appropriate marketing channel and recommend the most appropriate channel.

2. Make a cross-country comparison of McDonald's retail outlets. Identify the differences vis-à-vis your own country and make presentation in the class for discussions.

Project Assignments

1. Contact a firm in your city operating in international markets. Find out the marketing channels used by it in various markets. Identify the reasons for selecting these channels and their limitations. Discuss your findings in the class.
2. There has been a lot of resistance to opening up of Indian retail sector for foreign players. It is often argued that FDI in retail

is likely to hamper interests of small retailers in unorganized sector creating job losses. The issue has often been vehemently debated. Prepare your arguments for and against FDI in India and discuss in groups in the form of a debate in front of your class.

CASE STUDY: CHANNELS OF INTERNATIONAL DISTRIBUTION FOR CUT FLOWERS

Chandrika Flora, a Pune-based firm, had so far been a major supplier of roses to hotels and other corporates in Mumbai. In view of its strong production capabilities, Chandrika Flora has set up green house facilities and is exploring possibility of entering international markets. The firm has no idea about how to go about it. Therefore, Chandrika Flora engaged Dr Vidhu, an international floriculture marketing consultant, to explore various channels to enter international markets.

The excerpts of the report submitted after a detailed study and presentation made by Dr Vidhu to the marketing team of Chandrika Flora are as follows:

'Global Cut Flower Trade: An Overview

The global trade of cut flowers alone is estimated to be over US$9 billion. The world cut flower trade is dominated by Europe, the USA, and Japan. The worldwide consumption of commercially grown flowers is estimated to range between US$40–60 billion. The Netherlands is the highest producer of flowers in the world accounting for about 33 per cent of the world production followed

by Japan (24%), the USA (12%), Italy (11%), and Thailand (10%), whereas the rest of the countries account for only 14 per cent. Due to high cost of production in developed countries, the trend is to outsource flowers from developing countries such as Israel, Colombia, Ecuador, Kenya, and Ethiopia, where the cost of production is low. India has inherent advantage in production of cut flowers, primarily due to its favourable agro-climatic conditions, cheap labour, arable land, and availability of skilled manpower. Because of these reasons, India also has a good potential for export of cut flowers.

Total world exports of cut flowers increased significantly from US$3.8 billion in 2001 to US$9.1 billion in 2011 (Fig. C13.1). Netherlands is also the largest exporter of cut flowers with US$4.97 billion accounting for 54.9 per cent of world exports in 2011 followed by Colombia (13.8%,) Ecuador (7.5%), Kenya (5%), Belgium (2.9%), Ethiopia (1.9%), Malaysia (1.1%), Israel (1%), Italy (1%), Thailand (0.9%), and Germany (0.9%), whereas India's share remains a meagre 0.3 per cent. Over the last decade, there has been a shift towards developing

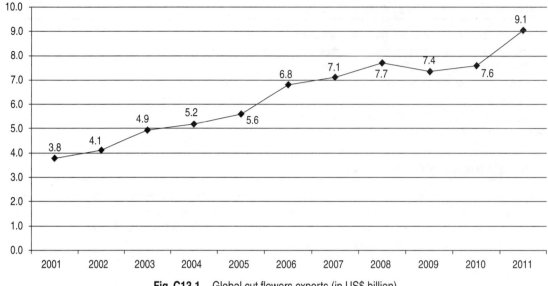

Fig. C13.1   Global cut flowers exports (in US$ billion)

Source: Trade Map, 2012

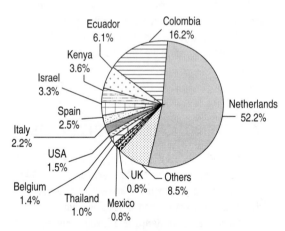

Fig. C13.2   World's major exporters of cut flowers, 2001

Source: Trade Map, 2002.

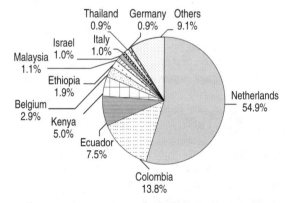

Fig. C13.3   World's major exporters of cut flowers, 2011

Source: Trade Map, 2012.

countries such as Ethiopia, Kenya, and Malaysia (Figs C13.2 and C13.3).

Major importing countries of cut flowers also reveal shifting trend from traditional markets such as Germany, the USA and the UK to new markets such as Russian Federation, Belgium, and others. However, Germany remains world's largest importer of cut flowers (Figs C13.4 and C13.5) with a share of 15.3 per cent followed by the USA (13.7%), the UK (12.7%), Netherlands (9.5%), Russian Federation (8.9%), France (6.1%),

Japan (5%), Belgium (4.4%), Italy (3.1%), Switzerland (2.5%), Austria (1.8%), Canada (1.6%), and Denmark (1.3%).

India's cut flower exports: an evaluation

India has about 1,90,000 hectare area[9] under floriculture cultivation in 2011–12 with estimated production of loose flowers at 1.03 million and of cut flowers at 690.27 million. This reveals a paradigm shift in India's floriculture industry from traditional flowers to cut flowers for exports. India's exports of cut flowers have grown considerably from merely US$2.74 million in 1993 to US$80.5 million in 2007. However, it later declined to US$ 21.86

---

[9] Agricultural and Processed Food Products Export Development Authority (APEDA), India, 2013.

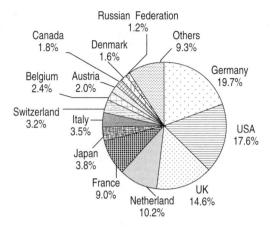

Fig. C13.4   World's major importers of cut flowers, 2001
Source: Trade Map, 2002.

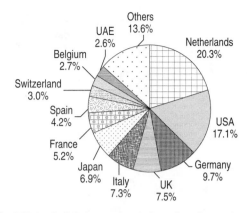

Fig. C13.6   India's top export markets of cut flowers (2001)
Source: Trade Map, 2002.

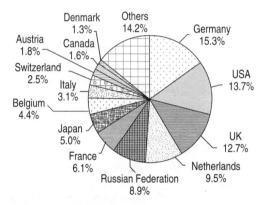

Fig. C13.5   World's major importers of cut flowers, 2011
Source: Trade Map, 2012.

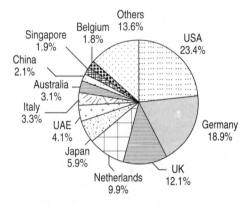

Fig. C13.7   India's top export markets of cut flowers (2011)
Source: Trade Map, 2012.

in 2009 but increased subsequently to US$ 31.3 million in 2011. Roses comprise 95 per cent of total cut flower exports from India besides lilies, carnations, and orchids.

India's major markets for floriculture in value terms are the USA with export worth US$7.3 million with the share of 23.4 per cent (Figs C13.6 and C13.7) followed by Germany with US$5.9 million (18.9%), UK with US$ 3.7 million (12.1%), Netherlands with US$3.09 million (9.9%), Japan with US$ 1.8 million (5.9%), UAE with US$1.2 million (4.1%), Italy with US $1.04 million (3.3%), Australia with US$0.95 (3.1%), China with US$0.6 million (2.1%), Singapore with US$0.58 million(1.9%), and Belgium with US$0.55 million (1.8%). India's exports to the Netherlands considerably declined from 20.3 per cent in 2001 (Fig. C13.6) to 9.9 per cent in 2011, indicating a rapid growth

of direct marketing channels to its major markets such as the USA, Germany, and the UK and reduction in use of traditional international trading hubs for cut flowers through the Netherlands. Besides, new markets such as the UAE, Australia, China, and Singapore have also emerged.

Channels of international distribution for flowers
As depicted in Fig. C13.8, the typical channels of international distribution for flowers,[10] involve auctions, agents, exporters, wholesalers, local wholesalers, purchase organizations, and retailers. The details of various channel intermediaries and their functions are given as follows.

Distribution options for flower producers   Producers mainly sell their cut flowers and plants via auctions and wholesalers. The auction system is particularly used in the Netherlands and

---

[10] *Floriculture: A Sector Study*, Occasional Paper No. 50, Export Import Bank of India, 1996, pp. 26–36

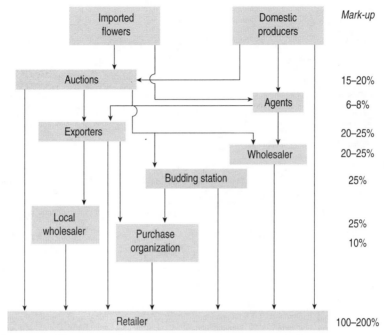

Fig. C13.8 Channels of international distribution for flowers

Source: Prepared from *Floriculture: A Sector Study*, Occassional Paper No. 50, Export Import Bank of India, 1996, pp. 26–36.

Japan. Auctions are less important in Canada, France, Italy, the USA, Belgium, Germany, Denmark, and Turkey. In other Western markets, growers sell their products directly to the wholesale trade or via wholesale markets. Some producers sell directly to the retail trade, this offers the advantage of being able to produce more specifically according to the buyers' needs. The disadvantage of direct sales to retailers is a great dependence on these buyers. So far, direct supplying has been more common among plant producers than among cut flower producers.

Auctions

Auctions are sales organizations for the growers. The growers try to obtain the highest possible price for their products via these sales organizations. In the Netherlands, the auctions are sales cooperatives of which the growers are members. The suppliers of flowers must be affiliated with the auction. The cooperatives aim at realizing the highest possible sales price for the affiliated members and the suppliers. In order to achieve this, the Dutch sales cooperatives make use of two sales methods as follows:

The auction The products supplied by the members of the sales cooperatives are sold via the auction. A clock is used for the purpose as an instrument for realizing the highest possible price for the product supplied. The buyers of a wholesale or retail store buy the auctioned products on the basis of the highest possible price. The price which the buyer pays for the flowers is closely related to the supply and demand on a specific day.

The supply per day depends on weather conditions and on the supply of local and foreign flowers.

In this form of sales, the producer does not have any actual control over the price. A producer can, however, try and realize a higher price by supplying flowers which meet the highest product requirements of the auctions. The flowers sold via the auction clock are also subjected to product inspections before being sold.

The mediating agency The mediating agency mediates on behalf of sales cooperatives in direct sales between the producer and the wholesaler or retailer. The mediating agency is an outlet, which is used by producers and traders to guarantee sales. In auctions before the clock, there is hardly any opportunity to match the needs of the producer to those of the buyer. The price and sales quantities are laid down in contracts. In doing so, the prices are based on that day's clock price, the orders received, the available supply, the hallmark and the packaging of the products.

In the Netherlands, the majority of the supply to the sales cooperatives is sold via the auction clock. In recent years information and communication technology has become integrated with sales cooperatives. This leads to a further separation between products and prices. Imported cut flowers and plants are sold via interactive media and an electronic auction clock.

The larger flower auctions in the Netherlands aim at the wholesale trade, whereas the smaller flower auctions cater to the

Fig. C13.9   A Dutch flower auction in progress

Source: www.flowersoftheworld.com/blog/category/dutch-flower-auction/, accessed on 17 August 2012.

retail trade. The two main flower auctions in the Netherlands are the VBA in Aalsmeer and Bloemenveiling Holland in Naaldwijk. The large Dutch flower auction (Fig. C13.9) with a space of over 10 million square metre and more than 4,800 suppliers and about 700 traders who buy flowers and plants is to the flower industry what the New York Stock Exchange is to Wall Street. As the auction continues, the price in a typical Dutch flower auction, actually lowers unlike many others. The bidders watch the price of flowers fall with the clock overhead and then stop the clock to get their blooms at the desired value. Most flowers in a typical Dutch auction are sold within hours by the noon and immediately get packed and shipped by air across the globe.

Besides the supply from their own members, the auctions also sell foreign flowers. The Dutch auctions apply a system of supply quotas with regard to imported flowers. This import restriction on the supply to the regular cooperative auctions has led to the establishment of a flower auction specialized in import flowers, which is the Tele Flower Auction (TFA).

Wholesalers

In countries which do not have auctions, flowers are sold to the wholesale and retail trade via producer markets. The wholesaler has both a collecting and a distributing function. The collecting function consists of purchasing a wide range of cut flowers and plants, whereas the distributing function consists of the wholesaler catering to the needs of his clients in their demand for flowers.

Various types of wholesalers in floriculture trade may be categorized as follows:

- Breeder/wholesaler: A breeder/wholesaler purchases and sells or auctions flowers of other producers to widen his own product range.
- Domestic wholesaler: Domestic wholesalers supply only to the domestic wholesale and retail trade.
- Cash-and-carry: A cash-and-carry is a cooled sales hall where both the wholesale and the retail trade may purchase cut flowers and plants in smaller numbers.
- Exporter: Exporting wholesalers supply a wide range of flowers to foreign florists, wholesalers and/or supermarkets.
- Door-to-door: Wholesalers who deliver to order are also known as 'flying Dutchman'. Deliveries may be made once or twice a day, seven days a week.
- Commission agent/importer: This type of wholesaler specializes in import flowers, bouquets, painted flowers and/or the sale of flowers which were purchased at other auctions.

Purchase by wholesalers

The wholesale trade purchases its cut flowers and plants from producers, auctions, foreign exporters and/or commission agents. To importers and wholesalers, the freshness of imported flowers is essential in respect of its sales value. The quantities of imported flowers purchased by wholesalersdepend on the domestic supply and on the price.

Sales by wholesalers

Cut flowers and plants of a wholesaler exporter may be intermediate products or end products for the customer. An intermediate product is one which is to be further processed into an end product by the customer. Its processing may consist of a flower being included in a bouquet or of retailers adding another product to the cut flower or plant before it is sold. An end product is, for instance, a bouquet, which a wholesaler has made suitable to sell directly in a shop. Some wholesalers make these bouquets themselves, while other wholesalers contract the making of bouquets to specialized businesses. The customers of a wholesaler may be provided with an intermediate or end product in accordance with their needs. The customers of the wholesaler/exporter are florists, supermarkets, and other wholesalers. The wholesalers in international markets may also specialize as follows:

- End-use specialist: Specializing in a certain consumer segment, like bouquets.
- Vertical level specialist: Specializing in deliveries to a specific link in the flower chain, such as supermarkets and florists.
- Geographic specialist: Sales only take place in a specific geographic area, such as the United Kingdom or Switzerland.
- Customer-size specialist: Exporters concentrate on segments which are 'neglected' by other exporters, such as cash-and-carry and garden centres.

Generally wholesalers are able to deliver to a retailer within a 1000-kilometre radius. Customers outside this radius are generally importers and/or wholesalers.

The wholesale trade is in touch with its customers on daily basis. The personal relationship between the customer and the seller is of great importance in the flower trade. Sales in the wholesale trade take place by telephone, fax, Internet or personal visits. The gross profit margins applied are 10–15 per cent for commission agents and approximately 15 per cent for other wholesalers. Deviations in margins depend on transport distances and customer needs. The wholesale trade is generally promoted, by means of trade fairs. Advertisements and trade names are hardly an issue in wholesale trade and among producers.

Processing

The wholesale trade bears always this in the top of their mind that cut flowers and plants are perishable products. Therefore, the wholesalers' approach is that cut flowers, even more than plants, must be sold on the same day they are purchased. The freshness of cut flowers is preserved by means of storage on water, cooling of the storage halls and means of transport, fast delivery and, suitable packaging.

Purchased flowers are controlled by the wholesaler by number on the basis of market demand. Then the cut flowers are stored in (cooled) storage halls. The flowers, which a customer wishes to purchase, are taken from these halls and put together. The flowers ordered are then packed according to the customer's requirements and placed in boxes or on water. The (water) boxes or buckets are then shipped to the wholesaler's own shipment department. From there, flowers are sent to the customers as per their order via their own or third-party transport.

Transportation

Cut flowers and plants are transported by road, water and air. The wholesale trade supplies to customers located within a 1,500-kilometre radius by truck. Cut flowers are transported in boxes or on water and plants in soil. The cut flowers are delivered to the customers either by their own trucks or by transporters. So far, transport by sea is used only for the export of a few plants.

Transport by air is used in inter-continental deliveries. The importance of transport by air has increased over the past years as a result of the increasing intercontinental trade in floriculture. A few airline companies offer door-to-door service or have a branch of their own at important wholesale markets or auctions. But, there are also companies that specialize in the transport of flower markets to the international airports.

Due care in packaging and transport is essential to wholesalers in order to preserve the freshness and otherwise to achieve a favourable price/volume ratio. International supplies may be hindered by lengthy customs formalities, phytosanitary inspections and unforeseen circumstances. With regard to the first two points, fast customs clearance and inspections are required. In order to limit the problems involved in lengthy phytosanitary inspections in the Japanese market, the Netherlands and Colombia have set up a pre-inspection system for Japan. Inspection takes place in the Netherlands and Colombia before the products are shipped to Japan. This reduces the export of inadequate cut flowers and plants that does not meet and speeds up the phytosanitary inspections at the destination.

Besides, cooling and distribution speed, packaging is also an important aspect in preserving the freshness of cut flowers and plants. In order to prevent damage and to preserve the optimal condition of cut flowers and plants, an exporter/wholesaler must pay attention to packaging. The packaging of an end product may also have a promotional significance or serve a practical purpose for the customer.

Retail trade

The retail trade is a link between the wholesaler and the consumer. The consumer may choose from four types of retailers for purchasing cut flowers and plants as follows.

Florist The florist supplies cut flowers and plants, besides a wide range of exclusive florists, there are also an increasing number of franchise florists in a number of countries. The exclusive florists distinguish themselves on the basis of service excellence and high prices. The franchise shops are positioned for a cheaper segment of the market than the specialist florists.

Supermarkets The importance of supermarkets in flower sales is increasing. In this sector, plants and cut flowers are sold at a low price without a great deal of service.

Street vendors Cut flowers and plants are sold by the street vendors at very competitive prices without a great deal of service.

Garden centres Cut flowers and plants are part of a wide range of garden products.

The market share, which these four groups may have in the flower retail trade, is different in each country. Exhibit C13.1 shows that florists are firmly established in Japan, Italy, the USA and Norway. In Germany, the garden centres are well established in the market. Supermarkets sell flowers and plants to many customers in Switzerland and Denmark. In the South European countries such as Spain, Italy, and Netherlands, sales via street vendors are substantial.

Thus, more cut flowers are generally sold at florists, in the market and at the supermarket. The garden centres and the supermarkets, on the other hand, are the main plant suppliers.

Supermarkets

Over the years, the importance of supermarkets in flower retail trade has been increasing especially in European market, the USA and Japan. This growth in supplying relatively cheap pre-packed flowers is expected to continue. The major supermarket chains dealing in cut flowers include the Swiss CO-OP, the German Aldi, the Dutch Albert Heyn, the French Carrefour, the Swiss Migros, and the British Sainsburys, and Marks & Spencer.

Purchase by retailers

Retailers generally purchase from several wholesalers. There are exclusive contracts, but they usually relate to specific products rather than to the entire range of flowers and plants. In Japan, the sale from producer to retailer involves relatively more channel intermediaries than in Europe and the USA.

Exhibit C13.1 Retail outlets per country by market share (in %)

Retail outlets	Florists	Garden centres	Super markets	Street vendors	Others
Austria	55	9	4	4	28
Belgium	52	6	6	17	19
Denmark	40	–	30	–	–
France	59	9	9	12	11
Germany	38	20	23	8	11
Italy	65	–	–	22	–
Japan	90	–	–	–	–
Netherlands	53	7	14	22	4
Norway	65	–	20	6	9
Spain	50	10	10	25	5
Switzerland	32	9	49	7	3
UK	50	10	19	13	8
USA	65	10	15	–	–

Source: PVS/BBH Floriculture: A Sector Study, Occasional Paper No. 50, Export Import Bank of India, New Age International, July 1996, pp. 27–40.

Sales by retailers

In Europe and Japan, the retail trade uses personal sales. In the USA, on the other hand, people are more familiar with the sale of cut flowers and plants by telephone. In telemarketing, a courier delivers the requested flowers to the desired address. Telemarketing is mainly concerned with the gift segment.

Consumer segmentation

Consumers can broadly be divided into two types: individual / households and the institutional. The latter group includes government institutions, hotels and other non-profit businesses'.

After making the presentation, Dr Vidhu left the decision to Chandrika Flora's management.

Questions

1. Critically evaluate the potential to export cut flowers from India to international markets.
2. As cut flowers are highly perishable in nature, identify the issues to be taken care by Chandrika Flora while managing logistics for international distribution.
3. Compare the distribution channels of floriculture in international markets vis-à-vis India. Identify the key differences.
4. Evaluate various channel alternatives for exporting flowers to the UK and Japan. Prepare a comprehensive distribution strategy for international markets in the form of a presentation to the class.

Communication Decisions for International Markets

INTRODUCTION

Effective communication is crucial to a firm's success in international markets. Firms attempt to convey a set of messages to the target customers through some communication channels in order to create a favourable response for their market offerings and regularly receive market feedback. In marketing terms, it is referred to as 'promotion', the fourth P of the marketing mix. Although marketing textbooks widely use the term 'promotion', 'marketing communication' is used in this book as this is much broader in scope and context.

Marketing communication in international market becomes highly complex and challenging due to differences in cultural contexts and legal framework. Neglecting nuances of different cultures lead not only to enormous costs on the marketing companies but also to market failures. Overlooking cross-country differences have resulted in much embarrassment in international markets even for the mighty transnational companies' global brands. For instance, when Coca-Cola was first introduced in China, it was named *Ke-Kou-Ke-La*. Later, the company found that the phrase translated in a Chinese dialect as 'bite the wax tadpole' or 'female horse stuffed with wax'. Subsequently, it found a close phonetic equivalent *Ko-Kou-Ko-Le*, which can roughly be translated as 'happiness in the mouth' after researching 40,000 Chinese characters.

In another incidence, Parker's slogan for its ball point pen, 'It won't leak in your pocket and embarrass you' also backfired in Latin America as its Spanish translation meant 'It won't leak and make you pregnant'. The company mistakenly translated 'embarrass' into 'embarazar' in Spanish. Chevrolet's highly popular US car Nova failed miserably in Latin America. Later, the company found that 'no va' means 'no go' in Spanish had to rename its car Caribe for the Spanish markets. The Swedish vacuum cleaner manufacturer Electrolux introduced the same print advertisement, which had

Learning Objectives

- To highlight the significance of communication decisions in international markets
- To explain the process of communication in international markets
- To elucidate the concept of international marketing communication mix
- To describe various tools of international marketing communication
- To discuss factors influencing international marketing communication decisions
- To examine the framework of international product-promotion strategy

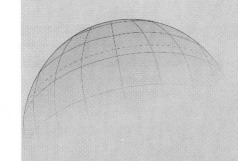

Fig. 14.1 Variation in interpretation of scripts across cultures may lead to marketing disasters

Copyright: Amin, Agha.

proved highly successful in Britain with its 'Nothing sucks like an Electrolux!' tag line in the US market. However, Electrolux found this to be a disaster in the USA as in American culture 'sucks' means 'really bad', that is, Electrolux is a 'really bad vacuum cleaner'.

Nike introduced its 'Air' line of basketball shoes in 1996 with a stylized flame like logo of the word 'Air' on the shoe's backside and sole (Fig. 14.1). A prominent Islamic organization, the Council for American–Islamic Relations (CAIR), irrationally declared that this logo could 'be interpreted' as the Arabic-script spelling of Allah. Nike initially protested its innocence.

But by June 1997, it had accepted multiple measures to ingratiate itself with the council. Nike

- 'apologized to the Islamic community for any unintentional offence to their sensibilities';
- 'implemented a global recall' of certain samples;
- 'diverted shipments of the commercial products in question from 'sensitive' markets';
- 'discontinued all models with the offending logo';
- 'implemented organizational changes to their design department to tighten scrutiny of logo design';
- promised to work with CAIR 'to identify Muslim design resources for future reference';
- took 'measures to raise their internal understanding of Islamic issues';

- donated $50,000 for a playground at an Islamic school; and
- recalled about 38,000 shoes and had the offending logo sanded off.

Later, the company reported that 'CAIR is satisfied that no deliberate offence to the Islamic community was intended' by the logo.[1]

In view of the above, it becomes pertinent for marketers to learn the basic concepts of international marketing communication and develop a thorough understanding of nuances under cross-country situations. This chapter explains the consumer response hierarchy models as the basis of customers' purchase decisions so as to enable a firm to make marketing communication decisions. It also describes the communication process in the context of international marketing to enable readers to appreciate its various constituents—sender, message, encoding, medium, decoding, receiver, noise, and feedback. Various international marketing communication tools such as advertising, sales promotion, direct marketing, personal selling, and public relations have also been dealt in detail in the chapter. As the firms from low-income countries have limited financial and other resources to invest in marketing communication strategies, participation in international trade fairs and other modes of two-way communication are often considered to be more cost-effective and feasible.

The environmental factors such as culture, government regulations, language, and media availability in multi-country marketing environment make international marketing communication decisions much more complex than domestic marketing decisions. This chapter also discusses the product-promotion strategies in international markets.

CONSUMER RESPONSE HIERARCHY MODELS

The objective of any marketing communication strategy is to induce the target customer segment to buy the product. This can be achieved by conveying various attributes and also the competitive edge of the product to the customers. The conveyed message is expected to change the customers' attitude towards the product and make them buy it. These response stages are known as cognitive, affective, and behavioural stages, respectively. Figure 14.2 depicts two such widely used hierarchy models.

'AIDA' Model

In this approach, the main objective of a firm is to make the customers aware of the product and seek their attention through effective marketing communication, such as through effective advertising. The awareness would, in turn, generate interest about the product in the consumers followed by the desire to own. The entire process would ultimately lead to purchase.[2]

Innovation-adoption Model

Another model on consumer adoption, developed by Rogers, especially in reference to a new product is the innovation-adoption model, depicted in Fig. 14.2. In the innovation-adoption model, a firm first creates awareness and generates interest before the customer gets a chance to evaluate it first-hand. The firm also gives a final trial to the new product before it is actually adopted by the customers.[3]

---

[1] Pipes, Daniel, 'How Terrorism has Failed the Cause of Radical Islam', *The Sun*, New York, 12 September 2006.

[2] Strong, E.K., *The Psychology of Selling*, McGraw-Hill, New York, 1925, p. 9.

[3] Rogers, Everett M., *Diffusion of Innovation*, Free Press, New York, 1962, pp. 79–86.

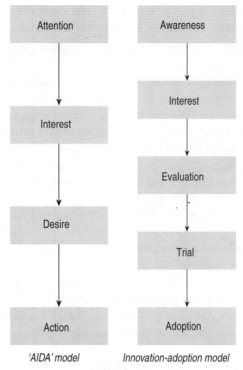

'AIDA' model   *Innovation-adoption model*

Fig. 14.2   Consumer response hierarchy models

MARKETING COMMUNICATION STRATEGIES

On the basis of promotional focus on market intermediaries in the distribution systems or the end customers, a firm has the following two options in marketing communication strategies.

Push Strategy

In push strategy, the promotional programme is primarily directed at the market intermediaries in the distribution system. It aims to motivate the market intermediaries to stock, promote, and sell the products to the ultimate customers, as depicted in Fig. 14.3. The market intermediaries, such as the distributors, wholesalers, and retailers, are offered a variety of incentives to push the product in the market. Generally, in push strategy, the distributors are motivated to promote the product to the wholesalers, who, in turn, promote the product to the retailers, who finally push the product to the consumers.

Fig. 14.3   Push strategy

The tools used in push strategy include personal selling and sales promotion, contests for salespeople, and trade shows. Push strategy is usually found to be more effective under the following situations:

- Lack of product differentiation
- Weak brand identity or brand clutter
- Low brand loyalty
- Difficulty in appreciating product benefits
- Industrial products
- Institutional sales

- Lack of access to advertising media
- Low promotional budget
- Short and direct marketing channels
- Low wages, that is, cost of employing salespeople is lower than the advertising cost

Firms with low promotional budgets often adopt push strategy to move their products through the distribution channels. Besides, commoditization of brands has made it difficult for the customers to differentiate between the competing brands, making push strategy more effective.

The biggest drawback of push strategy is that hardly any brand loyalty is created even after spending huge sums of money. Besides, the channel intermediaries become more demanding and ask for increase in their margins to support the product. In case the demand for a product is low, a marketer has to accede to the demands of channel intermediaries. This triggers an unhealthy competition among the marketers to offer more and more margins, which further squeezes their promotion budgets for advertising. In developing countries, the size of the retail outlets is small and a majority of them are managed by only one or two persons. Therefore, the customers come in direct contact with the sellers and often seek their opinion about the product. The margin of the seller on a particular product often determines her opinion. Under such situations, push strategy serves as an effective promotional tool.

Pull Strategy

The process of motivating the customers to buy the product from the retailers through promotional programmes, as given in Fig. 14.4, is referred to as pull strategy. A retailer asks for a product from a wholesaler and the wholesaler asks for the product from a distributor who gets the product from the firm.

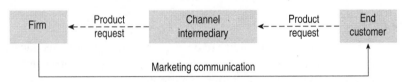

Fig. 14.4 Pull strategy

Pull strategy is more effective in the following situations:

- Perceived product differentiation
- Strong brand identity
- High brand loyalty
- High-involvement product category
- High promotional budgets
- Self-service in retail system, that is, supermarket culture

The promotional techniques used for pull strategy include advertising and sales promotion campaigns directed at consumers, such as discounts and gift vouchers, samples. In retail outlets where self-service is predominant, pull strategy is more effective. Besides, pull strategy also facilitates long-term brand loyalty among the customers.

However, in view of the market conditions and the aforementioned factors, a firm may use a judicial mix of pull and push strategies for market promotion.

PROCESS OF INTERNATIONAL MARKETING COMMUNICATION

Marketing communication aims at conveying a firm's message as effectively and accurately as possible. The basic process of marketing communication, as depicted in Fig. 14.5, involves the following constituents.

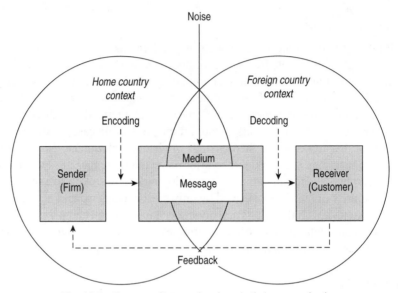

Fig. 14.5   Process of international marketing communication

Sender

It refers to the marketing firm that is conveying the message.

Encoding

Before a message can be sent, it has to be encoded. Putting thoughts, ideas, or information into a symbolic form is termed as encoding. Encoding ensures the correct interpretation of message by the receiver, who is often the ultimate customer. The use of words, signs, or symbols should be such that they become familiar to the target audience. Firms often use symbols for encoding messages that have a universal meaning. Language and cultural issues need to be taken care of while encoding the message.

Message

A message may be verbal or non-verbal, oral, written, or symbolic. A message contains all the information or meaning that the sender aims to convey. It is put into a transmittable form depending upon the channels of communication. From a semiotic perspective, every marketing message has three basic components: an object, a sign or symbol, and an interpretant. The object is the product that is the focus of the message (e.g., Marlboro cigarettes). The sign is the sensory imagery that represents the intended meaning of the object (e.g., the Marlboro cowboy). The interpretant is the meaning derived[4] (e.g., rugged, individualistic, American).

---

[4] Solomon, Michael, *Consumer Behaviour,* Fourth Edition, Upper Saddle River, Prentice Hall, NJ, USA, 1999, p.17.

Medium

The channel used to convey the encoded message to the intended receiver is termed as medium. The medium can be categorized in the following manner.

Personal

It involves direct interpersonal (face-to-face) contact with the target group. Salespeople serve as the channel of communication as they deliver the sales message to the target customers. Friends, peers, neighbours, and family members constitute social channels. 'Word of mouth' communication is a very powerful source of personal communication.

Non-personal

These are channels that convey the message without any interpersonal contact between the sender and the receiver. Since the message is communicated to many persons at a time, these channels are also referred to as mass media or mass communication channels. The non-personal channels of communication may further be broadly classified as follows:

- Print media: Newspapers, magazines, direct mails, etc.
- Electronic media: Radio and television

Decoding

It is the process of transforming the sender's message back into thought. Decoding is highly influenced by the self-reference criteria (SRC), which is unintended reference to one's own culture.

Receiver

It is the target audience or customers who receive the message by way of reading, hearing, or seeing. A number of factors influence how the message is received. These include clarity of the message, interest generated, translation, sound of words, and visuals used in the message.

Noise

The unplanned distortions or interference of the message is termed as 'noise'. A message is subjected to a variety of external factors that distort or interfere its reception. Technical snags, such as problems in telecommunication or signals, both at the sending and the receiving ends may cause distortion. The competitors' promotional activities often create confusion in the minds of the customers and are a major source of noise.

Feedback

In order to assess the effectiveness of the marketing communication process, feedback from the customers is crucial. The time needed to assess the communication impact depends upon the type of promotion used. For instance, an immediate feedback can be obtained by personal selling, whereas it takes much longer time to assess the communication effectiveness in case of advertisements.

In international markets, a firm has to communicate with the customers and the channel intermediaries located in overseas markets that have considerably different marketing environment characteristics. The differences in cultural environment, economic development of the market, regulatory framework, language, and media availability make the task of international marketing communications much more complex compared to domestic marketing.

CONCEPT OF INTERNATIONAL MARKETING COMMUNICATION MIX

The marketing communication mix involves advertising, sales promotion, public relations, personal selling, and direct and interactive marketing, as depicted in Fig. 14.6. A firm generally uses a mix of all these promotion tools after considering the firm's strategy and marketing requirements. Advertising is a paid form of non-personal communication carried out through newspapers, magazines, radio, television, and other mass media by an identified sponsor. Besides, it is also a non-personal form of communication. Sales promotion comprises short-term marketing measures, which stimulate quick actions of the buyers and result in immediate sale of the product. It includes rebates and price discounts, firm's catalogues and brochures, samples, coupons, and gifts. As a part of its image-building exercise, a firm invests in public relations. It may include sponsorship of sports and cultural events, press releases, and even lobbying at government level. Direct marketing is also an effective marketing communication tool, wherein a firm has direct interaction with the customers. Personal selling involves direct selling by a firm's sales force and is considered to be a two-way method of marketing communication, which helps in building strong customer relationships.

Fig. 14.6 International marketing communication mix

The communication mix for an international market is influenced by the following factors:

- Market size
- Cost of promotional activity
- Resource availability, especially finances
- Media availability
- Type of product and its price sensitivity
- Mode of entry into international market
- Market characteristics

An international communication programme may be internally focused or externally focused, as shown in Exhibit 14.1. The internally focused programmes integrate a firm's corporate identity, internal marketing communications, sales force, dealer and distributor training, retailer

Exhibit 14.1 Internal and external international communication programmes

Marketing programmes that influence communication programmes	International communication aims
Internally focused programmes	
Corporate identity	Consistency in company's logo, sign, and image
Internal marketing communications	Reinforce motivation through communicating to the staff about what is happening in the firm
Sales force, dealer, and distributor training and development	Training through conferences, manuals, and brochures
Retailer merchandising	Point of sale persuasion through displays and shelf facings
First-contact customer service	Welcome first contact through telephonist and receptionist training
After-sales service	Customer retention and satisfaction through staff training and brochures
Quality management	Assure a continuous quality approach in all programmes
Brand management	Achieve common brand standards and values
Externally focused programmes	
Product attributes	Offering innovative, high quality products
Distribution channel	Ensuring easy access to products and frequent customer encounters with the products
Price	Messages about quality and status
Product/Service promotion	Integration of the marketing mix communications
People	Using staff-customer interactions to reinforce the aims, standards, and values of the firm
Customer service process	Providing a satisfactory total experience through the service offer
Physical evidence for the service delivery	All contacts with the facilities reinforce the firm's messages

merchandising, first-contact customer service, after-sales service, quality management, and brand management, whereas the externally focused programmes integrate product attributes, distribution channels, price promotion, and staff–customer interaction.

TOOLS FOR INTERNATIONAL MARKETING COMMUNICATION

A firm has to use a mix of all these promotional tools that include advertising, sales promotion, public relations, personal selling, direct, interactive marketing, and trade fairs and exhibitions, taking into consideration the firm's strategy and marketing requirements. Each of these tools is discussed next in detail.

Advertising

Any paid form of non-personal communication by an identified sponsor is termed as advertising. It can be for a product, service, an idea, or organization. Non-personal communication uses a mass media such as newspapers, magazines, TV, or radio to transmit the message to a large number of individuals, often at the same time. Advertising is the most widely used form of promotion, especially for mass marketing.

Procter & Gamble (P&G) is the largest media spender worldwide[5] with US$11.4 billion, followed by Unilever, L'Oreal, General Motors, Nestlé, Toyota, Coca-Cola, Reckitt Benckiser, Kraft Foods, Johnson & Johnson (Fig. 14.7).

---

[5] *Reaching the Connected Consumer: Best Practices in Advertising Effectiveness*, PricewaterhouseCoopers, June 2012.

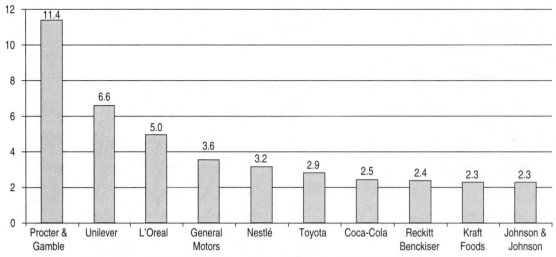

Fig. 14.7 World's top 10 media spenders (in US$ billion)

Source: 'Reaching the Connected Consumer: Best Practices in Advertising Effectiveness', PricewaterhouseCoopers, June 2012.

The global advertising after a decline from US$474 billion in 2007 to US$417 billion in 2009 due to global economic slump rose to US$442 billion in 2010 and is likely to grow consistently to US$ 578 billion in 2015, as shown in Fig. 14.8. North America's share in global advertising declined considerably from 46 per cent in 2006 to 41 per cent in 2010 and is likely to further drop to 38 per cent by 2015. The share of Latin America grew considerably from 4 per cent in 2006 to 5 per cent in 2010 and is likely to further rise by 2015. Asia Pacific is fast emerging as a major region for global advertising, which grew from 22 per cent in 2006 to 25 per cent in 2010 and is likely to rise to 27 per cent by 2015 mainly because of impressive growth in China and India.[6]

Advertising: standardization vs adaptation

An international marketing firm may either opt for a standardized advertising strategy or customize it, depending upon the needs of the target markets. Firms have to carefully scrutinize the decision to use standardized advertisements as these may face socio-legal problems when used in the context of another country. The adaptation of advertising may be either due to mandatory reasons like regulatory framework or voluntarily due to competitive market response.

Advertising standardization   Using the same advertising strategy across countries is termed as standardization. Adopting a standardized advertising strategy is gaining wider acceptance due to a large number of factors, which are as follows:

- The preferences and lifestyles of consumers are increasingly becoming homogeneous, enabling psychographic segmentation of markets that can be targeted through a uniform message.
- The consumer behaviour is increasingly getting similar in the urban centres across the world. The city dwellers exhibit similar working, shopping, travelling, and lifestyle patterns across countries.
- A sharp increase in international travel among customers has made standardized advertising strategy quite popular among the companies.

---

[6] *Global Entertainment and Media Outlook*, 2011–2015, PricewaterhouseCoopers, 2011.

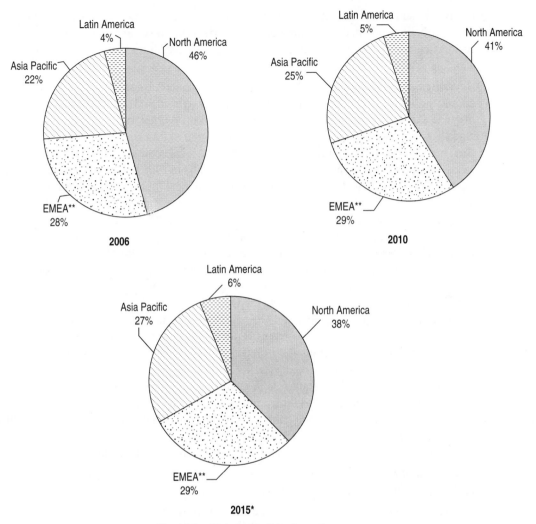

Fig. 14.8   Global advertising by region

*Projections
**Europe, Middle East, and Africa
Source: Global Entertainment and Media Outlook, 2011–2015, PricewaterhouseCoopers, 2011.

- International reach of media, such as television programmes, magazines, and some of the newspapers, has also boosted the use of standardized advertisements. For instance, programmes on channels such as Zee TV, Star Plus, ESPN, Discovery, BBC, and CNN are telecast and watched across the globe.
- Standardized advertising approach facilitates creation of uniform corporate image.
- A firm achieves economies of scale if it follows standardized advertising approach.

However, the extent of standardization varies under the following broad categories:

Advertisement with no change   The same advertisement is used with no change in theme, copy, or illustration except for translation. Benetton Group Spa, the Italy-based global clothing retailer, uses global advertising campaigns with the same theme 'The United Colours of Benetton'. However, Benetton's advertisements use shocking photos to attract public attention on global issues related to environment, terrorism, racism, and HIV. Many of Benetton's advertising campaigns have been under criticism and attack in a number of countries. But in so far an advertisement creates and sustains customers' interest, Benetton is moving ahead with its standardized shock advertising campaigns worldwide.

Advertisement with changes in illustration   Advertisements using local models worldwide maintaining the advertisement copy and the theme are also considered standardized advertisement. For instance, Lux has maintained a single advertising concept worldwide. It promotes the brand through cine stars. Lux has been positioned as the 'beauty soap of film stars'. However, adaptations have been made in different countries depending upon the local context. For example, it uses local film models in its advertisements. Lux was launched in India in 1905 before it started local manufacturing in 1934. It is believed that celebrities represent an ideal life and most people aspire and dream to be like cine stars. The cine actors are supposed to possess flawless skin and blemish-free face and their fans are always curious to know their beauty secrets. In India, Leela Chitnis was the first movie actor to endorse the brand. Since then, a host of movie actors such as Devika Rani, Nutan, Madhubala, Mala Sinha, and Sadhna have endorsed the brand. Presently, Katrina Kaif, Priyanka Chopra, Karishma Kapoor, Rani Mukherjee, and beauty queen Aishwarya Rai endorse Lux in the Indian subcontinent. Lux is endorsed by Sabitha Perera in Sri Lanka, Karishma Manadhar and Niruta Singh in Nepal, Zoe Tay and Phyllis Quek in Singapore, Maggie Cheung and Anita Yuen in Hong Kong, Sho Qi in China, and Bipasha Basu in Bangladesh. The Hollywood actors that have featured in Lux commercials have been Rita Hayworth, Marilyn Monroe, Brooke Shields, Dorothy Lamour, Sophia Loren, and Loretta Young. Figure 14.9 shows some of the actors who endorse Lux in their respective countries.

Advertising plays an important role in positioning a brand. Virginia Slims was always positioned as a women's cigarette, right from its inception in 1968. It later became an international market leader using a worldwide campaign, 'Find Your Voice', in which it used local models in different countries.

Universal appeals in international advertising are used[7] in the following situations:

Superior quality   The promise of superior quality may be used universally. For instance, BMW uses the slogan 'ultimate driving machine' worldwide.

New product/service   The worldwide launch of a product under the sprinkler approach is generally coupled with global communication campaign. For instance, Microsoft used such campaigns while launching its new versions of Windows.

Country of origin   Brands in product categories that have a strong country stereotype often leverage their route by emphasizing on 'made in …' cachet. The country of origin is often emphasized in case of luxury and fashion products.

Celebrities   Celebrities with universal appeal are engaged for global products, whereas the regional or national celebrities are employed for regional communication. Swiss watchmaker SMH International promoted its Omega brand with a TV commercial featuring actor Pierce Brosnan after the release of the James Bond movie *Golden Eye*. Sachin Tendulkar and Aishwarya Rai have been used in a number of their advertising campaigns in the south Asian region.

Lifestyle   A large number of global upscale brands use lifestyle advertisements to target customers regardless of the country.

---

[7] Kotabe, Masaaki and Helen Kristiaan, 'Communication with the World Consumer', *Global Marketing Management*, Second Edition, John Wiley & Sons Inc., Singapore, 2001, pp. 462–463.

Thailand

China

India

Fig. 14.9 Film stars endorse Lux worldwide as its uniform advertising concept with only adaptation by use of local film actors

Copyright: Unilever.

Global presence   In order to enhance the brand's image, firms project their 'global presence' by communicating to the target audience that the product is used worldwide and by using it they also would become a part of the global customers' community.

Market leadership   Brands with a strong country image often send a signal to the target audience that it is the most preferred brand in their home markets. The fact that the company is a market leader nationally, regionally, or internationally gives out a strong message to the customers.

Corporate image   Firms also use a common marketing communication approach to project a uniform corporate image.

The major benefits of standardized advertising include economies of scale and projection of uniform image in international markets. Such an approach can be adopted in the following marketing situations:

- The target market segmented on the basis of psychographic profile of the customers, such as their lifestyles, behaviour, and attitudes
- Cultural proximity among the customers

- Technology intensive or industrial products
- Similarity in marketing environment such as political, legal, and social

Advertising adaptation Modification in the advertisement message, copy, or content is termed as adaptation or customization. However, the emphasis on communication strategies varies between markets. For example, rich lather in bathtub and foamy experience is stressed in the advertising campaigns by Lux in Europe where it is primarily sold as a liquid soap, which may not be the case in other countries. Lux is mainly a shampoo in China, Taiwan, and the Philippines, soap in India, and everything from a soap to a shampoo in Japan. Hence, the benefits of the marketed product are emphasized in each of the markets. Communication adaptation is often needed in international markets due to the following reasons:

- Difference in cultural values among the countries
- Difficulties in language translation
- Variations in the level of education of the target groups
- Media availability
- Social attitudes towards advertising
- Regulatory framework of the target market

As the customer behaviour is greatly influenced by the cultural factors in the target market, it is difficult for a standardized communication strategy to be effective across different country markets. Therefore, to convey a similar concept across various cultures, a firm has to adapt its advertising campaigns in different markets in view of the different cultural contexts. For instance, in products with image-based positioning, such as Pepsi, an advertisement in Western countries may depict scantily clad women in swimsuites on a beach or in a bar, which is not feasible to adapt in Islamic countries due to the statutory framework and the cultural aspects.

However, global brands have a challenging task to build a global image while remaining sensitive to cultural nuances in different countries in their advertising strategy. The world's most popular male grooming brand, Axe, launched by Unilever in 1983 in France, is one of the rarest global brands that replicates its marketing mix across geographical boundaries. Although targeted at males aged 16–25, it really aims at 'naughty guys of all ages' and those 'young at heart'. The brand has an excellent track record of advertising honours, with several international advertising and marketing awards. Despite a globally uniform central theme, which revolves around seduction by the girls, the Axe advertising campaigns are adapted aptly to suit local cultures. In Western liberal societies, explicit advertisements are used to portray such scenarios, whereas brilliantly subtle advertisements are used to convey the theme in highly conservative societies, such as Saudi Arabia, as shown in Fig. 14.10. Such adaptations become crucial to marketing success for global brands in diverse cultural contexts.

Pepsi customizes its advertising campaigns to depict its core values of youthfulness (spirited, young, up-to-date, and outgoing) associated with 'generatioNext'. As celebrities enjoy a demigod status in India, Pepsi has used a number of celebrities, such as Shah Rukh Khan, Saif Ali Khan, Sachin Tendulkar, Amitabh Bachchan, Kajol, and Rani Mukherjee, in its advertisements. Music is a universal favourite with generatioNext. Pepsi had signed endorsement deals with Britney Spears and Ricky Martin. Pepsi invented a game called 'Pepsi Food', which could be played by exchanging short text messages over the phone in response to the wireless revolution by mobile phones in Finland. Besides music and soccer, emphasis is also given to family values in China. The Russian market has been in a transition phase from being a highly communist and conservative country to becoming a liberal capitalist country. As musicians make a dent into the society, especially the youth, Pepsi has used a rock band in its advertising campaign in Russia. Based

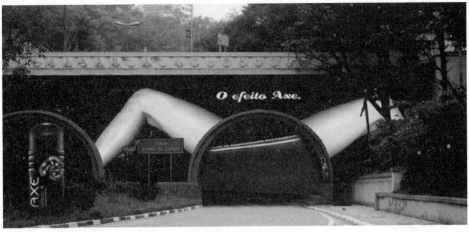

Brazil and Portugal

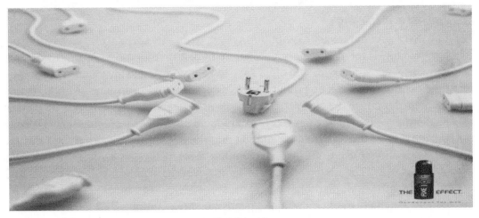

Saudi Arabia

Fig. 14.10 Brilliant adaptation of Axe advertisements in contrasting cultures to convey the uniform core theme globally

Copyright: Unilever.

on intense cross-country consumer research, Pepsi launched the 'Live for Now' campaign globally in May 2012. It did so by updating the Pepsi Pulse platform, making extensive use of social networking sites and encouraging customers to tweet, like, and pin items from the dashboard.

Direct Marketing

Selling products and services to customers, without using any market intermediary is termed as direct marketing. It deals with customers on a one-to-one basis directly, unlike conventional mass marketing that deals indirectly. Direct marketing has little dependence on mass promotion or advertising, whereas conventional marketing relies heavily on mass promotion. Technological advances, like proliferation of telecommunication and information technology, have facilitated direct marketing across the world. The fast growth of credit cards has increased payments over the Internet that has facilitated international sales transactions.

Direct marketing offers the following benefits over conventional marketing:
* Provides direct contact with the customers.
* Eliminates the market intermediaries.
* Facilitates finalization of sales deals through interaction.
* Helps in mass customization of a firm's market offerings rather than mass marketing.
* Facilitates effective and deeper market segmentation.
* Offers personalized service.
* Helps in building customer relationships.

Direct mailing

It involves sending letters, brochures or catalogues, emails, faxes, or even product samples directly to the consumers, who may, in turn, purchase the product through mail.

Door-to-door marketing

Receptivity of door-to-door marketing varies considerably among cultures. In Japan, even motorcars and stocks are sold door to door. Amway, Avon, and Tupperware are some of the largest firm relying on door-to-door marketing worldwide.

Multi-level marketing

It involves a revolutionary distribution system with little spending on advertising and infrastructure. In multi-level marketing, a core group of distributors are recruited, who generally pay the company a registration fee and often have to be introduced to the company by a sponsor. Each of these distributors picks up product worth a certain sum, for instance ₹1,000, with a mandate to sell them directly to the customer. The mark-up is generally pegged at 25–30 per cent. However, the distributor can charge a lower price, reducing the seller's commission. These core distributors appoint further distributors and get additional commission from the sales made by them too. The major global firms involved in multi-level marketing include Amway, Avon, Oriflame, and Mary Kay. The major benefits of multi-level marketing involve a rapid, continuous, and automatic growth of distribution networks. Besides, it is a quick and cost-effective marketing method. As the marketing system depends upon the continuity of the network, any snap in its linkage creates major setbacks for the entire distribution-cum-sale system. Since direct sellers repeatedly approach prospects, this is often a perceived irritant by prospects. The high-pressure tactics used to push the product many a time adversely affect the brand image. The firm has limited control over the sales force in terms of prices offered.

Personal Selling

It involves a firm's representatives personally meeting with customers. Personal selling is widely used for selling plants and machinery, heavy equipment, or high-value products to institutional buyers. As languages, customs, and business culture differ across international markets, personal selling becomes more complex. Generally, firms employ local salespeople for personal selling in international markets. Personal selling is generally employed in the following kinds of markets:

* It is highly cost-effective in low-income countries where wages are low compared to advertising.
* It is employed where customers are multi-linguistic, such as in India, where single language of communication hardly succeeds.
* It becomes an important tool to communicate in countries where literacy level is low.
* In oriental cultures, the sellers' one-to-one contact with the customers pays, as it facilitates the establishment of strong customer relationships.

Exhibit 14.2 Different buyer–seller relationships in different international markets

International market	Climate	Importance	Process	Decision-making
USA	Sometimes viewed as an aggressive or confrontational climate	Of less importance. Focus is on achieving desired results	Ordered process where each point is discussed in sequence	Can be either an individual or group decision process
Canada	Positive, polite climate. hard sell will not work here	Of less importance. Focus is on achieving desired results	Ordered process where each point is discussed in sequence	Can be either an individual or group decision process
Latin America	Positive and hospitable climate	Personal, one-one relationships very important	Relationship building through socialization will precede negotiations	A high-level individual usually makes decisions
UK	Traditional, polite climate. Hard sell will not work here	Of less importance. Focus is on achieving desired results	Ordered process where each point is discussed in sequence	Can be either an individual or group decision process
Germany/ Austria	Rigid, sober climate	Low, Germans remain aloof until negotiations conclude	Systematic process with emphasis on contractual detail	Even the most routine decisions are made by top-level officials
France/Belgium	Formal, bureaucratic climate. Hard sell will not work here	Formal, arm's-length relationships with attention to etiquette	French teams use argument to generate discussion	Usually, a group process headed by a senior negotiator
Japan	Formal polite climate with many idiosyncratic nuances	Great importance. Long-term relationships are what matter most	First all general items are agreed on, then details are discussed	A total group process with all levels involved in the final decision
China	Bureaucratic climate with an abundance of 'red tape'	Very important. Traditional, cultural courtesies are expected	Discussions are long and repetitive. Agreements must be in writing	Usually, a group process headed by a senior negotiator
Russia	Bureaucratic climate with an abundance of 'red tape'	Low, Russians will remain reserved until negotiations conclude	Cumbersome process due to bureaucratic constraints	Usually, a group process headed by a senior negotiator

Products such as plant and machinery, medicines with high value or high technology intensity, and B2B or institutional sales are often sold through personal selling. The differences in buyer–seller relationship in international markets influence the promotion strategy, as shown in Exhibit 14.2.

Personal selling has a special role to play in the Japanese market due to some peculiar socio-cultural features,[8] which are as follows:

- Individuality and independence are not as highly valued in Japan as they are in the West. Besides, Japanese marketers and salespeople are less inclined to take credit for successes or blame others for failures.
- Japanese companies rarely use non-financial incentives to recognize, praise, or reward salespeople for performing well. Good performance is simply expected, and special praise is deemed unnecessary.

---

[8] Kelly, Bill, 'Culture Clash: West Meets East', *Sales and Marketing Management*, July 1991, pp. 28–34.

- Loyalty to one's employer is a fundamental characteristic of Japanese society. Commissions are generally an unnecessary component of compensation packages. Salespeople consider it their duty to generate business for their companies. It is the honourable thing to do and no special compensation is required for doing what duty demands.
- The Japanese typically stay with one company throughout their careers. They have a greater tendency to focus on long-term goals than professionals from other countries.
- Japanese business people are more dedicated to their companies compared to their counterparts in other countries. Besides, they tend to have longer working hours and tend to socialize after office hours.

International firms should also provide periodic inputs to the distributors' sales force, such as periodic trainings, sales literature, and direct mailing; through such means the firm facilitates distributors' tasks and improves efficiency in personal selling.

Sales Promotion

Sales promotion entails various tools that are used as short-term incentives to induce a purchase decision. Due to increased competitive intensity in the market, firms make use of sales promotion to get short-term results. Besides, the buyers also expect some purchase incentives in view of competitors' offerings. It is estimated that manufacturers as a group spend about twice as much on trade promotion as they do on advertising, and an equal amount is spent on consumer promotions.[9] The promotional offer has a local focus and generally varies from country to country. The basic objectives of consumer promotion programmes are as follows:

- Solicit product enquiries.
- Generate trials for new or related products.
- Generate additional sales.
- Motivate customers for repeat purchase.

Types of sales promotions

Sales promotion can broadly be categorized as trade promotions and consumer promotions as follows.

Trade promotions   These are the promotional tools aimed at the market intermediaries. Due to increase in market competition and inter-firm rivalry, firms often offer promotional schemes to the market intermediaries to enhance the feeling of loyalty among the customers and push their products in the market. Various tools used for sales promotion include offering margins higher than the competitors, incentives for not keeping competitors' products, organizing joint promotions, providing financial assistance for promotional budgets, etc.

Consumer promotions   It refers to the promotional tools directed at the ultimate consumers. Various tools used for consumer promotion include discounts, free samples, contests, gifts, gift coupons, festival sales, special price offers for bulk purchase, etc. A cross-country comparison of regulatory framework for market promotion tools is given in Exhibit 14.3. The consumer-oriented promotion schemes are an integral part of a firm's pull strategy wherein the customer asks the retailer for the product with some sort of promotion offers.

Public Relations

In overseas markets, it is increasingly becoming important for a firm to be an 'insider'. Public relations aims at building corporate image and influencing media and other target groups to have

---

[9] Hume, Scot, 'Trade Promos Devour Half of All Marketing $', *Advertising Age*, 13 April 1992, p. 3.

Exhibit 14.3 Cross-country comparison of regulatory framework for market promotion tools

Country	Premiums	Games	Contests	Rebate/ Refunds	Gift vouchers	Database marketing	Product sampling
Argentina	Legal	Legal	Legal (if proof of purchase required, free option must be fixed)	Legal	Legal	Legal	Legal
Australia	Legal	Legal	Legal	Legal	Legal	Legal, but state privacy laws shortly anticipated	Legal, except therapeutics
Belgium	Legal, but with many restrictions Value may not exceed 5% of the main product value	Legal, but not when linked with purchase	Legal, but not when linked with purchase	Legal, but with many restrictions and conditions	Legal, but with many restrictions and conditions	Legal	Legal
Brazil	Legal, very popular	Legal, very popular. If requiring purchase or based on chance, approval from Consumer Defense Dept. required	Legal, very popular. If requiring purchase or based on chance, approval from Consumer Defense Dept. required	Legal, but not popular	Legal, popular	Legal, very popular. Mail must be discontinued at receiver's request	Legal, very popular
Chile	Legal	Legal	Legal	All consumers must have the same discount based on volume bought	Legal	Legal, but consumer can request to have names removed from database	Legal
Columbia	Legal	Legal, but games based on chance or luck require authorization	Legal, but contests based on chance or luck require authorization	Legal, but not popular	Legal	Legal	Legal
UK	Legal	Subject to compliance with Lotteries & Amusements Act	Subject to compliance with Lotteries & Amusements Act	Legal	Legal	Legal	Legal, but some restrictions on alcohol, tobacco, medicines, solvents and some food

(Contd)

Exhibit 14.3   *(Contd)*

Country	Premiums	Games	Contests	Rebate/Refunds	Gift vouchers	Database marketing	Product sampling
Finland	Legal, if gift has very small value or there is an evident material connection between the goods or services offered	Legal, when based on skill, purchase can be required. When based on chance, free method of entry is required	Legal, when based on skill, purchase can be required. When based on chance, free method of entry is required	Legal	Legal, if gift has very small value or there is an evident material connection between the goods or services offered	Legal, with many restrictions	Legal, some restrictions
France	Legal, if gift has a very small value or is identical to the good purchased Usually not allowed when the premium is free	Legal, but must be absolutely free and not connected to a purchase	Legal, but prize promotion must be skill, absolutely free, and not connected to a purchase	Legal	Legal, if gift has a very small value or is identical to the good purchased Usually not allowed when the premium is free	Legal	Legal
Germany	Buy one get one free not allowed	Legal, mechanics must be checked before practiced	Legal, mechanics must be checked before practiced	Legal, only to 3% maximum	Usually not allowed Some small-value give always are allowed, lawyers usually can find a way around the law	Legal, but consumer must consent first	Usually legal when only samples are used. No regular original retail products
Holland	Legal	Prize value not to exceed US$ 2500. Regulations currently under review	Prize value not to exceed US$ 2500. Regulations currently under review	Rebates-Legal Refunds-price restrictions	Legal	Legal, with some restrictions. Consumers can request to have name removed from database	Legal, except for alcohol, drugs and pharmaceuticals
Hungary	Legal, but only used between trade companies	Legal, must get approval from gambling supervision	Legal, must get approval from gambling supervision	Legal, but only used between trade companies	Legal, as long as gift has very small values	Legal, consumers can request to have names removed from database	Legal, except for pharmaceuticals, tobacco, alcohol, weapons or explosives

(Contd)

Exhibit 14.3   *(Contd)*

Ireland	Legal	Legal, if based on chance free entry required if winner is determined by skill, purchase can be required	Legal, if based on chance free entry required if winner is determined by skill, purchase can be required	Legal	Legal	Legal, but tobacco prohibited
Israel	Legal	Legal, but proof of purchase may be required	Legal, but proof of purchase may be required	Legal, but not popular	Legal, but cannot use private data such as credit card, bank, healthcare etc. info.	Legal
Italy	Legal, 20% tax on prize value. Govt. notification required	Legal, 45% tax on prize value Govt. notification required	Legal, 45% tax on prize value Govt. notification required	Illegal	Legal, but with use of personal data written permissions of consumer required	Legal
Japan	Legal, but very strict restrictions apply	Legal, but very strict restrictions apply	Legal	Legal	Legal	Legal, except medicine
Malaysia	Legal	Legal, but prize promotion must be skill, not chance	Legal, but prize promotion must be skill, not chance	Legal	Legal	Legal, except alcohol, cigarette to Muslims
Mexico	Legal	Legal	Legal	Legal	Legal	Legal
New Zealand	Legal	Legal	Legal	Legal, with restrictions	Legal, but protected by consumer privacy act	Legal
Poland	Legal	Legal, but games of chance restricted by law on games of chance & mutual bets	Legal, but games of chance restricted by law on games of Chance & mutual bets	Legal, but rebates are in use.	Legal, but significantly limited by the law on protection of personal data	Legal, except pharmaceuticals, alcoholic beverages

(Contd)

Exhibit 14.3   *(Contd)*

Country	Premiums	Games	Contests	Rebate/Refunds	Gift vouchers	Database marketing	Product sampling
Singapore	Legal	Legal, may require permission from authorities	Legal, may require permission from authorities	Legal	Legal	Legal	Legal
Spain	Legal, but you must ask for permission	Legal, you must register with the government	Legal, you must register with the government	Legal, you must register with the government	Legal, some restrictions	Legal, you must register database with data protection agency	Legal
Sweden	Legal, but exact details of offer must be revealed (closing date, conditions, value, etc.)	Legal, but government permit required	Legal, but promotion must be skill, not chance. Some restrictions to connect to a purchase. Exact details of offer must be revealed (closing date, conditions, value, etc.)	Legal, but exact details of offer must be revealed (closing date, conditions, value, etc.)	Legal, but exact details of offer must be revealed (closing date, conditions, value, etc.)	Legal, with some restrictions and a permit to maintain a list. The marketing offer must state from where the address was obtained	Legal
USA	Legal, but all material terms and conditions must be disclosed	Legal, but on-pack games subject to certain restrictions	Legal, some states prohibit requiring consideration. Bonafide skill must dominate and control final result. Various state disclosure requirements	Legal, must not be coupons	Legal, but cost of gift may not be built into the cost for purchased product	Legal, consumers may request to have name removed from industry, state and company lists	Legal, with restrictions on alcohol, tobacco, drugs and some agricultural products
Venezuela	Legal, some restrictions when with food. Must register with the government	Legal, must register with the government	Legal, must register with the government	Legal	Legal, some restrictions with food. Must register with the government	Legal	Legal, except cigarettes and alcohol to minor Must register with the government Some restriction when with food

a favourable publicity. Various methods used for public relations are as follows:

* Sponsorship of sports, cultural events, etc.
* Press release
* Contribution to awards and prices for sports and other events
* Publicity of a firm's promotional campaign
* Lobbying at government level

Public relations may aim at internal as well as external communication directed at employees, shareholders, suppliers of inputs and components, customers, and the general public. A firm attempts to create links with the media, politicians, bureaucrats, and other influential groups and persons in the target market to gain positive publicity. Professional PR firms offer specialized public relation services especially in high-income countries, whereas the 'word of mouth' mode of publicity is used widely in low-income countries.

Trade Missions

A trade mission consists of a group of business people travelling abroad to promote their business by meeting foreign companies or foreign government officials. The strategy of the mission might be to establish personal contacts with key decision-makers in the target country; to gather information and market intelligence on opportunities and prospects; or to promote the companies represented in the mission and convince the hosts to do business with those companies. Trade missions are generally facilitated by the following:

* The central and state governments
* Trade promotion organizations (TPOs) like India Trade Promotion Organization (ITPO) or export promotion organizations (EPOs)
* Trade and industry associations

Types of trade missions

Trade missions can be classified on the bases of orientation and focus.

On the basis of orientation

Inward trade missions   These missions focus on inviting buyers to home market. They are also known as buyer–seller meets. Generally, government agencies bear the cost of hospitality of foreign delegates as a part of their promotional activities.

Outward trade missions   The objective of these missions is to take exporters to international markets. They are also known as trade delegations.

On the basis of focus

General   These missions aim at creating awareness about the country and its supply potential. For example, missions organized by the ITPO and the Confederation of Indian Industries (CII).

Policy focused   These missions aim at promoting the country's image and capability by focusing on government policies and thus attract investment.

Industry focused   These missions focus on a particular industry, such as agriculture, food, or garments. Such missions are generally organized by specialized trade promotion organizations, such as Apparel Export Promotion Council (AEPC), Marine Products Export Development Authority (MPEDA), Export Promotion Council or Handicrafts (EPCH), and trade associations.

International Trade Fairs and Exhibitions

Trade fairs are organized gatherings where the buyers and the sellers meet and establish communication. These are the oldest and the most effective methods to explore marketing opportunities.

The main functions of international trade fairs are as follows:

- Provide an opportunity to get information on the competing products, their attributes, prices, etc. in the market.
- Help assess the customer's response to the firm's products.
- Serve as a meeting place for potential importers, agents, and distributors in the international markets.
- Provide publicity and generate goodwill.
- Provide opportunity to meet existing clients in the market and assess their performance vis-à-vis competitors.

Trade fairs may be international, regional, national, or provincial in terms of their scope and participants. Trade fairs may also be classified as follows.

General trade fairs   All types of consumer and industrial goods are exhibited in trade fairs. Such trade fairs are open both for general public and business persons. Generally, in less-developed countries, general trade fair is the only option.

Specialized trade fairs   Such trade fairs focus on a specific industrial or trade sector, such as apparels or food. Specialized trade fairs are targeted at business visitors but are usually also open for the general public on specific days and at specific times. Specialized trade fairs provide excellent opportunity to explore contacts in international markets, such as importers, agents, and distributors. Even established firms participate in specialized fairs in order to establish contacts.

Consumer fairs   Generally targeted at individual customers, the consumer fairs focus on household goods.

Minor trade fairs   These are fairs held at a small level, such as toy fairs or shoe fairs.

Solo exhibitions   Exhibitions held by a specific country or group. In these exhibitions, a number of dealers of a particular product field put up the show in a hotel, hall, or lounge.

Catalogue shows   As participation in trade fairs involves considerable cost and time, the display of catalogues, sometimes accompanied with trade samples, provides an opportunity to create market awareness about the firm's products. Generally, the government organizations and industry associations actively promote such catalogue shows.

Making Optimum Gains from Participation in International Trade Fairs

As participation in international trade fairs is comparatively costly and requires much larger resources, firms need to explore various trade fairs and select carefully the ones that meet its marketing goals and objectives. It needs to consider the following while selecting an international trade fair:

- Compatibility with the firm's product profile and marketing objectives
- Location of the fair
- Visitors' and participants' profile
- Performance of the fair in terms of the sales concluded, exhibitors participated, and the number of visitors during previous years
- Experience of previous business exhibitors
- Cost of participation vis-à-vis other promotional alternatives

Moreover, to make trade fair participation effective, marketers need to carry out thorough preparations while participating. In order to generate business and to make the participation in an international trade fair meaningful, the following issues need to be taken care of:

- Visit the overseas market in advance, one year to six months before the fair, to gather information about the markets, business dynamics, and to get oneself familiarized with the market.
- Carry out a market analysis in advance in terms of the social, cultural, linguistic, economic, legal, and political issues that influence the marketing opportunities.
- Prepare as detailed a plan of display before participation.
- Prepare exhibition materials, such as literature, promotional CD ROMs, videotapes, media kits, business cards, display items, signage, and promotional products.
- Immediate follow-up after participation in the fair is crucial to achieve business generation. Therefore, all queries should be answered as quickly as possible after the trade fair.

The effectiveness of the firm's participation in trade fairs may be assessed from the following:

- Securing business leads and contacts
- Volume of sales order
- Finding international trade partners
- Conducting market and competitor research
- Acquiring information about new products, processes, and technology
- Meeting with existing customers
- Creating awareness about the firm

ATA Carnet

For the ease of movement of imported duty-free goods, the International Chamber of Commerce (ICC), Paris, has evolved an international system of a document called the ATA carnet. The initials 'ATA' are an acronym of the French and English words '*Admission Temporaier*' and 'Temporary Admission', respectively. The ATA carnet is an international customs document that permits duty-free and tax-free temporary import of goods during its validity period. ATA carnets cover

- commercial samples,
- professional equipment, and
- goods for presentation or use at trade fairs, shows, exhibitions, and the like.

Each participating country appoints a national guaranteeing organization to administer carnets. All designated chambers in each country are authorized to issue or endorse a carnet. Thus, there is a chain of national chambers governed and controlled by ICC, Paris, which is authorized to issue such carnets or endorse the carnets of other designated national chambers issued for temporary importation of exhibits into their own country. The Federation of Indian Chambers of Commerce and Industry (FICCI) is the sole national guarantor chamber in India for issuing and endorsing foreign carnets for a fee. FICCI also endorses all ATA carnets issued by other notified chambers in the chain countries.

The obligation discharge requirements for ATA carnets include the following:

- Each carnet holder has to discharge the holder's obligations before its expiry date.
- To discharge the liability of an ATA carnet, the proof of re-exportation of goods covered or proof of payment of admissible duty on goods sold covered by an ATA carnet, if any, has to be submitted.
- Likewise, on all foreign carnets endorsed by their national, proof of re-exportation of goods has to be submitted to the home country's guaranteeing organization (i.e., FICCI in case of India) within its validity period.
- Non-fulfilment of discharge obligation of a carnet may cause forfeiture of the security deposit, besides other procedures as per law.

The ATA carnet system is for the facilitation of temporary duty-free import/export of goods and is currently in force in 71 countries including India, the USA, the UK, China, the UAE, France, Germany, and Japan. The ATA carnet services are available to business and sales executives, exhibitors, travelling professionals, and large and small companies. Virtually all goods can be included in the carnet except for disposable items or consumable goods, including food.

FACTORS INFLUENCING INTERNATIONAL COMMUNICATION DECISIONS

As the marketing environment across the countries varies considerably, there are various factors influencing international marketing communication.

Culture

Culture influences customers' behaviour across the country as discussed in detail in Chapter 5. Besides, customers are also very sensitive about the cultural aspects in marketing communications. Advertising in the USA and a number of Western countries reflects the direct approach, assertiveness, and competitiveness, whereas advertising themes in most oriental countries incorporating social acceptance, mutual dependence, respect for elders and traditions, harmony with nature, use of seasons, innovation and novelty, distinctive use celebrities, changing family role are often effective.[10]

Let us now illustrate some of the marketing blunders in international markets that occurred due to the faulty understanding of different cultures on the marketers' part.

- Procter & Gamble (P&G) showed an animated stork delivering Pampers diapers in its advertising campaigns in the USA. The same advertisement copy was used in Japan, only the language was changed. However, this advertisement did not work in Japan. The subsequent market research revealed that, unlike the Western folklore, storks, according to the Japanese folklore, are not expected to deliver babies. On the contrary, Japanese people believe that it is the giant peaches that float on the river that bring babies to the deserving parents. Subsequently, P&G changed the theme of the advertising campaign to 'expert mom', a nurse who is also a mother theme.
- Muhammad Ali is immensely popular in the Middle East. One of the car manufacturers used Muhammad Ali in its advertising campaign for the region. The advertisement theme was 'I am the greatest'. The advertisement backfired and offended the Muslims who regard only the God as great.[11]

Islamic countries impose certain restrictions on the presentation of women in advertisements, both print and electronic media. The most stringent laws regarding presentation of women are in Saudi Arabia where the TV commercials could show only a veiled woman or her back. For advertising Pert Plus Shampoo, P&G had to adopt an unusual strategy in Saudi Arabia. Since the focus had to be on the prospect's hair, the advertisement shows the hair of a woman from the back and another veiled woman from the front. Similar advertisement copies were aptly adapted by a number of hair product advertisers (Fig. 14.11) in Islamic markets with stringent laws on advertising in terms of depicting women.

The product Revital, which is a balanced combination of vitamins, minerals, and ginseng, from India's leading pharmaceutical company Ranbaxy Laboratory is promoted differently in different countries, primarily due to cultural sensitivities of the customers. In India, Revital

---

[10] Ricks, David A., *Blunders in International Business*, Cambridge, Blackwell Publishers, MA, USA, 1993.

[11] Harper, T., 'Polaroid Clicks Instantly in Moslem Markets', *Advertising Age*, 30 January 1986, p.12.

Fig. 14.11   Skilful adaptation of advertisements in Islamic markets to suit local culture and the law

Copyright: Unilever.

is promoted as a daily health-supplement diet defining the target customer as a 'regular man (urban office goer) who is able to do more in life and that too with a smile, after using Revital'. In Malaysia, it is targeted to young people and active sportsmen as a health supplement. It is marketed as a multi-vitamin supplement for expecting mothers in Nigeria. In countries such as Russia, Thailand, and South Africa, Revital is targeted at couples as a product promoting 'health and love', aimed at enhancing vitality and romance. In Southeast Asia and China, where ginseng is a highly desirable herb with numerous health benefits, the product packaging depicts a picture of the herb and prominently mentions in the local language, 'A combination of Korean Panax Ginseng extract with minerals and vitamins'. On the other hand, as ginseng is less known in India and South Africa, the picture of ginseng is not shown in the packaging.

Indians are highly fond of sweets and astonishing varieties of locally made sweets are available across the country. No celebration in India is complete without offering and consuming sweets. In response to the enormous customer demands for sweets, Nestlé promotes its chocolates as sweets in the Indian markets. As a result, the advertising campaign with the punchline '*Pappu pass ho gaya*' (Pappu cleared the examination), implying celebrating Pappu's success with Cadbury chocolates instead of sweets, became highly popular.

The cultural contexts

As discussed in Chapter 5, the culture has broadly been divided as high-context and low-context culture. Oriental countries such as Japan, China, India, and the Middle East generally have high-context cultures where the contextual background of communication is extremely significant unlike low-context countries. Therefore, marketing communication in high-context cultures has to be more implicit than explicit. The cultural contexts can be applied to international communications in the following manner.[12]

Conversational principles

- In high-context cultures, the customers look keenly at the details of the sales executives and the company. Therefore, any promotional or advertising campaign in such cases should aim at establishing the firm's credibility and background.
- There should be clarity in presentation. Jargons and slangs should be avoided. One should speak slowly and without a strong accent, unlike Western markets.
- Focus on identification with the international recipients by way of using phrases or words from the recipient language or use of historical or contemporary illustrations.
- Body language and tone of voice should be consistent with the message.

Presentation principles

- One should show respect for cultures that are more formal. It needs structured presentation in terms of format and content of communication.
- It should give due respect and appeal to different foreign audiences.
- One should be patient with the pace of different cultures. The length of message is often viewed as an indication of the importance the promoter attaches to its subject.

Return word principles

- In low-context cultures, communication is generally direct, to the point, and immediately stated. However, emphasis needs to be given on politeness and decorum of the message. Besides, proper translation in high-context cultures is very important. Modifications in slogans or branding are required so that the message does not offend the target audience.

Language

Translation from one language to another is crucial in international communication. Literal translation may fail to convey the desired message across countries due to cultural factors. For instance, the word 'yes' is understood differently across countries. In low-context societies, such as the USA and the Europe, 'yes' means 'yes' but in high-context societies, such as Japan, 'yes' means 'I am listening what you are saying' and not necessarily just a 'yes'. In Thailand, 'yes' means 'OK'. Such vast differences in inferring the meaning of 'yes' is due to the fact that in high-context cultures, the other person is given an opportunity to save her face and direct refusals are hardly appreciated by society.

Lack of understanding linguistic nuances has resulted in marketing blunders, as evident from the following instances:

- Pepsi's slogan 'Come Alive with the Pepsi Generation' backfired in Taiwan and China as it inadvertently translated to 'Pepsi will bring your ancestors back from the dead'.
- Parker pens' US marketing slogan for its ink 'Avoid Embarrassment—Use Quink' boomeranged in Latin America as its Spanish version 'Evite Embarazos—Use Quink' meant 'Avoid Pregnancy—Use Quink'.
- Much to its embarrassment, P&G learnt while introducing Vicks cough drops in Germany that 'v' is pronounced as 'f' in German leading to a vulgar connotation for the world 'vicks'. Consequently, it had to change the name to 'Wick' in the German market (Fig. 14.12).

---

[12] Dulek, R.E., J.S. Fielden, and J.S. Hill, 'International Communications: An Executive Primer', *Business Horizons*, January–February 1991, pp. 20–25.

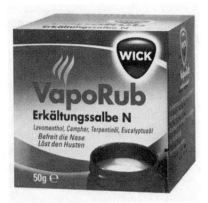

Fig. 14.12 As the global brand Vicks' pronunciation in German has a sexual connotation, P&G had to change its name to 'Wick' in German speaking countries

Copyright: Procter & Gamble.

Honda introduced its new car 'Fitta' in Nordic countries in 2001. Subsequently, it was found that 'Fitta' was an old vulgar word in Norwegian, Swedish, and Danish. Honda had to rename it as 'Honda Jazz'. Colgate's popular toothpaste in the USA 'Cue' miserably failed in France, as 'Cue' is the name of a French pornographic magazine.

Coping with translation problems

Communication decisions in international markets have to take into consideration not only the literal translation in the foreign language, but also subtle nuances. In order to avoid such mistakes in international marketing communication, the matter needs to be written perfectly and reviewed by native/s to the countries targeted. The problems related to translation may be overcome by using a variety of techniques, such as back translation, parallel translation, and decentring, as discussed next.

Back translation   The communiqué is translated from one language to another and then a second party translates it back into the original.[13] As a result, misinterpretations and misunderstandings are pinpointed beforehand.

Parallel translation   Due to commonly used idioms in both languages, back translations may not always ensure an accurate translation. In such cases, parallel translation is used wherein more than two translators are used for back translation. Subsequently, the results are compared, differences discussed, and the most appropriate translation is selected.

Decentring   It is a hybrid of back translation wherein a successive process of translation and retranslation of a questionnaire is used each time by a different translator. For instance, an English version of the matter is translated into the foreign language (e.g., Japanese) and then translated back to English by a different translator. Then the two English versions are compared and where there are differences, the original English version of the second iteration is modified and the process repeated. The process is repeated until the Japanese version can be translated into English and back to Japanese by different translators without any perceptible difference. The wording of the original matter undergoes change in the process but the final version of the instrument has equally comprehensive and equivalent terminologies in both languages.

---

[13] Iverson, Stephen P., *The Art of Translation*, World Trade, 2000, pp. 90–92.

Education

The level of literacy plays an important role in deciding a communication tool and message in international markets. Market segments with lower level of adult literacy needs to be addressed by way of more audio-visual content rather than a written message. It should be ensured that the visuals, rather than the text, convey the desired message.

Media Infrastructure

Availability of media, which varies widely across the countries, often influences advertisers' options for using a media. Outdoor advertisements are cost-effective and widely used, especially in low-income countries due to constraints related to media penetration. Movies, posters, puppet shows, mime, etc. are frequently used methods of communication in low-income countries that have lower levels of literacy. These methods are extremely popular in social marketing, such as anti-HIV campaigns, contraceptives, and family welfare and preventive health.

Outdoor advertisements are cost-effective and are widely used, especially in low-income countries due to constraints related to media penetration. Outdoor advertisements on buses, roadside hoardings, etc. are extremely popular in low-income countries. Movies, posters, puppet shows, mimes, etc. are frequently used methods of communication in low-income countries, which have a lower level of literacy. These methods are extremely popular in social marketing, such as anti-HIV campaigns, advertising campaigns for contraceptives, family welfare, etc.

An analysis of global advertising spend by media type (Fig. 14.13) reveals that the share of newspapers and magazines is considerably declining from 25.1 and 11.7 per cent respectively in 2006 to 19 and 9.6 per cent in 2010, which is further expected to decline to 15.8 and 9.1 per cent in 2015. The share of televising increased from 34.1 per cent in 2006 to 36.9 per cent in 2010 and is likely to show a marginal increase to 37.6 per cent in 2015. The Internet has emerged as a powerful advertising medium with a share of mere 8.2 per cent in 2006 to 15.3 per cent in 2010 and is likely to significantly grow to 21 per cent in 2015. Television will continue to dominate the share in advertising expenditure, whereas the share of Internet is expected to rise significantly, which would be at the cost of more traditional media, that is, newspaper, magazines, radio and directories.[14]

Government Regulations

The regulatory framework of a country influences the communication strategy in international markets. The government regulations in various countries relates to the following issues:

- Advertising in foreign language
- Use of pornography and sensuality
- Comparative advertising referring to competing products from rival firms
- Advertisements related to alcohol and tobacco
- Use of children as models
- Advertisements related to health food and pharmaceuticals

  Some of the advertising regulations in various countries[15] are summed up here:

- In Malaysia, the Ministry of Information's Advertising Code states that women should not be the principal objects of an advertisement or intend to attract sales unless the advertised product is relevant to women.
- The Ministry of Information in Saudi Arabia prevents any advertising depicting unveiled women.

---

[14] *Global Entertainment and Media Outlook*, 2011–2015, PricewaterhouseCoopers, 2011.

[15] Boddewyn, Jean J., 'Controlling Sex and Decency in Advertising around the World', *Journal of Advertising*, 20 December 1991, pp. 25–36.

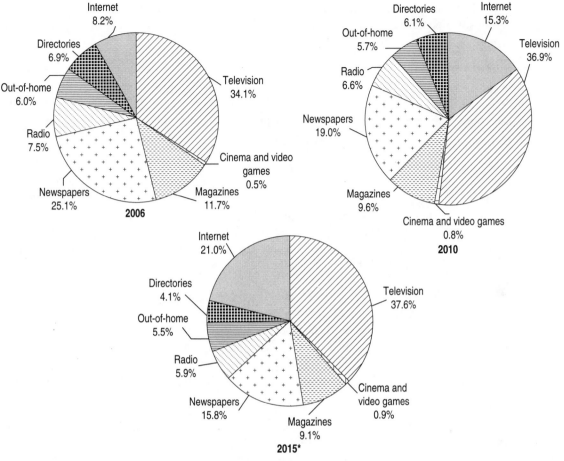

Fig. 14.13 Global advertising spend: by media type

*Projections
**Europe, Middle East, and Africa
Source: Global Entertainment and Media Outlook, 2011–2015, PricewaterhouseCoopers, 2011.

- Portuguese law prohibits sex discrimination or the subordination or objectification of women in advertising.
- The use of foreign words and expressions, when French equivalents can be found in the dictionary, are prohibited in France.
- Norway prohibits any advertising that portrays men or women in an offensive manner or imply any derogatory judgement of either sex.
- Most Arab countries prohibit explicit depiction of sensuality.

STRATEGIC FRAMEWORK FOR INTERNATIONAL PRODUCT-PROMOTION DECISIONS

Product and promotion decisions as to whether to offer a standardized product or adapt it for an overseas market are considerably influenced[16] by product function or need satisfied, the condition

---

[16] Keegan, Warren J., 'Multinational Product Planning: Strategic Alternatives', *Journal of Marketing*, January 1996, pp. 56–62.

of product use, and customers' ability to buy, as explained in Chapter 10. Under different marketing situations, the alternatives available with a firm either to extend or adapt product and/or promotion are discussed next.

Straight Adaptation

In cases when the need satisfied and the conditions of product use are the same, the product as well as the marketing communication is extended. Global brands, such as Pepsi, Coca-Cola, Gillette, Benetton, Heineken, and BMW often use a global product and global communication strategies.

Product Extension–Promotion Adaptation

When the condition of product use remains the same, whereas the needs satisfied or the product function is different, the product is extended as such but the promotion strategy is adapted. For instance, chewing gum is viewed primarily as a children's product in India, whereas it is considered a substitute to smoking in the USA. It is supposed to provide dental benefits in Europe while considered beneficial for facial fitness in Far Eastern countries. Under such situations, no changes are made in the product but the promotional strategy is customized so as to address the customers' needs.

Product Adaptation–Promotion Extension

When the need remains the same and the condition of the product use differs across markets, modifications are carried out in the product but the promotional strategy is often adapted. For instance, the electronic consumer durables such as TV and VCR serve the same purpose of recreation and information but the operating systems vary across countries. Therefore, product modification is needed in such cases and the communication process needs to be adapted too.

Dual Adaptation

A company has to customize both the product and the promotional strategies while marketing in countries where the functions of the product and need satisfied are different and the conditions for the product use is also different.

This chapter brings out the significance of communication decisions as one has to be quite prudent in international markets due to several contextual differences, especially culture and the legal framework. The concept of marketing communication mix that include advertising, sales promotion, direct and interactive marketing, personal selling, and public relations are also elucidated along with various market communication tools. This chapter also examines various factors influencing communication decisions in international markets. At the end, it presents a broad framework for international product-promotion strategy.

Summary

Communication is crucial to a firm's success in international markets. The consumer response hierarchy models provide a framework of the buying process that facilitates promotional decisions. The alternative marketing communication strategies, that is, pull and push strategies, are primarily based on targeting the channel intermediaries in the distribution system or the end customers. A firm adopts push strategy in marketing communication when there is lack of product differentiation, weak brand identity, low brand loyalty, lack of access to advertising media, and low promotional budgets and institutional sales. In cases where a product has considerable perceived product differentiation, strong brand identity, high brand loyalty, and high promotional budgets, the firms generally opt for a pull strategy. The firms need to adopt a judicial mix of pull and push in view of the competitive pressures and market characteristics.

The process of international marketing communication involves a sender, message, medium, and receiver. Besides, the firm has to take into consideration the 'noise' and the communication feedback so as to make modification in its communication strategy. The process of marketing communication becomes more complex in international context as the encoding and decoding of the message in different countries are influenced by a variety of factors, such as culture, regulatory framework, and media availability.

The marketing communication mix involves advertising, sales promotion, public relations, personal selling, and direct and interactive marketing. Advertising decisions in international markets often revolve around the issue of whether to opt for standardization or adaptation. It may be noted that even the term standardization varies quite considerably. It encompasses advertisements with no change as well as advertisements with changes in illustrations to communicate the basic concept. The emergence of global psychographic segments of the customers and breakthroughs in communication and transport has encouraged standardized advertising. Some of the global firms such as Avon, Amway, and Mary Kay, have successfully employed direct marketing in international markets. However, adaptation was necessitated due to market characteristics and government regulations in countries such as India and China.

International trade fairs and exhibitions serve as useful tools for market promotion and facilitate the establishment of contacts and communication among buyers and sellers from various countries. For small firms and most companies from low-income countries, international trade fairs and exhibitions are highly cost-effective promotional tools. Besides, catalogue shows and trade missions are other popular cost-effective trade promotion tools in low-income countries.

The factors influencing international communication decisions include culture, language, education, media infrastructure, and government regulations. Depending upon its marketing requirements, a firm is required to use a blend of these communication tools. Based on the product function or needs satisfied, the condition of product use and the customers' ability to buy, product and promotion may be either extended or adapted in international markets.

Key Terms

Advertising   Any paid form of non-personal communication by an identified sponsor.

ATA carnet   An international customs document that permits duty-free and tax-free temporary import of goods during its validity period.

Back translation   Translating from one language to another and then a second party translating this back into the original.

Decentring   A hybrid of back-translation, wherein a successive process of translation and re-translation of a questionnaire is used each time, by a different translator till there is no perceptible difference between the two versions.

Direct mailing   Sending letters, brochures, catalogues, emails, or faxes directly to the customers.

Direct marketing   Selling products and services to customers without using any market intermediary.

Marketing communication mix   Involves advertising, sales promotion, public relations, personal selling, and direct marketing.

Medium   Channels used to convey the encoded message to the intended receiver.

Message   All the information, verbal or non-verbal, that a sender aims to convey.

Multi-level marketing   A distribution system recruiting a core group of distributors who recruit sub-distributors and the distribution chain goes on.

Noise   Unplanned distortions or interference of the message.

Pull strategy   Promotional programmes directed to motivate the customers to ask for the product from the retailer.

Push strategy   Promotional programmes primarily directed at channel intermediaries in the distribution system.

Sales promotion   Various tools used as short-term incentives in order to induce a purchase decision.

Trade fairs   Organized gatherings wherein the buyers and the sellers come into contact and establish communication.

Trade missions   A group of business people travelling abroad to facilitate trade by meeting foreign companies or foreign government officials.

Concept Review Questions

1. Explain the process of marketing communication in the international context.
2. Distinguish between pull and push strategies. Explain the marketing situations that influence the decision-making process.
3. Examine the factors influencing the decisions for having a standardized vis-à-vis customized advertisement with suitable examples. Which one would you prefer and why?
4. What are the factors influencing international marketing communication decisions? Justify your answer with suitable illustrations.
5. Explain Keegan's framework for product promotion strategies in international markets with suitable examples.

Project Assignments

1. Carry out a cross-country comparison of the availability of various types of media and its costs. Examine factors influencing media selection decision in international markets.
2. Collect advertisement copies of an Indian firm in about four to six international markets. Compare them with the advertisement copy used in the domestic market and find out the differences. Evaluate the reasons for such differences and discuss your observations in the class.

Practice Exercises

1. Study the operations of a direct marketing international firm and find out the difficulties faced by it while operating in your country. Suggest the ways to overcome these bottlenecks.
2. Visit an international trade fair. Find out the profile of the participants and contact them to explore the reasons for their participation. Also, find out their experiences of participating in the international trade fair and how far have they been able to meet their marketing objectives.

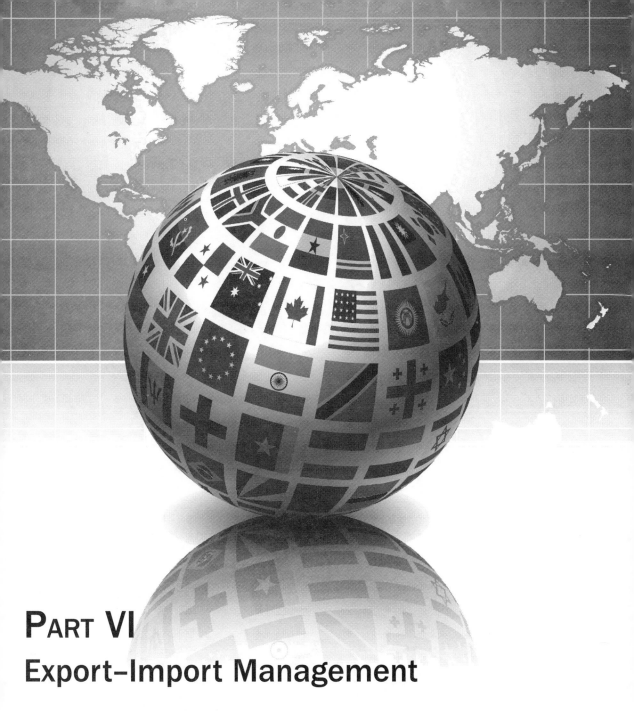

PART VI
Export–Import Management

Institutional Infrastructure for Export Promotion

INTRODUCTION

International marketing managers are expected to scan the international marketing environment, explore potential markets, and take a number of decisions before entering and operating in international markets depending upon the stage of their company's internationalization. These decisions pertain to identifying overseas market opportunities, product and packaging requirements, the pricing patterns, identifying international marketing channels, and marketing promotion opportunities. Most countries have established trade or export promotion organizations (TPOs/EPOs), meant to facilitate domestic companies to expand internationally. Therefore, managers entrusted with international marketing should develop a thorough understanding of the services offered by them and take their full advantage.

Individual countries do have independent TPOs at national level. Although the trade facilitation by national governments is primarily focused on export promotion, some countries with considerable imports do facilitate in sourcing imports by exclusive import promotion organizations. The International Trade Centre (ITC) headquartered at Geneva carries out a host of trade facilitation activities. Several international economic institutions established under the UN framework, already discussed in Chapter 2, also perform a variety of functions such as technical assistance for development, information collection and dissemination, training, economic surveillance, extending loans, promoting multilateral trade, and investment.

India has got a comprehensive set-up of export promotion both at central and state levels. Besides, the export promotion organizations, such as export promotion councils (EPCs) and commodity boards, are product-specific organizations that have specialized market knowledge as well as backward linkages of the products they deal in. They not only provide useful information but also facilitate

Learning Objectives

- To elucidate the significance of export promotion in international marketing
- To provide the conceptual framework of export promotion
- To outline the institutional set-up for export promotion in India
- To discuss the role of advisory bodies, commodity organizations, and service institutions in promoting exports
- To examine states' involvement in promoting exports
- To evaluate the strategic role of export promotion in emerging scenario

an international marketer's task in a variety of ways. Statutory requirements, such as registration-cum-membership certificates (RCMCs), quota administration, and disbursement of incentives through export promotion organizations, make it necessary for the marketers to approach these organizations. Moreover, participating in promotional activities, such as trade fairs, buyer–seller meets, trade delegations, and catalogue shows, through these export promotion organizations do make commercial sense for marketers.

This chapter elucidates the concept of export promotion and discusses various organizations involved in promoting international trade. It explains in detail and critically examines the institutional set-up available for export promotion in India, including the Department of Commerce, advisory bodies, commodity organizations, service organizations, and government trading organizations. Besides, the chapter critically evaluates the states' role in export promotion and elucidates the need for strategic reorientation under the emerging economic scenario.

THE CONCEPT OF EXPORT PROMOTION

A firm has to overcome several barriers in its process of internationalization. It, therefore, becomes necessary for an export manager to know about the institutional support available to him. All the countries realize and recognize the fact that exports are an integral part of their economic development. Hence, they readily assist the exporters in their efforts.

The functions of export promotion programmes are as follows:

- Creating awareness about exporting as an instrument of growth and market expansion
- Reducing and removing barriers to exporting
- Creating promotional incentives
- Providing various forms of assistance to potential and actual exporters

The export promotion[1] programmes initiated by the government are generally in the form of public policy measures, which focus on enhancing the export activities at the company, industry, or national level. Most countries actively promote exports as a part of their strategic thrust to increase exports and investment. The export promotion programmes are basically designed to assist firms in entering international markets and achieving optimum opportunities from their international business activities.

A firm has to overcome several barriers in its process of internationalization. It, therefore, becomes necessary for an export manager to know about the institutional support available to him. All the countries realize and recognize the fact that exports are an integral part of their economic development. Hence, they readily assist the exporters in their efforts.

In its process of internationalization, a company undergoes the transition from being a non-exporter to a regular exporter, as a result of which its requirement for export facilitation varies. Different export promotion tools are used depending upon the requirement of a firm, as depicted in Fig. 15.1. A non-exporter needs to be motivated by making him aware of the international marketing opportunities.[2] Once a company operating in the domestic market is motivated to enter international markets, it has to be convinced that better growth opportunities exist in exporting by way of market research, trade missions, and counselling. A first-time exporter has to be assisted in finding export marketing opportunities and may be supported on matters related to export policy, procedures, and documentations. An exporter who has already entered the international market and is now planning to expand his market base needs to be advised on selecting those foreign

---

[1] Root, F.R., *The Elements of Export Promotion*, International Trade Forum, July–September 1971, pp. 118–121.

[2] Seringhas, F.H. Rolf and Philip J. Rosson, *Government Export Promotion*, 1990, pp. 153–158.

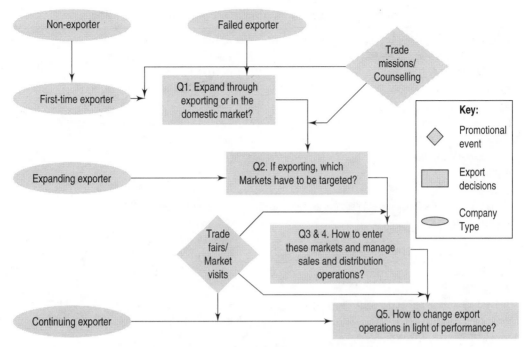

Fig. 15.1   Targeting export promotion

Source: Adapted from Seringhas, F.H. Rolf and Philip J. Rosson, *Government Export Promotion*, 1990, p. 179.

markets where one can derive optimum market opportunity. However, the established exporters consistently attempt to explore ways to improve their international marketing operations and need to be assisted by way of trade fairs, buyer–seller meets, and market promotion programmes.

As a part of their export promotion strategy, all national governments have established institutional set-ups to support export activities. The major objective of export promotion programmes is to create awareness about exports and make the people understand that it is one of the most crucial instruments of growth and market expansion. These programmes should focus on the reduction and removal of barriers to exporting, creation of promotional incentives, and development of some form of assistance to potential and actual exporters.

ORGANIZATIONS FOR INTERNATIONAL TRADE PROMOTION

Most countries have set up their own independent organizations for promoting international trade. Exhibit 15.1 lists the major country-wise organizations promoting international trade. These organizations broadly aim at promoting the respective country's international trade and investment. The activities carried out by these organizations vary considerably. However, such organizations usually carry out one or more of the following activities:

- Identifying trade and investment needs of local firms
- Keeping a watch on international business environment affecting the country's trade
- Gathering, compiling, and disseminating information
- Spotting opportunities for international trade and investment
- Matchmaking between buyers and sellers
- Organizing trade missions, trade delegations, buyer–seller meets, etc.
- Facilitating participation and organizing trade exhibitions

Exhibit 15.1   Country-wise organizations promoting international trade

Australia Australian Trade Commission (AUSTRADE) www.austrade.gov.au	*Malaysia* Malaysia External Trade Development Corporation (MATRADE) _ www.matrade.gov.my
Brazil Agêcia de Promoção de Exportações do Brasil http://www.apexbrasil.com.br	*Oman* The Omani Centre for Investment Promotion and Export Development (OCIPED) www.ociped.com
Canada International Trade Canada www.itcan-cican.gc.ca/	*Pakistan* Export Promotion Bureau (EPB) www.epb.gov.pk
China China Council for the Promotion of International Trade (CCPIT) www.ccpit.org	*Singapore* International Enterprise Singapore (IE Singapore) www.iesingapore.gov.sg
France The French Agency for International Business Development (UBIFRANCE) www.ubifrance.fr	*Sri Lanka* Sri Lanka Export Development Board (EDB) www.srilankabusiness.com
Hong Kong (Special Administrative Region of China) Hong Kong Trade Development Council www.tdctrade.com	*Sweden* Swedish Trade Council EXPORTRADET www.swedishtrade.se
India India Trade Promotion Organization (ITPO) www.indiatradepromotion.org	*Tanzania* United Republic of Board of External Trade (BET) www.bet.co.tz
Indonesia National Agency for Export Development (NAFED) www.nafed.go.id	*United Arab Emirates* Dubai Chamber of Commerce and Industry (DCCI) www.dcci.ae
Japan Japan External Trade Organization (JETRO) www.jetro.go.jp	*United Kingdom* UK Trade and Investment www.uktradeinvest.gov.uk
Kenya Export Promotion Council www.cbik.or.ke	*United States of America* U.S. Department of Commerce's Commercial Service www.export.gov
Korea Republic of Korea Trade-Investment Promotion Agency (KOTRA) www.kotra.or.kr/eng/	

- Networking with foreign trade promoting organizations
- Carrying out generic market promotion and marketing services

International Trade Centre

The International Trade Centre (ITC) is the focal point in the United Nations (UN) system for technical cooperation with developing countries in trade promotion. The ITC was created by the General Agreement on Tariffs and Trade (GATT) in 1964 and since 1968 has been operated jointly by GATT (now by the WTO) and the UN, the latter acting through the United Nations Conference on Trade and Development (UNCTAD). As an executing agency of the United Nations Development Programme (UNDP), the ITC is directly responsible for implementing

UNDP-financed projects in developing countries and economies-in-transition related to trade promotion. ITC's activities aim to

- facilitate the integration of its clients into the world trading systems;
- support national efforts to implement trade development strategies;
- strengthen key trade support services, both public and private;
- improve export performance in sectors of critical importance and opportunity; and
- foster international competitiveness of small and medium enterprises (SMEs).

To achieve these goals, the ITC offers a range of global programmes, advisory and training services, information sources, tools, and products. Global programmes, based on proven ITC methodologies, and incorporating advisory services, tools, and products, respond to the needs of partners in all regions. Global programmes are replicable and adaptable, and have a perceptible time-proven impact. The ITC also participates in major trade-related multi-agency programmes. Advisory and training services are offered in key areas of international trade. Needs assessment, tailor-made advisory activities, and customized training are designed and delivered to build capacity in partner countries in close cooperation with trade support institutions. Information sources for international trade and business development are largely accessible through the

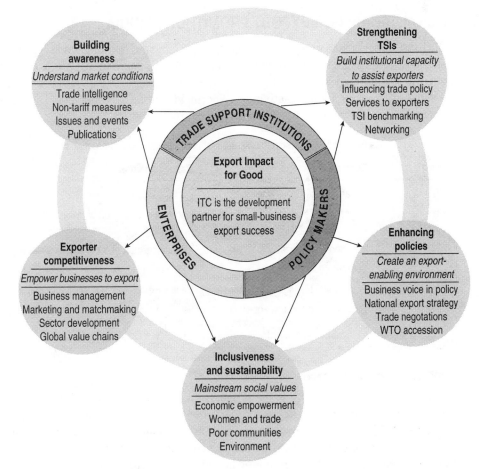

Fig. 15.2 An overview of ITC's support to developing countries in promoting exports

Source: www.intracen.org, accessed on 20 March 2013.

Internet. Tools and products support, sustain, and improve the delivery of trade support services through partner institutions. They include practical guides that can be adapted to local requirements, methodologies, and approaches for the development of review of trade support services, training materials, benchmarking, and assessment tools.

The ITC also supports developing and transitional economies, particularly their business sector, in their efforts to realize their full potential for developing exports and improving import operations (Fig. 15.2). ITC works in six areas, as follows:

- Product and market development
- Development of trade support services
- Trade information
- Human resource development
- International purchasing and supply management
- Needs assessment and programme design for trade promotion

Headquartered at Geneva, ITC is funded in equal parts by the UN and the WTO. It also finances general research and development on trade promotion and export development and information on international markets.

INSTITUTIONAL SET-UP FOR EXPORT PROMOTION IN INDIA

India has a comprehensive institutional set-up to promote international trade. The Department of Commerce is the prime agency of the country to promote international trade. It is supported by a massive institutional set-up (Exhibit 15.2) at the union and state government levels, carrying out a range of trade facilitation activities. Exporting firms need to understand and appreciate the institutions involved and the functions carried out by them.

Exhibit 15.2   Institutional set-up for international trade promotion in India

Tier levels	Bodies	Responsibilities
Tier I	Department of Commerce	Frame trade policy
Tier II	Advisory bodies	Coordinate discussion between industry and government for bringing in required changes
Tier III	Commodity organizations	Assist the export effort of specific product group
Tier IV	Service organizations	Facilitate and assist exporters to expand markets
Tier V	Government trading organizations	Handle export–import of specific commodity
Tier VI	State export promotion agencies	Facilitate export promotion from the states

Source: Ministry of Commerce and Industry, Government of India, New Delhi.

Department of Commerce

The Department of Commerce is the primary government agency responsible for developing and directing foreign trade policy and programmes, including commercial relations with other countries, state trading, various trade promotional measures and development, and regulation of certain export-oriented industries. The principal functional divisions of the Department of Commerce engaged in export promotion activities are discussed next.

The Economic Division is engaged in export planning, formulating export strategies, periodic appraisal, and review of policies. It also maintains coordination with and control over other divisions and various organizations set up by the Ministry of Commerce to facilitate export growth. Besides, the Economic Division monitors work related to technical assistance, management services for export, and overseas investment by Indian entrepreneurs.

The Trade Policy Division keeps track of development in international organizations, such as the WTO, UNCTAD, Economic Commission of Europe, Africa, Latin America, and Asia and Far East (ESCAP). The Trade Policy Division is also responsible for India's relationship with regional trading agreements, such as European Union (EU), North American Free Trade Agreement (NAFTA), South Asian Free Trade Area (SAFTA), and Commonwealth. It also looks after GSP and non-tariff barriers.

The Foreign Trade Territorial Division looks after the development of trade with different countries and regions of the world. It also deals with state trade and barter trade, organization of trade fairs and exhibitions, commercial publicity abroad, etc. Further, it maintains contact with trade missions abroad and carries out related administrative work.

The Export Product Division looks after problems connected with production, generation of surplus, and development of products for exports under its jurisdiction. However, for products wherein the administrative responsibility remains with concerned ministries, the Export Product Division keeps in close touch with them to ensure that the production is sufficient to realize the full export potential besides ensuring the home consumption. The division is also responsible for the working of export organizations and corporations, which deal with commodities and products under their jurisdiction.

The Exports Industries Division is responsible for development and regulation of rubber, tobacco, and cardamom. It is also responsible for handling export promotion activities related to textiles, woollens, handlooms, readymade garments, silk, cellulosic fibers, jute and jute products, coir and coir products, and handicrafts.

The Export Services Division deals with the problems of export assistance, such as export credit, export house, market development assistance (MDA), transport subsidies, free trade zones (FTZs), dry ports, quality control and pre-shipment inspection, and assistance to import capital goods.

The divisions mentioned above carry out their functions through EPCs, commodity boards, or other organizations, the details of which are given later in this chapter.

Subordinate Offices

In addition to these divisions, attached and subordinate offices are also involved in the promotion of foreign trade, as follows.

Directorate General of Foreign Trade

The directorate is responsible for framing and implementing India's foreign trade policy. It is headed by the Director General of Foreign Trade (DGFT). The directorate also looks after the work related to issuing of licenses and monitoring of export obligations. Its headquarters are at New Delhi and subordinate offices are located at Ahmedabad, Amritsar, Bengaluru, Baroda, Bhopal, Kolkata, Chandigarh, Chennai, Coimbatore, Cuttack, Ernakulam, Guwahati, Hyderabad, Jaipur, Kanpur, Ludhiana, Madurai, Moradabad, Mumbai, New Delhi, Panipat, Panaji, Patna, Pondicherry, Pune, Rajkot, Shillong, Srinagar (functioning at Jammu), Surat, Varanasi, and Vishakhapatnam.

Directorate General of Commercial Intelligence and Statistics

The Directorate General of Commercial Intelligence and Statistics (DGCIS), set up in 1962, is headquartered at Kolkata. It is responsible for collection, compilation, and dissemination of trade statistics and commercial information. The DGCIS also brings out a number of publications, mainly on inland and coastal trade statistics, revenue statistics, shipping, air cargo statistics, etc. Its main publications, such as *India Trade Journal* (weekly) and *Foreign Trade Statistics of India* (monthly), provide detailed information on export trade statistics. The DGCIS uses mainly daily trade returns (DTRs), an authentic source, for compiling and generating export–import statistics.

Directorate General of Anti-dumping and Allied Duties

Constituted in April 1998, the Directorate General of Anti-dumping and Allied Duties (DGAD) is responsible for carrying out anti-dumping investigations and to recommend wherever required, the amount of anti-dumping/countervailing duty under the Customs Tariff Act, on identified articles that would be adequate to remove injury to the domestic industry.

Advisory Bodies

Advisory bodies provide an effective mechanism for continued interaction with the trade and industry sector and increased coordination among various departments and ministries concerned with export promotion. The Government of India has set up the following advisory bodies for promoting international trade.

Board of Trade

In order to establish an effective mechanism for maintaining continuous dialogue with the trade and industry sector on issues related to international trade, the Board of Trade was set up under the chairmanship of the Union Minister of Commerce and Industry in May 1989. It was reconstituted on 1 April 2005 with an eminent representative from trade and industry as its chairperson.

The Secretaries of Commerce and Industry, Finance (Revenue), External Affairs (ER), Textile, Chairman of ITPO, Chairman/MD of ECGC, MD, Exim Bank, and Deputy Governor of Reserve Bank of India are official members of the board. Representatives from the Federation of Indian Chambers of Commerce and Industry (FICCI), Confederation of Indian Industry (CII), and Federation of Indian Export Organizations (FIEO) and various trade and industries sector, media, and other important eminent personalities in the field of import and export trade are also board members.

The broad terms of reference (ToR) of the Board of Trade are as follows:

- Advise the government on policy measures for preparation and implementation of both short-and long-term plans for increasing exports.
- Review the export performance of various sectors, identify constraints, and suggest industry-specific measures to optimize export earnings.
- Examine the existing institutional framework for exports and suggest practical measures for further streamlining to achieve the desired objectives.
- Review the policy instruments, package of incentives, and procedures for exports and suggest steps to rationalize and channelize such schemes for optimal use.
- Commence studies for promoting trade.

Thus, the Board of Trade ensures a continuous dialogue with trade and industry in order to advise the government on policy measures, to review export performance of various sectors, identify constraints, and suggest industry specific measures to optimize export specific earnings. It meets at least once every quarter and has the power to set up sub-committees, co-opt experts, and make recommendations on specific sectors.

Export Promotion Board

In order to provide greater coordination among concerned ministries involved in exports, the Export Promotion Board works under the chairpersonship of the Cabinet Secretary to provide policy and infrastructural support. The secretaries of all the ministries directly related to international trade are represented in this board, including secretaries of Departments of Commerce, Ministry of Finance, Department of Revenue, Department of Industrial Policy and Promotion, Ministry of Textile, Department of Agriculture and Cooperation, Ministry of Civil Aviation, Ministry of Surface Transport, and others, according to the requirements of inter-ministerial coordination. The coordinated approach of the Export Promotion Board provides the required impetus to the export sector and resolves inter-ministerial issues in promoting exports.

Commodity Organizations

In order to focus on the commodity- or product-specific exports, there are various commodity organizations such as EPCs, commodity boards, and autonomous bodies. These organizations look after sector-specific issues for promoting exports right from product development to export marketing.

Export promotion councils

Export promotion councils (EPCs) are non-profit organizations. They are supported by financial assistance from the central government. A complete list of EPCs is provided in Exhibit 15.3, whereas the details thereof are given in the online resource centre. The basic objective of EPCs is to develop and promote the country's export of specific products.

The major functions of EPCs are as follows:

- Providing commercially useful information and assistance to their members in developing and increasing their exports
- Offering professional advice to their members in areas such as technology upgradation, quality and design improvement, standards and specifications, product development, and innovation
- Organizing visits of delegations of their members abroad to explore overseas market opportunities
- Organizing participation in trade fairs, exhibitions, and buyer–seller meets in India and abroad
- Promoting interaction between the exporting community and the government, both at the central and state levels
- Building a statistical database and disseminate information

The EPCs also issue RCMCs to their members, which are mandatory for getting export incentives. Exhibit 15.4 gives a summary of services provided by the Synthetic and Rayon Textile

Exhibit 15.3   Export promotion councils in India

- Engineering Export Promotion Council
- Project Export Promotion
- Pharmaceutical Export Promotion Council
- Basic Chemicals, Pharmaceuticals and Cosmetics Export Promotion Council
- Chemicals and Allied Products Export Promotion Council
- Council for Leather Exports
- Sports Goods Export Promotion Council
- Gem and Jewellery Export Promotion Council
- Shellac Export Promotion Council
- Cashew Export Promotion Council
- Plastics Export Promotion Council
- Apparel Export Promotion Council
- Export Promotion Council for EOUs and SEZ units
- Carpet Export Promotion Council
- Cotton Textile Export Promotion Council
- Export Promotion Council for Handicrafts
- Handloom Export Promotion Council
- The Indian Silk Export Promotion Council
- Synthetic and Rayon Textile Export Promotion Council
- Wool and Woollens Export Promotion Council
- Powerloom Development and Export Promotion Council

Exhibit 15.4 Services provided by Synthetic and Rayon Textile Export Promotion Council

Service to overseas buyers

Helps the overseas buyers to source their requirements from India and performs a matchmaking function including the following:

- Introduces them to the right Indian manufacturers/exporters.
- Provides them with up-to-date product information.
- Circulates their trade inquiries.
- Organizes buyer–seller meets.
- Assists them in arranging travel and stay in India for their business visits.

Service to Indian exporters

- Introduces them to appropriate overseas buyers.
- Undertakes integrated export promotion programmes through special promotion displays, participation in trade fairs and exhibitions, and organizes buyer–seller meets.

- Conducts market studies and surveys and keeps the exporters updated on market information, trade opportunities, etc.
- Provides market-entry service by sponsoring delegations and sales teams to overseas markets.
- Conducts publicity abroad to build up goodwill for the Indian industry and products.
- Maintains liaison with the authorities to convey to them the requirements of the industry and trade and arranges adaptation of policy framework accordingly and assists the industry and trade in understanding the export policies and procedures.
- Provides information on the trends for product development and adaptation to suit the overseas market requirements.

Source: Synthetic and Rayon Textile Export Promotion Council, Mumbai, accessed on 22 March 2013.

Export Promotion Council to help the readers understand the role of EPCs. Other EPCs also carry out more or less similar activities.

Among the important roles of EPCs is to project India's image abroad as a reliable supplier of high-quality goods and services. In particular, the EPCs encourage and monitor the observance of international standards and specifications by exporters. The EPCs also keep abreast of the trends and opportunities in international markets for goods and services and assist their members in taking advantage of such opportunities in order to expand and diversify exports. Each council is responsible for the promotion of a particular group of products, projects, and services.

Commodity boards

In order to look after the issues related to production, marketing and development of commodities, there are nine statutory commodity boards as follows:

- The Tea Board
- The Coffee Board
- The Coir Board
- The Central Silk Board
- The All-India Handlooms and Handicraft Board

- The Rubber Board
- The Cardamom Board
- The Tobacco Board
- The Spice Board

The functions carried out by commodity boards are similar to those of export promotion councils. These boards broadly carry out the following functions:

- Providing an integrated approach for production development and marketing of the commodity under their purview
- Acting as a linkage between Indian exporters and importers abroad
- Formulating and implementing quality improvement systems, research and development programmes, education and training of farmers, producers, packers, and exporters on post-harvest management practices
- Acting as an interface between international agencies, such as the International Trade Centre (ITC), Geneva, Food and Agriculture Organization (FAO), and United Nations Industrial Development Organization (UNIDO), etc.

- Collecting and disseminating information on production, processing, and marketing of the products under their purview.
- Organizing export promotion activities, such as participation in international trade fairs, buyer–seller meets, inviting foreign delegations, and taking Indian delegations abroad.

Autonomous bodies

To promote international trade, certain organizations were established by the Government of India under the Ministry of Commerce and Industry, as discussed next.

Agricultural and Processed Food Products Export Development Authority   Set up under an Act of Parliament in 1986, the Agricultural and Processed Food Products Export Development Authority (APEDA) looks after the promotion of exports of agriculture and processed food products. It works as a link between Indian exporters and global markets. The products that fall under the purview of the APEDA, known as 'scheduled products', include fruits, vegetables and their products, meat and meat products, poultry and poultry products, dairy products, confectionary, biscuits and bakery products, honey, jaggery and sugar products, cocoa and its products, chocolates of all kinds, alcoholic and non-alcoholic beverages, cereal products, cashew nuts, groundnuts and *papads*, guar gum, floricultural products, and herbal and medical plants. The basic functions of APEDA are as follows:

- Development of database on products, markets, and services
- Publicity and information dissemination
- Inviting official and business delegations from abroad
- Organizing promotional campaigns abroad and visits of official and trade delegations abroad
- Participation in international trade fairs in India and abroad
- Organization of buyer–seller meets and other business interactions
- Distribution of annual APEDA awards
- Providing recommendatory, advisory, and other support services to the trade and industry sector
- Resolving issues and problems of its members related to government agencies and organizations, RBI, customs, import/export procedures, problems with importers through Indian missions abroad

Like export promotion councils, the APEDA registers its exporters and gives them RCMCs as a part of statutory requirement. The concept of agro-export zone (AEZ) to provide a focused approach to agro-exports has been widely appreciated amongst producers and exporters who also call for active involvement of the state government. Recently, the APEDA developed a system for grant of certification mark, that is, 'Quality Produce of India' on the basis of compliance with hygiene standards, implementation of quality assurance system, such as ISO 9000, food safety systems, such as the Hazard Analysis Critical Control Programme (HACCP), backward linkage, residue testing of pesticides and contaminants, and laboratory facilities. Under the National Programme for Organic Agriculture, the APEDA is also an accredited inspection and certification agency for organically produced foods. APEDA's agriXchange serves as a useful platform for buying and selling of agricultural and processed food products internationally (Fig. 15.3). It also provides financial support for export development under a number of schemes for infrastructure development, market development, quality development, R&D, and scheme for transport assistance.

Marine Products Export Development Authority   The Marine Products Export Development Authority (MPEDA), established in 1972, is an autonomous body under the Ministry of Commerce aimed at increasing export-oriented production, specifying standards, processing, and export

Fig. 15.3 APEDA's agriXchange—a useful platform for buying and selling agricultural and processed food products internationally

Source: APEDA website.

marketing of all kinds of fisheries and its products. It offers a comprehensive range of services to exporters so as to develop exports of marine products from India including market promotion. The basic functions of MPEDA are as follows:

- Conservation and management of fishery resources and development of offshore fishing
- Registration of exporters and processing plants
- Regulation of export of marine products
- Laying down standards and specifications
- Helping the industry in relation to market intelligence, export promotion, and import of essential items
- Imparting training in different aspects of the marine products industry, such as quality control, processing, and marketing
- Promotion of commercial shrimp farming
- Promotion of joint ventures in aquaculture, production, processing, and marketing of value added seafood

Some of the major activities undertaken by the MPEDA include promotion of export-oriented aquaculture, production of scampi, crabs, lobsters, molluscs, and finned fishes, establishment of the Integrated Development Programme for Sea Food Quality and Extension Services, a training programme on implementation of HACCP, and various schemes to promote value addition and diversification of marine products to facilitate higher unit value realization.

Service Institutions

A number of institutions and organizations have been established to meet the requirements of industry and trade. The fields in which these institutions are engaged include development of export management personnel, market research, export credit insurance, export publicity, organization of trade fairs and exhibitions, collection and dissemination of export-related information, inspection and quality control, development in packaging, etc. A brief review of the activities and functions of some of these institutions is as follows.

Indian Institute of Foreign Trade

The Indian Institute of Foreign Trade (IIFT) was set up in 1963 by the Government of India as an autonomous organization to induce professionalism in the country's foreign trade management. The institute has significantly contributed to India's foreign trade policies, rationalizing the framework of procedures and documentation, and developing the country's international trade strategy. The major objectives of the institute are as follows:

- Impart professional education in modern management techniques in the area of international business.
- Enable participants to appreciate the interrelationship between the diverse and complex tasks of international business.
- Develop capacities among business executives for improved understanding of various trade and economic issues.
- Conduct high-quality research that addresses domestic as well as world trade and business issues.

The institute conducts capacity building programmes and research apart from basic foundation programmes in international business (Fig. 15.4). It has achieved high standards of excellence and occupies the unique position today of being India's only premier institution that focuses on international business.

Fig. 15.4 Capacity building and research in international business constitute core activities of IIFT

India Trade Promotion Organization

The India Trade Promotion Organization (ITPO) is a premier trade promotion agency of India, which provides a broad spectrum of services to the trade and industry sector so as to promote India's exports. The major activities carried out by ITPO are as follows:

- Participating in overseas trade fairs and exhibitions
- Managing the extensive trade fair complex, Pragati Maidan, in Delhi
- Establishing linkages between Indian suppliers and overseas buyers
- Organizing buyer–seller meets and other exclusive Indian shows in India and abroad
- Organizing Indian promotions with department stores and mail order houses abroad
- Arranging product displays for visiting overseas buyers
- Organizing seminars/conferences/workshops on trade-related subjects
- Encouraging small- and medium-scale units in their export promotion efforts
- Conducting in-house and need-based research on trade and export promotion
- Trade information services through electronic accessibility at the Business Information Centre

ITPO maintains India's largest trade fair complex at Pragati Maidan, which is spread over 149 acre of prime land in the heart of Delhi having 62,000 sq. m. of covered exhibition space besides 10,000 sq. m. of open display area. ITPO has its regional offices at Bengaluru, Chennai, Kolkata, and Mumbai. Besides, ITPO also has overseas offices at New York, Frankfurt, Tokyo, Moscow, and Sao Paulo to promote India's international trade and investment.

Export Inspection Council

The Export Inspection Council (EIC) is responsible for the enforcement of quality control and compulsory pre-shipment inspection of various commodities meant for exports, notified under the Export (Quality Control and Inspection) Act, 1963. Headquartered in New Delhi, it functions through export inspection agencies (EIAs) located at Chennai, Delhi, Kochi, Kolkata, and Mumbai besides a network of 38 sub-offices and laboratories.

Indian Council of Arbitration

The Indian Council of Arbitration (ICA), set up under the Societies Registration Act, promotes arbitration as a means of setting commercial disputes and popularizes the concept of arbitration among traders, particularly those engaged in international trade. The Council, a non-profit service organization, is a grantee institution of the Department of Commerce. The main objectives of the council are to promote the knowledge and use of arbitration and provide arbitration facilities for amicable and quick settlement of commercial disputes with a view to maintain the smooth flow of trade, particularly export trade on a sustained and enduring basis.

National Centre for Trade Information

The National Centre for Trade Information (NCTI) was set up as a registered company in March 1995 with a view to create an institutional mechanism for collection and dissemination of trade data and improving information services to the business community, especially small and medium enterprises. It is a non-profit joint venture of the India Trade Promotion Organization (ITPO) and National Informatics Centre (NIC).

The major functions carried out by NCTI are as follows:

- Creating databases and disseminating information on trade and commerce at national and international levels for export promotion and import facilitation
- Maintaining constant communication with trade and commercial bodies throughout the world with a view to taking appropriate measures for promoting exports and facilitating imports

- Advising or representing government, local authorities, and trade and commercial bodies on matters related to standardization, access, and dissemination of information on trade and commerce
- Creating and maintaining databases/trade statistics for the nodal ministry and preparing region-/country-/product-specific analytical and value-added reports with a view to providing support for policy formulations and other strategic actions having bearing on the country's exports
- Keeping abreast of emerging information technologies and standardizing formats for collection and dissemination of trade information in user-friendly formats

Under UNCTAD's trade efficiency programme, NCTI is certified as an operational trade point in India. It uploads the trade leads on the World Trade Point Federations (WTPF) as per the United Nations rules for Electronic Data Interchange for Administration, Commerce and Transport (UN/EDIFACT) standard and provides value-added product/industry or country-specific information on international trade on the request of the customer on payment of a fee.

Export Credit Guarantee Corporation

Operating in the international market is far more risky than operating in domestic markets. Due to little predictability on political and economic changes, such as an outbreak of war and civil war, a coup or an insurrection, economic difficulties or balance of payment problems, commercial risks of insolvency, and protracted default of buyers may result into delayed payment, restrictions on transfer of payments and non-payment. The Export Credit Guarantee Corporation (ECGC) provides credit insurance in order to protect exporters from consequences of payment risks, both political and commercial, and to enable them to expand their overseas business without fear of loss. The type of insurance protection provided by ECGC may be grouped as follows:

- A range of credit risk insurance covers to exporters against loss in export of goods and services
- Guarantees to banks and financial institutions to enable exporters to obtain better facilities from them
- Overseas investment insurance to Indian companies investing in joint ventures abroad in the form of equity or loan

In addition to insurance protection to exporters against payment risks, ECGC facilitates the exporters by

- providing guidance in export-related activities;
- making available information on different countries with its own credit ratings;
- providing information on the credit-worthiness of overseas buyers;
- making it easy to obtain export finance from banks/financial institutions; and
- assisting exporters in recovering bad debts.

Export–Import Bank of India

The Export–Import (Exim) Bank of India was set up by an Act of Parliament in September 1981. It aims to provide financial assistance to exporters and importers, and to function as the principal financial institution for coordinating the working of institutions engaged in financing export and import of goods and services with a view to promoting India's international trade. It acts on business principles with due regard to public interest. The major services extended by Exim Bank for promoting exports are as follows:

1. It provides information and support services to Indian companies to help improve their prospects for securing business in multilateral agencies funded projects. These services include the following:
   - Disseminating business opportunities in funded projects
   - Providing detailed information on projects of interest

- Informing on procurement guidelines, policies, and practices of multilateral agencies
- Assisting with registration with multilateral agencies
- Advising Indian companies on preparation of expression of interest, capability profile, etc.
- Intervening in bids

2. In order to promote Indian consultancy, the bank has tie-ups with a number of international organizations, such as International Finance Corporation and Eastern and Southern African Trade and Development Bank.
3. It also serves as a consultant to various developing countries for promoting exports and exports finance.
4. It helps in knowledge-building by way of conducting seminars and workshops, and carrying out research studies on projects, sectors, countries, and macroeconomic issues relevant to international trade and investment. The bank has conducted sector-specific studies for identifying market potential for computer software, electric components, chemicals, floriculture, machine tools, pharmaceuticals, medicinal plants, sports goods, and financial services.
5. It gathers and disseminates information on exporters/importers, industry/market reports, trade regulations and laws, country reports, international quality standards, etc., so as to facilitate exporters.

Indian Institute of Packaging

Considering the existing deficiencies in the standard of packaging for eye appeal and the standards of packaging for safe transit, the Government of India, in collaboration with the industry, set up the Indian Institute of Packaging (IIP) in 1966.

The main objectives of the Institute are as follows:

- Undertake research on raw materials for the packaging industry.
- Keep India in step with international developments in the field of packaging.
- Organize training programmes on packaging technology.
- Stimulate consciousness of the need for good packaging.
- Organize consultancy services for the industry.

Its activities include effecting improvements in packaging standards and rendering testing facilities in respect of packaging.

Federation of Indian Export Organizations

The Federation of Indian Export Organizations (FIEO) is the apex body of various export-promotion organizations and institutions in India. Set up in 1965, the FIEO acts as a primary servicing agency to provide integrated assistance to government-recognized export houses/trading houses. It also acts as the central coordinating agency for promoting exports of consultancy services from India. Representing more than hundreds of thousand exporters from India, FIEO is not a product-specific organization and the member exporter may be from any export sector. Its basic functions are as follows:

- Maintaining linkages with international agencies and export promotion organizations in other countries
- Organizing visits of multi-product delegations to prospective overseas markets and hosting foreign business delegations in India
- Organizing buyer–seller meets in India and abroad
- Providing advisory services to its members as well as foreign buyers in international markets

- Maintaining a comprehensive database on India's export sector
- Acting as a nodal agency for promoting exports of consultancy and other services
- Disbursing market development assistance to export and trading houses
- Keeping track of export-related policy changes and acting as an interface between the government and the exporters so as to resolve the problems of its member exporters
- Interacting closely with the central bank, commercial banks, financial institutions, and the ECGC and take up issues and problems of its member exporters

Indian Government's Trade Representatives Abroad

The institutional arrangements that have been developed and strengthened within the country are supplemented by the Indian trade representatives abroad. The trade representations in the embassies and consulates are continually being strengthened to enable them to effectively support trade efforts being made within the country. India's commercial representatives are expected to monitor the commercial events and developments of their accreditation, identify products with export potential and other trade opportunities, and study tariff and non-tariff barriers, government procedures, and shipping facilities. The representatives should also take initiative in cultivating specific trade contracts, undertake all publicity activities for image-building, organize participation in trade fairs, stores promotion, etc., effectively guide trade visitors and missions, maintain a flow of timely commercial intelligence, and deal with all problems of commercial complaints and bottlenecks. Further, they are expected to provide facilities to the Indian trade delegations and exporters visiting foreign countries, and help procure and forward samples of exportable goods imported from other countries.

Government Participation in Foreign Trade

For supplementing the efforts of the private sector in the field of foreign trade, the Government of India has set up a number of trading corporations, namely the State Trading Corporation (STC), the Minerals and Metals Trading Corporation (MMTC), the Spices Trading Corporation Limited, and the Metal Scrap Trading Corporation (MSTC). The STC itself has a number of subsidiaries, namely the Handicrafts and Handlooms Export Corporation, the Projects and Equipment Corporation, the Tea Trading Corporation of India, and the Cashew Corporation of India. The Mica Trading Corporation is a subsidiary of the MMTC.

These corporations have provided the essential base for developing and strengthening efforts relating to specific commodities and products and diversifying the country's foreign trade. Briefly, their activities are as follows:

- Arranging for exports where bulk handling and long-term contracts are advantageous
- Facilitating exports of 'difficult to sell' items through various devices like linking essential imports with additional exports under counter-trade
- Organizing production to meet export demands and helping production units overcome difficulties of raw materials and other essential requirements to meet export orders and develop lines of export by various methods
- Undertaking import of such commodities where bulk purchase is advantageous

The corporations handle actual transactions. They also maintain offices abroad and function like any commercial unit in the corporate sector.

However, the government is now reducing its direct participation in trade. Therefore, a number of items, which were earlier canalized through government corporations, have been removed from the canalized list. New governmental policies are expected to intensify competition for the government corporations from private sector companies. As a result, the government is moving towards privatization of these corporations.

States' involvement in Promoting Exports

States being the prime centres for export production need to be involved actively in export promotion. The central and state governments therefore have enacted a number of measures to promote exports, which measures are discussed next.

Inter-state Trade Council

The Inter-state Trade Council has been set up in order to ensure a continuous dialogue between the state governments and union territories. It advises both the states as well as the centre on measures for providing a healthy environment for international trade with a view to boost India's exports.

States' Cell in Ministry of Commerce

As an attempt to involve states in export promotion, the Union Government has created a State's Cell under the Ministry of Commerce with the following functions:

- Acting as a nodal agency for interacting with state governments/union territories on matters concerning imports and exports
- Processing all references of general nature emanating from state governments and state export corporations, which do not relate to any specific problem pending in a division in the Ministry
- Monitoring proposals submitted by the state governments to the Ministry of Commerce and coordinate with other divisions in the Ministry
- Acting as a bridge between state level corporations, associations of industries and commerce, and export organizations, such as ITPO, FIEO, and export processing zones (EPZs)
- Disseminating information regarding export and import policy and export prospects to state governments and to other state-level organizations
- Providing guidance to state-level export organizations and assisting in the formation of export plans for each state, in cases where export possibilities remain untapped

Further, the Ministry of Commerce has nominated nodal officers for maintaining liaison with the state governments in export promotion matters.

Institutional infrastructure for export promotion by state governments

The state-level Export Promotion Committee headed by the Chief Secretary is the apex body promoting exports. It scrutinizes and approves projects and overseas implementation of union government's scheme on Assistance to States for Development of Export Infrastructure and Other Allied Activities (ASIDE).

Most of the problems of exporters relating to infrastructure, availability of power, water, supply of raw material from within the state and inter-state movement of raw material, and remission of taxes by the state governments are dealt by separate departments within the state. In order to resolve the problems of exporters emanating from multiplicity of departments within the state, most state governments have nominated a senior officer as the nodal officer or *niryat bandhu* at the level of Commissioner of Industries/Secretary of Industries.

The Department/s of Industries, Trade or Commerce in most states along with other industrial development organizations have shown interest in activities related to promoting exports of the goods produced in the states. There have been wide variations in the steps taken in this direction by various state governments.

Export promotion initiatives by state governments

The state governments undertake a number of policy measures to encourage industrial activity. These policies mainly relate to capital investment subsidy or subsidy for the preparation of feasibility report, project report, etc.; waiver or deferment of sales tax or providing loans for sales tax purposes; exemption from entry tax, octroi duty, etc.; waiver of electricity duty; power subsidy; exemption from taxes for certain captive power generation units; exemptions from stamp duties; provision of land at concessional rate, etc.

On examination of export promotion initiatives by the state governments, it is difficult to find any commonality among various states. However, some of the measures taken by the state governments are as follows:

- They provide information on export opportunities.
- They allot land for starting an export oriented unit (EOU).
- They plan for the development of export promotion industrial parks.
- They exempt entry tax on supplies to EOU/EPZ units.
- They exempt sales tax or turnover tax for supplies to EOU/EPZ units and inter-unit transfers between them.

States' impediments in export promotion

The states' initiatives to promote exports are not without hindrances. State governments are often reluctant to promote export activities due to a number of reasons especially the following:

- Exports never become the number one priority of a state agenda because the revenue generated from exports does not go to the state's coffers.
- The state governments generally do not distinguish between exporting units and domestic units, unlike the centre, since they do not get any direct gains from the foreign exchange earned.
- Additional facilities for export-oriented development mean more cost for the state governments in terms of capital costs incurred on providing infrastructure, research and development facilities, quality control equipment, and commercial information.
- Fiscal concessions and subsidies given to the exporters are considered as loss of revenue by the state governments. There is no provision for compensation by the centre against such losses.
- The planning commission makes state allocations on the basis of the Gadgil–Mukherjee formula, which does not take into account the states' export performance. It acts as a disincentive to the states for putting up resources for export promotion.
- The state governments generally lack the required expertise for export promotion.
- The information about international markets, export policy, and measures taken by the central government is lacking among the state administration and, therefore, awareness among the entrepreneurs and exporters is lacking.
- The municipal and local bodies and the state governments are under increasing pressure to raise resources on their own. Under such circumstances, they are forced to levy taxes on commercial activities. In view of the competing needs, states find it difficult to divert funds for export development activities.
- Multiplicity of taxes within the states for generating revenue diminishes their export competitiveness.
- The state governments have little say either in the formulation of international trade or export–import policy or in the design of the tariff measures.

However, the role of state governments is critical for influencing the factors for creating and sustaining export competitiveness of the states. Hence, proactive involvement of states in promoting exports becomes central to the success of their development strategies.

EXPORT PROMOTION IN INDIA: NEED FOR STRATEGIC REORIENTATION

India's trade strategy, since independence, largely focused on import substitution rather than export promotion. The protectionist measures of inward-oriented economy increased the profitability of domestic industries, especially in the import-substitution sector. Formidable tariff structures and trade policy barriers discouraged the entry of foreign goods into the Indian market. There was little pressure on domestic firms to be internationally competitive. However, with the introduction of economic liberalization in the country, foreign goods are finding their place in the Indian market. All this has put a lot of competitive pressure even on purely domestic companies.

The emergence of WTO has significantly affected the economic environment of international business the world over. The economic policies of nations are subject to stronger rules of international trade under the new regulatory framework after the Uruguay Round of multilateral negotiations. Opening up of national economies is a global phenomenon. As a result, the exporters presently face opportunities and challenges different from what they faced a few decades ago.

The WTO agreements, especially the Agreement on Subsidies and Countervailing Measures and on Agriculture, provide a framework for deciding the nature and scope of export promotion instruments.[3] It also limits our promotional efforts related to subsidies and countervailing measures.

The changing market scenario has increased the significance of export promotion programmes of the government as well as other trade promotion organizations. Today, their basic function is to bring about a smooth transformation of an inward-oriented economy into an outward-oriented economy and take advantage of the emerging market opportunities. Besides, the export promotion measures need to be conceptualized and implemented in such a manner so as to facilitate India's exporting community and make its goods competitive in international markets.

Summary

International marketing professionals are expected to familiarize themselves with the organizations involved in export promotion both at international and national levels. This chapter brings out the institutional framework available for export promotion in different countries as well as at international level. Besides, it also elaborates the institutional set-up for promoting exports in India. The Department of Commerce under the Ministry of Commerce is the main organization in India that formulates and guides the country's foreign trade policies. The Board of Trade facilitates direct interaction among the government, related organizations such as RBI, Exim Bank, ECGC, and ITPO, and the industry, while the Export Promotion Board provides institutional mechanism for coordination among the concerned ministries for promoting exports.

Export promotion councils (EPCs) promote sector-specific exports of a range of products such as engineering, overseas construction, electronics and computer software, plastics and linoleums, basic chemicals, pharmaceuticals, cosmetics, chemicals and allied products, gems and jewellery, leather, sports goods, cashew, shellac, apparel, synthetic and rayon, Indian silk, carpet, handicrafts, wool and woollens, cotton textiles, handloom, and powerloom. For commodities such as tea, coffee, coir, silk, handloom and handicraft, rubber, cardamom, tobacco, and spices, separate commodity boards are engaged in issues related to their production, marketing, and development. The government-owned trading corporations such as State Trading Corporation (STC) and its subsidiaries such as Handicrafts and Handlooms Export Corporation, Projects and Equipment Corporation, Tea Trading Corporation of India, Cashew Corporation of India, Minerals and Metals Trading Corporation (MMTC), Spices Trading Corporation, and Metal Scrap Trading Corporation (MSTC) have a special role to play in foreign trading of restricted items besides government's active participation in international trade. However, their significance has been consistently dwindling with the rapid pace of economic liberalization in the country.

The States' Cell in the Ministry of Commerce and the state government also involve themselves in export promotion activities. Since these export promotion institutions provide a number of useful services to exporters, such as gathering market information

---

[3] Raul, Saez, *Export Promotion as a Key of Development Strategy Executive Forum on National Export Strategies*, International Trade Centre, 1999.

and dissemination, organizing participation in international trade fairs, inviting foreign trade delegations, and organizing buyer–seller meets, and act as an interface between the exporters and the government, it makes commercial and professional sense for international marketing managers to get in touch and interact with them on a continuous basis.

Key Terms

EPC   Export promotion councils, set up by the Government of India, to promote sector-specific exports.

EPO   An organization (government or non-government) engaged in export promotion.

Export promotion   Public policy measures that actually or potentially enhance exporting activity at the company, industry, or national level.

Matchmaking   Bringing together of exporters and importers.

RCMC   Registration-cum-membership certificate is the certificate of registration and membership granted by an EPC or other competent authority as prescribed in the Exim policy in force from time to time.

Concept Review Questions

1. Explain the concept of export promotion in view of various decisions an international marketing manager is required to take before entering and operating in international markets.
2. As an entrepreneur wanting to export processed food products, identify the central export promotion organization you would approach. Briefly explain the promotional support you are likely to get from the organization.
3. What is the role of a two-service institution in international trade? Comment.
4. In view of the Government's emphasis on disinvestment of public sector, comment on the role of public sector trading corporations in promoting India's foreign trade.
5. Critically evaluate the role of states in export promotion and its impediments.

Practice Exercises

1. For a first-time exporter, participating in a trade fair is considered to be the most effective way to get an export order. Identify the organizations and services provided by them to facilitate your participation in an international trade fair.
2. Visit the website of Apparel Export Promotion Council (AEPC) at http://www.aepc.com and/or visit their nearest office. Critically evaluate the usefulness of the services provided from the point of view of apparel exporters.

Project Assignments

1. You have been asked to conduct a market survey for the export of leather garments from India. Proceed as follows:
   (a) Identify the secondary information you require to carry out the survey.
   (b) Shortlist the export promotion organizations you would get in touch with.
   (c) Record the information provided by the concerned EPOs for carrying out the market survey.
   (d) Identify the gaps between information provided by the EPC and information received.
2. Identify the organizations in your state that help exporters in pursuing their goals. Meet some of the officials and discuss the role and functions of the organization. Record your observations and critically evaluate the effectiveness of the facilities extended.
3. Make a visit to an export firm in your area. Enquire about the export promotion organizations the company has been in touch with. Document the facilities provided by these organizations to the exporters. Give your recommendations to the company about the EPOs the company should get in touch with.

16

Framework of International Trade Policy

INTRODUCTION

International marketing decisions of a firm are influenced significantly by various policy measures employed to regulate exports and imports by countries. Exportability and importability of a firm's goods are often determined by trade policies of the countries involved. Price competitiveness of traded goods is affected by import and export tariffs. The host country's trade and foreign direct investment (FDI) policies often influence entry decisions in international markets. High import tariffs and other import restrictions distort free market forces, guarding the domestic industry against foreign competition, and support indigenous manufacturing. Policy incentives help exporters increase their profitability through foreign sales.

The major decision areas in international marketing that are influenced by a country's trade policy are as follows.

Product selection   Trade policy provisions related to export prohibition and restriction in the exporting country's trade policy need to be examined for determining the exportability of a product.

Market selection   Import prohibitions and restrictions in the target markets need to be examined for determining the importability of the product.

Product customization for target market   It is specifically done to meet the trade policy provisions of both the exporting and the importing countries.

International market entry decisions   They decide whether to export or establish overseas manufacturing operations with regard to product importability or any other requirement, such as local content/value addition including policy provisions, and their effects on product and marketing costs.

International pricing decisions   They pertain to the effects of various incentives and concessions on import duty and other indirect taxes for inputs used in export production. Cost of export

production needs to be evaluated carefully to establish price competitiveness in the international markets and to take appropriate pricing decisions.

International market promotion decisions   Promotional campaigns in international markets are affected by the regulatory framework of the target markets, which should, therefore, be studied carefully. An exporter may choose from a variety of market promotion schemes of the exporting country, such as market development assistance (MDA), market access initiative (MAI), and Indian Brand Equity Fund (IBEF) in India, and integrate it into the firm's promotional plans for international markets.

International marketing strategy decisions   A thorough understanding of the trade policy provisions is essential for determining the overall international marketing strategy.

In view of the aforementioned points, a thorough understanding of a country's trade policy and incentives are crucial to the development of an effective strategy for international markets. India's foreign trade policy (FTP) is formulated under the Foreign Trade (Development and Regulation) Act, 1992 for a period of five years by the Ministry of Commerce, Government of India. The Government is empowered to prohibit or restrict, subject to conditions, export of certain goods for reasons of national security, public order, morality, prevention of smuggling, and safeguarding balance of payments.

This chapter elucidates the concept of international trade policy and provides a broad framework of India's FTP and major provisions, schemes, and incentives for trade promotion. Policy measures to promote international trade, such as schemes and incentives for duty-free and concessional imports, augmenting export production, and other export promotion measures are discussed in depth. Policy initiatives and incentives by the state government are also examined. This chapter also evaluates compatibility of India's trade policy measures with the multilateral trade regime under the WTO.

CONCEPT OF INTERNATIONAL TRADE POLICY

Trade policy refers to the complete framework of laws, regulations, international agreements, and negotiating stances adopted by a government to achieve legally binding market access for domestic firms. It also seeks to develop rules providing predictability and security for firms. Policy instruments affecting exports may also operate on both supply and demand sides. Initiatives for creating and expanding export production, developing transportation networks, port facilities, tax, and investment systems form parts of supply side policies. The demand side initiatives for export promotion include programmes to alert companies about the opportunities present in the international markets and to strengthen the commitment and skills of those involved. To be effective, the trade policy needs to be supported by domestic policies to foster innovation and international competitiveness. Besides, the trade policy should have flexibility and pragmatism.

Trade in developing countries is characterized by heavy dependence on developed countries, dominance of primary products, over-dependence on a few markets and a few products, and worsening of terms of trade and global protectionism, all of which make formulation and implementations of trade policy critical to their economic development. The strategic options for trade policy may either be inward- or outward-looking. As a result of liberalization and integration of national policies with WTO agreements, there has been a strategic shift in trade policies. Like other developing countries, India's trade policies also witnessed a gradual shift from highly restrictive policies with emphasis on import substitution to more liberal policies geared towards export promotion.

India followed a strong inward-oriented trade policy that primarily focused on conserving foreign exchange from the time it became independent to 1991. The entire focus of India's trade strategy was on import substitution rather than export promotion. Earning foreign exchange through exports and conservation thereof had always been the high priority task for various governments, irrespective of their political ideologies. In order to facilitate industrialization and thereby encourage import substitution, the government introduced a number of measures, such as outright ban on import of some commodities, quantitative restrictions, prohibitive tariff structure, which was one of the highest in the world, administrative restrictions like import licensing, foreign exchange regulations, local content requirements, and export obligations.

The protectionist measures of inward-oriented economy increased the profitability of domestic industries, especially in the import-substitution sector. The investments made to serve the domestic market were less risky due to proven demand potential by the existing level of imports. Formidable tariff structure and trade policy barriers discouraged entry of foreign goods into the Indian market. There had hardly been any pressure on domestic firms to be internationally competitive.

The policy makers of India had long believed that these policy measures would make the country a leading exporter with a comfortable balance of trade. In reality, however, these initiatives did not yield the desired results and rather gave rise to corruption, complex procedures, production inefficiency, poor product quality, and delay in shipment. All this led to a steep decline in India's share in world exports.

With the emergence and growth of economic liberalization during the last two decades, competitive pressure increased progressively even on purely domestic companies due to the presence of foreign goods in the Indian market. Consequently, export promotion got a major push in India's trade policies, in order to make exports the engine of growth, only in the last two decades. With the formulation of national trade policies and export promotion incentives in accordance with the WTO policies, promotional measures to encourage international marketing efforts rather than import substitution increasingly gained more importance.

Trade policies now aim at creating a friendly environment by eliminating redundant procedures, increasing transparency by simplifying the processes involved in the export sector, and moving away from quantitative restrictions. All this has improved the competitiveness of the Indian industries and has reduced the anti-export bias. Steps were also taken to promote exports through multilateral and bilateral initiatives. With the decline in restrictions on trade and competition, the constraints related to infrastructure and trade regulation became increasingly evident.

INDIA'S FOREIGN TRADE POLICY: AN OVERVIEW

In India, FTP is formulated and implemented mainly by the Ministry of Commerce and Industry, but also in consultation with other concerned ministries, such as finance, agriculture, textiles, and the central bank, that is, the Reserve Bank of India (RBI). The Directorate General of Foreign Trade (DGFT), under the Department of Commerce, is responsible for the execution of the FTP. The Directorate General of Anti-Dumping and Allied Duties, constituted in April 1998, carries out investigations and recommends levels of anti-dumping duty. The responsibilities of the Ministry of Finance include setting import duties and other border and internal taxes, surveying the working of customs, assisting and advising on implementation of the WTO Customs Valuation Agreement, and undertaking investigations to impose safeguard measures. The Ministry of Agriculture designs the National Agriculture Policy, which is aimed at ensuring an adequate supply of essential food at 'reasonable' prices, securing a reasonable standard of living for farmers and agricultural workers, developing agriculture and rural infrastructure, and helping the sector face the challenges arising out of globalization in a WTO-compatible manner. The Ministry of Agriculture and the Ministry of Commerce formulate India's proposals for WTO negotiations on agriculture. The Ministry of Textiles is in charge of promoting exports of textiles, and of managing quotas maintained by importing countries. The RBI manages the exchange rate policy and also regulates interest rates, for instance, for pre- and post-shipment export credit.

The Export–Import (Exim) Policy was earlier formulated under the Import and Export (Control) Act, 1947, which came into existence on 25 March 1947. Initially, the Act was for three years' duration, but was extended till 31 March 1977 for varying periods. Thereafter, it was extended for an indefinite period. In 1992, the Import and Export (Control) Act, 1947 was replaced by the Foreign Trade (Development and Regulation) Act, 1992, whereby the Chief Controller of Exports and Imports was designated as the DGFT.

Till 1985, the Exim Policy for each financial year used to be announced by means of public notice in the Gazette of India. In order to ensure continuity in operations and provide stability to the external sector, the Exim Policy was first announced for three years' duration during 1985–88. The objective of formulating long-term policy was to reduce unpredictability in the external trade regime with minimum changes of exceptional nature during the validity of the policy. However, the frequency of unabated changes has necessitated issuance of revised annual policies. The five-year Exim Policy (2002–07), launched co-terminus with the 10th Five Year Plan up to 31 March 2007, was terminated mid-length, and replaced with the FTP with effect from 1 April 2009 for a period of five years, to remain in force up to 31 March 2014.

The FTP outlines a country's export promotion measures, policies, and procedures related to foreign trade. India's FTP is built around the following two objectives:

* To make India a major player in world trade by 2020
* To arrest and reverse the declining trend of exports by providing additional support, especially to those sectors which have been hit badly by recession in the developed world

In order to achieve these objectives, the FTP is based on following seven broad principles:

(i) Give a focused thrust to employment intensive industry.
(ii) Encourage domestic manufacturing for inputs to export industry and reduce the dependence on imports.
(iii) Promote technological upgradation of exports to retain a competitive edge in global markets.
(iv) Persist with a strong market diversification strategy to hedge the risks against global uncertainty.
(v) Encourage exports from the North-Eastern region, given its special place in India's economy.
(vi) Provide incentives for manufacturing of green goods while recognizing the imperative of building capacities for environmental sustainability.
(vii) Endeavour to reduce transaction costs through procedural simplification and reduction of human interface.

India's FTP is published in four volumes, as follows.

Foreign Trade Policy Contains provisions and schemes related to exports and imports.

Handbook of Procedures: Volume I Contains export–import procedures to be followed by all concerned, such as an exporter or an importer, authorizing or any competent authority.

Handbook of Procedures: Volume II Contains Standard Input–Output Norms (SION) used for working out the proportion of various inputs used/required in manufacture of resultant products, so as to determine the advance authorization entitlement.

ITC (HS) Classification of Export and Import Items Serves as a comprehensive reference manual for finding out exportability or importability of products with reference to the FTP.

Export Prohibitions and Restrictions

Under the FTP, export prohibitions are maintained for environmental, food security, marketing, pricing and domestic supply reasons, and to comply with international treaties. Restrictions on exports on account of security concern through multilateral agreements are contained in the SCOMET (Special Chemicals, Organisms, Materials, and Equipment and Technologies) list. Export restrictions are GATT-compatible and permitted under Article XIX and XX (Security Exceptions). Since the SCOMET list is a negative one, licensing procedure is based on the presumption of denial. The SCOMET list is an aggregated outcome of the country's commitments to international efforts towards non-proliferation and the combined elements of multilateral arrangements, such as the Chemical Weapons Conventions (CWC) and the Biological and Toxins Weapons Convention (BTWC), and unilateral controls that a country exercises on dual use of goods and technologies, including nuclear materials and technologies.

Exports from India are free, except in cases where these are regulated by the provisions of FTP or any other law in force. Under the current FTP, export of wild animals, exotic birds, tallow, wood products, beef and offal of cows, oxen, and calves, undersized rock lobsters and sand lobsters, sandalwood products, certain species of sea shells, peacock tail feathers, including the handicrafts and other articles using them, manufactured articles and shavings from shed antlers of deer, human skeletons, certain endangered species of wild orchid and plants are prohibited. In addition to these export prohibitions, India also issues ad hoc prohibitions on export of sensitive products, for example, export prohibitions have been issued for non-basmati rice, wheat, pulses, edible oils, and sugar. Export prohibitions and export quotas are notified on an annual basis, and are usually in place for a specific period, during which they may be subject to change.

To ensure the domestic supply of certain products, export licensing is used as a policy tool. Export of restricted items is permitted only after obtaining authorization from DGFT. The export licensing requirements have been reduced considerably over the years, and the remaining restrictions on exports are essentially maintained for food safety and security reasons. The list of items restricted for exports include cattle, horses, camel, seaweed, and chemical fertilizers.

Quotas for wheat and wheat products, grain and flour of barley, maize, *bajra*, *ragi*, and *jowar*, butter, non-basmati rice and lentils, gram, and beans and flour made from them were removed in March 2002. Onions may be exported through designated state-trading enterprises, without quantitative ceiling, subject to conditions of quality laid out by the National Agricultural Co-operative Marketing Federation of India Ltd (NAFED) from time to time. In addition, quantitative ceilings are notified by the DGFT for sandalwood oil and sandalwood chips, recommended by the Ministry of Environment and Forests to conserve natural resources. All the quotas are allocated by the DGFT.

Trade with the Democratic People's Republic of Korea is prohibited. Additionally, the export and import of arms and related material to and from Iraq and the import of charcoal from Somalia are prohibited. Trade of all sorts of goods and technology related to nuclear facilities and its development to Iran is also prohibited. However, the earlier restrictions on exports to Libya, Fiji, and Iraq have now been lifted.

Export taxes

Presently, there is no tax on exports from India with the exception of tanned and untanned hide, skins and leathers, except for manufacturers of leathers, ranging from 10 to 20 per cent of freight on board (FOB) value. Quotas for wheat and wheat products, grain and flour of barley, maize, *bajra, ragi,* and *jowar,* butter, non-basmati rice and lentils, gram, and beans and flour made from them were removed in March 2002. However, in order to curb rapid price rise in the domestic markets and to discourage exports, an export duty of 15 per cent on semi-finished steel products, 5 per cent on galvanized sheets, and ₹8,000 per ton on basmati rice was imposed[1] in April 2008. An export duty of 5 per cent on export of iron ore fines[2] was introduced in the financial year 2010, which was raised to 20 per cent in 2011 and 30 per cent in 2012. To discourage export of bauxite, which is an important raw material for aluminium industry, India imposed 10 per cent export duty on bauxite[3] in April 2013. An export cess applied to various products including coffee, spices, tobacco, and other agricultural commodities has been repealed by the Cess Laws (Repealing and Amending) Act, 2005, enacted in 2006.

Import Prohibitions and Restrictions

The Indian Government is authorized to maintain import prohibitions and restrictions under Section 11 of the Customs Act, 1962, which allows the central government to prohibit imports and exports of certain goods either absolutely or subject to conditions by notifications in the Official Gazette.[4] The DGFT may adopt and enforce any restrictive measure in the trade policy[5] through a notification necessary for the following:

- Protection of public morals
- Protection of human, animal, or plant life, or health
- Protection of patents, trademarks, and copyrights, and the prevention of deceptive practices
- Prevention of use of prison labour
- Protection of national treasures of artistic, historic, or archaeological value
- Conservation of exhaustible natural resources
- Protection of trade of fissionable material or material from which they are derived
- Prevention of traffic in arms, ammunition, and implements of war

Trade policies subsequent to 31 March 2001, provide free importability status of goods, unless prohibited or restricted which can be freely imported by any person. This has been a reversal of the previous policies' open general licence (OGL) status of the freely imported items, which also needed permission from the licensing authorities who had discretion to modify, circumscribe, or deny permission on the grounds of regulating imports.

Import prohibitions may be made for a number of reasons, such as national security, public order, morality, prevention of smuggling, conservation of foreign exchange, and safeguarding balance of payment. Presently, only a few items are prohibited for imports[6] as follows:

- Tallow, fat and/or oils, rendered or unrendered of any animal origin
- Animal rennet

---

[1] 'Government Imposes Export Duty on Basmati Rise', *Business Standard*; and 'India to Impose Export Duty on Steel, Rice', *Financial Express*, 29 April 2008, New Delhi.

[2] 'India's Iron Ore Exports may Decline 72% This Year', *Business Standard*, 4 February 2013.

[3] 'Budget 2013: FM Proposes 10% Export Duty on Bauxite', *The Economic Times*, 28 February 2013.

[4] Under Section 11 (2), Customs Act, 1962.

[5] *Foreign Trade Policy*, 2009–14, Ministry of Commerce, Government of India, updated on 18 April 2013.

[6] Compiled from *Foreign Trade Policy*, 2009–14, Ministry of Commerce, Government of India, and related circulars.

- Wild animals, including their parts and products, and ivory
- Beef and products containing beef in any form
- Natural sponges
- Fish waste
- Domestic and wild birds, live pig; meat and meat products from avian species and pig; products from animal and bird origin intended for animal feed, agriculture, and industrial use
- Specified avian animal products from countries reporting the outbreak of highly pathogenic influenza
- Mobile handsets without international mobile equipment identity (IMEI) number or with all zeros; IMEI and code division multiple access (CDMA) mobile phones without electric serial number (ESN)/ mobile equipment identifier (MEID)

In view of integration of India's trade policy with the WTO, India was under obligation to remove import restrictions. However, India maintained import licensing measures under GATT article 18 b for balance of payment reasons. As a result of consultation under WTO, India agreed and implemented the phasing out of remaining restrictions by 1 April 2001.

Presently, the import restrictions are maintained only on a limited number of products for reasons of health, security, and public morals. These include a range of products from meat and offal of most wild animals, animal fats, and ivory powder. India banned import of certain avian livestock and livestock products for sanitary reasons and also prohibited import of milk and milk products from China[7] in 2008. Import of rough diamonds from Cote d'Ivoire and Bolivarian Republic of Venezuela was also banned under the Kimberly process. For the purpose of internal security, import of certain mobile handsets and mobile phones has been prohibited.

Import prohibitions include firearms and ammunition, certain medicines and drugs, poppy seeds, some products for preservation of wild life and environment. Besides, India's sanitary and phytosanitary laws require authorization for import of seeds for sowing and for agriculture and processed food products. The policy also restricts import of second-hand motor vehicles more than three years; old due to environmental reasons. The restricted items can only be imported subject to certain conditions stipulated in the FTP.

Policy Measures for Export Promotion

A large number of measures taken to promote export under the FTP include various schemes for duty-free and concessional imports for export production, schemes and incentives to augment export production, and other export promotion measures to facilitate marketing.

Schemes for duty-free and concessional imports

In order to reduce or remove the anti-export bias inherent in the system of indirect taxation, and to encourage exports, several schemes have been established allowing importers to benefit from tariff exemptions, especially on inputs. Such schemes include drawbacks for customs duty paid and exemptions from payment of import duty. To facilitate readers' understanding, schemes for duty-free and concessional imports are summarized in Table 16.1.

Export promotion capital goods scheme   In order to strengthen the export production base, the export promotion capital goods (EPCG) scheme was introduced in 1990 so as to enable import of capital goods at concessional rate of duty subject to an appropriate export obligation accepted by the exporter. The scheme aimed to reduce the incidence of high capital cost on

---

[7] DGFT Notification No. 46 dated 24 September 2008; 'India Extends Ban on Import of Chinese Milk, Milk Products', *The Economic Times*, 2 July 2012.

Table 16.1   Schemes for duty-free and concessional imports

Scheme	Eligibility	Concessions	Performance requirements
Export promotion capital goods (EPCG)	Manufacturer exporters with or without supporting manufacturers/ vendors; merchant exporters tied to supporting manufacturers and service providers.	0% duty on imports of capital goods spares, tools and consumables for existing plant and machinery imported/to be imported under the scheme.	Export obligation of six times the duty saved on capital goods imported to be completed in six years.
Duty exemption schemes			
Advance authorization *(previously advance licence)*	Manufacturer exporter or merchant exporter tied up with the manufacturer subject to actual user condition even after fulfillment of export obligation.	Zero duty on imports of inputs for export production. Duty-free import of spare parts required for the manufacture of the finished product may also be permitted up to 10% of of the c.i.f. value of authorization. Inputs may also be procured from 100% export-oriented units (EOUs), electronic hardware technology parks, software technology parks, biotechnology parks, and special economic zones (SEZs).	To qualify, exports must have a minimum value added of 15%, except for specified products, export obligation of positive value addition (except for certain products such as gems and jewellery and tea) and export of goods within 18 months from the date of issuance of the authorization.
Duty-free import authorization	Manufacturer exporter or merchant exporter tied up with the manufacturer subject to actual user condition until export obligation is fulfilled.	Zero duty on imports of inputs including fuel, energy, etc. that are consumed or utilized in the course of exports production.	Export obligation with minimum value addition of 20% (except for certain items such as gems and jewellery and tea) and export of goods within 12 months from the date of issuance of the authorization.
Duty remission scheme			
Duty entitlement passbook scheme (DEPB): Scheme phased out in June 2011	Merchant exporter or manufacturer exporter entitled to duty-free import (basic customs duty component only) of inputs used in the manufacture of goods. This is a post-export scheme and the certificate is freely transferable.	Neutralization of the incidence of basic customs duty on the import content of the export product by way of grant of duty credit against the export product.	Duty reimbursed as a percentage of exports as notified separately for different products in the DEPB schedule.
Deemed exports	Goods manufactured in India and supplied: against Advance Authorization/DFIA to EOUs, STPs, EHTPs, or BTPs; EPCG licence holders; projects financed by multilateral or bilateral agencies; projects notified by the Ministry of Finance; power projects and refineries; projects funded by UN agencies; nuclear power projects through competitive bidding; and the supply of marinefreight container by 100% EOUs provided they are exported within six months or a period permitted by customs.	*Pre-export duty neutralization schemes*—duty free import of inputs under advance authorization scheme. In addition, exemptions from excise duty by way of central excise exemption notification. *Post export duty neutralization schemes*—customs/excise duty neutralization by way of refund under deemed export drawback scheme, terminal excise duty refund scheme, etc.	Export obligation in terms of quantity and specified value added required. For post-export neutraization scheme, the duty component refunded is as per the actual exports and/or the notified rate schedule.

Source: *Foreign Trade Policy*, 2009–14, Ministry of Commerce, Government of India, updated on 18 April 2013.

export prices so as to make exports competitive in the international markets by way of reduced import duty on capital goods.

Initially, import of new capital goods up to a maximum cost, insurance, and freight (CIF) value of ₹10 crore were permitted at concessional rate of customs duty of 25 per cent. The general rate of customs duty was very high when the scheme was introduced. As the customs duties on capital goods were reduced, the import duty under EPCG scheme also reduced gradually. In 1992, import duty on capital goods was lowered to 15 per cent with export obligation of four times to be fulfilled in five years, which was further lowered to 10 per cent in 1997, 5 per cent in 2000, and 3 per cent in 2008. Foreign Trade Policy, 2009–2014, had EPCG scheme at 3 per cent duty for all sectors and zero per cent duty for a few sectors, which was rationalized in April 2013.

Manufacturing exporters with or without supporting manufacturers or vendors, merchant exporters tied to supporting manufacturers, and service providers are eligible for import of capital goods including spares, jigs, fixtures, dies, and moulds under the scheme. Besides, components of such capital goods for assembly or manufacture of capital goods and spares of existing plant and machinery can also be imported under the scheme. Import of capital goods is subject to the actual user condition till the export obligation is fulfilled. The manufacturing obligations under the scheme are in addition to any other export obligation undertaken by the importer except the export obligation for the same product under advance authorization, DFRC, DEPB, or drawback scheme.

Zero duty export promotion capital goods scheme Initially, FTP 2009–2014 had two variants under the EPCG scheme: zero duty EPCG scheme for a few sectors and 3 per cent duty EPCG scheme for all sectors. In April 2013, both these schemes were harmonized to one scheme: zero duty EPCG scheme, which covers all sectors. The salient features of the scheme are given as follows:

- Authorization holders will have export obligation of six times the duty saved amount to be completed in a period of six years.
- The period for import under the zero duty EPCG scheme would be 18 months.
- Export obligation discharge by export of alternate products as well as accounting of exports of group companies is not allowed.
- The exporters who have availed benefits under the technology upgradation fund scheme (TUFS) administered by the Ministry of Textiles, can also avail the benefit of zero duty EPCG scheme.
- The import of motor cars, super utility vehicles (SUVs), all purpose vehicles for hotels, travel agents, or tour transport operators, and companies owning/operating golf resorts is not allowed under the scheme.

Benefits
- For firms with export markets, the scheme provides an opportunity to import capital goods at zero import duty and substantial reduction in initial costs. Alternatively, a firm can opt for an export-oriented unit (EOU) and import capital goods duty free.
- The EPCG scheme is considered superior to EOUs, as there are no liabilities for customs duties after fulfilment of export obligation, whereas in case of EOUs, it is only deferment of import duties. However, customs duties are to be paid upon debonding at the depreciated value.
- Unlike EOUs, there are no restrictions on the quantum of domestic sales in case of imports under the EPCG scheme.

Limitations
- In case of failure to fulfil the export obligation, an exporter has to pay the customs duties saved in proportion of unfulfilled portion of export obligations, along with interest as prescribed by the customs authority.

Duty exemption schemes

Duty exemption schemes enable duty-free import of inputs required for export production. Under the duty exemption scheme, an advance authorization is used as follows.

Advance authorization   An advance authorization allows duty-free import of physical inputs incorporated in export products after making normal allowance in wastage. In addition, consumables such as fuel, oil, energy, and catalysts are also allowed under the scheme. Advance authorization can be issued for the following.

Physical exports (including exports to SEZs)   Advance authorization issued to manufacturer exporters or merchant exporters tied to supporting manufacturer(s) for import of inputs required for export production.

Intermediate supplies   Advance authorization issued for intermediate supplies to a manufacturer exporter for the import of inputs required for the manufacture of goods for supply to the ultimate exporter/deemed exporter holding another advance authorization.

Deemed exports   Advance authorization is also issued for deemed exports. The main contractor for import of inputs required in the manufacture of goods for supply to the specified categories.

Advance authorization is issued for duty-free import of inputs, subject to actual user conditions. Other than advanced authorization for deemed exports, they are exempted from payment of basic customs duty, additional customs duty, anti-dumping duty, and safeguard duty, if any. Advance authorization for deemed exports are exempted only from basic customs duty and additional customs duty. However, in case of supplies to EOUs/SEZs/EHTHs/STPs under advance authorizations, anti- dumping duty and safeguard duty are also exempted.

Input output and value addition norms   Input output norms are description of inputs required for production of particular products. The compiled SION are published in Volume II of the *Handbook of Procedures*. These norms are used for determining the proportion of various inputs, which are physically used and consumed for export production, and the packaging material.

The value addition is calculated as follows:

$$VA = \frac{A - B}{B} \times 100$$

where,

VA is value addition

A   is the FOB (free on board) value of the exports realized/FOR (free on rail) value of supply received.

B   is the CIF value of the imported inputs covered by authorization, plus any other inputs used on which the benefit of duty drawback is being claimed.

In SION, a duty-free authorization is required to maintain minimum value addition of 15 per cent except for certain specified products. The scheme also covers exports to SEZ units, supplies to developers and co-developers irrespective of currency of realization.

However, minimum value addition condition is not applicable on authorizations issued under the advance authorization scheme as in such cases the condition imposed is of positive value addition, which means *any* positive value addition. Thus, even 1 per cent value addition is sufficient. Exports for which payments are not received in freely convertible currency are subject to value addition of 15 per cent or the percentage of value addition indicated in SION, whichever is higher. In case of advance authorization for deemed exports, value addition to be maintained should be positive, and not 15 per cent which is applicable only for exports to rupee payment area (RPA), and is in no way linked to deemed exports.

The period for fulfilment of export obligations under advance authorization commences from the date of issue of the authorization. The export obligation is to be fulfilled within a period of 18 months. The validity of advance authorization/duty-free import authorization (DFIA) is reduced from the earlier period of 24 months to 12 months, with effect from April 2013.

Benefits and limitations of advance authorization Since advance authorization provides duty-free import of inputs and consumables for export production in advance, it is useful when large quantities of standard raw material are required for production.

As the import under advance authorization is allowed on actual-user condition, the authorization or material imported against it is not transferable even after discharge of export obligation. Merchant exporters are not eligible for the advance licensing scheme but can avail benefits under DFIA or duty drawback.

Duty free import authorization scheme The scheme, launched on 1 May 2006, replaced the duty free replenishment certificate (DFRC) scheme. Under the scheme, duty free import of inputs, including fuel, oil, energy sources, and catalysts is allowed for production of export products subject to manufacturer exporters, or merchant exporters tied up with the manufacturer for the import of inputs used in export production. It offers exemptions in respect of custom duty, additional duty, education cess, and anti-dumping or safeguard duties in force for inputs used in exports. The imported items or the authorization are subject to actual user conditions until the export obligation is fulfilled. The main difference between the DFIA and the advance authorization scheme is that the letter requires positive value added in exports, whereas the former requires minimum value added of 20 per cent.

Duty remission schemes

Duty remission schemes enable post-export replenishment of duty on inputs used for export production under various schemes, such as duty drawback, duty entitlement passbook scheme (discontinued in 2011), promotional measures for deemed exports, and schemes for concessional imports for the gems and jewellery sector.

Duty drawback Duty drawback is defined as the rebate of duty chargeable on any imported or excisable material used in the manufacture of goods exported from India. Duty drawback is admissible under the Customs Act, 1962, for re-export of goods on which import duty has been paid (Section 7), and for imported material used in the manufacture of exports (Section 75). The drawback consists of two components:

- The 'customs allocation', which includes the basic customs duty rate and the special additional duty
- The 'central excise allocation', which includes the additional duty and the excise duty on locally produced inputs

Drawback rates are drawn up annually and released soon after the annual budget is introduced in the parliament. The rates are based on parameters, including the prevailing prices of inputs, standard input–output norms published by the DGFT, share of imports in total inputs, and the applied rates of duty. In most cases, the drawback is less than 100 per cent of the import duty paid. Although the rates are based on a mixed classification, they are fully aligned with the HS nomenclature at the HS 4-digit level. The rates are expressed as a percentage of the FOB value of exports.

The drawback rates are fixed, either for any class of products manufactured, known as 'all industry rates', or for a product manufactured by a particular manufacturer, known as 'brand rates'.

All industry rates 'All industry rates' are calculated on the basis of broad averages of consumption of inputs, duties and taxes paid, quantity of wastages, and FOB prices of export products. The rates are either on quantity basis (e.g., per kg or per tonne), or on ad valorem basis, for example, percentage of FOB value. These are published in the form of notification by the Government every year, and are normally valid for one year. These rates are reviewed and revised periodically, taking into account variation in consumption pattern of inputs and duties offered thereon. It is estimated that all industry rates neutralize around 70–80 per cent of the total duty paid on the inputs for export production.

Brand rates/Special brand rates If all industry rates are unavailable, or if it is felt that duty drawback provides inadequate compensation for the import duty paid on inputs, the exporter may request the establishment of 'special brand rates'. The special brand rates are envisaged to neutralize up to 90–95 per cent of the total tax paid on inputs for export production.

While all industry rates are based on the average rates of consumption of inputs and the rates of duty paid, the special brand rate scheme is product- and exporter-specific, requiring the detailed submission of proof of duty payments by the exporter. Drawback is available on the following items:

- Raw materials and components used in the process of manufacture
- Materials and components used in the manufacture of goods
- Irrecoverable wastage that arises in the manufacturing process
- Material used for packing the finished export products
- Finished products

Drawback is also allowed on goods originally imported into India and exported within two years from payment of import duty under Section 74 of Customs Act, 1962. For goods exported without being used, 98 per cent of the import duty is refunded; for goods exported after use, the percentage of duty refunded varies depending on the period between import and export of the product. The rates range from 85 per cent of import duty for goods that remain in the country for up to six months, to 30 per cent for goods that remain in the country for between 30 and 36 months. Drawback under this provision is not allowed for apparel, tea chests, exposed cinematographic films passed by the Central Board of Film Certification in India, unexposed photographic films, paper and plates and X-ray films, and for cars that have been used for over four years. Drawback is admissible, irrespective of the mode of exports.

Duty drawback is an incentive widely used around the world with the objective to provide a level playing field to the country's exporters so as to exclude export production from the incidence of import duty and other indirect taxation. The duty drawback system has worked quite well in India, except for operational constraints faced by the exporters in getting drawback reimbursements.

Duty entitlement passbook scheme Under the DEPB scheme, grant of customs duty credit against the export product was provided on its import content. The scheme was introduced in 1997 wherein actual imports going into the export products were calculated on a case-by-case basis under actual user conditions. Under the DEPB scheme, merchant or manufacturer exporters were entitled to duty-free import (basic customs duty component only) of inputs used in manufacture of goods, as a specified percentage of FOB value of exports made in freely convertible currency. The scheme allowed naturalization of the incidence of basic customs duty on inputs used for export production. The holder of DEPB also had an option to pay additional customs duty, if any, in cash. It was valid for a period of 12 months from the date of its issuance. The transfer of DEPB was subject to import at the specified port in DEPB, or for the port from which exports were made. However, the scheme was discontinued from October 2011. The products that were earlier in the DEPB scheme are now being given appropriate rates of duty drawback, so that taxes suffered by the inputs for export production are offset.

Promotional measures for deemed exports Transactions in which goods supplied do not leave the country and payments for such supplies is received either in Indian rupees or in free foreign exchange are termed as 'deemed exports'. Under the FTP, the following categories of supplies of goods manufactured in India are considered 'deemed exports':

- Supply of goods against advance authorization/DFIA
- Supply of capital goods to holders of authorization under the EPCG scheme
- Supply of goods to EOUs, STPs, EHTPs, or BTPs
- Supply of goods to projects financed by multilateral or bilateral agencies under specified conditions of the Ministry of Finance
- Supply to projects funded by UN agencies
- Supply of goods to nuclear power projects through competitive bidding
- Supply of goods to power projects or refineries under specified conditions
- Supply of goods to any project or purpose where import of such goods at zero import duty is permitted
- Supply of 'stores' on board of foreign going vessel/aircraft subject to conditions specified in SION.

The manufacture and supply of goods qualifying as deemed exports are eligible for a number of benefits, including the following:

- Supply of goods against advance authorization or DFIA
- Deemed export drawback
- Exemption from terminal excise duty where supplies are made against international competitive bidding (ICB). In other cases, refund of terminal excise duty is given.

Schemes for concessional imports for gems and jewellery The gems and jewellery sector, one of the largest export sectors of India, is characterized by import of goods in rough or raw form of diamonds and semi-precious stones and gold and silver for value addition and conversion to finished products. Thus, this sector largely comprises export of services as a result of necessary skills and infrastructure available in India. The summary of sector-specific schemes for concessional imports in Table 16.2 indicates India's concern to nurture and promote exports from the gems and jewellery sector.

Schemes to augment export production

Development of export-related infrastructure and enclaves providing an environment conducive for export production is crucial to sustain export growth. The government has always supported creation and strengthening of enclaves for export production so as to 'immunize' the firms engaged in export production from constraints, such as infrastructural and administrative, from the rest of the economy. Schemes to augment export production are summarized in Table 16.3. These schemes attempt to reduce the burden of import duty and indirect taxation on capital goods and consumables and reduce operational hassles.

Table 16.2   Schemes of concessional imports for promoting gems and jewellery exports

Scheme	Eligibility	Concessions	Performance requirements
Replenishment authorization	Exporters of gems and jewellery; replenishment authorization granted against exports of gold, platinum, and silver jewellery and articles made thereof.	Post-export authorization for duty-free import of inputs precious stones, semi-precious and synthetic stones, and pearls and empty jewellery boxes up to 5% of the overall import value authorized and import of cut and polished preciuos stones other than emerald upto 10% of CIF value of authorization witinin its overall CIF value.	Quantity of duty-free inputs allowed as per the entitlement and value addition notified in the handbook.
Advance authorization schemes for gems and jewellery	Manufacturers of jewellery for export; inputs are based on the actual user conditions.	Duty-free purchase of precious metal inputs from nominated agencies (primarily banks) authorized by the Reserve Bank of India, MMTC Ltd, STC Ltd, Handicraft and Handloom Export Corporation, PEC. Certain categories of exporters are also allowed to import directly.	Export obligation subject to minimum value added ranging from 1.5% to 5% depending on the products and the wastage norms (0.25%–7%) to be exported within 120 days (extendable to 180 days) from the date of issue of authorization.

Source: Foreign Trade Policy, 2009–14, Ministry of Commerce, Government of India, updated on 18 April 2013.

Table 16.3   Schemes to augment export production

Scheme	Eligibility	Concessions	Performance requirements
Export-oriented units (EOUs), electronic hardware technology parks (EHTPs), software technology parks (STPs) and biotechnology parks (BTPs)	EOUs, or units set up in the EHTPs, STPs, or BTPs that undertake to export their entire production of goods and services (except permissible sales in domestic tariff area (DTA)). Trading units are not covered.	Duty-free imports of all types of goods, including new and second-hand capital goods, provided these are not prohibited for import including from the DTA or bonded warehouses.	All products and services to be exported, with some exceptions.
Special economic zones (SEZs)	Units based in the special economic zones.	Duty-free imports of all types of goods. Imports from DTA treated as deemed exports (see below). These units also benefit from tax holidays under the Income Tax Act.	Units based in SEZs have to be net foreign exchange earners, failing which punitive action can be taken. Performance is also evaluated on the basis of additional employment, investment, and infrastructure generation.
Free-trade and warehousing zones		As above	As above
Agricultural export zones (AEZs)	Exporters of products in the agriculture and allied sectors that are based in the AEZs	As for EPCG	

Source: Foreign Trade Policy, 2009–14, Ministry of Commerce, Government of India, updated on 18 April 2013.

Export-oriented units, electronic hardware technology parks, software technology parks, and biotechnology parks   A number of schemes were introduced for units engaged in export production of goods and services such as EOUs, electronic hardware technology parks (EHTPs), software technology parks (STPs), and biotechnology parks (BTPs). The schemes cover units engaged in manufacture of goods primarily for exports, including repair, re-making, recondi- tioning, re-engineering, and rendering of services, but excludes trading units, as discussed next.

Export-oriented units   The scheme was introduced under the recommendations of Prakash Tandon Committee, in early 1981. It is complementary to the export processing zone (EPZ) scheme, as it provides an internally competitive duty-free environment with better infrastruc- ture facilities for export production. As the FTZ/EPZ scheme introduced in the early 1960s had limitations of location, a large number of exporters could not be attracted to set up their units. The EOU scheme adopts the same production regime, but offers a wide option in locations with reference to factors such as source of raw materials, ports of export, hinterland facilities, availability of technological skills, existence of an industrial peace, and the need for a larger area of land for the project.

The exports of EOUs have increased from ₹2010.14 crore in 1992–93 to ₹1,76,923.02 crore in 2008–09, but declined thereafter significantly to ₹7,60,131.13 crore in 2010–11. However, it increased marginally to ₹79,343.28 crore in 2011–12 (Fig. 16.1). EOUs are mainly concentrated in textiles and yarn, food processing, electronics, chemicals, plastics, granites, and mineral ores.

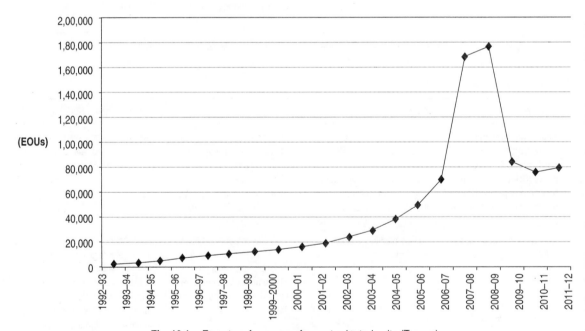

Fig. 16.1   Export performance of export-oriented units (₹ crore)

Source: Annual Report, 2012–2013, Ministry of Commerce, Government of India, pp. 178–179; indiastat.com, accessed in February 2013.

Software technology parks/Electronic hardware technology parks   In order to facilitate export- oriented production of computer software and hardware, units can be set up under the STPs and the EHTPs schemes, respectively. Both these schemes are monitored by the Ministry of Information Technology. A software technology park may be set up by the central government, state government, public or private sector undertaking, or a combination thereof.

Under the STP scheme, a software development unit can be set up for the purpose of software development, data entry and conversion, data processing, data analysis and control data management, or call centre services for exports. The major STPs have been set up at Pune, Bengaluru, Noida, Bhuneshwar, Hyderabad, Thiruvananthapuram, Gandhinagar, Guwahati, Kolkata, Mumbai, Chennai, and Gurgaon

Under the EHTP scheme, a unit can be set up for the purpose of manufacture and development of electronic hardware or electronic hardware and software in an integrated manner. For exports, the policy provisions for STP/EHTP are substantially the same as applicable to units under the EOU scheme. However, in view of the sector-specific requirements, the following provisions have specifically been made:

- STP/EHTP units are allowed domestic tariff area (DTA) sales through data communication/ telecommunication links.
- STP units are allowed telematic infrastructural equipment for creating a central facility for software exports without payment of duty.

Biotechnology parks In order to promote biotechnology exports, the DGFT notifies BTPs on the recommendation of the Department of Biotechnology under the Ministry of Science and Technology. The approval for units in BTP and other necessary approvals are granted by the designated officer from the department.

Benefits The major benefits enjoyed by EOUs/STPs/EHTPs/BTPs are as follows:

- Complementary to the SEZ scheme, providing the choice of locating the unit anywhere in India, unlike in case of the SEZ scheme.
- EOUs are required to be only net positive foreign exchange (NFE) earners[8] and the condition of export performance has been deleted with effect from 1 April 2004. The positive NFE is to be achieved over a period of five years from the date of commencement of business or commercial production. The value of goods imported by EOUs is allowed to be amortized uniformly over 10 years. Earlier, EOUs were allowed to sell in the domestic markets up to 50 per cent of FOB value of exports. Sales beyond this limit were made on payment of full duty. On the other hand, clearance from SEZ to DTA was allowed only at full rate of duty.
- Eligible for concession from payment of income tax for profit earners.
- Foreign direct investment in EOUs is allowed up to 100 per cent for manufacturing activities.
- Exempt from central excise duty in procurement of capital goods, raw materials, consumables, spares, etc.
- No authorizations are required for import or domestic procurement.
- Exemption of customs duty on import of capital goods, raw materials, consumables, spares, etc.
- Entitled for duty-free supply of furnace oil.
- Exempted even from anti-dumping duties.
- Reimbursement of central sales tax (CST) paid on domestic purchases.
- Complete freedom to sub-contract part of the production and production process in the domestic area.
- Supplies can be made to other EOUs/SEZs/EHTPs/STPs/BTPs unit without payment of duty and such supplies are counted towards fulfilment of export performance.

---

[8] Net foreign exchange (NFE) earnings is defined as the FOB value of exports minus the CIF value of all imported inputs, capital goods, and payments made in foreign exchange for royalties, fees, dividends, and interest on external borrowings during the first five-year period.

- Supplies from domestic area to EOUs are allowed deemed export benefits.
- Procurement of duty-free inputs for supply of manufactured goods to advance licence holders is allowed.
- Exempted from industrial licensing for manufacture of items reserved for the small-scale industrial sector.

Limitations
- Duty drawback is not allowed on exports affected by EOUs.
- Duty concession on import of capital goods is deferred only till the period for which the unit is working under the EOU scheme.

With substantial liberalization and rationalization of the EPCG scheme and lesser quantum of export obligation, no liability with respect to duty exemption on capital goods after completion of export obligation, and no restriction on sale in DTA, the attractiveness of the EOU scheme has declined. However, for capital intensive units also targeting domestic markets, the EOU scheme still remains viable and attractive.

Assistance to states for developing export infrastructure and other allied activities In order to involve states in export promotion efforts by providing assistance to state governments for creating infrastructure for development and growth of exports, the assistance to states for developing export infrastructure and other allied activities (ASIDE) scheme was launched in March 2002 as a comprehensive scheme. Under the scheme, assistance is given for setting up new export promotion parks and zones and complementary infrastructure, such as road links to ports, container depots, and power supply. The scheme provides an outlay for development of export infrastructure which is distributed to the states according to pre-defined criteria. The earlier export promotion industrial parks (EPIP), EPZ, and critical infrastructure balance (CIB) schemes have been merged with this new scheme. The scheme for export development fund (EDF) for the North-East and Sikkim (implemented since 2000) has also been merged with this scheme. After this merger, ongoing projects under the earlier schemes are funded by the states from the resources provided under this new scheme. Infrastructure-development activities can also be funded from the scheme, provided such activities have an overwhelming export content and their linkage with exports is fully established. During the 11th Five Year Plan (2007–12) ₹3,048 crore were spent, compared to ₹2,050 crore during the 10th Five Year Plan (2002–07).

Allocation of funds in ASIDE The outlay of the scheme has two components, as described here.

State component 80 per cent of the funds have been earmarked for allocation to the states on the basis of the following approved criteria:

- Creating new EPIPs/zones (including SEZs/agri-export zones (AEZs), and augmenting facilities in the existing ones
- Setting up electronic and other related infrastructure in export enclaves
- Equity participation in infrastructure projects including the setting up of SEZs
- Meeting requirements of capital outlay of EPIPs/EPZs/SEZs
- Developing complementary infrastructure, such as roads connecting the production centres with the ports, setting up inland container depots (ICDs), and container freight stations (CFS)
- Stabilizing power supply through additional transformers and islanding of export production centres
- Developing minor ports and jetties of a particular specification to serve exports
- Assistance for setting up common effluent-treatment facilities
- Projects of national and regional importance
- Activities permitted as per EDF in relation to North-East and Sikkim

Central component   The balance 20 per cent, and amounts equivalent to the un-utilized portion of the funds allocated to the states in the past year(s), if any, is retained at the central level for meeting the requirements of inter-state projects, capital outlays of EPZs, and activities relating to promotion of exports from the North-Eastern region. It can also be used for any other activity considered important by the central government from the regional or the national perspective.

Modus operandi for ASIDE   The state component is allocated to states in two tranches of 50 per cent each. The *inter se* allocation of the first tranche of 50 per cent to the states is made on the basis of export performance. This is calculated on the basis of the share of the state in the total exports. The second tranche of the remaining 50 per cent is allocated *inter se* on the basis of the share of the states in the average of the growth rate of exports over the previous year. The allocations are based on the data of exports of goods alone, and the export of services is not to be taken into account.

A minimum of 10 per cent of the scheme outlay is reserved for expenditure in the North-East and Sikkim. The funding of export development fund (EDF) for these regions is made out of this earmarked outlay and the balance amount is distributed inter se among the states on the basis of the laid-down export performance criteria. Allocation amongst North-Eastern states is also carried out on the basis of this criterion.

The export performance and growth of exports from states is assessed on the basis of the information available from the office of the Director General of Commercial Intelligence and Statistics (DGCI&S). The office of the DGCI&S compiles the state-wise data of exports from the shipping bills submitted by the exporter.

The states are required to set up a State Level Export Promotion Committee (SLEPC) headed by the Chief Secretary of the state, and consisting of the secretaries of concerned departments at the state level, and a representative of the States Cell of the Department of Commerce (DoC), the Joint Director General of Foreign Trade posted in that state/region, and the Development Commissioners of the SEZ/EPZ in the state. SLEPC scrutinizes and approves specific projects and oversees the implementation of the scheme. The funds are disbursed directly to a nodal agency nominated by the state government, where these are maintained under a separate head in the accounts of the nodal agency.

Revised ASIDE guidelines for 12th Five Year Plan (2012–17) include projectized basket approach wherein a general basket of 500–600 critical export infrastructure projects with visible and tangible impact for implementation shall serve as benchmark for the type and size of projects. States have been divided into four categories: large, medium, small, and North-Eastern states. To take up the tangible infrastructural projects, the ASIDE contribution would be a minimum of ₹5 crore for large states, and ₹2.5 crore for medium, small and North-Eastern states, including Sikkim. Moreover, 10 per cent of ASIDE outlay is reserved for incentivizing states for their better performance.

Critical infrastructure balance scheme   The Government of India launched the critical infrastructure balance (CIB) scheme, with an objective of balancing capital investments for relieving bottlenecks in infrastructure for export production and conveyance. Under the scheme, the proposals from state governments were considered for removing bottlenecks related to infrastructure at ports, roads, airports, export centres, etc. In addition, the scheme also covers investments that are in the nature of exigency and emergency and which could not be foreseen as part of initial plan scheme proposals of the Ministry of Commerce. The scheme had conceptually been a good beginning for involving states in removing infrastructural bottlenecks in the states, and a number of states have been benefited by improving the infrastructure. Presently, this scheme has also been merged with ASIDE.

Inland container depots and container freight stations   A large part of India is land-locked and a number of states are at a disadvantageous position with no seaport. For these states, accessible transport to the seaports is one of the major concerns and multimodal transport is a very effective solution to these logistics bottlenecks. The first inland container depot (ICD) in India was set up at Bengaluru in August 1981. Initially, the Container Corporation of India had been involved in establishing and managing ICDs and container freight stations (CFSs), mainly based on rail transport. Subsequently, ICDs and CFSs were established and managed by the Central Warehousing Corporation and some state corporations. There had been a major boost to containerized transportation of export cargo with the enactment of the Multimodal Transportation of Goods Act, 1993.

The central government later formulated a revised scheme for allowing the private sector to participate in setting up ICDs and CFSs across the country. The scheme of involving state governments in establishing and managing ICDs and CFSs not only led to increased involvement of the state governments, but also helped them to generate some revenue along with infrastructure development. Presently, this scheme has also been merged with ASIDE.

Export promotion industrial park scheme   With a view to involve the state governments in creation of infrastructural facilities for export-oriented production, the central government introduced the export promotion industrial park (EPIP) scheme in August 1995. The scheme provided that 75 per cent of the capital expenditure incurred towards creation of such facilities, ordinarily limited to ₹10 crore in each case, is met from a central grant to the state governments. In addition, a maintenance grant equivalent to 2 per cent of export turnover of each unit established therein is also given to state governments for a period of five years from the date of commercial production of that unit. The EPIPs are essentially industrial parks housing EOUs, which are expected to export at least 25 per cent of their total production.

The EPIP scheme was one of its kinds wherein the central government provides financial support to create infrastructure for export production. The basic infrastructure thus created could serve as a model for creating a planned export-oriented infrastructure in the states. From 1 April 2002, this scheme was also merged with ASIDE.

Free trade zones and export processing zones   In order to develop infrastructure for export production at internationally competitive prices and environment, the concept of EPZs was conceived. The EPZs, set up as special enclaves, separated from the DTAs by fiscal barriers, were intended to provide an internationally competitive duty-free environment for export production, at low costs, which enables the products of EPZs to be competitive, both quality-wise and in terms of price, in the international market. The EPZs aim at attracting foreign capital and technology to increase exports in particular and to contribute to economic development in general.

India's first EPZ was set up at Kandla (Gujarat) in 1965, followed by Santacruz (Mumbai) in 1973. Subsequently, EPZs were set up at Falta (West Bengal), Noida (UP), Cochin (Kerala), Chennai (Tamil Nadu), and Vishakhapatnam (Andhra Pradesh). The Santacruz Electronics Export Processing Zone (SEEPZ) deals exclusively with export of electronics and gem and jewellery items, whereas the other zones were multi-product zones. The incentives provided for investing in EPZs include income tax relief and tax holidays, exemption from customs duty for industrial inputs and export licenses, single window approval process, and exemption from payment of excise duty for inputs from DTA. The performance of EPZs in India has largely been very dismal. On the other hand, their performance in other Asian countries, such as South Korea, Malaysia, Taiwan, Philippines, China, and Sri Lanka, has been very impressive.

With the reduction of import tariffs during recent years in the post-WTO era, the significance and viability of these EPZs would mainly depend upon the quality of services and infrastructure provided in the EPZs as compared to units outside EPZs.

Private/Joint sector export processing zones The Government also permitted development of EPZs by the private, state, or joint sector since May 1994. These operated in the same regime as the EPZs, but could be developed and managed either privately, by the state governments or by private parties in collaboration with the state government or their agencies. The private investors could be Indian individuals, non-resident Indians (NRIs), and Indian and foreign companies. The viability of such a scheme largely depended upon the initiatives taken and conducive environment provided by the state governments.

Special economic zones With a view to provide an internationally competitive and hassle-free trade environment for export production, a scheme on SEZ has been introduced in the Exim Policy in April 2000. The SEZ is a designated duty-free enclave, to be treated as foreign territory for trade operations and duties and tariffs. SEZs may be set up in the public, private, or joint sector or by the state governments. Units for manufacture of goods and rendering of services may be set up in such zones. Besides, offshore banking units may also be set up in SEZs. All the import/export operations of the SEZ units are on self-certification basis. A unit in an SEZ should be a net foreign exchange earner but it is not subjected to any pre-determined value addition or minimum export performance requirements. However, sales made by SEZ units in the DTA are subjected to payment of full customs duty and import policy in force.

The distinguishing features of the SEZ policy are as follows:

- The zones are to be set up by the private or public sector or by the state government in association with the private sector. The private sector can also develop infrastructure facilities in the existing SEZs.
- State governments have a lead role in the setting up of an SEZ.
- An attempt is being made to develop a framework for creating special windows under existing rules and regulations of the central government and state governments for SEZ.

At the time of the conceptualization of the scheme, it was envisaged that the existing EPZs would be converted into SEZs. Subsequently, all the EPZs located at Kandla and Surat (Gujarat), Cochin (Kerala), Santa Cruz (Mumbai, Maharashtra), Falta (West Bengal), Chennai (Tamil Nadu), Visakhapatnam (Andhra Pradesh), and Noida (Uttar Pradesh) were converted into SEZs. The role of the states in developing SEZs has significantly increased as this scheme has been merged with ASIDE. Conceptually, the scheme appears very sound for promoting export-oriented production as it provides greater flexibility and the shortcomings of the earlier EPZ/SEZ scheme are significantly reduced. However, the effectiveness of SEZs largely depends upon further reducing operational hassles.

The multi-product SEZs can be set up by the government or private entities over a minimum contiguous area of 1,000 hectares, or at least 200 hectares in select states. The SEZs are self-contained economic parks providing advance infrastructure. All units operating in the SEZs are offered simplified customs, other administrative procedures, and basic facilities, such as electricity and water. Although SEZs are required to be NFEs, there are no minimum export requirements in contrast to EPZs and EOUs. In addition to the tax incentives already provided to the EPZs and EOUs, investors in SEZs are eligible for other incentives, such as exemption from service tax and minimum alternate tax, up to 100 per cent FDI in most activities, and a relaxation of certain requirements, including environmental impact assessment, labour laws, and residence requirements for foreign managing directors of the companies.

Similar to the EPZs, each SEZ is governed by a development commissioner. For establishing a unit in an SEZ, an application has to be made to the development commissioner of the SEZ along with supporting documents. The decision to the applicant must be provided by the

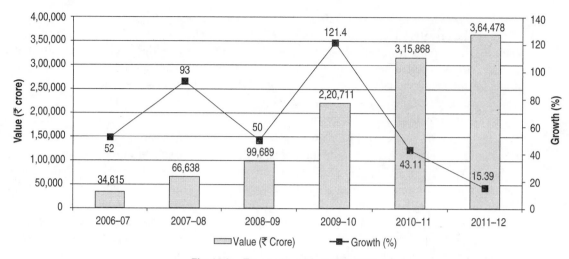

Fig. 16.2 Exports from functioning SEZs

Source: *Annual Report*, 2012–2013, Ministry of Commerce, Government of India.

approval committee within 15 days of the receipt of the application, whereas for applications requiring license, approval must be given within 45 days by the SEZ's Board of Approval in the Ministry of Commerce and Industry.

Though exports from SEZs increased significantly from ₹34,615 crore in 2006–07 to ₹3,53,195 crore in 2011–12, their growth, after reaching a peak of 121.4 per cent in 2009–10, declined to 15.39 per cent in 2011–12 (Fig. 16.2).

There has been a considerable debate over the effectiveness of SEZs in generating additional investment and employment. The geographical dispersion of the SEZs is mainly limited to seven states: Andhra Pradesh (20%), Maharashtra (17%), Tamil Nadu (14%), Karnataka (10%), Haryana (9%), Gujarat (8%), and Uttar Pradesh (5%), which account for nearly 92 per cent of SEZs established (Fig. 16.3). A sector-wise analysis indicates that out of 385 notified SEZs, IT and ITeS sectors accounted for 61 per cent of total SEZs (Fig. 16.4), whereas pharmaceutical and chemicals, biotechnology, and multi-product each accounted for 5 per cent, engineering (4%), and textiles (3%).

Moreover, most of the SEZs particularly in the IT and ITeS sectors have come up around major urban sectors. Besides, SEZs have also witnessed protests, sometimes violent, from farmers over land-acquisition issues that have significant socio-economic implications.

Agri-export zones The concept of agri-export zones (AEZs) was floated with a view to promote agricultural exports from India and providing remunerative returns to the farming community in a sustained manner. State governments are required to identify AEZs and also evolve a comprehensive package of services provided by all state government agencies, state agriculture universities, and all institutions and agencies of the union government for intensive delivery in these zones.

Services are expected to be managed and coordinated by state governments/corporate sector and include provision of pre-/post-harvest treatment and operations, plant protection, processing, packaging, storage and related research and development, etc. APEDA, the nodal agency that promotes setting up of AEZs, is expected to supplement, within its schemes and provisions, efforts of state governments for facilitating such exports. A web-based monitoring system has also been evolved to pursue more than 120 activities in each AEZ. Under this monitoring system, each

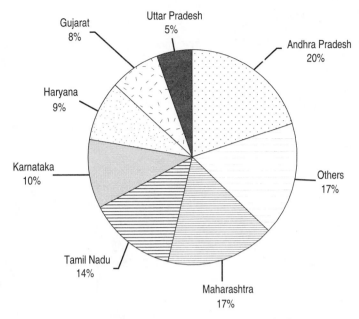

Fig. 16.3 State-wise distribution of notified SEZs

Source: *Annual Report*, 2012–13, Ministry of Commerce, Government of India.

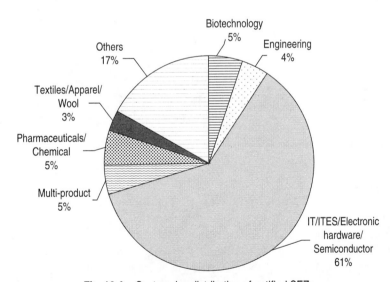

Fig. 16.4 Sector-wise distribution of notified SEZs

Source: *Annual Report*, 2012–13, Ministry of Commerce, Government of India.

activity is clearly defined, the agency responsible to undertake the activity is clearly indicated, and the time for performing that activity is clearly specified.

The emphasis in all the AEZs is on convergence. Thus, the objective is to utilize the ongoing schemes of various central and state government agencies in a coordinated manner to cover the entire value chain from farmer to consumer. The corporate sector with proven credentials are also encouraged to sponsor new AEZs or take over already notified AEZs or part of such zones

Table 16.4 India's agri-export zones* (AEZs)

States	AEZ projects
West Bengal	Pineapple, lychee, potatoes, mango, vegetables, Darjeeling tea
Karnataka	Gherkins, rose, onion, flowers, vanilla
Uttarakhand (earlier Uttaranchal)	Lychee, flowers, basmati rice, medicinal and aromatic plants
Punjab	Vegetables, potatoes, basmati rice
Uttar Pradesh	Potatoes, mangoes and vegetables, basmati rice
Maharashtra	Grape and grape wine, mango (Alphonso), *kesar* mango, flowers, onions, pomegranate, banana, oranges
Andhra Pradesh	Mango pulp and fresh vegetables, mango and grapes, gherkins, chilli
Jammu and Kashmir	Apple, walnuts
Tripura	Organic pineapple
Madhya Pradesh	Potatoes, onion, garlic, seed spices, wheat (Durham), lentil and grams, oranges
Tamil Nadu	Flowers, mangoes, cashew nut
Bihar	Lychee, vegetables, and honey
Gujarat	Mango and vegetables, value-added onion, sesame seeds
Sikkim	Flowers (orchids), cherry pepper, ginger
Himachal Pradesh	Apples
Orissa	Ginger and turmeric
Jharkhand	Vegetables
Kerala	Horticulture products, medicinal plant
Assam	Fresh and processed ginger
Rajasthan	Coriander, cumin

*as on May 2013.
Source: Agricultural Processed Export Development Authority.

for boosting agri-exports from the zones. Exporters under AEZs are also eligible for import of inputs, including fertilizers, pesticides, insecticides, and packaging material under advance authorization, DFIA, and DEPB schemes. Additionally, they may also avail the status of export houses or trading houses if the stipulated export performance is achieved.

The scheme has notified about 60 AEZs in 20 states for a wide range of agro products, as given in Table 16.4. However, the concept of AEZ could hardly take off, and 54 out of 60 approved AEZs reportedly failed to meet the targeted level of exports or attracted envisaged investment.[9]

Other export promotion measures

In addition to the tariff concessions and exemptions, the FTP provides a wide range of export promotion measures (Table 16.5), such as marketing assistance for export promotion, incentives to promote services exports, development of industrial clusters for export potential, promoting export generating employment in rural and semi-urban areas, and giving recognition to established exporters.

---

[9] 'Greenfield AEZs Needed for Food Security and Exports', *The Economic Times*, 8 August 2007.

Table 16.5 Other export promotion measures

Scheme	Eligibility	Concessions
Served from India scheme	All service providers listed in the *Handbook of Procedures* with total foreign exchange earnings of at least ₹1 million in the previous current financial year.	Duty-free imports of all goods including capital goods, office equipment, and consumables (except motor vehicles) up to 10% of the value of foreign exchange earnings of the previous financial year (up to 5% for hotels of one star and above).
Focus market and focus product scheme	Exports to notified countries under the focus market scheme and notified products to all countries under the focus product scheme.	Duty-free imports of up to 3% of the FOB value of exports in free foreign exchange of select markets and 2% or 5% of FOB value of exports for select products.
Special agriculture and village industry scheme *(Vishesh Krishi and Gram Udyog Yojana)*	Exporters of fruit, vegetables, flowers, minor forest products, dairy, poultry and their value added products, and *Gram Udyog* products.	Duty-free imports equivalent to 5% of the FOB value of exports (3.5% if the exporter has benefited from duty-free imports of agriculture under any other concessional entry scheme). Additional customs duty equivalent to excise duty to be adjusted as CENVAT credit or duty drawback according to the Department of Revenue rules.
Export and trading houses	Merchant and manufacturer exporters, service providers, EOUs, units located in SEZs, AEZs, EHTPs, STPs, and BTPs that meet certain prescribed export performance.	Authorization and customs clearances for both imports and exports on self-declaration basis, fixation of input-output norms on priority within 60 days, exemption from compulsory negotiation of documents through banks, 100 per cent retention of foreign exchange in EEFC account, enhancement in normal repatriation period from 180 to 360 days and exemption from furnishing of BG in schemes under FTP.

Source: *Foreign Trade Policy*, 2009–14, Ministry of Commerce, Government of India, updated on 18 April 2013.

Marketing assistance for export promotion The market assistance schemes under the FTP facilitate market promotion activities. The market development assistance (MDA) scheme supports efforts by the EPCs in their export promotion activities whereas the MAI scheme provides assistance for research on potential export markets, as well as incentives to improve quality, infrastructure, etc., related to agriculture through commodity boards and councils.

Market development assistance scheme In order to facilitate exporters to explore the overseas markets and to promote their exports, the MDA scheme of the Department of Commerce provides assistance for participation in export promotion seminars, trade fairs, and buyer–seller meets in India and abroad. Assistance is available to exporters with annual export turnover up to ₹150 million under specified conditions, as follows:

- Assist exporters for export promotion activities abroad.
- Assist EPCs to undertake promotional activities.

- Assist approved organization/trade bodies for carrying out non-recurring innovative activities for export promotion.
- Assist focus export promotion programmes in specific regions abroad, such as focus Latin American countries (LAC), focus Africa, focus CIS, and focus ASEAN programmes
- For other essential activities related with marketing promotion efforts abroad.

Financial assistance with travel grant is available to exporters travelling to Latin America, Africa, CIS region, ASEAN countries, Australia, and New Zealand. In other areas, financial assistance without travel grant is available. The scheme is implemented by EPCs and other export-promotion bodies, industry and trade associations (ITAs) on a regular basis every year. The annual expenditure under the scheme has been around ₹50–55 crore from 2006–07 to 2012–13.

Market access initiative   In order to supplement the MDA scheme and facilitate promotional efforts on a sustained basis, the MAI scheme was launched in 2001–02. The scheme is formulated on 'focus product' and 'focus market' approach to evolve specific strategy for specific market and specific product through market studies or survey.

Under the scheme, financial assistance is provided to

- identify the priorities of research relevant to the Department of Commerce and sponsor research studies consistent with the priorities;
- carry out studies for evolving WTO compatible strategy;
- support EPCs/trade promotion organizations in undertaking market studies/survey for evolving proper strategies;
- support marketing projects abroad based on the focus product–focus country approach. The activities funded include
  - opening of showrooms and warehouses;
  - display in international departmental stores;
  - publicity campaign and brand promotion;
  - participation in trade fairs abroad;
  - research and product development; and
  - reverse visits of the prominent buyers from the project focus countries.
- export potential survey of the states;
- registration charges for product registration abroad for pharmaceuticals, biotechnology, and agro-chemicals;
- testing charges for engineering products abroad;
- support cottage and handicrafts units; and
- support recognized associations in industrial clusters for marketing abroad.

Each of these export promotion activities can receive financial assistance from the Government, ranging from 25 per cent to 100 per cent of total cost, depending upon activity and implementing agency.

Under the scheme, financial assistance is provided to export/trade promotion organizations, national level institutions, research institutions, universities, laboratories, and exporters for enhancement of export through accessing new markets or through increasing the share in the existing markets. However, the assistance to individual exporters is available only for testing charges of engineering products abroad and registration charges of pharmaceuticals, biotechnology, and agro-chemicals. The proposals for assistance are examined by an empowered committee for a particular product and a particular market.

The MAI scheme provides an excellent opportunity, especially for public and private sector export promotion organizations to finance their marketing activities for the thrust products in the pre-identified markets. The scheme could not make the anticipated headway, mainly due to limited initiatives by the state and central government organizations, which were the targeted principal beneficiaries and also because of non-awareness among the target beneficiaries due to poor marketing of the scheme. However, expense under MAI scheme has increased from ₹40 crore in 2006–07 to ₹150 crore in 2011–12.

India brand equity foundation   It is a trust established and aimed to promote and create awareness of the 'Made in India' label in international markets and to disseminate information on Indian product and services. The trust promotes brand India and use digital technology by way of Internet and CDs.

Served from India scheme   In order to promote export of services from India, the served from India scheme (SFIS) was introduced in 2004. All service providers of select services, who have a free foreign exchange earning of at least ₹1 million or individual service providers with at least ₹0.5 million, are entitled to duty credit scrip equivalent to 10 per cent of free foreign exchange earned during the preceding year. However, hotels of one-star and above are entitled to duty credit scrip equivalent to 5 per cent. The scheme allows for import of any capital goods, including spares, office equipment and professional equipment, office furniture and consumables; that are otherwise freely importable under the trade policy relating to any service-sector business of applicant. Import entitlement/goods imported under the scheme are non-transferable and subject to actual user condition.

Towns of export excellence   The scheme aims at recognizing towns that have come up as industrial clusters with considerable exports so as to maximize their potential. The scheme notifies select towns producing worth ₹10 billion as towns of export excellence (TEE), whereas the threshold limit in the handloom, handicraft, agriculture, and fisheries sector is ₹2.5 billion. The TEE notified include Tirupur for hosiery, Ludhiana for woollen knitwear, Panipat for woollen blankets, Kanoor, Karur, and Madurai for handlooms, AEKK (Aroor, Ezhupunna, Kodanthuruthu and Kuthiathodu) for seafood, Jodhpur for handicrafts, Kekhra for handlooms, Dewas for pharmaceuticals, Alleppey for coir products, and Kollam for cashew products.

Recognized associations of units in the town of export excellence are allowed to access funds under the MAI scheme for creating focused technological services. Common service providers in these areas are also entitled for the EPCG scheme. However, such areas will receive priority for assistance under the ASIDE scheme.

Vishesh krishi and *gram udyog yojana* (**special agriculture and village industry scheme**)   In order to promote employment generation in rural and semi-urban areas, the *vishesh krishi upaj yojana* (special agricultural produce scheme) was launched. Subsequently, the scheme was expanded and renamed as *vishesh krishi* and *gram udyog yojana* (special agriculture and village industry scheme). The scheme aims to promote the agricultural produce, minor forest produce, village industries' products, and forest-based products. Under the scheme, duty credit scrip equivalent to 5 per cent of FOB value of exports is provided so as to compensate the high transport costs. The benefit is reduced to 3 per cent for exporters who have availed certain benefits under other schemes such as duty drawback, advance authorization, or DFIA scheme. A higher incentive in the form of duty credit scrip (agri infrastructure incentive scrip) equal to 10 per cent of FOB value of agricultural exports, limited to ₹100 crore per annum is given to status holders for import of capital goods and equipments for cold storage units, pack houses, etc.

Focus market scheme   In order to enhance India's export competitiveness to select strategic markets, the focus market scheme (FMS) was introduced on 1 April 2006. This scheme aims to offset high freight cost and other externalities by allowing duty credit scrip equivalent to 3 per cent of FOB value of exports in free foreign exchange for exports made from August 2009 onwards. It allows additional duty scrip of 1 per cent of FOB value for select markets. The scheme covers

119 countries as focus markets as on 15 April 2013 from Latin America, Africa, and CIS. Although the impact of the scheme remains to be evaluated, it appears to be too ambitious. By notifying a large number of countries as focus markets, there remains the concern of losing the very focus of the FMS. However, the scheme may help in broadening the destination profile of India's exports.

Focus product scheme   In order to provide incentives for export of select products that have high employment potential in rural and urban areas, the focus product scheme (FPS) was introduced on 1 April 2006. The scheme notifies a number of products from product categories such as value added leather products and leather footwear, handicrafts items, handloom products, value added fish and coir products, and some additional focus products. It aims to offset the inherent infrastructure bottlenecks and other associated costs involved in marketing of such products. The scheme initially allowed duty credit scrip equivalent to 1.25 per cent of FOB value of exports of each licensing year for notified products that was increased to 2 per cent or 5 per cent of FOB value of exports in free foreign exchange for exports made after August 2009. The scheme also provided for additional bonus benefits equivalent to 2 per cent of FOB value of exports of specified products for exports made after 1 April 2010.

The scrip and the items imported against both the focus market and focus product schemes are freely transferable. The duty credit may also be used for import of inputs or goods, including capital goods, provided the same is freely importable. Exporters have the option to avail of the benefits in respect of the same exported product/s under only one of the three schemes, that is, FMS, FPS, or *vishesh krishi* and *gram udyog yojana* (special agriculture and village industry scheme).

Incremental exports incentivization scheme   To incentivize export performance, an additional incentive in form of duty credit scrip of 2 per cent FOB value on the incremental growth of exports was introduced initially for three months from 1 January 2013 compared to the same period in the previous year has been extended for a period of one more year.[10]

Market-linked focus products scrip   A variant under FPS, called the market-linked focus products scrip (MLFPS), was introduced in April 2008 so as to give boost to market penetration for specific products in specified markets. Under the scheme, export of products with high export intensity or employment potential not covered under the FPS are incentivized by way of duty credit script of 2 per cent of FOB value of exports in free foreign exchange when exported to linked country markets. The scheme covers over 5,000 products at 8-digit level for various countries such as motor vehicles, auto-components, bicycles and parts, glass products, dyes and chemicals, household articles, machine tools, earth moving equipment, transmission towers, steel tubes and pipes, compressors, auto-components, and three wheelers. Countries covered under the scheme include Algeria, Egypt, Kenya, Nigeria, South Africa, Tanzania, Brazil, Ukraine, Australia, New Zealand, Cambodia, Vietnam, Japan, and China, among others.

Status holders incentive scrip   To promote investment in upgradation of technology, the status holders incentive scrip (SHIS) scheme started in 2009–10, entitles status holders of select sectors an incentive scrip of 1 per cent of FOB value exports with actual user condition. The scheme includes six sectors: leather, textile and jute, handicrafts, engineering, plastics, and basic chemicals.

National export insurance account   A separate fund, called the national export insurance account (NEIA), was set up in 2006 with a corpus of ₹2,000 crore as a public trust set up jointly by the Department of Commerce and the Export Credit and Guarantee Corporation (ECGC). It aims to promote exports from India, which may not take place without the support of credit risk insurance cover, which is difficult for ECGC to provide because of its own underwriting

---

[10] *Foreign Trade Policy*, 2009–14, Ministry of Commerce, Government of India, updated on 18 April 2013.

Table 16.6 Minimum annual export performance for trading houses

Category	Average FOB/FOR value* (in ₹)
Export house[11] (EH)	200 million
Star export house (SEH)	1 billion
Trading house (TH)	5 billion
Star trading house (STH)	25 billion
Premier trading house (PTM)	75 billion

*During current and preceding three licensing years; for export house (EH) status, at least two out of four years.
Source: *Foreign Trade Policy*, 2009–14, Ministry of Commerce, Government of India, updated on 18 April 2013.

capacity. It also provides risk cover for buyer credits, which may be extended by Exim Bank to overseas agencies. Projects that are backed by sovereign guarantees are covered up to 100 per cent of value, without recourse, to eligible exporters.

Export houses/Trading houses/Star trading houses/Super star trading houses   The objective of the scheme of export houses (EH), trading houses (TH), star trading houses (STH), and super star trading houses (SSTH) is to give recognition to the established exporters and large export houses to build up the marketing infrastructure and expertise required for export promotion. The registered exporters having a record of export performance over a number of years are granted the status of export/trading houses or STHs subject to the fulfilment of minimum annual average export performance in terms of FOB value on physical exports or services prescribed in the FTP (Table 16.6).

Besides, the following categories of exporters, both merchant and manufacturer, are eligible to get double weightage:

- Exporters in the small scale industry, tiny sector, cottage sector
- Units registered with KVICs and KVIBs
- Units located in North-Eastern states, Sikkim, and Jammu and Kashmir
- For exports of handloom, handicrafts, hand-knotted, or silk carpets
- For exports to Latin America, CIS, or Sub-Saharan Africa
- Units with ISO 9000 series, ISO 14000 series, WHOGMP, HACCP, SEI CMM Level-II and above status
- Exports of services and agro-products

The exporters who have been granted the status of EH/TH are entitled to a number of benefits under the FTP, including the following:

- Authorization and customs clearances for both import and exports on self declaration basis
- Fixation of input/output norms on priority within 60 days
- Exemption from compulsory negotiation of documents through banks. The remittance, however, would continue to be received through banking channels
- 100 per cent retention of foreign exchange in EEFC account
- Enhancement in normal repatriation period from 180 to 360 days
- Exemption from furnishing bank guarantee in schemes under the FTP

---

[11] For export house, export performance in at least any two out of current and preceding three years is required.

The export houses, trading houses, star trading houses, and super star trading houses scheme allow registered exporters certain additional benefits available to them under the policy.

POLICY INITIATIVES AND INCENTIVES BY STATE GOVERNMENTS

State governments generally do not distinguish between production for domestic market and production for export market. Therefore, few specific measures had been taken by state governments targeted at exporting units. However, state governments have taken a number of policy measures so as to encourage industrial activity in the state which mainly relate to

- capital investment subsidy or subsidy for preparation of feasibility report, project report, etc.;
- waiver or deferment of sales tax, or providing loans for sales tax purposes;
- exemption from entry tax, octroi duty, etc.;
- waiver of electricity duty;
- power subsidy;
- exemption from taxes for certain captive power generation units;
- exemptions from stamp duties; and
- provision of land at concessional rate.

These concessions extended by state governments vary among policies of individual state governments and are broadly based on the following criteria:

- Size of the unit proposed (cottage, small, and medium industries)
- Backwardness of the district or area
- Employment to weaker sections of society
- Significance of the sector, for example, software, agriculture
- Investment source, such as FDI or investment by NRIs
- Health of the unit (sick), etc.

Therefore, it may be noted that most of the exemptions tend to encourage capital- or power-intensive units though some concessions are linked to turnover. Most of the concessions in the state industrial policies have been designed keeping in view the manufacturing industries. An analysis of industrial policies of various states indicates that most state governments do compete among themselves in extending such concessions.

On examination of export promotion initiatives by the state governments, it is difficult to find commonality among various states. However, some of the measures taken by the state governments are as follows:

- Attempting to provide information on export opportunities
- Preference in land allotment for starting an EOU
- Planning for development of EPIPs
- Exemption from entry-tax on supplies to EOU/EPZ/SEZ units
- Exemption from sales tax or turnover tax for supplies to EOU/EPZ/SEZ units and inter-unit transfers between them

WTO AND INDIA'S EXPORT PROMOTION MEASURES

The emergence of the rule-based multilateral trading system under the WTO trade regime has affected India's trade policies and promotional efforts. It provides a rule-based framework as to which subsidies are prohibited, which can face countervailing measures, and which are allowed. The details on the WTO agreement are discussed in Chapter 3. However, the impact of the WTO agreements on trade policy and export promotion measures is examined here. The framework of the GATT is based on four basic rules.

Protection to domestic industry through tariffs   Even though GATT stands for liberal trade, it recognizes that its member countries may have to protect domestic production against foreign competition. However, it requires countries to keep such protection at low levels and to provide it through tariffs. To ensure that this principle is followed in practice, the use of quantitative restrictions is prohibited, except in a limited number of situations.

Binding of tariffs   Countries are urged to reduce and, where possible, eliminate protection to domestic production by reducing tariffs and removing other barriers to trade in multilateral trade negotiations. The tariffs so reduced are bound against further increase by being listed in each country's national schedule. The schedules are an integral part of the GATT legal system.

Most favoured nation treatment   This important rule of GATT lays down the principle of non-discrimination. The rule requires that tariffs and other regulations should be applied to imported or exported goods without discrimination among countries. Thus, it is not open to a country to levy customs duties on imports from one country, a rate higher than it applies to imports from other countries. There are, however, some exceptions to the rule. Trade among members of regional trading arrangements, which are subject to preferential or duty-free rates, is one such exception. Another is provided by the generalized system of preferences (GSP). Under this system, developed countries apply preferential or duty-free rates to imports from developing countries, but apply most favoured nation (MFN) rates to imports from other countries.

National treatment rule   While the MFN rule prohibits countries from discriminating among goods originating in different countries, the national treatment rules prohibit them from discriminating between imported products and equivalent domestically produced products, both in the matter of the levy of internal taxes and in the application of internal regulations. Thus, it is not open to a country, after a product has entered its markets on payment of customs duties, to levy an internal tax (for example, sales tax or VAT) at rates higher than those payable on a product of national or domestic origin.

The four basic rules are complemented by rules of general application, governing goods entering the customs territory of an importing country. These include rules which countries must follow

- in determining the dutiable value of imported goods where customs duties are collected on an ad-valorem basis;
- in applying mandatory product standards, and sanitary and phytosanitary regulations to imported products; and
- in issuing authorizations for imports.

In addition to the rules of general application just described, the GATT multilateral system has rules governing

- the grant of subsidies by governments;
- measures that governments are ordinarily permitted to take if requested by industry; and
- investment measures that could have adverse effects on trade.

The rules further stipulate that certain types of measures that could have restrictive effects on imports can ordinarily be imposed by governments of importing countries only if the domestic industry is affected by increased imports. These include

- safeguard actions and
- levy of anti-dumping and countervailing duties.

Under the safeguard action, the importing country is allowed to restrict imports of a product for a temporary period by either increasing tariffs or imposing quantitative restrictions. However, the safeguard measures can only be taken after it is established through proper investigation that increased imports are causing serious injury to the domestic industry.

The anti-dumping duties can be imposed if the investigation establishes that the goods are 'dumped'. The agreement stipulates that a product should be treated as being 'dumped' where its export price is less than the price at which it is offered for sale in the domestic market of the exporting country, whereas the countervailing duties can be levied in cases where the foreign company has charged low export price because its product has been subsidized by the government.

WTO's Trade Policy Review Mechanism

In order to enhance transparency of the members' trade policies and facilitate smooth functioning of the multilateral trading system, the WTO members established the trade policy review mechanism (TPRM) to review the trade policies of member countries at regular intervals. Under Annexure 3 of the Marrakesh Agreement, the four members with largest shares of world trade (that is, European communities, the USA, Japan, and China) are to be reviewed every two years, the next 16 to be reviewed every four years, and the other be reviewed every six years. For the least developed countries, a longer period may be fixed.

Reviews are conducted by the Trade Policy Review Body on the basis of a policy statement by the member under review and a report prepared by staff in the WTO Secretariat's Trade Policy Review Division. Although the secretariat seeks cooperation of the members in preparing the report, it has the sole responsibility for the facts presented and the views expressed.

The trade policy review (TPR) reports contain detailed chapters examining the trade policies and practices of the member and describing policymaking institutions and the macroeconomic situation. The members' subsidies contained in the TPR is of particular interest for the purpose of the report. Information on subsidies distinguished in the subsidiaries and countervailing measures (SCM) can be found in the following three parts of the TPR report:

- Measures directly affecting exports
- Trade policies and practices by sector
- Government incentives or subsidies that do not directly target imports and exports but nevertheless have an impact on trade flows

The contents of the report are mainly driven by the members' main policy changes and constraints rather than subsidy-related issues and problems. Besides, the coverage of the report is determined to a large extent by the availability of data. As a result, the amount of information contained in the reports varies from member to member. The TPR reports normally do not attempt to assess the effects of the subsidies on trade. Due to limited availability of detailed information, in many cases, it is difficult to identify the extent to which a benefit is actually being conferred or the identity of the recipient of the subsidy.

Despite shortcomings, especially with respect to cross-country comparability, the TPR report constitutes one of the few sources that systematically collects and compiles information on subsidies for a broad range of countries and economic activities.

This chapter brings out the significance of trade policy in international marketing decisions. Developing countries traditionally employed inward-looking trade strategy so as to protect their domestic industries from foreign competition. However, during the recent era of economic liberalization across the world, most countries gradually shifted their trade strategy to outward looking with greater integration with the world economy.

An overview of India's FTP, explaining various measures to promote international trade are discussed. The impact of the WTO agreements on trade policy and export promotion measures is also examined. Readers should develop an insight into the trade policy and regulatory framework as it considerably influences the international marketing decisions.

Summary

A thorough understanding of the country's trade policy and incentives is crucial to the development of a successful strategy for international markets. This chapter provides a broad framework of various provisions of FTP and incentives offered for exports. Till 1991, India followed a strong inward-oriented trade policy to conserve its foreign exchange. The major policy instruments used to promote import substitution industrialization included outright ban on import of some commodities, quantitative restrictions, prohibitive tariff structure, and a variety of administrative strictures.

India's FTP is formulated under the Foreign Trade (Development and Regulation) Act, 1992, for a period of five years by the Ministry of Commerce, which outlines a country's export promotion measures, policies, and procedures related to foreign trade. It is published in four volumes: *Foreign Trade Policy, Handbook of Procedures Volume I, Handbook of Procedures Volume II (Standard Input Output Norms)*, and *ITC (HS) Classification of Export and Import Items*.

India's FTP offers a variety of schemes for concessional imports by the exporters including duty drawback, export promotion capital goods scheme (EPCG), duty exemption scheme (DES), duty remission scheme (DRS), replenishment and imprest licence schemes for diamond, gems, and jewellery exports. A separate package of incentives including concessional or duty-free import is also given for export and trading houses, export-oriented units (EOUs) and units located in export processing zones (EPZs), software technology parks (STPs), electronic hardware technology parks (EHTP), and agri-export zones (AEZs).

For developing international markets, assistance is available under market development assistance (MDA), market access initiative (MIA), and India Brand Equity Fund (IBEF). Assistance to states for infrastructure development for exports (ASIDE) has been designed to increase states' participation in export promotion and provide support to state governments. A number of schemes for infrastructure support such as export promotion industrial park (EPIP), critical infrastructure balance (CIB) scheme, inland container depot (ICD)/container freight station (CFS), and export processing zone (EPZ) have been merged with ASIDE.

The WTO agreements, especially the agreement on subsidies and countervailing measures and on agriculture, provide a framework for deciding the nature and scope of export promotion instruments. They also limit promotional efforts of member countries as to which subsidies are prohibited, which can face countervailing measures, and which are allowed. It also provides for integration of trade policies of member countries with the WTO's multilateral trading system and an institutional framework for periodical review.

Key Terms

Agri-export zones (AEZs) A scheme involving comprehensive package of services in an identified zone by all related state and central government agencies, state agricultural universities, and related organizations so as to facilitate production and exports of agro products.

All industry rate Average industry drawback rates fixed by the Ministry of Finance from time to time.

ASIDE Scheme for providing assistance to states for developing export infrastructure and other allied activities by the Ministry of Commerce on the basis of pre-defined criteria. It includes earlier schemes of EPIP, EPZ, CIB, and export development fund for the North-East and Sikkim.

Brand rates Drawback incentive for exporters of manufactured goods determined on case-to-case basis for individual exporters on particular brands.

Critical infrastructure balance scheme (CIB) Assistance to states to facilitate balancing of capital investments for relieving bottlenecks in infrastructure for export production and conveyance.

Deemed exports Transactions in which goods supplied do not leave the country and payments for such supplies is received either in Indian rupees or in free foreign exchange.

Domestic tariff area (DTA) Area where normal import tariffs and taxes are applicable for the production and movement of goods.

Duty drawback An export incentive to refund customs duty paid on imports of inputs used in manufacture of goods subsequently exported.

Duty exemption pass book (DEPB) scheme Grant of credit on post-export basis as specified percentage of FOB value of exports made in freely convertible currency.

Duty exemption schemes (DES) Allows duty-free import of inputs required for export production subject to certain export obligations as stipulated in FTP.

Duty free import authorization (DFIA) scheme Offers exemptions in respect of custom duty, additional duty, education cess, and anti-dumping or safeguard duties for inputs used in exports.

Export promotion industrial park (EPIP) Assistance given to the states to create infrastructure facilities for export-oriented production.

Export promotion capital goods (EPCG) Allows for the import of capital goods at concessional rate of duty subject to an appropriate export obligation accepted by the exporter.

Export-oriented units (EOUs) Complementary to EPZ scheme for units located in DTA.

Input–output norms (SION) Description on inputs required for production of particular products. These norms are published in Volume II of the *Handbook of Procedures*.

Inward looking strategy (import substitution) Systematic encouragement of domestic production of those goods and services which are otherwise imported. Emphasis is laid on extensive use of trade barriers to protect domestic industries from import competition.

Market access initiative (MAI) Scheme to support market promotion efforts of exporters and export promotion organizations based on focus product-focus country approach.

Market development assistance (MDA) Assistance given to exporters and export promotion organizations for market exploration and export promotion on cost-sharing basis.

NFE Net foreign exchange earnings is defined as the FOB value of exports minus the CIF value of all imported inputs, capital goods, and payments made in foreign exchange for royalties, fees, dividends, interest on external borrowings during the first five-year period.

Outward looking strategy (export-led growth) Aims at linking the domestic economy to the world economy, promoting economic growth, through exports involving incentives to promote exports, rather than import restrictions.

Special economic zones (SEZs) Duty-free enclaves to be treated as foreign territory for trade operations so as to provide an internationally competitive and hassle-free environment for export production. It further reduces the operational hassles associated with earlier export processing zones (EPZs) and free trade zones (FTZs).

Concept Review Questions

1. Why does a manager operating in international markets need to have a thorough knowledge of foreign trade policy (FTP) and incentives? Justify your answer with suitable reasons.
2. Briefly explain the major provisions of the FTP currently in force.
3. Briefly explain the prohibitions and restrictions on exports and imports in India's FTP currently in force.
4. Briefly describe various measures to promote exports from your country under the FTP.
5. Explain the concept of SEZ, and identify the constraints in their effective operation.

6. Describe the policy measures taken by the state governments to promote exports.
7. How does the WTO affect the FTP and export incentives? Critically evaluate WTO's compatibility with export incentives from your country.
8. Write down short notes on the following:
   (a) Export promotion capital goods (EPCG) scheme
   (b) Advance authorization scheme
   (c) Duty free import authorization (DFIA) scheme
   (d) ASIDE

Practice Exercises

1. Select a product and a target market of your interest. Pick up the latest FTP of your country from your library or explore it from the Internet. Find out the policy provisions relevant for making international marketing decisions and discuss the same in the class.
2. The management of a well-established brand in India, which had been catering to the international markets infrequently, is

serious about making a sustained presence in the international markets, but is facing financial constraints. You have been hired to take charge of the firm's expansion plan in international markets. Suggest suitable schemes for getting assistance for its market promotion campaign.

Project Assignments

1. Visit an export-oriented unit located near your place. Find out incentives availed of by the EOU and the constraints faced. Identify the key factors that have affected the viability of the unit.
2. Contact a trading house located in your city and find out the difficulties faced. Critically evaluate the effectiveness of the policy incentives received.

3. Visit a unit located in an SEZ. Find out the incentives availed and constraints faced in its operation. Identify the key factors that have affected its operational viability.

Export Procedures and Documentation

INTRODUCTION

Proper export procedures and documentation is crucial to international marketing, as both exporters and importers are situated in two different countries, and are governed by different legislative frameworks. The export transaction chain consists of a number of entities, which are integral to the entire system. A number of government regulatory agencies, such as the Directorate General of Foreign Trade (DGFT) in India, inspection agencies, insurance companies, customs and central excise authorities, banking institutions, clearing and forwarding (C&F) agents, shipping companies or airlines, and carriers for inland transportation, facilitate trade transactions between the exporters and importers. These entities facilitate hassle-free transactions between the exporters and the importers. The exporters have to comply with the rules, regulations, and trade customs of all these organizations.

To carry out an international trade transaction, one has to follow various international commercial practices and laws, such as the Carriage of Goods by Sea Act, 1924, Uniform Customs and Practices for Documentary Credit (UCPDC), 1993, International Commercial Terms (INCOTERMS), 2000, and any amendments thereof from time to time. In case of India, the relevant laws/Acts include Insurance Act, 1938, Central Excise Act, 1944, Customs Act, 1962, Marine Insurance Act, 1963, Export (Quality Control and Inspection) Act, 1963, Foreign Trade (Development and Regulation) Act, 1992; Foreign Exchange Management Act, 1999, Central Excise Rules, 2001, Foreign Trade Policy, and Handbook of Procedures, and amendments thereof brought out from time to time by the DGFT, etc. Therefore, an export manager has to develop a thorough understanding of the various legislations governing international trade in the exporting as well as the importing country.

Apart from all this, an exporter has to also assure of receiving timely payment, while the importer has to ensure that he receives

Learning Objectives

- To explain the framework of export transactions
- To discuss the significance of export documentation
- To explicate the commercial documents needed in export transactions
- To discuss regulatory documents required in export transactions
- To outline the procedures involved in an export–import transaction
- To elucidate the electronic processing of export documents

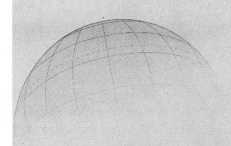

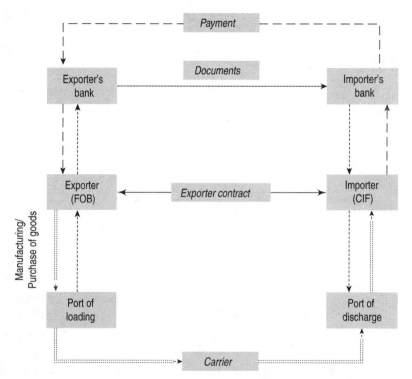

Fig. 17.1 Export transaction framework

the imported cargo in good condition and on time. Besides, the cargo is exposed to a number of risk factors, such as damage due to fire or loss, or maritime damage, due to various sea perils.

To facilitate the flow of export cargo from the exporter to the importer and to ensure the receipt of payment from the importer, international transactions evolved a customary and regulatory framework over a period of time. An illustrative framework of export transactions is depicted in Fig. 17.1 in a simplified form to make the readers appreciate the process. For entering into international markets, an exporter has to identify an importer and strike a deal with him. The export contract should explicitly indicate the description of goods, the price of each item, net and gross shipping weights, the terms of delivery, the terms of payment, insurance and shipping costs, the currency of sales, the port of loading, the port of discharge, the estimated shipping date, and the validity period of the contract.

As the documentary requirements and procedure for export transaction is considerably complex, the exporter generally utilizes the services of the C&F agents at the ports who specialize in these operations. Depending upon the terms of the export contract, the export cargo is delivered to the carrier against the receipt of the bill of lading (B/L). The ocean B/L serves as a receipt of cargo by the shipping company, the contract of transport (or carriage), and a negotiable 'document of title'. Therefore, the goods can be claimed at the destination only by the lawful holder of the B/L. As a part of the international commercial practices, the B/L is handed over to the importer by the importer's bank only after the payment has been made or in case of usance documents, the importer commits to make the payment at a future date. This process ensures the receipt of payment to the exporter on one hand and receipt of cargo to the importer on the other. Therefore, an international marketing manager has to have a thorough understanding of the export procedures and documentation practices in international trade.

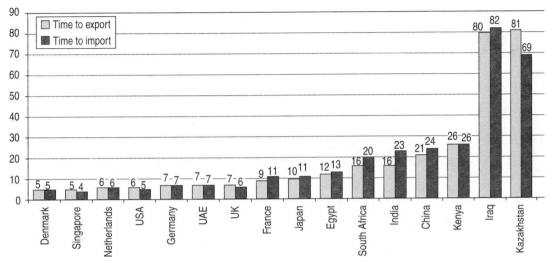

Fig. 17.2 Time required for international trade transaction

Source: 'Trading Across Borders', *Doing Business: 2013*, The International Bank for Reconstruction and Development/World Bank, Washington D.C., 2013.

Considerable time is required to export or import merchandise, as it consists of obtaining all the documents, inland transport, customs clearance and inspections, and port and terminal handling procedures, whose length vary across countries. It takes only five days to export and import each from Denmark, five days to export and four days to import from Singapore, six days each from Netherlands, six and five days from the USA, seven days each from Germany, seven days each from the UAE, seven and six days from the UK, 9 and 11 days from France, 10 and 11 days from Japan,12 and 13 days each from Egypt, 16 and 20 days from South Africa, 16 and 23 days from India, 21 and 24 days from China and 26 days each from Kenya for exports and imports respectively, as shown in Fig. 17.2. On the other hand, it takes 80 days to export and 82 days for import from Iraq, and 81 and 69 days for exports and imports respectively from Kazakhstan. The time taken to effect an export shipment is crucial, as each additional day that an export product is delayed is reported to reduce a country's exports by more than 1 per cent. In case of time-sensitive agricultural products, reduction in delays by 10 per cent increases exports of the firm by more than 30 per cent.[1]

To effect export or import, various costs are incurred for obtaining documents, administrative fees for customs clearance and technical control, terminal handling charges, and inland transport. A cross-country comparison indicates that the cost incurred in exports and imports is the lowest, at US$435 and US$420 per container, in Singapore, as shown in Fig. 17.3, while it is the highest in Tajikistan at US$8,450 and US$9,800, respectively.

Therefore, a thorough understanding of the procedures and documents involved facilitate decision-making while handling an international transaction. This chapter discusses in detail the important regulatory and auxiliary documents, such as commercial invoice, packing list, transport documents such as B/L, airways bill, combined transport documents, certificate of origin (CoO), inspection certificate, insurance certificate, bill of exchange, shipping bill, bill of entry, mate's receipt, and exchange control declaration forms. Subsequently, the step-by-step

---

[1] Djankov, Simeon, Caroline Freund, and Cong Pham, 'Trading on Time', *Policy Research Working Paper 3909*, World Bank, Washington, D.C., 2007, pp. 2–23.

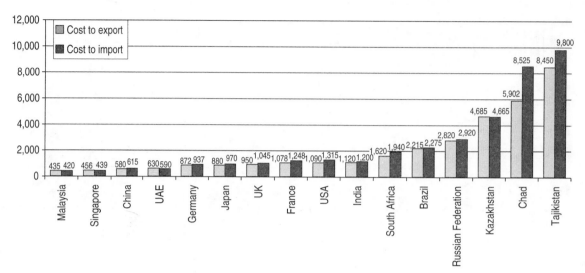

Fig. 17.3   Cost incurred in an international trade transaction

Source: 'Trading across Borders', *Doing Business: 2013,* The International Bank for
Reconstruction and Development/World Bank, Washington D.C., 2013.

procedure for executing an export order has also been discussed. Readers may also refer to the
sample copies of each of the documents used in international trade transactions given in the
online resource centre.

EXPORT DOCUMENTATION

Export documentation is considered to be a critical constituent of international marketing, as
export transactions involve complex documentation work. Export documentation facilitates
international transactions, and protects the interest of the exporters and importers located
in two different countries governed by different statutory and legislative frameworks. The
successful execution of an export order, ensuring physical delivery of goods and remittance of sales proceeds, is as important as procurement of an export order and sourcing or
production of goods for exports.

The number of documents required for exports and imports vary considerably across countries.
Merely two documents are required each for exports and imports[2] from France, as shown in Fig. 17.4,
whereas three and five from Japan, four documents each from Singapore and the UK, four and five
each from Switzerland, UAE and the USA, six and seven from Australia and South Africa, seven
and eight from Brazil, eight and five from China, eight and nine from Egypt, eight and eleven from
Russian Federation and nine and eleven from India. However, 10 documents each for exports and
imports are required from Nigeria, and 13 and 14 documents from Uzbekistan.

As far as the customs and conventions of international trade are concerned, there are certain
other documents that are essential in export trade. Besides, some documents are required to fulfil
the statutory requirements of the exporting and the importing countries, such as export–import
trade control, foreign exchange regulations, pre-shipment inspections, and central excise and
customs requirements.

---

[2] 'Trading across Borders', *Doing Business: 2013,* The International Bank for Reconstruction and Development/
World Bank, Washington D.C. 2013.

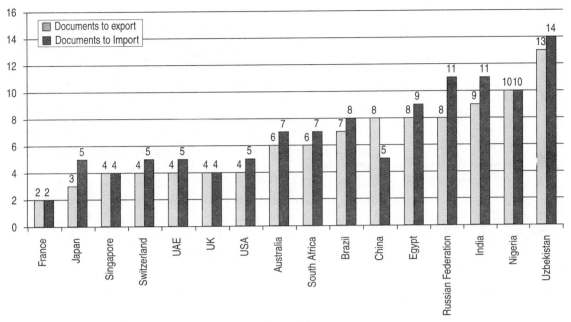

Fig. 17.4 Number of documents required for exports and imports (in numbers)

Source: 'Trading across Borders', *Doing Business: 2013*, The International Bank for Reconstruction and Development/ World Bank, Washington D.C.

In an export transaction, a number of trade intermediaries and government authorities are inevitably involved,[3] such as the DGFT, export promotion councils, export inspection agencies, shipping companies, freight forwarders, insurance companies, banks, port trusts, and central excise and customs authorities, which have their own documentary requirements. Strict compliance with procedural formalities and documentary requirements requires meticulous planning and desired skills for the successful completion of an export order.

Consequences of Poorly Completed Documentation

An export manager should carry out the documentation work meticulously to avoid problems related to the smooth flow of goods and getting remittances from the overseas importers. Poor documentation may result in a number of problems in executing an export order, which may lead to additional costs to the exporter. These costs[4] may be of the following three types:

- The cost of interest charges incurred by the exporters as a result of delays in receiving payment.
- The cost of putting the problem right, such as telephone bills, courier charges for sending replacement documents, and bank charges for amending documents like letter of credit (L/C) and, possibly, loss of credit insurance cover.
- Perhaps the most serious, but also the most difficult to quantify, is the cost to the relationship between the exporter and the customer. More often than not, a new customer will be so upset by poor documentation and the problems it causes, that she will be reluctant to do further business with such an exporter.

---

[3] *Standardized Pre-shipment Export Documentation*, Export Facilitation Committee of India, Ministry of Commerce, 1990.
[4] *ITC Training Handbook of Export Documentation*, International Trade Centre, UNCTAD/GATT, 1994.

Adaptation of Aligned Documentation System in India

Prior to 1990, the form of documents and related formalities, which had been developed by different government agencies and authorities in India, were aimed to suit their own individual requirements with little regard to the interrelationship of different documents, and their effects on the total documentation burden in an export transaction. For instance, quotations and invoices made by various exporters used to differ widely. Even the regulatory documents used by different government departments had little synergy.

Moreover, all these documents were prepared individually and separately, and were highly prone to errors and discrepancies. As a result, it made export documentation in India extremely complicated and overlapping in nature.

The aligned documentation system (ADS) is a methodology of creating information on a set of standard forms printed on a paper of same size in such a way that the items of identical specification occupy the same position on each form. The basic objectives of ADS may be summarized as follows:

- It simplifies and prioritizes information required by various commercial interests and government agencies, and aligns it in a standardized format.
- It achieves economy of time and effort involved in the prevailing methodology of export documentation.

An ADS requires the preparation of only one 'master document' containing the information common to all documents included in the aligned series. The system is mainly based on Master Document I (Annexure 17.1 given in the online resource centre) for preparing commercial documents and Master Document II (Annexure 17.2 given in the online resource centre) for preparing regulatory documents.

Earlier, documents under ADS were prepared using masks, which were intended to blank out all the information not required in a particular document. Thus, all the aligned documents could be prepared by photocopying, using masks along with the master documents. Any additional information specific to a document could either be pre-printed, or added as and when required. However, the widespread availability of numerous software programs nowadays has replaced the use of masks for the preparation of export documents.

The commercial documents under ADS are prepared on a uniform and standard A4-size paper (210 mm × 297 mm), while the regulatory document papers are prepared on a full-scale paper (34.5 cm. × 21.5 cm.). All the documents are aligned to one another in such a way that the common items of information are given in the same relative slots in each of the documents included in the system. Based on the UN layout key, the ADS provides an effective alternative to repetitive dilatory and unproductive method of preparation of export documents.

Sweden was the first country to introduce pre-shipment export trade documents in standard layout in 1956 followed by Denmark, Finland, and Norway. Encouraged by the experience of these Scandinavian countries, the United Nation Economic Commission for Europe (UNECE) set up a committee in 1960 comprising European countries, the USA, and several other organizations related to international trade and transport. By 1963, the UNECE agreed to use A4-size paper (210 mm × 297 mm) as the standard size of international trade documents. It also agreed on the standard layout as a basis for the aligned series of export documents. This is known as the UN layout key. Most of the European countries, the USA, Australia, Hong Kong, Singapore, etc. have already adapted the UN layout key. In India, the Indian Institute of Foreign Trade (IIFT) brought out the simplified and standardized versions of a number of pre-shipment export documents. These documents were later reviewed and updated at the

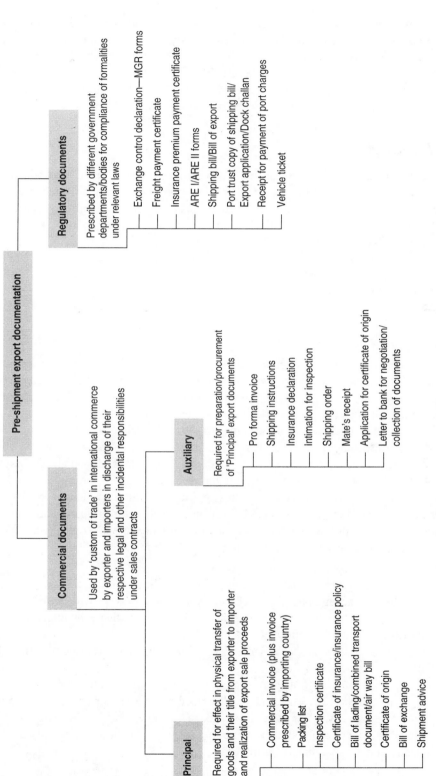

Fig. 17.5　Framework of international trade documentation

Source: Standardized Pre-shipment Export Documentation, Export Facilitation Committee of India, Ministry of Commerce, Government of India, 1990.

instance of the Ministry of Commerce by various government departments and trade associations concerned with international trade. Consequently, the ADS documentation system in India was implemented in 1990–91.

On an average, about 25 documents have to be prepared for an export shipment. An overview of pre-shipment export documents is summarized in Fig. 17.5. For the purpose of understanding of an export manager, these documents can be divided into the following categories.

COMMERCIAL DOCUMENTS

Commercial documents are those documents which, as per customs of the trade, are required to be prepared and used by the exporters and importers in discharge of their respective legal and other incidental responsibilities under the sales contract. These are required for effecting physical transfer of goods and their title from the exporter to the importer as well as for realizing the exports sales proceeds. These documents have to be prepared strictly as per the terms of the L/C, which has been discussed separately. It should also be kept in mind while carrying out documentation work that banks deal in documents and not goods.[5] Therefore, the documents have to be prepared meticulously, and with due diligence. The principal commercial documents are discussed next.

Commercial Invoice

Commercial invoice is the key document for an export transaction, and it must be prepared by the exporter. Since it is the basic export document, it should provide information as comprehensively as possible. Besides, the information provided should be mentioned clearly and accurately.

A commercial invoice contains information on the exporter, the consignee's details, country of origin of goods, country of final destination, terms of delivery and payment, vessel/flight number, port of loading, port of discharge, final destination, marks and numbers, number and kind of packaging, detailed description of goods, quantity, rate, and total amount payable. As a customary trade practice, soon after striking an export deal, the exporter prepares a pro forma invoice (Annexure 17.3 given in the online resource centre), and sends it to the importer. Once the importer accepts and countersigns the pro forma invoice, it becomes a part of an export contract. A pro forma invoice also helps the importer in arranging finances and opening the L/C.

Commercial invoice serves the following three main functions:

1. As a *document of content*, a commercial invoice provides
   - *identification of the shipment* by recording the leading identification marks and numbers given on the package being shipped. Every shipment must provide marks in the form of words. Besides, every shipment must have numbers to indicate the total number of packs or any other unit of account.
   - *detailed description of goods*, which corresponds with the description given in the L/C or contract, as the case may be.
   - *description of quantity* in the commercial invoice must tally with the specifications mentioned in the L/C. The quantity described should neither be less nor more than the contracted quantity. An exporter has to take care while finalizing the export deed that part shipments are not prohibited. The exporter should ship and mention only the contracted quantity, unless specifically permitted.

---

[5] *Uniform Customs and Practices for Documentary Credit (UCPDC)*, ICC Publication No. 600, International Chamber of Commerce, 2007.

2. As a *seller's bill*, it should indicate the net price (net of commission or discount), unless otherwise required under the contract. Generally, the detailed break-up of price is also required to be given in the invoice as per the contractual requirement.
3. As a *packing list*, the description of goods and quantity thereof is given in detail; the commercial invoice can also serve as a packing list, especially when the packaging is simple or in a standard pack.

Some importing countries may need specific commercial invoices, as follows.

Legalized invoice   Some of the importing countries, like Mexico, require legalized invoice wherein the commercial invoice is certified by the local chamber of commerce of the exporting country to verify that the invoice and declaration in the invoice are correct.

Consular invoice   It is a specific invoice verified by the counsel of the importing country. Some of the countries in the Middle East require the invoice to be verified by the commercial section of their embassy in the exporting country (i.e., in India) that the facts mentioned in the invoice are correct. The certification or legalization is done by way of stamp or seal for payment of processing fee. The process may take about a week's time. However, the consular invoice is a form of non-tariff barrier.

Customs invoice   Some countries, such as the USA and Canada, require customs invoice to be prepared in the prescribed format primarily for their actions related to anti-dumping. The customs invoice varies in format, but contains similar information. The customs invoice is self-certified by the exporter. However, certain countries need completed customs invoice from the importers rather than exporters for the purpose of customs clearance.

Certain importing countries require the commercial invoice and the packing list to be prepared or translated to the language of the importing country, for example, in Italian for shipment to Italy, in French to France, and in Spanish to Mexico and Venezuela.

In order to make the readers appreciate the process of export documentation, a sample invoice has been shown in Annexure 17.4, given in the online resource centre. An exporting manager should take due diligence of the following while preparing a commercial invoice:

Exporter   This box should indicate the exporter's name and address along with the details of the city, state, country, and exporter's phone and fax numbers. This box is captioned as shipper in the mate's receipt and the B/L to indicate the identity of the shipper. The same box is captioned as 'drawer' in the letter to the bank for negotiation and collection of documents to indicate the identity of the person/firm who draws the bill of exchange on importer.

Consignee   This box should contain the name and address of the party to whom goods are to be delivered.

Buyer   Generally, buyer is the person to whom goods are consigned. In case the buyer is different from the consignee, the name and address of the buyer should be indicated in this box.

References   Suitable references, such as invoice number, buyer's order number and date, and exporter's reference have to be correctly filled up in these boxes.

Country of origin of goods   This box should indicate the identity of the country where goods have been produced as per the CoO issued by the competent authority. However, this box is generally filled only if the importer requires the details of the country of origin to be furnished.

Country of final destination   It should contain the name of the country where the goods are to be finally delivered.

Terms of delivery and payment   This box should indicate the details of delivery terms, such as free on borad (FOB), cost and freight (CFR), and cost, insurance, and freight (CIF), and the payment terms, such as the documentary L/C, delivery against acceptance (D/A), and delivery against payment (D/P).

Pre-carriage by   This box should indicate the name of the carrier/mode of transport used for transporting the goods from the point of origin where they were accepted for carriage by the pre-carrier.

Place of receipt by pre-carrier   It should indicate the name of the place where goods were received for carriage by the pre-carrier.

Vessel/Flight number   It indicates the details of the vessel or flight number by which the goods are exported including the name of vessel/air carrier, using internationally accepted codes or abbreviations.

Port of loading   This box should indicate the name of the seaport/airport where the goods were loaded.

Port of discharge   This box indicates the name of the seaport/airport where the exported goods are to be unloaded.

Final destination   It indicates the name of the place where the goods are to be finally delivered, in case the final destination is different from the place of discharge. In case of contracts where any movement of export cargo involves trans-shipment or own carriage subsequent to first discharge, the name of the place of the final destination has to be shown.

Mark numbers/Container numbers   It indicates marks and numbers appearing on the packages comprising the consignment as agreed between the exporter and the importer. In case of containerized cargo, it should indicate container number.

Number and kind of packages   This box indicates the total number and nature of packaging in which goods are shipped, such as bags, bales, crates, drums, and bundles.

Description of goods   It gives the description of goods as per the contract. Separate description of different types of goods for the same consignment should be given against related, number, and kind of packages.

Quantity, rate, and amount   These boxes should indicate in respect of each type of goods comprising the consignment, the respective quantity and rate as per the contract, and the amount payable.

Signature and date   Each copy of the commercial invoice should contain in ink the dates and signature of the authorized person to make it legally acceptable.

It has been observed that smooth flow of export transaction is hindered by errors made inadvertently by clerical negligence. Therefore, an export manager should take extra care to avoid these errors and the subsequent problems while preparing the export documents. The consequences of errors while preparing commercial invoice could be significant including the following:

- If the boxes (No. 1, 2, and 3, if any) are incomplete, incorrect, or do not contain all the required details, it may lead to delay in the delivery of documents.
- When the buyer's purchase reference is not shown, payment may get delayed.
- If the quantity of goods covered by the invoice is not correctly shown, it may be difficult for custom officials or importers to check the goods.
- If the description of goods is not complete, it may be difficult to identify individual items at the importer's end.
- If the currency used for invoice is not stated, misunderstandings may arise, and may result in cost for the exporter.

- If the values of the individual items covered by the invoice are not shown, the invoice may be difficult to check.
- If the FOB value is not shown separately, the importer may pay more import tax than he should.
- If the details of the freight charges are not furnished, misunderstandings may arise, bringing about extra costs for the importer.
- If the carrier and the date of shipment are omitted, it will become difficult to trace the consignment.
- If each original and copy invoice is not signed, it may not be accepted by the customs authorities at the port of importation.

In order to enable the readers to understand the nitty-gritty of export documentation, the detailed illustration has been given only for the commercial invoice. It may also be noted that the items to be filled in while completing other documents occupy same amount of space under the ADS. The readers can fill up these documents on their own.

Packing List

Packing list provides details of how the goods are packed, the contents of different boxes, cartons, or bales, and details of the weights and measurement of each package in the consignment (Annexure 17.5 given in the online resource centre). Packing list is used by the carrier while deciding on the loading of the consignment. Besides, this is an essential document for the customs authority. It also helps the importer to check the inventory of the merchandise received.

When the consignment is small or consists of a simple product in a standard pack, the packing information is generally incorporated in the commercial invoice. However, as a general trade rule, it is better to provide financial and packing information separately in invoice and packing list, respectively.

Transport Documents

All the documents that evidence shipment of goods, like the B/L (in ocean transport), combine transport document (in multi-modal transport), way bill, or consignment note (for rail, road, air, or sea transport), and receipt (in postal or courier delivery) are collectively known as transport documents.

Ocean (Marine) Bill of Lading

It is a transport document issued by the shipping company to the shipper for accepting the goods for the carriage of merchandise. This document has got a unique significance in shipping, and is known as the *document of title*, which means that the legitimate holder of the document is entitled to claim the ownership of the goods covered therein. Therefore, it would be impossible for the importers to obtain the possession of the cargo, unless they surrender a signed original B/L to the shipping company at the destination.

Thus, a B/L (Annexure 17.6 given in the online resource centre) serves the following three purposes:

- The receipt of cargo by the shipping company
- A document of title
- The contract of carriage (or transport)

A document of title means that a lawful holder of a B/L has the right to claim goods from the carrier at the destination. Besides, the B/L becomes a *negotiable* document by endorsing it, in which case the goods specified in it can be transferred from one party to another. The negotiability is created in the B/L by mentioning *to order* B/L. An exporter should insist upon to order B/L in which case any cargo would be released on presentation of an original of to order B/L. On the other hand, the *consignee-named* B/L is prepared in the name of a specific party and it cannot be negotiated (transferred). The consignee named B/L should be accepted by an exporter only in case he is confident of receiving timely payment, as in the case of either advance payment or an irrevocable L/C.

If the B/L includes the trans-shipment clause, the carrier has the right to trans-ship even if the L/C prohibits it. Besides, the B/L should not indicate whether the cargo is loaded or has been loaded on the deck, unless otherwise stated in the L/C. In case of modern cellular vessels, they may carry one-third of the containers on deck. If there is a provision in the B/L that the cargo may be carried on the deck, the loading on the dock is acceptable even if L/C stipulates otherwise, provided that the B/L does not specifically mention that the cargo is, or will be, loaded on the deck.

There can be a number of variants of B/L as follow:

On board or shipped B/L   It indicates that the goods have been placed 'on board' the carrier.

Received for shipment B/L   It indicates that goods have been received by the shipping company, and pending shipment and cargo are under the custody of the carrier. In case of shipment on free alongside ship (FAS) terms, a *received for shipment* B/L is required, while for FOB shipment, *on board ship* B/L is required.

Clean B/L   It does not contain any adverse remarks on the quality or condition of package of the cargo received. In fact, all importers insist upon a clean B/L.

Dirty (claused) B/L   In case a shipping company puts remarks about the damage of cargo or its packaging on the B/L, it becomes dirty or claused B/L. Generally, claused B/L is not accepted by most importers, unless otherwise explicitly stipulated in the export contract.

Stale B/L   It is a B/L that is presented after the vessel has sailed and the goods have arrived at the port of discharge. It may lead to delay in customs clearance of goods, payment of warehousing charges, and the risk of loss or damage to the cargo at the destination. However, the issuing bank may issue the importer a guarantee for delivery of goods and a bond, both of which need to be countersigned by the issuing bank for getting the goods cleared through customs in the absence of the B/L. However, an importer is required to surrender the properly endorsed B/L upon its receipt, or replace it in case of its loss.

Through B/L   This is issued when cargo is to be moved from one carrier to another. It is a form of combined transport document where the first carrier acts as the principal carrier and is responsible for the total voyage, and is liable in the event of any loss or damage to the cargo.

Trans-shipment B/L   It is issued when trans-shipment of cargo is required, but the first carrier issuing the B/L acts as an agent in the subsequent stages of the voyage. Hence, the first carrier cannot be held liable for any loss or damage in the subsequent stages of transport by the holder of trans-shipment B/L.

Therefore, importers generally prefer a through B/L. However, from the exporter's point of view, they should insist that presentation of trans-shipment B/L should not be prohibited at the time of finalizing the export contracts.

House or freight forwarders' B/L   It is issued by the freight forwarder, consolidator, or non-vessel carrier (NVC). Under the Carriage of Goods by Sea Act, 1971, it is a non-negotiable document and is not subject to the Hague Rules relating to the B/L, where the non-negotiable documents provide evidence that they relate to the contracts of carriage of goods by sea.

Short forms B/L   It has got all the attributes of a B/L except that it does not contain all the conditions of contract of affreightment. Unless specifically prohibited, banks accept short forms B/L.

Charter party B/L   It is issued by the carrier or its agent in case of charter shipping. The charter party B/L is not accepted for L/C negotiation, unless otherwise authorized in the L/C.

The B/L may be marked 'freight paid' or 'freight to pay'. If the freight is pre-paid by the exporter, the B/L is marked or stamped as 'freight paid', while in case the freight has not been paid, 'freight to pay' or 'freight collect' is marked on the B/L. A B/L is issued by the shipping company in exchange for mate's receipt (Annexure 17.7 given in the online resource centre). Therefore, the shipping company ensures that all the clauses appearing on the mate's receipt are reproduced on the B/L prior to signing and issuing it.

Airway Bill

Airway bill (AWB) is also known as the air consignment note or airway B/L. The airway bill is a receipt of goods and an evidence of the contract of carriage, but unlike the ocean B/L, it is not a document of title and, therefore, is non-negotiable. The goods are consigned directly to the named consignee, and are delivered to the consignee (i.e., the importer) without any further formality once the customs clearance is obtained at the destination. Therefore, it is risky to consign the goods directly to the importer, unless the exporter has ensured the receipt of the payment of goods. Alternatively, the exporter may insist upon a provision in the L/C to consign the goods to a third party, like the issuing bank, or arrange for receiving the payment on cash on documents basis.

The International Air Transport Association (IATA) airway bill is issued in a set of 12 copies, three of which are originals, all having the same validity and commercial significance as follows.

Original 1 (Green)   For the issuing carrier, which is to be signed by the consignor or his agent.

Original 2 (Pink)   For the consignee, which accompanies the goods to the destination, and is signed by the carrier or his agent.

Original 3 (Blue)   For the shipper, is signed by the carrier and handed over to the consigner or his agent after goods have been accepted by the carrier. In cases where the L/C requires a full set of original document to be submitted, the bank requirement is satisfied by presenting the Original 3, that is, the shipper's copy.

It is generally impossible to trace the consignment and get it cleared through customs without an airway bill or its reference number. In case the airway bill indicates a trans-shipment clause, the trans-shipment will or may take place even if it is not allowed under the L/C. The split shipment mentioned in an airway bill means that a part of shipment would enter the importing country at different times.

Combined Transport Document

With the container shipments (Fig. 17.3) becoming popular, combined transport document (CTD) is increasingly being used. The CTD covers the movement of cargo from the place of containerization to the place of destination using multi-modal transport. Under the aligned documentation system, Annexure 17.6 (given in the online resource centre) may also be used as a combined transport document. While making shipments from inland container depots (ICD), the exporters can stuff the goods in the containers and get them examined and sealed by the customs authorities for dispatch to gateway ports in customs-sealed containers. In cases where goods are exported from inland container depots and the L/C does not require a marine B/L, the CTD, to be drawn as per the Foreign Exchange Dealers Association of India (FEDAI) rules, is accepted by the authorized dealers.

In situations where the L/C does not allow the acceptance of the combined transport document or specifically requires ocean B/L, the authorized dealers may accept the CTD drawn as per the FEDAI regulations with an undertaking from the combined transport operator (CTO) stating that the CTD would be replaced by the ocean B/L soon after the cargo is loaded on board the vessel. However, only after the submission of the ocean B/L, the documents are negotiated by the authorized dealer.

Certificate of Origin

The certificate of origin (CoO) is a document used as an evidence of the origin of goods in the importing country. It includes the details of the goods covered and the country where the goods are grown, produced, or manufactured. The manufactured goods must have substantial value addition in the exporting country. Operations such as packaging, splitting, assembling, or sorting may not be sufficient for qualifying the country of origin. It is also needed for deciding whether the import from the country of origin is partially or completely prohibited. The CoO is required for deciding the liability and the rate of import duty in the importing country. Besides, it is also used for granting preferential duty treatment to goods originating in the importing country, for example, in case of the Generalized System of Preference (GSP) certificate. The CoO is of two types.

Preferential CoO

The preferential certificates of origin are required by the countries offering tariff concessions on imports from certain countries. For exports from India, presently, preferential CoO includes:

Generalized system of preferences (GSP)   It is a non-contractual instrument by which developed countries unilaterally, and on the basis of non-reciprocity, extend tariff concessions to developing countries. The countries extending preferences under their GSP scheme include the USA, Japan, Hungary, Belarus, European Union, Norway, Switzerland, Bulgaria, Slovakia, Canada, Russia, Poland, Czech Republic, and New Zealand.

GSP schemes of these countries mention in detail the sectors/products and tariff lines under which these benefits are available, besides the conditions and the procedures governing the benefits. These schemes are renewed and modified from time to time. Normally, the customs of GSP-offering countries require information in a prescribed GSP form (Annexure 17.8 given in the online resource centre).

Global system of trade preference (GSTP)   In the GSTP, trade concessions are exchanged among developing countries that have signed the agreement. The 43 GSTP participating economies represent nearly 20 per cent of total world trade and a market valued in 2010 at US$11 trillion.[6] The Export Inspection Council (EIC) is the sole agency authorized to issue the CoO under GSTP.

Non-preferential CoO

It merely evidences the origin of goods from a particular country and does not bestow any tariff benefits on exports to the importing nations. Generally, such a CoO is issued by the local chamber of commerce. An exporter has to make an application to the local chamber of commerce in the prescribed format (Annexure 17.9 given in the online resource centre) for getting the CoO (Annexure 17.10 given in the online resource centre).

---

[6] *Members of Global System of Trade Preferences Reaffirm Their Strong Commitment to South-South Trade Cooperation*, UNCTAD Press Release No. 27, Doha, 2012.

It is a significant document, which helps in deciding upon the importability and tariff in a number of importing countries. Therefore, an exporter should complete the CoO carefully and accurately as per the rules of the importing country.

Inspection Certificate

Under the Export (Quality Control and Inspection) Act, 1963, it is mandatory to obtain an export inspection certificate for a number of products by the notified agency. The agencies entrusted with compulsory pre-shipment quality inspection include Export Inspection Agency (EIA), Bureau of Indian Standard (BIS), Agricultural Marketing Advisor (AgMark), Drugs Controller, Tea Board, Coffee Board, etc.

Generally, an importer wants the inspection to be carried out by a private agency (namely SGS, Geochem, etc.) nominated by him to ensure the quality of merchandise as per the export contract. The exporter has to submit the intimation for inspection in a prescribed format (Annexure 17.11 given in the online resource centre), and the inspection certificate is issued (Annexure 17.12 given in the online resource centre) by the inspecting agency for payment of a fee.

Insurance Policy/Certificate

Since the carrier and other intermediaries, such as the C&F agents, port authorities, and warehousing operators, have only limited liability during the process of cargo movement from the exporter to the importer, they cannot be held responsible in the event of loss due to a situation beyond their control, such as man-made accidents and natural calamities (Act of God). Therefore, in order to provide protection to the cargo-owner, an insurance cover is necessary while the cargo is in transit from the consignor to the consignee.

The risk to be covered under a cargo insurance policy is governed by the international practice to write policies on standard forms devised by the Institute of London Underwriters. Usually, the insurance policy uses Institute Cargo Clauses, Institute War Clauses, and Institute Strike Clauses. A policy with Institutional Cargo Clauses 'A' plus Institute War Clauses and Institute Strike Clauses provides maximum insurance cover, while a policy with Institutional Cargo Clause 'C' provides minimum cover to various types of risks related to international trade. The details of risks in an international transaction are discussed in Chapters 19 and 20 on international trade finance and risk management. In view of the various factors, such as the nature of cargo, the mode of transport, and port conditions, one has to select the most appropriate cargo insurance policy.

Usually, regular exporters obtain an open cover or open insurance policy with the insurance company. As and when the shipments are made, the exporter gives a marine insurance declaration (Annexure 17.13 given in the online resource centre) to the insurance company, which later issues the insurance certificate (Annexure 17.14 given in the online resource centre). Insurance certificate is a negotiable instrument. Thus, it saves time for the regular exporters in taking the insurance policy. Many a time, the export contract requires submission of insurance certificate instead of the policy.

Mate's Receipt

On receipt of cargo on board, the master of the vessel issues the mate's receipt (MR) (Annexure 17.7 given in the online resource centre) for every shipment taken on board. The port authorities collect the MR from the master or chief officer of the vessel. They do not accept any *claused* MR unless authorized by the shipper. The shipper or his agent has to collect the MR from the port authorities after the payment of all port dues. After receiving the MR, the shipper or his agent prepares a B/L, as per the MR, on blank forms supplied by the shipping company, and presents 2–3 originals and some non-negotiable copies along with the original MR to the shipping company for signature of the authorized officer of the shipping company. An MR is merely a receipt of goods shipped. It is not a document of 'title'. The MR is an important document because the shipping company issues the B/L in exchange of the MR. Therefore, the exporter must collect the MR soon after its receipt from the shed superintendent to avoid any problems and delays in getting the B/L.

Bill of Exchange (Draft)

It is an unconditional order in writing prepared and signed by the exporter and addressed to the importer, requiring the importer to pay on demand (sight bill of exchange) or at a future date (usance bill of exchange) a certain sum of money (contract value) to the exporter or his or her nominee (or endorsee). The maker of the bill (i.e., the exporter) is known as the 'drawer', whereas the person receiving the bill (i.e., the importer) is called the 'drawee'. Sight drafts (or bills of exchange) are used when payment is received by document against payment (D/P), while the usance drafts are used in document against acceptance (D/A). In case of usance bills of exchange, the drafts are drawn for 30–180 days and are negotiable instruments, which can be bought and sold.

A bill of exchange is invariably prepared in two original copies. Both the copies refer each other, and are equally valid. The two original copies are sent by different airmails and the one that reaches earlier is used for exchanging the title documents and the sale amount. Once an original bill of exchange has been honoured, the other becomes redundant. The exporter should ensure before sending the bill of exchange that the details mentioned therein tallies with the other documents, the amount is invariably mentioned in words, and it is signed out in the same way as a cheque is signed by an authorized representative of the exporting firm.

As a bill of exchange does not provide security to the exporter on its own, therefore, as a matter of customary practice, it is used in international trade in conjunction with an L/C. An L/C guarantees that a bill of exchange would be honoured.

Shipment Advice

Soon after the shipment has taken place, the shipment advice (Annexure 17.15 given in the online resource centre) is sent to the importer informing him of the details of the shipment. The shipment advice indicates details of the vessel or flight number, port of discharge and destination, export order or contract number, description of cargo, quantity, etc. This gives advance information to the importer about the details of shipment to enable him to make arrangements to take delivery of the goods at destination. Generally, the importers insist upon sending the copy of shipping advice by fax followed by the first airmail. A non-negotiable copy of the B/L, commercial invoice, customs invoice, if any, and packing list should also to be attached to the shipping advice.

REGULATORY DOCUMENTS

Regulatory documents fulfil the statutory requirements of both the importing and the exporting countries. These documents are related to various government authorities, such as the Directorate General of Foreign Trade (DGFT), the Reserve Bank of India (RBI), export promotion councils, export inspection agencies, banks, and customs and central excise authorities.

Exchange Control Declaration Forms

Under the Foreign Exchange Management (Export of Goods and Services) Act (FEMA), 2000, for every export activity taking place out of India, the exporter has to submit an exchange control declaration form in the prescribed format. Exports to Nepal and Bhutan are exempted from such declarations. The basic objective of a declaration form is to ensure the realization of export proceeds by the exporter, as per the provisions of India's foreign exchange regulations.

The various types of forms used for foreign exchange declaration are as follows.

GR form   Guaranteed remittance (GR) forms are for all types of physical exports, (Annexure 17.16 given in the online resource centre), including software exports in physical form by using magnetic tapes or paper (to be filled in duplicate).

SDF form   For all such exports (Annexure17.17 given in the online resource centre) where the customs authority has the facility for electronic data interchange (EDI), processing of a shipping bill and is attached in duplicate with the shipping bill.

PP form   Postal parcel (PP) forms are for all exports (Annexure 17.18 given in the online resource centre) by post (in duplicate).

SOFTEX form   Software export declaration (SOFTEX) forms for software exports in non-physical form (Annexure 17.19 given in the online resource centre), such as data transmission through satellite link.

The declaration forms should explicitly contain the following details:

• Analysis of the full export value of goods shipped, including the FOB value, freight, insurance, etc.
• Clear indication whether the export is on 'outright sales basis' or 'consignment basis'
• Name and address of the dealer through which export proceeds have been realized or would be realized
• Details of commission or discount due to the foreign agent or buyer

As per FEMA 2000, all the documents relating to export of goods from India should be submitted to the authorized dealer in foreign currency within 21 days, and the amount representing the full export value must be realized within six months from the date of shipment.

GR forms have to be submitted to the customs in duplicate at the port of shipment. The customs authorities verify the declared value, and record the assessed value. The original copy of a GR form is directly sent by the customs to the RBI. At the time of actual shipment, the customs certifies the quantity passed for shipment, and returns it to the exporter. The exporter is required to submit the customs-certified copy of the GR form to the authorized dealer. Once the export proceeds are received, the authorized dealer makes his endorsement and sends it to the RBI.

Shipping Bill/Bill of Export

Shipping bill is the main document required by the customs authorities. The export cargo is allowed to be carted on port sheds and docks only after the shipping bill has been stamped by the customs authorities. The shipping bill mentions the description of goods, marks, numbers, quantity, FOB value, name of the vessel or flight number, port of loading, port of discharge, country of destination, etc. In case of shipment by sea/air/ICD, the document is known as the shipping bill, while in case of shipment by land, the document is known as the bill of exports. Under Section 50 of Customs Act, 1962, the shipping bill has to be submitted to the customs for seeking their permission. The main types of shipping bills are as follows:

• Shipping bill for dutiable goods (Annexure 17.20 given in the online resource centre)
• Shipping bill for duty-free goods (Annexure 17.21 given in the online resource centre)
• Shipping bill for goods claiming duty drawback (Annexure 17.22 given in the online resource centre)

An exporter is required to submit the appropriate shipping bills for customs clearance depending upon the nature of goods.

Bill of Entry

After unloading, the imported cargo is transferred to the custody of an authorized agency, such as the Port Trust Authority, or Airport Authority of India, or any other customs-approved warehouse prior to its customs examination, duty payment, and handing over to the importer. For getting customs clearance on the imported cargo, bill of entry is required to be submitted in four copies by an importer or his agent to the customs authority. The format of bill of entry has been standardized by the Central Board of Customs and Central Excise. There are three types of bills of entry.

Bill of entry for home consumption (white-coloured) It is used to get goods cleared (Annexure 17.23 given in the online resource centre) in one lot by the importer.

Bill of entry for warehousing (yellow) Using 'into bond' bill of entry, an importer can get the goods shifted to a warehouse and get them cleared in small lots. It is especially useful when the importer has shortage of warehousing space or is unable to pay the import duty at one go.

Ex-bond bill of entry (green) For removing goods from the warehouse, an importer has to use ex-bond bill of entry.

While importing by post, there is no bill of entry. The foreign post office prepares a way bill for the assessment of import duty.

Documents for Central Excise Clearance

An exporter has to prepare certain documents and comply with central excise regulations for getting exemptions on export of goods, as discussed next.

Invoice

The goods are delivered against a document known as invoice under Rule 11 of Central Excise (No. 2) Rules, 2001. It is issued by the manufacturer in a set of three copies. The original copy is for the buyer, the duplicate for the transporter, and the triplicate for the assessee. Transportation of goods without invoice is considered to be a violation of rules.

Personal ledger account

When the goods are removed after the payment of duty, a personal ledger account (PLA) is required to be maintained by the exporter. The estimated amount of excise duty to be paid by the exporter is deposited to the nationalized bank or treasury. The amount deposited in the bank is shown as credit in the PLA on the basis of the proof of deposit. At the time of the removal of consignment, the amount of duty actually levied is shown as debit entry. An equivalent amount is again re-credited after the proof of export is received. Thus, debit and credit entries are continuously maintained in the PLA. However, in case of exports against bond or legal undertaking (LUT), where the duty is not actually paid, the exporters are not required to maintain a PLA.

ARE-1 (Application for removal of excisable goods-1)

This document is in the form of an application to the jurisdictional central excise superintendent made by the exporter while removal of the goods. It mentions separately (Annexure 17.24 given in the online resource centre) all the details of the consignment, such as the value of the consignment and the amount of duty involved. An exporter has to submit the ARE-1 form 24 hours in advance from the time of removal of the goods, in four copies. Once the goods are handed over to the carrier, the ARE-1 form is endorsed by the customs and it becomes the proof of exports.

ARE-2 (Application for removal of excisable goods-2)

This document is used for the refund of excise duty paid on the finished goods as well as the production inputs used (Annexure 17.25 given in the online resource centre) in the manufacture of final products. Since the refund of central excise duty on the finished products is obtained against the ARE-1 formalities, the ARE-2 is a consolidated application for removal of goods for exports under claim for rebate of duty paid on excisable material used in the manufacture and packaging of such goods and removal of excise dutiable goods for export under rebate claim at the finished stage or under bond without payment of excise duty. However, due to the cumbersome procedure involved, ARE-2 formalities have not gained any popularity among the exporters.

CT-1

This document is used for the procurement of excisable goods without the payment of excise duty for exports. It gives details such as the description of goods, quantity, value, and the excise duty payable on goods to be removed duty-free on the basis of information furnished by the exporter. The CT-1 form (Annexure 17.26 given in the online resource centre) is issued by the designated central excise authority with which the manufacturer exporter or merchant exporter executes the LUT or bond, respectively.

Blacklist Certificate

Countries that have strained political relations or are at war with another country require the blacklist certificate as an evidence of the following:

- The point of origin of goods is not a particular country.
- The parties involved, such as the manufacturer, bank, insurance company, and shipping line, are not blacklisted.
- The ship or aircraft would not call at ports of such a country unless forced to do so.

It is required to be furnished by the exporter only when specifically asked for by the importer for exports to certain countries.

Health/Veterinary/Sanitary Certificate

The importer or the importing county's customs department sometimes requires a certificate for the export of foodstuff, livestock, marine products, hides and skins, etc. from health, veterinary, or sanitary authorities. This is done to ensure that imported cargo is not contaminated by any disease or health hazard.

ELECTRONIC PROCESSING OF EXPORT DOCUMENTS

As discussed in the previous sections, export documentation and processing through various regulatory and commercial agencies has always been highly complex, tedious, time consuming, and adds to the cost of export transaction. The introduction of information technology in the field of international business has facilitated computerized generation and processing of export documents.

For the preparation of documents, a number of software packages are available in the Indian market, such as Visual X-Port, Frontline ExMs, and StarExim, which carry out a number of functions, such as the preparation of pre-shipment or post-shipment documents, generation of MIS reports relating to inquiries, pending inquiries, pending/executed order, pre-shipment, post-shipment, drawback, DEEC, DEPB, and ECGC, and maintaining export–import data.

Exhibit 17.1 Illustrative list of functions carried out by an export documentation software

- Maintains export data right from inquiries received to payment realization.
- Data flows from inquiry to order, from order to pre-shipment, and from pre-shipment to post-shipment; hence, there is no duplication of work.
- Master database for buyers, bankers, custom house agents, and EPCs.
- Databases such as currency, country, unit, and packages are provided for exporters' convenience.
- Products can be categorized or sub-categorized as per requirements and can be stored with all the relevant details such as its price, HS codes, drawback rates, DEPB rates, and export duties.
- Facility is provided for auto number generation for transaction, based on exporter's own format.
- Can generate quotations for the inquiries received.
- Order confirmations and/or pro forma invoices can be generated once the order is confirmed.
- All the pre-shipment documents such as invoice, packing list, CoO, GSP form, shipping instructions, shipping bill, EDI annexure, and GR form can be generated.
- All the post-shipment documents such as invoice, packing list, CoO, GSP form, B/L (generic format), shipment advice,

negotiation letter to bank, bank draft, and bill of exchange can be generated.
- Packing list for pre-shipment and post-shipment can be printed as per exporter's own format.
- Documents can be printed on standard pre-printed stationery or on a plain paper.
- Facility has been provided to edit the documents on screen before printing.
- Keeps a track of exporters' advance licenses and corresponding reports can be generated to check the status of licenses.
- Generates DEPB application and register for a particular port.
- Drawback register can be generated showing amount of drawback claimed, received, and pending.
- Maintains ECGC policy details and gives exporter the register showing details of overall and buyer-wise credit available and used.
- Generates customer-wise, country-wise, product-wise, category-wise inquiry register, order register, pre-shipment register, post-shipment register, and financial register.
- Reports such as pending inquiries and orders can be generated for a particular buyer, country, category, and product.
- Generates monthly, quarterly, and yearly shipment register.

Source: Visual X-Port, Softlink Impex Services Pvt. Ltd, Mumbai.

An illustrative list of functions carried out by an export software program is given in Exhibit 17.1. These documentation software programs provide a single entry point for all shipment data and, therefore, save a lot of effort, time, and cost.

PROCEDURE FOR EXPORT–IMPORT

The execution of an export order involves a complex procedure in which the exporter comes across a number of regulatory authorities and trade agencies. The export procedure involves compliance with the exporting country's legal framework, concluding an export deal, arranging export finance, procuring or manufacturing of goods, appointing C&F agent, arranging cargo insurance, book shipping space, sending documents and goods to C&F agent, customs clearance and port procedures for cargo shipment, submitting documents to bank, and receiving payment from the importer, and export incentives. In order to facilitate the understanding of the readers, the export procedures are summarized in Fig. 17.6

Compliance with Legal Framework

Each country has its own legal framework for export–import transactions, which need to be complied by those entering into international trade. In the process of executing an export order, an exporter needs to interact with the DGFT, customs and central excise authorities, the RBI, banks, port trust authorities, insurance company, shipping or airline, freight forwarders, chamber of commerce, inspection agencies, export promotion council or authority, etc. In India, the exporter has to fulfil all legal requirements in a manner depicted in Fig. 17.7.

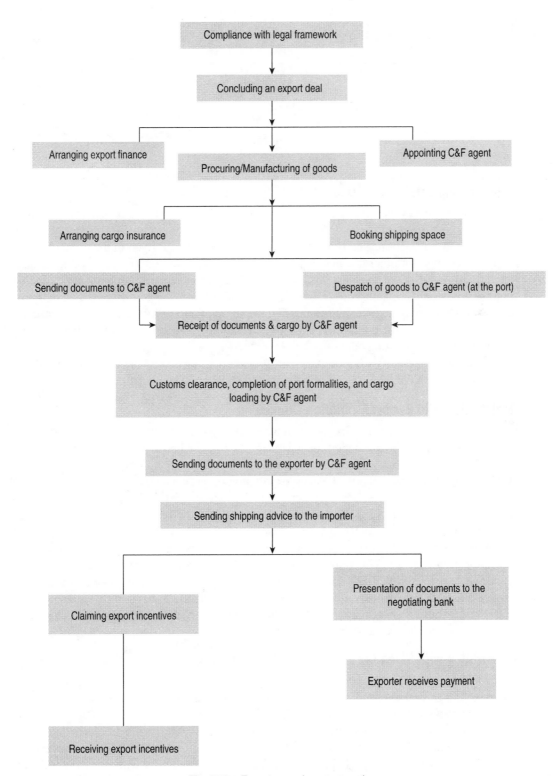

Fig. 17.6   Export procedure: an overview

Fig. 17.7 Compliance with legal framework in India

Obtaining Import–Export Code Number

It is mandatory for every exporter to hold a valid import–export (IE) number for exporting or importing goods from India or into India, without which Indian customs would not permit the export–import transaction. The IE code number (Annexure 17.27 given in the online resource centre) is required for other documents prescribed under the Foreign Trade (Development and Regulation) Act, 1992 or the Customs Act, 1962. The export–import number can be obtained from the Regional Licensing Authority (RLA). This number needs to be mentioned in a number of international trade documents including the shipping bill or bill of entry as the case may be. It is also required for the foreign exchange declaration forms, such as the GR form, to be submitted to the negotiating bank.

In its efforts to simplify the export–import procedures, since 1997 the Government of India has dispensed with the requirement of obtaining the RBI code number from the RBI.

Registration with Export Promotion Council

For obtaining benefits under the export–import policy, an exporter is required to get himself registered with an appropriate export promotion council relating to his main line of exports. The application for registration has to be accompanied by a self-certified copy of the export–import code number issued by the regional licensing authority. Besides, export promotion councils, the registration authorities also include the Marine Export Development Authority (MPEDA), Agricultural and Processing Food Development Authority (APEDA), Commodity Boards such as the Tea Board, Coffee Board, Spices Board, Jute Commission, Khadi and Village Industry Commission, Development Commissioners of free trade zones (FTZs), export processing zones (EPZs), special economic zones (SEZs), and Federation of Indian Export Organization (FIEO). The export houses or trading houses need to get themselves registered with FIEO. Export promotion agencies issue a registration-cum-membership certificate (RCMC), which is valid for five years (Annexure 17.28 given in the online resource centre). The exporters are required to submit the regular export returns (Annexure 17.29 given in the online resource centre) to the registration agency.

Registration with Sales Tax and Central Excise Authorities

Goods that are shipped out of a country are eligible for exemption of states' sales tax, central sales tax, and central excise duties. Therefore, they are required to get themselves registered with the sales tax authority of the state under the Sales Tax Act, 1956.

Both the manufacturers and the merchant exporters have the option to either deposit the central excise duty at the time of taking goods out of the factory and avail of its refund later, or take the goods out by signing a bond with the central excise authority without paying the duty. Once the central excise authorities receive the proof of shipment along with the B/L, shipping bill, and ARE1/ARE2 form, exporters running bond account is credited.

Concluding an Export Deal

While concluding an export deal, an exporter should negotiate the terms of the deal in detail, including the price, the product description, packaging, port of shipment, delivery, and payment terms. The process of concluding an export deal is summarized in Fig. 17.8. It is recommended that the export activity should comply with the written contract rather than relying on verbal agreements to avoid future disputes. However, a substantial amount of exports from India, especially in case of gems and jewellery, garments, handicrafts, handloom, etc., is carried out without written contracts.

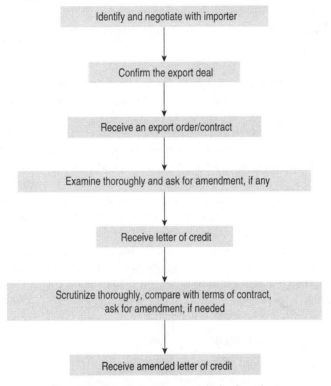

Fig. 17.8   Concluding an export deal: a flow chart

In case there is no written contract, considerable communication between exporter and importer does take place by way of fax, telex, letters, pro forma invoice, L/C, commercial invoice, etc. Under such situations, a 'constructed contract' comes into existence. Thus, under a constructed contract, the existence of the contract can be inferred from relevant documents such as fax, telex, pro forma invoice, L/C, and commercial invoice. However, in such cases, an exporter is required to keep all these documents carefully.

Depending upon the export product and the importing country, the export contracts may differ, but an exporter should take care of the following aspects:

- Details of the contracting party
- Description of products, including quality specifications
- Quantity
- Unit price and the total value of the contract
- Packaging
- Marking and labelling
- Inspection of quality, quantity, and packaging by the inspection agency

- Shipment details such as the choice of carrier, place of delivery, date of shipment/ delivery, port of shipment, and trans-shipment
- Payment terms including currency, credit period, if any, and mode of payment such as the L/C (including type of L/C such as revocable, irrevocable, confirmed, unconfirmed, registered, and unregistered)
- Insurance requirement and risk liabilities
- Documentary requirement for payment realization include the number and type of invoices, certificate of inspection, CoO, insurance policy, transport document, bill of exchange, etc.
- Last date of negotiating documents with bank
- Force *majeure* in case of non-performance of contract
- Arbitration
- Jurisdiction

For the convenience of exporters, the model export contract drafted by the Indian Council of Arbitration is given in Annexure 17.30 given in the online resource centre. Once an exporter receives an export order, she should examine it carefully to ensure that it serves her capability and interest to execute the export deal. The exporter should also scrutinize carefully the commercial and legal provisions of the exporting and importing countries. In case an exporter finds it difficult to fulfil the contractual obligations, such as the quality specifications, delivery schedule, mode of payment, and availability of the inspection agency, she should ask for an amendment from the importer.

Export contracts are concluded between two private firms, and the government does not interfere in such contracts. However, these contracts should abide by the legislative provisions of both exporting and importing countries.

Generally, an exporter prepares a pro forma invoice mentioning the details of the description of goods, number and kind of packaging, marks and container numbers, quantity, rate, amount, etc. as per the contract. The importer returns the signed copy of the pro forma invoice, which becomes part of an export contract. The exporter should also examine the L/C for any discrepancy and ask for amendment, if needed.

Arranging Export Finance

The exporters may avail of packing credit facility from commercial banks in India at concessional rates for manufacturing, purchasing, and packaging of goods. Export credit is extended to the exporters to meet their working capital requirements. The pre-shipment credit is generally provided for the following activities:

- Packing credit or shipping loan in rupee
- Packing credit advance in foreign currencies
- Advances against export incentives
- Import financing for opening L/C for the importing goods needed as input for manufacture of export goods
- Export credit is normally given on collateral security through a third-party guarantee or mortgage of immovable property

The working capital requirement may be at the pre-shipment or post-shipment stage, as depicted in Fig. 17.9.

The procedure followed for disbursement of export credit is as follows:

- The exporter submits an evidence of export like an irrevocable L/C issued by a reputed international bank or confirmed order placed by a foreign buyer.
- The bank calculates the amount of packing credit to be granted, which generally does not exceed FOB value of the goods.

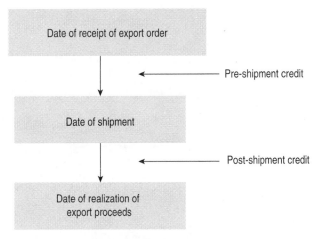

Fig. 17.9 Need for export finance

- Generally, banks fix 10–25 per cent as margin (i.e., exporters' contribution) and release the funds debiting to the packing credit amount and crediting to the exporters' account.
- The exporter would be required to send the goods through approved transport and forwarding agency.
- Besides, exporters are also required to take adequate insurance while warehousing and transport of goods.

The details of export credit are discussed in Chapter 19.

Procuring or Manufacturing of Goods

After receiving a confirmed export order, the exporting firm should make preparation for the procurement or production of goods (Fig. 17.10), as the case may be, for the merchant or manufacturing exporter, respectively. Different companies have different internal communication systems, which generally involve sending a 'delivery note' in duplicate to the factory for the manufacture and dispatch of goods to the given port of shipment. The delivery note should mention in clear terms the description of goods, the quantity, quality specification, packaging and labelling requirement, the date by which the goods should be manufactured, and the details of formalities such as pre-shipment inspection and central excise clearance. Similar activities follow in case of procurement of goods. However, in case of production of goods by the merchant exporter, the subsequent activities differ.

Pre-shipment inspection

At the time of exports, before clearing the shipment, the customs authorities require submission of an inspection certificate in compliance with the Government of India's rules and regulations under force regarding compulsory quality control and pre-shipment inspection. Under the Export Quality Control and Inspection Act, 1963, about 1,000 commodities, under the major group of fisheries, food and agriculture, organic and inorganic chemicals, jute products, light engineering, cost of products, etc. are subject to compulsory pre-shipment inspection. Inspection of export goods may be carried out in the following manner:

- In-process quality control
- Consignment-wise quality control
- Self-certification

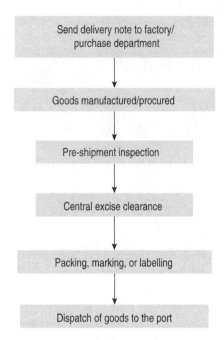

Fig. 17.10 Procuring or manufacturing of goods for exports: flow chart

The pre-shipment inspection should be completed before the consignment is sealed by the excise authorities. The exporter has to apply to the nominated export inspection agency for conducting the pre-shipment and quality-control inspection for the export consignment (Annexure 17.11 given in the online resource centre), and obtain an inspection or quality certificate (Annexure 17.12 given in the online resource centre) conforming to the prescribed specifications. This inspection certificate would be required for customs clearance of cargo before shipment.

Central excise clearance on goods for exports

The exports are free from the incidence of indirect taxes as per internationally accepted practice. Therefore, all goods exported from India are exempt from payment of central excise duties. The Central Excise Act, 1944 also provides rebate on excise duty levied both on inputs used for manufacture of export products and the final export production under the 'Export under Rebate/Exemption' Scheme under Rule 18 of Central Excise (No. 2) Rules, 2001. Soon after manufacturing the goods, for getting the central excise clearance, the exporter has to adopt any one of the following options available.

Option 1: Export of goods under claim for excise duty rebate Under this procedure, the exporter first makes payment on the excise duty, and subsequently gets refund (Rule 18). Complete refund of excise duty paid on raw materials used for exports and excisable finished goods for exports is allowed, except for exports to Nepal and Bhutan. However, in case the exporter has availed the benefits under the Duty Drawback Scheme or the Central Value Added Tax Credit (CENVAT) on excisable inputs, he is not eligible for refund of the excise duty paid.

The exporter has an option to get the goods examined and sealed by central excise authorities at his own premises before removal of goods for exports, so that the goods are not examined at the port/airport by the customs authorities. The exporter prepares six copies of ARE1/ARE2 forms and submits them to the superintendent of central excise having jurisdiction over the premises of the exporter. The superintendent may depute an inspector of central excise, or may in person carry out inspection and ceiling of export cargo. The central excise authorities put their seal on the cargo after its examination, and their satisfaction.

Option II: Export of goods under bond   Exporters are allowed to remove export excisable goods or inputs for export production form the place of manufacture or warehouse without payment of excise duty, under Rule 19 using the following procedure.

Examination of goods at the place of dispatch   The exporter submits four copies of ARE-1 to the jurisdictional central excise authority. However, the exporter has an option to submit fifth copy of ARE-1 for availing any export facility for his record. On the basis of the furnished information, the concerned central excise authority identifies and examines the goods in accordance with rules and regulations laid down in the export–import policy and other related regulations in force. After conforming to these requirements, the goods are allowed to be sealed and an endorsement is made on all the copies of the ARE-1 form that the goods have been examined, sealed, and are permitted for exports.

The original and duplicate copies of the ARE-1 form are given to the exporter, the triplicate is sent to the central excise (bond) authority, and the quadruplicate copy is for the purpose of central excise records. At the time of shipment, the exporter encloses the original and duplicate copy of the ARE-1 form with the shipping bill to the customs at the port of loading. Customs authorities verify the examination report and the seal on the goods, and permits goods for loading on board the carrier. Subsequently, an endorsement is made on the original and duplicate copies of ARE-1 by the customs. The original endorsed copy is handed over to the exporter and the duplicate is sent to the concerned central excise authorities. The exporter submits the original copy endorsed by customs to the concerned central excise authorities as a proof of exports and gets his obligation under the LUT or bond discharged.

Removal of goods under self-certification   An exporter can move the goods from the factory or warehouse under self-certification in the ARE-1 forms. The original and duplicate copies are sent along with the goods while the third and fourth copies are sent to the concerned central excise authorities within 24 hours of removal of goods for verification and records. The endorsement is made by the customs on ARE-1 and export is allowed. The exporter submits the original and duplicate to the customs as a proof of exports, and discharges his obligation under LUT or bond.

Examination of goods at the place of export   This is similar to the procedure discussed in the preceding section, but in this case, the physical examination of goods is carried out by the customs authorities as per the information furnished in the ARE-1 form. Subsequently, goods are allowed to be exported and the exporters' obligation under LUT or bond is discharged.

However, the following conditions need to be observed for central excise clearance:

* The central excise duty leviable on the goods should not exceed the bond amount.
* The goods meant for exports must be exported within a period of six months after clearance. However, the period can be extended by the competent central excise authority in special cases.
* Proof of export of goods is mandatory for getting LUT or bond discharged.

Removal of excisable inputs for export production   The central excise rules provide facility for procurement of excisable goods without payment of excise duty to be used as input in export production. To avail this facility, the manufacturer exporter is required to register under Rule 9 of Central Excise (No. 2) Rule, 2001. The manufacturer exporter has to furnish details of input–output ratio and the rate of excise duty on such excisable goods. After verification and countersigning by the competent central excise authority, the exporter may avail benefit of removing the goods used as inputs for production without payment of duty. The goods are exported under this case using ARE-2 formalities, which are similar to ARE-1.

As a rule, central excise authorities are required to settle all claims within three months from the date of acceptance. For any delay beyond three months, the exporter becomes eligible for getting interest.

Packaging, Marking, and Labelling of Goods

Proper packaging of export cargo facilitates in minimizing transit and delivery costs and losses. Besides, the insurance companies also insist upon adequate packaging for settling the claims. After packaging, marking of the packages is done to ensure easy identification of goods during handling, transportation, and delivery. Labelling contains detailed instructions, and is done by affixing labels on the packs or by stencils. Packaging tips for air cargo are given in Exhibit 17.2.

Exhibit 17.2 Packaging tips for air cargo

Dos

- Choose the size of the package according to its content. Under-filled boxes are likely to collapse; overloaded ones may burst.
- Always use high quality materials for your shipments. Consider strength, cushioning, and durability while selecting your wrapping supplies.
- Choose boxes made of corrugated cardboard with good quality outer liners. Use heavy-duty double-layered board for valuable items.
- Make use of cushioning materials, especially to stop your package contents from moving.
- Use strapping, when suitable, as a good way to seal and secure your box. Use strong tape if a strapping machine is not available.
- Put fragile goods in the centre of a package, ensuring they don't touch the sides. Your item should be well cushioned on all sides.
- Ensure liquids are stored in leak-free containers, packed with a lightweight, strong, internal material (for example, Styrofoam), and sealed with a plastic bag. Always remember that bad packaging may cause damage to surrounding items.
- Seal semi-liquids, greasy, or strong-smelling substances with adhesive tape, then wrap in grease resistant paper. Always remember that bad packaging may cause damage to surrounding items.
- Place powders and fine grains in strong plastic bags, securely sealed and then packed in a rigid fiberboard box.

- Use 'arrow-up' label for non-solid materials.
- Repack your gifts properly. Many goods sold in attractive packaging may not be suitable for shipping.
- Use triangular tubes, not round tube-type cylinders, to pack rolled plans, maps, and blueprints.
- Always remember to pack small items in flyers appropriately.
- Protect your data discs, audio and video-tapes with soft cushioning material around each item.
- Complete the address clearly and completely using uppercase letters when handwriting labels to improve readability.
- When shipping sharp items, such as knives or scissors, ensure that you fully protect the edges and points. Heavy cardboard is suitable for this. Fix the protective material securely so that it is not accidentally removed in transit.
- Always use cardboard dividers when sending flat, fragile materials (such as vinyl records).
- When re-using a box, remove all labels and stickers. Ensure that the box is in good shape and not worn out.

Don'ts

- Do not use bags made of fabric or cloth.
- Do not over seal your package. Remember that all shipments can be opened by customs authorities for inspection.
- Do not use Cellophane tape or rope to seal your shipment.
- Do not consider 'Fragile' and 'Handle with care' labels as a substitute for careful packaging. They are only appropriate for information purposes.

Appointment of Clearing and Forwarding Agents

The clearing and forwarding (C&F) agents or freight forwarders (Fig. 17.10) are essential links in international trade operations. They carry out a number of functions, including the following:

- Advising exporters on choice of shipping routes
- Reservation of shipping space
- Inland transportation at port
- Packing
- Studying provisions of L/C or contract and taking necessary action accordingly
- Warehousing insurance
- Port, shipping, and customs formalities
- Arranging overseas transport service
- Rendering assistance in filing claims
- Monitoring movements of goods to importer
- General advisory services

The export department prepares detailed instructions regarding the shipment of consignment, and sends the following documents to the C&F agent:

- Original export order/export contract
- Original L/C
- Commercial invoice
- GR forms (original and duplicate) indicating the IE code number
- Certificate of origin (CoO)
- Inspection/quality-control certificate
- Purchase memo (in case of merchant exporters)
- Railway/Truck/Lorry receipt
- Consular/Customs invoice (if required)
- ARE-1/ARE-2 forms
- Declaration form (three copies) by the exporter that the value, specifications, quality, and description of goods mentioned in the shipping bill are in accordance with the export contract and the statement made in the shipping bill is true.

Arranging Cargo Insurance

The marine insurance cover is arranged by the export department soon after receiving the documents and obtains insurance policy in duplicate. The liability to take the insurance cover is determined by the conditions mentioned in the export contract. In case of FOB and CFR contracts, the importer has to obtain the insurance cover once the cargo is loaded 'on board' the vessel. While in case of CIF contracts, the insurance is arranged by the exporter but the policy is endorsed in favour of the importer. The nature of risk coverage and insurable value is also specified in the export contract. Other procedural formalities such as arranging ECGC cover, CoO, and consular invoice are finalized at this stage.

Booking Shipping Space

While getting the excise clearance and pre-shipment inspection by the manufacturing office, the export department gets the shipping space reserved in the vessel by sending shipping instructions (Annexure 17.31 given in the online resource centre) through the C&F agent, or through the freight broker who works on behalf of the shipping company. Once the space is reserved, the shipping company issues a shipping order as a proof of space reservation.

Dispatch of Goods to the Port

On getting information on the reservation of shipping space, the production department makes arrangements for transport of goods to the port of shipment by either road or rail. The goods are generally consigned to the port town in the name of the C&F agent. The Indian railway allots wagons on a priority basis for the transportation of export cargo to the port of shipment for which the following documents are submitted:

- Forwarding note (a railway document)
- Shipping order (proof of booking shipping space)
- Receipt of wagon registration fee

After the loading of goods is completed in the allotted wagons, the railway department issues railway receipt (RR). At this stage, the manufacturing officer prepares a 'dispatch advice' and sends it to the export department along with the following documents:

- Railway/Lorry/Truck receipt
- ARE-1/2 form
- Inspection certificate

Port Procedures and Customs Clearance

At the port town, the procedure for customs clearance and other port formalities is relatively complex, which requires not only the knowledge of export procedures, but also the ability to get the shipment speedily with least hassles. Therefore, exporters generally avail of the services of C&F agents. The activities related to port procedures and customs clearance are summarized in Fig. 17.11.

After receiving the documents, the C&F agent takes delivery of the consignment from the road transportation company or the railway station. The cargo is stored in the C&F agent's warehouse till shipment. Soon after receiving the cargo, the C&F agent initiates action to obtain customs clearance and seeks permission of port authorities for bringing the cargo to the shipment shed.

In all countries, the customs department is entrusted with the control of export–import of goods in accordance with the law of the land. The basic objectives of customs control are as follows:

- Ensure that goods exported out of the country or imported in the country comply with various regulations related to export–import.
- Ensure the authenticity of the value of goods in the export–import trade and check under-invoicing or over-invoicing.
- Accurately assess and collect the customs duty, wherever applicable.
- Compile data.

The customs department makes both documentary check and physical examination of goods before clearance. The C&F agent prepares the shipping bill and submits the following documents to the customs house for their clearance:

- Shipping bill (4–5 copies)
- Export order/contract
- L/C (original), where applicable
- Commercial invoice (one each for shipping bill)
- GR form (original and duplicate)
- Inspection certificate (original)
- ARE-1/ARE-2 form (original and duplicate)
- Packing list, if required
- Any other document needed by the customs

These documents are examined by the customs appraiser for the following:

- Compliances to the rules, regulations, and other procedural requirements for exports
- Declaration of value and quantity in the shipping bill vis-à-vis export order or L/C

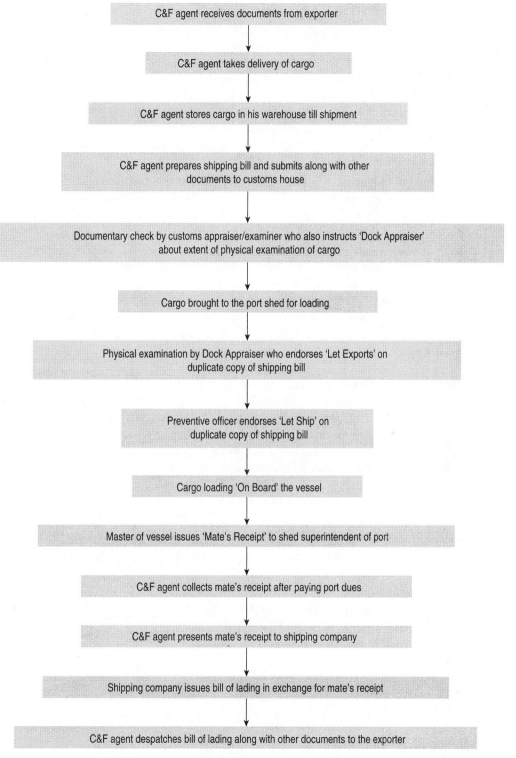

Fig. 17.11 Port procedures and customs clearance: a flow chart

After value appraisal and examination of documents, the customs appraiser/examiner makes an endorsement on the duplicate copy of the shipping bill and gives direction to the dock appraiser to the extent of physical inspection required to be made at the docks. Except for the original shipping bill, original GR form, and a copy of commercial invoice, all documents are returned to the C&F agent.

The C&F agent submits the port trust copy of the shipping bill to the shed superintendent of the port trust and obtains order for carting the cargo in the transit shed for physical examination by the dock appraiser. In case of shed cargo, a separate dock *chalan* is prepared, while in case of ship loading over-side, no separate dock *chalan* is needed, and the dock charges are mentioned in the shipping bill itself. For getting the physical examination done by the dock appraiser, the following documents need to be submitted:

- Shipping bill (duplicate, triplicate, and export promotion copies)
- Commercial invoice
- Packing list
- Inspection certificate (original)
- ARE-1/ARE-2 form
- GR form (duplicate)

After conducting the physical examination, the dock appraiser endorses 'let export' on the duplicate copy of the shipping bill and hands it over to the forwarding agent along with all other documents. The forwarding agent then presents these documents to the preventive officer of the customs department. The officer supervises the cargo loading on the vessel, examines and checks content, weight, etc., and makes an endorsement 'let ship' on the duplicate copy of the shipping bill. It authorizes the shipping company to accept the cargo in the vessel for shipment.

After loading 'on board', the master of the vessel issues 'mate's receipt' to the shed superintendent of the port. The C&F agent takes the 'mate's receipt' after the payment of port charges to the port authorities. The mate's receipt is presented to the preventive officer, who certifies that shipments have taken place and mentions it on all the copies of the shipping bill, original and duplicate copies of ARE-1/ARE-2 form, and all other copies which need post-shipment endorsement from the customs. The mate's receipt is presented to the shipping company, which in turn issues the B/L (two or three negotiable in original and about 10 non-negotiable copies) in its exchange.

The B/L is prepared in strict accordance with the mate's receipt. The exporter has to ensure that the B/L is 'clean on board', since 'claused' or 'dirty' B/L are generally not acceptable to the importer, unless specifically stipulated in the L/C.

Dispatch of Documents to the Exporter

Soon after obtaining the B/L from the shipping company, the C&F agent sends the following documents to the exporter:

- Full set of *clean on board* B/L
- Copies of commercial invoice attested by customs
- Duty drawback copy of shipping bill
- Original export order/export contract
- Original L/C
- Copies of consular invoice/customs invoice, if any
- ARE-1/ARE-2 forms
- GR form (duplicate)

Sending Shipment Advice

Soon after the shipment, the exporter sends a shipment advice (Annexure 17.15 given in the online resource centre) to the importer intimating the importer about the date of shipment, name of the vessel, and its expected time of arrival (ETA) at the port of discharge. The shipment advice is accompanied by the commercial invoice, packing list (if any), and a non-negotiable copy of B/L to enable the importer to take delivery of the shipment.

Presentation of Documents at the Negotiating Bank

Soon after the shipment, an exporter has to present the following documents to the negotiating bank in the format shown in Annexure 17.32 given in the online resource centre:

- Bill of exchange (first and second of original)
- Commercial invoice (two or more copies as required)
- Full set of clean on board B/L (all negotiable and non-negotiable, as required)
- GR Form (duplicate)
- Export order/contract
- L/C (original)
- Packing list
- Marine insurance policy (two copies)
- Consular and/or customs invoice, if required
- Bank certificate (in the prescribed form)

The negotiating banks scrutinize all the documents thoroughly as per the terms of the L/C. The bank sends a set of documents to the issuing (importer's) bank by two consecutive airmails to ensure timely delivery of documents to the importer's bank, and subsequently the importer to enable him to take delivery of the cargo at the destination. The documents that are sent by the negotiating bank to the issuing bank are as follows:

- Bill of exchange
- Commercial invoice
- Negotiable B/L
- Insurance policy
- Customs/Consular invoice, if any
- Packing list, if any
- Inspection/Quality control certificate
- Certificate of origin (CoO)

The payment is made by the negotiating bank on receipt of these documents. Once the payment is received from the importer's bank, the duplicate copy of the GR form is directly transmitted by the negotiating bank to the Exchange Control Department of the RBI. The exporter is returned the original copy of the bank certificate along with the attested copies of the commercial invoice. The authorized dealer forwards the duplicate copy of the bank certificate to the jurisdictional DGFT office.

Claiming Export Incentives

Soon after shipment, the exporter files claims for getting export incentives.

Claiming excise rebate

After shipment, the exporter or his C&F agent files claim with the maritime commissioner of the central excise authority in the port town or jurisdictional central excise authorities for getting refund of the excise duty paid, credit in the personal ledger account (PLA), and discharge of bond liabilities. The duplicate copy ARE-1/ARE-2 certified by the customs authority and a non-negotiable copy of the B/L or shipping bill are the only documents required for the purpose.

Receiving duty drawback

The exporter has to file duty drawback claim with the drawback department of the customs by submitting drawback claim pro forma, bank or customs-certified copy of commercial invoice, and non-negotiable copy of the B/L. After examining the exporter's claim, the duty drawback claim amount is sent to the exporter's bank under his intimation.

ELECTRONIC PROCESSING OF INTERNATIONAL TRADE DOCUMENTS

Traditionally, exporters and importers were required to prepare multiple copies of trade documents on paper, and physically deliver them to various government agencies for processing and clearances, as depicted in Fig. 17.12. Such a system was not only tedious but also involved delays ranging from a few hours to several days, lack of transparency, and widespread unethical corrupt practices among government officials. Besides, enormous paperwork led to additional business costs for both the government and the traders.

Rapid growth of international trade volume tends to reduce considerably the speed of traditional paper-based document processing systems, besides enhancing the chances of error. Such systems are also vulnerable to corruption, besides lack of transparency and unpredictability.

Electronic Trade Documentation System

The manual ways of trade documentation and its processing are being transformed into paperless means by way of introduction of the electronic data interchange (EDI) trade system. Besides, trade procedures are also being streamlined and automated, so that a single form could be used for all trade documentation requirements. An ideal single electronic window system should provide a single point of data entry to achieve a number of completed transactions with the multiple government agencies. The conceptual framework of single electronic window for trade facilitation, as depicted in Fig. 17.13 reveals that the traders, freight forwarders, and brokers may send their documents to a single electronic window, which carries out the sorting of the documents and in turn transmits them electronically to various government agencies, such as customs, port authorities, and certification agencies. However, the extent of implementation of the Electronic Trade Documentation System (ETDS) varies considerably among the countries. The clearances/approvals of various governments are transmitted electronically to a single electronic window, which in turn transmits such approvals/clearances back to the traders, freight forwarders, and brokers.

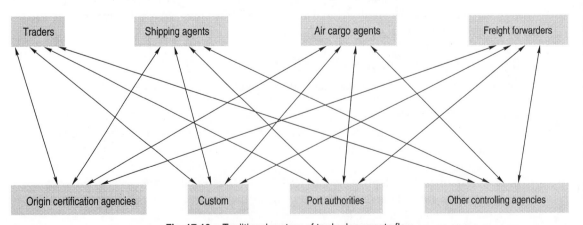

Fig. 17.12 Traditional system of trade documents flow

Source: Joshi, Rakesh Mohan, *International Business*, Oxford University Press, New Delhi, 2009, p. 839.

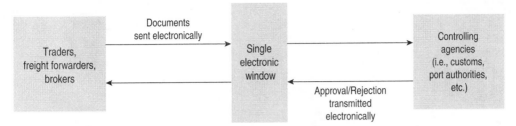

Fig. 17.13 Conceptual framework of single electronic window for trade facilitation

Source: Joshi, Rakesh Mohan, *International Business*, Oxford University Press, New Delhi, 2009, p. 840.

The introduction of electronic processing of export documentation reduces not only the transaction time and cost, but also discretionary approach by the officials concerned. Effective electronic and automated trade documentation systems enhance transaction speed and make regulatory system more transparent and predictable. For instance, traders can apply for necessary regulatory permissions and approvals round the clock and obtain these instantaneously rather than in weeks or days. E-payment systems also allow making online payments of customs duties and settling the trade transactions electronically within seconds. Thus, implementation of an ETDS makes the regulatory process seamless.

Major concerns about the ETDS relate to security aspects and legal framework, and need to be tackled both at national and multilateral levels.

Singapore's Electronic Trade Documentation System

Given its geographical size constraint, the Government of Singapore recognized that the key to providing opportunities for its economy and attaining competitiveness lay in enhancing operational efficiency of all economic activities by way of integrating them with information technology. To this end, it established the Committee on National Computerization (CNC) in 1979. Consequently, under this computerization project, several government agencies were brought under computerization and exemplary systems for electronic trade documentation established.

TradeNet

Since 1989, the TradeNet system has been operational in Singapore. It is an EDI system that allows computer-to-computer exchange of inter-company business documents in an established format between connected members of the Singapore trading community (Fig. 17.14). It links multiple parties involved in international trade transactions, including 35 government institutions, to a single point of transaction for most trade documentation tasks. It is an electronic trade clearance system that allows customs brokers, traders, ports, banks, customs, and other government agencies to exchange structured trade messages and information electronically. It integrates import, export, and trans-shipment documentation processing procedures, resulting in a reduction in cost and turnaround time for the preparation, submission, and processing of trade and shipping documents. The benefits of the TradeNet system are summarized in Exhibit 17.3.

TradeXchange

TradeXchange is the world's first nationwide electronic trade documentation system that offers a single point of data entry to achieve a number of completed transactions with the government. It is a multi-agency initiative launched in October 2007 that processes 100 per cent of all trade declarations and integrates the requirements of all 35 controlling units in Singapore.

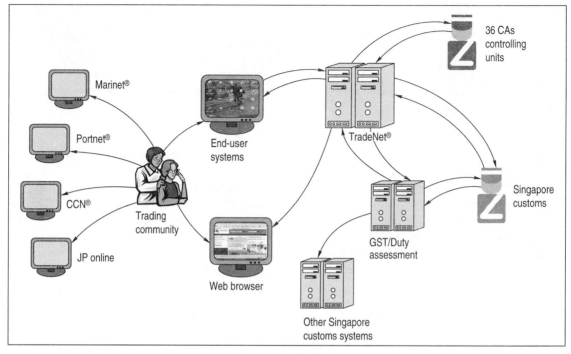

Fig. 17.14   Singapore's TradeNet system

Exhibit 17.3   Benefits of the TradeNet system

Characteristics	Previous manual process	TradeNet
Submission of document	Via expensive dispatch clerks/couriers	Electronically from comforts of office (or home)
Time of submission	Within office hours	Available 24 hours
Trips per controlling agency per document	At least two trips or more	No trips required
Copies of document	Multiple copies	Single copy
Turnaround time for approval	From 4 hours to 2–7 days	Within two minutes (general goods handling)
Dutiable goods handling	Separate documents sent to different controlling agencies for processing	Same electronic document routed to controlling agencies for processing
Customs duties collection	By cheque	Automatic bank account deduction

Source: Based on information from CrimsonLogic, Singapore, accessed on 22 March 2013.

In addition to TradeNet, which connects users to government agencies, TradeXchange also provides seamless inter-connectivity among commercial and regulatory systems for the Singapore trade and logistics community. Moreover, it offers a single electronic window for integrated workflow, submission, and enquiries to seaports, airports, maritime authorities, customs, and controlling agencies. It also provides connectivity to commercial and regulatory systems in other

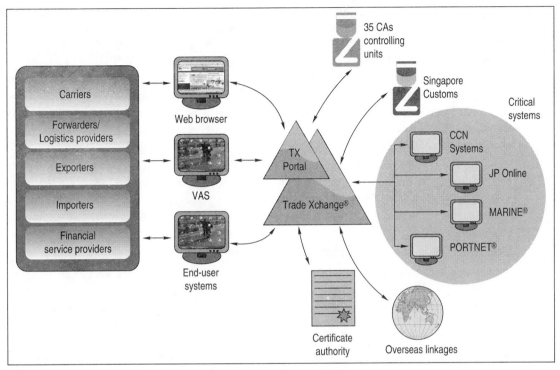

Fig. 17.15   Singapore's TradeXchange

countries. Besides, a number of value-added service providers also offer application services to the trade and logistics community in areas, such as trade document preparation, supply chain management, logistics and freight management, trade finance, and insurance.

The earlier TradeNet facilitated business only to government transactions and users had to access disparate, stand-alone systems to perform trade transaction as shown in Fig. 17.15. The TradeXchange system offers a neutral and secure IT platform that enables information exchange between commercial entities and government through a comprehensive suite of trade services summarized as follows.

Shipping line linkages   The shipping line linkages facilitate sending and receiving relevant messages to and from shipping lines. Messages include vessel schedule, cargo booking, draft bills of lading, and track and trace status (for example, loaded on vessel, carrier release, and container out gate).

Overseas highway customs   They enable sending data for customs clearance via the Pan Asia e-commerce Alliance (PAA) network to Malaysia, Taiwan, Korea, Macau, Shanghai, Hong Kong, Philippines, and Thailand, besides direct customs clearance connection to Australia, Canada, etc.

Title registry   End users and providers of value-added services can leverage on electronic title registry to facilitate secured registration and transfer of title of the goods, and to allow secured access to the title record as needed in the entire export–import process.

Overseas highway manifest   Global linkages facilitate sending advanced manifest data electronically to other countries, such as the USA (Automated Manifest System, AMS), Canada (Advance Commercial Information, ACI), and Australia (Integrated Cargo System, ICS).

Integrated multimodal solution (IMS)   Integrated Multi-modal Solution (IMS) interface with Cargo Community Network (CCN) and Port Net provides sea/air schedule and tracking modules to critical system services.

TradeXchange was developed as a public–private partnership project (PPP) with CrimsonLogic Pte Ltd, which is also responsible for its operations and maintenance. Exporters and importers can deposit, extract, and transmit information to trade exchange through value-added service solutions. TradeXchange has greatly facilitated Singapore's trade processes in a number of ways including the following:

- Providing single interface for users
- Improving trade documentation process by way of business process re-engineering
- Simplifying permit declaration requirement
- Reducing errors from repeated data entry
- Enhancing economic competitiveness by positioning Singapore as a global trading hub

Electronic Trade Documentation System in India

India's Ministry of Commerce launched a coordinated EC/EDI implementation project involving a number of government agencies, such as customs and central excise, DGFT, Apparel Export Promotion Council (AEPC), Cotton and Textile Export Promotion Council (TEXPROCIL), Port Trusts, Airport Authority of India (AAI), Container Corporation of India (CONCOR), RBI, scheduled banks, airlines, Indian Railways, and customs house agents (CHA)/freight forwarders. Presently, all 33 DGFT offices have been computerized and networked through high-speed VSATs/leased lines. The DGFT website contains web-based e-commerce modules for all export promotion schemes, so that exporters could submit online imports/exports applications. The launch of digital signature and electronic fund transfer systems in the offices of DGFT in January 2004 enabled exporters to submit online export/import applications. The Ministry of Commerce has also made arrangements with a few banks such as ICICI, HDFC, and State Bank of India for providing electronic fund transfer facility for depositing the import–export license fee. Besides, the DGFT has also reduced the licensing fee considerably for online digitally signed applications with electronic fund transfer.

For electronic filing and processing of documents, the Indian Customs and Central Excise Electronic Commerce/electronic data interchange (EC/EDI) gateway has been created, popularly known as ICEGATE. The ICEGATE runs on a software program that offers a variety of technological options with regard to communication and messaging standards. The software also ensures efficient management of all incoming and outgoing messages/documents. It offers the facility of filing shipping bills, bill of entry and related electronic messages between the customs, port authority, and traders through communication facilities like the communication protocols commonly used on the Internet. This facility ensures smooth flow of data between customs authorities and various regulatory agencies.

All electronic documents/messages handled by the ICEGATE are processed at the customs' end by the Indian Customs EDI System (ICES), which is running in 23 customs locations, handling nearly 75 per cent of India's international trade in terms of import and export consignment. The electronic processing of documents by ICES has three systems components, which are as follows.

Indian Customs EDI System (ICES)   ICES has to automatically receive and process all incoming messages at all its 23 operational locations. It generates all outgoing messages automatically at the appropriate stage of the clearance process.

Message exchange servers (MES) These are computers installed in the custom houses alongside the ICES computers, and act as intermediate stations, which hold incoming and outgoing messages.

Indian Customs and Central Excise Gateway, and Indian Customs and Central Excise Network (ICEGATE and ICENET) ICENET is a network of all ICES at 23 locations, Central Board of Excise and Customs (CBEC), Directorate of Valuation, National Informatics Centre (NIC), and DGRI (Directorate General of Revenue Intelligence).

The entire network of the three systems (ICES, ICEGATE/ICENET) and MES have been divided into five service areas as depicted in Fig. 17.16.

The ICES performs the following functions:

- Internal automation of the custom house for a comprehensive, paperless, fully automated customs clearance system
- Online, real-time electronic interface with the trade, transport, and regulatory agencies concerned with customs clearance of import and export cargo

The exporter may use any of the following options for submitting data (shipping bill/bill of entry) to the custom house:

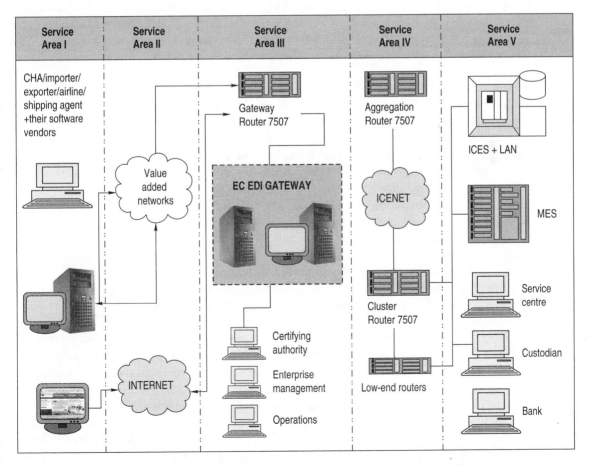

Fig. 17.16 Framework for electronic processing of trade documents in India

Using SMTP (Simple Mail Transfer Protocol) Option

While filing on SMTP, the security aspects are taken care of by using digital signature certificate. The following steps have to be taken:

- Create the appropriate electronic message (bill of entry/shipping bill) by using the remote EDI system (RES) or local application to generate the electronic message.
- Install SMTP Client by using Netscape Messenger, which is the default SMTP client used by the CHA/importer/exporter for sending and receiving emails on ICEGATE.
- Configure the SMTP client.
- Receive electronic messages on ICEGATE.

The importer/exporter/CHA receives emails from ICEGATE on an email address established at the time of membership registration. Upon receipt of the documents submitted by the importer/exporter/CHA at ICEGATE, an immediate email confirmation message is sent to importer/exporter/CHA stating receipt of the file (bill of entry/shipping bill) at ICEGATE. If it is a batch processing where more than one file (bill of entry/shipping bill) is submitted, then the batch key is also displayed in the same email. The message received is as follows:

- Your message has been successfully received by server at ICEGATE.
- You should receive a confirmation message from ICES shortly.

The shipping bill/bill of entry is submitted to the ICES at the customs house. The validation of the messages would be carried out by the ICES server, after which ICES will send a message confirming the file has been processed. This message is the acknowledgement message of ICES, and is the proof that the document has actually been submitted to ICES.

Using the File Upload Option

It can be used by creating the appropriate electronic message (bill of entry/shipping bill), using the RES or his local application to generate the electronic message.

The ICES is designed to exchange/transact customs clearance electronically using EDI. A large number of documents that trade, transport, and regulatory agencies (collectively called trading partners) are required to submit/receive in the process of physical customs clearance are now being processed online.

The nature of information exchanged through EDI and the number of messages needed for trading partners for an export transaction are summarized in Exhibit 17.4.

In view of widespread computerization, more and more exporters and freight forwarders are making use of software for document preparation. It is reported that a large number of exporters are using the online facility for submitting IE code number applications to DGFT.

The introduction of electronic processing of export documentation not only reduces the transaction time and cost but also impart much needed transparency and reduce discretionary approach by the officials concerned. The export managers in future would experience significant changes in the way the export documentation and its processing are carried out.

Efforts have been made around the world to deal with the legal and security aspects of processing export documents electronically, including recognition of digital signature and amendments in the laws related to evidence. However, the basic purpose and spirit of these documents remain more or less unchanged. Therefore, an international marketing manager needs to have a thorough understanding of the nitty-gritty of each of these documents and its procedural implications.

This chapter brings out the significance of procedure and documentation involved in international trade transaction in view of the different regulatory frameworks of the buyer and the seller. In order to assure the exporter about the receipt of payment and to the importer of the

Exhibit 17.4   Summary of customs EDI trading partners

S. No.	EDI trading partner	Nature of information exchanged through EDI	No. of messages (approx.)
1.	Importers/Exporters/ Customs house agent	Bills of entry/Shipping bills and related messages	13
2.	Airlines/Shipping agents	Manifests and cargo logistics messages	26
3.	Air custodians	Cargo logistics messages	AAI-17
4.	Sea custodians	Cargo logistics messages	Port-30
5.	ICDs	Cargo logistics messages	CONCOR-12
6.	Banks	Financial messages—duty drawback disbursal and customs duty payment	30
7.	Directorate General of Foreign Trade	License, shipping bills, and IE code data	13
8.	The Reserve Bank of India	Forex remittance data	1
9.	DGCI&S	Trade statistics	2
10.	Directorate of Valuation	Valuation data	2

Source: Department of Customs, Ministry of Finance, Government of India.

transfer of the title of the goods, banking channels are commonly involved in international trade transactions for routing the payments and documents as well.

Significance of export documentation in view of much greater risk and number of intermediate trade and regulatory entities involved is also discussed. The detailed procedure for international trade transaction is also explained in a simplistic way with the help of flow charts so as to facilitate readers' understanding about the complex process.

Summary

The export procedures and documentation is a crucial activity of international marketing. Although the time required and the cost incurred in an international trade transaction vary among countries, this chapter provides a broad outline of international trade procedures and documentation involved. In an international trade transaction, the exporter and importer situated in different countries are governed by distinct regulatory frameworks of their own countries. The payment in an export transaction is generally routed through banking channels to assure the exporter about the receipt of payment, whereas the importer is assured of the transfer of the title of the goods.

The aligned documentation system (ADS) is a methodology of creating information on a set of standard forms printed on a paper of the same size in such a way that items of identical specification occupy the same position on each form. Commercial documents are those documents which by customs of trade are required to be prepared and used by the exporters and importers in discharge of their respective legal and other incidental responsibilities under the sales contract. Commercial documents include commercial invoice, packing list, transport document, such as ocean B/L, airways bill, combined transport documents (CTD), CoO, inspection certificate, insurance policy certificate, mate's receipt, bill of exchange (draft), and shipment advice. The documents required to fulfil the statutory requirements of both exporting and importing countries, such as export–import trade control, foreign exchange regulation, pre-shipment inspection, central excise, and customs requirements, are known as regulatory documents. These documents include the exchange control declaration form, shipping bill, bill of export, bill of entry, documents for central excise clearance, such as personal ledger account (PLA), ARE 1, ARE 2, CT 1, and black list certificate.

The execution of an export transaction is a complex procedure and involves interaction with a number of regulatory and trade agencies. It involves compliance with legal framework, such as obtaining IE code number, registration with export promotion councils, registration with sales tax and central excise authorities, concluding an export deal, arranging export finance, procuring or manufacturing of goods, pre-shipment inspection, central excise clearance, packaging, marking and labelling, booking shipping space, appointment of C&F agent, dispatch of goods to the port, arranging cargo insurance, port procedures and customs clearance, sending shipment advice, presentation of documents at the negotiating banks, and claiming export incentives.

The introduction of information technology has facilitated computerized generation and processing of export documents.

For the preparation of documents, a number of software packages are available in the market. Indian customs and central excise has created an electronic commerce/electronic data interchange (EC/EDI) gateway popularly known as ICEGATE for electronic filing and processing of documents. The emergence of electronic processing of export documentation is likely to reduce transaction time and cost besides imparting much need transparency and reduction of discretionary approach of the officials concerned.

Key Terms

Affreightment   A contract for the carriage of goods by sea for shipment expressed in charter party or bills of lading.

Airway bill   It also known as air consignment note issued by the carrier as an evidence of contract of carriage.

Aligned documentation system (ADS)   A methodology of creating information on a set of standard forms printed on a paper of same size in such a way that the items of identical specification occupy the same position on each form.

Bill of entry   A document needed for customs clearance of imported cargo.

Bill of exchange   An unconditional order in writing prepared and signed by the exporter, addressed to the importer requiring the importer to pay a certain sum of money to the exporter or his nominee.

Bill of lading   A transport document issued by the shipping company to the shipper for accepting the goods for carriage.

Clean bill of lading   A bill of lading that does not have superimposed claused expressly declaring a defective condition of packaging or goods.

Clearing and forwarding (C&F) agent   An essential link in international trade operations who carries out a number of functions, including cargo handling, documentation, and customs clearance for shipment.

Combined/multimodal transport document (CTD/MTD)   Used in place of bills of lading in case of multi-modal transportation of cargo.

Commercial documents   Those documents which by customs of trade are required to be prepared and used by exporters and importer in discharge of their respective legal and other incidental responsibilities under the sales contract.

Consignor   The party sending the consignment, that is, the shipper.

Consignee   The party to whom goods are to be delivered.

Consul   Commercial representative of a country residing officially in a foreign country who is primarily responsible for facilitating commercial transactions.

Counsular invoice   An invoice verified by the counsel of the importing country.

Customs invoice   An invoice to be prepared in the prescribed format provided by the importing country.

Dirty (claused) bill of lading   A bill of lading stating damage of cargo or its packaging.

Drawee   The party to whom a draft is addressed and who is expected to honour it.

Drawer   The party who issues a draft. Generally the beneficiary of the credit.

Drawing   The presentation of documents under a credit.

Endorsement   Signing of a document, (i.e., draft, insurance document, or bills of lading) usually on the reverse to transfer title to another party. Generally, the documents are endorsed in blank so as to permit in future the holder to gain title.

Generalized system of preferences (GSP)   A non-contractual instrument by which developed countries unilateral and on the basis of non-reciprocity extend tariff concessions to developing countries.

Globalized system of trade preference (GSTP)   A preferential tariff system in which the member developing countries exchange tariff concessions among themselves.

Import–Export (IE) code number   Number issued by regional licensing authority needed for completing export documentation.

Indemnity   Compensation for loss/damage or injury.

Legalised invoice   A variant of commercial invoice, certified by the local chamber of commerce of the exporting country so as to confirm the accuracy of furnished information.

Mate's receipt   A cargo receipt issued by the master of the vessel for every shipment taken on board.

Port of discharge   Seaport/airport at which the exported goods are to be unloaded.

Port of loading Seaport/airport at which the goods are loaded.

Shipping bill/bill of export The principal document required by customs authority mentioning details of shipment for exports.

Stale bills of lading In banking practices, bills of lading are presented after the cargo has arrived at the port of discharge.

Transport documents All the documents that evidence shipment of goods, such as Bills of Lading, combined transport document, waybill, and consignment note.

Waybill A receipt of goods and evidence of the contract of carriage but not a document of title.

Concept Review Questions

1. 'Documentation is a crucial activity of an export transaction.' Critically examine the statement and discuss the consequences of incomplete or faulty documentation.
2. As a newly appointed export manager, you have received an export order for export of basmati rice to Saudi Arabia. Write down the steps you will take for executing the export order.
3. What is a GSP CoO? Identify the agencies that issue such certificates in India.
4. Explain the significance of marine B/L. Identify its unique features, which make it different from an airway bill.
5. Electronic preparation and processing of documents is an emerging area in developing countries. Explaining the concept of electronic processing of documents, discuss its benefits and limitations.
6. Distinguish between the following:
   (a) Legalized invoice and consular invoice
   (b) Dirty and stale B/L
   (c) Preferential and non-preferential CoO
   (d) Shipping bill and bill of entry
7. Write short notes on the following:
   (a) Consequences of poor documentation for export transaction
   (b) Aligned documentation system (ADS)
   (c) Types of commercial invoices
   (d) Bill of lading (B/L)

Practice Exercises

1. Explore the Internet and prepare a list of documents required for exports from the USA, China, India, and Russia. Critically evaluate the similarity and differences in export documentation needed.
2. Take a printout of marine bills of lading, airway bill, and combined transport document (CTD) from the online resource centre, and identify the differences between the above three transport documents. Critically evaluate legal implications for each.
3. Prepare a packing list for the following consignment.
   Invoice No. 53478 dated 17 February 2013
   Consignment consisting of hand-woven carpets in three sizes. The carpets are patterned and each carpet is in three colours: red, green, and yellow.
   (a) 2.0 m × 1.0 m, net weight 10.12 kg each
   (b) 2.3 m × 12 m, net weight 13.25 kg each
   (c) 3.0 m × 1.5 m, net weight 21.37 kg each
   They are packed in wooden packing cases as follows:
   (a) 16 carpets in each case

External measurement: 105 cm × 105 cm × 125 cm
Gross weight: 152 kg
   (b) 10 carpets in each case
External measurement: 125 cm × 85 cm × 125 cm
Gross weight: 132 kg
   (c) 10 carpets in each case
External measurement 155 cm × 105 cm × 125 cm
Gross weight: 212 kg
The cases are numbered from 1 up and each case is marked with the following.
   Chandrika International,
   12, Adan Bagh,
   Agra–282004, India
The consignment is made up of equal quantities of the three colours in the following total quantities:
   (a) 64 carpets
   (b) 40 carpets
   (c) 40 carpets

Project Assignments

1. Visit an exporter in your vicinity and carry out the following activities.
   (a) Make a list of documents prepared by the exporter.
   (b) Prepare a flow chart of the procedure followed by the exporter in executing an export order.

Review the field information collected by you in view of what you have already learnt in the present chapter, and discuss the same in the class.

2. Make a visit to the nearest seaport/airport or inland container depot (ICD), and contact the local customs officials. Find out

the common discrepancies in export documentation which lead to delayed shipment. Prepare a list of common errors. These may be discussed in groups in the class.

3. Meet the local customs authority in your vicinity at any of the two customs check points: seaport, air cargo complex, or land customs stations. Find out the customs documents used for exports and imports, and identify the similarities

and differences in customs documents for different modes of transport.

4. Contact an exporter in your city and find out the extent of computerization being used for preparing and processing of documents. Find out his experiences regarding any problem faced by him due to switching over to the computerized system. Discuss these problems in the class, and evolve remedial measures.

CASE STUDY: EXAMINING A LETTER OF CREDIT

As an export manager at Taj Mahal International, you have received the following letter of credit:

Letter of Credit

From	: Standard Chartered Bank Hong Kong Main Office, Hong Kong
To	: State Bank of Bikaner and Jaipur Head Office, P. O. Box 154, Tilak Marg, Jaipur 302 003, India
Date	: 030228
Form of Documentary Credit	: Irrevocable
Documentary Credit Number	: 253010449748-A
Date and place of expiry	: 030324, India
Applicant	: Cargil Hong Kong Limited, 36/F, One Pacific Place, 68 Queensway, Central Hong Kong
Beneficiary	: Taj Mahal International, 452, Barkat Nagar, Jaipur (India)
Percentage Credit Amount Tolerance	: 02/02
Available With...by	: Any Bank By Negotiation
Draft at	: Sight in Duplicate
Drawee	: Cargil Hong Kong Limited, 36/F, One Pacific Place, 68 Queensway, Central Hong Kong

Partial shipment	: Permitted
Trans-shipment	: Permitted
Loading on board/ Dispatch/Taking in charge at/from	: Bedibunder, India
For Transportation to	: Asian Port(S)
Latest date of shipment	: 170714
Description of goods and/or services:	
Cargo description	: Indian toasted yellow soya bean extraction in bulk
Specifications	:
Protein (Albuminoids)	: 48.0 PCT MIN Up to 46 PCT with rebates, Rejectable below 46 PCT 48 PCT–47 PCT 1:1 or fraction basis 47 PCT–46 PCT 1:2 or fraction basis
Fat	: 1.5 PCT MAX
Sand/Silica	: 2.0 PCT MAX UP TO 2.5 PCT Acceptable 2.0 PCT to 2.5 PCT 1:1 or fraction basis
Fibre	: 6.0 PCT MAX Rejectable : above 6.0 PCT at Buyer's Option
Moisture	: 12.0 PCT Max Rejectable: above 12 PCT at Buyer's Option
Urease activity	: 0.30 MG N2/GM maximum at 30 degree Celsius,

Acceptable by buyer up to 0.35;
Rebate 0.3 to 0.35 on 0.1 PCT for each 0.1 unit

Quantity : 1,000 Metric Tons

Unit Price : US$200.50 per Metric Ton FAS Bedibunder in Bulk

Documents Required

(a) Signed commercial invoice in three copies containing the number of this credit and contract number.

(b) Full set of 3/3 Original Clean 'On Board Shipped' bills of lading made out to order blank endorsed marked 'Freight payable at destination', and notify Cargill Hong Kong Ltd, 36/F, One Pacific Place, 68, Queensway, Central Hong Kong.

(c) Certificate of weight issued by SGS or Geo Chem. Surveyor at the port of loading in one original and two copies.

(d) Certificate of quality issued by SGS or Geo Chem. Surveyor at the port of loading in one original and two copies.

(e) Fumigation and Disinfestation Certificate issued by Pest Mortem (India) Ltd. at the port of loading in one original and two copies.

(f) Phytosanitary certificate issued by plant protection service of Government of India at port of loading in one original and two copies.

(g) Beneficiary's certified telex to applicant within eight working days from B/L date advising B/L Number, B/L date, vessel name, commodity, and total net shipped weight and contact number.

(h) Beneficiary's certificate that full set of non-negotiable shipping documents have been sent to applicant within eight working days after shipment. The relative courier receipt to accompany above documents.

(i) Both original fumigation and disinfestations certificate must be handed over to Arian Maritime and Logistics Ltd, Bombay, India and an acknowledgement receipt of the same to be attached for presentation.

Additional Conditions

Each set of documents presented with discrepancies under this L/C will be subject to a US$30.00 discrepancy charge and should be deducted from your drawing on the reimbursing/paying bank. In addition, telex expenses, if any, incurred by us as a result of discrepancies will also be for beneficiary's account.

(i) Insurance to be arranged by the ultimate buyer.

(ii) Third-party documents except invoice and drafts acceptable.

(iii) Charter party B/L acceptable.

(iv) Consignee in all certificates must be left in blank or made out 'To Whom it May Concern'.

(v) All documents except invoice, draft, and discrepancy telex must not show this credit number or contract number or any reference number.

(vi) Any marks or distinguishing marks and the number of bags must not be indicated in the documents.

(vii) Delivery term and contract number must not be indicated in all documents except invoice.

(viii) Bill of lading must be issued by a named carrier or his agent. In the latter case, the words 'as agents' must be shown with the signatory and officially stamped by the issuing party.

This L/C is as per contract number CI/101/13-14, and is only for your reference.

Two per cent more or less in credit amount and quantity acceptable.

Full address of beneficiary	:	Taj Mahal International, 452, Barkat Nagar, Jaipur (India)
Charges	:	All bank charges outside Hong Kong and our reimbursement charge of US$25 for each drawing (or equivalent therefore) and our telex charges are for the account of beneficiary.
Period of presentation	:	Documents to be presented within 15 days after the date of issuance of the transport document(s) but within the validity of the credit.
Confirmation instructions	:	Without
Reimbursement bank	:	Standard Chartered Bank 14/F, Standard Charted Building, 4-4 A Des Voeux Road Central, Hong Kong

Instructions to the negotiating bank

- Documents to be dispatched to Standard Chartered Bank; 14/F, Standard Charted Building; 4-4 A Des Voeux Road Central, Hong Kong in one lot by DHL courier services.
- We shall remit the payment upon receipt of documents complying with the credit terms.
- This credit is subject to ICC 600.
- This mail is the operative instruction, and no mail confirmation will follow.

Questions

Carefully examine the above L/C and carry out the following:

(i) List out the salient features of the L/C that have to be observed while executing the export order.

(ii) Make necessary assumptions and prepare a complete set of commercial and regulatory documents for the shipment.

Trade Logistics and International Shipping

INTRODUCTION

In order to offer value to its customers, a firm needs to manage its logistics, operations, marketing, and services functions in an integrated manner. The efficiency and effectiveness of a firm to procure raw materials and inputs in order to make its finished products available to the ultimate customers in the most cost-effective and efficient manner is crucial to a firm's competitive advantage in international markets.

Effective and efficient management of the logistics system is crucial for achieving competitiveness in international markets. As the pricing decisions are dependent on the cost of logistics and the sales contracts go hand in hand with shipping contracts, managers wanting to operate in international markets need to develop a thorough understanding of international logistics. The integrated system comprising inbound and outbound logistics is nowadays referred to as supply chain management. If the unit value of the product is low, the cost of transportation of inputs and final product has proportionately greater impact on the final cost of the product.

Managing logistics in international markets is much more complex due to physical distance, differences in logistics systems and their compatibility, different legal systems, and numerous intermediaries involved. However, the principal objective of any logistics system remains that the goods reach the final customers in the following manner:

- In correct quantity
- At desired location
- At right time
- In usable condition
- In the most cost-efficient manner

All these logistics objectives are interrelated and may be achieved by a firm's integrated logistics management strategy. Efficient management of international supply chain in an integrated manner has

Learning Objectives

- To explain the concept of international trade logistics
- To learn how to manage logistics and cargo shipping
- To discuss key concepts and issues of maritime transportation in international trade
- To elaborate containerization and multi-modal transportation
- To discuss institutional framework for maritime transport in India

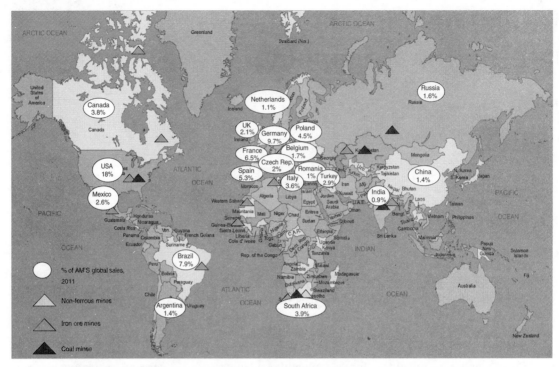

Fig. 18.1 Worldwide integrated logistics system of ArcelorMittal, world's largest steel producer

Source: 'Core Strengths, Sustainable Returns', *ArcelorMittal, Annual Report*, 2011, published in April 2012.

been instrumental in the success of the world's largest mining and steel company, ArcelorMittal, which operates in over 60 countries and produces 91.9 million tonnes of steel annually with the revenue of US$94 billion, as depicted in Fig. 18.1. Proximity to inputs and markets and efficiency in integrated logistics worldwide are critical to ArcelorMittal's success.

This chapter elucidates the concept of logistics management and elaborates the main constituents of a typical logistics system include warehousing, transportation, inventory, packaging and unitization, and information and communication. Transportation, an important part of international logistics comprising various modes such as air, road, rail, and ocean, has been dealt in separately. Moreover, as shipping is not only the oldest and the most effective, but also the most widely used form of transport employed in international trade. This has been discussed separately later in the chapter.

CONCEPT OF INTERNATIONAL LOGISTICS

The word 'logistics' is derived from a French word *loger* that means the art of transport, supply, and quartering of troops. Thus, logistics was conceptually designed for use in military so as to ensure meticulous planning and implementation of supply of weapons, food, medicines, and troops in the battlefield. However, logistics has presently become an integral part of business.

Conceptualization, design, and implementation of a system for direct flow of goods and services across national borders is termed as 'international logistics'. Thus, logistics consists of planning and implementing the strategy for procuring inputs for the production process to make goods and services available to the end customers. As depicted in Fig. 18.2, logistics has two distinct components, namely materials management and physical distribution.

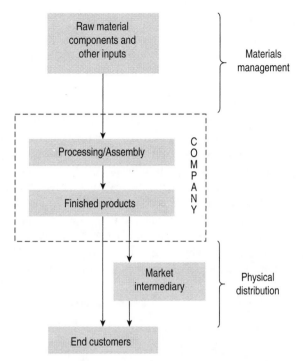

Fig. 18.2 Concept of international logistics

Materials management

It involves procurement of inputs such as raw materials and components for processing or value addition by the firm. This is also known as inbound logistics. Procurement of inputs is no longer limited to national boundaries or neighbouring countries for international companies. Instead, globally integrated sourcing of inputs, through most cost-effective and efficient sources, known as global sourcing has become crucial for achieving global business competitiveness.

Global sourcing As the firm expands its business operations internationally, market forces compel a firm to evolve ways to reduce costs and improve quality to remain competitive. Instead of manufacturing a product or delivering a service itself, the international company often resorts to outsourcing and procures its inputs from the most cost effective diverse sources across the globe. Global sourcing refers to procurement of inputs for production of goods and delivery of services globally from the most optimal sources. The major reasons for global outsourcing include the following:

- Price differentials leading to lower prices from foreign sources
- Need for foreign products not available domestically
- Global strategy and operations of the company
- Need for technology- and R&D-intensive foreign products
- Requirement for superior quality overseas products

A firm may use a number of global sourcing arrangements, as already discussed in Chapter 9, such as imports from a foreign manufacturer, overseas contract manufacturing, international joint venture, and wholly owned subsidiaries.

Physical distribution

It involves all the activities such as transportation, warehousing, and inventory carried out to make the product available to the end customers. This is also known as outbound logistics. Physical distribution has already been discussed in detail in Chapter 13.

Logistics and the Value Chain Concept

The objective of any business firm is to create value by way of performing a set of activities such as to conceptualize, design, manufacture, market, and service its market offerings. This set of inter-related activities is termed as value chain. To gain competitive advantage over its rivals, a firm must provide comparable buyer value by performing activities more efficiently than its competitors (lower cost) or by performing activities in a unique way that creates greater buyer value and commands a premium price (differentiation) or accomplishes both. Figure 18.3 gives the basic framework of Michael Porter's concept of value chain to carry out these interrelated activities. The primary activities include inbound logistics, operations (manufacturing), outbound logistics, marketing and sales, and after-sales services, whereas the support activities include firm's infrastructure (finance, planning, etc.), human resource management, technology development, and procurement.

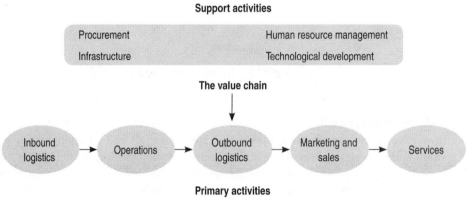

Fig. 18.3   Logistics and the value chain

The model suggests that there are two primary activities related to logistics: procurement of inputs, components, raw materials, parts and related services, (inbound logistics) and transfer of finished products to the end consumers. Therefore, the competitive advantage of a firm is dependent upon its ability to organize and perform discrete activities. Firms create value for their buyers by performing these activities in a competitive manner. The ultimate value created by a firm is measured by the amount buyers are willing to pay for its products and services. If the value of performing the required activities exceeds the collective costs, the firm becomes profitable. Thus, achieving competitive advantage in logistics becomes crucial to the success of a business firm.

Managing logistics is also crucial to a firm's competitive advantage, as explained in Fig. 18.3, and it is hardly feasible to create efficient and effective marketing channels without a thorough understanding of international logistics.

Logistics Performance Index

The ability of firms to move goods across borders rapidly, reliably, and at lower costs is crucial to success in integrating global supply chains. The Logistics Performance Index (LPI) developed by the World Bank is a benchmarking tool to measure performance along the logistics supply chain among countries.[1]

The LPI developed by the World Bank serves as a useful tool to enable international managers to carry out an empirical assessment of logistics gaps and constraints and allow comparisons across 150 countries. The index comprises several areas of supply chain performance elaborated, such as customs procedures, logistics costs, quality of infrastructure, the ability to track and trace shipments, timeliness in reaching destination, and the competence of the domestic logistics industry. The LPI is built upon a web-based questionnaire completed by more than 800 professionals worldwide and more than 5,000 country evaluations, based on seven areas of performance as follows:

- Efficiency of the clearance process by customs and other border agencies
- Quality of transport and information technology infrastructure for logistics
- Ease and affordability of arranging international shipments
- Competence of the local logistics industry
- Ability to track and trace international shipments
- Domestic logistics costs
- Timelines of shipments in reaching destination

A cross-country comparison of LPI (Fig. 18.4) reveals that Singapore ranks at the top with a score of 4.13 on a five-point scale, being the major global transport and logistics hub, compared to Hong Kong (4.12), Finland (4.05), Germany (4.03), Netherlands (4.02), Denmark (4.02), Japan (3.93), the USA (3.93), the UK (3.9), France (3.85), UAE (3.78), Australia (3.73), China (3.52), India (3.08), and Russian Federation (2.58), whereas Burundi (1.61) ranks at the last.[2]

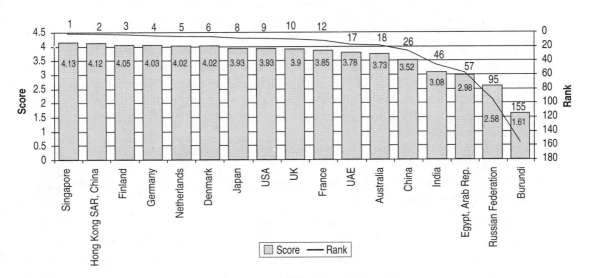

Fig. 18.4   Logistics Performance Index, 2012

Source: Based on data from *Connecting to Compete: Trade Logistics in the Global Economy*, World Bank, Washington DC, 2012, p. viii.

---

[1] *Connecting to Compete: Trade Logistics in the Global Economy*, World Bank, Washington DC, 2012, p. viii.
[2] Based on *Connecting to Compete: Trade Logistics in the Global Economy*, World Bank, Washington DC, 2012.

MANAGING INTERNATIONAL LOGISTICS

A typical logistics system consists of warehousing, transportation, inventory, packaging and unitization, and information and communication which are explained in this section. As transportation, especially ocean transport, is crucial to international trade, it is discussed at length later in the chapter.

Warehousing

A firm is required to store the goods so as to bridge the time gap between the production and meeting the customer demand. The major functions of warehousing are as follows.

Storage of goods   The basic function of warehouses is to store inventories in safe and orderly conditions till the time of export shipment. Besides, the storage facilities at overseas locations facilitate holding inventories that are released as and when demanded by the market.

Consolidation   Storage is used to consolidate cargo from various locations or shippers before it is loaded on board the vessel. Besides, warehouses are also used to consolidate the less than container load (LCL) cargo for stuffing in the container before despatching the container to the port of shipment or destination.

Breaking bulk   In the overseas markets, the import cargo either received in container load or bulk is divided into several small parts in the warehouse before despatching it to wholesalers or distributors.

Mixing or assembly   A shipper may procure the goods from various suppliers and mix them before shipment. Similarly, an importer may import the goods from a number of exporters located in different countries and mix them before despatch to wholesalers and distributors. Assembly is an equivalent term used for mixing in case of industrial or semi-manufactured goods in completely knocked down (CKD) or semi-knocked down (SKD) condition.

Various types of warehouses include commodity bulk storage, refrigerated, or general merchandise warehouse. In India, Central Warehousing Corporation (CWC) provides custom-bonded warehouses at ports and air cargo complexes. A firm has an option to use its own warehouse or a leased private warehouse or may use a public warehouse depending upon its requirements and availability. Various factors affecting selection of warehouse include the inventory level to be maintained by the firm, location of the warehouse, the level of customer service provided, and the warehousing costs.

Inventory Management

Maintaining inventories is an integral part of supply chain management. The principal reasons for holding inventories are as follows.

To maintain uninterrupted supply   In order to meet the demand fluctuations in the markets, a firm has to maintain inventories so that its supply to market remains uninterrupted.

To optimize buying costs   A firm has to hold certain level of inventory so as to optimize the administrative costs associated with procuring the goods. A widely used classical technique is economic order quantity (EOQ) for inventory decisions for cost optimization.

To economize production costs   Inventories facilitate continued production runs that help in keeping production costs lower due to optimum utilization of fixed costs.

To take advantage of quantity discounts   Firms usually get quantity discounts for buying products in bulks.

To cope-up with seasonal fluctuations   Demand and supply patterns for most products in the markets are cyclical in nature. In order to maintain continued production and cope up with seasonal demand variations in the market, a firm is required to carry inventory.

Packing and Unitization

Packaging of export cargo is an important logistics activity as it facilitates safe and smooth shipment of goods. Besides, packaging facilitates unitization of export cargo that facilitates cargo-handling during transit. Standardized practices for cargo unitization are used so as to increase its acceptability internationally in various markets. Sling load and pallets are widely accepted unitized cargo in air transport while containers with 20 or 40 ft length, 8 ft height, and 8 ft width are widely used for ocean transport. A container is an article of transport equipment, strong enough for repeated use, to facilitate handling and carriage of goods by one or more modes of transport. Containerization increases the size of unit load and facilitates handling and transportation of cargo.

Transporting the cargo by containers offers the following benefits to shippers:

- Facilitates door-to-door delivery.
- Reduces cost of packing as the container acts as a strong protective cover.
- Reduces documentation work.
- Lowers warehousing and inventory costs.
- Prevents pilferage and theft.
- Reduces susceptibility to cargo damage.

Information and Communication Technology

Developments in information and communication technology (ICT) have revolutionized the entire concept of logistics management. It has evolved new areas of logistics management, such as just-in-time (JIT) management wherein the emphasis is on continued and reliable supply with much lower level of inventories holdings. Firms have to develop an integrated logistics management system with meticulous conceptualization, planning, coordination, and implementation so as to create competitive advantage in the marketplace.

Transportation

Transportation is an important part of international logistics. Various modes of transport used are as follows.

Air   Transportation of goods by air accounts for only 1 per cent in terms of volume but about 20 to 30 per cent in terms of value of the total world trade. Thus, it is the most preferred mode of transport for high-value goods. Besides, due to the increase in market competition and increasing availability of air cargo services, air transportation is rapidly gaining popularity in international trade. The major benefits of transporting cargo by air are as follows:

- Speedier delivery.
- Highly suitable for perishable goods, such as foods, fresh fruits and vegetables, flowers, and meat.
- Does not require robust packaging as in case of ocean transport.
- Low risk of pilferage or cargo damage with competitive rate of insurance.
- The system of documentation for air transport is simple and, therefore, cost-effective.
- Low inventory and storage cost.
- Reliability of service.

However, the limitations associated with air transport are as follows:

- As air freight is more expensive compared to ocean transport, the value of the cargo or the significance of speed of delivery should justify the cost incurred.
- Limited capacity with air freighters.
- The packaging needs to be small so as to fit in the air carrier.
- Air services are vulnerable to disruption by weather.

Road   Transport by road provides flexibility to the exporter. However, this can be used only to the bordering countries. The major advantages of road transport are as follows:

- Facilitates door-to-door delivery with little intermediate handling.
- Flexibility of operation.
- Competitive for small distances compared to air freight in respect of transit time and freight.
- Economy on packaging cost compared to conventional ocean shipping.
- Lower risk of cargo damage during transit.

A firm has the option to use its own private carriers, contract carriers (with formal agreement to transport, such as oil or milk tankers), or public carriers (that can be used by anyone). Road transportation is common for cross-country trade in land-locked nations and countries with strong economic groupings, such as European Union and NAFTA. In India, the major land customs stations notified for cross-border trade include Attari in Punjab at the Indo-Pak border, Petrapole in West Bengal, Dwaki in Meghalaya at the Indo-Bangladesh border, and Moreh in Manipur at the Indo-Myanmar border.

Rail   India has the distinction of having a highly developed rail transport system in the world, but it can be used only to transport goods to bordering countries. The major benefits of using rail for cargo transport are as follows:

- Economic vis-à-vis road transport
- Bulk cargoes can be handled in higher volumes

The major limitations in transporting the cargo by rail include limited availability of the railway network and the trade relations between India and its neighbouring countries. The major railway networks for international trade in India are Attari in Punjab at Indo-Pak border and Petrapole in West Bengal that links Benapole in Bangladesh. However, the transport of cargo through railway is widely used in European Union, NAFTA, i.e., Canada, USA, and Mexico, and CIS countries that not only have good railway network but also much liberalized trade relations.

Ocean   Transportation of cargo by sea is the largest means of transportation in international trade. Operation of merchant ships is estimated to generate over US$500 billion in freight rates, representing about 5 per cent of the total global economy. The shipping industry presents healthy competition among over 10 thousand individual shipping companies involved in international trade operating over 50,000 ships. The deep sea trade is served by over 3,000 ports and the cargo carried by the shipping industry consists of many millions of separate consignments, of different sizes, and with different physical characteristics. In view of high significance of ocean transport in international trade, it has been discussed at length later in the chapter.

THIRD PARTY LOGISTICS

Since the advent of modern trade several centuries ago, the international movement of goods has been primarily organized by freight forwarders, typically large networks of companies with worldwide coverage, capable of handling and coordinating diverse actions required to move goods across long distances and international borders. The rapid rise of express carriers and third party logistics (3PL) providers has expanded the scope of services available to traders.

Third party logistics provider refers to a company that provides multiple logistics services for its clients and customers. Thus, outsourcing of more sophisticated logistics and supply chain services, especially on a global scale may be defined as 3PL. In recent years, many freight forwarders have developed their operations to introduce value-added services at both ends of the supply chain to become globally integrated service providers. Europe is the largest market for freight forwarding and logistics services with a share of just over a third followed by Asia Pacific (29%) and North America (27%). The global logistics and freight forwarding market is in the process of rationalization and consolidation with a handful of major players that have global coverage. DHL Global Forwarding, with 9 per cent share, is the largest logistics provider, followed by Kuehne and Nagel (7 %), Schenker (6 %), Panalpina (4 %), and others.

MARITIME TRANSPORTATION IN INTERNATIONAL TRADE

Since ocean transport is responsible for carriage of 90 per cent of world trade, making it the largest means of transport in international trade, it is elucidated separately. The bulk transport of raw material for import and export of affordable food and manufactured goods would not have been possible without shipping. It is the low-cost availability and efficiency of maritime transport that has made it possible to shift industrial production to low-cost countries. Costs of ocean transport are very competitive due to continuous improvements in technology and efficiency. To illustrate, the typical cost of transporting a 20 ft container from Asia to Europe, carrying over 20 tonnes of cargo is about the same as the economy journey for a single passenger on the same journey. Table 18.1 reveals that the typical international shipping costs from Asia to the USA or Europe are minuscule compared to products' shelf-price. Moreover, over the last 50 years, bulk shipping costs have increased only by 70 per cent, whereas the retail prices have grown by more than 800 per cent.

Since ocean transport is the oldest mode of international business, a large number of shipping practices are derived by the customs of trade. An international sales agreement and arrangement of transport goes hand in hand. Therefore, managers operating in international markets need to develop a thorough understanding of the shipping practices. The basic concepts of international shipping practices have been discussed in this chapter.

Table 18.1 An overview of typical ocean freight costs (Asia–US or US–Asia)

Product	Unit	Typical shelf price (US$)	Shipping costs (US$)
TV set	per unit	700	10.00
DVD/CD player	per unit	200	1.50
Vacuum cleaner	per unit	150	1.00
Scotch whisky	per bottle	50	0.15
Coffee	per kg	15	0.15
Biscuits	per tin	3	0.05
Beer	per can	1	0.01

Source: *International Shipping Carrier of World Trade*, Maritime International Secretariat Services Ltd, London, 2007, pp. 2–6.

Types of Ocean Cargo

Maritime cargo may be broadly classified as bulk and containerized as explained next.

Bulk cargo

Cargo that is loaded and carried in bulk, without mark or count, in a loose unpackaged form, having homogenous characteristics is termed as bulk cargo. To be loaded on a containership, bulk cargo is put in containers first. It could also be stowed in bulk instead of being loaded into containers. Examples of such cargo are coal, iron ore, fertilizers, grains, oil, etc.

Break-bulk   It refers to packaged cargo that is loaded and unloaded on a piece-by-piece basis, that is, by number or count. This can be containerized or prepared in groups of packages covered by shrink wrap or shipment. Examples are coffee, rubber, steel, etc.

Neo-bulk   Certain types of cargo that are often moved by specialized vessels, for example, auto, and logs are termed as neo-bulk.

The physical form of cargo and the way it is shipped is shown in Exhibit 18.1. Both dry and bulk commodities can be shipped in unit loads, break-bulk, and as bulk cargo.

Exhibit 18.1   Physical form and the way of shipping

The way of shipping/ Physical form	General cargo		Bulk cargo
	Unit load	Break-bulk	
Dry cargoes	e.g., bagged rice in whole load	e.g., machinery parts in crates and boxes	e.g., loose grain in holds
Liquid cargoes	e.g., whole load of oil in drums	e.g., part loads of wine in cases	e.g., crude oil in tank vessels.

Source: 'Use of Maritime Transport', *Economic and Social Commission for Asia and the Pacific*, vol. 1, United Nations, p. 50.

Containerized cargo

Cargo loaded at a facility away from the pier or at a warehouse into a metal container usually 20 to 40 ft long, 8 ft high, and 8 ft wide is known as containerized cargo. The container is then delivered to a pier and loaded onto a 'containership' for transportation. Some cargoes cannot be containerized, for example, automobiles, live animals, bulk products, etc.

Types of Commercial Vessels

As international managers are expected to handle international shipping operations too, various types of vessels used in international trade have been briefly elucidated. To explain in simple terms, a ship is made up of two main parts, that is, hull and machinery. The hull is the shell, including the superstructure. Most often the hull is divided into two sections, that is, holds or tanks, especially in larger vessels. The machinery includes engines, auxiliary equipment, serving electrical installations.[3] The cost of operation of vessels is influenced by the type of machinery that interests a shipper.

The classification of ships on the basis of size is generally based on their capacity expressed in tonnage. A variety of ways customarily used to express tonnage in the shipping industry often

---

[3] Branch, A. E., *Elements of Shipping*, Chapman & Hall Ltd, London, 1981, p. 3.

Exhibit 18.2   Measurement units used to express vessel capacity

Dead weight tons (dwt)
Dead weight ton (dwt) refers to the maximum weight of cargo a vessel can carry, which is also known as 'tonnage'. The dwt of a ship includes both the bunker (the fuel carried on board the vessel for travel) and the stores (supplies carried on board needed to function). The dwt is measured by using the weight of the difference in water displacement when the ship is empty and when it is fully loaded to its maximum.

Gross registered tonnage (GRT)
This represents the total volume of a vessel's carrying capacity, measured as the space available below the deck expressed in hundreds of cubic feet. It means one gross register ton (GRT) equals to a volume of 100 cubic feet (2.82 m³).

Net registered tonnage (NRT)
This represents the volume of cargo a vessel can carry. It is arrived by subtracting the volume of space that would not hold the cargo such as engine room, the crew space, etc., from the GRT.

Displacement tonnage
It refers to the total volume of the ship, when fully loaded. It is measured by the weight of the volume of water displaced by the fully loaded vessel.

Light tonnage
It refers to the total weight of the ship, when empty. It is measured by using the weight of the water displaced by the empty vessel.

makes it difficult to comprehend. A brief description of various types of tonnage used to describe vessel capacity is given in Exhibit 18.2.

On the basis of registry groupings

The review of maritime transport prepared by UNCTAD categorizes vessels into five groups[4] that cover 20 principal types of vessel categories. The composition of the present world fleet by vessel types (Fig. 18.5) consists of oil tankers (34%), dry bulk carriers (38%), container ships (13%), general cargo carriers (8%), and other vessels (7%).

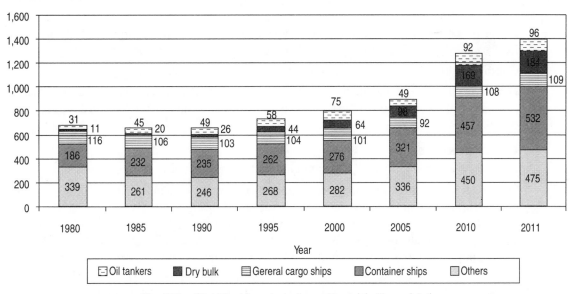

Fig. 18.5   World fleet (by principal vessel types) (millions of dwt)

Source: *Review of Maritime Transport, 2011*, United Nations Conference of Trade and Development, New York and Geneva, 2011, pp. 23–37.

---

[4] *Review of Maritime Transport, 2011*, United Nations Conference of Trade and Development, New York and Geneva, 2011, p. xiv.

Oil tankers   These are vessels that carry oil. Crude oil tankers are further classified into the following categories on the basis of dwt:[5]

ULCC (Ultra-large crude carriers)
    Double hull   above 3,50,000 dwt
    Single hull   above 3,20,000 dwt
VLCC (Very large crude carriers)
    Double hull   2,00,000–3,49,999 dwt
    Single hull   2,00,000–3,19,999 dwt
Suezmax crude tanker   1,25,000–1,99,999 dwt
Aframax crude tanker   80,000–1,24,999 dwt; moulded breadth > 32.31 m
Panamax crude tanker   50,000–79,999 dwt; moulded breadth < 32.31 m

Bulk carriers   These ore and bulk carriers and also ore/bulk/oil carriers. Vessels carrying dry bulk cargo are known as dry bulk carriers, which may further be classified as follows.

Cape size   These are ships above 80,000 dwt and too wide to pass through the Panama Canal and hence through the Cape of Good Hope from Pacific to Atlantic and vice versa. These ships mainly carry iron ore, coal, and to a lesser extent, grain, and have limited gears restricting them to the largest well-equipped ports.

Panamax   These are ships of 50,000–79,999 dwt and maximum beam of 32.2 m, the largest that can pass through Panama Canal, mainly carrying grain and coal and have limited gears, restricting them to largest well-equipped ports.

Handymax   Ships of 35,000–54,999 dwt, mostly with gears making them independent of shore facilities, are included in this category.

Handysize   These ships are of 10,000–34,999 dwt, mostly with gears (cranes or derricks) making them independent of shore facilities.

General cargo   These include vessels designed to carry refrigerated cargo, specialized cargo, Ro-Ro cargo, general cargo (single and multi-deck), general cargo/passengers.

Container ships   These are fully cellular vessels that carry container cargo.

Other vessels   These include oil chemical tankers, chemical tankers, other tankers, liquefied gas carriers, passenger Ro-Ro, passenger, tank barges, general cargo barges, fishing, offshore supply, and all other types of vessels.

On the basis of decks

Ships may be classified on the basis of number of decks[6] as follows.

Single-deck   Such vessels have one continuous deck as depicted in Fig. 18.6. Easy access with one hatch for each hold means economic loading and discharging. Many single-deck vessels have very large hatches, and some are known as 'self-trimmers' because of provisions for the cargo to flow into all corners of the hold. This reduces loading costs and time spent in ports.

The most suitable cargoes for single-deck vessels are heavy bulk cargoes, such as coal, grain, and iron ore. However, these vessels also carry light cargoes, like timber, which can be stowed on deck as well as below. Single-deck vessels are not suitable for general cargoes, because there are few means of separating cargo tiers and lots.

---

[5] *Review of Maritime Transport, 2011*, United Nations Conference of Trade and Development, New York and Geneva, (2007), p. xiv.

[6] Cufley, C.F.H., *Ocean Freights and Chartering*, Crosby Lockwood Staples, London, 1970, pp. 232–238; *Use of Maritime Transport*, vol. I, Economic and Social Commission for Asia and the Pacific, United Nations, p. 73.

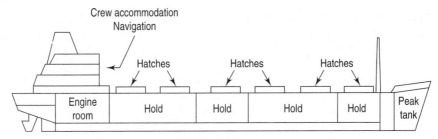

Fig. 18.6 A single-deck vessel (gearless bulk carrier)

Tween-deck It has additional deck (tween decks) below the main deck as depicted in Fig. 18.7, all running the full length of the ship. A vessel with tween decks is suitable for general cargo, because the cargo space is divided into separate tiers, and the decks eliminate risks of cargo damage by preventing too much weight to be placed on the cargo at the bottom.

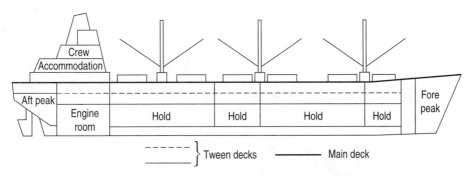

Fig. 18.7 A tween-deck vessel (with cargo gear)

Shelter-deck Shelter-deck vessels (Fig. 18.8) have an additional deck above the main deck—a shelter deck. The advantage of the shelter deck is that it provides more under-deck space for carrying light cargoes. There are two types of shelter-deck vessels, the closed and the open. The difference relates to the measurement of the ship. For new tonnage, the difference has been abolished through changes in the measurement rules.

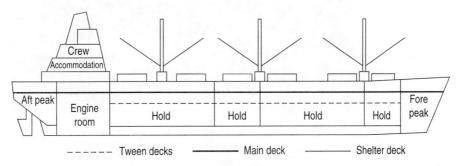

Fig. 18.8 A shelter-deck vessel

In addition to traditional single-deck, also called full-scantling ships, and tween and shelter deckers, there exists a multitude of specialized cargo carrying vessels. These include gas carriers, wood carriers, refrigerated ships, oil tankers, container ships, and roll-on/roll-off vessels.

Container   For shipping containerized cargo as in case of multi-modal transportation, a container vessel (Fig. 18.9) is used, which is designed to load, stack, and unload containers.

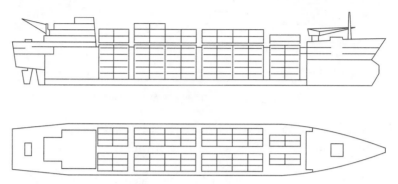

Fig. 18.9   A typical container vessel

On the basis of type of cargo
Vessels may be classified on the basis of the type of cargo, as follows.

Container ships   These are vessels carrying most of the world's manufactured goods and products, usually on scheduled liner services. The latest generation of container ship can carry equivalent of 10,000 heavy trucks (Fig. 18.10).

Fig. 18.10   Container ship

Source: http://all-free-download.com/free-photos/ship_containers_products_214224_
download.html, accessed on 2 April 2014.

Tankers   Tankers are vessels designed to carry liquid cargo, such as crude oil, chemicals, and petroleum products in large tanks (Fig. 18.11). More than 70 per cent of ocean-going tankers have double hulls. The largest tankers can carry over 3,00,000 tonnes of oil. They can be modified to carry other types of cargo, such as grain or coffee.

Fig. 18.11　Tanker ship

Source: http://en.wikipedia.org/wiki/MV_Sirius_Star, accessed on 2 April 2014.

Bulk carriers　These are vessels that carry a variety of bulk cargo, such as iron ore, coal, and food-stuff and are identifiable by the hatches raised above deck level which cover the large cargo holds (Fig. 18.12). The largest bulk carriers can transport enough grain to feed nearly four million people for a month.

Fig. 18.12　Bulk carrier

Source: http://www.flickr.com/photos/trekman/2872892647/, accessed on 2 April 2014.

Neo-bulk carriers   These are vessels designed to carry specific types of cargo.

Combination carriers   These are vessels that carry passengers and cargo, oil and dry bulk, or containers and bulk cargo. Other combinations are also possible.

General cargo vessels

Roll-on and roll-off (Ro/Ro) vessels   These are vessels that allow rolling cargo such as tractors and cars to be driven aboard the vessel (Fig. 18.13).

Fig. 18.13   Roll-on/Roll-off (Ro-Ro) vessel (loading cars for exports)

Source: http://en.wikipedia.org/wiki/file:Roro_faehre.jpg, accessed on 2 April 2014.

LASH (lighter aboard ship) vessels   These are vessels that can carry very large containers, like barges. They enable cargo to be loaded on barges in shallow waters and then loaded on board a vessel.

Barges   These are unmanned vessels generally used for oversized cargo and towed by a tugboat.

Other vessels   These are specialist vessels, such as car carriers, gas carriers, heavy lift vessels, salvage tugs, ice breakers, research vessels, and ships for off-shore drilling. They also include general cargo vessels and a large number of small vessels.

Alternates for Ocean Shipment

A firm has specific requirements for ocean transport of cargo. The size, type, unit value, and frequency of shipment often determine alternative forms of ocean transport. The basic types of ocean shipping operations, that is, charter shipping, liners, and multi-modal transport may be summarized as follows.

Charter Shipping

For shipment of bulk cargo, such as grain, coal, ores, fertilizers, and oil, which are to be carried in complete ship-loads, charter shipping is often used. It is also known as trump shipping. The charter vessel does not have any fixed itinerary or fixed sailing schedule. These can be hired or engaged to ship the firm's cargo on charter basis as per the terms and conditions of the charter party. The contract made between the charterer and the ship owner is known as charter party that contains details of the ship, routes, and methods of cargo handling, port of call, etc. A shipper may pay charter rates either on the basis of the amount of cargo shipped or fixed prices. The chartering services are generally offered in auction markets. The rates are negotiated with the help of brokers or charter agents to get the lowest market price.

Forms of chartering
Various forms of chartering the ships for carriage of bulk cargoes follow.

Voyage charter   Contract of carriage in which a vessel is hired for transport of a specified cargo from one port to another is termed as voyage charter. The ship owner pays for all the operating costs of the ship, while payment for port and cargo-handling charges are the subject of agreement between the parties. Freight is generally paid per unit of cargo (per tonne) based on an agreed quantity or as a lump sum, irrespective of the quantity loaded. Terms and conditions are set down in a document, which is called a charter party. The ship is said to be on 'voyage charter'.

Time charter   Time charter refers to hiring of a ship from a ship owner for a period of time, whereby the ship owner places the ship with the crew and the equipment at disposal of the charterer, in exchange of hired money. Subject to restrictions in the contract, the charterer decides on the type and quantity of cargo to be carried and ports of loading and discharging and is responsible for supplying ships with bunkers and for payment of cargo, handling operations, port charges, pilotage, towage, and ship's agency. The technical operation and navigation of the ship remain the responsibility of the ship owner. The ship is said to be on time charter.

Bare boat charter (demise charter or charter by demise)   In a bare boat charter, the hiring or leasing of a ship is for a period of time during which the ship owner provides only the ship, while the charterer provides the crew along with all stores and bunkers and pays for all operating costs. The ship is said to be on 'bare boat' or 'demise' charter.

Other charter types   There are a few other types of charters, as follows.

Back-to-back charter   This involves a contract between a charterer and a sub-charterer, whose terms and conditions are identical to the contract (charter) between the charterer and the ship owner. Identical terms mean any money for which the charterer may be liable to the sub-charterer and which is recoverable from the ship owner.

Trip time charter   A charterer hires the vessel for a single voyage or a round trip on terms and conditions similar to that of time charter.

Contract of affreightment   A contract of affreightment is a long-time agreement to carry a certain amount of cargo between two ports. The choice of vessel and timing will usually be at the ship owner's discretion. Alternatively, the contract may specify a certain amount of shipping that must be completed within a specific time period.

Contract terms used in vessel chartering
Various alternative arrangements for loading and unloading of cargo between the vessel owner and the charterer used in charter party are as follows.

Gross terms   As per gross terms, the ship owner is responsible for the cost of loading, stowing, trimming, and unloading of the vessel.

Net terms   The ship owner is not responsible for the cost of loading and discharge. Typically, net terms are used in voyage charter parties, as the ship owner has no control over loading and discharging. There are suitable clauses for laytime and demurrage to allow for delays at the loading and discharging ports. The specific terms used for net terms are as follows.

Free in and out (FIO) It confers the responsibility to the charterer or shipper to arrange the stevedores and to load/discharge the cargo on the charterer's own account, that is, free of expense to the ship owner, who is still accountable for the port charges.

Free in and out stowed and trimmed (FIOST) This is similar to FIO, but here, the charterer is also responsible for bearing the expenses of stowing and trimming, that is, free to the ship owner.

Shared responsibilities The charterer and the ship owner both have shared responsibilities in the following terms:

Free in liner out (FILO) The ship owner is not responsible for the cost of loading but is responsible for the cost of unloading.

Liner in free out (LIFO) The ship owner is responsible for the cost of loading but not for vessel unloading.

Laytime In addition, the charterer's responsibility in terms of agreed time frame known as 'laytime' is included in the charter party. This can be expressed in days, hours, tonnes per day, etc. The charterer has to pay 'demurrage' to the ship owner by way of financial compensation for delays in exceeding allowed laytime. However, accomplishing loading and/or discharge in less than the agreed time is often rewarded financially by the ship owner by a payment called 'dispatch'. Usually, dispatch is paid at half the demurrage rate.

As a matter of shipping trade practices, certain terms are used for accounting laytime in a charter party. Sundays and holidays are generally excluded for calculation of 'laycan' in most countries where Sunday is a weekly public holiday. However, in case of Middle East and some other Islamic countries where Friday is a holiday, it is excluded for computing 'laycan'.

The terms used in charter party for such exclusions are as follows.

Other terms Some other terms used in charter party are as follows:

As fast as the vessel can (FAC) Maximum rate at which a vessel can load/unload.

Notice of readiness (NOR) Formal advice that the vessel is ready for loading/unloading.

Running days Days that run consecutively after each other.

Weather permitting Inclement weather is excluded from laytime.

Weather working day (WWD) A day or part of a day when weather does not prevent loading/unloading.

SHEX Sundays and holidays excluded.

SHINC Sundays and holiday included.

FHEX Fridays and holidays excluded.

FHINC Fridays and holidays included.

Terms of sales as agreed between the buyer and the seller, as per INCOTERMS 2011, also influence the charter party terms regarding vessel loading and unloading negotiated between the ship owner and the charterer.

- Free alongside (FAS) requires the seller to place the goods alongside the vessel, whereas free on board (FOB) requires the seller to load them. When the vessel is chartered by the buyer, the seller generally prefers FAS as he is often unwilling to become involved in vessel loading. On the other hand, a buyer who is not very familiar with the port of loading may ask the seller to arrange loading by requesting FOB. Besides, sellers may prefer to arrange vessel loading by them if they control or own their own loading facility at the port of shipment.

- In cases where the seller charters the vessel and goods are sold on the basis of 'Delivered ExQuay' (DEQ) and 'Delivered ExShip' (DES), the seller is responsible for unloading in DEQ converacts, whereas he is not responsible for unloading in DES contracts. As sellers have little familiarity with the port of discharge, they generally prefer DES and the buyer has to take care of and bear the expenses of unloading operations.

Liner Shipping

Regular scheduled vessel services between two ports are termed as liner shipping. Generally, liner shipping is used for cargo with higher unit value and manufacture and semi-manufacture goods. The shipping lines offer speedier shipping services, that is, services useful for goods that are prone to market fluctuations due to changes in fashion, designs, season, technology, etc.

In liner shipping, for determining responsibilities of shipper and ship owner regarding cargo loading and discharge, liner terms are used. Under liner terms, shippers have no responsibility to the ship other than to have cargo delivered to the terminal, ready for loading prior to cut-off date, and the consignees are responsible for collecting their arrived cargo in a timely manner.

The major difference between charter and liner shipping are given in Exhibit 18.3.

Cost calculations for liner shipping

For liner shipping, the cost of freight is calculated from the commodity-based published price list of shipping companies. These lists indicate the cost of pure freight, also known as 'based rate' and any applicable surcharges, that is, 'accessorial charges'. The base rate is often commodity-specific,

Exhibit 18.3   Charter vs liner shipping

Charter shipping	Liner shipping
Single-deck gearless vessels are used.	Tween- or shelter-deck vessels with cargo gears are used.
As used for moving bulk cargo, vessels with larger size, generally 75,000 DWT or more are engaged.	As liner ships sail more frequently, smaller ships are engaged.
Speed of operation is not of much significance.	Speed and early delivery are crucial to liner operators for providing them a competitive edge.
Carries bulk homogeneous or single low value cargo.	Carries large variety of manufactured and semi-finished goods.
A charter vessel is engaged by a single shipper at a time.	A liner ship provides service to large number of shippers.
Generally cargo is shipped in bulk as loose.	Cargo is packed in parcels, packages, cases, rolls, etc.
Non-scheduled service.	Operates regularly on a fixed schedule.
Vessels are hired through ship brokers or agents.	Cargo booking is done through freight forwarders.
Market forces determine the freight rates.	Liner vessels have pre-determined tariff structure.
Rates fluctuate frequently.	Rates are generally stable.
'Charter party' used as the document of transport contract.	'Bills of lading' used as document of transport contract.
No cartel or association so as to ensure cargo availability.	Liner vessels generally operate as conferences or cartels so as to eliminate competition and ensure cargo availability.

calculated on a billing unit known as a revenue term. Revenue terms are calculated by comparing a shipment's size (measurement terms) versus its gross shipping weight. Various methods used for determining the total number of revenue terms in a given shipment are as follows:

Metric   The greater of the total number of cubic metres versus the total number of metric tons

40-short ton   The greater of total cubic feet/40 versus the total gross weight in pounds/short ton.

40-long ton   The greater of total cubic feet/40 versus the total gross weight in pounds/long ton.

In addition to the base rate just mentioned, some other surcharges that reflect extra costs over which the carrier has little direct control are also to be paid. The major surcharges include the following:

Bunker adjustment factor (BAF)   It reflects the cost of fuel (called bunkers). It is handled separately, as fuel is subject to frequent price fluctuations.

Currency adjustment factor (CAF)   It reflects changes in the exchange rate of the currency in which the freight costs are billed. It is handled separately because exchange rates fluctuate more often than freight costs.

Port congestion surcharge   It reflects additional expenses that ship lines incur when calling at congested ports.

Terminal handling charge (THC)   It covers vessel-loading and unloading and cartage within the port area. It is handled separately as such costs are port-specific.

Container positioning   It is an additional fee for the use of the carrier's container, imposed for destinations with little return cargo or high risk of loss or damage to the container.

Arbitrary   It is an additional fee that ship lines charge for serving markets outside the hinterlands of their normal ports of call. For instance, an Irish arbitrary is often applied to shipments made through hub ports in the UK.

Liner or shipping conferences

When two or more shipping companies collaborate to operate vessels in the same trade lanes, legally agree not to compete on price, and charge the same freight for the same type of cargo and the same voyage, it is referred to as 'liner' or 'shipping conference'. Thus, under a 'conference', the members agree to a set of tariffs, conference terms and conditions of carriage, the number and type of ships, that each member will contribute, and the timetable for sailing. Besides, setting the freight rates, the shipping conferences also adopt a wide number of policies, such as allocation of customers, loyalty contracts, open pricing contracts, etc. A secretariat, often run by one of the members, coordinates the activities.

Liner Shipping Connectivity Index

Connectivity to maritime shipping is often captured by the Liner Shipping Connectivity Index (LSCI) developed by UNCTAD (Fig. 18.14). The LSCI can be considered as a proxy of accessibility to global trade. The index is calculated on the basis of four major components: containership deployment, container carrying capacity, number of shipping companies, liner services and vessels per company and average and maximum vessel size. The higher the index, the easier it is to access a high capacity and frequency global maritime freight transport system and thus effectively participate to international trade. Generally, countries that have the highest LSCI values are actively involved in trade. China ranks at the top of LSCI as the single most connected country, followed by Hong Kong SAR (115.27) and Singapore (105.02) as being global transhipment hubs. Besides, major traders such as Germany (93.32), UK (87.46), USA (81.63), France (71.84), and Japan (67.81) also rank among the top 15.

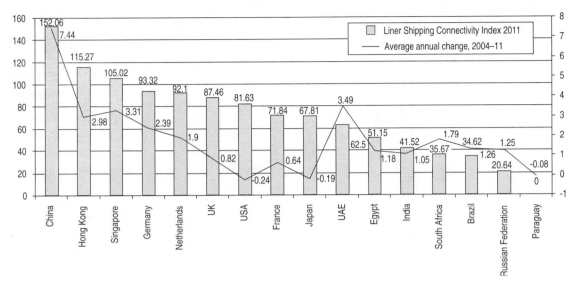

Fig. 18.14   UNCTAD's Liner Shipping Connectivity Index

Source: *Review of Maritime Transport, 2011*, United Nations Conference on Trade and Development, New York and Geneva, 2011.

CONTAINERIZATION AND MULTI-MODAL OR INTER-MODAL TRANSPORTATION

Containerization has been the most significant development in cargo transportation and industry. International 'multi-modal' or 'inter-modal' transport means transport of goods by at least two different modes of transport, such as rail, road, sea, or air on the basis of a multi-modal transport contract, from a place in a country at which the goods are taken in charge by the multi-modal transport operator to a place designated for delivery situated in different countries. Multi-modal transportation has revolutionized the carriage of goods in international trade. It covers the door-to-door movement of goods under the responsibility of a single transport operator. The Multi-modal Transportation of Goods Act, 1993, and the Amendment Act, 2000 provide a regulatory framework for use of containers and multi-modal transportation of goods in India.

Multi-modal transport operators (MTO) are people who on their own behalf or through another person acting on their behalf conclude a multi-modal transport contract and act as principals and not as agents or on behalf of the consumer or of the carriers participating in the multi-modal transport operations and who assume responsibility for the performance of the contract.

Multi-modal transportation of goods developed with the container revolution initiated in the late 1950s by Malcom McLean and his trucking operations. Containerization accounts for over 50 per cent of the world merchandise trade and is expected to grow up further. Informational and technological progress has contributed to rapid growth of container traffic facilitating transnational movement of highly perishable goods. Major benefits offered by transportation through containers include the following:

- Substantial reduction in risk of damage to the goods during transport due to pilferage or mishandling
- Cargo arrival in good condition at final destination creating a positive impact on the buyer's perception
- No cargo damage due to mishandling during trans-shipments

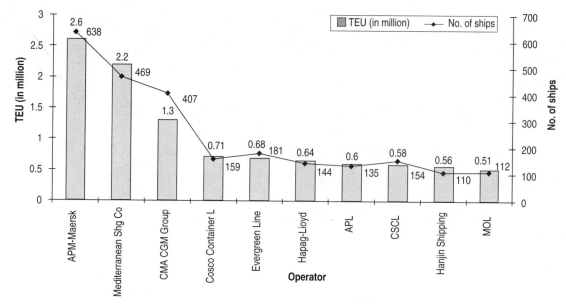

Fig. 18.15   World's top 10 container ship companies
*As on 23 July 2012.
Source: Alphaliner.

Growing significance of containerization is reflected by rising fleet of containers in sea-borne trade from about 7 million twenty-feet equivalent units (TEUs) in 1991 to 20 million TEUs in 2011. Moreover, efficiency of container deployment has also improved significantly in terms of increased transhipment, faster ships, improved port handling, and faster customs clearance.

APM-Maersk, with 15.9 per cent share, is the largest container ship company in the world[7] (Fig. 18.15) followed by Mediterranean Shipping Company with 13.3 per cent share, CMA CGM Group with 8.2 per cent, COSCO Container Ltd with 4.3 per cent, and Evergreen Line with 4.1 per cent in TEUs. APM-Maersk also owns the highest number (638) of containerships in the world, followed by CMA CGM Group (407), Mediterranean Shipping Company (374), Evergreen Line (181), and COSCO Container Ltd (159).

The container traffic handled by major Indian ports has shown a rising trend over the years. Container traffic handled at India's major ports increased from 5.54 million TEUs (73.5 million tonnes) in 2006–07 to 7.78 million TEUs (77.8 million tonnes) in 2011–12 (Fig. 18.16). Jawaharlal Nehru Port Trust (JNPT) at Mumbai is India's largest container port handling 55.6 per cent of container traffic followed by Chennai (20%), Kolkata (7.1%), and Tuticorin (6.1%).

Types of Containers

Containerization has been the most significant development in transportation of goods that has made 'multi' or 'inter'-modal transport of cargo possible. Containers may be classified into two main categories.

---

[7] Alphaliner, 23 July 2012.

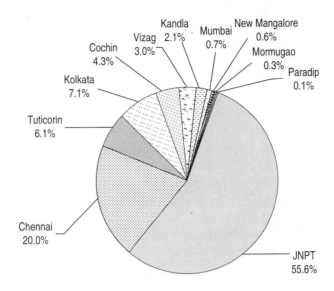

Fig. 18.16 Container traffic at major ports in India (in TEUs)
(2011–12)

Source: 'Update on India's Shipping Sector', Ministry of Road Transport
and Highways, March 2012.

ISO containers

Since these containers conform to the specification of the International Organization for Standardization (ISO), Geneva, these are also referred as standard or inter-modal containers. ISO containers are manufactured in standard sizes as follows:

- Width: 8 ft
- Height: 8 ft 6 in. and 9 ft 6 in.
- Length: 20 ft and 40 ft

Besides, some less common lengths of standard containers include 24, 28, 44, 45, 46, 48, 53, and 56 ft.

The main configurations of ISO containers are as follows:

Dry containers   These are totally closed box-type containers used for general purpose transportation. Manufactured with a standard height of 8 ft 6 in., these are also known as 'cube' containers. These can also be extended to 9 ft 6 in. height, known as 'high cube' containers.

Insulated or thermal containers   These containers have thermal insulation of their wall but not their own refrigeration units. Such containers are used to transport products sensitive to temperature, such as food products and sensitive pharmaceutical products, in chilled or frozen conditions.

Refrigerated or reefer containers   These containers have their own refrigeration units so as to maintain a constant temperature during the voyage. An outside power source (electricity) is required for their functioning during the course of their multi-modal transportation. Most container-ships nowadays have got power facilities to accommodate 'reefer' containers. Such containers are required for transport of highly perishable food products, such as meat, fish, fresh fruits, and vegetables.

Open top containers   In order to hold cargo that is larger than the standard container size of 8 ft, open top containers are required. These containers are designed to hold cargo too large to fit through the doors of a regular container. Therefore, the cargo needs to be loaded in open top containers from the top and then covered with a tarpaulin. Since another container cannot be stacked above an open top container, these containers are always stacked at the top of the stack either above or under the deck.

Liquid bulk containers   Such containers are designed in the shape of a cylindrical tank mounted within a rectangular steel framework to transport liquid cargo. They have the same standard dimension as other inter-modal containers and can also be stacked with standard containers.

Dry bulk containers   In order to save packaging space in drums or bags, such containers are designed to hold dry bulk cargo, such as food grains or polymer pallets, which may have the same dimensions as standard containers.

Flat racks and platforms   To transport heavy machinery, open-sided containers are used that have no side walls but may have end bulkheads that can be folded down when the rack is empty. Nowadays, flat rack containers, which are collapsible, are also available.

Swap bodies

In most of Europe, 'swap bodies' are used which have many characteristics of inter-modal containers but are not standard ISO containers. Strong bottom and a minimal upper body constitute their major characteristics. These can also have an open top, which allows them to be transferred from road to rail mode. Swap bodies cannot be stacked and can only be bottom-lifted. They also have bottom fittings so that they can be locked onto either a road chassis or a rail car.

FCL vs LCL Containers

A shipper has option either to use an entire container, known as full container load (FCL) or partial space in a container, known as less than container load (LCL) of a liner operator. The major advantages of FCL over LCL containers are as follows:

- The freight cost of FCL is more economical than that of LCL.
- As the FCL has a common origin and destination, there is no loss of time once the FCL is loaded and sealed.
- FCL provides ease of handling as the final destination is one.
- Much lower chances of mishandling and pilferage of cargo are present in FCL as handling is only at the time of loading at origin.
- As there is no transit handling, FCL facilitates in avoiding transit damages.
- There is effective utilization of containers both in weight and volume terms.
- There is easy tracking of FCL cargo.

  However, certain limitations associated with FCL cargo are as follows:

- FCL is cost-effective only when the cargo has a load of more than 75 per cent.
- Since container is to be stuffed and sealed at the factory in presence of a local excise official, the firm's responsibility becomes much higher.
- The utilization of the FCL container by weight and volume must be to the maximum for attaining the freight efficiencies.

INTERNATIONAL ORGANIZATIONS ASSOCIATED WITH INTERNATIONAL MARITIME TRANSPORTATION

International shipping has a framework of global regulations on matters, such as construction standards, navigational rules, and crew qualifications. These are common to all ships in international trade. When a ship sails from Mumbai to Rotterdam or Singapore to New York, the same rule applies during the voyage. Shipping is highly regulated at the global level by a number of organizations as discussed here.

International Maritime Organization

The International Maritime Organization (IMO) is a specialized agency of the United Nations (UN) responsible to develop and maintain a comprehensive regulatory framework for shipping, which includes maritime security and safety, environmental concerns, legal matters, technical cooperation, and the efficiency of shipping. Presently, it has 170 member states and three associate members. The convention establishing the organization was held in Geneva in 1948 and the IMO first met in 1959. The IMO keeps legislation up-to-date and ensures that it is ratified by as many countries as possible. Presently, many conventions apply to more than 98 per cent of the world merchant shipping tonnage. The IMO also considers proposals to integrate appropriate cargo security procedures based on or compatible with the standards of various conventions. The three key IMO conventions include the following:

- The International Convention for the Safety of Life at Sea (SOLAS)
- The Standards of Training, Certification, and Watch-keeping Convention (STCW)
- The International Convention for the Prevention of Pollution from Ships (MARPOL)

The International Ship and Port Facility Security (ISPS) code was introduced in 2004 as a fallout of 11 September 2001 in the USA when the need to tighten up security for all modes of transport, which can be potential threat to the national security, was realized. The ISPS code provides for the international framework through which ship and port facilities can cooperate to detect and deter acts which threaten security in the maritime transport sector. The code has been implemented with effect from 1 July 2004 with respect to all contracting parties, including India. The IMO regulations are enforced on a global basis and nations have the power to detain foreign ships that do not conform to international rules.

United Nations Conference on Trade and Development

As a part of its mandate, the United Nations Conference on Trade and Development (UNCTAD) monitors development in the field of transport security and disseminates information's in form of various reports and its annual 'Review of Maritime Transport'. There are a number of international conventions affecting the commercial and technical activities of maritime transport. A brief overview of such conventions under the auspices of UNCTAD is shown in Exhibit 18.4.

World Customs Organizations

In June 2005, the World Customs Organization (WCO) unanimously adopted the Framework of Standards to Secure and Facilitate Global Trade (SAFE Framework), which provides broad outlines and overarching principles concerning security and facilitating global supply chain, based on two main pillars: customs-to-customs cooperation and customs-to-business partnership. Its four core elements are as follows:

- Harmonizing advance electronic cargo information requirements concerning inbound, outbound, and transit shipments
- Developing and implementing a common risk management approach
- Using non-intrusive detection equipment to conduct inspection of high-risk containers and cargo
- Defining benefits for businesses that meet minimal supply-chain security standards and best practices

Exhibit 18.4 Major conventions on maritime transport[8]

Title of convention	Date of entry into force or conditions for entry into force	Contracting states
United Nations Convention on a Code of Conduct for Liner Conferences, 1974	Entered into force on 6 October 1983	81 countries (including Bangladesh, Belgium, China, Chile, Denmark, Egypt, Ethiopia, Finland, France, Germany, India, Jamaica, Kenya, Mauritius, Norway, Portugal, Russian Federation, Saudi Arabia, Spain, Sweden, UK, Venezuela)
United Nations Convention on the Carriage of Goods by Sea, 1978 (Hamburg Rules)	Entered into force on 1 November 1992	33 countries (including Austria, Egypt, Hungary, Jordan, Kenya, Romania, Tanzania, Tunisia)
International Convention on Maritime Liens and Mortgages, 1993	Entered into force on 5 September 2004	12 countries (including Ecuador, Russian Federation, Peru, Spain, Tunisia, Ukraine)
United Nations Convention on International Multi-modal Transport of Goods, 1980	Not yet in force—requires 30 contracting parties	11 countries (including Chile, Georgia, Lebanon, Mexico, Morocco, Senegal, Zambia)
United Nations Convention on Conditions for Registration of Ships, 1986	Not yet in force—requires 40 contracting parties with at least 25% of the world's tonnage	14 countries (including Bulgaria, Egypt, Georgia, Hungary, Iraq, Mexico, Oman)

Source: Review of Maritime Transport, 2007, United Nations Conference of Trade and Development, New York and Geneva, 2007, p. 112.

International Organization for Standardization

In order to enhance supply chain security, consistent with ISPS code, and the WCO framework of standards, the International Organization for Standardization (ISO) has developed certain procedures and standards. Although ISO standards are voluntary, they are developed in response to market demand based on consensus of interested parties. Besides, the ISO standards for containers, as discussed earlier, are also used worldwide in multi-modal transportation.

International Labour Organization

Standards of employment and working conditions for seafarers are established by the International Labour Organization (ILO). It is also adopted by the Maritime Labour Convention (MLC) to provide a level playing field on a global basis with regard to seafarers' employment standards.

INSTITUTIONAL FRAMEWORK FOR MARITIME TRANSPORT IN INDIA

To regulate maritime transport, India has a comprehensive set of institutions that often complement each other's activities as follows.

---

[8] As on 30 September 2007, *Review of Maritime Transport, 2007,* United Nations Conference of Trade and Development, New York and Geneva, 2007, p. 112.

Ministry of Shipping

Although the nomenclature of the Ministry of Shipping has changed several times as in other government departments, but the function, by and large, remains the monitoring and development of maritime transport infrastructure in the country. Presently, the Department of Shipping under the Ministry of Shipping, Road Transport, and Highways is responsible for formulating policies and programmes for development of shipbuilding, ship-repair, major ports, and inland water transport.

National Shipping Board

To advise the Government of India on matters related to shipping and its development, the National Shipping Board is a permanent statutory body established in 1959 under Section 4 of the Merchant Shipping Act, 1958. The board comprises six members of parliament, five representatives from central government, three representatives each of shipowners and seamen, and five representatives of other interest, and is re-constituted after every two years.

Directorate General of Shipping

It is a statutory organization under the Ministry of Shipping, Road Transport, and Highways, established in 1949. Its basic functions include administration of the Indian Merchant Shipping Act, 1958, on all matters related to shipping policy and legislation, implementation of various international conventions relating to the safety, prevention of pollution and other mandatory regulations of the International Maritime Organizations, promotion of maritime education and training, examination and certification, supervision of subordinate offices, etc.

Shipping Corporation of India Ltd

The Shipping Corporation of India Ltd (SCI) was formed on 2 October 1961 by the amalgamation of Eastern Shipping Corporation Ltd (ESC) and Western Shipping Corporation of India Ltd (WSC) with a paid up capital of ₹23.5 crore. The highly diversified fleet of SCI includes bulk carriers, crude and product tankers, combination carriers, general cargo vessels, cellular container vessels, LPG/ammonia carriers, phosphoric acid/chemical carriers, offshore supply vessels, and passenger-cum-cargo vessels.

Container Corporation of India

The Container Corporation (CONCOR) of India was set up in 1988 with the objective of developing multi-modal logistics support for India's international and domestic containerized cargo and trade. The task was to provide customers with the advantages of direct interaction and door-to-door services while capitalizing on the Indian Railway network. CONCOR currently provides the only means by which shippers may obtain containerized freight transportation by rail in India. Though rail is the mainstay of CONCOR's transportation plan, road services are also provided according to market demand and operational exigencies. CONCOR also operates container terminals across the country to cater to the needs of trade. The major services offered by CONCOR are as follows:

- Transit warehousing for import and export cargo
- Bonded warehousing, which enables importers to store cargo and ask for partial releases, thereby deferring duty payment
- Less than container load (LCL) consolidation, and reworking of LCL cargo at nominated hub
- Air cargo clearance using bonded trucking

INDIA'S INTERNATIONAL SHIPPING ACTIVITIES

About 95 per cent by volume and 70 per cent by value of India's merchandise trade is carried out through maritime transport. India's maritime transport sector comprises ports, shipping, shipbuilding, ship-repair, and inland water transport systems. India has a long coastline of about 7,517 km. India is among the top twenty merchant fleets all in the world with over 1,400 vessels and 15.28 million gross tonnage (GT) and 13.92 dead weight tons (dwt) under the Indian flag.[9]

India has 13 major ports that handle about 76 per cent of the traffic, whereas its 187 minor ports handle only 24 per cent of cargo. The major ports are managed by the port trusts under the central government, whereas the minor ports are developed and managed by the concerned state governments. The major ports are Kandla, Mumbai, JNPT, Mormugao, New Mangalore, Cochin, Tuticorin, Chennai, Ennore, Visakhapatnam, Paradip, Kolkata, and Haldia. Traffic handled at major ports grew from 464 million tonnes in 2006–07 to 560 million tonnes in 2011–12 (Figs 18.17 and 18.18). Kandla is the largest port handling 14.7 per cent of traffic handled by major ports in 2011–12, followed by Vizag (12%), JNPT (11.7%), Mumbai (10%), Chennai (9.9%), and Paradip (9.7%).

Energy imports consisting of petroleum, oil, and lubricants (POL) and coal constituted 46 per cent of the total cargo traffic at India's major ports in 2011–12 followed by containers (21%), iron ore (11%), and fertilizers (4%). Commodity composition and traffic handled did hardly undergo any significant change from 2006–07 (Figs 18.19 and 18.20).

Non-major ports are crucial to India's maritime transport as they help alleviate the congestion at major ports. Among the 187 minor ports, only 61 ports are functional. Only some minor ports provide round-the-year berthing facilities. Traffic handled by major ports grew from 185 million

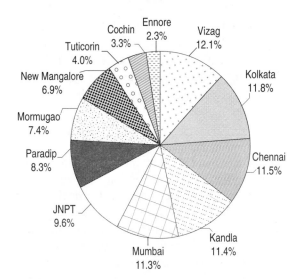

Fig. 18.17   India's major ports: traffic handled (2006–07)

Source: Update on India's Shipping Sector, Ministry of Road Transport and Highways, March 2012.

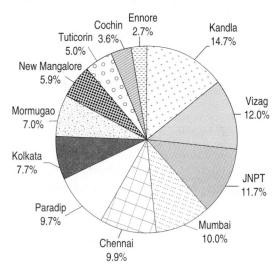

Fig. 18.18   India's major ports: traffic handled (2011–12)

Source: Update on India's Shipping Sector, Ministry of Road Transport and Highways, March 2012.

---

[9] *Review of Maritime Transport, 2011*, United Nations Conference on Trade and Development, New York and Geneva, 2011, p. 47.

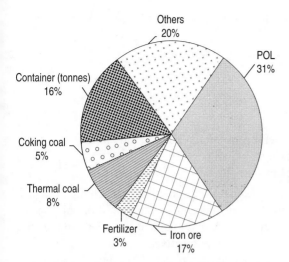

Fig. 18.19 Commodity-wise traffic at major ports (2006–07)

Source: 'Update on India's Shipping Sector', Ministry of Road Transport and Highways, March 2012.

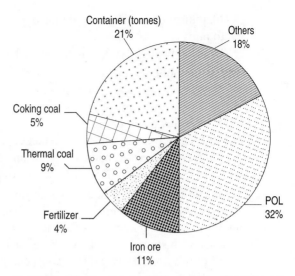

Fig. 18.20 Commodity-wise traffic at major ports (2011–12)

Source: 'Update on India's Shipping Sector', Ministry of Road Transport and Highways, March 2012.

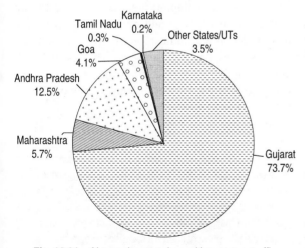

Fig. 18.21 Non-major ports in maritime states: traffic handled (2011–2012)

Source: 'Update on India's Shipping Sector', Ministry of Road Transport and Highways, March 2012.

tonnes in 2006–07 to 352 million tonnes in 2011–12. Gujarat with 259 million tonnes of cargo accounted for 73.7 per cent of the traffic handled by non-major ports followed by Andhra Pradesh (12.5%), Maharashtra (5.7%), and Goa (4.1%) in 2011–12 (Fig. 18.21).

All ports in India are governed by the statutory framework of Indian Ports Act, 1908. Major ports in India are administered by a 'Port Trust' and are under purview of the central government, whereas non-major ports are under purview of the state governments. Maritime States Development Council (MSDC) was constituted in May 1997 to have an integrated approach for development of ports in India. India encourages private investments and public–private partnership (PPP) for port development and handling. It also allows FDI up to 100 per cent for construction and maintenance of ports and harbours.

The Ministry of Shipping has come out with a Maritime Agenda 2010–20 for the next 10 years which focuses on the following issues:

Agenda for port development
- Develop two new major ports, one each on east and west coasts.
- Full mechanization of cargo handling and movement.
- Major ports to have draft of not less than 14 m and hub ports 17 m

- Identification and implementation of projects for rail, road, and inland waterway connectivity to ports
- Development of two hub ports on each of the west and the east coasts

Maritime policy measures
- New land policy for major ports
- New policy on captive berths
- New policy on dredging
- Shifting of trans-shipment of Indian containers from foreign ports to Indian ports
- Policy on cooperation and competition amongst Indian ports
- Establishing 'Indian Ports Global' for overseas investments by Indian ports

The principal objective of any logistics system is that the goods should reach the final customers in correct quantity, at desired location, at right time, in usable condition, and in the most cost-efficient manner. A firm needs to conceptualize and implement an integrated logistics management strategy to achieve these interrelated business objectives.

Logistics involves two distinct aspects: procurement of raw material or inputs for manufacturing/processing known as materials management, and making goods and services available from the place of production to the ultimate customers termed as physical distribution. Michael Porter suggests in his concept of value chain that both inbound and outbound logistics are critical to a firm for value creation.

Since maritime transport is the oldest and the most cost-effective means of transport used in international trade, it is governed by a large number of shipping practices derived by the customs of trade. Depending upon the size, type, and nature of trade operations, a firm may either opt for charter or liner shipping. Containerization and multi-modal transport facilitate cargo exports from inland locations using more than one means of transport. The international shipping industry often uses a framework of global regulations on matters such as constructions standards for ships, navigational rules, and crew qualifications. Various international and national organizations associated with maritime transport are briefly discussed.

Summary

Effective and efficient management of logistics system is crucial for achieving competitiveness in international markets. The set of activities from procurement of inputs for the production process to making goods and services available to the ultimate customers is termed as logistics. The procurement of inputs and marketing of products beyond country boundaries is referred to as international logistics.

A typical logistics system consists of transportation, inventory, packaging, and unitization and information and communication technology. Transportation is an important part of international logistics comprising various modes such as air, road, rail, and ocean. Transportation by sea constitutes over 99 per cent of cargo shipment in volume terms in international trade. Various types of ocean cargo include bulk, break-bulk, neo bulk, and containerized. An exporter may use either a charter or a liner vessel for international shipments. Various forms of chartering include voyage charter, time charter, bare boat charter, back-to-back charter, trip time charter, and contract of affreightment. Containerization has facilitated multi-modal transportation of goods facilitating cargo handling and transport besides enabling door-to-door delivery of goods in international markets. Outsourcing of more sophisticated logistics and supply chain services, especially on a global scale, defined as third party logistics (3PL), has grown rapidly during the recent years.

International organizations associated with international maritime transportation include International Maritime Organization (IMO), International Labour Organization (ILO), World Customs Organizations (WCO), United Nations Conference on Trade and Development (UNCTAD), and International Organization for Standardization (ISO). Institutional framework associated with promotion of maritime transport in India includes Ministry of Shipping, National Shipping Board, Directorate General of Shipping, Shipping Corporation of India Ltd (SCI), and Container Corporation (CONCOR) of India.

Key Terms

Back-to-back charter Contract between a charterer and a sub-charterer, whose terms and conditions are identical to contract (charter) between the charterer and the shipowner.

Bare boat (demise) charter Hiring of a ship for a period of time during which the shipowner provides only the ship, whereas the charterer has to provide the crew together with all stores and bunkers and pays for all operating costs.

Barges Unmanned vessels generally used for oversized cargo and towed by a tugboat.

Break-bulk Packaged cargo that is loaded and unloaded on a piece-by-piece basis, that is, by number or count.

Bulk cargo Cargo with homogeneous characteristics in loose, unpackaged form without mark or count, loaded and carried in bulk.

Bulk carriers Vessels carrying a variety of bulk cargo, such as iron ore, coal, and foodstuff, and are identifiable by the hatches raised above the deck level that cover the large cargo holds.

Captive off-shoring Relocating business processes to a low-cost location and delivering from a shared service centre owned by the company itself.

Charter vessel A ship that does not have any fixed itinerary or sailing schedule and can be engaged to ship the firm's cargo from one port to another port.

Combination carriers Vessels carrying passengers and cargo, oil and dry bulk, or containers and bulk cargo.

Container ships Vessels carrying manufactured goods and products, usually on scheduled liner services.

Container Transport equipment, strong enough for repeated use, to facilitate handling and carriage of goods by one or more modes of transport.

Contract of affreightment A long-time agreement to carry a certain amount of cargo between two ports.

Dead weight tons (dwt) The maximum weight of the cargo a vessel can carry, also known as tonnage, including both bunker and the stores.

Displacement tonnage Weight of the ship, when fully loaded, measured by the weight of the volume of water displaced by the fully loaded vessel.

Free in and out (FIO) The charterer has to arrange the stevedores and to load/discharge the cargo on his own account.

Free in and out stowed and trimmed (FIOST) Similar to FIO, but the charterer is also responsible and bears the expenses of stowing and trimming.

Free in liner out (FILO) The shipowner is not responsible for the cost of loading but is responsible for cost of unloading

Full container load (FCL) Use of an entire container.

Global integration Coordination of activities across the country to build efficient operations network and take optimal advantage of internalized synergy at similarities across the operational locations.

Global sourcing Procurement of inputs for production of goods and delivery of services globally from the most optimal sources.

Gross registered tonnage (GRT) The total volume of a vessel's carrying capacity, measured as the space available below the deck expressed in hundreds of the cubic feet.

Gross terms The shipowner is responsible for the cost of loading, stowing, trimming, and unloading of the vessel.

ISO containers Containers that conform to the specifications of the International Organization for Standardization (ISO).

LASH (lighter aboard ship) vessels Vessels carrying very large containers like barges. It enables cargo to be loaded on barges in shallow water and then loaded on board a vessel.

Less than container load (LCL) Use of partial space in a container.

Light tonnage The total weight of the ship, when empty, is measured by using the weight of the water displaced by the empty vessel.

Liner in free out (LIFO) The shipowner is responsible for the cost of loading but not for vessel unloading.

Liner shipping Regular scheduled vessel services between two ports.

Local responsiveness Response by a firm to specific needs within various host countries.

Materials management Procurement of inputs such as raw materials and components for processing or value-addition by the firm.

Near-shoring Relocation of business process to a country within the same geographical region.

Neo-bulk carriers Vessels carrying specific types of cargo.

Neo-bulk Certain types of cargo that are often moved by specialized vessels, namely auto, logs, etc.

Net registered tonnage (NRT) The volume of cargo a vessel can carry arrived by subtracting the volume of space that would not hold the cargo from the GRT.

Net terms The shipowner is not responsible for the cost of loading and discharge.

Off-shoring Relocation of business processes to a low-cost location by shifting the task overseas.

Operations The process that transforms inputs, such as materials, machines, labour, capital, and management, into output (i.e., goods and services).

Roll-on-roll-off (Ro/Ro) vessels   Vessels that allow rolling cargo such as tractors and cars to be driven aboard the vessel.

Tankers   Vessels carrying liquid cargo such as crude oil, chemicals, and petroleum products in large tanks.

Third party off-shoring/outsourcing   Relocation of business processes from within the client country to an outside vendor operating at a low-cost location.

Time charter   Hiring of a ship for a time period whereby the shipowner places the ship with crew and equipment at the disposal of the charterer.

Trip time charter   A charterer hires the vessel for a single voyage or a round trip on terms and conditions similar to time charter.

Voyage charter   Contract of carriage in which a vessel is hired for transport of a specified cargo from one port to another port.

Concept Review Questions

1. Explain the concept of international logistic and its significance in international marketing.
2. Briefly explain the concept of international trade logistics.
3. Write short notes on the followng:
   (a) Contract of affreigtment
   (b) International Maritime Organization (IMO)
   (c) Shipping Corporation of India Ltd
   (d) CONCOR

4. Differentiate between the following:
   (a) Charter vs liner shipping
   (b) Voyage vs time charter
   (c) FIO vs FIOST
   (d) FILO vs LOFO
   (e) LCL vs FCL container

Critical Thinking Questions

1. Browse the Internet and explore the services provided by various liner shipping companies from your nearest seaport especially for the products of your interest.

2. Identify a few companies providing 3PL services located near your place and compare the services provided and the costs involved.

Project Assignments

1. Visit a seaport and explore the various types of vessels used for cargo shipment.
2. Visit an inland container depot (ICD) or terminal and find out the various activities carried out. Meet and discuss various issues and problems associated with international cargo shipment using containers.

3. Visit an international trading company and find out the various forms of ship chartering used by it and try to find out the reasons for the same.

Modes of Payment and International Trade Finance

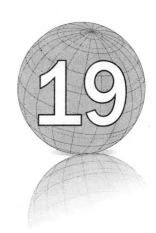

INTRODUCTION

The risks involved in an export–import transaction are much higher as the exporter and the importer are situated in two different countries and governed by two different legal systems. The exporter has to assure of receiving timely payment, while the importer has to ensure that he receives the imported cargo in good condition and on time. This requires extra diligence on part of both the exporter and the importer so as to ensure a smooth transaction. Over a period of time, as customs of trade, well-defined international procedures for export–import, system of documentation, shipping practices, and risk management have evolved, which are discussed at length in Chapters 17, 18, and 20.

A firm has to decide the 'modes' or 'terms' of payment while executing an export order so as to decide on the conditions for transfer of money from the seller to the buyer. The mode of payment differs widely, depending upon the nature of market competition, type of products dealt in, credit worthiness of buyers, and exporters' relationship and experience with the importer.

Since there is a considerable time lag between the procurement of inputs for export production and the realization of payments from the overseas importer, a sizable amount of finance gets blocked for export production and other activities thereafter before the payment is received. This makes hassle-free availability of export credit at easy rates crucial to export competitiveness.

This chapter brings out the concept of modes of payments in international markets. It also elucidates alternative modes of payment used in international trade so as to make readers appreciate, evaluate, and select the most suitable option depending upon the speed, security, cost, market competition, and risks associated. Various instruments used for financing international trade, including export credit schemes, have also been elaborated. Lastly, this chapter examines compatibility of trade finance schemes under the multilateral provisions of the WTO.

Learning Objectives

- To elucidate the significance of payments and financing in international trade
- To explain the concept of 'modes' or 'terms' of international payments
- To discuss various modes of payment
- To explicate the concepts of pre- and post-shipment credits
- To evaluate various financing options for international trade
- To examine the WTO compatibility of trade finance schemes

MODES OF PAYMENT IN INTERNATIONAL TRADE

The 'modes' or 'terms' of payment describe how and when the money is transferred from the buyer to the seller. Various modes of payments in international trade include advance payment, documentary credit with letter of credit (L/C), sight and time drafts, consignment sales, and open account. The problem faced in realizing the payment varies from case to case. Various factors affecting the choice of terms of payment include the risk associated, speed, security, cost, and the market competition.

The costs incurred to the importer and the risks associated to the exporter vary widely among different payment modes. As a matter of thumb rule, the lower the risk to the exporter, the higher is the cost to the importer (Fig. 19.1). While agreeing to the payment mode, both the exporter and the importer have to carry out a trade-off between the risks to the exporter and costs to the importer.

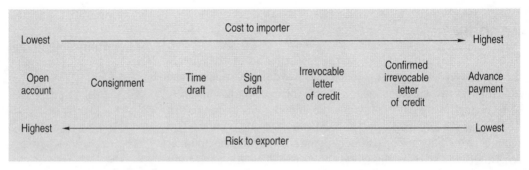

Fig. 19.1 Risk-cost trade-off for international payment modes

Source: Joshi, Rakesh Mohan, *International Business*, Oxford University Press, New Delhi, 2009, p. 659.

Advance Payment

In this mode, the payment is remitted by the buyer in advance, either by a draft mail or telegraphic transfer (TT). Generally, such payments are made on the basis of a sample receipt and its approval by the buyer. The clean remittance is made after accepting the order, but before the shipment, through banking channels.

Advance payment is the simplest and least risky form of payment from the exporter's point of view. Besides, no post-shipment finance is required if the payment is received in advance. There is no payment of interest on the funds and no commission is required to be paid as in other modes of payment, which makes it the cheapest mode of receiving payment. As it involves the highest level of risk for the buyer, the advance payment option is used only in cases where the exporter is in a position to dictate his terms. For instance, the advance payment option is often used if the product supplied is unique or has some sort of monopolistic power. However, such form of payment is common, mainly in case of overseas affiliates of the exporting firm.

Documentary Credit

In a typical international transaction, an exporter deals with an overseas buyer who is situated in a significantly different regulatory and business environment. The exporter is unwilling to part with his goods unless he is assured of receipt of the payment from the importer. On the other hand, the importer is unwilling to part with the money unless assured of receiving the goods. In such a situation, the bank plays a crucial role of an intermediary, providing assurance to both the importer and the exporter in an international transaction.

The payment collection mechanism that allows exporters to retain ownership of the goods or reasonably ensures their receiving is known as 'documentary collection'. The bank acts as the exporter's agent in a documentary collection and regulates the timing and the sequence of the exchange of goods for value by holding the title of the documents until the importer fulfils his obligation as given in the Uniform Customs and Practices of Documentary Credits (UCPDC), brought out by the International Chamber of Commerce (ICC) in its publication no. 600, widely known as UCPDC 600, implemented on 1 July 2007.

The two principal documents used in documentary collection are the bills of lading (B/L) issued by the shipping company and the draft (bill of exchange) drawn by the exporter. The B/L is issued by the shipping company to the shipper for accepting the merchandise for the carriage. As the 'document of title', it has a unique significance in shipping that only its legitimate holder is entitled to claim ownership of the goods covered therein. The importer cannot take possession of the goods unless the B/L is surrendered in original to the shipping company at destination. The procedure and the process involved in documentary credit employing banking channels assures both the exporter and the importer that the former gets the payment and the latter receives the goods.

The draft, commonly known as the bill of exchange, is used as an instrument to effect payment in international commerce. It is an unconditional order in writing signed by the seller (exporter), also known as drawer, addressed to the buyer (importer) or importer's agent, also known as drawee, ordering the importer to pay on demand or at a fixed or determinable future date the amount specified on its face. The draft provides written evidence of a financial obligation in clear and simple terms. Besides, it is a negotiable and unconditional instrument, which means payment must be made to any holder in due course despite any disputes over the underlying commercial transaction. Using a draft enables an exporter to employ its bank as a collection agent. The exporter's bank forwards the draft or the bill of exchange to the importer, generally through a correspondent bank, collects the draft, and then remits the proceeds to the exporter. Thus, in the process, the bank has all the necessary documents for control of the merchandise, which are handed over to the importer only when the draft has been paid or accepted in strict accordance with the exporter's instructions.

Documentary credit with letter of credit

A documentary credit represents a commitment from a bank to pay a certain amount to the seller of goods or services, provided the seller presents stipulated documents evidencing the shipment of goods or performance of services within a specified period. The modus operandi of an L/C is depicted in the form of a self-explanatory diagram in Fig. 19.2. The exporter gets in touch with the importer, and based on mutual communication, either by telephone, fax, or electronic messaging, mutually agrees on terms of sale and enters into a sales contract. (1) The importer, also known as applicant, applies to the issuing bank located in his country (2) for opening an L/C in accordance with the terms already agreed upon between the buyer and the seller in the sales contract. The issuing bank opens the L/C and delivers it (3) to the corresponding bank located in the exporter's country, which in turn advises (4) it to the exporter, also known as beneficiary. The exporter carefully scrutinizes the L/C and ensures all the terms and conditions agreed upon in the sales contract are mentioned. In case there is any variation or discrepancy, it is brought to the notice of the applicant (i.e., importer) and rectified.

Once the exporter is satisfied of the terms and conditions contained in the L/C, the shipment is sent (5). Soon after delivering goods to the shipping company, the B/L is obtained (6), which serves as the cargo receipt, contract of carriage, and the document for title of the goods. The shipment procedure requires a number of documents, both commercial and regulatory,

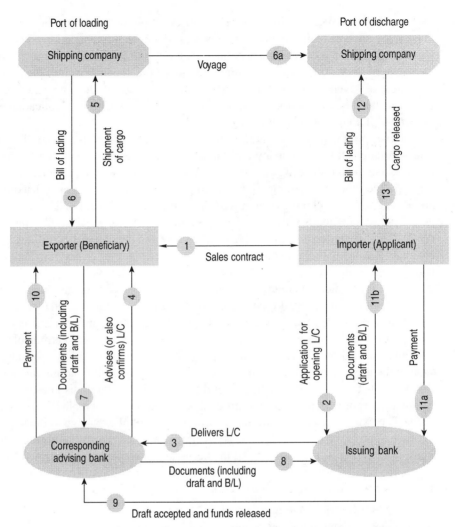

Fig. 19.2 Operation of an L/C: a schematic diagram

Source: Joshi, Rakesh Mohan, *International Business*, Oxford University Press, New Delhi, 2009, p. 661.

to be prepared, which are dealt in detail in Chapter 18. The exporter submits the complete set of documents as mentioned in the L/C, including the B/L along with the draft drawn by the exporter (7), to the advising bank, which in turn sends it to the issuing bank (8). The issuing bank scrutinizes the documents, and if found in accordance with the terms and conditions contained in the L/C, it accepts the documents and in case of a sight L/C releases the payment (9) to the issuing bank. The issuing bank in turn makes the payment to the exporter (10). However, in case of a usance L/C, the payment is made at a later date as contained in the L/C. The issuing bank presents the draft to the applicant (i.e., importer), who releases the payment (11a) upon which it handovers the B/L along with other documents (11b) to the importer, who in turn handovers the B/L (12) to the shipping company at the destination and takes delivery of the cargo (13).

As discussed, the operation of L/C is governed by the UCPDC of the ICC. As per the UCPDC, payment is made only if the documents strictly conform to the terms and conditions of the documentary credit. Under article 4 of the UCPDC, banks deal in documents and not in goods and services. An exporter should carefully examine the L/C and ensure that

- the names and addresses are complete and spelled correctly;
- the L/C is irrevocable and preferably confirmed by the advising bank, conforming to sales contract. However, the confirmation of an L/C, although preferable by the exporter, depends upon the terms of the sales deal;
- the amount is sufficient to cover the consignment;
- the description of goods is correct;
- the quantity is correct;
- the unit price of goods, if stated in the L/C, conforms to the contract price;
- the latest date for shipment or the shipping date is sufficient to dispatch the consignment;
- the latest date for negotiation or the expiry date is sufficient to present the documents and draft(s) to the bank;
- the port (or point) of shipment and the port (or point) of destination are correct;
- the partial shipment/drawing is permitted or prohibited;
- the transhipment is permitted or prohibited;
- the L/C is transferable or non-transferable;
- the type of risk and the amount of insurance coverage, if required, are included in the L/C;
- the documents required are obtainable;
- the following words, or similar, are present in the L/C:
  'Unless otherwise expressly stated, this credit is subject to the Uniform Customs and Practice for Documentary Credits, International Chamber of Commerce Publication No. 600.'

Under a documentary credit, a debt relationship exists between the issuing bank and the beneficiary. Therefore, it is advisable to assess the issuing bank's standing besides the sovereign and transfer risk of the importing country.

The issuing bank authorizes a corresponding bank in the beneficiary's country to honour the documents in its place. Under the UCPDC, unless the credit stipulates that it is available only with the issuing bank, all credits should nominate the bank (the 'nominated bank'), which is authorized to pay (to incur a deferred payment undertaking to accept drafts) or negotiate. However, in a freely negotiable credit, any bank is treated as a nominated bank.

An L/C may be of various types.

Irrevocable The issuing bank irrevocably commits itself to make payment if the credit terms as given in the L/C are satisfied under article 9A of UCPDC. A unilateral amendment or cancellation of an irrevocable L/C is not possible.

Revocable A revocable L/C is highly risky for the exporters, as it can be revoked any time without consent of or notice to the beneficiary. For an L/C to be revocable, it should explicitly indicate as 'revocable', otherwise under article 6C of UCPDC, in absence of any explicit indication that the credit is revocable, it is deemed as irrevocable. Nowadays, revocable L/Cs are rare, although these were not uncommon in the 1970s and earlier, especially when dealing with less-developed countries.

Confirmed The confirming bank (generally a local bank in the exporter's country) commits itself to irrevocably make payment on presentation of documents under a confirmed L/C. The issuing bank asks the corresponding bank to confirm the L/C. Consequently, the corresponding bank confirms the L/C by adding a clause, 'The above credit is confirmed by us and we hereby undertake to honour the drafts drawn under this credit on presentation provided that all terms and conditions of the credit are duly satisfied.' A confirmed L/C provides additional protection to the exporter by localizing the risk of payment. Thus, the exporter enjoys two independent recognitions: that of the issuing bank and the confirming bank. However, the confirming banks require the following criteria to be fulfilled:

- The L/C should be irrevocable.
- The credit should clearly instruct or authorize the corresponding bank to add its confirmation.
- The credit should be available at the confirming bank.
- The contents of credits should be unambiguous and free of 'stop' clauses (that allow the buyer to prevent the terms of credit being fulfilled).

Unconfirmed   Under such credit, the issuing bank asks the corresponding bank to advise about the L/C without any confirmation on its part. It mentions, 'The credit is irrevocable on the part of the issuing bank but is not being confirmed by us.'

Types of credit according to methods of payment

Sight   The beneficiary receives payment upon presentation and examination of documents in a sight L/C. However, the bank is given a reasonable time (generally not more than seven banking days) to examine the documents after its receipt.

Term credits   Term credits are used as financing instruments for the importer. During the deferred time period, the importer can often sell the goods and pay the due amount with the sales proceeds.

Acceptance credit   The exporter draws a time draft, either on the issuing or confirming bank or the buyer or on another bank depending upon the terms of credit. When the documents are presented, the draft is accepted instead of payment being made. For instance, the payment date may be 60 or 90 days after the invoice date or the date of transport documents.

Deferred payment credit   Such credits differ from the time draft in terms of lack of acceptance of a draft. The bank issues a written promise to make the payment on due date upon presentation of the documents. The due date is calculated on the basis of the terms of the credit. The deferred payment credit is generally more economical from the point of view of commission than the credit with time draft. However, an advance payment of credit amount may normally be obtained only from the issuing or confirming bank, whereas there are various possibilities for discounting a draft.

Revolving credit   Under 'revolving letters of credit (L/Cs)', the amount involved is reinstated when utilized, that is, the amount becomes available again without issuing another L/C and usually under the same terms and conditions.

Back-to-back credit   Back-to-back L/Cs are used when an exporter uses them as a cover for opening a credit in favour of the local suppliers. As the credits are intended to cover the same goods, it should be ensured that the terms are identical except that the price is lower and validity is different from the earlier one.

Documentary credit without letter of credit

Documents are routed through banking channels that also act as the seller's agent along with the bill of exchange. The major documents should include a full set of B/L, commercial invoice, marine insurance policy, and other stipulated documents. The bill of exchange (draft) is an unconditional order in writing signed by one person and requiring the person to whom it is addressed to pay a certain sum of money on instructions at a specified time. The major types of bills of exchange can either be sight or usance.

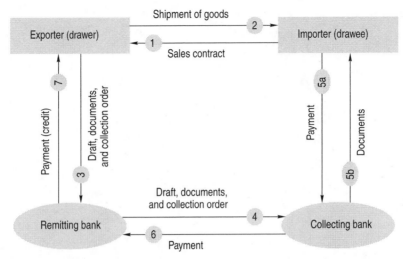

Fig. 19.3 Operation of sight draft (documents against payment): a schematic diagram

Source: Joshi, Rakesh Mohan, *International Business*, Oxford University Press, New Delhi, 2009, p. 665.

Sight draft (documents against payment) Similar to an L/C, just discussed, the exporter and the importer enter into a sales contract (1) on mutually agreed terms. Upon finalization of the contract, the exporter (drawer) ships (2) the goods and submits the documents along with the bill of exchange through his bank, also known as the remitting bank (3) to the corresponding bank, also known as the collecting bank (4) in the importer's country. The corresponding bank presents the draft to the importer (drawee), who makes payment at sight (5a) and thereafter the documents (5b) are handed over. The collecting bank transfers the payment (6) to the remitting bank in the exporter's country, which in turn makes payment (7) to the exporter (Fig. 19.3).

Thus, under 'documents against payment', the importer can take physical possession of the goods only when he has made the payment before getting documents from the bank. Sight drafts are generally considered safer as the exporter has possession and title of the goods till the time payment is made.

Usance or time draft (documents against acceptance) Once a sales contract (1) is signed between the exporter and the importer, the exporter (drawer) ships the goods (2) and submits the draft along with documents and the collection order (3) to the bank located in his country, also known as the remitting bank, which in turn sends (4) the draft along with documents to a corresponding bank, also known as the collecting bank, in the importer's country. The collecting bank presents the draft to the importer (drawee) who indicates his or her acceptance of the payment obligations (5a) by signing the draft upon which the B/L along with other documents is handed over to the importer (5b) for taking delivery of the goods.

The payment under time draft is usually to be made at a later date after 30, 60, 90, or more days. However, the bill of exchange already accepted by the drawee (i.e., importer) is again presented to the buyer (6a) on the due date, who in turn releases the payment (6b). The collecting bank transfers the funds to the remitting bank (7) for onward payment to the exporter (8) (Fig. 19.4).

This mode of payment poses a much greater risk as the documents are delivered to the importer, who subsequently takes title of the goods before the payment is released. In case the importer fails to make the payment, the recovery of sales proceeds is difficult and involves a cumbersome process.

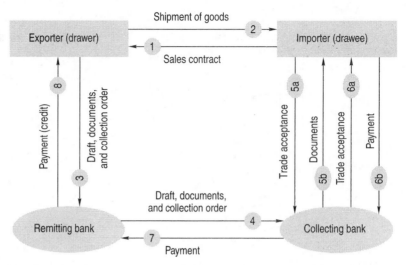

Fig. 19.4   Operation of usance or time draft (documents against acceptance): a schematic diagram

Source: Joshi, Rakesh Mohan, *International Business*, Oxford University Press, New Delhi, 2009, p. 666.

Consignment Sales

Under the consignment sales, the shipment of goods is made to the overseas consignee and the title of goods is retained with the exporter until it is finally sold. As the title of goods lies with the exporter, the funds are blocked and the payment period is uncertain. Consignment sales involve certain additional costs, such as warehousing charges, insurance, interest, and commission of the agents. Besides, the liability and risks lie with the exporter unless the consignment is sold. The risk of violating the terms of consignment is much higher in consignment sales. Besides, the price realization is also uncertain, over which the exporter has little control.

Selling goods on consignment basis in international markets also provides opportunity to the exporter to realize higher prices based on the buyers' satisfaction. Generally, such a mode of payment is restricted to dealing with trusted counterparts in the overseas markets. The export of precious or semiprecious stones and cut flowers is generally made on consignment basis. However, the exporters are required to declare the expected value of consignment on the guaranteed remittance (GR) form.

Open Account

The exporter and the importer agree upon the sales terms without documents calling for payments. However, the invoice is prepared by the exporter and the importer can take delivery of goods without making the payment first. Subsequently, the exporting and importing firms settle their accounts through periodic remittances.

As the payment is to be released later, it serves as an instrument to finance the importer for the transaction and the importer saves the cost of getting bank finances. It requires sufficient financial strengths on the part of the exporter. The operation of open account is hassle free and simple. The major drawback of an open account is the lack of safeguard measures against non-payment by the importer. Therefore, an open account is generally restricted to firms with longstanding dealing and business relationship and intra-company transactions among subsidiaries and affiliates. The statutory provisions related to foreign exchange often restrict using open account for receiving payments in international transactions. Generally, the central banks in most countries permit open accounts to foreign firms operating in their country and restrict them to domestic firms.

INTERNATIONAL TRADE FINANCE

Access to adequate finance at competitive rates is crucial to successful completion of an export transaction. Finances are required to complete an export trade cycle right from receiving the export order till the realization of final payment from the importer (Fig. 19.5). A firm has to procure raw materials, inputs, spares, or capital equipment for export production. Many a time, the exporting firm is required to import the inputs or spares required for export production and finances are needed in much advance. Export credit is extended both at pre-shipment and post-shipment stages.

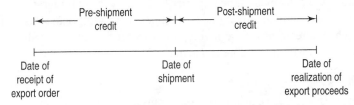

Fig. 19.5 Pre-shipment vs post-shipment credit

International managers need to understand various alternatives available for trade finance as discussed in this chapter. However, the choice of trade finance strategy depends upon several factors:

- Financing alternatives available
- Nature of goods sold: Capital goods require long-term financing, whereas perishables or consumer goods require short-term financing
- Intensity of market competition: Exporters are expected to offer long-term credit to importer in buyers' market, whereas it is the reverse case in sellers' market
- Relationship between the exporter and the importer

Various types of international financing alternatives available include banker's acceptance, discounting, accounts receivables, financing, factoring, forfaiting, L/C, and counter-trade. Besides, commercial banks also extend export finance at subsidized rates under the guidelines of the country's central bank.

Banker's Acceptance

Since centuries, banker's acceptance (BA) has been widely used in financing international trade. BA is the time draft or the bill of exchange drawn on and accepted by a bank. By 'accepting' the draft, the bank makes an unconditional promise to pay the holder of the draft the specified amount of money on maturity. Thus, the bank effectively substitutes its own credit with that of a borrower. The BA is a negotiable instrument that can be freely traded. The bank buys (discounts) the BA and pays the drawer (exporter) a sum less than the face value of the draft followed by selling (rediscounting) to an investor in the money market. The discount reflects the time value of money. The bank makes full payment at maturity to the investor who presents it. Banker's drafts, by definition, are time drafts with varying maturity of 30, 60, 90, or 180 days. The fee charged by the accepting bank varies depending upon the maturity period and the creditworthiness of the borrower.

Rediscounting

Exporters can convert their credit sales into cash by way of 'discounting' the draft even when it is not accepted by the bank. The draft is discounted by the bank on its face value minus interest and commissions. The discounting may be 'with' or 'without' recourse. If the importer fails to pay, the bank can collect from the exporter in case of 'with recourse' discounting, whereas the collection risk is borne by the bank in case of 'without recourse' discounting. Usually, the discounting rates are lower than other means of financing, such as loans and overdraft, mainly due to the government's export promotion schemes and subsidies.

Accounts Receivable Financing

In an open account shipment or time draft, goods are shipped to the importer without assurance of payment from a bank. Banks often provide loans to the exporter based on its credit worthiness secured by an assignment of the accounts receivables. The exporter is responsible for repaying the loan to the bank even if the importer fails to pay the exporter, for whatever reasons. Usually, the period of such financing is one to six months. As additional risks such as government control and exchange restrictions are involved in case of foreign receivables, banks often insist upon export credit insurance before financing.

Factoring

Factoring is widely used in short-term transactions as a continuous arrangement. It involves purchase of export receivables by the factor at a discounted price, that is, generally 2–4 per cent less than the full value. However, the discount depends upon a number of other factors such as the type of product and terms of the contract. Generally, factors advance up to 85 per cent of the value of outstanding invoices. The factoring service may be undertaken by the factor *with recourse* to the seller, wherein the exporter remains exposed to the risk of non-payment by the importer. Besides, the factoring may be *without recourse*, wherein the factor assumes the credit and non-payment risks.

The operation of export factoring is depicted in Fig. 19.6, which involves the following steps:

- The importer and the exporter enter into a sales contract and agree on the terms of sale (i.e., open account) (1).
- The exporter ships the goods to the importer (2).
- The exporter submits the invoice to the export factor (3).
- The export factor pays cash in advance to the exporter against receivables until the payment is received from the importer (4). However, the exporter pays interest to the factor on the money received or the factor deducts commission charges before making payment to the exporter.

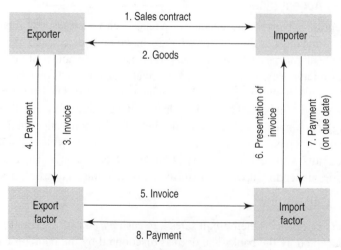

Fig. 19.6   Operational mechanism of factoring

- The export factor transfers the invoice to the import factor, who in turn assumes the credit risks and undertakes administration and collection of receivables (5).
- The import factor presents the invoice to the importer on the due date for payment (6).
- The importer makes payment to the import factor (7).
- The import factor in turn pays to the export factor (8).

Benefits to Exporters

The benefits of using a factoring service for the exporter are as follows:

- It facilitates expanding sales in international markets by offering prospective customers the same terms and conditions as local competitors.
- It facilitates immediate payment against receivables and increases working capital.
- Tasks related to credit investigations, collecting account receivables from the importer, and providing other bookkeeping services are carried out by the factors.
- In the event of buyer's default or refusal to pay, factors assume credit risk.
- Factoring often serves as a good substitute for the bank credit especially when the bank credit is either uneconomical or too restrictive.

  Besides, factoring is also beneficial for the importers as it

- increases their purchasing power without drawing on bank credit lines and
- facilitates procurement of goods with little hassles.

Forfaiting

The term 'forfaiting' is derived from the French word *forfait*, which means to relinquish or surrender the rights. Thus, forfaiting refers to the exporter relinquishing his rights to a receivable due at a future date in exchange for immediate cash payment at an agreed discount, passing all risks and responsibility for collecting the debt to the forfaiter. Forfaiting is particularly used for medium-term credit sales (1–3 years) and involves the issue of bill of exchange by the exporter or promissory notes by the buyer on which a bank and the buyer's country guarantee payment.

Forfaiting is the discounting of receivables, typically by negotiating bills drawn under an L/C or co-accepted bills of exchange. Generally, forfaiting is applicable in cases where export of goods is on credit terms and the export receivables are guaranteed by the importer's bank. This allows the forfaiting bank to buy the risk 'without recourse' to the exporter. The financing terms mainly depend on country risk of the buyer, size of contract, financial standing of the L/C opening bank or guarantor bank.

By forfaiting, the exporter surrenders without recourse the right to claim for payment of goods exported in return for immediate cash payment. As a result, an exporter can convert a credit sale into a cash sale on a no-recourse basis. Thus, forfaiting is a mechanism for financing exports

- by discounting export receivables evidenced by bills of exchange or promissory notes;
- on a fixed rate basis (discount);
- without recourse to the exporter;
- carrying medium- to long-term maturities (usually over 120 days); and
- up to 100 per cent of the contract value.

Avalization (co-acceptances)   Avalization or co-acceptance is a means of non-fund-based import finance whereby a bill of exchange drawn by an exporter on the importer is co-accepted by a bank. By co-accepting the bill of exchange, the bank undertakes to make payment to the exporter even if the importer fails to make payment on the due date.

Operation of a forfaiting transaction

Receivables under a deferred payment contract for export of goods, evidenced by bills of exchange or promissory notes (pro notes), can be forfaited. Bills of exchange or pro notes backed by avalization (co-acceptance) of the importer's bank are endorsed by the exporter, without recourse, in favour of the forfaiter in exchange for discounted cash proceeds. Some transactions are taken without such a guarantee or co-acceptance, provided the importer is of an acceptable standing to the forfaiter.

Step I: Pre-shipment stage
- As the exporter is in the process of negotiating a contract with the overseas buyer, she provides the bank the following details to enable it to give an 'indicative quote':
  - Name and full address of the foreign buyer
  - Details of goods (quantity, base price, etc.)
  - Amount of the contract
  - Number and expected dates/period of shipments
  - Security banker's name (under L/C or bills of exchange avalized by bank)
  - Repayment schedule
  - Country to which exports are to be made
- Based on the details provided, the bank contacts the forfaiting agencies/Exim Bank, who are given an indicative quote with details of discounting cost, commitment fees, etc.
- After confirming that the terms are acceptable, the exporter informs the bank, who accordingly calls for the final quote.
- After confirming acceptance of the forfaiting terms to the bank, the exporter signs off the commercial contract with her buyer. The contract must provide for the buyer to furnish avalized bills of exchange. Simultaneously, a forfaiting contract is entered into with the forfaiting agency through the bank.
- Once the forfaiting contact is duly signed, the bank will issue the following certificates:
  - A certificate giving permission to the exporter to remit commitment fees
  - A certificate showing the discount payable by the exporter to the forfaiting agency to enable them to declare the same on the GR form. Otherwise, the customs clearance of the goods would be held up

Step II: Post-shipment stage
- On shipment of goods, the exporter presents the documents to the bank, which in turn forwards those to the buyer or the buyer's bank. The set of documents being forwarded must contain the bills of exchange for the total amount (inclusive of the forfaiting cost drawn on the importer or importer's bank).
- The importer's bank would accept, co-accept, or avalize the bill of exchange and send it back to the exporter's bank.
- The exporter's bank would ensure that the bill of exchange is endorsed 'without recourse' in favour of the forfaiting agency.
- After checking the documents, the forfaiter would deposit the forfaited proceeds in the specified account.
- The bank, after checking the proceeds, would issue an FIRC and the GR form.

  A forfaiting transaction generally has three cost elements:

Commitment fee   The commitment fee is payable by the exporter to the forfaiter for her commitment to execute a specific forfaiting transaction at a discount. Generally, the commitment fee ranges from 0.5–1.5 per cent per annum of the utilized amount to be forfaited. Besides, the commitment fee is payable regardless of whether or not the export contract is ultimately executed.

Discount fee It is the interest payable by the exporter for the entire period of credit involved and is deducted by the forfaiter from the amount paid to the exporter against the analysed promissory notes or bills of exchange. The discount fee is based on the market interest rates as determined by the prevailing London Inter-Bank Offered Rate (LIBOR) for the credit period and the currency involved plus a premium for the risk assumed by the forfaiter. The discount rate is agreed upon at the time of executing the contract for forfaiting.

Documentation fee Generally, no documentation fee is incurred in straight forfait transaction. However, a documentation fee may be levied in case extensive documentation and legal work is required.

Benefits to the exporter

The major advantages of forfaiting to exporters are listed here:

- In India, post-shipment finance extended by bankers is limited to 180 days at subsidized rates. The exporter converts a deferred payment export into a cash transaction, improving liquidity and freeing the balance sheet of debt, thus also improving leverage.
- Forfaiting frees the exporter from cross-border political risks and commercial risks associated with export receivables. There is no contingent liability in the balance sheet of the exporter.
- As forfaiting offers 'without recourse' finance, it does not impact the exporter's borrowing limits. It represents an additional source of finance, outside working capital limits, providing a convenient option if funded limits are not sufficient.
- Since it is fixed rate finance, it hedges against interest and exchange risk arising out of deferred export payments.
- The exporter saves on insurance costs as forfaiting obviates the need for export credit insurance.
- Forfaiting is transaction-specific as the exporter need not have a long-term relationship with the forfaiting agency abroad.
- There is simplicity of documentation as the documents being submitted are readily available with the exporter.
- Forfaiting is not bound by any retention percentages. It offers 100 per cent financing and there is no restriction on the type, condition, or age of the products.

Letters of Credit

One of the oldest forms of international finance, L/Cs are still used in international transactions. As discussed in detail earlier in this chapter, in an L/C, the issuing bank undertakes a written guarantee to make the payment to the beneficiary, that is, the importer, subject to the fulfilment of its specified conditions. In the process, a debt relationship exists between the issuing bank and the beneficiary. Terms credit is often used as a financing instrument for the importer who gets delivery of the goods without making payment to the exporter.

Counter-trade

Counter-trade is used to combine trade financing and price setting in one transaction. It involves various forms of reciprocal transactions such as barter, clearing arrangements, switch trading, counter purchase, buy-back, and off-set, as already discussed in Chapter 12. Counter-trade finance imports in form of reciprocal commitments from countries that have payment problems, especially in hard currencies.

Export Finance

In order to be competitive in markets, exporters are also expected to offer attractive credit terms to their overseas buyers. Extending such credit to foreign buyers puts considerable strain on the liquidity of the exporting firm. It makes adequate trade finances from external sources at competitive terms during the post-shipment stage. Unless competitive trade finance is available to the exporters, they often try to quote lower prices to compensate their inability to offer competitive credit terms. Therefore, finances are provided to the exporters, generally at concessional rates, by the national governments in most countries, both at pre-shipment and post-shipment stages, through commercial banks.

Export Credit in India

In India, export credit is available both in Indian rupees and foreign currency. The following sections discuss this in detail.

Export credit in Indian rupees   The Reserve Bank of India (RBI) prescribes a ceiling rate for the rupee export credit linked to benchmark prime lending rates (BPLRs) of individual banks available to their domestic borrowers. However, the banks have freedom to decide the actual rates to be charged with specified ceilings. Generally, the interest rates do not exceed BPLR minus 2.5 percentage points per annum for the specified categories of exports[1] as given in Exhibit 19.1.

Pre-shipment credit   Pre-shipment credit means any loan or advance granted by a bank to an exporter for financing the purchase, processing, manufacturing, or packing of goods prior to shipment. It is also known as packing credit. As the ultimate payment is made by the importer, her creditworthiness is important to the bank. Banks often insist upon the L/C or a confirmed order before granting export credit. The banks reduce risk of non-payment by the importer by collateral or supporting guarantee.

Period of advance   The period of packing credit given by the bank varies from case to case depending upon the exporter's requirement for procurement, processing, or manufacturing and shipping of goods. Primarily, individual banks decide the period of packing credit for exports. However, the RBI provides refinance to the banks only for a period not exceeding 180 days. If pre-shipment advances are not adjusted by submission of export documents within a period of 360 days from the date of advance, the advance ceases to qualify for concessive rate of interest ab initio. Banks may release the packing credit in one lump sum or in stages depending upon the requirement of the export order or the L/C.

Liquidation of packing credit   The pre-shipment credit granted to an exporter is liquidated out of the proceeds of the bills drawn for the exported commodities on its purchases, discount, etc., thereby converting pre-shipment credit to post-shipment credit. The packing credit may also be

Exhibit 19.1   Export credit in Indian rupee

1. Pre-shipment credit (from the date of advance)	(i) Up to 180 days
(a) Up to 270 days	(ii) Up to 365 days for exporters under the Gold Card
(b) Against incentives receivable from the government	scheme
(covered by ECGC Guarantee) up to 90 days	(c) Against incentives receivable from government
2. Post-shipment credit (from the date of advance)	(covered by ECGC Guarantee) up to 90 days
(a) On demand bills for transit period (as specified by FEDAI)	(d) Against undrawn balances (up to 90 days)
(b) Usance bills (for total period comprising usance	(e) Against retention money (for supplies portion only)
period of export bills, transit period as specified by	payable within one year from the date of shipment
FEDAI, and grace period, wherever applicable)	(up to 90 days)

Source: Rupee/Foreign Currency Export Credit and Customer Service to Exporters, Master Circular, RBI/2012–13/74.

---

[1] *Rupee/Foreign Currency Export Credit and Customer Service to Exporters*, Master Circular, RBI/2012–13/74.

repaid or prepaid out of the balances in the Exchange Earners' Foreign Currency (EEFC) account. Moreover, banks are free to decide the rate of interest from the date of advance.

Running account facility Generally, pre-shipment credit is provided to exporters on lodgement of L/Cs or firm export orders. It has also been observed that in some cases the availability of raw material is seasonal, whereas the time taken for manufacture and shipment of goods is more than the delivery schedule as per the export contracts in others. Besides, often the exporters have to procure raw material, manufacture the export products, and keep the same ready for shipment, in anticipation of the receipt of firm export orders or L/Cs from overseas buyers. In view of these difficulties faced by the exporters in availing the pre-shipment credit in such cases, banks are authorized to extend the pre-shipment credit 'running account facility'. Such running account facility is extended in respect of any commodity without insisting upon prior lodgement of firm export orders or L/Cs depending upon the bank's judgement.

Post-shipment credit Post-shipment credit means any loan or advance granted or any other credit provided by a bank to an exporter of goods from the date of extending credit after shipment of goods to the date of realization of export proceeds. It includes any loan or advance granted to an exporter, in consideration of any duty drawback allowed by the government from time to time. Thus, the post-shipment advance can mainly take the form of

- export bills purchased, discounted, or negotiated;
- advances against bills for collection; and/or
- advances against duty drawback receivable from government.

    Post-shipment finance can be categorized into the following:

- Advances against undrawn balances on export bills
- Advances against retention money
- Exports on consignment basis
- Exports of goods for exhibition and sale
- Post-shipment credit on deferred payment terms

    Post-shipment credit is to be liquidated by the proceeds of export bills received from abroad in respect of the goods exported.

Period of post-shipment credit In the case of demand bills, the period of advance is the normal transit period (NTP) as specified by the Foreign Exchange Dealers Association of India (FEDAI). An NTP means the average period normally involved from the date of negotiation, purchase, or discount till the receipt of bill proceeds in the Nostro account of the bank concerned, as prescribed by the FEDAI from time to time. It is not to be confused with the time taken for the arrival of goods at an overseas destination.

    The demand bill is not paid before the expiry of the NTP, whereas the usance bill is paid after the due date and is also termed as an overdue bill. In case of usance bills, credit can be granted for a maximum duration of 365 days from the date of shipment inclusive of NTP and grace period, if any. However, banks closely monitor the need for extending post-shipment credit up to the permissible period of 365 days and also influence the exporters to realize the export proceeds within a shorter period.

Export credit in foreign currency In order to make credit available to the exporters at internationally competitive rates, banks (authorized dealers) also extend credit in foreign currency[2] (Exhibit 19.2) at London Interbank Offered Rates (LIBOR), LIBOR dominated in Euro (EURO LIBOR), or Euro Interbank Offered Rates (EURIBOR). LIBOR is a daily reference rate based

---

[2] *Rupee/Foreign Currency Export Credit and Customer Service to Exporters*, Master Circular, RBI/2012–13/74.

Exhibit 19.2   Export credit in foreign currency

Type of credit	Interest rate (per cent per annum)
(i) Pre-shipment credit	
(a) Up to 180 days	Not exceeding 350 basis points over LIBOR/EURO LIBOR/EURIBOR
(b) Beyond 180 days and up to 360 days	Rate for initial period of 180 days prevailing at the time of extension plus 200 basis points, i.e., (i) (a) above plus 200 basis points
(ii) Post-shipment credit	
(a) On demand bills for transit period (as specified by FEDAI)	Not exceeding 350 basis points over LIBOR/EURO LIBOR/EURIBOR
(b) Against usance bills (credit for total period comprising usance period of export bills, transit period as specified by FEDAI, and grace period wherever applicable) Up to 6 months from the date of shipment	Not exceeding 350 basis points over LIBOR/EURO LIBOR/EURIBOR
(c) Export bills (demand or usance) realized after due date but up to date of crystallization	Rate for (ii) (b) above plus 200 basis points

Source: Rupee/Foreign Currency Export Credit and Customer Service to Exporters, Master Circular, RBI/2012–13/74.

on the interest rates at which banks offer to lend unsecured funds to other banks in the London wholesale (or 'interbank') money market. The rate paid by one bank to another for a deposit is known as London Interbank Bid Rate (LIBID).

Pre-shipment credit in foreign currency   To enable the exporters to have operational flexibility, banks extend pre-shipment credit in foreign currency (PCFC) in any one of the convertible currencies, such as US dollars, pound sterling, Japanese yen, or euro, in respect to an export order invoiced in another convertible currency. For instance, an exporter can avail of PCFC in US dollar against an export order invoiced in euro. However, the risk and cost of cross-currency transaction are that of the exporter. Under this scheme, the exporters have the following options to avail export finance:

- To avail of pre-shipment credit in rupees and then the post-shipment credit either in rupees or discounting/re-discounting of export bills under Export Bills Abroad (EBR) scheme
- To avail of pre-shipment credit in foreign currency and discount or rediscounting of the export bills in foreign currency under EBR scheme
- To avail of pre-shipment credit in rupees and then convert at the discretion of the bank

Banks are also permitted to extend PCFC for exports to Asian Currency Union (ACU) countries. The applicable benefit to the exporters accrues only after the realization of the export bills or when the resultant export bills are rediscounted on 'without recourse' basis. The lending rate to the exporter should not exceed 1.0 per cent over LIBOR, EURO LIBOR, or EURIBOR, excluding withholding tax.

Post-shipment export credit in foreign currency   The exporters also have options to avail post-shipment export credit either in foreign currency or domestic currency. However, the post-shipment credit has also to be in foreign currency if the pre-shipment credit has already been availed in foreign currency so as to liquidate the pre-shipment credit. Normally, the scheme covers bills with usance period up to 180 days from the date of shipment. However, RBI approval needs to be obtained for longer periods. Similar to the PCFC scheme, post-shipment credit can also be obtained in any convertible currency; however, most Indian banks provide credit in US dollars.

Under the rediscounting of Export Bills Abroad Scheme (EBR), banks are allowed to rediscount export bills abroad at rates linked to international interest rates at post-shipment stage. Banks may also arrange a Banker's Acceptance Facility (BAF) for rediscounting the export bills without any margin and duly covered by collateralized documents. Banks may also have their own BAF limits fixed with an overseas bank, a rediscounting agency, or a factoring agency on 'without recourse' basis.

Exporters also have the option to arrange for themselves a line of credit on their own with an overseas bank or any other agency, including a factoring agency for rediscounting their export bills directly.

Financing to overseas importers   Generally, commercial banks extend exports credit, often at concessional rates, to finance export transactions to the exporters as a part of their export promotion measures. In addition, credit is also available to overseas buyers so as to facilitate import of goods from India, mainly under the following two forms.

Buyer's credit   It is a credit extended by a bank in the exporter's country to an overseas buyer enabling the buyer to pay for machinery and equipment that she may be importing for a specific project.

Line of credit   It is a credit extended by a bank in the exporting country (e.g., India) to an overseas bank, institution, or government for the purpose of facilitating import of a variety of listed goods from the exporting country (India) into the overseas country. A number of importers in the foreign country may be importing the goods under one line of credit.

Commercial banks carry out the task of export financing under the guidelines of the central bank (e.g., RBI). The export financing regulations are modified from time to time. Most countries have an apex bank coordinating the country's efforts of financing international trade. For instance, the Export–Import (Exim) Bank of India is the principal financial institution coordinating the working of institutions engaged in export–import finance in India, whereas the USA too has the Export–Import Bank of the United States for carrying out similar activities. The major categories of export finances provided by the Exim Bank are as follows:

- Credits for exports of Indian machinery, manufactured goods, consultancy, and technology services on deferred payment terms
- Lines of credit or buyer's credits to overseas entities, that is, governments, central banks, commercial banks, development finance institutions, and regional development banks for financing export of goods and services from India
- Project finance
- Trade finance

The exporters also have the option to arrange for themselves a line of credit with an overseas bank or any other agency, including a factoring agency, for rediscounting their export bills directly.

WTO COMPATIBILITY OF TRADE FINANCE SCHEMES

The multilateral trade regime under the WTO sets the framework for the types of subsidies that can be provided by a country for export promotion. As discussed in Chapter 3, the agreement on Subsidies and Countervailing Measures (SCM) prohibits national governments to provide subsidies that are contingent upon export performance or upon the use of domestic goods over the imported ones. Among the prohibited subsidies in the first category are direct subsidies to a firm or industry contingent on export performance, such as

- currency retention schemes giving a bonus to the exporter;
- internal transport and freight charges on export shipments on more favourable terms than for domestic shipment;
- the provision of subsidized inputs for the production of exported goods; and
- remission or exemptions from direct taxes and charges for export products.

The SCM agreement also constrains government intervention in the area of export financing and insurance. In particular, it prohibits the provision of export credits at conditions more favourable than those set in international capital markets and the extension of export credit insurance and guarantee programmes at subsidized premium rates.

This chapter elucidates the significance of payment terms and financing in international markets. Various modes of payment employed in international trade transaction are also elaborated. The chapter also deals with alternative options available to exporters for trade finance.

Summary

As the exporter and the importer are situated in two different countries, governed by two legal systems, the risk involved in international transaction is much greater than the domestic one and requires extra diligence for a smooth transaction.

The mode of payment describes how and when the money is transferred from the buyer to the seller. Exporters find advance payment as the simplest and the least risky method of receiving payment, but this involves a high level of risk for the importer. Therefore, importers are unwilling to remit advance payment unless the exporter enjoys monopolistic power in the market. Other modes of payment such as open account, consignment, and documentary credit have also been discussed. From exporters' point of view, a confirmed, irrevocable, and payable at sight L/C is considered highly secure. Exporters need to evaluate various alternative payment options and select the most suitable one depending upon the speed, security, cost, market competition, and risks associated.

Access to adequate finance at competitive terms is crucial to successful completion of an export transaction. Exporters do need credit to complete the export cycle right from receiving the export order till final payment is realized. Export credits are made available at concessional rates by national governments both at pre- and post-shipment stages. Major options available to exporters for international trade finance include banker's acceptance, discounting, accounts receivables financing, factoring, forfaiting, L/C, and counter-trade. Export credit similar to that provided by many other countries is available in India too at concessional rates in Indian and foreign currency for both pre-shipment and post-shipment credits.

However, the SCM agreement under WTO prohibits national governments to extend export credits at conditions more favourable than those set in international capital markets and the extension of export credit insurance and guarantee programmes at subsidized premium rates.

Key Terms

Back-to-back L/C An L/C used by an exporter for opening a credit in favour of local suppliers.

Bill of exchange (draft) An unconditional order in writing signed by one person and requiring the person to whom it is addressed to pay a certain sum of money on instructions at a specified time.

Confirmed L/C An L/C in which a confirming bank (generally a local bank) commits itself to make payment on presentation of documents.

Factoring Purchase of receivables by the factor at a discounted price.

Forfaiting Discounting of the receivables, typically by negotiating bills drawn under a letter or credit or co-accepted bills of exchange.

Irrevocable L/C An L/C that can be neither amended nor cancelled by the importer unilaterally.

LIBOR London Inter-Bank Offer Rate that serves as the base cost of funds for the prime banks.

Post-shipment credit Any loan or advance granted to an exporter from the date of shipment till the realization of export proceeds.

Pre-shipment credit Any loan or advance granted to the exporter for financing the purchase of inputs, raw material, etc., for processing, manufacturing, or packaging of goods prior to shipment.

Revocable L/C   An L/C that can be revoked any time by the importer without consent of or notice to the beneficiary.

Revolving L/C   An L/C wherein the amount involved is reinstated when utilized.

Sight draft   Draft for which payment is made by the importer at sight before taking delivery of the documents.

Time draft   Draft for which payment is made by the importer at an agreed later date.

Concept Review Questions

1. Explain the concept of 'modes' or 'terms' of payment in an international trade transaction.
2. Explain with the help of a suitable diagram the modus operandi of an L/C.
3. Distinguish between the 'sight' and 'time' drafts and its implications in international trade.
4. Discuss the significance of the availability of trade finance on competitive terms in international marketing.
5. Explaining the operational mechanism of forfaiting, enumerate its benefits for exporters.

6. Describe various pre-shipment and post-shipment credit schemes available in India.
7. Write short notes on the following:
   (a) Banker's acceptance
   (b) Rediscounting
   (c) Factoring
   (d) Counter-trade

Project Assignments

1. Meet a local exporter and find out the mode of payment used for realization of export proceeds. Identify the problems being faced by him in payment realization and share your experience in class. You may also make some recommendations to overcome these problems.

2. Explore the Internet to find out export credit schemes at subsidized rates offered in your country and compare with those of other countries. Identify the significant differences and assess its implications on exports.

Field Assignment

Contact a local bank dealing in international transactions and find out the various types of payment modes used in export transactions through the banking channels. Discuss the pros and cons of each of the payment mode used.

CASE STUDY: EXIM BANK'S CREDIT TO FACILITATE IMPORTS FROM INDIA

Mamta Engineering, an Indian firm, is in the process of manufacturing and marketing oil expellers and machinery for edible oil mills. The firm has received an unsolicited export order from a Kenya-based firm, Akitu Oils, for import of oil expellers and some related machinery valued at about US$70,000. A team of technical experts from Akitu Oils visited the firm's manufacturing facility at Kota and are satisfied with the technical parameters. However, the team indicated the firm's inability to make immediate payment. Akitu Oils even approached the Kenya-based banking institutions, but found it difficult to arrange finance at reasonable terms.

However, the Chief Executive of Mamta Engineering, Mrigank, is in no mood to let this order slip. He has instructed the finance department to carry out a comprehensive study and explore alternative ways to facilitate financing to Akitu Oils. The excerpts of the detailed report on various financing options prepared by Pragya, the Vice-President (Finance), are as follows:

'In order to facilitate exports, a number of financial institutions are involved in export financing that also include financing at easy terms to overseas importers. A typical institutional structure for export finance in most countries is depicted in Exhibit C19.1. Generally, it consists of a central bank that controls the monetary policy of the country administering interest rates. Short-term finances are monitored by commercial banks, whereas medium- and long-term finances are dealt by an export–import bank. Besides, most countries have an export credit insurance agency providing export credit insurance to exporters and guarantees to banks.

In order to respond to the competitive international markets, export credit agencies offer a gamut of other services, besides their traditional role in extending export credit. For instance, the Japan Bank for International Cooperation (JBIC) invests in equity in overseas projects of Japanese companies; the US Exim Bank also operates in the area of leasing of capital equipment and

Exhibit C19.1 Institutional set-up for trade finance

Institution	Role
Central bank	• Ensuring through conduct of monetary policy, adequate liquidity for financing exports • Administering interest rates/interest equalization schemes. In some countries, governments directly provide the support.
Commercial banks	• Providing short-term finance for exports typically up to 6 months/12 months
Exim bank	• Providing medium- and long-term finance for exports typically for 1–15 years
Export credit insurance agencies	• Providing export credit insurance to exporters, guarantees to banks

related services; whereas the Exim Bank of People's Republic of China administers the Chinese government concessional rules and lends foreign government rules. A comparative overview of the range of services provided by export credit agencies across major exporting countries is given in Exhibit C19.2.

The Exim Bank of India offers a variety of trade financing options to commercial banks, importers, as well as exporters to promote exports from India.

Exim Bank's Major Trade Financing Facilities
In India, the Exim Bank offers the following trade financing options to suit its various clients:

- Export credit
- Lines of credit
- Buyer's credit
- Supplier's credit
- Equipment finance
- Overseas investment finance
- Pre-shipment and post-shipment credit in Indian rupee
- Finances for consultancy and technology services
- Re-finance to commercial banks
- Guarantees

Lines of credit and buyer's credit are extended to overseas entities, that is, governments, central banks, commercial banks, development finance institutions, and regional development banks for financing export of goods and services from India.

Lines of Credit
The Exim Bank extends lines of credit to overseas governments/agencies nominated by them or overseas financial institutions, to enable buyers in those countries to import capital, engineering goods, industrial manufactures, and related services from India on deferred payment terms. This facility enables importers in those countries to import from India on deferred credit terms as per the terms and conditions already negotiated between the Exim Bank and the overseas agency. The Indian exporters can obtain payment of eligible value from the Exim Bank against negotiation of shipping documents, without recourse to them.

Features
The lines of credit are denominated in convertible foreign currencies or Indian rupees and extended to sovereign governments/agencies nominated by them or financial institutions. Such governments, agencies, or institutions are the borrowers and the Exim Bank the lender. Terms and conditions of different lines of credit are varying. It would need to be ascertained from time to time that the lines of credit have come into effect and uncommitted balance is still available for utilization. Indian exporters also need to ascertain the quantum of service fees payable to the Exim Bank on account of prorate export credit insurance premium and/or interest rate differential cost that they can then pay in their prices to their importers.

Modus operandi
The modus operandi of line of credit, as depicted in Fig. C19.1, is as follows:

- The Exim Bank signs agreement with the borrower (1).
- The buyer arranges to obtain allocation of funds under the credit line from the borrower. The exporter then enters into contract with the buyer (2), for the eligible items covered under the line of credit. The contract would need to conform to the basic terms and conditions of the respective credit lines.
- The delivery period stipulated in the contracts should be such that the credit can be drawn from Exim Bank within the terminal disbursement date stipulated under the respective line of credit agreements. Also, all contracts should provide for pre-shipment inspection by the buyer or agent nominated by the buyer.
- The buyer arranges to comply with procedural formalities as applicable in his country and then submits the contract to the borrower (3) for approval. The borrower in turn forwards copies of the contract to the Exim Bank for approval.
- The Exim Bank advises approval of the contract to the borrower (4), with a copy to the exporter, indicating approval

Exhibit C19.2 Cross-country comparison of products offered by export credit agencies

Countries	ECAs/other government agencies	Short-term insurance	Medium/long-term export credit schemes	Fixed rate financing (CIRR)	Foreign exchange risk cover	Direct lending	Investment insurance	Bond support scheme/issuance	Unfair calling insurance	L/C guarantee scheme	Working capital facility	Score
Canada	EDC	✓	✓	✓	✓	✓	✓	✓	✓	✓	✓	10
USA	Ex-IM/OPIC	✓	✓	✓	✓	✓	✓	✓	✓	✓	✓	10
France	Coface	✓	✓	✓	✓	✗	✓	✓	✓	✓	✓	9
South Korea	KEIC/KEXIM	✓	✓	✓	✓	✓	✓	✓	✓	✗	✓	9
Australia	EFIC	✗	✓	✓	✗	✓	✓	✓	✓	✓	✓	8
Germany	Euler Hermes/KfW	✓	✓	✓	✗	✓	✓	✓	✓	✓	✗	8
India	ECGC/Exim Bank	✓	✓	✗	✓	✓	✓	✓	n.a.	✓	✓	8
Italy	SACE/SIMEST	✓	✓	✓	✗	✗	✓	✓	✓	✓	✓	8
Japan	NEXI/JBIC	✓	✓	✓	✗	✓	✓	✗	✓	✗	✓	7
Malaysia	Exim Bank	✓	✓	✗	✗	✗	✓	✓	✓	✓	✓	7
Netherlands	Atradius	✓	✓	✗	✓	✗	✓	✓	✓	✓	✗	7
South Africa	ECIC SA	✓	✓	✓	✓	✗	✓	✓	✓	✗	✗	7
Switzerland	SERV	✓	✓	✓	✗	✗	✗	✓	✓	✓	✓	7
China	Sinosure	✓	✓	✗	✗	✗	✓	✗	✗	✓	✓	6
Singapore	ECICS	✓	✓	✓	✗	✗	✓	✗	✓	✗	✓	6
UK	ECGD	✗	✓	✓	✗	✗	✓	✗	✓	✓	✗	5
Brazil	SBCE	✓	✓	n.a.	n.a.	✓	n.a.	✗	n.a.	n.a.	n.a.	3

Source: Annual reports of various export credit agencies, 2013.

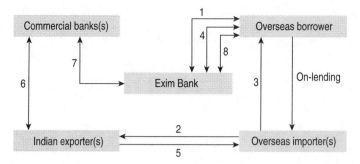

Fig. C19.1 Lines of credit

Source: Exim Bank.

number, eligible contract value, last date for disbursement, and other conditions subject to which approval is granted.

- The buyer, on advice from the borrower, establishes an irrevocable sight L/C. A single L/C is to be opened, covering the full eligible value of the contract including freight and/or insurance as laid down in the contract.
- The L/C is advised through a bank in India designated by the Exim Bank.
- The exporter ships the goods (5) covered under the contract and presents documents for negotiation to the designated bank. The bank forwards negotiated documents to the buyer.
- On receipt of a clean non-negotiable set of shipment documents (6) along with the relative invoices, inspection certificate, and a certificate that documents negotiated are as per terms of L/C and without reserve from the negotiating bank and after having satisfied itself that all formalities have been complied with in conformity with the terms of the Credit Agreement, the Exim Bank reimburses (7) the eligible value of shipment in equivalent rupees at spot exchange rate to the negotiating bank for payment to the exporter.
- The Exim Bank debits the borrower's account (8) and arranges to collect interest and principal receivable on due dates as per the terms of the line of credit agreement between the Exim Bank and the borrower.

However, under a line of credit,

- any bank charges, commission expenses payable in India, as also pro-rata export credit insurance premium, and/or interest rate differential cost, as may be applicable, shall be to the account of the exporter. The exporter should ascertain from the Exim Bank the amount service fee payable by the exporter before entering into commercial contract with the overseas buyer; and
- the Exim Bank is not liable to pay interest for the period between dates of negotiation and actual reimbursement from the Exim Bank.

Overseas Buyer's Credit

Under this scheme, credit is offered by the Exim Bank to an overseas buyer to facilitate import of Indian goods.

Supplier's Credit for Deferred Payment Exports

The Exim Bank offers supplier's credit in rupees or in foreign currency at post-shipment stage to finance the export of a number of specified goods and services on deferred payment terms. It includes an exhaustive list of capital goods and machinery besides other goods. Supplier's credit is available both for supply contracts as well as project exports; the latter include construction, turnkey, or consultancy contract undertaken overseas.

Exporters can seek supplier's credit in rupees or foreign currency from the Exim Bank in respect of export contracts on deferred payment terms irrespective of the value of export contracts.

The modus operandi of supplier's credit is depicted in Fig. C19.2, as follows:

- Extent of supplier's credit: 100% of post-shipment credit extended by exporter to overseas buyer (1).
- Currency of credit: Supplier's credit from the Exim Bank is available in Indian rupees or in foreign currency.
- Rate of interest: The rate of interest for supplier's credit in rupees is a fixed rate and is available on request. Supplier's credit in foreign currency is offered by the Exim Bank on a floating rate basis at a margin over LIBOR dependent upon cost of funds.

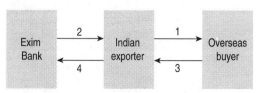

Fig. C19.2 Post-shipment supplier's credit

Source: Exim Bank.

- Security: Adequate security by way of acceptable L/C and/ or guarantee from a bank in the country of import or any third country is necessary, as per RBI guidelines.
- Period of credit and repayment: Period of credit is determined for each proposal having regard to the value of contract, nature of goods covered, security, and competition. The repayment period for supplier's credit facility is fixed coinciding with the repayment of post-shipment credit extended by Indian exporter to overseas buyer. However, the Indian exporter will repay the credit to the Exim Bank as per the agreed repayment schedule, irrespective of whether or not the overseas buyer has paid the Indian exporter.

Utilization of credit

The Exim Bank enters into supplier's credit agreement (2) with the Indian exporter as also with the exporter's commercial bank in the event of the latter's participation in the supplier's credit. The agreement covers details of drawdown, repayment, and includes an affirmation by the Indian exporter that repayment to Exim Bank would be made on due date, regardless of whether due payments have or have not been received from the overseas buyer.

- Negotiation of documents: The commercial bank negotiates export documents and seeks reimbursement of supplier's credit amount.
- Supplier's credit claims: The commercial bank seeks reimbursement of supplier's credit from the Exim Bank along with
    — annexure containing particulars of shipment/s made;

— copies of shipping documents. On satisfying itself that the disbursement claim is in order, the Exim Bank either credits (3) the amount in rupees under rupee supplier's credit into the account of the commercial bank, maintained with RBI at Mumbai, or the commercial bank's Nostro account under foreign currency supplier's credit and advises details of the account credited to bank/ exporter.

- Repayment of supplier's credit: The exporter repays principal amount (4) of credit to the Exim Bank as per agreed repayment schedule. Interest amounts are payable to the Exim Bank half yearly without any moratorium.

Regulatory norms for supplier's credit

The RBI has laid down guidelines for project exports and export of goods from India on deferred payment terms.'

Pragya made a presentation of the report on financing options available to the senior officers of Mamta Engineering, who are in the process of brainstorming to arrive at a consensus.

Questions

1. Critically examine various options available with Mamta Engineering to finance Akitu Oils. Identify the pros and cons of the various options.
2. Select the most suitable financing option to facilitate import by Akitu Oils. Give reasons to justify your choice.
3. Carry out an exploratory study to find out more financing options available for imports from the countries of competing suppliers.

Managing Risks in
International Trade

Learning Objectives

- To highlight the significance of risk management in international markets
- To explain various types of risks in international markets
- To discuss the tools and techniques for measuring risks
- To elaborate upon various options available for managing international marketing risks

INTRODUCTION

The level of complexity of operating in international markets is much higher than that in a domestic market because of the considerable differences in the political, legal, and economic systems of trading partners, and the distances involved. It offers far greater level of risks, as compared to domestic markets, which adversely affects a firm's smooth operations. Therefore, mangers operating in international markets need to develop a thorough understanding of various risks and options available to manage them, as elucidated in this chapter.

International managers are required to operate under different political conditions in various country markets where the level of political sensitivity and risks associated to business varies significantly. Political decisions often distort demand and supply in international markets and hamper free flow of goods and services. Political considerations often play an important role in determining the type and extent of concessions and protection granted to certain industries, labour, investment, and monitory policies. In addition, political stability in the host country also influences continuity of economic policies and a predictable business environment. Conceptual understanding of subtle differences in political and legal environment across the countries and associated risks facilitate in formulating and implementing effective strategy for international markets.

The legal framework of countries' trade policies differ significantly in terms of restrictions on export–import, participation of foreign firms in the local economy, norms for foreign direct investment (FDI), local content requirements for production, controls on foreign exchange, etc., which contribute to economic risks. Country risk ratings provided by a number of international agencies provide useful insights into risk factors associated with target markets, as discussed in this chapter.

An exporter is concerned about receiving the payment, that is, payment risk, whereas an importer is concerned about getting delivery of goods in the right condition and within the stipulated time, that is, performance risk. Exporters may protect themselves against political and commercial risks by getting credit risk insurance, whereas transit risk can be managed by marine cargo insurance, which is explained later in the chapter.

Before agreeing to finance a firm's export transactions, banks need to be assured about the ability of the borrowers to repay the loan. Once the perceived risks of default are reduced, banks are often willing to grant exporters favourable terms of credit. Generally, banks insist on adequate collateral before sanctioning export finance. Insurance policies and guarantees provided by export credit agencies like the Export Credit Guarantee Corporation (ECGC) can be used as collateral for trade financing. Thus, in addition to funding for exports, export finances also limit the risks involved in international transactions.

This chapter elaborates the various types of risks a company faces in international markets, the tools and techniques available to measure them, and several ways and instruments to manage such risks.

TYPES OF RISKS IN INTERNATIONAL MARKETS

The major types of risks in international markets include political, economic, commercial, and transit risks.

Political Risk

The possibility of political decisions, events, or conditions in an overseas market or country that adversely affect international business is termed as political risk. Such risks occur due to discontinuities in the business environment that are difficult to anticipate resulting from political change.[1] Confiscation of goods by a foreign government is considered to be the most severe form of political risk. Other forms of political risks may arise due to changes in government regulations and controls, which may directly affect the performance of business activities. The major types of political risks are as follows.

Confiscation   It refers to the process of taking over a property without any compensation.

Expropriation   It refers to the taking over of a company's goods, land, or other assets by a foreign government, and offering some kind of compensation in return. However, the compensation paid is generally much lower than the market value of the assets taken over.

Nationalization   It refers to the taking over of the assets and property by the government, and operating the business taken over under its ownership.

Domestication   It refers to a foreign company's relinquishing control and ownership to the nationals.

Over the recent years, the political risks of explicitly unjustifiable measures, such as confiscation and expropriation, have considerably reduced as countries are competing with each other for promoting foreign investments. However, countries often resort to *creeping expropriation* that refers to a set of actions whose cumulative effect is to deprive foreign investors of their fundamental rights in the investment. The economic impact is due to the fact that laws that affect corporate ownership, control, profit, and reinvestment can be enacted. Companies thus need to adopt adequate safeguards against these measures. Strategic alliance or joint ventures are often strategically used to mitigate the risks of confiscation or expropriation of a firm's assets in overseas locations.

---

[1] Robock, Stefan, 'Political Risk: Identification and Assessment', *Columbia Journal of World Business*, July–August 1971, pp. 6–20.

Economic Risk

Countries often impose restrictions on business activities on the grounds of national security, conserving human and natural resources, scarcity of foreign exchange, to curb unfair trade practices, and to provide protection to domestic industries. The balance of payment position of a country greatly influences the economic restrictions imposed on international business activities. The principal economic risks in international markets include import restrictions, local content requirements, exchange controls, and foreign exchange risks and exposures as elucidated next.

Import restrictions

In order to protect the domestic industry, national governments often impose selective restrictions on the import of goods. Such restrictions vary from a total ban on imports to quota restrictions. Firms with operations in countries with import restrictions often have to source locally available inputs at higher costs, thereby compromising the product quality.

Local content requirements

Trade policies often make provisions for local content requirements for extending export incentives or putting a country-of-origin label. For instance, the European Economic Community (EEC) discouraged assemblers and termed them as 'screw-driver operations' imposing a local content requirement of 45 per cent. For all cars manufactured in member countries, the North American Free Trade Agreement (NAFTA) imposes 62 per cent as local content requirement.

Exchange controls

In view of the scarcity of foreign exchange, countries often adopt stringent exchange control measures. These measures adversely affect the repatriation of profits and sales proceeds to the home country. Certain countries have multiple exchange rates for international transactions. For instance, Myanmar has three exchange rates for their currency Kyat (Kt), that is, the official rate (Kt6.51: US$1), the market rate[2] (Kt856: US$1), and an import duty rate (Kt450: US$1).

FOREIGN EXCHANGE RISKS AND EXPOSURE

A company operating in international markets is required to deal with multiple exchange rate regimes and cash flow across countries, making it vulnerable to foreign exchange fluctuations. In an international transaction, exporters and importers are both exposed to foreign exchange risks, as the payment of a specific amount already agreed under the contract is to be received or made in foreign currency at a future date. While managing international finances, one should develop a clear conceptual understanding of the following two distinct concepts.

Foreign Exchange Risk

Foreign exchange risk refers to the variance of domestic currency value of assets, liabilities, or operating income attributable to unanticipated changes in exchange rates. Thus, it refers not to the unpredictability of foreign exchange rates, but to the uncertainty of the values of a firm's assets, liabilities, and operating income due to unanticipated changes in exchange rates. Therefore, exchange risks arise only if the changes in exchange rates translate into volatility in domestic currency value of assets, liabilities, and operating income. Unless 'exposed' to foreign exchange fluctuations, a firm may not face foreign exchange risk. Thus, foreign exchange risk becomes dependent on foreign exchange exposure.

---

[2] As on 1 March 2013.

Exhibit 20.1   Impact of exchange rate fluctuations on a firm

	Home currency strengthens	Home currency weakens
Direct economic exposure		
Sales abroad	Unfavourable—Revenue worth less in home currency terms	Favourable—Revenue worth more
Source abroad	Favourable—Inputs cheaper in home currency terms	Unfavourable—Inputs more expensive
Profits abroad	Unfavourable—Profits worth less	Favourable—Profits worth more
Indirect economic exposure		
Competitor that sources abroad	Unfavourable—Competitor's margins improve	Favourable—Competitor's margins decrease
Supplier that sources abroad	Favourable—Supplier's margins improve	Unfavourable—Supplier's margins decrease
Customer that sells abroad	Unfavourable—Customer's margins decrease	Favourable—Customer's margins improve
Customer that sources abroad	Favourable—Customer's margins improve	Unfavourable—Customer's margins decrease

Source: Pringle, John J. and Robert A. Connolly, 'The Nature and Causes of Foreign Currency Exposure', *Journal of Applied Corporate Finance*, vol. 6, no. 3, Fall 1993, pp. 61–72.

Foreign Exchange Exposure

This refers to the sensitivity of the real value of assets, liabilities, and operating income to unanticipated changes in exchange rates expressed in its functional currency. The exposure includes 'real' value, which means the value has been adjusted by a country's inflation. The functional currency is the primary currency of a firm in which its financial statements are published. The domestic currency of a firm's home country is often the functional currency for most companies.

The impact of foreign exchange fluctuations depends on how the firm reacts, and also on how the firm's competitors, customers, and suppliers react. Exhibit 20.1 summarizes the direct and indirect impact of exchange rate fluctuations on a firm.

Thus, foreign exchange risk is a function of variance both in unanticipated changes in exchange rates and foreign exchange exposures. Unanticipated changes in exchange rates do not imply foreign exchange risk for items which are not exposed. Similarly, if exchange rates are precisely predictable with accuracy, exposure on its own does not mean foreign exchange risk. Although it is difficult to forecast the exchange rates with precision, an international company can at least measure its exposure to exchange rate fluctuations, and use available tools and techniques. Exchange rate fluctuations can lead to three types of exposures, as discussed next.

Transaction exposure

This is the effect of exchange rate fluctuations on the value of anticipated cash flows, denominated in home or functional currency terms, relating to transactions already entered in foreign currency terms. Transaction exposure may arise due to conversion of currency in order to

- make or receive payments for import or exports of goods and services;
- repay a loan; and/or
- make interest payment or pay dividends.

Transaction exposure arises due to various transactions denominated in foreign currency, including foreign-currency denominated assets (export receivables or bank deposits), liabilities (account payable or loans), revenues (expected future sales), expenses (expected purchase of goods), or income (dividends). An exporting firm has a transaction exposure from the time it accepts an export order till the time the payment is received and converted into domestic or functional currency. Thus, a company makes 'exchange gain' if a currency has appreciated between the receivables booked and the payments received, and 'exchange loss' if the currency has depreciated.

Strategies used to manage the transaction exposure include hedging with financial instruments forward, futures or options markets, and hedging with contract invoicing, such as home currency and mix currency invoicing or using price escalation clause.

Economic exposure

The effect of exchange rate fluctuations on a firm's future operating cash flows, that is, its future costs and revenues, is termed as operating exposure. Any business enterprise whose revenue and costs are affected by currency fluctuations has operating exposure even if it solely operates domestically and has all its cash flows denominated in the home currency.

In technical terms, both the operating and transaction exposures equal a firm's economic exposure. Economic exposure assesses the effect of exchange rate changes on future revenue costs, cash flows, and profits of the firm.

Economic exposure refers to the effect of the present value of future cash flows influenced by unanticipated changes in exchange rates and macroeconomic factors, such as unexpected changes in inflation rates and interest rates. The economic exposure of a firm is determined by localization of production inputs and export-orientation, flexibility in pricing, and the firm's ability to shift production and sourcing of inputs among countries.

Strategies used to manage economic exposure include financial initiatives, such as leads and lags, netting, matching, and intra-company re-invoicing, apart from production initiatives, such as input outsourcing in the same currency as the one used for exports and adjusting production quantity and location. 'Lead' refers to making payments early by using soft currency to pay the hard currency debts before the soft currency drops in value. Conversely, 'lag' refers to paying late, when a firm holds a hard currency with debts denominated in a soft currency, which decelerates by paying late. It reduces the transaction exposure too. Netting refers to settlement of inter-subsidiary debts for the net amount within affiliates of a multinational enterprise (MNE), as discussed later in this chapter. The mechanism of matching a firm's foreign currency inflows with its foreign currency outflows in respect of amount currency unit and timing is termed as 'matching'.

Translation exposure

Also known as accounting exposure, translation exposure arises due to conversion or translation of financial statements of foreign subsidies and affiliates denominated in foreign currencies into consolidated financial statements of an MNE in its functional or home currency. Fluctuations in exchange rates affect the earnings of subsidiaries and affiliates, and get translated into a consolidated income statement. Translation exposure depends upon the share of a firm's business from overseas operations, location of foreign subsidies, and accounting methods used.

Commercial Risk

In an international trade transaction, a firm has to deal with an overseas buyer operating in a different legal and political environment, thereby increasing the risks to smooth conduct of the commercial transaction. The major commercial risks involved in international trade transactions are as follows:

* Non-payment by the importer at the end of the credit period or after some specified period following the expiry of credit term
* Non-acceptance of goods by the importer despite his compliance with the export contract
* Insolvency of the purchaser

It has been observed that commercial risks have resulted in more losses in international transactions, as compared to political risks.

Transit Risk

The distance involved for cargo transport in international trade is much larger compared to domestic shipments, and it has to pass through either sea, air, or land through boundaries of several sovereign countries and perils of transport. Thus, the transit risk not only becomes greater, but also gets affected by international trade laws. Moreover, in international trade transaction, one is genuinely concerned about the reliability of the counter party. Therefore, developing a conceptual understanding of cargo transit risks, various types of transit losses, and marine cargo insurance becomes crucial, and an integral part to international shipment decisions.

Types of transit risk

The managers involved in international trade transactions need to develop a conceptual understanding of the various types of risks or perils involved in the transit of the cargo. The basic types of cargo risks are categorized in the following manner:

Maritime risk The damage or loss of the cargo in transit is caused by an 'act of God', that is, a natural calamity, or by an 'act of man', that is, a man-made event that may occur due to negligence or connivance. The possibility of a natural calamity or a man-made event is termed as maritime peril/risk. Natural calamities include events such as earthquakes, volcanic eruptions, lightning, flooding of a ship with sea water, damage of cargo with either sea water or rainwater, whereas explosion, fire, smoke, water used to extinguish fire, piracy, and deliberate damage are man-made perils.

Extraneous risk It includes incidental perils to which the cargo is exposed during transit, such as faults in loading, keeping, carrying, unloading of cargo, losses due to rough handling, breakage and leakage, improper stowage, hook and sling damage, contact with mud, theft, pilferage, and non-delivery.

War peril Risks related to war or warlike acts during or even after the war as covered by the Institute War Clauses (see *Institute Clauses* in Key Terms) include

* war, civil war, revolution, rebellion, insurrection or civil strife, or any hostile act by or against a belligerent power;
* capture, seizure, arrest, restraint, or detainment of carrier or craft due to above events (thus, confiscation of goods being smuggled by the customs authorities does not fall under this category and, therefore, cannot be insured); and
* derelict (abandoned) mines, torpedoes, bombs, or other derelict weapons of war.

Strike peril It includes the perils covered in the Institute Strike Clauses, which include damage or loss of cargo caused by

* strikers, locked-out workmen, or persons taking part in labour disturbances, riots, or civil commotion and
* a terrorist or any person acting from a political motive.

Types of cargo losses

Various types of cargo losses may occur in transit. There may be either a total loss or a partial loss.

Total loss   Total loss may be either actual or constructive.

Actual total loss   Under actual total loss (ATL), goods are completely damaged or destroyed, or undergo such a marked change in their nature that they become unmarketable. Actual total loss may take place in the following ways:

- When the cargo insured is physically destroyed, for instance, by a fire or sinking of the ship in deep waters with no possibility of salvation.
- The cargo insured is damaged to such an extent that it ceases to be insured. For instance, cement when damaged by sea water turns into concrete, and has little commercial value.
- Cargo is irretrievably lost and there is no hope of its recovery.

Constructive total loss   Under constructive total loss (CTL), the actual loss is inevitable as the cost of saving, repairing, or reconditioning of insured goods is more than the value of goods. Therefore, it is considered as total loss. While claiming constructive total loss, the insured is required to abandon his interests in the insured cargo in favour of the insurance company.

Partial loss   Partial loss may be general average, particular charges, or particular average.

General average   General average (GA) is the loss specific to marine cargo insurance. The concept of general average is centuries old. It operates on the principle that the cost of those goods that have been sacrificed to save the entire cargo shall be borne by all those whose goods have been saved. Therefore, if a vessel is in danger and the only way to prevent it from sinking is to throw one person's cargo overboard, then the rest of the cargo owners and the vessel owner will make up for the loss to that person in proportion to the value of their goods in relation to the total amount saved. It also includes the sacrifices made, such as pouring of water on cargo to extinguish fire or expenses incurred to tow a ship safely to the port and prevent it from sinking.

If a general average is declared on a voyage, a general average adjuster is appointed to determine the extent of loss and each party's contribution. All cargo owners must place a suitable general average security in order to obtain their cargo. Since general average is covered by marine cargo insurance, it becomes the insurer's responsibility to look after the insured shipments.

Particular charges   Particular charges (PC) are the expenses incurred to prevent loss or damage to the insured cargo from the risk that it is insured against. For instance, expenses incurred to feed the cattle during ship repair, for any ship damage that may have occurred due to a hurricane hitting the ship—any such eventuality is covered under the policy.

Particular average   Particular average (PA) includes partial loss or damage that is not covered by general average and particular charges. As particular average is not covered under general average, it is payable only when covered under the insurance policy.

MEASURING RISKS IN INTERNATIONAL MARKETS

A number of risk analysis agencies provide specialized services for country risk ratings. The most significant and widely used country risk ratings include Business Environment Risk Intelligence (BERI) index, Economist Intelligence Unit (EIU) indices, and PRS Group's International Country Risk Guide. These country risk ratings generally use different criteria to arrive at political, financial, economic, and overall risks. These ratings may be subscribed by international firms.

Business Environment Risk Intelligence Index

The BERI index provides risk forecasts for about 50 countries throughout the world and provides a broad assessment of the country's business climate. The index was developed by Frederich Haner, of the University of Delaware in the USA. It has since expanded into country-specific forecasts and country risk forecasts for international lenders, but its basic service is the Global Subscription Service. BERI's Global Subscription Service assesses about 50 countries, three times a year, on 15 economic, political, and financial factors on a scale from zero to four. As shown in Exhibit 20.2, zero indicates unacceptable conditions for investment in a country, one equates with poor conditions, two with acceptable or average conditions, three with above average conditions, and four with superior conditions. The key factors are individually weighted according to their assessed importance.

Exhibit 20.2   BERI index: a computational framework

Criteria	Weights	Multiplied with the score (rating) on a scale of 0–4[a]	Overall BERI index[b]
Political stability	3		
Economic growth	2.5		
Currency convertibility	2.5		
Labour cost/productivity	2		
Short-term credit	2		
Long-term loans/venture capital	2		
Attitude towards the foreign investors and profits	1.5		
Nationalization	1.5		
Monetary inflation	1.5		
Balance of payments	1.5		
Enforceability of contracts	1.5		
Bureaucratic delays	1		
Communications: phone, fax, Internet access	1		
Local management and partner	1		
Professional services and contractors	0.5		
Total	**25**		
		x 4 (max.)	= max. 100

[a]0 = unacceptable; 1 = poor; 2 = average conditions; 4 = superior conditions.
[b]*Total points:*
  More than 80 : favourable environment for investors, advanced economy
  70–79 : not so favourable, but still an advanced economy
  55–69 : an immature economy with investment potential, probably a newly industrialized country (NIC)
  40–54 : a high-risk country, probably a less developed country (LDC); quality of management has to be superior to realize potential
  Less than 40 : very high risk, would only commit capital if there exists some extraordinary justification
Source: www.beri.com, accessed on 13 July 2013.

Economist Intelligence Unit's Risk Indices

The EIU brings out indices to monitor business environment ranking so as to facilitate assessment of countries for doing business. It also monitors operational risks for 150 countries on a scale of 0 to 100, where 0 indicates the least risky and 100, the most risky place to operate. The overall score includes an aggregate of 10 categories of risks, such as security, political stability, government effectiveness, legal and regulatory, macroeconomic, foreign trade and payments, financial, tax policy, labour markets, and infrastructure. Switzerland (10), Singapore (11), Liechtenstein (11), Norway (12), Sweden (13), Hong Kong (14), Finland and Denmark (15) rank as the safest places to operate compared to Germany (21), USA and France (22), the UK (26), Qatar and Japan (27), the UAE (33), China (46), and India (53), whereas Russia (54), Angola (55), Kazakhstan (61), Ethiopia (61), Algeria (62), Pakistan (65), Sudan (79), Guinea (81), Syria (82), and Somalia (87) are the most risky countries to carry out business[3] (Fig. 20.1).

Global Risk Index

A cross-country comparison of external risks to the business may be carried out using the Global Risk Index (GRI) developed by the UK-based Maplecroft, which also monitors risks in international markets. This enables one to assess, quantify, and compare global risks across 179 countries based on 36 risk issues. These issues are clustered into two main categories:

- *global risks exposure* (i.e., macroeconomic risk, security risk, resource security, climate change, and pandemics and infectious diseases)
- *global risks resilience* (i.e., governance risks and societal resilience)

Somalia is reported to have the highest level of global risk followed by Sudan, Congo, D.R., Afghanistan, South Sudan, Central African Republic, Myanmar, Pakistan, Cote d'ivoire, and Syria.

Failed States Index

The Failed States Index, presented by Fund for Peace, an independent organization and foreign policy magazine is a useful tool to carry out a cross-country comparison of the world's weakest states. It uses 12 social, economic, political, and military indicators, and ranks on a scale of 0–120 (0 being the most stable and 120 the least stable) to assess about 177 states in order of their vulnerability to violent internal conflict and societal deterioration. The 12 indicators cover a wide range of the elements of the risk of state failure, such as extensive corruption and criminal behaviour, inability to collect taxes or draw on citizen support, large-scale involuntary dislocation of the population, sharp economic decline, group-based inequality, institutionalized persecution or discrimination, severe demographic pressures, brain drain, and environmental decay. States can fail at varying rates through explosion, implosion, erosion, or invasion over different time periods.

Somalia tops the list of the world's failed states[4] (Fig. 20.2) with a score of 114.9, followed by Congo, D.R. (111.2), Sudan (109.4), South Sudan (108.4), Chad (107.6), Zimbabwe (106.3), Kenya (98.4), Ethiopia (97.9), and Egypt (90.4), compared to Russia (77.1), India (78) and China (78.3). Incidentally, India is surrounded by some of the world's highly unstable countries, such as Afghanistan (106), Pakistan (101.6), Bangladesh (92.2), Myanmar (96.2), Nepal (93), and Sri Lanka (92.2). This severely restrains India's international marketing opportunities with its neighboring countries. Finland (20), Sweden (21.3), Denmark (23), Switzerland (23.3), Luxembourg (25.5), Australia (29.2), the USA (34.8), the UK (35.3), and Japan (43.5) rank among the most stable countries of the world.

---

[3] *Risk Briefing*, Economic Intelligence Unit, 2013.
[4] *The Failed States Index, 2012*, Fund for Peace.

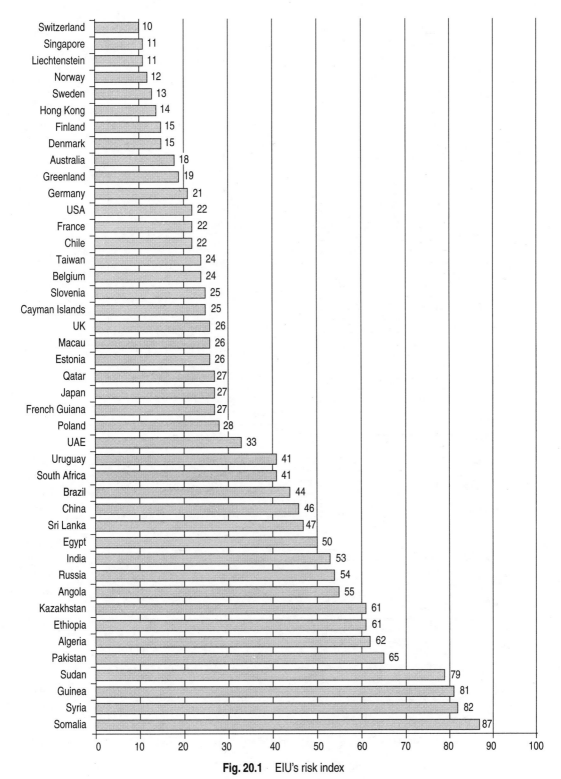

Fig. 20.1 EIU's risk index

Source: Risk Briefing, Economic Intelligence Unit, 2013.

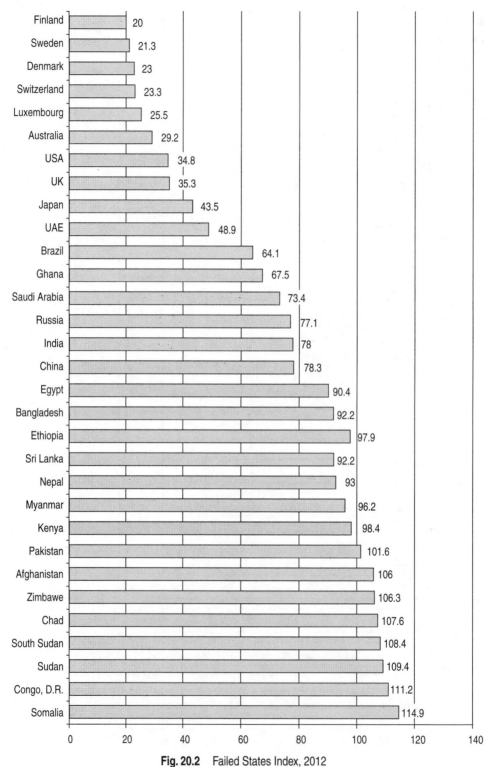

Fig. 20.2 Failed States Index, 2012

Source: The Failed States Index, 2012, Fund for Peace.

Among the wide range of reasons that contribute to a state's failure are rampant corruption, severe ethnic or religious divisions, predatory elites who have long monopolized power, and an absence of the rule of law. The world's weakest states are also the most religiously intolerant. The state's failure is contagious to neighboring states mainly due to porous borders, cultural affinity, and widespread underdevelopment.

MANAGING RISKS IN INTERNATIONAL MARKETS

International managers need to develop basic understanding of various strategic options available to manage international marketing risks. 'Insurance' and 'guarantees' allow an international firm to shift the risks to a third party as discussed next, besides other techniques of risk management.

Managing Political Risks

Political risks in international business may be managed either through 'avoidance' or 'insurance'. 'Avoidance' means screening out the countries with higher political risks by carrying out a cross-country analysis.

Strategic management of political risks

Political risks are beyond the control of a business firm, yet, in order to minimize them, certain measures can be employed.

Employing locals   An international firm should never make the costly mistake of underestimating the potential of locals in terms of their suitability of skills, competence, motivation, and education. Instead, it should strategically employ locals who have a much better understanding of local politics, and are accustomed to operate in their own environments.

Sharing ownership   In countries with higher level of risks, internationalizing firms should form joint ventures with local companies and share the risks, instead of operating alone.

Increasing perceived economic benefits to the host country economy   Countries often welcome foreign firms that have potential to provide economic benefits. FDI laws often encourage investment that provides employment to the local work-force, sources local inputs, such as raw materials or components, and increases the country's exports or substitutes import requirements. Therefore, an international firm should attempt to stimulate the benefits to the host economy.

Follow political neutrality   An international firm needs to be politically neutral so as to avoid any political controversy in a foreign country. It must maintain equal distance from all political parties and interest groups in the host country. The international firms also make it clear that it does not have anything to do with the national politics of the host country and is solely in the economic business.

Assuming social responsibility   In the long-term interest of an international firm, it should carry out business activities in a socially responsible manner. Foreign multinationals are often under criticism and considered to be exploiting national resources by nationalistic forces across the world. Therefore, in order to change its negative perception in the host country, it needs to operate in a socially responsible manner and take up projects involving social welfare of the masses.

Adapting to local environment   Business firms must adapt to local environment and local character so as to be perceived as local rather than foreign entities. For instance, McDonald's hires local staff and brings out products suited to local tastes, such as McVeggie, McAloo Tikki, Veg McCurry Pan, and Chicken Maharaja Mac, in India.

Insurance and guarantees

The political and commercial risks involved in international business can be managed by way of insurance and guarantees. The World Bank's subsidiary Multilateral Investment Guarantee Agency (MIGA) guarantees against non-commercial risks (i.e., political) at the multilateral level, whereas most countries have central level export credit agencies (ECA) to cover both political and commercial risks.

MIGA's guarantees against non-commercial (political) risks   MIGA, a World Bank Group subsidiary, helps foreign investors cover political risks by offering guarantees against the following types of coverage.

Currency transfer restrictions   The coverage protects against losses arising from an investor's inability to convert local currency (for example, capital, interest, principal, profits, royalties, or other monetary benefits) into foreign exchange for transfer outside the host country. The coverage also insures against excessive delays in acquiring foreign exchange caused by the host government's actions or failure to act. However, it does not cover risks arising due to currency devaluation.

Expropriation   The coverage offers protection against loss of the insured investment as a result of acts by the host government that may reduce or eliminate ownership of, control over, or rights to the insured investment. This policy also covers partial losses, as well as the 'creeping' effect. However, bona fide, non-discriminatory measures taken by the host government in the exercise of its legitimate regulatory authority are not considered expropriatory.

War and civil disturbance   The coverage protects against loss due to the destruction, disappearance, or physical damage to tangible assets caused by politically motivated acts of war or civil disturbance, including revolution, insurrection, and coups d'état. Terrorism and sabotage are also covered. It also extends to events that result in the total inability of the project enterprise to conduct operations essential to its overall financial viability.

Breach of contract   Coverage protects against losses arising from the host government's breach or repudiation of a contractual agreement with an investor. In the event of such an alleged breach or repudiation, the investor must be able to invoke a dispute resolution mechanism (e.g., arbitration) under contract and obtain an award for damages. If the payment is not received even after a specified period of time, the investor may file for a claim.

MIGA's guarantee premiums are based on a calculation of both county and project risk ranging from 0.45 per cent to 1.75 per cent basis points per year for three coverages. Investors may choose from any combination of the four types of coverage just discussed. Equity investment can be covered up to 90 per cent and debt up to 95 per cent. MIGA may insure up to US$200 million.

Managing Commercial Risks

Exporters are subject to risk of receiving payments from overseas buyers. Due to the fast-emerging and far-reaching political and economic changes, the payment risks in international transactions have considerably increased. An outbreak of war or civil war may block or delay payment for goods exported. A coup or an insurrection may also bring about the same result. Economic difficulties or balance of payment problems may lead a country to impose restrictions on either import of certain goods or on transfer of payments for goods imported. In addition, exporters have to face commercial risks of insolvency or protracted default of buyers. The commercial risks of a foreign buyer going bankrupt or losing his capacity to pay are aggravated due to political and economic uncertainties.

Credit risk insurance

Credit risk insurance provides protection to the exporters who sell their goods on credit terms. It covers both political and commercial risks. Credit insurance also facilitates exporters in getting export finances from commercial banks. The benefits provided by credit insurance to the exporters are as follows:

- Exporters can offer competitive payment terms to their buyers.
- It protects the exporters against the risk and financial costs of non-payment.
- Exporters also get covered against further losses from fluctuations in foreign exchange rates after the non-payment.
- It provides exporters a freer access to working capital.
- The insurance cover reduces exporters' need for tangible security while negotiating credit with their banks.
- Credit insurance provides exporters a second check on their buyers.
- Exporters get access to and benefit from the credit insurer's knowledge of potential payment risks in overseas markets and their commercial intelligence, including changes in their import regulations.

Most countries have central level ECAs to cover credit risks offering a number of schemes to suit varied needs of the exporters for export credit and guarantee. Examples are ECGC in India, Export Credit Guarantee Department (ECGD) in the UK, Export Risk Insurance Agency (ERIA) in Switzerland, and Export Finance and Insurance Corporation in Australia.

Insurance policies and guarantees extended by export credit agencies like ECGC can be used as collateral for trade financing. Once the perceived risks of default are reduced, banks are often willing to grant favourable terms of credit to the exporters. Thus, in addition to funding for exports, export finances also limit the firm's risk of international transactions.

Export credit guarantee corporation The ECGC of India, established in 1957 by the Government of India, is the principal organization for promoting exports by covering the risk of exporting on credit. It functions under the administrative control of the Ministry of Commerce. It is the world's fifth largest credit insurer of the world in terms of coverage of national exports. The ECGC mainly

- provides a range of credit risk insurance covers to exporters against loss in export of goods and services;
- offers guarantees to banks and financial institutions to enable exporters to obtain better facilities from them; and
- provides overseas investment insurance to Indian companies investing in joint ventures abroad in the form of equity or loan.

Credit insurance and guarantee schemes of ECGC The ECGC offers a variety of credit insurance and guarantee schemes of varying duration for exporters and banks as well, as shown in Fig. 20.3. Besides, there are a number of special schemes, as briefly discussed next.

Export Credit Insurance for Exporters ECGC offers two types of export credit insurance for exporters (ECIE): short-term and medium- and long-term, as briefly outlined next.

A. *Short-term (ECIE-ST) policies for exporters* Such policies may be based on either turnover or exposure. Some of the most popular policies of ECGC such as the Standard Policy, Small Exporter Policy, and Specific Shipment Policy—Short-term are discussed at length along with other policies offered by ECGC.

I. Turnover-based policies

    1. Shipment Comprehensive Risk (SCR) policy: This policy, also known as the *Standard Policy*, is the most popular policy, and is ideally suited to cover risks in respect of

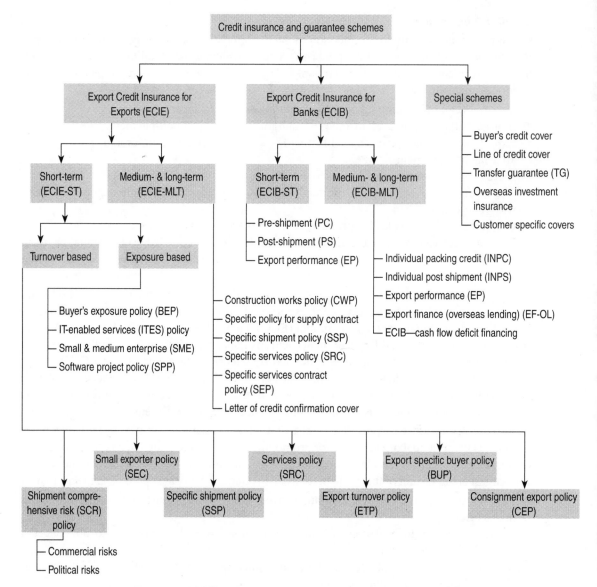

Fig. 20.3 ECGC's credit insurance and guarantee schemes: an overview

goods exported on short-term credit, that is, credit not exceeding 180 days. It is issued to exporters whose anticipated export turnover for the next 12 months is more than ₹5,00,000. This policy covers both commercial and political risks from the date of shipment especially the following risks:

(a) *Commercial risks*
  (i) Risks covered on the overseas buyers:
  - Insolvency of the buyer
  - Failure of the buyer to make the payment due within a specified period, normally four months from the due date
  - Buyer's failure to accept the goods, subject to certain conditions

    (ii) Risks covered on the L/C opening bank
- Insolvency of the L/C opening bank
- Failure of the L/C opening bank to make the payment due within a specified period normally four months from the due date
- Insolvency of the L/C opening bank

(b) *Political risks*
- Imposition of restriction by the government of the buyer's country or any government action, which may block or delay the transfer of payment made by the buyer
- War, civil war, revolution, or civil disturbances in the buyer's country. New import restrictions or cancellation of a valid import license in the buyer's country
- Interruption or diversion of voyage outside India resulting in payment of additional freight or insurance charges, which cannot be recovered from the buyer
- Any other cause of loss occurring outside India not normally insured by general insurers, and beyond the control of both the exporter and the buyer

The standard policy is meant to cover all the shipments made by an exporter on credit terms during the period of 24 months after the issue of the policy. An exporter may exclude shipments made against advance payment or those which are supported by irrevocable letters of credit, which carry the confirmation of banks in India, since he faces no risk in respect of such transactions. ECGC normally pays 90 per cent of the loss, whether it arises due to commercial risks or political risks. The remaining 10 per cent has to be borne by the exporter himself.

2. Small Exporter (SEC) policy: In order to encourage small exporters to obtain and operate an insurance policy, the small exporters' policy is issued to the exporters whose anticipated export turnover does not exceed ₹5,00,000 for one year. This policy is basically similar to the standard policy with some improvements in terms of cover especially the following:

(a) *Period of policy*　Small exporters' policy is issued for a period of 12 months, as against 24 months in the case of standard policy.

(b) *Minimum premium*　Minimum premium payable for a small exporters' policy is equal to ₹2,000 as against ₹10,000 for the standard policy.

(c) No claim bonus in the premium rate is granted every year at the rate of 5 per cent, as against once in two years for standard policy at the rate of 10 per cent.

(d) *Declaration of shipments*　Shipments need to be declared every quarter instead of every month as in the case of standard policy.

(e) *Declaration of overdue payments*　Small exporters are required to submit monthly declarations of all payments remaining overdue by more than 60 days from the due date, as against 30 days in the case of exporters holding the standard policy.

(f) *Percentage of cover*　For shipments covered under the small exporters' policy, ECGC will pay claims to the extent of 95 per cent where the loss is due to commercial risks, and 100 per cent if the loss is caused by any of the political risks. However, under standard policy, the extent of cover is 90 per cent for both commercial and political risks.

(g) *Waiting period for claims*　The normal waiting period of four months under the standard policy has been halved in the case of claims arising under the small exporters' policy.

(h) *Change in terms of payment of extension in credit period* In order to enable the small exporters to deal with their buyers in a flexible manner, the following facilities are allowed:
  - A small exporter may, without the prior approval of ECGC, convert a D/P bill into a D/A bill, provided that he has already obtained suitable credit limit on the buyer on D/A terms.
  - Where the value of this bill is not more than ₹3,00,000, conversion of D/P bill into a D/A bill is permitted even if credit limit on the buyer has been obtained on D/P terms. However, only one claim can be considered during the policy period on account of losses arising from such conversions.
  - A small exporter may, without the prior approval of ECGC, extend the due date of payment of a D/A bill provided that a credit limit on the buyer on D/A terms is in force at the time of such extension.

(i) *Resale of unaccepted goods* If, upon non-acceptance of goods by a buyer, the exporter sells the goods to another buyer, without obtaining the prior approval of ECGC even when the loss exceeds 25 per cent of the gross invoice value, ECGC may consider the payment of claims up to an amount considered reasonable, provided that ECGC is satisfied that the exporter did his best under the circumstances to minimize the loss.

3. Specific Shipment Policy (SSP)—Short-term: These policies provide cover to Indian exporters against commercial and political risks involved in export of goods on short-term credit not exceeding 180 days. Exporters can take cover under these policies for either a shipment or a few shipments to a buyer under a contract. These policies can be obtained by
   - exporters who do not hold SCR policy and
   - exporters having SCR policy in respect of shipments permitted to be excluded from the purview of the SCR policy.

The specific shipment policies offered by ECGC include
   - specific shipments (commercial and political risks) policy—short-term;
   - specific shipments (political risks) policy—short-term; and
   - specific shipments (insolvency and default of L/C opening bank and political risks) policy—short-term.

The exporter can opt to cover one or more shipments under a particular contract. He can also choose to cover shipments made during a given period within the validity of the contract. For example, if an exporter has received a contract for the supply of goods within a specific period, say 90 days or 180 days, he may also opt to cover further shipments under another specific policy at a later date.

The percentage of cover normally available under the policy is 80 per cent of the gross invoice value of the shipments covered in respect of countries in open cover. The maximum liability (ML), which is the limit up to which ECGC would accept liability under the policy, is arrived at by applying the agreed percentage of cover to the gross invoice value of the shipments covered under the policy.

4. Service (SRC) policy: It covers risk of non-payment to Indian companies entering into contract with foreign principals for providing them with technical or professional services.

5. Export Turnover Policy (ETP): It is a variation of the standard policy with additional discounts and incentives available to exporters who contribute not less than ₹1,00,000 per annum towards premium.

6. Export (Specific Buyers) Policy (EWP): It provides cover to Indian exporters against commercial and political risks involved in export of goods on short-term credit to a particular buyer.

7. Consignment Export Policy (CEP): It covers the Indian exporters from possible losses when selling goods to ultimate buyers. There are two policies available for covering consignment export, that is, Stock-holding Agent and Global Entity Policy.

II. Exposure-based policies

1. Buyer Exposure Policies (BEP): These are the policies that cover risk in respect of shipments to a single and multiple buyer(s), and on which premium would be charged on the basis of the expected level of exposure.

2. IT-enabled Services (ITES) policy: It is issued to cover the commercial and political risks involved in rendering IT-enabled services to a particular customer.

3. Small and Medium Enterprise (SME) policy: This policy covers the political and commercial risks that provide the SME sector easy administrative and operational convenience.

4. Software Projects Policy (SPP): It provides a credit insurance cover to meet the needs of software exporters, namely software projects policy where the payments will be received in foreign exchange.

B. *Medium- and long-term (ECIE-MLT) policies for exporters*   This type includes the following policies:

I.   Construction Works Policy (CWP): It is designed to provide cover to an Indian contractor who executes a civil construction job abroad.

II. Specific Policy for Supply Contract: It is a whole turnover policy designed to provide a continuing insurance for the regular flow of an exporter's shipments, for which credit period does not exceed 180 days.

III. Specific Shipment Policy (SSP): The Specific Shipments Policy can be obtained by exporters who have secured contract for supply of capital goods such as machinery or equipments on deferred terms of payment. The cover provides protection against non-receipt of payments due to commercial and/or political risks.

IV. Specific Services Policy (SRC): Where Indian companies conclude contracts with foreign principals for providing them with technical or professional services, payments due under the contracts are open to risks similar to those under supply contracts. In order to give a measure of protection to such exporters of services, ECGC has introduced the Services Policy. A wide range of services such as technical or professional, hiring or leasing can be covered under these policies.

V.   Specific Services Contract (SCP) policy: The Standard Policy is a whole turnover policy designed to provide a continuing insurance for the regular flow of an exporter's shipments for which credit period does not exceed 180 days. Contracts for export of capital goods, turnkey projects, construction works, and rendering services abroad are not of a repetitive nature, and they involve medium/long-term credits. Such transactions are, therefore, insured by ECGC on a case-to-case basis under specific policies.

VI. Letter of Credit Confirmation Cover: This policy covers a risk of non-payment by a bank that has issued a letter of credit to the exporter. The insured is the confirming bank.

Export Credit Insurance for Banks (ECIB)   A guarantee from ECGC ensures that the liabilities of a debtor are met even when he fails to settle it himself. The duration for the period of cover is 12 months and all packing credit advances as per the Reserve Bank of India (RBI) guidelines are eligible. There are two types of export credit insurance for banks:

1. Short-term (ECIB-ST) credit insurance: Such policies provides protection to the banks against the losses that may be incurred in extending packing credit advances due to protracted default or insolvency of the exporter client. They also give insurance to banks for both on pre-shipment (PC) and post-shipment (PS) credits and export performance (EP) as well.

2. Medium- and long-term (ECIB-MLT) credit insurance: These policies cover banks for their medium- and long-term credits such as Individual Packing Credit (INPC), Individual Post Shipment (INPS) Credit, Export Performance (EP), Export Finance-Overseas Lending (EF-OL), and ECIB-Cash Flow Deficit Financing.

Special schemes   These include the following:

1. Buyer's credit cover: It covers risks in respect of credit extended by a bank in India to an overseas buyer to pay for machinery and equipment to be imported from India for a specific project.

2. Lines of credit cover: It covers the credit extended by a bank in India to an overseas bank, institution, or government for the purpose of facilitating import of a variety of listed goods from India into the overseas country, popularly known as line of credit.

3. Transfer guarantee: Transfer guarantee indemnifies the insured bank for any loss due to the insolvency or default of the foreign bank opening letter of credit or due to certain political risks such as war, transfer delays, or moratorium, which may delay or prevent the transfer of funds to the bank in India.

4. Overseas investment guarantee: It provides protection for Indian investments abroad by covering the risks on account of war, expropriation, or restriction on remittances to Indian investments made by way of equity capital or untied loan for the purpose of setting up or expansion of overseas projects.

5. Customer specific policy cover: In order to cater to the specific need for export credit insurance cover of reputed large value exporters, which otherwise could not be fully addressed under any one of standard products, the customer specific policies have been introduced, and are issued to large exporters on a selective basis on the merits respective requests for such cover.

Managing Foreign Exchange Risks

A company operating internationally has to deal in multiple currencies and exchange rate regimes, which makes it vulnerable to foreign exchange risks and exposures. 'Hedging' is a common terminology in foreign exchange management that refers to the avoidance of foreign exchange risk and covering an open position. In international operations, firms often receive payments in a foreign currency at a future date, which is a cause for concern due to the changes in the spot rate that may cause them to make higher payment or receive less than expected in terms of their domestic currency. This may significantly affect the anticipated profits. Among the various hedging techniques available, the principal techniques include contracts, options, and swaps.

Foreign exchange contracts

A commitment to buy or sell foreign exchange is known as foreign exchange contract. It may either be a forward or a future one.

Forward contracts   A forward contract is a commitment to buy or sell a specific amount of foreign currency at a later date or within a specific time period, and at an exchange rate stipulated when the transaction is struck. The delivery or receipt of the currency takes place on the agreed forward value date. A forward transaction cannot be cancelled, but can be *closed* out at any time by the repurchase or sale of the foreign currency amount on the value date originally agreed upon. Any resultant gains or losses are realized on this date.

Generally, there is variation in the *forward* price and *spot* price of a currency. In case the forward price is higher than the spot price, a forward premium is used, whereas if the forward price is lower, a forward discount is used. To compute annual percentage premium or discount, the following formula may be used:

Forward premium or discount = (Forward rate – Spot rate)/Spot rate
× 360/ Number of days under the forward contract

In this formula, the exchange rate is expressed in terms of domestic currency units per unit of currency. To illustrate, if the spot price of 1 US dollar is ₹39.3750 in terms of Indian currency on a given date and its 180-day forward price quoted is ₹39.8350, the annualized forward premium works out to 0.92, as under:

Forward premium/Discount = (39.8350 – 39.3750) × 360/180 = 0.92

The forward differential is known as swap rate. By adding the premium (in points) to, or subtracting the discounts (in points) from the spot rate, the swap rate can be converted into an outright rate.

These forward premiums and discounts reflect the interest rate differentials between the respective currencies in the inter-bank market. If a currency with higher interest rates is sold forward, sellers enjoy the advantage of holding on to the higher earning currency during the period between agreeing upon the transaction and its maturity—buyers are at a disadvantage since they must wait until they can obtain the higher earning currency. The interest rate disadvantage is offset by the forward discount. In the forward market, currencies are bought and sold for future delivery usually a month, three months, six months, or even more, from the date of transaction.

Future contracts Commonly used by MNEs as hedging instruments, future contracts are standardized contracts that trade on organized future markets for only specific delivery dates only. The major differences in forward and future markets are summarized as follows:

- Forward contract does not have a lot size and is tailored to the need of the exporter, whereas the futures have standardized round lots.
- Date of delivery in forward contracts is negotiable, whereas future contracts are for only particular delivery dates.
- Contract costs in forward contracts are based on the bid/offer spread, whereas brokerage fee is charged for futures trading.
- Settlement of forward contracts is carried out only on the expiration date, whereas profits or losses are paid daily in case of futures at the close of trading.
- Forward contracts are issued by commercial banks, whereas international monetary markets (for example, of the Chicago Mercantile Exchange) or foreign exchanges issue futures contracts.

Options

Foreign currency options provide the holder the right to buy or sell a fixed amount of foreign currency at a pre-arranged price, within a given time. An option is an agreement between a holder (buyer) and a writer (seller) that gives the holder the right, but not the obligation, to buy or sell financial instruments at a time through a specified date. Thus, under an option, although the buyer is under no obligation to buy or sell the currency, the seller is obliged to fulfil the obligation.

This provides flexibility to the holder of a foreign currency option not to buy or sell the foreign currency at the pre-determined price unlike in a forward contract, if it is not profitable. The price at which the option is exercised, that is, at which a foreign currency is bought or sold, is known as strike price. Both currency call and put options can be purchased on an exchange. There are two types of foreign currency options:

- *Call option* gives the holder the right to buy foreign currency at a pre-determined price. It is used to hedge future payables.
- *Put option* gives the holder the right to sell foreign currency at a pre-determined price. It is used to hedge future receivables.

Foreign currency options are used as effective hedging instruments against exchange-rate risks as they offer more flexibility than forward or future contracts because no obligation is required on the part of the buyer under the currency options.

Swap

In order to hedge long-term transactions to currency rate fluctuations, currency swaps are used. An agreement made to exchange one currency for another at a specified exchange rate and date is termed as currency swap. Currency swaps between two parties are often intermediated by banks or large investment firms. Foreign exchange swap accounts for about 55.6 per cent of the average daily foreign exchange turnover of the world, whereas spot deals account for 32.6 per cent and outright forward for 11.7 per cent.

Buying a currency at a lower rate in one market for immediate resale at higher rate in another with an objective to make profit from divergence in exchange rates in different money markets is known as 'currency arbitrage'. To capitalize on discrepancy in quoted prices, arbitrage is often used to make risk-less profits.

Managing Transit Risks: Marine Cargo Insurance

Marine cargo insurance plays a pivotal role in transport of cargo in international trade. Regardless of the mode of transport, marine cargo insurance covers agreed risks of goods shipped in international trade. Marine cargo insurance provides protection against unanticipated and accidental losses in international business.

Concept of marine cargo insurance

Marine cargo insurance covers the risks of damage or loss of cargo during transit from the seller to the buyer. Both the legal and commercial aspects of marine cargo transport and its insurance are now discussed.

Legal aspects   During transit from the exporter to the importer, the custody of goods gets transferred at various stages to different authorities and agencies such as the carriers, clearing and forwarding agents, and customs and port authorities. The liability of these intermediaries is extremely limited in the event of damage or loss of the cargo. Besides, in the event of natural calamities, strike, or war, these intermediaries may not be held responsible.

International transportation of cargo by sea is mainly governed by the Hague Rules, 1924 and their subsequent modifications, such as Hague–Visby Rules, 1968 and Hamburg Rules, 1978. These rules apply to all bills of lading issued in any of the contracting countries. If the parties agree to incorporate any one of the previous rules in their contract, such rules govern the contract of carriage even when the countries where the parties reside subscribe to different rules. A carrier transporting goods under a bill of lading is required to exercise 'due diligence' in

- making the ship seaworthy;
- properly manning, equipping, and supplying the ship;

- making the ship (holds, refrigerating chambers, etc.) fit and safe for reception, carriage, and preservation of the goods; and
- properly and carefully loading, handling, stowing, carrying, and discharging the goods.

Thus, whenever loss or damage results from some unseaworthiness, the burden of proving the exercise of due diligence falls on the carrier. When different modes of transportation are used, the issuer of the bill of lading undertakes to deliver the cargo to the final destination. In the event of loss or damage to merchandise, liability is determined according to the law relative to the mode of transport that is responsible for the loss. If the means of loss is not determinable, it will be assumed to have occurred during the sea voyage.

As per the prevailing practices in most countries, the maximum amount of loss recovery from the carriers or intermediaries is limited to the amount prescribed by their law. For instance, the maximum liability of ship owners is SDR 666.67 per package or unit, or SDR 2 per kg of gross weight, whichever is higher for the goods carried by the Indian shipping companies. In case the cargo value is more than the maximum recoverable amount, the cargo owners have to bear the loss. Therefore, cargo insurance provides exporters protection against such losses.

The Warsaw Convention, 1929 and its subsequent amendments govern the international transportation of goods by air. In case of air transport, an airway bill (consignment note) is the document issued by the air carrier to a shipper that serves as a receipt of goods and evidence of the contract of carriage. However, an airway bill is not a document of title to the goods, as is the case with the bill of lading. The carrier requires the consignor to make out and hand over the airway bill with the goods. The consignor is responsible for the accuracy of the statements relating to the goods mentioned in the airway bill. Soon after the arrival of goods at the destination, the carrier notifies the consignee and hands over the airway bill upon compliance of the conditions of the carriage by the consignee. The carrier is liable for the loss or damage of cargo arising from delay unless it proves that the damage was due to negligent handling of the aircraft and the carrier and its agents have taken all necessary measures to avoid such damage. In case the airline proves that the shipper was negligent, it can escape its liability regardless of its own negligence. However, the carrier's liability is limited to US$20 per kg, unless the consignor has declared a higher value and paid a supplementary charge.

Besides, the rights and responsibilities of trading partners have been delineated in INCOTERMS, explained in Chapter 12. Out of 11 INCOTERMS, only two (i.e., CIF and CIP) require either party to insure. Even under CIF and CIP (carriage and insurance paid), the cargo has to be insured by the sellers but their obligation extends only to minimum cover, that is, London Institute Cargo clause 'C' coverage. As this is the minimum level of coverage and is inadequate for most shipments, sellers and buyers need to address this issue by taking additional insurance coverage.

Commercial aspects   In contracts where the cargo is shipped on free on board (FOB) terms but the payment is received on documents against payment (D/P) or documents against acceptance (D/A) terms, the negotiating banks do insist upon an appropriate insurance policy for advancing post-shipment credit.

Regulatory framework of marine cargo insurance

A marine cargo insurance policy consists of universally acceptable uniform rules governing insurance in different countries. This makes cargo insurance policies international in character, which means that a policy taken in one country will be acceptable in another country. In India, the marine insurance is subject to legislations such as the Insurance Act, 1938, Insurance Rules, 1939, and Marine Insurance Act, 1963.

Marine insurance contract is defined as an agreement whereby the insurer undertakes to identify the assured in the manner and to the extent thereby agreed against marine losses, that is to say, losses incidental to marine adventure. Although the word 'marine' is used in this definition, the cargo insurance principles are equally applicable to all modes of transport and not specifically to carriage by sea.

In an insurance contract, there are two parties—the insurer and the assured or insured. The insurer is the insurance company, also known as the underwriter, which assumes the liability when the loss takes place. The insured or assured, on the other hand, is one who procures the insurance policy or is its beneficiary.

Under the Indian Marine Insurance Act, 'There must be a physical object exposed to marine perils and that the insured must have some legal relationship to the object, in consequence of which he benefits by its preservation and is prejudiced by loss or damage happening to it or where he may incur liability in respect thereof.' Therefore, a marine insurance contract covers only physical objects and not the intangible. Besides, the insured should have some legal relationship with the goods as either a loser or a gainer by safe or unsafe arrival of cargo at the destination. For instance, exporters, importers, their agents, suppliers, financiers, or bankers have insurable interest in the goods and, therefore, can obtain insurance cover.

Coverage under marine cargo insurance

The main coverage provided against risks to cargo is on the basis of Institute Cargo Clauses A, B, and C. These were introduced by the London market, but have been adopted in India. However, for insurance coverage on internal movements within India, Inland Transit Clauses are used. The covers available under Institute Cargo Clauses are summarized as follows.

Institute Cargo Clause 'C' or ICC 'C'   This is the most restricted coverage and is subject to certain listed exclusions. It covers loss or damage to the insured cargo caused by

- fire or explosions;
- stranding, grounding, sinking, or capsizing;
- overturning or derailment;
- collision or contact of vessel craft or conveyance with any external object other than water;
- discharge of cargo at the port of distress;
- general average losses; and
- jettison.

This clause covers major casualties during land or sea transit, and tends to be used for cargo that is not easily damaged, such as scrap steel, coal, and oil in bulk.

Institute Cargo Clause 'B' or ICC 'B'   This cover is wider and apart from the risks covered under ICC 'C', it also covers loss or damage to cargo caused by

- earthquake, volcanic eruption, or lightning;
- damage of cargo by the entry of sea or river water in the ship;
- total loss of package lost overboard; and
- total loss of package dropped during loading and unloading.

There is significant additional coverage against wet damage from sea, lake, or river water and accidents in loading and discharging are covered, but there is no coverage for theft, pilferage, shortage, and non-delivery.

Institute Cargo Clause 'A' or ICC 'A'   This option is the widest of all three and is generally summed up as 'all risks' of loss or damage to the insured cargo. The words 'all risks' have been the subject of careful examination in legal cases over the years and should be understood in the context of Clause 'A' to cover fortuitous loss, but not the loss that occurs inevitably. Besides covering all the provisions under ICC 'C' and 'B', the Institute Cargo Clause 'A' also covers

- breakage;
- scratching, chipping, denting, and bruising;
- theft, malicious damage, and non-delivery; and
- all water damages including rainwater damage.

Additional clauses It includes Institute War Clauses and Institute Strike Clauses that are generally added to a marine insurance policy so as to provide an additional cover against the risk of war, strikes, riots, and civil commotion. Under the strike clauses, terrorism cover is granted when the goods are in ordinary course of transit. For most cargoes, the covers mentioned in the above basic clauses offer adequate cover. However, special market rate clauses are used for some commodities, goods, and situations.

Coal:	Institute Coal Clauses
Frozen meat:	Institute Frozen Meat Clauses
Cocoa, coffee, cotton, fats, oils not in bulk, hides, skins and leather, metals, oil seeds, sugar (raw or refined), and tea:	Institute Commodity Trade Clauses (A)

Exclusions under Institute Cargo Clauses

The Institute Cargo Clauses incorporate the following exclusions in the context of cover.

Wilful misconduct of the assured Even if the loss is proximately caused by an insured peril, it is excluded if it is attributable to the wilful misconduct (deliberate damage) of the assured.

Ordinary leakage, ordinary losses in weight or volume, or ordinary wear and tear Examples of the losses excluded in this category include evaporation, natural shrinkage, and pre-existing damages, for instance, machinery and second-hand motor cars.

Insufficiency or unsuitability or packing or preparation of packing of the insured cargo It is the duty of the insured to act as if he is uninsured. Clearly, if goods are sent insufficiently packed to withstand the normal handling anticipated during transit, then any loss that arises as a result should not be for insurance companies to pay.

Inherent vice or nature of the cargo Examples of excluded loss include blowing of tins containing foodstuff or spontaneous combustion of a cargo liable for self-heating.

Delay The insurance company is not responsible for any loss, damage, or expense caused by delay although the delay is caused by a peril insured against. Losses through delay could include loss of market or deterioration in respect of perishable goods that would be irrecoverable even if the cause of delay was a peril that was insured against, such as a collision.

Insolvency or financial default of carriers This exclusion was introduced to discourage the assured from shipping their goods on vessels whose owners, managers, charterers, or operators might be in financial distress. In practice, the clause would exclude all types of claims for recovery and forwarding of goods arising from abandonment of an insured voyage where the proximate cause was the financial distress of one of these parties.

Unseaworthiness and unfitness of the vessel This only applies in cases where the assured or their agents were privy to this information prior to loading.

War, strikes, riots, and civil commotion These risks are excluded under all the clauses, but can be insured by payment of an additional premium.

Premium

Marine insurance business in India is largely non-tariff based. Although certain guidelines provide chargeable premium rates, insurance companies normally take into account certain important factors while charging the premium rates. The nature of goods, their size, weight, and packing are taken into consideration. Hazardous and fragile goods attract a higher rate than normal cargo. The voyage to be undertaken is also an important factor. Some locations may be difficult to reach because of a poor or deteriorated infrastructure or due to trans-shipment during the voyage. The quality of the vessel or conveyance is also of great significance. Risks increase considerably when an old or substandard vessel or a vessel of poor classification is used for transporting the cargo. Shipment by such vessels involves loading at a premium rate.

The conditions of the insurance policy also have a bearing on the premium rates. The wider the cover sought, the more the premium. In certain cases, excesses or deductibles are imposed to avoid small losses. For higher excesses volunteered by the assured, a reduction in the rate is allowed. The loss prevention methods adopted, such as sending goods in containers, also merit discount in the premium. Further, the loss experience of the insured, if favourable to the insurer, also enables a discount in the premium rate.

Types of cargo insurance policies

The major types of marine cargo insurance policies available in the Indian market are as follows.

Specific voyage or time policies   These policies are issued to firms that require coverage for a specific voyage. It is suitable for firms that seldom require marine cargo policies in the course of their trade. These policies are issued on a 'from and to' basis, and the cover commences once the goods leave the place of origin named in the policy and terminates on delivery at the place of destination. Sometimes these policies are also issued in terms of duration of the voyage, in which case the cover commences on the date and time specified for the same in the policy.

Open policies   Exporters, importers, firms, and companies that handle a large turnover of goods take open marine insurance policies. It becomes extremely cumbersome for them to take specific voyage policies each and every time they transport their goods, as they have to handle innumerable transactions during a given period of time. The open policy is normally issued for a period of one year. A firm insures a part of its annual turnover at the beginning of the policy and goes on declaring the value of its consignments to the insurance company for each shipment.

For instance, an exporter's annual turnover is ₹120 million per year and approximately ₹10 million worth of goods is exported every month. Each consignment is valued at ₹5,00,000. There are about 20 trips every month. It is impracticable for him to take 20 specific voyage policies every month and so he takes an open policy of ₹20 million, and goes on sending declaration slips, giving certain details about the transit and its value, to the insurance company. Every time the exporter sends a declaration, the sum assured under the policy is reduced by the said amount. Before the entire sum assured is exhausted, the exporter again pays the premium to cover another ₹20 million, and reinstates the sum assured and continues like this. At the end of the policy term, it is likely that a certain balance amount of sum assured remains pending, in which case the premium corresponding to the balance amount left is refunded to him.

In open policies, it is a condition precedent to liability that each and every transit of the assured are declared for insurance. This is essential since the policy gives an automatic protection to the transit of the assured, and in case he forgets to declare a particular transit and a loss takes place in that particular transit, the insurance company accepts the loss as covered in the policy, provided there is sufficient balance of sum assured at that time.

Special declaration policy This is a variant of the open policy. This policy can only be taken by firms with an annual turnover of ₹20 million and above. In this policy, the entire annual turnover has to be declared at the commencement of the policy and the entire premium is paid in advance. Since the assured has to pay the premium in advance, he gets a discount ranging from 20–50 per cent on the premium. This policy is suitable for firms having a very large turnover and it becomes administratively difficult for them to keep track of the sum assured for the purpose of reinstating the same, once exhausted. In such policies, the assured is allowed to make his declarations on a monthly or even quarterly basis.

Duty insurance policy Customs duties form a major part of the cost of imported goods. Once the goods land at the port of destination, custom duty becomes payable. In case the goods are damaged during transit from the port to the importer's warehouse, the cost, insurance, and benefit (c.i.f.) value is not sufficient to represent the actual value of the goods since the custom duties have already been paid. This additional element of cost can be covered by a duty insurance policy. Claims under a duty policy are only payable if the claim is otherwise admissible in the marine cargo policy covering the goods.

Seller's contingency policy In almost all export transactions where credit is allowed by the seller to the buyer and the goods are not exported on c.i.f. basis, responsibility for the goods passes to the buyer when the goods are loaded on the overseas vessel. However, ownership does not change until the buyer accepts the goods and the relative documents. Thus, sellers allow credit to the buyers and ship goods on FOB terms, where the responsibility for loss or damage to the goods is passed to the buyer when the goods are loaded on the overseas vessel. Thus, the seller has no control over the conditions of the insurance cover arranged by the buyer.

In event of loss or damage to the goods in transit from a peril insured against, and the buyer refuses to pay for such loss or damage, the seller could stand to lose financially. The seller's interest or contingency interest cover could help to prevent this. The cover is normally arranged as an extension of FOB cover. The seller's interest cover, in effect, retrospectively reinstates cover, as per the Institute Cargo Clauses, provided for in the policy and allows the seller to be protected in an area where he has no control over the insurance arrangement.

Settlement of marine insurance claims

Once damage is discovered, the assured should make every effort to reduce the loss and/or prevent further loss to the consignment as provided in the policy. This could include re-bagging, re-cooperating barrels, separating wet cargo from dry, etc. Reasonable expenses incurred in taking such steps are reimbursable by the insurance company in addition to the payment of the claim itself. It means that the insurance company expects the assured to do exactly what he would have done if the shipments were uninsured.

The assured should notify the insurance company after these steps have been taken, so that the survey of the damage can be arranged promptly, if necessary. As stipulated in the Insurance Act, all claims amounting to ₹20,000 and above are required to be surveyed by a licensed surveyor. A survey report issued by the surveyor will give a detailed report of the circumstances, nature, origin, cause, and the extent of loss and damage. The carrier or his agent should also be notified immediately and advised of the time and place of the survey so that they can be represented.

It is also essential that a monetary claim be notified immediately in writing against the carrier, port trust, or any other responsible party in whose custody the consignment was at the time of loss as soon as the loss is known, or on taking delivery. This must include the full transit details, a description of the loss or damage, and should state that the carriers or other party will be held responsible for the loss or damage with an indication of the estimated amount of loss.

After payment of a claim on the basis of a subrogation letter and a power of attorney obtained from the assured, the insurance company proceeds against the carriers or any other responsible party for recovery of the amount as per the laws laid down. If the rights of recovery against the liable parties are not protected, the amount recoverable from the liable party, but prejudiced by the assured, will be deducted from the claimed amount and the balance amount will be paid. In case the amount of recovery prejudiced is not ascertainable, the claim will be settled on non-standard basis for an amount not exceeding 75 per cent of the assessed loss.

This chapter brings out the significance of understanding risks in international marketing operations. Various types of risks are explained along with tools and techniques available to measure the same. Instruments and options available to measure the risks are also elaborated in the chapter.

Summary

The level of complexity of operations in international markets offers much greater level of risks compared to that in the domestic market. The major types of risks involved in international markets include commercial, economic, foreign exchange, political, and transit risks.

Political risks may vary from confiscation of goods by a foreign government without paying any compensation to other forms such as expropriation, nationalization, and domestication. The major economic risks relate to import restrictions, local content requirements, and exchange controls. An exporter looks for some assurance that he would be paid for his goods, whereas the importer would like to be sure that the exporter would deliver the contracted goods. Cargo is exposed to maritime risks, extraneous risks, war perils, and strike perils during transit. International firms may use various risk analysis indices, such as Business Environment Risk Intelligence (BERI) index, EIU's risk indices, Maplecroft's Political Risk Index, and Failed States Index.

Political risks can strategically be managed by employment nationals, sharing ownership, increased perceived economic benefits to the host country economy, following political neutrality, assuming social responsibility, and adapting to local environment. To manage political risks, managers may use either 'avoidance' strategy by screening out the countries with higher political risks or 'insurance' by national, like ECGC, or multilateral agencies, like MIGA.

Credit risk insurance protects the exporters against the risk and financial costs of non-payment enabling them to offer competitive terms to their buyers. Most countries have central level export credit agency (ECA) to cover credit risks. ECGC is the principal organization of India offering a variety of export credit and guarantee schemes. The major credit insurance policies offered by ECGC include shipment (comprehensive risks) policy, specific shipment policy (short-term), small exporters' policy, turnover policy, consignment exports policy, buyer-wise policy, etc. Besides, ECGC also offers a variety of guarantees to the banks for extending export credit to the banks.

During transit from the exporter to the importer, the custody of goods gets transferred at various stages to different authorities and agencies, such as carriers, cleaning and forwarding agents, and customs and port authorities. The liability of these intermediaries is extremely limited in the event of damage or loss of cargo. Therefore, marine cargo insurance provides protection against anticipated and accidental losses in international business. The risk coverage under marine cargo insurance is governed by the London Institute Cargo Clauses 'A', 'B', and 'C' offering varying levels of risk coverage. The major types of marine cargo insurance policies available in the Indian market include specific voyage or time policies, open policies, special declaration policy, duty insurance policy, and seller's contingency policy.

Key Terms

Actual total loss   Occurs when goods are completely damaged or destroyed or undergo such a marked change that they no longer remain marketable.

Call option   Gives the holder the right to buy foreign currency at a pre-determined price.

Commercial risks   Risks such as non-acceptance of goods, non-payment, or insolvency of the importer.

Confiscation   The process of taking over of a property without any compensation.

Constructive total loss (CTL)   The actual loss is inevitable as the cost of saving, repairing, or reconditioning of insured goods is greater than the value of goods and is known as constructive total loss.

Creeping expropriation   A set of actions whose cumulative effect is to deprive investors of their fundamental rights in the investment.

Currency depreciation   An increase in domestic price of the foreign currency.

Domestication   A foreign company's relinquishing of control and ownership to the nationals.

Economic exposure   The effect of exchange rate fluctuations on a firm's future operating cash flows.

Economic risks   Restrictions imposed on business activities on the grounds of national security, conserving human and natural resources, scarcity of foreign exchange, to curb unfair trade practices, and to provide protection to domestic industries.

Expropriation   A foreign government's taking over of company's goods, land, or other assets offering some kind of compensation that is generally much lower than the market value of the assets taken over.

Foreign currency option   Providing the holder the right to buy or sell a fixed amount of foreign currency at a pre-arranged price, within a given time.

Foreign exchange exposures   The sensitivity of the real value of assets, liabilities, and operating income to unanticipated changes in exchange rates expressed in its function currency.

Foreign exchange risk   The variance of domestic currency value of assets, liabilities, or operating income attributable to unanticipated changes in exchange rates.

Foreign exchange   Any type of financial instrument that is used to make payments between countries such as foreign currency notes, monetary gold, and special drawing rights (SDRs).

Forward rate   The price at which the foreign exchange rate is quoted for delivery at a specified date after two business days.

Forward transactions   A commitment to buy or sell a specific amount of foreign currency at a later date, and at an exchange rate stipulated when the transaction is struck.

General average (GA)   A loss specific to marine cargo insurance.

Hedging   The avoidance of foreign exchange risk and covering an open position.

Institute clauses   Institute clauses of the Institute of London Underwriters, often referred to as the London Clauses or English Clauses, form the basis of the cargo insurance contract in many countries. The most common Institute Clauses include the Institute Cargo Clauses, Institute War Clauses, Institute Strike Clauses, and Institute Air Cargo Clauses.

Maritime risks   The damage or loss to the cargo in transit is caused either by an 'act of God', that is, natural calamity or an 'act of man', that is, man-made event that may occur due to negligence or connivance.

Nationalization   Government's taking over of the assets and property and operating the business taken over under its ownership.

Particular average   Partial losses or damage that is not covered by general average and particular charges.

Payment risk   Risk to exporters that they would be paid.

Performance risk   Risk to importers that the exporter would deliver.

Political risks   Possibility of political decisions, events, or conditions in an overseas market or country that adversely affect the international business that include confiscation, expropriation, nationalization, and domestication.

Price risk   Risk of a change in the cost of, or the revenues from, a transaction, and the impact of such a change.

Put option   Gives the holder the right to sell foreign currency at a pre-determined price.

Spot rate   Price agreed for purchase or sale of foreign currency with delivery and payment to take place not more than two business days after the day the transaction has been concluded.

Transaction exposure   The effect of exchange rate fluctuations, on the value of anticipated cash flows, denominated in home or functional currency terms relating to transactions already entered in foreign currency terms.

Concept Review Questions

1. Briefly explain the significance of risk management in international marketing.
2. Discuss various types of political risks in international markets and strategic options available with a firm to manage the same.
3. Differentiate between foreign exchange risks and exposure.
4. Briefly discuss the various credit insurance and guarantee schemes of ECGC.
5. Describe the various types of transit risks involved in international trade.
6. Write short notes on the following:
   (a) BERI index
   (b) MIGA
   (c) General average
   (d) Institute Cargo Clauses

Practice Exercises

1. Visit your library and also browse the Internet to find out the country risk ratings carried out by an agency based in your country, like ECGC. Compare these ratings with that of an international agency such as the EIU or BERI index.

2. Explore the Internet and carry out cross-country analysis of political risks in the top three export markets of your country.

Project Assignments

1. Contact a firm that operates in a country with high incidence of terrorism, crime, and violence. Explore the strategies adapted by the firm to operate in such countries and compare it with the strategic management of political risks learnt in the chapter. Discuss your findings in class.

2. Meet an exporting firm and find out the measures taken by it to manage commercial risks related to international transactions. List out the adequacy of such measures and discuss the bottlenecks.

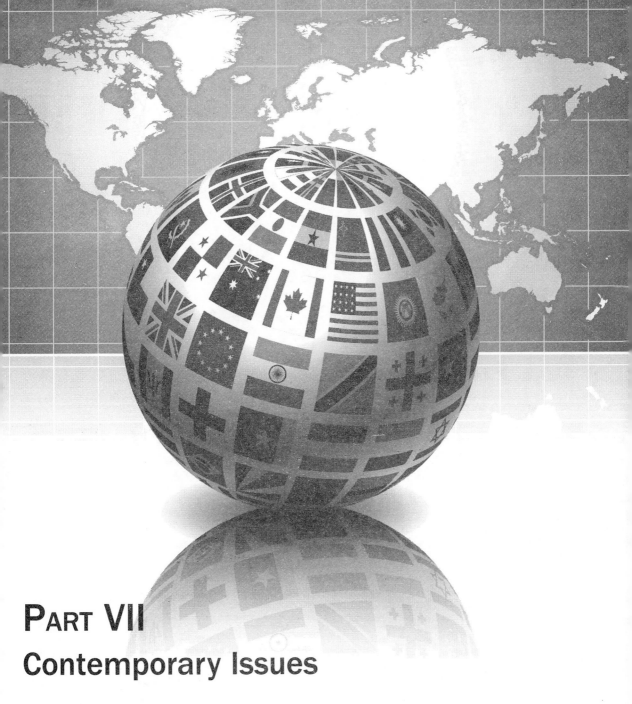

PART VII
Contemporary Issues

Global E-marketing

INTRODUCTION

The breakthroughs in information and communication technology (ICT), especially the advent of the Internet and the World Wide Web (www), have significantly changed the way people communicate and manage their daily lives across the world. The Internet is becoming increasingly integrated with day-to-day activities both in developed and developing economies. It has revolutionized relationships within and between organizations and individuals. In markets where there are many more mobile phones in hands than personal computers (PCs) on desks, including most of the developing world, wireless devices are becoming delivery mechanisms for Internet services.

The use of ICT is gaining significance as a strategic tool to increase productivity, reduce costs, enable mass customization, and encourage greater customer participation. The advent of the Internet and web-based technology has brought down the distinctions between traditional marketplaces and the global electronic market space. The name of the game is strategic positioning, the ability of a company to determine emerging opportunities, and utilize the necessary human capital skills (like intellectual resources) to make the most of these opportunities through an e-marketing strategy that is simple, workable, and practicable within the context of a global information milieu and new economic environment.[1]

Companies are progressively integrating ICT in their traditional ways of marketing and moving towards e-marketing to achieve business competitiveness. Businesses that fail to recognize the rapidly growing competitive strengths of rivals as a result of technological integration are likely to vanish, as illustrated in Exhibit 21.1.

In view of the growing significance of digital technology, especially as a tool to achieve and sustain competitiveness, a thorough

Learning Objectives

- To discuss the growing significance of ICT on global marketing
- To elucidate the conceptual framework of e-marketing
- To examine e-marketing technology and environment
- To explain various e-marketing models and strategic options
- To discuss e-enabled marketing process transformation and challenges
- To evaluate policy framework for global e-marketing

---

[1] Andam, Zorayda Ruth, 'e-Commerce and e-Business', e-ASEAN Task Force, *UNDP-APDIP*, May 2003, p. 5.

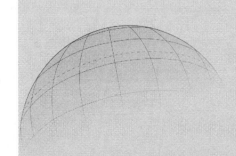

Exhibit 21.1 Death of *Encyclopaedia Britannica* and rise of Wikipedia

The world's first and the most famous encyclopaedia since 1768, *Encyclopaedia Britannica*, synonymous with erudition and wealth of knowledge, was the most accessible brand name in the publishing world. The reputation of brand Britannica was built over two centuries and its sales peaked at all time-high of US$650 million in 1990.

In 1990, Microsoft bought the rights to an encyclopaedia by Funk & Wagnalls, a third-rate product with hardly any brand recognition. Microsoft produced its multi-media version, renamed it Encarta and released in the form of a CD-ROM in 1993. The marginal cost to produce a copy of Encarta was US$1.5 and it was distributed free with new PCs. On the other hand, the marginal reproduction cost of *Encyclopaedia Britannica* was about US$250 per copy plus a sales commission of about US$500 to US$600 for each copy sold. It was sold at a market price of US$1500 to US$2200, depending upon the quality of binding.

Initially, Britannica grossly undermined the product strength of Encarta considering it a frivolous toy that was no match to Britannica's own profile of a scholastic classic. However, contrary to Britannica's market analysis, the sales of the mighty brand plummeted measurably. Compared to 1,17,000 in 1990, only 40,000 hard copies were sold in 1996, which later declined to 8,000 in 2009. In order to arrest the steep decline in sales, Britannica also brought out a text-only CD-ROM version. Since its salesforce received huge commissions on sales of the printed copies, it vehemently protested the CD-ROM version. To appease its salesforce, Britannica decided to offer the CD-ROM as a gift with the printed version. Moreover, the price of the stand-alone CD-ROM was kept a whopping US$1,000. Britannica had to put its version online in 1994. In 2012, Britannica announced the end of any further print after its 2010 edition.

In 2001, a web-based multilingual free content encyclopaedia, Wikipedia was launched, which presently contains more than 22 million articles in about 285 languages and has over 77,000 active contributors. Availability of exhaustive content for free and ease of use made it rapidly popular among Internet users across the world with over 470 million visitors monthly by 2012.

The 2010 version of the 15th edition of *Encyclopaedia Britannica* had 32 volumes weighing 129 pounds against the iPad weighing 1.44 pounds. Presently, online access to Britannica is available at US$70 a year, the iPad edition costs US$1.99 a month compared to the high price of print edition at US$1,395, whereas Wikipedia is available for free. Moreover, the online edition of Britannica consists of 65,000 articles compared to 38,90,000 articles in Wikipedia. Interestingly, sale of 8,000 sets of the 2010 print version of the Britannica generated revenue of US$11 million, which was much lower compared to over US$60 million contribution to fund Wikipedia and its other projects.

Thus, the rapid integration of technology in the publishing industry has seriously threatened the two-century-old unrivalled brand of encyclopaedia, leaving several lessons to learn, for others too.

Source: '*Encyclopaedia Britannica* Stops Printing after More than 200 Years', *The Telegraph*, 12 March 2012; 'The Death of *Encyclopaedia Britannica*: No Big Deal?', *The Week*, 15 March 2012; http://www.microsoft.com/uk/encarta; '*Encyclopaedia Britannica* Changes to Survive', *BBC News*, 17 December 1997.

conceptual understanding of e-marketing becomes crucial for managing global marketing effectively. This chapter brings out the significance of integration of ICT to marketing processes in achieving competitiveness. The conceptual framework that facilitates readers to understand e-enabled marketing systems vis-à-vis traditional marketing systems has been examined. The prerequisites for e-business transactions, e-enabled transformation in marketing processes, and the major challenges involved have been elucidated. The chapter also explains the principal technological arenas of e-business, such as electronic data interchange (EDI), Internet, extranet, and intranet. Further, this chapter elaborates various e-marketing models and alternative strategies. Global e-marketing and e-services have been separately discussed at length. Use of digital technology in trade documentation, which considerably contributes to efficiency and increases process transparency, has also been elucidated.

CONCEPTUAL FRAMEWORK OF E-MARKETING

Prefixing 'e' to any word implies an 'electronic' involvement or integration of ICT. Examples of such terms include e-business, e-shopping, e-learning, e-governance, e-logistics, etc. Thus, in simple terms, e-marketing refers to integration of ICT with marketing processes. Moreover, competitive pressures have compelled most companies to integrate online marketing with their traditional strategies. The major reasons for companies making online presence include the following:

- Expanding global market reach
- Creating worldwide virtual presence
- Improving business visibility
- Increasing responsiveness to customers and business partners
- Reduction in marketing cost
- Nurturing and strengthening relationships with customers and business partners

ICT is employed to collect information at the point of sales and to transmit it instantaneously from the retailer to the manufacturer. The Web has transformed the entire world into a virtual local market. It has transformed the markets from 'physical marketplace' to 'virtual marketspace' leading to basic alteration in the consumer-decision process. The way of offering services across geographical boundaries has also been revolutionized by ICT.

Traditionally a marketing system, as depicted in Fig. 21.1, consists of basic 4Ps of marketing, namely product, price, place, and promotion. The traditional marketing strategy requires dividing the heterogeneous universe of customers into homogeneous sub-groups, known as market segmentation, who would respond more or less similarly to a given marketing strategy under the traditional marketing approach. A business enterprise generally adopts a uniform strategy

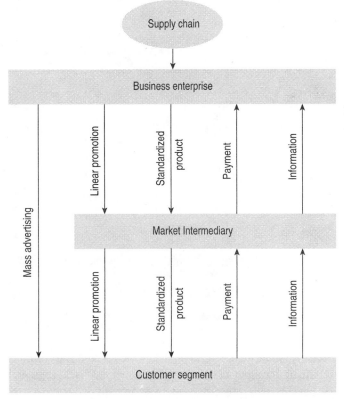

Fig. 21.1 Traditional marketing system

Source: Joshi, Rakesh Mohan, *International Business,* Oxford University
Press, New Delhi, 2009, p. 814.

for a given market segment. Thus, advertising, promotion, product, and the marketing channel remain the same for all the customers in a given market segment. Distribution channels are often elaborate and market intermediaries play a crucial role in sales transactions.

The e-marketing system facilitates business enterprises to leverage upon ICT to achieve competitiveness. In an e-business-based marketing system (Fig. 21.2), firms can target an individual customer and adopt customized marketing strategies targeting a single-customer segment, also known as 'segment size of one'. This is after referred to as 'one-to-one' or 1:1 marketing. Instead of discrete flow of information under the traditional marketing system, the e-marketing system facilitates a business enterprise to have elaborate knowledge management and database management systems that can be used to design individualized market promotion and customized products. Contrary to the traditional marketing system that often has several intermediaries for making its products available to the end customers, electronic marketing systems are either direct or have shorter channels of distribution, often dominated by facilitators. In an e-enabled system, the payments flow from end customers to the seller directly takes place electronically unlike through market intermediaries in a traditional system. Moreover, e-based marketing systems greatly contribute to speed and efficiency of business operations, adding to effective customer relationship management (CRM).

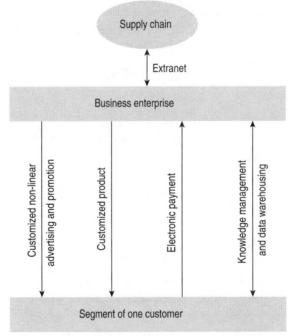

Fig. 21.2   The e-business-based marketing system

Source: Joshi, Rakesh Mohan, *International Business*, Oxford
University Press, New Delhi, 2009, p. 814.

Unlike the traditional marketing approach, which is based on customer segmentation, e-marketing enables a company to target an individual customer, that is, a 'segment size of one'. By integrating technology, business enterprises may adopt a company-led approach to target individual customers and adopt a marketing strategy customized to the segment of even one customer.

Integration of information technology also allows businesses to estimate lifetime value of customer (LVC) that may be used to facilitate marketing decision-making. LVC refers to the estimate of potential profit a company is likely to derive from a customer during her lifetime. It is arrived at by subtracting lifetime costs, such as costs of customer acquisition, operating expenses, customer service, etc., from the lifetime earnings from a customer. For instance, if the total costs of maintaining a customer exceed her lifetime value, the company needs to take a decision either to drop the customer or charge higher prices.

The major factors contributing to the growth of e-marketing may be summarized as follows:

- Advent of the Internet and www that offers cost-effective alternative to proprietary and value-added networks
- Cost savings through integrating marketing processes with network-based technology
- Growing use of the Internet as marketing channel
- Opportunities to enhance supply-chain efficiency and cost-effectiveness
- Improved customer service in the form of round-the-clock online access to the company that contributes to enhancing relationship with its customers

However, rapid growth of ICT enabled marketing has also threatened a number of traditionally well-established market intermediaries, especially the following:

Travel agents   Airlines and railways across the world are selling tickets online; some are even offering discounts to direct customers and cutting commissions to travel agents.

Wholesalers   Traditional wholesalers hardly add value to the exchange processes.

Insurance agents   Although most insurance companies are reluctant to alienate their existing massive agent structure, they are simultaneously making attractive online offers for direct insurance.

Marketing applications of digital technology have given rise to an era of information asymmetry where customers are much better informed, information is controlled by customers, and customers also initiate market exchanges. Moreover, since integration of ICT with business operations provides a level playing field, it enables small and medium enterprises to compete with large and capital-based businesses. The basic concepts of e-commerce, e-business, and m-marketing are discussed next.

E-commerce

Commerce is a basic economic activity involving trading or the buying and selling of goods. An electronic transaction primarily involves three stages, namely searching and deciding upon products to be bought, ordering and making payments, and delivery of products bought. E-commerce involves exchange among customers, business partners, and vendors. Thus, in simple terms, e-commerce refers to buying and selling of goods or services through a computer-mediated network. It includes all forms of business transactions in which the transacting parties interact electronically over digital networks rather than by physical exchanges or physical contact.

As shown in Fig. 21.3, a conceptual framework of e-commerce reveals that it involves electronic exchange of information or 'digital content' between two or more parties, that is, the business enterprise and the buyer or the supplier. In order to operationalize an e-commerce system, the seller is required to produce the content, and its digitization (i.e., conversion of the content into digital format), storage of digital content, and linking to electronic network and electronic payment system (EPS) and electronic delivery for information goods or arranging for physical manufacturing and delivery for physical goods. An EPS refers to a system of financial exchange between buyers and sellers in the online environment that is facilitated by a digital financial instrument (such as encrypted credit card numbers, electronic checks, or digital cash) backed by a bank, an intermediary, or by legal tender. On the other hand, the buyer also has to

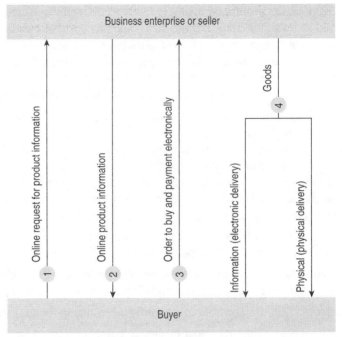

Fig. 21.3 Conceptual framework of e-commerce

Source: Joshi, Rakesh Mohan, *International Business*, Oxford University Press, New Delhi, 2009, p. 811.

link to an electronic network, search and locate content on network, retrieve information from network, display information, place a purchase order, and link to an EPS.

In an e-commerce system, several disparate technologies are required to make an 'any information-anywhere' system operational. These include the following.

Content production Word processors, video cameras, music synthesisers, and editing software

Digitization Dictation software, digital cameras, scanners, etc.

Storage Floppy disk, CD-ROMs, tapes, memory sticks or pen drives, hard disk drives

Network communications Electricity cables, telephone cables, dedicated lines, mobile phones, etc.

Network connections Personal computers, modem or broadband connections, televisions and set-up boxes

Information search and retrieval mechanisms Search engines and directories

Display devices TV, PC monitor, mobile phones,[2] etc.

E-business

Although the terms 'e-commerce' and 'e-business' are often used interchangeably, these are two distinct concepts. E-commerce includes inter-business or inter-organizational transactions (i.e., transactions between and among firms or organizations) and business to customers transactions (i.e., transactions between firms/organizations and individuals). On the other hand, e-business refers to integration of ICT with business processes so as to enhance an organization's competitive strength.

---

[2] Chen, Stephen, *Strategic Management of E-business*, John Wiley & Sons Ltd, Singapore, 2004, pp. 3–6.

The term e-business encompasses a broad frame of business activities, whereas e-commerce is confined to buying and selling over electronic media. In addition to online buying and selling, e-business also involves collaborating with a firm's business partners and servicing its customers with the use of ICT over the Internet. It includes both front- and back-office applications to redefine traditional business processes with the help of technology so as to maximize customer value. E-commerce is indeed a subset of e-business that deals with commercial activities, such as buying and selling of goods and services using the Internet and other information and communication technologies. However, in practice, the terms 'electronic' and 'Internet' commerce are often used interchangeably.

E-business refers to the performance of business activities, such as designing products, managing supply chain, operations, marketing, and offering services to various stakeholders through extensive use of electronic technology. Thus, e-business leads to transformation of an organization's business processes so as to deliver additional customer value through application of technology and processes. It usually enhances three primary processes:

- *Production processes*, which include procurement, ordering and replenishment of stocks; processing of payments; electronic links with suppliers; and production-control processes, among others
- *Customer-focused processes*, which include promotional and marketing efforts, selling over the Internet, processing of customers' purchase orders and payments, and customer support, among others
- *Internal management processes*, which include employee services, training, internal information sharing, videoconferencing, and recruiting. Electronic applications enhance information flow between production and sales forces and improve their productivity. Work-group communications and electronic publishing of internal business information are likewise made more efficient.[3]

Hence, e-business may be defined as the process of carrying out business activities using electronic technologies. It includes the use of technology for online buying and selling and to forge and foster linkages with various stakeholders, such as customers, suppliers, government, and other business partners. E-business integrates traditional business practices and information systems with worldwide reach of the Web and connects its various stakeholders.

Thus, e-business is a much broader concept, which involves the use of *extranets*, the Internet links between the business suppliers and purchasers, and *intranets,* the Internet links within a business. It also includes the strategic adaptations of business practices integrating the use of technology. It comprises generating business needs, providing sales support, and integrating business partners; linking various aspects of business operations to distributors and suppliers through extranets; and carrying out communications within the organization control through intranets.

M-marketing

Although conduct of marketing transactions through computers has greatly facilitated marketing activities, the use of wireless technology relieves all the stakeholders in the business from the constraints of time and place, greatly enhancing convenience and accessibility. M-marketing is defined as the conduct of marketing activities through use of wireless technology, such as mobile phones, personal digital assistant (PDA), and telematics. M-marketing facilitates interaction

---

[3] Kalakota, Ravi and Andrew B. Whinston, *Electronic Commerce: A Manager's Guide*, Addison Wesley, USA, 1997, pp. 2–32.

among business stakeholders with the Web, irrespective of location-specific context. It also enables marketing communication through mobile devices and text applications such as SMS, using email, and through the Web.

To illustrate, mobile banking alerts keep its customers alerted when the event, the customer has subscribed to, get triggered. Customers can subscribe for receiving SMS alerts for a number of transactions, such as when an amount is credited, an amount over a specified amount gets debited/credited, balance falls below/goes above a specified limit, or when a cheque bounces. Under the alert facility, customers get alerts only when the events they have subscribed to occurs, unlike the request facility where the customer requests for information as and when desired.

M-commerce finds enormous applications in various businesses, especially the following:

Financial services   Mobile banking and stock investment carried out over wireless devices

Retail   Placing orders and making payments over wireless devices for retail purchase

Telecommunication   Single wireless device for getting account status, changing services, and making payment

Information services   Delivery of news, stock reports, sports figures such as cricket or football scores, entertainment such as jokes, ringtones, astrological predictions, etc.

Worldwide mobile penetration with about 87 per cent is far ahead of fixed line penetration of merely 17 per cent in 2012. Developing countries with 118 per cent mobile penetration indicates more than one mobile connection per person compared to 40 per cent fixed line connections, whereas mobile connections in developing countries is 79 per cent compared to merely 12 per cent fixed line connections.[4]

China has the largest number of mobile subscriber connections in the world (1,092 million), followed by India (907 million), the USA (322 million), Indonesia (260 million), Brazil (259 million), Russian Federation (227 million), Japan (128 million), Pakistan (120 million), and Germany (114 million), whereas the market penetration rate was highest at 160 per cent in Russian Federation, followed by Germany (140%), Brazil (132%), Indonesia (107%), the USA (103%), Japan (100%), China (81%), India (73%), and Pakistan (69%).

Global mobile connection is expected to rise at 7.6 per cent CAGR from 6.8 billion in 2012 to 9.7 billion in 2017, whereas the mobile broadband is likely to grow from 1.6 billion to 5.1 billion with a CAGR of 26 per cent during the same period. Interestingly, global mobile subscribers are expected to grow four times faster than global population during 2012 and 2017 making m-marketing even more significant.[5] Japan is the global leader in m-commerce. It is believed that m-commerce may surpass wireless e-commerce for digital commercial transactions, as the content delivery over wireless devices become faster, scalable, and more secure.

E-MARKETING TECHNOLOGY AND ENVIRONMENT

In the initial phases of development of e-commerce, proprietary networks were often used under an EDI framework. The advent of the Internet, which interlinks millions of networks across the world and offers a much wider platform for marketing transactions at a global scale, has largely replaced the earlier EDI systems. Intranets provide platforms for communications within organizations, whereas extranet links a business organization with its various stakeholders.

---

[4] International Telecommunication Union, 2012.
[5] *The Mobile Economy 2013*, GSMA; A.T. Kearney, London, 2013.

Electronic Data Interchange

Electronic data interchange (EDI) was the first approach used for information sharing and business transactions. It began in the 1970s and predates the Internet. It refers to the exchange of information through computers between organizations in a standard, computer-processable, and universally accepted format using proprietary networks (Fig. 21.4). EDI had generally been used to eliminate paperwork in supply chain management and getting regulatory clearances from government authorities. The major components required to send and receive EDI messages are as follows:

- EDI standards
- EDI software
- Third party networks for communication

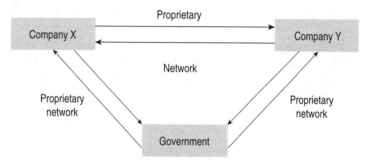

Fig. 21.4   Electronic data interchange (EDI)

The United Nations defined a set of rules in 1987 for electronic data interchange for administration, commerce, and transport, known as UN/EDIFACT. EDI has been the dominant technology used by large business firms, such as Walmart, Ford, Suzuki, and General Motors, to exchange information with their business partners, especially for managing supply chains. Besides, it also facilitated information sharing within different departments of a firm.

Internet

The advent of the Internet has facilitated almost-instantaneous worldwide communication and metamorphosed traditional communication processes. The Internet refers to a 'network of networks' or 'interconnected computer networks' comprising millions of small domestic, business, academic, and government networks linked by copper wires, optical fibre cables, or wireless connections. Internet or *Inter*connected *Net*work began as a sponsored project to link computing systems by the US government. The ability to transmit information packets between widely dispersed computer networks was perceived as a means of lowering the computing costs. The original project in 1969 was called ARPANET, the grandparent of today's Internet. The National Science Foundation incorporated the ARPANET into its own network, the NSFNET, by the 1980s, which became the core of the US Internet, until its privatization and ultimate retirement in 1995. The US Federal Networking Council unanimously passed a resolution defining the term 'Internet' on 24 October 1995.

The World Wide Web (www) or the Web is relatively a new addition to the Internet. It is the universe of network-accessible information. The www uses the Internet as a backbone to send information from servers or repositories of file information, to browsers, or to software designed to display the files. It also facilitates the transfer of hypermedia-based files, allowing links to other pages, places, or applications.

The Internet can be accessed round the clock from all over the world. Besides, it is easy to use and involves extremely low transaction costs. The two-way communication over the Internet facilitates businesses to instantaneously customize marketing mix and integrate business processes. The Internet has made mass customization possible for different users so as to create individualized web pages, products, and services. The customized web page not only offers the preferred layout of the customer, but also provides the company with useful information about its customers in terms of their individual interests. This allows a firm to work out a proactive customized marketing strategy to suit the needs of individual customers and make customized market promotions and product offerings.

Although it provides a good medium for electronic transactions, not everything can be sold effectively over the Internet:

- As far as 'high-touch' products, such as clothes, jewellery, and fashion goods are concerned, customers like to touch, feel, or experience first-hand the product before making a buying decision.
- The diverse geographical spread of customers may render product delivery difficult, especially in the countryside where the 'Brick & Mortar' model is more effective.
- Bulky products with high transportation costs are difficult to sell over the Internet.
- Services that require face-to-face interactions like healthcare wherein the doctor would physically need to medically examine the patient, or aesthetics wherein a beautician needs the physical presence of her clients are also not effectively sold over the Internet.

China has the highest number of Internet users (538 million) in the world, followed by the USA (245 million), India (137 million), Japan (101 million) , Brazil (88 million), Russia (68 million), Germany (67 million), Indonesia (55 million), UK (52.7 million), and France (52.2 million).[6]

Moreover, the level of Internet penetration varies considerably across countries. Iceland has the highest percentage of Internet penetration with 95 per cent followed by Norway (94%), Netherlands (92.3%), Sweden (91%), compared to the UK (83.6%), Germany (83%), France (79.6%), Japan (79.5%), the USA (78.1%), Singapore (75%), UAE (70%), Russian Federation (47.7%), Brazil (45.6%), China (40.1%), Egypt (35.6%), South Africa (21%), India (11.4%), and very low in Ethiopia (1.1%) and Sierra Leone (0.3%). Interestingly, despite India's ranking third in terms of total number of Internet users, its level of penetration is merely 11.4 per cent. Such wide variation in these two parameters is due to considerable differences in Internet users among the urban and rural population.

English is the highest used language on the Web[7] with 26.8 per cent of total users, followed by Chinese (24.2%), Spanish (7.8), Japanese (4.7%), Portuguese (3.9%), German (3.6%), Arabic (3.3%), French (3%), Russian (3%), Korean (2%), whereas other languages account for 17.8 per cent. Arabic has been the fastest growing language on the Web with 2,501 per cent growth followed by Russian (1,825%), Chinese (1,478%), Portuguese (990%), Spanish (807%), French (398%), English (301%), German (174%), Japanese (111%), and Korean (107%) during the past 10 years.

Extent of Internet use in business

The extent to which companies use Internet for their business activities such as buying and selling goods and interacting with customers and suppliers varies significantly across countries. Sweden has the highest use of Internet for business purposes in the world with a score of 6.5 on a seven-point scale (Fig. 21.5), followed by Korea (6.4), Estonia (6.3), UK (6.3) in comparison

---

[6] International Telecommunication Union, 2012.
[7] International Telecommunication Union, 2012.

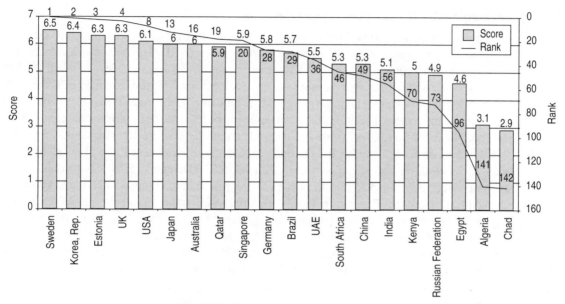

Fig. 21.5 Extent of Internet use in business

Source: The Global Information Technology Report, 2012, World Economic Forum, Geneva.
1 = not at all; 7 = extensively

to the USA (6.1), Japan (6), Qatar (5.9), Singapore (5.9), Germany (5.8), Brazil (5.7), UAE (5.5), South Africa (5.3), China (5.3), India (5.1), Kenya (5), Russian Federation (4.9), Egypt (4.6), Algeria (3.1), and Chad (2.9).

The term 'Internet economy' comprises physical ICT infrastructure, business infrastructure, and commerce. It pertains to all economic activities using electronic networks as a medium for commerce or activities involved in both building the networks linked to the Internet and purchasing application services, such as the provision of enabling hardware and software and network equipment for web-based online retail and shopping malls (e-malls).

Extranet

It is an Internet-based network between a business enterprise and its suppliers, distributors, and business partners, which is not open to the general public. Such systems are replacing the earlier EDI systems. It consists of two intranets connected via the Internet, whereby two organizations are allowed to view each other's confidential information. Generally, only a small portion of information, required to conduct business, is made available through the extranet to its business partners. Interestingly, such business-to-business (B2B) networks have existed since long before the present-day Internet.

Intranet

It refers to an internal private network used to link various divisions of a business around the world into a unified communication network using the same types of software, hardware, and connections as the Internet. It uses Internet standards for electronic communication within the organization, separating these websites from the rest of the world by firewalls and other security measures.

In technical terms, there is hardly any difference between the Internet, the extranet, and the intranet. Since intranet and extranet can be viewed by specific groups, these also form subsets of Internet.

Leveraging ICT to Enhance Competitiveness

The degree to which economies across the world leverage ICT for enhanced competitiveness may be objectively measured using Networked Readiness Index (NRI). This serves as a valuable tool for assessing and leveraging technology for enhancing competitiveness and development. The NRI comprises four sub-indices that measure the environment for ICT; the readiness of a society to use ICT; the actual usage of all main stakeholders; and, finally, the impacts that ICT generates in the economy and society. The three first sub-indexes can be regarded as the drivers that condition the results of the fourth sub-index. These four sub-indexes are divided into 10 pillars and 53 variables.

On a scale of seven, Sweden has the highest Networked Readiness Index (Fig. 21.6) with a score of 5.94 followed by Singapore (5.66), Finland (5.81), Denmark (5.70), Switzerland (5.61), in comparison to the USA (5.56), the UK (5.50), Japan (5.25), France (5.12), the UAE (4.77), China (4.11), Russian Federation (4.02), Brazil (3.92), India (3.89), South Africa (3.87), Egypt (3.77), Kenya (3.51), Bangladesh (3.20), Yemen (2.41), and Haiti (2.27). India is a shining example of an emerging market for its famed IT-enabled services sector that contributed significantly to its economy. Besides, India's success story has been replicated throughout the region. This has transformed Asia into an emblem of borderless economy.

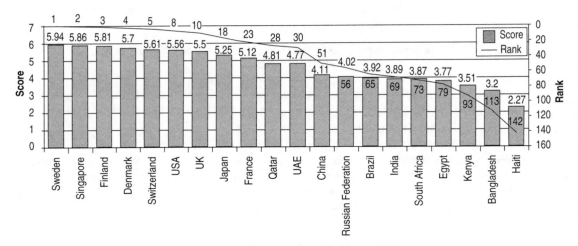

Fig. 21.6   The Networked Readiness Index, 2012

Source: The Global Information Technology Report, 2012, World Economic Forum, Geneva. 1 = worst; 7 = best

PREREQUISITES FOR EFFECTIVE E-MARKETING TRANSACTIONS

The scope of e-marketing goes far beyond hosting a website for buying and selling of goods over the Internet. In order to make e-marketing function effectively, a number of interrelated factors and prerequisites involved in the transaction loop[8] need to be put in place. The principal players in an e-commerce transaction and the corresponding requisites are summarized next.

Marketing enterprise or seller
- A corporate website with e-commerce capabilities to conduct secured transactions
- A corporate intranet so that orders are processed promptly and efficiently
- Workforce with IT proficiency to manage and sustain the e-commerce system

---

[8] Based on Andam, Zorayda Ruth, 'E-commerce and E-business', e-ASEAN Task Force, *UNDP-APDIP*, May 2003, pp. 16–18.

Transaction partners

- Financial institutions offering online transaction services, such as processing payments over credit cards and electronic funds transfer
- Logistics service providers linked electronically and providing efficient physical movement of cargo
- Authentication authority that serves as a trusted third party to ensure the integrity and security of transactions

Consumers (in business-to-consumer or B2C transactions)

- They should form a critical mass of the population with access to the Internet and disposable income enabling widespread use of credit cards.
- They should possess a mindset for purchasing goods over the Internet rather than by physically inspecting items.

Companies/Businesses (in business-to-business or B2B transactions)

- They should together form a critical mass of companies (especially within supply chains) with Internet access and the capability to place and take orders over the Internet.

Government

- It should establish a legal framework governing e-commerce transactions (including electronic documents, signatures, and the like).
- It needs to set up legal institutions that would enforce the legal framework (laws and regulations) and protect consumers and businesses from fraud, among others.

Companies

- They should have a robust and reliable Internet infrastructure.
- They need a pricing structure that does not discourage consumers from spending time on and buying goods over the Internet.

GLOBAL E-MARKETING

Conduct of marketing transactions, such as buying, selling, distributing, or delivering goods or services using electronic methods is termed as e-marketing. It includes use of electronic data and its applications for conceptualization, planning, pricing, and distribution and promotion of goods and services to create exchanges to satisfy customer needs. Global e-marketing involves marketing transactions through electronic methods across the world.

Earlier, EDI used proprietary-dedicated networks to transmit highly structured machine-readable data. However, the Internet has facilitated creating an electronic marketspace as depicted in Fig. 21.7, where buyers and sellers can exchange information through emails, video, voice, and image, in a cost-effective manner.

Although Internet-based e-marketing networks are highly cost-effective, the transactions are less secure as these are open networks. B2B e-commerce adds to the efficiency of marketing transactions. It facilitates greater access to information to the buyers about the sellers world-wide. As the prices have become more transparent through the Internet, it has increased price pressures on undifferentiated commodities. At the same time, it provides greater information on highly differentiated brands.

The traditional approach to marketing calls for market segmentation, that is, dividing the customers into sub-groups, who would respond similarly to a given marketing strategy, and target a group of customers with a uniform marketing strategy. 'Personalization' implies market targeting to the extreme by using a unique marketing mix for each customer. The term 'customization' refers to manufacturing systems and is a 'company-led approach' and focuses on

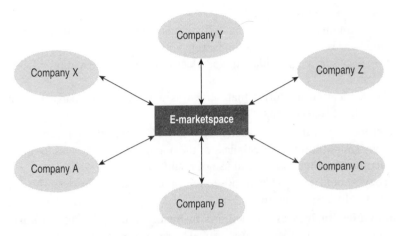

Fig. 21.7   Internet-based virtual e-marketspace

developing production systems to provide unique products to individual customers, whereas 'personalization' is more appropriate for e-commerce as it incorporates both the customer-led and company-led approaches to target a customer segment size of one. Thus, digital technology is increasingly harnessed to create and offer a highly personalized marketing mix and to develop effective and sustainable CRM.

Michael Dell, the founder of Dell computers, was among the first to adopt innovative business processes that integrated digital technology with marketing, as illustrated in Exhibit 21.2. These processes have made Dell computers the largest seller of PCs in the USA.

Exhibit 21.2   Dell's global e-marketing strategy

Michael Dell began to assemble computers in 1983 in his college dormitory as a student at the University of Texas at Austin with a capital of US$100. As his business grew, he pioneered the direct sale of computers over the telephone. In 1996, Dell started selling computers over the Internet through its own website.

Leading computer manufacturers such as IBM and Compaq had built extensive worldwide distribution networks and relied heavily on resellers for sale of their products. Dell's decision to sell directly to customers through its new e-marketing model could have alienated market intermediaries. However, Dell effectively overcame the resellers' threat by mass customization of its computers for each of its customers. This resulted in much higher customer satisfaction on one hand and cost savings by elimination of middlemen on the other.

As a result, Dell had become the largest seller of PCs in the USA in 1999, overtaking Compaq. It ranked as the 25th largest company in the Fortune 500 list in 2006, however slipped to 44th place in 2012 list with a revenue of US$62.07 billion.

Source: 'Dell Changed the Industry with Direct Sales', *The Statesman*, 3 May 2004; 'Business: The Company File: Dynamic Dell', BBC News, 20 August 1998; *Fortune 500*, 2006 and 2012 issues.

E-marketing Communication

To communicate with various stakeholders, businesses traditionally used various methods of 'linear' communication such as print media (i.e., newspapers, magazines, journals, etc.), electronic media (i.e., television and radio), telephone, direct sales, etc. The advent of the Internet and the Web has fostered a 'hypermedia' environment, making it possible to deliver targeted messages to specific audiences. This environment allows 'non-linear' communication using hyperlinks with search and retrieval processes to collect information.[9] Hypermedia advantage

---

[9] Hoffman, Donna L. and Thomas P. Novak, 'Marketing in Hypermedia Computer-mediated Environments: Conceptual Foundations', *Journal of Marketing*, vol. 60, July 1996, pp. 50–68.

Exhibit 21.3 Measurement of hypermedia advertising

Measurement method	Definition	Comments
Hit count	Measures the number of items a page is requested but not necessarily seen or displayed at the user's browser.	Provides information on actual hits, but there could be multiple hits counted for every click of the mouse or page refresh. Records activity regardless of the viewer's location, such as workplaces, homes, schools, or other countries. Provides no information on users.
Page view	Tracks the number of individual pages sent to web viewers.	Gives no indication of how many users receive or view pages and no profile data on users.
Click through	Tracks the number of times an online ad is clicked on.	Gives no information about the customers. Customers who click through may dump a page before it loads.
Unique visitors	Allow tracking by the IP address of the viewer.	Many people use the same IP address to access a site.
Reach	Measures sampled group's visits (if 25% of sample has visited site, reach obtained 25%).	Requires the use of panels or surveys. This can pair information on the individual's background with individual behaviour. These panels may be narrow in scope and not account for all web surfers, such as those at work or from other countries.
New measures	Include linking individuals by demographic data, loyalty, site behaviour, and other measures.	May allow online, constant measures like people who visit a site and how long they stay at a site.

Source: 'Fast Principles of Online Media Audience Measurement', FastInfo.org, http://www.fastinfo.org/measurement/pages/index.cgi/audiencemeasurement, 22 September 1999; Vonder Haar, Steven, 'Web Metrics: Go Figure', *Business 2.0*, June 1999, pp. 46–47.

may be measured by various methods (Exhibit 21.3), such as hit count, page view, click through, unique visitors, and reach.

E-marketing Research

The uses of electronic surveys for marketing research have increased tremendously in the last decade. Due to variation in the extent of availability of personal computers and Internet penetration, mass electronic surveys are possible only in a few developed countries, while stratified sampling for select market segments can also be carried out in developing countries. With the intensification of cyber cafes in India and other emerging economies, the Internet has come to the reach of far greater population than that captured in most multilateral surveys and publications. Market and institutional surveys are gaining popularity even in the developing countries. Although electronic surveys are cost-effective and quick, the sample surveyed may not be representative of the population and may lead to faulty inferences. Therefore, due care is to be taken while selecting samples for electronic surveys.

GLOBAL E-MARKETING OF SERVICES

ICT has revolutionized the way services are offered breaking geographical boundaries. With digitization, the Internet, and high-speed data networks as the driving forces, all kinds of knowledge-related work can now be done almost anywhere in the world. Corporate downsizing in the USA and Europe is also helping create more high-skilled jobs in developing countries. This covers a wide range of professions, such as life sciences, legal services, art and design, management, business operations, computing, architecture, sales, and office support.

The Indian BPO business began with basic data entry and transcription of medical records. Gradually, it moved up the ladder to rules-set based processing where agents made judgements based on rules set by the customer, for instance, upgrading travellers from economy to business class. Further up the ladder, offshore ITeS included troubleshooting by BPO agents, such as the discretion to enhance credit card limits. Direct customer interaction requires BPO workers to handle more elaborate transactions with a client's customers. Collecting delinquent payment from credit-card customers or sorting out computer snags.

Companies are increasingly offshoring knowledge intensive activities, such as engineering drawings and design, marketing, research, and legal services, which transforms the role of traditional BPO vendor to a knowledge processing outsourcing (KPO) vendor. Over recent years, the scope of IT-enabled services has expanded considerably to include the increasingly complex processes involving rule-based decision-making and even research services requiring informed individual judgement. The rapid expansion in scope of BPOs has been accompanied by an equally rapid adoption across a range of vertical industries. The various IT-enabled services may be categorized as follows:

Finance and accounting (F&A) services   These include activities, such as general accounting, transaction management (accounts receivables and payables management), corporate finance (for example, treasury and risk management, and tax management), and compliance management and statutory reporting.

Customer interaction services   These include all forms of IT-enabled customer contact; inbound or outbound, voice or non-voice based support used to provide customer services, sales and marketing, technical support and help-desk services.

Human resource administration services   These include payroll and benefit administration, travel and expense processing, talent acquisition and talent management services, employee communication design, and administration.

Other vertical specific and niche services   These include innovation of the underlying business processes being outsourced, improved competitive positioning, managing customer expectations, elevation of the strategic role of the retained organization, optimal resource allocation, support for globalization of businesses, and technology support and access.

With an abundance of professional manpower at much lower cost compared to developed economies, India has emerged as the most preferred location for expert knowledge service. GE's former CEO Jack Welch brought out a 70:70:70 vision, which means GE would outsource 70 per cent of its work, 70 per cent of that will be offshored, and 70 per cent of the offshored tasks will be done out of India.

E-MARKETING MODELS

The basic process flow and linking together of diverse marketing functions is termed as a 'marketing model'. The principal e-marketing models (Fig. 21.8) can basically be categorized, as follows.

Business-to-business

It involves inter-firm transactions using an electronic network. Business-to-business (B-to-B or B2B) transactions account for about 80 per cent of total electronic transactions and are predicted to move faster compared to the B2C segment. B2B e-business comprises two primary components.

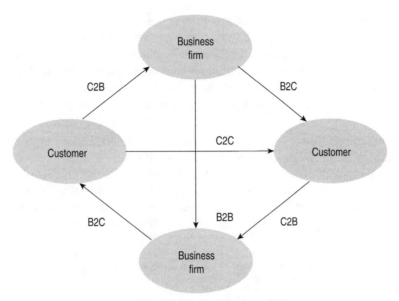

Fig. 21.8   Types of e-marketing models

E-infrastructure   It is the architect of B2B that primarily consists of the following:

- Logistics that include transportation, warehousing, and distribution (e.g., Procter & Gamble)
- Application service providers that include deployment, hosting, and management of packaged software from a central facility (e.g., Oracle)
- Outsourcing of functions in the process of e-commerce, such as web hosting, security, and customer-care solutions (e.g., outsourcing providers, such as eShare and NetSales)
- Auction solutions software for the operation and maintenance of real-time auctions over the Internet (e.g., Moai Technologies and OpenSite Technologies)
- Content management software for the facilitation of website content management and delilvery (e.g., Interwoven and ProcureNet)
- Web-based commerce enablers (e.g., Commerce One, a browser-based, XML-enabled purchasing automation software)[10]

E-markets   It includes web portals where buyers and sellers interact with each other and conducts transactions, for instance, Hewlett-Packard (HP), IBM, Cisco, etc.

The major areas of B2B applications include supplier management (especially purchase-order processing), inventory management (i.e., managing order-ship-bill cycles), distribution management (especially in the transmission of shipping documents), channel management (i.e., information dissemination on changes in operational conditions), and payment management (for example, EPS).

Benefits of B2B e-marketing

The benefits of B2B e-marketing are as follows.

Reduction in transaction costs   Conduct of B2B e-business reduces costs in the following areas:

- Cost reduction in search for alternatives, as buyers need not go through multiple market intermediaries as in the traditional supply chain, to search for information about supplier's

---

[10] 'E-Commerce/Internet: B2B: 2B or Not 2B?', *Goldman Sachs Investment Research*, vol. 1.1, 16 November 1999, pp. 68–71.

products and prices. Besides, the Internet is a more efficient channel in terms of effort, time, and money spent compared to its traditional counterparts.

* Cost of processing transactions (invoices, purchase orders, and payment schemes), as B2B allows for the automation of transaction processes and therefore, the quick implementation of the same compared to other channels (such as, telephone and fax). Efficiency in trading processes and transactions is also enhanced by way of processing sales through online auctions.

Disintermediation The process of eliminating the middlemen from the exchange processes is known as 'disintermediation'. The B2B transactions enable suppliers to interact and transact directly with buyers, thereby eliminating intermediaries and distributors (Fig. 21.9). Most middlemen who survived merely on knowledge about the requirements of buyers and sellers and hardly added value to the exchange processes face extinction in a variety of industries, such as insurance, real estate, travel agencies, and stock brokerages.

Fig. 21.9 Process of disintermediation

Source: Joshi, Rakesh Mohan, *International Business*, Oxford University Press, New Delhi, 2009, p. 828.

Transparency in pricing Collective participation of multiple buyers and sellers in a single e-market reveals market price information and transaction processing to all the participants. This not only increases transparency in prices but also pulls down the prices.

Economies of scale and network effect B2B e-marketing brings together a large number of buyers and sellers who provide demand side economies of scale and network effects. Each additional incremental participant in the e-market creates value for all participants in the demand side. More participants form a critical mass, which is crucial to attract more users to an e-market.

Business-to-consumer

Business-to-consumer (B-to-C or B2C) transaction is the second largest and the earliest form of e-business, the origin of which can be traced to e-tailing or online retailing. The B2B e-commerce is often used for purchasing products and information, mainly personal finances and investments, with the use of online banking and investment tools. Business transactions between companies and consumers involve customers gathering information, purchasing physical goods (i.e., tangibles, such as books or consumer products) or information goods (goods of electronic material or digitized content, such as software or e-books), and for information goods, receiving products over an electronic network.[11]

The Internet has greatly facilitated the proliferation of B2C e-commerce during the recent years. It is estimated that the major items purchased[12] online include books (58%), music (50%), software (44%), air tickets (29%), PC peripherals (28%), clothing (26%), videos (24%), hotel reservations (20%), toys (20%), flowers (17%), and consumer electronics (12%). However,

---

[11] Based on Lallana, Quimbo, C. Andam, Ravi Kalakota, and Andrew B. Whinston, *Electronic Commerce: A Manager's Guide*, Addison Wesley Longman, Inc., USA, 1997, pp.19–20.

[12] Kotler, Philip, *Market Management*, 11th Edition, Prentice Hall, New Delhi, 2002, p. 40.

e-marketing transactions are less popular in product categories that need to be physically touched and examined by the buyers, such as clothes and furniture. Consumers buying online tend to be relatively younger, better educated, and generally affluent. B2C e-marketing leads to an exchange process initiated and controlled by customers. Until customers invite marketers to participate in their exchange processes, marketers have to wait. Moreover, the rules of marketing engagement are also determined by the end customers.

The world's most favoured online retailers (Table 21.1) include Amazon, eBay, Walmart, Best Buy, Target, Netflix, IKEA, Macy's, Newegg, and Sears. The sales of Amazon grew at a very rapid rate compared to other e-retailers, with its stellar 93 per cent annual growth rate. Its virtual marketing channel made it 'the earth's biggest book store' in July 1995. Since then, it has expanded into broad range of product lines. Dell sells PCs directly through the Internet to its global customers on a 'build to order' basis rather than a 'build to forecast' basis. However, the firm has very efficient supply chain management so as to ship PCs on local or regional basis.

Table 21.1   World's favourite online retailers

Retailers	Headquarter	Main Product
Amazon	Seattle, USA	Books
eBay	California, USA	Online auction and shopping
Walmart	Arkansas, USA	General merchandise
Best Buy	Minnesota, USA	Electronics
Target	Minneapolis, USA	General merchandise
Netflix	California, USA	Movie rental
IKEA	Delft, Netherlands	Furniture and household
Macy's	New York, USA	Clothing and accessories
Newegg	California, USA	Computer hardware and software
Sears	Illinois, USA	General merchandise

Consumer-to-business

In a complete reversal of traditional business models, consumer-to-business (C2B) e-business allows individuals, especially professionals, such as lawyers and accountants, to offer their services to businesses as well as sites that allow individuals to offer their services or products to businesses. Under C2B transactions, 'reverse auctions' are often involved, where customers, rather than the seller, initiate market transactions. It includes tendering by the buyers, inviting suppliers to put forward their bids.

Consumer-to-consumer

Consumer-to-consumer (C2C) involves horizontal interaction between consumers, who generally share their experiences with the product by way of chat rooms. C-to-C or C2C e-commerce takes place through the following:

- Auctions facilitated at a portal, like eBay, which allows online real-time bidding. eBay's person-to-person trading in a web-based community is the world's largest and the most popular. It pioneered online person-to-person trading by developing a web-based community wherein the buyers and sellers transact personal items. eBay permits sellers to list items for sale, buyers to bid on the items of their interest, and all eBay users to browse through listed items on easy-to-use online services. Items generally transacted under eBay include apparel and accessories, books and magazines, computers and peripherals, fitness and sports, jewellery and watches, music and instruments, stamps, coins and hobbies, consumer electronics, mobiles and accessories, movies and videos, etc.

- Peer-to-peer systems, like the Napster model, a protocol of sharing files between users used by chat forums, and other file exchanges
- Classified ads at portal sites, such as e-class, click India, e-classifieds, and classified e-ads.

ALTERNATIVE E-MARKETING STRATEGIES

Depending upon the integration of Internet technologies with the firm's marketing strategies, a firm may opt any of the following alternatives.

Brick and Mortar

The phrase 'brick and mortar' refers to tangible physical assets, such as a manufacturing unit or building, or a storage facility. This is the traditional marketing model wherein websites are used only as company brochures. Brick and mortar firms generate their total revenue from traditional means of sale, whereas the website is only used to provide information. However, such brick and mortar firms, consequent to a favourable market feedback, often develop as brick and click companies.

Pure Click

Under this model, all marketing transactions are carried out online with little physical presence. Such firms are also known as 'dotcoms' or 'pure-plays'. Such 'pure-click' firms include search engines, commercial sites, Internet service providers (ISPs), transaction sites, content sites, and enabler sites. Engines, such as Google, Yahoo, Sify, and AltaVista, primarily started as search engines, now also provide a variety of services such as free mails, weather reports, news, and entertainment. The commercial sites of pure click companies, such as amazon.com and indiatimes. com, sell books and other products. eBay provides platform for auction for any commission on transaction conducted on the sites. In the late 1990s, pure click firms achieved a very high level of market capitalization and were considered a major threat to traditional marketing. However, the hype of dotcoms was short-lived and went bust in 2000.

Brick and Click

Under this model, a firm conducts marketing activities and transactions, both online and offline. Firms using the brick and click model need to be cautious that their online sales do not cannibalize existing sales through traditional marketing channels. Such firms also emphasize reduction of channel conflicts between their own channel intermediaries and online sales. Firms such as Avon and Compaq evolved models so that their e-marketing activities became complimentary, rather than competitive, to the traditional marketing model. In January 2000, Walmart.com was founded as a subsidiary of Walmart stores, which provides easy access to more than 1 million products available online. It combines technology and world-class retailing aimed at gaining customers and offers a wide assortment of products round the clock.

Today, the Internet is extensively used by businesses to communicate with their external and internal audiences. External audiences include stockholders, customers, the general public, etc., whereas both suppliers and employees constitute a firm's internal audiences. Suppliers and employees often use the intranet for communicating within the organization. Unlike the linear communication that follows a scripted flow, hypermedia communication over the Internet allows a free flow and exchange of information.

E-ENABLED MARKETING PROCESS TRANSFORMATIONS AND CHALLENGES

Integration of digital technology into the marketing processes has considerably transformed the traditional ways of marketing. Some of the changes brought about by e-marketing are as follows.

Physical marketplace to virtual marketspace   The Internet has transformed the traditional ways of buying and selling of goods at physical marketplaces into virtual marketspace enabling almost unlimited movements beyond physical borders.

Physical products to digital products   Breakthroughs in ICT have made possible selling and buying some products online. For instance, computer software, music, movies, video games, drawings, designs, research papers, reports, and even books can be accessed, evaluated, bought, and downloaded over the Net.

Mass production of standardized products to mass customization   Consequent to industrial revolution in the 18th century, the large-scale production of standardized products was used as the most significant tool to achieve scale economies and competitiveness. Advent of electronic technology and Internet facilitated real-time interaction and information-sharing between the businesses and their various stakeholders, especially the customers and suppliers that made it possible to integrate manufacturing systems to produce customized products for different customers.

Fixed pricing to dynamic pricing   E-marketing models offer flexibility in price determination in several ways, such as buyer-determined customized pricing and dynamic pricing by way of online auctions, unlike the traditional fixed-pricing approach.

Mass marketing techniques to customized marketing   Traditional marketing heavily relied upon mass marketing techniques with some adaptations for different market segments. The advent of ICT has facilitated businesses to gather information about individual customers' tastes and preferences, their buying behaviour, and customized marketing strategy to cater to each customer.

Hierarchal organizations to network organizations   The traditional 'hierarchal organizational structures' are transforming into 'network organizational structures' so as to take benefit of emerging e-business opportunities and meet the potential challenges.

However, businesses going online face several challenges, as follows:

- As most businesses are making their online presence, the market competition has grown multi-fold from local to global level.
- Online buying and selling of goods often result in elimination of market intermediaries; the process is frequently referred to as 'disintermediation' and leads to channel conflict.
- Increase in availability of information online on the public domain augments the chances of its copying with competitors who make its use for their own benefits.
- Since the Internet can be accessed from across the world, there is no single binding legal framework.
- Most businesses and customers often fear breach of security in terms of both the theft and misuse of classified and personal information over the Internet.
- A large segment of customers are resistant to carrying out marketing transactions over the Internet.
- Viability of carrying out marketing transactions differs across firms, depending upon their nature of business and resource availability.

IMPACT OF ICT ON NEW PRODUCTS AND SERVICES

ICT often creates new business models, services, and products that differ considerably in various countries. It has the most significant impact on creating new products, services, and business models in Sweden with a score of 6.2 (Fig. 21.10) on a scale of one to seven, followed by Korea (5.9), the UK (5.9), Taiwan (5.8), Singapore (5.8), France (5.7) in comparison to Switzerland (5.6), the USA (5.6), the UAE (5.4), Qatar (5.4), Germany (5.4), Japan (5.2), Brazil (5.2), India (5), China (5), Kenya (4.7), South Africa (4.7), Egypt (4.2), Russian Federation (3.8), Syria (2.9), and Yemen (2.2).

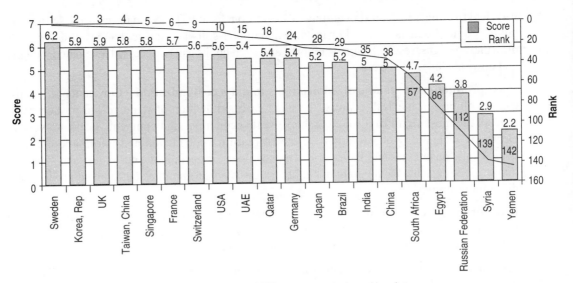

Fig. 21.10   Impact of ICT on new products and services

Source: The Global Information Technology Report, 2012, World Economic Forum, Geneva. 1 = no impact; 7 = significant impact

IMPACT OF ICT ON CONSUMER PURCHASE DECISION PROCESS

E-marketing has also transformed the marketing process from a physical marketplace to a virtual 'marketspace', which has considerably altered the consumer buying behaviour. Integrating ICT applications with marketing has led to considerable changes in the consumer purchasing-decision process,[13] briefly summarized next.

Problem Recognition

Conventional marketing communications stimulate market demand via conventional media, that is, advertisements in print media, radio, or television. Communication strategy on the Internet should be user-specific rather than a mass-communication approach as used in traditional media. Thus, the communication strategy has undergone a fundamental change with an increased focus on the customized communication approach targeting individual customers.

Information Search

In traditional marketing systems, customers gather information through either internal or external sources, including peer group discussions, company brochures, etc. The availability of

---

[13] Butler, P. and J. Peppard, 'Consumer Purchasing on the Internet: Process and Prospects', *European Management Journal*, vol. 16, no. 5, 1998, pp. 600–610.

market information varies widely between the firms and the customers. However, in the virtual marketspace, customers can scan information on the Internet and make comparisons to suit their individual requirements. The intermediary function performed by Internet sites is mainly related to providing information and exchange. For instance, airlines, railways, tour operators, etc. provide online booking that bypasses traditional market intermediaries, like travel agents. Internet websites also provide links with other websites that help customers gather more information.

Evaluation of Alternatives

In a traditional marketplace, the evaluation of alternatives is greatly influenced by the peer groups, family members, friends, and publicity through word of mouth, whereas in an electronic marketspace, the virtual community has taken up the role of traditional reference groups. Various discussion groups and consumer forums share their experiences with each other over the Net.

Purchase Decision

The decision to select a seller for a purchase is traditionally based on previous experiences of the buyer with the seller, her proximity, range of products offered, and the price charged. However, in the electronic marketspace, sellers often attract buyers by way of creating interesting websites, competitive prices, and superior purchasing experience to induce purchase decisions. In Internet transactions, the payment is usually through credit cards but delivery mechanisms differ depending upon the product type. It may be in the form of either online delivery or physical delivery. For instance, software, music, design, etc. may be delivered online, whereas physical goods have to be delivered physically.

Post-purchase Behaviour

In traditional markets, a firm should respond to customer complaints and enquiries through the marketing channels. However, in an electronic marketspace, the emphasis is on ICTs, such as continuous updating of websites, and on satisfying customer needs. A firm should endeavour to offer value to its customers through its websites by promptly responding to their queries and providing latest information to encourage new purchases.

EMERGENCE OF REVERSE MARKETING

Earlier, the information flow between the companies and the customers was generally a one-way process. The information was market controlled, customers were ill informed, and the exchanges were market initiated.[14] The industrial era was known as the era of information asymmetry. With breakthroughs in ICT, information has become affordable and universal. The ease of access and availability of information about a firm's products and those of its competitors to the customers have greatly increased around the world. This has resulted in a shift of power from manufacturers to customers. This has led not only to customer-oriented marketing but also to customer-initiated marketing. The use of the Internet has empowered buyers significantly. Today, the buyers can[15]

- get information about the manufactures of the products and brands around the world;
- carry out comparison of product features, quality, prices, etc., from a variety of sources;
- initiate requests for advertising and information from the manufacturers;
- design market-offerings;

---

[14] Sawhney, Mohanbir and Philip Kotler, 'Marketing in the Age of Information Democracy', *Kellogg on Marketing*, (ed.) Iacobucci, Dawn, John Wiley & Sons, New York, p. 401.

[15] Sawhney, Mohanbir and Philip Kotler, 'Marketing in the Age of Information Democracy', *Kellogg on Marketing*, (ed.) Iacobucci, Dawn, John Wiley & Sons, New York, p. 401.

- hire buying agents and invite market offers from multiple sellers; and
- buy ancillary products and services from a specialized third party.

Earlier, the marketers used to initiate the marketing activities, but the breakthroughs in ICT have metamorphosed the marketing system, enabling customers to initiate marketing activities. The phenomenon is termed as *reverse marketing* wherein the customers initiate the exchanges and gather the required information.[16] The customers can now initiate and carry out the following activities.

Reverse promotion   A customer may search for product information and solicit promotion from the marketers or through the intermediaries. These intermediaries relay customer requests to the marketers without divulging personal information and block unwanted offers.

Reverse advertising   Traditionally, firms used to push advertisements to the customers, generally as a mass communication tool. ICT has now enabled customers to request for more information from manufacturers and click on the advertisements they are interested in. Thus, advertising becomes customer-initiated as it can be pulled by customers.

Reverse pricing   Buyers can place their offer for bidding and set the prices. A number of e-marketing firms like indiatimes.com allow the customers to set their own price. Buyers can specify the price and model options. A variety of branded consumer durables are also available for auction on such sites.

Reverse product design   The e-marketing firms enable customers to customize the products of their own choice. HMV's HamaraCD.com enables customers to customize their own CD with their own titles.

Reverse segmentation   Traditionally, the marketing firms used customer purchase history to create customized offer. However, under e-marketing, customers are self-select and co-customize offers with marketers.

POLICY FRAMEWORK AND ICT LAWS FOR GLOBAL E-MARKETING

From a policy perspective, electronic delivery of goods is the most challenging aspect as such trade is rising rapidly without any global regulatory framework and hardly any national or international legislation. In view of the growing significance of e-commerce in international trade, the Second Ministerial Declaration of the WTO at Geneva adopted a declaration on global electronic commerce on 20 May 1998, which directed the WTO General Council to establish a comprehensive work programme to examine all trade-related issues arising from electronic commerce. The work programme includes issues such as characterization of electronic transmission as goods or services or something else; market access involving the method of application of customs duties to electronic transmission; classification of digitized products under the existing harmonized system (HS) of trade classification; rules of origin; standardization; and development dimensions involving the effect on revenue and fiscal positions of developing countries in future. The 1998 declaration also included a so-called moratorium stating that 'members will continue their current practice of not imposing customs tariffs on electronic transmissions'.

The penetration of B2C e-marketing is of high significance for developing countries as the ban on customs duty is applicable to digitized products that mostly fall in this category. Traditional trade transactions of digital products through a carrier media in the form of diskettes, tapes, CDs etc. were subjected to customs duties in the importing countries. However, the breakthroughs in ICT have made it possible to transmit these products through electronic networks that are not subject to customs duties.

---

[16] Sawhney, Mohanbir and Philip Kotler, 'Marketing in the Age of Information Democracy', *Kellogg on Marketing*, (ed.) Iacobucci, Dawn, John Wiley & Sons, New York, pp. 386–408.

With rapid growth in international trade of digital products, such as printed matter, software, music and other media, films, and video games, most developing countries are becoming net importers of digitized products. The revenue implications of e-commerce have made both developed and developing countries equally concerned, although they differ in terms of the type of tax that can be addressed to stop erosion of revenue. Consumption taxes are important sources of revenue for developed countries; therefore, OECD countries decided to impose VAT at a 1998 conference in Ottawa, whereas developing countries are more dependent on customs duties and moratorium on customs duties on digitized products has caused significant losses.

Since e-commerce differs from normal trade in goods, the trade policy requirement also differs for transactions involving digital transmission. Therefore, a specific trade policy is required for international trade electronically.

The technological breakthroughs are likely to transform a large portion of present day 'non e-trade' into 'e-trade' in the near future both in B2B and B2C segments. Besides, increase in FDI and growth in inter-corporate transfers could increase the scope of B2B form of e-commerce also for developing countries. In view of the rapidly growing significance of e-commerce, the national commitments under the GATS agreement would also be required to be reviewed.

Moreover, laws related to the use of ICTs (e.g., electronic commerce, digital signatures, and consumer protection) differ in various countries all over the world. Sweden has the most developed ICT laws in the world with a score of 5.9 (Fig. 21.11) on a seven-point scale, followed by Singapore (5.9), Estonia (5.8), Denmark (5.8), Luxembourg (5.7), compared to the UK (5.4), the USA (5.3), Qatar (5.3), France (5.2), the UAE (5.1), South Africa (5), Germany (5), Japan (4.7), Brazil (4.4), China (4.4), India (4.4), Kenya (4.2), Egypt (3.7), Russian Federation (3.5), and Yemen (1.9).

This chapter elucidates the conceptual framework of e-marketing and related technologies. Various applications of e-marketing are also elaborated. Besides, various e-marketing models and alternative strategic options are discussed. This chapter also brings out e-enabled business process transformation, global e-marketing, and e-services. The process changes brought out by digital technology in international trade documentation system are also explicated. The policy framework and related concerns in implementing e-enabled marketing processes are also examined.

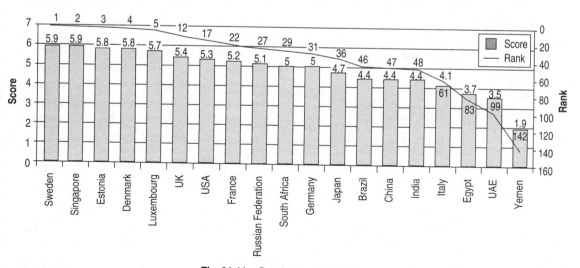

Fig. 21.11 Development of ICT laws

Source: The Global Information Technology Report, 2012, World Economic Forum, Geneva. 1 = non-existent; 7 = well developed

Summary

Rapid economic globalization and advances in information and communication (ICT) technology has made e-marketing an essential component of a firm's business strategy. The term e-commerce is confined to buying and selling of goods over electronic media, whereas e-business encompasses a broad framework of business activities. In addition to traditional commercial activities of buying and selling, it also involves collaborating with business partners and servicing customers.

The major changes brought about by integration of digital technology to marketing processes include physical marketplace to virtual marketspace, physical products to digital products, mass production of standardized products to mass customization, fixed pricing to dynamic pricing, mass marketing techniques to customized marketing, and hierarchal organizations to network organizations.

The former system of exchange of information between the organizations through computers using proprietary networks, known as EDI, has now been widely replaced by the Internet. The network between business enterprises and their suppliers, distributors, and supplier partners, which is not open to public, is known as extranet, whereas intranet refers to the internal network within an organization across geographical boundaries.

The major types of e-marketing models include business-to-business (B2B), business-to-consumer (B2C), consumer-to-business (C2B), and consumer-to-consumer (C2C). Alternative e-marketing strategies include brick and mortar, pure click, and brick and click.

Conduct of marketing transactions, such as buying, selling, and distributing or delivering goods or services using electronic methods, is termed as e-marketing. Use of electronic methods for marketing transactions across the world is termed as global e-marketing. E-marketing has transformed the marketing process from physical marketplace to virtual marketspace that has changed considerably the process of consumers' purchasing decisions. E-marketing has also given rise to reverse marketing wherein marketing activities are initiated by the customers rather than marketing firms. The ICT has revolutionized the ways services are offered across geographical boundaries.

There exists hardly any global regulatory framework for conduct of electronic transactions across borders and limited national or international legislation on e-business, that too with wide variations.

Key Terms

Brick and click Conduct of commercial activities and transactions both online and offline.

Brick and mortar Conduct of marketing activities through tangible physical assets, such as manufacturing unit or building, or a storage facility.

Business-to-business (B2B) e-commerce Intra-firm transactions using an electronic network.

Disintermediation A process that enables suppliers to interact and transact directly with buyers, thereby eliminating intermediaries and distributors.

E-business Performance of business activities, such as designing products, managing supply chain, operations, marketing, and offering services to various stakeholders using electronic technologies.

E-commerce Buying and selling of goods or services through computer-mediated networks.

Electronic data interchange (EDI) The exchange of information between organizations through computers using proprietary networks.

Electronic payment system (EPS) A system of financial exchange between buyers and sellers in the online environment that is facilitated by a digital financial instrument.

E-readiness Measures a country's e-business environment indicating how amenable a market is to Internet-based opportunities.

E-tailing Retailing through the Internet.

Extranet An Internet-based network between a business enterprise and its suppliers, distributors, and business partners, which is not open to the general public.

Global e-marketing Conduct of marketing transactions such as buying, selling, distributing, or delivering goods or services using electronic methods.

Intranet An internal private network used to link various divisions of a business around the world into a unified communication network.

Lifetime value of a customer (LVC) The estimate of potential profit a company is likely to derive out of a customer during his lifetime.

M-marketing Conduct of marketing activities through use of wireless technology such as mobile phones, personal digital assistant (PDA), or telematics.

One-to-one (1:1) marketing Marketing targeted to individual customer, that is, 'segment size of one'.

Personalization Market targeting to the extreme by using a unique marketing mix for each customer.

Pure click All commercial transactions are carried out online with little physical presence.

Reverse marketing Marketing system wherein the customer initiates the exchanges and pulls the required information.

Concept Review Questions

1. Explain the significance of integrating information and communication technology (ICT) with marketing processes.
2. Elucidate the conceptual framework of e-marketing. Identify the significant changes it has brought to marketing processes.
3. Describe the prerequisites for conducting effective e-marketing transactions.
4. Describe the impact of ICT on consumers' purchase decision process.
5. Write short notes on the following:
   (a) Electronic data interchange (EDI)
   (b) Internet
   (c) Extranet and intranet

Critical Thinking Questions

1. Explore the Internet and find out three companies employing the following marketing models:
   (a) Business-to-business (B2B)
   (b) Business-to-consumers (B2C)
   (c) Consumer-to-business (C2B)
   (d) Consumer-to-consumer (C2C)
2. Find out the salient features of the regulatory framework for e-marketing transactions in your country and compare it with any two other countries that have relatively higher level of online marketing transactions.

Project Assignments

1. Select a firm in your country operating internationally with use of e-enabled marketing processes. Find out its constraints and strengths and its impact on the company's marketing competitiveness.
2. Recall your experience of an online purchase preferably involving an online transaction. Share your experience with your colleagues in the class and prepare a comprehensive list of pros and cons of online purchase based on their experience.

Emerging Issues

INTRODUCTION

The marketing environment across the world witnessed unprecedented changes in the last few decades that have metamorphosed the very approach to marketing. Rising income levels in all parts of the world except for Sub-Saharan Africa combined with reduction in trade barriers accelerated the growth of global markets. The advent of information and communication technology (ICT) and the rapid development of the transport sector not only bridged the gaps in diverse markets but also made distances irrelevant.

Moreover, ICT has revolutionized the entire marketing process and has become an integral part of the firms' marketing strategies. Buyers can obtain information about manufacturers around the world, carry out comparisons of product features, quality, prices, etc. from a variety of sources, customize their own market offerings, and invite market offers from multiple sellers.

The technological advances and the growing customer demands consistently put pressure on firms to develop new products at a very fast pace resulting in product proliferation in the markets and shortening of product life cycles. The strength of the retailers is growing progressively the world over that led to accelerated pace of growth of private labels and increased the pressure on manufacturers' margins.

The role of information and knowledge as inputs in achieving a firm's competitiveness has considerably increased in the changed global scenario. The agreement on Trade-Related Intellectual Property Rights (TRIPS) under the WTO generated intense debate among the high- and low-income countries. Customers' sophistication has also witnessed a dramatic rise, forcing the firms to address the needs of new customer segments. As markets in high-income countries are increasingly getting saturated for most consumer goods, firms are exploring new markets in middle- and low-income countries.

Even in these countries, firms are required to capture the market beyond the urban middle class with innovative marketing strategies so as to sustain and grow.

Recent years witnessed rapid rise as well as growing concern over unethical marketing practices such as circumventing product attributes and benefits, making false claims, counterfeiting and piracy, bribery, smuggling, and rising concern for corporate social responsibility (CSR). CSR has become a strategic tool for growth and survival of firms' operations across the world markets.

Emerging economies are projected to grow at 4 per cent, which is double the rate of 2 per cent in the developed economies during 2011–50, implying their growing significance in future marketing. Multinationals are finding it difficult to capture marketing opportunities in emerging markets with products developed for the American and European mass markets in view of their vastly different purchasing power. They need to maintain a delicate balance while serving bi-polar needs of developed and developing markets as wide ranging as the USA and Ethiopia. Presently, global marketers are increasingly in desperate search for value for money offerings. Therefore, in today's rapidly changing marketing scenario, regular interactions on emerging opportunities and challenges in international markets and re-orientation of strategies become crucial to success (Fig. 22.1).

Fig. 22.1   An interactive session with the author, Prof. Joshi, on emerging challenges and opportunities in international markets

In the aftermath of economic recession in the developed world, both MNCs and consumers across the world are hunting for value. Consumers, even in developed markets, are exhibiting a shift in their behaviour; there is lifestyle change not to overspend but to seek the same value at lower prices. So far, customers in developed countries were hardly given the option of low-cost products. The entire cost structure in developed markets prevented the customers from having access to products priced economically.

Transnational companies are finding it worthwhile to change their business strategies: if any innovation helps reduce operational and manufacturing costs, it will go global. Innovative ideas are hardly a proprietary of rich countries. Emerging economies like India and China are increasingly providing reverse learning in varied aspects of business to multinationals to be used in other parts of the world. India presents a unique combination of low-price talent pool at a fraction of the cost vis-à-vis developed countries and a mass market making it a fast emerging innovation destination in the world. Products designed and developed in emerging markets like India are finding their ways to the rest of the world (refer to Exhibit 10.5 in Chapter 10).

The future marketing challenges lie in understanding and adapting to local rules, regulations, and customs, identifying right partners and forging alliances, developing good relations with host country governments and regulatory bodies. In some cases, the optimal production location may not be the same as the largest consumer markets. For instance, investing in Malaysia, Indonesia, or Vietnam could be a gateway to China or India or Poland as a gateway to Russia.

This chapter provides an overview of contemporary issues in international markets and examines the emerging issues such as accelerated growth of global markets, pervasiveness of globalization, rapid integration of global markets, breaking down of marketing boundaries, emerging new marketing barriers, emergence of global customer segment, product proliferation and shortening product life cycles, growing strength of retailers, emergence of knowledge economy, growing customer expectations, and emergence of global e-marketing. ICT revolutionizes marketing of services and customer relationship marketing (CRM). Ethical issues in international marketing such as counterfeiting, piracy, bribery, smuggling, and CSR are also elucidated. At the end, the chapter brings out India's emergence at the global stage, its rising soft power, internationalization of Indian firms, its changing demographics, and its potential to become world's biggest consumer market.

EMERGING ISSUES IN INTERNATIONAL MARKETING

The fast changing environmental factors have significantly influenced the global marketing activities. The major emerging issues in international markets may be summarized as follows.

Accelerated Growth of Global Markets

Rapid rise in income levels and the growing consumer class across the world are opening up new marketing opportunities. The World Bank estimates that in coming years, the per capita income is likely to increase in all regions of the world except in Sub-Saharan Africa. Markets worldwide are likely to grow at a much higher rate than anticipated. International trade has become the locomotive of growth of world economy and has also been instrumental in increasing the global economic integration. The advent of technology has greatly facilitated a firm's ability to access international markets.

Pervasiveness of Globalization

Globalization has become a catchphrase for politicians, journalists, and the public at large who appear to be baffled about the term and its implications. They try to attribute globalization for all the ills or happenings around in their own way and rationalize their actions. The forces of globalization have considerably narrowed down the gap of time and space. This has led to significant increase in interactions among the people from across the world.

Rapid Integration of Global Markets

The marketing boundaries are fast disappearing consequent to economic liberalization and integration with the WTO. At the same time, the state-driven marketing systems in the

Commonwealth of Independent States (CIS) and China are fast moving towards free-market regimes. The economic integration of most countries with the WTO has led to reduction in tariffs and restrictions on imposing explicit non-tariff marketing barriers. However, these drastic changes have resulted in the imposition of new marketing barriers such as strict quality norms, technical specifications, and environmental concerns and regulations to discourage human exploitation and child labour.

Economies are increasingly getting interdependent. This was experienced during the economic crisis of 2008, which emanated from the USA but later engulfed Europe and other parts of the world. In 2012, the Eurozone crisis not only adversely affected the demand of imported goods in Europe but also decelerated economies of the USA, India, China, Japan, and Brazil as its far reaching impact. Moreover, the slowdown in these critical economies adversely impacted their neighbourhood. For instance, the slowdown in China adversely affected several East Asian countries. Thus, countries across the world would find it increasingly difficult to isolate themselves from global economic upheavals.

Consolidation of markets across the world exhibit more or less similar patterns. When China opened up its market, there were lot of local companies. Consequent to entry of foreign companies, a lot of consolidation has taken place in the Chinese industry as it has a lot of similarity with the Indian market.

Breaking Down of Marketing Boundaries

The markets across countries are becoming global as the marketing boundaries are fast disappearing. The major reasons for breaking down of marketing boundaries include economic liberalization, move towards market-driven systems, and rapidly narrowing down of distances as discussed next.

Economic liberalization
Economic liberalization in India and other developing countries as well, in terms of regulations, market access, and tariff structures, greatly contributed to the breakdown of international marketing boundaries. Dismantling of the industrial licensing system, introduction of current account convertibility, removal of quantitative restrictions on imports and foreign exchange, and reforms of capital markets facilitated Indian companies to expand their capacities and compete in international markets.

The emergence of the multilateral trade regime under the WTO has facilitated the reduction of tariff and non-tariff marketing barriers. Besides, there has also been a proliferation in regional trade agreements that facilitated reduction of marketing barriers among the member nations. For instance, the European Union (EU) has become a powerful economic union considerably affecting a firm's marketing strategy for the European market.

Path to free markets
The marketing systems under planned economies witnessed a worldwide collapse, thus paving way to capitalist market-driven systems. Over the years, CIS countries and China opened up and are moving towards market-driven economic systems at a fast pace. However, presently the exceptions to free market systems are only a few autocratic countries, such as North Korea and Cuba.

Death of distance
Geographical proximity of markets had traditionally been a significant criterion for selecting target markets. The advents of ICT and rapid strides in the means of transport have considerably

undermined the significance of distance in market selection. Besides, air travel has become much faster and cheaper. Over the years, there has also been a considerable reduction in the international telecommunication tariff rates due to the advent of new technology and increased competition.

With the arrival of the Internet, the transaction costs of transferring ideas and information have declined enormously. 'Global village' is the term increasingly used to describe the collapse of space and time barriers in human communication, especially the Web enabling people to interact on a global scale.

Emerging New Marketing Barriers

The integration of national economies under the multilateral trade regime of the WTO has restrained countries from increasing tariffs and imposing explicit non-tariff marketing barriers. However, the member countries consistently evolve innovative marketing barriers that are WTO compatible to protect their national interests and retain competitiveness of their goods and services. Such barriers include quality and technical specifications, environmental issues, regulations related to human exploitation, like child labour, etc. Innovative technical jargons and justifications are consistently evolved often on the grounds of health, safety, environment, etc. especially by high-income countries to impose such barriers to restrict the import of goods from low-income countries, which find it very hard to defend such measures.

Emergence of Global Customer Segment

The process of globalization has given rise to a global customer segment exhibiting similar tastes and preferences across the geographical boundaries. Customers around the world are exhibiting convergence of tastes and preferences in terms of their product likings and buying habits. The automobiles, fast-food outlets, music systems, and even fashion goods are becoming amazingly similar across the countries. The proliferation of transnational satellite television and telecommunication has accelerated the process of cultural convergence. Traditionally, the cultural values were transmitted through generations by parents, grandparents, or other family members. However, the emergence of nuclear families, with both the parents working, has made television and Internet the prominent source of acculturation not only in the Western countries but also in the oriental countries. Besides, the advances in the modes of transport and increased international travel have greatly contributed to the growing similarity in customer preferences across the countries. Thus, the process of globalization has encouraged firms to tap the global markets with increased product standardization. This has also given rise to a rapid proliferation of global brands for the fast emerging global customers.

Growing Customer Expectation

Although the emphasis on launching global products has gained popularity among the global transnational corporations, the market response hardly supports this uniform approach. Consequent to the liberalization of the Indian economy, most multinationals entered India with the belief that anything with a foreign label could be sold to the Indian consumers like hot cakes. They failed to understand the extent to which the preferences between India and the West converge. Indian customers are making a distinct market segment as they want to enjoy the latest technology/products but, at the same time, they prefer some degree of customization that suits local conditions and tastes.

With the increasing levels of customer sophistication, products need to be customized for the target markets. Cell phones were introduced in India about a decade ago with the presumption that their use would be restricted to the upper segment of the Indian market. The Western manufacturers simply shipped European models to India. However, cell phones became a mass product consequent to the mobile revolution that started in 2000. It necessitated product adaptation for Indian market. In early 2004, Nokia launched its model 1100, which had a host of unique features, such as special grip and torchlight, to suit the needs of its target segment—the Indian truckers. The Reliance code division multiple access (CDMA) phones (from LG and Samsung) have been made especially for India, with unique polyphonic rings and colour displays.

Indian families typically watch TV together in the evening and most of their viewing revolves around Hindi films and serials that have a considerable component of music, songs, and dance. Therefore, a large number of Indian customers prefer big boom and sound output features in their televisions. In order to cater to such needs of the Indian customers, Samsung introduced the Metallica and Woofer series especially for the Indian market. Based on the feedback that Indian housewives were not technology-friendly and were uncomfortable with many washing programmes fed in their washing machines, Electrolux Kelvinator Ltd launched the world's first talking washing machine—the 'Washy Talky' in Hindi for the Indian market. The machine has been developed indigenously and is equipped with a 'digital vigilante' feature, which consists of an interactive voice response system. This system guides the user step-by-step during the entire washing process. It even warns the user of any operating errors. Using artificial intelligence through 'Intelli Clean Logic', the machine can also sense the load weight and choose the optimum programme.

Product Proliferation and Shortening Product Life Cycles

The technological advances have accelerated the process of new product development. Besides, the ever-growing demands of the customers have necessitated firms to innovate and customize their products. This has triggered competitive pressure to add new features to the firms' existing products or develop new products so as to maintain and increase their market share. The proliferation of products has increased the complexity of firms to maintain their unique marketing proposition (UMP) and sustain their market share.

The growing competitive pressures on the one hand and technological breakthroughs on the other have considerably shortened the life span of products. For example, manual typewriters survived the market for more than a century, whereas electronic typewriters survived merely for a decade. Today, the breakthroughs in computer technology have reduced the life span of computers and their components and software to only a few months rather than a year. Since a firm cannot afford to lag behind its competitors who are constantly coming out with new products, it has no other option but to innovate. As new product development involves considerable investment of resources, firms are under intense pressure to recover their investment as early as possible and often resort to adopting market skimming strategies. Besides, the new products are designed with built-in obsolescence features so as to pave the way for launching a firm's new products. Intel's new microprocessors and Microsoft's software are good examples of built-in product obsolescence enabling the marketers to replace their own existing products with newer ones.

Emergence of Knowledge Economy

Knowledge or information is gaining significance to achieve competitiveness in a firm. The Industrial Revolution that led to economic growth in Europe was primarily based on the invention of steam engine and its successor, the internal combustion engine. Both required coal and petroleum as fuel. Once the industrialized countries exhausted their own supply sources, they explored and identified alternative sources in the Middle East. This search resulted in a massive boost to economic growth of the region.

In the 19th century, some of the world's wealthiest people, from John Rockefeller to the Sultan of Brunei, were associated with oil. Today, Bill Gates is the richest person on earth due to his hold on the information technology segment. The industries with the highest level of growth today, such as biotechnology, electronics, ICT, and designing, are primarily knowledge-based.

However, in the 1990s, the US growth rates were primarily attributed to increased productivity enabled by a highly skilled workforce. Ironically, the developed countries are now experiencing shortage of skilled professionals, who serve as the key fuel to sustain economic growth. Therefore, developed countries are now looking towards developing nations to make up for this shortfall.

Firms increasingly derive their competitive advantage based on their intellectual property. The agreement on TRIPS under the WTO has generated considerable debate among the high- and low-income countries about the legislations related to the protection of intellectual property. The knowledge-based industries are bound to flourish globally in the 21st century. India, with the strength of its brainpower of technical and professional personnel, is likely to achieve much higher growth for its products in international markets.

Emergence of Global E-marketing

The introduction of e-marketing has transformed the 'physical marketplace' to a 'virtual marketspace', which has significantly altered the consumer purchasing decision process. This has led to a customer revolution with collision of virtual and physical worlds fundamentally changing consumers' buying behaviour. The IT-based new marketing system enables the customers to initiate the marketing activities, giving rise to the concept of reverse marketing, as discussed in Chapter 21.

The Internet is becoming increasingly integrated with day-to-day activities both in the developed and the developing economies.

Earlier, the information flow between the companies and the customers was generally a one-way process. The information was market-controlled, customers were ill-informed, and the exchanges were market-initiated. The industrial era was known as the era of information asymmetry. With the breakthroughs in ICT, information has become affordable and universal. The ease of access and availability of information about a firm's products and those of its competitors to the customers have greatly increased around the world. This has resulted in a shift of power from the manufacturers to the customers. This has led to not only customer-oriented marketing but also customer-initiated marketing.

In markets where there are many more mobile phones in hands than PCs on desks—including most of the developing world—wireless devices are becoming delivery mechanisms for IT-enabled services. It is not surprising that mobile banking services are more developed in the Philippines and China than in the USA.

Moreover, the collision of physical and virtual world is rapidly changing consumers' purchase behaviour. Consumers are increasingly seeking an integrated shopping experience.

ICT Revolutionizes Marketing of Services

Breakthroughs in ICT have revolutionized the ways services are offered breaking geographical boundaries. Services such as e-learning, IT, and medical services now increasingly make use of ICT. The Apollo Hospitals in India provide a number of Internet-based services to the patients who are its customers, such as information search about medical specialists, booking of appointments, periodic check-ups, and location of Apollo speciality hospitals. It has also set up a telemedicine network (Fig. 22.2) catering to a population of 50,000 villages in India and its neighbouring countries. It provides a wide range of services through telemedicine applications, which includes

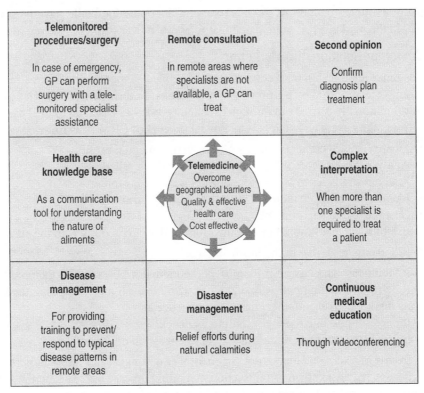

Telemonitored procedures/surgery	Remote consultation	Second opinion
In case of emergency, GP can perform surgery with a tele-monitored specialist assistance	In remote areas where specialists are not available, a GP can treat	Confirm diagnosis plan treatment
Health care knowledge base	**Telemedicine** Overcome geographical barriers Quality & effective health care Cost effective	**Complex interpretation**
As a communication tool for understanding the nature of aliments		When more than one specialist is required to treat a patient
Disease management	**Disaster management**	**Continuous medical education**
For providing training to prevent/ respond to typical disease patterns in remote areas	Relief efforts during natural calamities	Through videoconferencing

Fig. 22.2 ICT revolutionizes marketing of services: telemedicine applications in Apollo Hospitals

Source: www.apollohospitals.com, accessed on 13 April 2011.

remote consultation, obtaining second opinion from specialists, complex interpretations by a panel of specialists, medication education, disease management, and communication of health care knowledge. Besides, the tele-monitored surgical procedure also enables a general practitioner (GP) to perform surgery with assistance from a tele-monitor specialist. Thus, telemedicine provides cost-effective and quality health-care services overcoming geographical barriers.

Growing Strength of Retailers

Retailers have shown an increasing strength in terms of their size and the sales the world over. This has encouraged the large retailers to put their private labels on the merchandise. The retailers buy products directly from the manufacturers and put their own labels, which results in higher margins for them. Besides, the private labels offer tough competition to the manufacturers of branded products. The private labels have witnessed a rapid increase over the years.

Overall retail contributes to 14 per cent of India's GDP, penetration of organized retail remains low at 5–6% indicating a high growth potential in organized retail. In 2011, India allowed 100 per cent FDI in single brand retail with a constraint of 30 per cent local sourcing. Companies such as Gap, IKEA, Abercrombie & Fitch, LVMH, Zara, Marks & Spencer, and Mango are entering the Indian market. Starbucks partnered with Tata Group to own and operate cafes and Dunkin' Donuts also opened their first stores in Delhi. Later with the opening of FDI in multi-brand retail, the Indian market is likely to witness entry of mega retailers such as Walmart, Metro, and Carrefour.

The growing power of retailers has given rise to the adoption of push strategies by the firms where the retailers wield their muscles to get more and more margins on one hand and squeeze the promotional budgets of the marketers on the other that could have been used for creating pull in the markets. It is anticipated that retailers' power is likely to grow in future.

Customer Relationship Marketing

Customer relationship marketing (CRM) is defined as the process of creating and maintaining business relationship by a firm with its customers. In the oriental countries, marketing activity was traditionally carried out through exchange processes based on mutual trust and relationship between the buyers and sellers. The typical process of CRM is as follows:

- Identify key customers in terms of long-term potential profits.
- Analyse the expectations of the customers and the sellers.
- Find out strategies to work more closely with the customers.
- Identify the changes required in the operating procedures.
- Customize the marketing mix.
- Establish an institutional mechanism for regular interactions with the customers.

ICT facilitates CRM in the following manner:

- It facilitates mass customization of marketing messages and also the product.
- It helps in initiating two-way dialogues with the customers, allowing the firm to customize its market offerings to meet the customers' needs.
- It makes it possible to receive online feedback.
- It provides incentives to the customers to engage in dialogues.

In case of traditional marketing, the focus was on single sales transactions between a firm and its customers, also known as transaction marketing. In case of CRM, on the other hand, greater emphasis is laid on retaining existing customers than on acquiring new ones. It is well known that it is much easier for a firm to retain its existing customers than acquiring new ones. Such relationships were also an integral part of high cultural context of oriental markets. However, with the advent of the Internet, the concept of relationship marketing has become highly popular in the Western markets.

ETHICAL ISSUES IN INTERNATIONAL MARKETING

Marketers often resort to a wide range of unethical practices, such as corruption and bribery, financial misappropriations, circumventing law enforcement, evading taxes and duties, dumping, making exaggerated and even false claims, exploiting customers, flouting basic norms of civil decency, and even manufacturing and distributing pirated and fake products. Such marketing practices are detrimental not only to customers but also to civil society at large.

Rising Concern for Unethical Marketing Practices

The axiom 'everything is fair in love and war' is often endorsed by marketers since marketing is also considered to be a strategic war fought against competitors, though in a civilized manner. Companies often resort to several ways and means, even if these violate basic ethics, to establish the edge of their products and services over competitors. Therefore, businesses often adopt means and ways, both fair and unfair, to entice customers and establish their supremacy in the marketplace. Companies barely hesitate to make exaggerated and sometimes even false claims about their products and uses to win fierce marketing rivalries.

Multinational companies are frequently accused of adopting unethical business practices to achieve and retain their competitive edge. Nestlé has long been accused of promoting its infant food products in low-income countries by projecting them as key to infants' health and grossly undermining the importance of breastfeeding. The situation worsened, especially in low-income countries with poor quality of potable water and widespread illiteracy among expectant and nursing mothers. The company adopted aggressive strategies to convince mothers about the benefits of its infant formulae that would make their babies healthy and chubby. This has been in violation to globally accepted norms that the infant should mainly be breastfed in its initial few months. The World Health Organization (WHO) estimates that over 1.5 million infants die every year around the world because they are not breastfed. In countries where water in unsafe, a bottle-fed child is up to 25 times more likely to die as a result of diarrhoea than a breastfed child. Despite this, companies manufacturing baby food continue to market their products in ways that grossly undermine breastfeeding.

Soft drink companies are often accused of selling sub-standard drinks with high levels of pesticide content, polluting groundwater and soil around bottling plants, causing severe water shortages in communities, and distributing toxic waste as fertilizer to farmers. The Centre for Science and Environment (CSE), New Delhi, released a report in 2003 revealing that soft drinks sold in India contained unacceptable levels of pesticides and other harmful chemicals. In response, the soft-drink lobby led by Pepsi and Coca-Cola sought to completely discredit the report, accusing the role of the clandestine hand of European lobbies in maligning US multinationals.

Three years later, another CSE investigation which was even more widespread and scientifically rigorous, made the shocking revelation that average pesticide residues in all brands of PepsiCo were 25 times and Coca-Cola 22 times higher than the norms set by the Bureau of Indian Standards (BIS). Moreover, the concentration of lindane, a confirmed cancer-causing chemical, was found 54 times the standards set by BIS, adding to consumers' nightmare.

In March 2006, the news of an Indian consumer court fining Pepsi for ₹1,00,000 because a condom was found in its bottle,[1] aggravated consumers' concerns. The incident revealed the lackadaisical attitude of multinationals in developing countries. Such irresponsible behaviour of mega-corporations may be largely attributed to the fact that in developing countries like India they remain largely unpunished unlike in the USA where the corporate entities are often imposed huge penalties. The strong nexus of unethical practices between corporates, bureaucrats, and politicians adds to the woes of consumers in low-income countries. Besides, the complicated judiciary system in such countries takes several years to arrive at the final outcome. Moreover, the maximum penalty of a fine ranges from ₹1,00,000 to ₹7,00,000, which is too meagre to be of any consequence to the mighty global corporations.

Counterfeiting and Piracy

Counterfeiting means imitating something with the intent to deceive or defraud. Counterfeiting accounts for 5 to 7 per cent of world trade, worth an estimated US$ 600 billion a year. It has grown by over 10,000 per cent in the past two decades. A wide range of products such as consumer goods, currency, and documents are counterfeited internationally. Customers find it difficult to differentiate between a genuine and a counterfeit product. Wider the price difference between branded and generic products, more lucrative becomes the business of counterfeit products.

Counterfeiting, one of the fastest growing economic crimes of modern times, presents companies, governments, and individuals with a unique set of problems and poses a serious threat to global health and safety. It is also one of the most significant threats to free market systems. Counterfeiting not only steals the value of intellectual capital, but also stifles innovation and robs

---

[1] 'Condom in Bottle Costs Pepsi ₹1 Lakh', *The Times of India,* 26 April 2006.

Exhibit 22.1   Driving factors for counterfeit and pirate activities

Supply drivers	Demand drivers
Market characteristics High unit profitability Large potential market size Genuine brand power	*Product characteristics* Low prices Acceptable perceived quality Ability to conceal status
Production, distribution, and technology Moderate need for investments Moderate technology requirements Unproblematic distribution and sales High ability to conceal operation Easy to deceive the consumers	*Consumer characteristics* No health concerns No safety concerns Personal budget constraint Low regard for IPR
Institutional characteristics Low risk of discovery Legal and regulatory framework Weak enforcement Penalties	*Institutional characteristics* Low risk of discovery and prosecution Weak or no penalties Availability and ease of acquisition Socio-economic factors

Source: The Economic Impact of Counterfeiting and Piracy, OECD, 2007, pp. 10–15.

customers of the quality they expect from a brand.[2] It devalues corporate reputations, hinders investment, funds terrorism, and costs hundreds of thousands of people their livelihood every year. What was once a cottage industry has now become a highly sophisticated network of organized crime with the capacity to threaten the very fabric of national economies. Counterfeiters are often hardened criminals, exploiting consumers, businesses both large and small, inventors and artists, and children labouring in sweatshops, especially in third world countries.

Counterfeit and pirate activities are driven by a separate but related set of both supply and demand side drivers, as shown in Exhibit 22.1. Supply-side drivers include market opportunities, associated technological and distribution challenges, and the risks involved. The demand for such products is driven by product characteristics, individual consumer characteristics, and institutional environment in which the consumer operates.

The markets for counterfeit and pirated products are distinctly segmented into two interrelated sub-markets as follows.

Primary markets   Consumers demand genuine goods, but the counterfeiters sell their products deceptively to customers, portraying their products as legitimate items and compete with genuine products. For instance, markets for fake medicines, food products, luxury goods, etc.

Secondary markets   Consumers are willing to purchase counterfeit products, generally at a low price knowing well the product is not legitimate. For instance, markets for pirated CDs, software, etc.

Free trade zones (FTZs) and free ports are often used by counterfeiters to carry out the following three types of illegal operations:

- 'Merchants' import shipments of counterfeit goods into the warehouses in FTZs and then re-export them to other destinations. Thus, FTZs become 'distribution points' in the supply chain of counterfeit goods in addition to being used to 'sanitize' shipments and documents so as to disguise their original point of manufacturer or departure.

---

[2] *Managing the Risks of Counterfeiting in the Information Technology Industry*, KPMG, 2005.

- Counterfeiters import unfinished goods and then 'further manufacture' them in the FTZs by adding counterfeit trademarks, or repackaging or re-labelling the goods, and then export those 'finished' counterfeit goods to other countries.
- FTZs are also used for complete manufacturing of counterfeit goods.[3]

The levels of counterfeit products vary across countries. It is estimated that China is the world's largest source and market for counterfeit goods,[4] causing great losses to consumers and original producers. Counterfeits and lookalikes are common in most industries: pharmaceuticals, cosmetics, software, computer peripherals, auto components, audio and video cassettes, food, soft drinks, liquor, watches, clothing, and even currency.

The market for counterfeit products in India was estimated at around ₹150 trillion.[5] While the problem of fake products is witnessed across the country, counterfeiting is particularly rampant in the states of Delhi, Punjab, Haryana, and Uttar Pradesh. Among the other industries hard-hit by counterfeit products include all major brands of soap, shampoo, toothpaste, hair oil, biscuits, soft drinks, confectionery, batteries, and so on. The counterfeit products are available under slightly altered names: Fair & Lovely could be Pure & Lovely or Parachute could be Parashudh. A study by ORG, a market research agency, revealed 113 lookalikes for Fair and Lovely, nine lookalikes for Colgate toothpaste, 128 for Parachute oil, 44 for Vicks VapoRub, and 38 for Clinic Plus shampoo. These brands are popular with counterfeiters because they have wide appeal and are easily reproduced.

India is also one of the largest markets in the world for fake drugs, according to a WHO survey. An estimated 15–20 per cent of all medicines on pharmacy shelves across the country are fake, ranging from cough syrups to drugs for treatment of life-threatening illnesses. Procter & Gamble (P&G), for example, has found that 54 out of every 100 strips of its popular Vicks Action 500 brand of cough medicine being sold in the market are counterfeits.[6]

Piracy

The term 'piracy' refers to the use of illegal and unauthorized means to obtain goods. It includes use or reproduction of patented or copyrighted matter such as software, music, movies, and computer games. Piracy activities are directly influenced by the intellectual property regime within a country. Protection of intellectual property and its enforcement in 2013–14 is the strongest in Finland (Fig. 22.3) with a score of 6.3 on a seven-point scale, followed by Singapore (6.1), New Zealand (6.1), as compared to the UK (5.9), France (5.6), Germany (5.6), Japan (5.4), South Africa (5.3), the UAE (5.2), the USA (5), China (3.9), India (3.7), Brazil (3.5), Kenya (3.1), Venezuela (1.7), and Haiti (1.6).

Bribery

Bribe may be defined as any voluntary offering of an object of some value, such as money, gifts, and privilege, with an objective to influence the action of the receiver who is generally a government official or a person with power. It refers to an offer or receipt of any gift, loan, fee, reward, or other advantage to or from any person as an inducement to do something which is dishonest, illegal, or a breach of trust, in the conduct of the enterprise's business. A bribe becomes extortion[7]

---

[3] *The International Anti-Counterfeiting Directory 2008: Protecting the World Against the Plague of Counterfeiting*, ICC Counterfeiting Intelligence Bureau, London, p. 7.

[4] Asia Pulse, 24 June 2005.

[5] 'The ₹15,000 crore Fake Market', *Outlook Business*, 5 July 2006.

[6] 'Indian Industry: Laws on Counterfeiting are Ineffective', *EIU Business—New Analysis,* 28 February 2005.

[7] *The OECD Guidelines for Multinational Enterprises*, Paris, 2000; *OECD Observer*, June 2003, pp. 1–7.

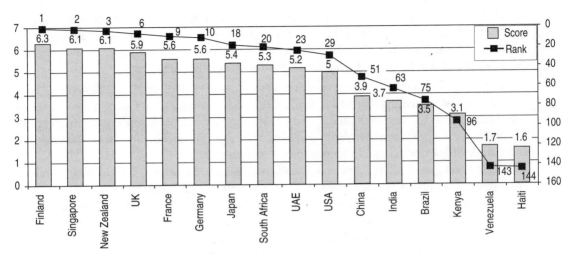

Fig. 22.3 Intellectual property protection

Source: The Global Competitiveness Report, 2013–14, World Economic Forum, Geneva, 2013.

when this demand is accompanied by threats that endanger the personal integrity or the life of the private actors involved.

The scope of bribery in international marketing transactions is much wider as it covers public sector bribery, bribery involving political parties as well as both the active and passive sides of private sector bribery. It also covers solicitation and extortions of bribes. Payment of bribe has become a business tool as revealed in a survey carried out by the international organization Transparency International. 43 per cent of the respondents from companies operating internationally believed that their companies failed to win a contract or gain new business because a competitor paid bribe in the last five years, whereas one third of the respondents believed that they lost their business due to non-payment of bribe in the last 12 months.

Given their financial strength and widespread global networking, international firms are often accused of paying bribes in the countries of operations. Transparency International has developed Bribe Payers Index (BPI) to rank world's 28 largest economies as per the propensity of firms with headquarters in those countries to bribe when operating abroad. It is based on the responses of more than 3,000 business executives from companies in 125 countries. As shown in Fig. 22.4, a higher score reveals a lower propensity of companies from a country to offer bribes or undocumented extra payments when doing business abroad. On a 10-point scale of one (bribes are common) to 10 (bribes never occur), Netherlands and Switzerland top the list each at 8.8, compared to Belgium (8.7), Germany (8.6), Japan (8.6), Singapore (8.30, the UK (8.3), the USA (8.1), France (8), Brazil (7.7), South Africa (7.6), India (7.5), Saudi Arabia (7.4), the UAE (7.3), Indonesia (7.1), China (6.5), and Russia[8] (6.1). As all countries fall short of the perfect score of 10, there is considerable propensity of companies of all nationalities to bribe when operating abroad.

International companies often circumvent anti-bribery legislations by using intermediaries, such as commercial agents or joint venture partners, to pay bribe on their behalf. This is despite the fact that OECD Convention on Combating Bribery of Foreign Public Officials in International Business prohibits bribes paid 'directly' or 'indirectly' and national laws, like the Foreign Corrupt Practices Act (FCPA) of the USA, have successfully prosecuted companies paying bribe via middlemen.

---

[8] *Bribe Payers Index,* 2011,Transparency International, Cambridge University Press, UK, 2011, p.4.

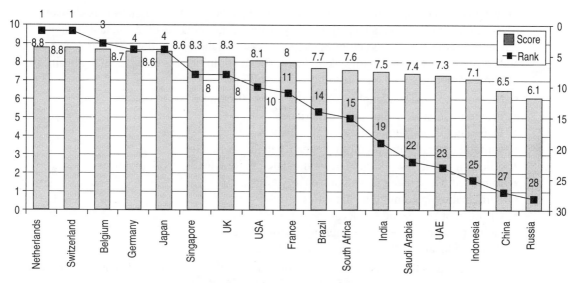

Fig. 22.4   Bribe payers index 2011

Source: *Bribe Payers Index*, 2011, Transparency International, Cambridge University Press, UK, 2011.

Smuggling

Smuggling refers to surreptitious trade across the borders aimed at circumventing enforcement of regulatory prohibitions and restrictions and evading payment of legitimate customs duties. Smuggling may have both financial and non-financial motives. Smuggling implies either ill-formulated national policies or their ineffective implementation or a combination of the two. Products with higher prohibition and restrictions such as liquor, cigarettes, drugs, arms, and ammunitions are generally appealing to smugglers. Due to restrictive immigration laws, organized gangs smuggle in millions of illegal immigrants into USA and Europe with the promise of lucrative jobs.

The incentive to smuggle generally increases with rise in customs duties and other restrictions and vice versa. To illustrate, smuggling flourished as a full-fledged industry in most developing countries a few decades back, when the customs duties and other import restrictions were very high. As a result, a few markets in India, such as Palika Bazar in Delhi, Chor Bazar (Thief Market) in Mumbai, and Moreh Market in Imphal, became famous (or infamous) for smuggled goods. Hefty margins in smuggling became so lucrative, implying lavish lifestyles that smuggling even became the preferred theme for Bollywood movies. As import restrictions were eased and duties declined, the incentive to smuggle also diminished considerably.

Smuggling has a detrimental effect on national trade policies and their implementation. Besides, the competition from smuggled goods severely hampers fair market competition by legitimate importers. Counterfeit and pirated goods also find their way into the distribution channels of smuggled goods, tarnishing manufacturers' image.

Growing Awareness of Corporate Social Responsibility

Charity for charity's sake is passé in today's business environment. Corporate business responsibility makes sound business sense. A growing number of business organizations the world over link their growth and survival schemes with a firm's overall corporate objectives.

CSR refers to the commitment of business enterprise to work with employees, their families, the local communities, and society at large so as to improve their quality of life and contribute to sustainable economic and social development. It is the process of assuming responsibility by a business enterprise across its entire supply chain for the social, ecological, and economic consequences of the company's activities, prepare reports on these activities and their consequences, and constructively engage with stakeholders. The major initiatives undertaken[9] by businesses to promote corporate social responsibility are as follows:

- Measures to improve employees' health and well-being
- Providing internship and work experience
- Donating to community causes and charity
- Cultural diversity and promoting equality in the workplace
- Allowing flexible working to accommodate family-friendly work practices
- Improved waste management and energy efficiency
- Participation in community activities
- Changed products and services
- Helping other businesses to improve performance
- Sourcing local or ethical products and services

CSR facilitates the firms to fulfil their roles as socially responsible citizens while promoting their own business interests. Small companies traditionally have fewer stakeholders to satisfy, with greatest concern regarding their customers, and their own ability to satisfy the demand for products effectively. Well-managed CSR actually supports business objectives, especially among large companies, where improved compliance, reputation, and relationships tend to increase shareholders' value and profitability.

For instance, Pfizer's Indian subsidy has sponsored diagnostic centres and X-ray clinics for the poor. These centres would eventually act as referral centres for Pfizer products. Similarly, Hindustan Unilever Limited (HUL) promoted its health-care programmes in the villages of Kerala as part of its plan to expand its market for personal care products in rural India. Lafarge, the global building materials manufacturer, build low-cost concrete houses.

Moreover, businesses operating ethically and in a socially responsible manner have a greater chance of sustainability and success. Firms are increasingly associating CSR as a strategic tool for their operations in global markets. Multinational enterprises (MNEs) are increasingly taking numerous proactive measures to boost their CSR image.

GROWING SIGNIFICANCE OF EMERGING ECONOMIES IN INTERNATIONAL MARKETING

The global rates of development, from a historical perspective, have been increasing for more than a century. The dramatic rise of Japan and the East Asian tigers (namely Hong Kong, Singapore, South Korea, and Taiwan), and most recently China are illustrative of this point. An objective assessment reveals that all the major engines of economic growth that have accelerated growth until now will be present in greater abundance in the coming years than they had been in the past. The world economy is projected to grow at an average rate of over 3 per cent per annum from 2011 to 2050, doubling in size by 2032 and doubling again by 2050. Interestingly, emerging economies are likely to grow at 4 per cent per annum or more, whereas advanced economies are projected to grow at 2 per cent or less during 2011–50.

China is likely to overtake the USA as the world's largest economy by 2017 in purchasing power parity (PPP) terms and by 2027 in market exchange rate (MER) terms. Russia could overtake

---

[9] *Corporate Social Responsibility: a Necessity Not a Choice*, International Business Report, Grant Thornton International, 2008, pp. 1–20.

Germany to become the largest European economy before 2020 in PPP terms and by around 2035 at MERs. India remains the third largest economy of the world in terms of PPP and its gap with leading economies such as the USA and China is likely to narrow down significantly by 2050. Emerging economies such as Mexico and Indonesia could be larger than the UK and France by 2050 and Turkey larger than Italy. Moreover, Vietnam, Malaysia, and Nigeria also have long-term growth potential, while Poland may outpace the large Western economies in a couple of decades.

GDP at PPP is a better indicator of average living standards or volumes of outputs and inputs as it corrects for price differences across countries at different levels of development, whereas GDP at MERs may be a better measure of the relative size of the economies from a business perspective, at least in the short term. As price levels in emerging markets are in general lower than advanced economies, GDP at PPP comparison helps narrow the income gap with advanced economies compared to using MERs. For long run business planning or investment appraisal purposes, it is crucial to factor in the likely rise in real MERs in emerging economies towards their PPP rates. This could occur either through relatively higher price inflation in these emerging economies, or through nominal exchange rate appreciation, or a combination of both.

China is projected to overtake the USA as the largest economy of the world in terms of GDP at MERs, while India moves to a clear third place by 2030 well ahead of Japan and Brazil as shown in Table 22.1.

Table 22.1 India projected to become the third largest economy by 2030 (in MERs)

	2011		2030		2050	
MER rank	Country	GDP at MER (2011 US$ bn)	Country	Projected GDP at MER (2011 US$ bn)	Country	Projected GDP at MER (2011 US$ bn)
1	USA	15,094	China	24,356	China	48,477
2	China	7,298	US	23,376	US	37,998
3	Japan	5,867	**India**	**7,918**	**India**	**26,895**
4	Germany	3,571	Japan	6,817	Brazil	8,950
5	France	2,773	Brazil	4,883	Japan	8,065
6	Brazil	2,477	Germany	4,374	Russia	7,115
7	UK	2,432	Russia	4,024	Mexico	6,706
8	Italy	2,195	France	3,805	Indonesia	5,947
9	Russia	1,858	UK	3,614	Germany	5,822
10	**India**	**1,848**	Mexico	2,830	France	5,714
11	Canada	1,736	Italy	2,791	UK	5,598
12	Spain	1,491	Indonesia	2,465	Turkey	4,486
13	Australia	1,372	Canada	2,414	Italy	3,867
14	Mexico	1,155	Spain	2,310	Spain	3,612
15	South Korea	1,116	Turkey	2,106	Canada	3,549
16	Indonesia	847	South Korea	2,078	Nigeria	3,451
17	Turkey	773	Australia	1,898	South Korea	3,315
18	Saudi Arabia	577	Saudi Arabia	1434	Saudi Arabia	2,977
19	Poland	514	Argentina	1,052	Australia	2,603
20	Argentina	446	South Africa	935	Argentina	2,333

Source: World in 2050: The BRICS and Beyond: Prospects, Challenges and Opportunities, PricewaterhouseCoopers, January 2013.

China's economic growth rate is likely to cool down progressively during the period 2020–50 as its economy matures. It is expected to witness transition from being an export-oriented economy to more of a consumption-driven economy mainly due to rapidly rising real labour costs and aging population, accentuated by its one child policy for the past 30 years. As a result, Chinese exporters would be required to compete more on the basis of quality rather than price in their key US and European markets.

Emerging markets are likely to open up numerous opportunities for global marketers especially in the following sectors:

- Multinationals with global brands
- Global retailers with strong franchise models
- Health-care and educational services
- Financial services
- Manufacturers with high value addition especially in niche segments
- Creative industries

However, certain challenges foreseen in the emerging markets include the following:

- Manufacturers of mass products not only of low-tech products but also of high-tech as the countries such as China and India move up the value chain
- Emerging markets being too complex for global marketers to penetrate on their own, forging and maintaining alliance with a right local partner is the key to success
- Financial services companies with high exposure in their domestic markets especially in advanced economies

Emerging markets such as China, India, and Brazil are likely to become not just low-cost production locations but also increasingly large consumer markets. As the economic growth in developed markets is likely to be about half of that in emerging markets, global marketers would increasingly be required to target emerging markets for sustaining their future growth.

However, the USA and the EU are likely to remain attractive markets for higher value products and services given their more affluent consumers. Multinationals from emerging markets would increasingly achieve stronger positions in developed markets as they move up the value chain.

INDIA: EMERGES AT THE GLOBAL STAGE

India is a young developing nation. It has a rich and illustrious history as one of the longest living civilizations in the world. In 1835, the British historian and politician, Lord Macaulay, admitted[10] before the British Parliament: 'I have travelled across the length and breadth of India and I have not seen one person who is a beggar, who is a thief. Such wealth I have seen in this country, such high moral values, people of such calibre, the very backbone of this nation, which is her spiritual and cultural heritage.' India's unique approach to development is preparing it to overtake China in the economic growth race.[11]

Moreover, India's soft power and its presence are its greatest assets. India's remarkable innovations include Nano, the world's cheapest car, and Akash, the world's cheapest tablet PC at a price of US$46.

---

[10] *The Awakening Ray*, vol. 4, no. 5, The Gnostic Centre, Report of the Committee on India Vision 2020, Planning Commission, Government of India, New Delhi, December 2002, p.17.

[11] *Far Eastern Economic Review*, 15 April 2004.

India is not only the most populous democracy in the world but it is also the largest producer of milk, largest consumer of sugar, spices, and even gold. A snapshot of India's strengths in international markets[12] is as follows:

- India is the largest whisky manufacturer in the world.
- Parachute is the world's largest coconut oil brand.
- Coal India is the largest coal miner in the world.
- Bangalore has more Grade-A offices than Singapore.
- India is the largest diamond cutting and polishing centre in the world.
- India is the largest sugar consumer in the world.
- Ireland's richest person is an Indian—Pallonji Mistry.
- Parle-G is the world's largest selling biscuit brand.
- KEC is the global leader in tower production capacity.
- Tata Group is the largest manufacturing employer in the UK.

India is fast emerging as one of the largest consumer markets in the world. Political empowerment and economic trickle-down effect have now fuelled ambitions and aspirations in more Indians than at any other point of time in Indian history. The British East India Company, world's first multinational that created history, has now been acquired by a London-based businessman of Indian origin (Exhibit 22.2). The analysis of various environmental factors carried out in the

Exhibit 22.2   The British East India Company is now truly Indian

The world's first multinational, the British East India Company, which evokes a lot of emotions in the Indian sub-continent for centuries had a profound impact on the development of international trade. By 1801 AD, its trade volume soared to 7.5 million British pounds. At the time of the company's glory, it controlled about half of the world trade and employed a third of the British workforce. It ruled the Indian sub-continent for over 200 years, which made East India Company the world's first truly global brand.

The company was established on 31 December 1600 when the British Queen Elizabeth I granted a group of merchants monopoly trading rights with what was called the East Indies under a charter named 'The Company of Merchants of London Trading into the East Indies'. During the British Queen Elizabethan period, the company was responsible for taking tea, coffee, and luxury goods to the West and trading spices across the globe.

The company's first ships arrived in India on the coast of Surat, Gujarat, in 1608. Sir Thomas Roe managed to gain trading rights from the Mughal Emperor Jahagir in 1615. The expansion of the company in India was rapid with several trading posts coming along the coast in Bengal (now West Bengal), Bombay (now Mumbai), and Madras (now Chennai).

The transition of East India Company from a transnational commercial entity to a ruling power took place after Robert Clive defeated the Nawab of Bengal Sirajuddaulah in 1757, at the Battle of Plassey. By 1757, the company had become a powerful arm of British imperial might, with its own army, navy, shipping fleet, and currency, and control over key trading posts in India. In 1773, the company was brought under the British Parliament and a Governor General was appointed to oversee its activities. Territories were annexed ruthlessly and the Sikhs, Marathas, and Tipu Sultan of Mysore were defeated.

The last major violent Indian uprising was quelled in 1857. Harsh revenue policies, a bleeding economy, starving peasantry, which led to brutal wars, finally forced Queen Victoria to intervene. The company was disbanded in 1858 and India was brought under the direct rule of the Crown with a Viceroy at the helm. In 1874, the British government nationalized the company, opportunistically blaming the 1857 uprising on its excesses. But the East India Company army, brought under the command of the Crown, retained its all-powerful presence in India.

The company became truly Indian in 2005 when it was bought by a Mumbai-born London-based businessman of Indian origin, Sanjiv Mehta. With a worldwide brand recall, the company aims to pitch itself against established brands ranging from tea, spices, coffee, cocoa, sweets, champagnes, chocolates, sauces, marmalades, and other exotic offerings and regain its lost glory to become a present-day transnational.

Source: 'Mahindra Buys Stake in East India Company', *Business Standard*, 25 January 2011;'The East India Company is Now Truly Indian', *Khaleej Times*, 22 February 2010; 'An Indian Now Owns East India Company', *SME Times*,15 February 2010.

---

[12] 'Brand India Saving Grace in Time of Crisis', *The Times of India,* 4 April 2012.

chapter suggests that India is likely to emerge as a major marketing force and the world's third largest economy by 2050.

It is interesting to understand as to how India emerged as an economic superpower and a political counterweight to China. India not only has the second highest population in the world but is also the fourth largest consumer market with an impressive rate of growth that hardly a company aspiring to become transnational can afford to ignore.

In the 1990s, India was seen as holding world records in starvation and poverty and a bottomless pit for foreign aid. It tried to project itself as a third-world leader at international forums. Many other developing countries outpaced India and it was generally seen not as an economic or political role model but as an expert drafter of documents.

India's global positioning today is the result of individual Indians, entrepreneurs, and corporates rather than the government. Individual and corporate relations boomed even during the days of the Cold War between India and the USA and it became India's largest trading partner. Over a million Indians migrated to the USA and hundreds of thousands flooded Western universities. On the contrary, only very few, if any, Indians migrated to the USSR, despite its friendly relations with India.

Once the Cold War ended and the economic liberalization began in India, it was the private initiatives that spearheaded the transformation of India's global impact. Private initiatives by individuals and Indian corporates have been a parallel initiative rather than privatization or liberalization of the India foreign policy. At the best, the government's role may be termed as supportive rather than leading unlike China.

Rapid rise of India's IT capabilities instils fear in the developing countries' workforce, analysts, and politicians. This has inspired a TV series 'Outsourced' and a new word 'Bangalored' has entered the dictionary. India, with over 100 companies of over a billion dollar market cap, has established its position globally that made GE set up its first R&D centre outside the USA in Bangalore (now Bengaluru).

International acquisitions have made Indian business houses global giants. Lakshmi Niwas Mittal is the world's largest steel producer. Tata Steel took over Corus, which was six times its size. Tata Motors acquired and turned around Jaguar Land Rover, reviving world famous brands that had earlier languished under Ford and BMW. Birla became a global name in aluminium with the takeover of Novelis.

India became globally famous in the automobile industry with the innovation of Tata's Nano, manufacturing and selling a passenger car only for US\$2,500. On the other hand, there is the North-South technical relationship between Bajaj Auto, which has been entrusted for R&D to bring out a rival, and its collaborator Renault-Nissan.

India's economic rise has translated into political clout, and explains why the Western powers have decided to waive the nuclear rules for India and back its bid for permanent membership in the UN Security Council.[13]

Manufacturing

A study conducted by Deloitte and the US Council on Competitiveness reveal that India is ranked second behind China in manufacturing competitiveness and will only narrow the gap over the next few years.[14] India is fast establishing itself as a global manufacturing hub. Contributing close to a fourth of the GDP, India's manufacturing sector has a diversified base of world-class capabilities

---

[13] Aiyar, Swaminathan Ankalesaria, 'India's Global Image is Driven by Private Initiative', *The Times of India*, 9 January 2011.

[14] 'India Ranks Second in Manufacturing Competitiveness', *The Times of India,* 3 December 2010.

using state-of-the-art technologies. Global corporations are leveraging India's acknowledged strengths in product design, reconfiguration, and customization with creativity, assured quality, and value additions, and all those factors that outweigh mere cost considerations.

Services

Growing consistently, the services sector currently accounts for over half of India's GDP. Global investment banks, brokerages, and accounting firms have set up large research establishments in India. A growing number of US companies are hiring Indian mathematics experts to devise models for risk analysis, consumer behaviour, and industrial processes. India's strategic strength in offering services to international markets lies both in individual and corporate services, as depicted in Fig. 22.5.

Channels of services

	Remote servicing	'Importing' the customers
Individual	*Telemedicine* D-I-Y support • Tele-plumbing • Auto repairs • Text advisory services • Horoscope reading *E-learning* • Home-schooling • Adult professional courses-re-skilling Personal privacy services providing server space to individual for record maintenance	*Tourism* • Medical tourism, spiritual tourism, adventure tourism, etc. • 'Dollar' shopping centres duty-free shopping zones *Education* • Higher education for developed and developing countries • Training courses revolving around India's heritage—Ayurveda, cuisine, yoga, etc. *Nursing houses and retirement services* • Ashram model • Settlements near university towns
Targets **Corporates**	*IT services* • IT consulting • Software application development • Knowledge networking *IT-enabled services* • Data analysis and database consulting • HR and admin outsourcing • Digital media and content development (E-learning content, publishing, entertainment, etc.) • CAD/CAM design • Animation • Bio-informatics • Oil-shore financial services • Real-estate management-security services *Others* • R&D across industry verticals-semiconductor technology, drug research, etc. • Legal/Advisory services for MNCs	Tourism for corporate clients Education services for corporate clients

Fig. 22.5   India's strategic strengths for offering services to international markets

Copyright: The Boston Consulting Group

A unique feature of India's exports is its services-based export composition. India's services export accounts for 31 per cent of total exports, which is even higher than those of even the USA (29%), Brazil (13%), and China[15] (9%), whereas the share of merchandise exports from India

---

[15] International Monetary Fund database.

as a percentage of total exports remain 69 per cent compared to the USA (71%), Brazil (87%), and China (91%).The Indian mythological serial 'Ramayan', produced by Ramanand Sagar, was viewed by over 650 million people worldwide, out of which 40 million Indians regularly watched it on its first telecast, according to a BBC report. Moreover, the serial had repeat telecast on 20 channels in 17 countries in all five continents at different times.[16]

The major potential for remote servicing to individual customers lies in telemedicine, e-learning, record keeping, and tax advisory services. IT and IT-enabled services such as IT counselling, software application development, data analysis, digital media, content development, and bioinformatics are mainly targeted at corporate customers. Besides, tourism, education, health, nursing, etc. are the services that can be targeted mainly at individual customers who are going to visit India.

Indian firms are on a global shopping spree of overseas companies during recent years. Now, they are expanding their merger and acquisition (M&A) activities into new markets such as Spain, Brazil, South America, and Europe.

Foreign Direct Investment

India offers a unique blend of talent and low cost that fits well with the perspective of global corporations increase profits and ensures business continuity through multi-country strategies. India has also emerged as a global R&D hub. Companies in the manufacturing and communication services sector feel bullish about India, ranking it the second most attractive market globally. The companies in these industries represent mostly knowledge-intensive segments such as semiconductor manufacturers, pharmaceuticals, and scientific instruments.

After China, India has the fastest growing mobile market. Finnish Nokia and Chinese Huawei Technologies established their R&D centres in India in 2004. The implementation of the WTO rules covering Intellectual Property Rights (TRIPS), combined with a highly talented pool of pharmaceutical scientists, positioned India to become an R&D player in the drug development field.

India and China: David and Goliath

The global investors view India and China as distinctly different markets. China is viewed as the world's leading manufacturer and the fastest growing consumer market. India, on the other hand, is viewed as the world's business process and IT services provider with long-term market potential. China leads for manufacturing and assembly, while India leads for IT business processing and R&D investments. Investors favour China over India for its market size, access to export markets, favourable cost structure, infrastructure, and macroeconomic climate. However, the same investors cite India's highly educated workforce, management talent, state policies and rules, transparency, cultural affinity, and regulatory environment as more favourable than what China presents. China's FDI flows were larger (US$220 billion) and primarily capital-intensive, while Indian FDI flows were smaller[17] (US$32 billion) in 2011 and skill-intensive, concentrated in information and technology areas.

China's export-manufacturing FDI framework brought capital-intensive industries, while India's import-substitution regime led to higher technology-oriented FDI. India's previously restrictive FDI regime limited foreign participation in the economy to mostly licensing and other contractual agreements instead of FDI. This also explains the foreign companies using a third-party service provider in India rather than investing as a mode of market entry. 'India's model should prove more sustainable than the typical East Asian strategy adopted by China. India is developing more efficient corporate, healthier banks, more robust service industries, and a bigger consumption base.'[18]

---

[16] headlines.sify.com, accessed on 19 January 2011.
[17] World Bank database as updated in June 2013.
[18] Fineman, Dan,'Growth Model', *Far Eastern Economic Review*, April 2004.

Internationalization of Indian Firms

The emerging markets in Asia and Africa with low to medium penetration of some of the fast moving consumer goods (FMCG) categories offers significant opportunities for growth in the medium-term. Favourable macroeconomic environment, progressive policies of governments, and changing attitude of the customers also make these markets attractive destinations especially for products from developing countries such as India and China. Some of them offer inorganic growth possibilities that can create access to mainstream distribution, manufacturing, and talent.

Indian companies are now making big impact in the markets of Africa and Latin America. Besides several IT companies, pharmaceutical and automobile manufacturers are entering into this market unexplored so far. Jindal Steel is setting up Bolivia's first steel plant. Consequent to takeover of Zain, Bharti Airtel is providing mobile services in over 150 countries. A number of Indian companies are queuing up to exploit newly discovered coal deposits in Mozambique. Sterlite acquired Zambia's Konkola mine, the biggest in Africa and turned it around after an Anglo-American multinational failed to revive it.

Reaping India's Demographic Dividend

India is at an inflection point at which the increase in its share of the labour force is set to accelerate. The decline in India's population growth rate is mainly attributed to a fall in the birth rate (per 1,000) from 33.9 per cent in 1981 to 29.5 per cent in 1991, 25.2 per cent in 2001, and around 20.6 per cent in 2012. This decline in birth rate has so far been reflected in a very gradual increase in the share of population of working age. Therefore, India is entering the second stage of demographic transition where the share of its working age population is expected to increase over the next three decades. Most other Asian economies entered these demographic stages decades ago and some, especially Japan, have entered the next stage and are now aging rapidly. The share of working age population in India is likely to overtake that of China by 2030 as shown in Fig. 22.6, whereas the working population in Japan is likely to decline considerably.

India is likely to have a unique competitive advantage in terms of surplus workforce and its quality in terms of productivity, cost-effectiveness, and English language skills, as depicted in Fig. 22.7.

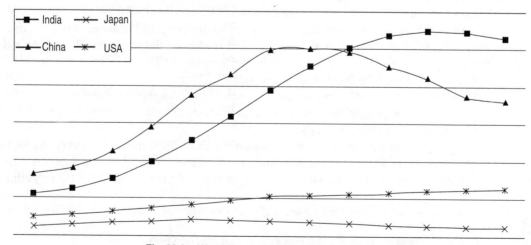

Fig. 22.6   Working age population (15–64 years)

Source: United Nations World Population Prospects, accessed in June 2013.

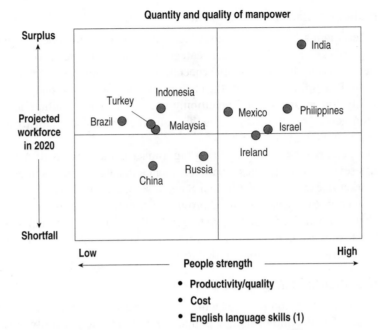

Fig. 22.7   India's competitive advantage in workforce

(1) Over 50% of shortages expected from English-speaking countries
Note: Pakistan, Bangladesh, and Vietnam have not been represented for lack of reliable data on productivity and cost of service employees.
Source: *World Competitiveness Yearbook 2001*, *Britannica Yearbook*, 'India's New Opportunity—2020', All India Management Association, The Boston Consulting Group, 2003, p. 19.
Copyright: The Boston Consulting Group

India Posed to be the World's Biggest Consumer Market

Over the years, spending power has steadily increased in India. Its middle class population is growing rapidly and is likely to be soon larger than the entire US population. The middle class population in India is estimated to be about 586 million by 2025 compared to the total population of 350 million of the US.[19] The growth of the middle class leads to an overall market growth, especially in education, healthcare, housing, retailing, and financial services. Given the large size of Indian population, the consumption growth by the rising middle class in India is unprecedented. OECD estimates India to be the third largest consumer market in the world by 2030 and the largest[20] by 2050 as shown in Table 22.2.

Rapid growth of middle class in India implies huge consumption spending in terms of the demand for mobile phones, televisions, scooters, cars, and credit goods and a consumption pattern associated with rising incomes.

India is likely to witness continued urbanization. Until 1988, India with an urban population of 25 per cent was actually ahead of China in urbanization. The urban population is expected to rise from 31 per cent in 2010 to 52 per cent of the total population[21] by 2050 exhibiting the

---

[19] *The Rise of Indian Consumer Market*, McKinsey Global Institute, May 2007; United Nations World Population Prospects, 2012.
[20] *OECD Development Centre Working Paper No. 285 DEV/DOC (2010) 2.*
[21] *World Urbanization Prospects: The 2011 Revision*, United Nations, Department of Economics and Social Affairs, Population Division, 2011.

Table 22.2　India is likely to be the world's biggest consumption market by 2030 (Middle class consumption in trillions of 2005 PPP $)

	2009		2020		2030	
1	USA	4.4	China	4.5	India	12.8
2	Japan	1.8	USA	4.3	China	10
3	Germany	1.2	India	3.7	USA	4.0
4	France	0.9	Japan	2.2	Indonesia	2.5
5	UK	0.9	Germany	1.4	Japan	2.3
6	Russia	0.9	Russia	1.2	Russia	1.4
7	China	0.7	France	1.1	Germany	1.3
8	Italy	0.7	Indonesia	1.0	Mexico	1.2
9	Mexico	0.7	Mexico	1.0	Brazil	1.2
10	Brazil	0.6	UK	1.0	France	1.1
	World	**21.3**	**World**	**35.0**	**World**	**55.7**

Source: OECD Development Centre Working Paper No. 285 DEV/DOC (2010) 2, Brookings Institution.

growth rate of 21 per cent, whereas the urban population in China is expected to rise from 49 per cent to 77 per cent during the same period with a growth rate of 28 per cent. Future growth is likely to be concentrated in and around 60 to 70 large cities having a population of one million or more. This profile of concentrated urban population will facilitate greater customer access.

This chapter brings out major contemporary issues in global marketing. Globalization, accelerated growth of global markets in all parts of the world, rapidly disappearing global boundaries, emerging global market segment, product proliferation, integration of ICT in marketing and CRM, and ethical issues in international marketing are discussed. The chapter also discusses the increasing significance of emerging economies and emergence of India at the global stage.

Summary

The marketing environment has witnessed unprecedented changes during the last few decades. This chapter examines the emerging issues in international markets, such as accelerated growth of global markets, pervasiveness of globalization, rapid integration of global markets, breaking down of marketing boundaries, emerging new marketing barriers, emergence of global customer segment, growing customer expectation, product proliferation and shortening product life cycles, emergence of knowledge economy, growing strength of retailers, and emergence of global e-marketing.

The ICT has revolutionized the ways services are offered across geographical boundaries. The increasing use of ICT is being made in offering cross-border services in the fields of IT, health, and e-learning. The process of creating and maintaining business relationship by a firm with its customers, known as customer relationship management (CRM), has gained significance as it greatly facilitates the retention of existing customers.

In order to attain long-term sustainability and success in business, adoption of ethical and socially responsible marketing practices becomes a fundamental condition. In their quest to win over customers, companies frequently make exaggerated claims about their products and services and many a time even cross all the limits of basic social decency while advertising. This chapter discusses unethical marketing practices such as counterfeiting, piracy, bribery, and smuggling. Carrying out business in a socially responsible manner, known as CSR, has become crucial to success, long-term sustainability, and even survival.

Emerging markets are gaining increasing significance with a considerably higher growth compared to developed markets. India has fast emerged at the global marketplace as the third largest economy in PPP terms and a global soft power. India is likely to have an increase in the ratio of working age adults to total population, whereas it is likely to decline in the most developed countries and even in the next few decades. India's competitive advantage in workforce comes from its workforce strength in terms of productivity, cost, and English language skills, besides surplus workforce by 2020. Moreover, India is projected to be the biggest consumption market in the world by 2030.

Key Terms

Bribe Any voluntary offering of an object of some value, such as money, gift, and privilege, with an objective to influence the action of the receiver.

Corporate social responsibility (CSR) Carrying out business activities in a socially responsible manner.

Corruption Abuse of entrusted power for private gains.

Counterfeiting Imitating something with an intent to deceive or defraud.

Customer relationship management (CRM) The process of creating and maintaining business relationship by the firm with its customers.

Ethics Study of moral conduct and its evaluation as to what is right or wrong.

Global e-marketing Marketing transactions through electronic methods across the world.

Grey marketing Import or export of goods and distributing them through unauthorized channels.

Smuggling Surreptitious trade across borders aimed at circumventing enforcement of regulatory prohibitions and restrictions and evading payment of legitimate customs duties.

Concept Review Questions

1. As emerging markets are growing much faster compared to developed countries, multinationals from developed economies are finding it difficult to compete and are in desperate search of value for money offerings. Critically evaluate the opportunities and challenges for companies from emerging economies in the present scenario.
2. 'Marketing boundaries across the countries are fast disappearing.' Critically examine this statement with suitable examples.
3. Explain the significance of ethical practices in business transactions. Examine briefly the unethical practices adopted in international marketing.
4. Critically evaluate India's rise on the global stage and identify international marketing opportunities from India.
5. Write short notes on the following:
   (a) Piracy
   (b) Smuggling
   (c) Customer relationship management (CRM)
   (d) Corporate social responsibility (CSR)

Practice Exercise

Identify a few Indian firms that have expanded internationally. Find out key opportunities and challenges for these companies in the next five years.

Project Assignments

1. Explore the magnitude of counterfeit and pirated goods in your country. Also attempt to assess its category or industry-wise break-up. Find out the major distribution centres of such goods in your country.
2. Identify a local firm operating in international markets that has implemented customer relationship marketing (CRM). Study the process and find out the firm's experience in implementing CRM.

Index

About the Author

Rakesh Mohan Joshi is presently Professor, International Business and International Marketing, and Chairperson, International Collaborations and Research, Indian Institute of Foreign Trade, New Delhi. A distinguished academician, an eminent author, a celebrated speaker on electronic media and other fora, and a renowned management expert having varied experience in teaching, research, and consultancy, Dr Joshi has authored numerous research papers in leading journals. Some of his case studies have been awarded by London Business School and published internationally, besides having been recipient of several other approbations.

Dr Joshi regularly conducts training programmes for corporate executives, government officials, and diplomats in India as well as abroad including China, USA, Russia, UAE, Singapore, France, Hong Kong, Thailand, South Africa, Uganda, Egypt, Tanzania, Oman, Bangladesh, Ethiopia, Botswana, Namibia, Burkina Faso, Sudan, Mauritius, Seychelles, and Niger. He has extensive transnational exposure and has been associated with several multilateral organizations such as the World Bank and the Asian Development Bank. He is also on the Board of Governors, Indian Institute of Forest Management, Ministry of Environment and Forests, Government of India, and Board of Management, Rajasthan Technical University.

Dr Joshi is also the author of *International Business*, published by Oxford University Press, India, in 2009. He may be contacted at the email ID rakeshmohanjoshi@gmail.com or through his website www.rakeshmohanjoshi.com.

Related Titles

ADVERTISING MANAGEMENT, 2E [9780198074120]

Jaishri Jethwaney, *Professor, Indian Institute of Mass Communication, JNU, New Delhi* and **Shruti Jain**, *Chief Communications Officer and Global Head–CSR, EXL Service*

The second edition of *Advertising Management* is a comprehensive textbook tailored to meet the syllabi requirements of management students, mass media, and stand-alone courses on advertising. Interspersed with examples, exhibits, and real-life cases, the book provides an in-depth coverage of the key components, namely advertising and promotions, media strategy and planning, and agency relationships.

The book includes topics such as consumer behaviour and advertising research, advertising agencies, creative strategy and development, structure and management, and advertising classification. Further, topics of current relevance such as digital advertising, advertising laws and ethics, and advertising in rural and global contexts in India have also been included. With dedicated chapters on sales promotion and direct marketing, the book lays emphasis on all major channels of marketing communication.

Key Features

- Examines the advertising strategies followed by business organizations
- Explores the emerging issues in advertising management from an Indian perspective
- Contains cases and examples in the key areas of advertising management

BRAND MANAGEMENT: PRINCIPLES AND PRACTICES (WITH CD) [9780198069867]

Kirti Dutta, *Bhartiya Vidya Bhavan's Usha and Lakshmi Mittal Institute of Management, New Delhi*

Brand Management: Principles and Practices is a comprehensive textbook designed for students of postgraduate management programmes specializing in marketing. It explores the core concepts of branding and illustrates them through numerous examples, exhibits, figures, images, case studies, and videos.

Key Features

- Includes exclusive chapters on creating a brand, understanding organizational culture, consumer behaviour, e-branding, and managing brand architecture

- Provides rich learning from brand practices of Indian brands like Kingfisher, Maggi, Airtel, Aircel, Micromax, ITC, and LIC
- Each chapter is linked with the CD and contains videos and presentations that explain the key concepts and includes exercise(s) for enhancing decision-making abilities

SALES AND DISTRIBUTION MANAGEMENT, 2E [9780198077046]

Tapan K. Panda, *Great Lakes Institute of Management Studies, Chennai* and **Sunil Sahadev**, *University of Sheffield, UK*

Sales and Distribution Management, 2/e is a textbook specially designed to meet the requirements of management students specializing in sales and marketing. This book gives a balanced presentation of the concepts of sales and distribution through examples and cases.

Key Features

- Contains classroom-tested cases from Indian as also international business organizations
- Includes examples and boxed exhibits in key areas of sales and distribution management

MARKETING RESEARCH [9780195676969]

Sunanda Easwaran, *Dean, ICFAI Business School, Mumbai* and **Sharmila Singh**, *National Qualitative Head and Director, Mode Modellers Pvt. Ltd, Mumbai*

Marketing Research is a comprehensive textbook specially designed to meet the needs of management students. It combines the quantitative and qualitative aspects of marketing research, and addresses its utility for both the researcher and the end-user.

Key Features

- Addresses both the quantitative and qualitative research aspects of marketing management
- Provides practical guidelines on the relationship between the researcher and the manager, the scope of research, and what the user may expect from research
- Includes step-wise SPSS commands for conducting discriminant analysis, factor analysis, cluster analysis, and multidimensional scaling

---

Other Related Titles